BUSINESS MATHEMATICS

BUSINESS MATHEMATICS

Second Edition

Qazi Zameeruddin

VK Khanna and **SK Bhambri**

Department of Mathematics, Kirori Mal College,
University of Delhi, Delhi

VIKAS®

VIKAS® PUBLISHING HOUSE PVT LTD

VIKAS® PUBLISHING HOUSE PRIVATE LIMITED
E-28, Sector-8, Noida-201301 (UP), India
Phone: +91-120-4078900 • Fax: +91-120-4078999
VIKAS® Registered Office: A-27, 2nd Floor, Mohan Co-operative Industrial Estate, New Delhi-110044
E-mail: helpline@vikaspublishing.com • Website: www.vikaspublishing.com

SALES AND BRANCH OFFICES OF VIKAS® AND S CHAND AND COMPANY LIMITED

Chennai	:	Ph: 044-2363 2120, chennai@schandpublishing.com
Guwahati	:	Ph: 0361-2738 811, 2735 640, guwahati@schandpublishing.com
Hyderabad	:	Ph: 040-4018 6018, hyderabad@schandpublishing.com
Jalandhar	:	Ph: 0181-4645 630, jalandhar@schandpublishing.com
Kolkata	:	Ph: 033-2335 7458, 2335 3914, kolkata@schandpublishing.com
Lucknow	:	Ph: 0522-4003 633, lucknow@schandpublishing.com
Mumbai	:	Ph: 022-2500 0297, mumbai@schandpublishing.com
Patna	:	Ph: 0612-2260 011, patna@schandpublishing.com

Business Mathematics
ISBN: 978-81259-2841-6 Product Code: V8BMA60MATH10ENAB09O

Second Edition 2009
Reprinted several times 2022 (Thrice)
Reprint 2024

PRINTED IN INDIA
By Vikas Publishing House Private Limited, Plot 20/4, Site-IV, Industrial Area Sahibabad, Ghaziabad-201010 and Published by Vikas Publishing House Private Limited, E-28, Sector-8, Noida-201301

Preface to the Second Edition

A revision of the book was probably long due which has finally been accomplished. Although in some of the chapters it might look like a mere rehash of the previous edition, a sizeable expansion has been done in others. Besides a new chapter on Linear Programming a major impact of the revision can be felt in the applications part to commerce & economics, especially under matrices and calculus. Instead of confining the applications part to one single chapter, the material has now been put at appropriate places in the related chapters with an eye on making it more reader friendly.

There is a wealth of examples and exercises of varying difficulty covering the entire range in the text. Every effort has been made to keep the book free of errors. Suggestions from readers regarding any improvement would be most welcome.

Authors

Preface to the First Edition

For the last two decades or so the use of mathematical techniques has been gaining popularity in social and biological sciences and as well as in the field of commerce and management. In fact the exactness and precision of mathematical language and methods have made it possible to explore large areas of research in these subjects which remained hidden so far from the keen eyes of the researchers. Today, one could say that mathematics is probably the most convenient shoulder to lean on for not only pure sciences but subjects like commerce and economics also.

The present volume has been designed keeping in view the needs of the students of commerce, economics and pharmacy. Starting from set theory, logic and number system the book also covers a vast field embracing in its fold algebra (both classical and modern), geometry, trigonometry, matrices, vectors, calculus (both differential and integral). A chapter on applications to economics has also been added.

Different concepts have been explained with the help of carefully selected examples and a large number of exercises have been added to make the students work on their own. Most of the problems have been picked up from different examination papers.

All efforts have been made to keep the book free from errors and we hope that the book will prove helpful to all those interested in the field. We shall be only too glad to receive suggestions and comments for the betterment of the book.

Authors

Contents

4. REAL NUMBERS AND MATHEMATICAL INDUCTION 94-115

5. LINEAR EQUATIONS AND INEQUALITIES 116-124

6. SOLUTION OF EQUATIONS — QUADRATIC AND SIMULTANEOUS 125-159

7. PROGRESSIONS (AP, GP and HP) 160-203

8. SURDS AND INDICES 204-230

9. CUBIC AND BIQUADRATIC EQUATIONS 231-242

10. PERMUTATIONS AND COMBINATIONS 243-264

11. BINOMIAL THEOREM 265-293

12. SEQUENCES AND INFINITE SERIES 294-315

13. LOGARITHMS 316-340

14. INTEREST AND ANNUITIES 341-363

15. MEASUREMENT OF ANGLES 364-374

22. THE STRAIGHT LINE 493-521

23. THE CIRCLE 522-542

24. CONIC SECTIONS 543-593

25. DIFFERENTIATION 594-651

26. APPLICATIONS OF DIFFERENTIATION 652-723

27. INTEGRATION — DIFFERENT METHODS 724-772

28. REDUCTION FORMULAS, DEFINITE INTEGRALS AND APPLICATIONS 773-814

29. MATRICES AND DETERMINANTS 815-911

CHAPTER 1

LOGIC

1. LOGIC

Logic is analysis of language and its study involves the learning of the principles and methods employed in distinguishing valid arguments from those that are not valid. We start our discussion by first examining what we mean by a statement.

2. STATEMENT

In our everyday language we come across statements that may be interrogative, declarative or exclamatory. In Mathematics, however, a declarative sentence which is either true or false is called a *statement.*

Example 1. *Each of the following is a statement:*

(*i*) *Two is an even integer.*

(*ii*) *A quadrilateral is a square.*

(*iii*) *There is no real number x such that* $x^2 = -1$.

(*iv*) *A triangle has four sides.*

Example 2. *None of the following is a statement:*

(*i*) *May God bless you!*

(*ii*) *Who are you?*

The statements in Example 1 are all *simple statements*. A statement which is made up of two or more simple statements is called a *compound statement*. For example, "The sum of three angles of a triangle is equal to two right angles and the sum of the lengths of two sides of a triangle is greater than the length of the third side" is a compound statement.

In the study of logic, letters such as *p*, *q*, *r*, ... are used to represent statements.

3. CONNECTIVES

There are many ways of combining statements *p*, *q*, *r*, . . . to form a compound statement. The words which combine simple statements to form a compound statement are called *connectives*. There are five connectives which are used frequently. These are (*a*) "and" denoted by $\wedge$, (*b*) "or" denoted by $\vee$, (*c*) "not" denoted by ~, (*d*) "implies" denoted by $\Rightarrow$, (*e*) "if and only if " denoted by $\Leftrightarrow$.

NOTES: 1. The connective '$\wedge$' is also called a conjunction.
2. The connective '$\vee$' is also called a disconjunction.
3. The connective '~' is also called a negation.

The connectives $\wedge$ and $\vee$ may be placed between any two statements p and q to form the compound statements $(p \wedge q)$ and $(p \vee q)$ respectively. The compound statement $p \wedge q$ is true if and only if both p and q are true. So, if p is false or q is false or both p and q are false, then $p \vee q$ is true and conversely also.

Again, the compound statement $p \vee q$ is false if and only if both p and q are false. So, if p is true or q is true or both p and q are true, then $p \vee q$ is true and conversely too.

Further, the statement $\sim p$ is true when p is false and $\sim p$ is false when p is true.

4. TRUTH VALUES

If a statement is true, we say its truth value is *T* and if it is false we say its truth value is *F*.

5. TRUTH TABLES

A table that gives truth value of a compound statement is called *Truth Table*. It consists of rows and columns. In the initial columns, we write the possible truth values of the constituent statements and in the last column the truth value of the compound statement is written (which, of course, depends upon the values written in the initial columns). If a compound statement is made up of two simple statements then number of rows will be 2^2 and if it is made up of three statements, then number of rows will be 2^3 (=8) and so on.

Example 3. *Let p be a statement. Construct the truth table for ~p.*

Solution. We know that $\sim p$ is true when p is false and $\sim p$ is false when p is true. We record these facts in the following truth Table 1.

Table 1

p	$\sim p$
T	*F*
F	*T*

Example 4. *Let p and q be two statements. Construct the truth table for the compound statement* $p \wedge q$.

Solution. We know that $p \wedge q$ is true if and only if p is true and q is true. The truth Table 2 of $p \wedge q$ will then be

Table 2

p	q	$p \wedge q$
T	T	T
T	F	F
F	T	F
F	F	F

Example 5. *Construct the truth table for the compound statement* $p \vee q$.

Solution. We know that $p \vee q$ is false if and only if p is false and q is false. The truth Table 3 of $p \vee q$ will then be

Table 3

p	q	$p \vee q$
T	T	T
T	F	T
F	T	T
F	F	F

Example 6. *Construct the truth table for the compound statement*

$$\sim[(\sim p) \wedge (\sim q)]$$

Solution. In the following truth Table 4, the first two columns record all cases for truth values of p and q. To obtain the entries in the third and fourth columns, we use Table 1. The entries in fifth column are obtained by using Table 2. Finally, the entries in fifth column and Table 1 give the entries in sixth column—the truth values of $\sim[(\sim p) \wedge (\sim q)]$.

Table 4

p	q	$\sim p$	$\sim q$	$(\sim p) \wedge (\sim q)$	$\sim[(\sim p) \wedge (\sim q)]$
T	T	F	F	F	T
T	F	F	T	F	T
F	T	T	F	F	T
F	F	T	T	T	F

Example 7. *Construct the truth table for the compound statement*

$$(p \wedge q) \wedge \sim p$$

Solution. In the following truth Table 5 the first two columns record all cases for truth values of p and q. The entries in third and fourth columns are obtained by using Table 2 and Table 1 respectively. Finally, the entries in fifth column are obtained by using third and fourth columns and Table 2.

Table 5

p	q	$p \wedge q$	$\sim p$	$(p \wedge q) \wedge \sim p$
T	T	T	F	F
T	F	F	F	F
F	T	F	T	F
F	F	F	T	F

Example 8. *Construct the truth table for the compound statement*

$$\sim[(\sim p) \vee (\sim q)]$$

Solution. With the help of Table 1 and Table 3, we record the entries in the following truth Table 6 of $\sim[(\sim p) \vee (\sim q)]$.

Table 6

p	q	$\sim p$	$\sim q$	$\sim p \vee \sim q$	$\sim[\sim p \vee \sim q]$
T	T	F	F	F	T
T	F	F	T	T	F
F	T	T	F	T	F
F	F	T	T	T	F

Example 9. *Let p be the statement "The South-west monsoon is very good this year" and q, the statement "rivers are rising." Give the verbal translations for*

(a) $p \vee \sim q$ *(b)* $\sim(\sim p \vee \sim q)$

Solution. *(a)* $\sim q$ means "rivers are not rising". So, $p \wedge \sim q$ means "South-west monsoon is very good this year and rivers are not rising."

(b) $\sim p \vee \sim q$ means "neither South-west monsoon is very good this year nor rivers are rising." So $\sim(\sim p \vee \sim q)$ means. "It is not true that neither South-west monsoon are very good this year nor rivers are rising."

6. EQUIVALENT STATEMENTS

Two statements p and q are said to be equivalent if they have same truth values for all logical possibilities. In this case we write $p \equiv q$. In other words, two statements are equivalent if they have same truth table. For example, the truth tables of $p \vee q$ (Table 3) and $\sim(\sim p \wedge \sim q)$ (Table 4) are same, implying that

$$p \vee q \equiv \sim(\sim p \wedge \sim q)$$

Example 10. *Prove the following relations:*

(a) $\sim(p \vee q) \equiv \sim p \wedge \sim q$ *(b)* $\sim(p \wedge q) \equiv \sim p \vee \sim q$

These are called De Morgan's Laws.

Solution. The following truth Tables 7 and 8 prove the relations (*a*) and (*b*).

Table 7

p	q	$p \vee q$	$\sim(p \vee q)$	$\sim p$	$\sim q$	$\sim p \wedge \sim q$
T	T	T	F	F	F	F
T	F	T	F	F	T	F
F	T	T	F	T	F	F
F	F	F	T	T	T	T

Table 8

p	q	$p \wedge q$	$\sim(p \wedge q)$	$\sim p$	$\sim q$	$\sim p \vee \sim q$
T	T	T	F	F	F	F
T	F	F	T	F	T	T
F	T	F	T	T	F	T
F	F	F	T	T	T	T

Example 11. *Prove the following relations:*

(a) $\sim(\sim p) \equiv p$ *(b)* $\sim(p \vee \sim q) \equiv \sim p \wedge q$

(c) $\sim(\sim p \wedge q) \equiv p \vee \sim q$ *(d)* $\sim(\sim p \vee \sim q) \equiv p \wedge q$

Solution. (*a*) There are two logical possibilities, namely, p is true or p is false. Now, when p is true, $\sim p$ is false, and so $\sim(\sim p)$ is true. Also, when p is false, $\sim p$ is true and so $\sim(\sim p)$ is false.

Therefore p and $\sim(\sim p)$ have same truth values. This proves (*a*).

(*b*) By De Morgan's Law

$$\sim(p \vee \sim q) \equiv \sim p \wedge \sim(\sim q) \equiv \sim p \wedge q \text{ by } (a).$$

(*c*) Also, by De Morgan's Law

$$\sim(\sim p \wedge q) \equiv \sim(\sim p) \vee \sim q \equiv p \vee \sim q \text{ by } (a).$$

(*d*) Again, using De Morgan's Law

$$\sim(\sim p \vee \sim q) \equiv \sim(\sim p) \wedge \sim(\sim q) \equiv p \wedge q \text{ by } (a).$$

Example 12. *If p stands for "He is honest" and q stands for "He is hard working" then give verbal translation for the following compound statements*

(*a*) $\sim(p \wedge q)$ (*b*) $\sim(p \vee q)$

Solution. (*a*) $p \wedge q$ means "He is both honest and hard working. So $\sim(p \wedge q)$ will mean "It is not true that he is both honest and hard working."

(*b*) The verbal translation of $\sim(p \vee q)$ as such is complicated. We know by De Morgan's Law $\sim(p \vee q) \equiv \sim p \wedge \sim q$. So, verbal translation of $\sim(p \vee q)$ in equivalent form is "He is neither honest nor hard working."

7. We will now discuss the other two connectives "⇒" and "⇔".

Consider the statement

"If you work hard you will be successful." Suppose p stands for "You work hard" and q stands for "You will be successful." In symbols, the above statement can be written as $p \Rightarrow q$.

Such statements are called *Conditional Statements*. Here q depends upon p, but p need not depend upon q.

The compound statement $p \Rightarrow q$ is true in every case except when p is true and q is false.

Example 13. *Construct truth table for* $p \Rightarrow q$.

Solution. The truth table of $p \Rightarrow q$ will be

Table 9

p	q	$p \Rightarrow q$
T	*T*	*T*
T	*F*	*F*
F	*T*	*T*
F	*F*	*T*

Example 14. *Suppose p stands for "The triangle is isosceles" and q stands for "Two sides of the triangle are of equal length". Translate the following compound statement into a symbolic form and give its equivalent statement, both in words and symbols.*

"If the triangle is isosceles then two sides of the triangle are of equal length."

Solution. The above compound statement in symbolic form is "$p \Rightarrow q$".

We show that $(p \Rightarrow q) \equiv (\sim q) \Rightarrow (\sim p)$. The following truth Table 10 proves our assertion.

Table 10

p	q	$p \Rightarrow q$	$\sim q$	$\sim p$	$\sim q \Rightarrow \sim p$
T	T	T	F	F	T
T	F	F	T	F	F
F	T	T	F	T	T
F	F	T	T	T	T

So, the equivalent statement in words will be "If two sides of the triangle are not of equal length then the triangle is not isosceles."

Example 15. *Are the following statements equivalent?*

"If the traders do not reduce the prices then the government will take action against them."

"It is not true that the traders do not reduce the prices and government does not take action against them."

Solution. Suppose p stands for "traders do not reduce the prices" and q stands for "government takes action against them."

The first statement in symbolic form is $p \Rightarrow q$ and the second statement is $\sim(p \wedge \sim q)$. We prove their equivalence by constructing the following truth Table 11.

Table 11

p	q	$\sim q$	$p \wedge \sim q$	$\sim(p \wedge \sim q)$	$p \Rightarrow q$
T	T	F	F	T	T
T	F	T	T	F	F
F	T	F	F	T	T
F	F	T	F	T	T

Consider the following statements

"He will be successful if and only if he works hard."

Suppose p stands for "He works hard" and q stands for "He is successful."

Then, the above compound statement in symbolic form will be $p \Leftrightarrow q$.

Such statements are called *Biconditional Statements.*

The compound statement $p \Leftrightarrow q$ is true if and only if both $(p \Rightarrow q)$ and $(q \Rightarrow p)$ are true.

As a consequence of this, we construct the truth table of $p \Leftrightarrow q$.

Example 16. *Construct the truth table for* $p \Leftrightarrow q$.

Solution.

Table 12

p	q	$p \Rightarrow q$	$q \Rightarrow p$	$p \Leftrightarrow q$
T	T	T	T	T
T	F	F	T	F
F	T	T	F	F
F	F	T	T	T

Example 17. *A firm of Chartered Accountants makes the following declaration: An articled clerk from the firm passing the final C.A. examination in the first attempt will be awarded a prize of Rs 100. Five clerks P, Q, R, S, U appeared in the examination and only P, Q could pass. The firm awards prizes not only to them but to R and S also. Is this action logically justified? U claims the prize comparing himself with R and S but the firm refuses. Is this refusal logically justified? How should the statement be worded so that only P and Q will be entitled for the prize.*

Solution. Suppose p stands for "passing the examination in first attempt" and q stands for "getting a prize," then declaration of the firm is a conditional statement $p \Rightarrow q$. It is very clear from truth table of $p \Rightarrow q$ (*see* Table 9) that relationship $p \Rightarrow q$ is false only when p is true and q is false. In other words, if R and S get a prize, the action is logically justified by looking at 3rd row of the truth table. Again U does not get a prize implies statement q is false for U. Since "U has not passed the examination" implies p is false for U, so, 4th row suggests that action is logically justified. Also P and Q get a prize implies q is true for P and Q. Since P and Q have passed the examination implies p is true for P and Q. So, first row suggests that action, P, Q get a prize is logically justified.

Now consider the truth table of $p \Leftrightarrow q$ (*see* Table 12). Since R, S, U fail in the examination implies p is false for R, S, U. If they get a prize, then q is true for them. Third row suggests, it is not correct. If R, S, U do not get a prize, then q is false for them and 4th row suggests it is correct. So, truth table of $p \Leftrightarrow q$ shows that if a person fails, he cannot get a prize. Finally, if

P, Q get a prize then p, q are true for both P and Q and by first row, it is correct. If P, Q do not get a prize, then q is false for P and Q and so by 2nd row, it is not true. So, the truth table of $p \Leftrightarrow q$ shows that only P and Q can get a prize.

Hence the statement should be "Those and only those persons who pass the examination in first attempt will get a prize of Rs 100."

Example 18. *Are the following statements equivalent? Justify! "It is not true that Ashok will get a job if and only if he secures first division."*

"Ashok will not get a job if and only if he secures first division."

Solution. Suppose p stands for "Ashok gets a job" and q stands for "Ashok secures first division." The two statements in symbolic form will then be

$$\sim(p \Leftrightarrow q), \sim p \Leftrightarrow q$$

We prove their equivalence by constructing the truth Table 13.

Table 13

p	q	$\sim p$	$\sim p \Leftrightarrow q$	$p \Leftrightarrow q$	$\sim(p \Leftrightarrow q)$
T	T	F	F	T	F
T	F	F	T	F	T
F	T	T	T	F	T
F	F	T	F	T	F

7. TAUTOLOGY AND CONTRADICTION

A statement is said to be a *tautology* if it is true for all logical possibilities.

A statement is said to be a *contradiction* if it is false for all logical possibilities.

Example 19. *Prove that the statement $p \vee \sim p$ is a tautology while $p \wedge \sim p$ is a contradiction.*

Solution. If p is false then $\sim p$ is true. So, $p \vee \sim p$ is true and $p \wedge \sim p$ is false. If p is true then $\sim p$ is false. So $p \vee \sim p$ is true and $p \wedge \sim p$ is false. These are the only logical possibilities and in each case $p \vee \sim p$ is true while $p \wedge \sim p$ is false. This proves our assertion.

Example 20. $(p \wedge q) \Rightarrow (p \vee q)$ *is a tautology.*

Solution. The following truth Table 14 shows that the compound statement $(p \wedge q) \Rightarrow (p \vee q)$ has truth value T for all logical possibilities and so, it is a tautology.

Table 14

p	q	$p \wedge q$	$p \vee q$	$(p \wedge q) \Rightarrow (p \vee q)$
T	T	T	T	T
T	F	F	T	T
F	T	F	T	T
F	F	F	F	T

Example 21. *$(p \wedge q) \wedge \sim(p \vee q)$ is a contradiction.*

Solution. The following truth Table 15 shows that the compound statement $(p \wedge q) \wedge \sim(p \vee q)$ has truth value F for all logical possibilities and so, it is a contradiction.

Table 15

p	q	$p \wedge q$	$p \vee q$	$\sim(p \vee q)$	$(p \wedge q) \wedge \sim(p \vee q)$
T	T	T	T	F	F
T	F	F	T	F	F
F	T	F	T	F	F
F	F	F	F	T	F

Example 22. *$(p \Rightarrow q) \wedge (q \Rightarrow r) \Rightarrow (p \Rightarrow r)$ is a tautology. This is called* **Transitive law.**

Solution. We construct the truth Table 16 of given compound statement to prove our assertion.

Table 16

p	q	r	$p \Rightarrow q$	$q \Rightarrow r$	$p \Rightarrow r$	$(p \Rightarrow q) \wedge (q \Rightarrow r)$	$(p \Rightarrow q) \wedge (q \Rightarrow r) \Rightarrow (p \Rightarrow r)$
T	T	T	T	T	T	T	T
T	T	F	T	F	F	F	T
T	F	T	F	T	T	F	T
T	F	F	F	T	F	F	T
F	T	T	T	T	T	T	T
F	T	F	T	F	T	F	T
F	F	T	T	T	T	T	T
F	F	F	T	T	T	T	T

Example 23. *If t denotes tautology and p is any statement, then*

(i) $p \wedge t \equiv p$ *(ii)* $p \vee t \equiv t$.

Solution. (*i*) When p is true, $p \wedge t$ is also true (as t is always true) and when p is false, $p \wedge t$ is false. So, p and $p \wedge t$ are equivalent statements.

(*ii*) When p is true, $p \vee t$ is also true and when p is false, $p \vee t$ is true. So, $p \vee t$ is always true. Hence $p \vee t$ and t are equivalent statements.

Example 24. *If c denotes a contradiction and p be any statement, then*

(*i*) $p \vee c \equiv p$ (*ii*) $p \wedge c \equiv c$.

Solution. (*i*) If p is true then $p \vee c$ is clearly true and if p is false, then $p \vee c$ is false (as c is always false). So, $p \vee c$ and p are equivalent statements.

(*ii*) If p is true then $p \wedge c$ is false and again p is false implies $p \wedge c$ is false. So, $p \wedge c$ is a contradiction. Hence $p \wedge c$ and c are equivalent statements.

8. ALGEBRA OF STATEMENTS

We list below some important laws of statements.

(1) **Commutative law.** If p and q are two statements, then $p \vee q \equiv q \vee p$ and $p \wedge q \equiv q \wedge p$

Proof. Obvious.

(2) **Associative law.** If p, q, r are three statements, then

$$(p \vee q) \vee r \equiv p \vee (q \vee r)$$
$$(p \wedge q) \wedge r \equiv p \wedge (q \wedge r)$$

Proof. The following truth Table 17 proves their equivalence.

Table 17

p	q	r	$p \vee q$	$q \vee r$	$p \wedge q$	$q \wedge r$	$(p \vee q) \vee r$	$p \vee (q \vee r)$	$(p \wedge q) \wedge r$	$p \wedge (q \wedge r)$
T	T	T	T	T	T	T	T	T	T	T
T	T	F	T	T	T	F	T	T	F	F
T	F	T	T	T	F	F	T	T	F	F
T	F	F	T	F	F	F	T	T	F	F
F	T	T	T	T	F	T	T	T	F	F
F	T	F	T	T	F	F	T	T	F	F
F	F	T	F	T	F	F	T	T	F	F
F	F	F	F	F	F	F	F	F	F	F

(3) **Identity law.** If t denotes a tautology and c, a contradiction, then for any statement p

$$p \vee t \equiv t, \qquad p \wedge t \equiv p$$
$$p \vee c \equiv p, \qquad p \wedge c \equiv c$$

Proof. See Examples 23 and 24.

(4) **Complement law.** For any statement p,

$p \vee \sim p \equiv t, \qquad p \wedge \sim p \equiv c$

Proof. See Example 19.

(5) **Distributive law.** If p, q, r are three statements, then

(*i*) $p \wedge (q \vee r) \equiv (p \wedge q) \vee (p \wedge r)$

(*ii*) $p \vee (q \wedge r) \equiv (p \vee q) \wedge (p \vee r)$

Proof. We prove (*i*) and leave (*ii*) for the reader to prove the equivalence.

The following truth Table 18 proves our assertion.

Table 18

p	q	r	$p \wedge q$	$p \wedge r$	$q \vee r$	$p \wedge (q \vee r)$	$(p \wedge q) \vee (p \wedge r)$
T	T	T	T	T	T	T	T
T	T	F	T	F	T	T	T
T	F	T	F	T	T	T	T
T	F	F	F	F	F	F	F
F	T	T	F	F	T	F	F
F	T	F	F	F	T	F	F
F	F	T	F	F	T	F	F
F	F	F	F	F	F	F	F

(6) **Idempotent law.** For any statement p

$p \vee p \equiv p, \qquad p \wedge p \equiv p$

Proof. Obvious.

(7) **DeMorgan's laws.** If p and q are two statements, then

$\sim(p \wedge q) \equiv \sim p \vee \sim q$

$\sim(p \vee q) \equiv \sim p \wedge \sim q$

Proof. See Example 10.

(8) **Contrapositive law.** For any statements p and q,

$$(p \Rightarrow q) \equiv (\sim q \Rightarrow \sim p)$$

Proof. See Example 14.

(9) **Law of double negation.** For any statement p, $\sim(\sim p) = p$

Proof. See Example 11.

(10) **Transitive law.** For any statements p, q, r,

$$(p \Rightarrow q) \wedge (q \Rightarrow r) \Rightarrow (p \Rightarrow r) \text{ is a tautology.}$$

Proof. See Example 22.

(11) **Law of addition.** If p and q are two statements, then $p \Rightarrow (p \vee q)$ is a tautology.

Proof. The following truth Table 19 establishes our assertion.

Table 19

p	q	$p \vee q$	$p \Rightarrow (p \vee q)$
T	T	T	T
T	F	T	T
F	T	T	T
F	F	F	T

(12) **Law of simplification.** If p and q are two statements, then

(*i*) $p \wedge q \Rightarrow p$ is a tautology

(*ii*) $p \wedge q \Rightarrow q$ is a tautology

Proof. We leave the proofs to the reader as exercises.

NOTE: Transitive law may also be stated as "If $p \equiv q$ and $q \equiv r$ then $p \equiv r$, for any statements p, q, r."

9. DEDUCTIVE REASONING

The 12 laws listed in "Algebra of Statements" are very useful tools for proving the equivalence of different statements. In this section, we shall prove the equivalence of statements by using these laws only. The method of proof so used is called *deductive method* or *deductive reasoning.*

Example 25. *Prove the following tautology by deductive method* $p \wedge (p \Rightarrow q) \Rightarrow q$.

Solution. We shall assume the following as definition of $p \Rightarrow q$

$(p \Rightarrow q) \equiv \sim(p \wedge \sim q)$ (See Example 15)

Now $p \wedge (p \Rightarrow q) \Rightarrow q$

$\equiv \sim[\{p \wedge (p \Rightarrow q)\} \wedge \sim q]$

$\equiv \sim[\{p \wedge \sim(p \wedge \sim q)\} \wedge \sim q]$

$\equiv \sim[\{p \wedge (\sim p \vee q)\} \wedge \sim q]$ by De-Morgan's law and law of Double Negation

$\equiv \sim[\{(p \wedge \sim p) \vee (p \wedge q)\} \wedge \sim q]$ by Distributive law

$\equiv \sim[\{(c \vee (p \wedge q)\} \wedge \sim q]$ by Complement law

$\equiv \sim[(p \wedge q) \wedge \sim q]$ by Identity law

$\equiv \sim[p \wedge (q \wedge \sim q)]$ by Associative law

$\equiv \sim[p \wedge c]$ by Complement law

$\equiv \sim c$ by Identity law

$\equiv t$

Therefore $p \wedge (p \Rightarrow q) \Rightarrow q$ is a tautology.

Example 26. *Prove by deductive reasoning that following is a tautology.*

$$(p \vee q) \wedge \sim p \Rightarrow q$$

Solution. By definition (as stated in Example 25)

$(p \vee q) \wedge \sim p \Rightarrow q \equiv \sim[\{(p \vee q) \vee \sim p\} \wedge \sim q]$

$\equiv \sim[\{(p \wedge \sim p) \vee (q \wedge \sim p)\} \wedge \sim q]$ by Distributive law

$\equiv \sim[\{c \vee (q \wedge \sim p)\} \wedge \sim q]$ by Complement law

$\equiv \sim[(q \wedge \sim p) \wedge \sim q]$ by Identity law

$\equiv \sim[(\sim p \wedge q) \wedge \sim q]$ by Commutative law

$\equiv \sim[\sim p \wedge (q \wedge \sim q)]$ by Associative law

$\equiv \sim[\sim p \wedge c)]$ by Complement law

$\equiv \sim[c]$ by Identity law

$\equiv t$

Therefore $(p \vee q) \wedge \sim p \Rightarrow q$ is a tautology.

10. ARGUMENT

An argument is the assertion that a statement, called the *conclusion,* follows from other statements, called the *hypotheses*. For example, consider the following three statements.

(1) If he works hard, he will be successful.

(2) He was not successful.

(3) Therefore, he did not work hard.

These three statements, taken together constitute an argument in which the first two statements are hypotheses and the last statement is the conclusion.

If p stands for "He works hard" and q stands for "He is successful," then above argument may be symbolized as:

$$(p \Rightarrow q) \wedge \sim q \Rightarrow \sim p$$

If an argument is a tautology, we say it is *valid argument*.

If an argument is not a tautology, we say it is *invalid argument*.

The following examples will illustrate our point:

Example 27. *Prove that the following argument is valid.*

"If he works hard, he will be successful. He was not successful. Therefore, he did not work hard."

Solution. Suppose p stands for "He works hard" and q stands for "He is successful." The above argument may be symbolized as

$$(p \Rightarrow q) \wedge {\sim}q \Rightarrow {\sim}p$$

We draw the truth Table 20 for this argument and show that it is a tautology. This will prove that the given argument is valid.

Table 20

p	q	${\sim}p$	${\sim}q$	$p \Rightarrow q$	$(p\Rightarrow q) \wedge {\sim}q$	$(p\Rightarrow q) \wedge {\sim}q \Rightarrow {\sim}p$
T	T	F	F	T	F	T
T	F	F	T	F	F	T
F	T	T	F	T	F	T
F	F	T	T	T	T	T

Example 28. *Prove that the following argument is not valid.*

"If it rains, crops will be good. It did not rain. Therefore, crops were not good."

Solution. Suppose p stands for "It rains" and q stands for "crops are good."

The above argument may be symbolized as

$$(p \Rightarrow q) \wedge {\sim}p \Rightarrow {\sim}q$$

We draw the truth Table 21 for this argument and show that it is not a tautology. This will prove that the given argument is invalid.

Table 21

p	q	${\sim}p$	${\sim}q$	$p \Rightarrow q$	$(p\Rightarrow q) \wedge {\sim}p$	$(p\Rightarrow q) \wedge {\sim}p \Rightarrow {\sim}q$
T	T	F	F	T	F	T
T	F	F	T	F	F	T
F	T	T	F	T	T	F
F	F	T	T	T	T	T

Example 29. *Test the validity of following argument. "If my brother stands first in the class, I give him a watch. Either he stood first or I was out of station I did not give my brother a watch this time. Therefore, I was out of station.*

Solution. If p stands for "My brother stands first" and q stands for "I give him a watch" and ~ stands for "I was out of station," then given argument may be written as

$$(p \Rightarrow q) \wedge (p \vee r) \wedge (\sim q) \Rightarrow r$$

This can be proved to be a tautology by drawing a truth table. Hence, given argument is valid.

11. JOINT DENIAL

We introduce a new connective '↓' called *Joint Denial*. If p and q are two statements; then $p \downarrow q$ will be read as 'neither p nor q." The compound statement $p \downarrow q$ is true if and only if both p and q are false.

In the following examples, we will prove that the compound statement in which connective like ∧, ∨, ~ appear, can all be replaced by a single connective ↓. So, the resulting compound statement will have only one connective, namely ↓. This proves very useful in the designing of a computer, as it is much more simple and economical to design a computer where only one operation is to be performed.

Example 30. *Construct the truth table for the compound statement* $p \downarrow q$.

Solution.

Table 22

p	q	$p \downarrow q$
T	T	F
T	F	F
F	T	F
F	F	T

Example 31. *Prove that the following statements are equivalent:*

(i) $\sim p$ *(ii)* $p \downarrow p$.

Solution. The following truth Table 23 will prove that $\sim p$ and $p \downarrow p$ are equivalent.

Table 23

p	$\sim p$	$p \downarrow p$
T	F	F
F	T	T

Example 32. *Show that* $p \downarrow q$ and $\sim p \wedge \sim q$ *are equivalent.*

Solution. The following truth Table 24 will prove our assertion.

Table 24

p	q	$\sim p$	$\sim q$	$\sim p \wedge \sim q$	$p \downarrow q$
T	*T*	*F*	*F*	*F*	*F*
T	*F*	*F*	*T*	*F*	*F*
F	*T*	*T*	*F*	*F*	*F*
F	*F*	*T*	*T*	*T*	*T*

Example 33. *Prove that the following statements are equivalent:*

(*i*) $p \wedge q$ and $(p \downarrow p) \downarrow (q \downarrow q)$ (*ii*) $p \vee q$ and $(p \downarrow q) \downarrow (q \downarrow p)$.

Solution. We draw the truth Tables 25, 26 of (*i*) and (*ii*) to prove the equivalence of the given statements.

Table 25

p	q	$p \wedge q$	$p \downarrow p$	$q \downarrow q$	$(p \downarrow p) \downarrow (q \downarrow q)$
T	*T*	*T*	*F*	*F*	*T*
T	*F*	*F*	*F*	*T*	*F*
F	*T*	*F*	*T*	*F*	*F*
F	*F*	*F*	*T*	*T*	*F*

Table 26

p	q	$p \vee q$	$p \downarrow q$	$(p \downarrow q) \downarrow (p \downarrow q)$
T	*T*	*T*	*F*	*T*
T	*F*	*T*	*F*	*T*
F	*T*	*T*	*F*	*T*
F	*F*	*F*	*T*	*F*

Example 34. *Give an equivalent statement of* $p \Rightarrow q$ *in terms of the connective* $\downarrow$ *only.*

Solution. We know $(p \Rightarrow q) \equiv \sim(p \wedge \sim q)$

By Example 31, $\sim(p \wedge \sim q) \equiv (p \wedge \sim q) \downarrow (p \wedge \sim q)$

and by Example 33, $(p \wedge \sim q) \equiv (p \downarrow p) \downarrow (\sim q \downarrow \sim q)$

Again, by Example 31, $\sim q \equiv q \downarrow q$

Combining these, we have

$(p \Rightarrow q) \equiv \sim(p \wedge \sim q) \equiv (p \wedge \sim q) \downarrow (p \wedge \sim q)$

$$\equiv (p \downarrow p) \downarrow (\sim q \downarrow \sim q) \downarrow (p \downarrow p) \downarrow (\sim q \downarrow \sim q)$$
$$\equiv (p \downarrow p) \downarrow \{(q \downarrow q) \downarrow (q \downarrow q)\} \downarrow (p \downarrow p) \downarrow [(q \downarrow q) \downarrow (q \downarrow q)]$$

12. In the preceding sections, we have been constructing the truth table for a given compound statement. It is also interesting to consider the converse problem, given a truth table to find one or more compound statements having this truth table. We illustrate this by following examples.

Example 35. *Construct one or more compound statements having following truth Table 27.*

Table 27

p	q	r	
T	T	T	T
T	T	F	F
T	F	T	T
T	F	F	F
F	T	T	F
F	T	F	F
F	F	T	T
F	F	F	F

Solution. In last column there are three Ts. Consider the statement $p \wedge q \wedge r$. It satisfies first row. Similarly $p \wedge \sim q \wedge r$ satisfies third row and $\sim p \wedge \sim q \wedge r$ statisfies seventh row. Each of these statements is true only in first, third and seventh row respectively. In all other cases, these statements are false. So, if we consider the compound statement

$$(p \wedge q \wedge r) \vee (p \wedge \sim q \wedge r) \vee (\sim p \wedge \sim q \wedge r)$$

then the truth table of this compound statement will be as given in the problem.

Example 36. *Construct one or more compound statements for the following truth Table 28.*

Table 28

p	q	
T	T	T
T	F	F
F	T	F
F	F	T

Solution. The first row is clearly satisfied by the statement $p \wedge q$ and last row by the statement $\sim p \wedge \sim q$. Each of these statements is true only in first row and fourth row respectively. So, the compound statement

$$(p \wedge q) \vee (\sim p \wedge \sim q)$$

will have the same truth table as shown in the problem.

Note that $p \Leftrightarrow q$ also has the same truth table as given in the problem.

Example 37. *A student is confronted with a true-false exam, consisting of five questions. He knows that his instructor always has more true than false questions and he never has three questions in a row with the same answer. From the nature of first and last question he knows that these must have the opposite answers. The only question to which he knows the answer is number two and this assures him of having all answers correct. What did he know about question two? What are the answers to the five questions?*

Solution. It is very clear that three questions have answers "True" and two have answers "False". Let p be the statement "The answer to question 3 is true," and q, the statement "The answer to question 4 is true." Now, suppose the answer to question number 2 is true. Then p is true (Because if p is false, then there will be two correct answers namely *TTFTF* and *FTFTT*. This is not possible as the answer to question 2 assures him of having all the answers correct). Similarly, if the answer to question 2 is false, then p is false. So, we have the following Table 29.

Table 29

p	*Answer to question 2*
T	*True*
F	*False*

T and *F* indicate truth values of p. Again, if the answer to question 2 is true, then truth value of q is either *T* or *F*.

If truth value of q is *T*, then there will be two correct answers namely *TTFTF* and *FTFTT*.

This is not possible. So, the truth value of the resulting statement is *F*. Again, if truth value of q is *F*, then there will be only one correct answer namely *FTTFT*. So, the truth value of the resulting statement is *T*. Similarly if answer to question number 2 is false, the truth value of resulting statement will be *F* (whatever the truth value of q may be). So, we have the following truth Table 30.

Table 30

p	q	*Answer to question* 2	
T	T	*True*	F
T	F	*True*	T
F	T	*False*	F
F	F	*False*	F

The statement $p \wedge \sim q$ has the truth table as above. So, the student finds that "The answer to question 3 is true and to question 4 is false." This shows answer to question 5 is true which in turn means answer to question 1 is false. Hence answer to question 2 is true.

12. APPLICATIONS TO SWITCHING CIRCUITS

We will now discuss how the theory of compound statements can be applied in Electrical Engineering. As an example we shall develop a theory of simple *switching networks.*

A switching network is an arrangement of wires and switches which connects together two terminals T_1 and T_2. Each switch has two states, "open" and "closed." A closed switch allows the current to pass while the open switch prevents the flow of current. In the following Fig. 1, terminals T_1 and T_2 are connected by a single wire containing a switch S_1. If S_1 is closed, then the current will flow between T_1 and T_2 otherwise it does not flow.

Fig. 1

In the following Fig. 2, the network has two switches S_1 and S_2 in series. The current will flow when both S_1 and S_2 are closed.

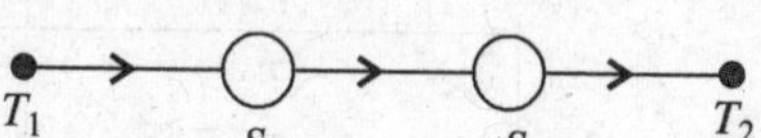

Fig. 2

In the Fig. 3 switches S_1 and S_2 are placed in parallel. The current will flow if any one of S_1 and S_2 is closed.

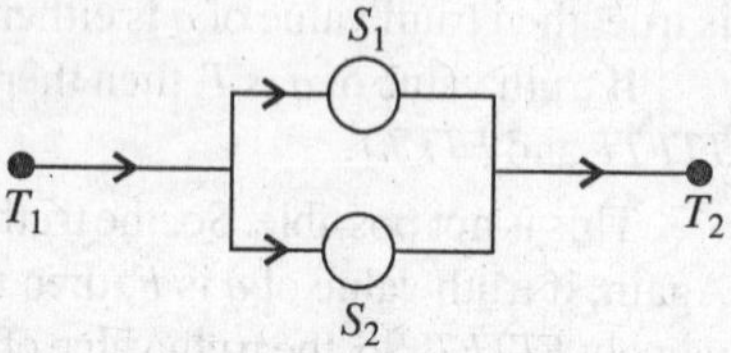

Fig. 3

We now see how the theory of logic can explain the networks shown in Figures 1 to 3. Let p be the statement "S_1 is closed" and q the statement "S_2 is closed." Then in Fig. 1, current will flow if and only if p is true. In Fig. 2, the current will flow if and only if both p and q are true and Fig. 3, the current will flow if and only if at least one of the statements p or q is true.

The network in Fig. 1 is represented by p and in Fig. 2 by $p \wedge q$ and in Fig. 3 by $p \vee q$.

Switches need not always act independently of each other. It is possible that two (or more) switches may be linked together so that they may open or close simultaneously. We denote these switches by the same letter in diagrams. If we represent two switches by letters S_1 and S_1' then it means whenever S_1 is open, S_1' is closed and conversely, whenever S_1' is open, S_1 is closed.

Consider the following network of switches:

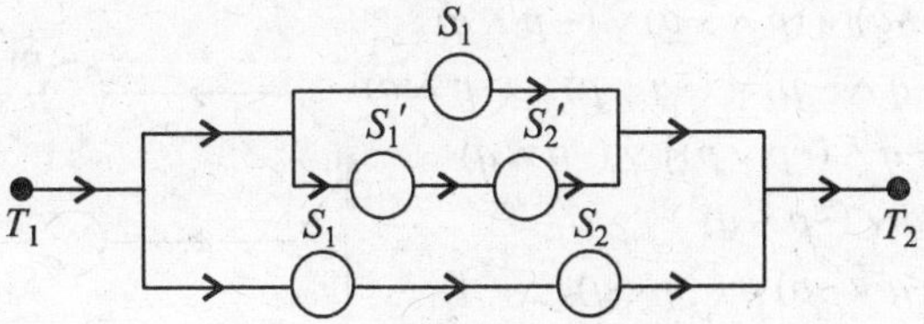

Fig. 4

If p denotes "Switch S_1 is closed" and q denotes "Switch S_2 is closed", then the network in Fig. 4 may be expressed in symbolic form of logic as

$$p \vee (\sim p \wedge \sim q) \vee (p \wedge q)$$

It is very clear from the figure that current will flow if and only if the compound statement $p \vee (\sim p \wedge \sim q) \vee (p \wedge q)$ is true.

These are also switching networks which are placed in series (as networks). For example, in Fig. 5 there are two networks placed in series.

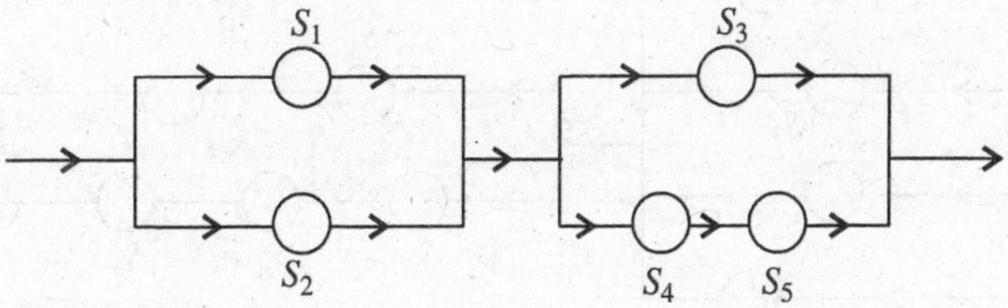

Fig. 5

This may be expressed as

$$(p \vee q) \wedge [r \vee (s \wedge t)]$$

Example 38. *Give an alternate arrangement of the following network such that new network has two switches.* (**L** *is light*).

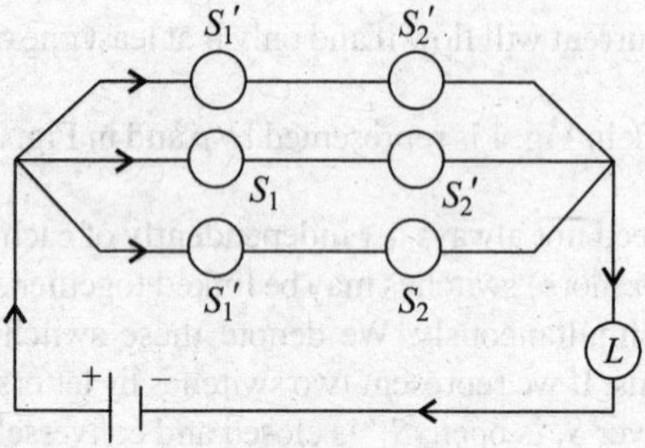

Fig. 6

Solution. The given network may be expressed as

$(\sim p \wedge \sim q) \vee (p \wedge \sim q) \vee (\sim p \wedge q)$

$\equiv (\sim q \wedge \sim p) \vee (\sim q \wedge p) \vee (\sim p \wedge q)$

$\equiv \{\sim q \wedge (\sim p \vee p)\} \vee (\sim p \wedge q)$

$\equiv \sim q \vee (\sim p \wedge q)$

$\equiv (\sim q \vee \sim p) \wedge (\sim q \vee q)$

$\equiv (\sim q \vee \sim p)$

So, two open switches in parallel, will be an alternate arrangement of the given network. The following Fig. 7 shows the alternate arrangement.

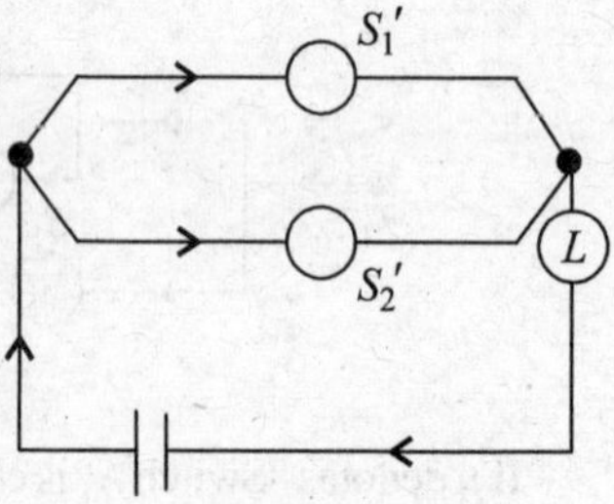

Fig. 7

Example 39. *In the following network there are 10 switches. Give an alternate arrangement with two switches only.*

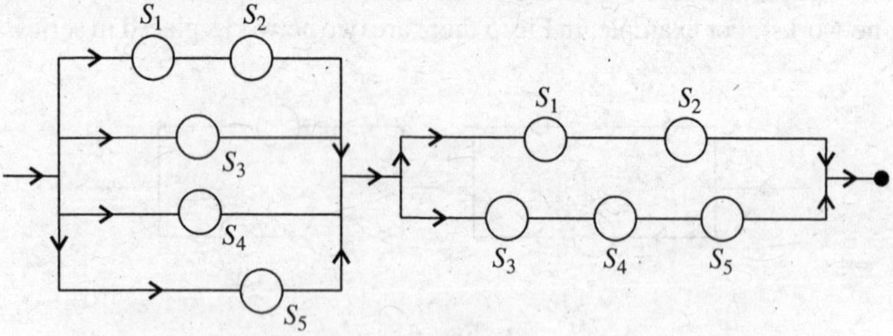

Fig. 8

Solution. If p, q, r, s, t denote "Switches S_1 to S_5 are closed" respectively, then the given network may be expressed as

$$[(p \wedge q) \vee (\sim r \vee \sim s \vee \sim t)] \wedge [(p \wedge q) \vee (r \wedge s \wedge t)]$$

$$\equiv (p \wedge q) \vee [(\sim r \vee \sim s \vee \sim t) \wedge (r \wedge s \wedge t)]$$
$$\equiv (p \wedge q) \vee [\sim(r \wedge s \wedge t) \wedge (r \wedge s \wedge t)] \equiv (p \wedge q)$$

Hence the given network is equivalent to the following:

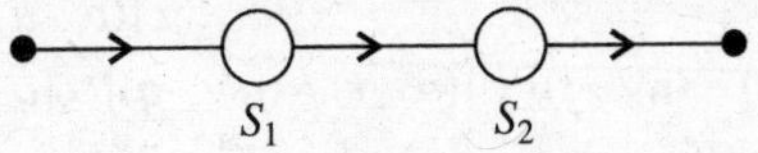

Fig. 9

Note that in this problem there are two networks which have been placed in series.

Example 40. *Construct a network for the following statement:*

$$(p \wedge q \wedge \sim r) \vee [\sim p \wedge (q \vee \sim r)]$$

Solution. Since $p \wedge q \wedge \sim r$ is a network in series which is parallel with $\sim p \wedge (q \vee \sim r)$ which in turn is $\sim p$ in series with a parallel network of $q \vee \sim r$, Fig. 10 illustrates the given network.

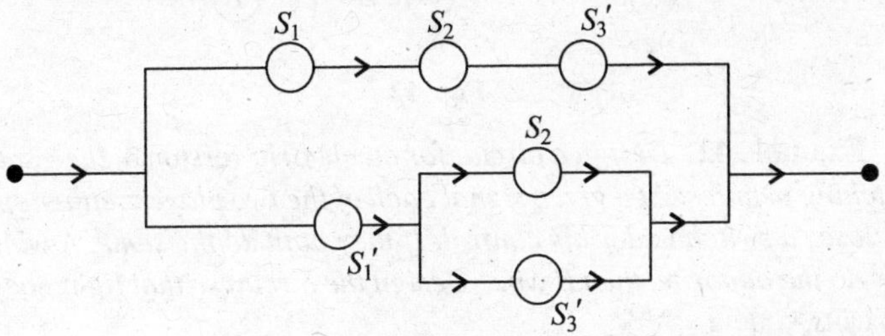

Fig.. 10

Example 41. *Give an alternate arrangement of the following network such that the new arrangement has only five switches.*

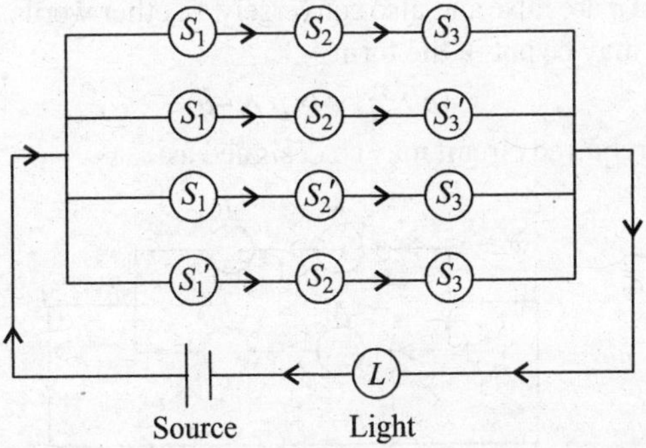

Fig. 11

Solution. The given network may be expressed as

$$(p \wedge q \wedge r) \vee (p \wedge q \wedge \sim r) \vee (p \wedge \sim q \wedge r) \vee (\sim p \wedge q \wedge r)$$
$$\equiv [(p \wedge q \wedge r) \vee (p \wedge q \wedge \sim r)] \vee [(p \wedge q \wedge r) \vee (p \wedge \sim q \wedge r)]$$
$$\vee [(p \wedge q \wedge r) \vee (\sim p \wedge q \wedge r)]$$
$$\equiv [(p \wedge q) \wedge (r \vee \sim r)] \vee [(p \wedge r) \wedge (q \vee \sim q)] \vee [q \wedge r) \wedge (p \vee \sim p)]$$
$$\equiv (p \wedge q) \vee (p \wedge r) \vee (q \wedge r) \equiv [p \wedge (q \vee r)] \vee (q \wedge r)$$

In this equivalent statement, there are only five switches. This equivalent statement may be expressed by the diagram

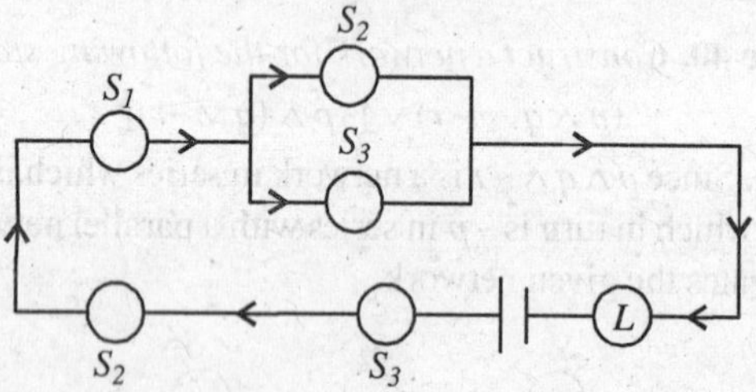

Fig. 12

Example 42. *Design a circuit for an electric version of the game of matching pennies: At a given signal each of the two players either opens or closes a switch under his control. If they both do the same, A wins; if they do the opposite, then B wins. Design the circuit so that light goes on if A wins.*

Also, write in symbolic form the circuit so obtained.

Solution. Suppose p stands for "A opens the switch" and q for "B opens the switch." It is given that light goes on when both p and q are true or both p and q are false and also conversely. In other words, the circuit to be designed may be put in the form

$$(p \wedge q) \vee (\sim p \wedge \sim q)$$

So, the required circuit may be designed as:

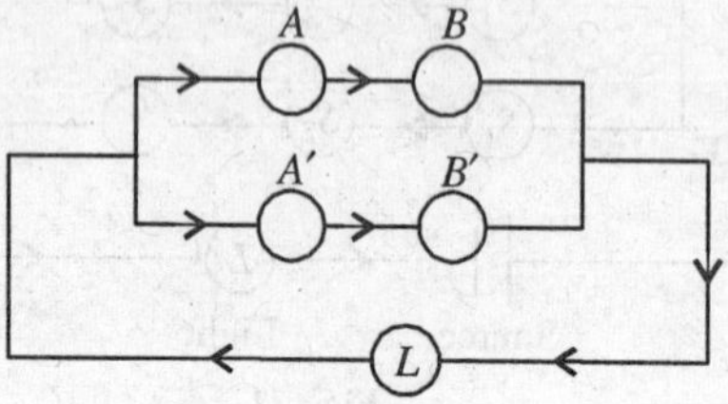

Fig. 13

EXERCISES

1. In each of the following sentences, determine which is a statement (*S*), or not (*N*)
   (*i*) Every rectangle is a square.
   (*ii*) The sum of three angles of a triangle is 180°.
   (*iii*) How are you?
   (*iv*) $2 + 1 = 3$
   (*v*) $\sqrt{2}$ is a rational number.
2. Among the statements in Problem 1, indicate the statements which are true (*T*) or false (*F*).
3. In each of the following, translate the given compound statement into a symbolic form
   (*i*) It is not true that I am not friendly to you.
   (*ii*) The sky is blue and grass is green.
   (*iii*) Ashok reads Indian Express or Statesman.
   (*iv*) If it rains then we will not go to school.
   (*v*) He will be successful if and only if he works hard.
4. Is the statement $p \Rightarrow q$ equivalent to the statement $\sim p \vee q$?
5. Is the statement $p \Leftrightarrow q$ equivalent to the statement $(\sim p \vee q) \wedge (\sim q \vee p)$?
6. If c is a contradiction, prove that $(p \wedge \sim q) \Rightarrow c$ is equivalent to $p \Rightarrow q$.
7. Is the statement $p \wedge (p \Rightarrow q) \wedge (p \Rightarrow \sim q)$, a contradiction?
8. Prove that $(p \Rightarrow q) \Rightarrow [(p \vee r) \Rightarrow (q \wedge r)]$ is a tautology.
9. Is the statement $p \wedge (p \vee r)$ equivalent to p?
10. Prove that $p \vee (p \wedge q)$ is equivalent to p.
11. Is the statement $[(p \wedge \sim q) \Rightarrow (q \wedge \sim q)]$ equivalent to $p \Rightarrow q$?
12. Prove that $\sim(p \wedge q \wedge r) \equiv \sim p \vee \sim q \vee \sim r$.
13. Prove that $\sim(p \vee q \vee r) \equiv \sim p \wedge \sim q \wedge \sim r$.
14. Is the statement $p \Rightarrow q$ equivalent to $(p \wedge r \Rightarrow q \wedge r)$?
15. Is the statement $p \Rightarrow q$ equivalent to $(p \vee r \Rightarrow q \wedge r)$?
16. Prove that $p \Leftrightarrow q$ is equivalent to $(p \wedge q) \vee (\sim p \wedge \sim q)$.
17. Are the following statements equivalent?
    "It is false that she is both beautiful and intelligent."
    "If she is beautiful, she can't be intelligent." **[Hint:** Use Problem 6]
18. Prove that $p \Rightarrow q$ is equivalent to $p \Rightarrow p \wedge q$.
19. Is the statement $p \Rightarrow q$ equivalent to $(p \vee q) \Rightarrow q$?
20. Is the statement $p \Rightarrow q$ equivalent to $\sim p \vee q$?
21. Prove that $(p \Rightarrow q) \vee (p \Rightarrow \sim q) \equiv \sim p$.
22. Prove that $(p \Rightarrow q) \vee (p \Rightarrow r) \equiv p \Rightarrow (q \vee r)$.
23. Prove that $(p \Rightarrow r) \vee (q \Rightarrow r) \equiv (p \wedge q) \Rightarrow r$

24. If p stands for "He is rich" and q stands for "He is hard working," then give a verbal translation of the following

$$\sim(p \wedge \sim q),\ \sim(q \wedge \sim p),\ \sim p \wedge \sim q.$$

25. Prove that $[(p \wedge q) \Rightarrow r] \equiv [p \Rightarrow (q \Rightarrow r)]$ by the deductive method.
26. Prove that $(p \Rightarrow r) \vee (q \Rightarrow s) \equiv [(p \wedge q) \Rightarrow (r \vee s)]$ by deductive reasoning.
27. Prove by deductive method that $(p \vee q) \wedge \sim p \Rightarrow q$ is a tautology.
28. Prove by deductive method that $(p \Rightarrow q) \Leftrightarrow \sim p \vee q$ is a tautology.
29. Prove that following argument is valid:

    "If he is honest then he will be happy. He is not happy. Therefore he is not honest."
30. Prove that the following argument is invalid:

    "If the sun is shining, he will play tennis. Sun was not shining. Therefore, he did not play tennis."
31. Is the following argument valid?

    "If he studies medicine, he will get a good job. If he gets a good job, he will get a good wife. He did not get a good wife. Therefore he did not study medicine."
32. A teacher made the following announcement in the class:

    "Those students who secure first division will get a prize."

    10 students got first division. But the teacher gave away prizes to 15 students. Is this action logically justified? How should the statement be worded so that only 10 students get prizes?
33. Prove that a contradiction is equivalent to $(p \downarrow p) \downarrow p$.
34. Prove that a tautology is equivalent to $[p \downarrow (p \downarrow p)] \downarrow [p \downarrow (p \downarrow p)]$.
35. Prove the following relations

    $\sim(p \wedge q) \equiv [(p \downarrow p) \downarrow (q \downarrow q)] \downarrow [(p \downarrow p) \downarrow (q \downarrow q)]$

    $\sim(p \vee q) \equiv [(p \downarrow q) \downarrow (p \downarrow q) \downarrow [(p \downarrow q) \downarrow (p \downarrow q)]$.
36. Construct one or more compound statements having following truth table.

p	q	r	
T	T	T	F
T	T	F	F
T	F	T	F
T	F	F	T
F	T	T	F
F	T	F	F
F	F	T	F
F	F	F	F

37. Find a statement (consisting of three statements p, q, r) whose truth table has *T*s in the first, second, and last rows and *F*s in other rows.
38. A logician is captured by a tribe of savages and placed in a jail having two exits. The savage chief offers the captive the following chance to escape: "One of the doors leads to a certain death and the other to freedom. You can leave by either

door. To help you in making a decision, two of my warriors will stay with you and answer any one question which you wish to ask of them. I must warn you, however, that one of the warriors is completely truthful while the other always lies." The chief then leaves, believing that he has given his captive only a sporting chance to escape.

After thinking a moment, our quick-witted logician asks one question and then chooses the door leading to freedom. What question did he ask?

[**Hint:** Let p be the statement "The first door leads to freedom" and q the statement "You are truthful."]

ANSWERS

1. (*i*) *S* (*ii*) *S* (*iii*) *N* (*iv*) *S* (*v*) *S*.
2. (*i*) *F* (*ii*) *T* (*iii*) *T* (*iv*) *T* (*v*) *F*.
3. (*i*) $\sim(\sim p)$ where p stands for "I am friendly to you".
   (*ii*) $p \wedge q$ (*iii*) $p \vee q$.
   (*iv*) $p \Rightarrow q$ where p stands for "It rains" and q stands for "We will not go to school."
   (*v*) $p \Leftrightarrow q$.

4. Yes. 5. Yes. 7. Yes. 9. Yes.
11. Yes. 14. Yes. 15. No. 17. Yes.
19. Yes. 20. Yes.

24. "If he is rich, then he is hard working."
    "If he is hard working then he is rich."
    "He is neither rich nor hard working."
31. No.
32. Yes. "A student will get a prize if and only if he secures first division."
36. $p \wedge \sim q \wedge \sim r$.
37. $(p \wedge q \wedge r) \vee (p \wedge q \wedge \sim r) \vee (\sim p \wedge \sim q \wedge \sim r)$.
38. "Does the first door lead to freedom if and only if you are truthful?"

CHAPTER 2

SETS

1. SETS

This chapter deals with the most fundamental items in Mathematics — the Sets. The reader may be disappointed when he learns that ultimate object of study will not be defined here. There is a treatment in set theory in which sets are studied axiomatically. But that axiomatic approach to set theory is beyond the scope of this book. So, in this chapter we shall develop theory relating to sets without defining the notion of a set. But, then such a situation does occur in plane geometry, where we prove theorems about points and lines without precise definitions of these terms. We shall, therefore, content ourselves by accepting the following:

"A *set* is any collection of objects such that given an object, it is possible to determine whether that object belongs to the given collection or not."

Example 1. (*i*) *The set of all integers.*

(*ii*) *The set of all students of Delhi University.*

(*iii*) *The set of all letters of the alphabet.*

(*iv*) *The set of even integers 2, 4, 6, 8.*

Example 2. *Let M be the collection of all those men (and only those men) in a village who do not shave themselves. Given that (i) All men in the village must be clean shaven. (ii) The village barber shaves all those men who do not shave themselves.*

Suppose b denotes the village barber. If b belongs to M, then b does not shave himself. Then by (*ii*) *b shaves himself, a contradiction.*

If b does not belong to M, then b shaves himself. Then by (*ii*) *b does not shave himself, again a contradiction.*

Since we cannot answer "Yes" or "No" to the question, "Is barber himself a member of M?" we conclude that M is not a set.

2. The members of a set are called *elements*. We shall use capital letters to denote sets and small letters to denote elements. If a is an element of the set A, we write $a \in A$ (read as "a belongs to A") and if a is not an element of the set A, we write $a \notin A$ (read as "a does not belong to A"). There are different ways of describing *a* set. For example, the set consisting of elements 1, 2, 3, 4, 5 could be written as $\{1, 2, 3, 4, 5\}$ or $\{1, 2, \ldots, 5\}$ or $\{x \mid x \in N, x \leq 5\}$ where N = set of natural numbers. In fact we always use $\{\ \}$ brackets to denote a set. A set which has finite number of elements is called a *finite set.* Otherwise, it is called an *infinite set.* For example, if A is the set of all integers, then A is an infinite set denoted by $\{\ldots, -2, -1, 0, 1, 2, \ldots\}$ or $\{x \mid x \text{ is an integer}\}$.

3. SINGLETON

A set having only one element is called Singleton. If a is the element of the singleton A, then A is denoted by $A = \{a\}$. Note that $\{a\}$ and a do not mean the same; $\{a\}$ stands for the set consisting of a single element a while a is just the element of $\{a\}$.

4. EQUALITY OF SETS

Two sets A and B are said to be *equal* if and only if every member of A is a member of B and every member of B is a member of A. We express this by writing $A = B$, logically speaking $A = B$ means $(x \in A) \equiv (x \in B)$ or the biconditional statement $(x \in A) \Leftrightarrow (x \in B)$ is true for all x.

NOTES: 1. The order of appearance of the elements of a set is of no consequence. For example, the set $\{1, 2, 3\}$ is same as $\{2, 3, 1\}$ or $\{3, 2, 1\}$ etc.

2. We always write each element of a set only once. For example, $\{2, 2, 3\}$ is not a proper way of writing a set and it should be written as $\{2, 3\}$.

5. SUBSET

Let A and B be two sets. If every element of A is an element of B then A is called a subset of B and we write $A \subseteq B$ or $B \supseteq A$ (read as "A is contained in B" or "B contains A").

Logically speaking, $A \subseteq B$ means $(x \in A) \Rightarrow (x \in B)$ is true for every x.

NOTES: 1. If $A \subseteq B$ and $A \neq B$, we write $A \subset B$ or $B \supset A$ (read as: A is a *proper subset* of B or B is a *proper superset* of A).

2. Every set is a subset and a superset of itself.

3. If A is not a subset of B, we write $A \not\subseteq B$.

6. EMPTY SET OR NULL SET

A set which has no element is called the *null set* or *empty set.* It is denoted by the symbol ϕ.

Example 3. *Each of the following is a null set:*

(*a*) *The set of all real numbers whose square is –1.*

(*b*) *The set of all those integers that are both even and odd.*

(*c*) *The set of all rational numbers whose square is 2.*

(*d*) *The set of all those integers x that satisfy the equation $2x = 5$.*

Example 4. *The empty set ϕ is a subset of every set.*

Solution. Suppose ϕ is not a subset of the set A. This means there exists $a \in \phi$ such that $a \notin A$. This is impossible as ϕ has no element. So, ϕ is a subset of every set.

Aliter. Logically speaking, we want to prove that the conditional statement $(x \in \phi) \Rightarrow (x \in A)$ is true for every x. Since ϕ has no element, the statement "$x \in \phi$" is false. So, the conditional statement $(x \in \phi) \Rightarrow (x \in A)$ is true, which proves the result.

Example 5. *List the following sets (here N denotes the set of natural numbers and Z, the set of integers).*

(*i*) $\{x \mid x \in N \text{ and } x < 10\}$ (*ii*) $\{x \mid x \in Z \text{ and } x < 6\}$

(*iii*) $\{x \mid x \in Z \text{ and } 2 < x < 10\}$.

Solution. (*i*) We have to find the natural numbers which are less than 10. They are 1, 2, 3, 4, 5, 6, 7, 8, 9. So (*i*) can be described as {1, 2, 3, 4, 5, 6, 7, 8, 9}.

(*ii*) We have to find integers which are less than 6. They are all negative integers and the integers 0, 1, 2, 3, 4, 5. So (*ii*) may be described as {. . . , –3, –2, –1, 0, 1, 2, 3, 4, 5}.

(*iii*) We have to find integers lying between 2 and 10. They are 3, 4, 5, 6, 7, 8, 9. So (*iii*) may be described as {3, 4, 5, 6, 7, 8, 9}.

Example 6. *Give the verbal translation of the following sets:*

(*i*) {2, 4, 6, 8} (*ii*) {1, 3, 5, 7, 9, . . .} (*iii*) {–1, 1}.

Solution. (*i*) It consists of all positive even integers less than 10.

(*ii*) It consists of all positive odd integers.

(*iii*) It consists of those integers x which satisfy $x^2 - 1 = 0$.

Example 7. *If $a_1 \neq b_1$ and $\{a_1, b_1\} = \{a_2, b_2\}$ then show that $a_2 \neq b_2$.*

Solution. Let $a_2 = b_2$. Then $a_1 \in \{a_1, b_1\}$ means $a_1 \in \{a_2, b_2\} = \{a_2\}$. So $a_1 = a_2$. Also $b_2 \in \{a_1, b_1\}$ means $b_1 \in \{a_2, b_2\} = \{a_2\}$. So, $b_1 = a_2$. Therefore $a_1 = b_1$ which is wrong, thus $a_2 \neq b_2$.

Example 8. *If $A \subseteq B$ and $B \subseteq C$, then $A \subseteq C$.*

Solution. Let $a \in A$ be any element of A. Then as $A \subseteq B$, $a \in B$.

Also $B \subseteq C \Rightarrow a \in C$.

Thus every element of A belongs to $C \Rightarrow A \subseteq C$.

Aliter. Logically speaking, we want to prove that

$[(x \in A) \Rightarrow (x \in B)] \wedge [(x \in B) \Rightarrow (x \in C)] \Rightarrow [(x \in A) \Rightarrow (x \in C)]$

is true for every x. This follows from transitive Law, (in logic).

Example 9. *If $A \subseteq B$ and $B \subseteq A$, then $A = B$.*

Solution. Since $A \subseteq B$, every element of A is an element of B. Also $B \subseteq A$, means every element of B is also an element of A. This proves $A = B$.

Aliter. Logically speaking, we want to prove

$[(x \in A) \Rightarrow (x \in B)] \wedge [(x \in B) \Rightarrow (x \in A)] \Rightarrow [(x \in A) \Leftrightarrow (x \in B)]$

is true for every x. In other words, $[(p \Rightarrow q) \wedge (q \Rightarrow p)] \Rightarrow (p \Leftrightarrow q)$ is true. Since $p \Rightarrow q$ is true and $q \Rightarrow p$ is true, $(p \Rightarrow q) \wedge (q \Rightarrow p)$ is also true. This also means $p \Leftrightarrow q$ is true. So, $[(q \Rightarrow q) \wedge (q \Rightarrow p)] \Rightarrow (p \Leftrightarrow q)$ is true. This proves the result.

Example 10. *If $A \subset B$ and $B \subseteq C$, then $A \subset C$.*

Solution. If $A = C$, then every element of B is also an element of A (as $B \subseteq A$). But $A \subset B$ means every element of A is also an element of B. Combining these facts, we get $A = B$ which is a contradiction (as A is a proper subset of B). So, $A \neq C$. Clearly every element of A is also an element of C. Therefore, A is a proper subset of C.

Aliter. If $A = C$, then $B \subseteq A$. This means $(x \in B) \Rightarrow (x \in A)$ is true for all x.

Also $A \subset B$ means $(x \in A) \Rightarrow (x \in B)$ is true for all x. Therefore, $(x \in A) \Leftrightarrow (x \in B)$ is true for every x. So, $A = B$, which is not possible as A is proper subset of B. Thus $A \neq C$. A is subset of C, follows from Example 6.

Example 11. *Find all possible solutions for x and y in each of the following cases*

(*i*) $\{2x, y\} = \{4, 6\}$ (*ii*) $\{x, 2y\} = \{1, 2\}$ (*iii*) $\{2x\} = \{0\}$.

Solution. (*i*) Let $A = \{2x, y\}$ and $B = \{4, 6\}$.

Now $2x \in A$ means $2x \in B$. So, $2x = 4$ or $2x = 6$. If $2x = 4$ then $x = 2$. Also $y \in A$ means $y \in B$. So, $y = 4$ or $y = 6$. y cannot be equal to 4. For then A will have only element 4 while B has 4 and 6. Therefore, one solution is $x = 2$ and $y = 6$. If $2x = 6$, then $x = 3$. y cannot be 6. For then, A will have only the element 6. So y must be 4. Therefore, another solution is $x = 3$ and $y = 4$.

(*ii*) Let $A = \{x, 2y\}$ and $B = \{1, 2\}$

$x \in A$ means $x \in B$.

So, $x = 1$ or $x = 2$

If $x = 1$, then $2y = 2$. So, one solution is $x = 1$ and $y = 1$.

If $x = 2$, then $2y = 1$. So, another solution is $x = 2$ and $y = \frac{1}{2}$.

(*iii*) Let $A = \{2x\}, B = \{0\}$

$2x \in A$ means $2x \in B$

So, $2x = 0$ which means $x = 0$.

Therefore there is only one solution $x = 0$.

Example 12. *Find at least one set A such that*

(*i*) $\{1, 2\} \subseteq A \subset \{1, 2, 3, 4\}$ (*ii*) $\{0, 1, 2\} \subset A \subset \{2, 3, 0, 1, 4\}$

Solution. (*i*) Since $\{1, 2\} \subset A$, it means A must have 1, 2 as its elements and some extra member. Again, $A \subset \{1, 2, 3, 4\}$ means that the extra member should be 3 or 4. So $A = \{1, 2, 3\}$ or $A = \{1, 2, 4\}$.

(*ii*) Proceeding as in (*i*), there are two possibilities. Either $A = \{0, 1, 2, 3\}$ or $A = \{0, 1, 2, 4\}$.

Example 13. *Show that the set* $A = \{x \mid x$ *is a real number,* $x^2 = 16$ *and* $2x = 6\}$ *is an empty set.*

Solution. If $x \in A$, then $x^2 = 16 \Rightarrow x = 4$ or -4. Also $2x = 6 \Rightarrow x = 3$. But $x = 4$ or -4. So, A has no element. Thus $A = \phi$.

EXERCISES

1. Write the following sets by listing elements enclosed in brackets { },
   (*i*) A is the set whose elements are first five letters of the alphabet.
   (*ii*) B is the set of all odd integers.
   (*iii*) X is the set of all two digit positive numbers which are divisible by 15.
2. Write the following sets using a statement to designate each:
   (*i*) $A = \{3, 6, 12, 15, 18\}$ (*ii*) $B = \{s, t, u, v, w, x, y, z\}$
   (*iii*) $C = \{1, 3, 5, 7, ..., 2n - 1, ...\}$ (*iv*) $D = \left\{\frac{1}{1}, \frac{1}{2}, \frac{1}{3}, \frac{1}{4}, ..., \frac{1}{n}, ...\right\}$.
3. Determine which of the following sets are equal:
   $A = \{1, 2, 4\}$, $B = \{2, 4, 1\}$, $C = \{4, 1, 2\}$
   $D = \{x \mid x$ is a positive integer less than $5\}$
   $E = \{1, 2, 3, 4\}$.
4. Indicate which of the following sets are finite:
   (*i*) $A = \{x \mid x$ is a positive integer$\}$
   (*ii*) $B = \{x \mid x$ is an even integer lying between 2 and $10\}$
   (*iii*) $C = \{x \mid x$ is a letter of the alphabet$\}$
   (*iv*) D = the set of all students of Delhi University
   (*v*) $E = \{x \mid x$ is an integer less than $10\}$.

5. Let A be the set { 1, 3, 5, 7, 9, 11, 13, 15, 17, 19}. List the following sets:
   (i) $\{x \mid x$ is an element of A and $x + 1$ is even$\}$
   (ii) $\{x \mid x$ is an element of A and $2x$ is an element of $A\}$
   (iii) $\{x \mid x$ is an element of A and $2x < 20\}$.
   (iv) $\{x \mid x$ is not an element of A and $0 < x < 21\}$.
6. Find at least one set A such that
   (i) $\{2, 1, 3\} \subset A \subset \{1, 2, 3, 4, 5\}$ (ii) $\{0, 1, 2\} \subset A \subset \{-1, 0, 1, 2, 3\}$.
7. Find all possible solutions for x and y in each of the following cases:
   (i) $\{2, 3\} = \{2x, y\}$ (ii) $\{x, y\} = \{1, 2\}$ (iii) $\{x, x^2\} = \{9, 3\}$.
8. Show that if $a_1 \neq b_1$, $a_1 \neq a_2$ and $\{a_1, b_1\} = \{a_2, b_2\}$ then $b_1 = b_2$.
9. Show that $\{a\} = \{b, c\}$ if and only if $a = b = c$.
10. List all the subsets of $\{1, 3, 5\}$.
11. List all the subsets of a singleton and the empty set.
12. State the relation if any, between sets A and B in the following:
    (i) $A = \{1, 3, 5, 7, 9, \ldots\}$
    $B = \{3, 9, 15, 21, \ldots, 3(2n - 1), \ldots\}$
    (ii) $A = \{2, 4, 7, 12, 18, 24\}$
    $B = \{1, 3, 7, 11, 16, 22, 29\}$
    (iii) $A = \{1, 2, 3\}$
    $B = \phi$
    (iv) $A = \{x \mid x$ is an even natural number less than $20\}$
    $B = \{x \mid x$ is natural number less than 20 which is divisible by $2\}$
    (v) $A = \{x \mid x$ is an even integer$\}$
    $B = \{x \mid x$ is an integer divisible by $3\}$.
13. Disprove the following statement for any two sets A and B:
    "If $A \subseteq B$, then $B \subseteq A$."
14. Prove that $A \subseteq B$ and $B \subset C$ implies $A \subset C$.
15. Prove that $A \subseteq \phi$ implies $A = \phi$.

ANSWERS

1. (i) $A = \{a, b, c, d, e\}$ (ii) $B = \{\ldots, -5, -3, -1, 1, 3, 5, 7, \ldots\}$
   (iii) $X = \{15, 30, 45, 60, 75, 90\}$
2. (i) $A = \{x \mid x$ is a positive integer less than 19 and multiple of $3\}$
   (ii) $B = \{x \mid x$ is one of the last 8 letters of the alphabet$\}$
   (iii) $C = \{x \mid x$ is a positive odd integer$\}$
   (iv) $D = \{x \mid x$ is a positive real number less than 1 and $x = \frac{1}{n}$ where n is natural number.$\}$
3. $A = B = C$, $D = E$. 4. B, C, D are finite sets.
5. (i) A (ii) ϕ (iii) $\{1, 3, 5, 7, 9\}$ (iv). The set of all real number lying between 0 and 21, except all odd integers between 0 and 20.

6. (*i*) $A = \{1, 2, 3, 4\}$, (*ii*) $\{0, 1, 2, 3\}$.

7. (*i*) $x = 1$, $y = 3$ or $x = \frac{3}{2}$, $y = 2$ (*ii*) $x = 1$, $y = 2$ or $x = 2$, $y = 1$ (*iii*) $x = 3$.

10. ϕ, $\{1\}$, $\{3\}$, $\{5\}$, $\{1, .3\}$ $\{.1, 5\}$, $\{3, 5\}$, $\{1, 3, 5\}$.

11. (*i*) Singleton and ϕ (*ii*) ϕ.

12. (*i*) $B \subseteq A$ (*ii*) no relation (*iii*) $B \subseteq A$ (*iv*) $A = B$ (*v*) no relation.

7. POWER SET

The set of all subsets of a given set A is called the *power set* of A and is denoted by $P(A)$. The name power set is motivated by the fact that "if A has n elements then its power set $P(A)$ contains exactly 2^n elements."

Example 14. *Let* $A = \{1, 2\}$. *Find* $P(A)$.

Solution. Now ϕ is a subset of A. A is also subset of A. $\{1\}$ and $\{2\}$ are also subsets of A. These are all subsets of A. So $P(A) = \{\phi, \{1\}, \{2\}, A\}$. Note $P(A)$ has 2^2 (= 4) elements.

Example 15. *Let* $A = \{1, 2, 3\}$. *Find* $P(A)$.

Solution. Now subsets consisting of one element only are $\{1\}$, $\{2\}$, $\{3\}$. Subsets consisting two elements only are $\{1, 2\}$, $\{2, 3\}$, $\{1, 3\}$. Also ϕ and A are subsets of A.

So $P(A) = \{\phi, \{1\}, \{2\}, \{3\}, \{1, 2\}, \{2, 3\}, \{1, 3\}, A\}$ and the number of elements in $P(A)$ is 2^3 (= 8).

Example 16. *Two finite sets have m and n elements. The number of subsets of the first set is 30 more than the number of subsets of the second. Find m and n.*

Solution: Given: $2^m - 2^n = 30$

Then $m = 5, n = 1$ satisfy above equation.

So, $m = 5, n = 1$.

Example 17. *Let B be a subset of A. Let* $P(A : B) = \{X \in P(A) \mid B \subseteq X\}$. *If* $B = \{1, 2\}$ *and* $A = \{1, 2, 3, 4, 5\}$, *list all the members of* $P(A : B)$.

Solution. Clearly $B \subseteq \{1, 2\}$, $B \subseteq \{1, 2, 3\}$, $B \subseteq \{1, 2, 3, 4\}$, $B \subseteq \{1, 2, 3, 4, 5\}$, $B \subseteq \{1, 2, 4\}$, $B \subseteq \{1, 2, 5\}$, $B \subseteq \{1, 2, 3, 5\}$, $B \subseteq \{1, 2, 4, 5\}$. These give all the elements of $P(A : B)$.

8. OPERATIONS WITH SETS

The reader is familiar with the operations of addition and multiplication in Arithmetic. Given any two numbers, the operations of addition and multiplication associate another number called sum or product of two numbers respectively. In the chapter on logic, the connectives $\wedge, \vee, \sim, \Rightarrow$, $\Leftrightarrow$ were used to associate with any two given statements a new statement called a compound statement. In this section, we will define three operations for associating to any two given sets, a third set. These three operations namely, union, intersection and complementation will be, loosely speaking, analogous to the operations of addition, multiplications and subtraction of numbers respectively.

9. UNION

The union of any two sets A and B is the set of all those elements x such that x belongs to at least one of the two sets A and B. It is denoted by $A \cup B$. Logically speaking, if the biconditional statement $(x \in C) \Leftrightarrow (x \in A) \vee (x \in B)$ is true for all x, then $C = A \cup B$. In other words $(x \in A \cup B) \equiv (x \in A) \vee (x \in B)$.

Example 18. *If* $A = \{1, 2, 3\}$ *and* $B = \{3, 4\}$ *then* $A \cup B = \{1, 2, 3, 4\}$.

Example 19. *Prove that for any sets A and B (i)* $A \subseteq A \cup B$, *(ii)* $B \subseteq A \cup B$.

Solution. (*i*) $x \in A$ means $x \in A \cup B$ by definition. So $A \subseteq A \cup B$

(*ii*) $x \in B$ means $x \in A \cup B$ by definition. So $B \subseteq A \cup B$.

Aliter. (*i*) We want to prove that the conditional statement

$$(x \in A) \Rightarrow (x \in A \cup B) \text{ is true}$$

But this statement is false if only if $(x \in A)$ is true and $(x \in A \cup B)$ is false. Such a situation cannot occur, for $(x \in A)$ is true means $(x \in A) \vee (x \in B)$ is true. Therefore $(x \in A) \vee (x \in B)$ is true and $(x \in A \cup B)$ is false. It means $(x \in A) \vee (x \in B) \Rightarrow (x \in A \cup B)$ is false. This is impossible by definition of $A \cup B$. Similarly, we can prove (*ii*).

Example 20. *If* $A \subseteq B$, *then* $A \cup B = B$ *and conversely, if* $A \cup B = B$, *then* $A \subseteq B$.

Solution. Suppose $A \subseteq B$. Let $x \in A \cup B$. Then $x \in A$, or $x \in B$ or $x \in$ both A and B. If $x \in A$, then $x \in B$ (as $A \subseteq B$). In any case $x \in A \cup B$ means $x \in B$. So, $A \cup B \subseteq B$. We have already proved $A \subseteq A \cup B$. Therefore, $A \cup B = B$ conversely, let $A \cup B = B$. Let $x \in A$. Then $x \in A \cup B$, which means $x \in B$. So $A \subseteq B$.

Aliter. Suppose $A \subseteq B$. We want to show that the biconditional statement $(x \in B) \Leftrightarrow (x \in A) \vee (x \in B)$ is true for every x. But this statement is false if and only if $(x \in B)$ is false and $(x \in A)$ is true. Such a situation cannot occur as $A \subseteq B$.

This proves $A \cup B = B$.

Conversely, if $A \cup B = B$, then we want to show that the conditional statement $(x \in A) \Rightarrow (x \in B)$ is true for every x. This is false if and only if $(x \in A)$ is true and $(x \in B)$ is false. Now $(x \in A)$ is true means $(x \in A) \vee (x \in B)$ is true. Therefore $(x \in A) \vee (x \in B) \Rightarrow (x \in B)$ is false. This is impossible as $B = A \cup B$. This proves $A \subseteq B$.

Example 21. *If $A \subseteq C$ and $B \subseteq C$, then $(A \cup B) \subseteq C$.*

Solution. We want to show that $(x \in A \cup B) \Rightarrow (x \in C)$ is true for every x. This is equivalent to saying that $(x \in A \cup B)$ is true and $(x \in C)$ is false cannot occur together. Suppose $(x \in A \cup B)$ is true. Then $(x \in A) \vee (x \in B)$ is true. This means $(x \in A)$ is true or $(x \in B)$ is true. If $(x \in A)$ is true then $(x \in C)$ is true as $A \subseteq C$. If $(x \in B)$ is true then $(x \in C)$ is true as $B \subseteq C$. In any case $(x \in C)$ is true. So, when $(x \in A \cup B)$ is true, $(x \in C)$ should also be true. This proves our assertion.

Aliter. Let $x \in A \cup B$. This means $x \in A$ or $x \in B$ or $x \in$ both A and B. If $x \in A$, then $x \in C$ (as $A \subseteq C$). If $x \in B$, then $x \in C$ (as $B \subseteq C$). In any case, $x \in C$. So, $x \in A \cup B$ means $x \in C$.

This proves $A \cup B \subseteq C$.

10. INTERSECTION

The intersection of two sets A and B is the set of all those elements x such that x belongs to both A and B and is denoted by $A \cap B$. If $A \cap B = \phi$, then A and B are said to be *disjoint*.

Logically speaking, if the biconditional statement $(x \in C) \Leftrightarrow (x \in A) \wedge (x \in B)$ is true for all x, then $C = A \cap B$. In other words,

$$(x \in A \cap B) \equiv (x \in A) \cap (x \in B)$$

Example 22. (*i*) *If $A = \{1, 2, 3, 4\}$, $B = \{1, 2\}$* then

$$A \cap B = \{1, 2\}$$

(*ii*) *If $A = \{1, 2, 3\}$, $B = \{4, 5\}$*, then

$$A \cap B = \phi$$

Example 23. (*i*) $A \cap B \subseteq A$ (*ii*) $A \cap B \subseteq B$ *for any sets A and B.*

Solution. Let $x \in A \cap B$. Then, by definition $x \in A$ and $x \in B$. So, $A \cap B \subseteq A$ and $A \cap B \subseteq B$.

Aliter. (*i*) We want to show that

$$(x \in A \cap B) \Rightarrow (x \in A) \text{ is true for all } x.$$

We have to only consider the case when $(x \in A \cap B)$ is true and $(x \in A)$ is false. Now $(x \in A)$ is false shall mean $(x \in A) \cap (x \in B)$ is false and so $(x \in A \cap B) \Rightarrow (x \in A) \cap (x \in B)$ is also false which is impossible by definition of $(A \cap B)$. This proves the result.

(*ii*) We want to show that

$$(x \in A \cap B) \Rightarrow (x \in B) \text{ is true for all } x.$$

The only doubtful case is when $(x \in A \cap B)$ is true and $(x \in B)$ is false. Such a case is not possible as above by definition of $A \cap B$. This proves (*ii*).

Example 24. *If $A \subseteq B$ and $A \subseteq C$, then*

$$A \subseteq (B \cap C).$$

Solution. Let $x \in A$. Then $x \in B$ and $x \in C$ (as $A \subseteq B$ and $A \subseteq C$). So, $x \in B \cap C$.

This proves $A \subseteq B \cap C$.

Aliter. We want to show that

$$(x \in A) \Rightarrow (x \in B \cap C) \text{ is true for all } x.$$

The only doubtful case is when $(x \in A)$ is true and $(x \in B \cap C)$ is false.

Now $(x \in A)$ is true means $(x \in B)$ is also true (as $A \subseteq B$). Also $(x \in C)$ is true (as $A \subseteq C$). This mens $(x \in B) \cap (x \in C)$ is true and so $(x \in B \cap C)$ is true. This proves the result.

Example 25. $A \cup B = A \cap B$ if and only if $A = B$.

Solution. Suppose $A \cup B = A \cap B$. Let $x \in A$. Then $x \in A \cup B$ and so $x \in A \cap B$. Therefore, $x \in B$. This proves $A \subseteq B$. Similarly $B \subseteq A$ and so $A = B$.

Aliter. Suppose $A \cup B = A \cap B$

Then $(x \in A) \equiv (x \in A) \cap [(x \in A) \vee (x \in B]$ Absorption law

$$\begin{aligned}
&\equiv (x \in A) \wedge [(x \in A \cup B)] \\
&\equiv (x \in A) \wedge [x \in A \cap B)] \\
&\equiv [(x \in A) \wedge (x \in A)] \wedge (x \in B) \\
&\equiv (x \in A) \wedge (x \wedge B) \\
&\equiv (x \in A \cap B) \\
&\equiv (x \in A \cup B) \\
&\equiv (x \in B) \vee (x \in A) \\
&\equiv (x \in B) \vee [(x \in A) \cup (x \in A)] \\
&\equiv (x \in B) \vee [(x \in B \cup A] \\
&\equiv (x \in B) \vee [x \in A \wedge B] \\
&\equiv (x \in B) \vee [x \in A) \wedge (x \in B)] \\
&\equiv [(x \in B) \vee (x \in A)] \wedge (x \in B] \\
&\equiv (x \in B) \text{ Absorption law}
\end{aligned}$$

This proves $A = B$.

Conversely, if $A = B$, then

$$\begin{aligned}(x \in A \cup B) &\equiv (x \in A) \cup (x \in B)\\ &\equiv (x \in B) \cup (x \in B)\\ &\equiv (x \in B)\\ &\equiv (x \in B) \cap (x \in B)\\ &\equiv (x \in A) \cap (x \in B)\\ &\equiv (x \in A \cap B)\end{aligned}$$

NOTE: Absorption laws in logic mean the following:

(i) $p \cap (p \cup r) \equiv p$ (ii) $p \cup (p \cap r) \equiv p$.

Example 26. *If* $A \cup B = A \cup C$ *and* $A \cap B = A \cap C$, *show that* $B = C$.

Solution: Let $b \in B$. Then $b \in A \cup B \Rightarrow b \in A \cup C$. So, $b \in A$ or $b \in C$. If $b \in A$, then $b \in A \cap B \Rightarrow b \in A \cap C \Rightarrow b \in C$.

Therefore, $B \subseteq C$. Similarly $C \subseteq B$. Thus, $B = C$.

Example 27. *Let* $A = \{2n \mid n \text{ is an integer}\}, B = \{3m \mid m \text{ is an integer}\}$ *Show that* $A \cap B = \{6r \mid r \text{ is an integer}\}$.

Solution: $x \in A \cap B \Rightarrow x \in A$ and $x \in B \Rightarrow 2$ divides x and 3 divides $x \Rightarrow 6$ divides $x \Rightarrow x$ is an integral multiple of $6 \Rightarrow x \in \{6r \mid r \text{ is an integer}\}$. Conversely, let $x = 6r$. Then 2 divides x and 3 divides $x \Rightarrow x$ is multiple of 2 as well as $3 \Rightarrow x \in A \cap B$.

11. UNIVERSAL SET

Throughout this book, whenever we talk of a set, we shall assume it to be a subset of a fixed set U. This fixed set U will be called The Universal Set.

12. COMPLEMENTS

If A and B are two sets then complement of B relative to A is the set of all those element $x \in A$ such that $x \notin B$ and is denoted by $A - B$. Logically speaking, if for a set C the biconditional statement $(x \in C) \Leftrightarrow (x \in A) \cap (x \notin B)$ is true for all x, then $C = A - B$. In other words, if $(x \in C) \equiv (x \in A) \wedge (x \notin B)$ then C is called the complement of B relative to A.

NOTES: 1. It is very clear from the above definition that $A - B$ is a subset of A.

2. Whenever we say complement of B we mean, complement of B relative to the universal set U. In such case, we denote complement of B by B'.
So, $B' = U - B$.

Example 28. *If* $A = \{1, 2, 3, 4\}$ *and* $B = \{3, 4, 5\}$ *then* $A - B = \{1, 2\}$.

Example 29. *Show that* $A - B = A \cap B'$.

Solution. Let $x \in A - B$. This means $x \in A$ and $x \notin B$. By definition of the universal set $A - B \subseteq U$. So, $x \in U$. Therefore $x \in U$, $x \notin B$, implies $x \in B'$. This proves $A - B \subseteq A \cap B'$. Again if $x \in A \cap B'$, then $x \in A$ and $x \in B'$. Now $x \in B'$ implies $x \notin B$. So $x \in A - B$. This proves $A \cap B' \subseteq A - B$.

Therefore $A - B = A \cap B'$.

Aliter.
$$\begin{aligned} (x \in A - B) &\equiv (x \in A) \wedge (x \notin B) \\ &\equiv (x \in A \wedge U) \wedge (x \notin B) \text{ as } A \wedge U = A \\ &\equiv [(x \in A) \wedge (x \in U)] \wedge (x \notin B) \\ &\equiv [(x \in A) \wedge [(x \in U) \wedge (x \notin B)] \\ &\equiv [(x \in A) \wedge (x \in B')] \end{aligned}$$

This proves $A - B = A \cap B'$.

Example 30. $A \subseteq B$ *if and only if* $B' \subseteq A'$.

Solution. Suppose $A \subseteq B$. Let $x \subseteq B'$. Then $x \in U$ and $x \notin B$. Now $x \notin B$ implies $x \notin A$ (as $A \subseteq B$). Therefore $x \in U$ and $x \notin A$ implies $x \in A'$. This proves $B' \subseteq A'$. Conversely, let $B' \subseteq A'$. Let $x \in A$. Then $x \notin A$. Now $x \notin A'$ implies $x \notin B'$ (as $B' \subseteq A'$). This means $x \in B$. So, $A \subseteq B$.

Aliter. Now $(x \in A) \Rightarrow (x \in B)$
$$\begin{aligned} &\equiv \sim (x \in B) \Rightarrow \sim (x \in A) \\ &\qquad \text{(by Contrapositive law in logic)} \\ &\equiv (x \notin B) \Rightarrow (x \notin A) \\ &\equiv (x \in B') \Rightarrow (x \in A') \end{aligned}$$

Suppose $A \subseteq B$. Then $(x \in A) \Rightarrow (x \in B)$ is true for all x. By above, $(x \in B') \Rightarrow (x \in A')$ is true for all x. This means $B' \subseteq A'$. Conversely, suppose $B' \subseteq A'$. Then $(x \in B') \Rightarrow (x \in A')$ is true for all x. By above $(x \in A) \Rightarrow (x \in B)$ is true for all x. This implies $A \subseteq B$. Hence the result follows.

EXERCISES

1. If a set A has 101 elements, find the number of subsets of A having odd number of elements.
   [**Hint.** Use the fact that $C_0 + C_2 + C_4 + \ldots = C_1 + C_3 + \ldots$]
2. What are the elements of the power set of the set $\{1, \{2, 3\}\}$?
3. Perform the indicated operations on
   $$A = \{a, b, c, d, e, f\}$$

$B = \{a, e, i, o, u\}$

$C = \{m, n, o, p, q, r, s, t, u\}$

(*i*) $A \cup B$ (*ii*) $A \cap B$ (*iii*) $A \cup B \cup C$ (*iv*) $A \cap B \cap C$.

4. If $A = \{1, 2, 3, 4, 5\}$, $B = \{2, 4, 6, 8, 10\}$, $C = \{3, 6, 9, 12, 15\}$
find (*i*) $(A \cup B) \cap C$
(*ii*) $A \cup (B \cap C)$
(*iii*) $(A \cap C) \cup B$.

5. If $A = \{1, 2, 3, 4\}$, $B = \{3, 4, 5, 6\}$, $C = \{4, 5, 6, 7\}$
find (*i*) $A - B$ (*ii*) $(A \cup B) - C$
(*iii*) $A - (B \cap C)$ (*iv*) $(A \cap B) - (B \cup C)$.

6. If $U = \{1, 2, 3, 4, 5, 6, 7, 8, 9, 10\}$
$A = \{1, 4, 7, 10\}$
$B = \{2, 5, 8\}$
find (*i*) A' (*ii*) B' (*iii*) $A \cap B'$ (*iv*) $A' \cap B$ (*v*) $A' \cap B'$.

7. Prove that $(A \cap B) \cup C = A \cap (B \cup C)$ if and only if $C \subseteq A$.

8. Prove that if $A \subseteq B$ then $P(A) \subseteq P(B)$.

9. If A and B are two sets, prove that $A - B = A - (B \cap A)$.

10. For any sets A and B, prove or disprove that
$P(A) \cap P(B) = P(A \cap B)$
$P(A) \cup P(B) = P(A \cup B)$.

ANSWERS

1. 2^{100}.
2. ϕ, $\{1\}$, $\{2, 3\}$, $\{\{1\}, \{2, 3\}\}$
3. (*i*) $\{a, b, c, d, e, f, i, o, u\}$, (*ii*) $\{a, e\}$
(*iii*) $\{a, b, c, d, e, f, i, o, u, m, n, p, q, r, s, t\}$, (*iv*) ϕ
4. (*i*) $\{6\}$, (*ii*) $\{1, 2, 3, 4, 5, 6\}$, (*iii*) $\{2, 3, 4, 6, 8, 10\}$
5. (*i*) $\{1, 2\}$, (*ii*) $\{1, 2, 3\}$, (*iii*) $\{1, 2, 3\}$
6. (*i*) $\{2, 3, 5, 6, 8, 9\}$, (*ii*) $\{1, 3, 4, 6, 7, 9, 10\}$
(*iii*) $\{1, 4, 7, 10\}$, (*iv*) $\{2, 5, 8\}$, (*v*) $\{3, 6, 9\}$.

13. ALGEBRA OF SETS

We list below some of the important laws of sets.

1. *Laws of Idempotence.* For any set A

$$A \cup A = A \text{ and } A \cap A = A$$

Proof. Obvious.

2. *Commutative laws.* For any sets A and B

$$A \cup B = B \cup A, A \cap B = B \cap A$$

Proof. Obvious.

3. *Associative laws.* For any three sets *A*, *B*, *C*

(*i*) $A \cup (B \cup C) = (A \cup B) \cup C$

(*ii*) $A \cap (A \cap C) = (A \cap B) \cap C.$

Proof. (*i*) We want to show that

$$[x \in A \cup (B \cup C)] \Leftrightarrow [x \in (x \cup B) \subset C] \text{ is true for all } x$$

Now by definition,

$$[x \in A \cup (B \cup C)] \equiv [x \in A) \cup \{x \in B) \cup (x \in C\}]$$

and $\quad [x \in (A \cup B) \cup C] \equiv [\{x \in A) \cup (x \in B)\} \cup (x \in C)]$

So, by associative law in logic, the result (*i*) follows.

Similarly, we can prove (*ii*).

We leave it to the reader to give an alternative proof of the above without using logic.

4. *Distributive laws.* For any three sets *A*, *B*, *C*

(*i*) $A \cap (B \cup C) = (A \cap B) \cup (A \cup C)$

(*ii*) $A \cup (B \cap C) = (A \cup B) \cap (A \cup C)$

Proof. (*i*) Let $x \in A \cap (B \cup C)$. This implies $x \in A$ and $x \in B \cup C$. Now, $x \in B \cup C$ implies $x \in B$ or $x \in C$ or $x \in$ both *B* and *C*. If $x \in B$, then $x \in A \cap B$. If $x \in C$, then $x \in A \cap C$. In any case $x \in (A \cap B) \cup (A \cap C)$.

So $A \cap (B \cup C) \subseteq (A \cap B) \cup (A \cap C)$.

Similarly $(A \cap B) \cup (A \cap C) \subseteq A \cap (B \cup C)$. This proves (*i*).

Similarly, we can prove (*ii*)

Aliter. $x \in [A \cap (B \cup C)] \equiv [(x \in A) \wedge (x \in B \cup C)]$

$\equiv [(x \in A) \wedge \{(x \in B) \vee (x \in C)\}]$

$\equiv [(x \in A) \wedge (x \in B)] \vee [(x \in A) \subset (x \in C)]$

by distributive law of logic

$\equiv [x \in (A \cap B)] \cup [x \in (A \cap C)]$

$\equiv [x \in (A \cap B) \cup (A \cap C)]$

So, $\qquad A \wedge (B \cup C) = (A \cap B) \cup (A \cap C)$

Similarly we can prove (*ii*) by logic.

5. *De-Morgan's laws.* For any two sets *A* and *B*.

(*i*) $(A \cup B)' = A' \cap B'$

(*ii*) $(A \cap B)' = A' \cup B'$

Proof. (*i*) Let $x \in (A \cup B)'$. This implies $x \notin A \cup B$ and $x \in U$. Now $x \notin A \cup B$ implies $x \notin A$ and $x \notin B$. But $x \notin A$ and $x \in U$ implies $x \in A'$ and $x \notin B$ and $x \in U$ implies $x \in B'$. Therefore, $x \in A' \cap B'$ and so $(A \cup B') \subseteq A' \cap B'$. Similarly $(A' \cap B') \subseteq (A \cup B)'$.

This proves $(A \cup B)' = A' \cap B'$.

Alternative proof of (*i*) using logic:

Now $$x \in (A \cup B)' \equiv \sim[(x \in (A \cup B)]$$
$$\equiv \sim [(x \in A) \vee (x \in B)]$$
$$\equiv \sim (x \in A) \wedge \sim (x \in B)$$
$$\equiv (x \notin A) \wedge (x \notin B)$$
$$\equiv (x \in A') \wedge (x \in B')$$
$$\equiv (x \in A' \cap B')$$

Therefore, $(A \cup B)' = A' \cap B'$.

We leave the proof of (*ii*) for the readers.

Example 31. *Let A, B, C be any three sets. Prove that*

$$A \cap (B - C) = (A \cap B) - (A \cap C).$$

Solution. $(A \cap B) - (A \cap C) = (A \cap B) \cap (A \cap C)'$

$= (A \cap B) \cap (A' \cup C')$

by De Morgan's law

$= [(A \cap B) \cap A'] \cup [(A \cap B) \cap C']$

Distributive law

$= [(A \cap A') \cap B] \cup [(A \cap B) \cap C']$

Associative law

$= [\phi \cap B] \cup [A \cap (B \cap C')]$

$= \phi \cup [A \cap (B \cap C')]$

$= A \cap (B \cap C') \equiv A \cap (B - C)$.

Example 32. *For any sets A and B, show that*

$$(A - B) \cup (B - A) = (A \cup B) - (A \cap B).$$

Solution. $(A - B) \cup (B - A) = (A \cup B) \cap (A \cap B)'$

$= (A \cup B) \cap (A' \cup B')$

De-Morgan's law

$= [(A \cup B) \cap A'] \cup [(A \cup B) \cap B']$

Distributive law

$= [(A \cap A') \cup (B \cap A')] \cup [(A \cap B') \cup (B \cap B')]$

$= [\phi \cup (B \cap A')] \cup [(A \cap B') \cup \phi]$

$= (B \cap A') \cup (A \cap B')$

$= (B - A) \cup (A - B)$

$= (A - B) \cup (B - A)$, Commutative law

14. VENN DIAGRAMS

To illustrate the various set operations, we introduce diagrams called *Venn diagrams* after John Venn (1834 – 1883). We shall represent the Universal Set by the points in and on a rectangle and subsets *A*, *B*, *C*, . . .by points in and on the circles or ellipses drawn inside the rectangle. In Fig. 1, the shaded portion represents $A \cap B$.

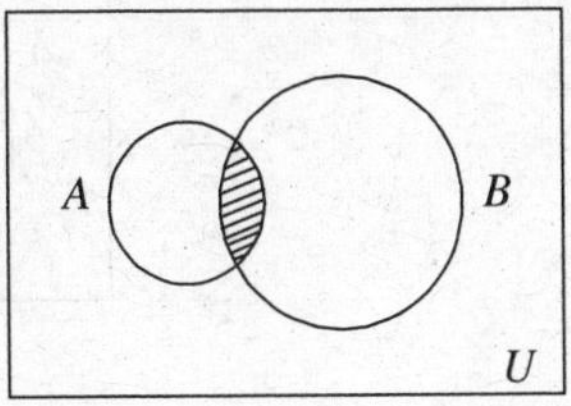

Fig. 1

In Fig. 2, the shaded portion represents $A \cup B$.

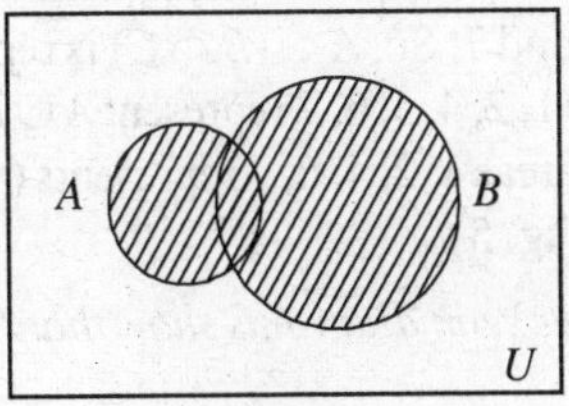

Fig. 2

In Fig. 3, the shaded portion represents A'.

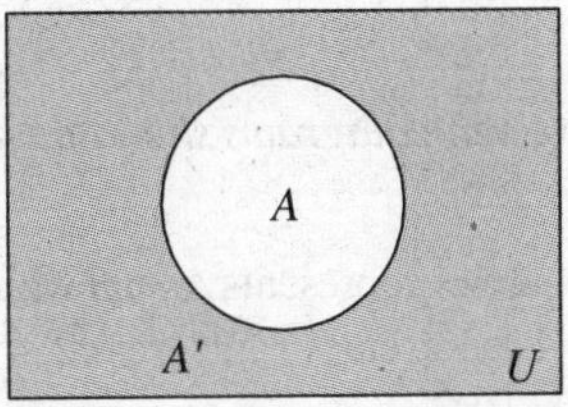

Fig. 3

In Fig. 4, the shaded portion represents $A - B$.

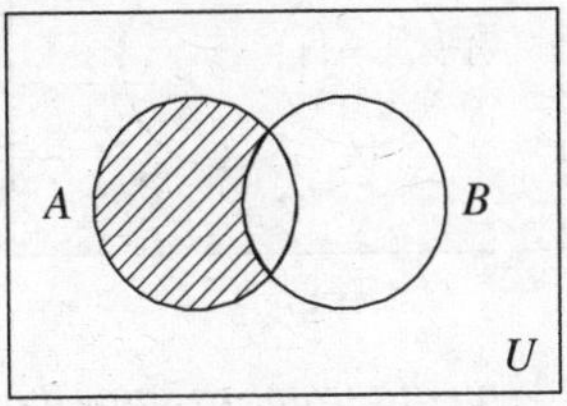

Fig. 4

In Fig. 5, three sets *A*, *B*, *C* divide the universal set *U* into 8 parts, 8th part not numbered in the diagram.

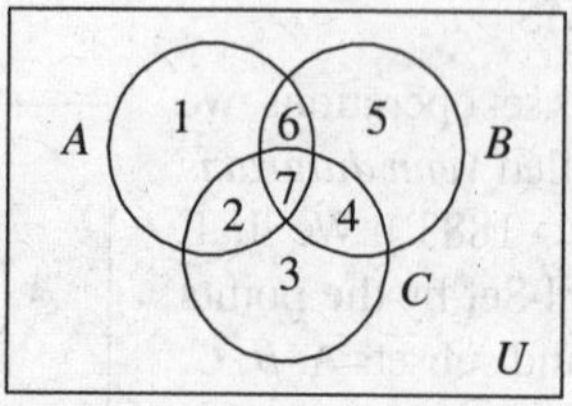

Fig. 5

Example 33. *Prove that* $A \cup (B \cap C) = (A \cup B) \cap (A \cup C)$ *using Venn diagrams.*

Solution. Now $B \cap C$ is represented by areas 4 and 7, and A is represented by areas 1, 2, 6 and 7. So, $A \cup (B \cap C)$ is represented by areas 1, 2, 4, 6 and 7. Again, areas 1, 2, 4, 5, 6, 7 represent $A \cup B$ and areas 1, 2, 3, 4, 6, 7 represent $A \cup C$. So, areas 1, 2, 4, 6, 7 represents $(A \cup B) \cap (A \cup C)$. This proves our assertion (Fig. 5).

Example 34. *Using Venn diagrams show that* $A - (B \cup C) = (A - B) \cup (A - C)$.

Solution. In Fig. 5, areas 2, 3, 4, 5, 6, 7 represent $B \cup C$. Therefore area 1 represents $A - (B \cup C)$. Now areas, 1, 2 represent $A - B$ and areas 1, 6 represent $A - C$. So, area 1 represents $(A - B) \cap (A - C)$. This proves the result.

Example 35. *Using Venn diagrams show that for any two sets A and B* $(A \cup B)' = A' \cup B'$.

Solution. In Fig. 6, area 1 represents $A \cap B$ while areas 2, 3, 4 represent $(A \cap B')$. Again areas 3, 4 represent A' and areas 2, 4 represent B'. Therefore areas 2, 3, 4 represent $A' \cup B'$.

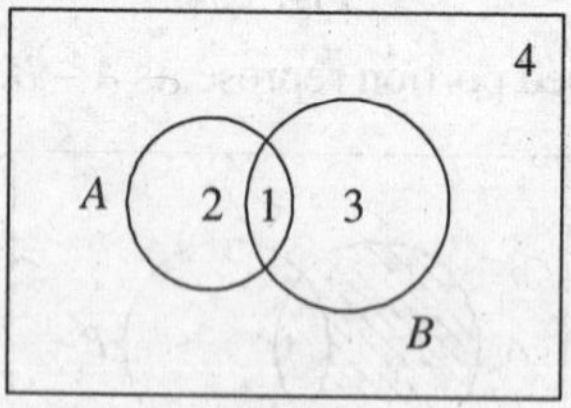

Fig. 6

Example 36. *Use Venn diagrams to show that for any sets A and B*

$$A \cup B = A \cup (B - A)$$

Solution. In Fig. 6, areas 1, 2, 3 represent $A \cup B$. Also areas 1, 2 represent A and areas 3 represents $B - A$. So, areas 1, 2, 3 represent $A \cup (B - A)$. This proves the result.

15. APPLICATIONS OF SET THEORY

If A is a finite set, then we shall denote the number of elements in A by $n(A)$. If A and B are two finite sets, then it is very clear from the Venn diagram of $A - B$ that

$$n(A - B) = n(A) - n(B \cap A)$$

Suppose A and B are two finite sets such that $A \cap B = \phi$. Then clearly, the number of elements in $A \cup B$ is the sum of number of elements in A and the number of elements in B

i.e., $$n(A \cup B) = n(A) + n(B) \text{ if } A \cap B = \phi$$

To find the number of elements in $A \cup B$, in case $A \cap B \neq \phi$, we proceed as follows: We know that for any two sets A and B

$$A \cup B = A \cup (B - A) \qquad \text{(See Example 36)}$$

Here $A \cap (B - A) = \phi$

Therefore, $n(A \cup B) = n(A) + n(B - A)$

$$= n(A) + n(B) - n(A \cap B)$$

Note that, from the definition of empty set it follows that $n(\phi) = 0$.

So, we have proved the following:

"If A and B are two finite sets, then

$$n(A \cup B) = n(A) + n(B) - n(A \cap B)\text{"}$$

Similarly, if A, B, C are three finite sets, then

$$\begin{aligned} n(A \cup B \cup C) &= n(A \cup B) + n(C) - n[(A \cup B) \cap C] \\ &= n(A) + n(B) - n(A \cap B) + n(C) - n[(A \cup B) \cap C] \\ &= n(A) + n(B) + n(C) - n(A \cap B) - n[(A \cap C) \cup (B \cap C)] \\ &= n(A) + n(B) + n(C) - n(A \cap B) - [n(A \cap C) \\ &\qquad + n(B \cap C) - n[(A \cap C) \cap (B \cap C)]] \\ &= n(A) + n(B) + n(C) - n(A \cap B) - n(A \cap C) - n(B \cap C) \\ &\qquad + n(A \cap B \cap C) \text{ as } A \cap C \cap B \cap C = A \cap B \cap C \end{aligned}$$

We now make use of these two results in the following problems.

Example 37. *In a recent survey of 400 students in a school, 100 were listed as smokers and 150 as chewers of gum; 75 were listed as both smokers and gum chewers. Find out how many students are neither smokers nor gum chewers.*

Solution. Let U be the set of students questioned. Let A be the set of smokers, and B the set of gum chewers.

Then $n(U) = 400, n(A) = 100, n(B) = 150, n(A \cap B) = 75$

We want to find out $n(A' \cap B')$

Now $A' \cap B' = (A \cup B)' = U - (A \cup B)$

Therefore,

$$n(A' \cap B') = n\,[U - (A \cup B)]$$
$$= n(U) - n[A \cup B) \cap U]$$
$$= n(U) - n(A \cup B)$$
$$= n(U) - n(A) - n(B) + n(A \cap B)$$
$$= 400 - 100 - 150 + 75 = 225$$

Example 38. *Out of 500 car-owners investigated, 400 owned Fiat cars and 200 owned Ambassador cars; 50 owned both Fiat and Ambassador cars. Is this data correct?*

Solution. Let U be the set of car owners investigated. Let A be the set of those persons who own Fiat cars, B the set of persons who own Ambassador cars; then $A \cap B$ is the set of persons who own both Fiat and Ambassador cars.

$n(U) = 500, n(A) = 400, n(B) = 200, n(A \cap B) = 50$

Therefore, $n(A \cup B) = n(A) + n(B) - n(A \cap B)$

$$= 400 + 200 - 50 = 550$$

This exceeds the total number of car-owners investigated.

So, the given data is not correct.

Example 39. *In a certain government office there are 400 employees; there are 150 men, 276 university graduates, 212 married persons. 94 male university graduates, 151 married university graduates, 119 married men, 72 married male university graduates. Find the number of single women who are not university graduates.*

Solution. Let U = set of employees.

A = set of men.

B = set of married persons.

C = set of university graduates.

Then $A \cap B$ = set of married men.

$A \cap C$ = set of male university graduates

$B \cap C$ = set of married university graduates

$A \cap B \cap C$ = set of married male university graduates

Now $n(U) = 400, n(A) = 150, n(B) = 212, n(C) = 276, n(A \cap B) = 119,$ $n(A \cap C) = 94, n(B \cap C) = 151, n(A \cap B \cap C) = 72$

We want to find out $n(A' \cap B' \cap C')$

Now $(A' \cap B' \cap C') = (A \cup B \cup C)'$

$$= U - (A \cup B \cup C)$$

Therefore,

$$\begin{aligned} n(A' \cap B' \cap C') &= n(U) - n[(A \cup B \cup C) \cap U] \\ &= n(U) - n[A \cup B \cup C] \\ &= n(U) - [n(A) + n(B) + n(C) - n(A \cap B) \\ &\quad - n(A \cap C) - n(B \cap C) + n(A \cap B \cap C)] \\ &= 764 - 710 = 54 \end{aligned}$$

So, the number of single women who are not university graduates is 540.

Example 40. *A market research group conducted a survey of 1000 consumers and reported that 720 consumers liked product A and 450 consumers liked product B. What is the least number that must have liked both products?*

Solution. Let U = set of consumers questioned

S = set of consumers who liked product A

T = set of consumers who liked product B

Then $S \cap T$ = set of consumers who liked both products

Now, $n(U) = 1000, n(S) = 720, n(T) = 450$

Therefore, $n(S \cup T) = n(S) + n(T) - n(S \cap T)$

$= 1170 - n(S \cap T)$

So, $n(S \cap T) = 1170 - n(S \cup T)$

Now $n(S \cap T)$ is least when $n(S \cup T)$ is maximum. But $S \cup T \subseteq U$ implies $n(S \cup T) \leq n(U)$

This implies maximum value of $n(S \cup T)$ is 1000.

So, least value of $n(S \cap T) = 170$.

Hence the least number of consumers who liked both products is 170.

Example 41. *Out of 1000 students who appeared for C.A. Intermediate Examination, 750 failed in Maths, 600 failed in Accounts and 600 failed in Costing, 450 failed in both Maths and Accounts, 400 failed in both Maths and Costing, 150 failed in both Accounts and Costing. The students who failed in all the three subjects were 75. Prove that the above data is not correct.*

Solution. Let U = set of students who appeared in the examination.

A = set of students who failed in Maths.

B = set of students who failed in Accounts.

C = set of students who failed in Costing.

Then $A \cap B$ = set of students who failed in Maths and Accounts.

$B \cap C$ = set of students who failed in Accounts and Costing.

$A \cap C$ = set of students who failed in Maths and Costing.

$A \cap B \cap C$ = set of students who failed in all three subject.

Now $n(U) = 1000, n(A) = 750, n(B) = 600\ n(C) = 600, n(A \cap B) = 450,$
$n(B \cap C) = 150, n(A \cap C) = 400, n(A \cap B \cap C) = 75.$

Therefore $n(A \cup B \cup C) = 750 + 600 + 600 - 450 - 150 - 400 + 75$
$= 1025.$

This exceeds the total number of students who appeared in the examination.

Hence, the given data is not correct.

Example 42. *In a survey of 100 families, the number that read recent issues of a certain monthly magazine were found to be: September only 18, September but not August 23; September and July 8; September 26; July 48; July and August 8; none of the three months 24. With the help of set theory find*

(*a*) *How many read August issue?*

(*b*) *How many read two Consecutive issues?*

(*c*) *How many read the July issue, if and only if they did not read the August issue?*

(*d*) *How many read the September and August issues but not the July issue?*

Solution. Let A = set of those families that read the September issue.

B = set of those families that read the August issue.

C = set of those families that read the July issue.

Then $A - B$ = set of those families that read September issue but not August.

$A \cap C$ = set of those families that read both September and July issue.

$A \cap B$ = set of those families that read both September and August issue.

$A' \cap B' \cap C'$ = set of those families that read none.

$A - (B \cup C)$ = set of those families that read September issue only.

Now $n(A) = 26, n(C) = 48, n(A - B) = 23, n(A \cap C) = 8, n(B \cap C) = 8,$
$n(A' \cap B' \cap C') = 24, n[A - (B \cup C)] = 18$

Now $n(A - B) = n(A) - n(A \cap B)$

So, $23 = 26 - n(A \cap B)$

Therefore $n(A \cap B) = 3.$

Again $n[A-(B\cup C)]=n(A)-n[A\cap(B\cup C)]$

So, $18=26-n[(A\cap B)\cup(A\cap C)]$

$=26-n(A\cap B)-n(A\cap C)+n(A\cap B\cap C)$

$=26-3-8+n(A\cap B\cap C)$

Therefore, $n(A\cap B\cap C)=3$

Also $A'\cap B'\cap C'=(A\cup B\cup C)'$

$=U-(A\cup B\cup C)$

where U = set of those families that are questioned and $n(U)=100$.

So, $n(A'\cap B'\cap C')=n(U)-n(A\cup B\cup C)$

$24=100-n(A\cup B\cup C)$

Therefore $n(A\cup B\cup C)=76$.

Now $n(A\cup B\cup C)=n(A)+n(B)+n(C)-n(A\cap B)-n(A\cap C)$

$-n(B\cap C)+n(A\cap B\cap C)$

implies $76=26+n(B)+48-3-8-8+3$

So, $n(B)=18$

This gives the number of families that read the August issue.

Now $(A\cap B)\cup(B\cap C)$ = set of those families that read two consecutive issues.

So, $n[(A\cap B)\cup(B\cap C)]=n(A\cap B)+n(B\cap C)-n(A\cap B\cap C)$

$=3+8-3=8.$

Again $C-B$ = set of those families that read the July issue but not the August issue.

Then $n(C-B)=n(C)-n(B\cap C)$

$=48-8=40.$

Now $(A\cap B)-C$ = set of those families that read the September and August issues but not July.

So, $n[(A\cap B)-C]=n(A\cap B)-n(A\cap B\cap C)$

$=3-3=0$

Therefore, $(A\cap B)-C=\phi$.

Hence there is no family that read both the September and August issue but not the July issue.

Example 43. *A factory inspector examined the defects in hardness, finish and dimensions of an item. After examining 100 items he gave the following report:*

All three defects 5, defects in hardness and finish 10, defects in dimension and finish 8, defects in dimension and hardness 20. Defects in finish 30, in hardness 23, in dimension 50. The inspector was fined. Why?

Solution. Suppose H represents the set of items which have defect in hardness, F represents the set of items which have defect in finish and D represents the set of items which have defect in dimension.

Then $n(H \cap F \cap D) = 5, n(H \cap F) = 10, n(D \cap F) = 8$

$n(D \cap H) = 20, n(F) = 30, n(H) = 23, n(D) = 50$

So, $n(H \cup F \cup D) = 30 + 23 + 50 - 20 - 10 - 8 + 5 = 70$

Now $n(D \cup F) = n(D) + n(F) - n(D \cap F)$

$= 50 + 30 - 8 = 72.$

$D \cup F \subseteq D \cup F \cup H$ implies $n(D \cup F) \leq n(D \cup F \cup H)$ *i.e.*, $72 \leq 70$.

Hence, there is an error in the report and for this reason inspector was fined.

Example 44. *In a survey of 100 families the numbers that read the most recent issues of various magazines were found to be as follows:*

Readers Digest	*28*
Readers Digest and Science Today	*8*
Science Today	*30*
Readers Digest and Caravan	*10*
Caravan	*42*
Science Today and Caravan	*5*
All the three Magazines	*3*

Using set theory, find

(*a*) *How many read none of the three magazines?*

(*b*) *How many read Caravan as their only magazine?*

(*c*) *How many read Science Today if and only if they read Caravan?*

Solution. Let S = set of those families that read Science Today

R = set of those families that read Readers Digest

C = set of those families that read Caravan.

(*a*) We want to find $n(S' \cap R' \cap C')$

Let U = set of the families questioned.

Now $S' \cap R' \cap C' = (S \cup R \cup C)'$

$= U - (S \cup R \cup C)$

Therefore $n(S' \cap R' \cap C') = n(U) - n(S \cup R \cup C)$

$= 100 - n(S \cup R \cup C)$

Now $n(S \cup R \cup C) = 30 + 28 + 42 - 8 - 10 - 5 + 3 = 80.$

So, $n(S' \cap R' \cap C') = 100 - 80 = 20.$

(*b*) We want to find $n[C-(R\cup S)]$

Now $\quad n[C-(R\cup S)] = n(C)-n[C\cap(R\cup S)]$

$= n(C)-n[(C\cap R)\cup(C\cap S)]$

$= n(C)-n(C\cap R)-n(C\cap S)+n(C\cap R\cap S)$

$= 42-10-5+3=30.$

(*c*) We want to find $n[(S\cap C)-R]$

Now $\quad n[(S\cap C)-R] = n(S\cap C)-n(S\cap C\cap R)$

$= 5-3=2.$

Example 45. *In a survey conducted of women it was found that*

(*i*) *there are more single than married women in South Delhi,*

(*ii*) *there are more married women who own cars than unmarried women without them.*

(*iii*) *there are fewer single women who own cars and homes than married women without cars and without homes.*

Is the number of single women who own cars and do not own homes greater than number of married women who do not own cars but own homes?

Solution. Let A = set of married women,

B = set of women who own cars,

C = set of women who own homes.

Then, the given conditions are

(*i*) $n(A')>n(A)$

(*ii*) $n(A\cap B)>(A'\cap B')$

(*iii*) $n(A\cap B'\cap C')>n(A'\cap B\cap C)$

We want to find $n(A'\cap B\cap C')$ and $n(A\cap B'\cap C)$

Let U = set of all women questioned.

Now $A' = A'\cap U = A'\cap(B\cup B') = (A'\cap B)\cup(A'\cap B')$

$A = A\cap U = A\cap(B\cup B') = (A'\cap B)\cup(A\cap B')$

So, $n(A') = n(A'\cap B)+n(A'\cap B')$

$n(A) = n(A\cap B)+n(A\cap B').$

By (*i*), we have

$$n(A'\cap B)+n(A'\cap B')>n(A\cap B)+n(A\cap B')$$

and by (*ii*)

$$n(A'\cap B)+n(A'\cap B')>n(A\cap B)+n(A\cap B')>n(A'\cap B')+n(A\cap B')$$

Therefore,

$$n(A'\cap B)>n(A\cap B').$$

Also $A' \cap B = (A' \cap B) \cap (C \cup C')$

$= (A' \cap B \cap C) \cup (A' \cap B \cap C')$.

and $A \cap B' = (A \cap B') \cap (C \cup C')$

$= (A \cap B' \cap C) \cup (A \cap B' \cap C')$

So, $n(A' \cap B) = n(A' \cap B \cap C) + n(A' \cap B \cap C')$.

$n(A \cap B') = n(A \cap B' \cap C) + n(A \cap B' \cap C')$.

This gives, using (*iii*)

$$n(A \cap B \cap C) + n(A' \cap B \cap C') > n(A \cap B' \cap C) + n(A' \cap B \cap C)$$

i.e., $n(A' \cap B \cap C') > n(A \cap B' \cap C)$.

So, the number of single women who own cars and do not own a home is greater than the number of married women who do not own cars but own homes.

EXERCISES

1. In a survey of 100 students, the numbers studying various languages were found to be: Spanish 28; German 30; French 42; Spanish and French 10; Spanish and German 8; German and French 5; all the three languages 3.
   (*i*) How many students were studying no language?
   (*ii*) How many students had French as their only language?
   (*iii*) How many students studied German if and only if they studied French?
2. In a latter survey of the 100 students (see exercise 1), the numbers studying the various languages were found to be:
   German only 18; German but not Spanish 23; German and French 8; German 26; French 48; French and Spanish 8; no language 24.
   (*i*) How many students took Spanish?
   (*ii*) How many took German and Spanish but not French?
   (*iii*) How many took French if and only if they did not take Spanish?
3. If A and B are two sets, prove that number of elements in $A \cap B'$ is equal to (number of elements in A — number of elements in $A \cap B$).
4. The report of one survey of 100 students (see exercise 1) stated that the numbers studying the various languages were; all three languages 5; German and Spanish 10; French and Spanish 8; German and French 20; Spanish 30; German 23; French 50. The surveyor who turned in this report was fired. Why?
5. In a recent survey of 5000 people, it was found that 2800 read Indian Express and 2300 read Statesman while 400 read both the papers. How many read neither Indian Express nor Statesman?
6. In a survey of 30 students, it was found that 19 take Mathematics, 17 take Music, 11 take History, 7 take Mathematics and History, 12 take Mathematics and Music, 5 take Music and History and 2 take all three courses. Find (*i*) the number of students that take Mathematics but do not take History (*ii*) the number that take exactly two of the three courses.

7. In a Chemistry class there are 20 students, and in a Psychology class there are 30 students. Find the number either in a Psychology class or Chemistry class if
   (*i*) the two classes meet at the same hour.
   (*ii*) the two classes meet at different hours and 10 students are enrolled in both courses.
8. On an Air India flight, there are 9 boys, 5 Indian children, 9 men, 7 foreign boys, 14 Indian, 6 Indian males and 7 foreign females. What is the number of people in this plane?
9. A college awarded 38 medals in Football, 15 in Basket ball and 20 in Cricket. If these medals went to a total of 58 men and only three of these men got medals in all the three sports, how many men received medals in exactly two of the three sports?
10. Suppose that in survey concerning the reading habits of students it is found that:
    60 per cent read magazine *A*,
    50 per cent read magazine *B*,
    50 per cent read magazine *C*,
    30 per cent read magazines *A* and *B*,
    20 per cent read magazines *B* and *C*,
    30 per cent read magazines *A* and *C*,
    10 per cent read all three magazines.
    (*i*) What per cent read exactly two magazines?
    (*ii*) What per cent do not read any of the magazines?
11. In a survey of 500 consumers, it was found that 425 liked product *A* and 375 liked product *B*. What is the least number of consumers that must have liked both products assuming that there may be consumers of products different from *A* and *B*.

ANSWERS

1. (*i*) 20 (*ii*) 30 (*iii*) 38.
2. (*i*) 18 (*ii*) None (*iii*) 50.
5. 300.
6. (*i*) 12.
7. (*i*) 50 (*ii*) 40.
8. 33.
9. 9
10. (*i*) 50 (*ii*) 10.
11. 300

16. CARTESIAN PRODUCT OF TWO SETS

Let *A* and *B* be two sets. The set of all ordered pairs (*a*, *b*) such that $a \in A$, $b \in B$ is called the Cartesian product of *A* and *B* and is denoted by $A \times B$.

NOTES: 1. The ordered pair (*a*, *b*) is not the same as the set {*a*, *b*}
2. Two ordered pairs (*a*, *b*) and (*c*, *d*) are equal if and only if $a = c$ and $b = d$.
3. For the ordered pair (*a*, *b*), *a* is called the first coordinate and *b* is second coordinate.

Example 46. *Let* $A = \{1, 2, 3\}, B = \{4, 5\}$. *Then* $A \times B = \{(1, 4), (1, 5), (2, 4), (2, 5), (3, 4), (3, 5)\}$ *and* $B \times A = \{(4, 1), (5, 1), (4, 2), (5, 2), (4, 3), (5, 3)\}$. *This shows that* $A \times B \neq B \times A$.

Example 47. *Let A be any set. Then* $A \times \phi$ *and* $\phi \times A$ *are empty sets.*

Solution. Suppose if possible $A \times \phi$ be not empty.

Then there is some $x \in A \times \phi$

By definition $\quad x = (a, b) \quad$ where $a \in A, b \in \phi$.

This is absurd as ϕ is empty.

Hence $A \times \phi = \phi$. Similarly $\phi \times A = \phi$.

Example 48. *Let A, B, C be three sets. Then*

$$A \times (B \cup C) = (A \times B) \cup (A \times C).$$

Solution. Let $x \in A \times (B \cup C)$.

Then $x = (a, d)$ where $a \in A, d \in B \cup C$

Now, if $d \in B$, then $x \in A \times B$

and if $d \in C$, then $x \in A \times C$

In any case $x \in (A \times B) \cup (A \times C)$

Therefore, $A \times (B \cup C) \subseteq (A \times B) \cup (A \times C)$

Similarly, $(A \times B) \cup (A \times C) \subseteq A \times (B \cup C)$

This proves the result.

Example 49. *Let A, B, C be three sets. Then*

$$A \times (B - C) = (A \times B) - (A \times C).$$

Solution. *Let* $(a, d) \in A \times (B - C)$

Then $a \in A, d \in B$ and $d \notin C$

So, $(a, d) \in A \times B$ and $(a, d) \notin A \times C$

Therefore $(a, d) \in (A \times B) - (A \times C)$

This proves $A \times (B - C) \subseteq (A \times B) - (A \times C)$.

To prove the other side containment we proceed as under

Let $\quad x \in (A \times B) - (A \times C)$

Then x is an element of $A \times B$ but it does not belong to $A \times C$. This means that $x = (a, b)$ where $a \in A, b \in B$ but $b \notin C$,

otherwise $\quad x = (a, b) \in A \times C$

This implies that $\quad b \in B - C$.

Therefore $\quad x \in A \times (B - C)$

Hence $\quad (A \times B) - (A \times C) \subseteq A \times (B - C)$.

Example 50. *If the set A has m elements and the set B has n elements, how many elements does A × B have?*

Solution. Let $a \in A$. Then number of elements of $A \times B$ with first coordinate as a is n. But a can be chosen in m ways. So, the number of distinct elements of $A \times B$ is mn.

Example 51. *If* $A = \{1, 4\}, B = \{4, 5\}, C = \{5, 7\}$

Find (*i*) $(A \times B) \cup (A \times C)$

(*ii*) $(A \times B) \cap (A \times C)$

Solution. (*i*) By Example 48, $(A \times B) \cup (A \times C) = A \times (B \cup C)$

Now $B \cup C = \{4, 5, 7\}$

So $A \times (B \cup C) = \{(1, 4), (4, 4), (1, 5), (4, 5), (1, 7), (4, 7)\}$

$= (A \times B) \cup (A \times C)$

(*ii*) Now $A \times B = \{(1, 4), (4, 4), (1, 5), (4, 5)\}$,

$A \times C = \{(1, 5), (1, 7), (4, 5), (4, 7)\}$

So $(A \times B) \cap (A \times C) = \{(1, 5), (4, 5)\}$.

17. RELATION

Let A and B be two sets. A relation R from A to B is a subset of the Cartesian product $A \times B$. If $(a, b) \in R$, then it is also denoted by aRb and conversely aRb means $(a, b) \in R$. The symbol aRb is read as "a is related to b". If $A = B$, we shall say R is a relation in A instead of "from A to A".

Let $A = \{1, 2\}, B = \{3\}$,

then $R_1 = \{(1, 3), (2, 3)\}, R_2 = \{(1, 3)\}, R_3 = \{(2, 3\}$, are different relations from A to B.

Let now, A be a non empty set. A relation R in A is called

Reflexive: if $(a, a) \in R$ for all $a \in A$

Symmetric: if whenever $(a, b) \in R$ then $(b, a) \in R$

Anti-Symmetric: if $(a, b) \in R, (b, a) \in R \Rightarrow a = b$

Transitive. if whenever $(a, b), (b, c) \in R$ then $(a, c) \in R$

A relation R is called an equivalence relation if it is reflexive, symmetric and transitive.

A relation R on a set A is called a partial order relation, if it is reflexive anti-symmetric and transitive.

Example 52. *If* $A = \{1, 2, 3\}$ *then*

$R_1 = \{(1, 1), (2, 2), (3, 3), (1, 3)\}$ *is reflexive*

$R_2 = \{(1, 1), (2, 2\}$ *is not reflexive*

$R_3 = \{(1, 2), (2, 1)\}$ is symmetric but not reflexive

$R_4 = \{(1, 1), (1, 2)\}$ is neither reflexive nor symmetric but is transitive.

Example 53. *Let A be the set of all lines in a plane. Let* $R \subseteq A \times A$ *where* $R = \{(l, m) \mid l, m \in A, l \parallel m\}$ *then R is*

Reflexive, as $(l, l) \in R$ for all $l \in A$

as $l \parallel l$ for all $l \in A$

Symmetric, as if $(l, m) \in R$

then $l \parallel m$

$\Rightarrow$ $m \parallel l$

$\Rightarrow$ $(m, l) \in R$

Transitive, as if $(l, m) \in R, (m, n) \in R$

then $l \parallel m, m \parallel n$

$\Rightarrow$ $l \parallel n \Rightarrow (l, n) \in R$

Thus; relation of parallelism is an equivalence relation.

Example 54. *Let Z = set of integers then the usual* $\leq$ *is a partial order relation on Z as it is*

Reflexive, as $a \leq a$ for all $a \in Z$

Anti-Symmetric, as $a \leq b, b \leq a \Rightarrow a = b$

Transitive, as $a \leq b, b \leq c \Rightarrow a \leq c$.

Example 55. *Let* $R = \{(m, n) \mid m, n \in Z, m \mid n\}$ *then R is partial order relation. Verify?*

Where by $x \mid y$ (x divides y) we mean , $\exists z$, *s.t.*, $y = xz$.

Example 56. *The relation of equality on integers is an equivalence relation.*

18. REPRESENTATION OF A RELATION BY A MATRIX

Sometimes, a relation is represented by a matrix (see for definition etc. under Matrices) where first we draw a table. Suppose, R is a relation from a finite set A to a finite set B. We first construct a table by writing all the elements of A as a column on left and all the elements of B as the top row. Now if $(a_i, b_j) \in R$, *i.e.*, $a_i R b_j$ then we write 1 in the ith row and jth column. If $(a_i, b_j) \notin R$ we write 0. We illustrate this by the following example.

Suppose, $A = \{a_1, a_2, a_3, a_4\}$, $B = \{b_1, b_2, b_3\}$. Then

$$A \times B = \{(a_1, b_1), (a_1, b_2), (a_1, b_3), (a_2, b_1), (a_2, b_2), (a_2, b_3), (a_3, b_1), (a_3, b_2), (a_3, b_3), (a_4, b_1), (a_4, b_2), (a_4, b_3)\}$$

Suppose, $R = \{(a_1, b_1), (a_1, b_2), (a_2, b_2), (a_3, b_3), (a_4, b_1)\}$

The table and the corresponding relation matrix of R is given by

	b_1	b_2	b_3
a_1	1	1	0
a_2	0	1	0
a_3	0	0	1
a_4	1	0	0

$$\begin{bmatrix} 1 & 1 & 0 \\ 0 & 1 & 0 \\ 0 & 0 & 1 \\ 1 & 0 & 0 \end{bmatrix}$$

The above representation of a relation by the relation matrix has an advantage in as far as a look at it gives us some information regarding the relation. For instance, if the diagonal entries in the matrix are all 1 then the corresponding relation is reflexive. Again if the relation matrix is symmetric the corresponding relation is also symmetric. Similarly, if the relation happens to be anti-symmetric then in the relation matrix if $a_{ij} = 1$ then $a_{ji} = 0 \ (i \neq j)$.

19. DIAGRAMMATICAL REPRESENTATION OF A RELATION

Sometimes a relation is represented with the help of a diagram called the graph of the relation. All we do in this representation is that we represent the elements by small circles (or dots) called nodes and if *aRb* we join *a* and *b* by a line (or an arc) and put an arrow form *a* to *b*. In case *bRa* also holds we draw another arc form *b* to *a* and put an arrow from *b* to *a*. If *aRa*, we draw a circular arc showing *a* being joined to *a* (which will look like a loop). Thus, if a relation is reflexive, there will be loops at all the nodes.

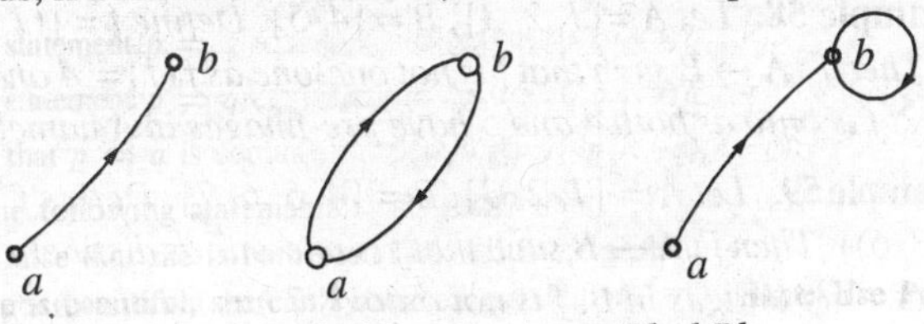

aRb   *aRb, bRa*   *aRb, bRb*

Fig. 7

20. MAPPING OR FUNCTION

Let A and B be two sets. **A mapping** or (**function**) f from A *to* B is a relation from A to B such that to each $a \in A$ there exists a unique $b \in B$. In other words, f is a subset of $A \times B$ such that $(a, b_1) \in f$ and $(a, b_2) \in f \Rightarrow b_1 = b_2$

and for each $a \in A$, there is some $b \in B$ such that $(a, b) \in f$. A mapping f from A to B is denoted by $f : A \to B$.

A is called **Domain** of f.

B is called **Co-domain** of f.

Image of f is the set of those elements $b \in B$ such that $(a, b) \in f$ for some $a \in A$. It is denoted by $Im\,(f)$.

NOTES: 1. If $f : A \to B$ and $(a, b) \in f$, then we write $b = f(a)$ and b is called the image of a under f. Also, a is called preimage of b under f.

2. Image of every element in A is unique.

Example 57. *Let* $A = \{1, 2, 3\}$, $B = \{4, 5\}$. *Define* $f = \{(1,4), (2, 5), (3, 4)\}$. *Then* f *is a mapping from* A *to* B.

But $g = \{(1, 4), (2, 5), (3, 5), (1, 5)\}$ *is not a mapping from* A *to* B *as two elements 4 and 5 in* B *are assigned to the element* $1 \in A$.

Again $h = \{(1,4), (2, 5)\}$ *is not a mapping as* $Dom\,(h) = \{1, 2\} \neq A$.

21. ONE-ONE MAPPING

A mapping $f: A \to B$ is said to be *one-one* if $f(a_1) = f(a_2)$ implies $a_1 = a_2$ where $a_1 \in A$, $a_2 \in A$. This is also sometimes called *injective mapping*. In other words, a mapping $f : A \to B$ is one-one if and only if whenever $a_1 \neq a_2$ $(a_1 \in A, a_2 \in A)$ then $f(a_1) \neq f(a_2)$ *i.e.*, images of distinct elements in A are distinct.

22. ONTO MAPPING

A mapping $f : A \to B$ is said to be *onto* if given $b \in B$ there exists $a \in A$ such that $f(a) = b$. It is also sometimes called *surjective mapping*.

Example 58. *Let* $A = \{1, 2, 3\}$, $B = \{4, 5\}$. *Define* $f = \{(1, 4), (2, 4), (3, 5)\}$. *Then* $f: A \to B$ *such that* f *is not one-one as* $f(1) = 4$ *and* $f(2) = 4$. *But* $1 \neq 2$. f *is onto as both 4 and 5 have pre-images in* A *namely 1 and 3.*

Example 59. *Let* $A = \{1, 2, 3\}$, $B = \{4, 5, 6, 7\}$. *Define* $f = \{(1, 4), (2, 5), (3, 6)\}$. *Then* $f: A \to B$ *such that* f *is one-one as distinct elements in* A *have distinct images in* B. f *is not onto as 7 has no pre-image in* A.

Example 60. *Let* $A = \{1, 2, 3\}$, $B = \{4, 5, 6\}$. *Define* $f = \{(1, 6), (2, 4), (3, 5)\}$.

Then $f: A \to B$ *such that* f *is neither one-one nor onto.*

Example 61. *Let* $A = \{1, 2, 3\}$, $B = \{4, 5, 6\}$. *Define* $f = \{(1, 4), (2, 4), (3, 5)\}$.

Then $f: A \to B$ *such that* f *is neither one-one nor onto.*

Example 62. *If $f: A \to B$ such that f is onto, then Im $(f) = B$.*

Solution. By definition, Im $f \subseteq B$. Let $b \in B$. Then there exists $a \in A$ such that $f(a) = b$ (as f is onto). This implies $b \in$ Im (f). So, $B \subseteq$ Imf.

Hence Im$(f) = B$.

23. BINARY COMPOSITION

A binary composition (or binary operation) on a set S, is a rule which assigns to each pair of elements a, b of S a unique element c of S.

24. BOOLEAN ALGEBRA

A *Boolean Algebra* is a set B of elements $x, y, z, \ldots$ together with two binary operations + and . on B such that the following axioms hold:

B1. Commutative laws. For any $x, y \in B$

$$x + y = y + x \text{ and } x.\, y = y.\, x$$

B2. Distributive laws. For any $x, y, z \in B$

$$x \,.\, (y + z) = x \,.\, y + x \,.\, z$$

and
$$x + (y \,.\, z) = (x + y) \,.\, (x + z)$$

B3. Identity. There exist $0 \in B$ and $1 \in B$ (called the *zero* element and the *unit* element respectively) such that for all $x \in B$.

$$x + 0 = x \text{ and } x \,.\, 1 = x$$

B4. Complement. For each $x \in B$, there exists $x' \in B$ (called the *complement* of x) such that

$$x + x' = 1 \text{ and } x \,.\, x' = 0$$

In the following examples, we first prove some results which can be easily deduced from the definition of Boolean Algebra.

Example 63. *Both identity elements, 0 and 1 of B are unique.*

Solution. Suppose there exist two zero elements 0_1 and 0_2. Then $0_1 + 0_2 = 0_1$ and $0_2 + 0_1 = 0_2$. So, by commutative law $0_1 = 0_2$. Hence zero element of B is unique. Similarly, we can prove uniqueness of unit element.

Example 64. *Any complement x' for x in B is unique.*

Solution. Suppose x_1' and x_2' are two complements of x in B. Then

$$x + x_1' = 1, \qquad x + x_2' = 1$$

and
$$x \,.\, x_1' = 0, \qquad x \,.\, x_2' = 0$$

Therefore,

$$x_1' = x_1' \,.\, 1 \qquad \text{(using } B3)$$

$$= x_1' \,.\, (x + x_2')$$

$= (x_1'.x) + (x_1'.x_2')$ (using $B2$)
$= (x.x_1') + (x_1'.x_2')$ (using $B1$)
$= 0 + (x_1'.x_2')$
$= (x_1'.x_2') + 0$ (using $B1$)
$= (x_1'.x_2')$ (using $B3$)

Similarly,

$x_2' = x_2'.1$ (using $B3$)
$= x_2'.(x + x_1')$
$= (x_2'.x) + (x_2'.x_1')$ (using $B2$)
$= (x.x_2') + (x_1'.x_2')$ (using $B1$)
$= 0 + (x_1'.x_2')$
$= (x_1'.x_2') + 0$ (using $B1$)
$= x_1'.x_2$ (using $B3$)

This shows $x_1' = x_2'$ i.e., complement of any element in B is unique.

Example 65. *Each of the identity elements in B is the complement of the other.*

Solution. We want to show that $0' = 1$ and $1' = 0$.

Now $0' + 0 = 0'$ and $0 + 0' = 1$
using $B1$, it follows that $0' = 1$.

Also $1'.1 = 1'$ and $1.1 = 0$
using $B1$, it follows that $1' = 0$.

Example 66. *For any x in B,* $(x')' = x$

Solution. Now $x + x' = 1$ and $x.x' = 0$ implies $x' + x = 1$ and $x'.x = 0$ (using $B1$).

This means x is complement of x'. *i.e.* $(x')' = x$.

Example 67. *Prove the idempotent laws* (*i*) $x + x = x$ (*ii*) $x.x = x$ *for all x in B.*

Solution. (*i*) Now $x = x + 0 = x + (x.x')$
$= (x + x).(x + x')$
$= (x + x).1 = x + x$

we leave the proof of (*ii*) to the reader as an exercise.

Example 68. *Show that* (*i*) $x + 1 = 1$ (*ii*) $x.0 = 0$ *for any x in B.*

Solution. (*i*) $x + 1 = (x + 1)$
$= 1.(x + 1)$ using $B1$

$$= (x + x') \,.\, (x + 1)$$

$$= x + (x' \,.\, 1) \qquad \text{using } B2 \text{ and Example 68}$$

$$= x + x' = 1$$

Similarly $\quad x \,.\, 0 = (x \,.\, 0) + 0$

$$= 0 + (x \,.\, 0)$$

$$= (x \,.\, x') + (x \,.\, 0)$$

$$= x \,.\, (x' + 0)$$

$$= x \,.\, x' = 0$$

This proves (*ii*).

Example 69. *Prove the absorption laws*

(*i*) $x + (x \,.\, y) = x$ $\qquad$ (*ii*) $x \,.\, (x + y) = x$

for all x, y in B.

Solution. (*i*) $x + (x \,.\, y) = (x \,.\, y) + x$ (using $B1$)

$$= (x \,.\, y) + (x \,.\, 1) \qquad \text{(using } B3\text{)}$$

$$= x \,.\, (y + 1) \qquad \text{(using } B2\text{)}$$

$$= x \,.\, 1 = x$$

(*ii*) $x \,.\, (x + y) = (x + y) \,.\, x$ (using $B1$)

$$= (x + y) \,.\, (x + 0) \qquad \text{(using } B3\text{)}$$

$$= x + (y \,.\, 0) \qquad \text{(using } B2\text{)}$$

$$= x + 0 = x.$$

Example 70. *If* $x + z = y + z$ *and* $x \,.\, z = y \,.\, z$

then $x = y$ *where* $x, y, z \in B$.

Solution. $x = x \,.\, (x + z)$ (using Absorption law)

$$= x \,.\, (y + z)$$

$$= x \,.\, y + x \,.\, z \qquad \text{(using } B2\text{)}$$

$$= x \,.\, y + y \,.\, z$$

$$= y \,.\, x + y \,.\, z \qquad \text{(using } B1\text{)}$$

$$= y \,.\, (x + z) \qquad \text{(using } B2\text{)}$$

$$= y \,.\, (y + z)$$

$$= y. \qquad \text{(using Absorption law)}$$

Example 71. *If* $y \,.\, x = z \,.\, x$ *and* $y \,.\, x' = z \,.\, x'$

then, $y = z$ where $x, y, z \in B$.

Solution. $y = y \,.\, 1$ (using $B3$)

$$= y \,.\, (x + x') \qquad \text{(using } B4\text{)}$$

$$= y \,.\, x + y \,.\, x' \qquad \text{(using } B2\text{)}$$

$$= z \,.\, x + z \,.\, x'$$

$$= z \,.\, (x + x') \qquad \text{(using } B2\text{)}$$

$$= z \,.\, 1 \qquad \text{(using } B4\text{)}$$

$$= z.$$

Example 72. *Prove the associative laws for B*

(*i*) $x + (y + z) = (x + y) + z$

(*ii*) $x \,.\, (y \,.\, z) = (x \,.\, y) \,.\, z$

for all x, y, z in B.

Solution. *Let* $X = x + (y + z)$

$$Y = (x + y) + z$$

Then $X \,.\, x = [x + (y + z)] \,.\, x$

$$= x \,.\, [x + (y + z)] = x \qquad \text{(by Absorption laws)}$$

and $Y \,.\, x = [(x + y) + z] \,.\, x$

$$= (x + y) \,.\, x + z \,.\, x$$

$$= x \,.\, (x + y) + z \,.\, x$$

$$= x + z \,.\, x$$

$$= x + x \,.\, z$$

$$= x \,.\, 1 + x \,.\, z$$

$$= x \,.\, (1 + z)$$

$$= x \,.\, 1 = x$$

So $X \,.\, x = Y \,.\, x$

Also $X \,.\, x' = [x + (y + z)] \,.\, x'$

$$= x \,.\, x' + (y + z) \,.\, x'$$

$$= 0 + (y + z) \,.\, x'$$

$$= (y + z) \,.\, x'$$

and $Y \,.\, x' = [(x + y) + z] \,.\, x'$

$$= (x + y) \,.\, x' + z \,.\, x'$$

$$= [x \,.\, x' + y \,.\, x'] + z \,.\, x'$$

$$= [0 + y \,.\, x'] + z \,.\, x'$$

$$= y \,.\, x' + z \,.\, z' = (y + z) \,.\, x'$$

So $X \,.\, x' = Y \,.\, x'$

By the previous Example (*i*) follows. We leave (*ii*) to the reader as an exercise.

Example 73. *Prove De Morgan's Law for B*

(*i*) $(x + y)' = x' \,.\, y'$ (*ii*) $(x \,.\, y)' = x' + y'$.

Solution. (*i*) We want to show that $x' \cdot y'$ is the complement of $(x+y)$

Consider $(x+y)+(x' \cdot y')$

$$= [(x+y)+x'] \cdot [(x+y)+y'] \quad \text{(using } B2\text{)}$$
$$= [x'+(x+y)] \cdot [x+(y+y')]$$
$$= [(x'+x)+y] \cdot [x+1]$$
$$= [(x+x')+y] \cdot 1$$
$$= (x+x')+y$$
$$= 1+y = y+1 = 1$$

Also $(x+y) \cdot (x' \cdot y')$

$$= (x' \cdot y') \cdot (x+y)$$
$$= [(x' \cdot y') \cdot x] + [(x' \cdot y') \cdot y]$$
$$= [x \cdot (x' \cdot y')] + [x' \cdot (y' \cdot y)]$$
$$= [(x \cdot x') \cdot y'] + [x' \cdot (y \cdot y')]$$
$$= [0 \cdot y'] + [x' \cdot 0]$$
$$= 0 + 0 = 0.$$

This shows $x' \cdot y'$ is a complement of $(x+y)$. But every element in B has a unique element. So (*i*) follows.

(*ii*) We leave it as an exercise for the reader.

25. It can be easily shown that the Algebra of statements under the binary relations '$\wedge$' and '$\vee$' is a Boolean Algebra. Also, the algebra of sets under the binary operations '$\cap$' and '$\cup$' is a Boolean Algebra. We give below a table showing the similarity in logic, theory of sets and Boolean Algebra.

	Logic	*Sets*	*Boolean Algebra*
Statements	$p, q, r, \ldots$	$A, B, C, \ldots$	$x, y, z, \ldots$
Operator *OR*	$p \vee q$	$A \cup B$	$x + y$
Operator *AND*	$p \wedge q$	$A \cap B$	$x \cdot y$
Operator *NOT*	$\sim p$	A'	x'
Tautology	T	Universal set	1
Fallacy	F	ϕ	0
Implication	$p \Rightarrow q$ or $[\sim(p \wedge \sim q)]$	mapping	$x' + y$
Equivalence	$p \Leftrightarrow q$ $(p \equiv q)$	One-One mapping	$x \cdot y + x' \cdot y'$

Example 74. *Using Boolean Algebra, prove that*

$p \wedge (p \Rightarrow q) \Rightarrow q$ is a tautology.

Solution. Using symbols '+' and '.' of Boolean Algebra, the given statement can be written as

$$\begin{aligned}[x\,.\,(x'+y)]'+y &= [x\,.\,x'+x\,.\,y]'+y\\ &= [0+x\,.\,y]'+y\\ &= (x\,.\,y)'+y\\ &= (x'+y')+y\\ &= x'+(y'+y)\\ &= x'+1=1 \qquad \text{(which is a tautology)}\end{aligned}$$

Example 75. *Using Boolean Algebra, show that*

$\sim q \wedge (p \Rightarrow q) \Rightarrow \sim p$ is a tautology.

Solution. Now the given statement can be written as

$$\begin{aligned}[y'\,.\,(x'+y)]'+x' &= [y'\,.\,x'+y'\,.\,y]'+x'\\ &= [y'\,.\,x'+0]'+x'\\ &= [y+x]+x'\\ &= y+(x+x')\\ &= y+1=1 \qquad \text{(which is a tautology)}\end{aligned}$$

Example 67. *Using Boolean Algebra determine the validity of the following argument:*

"The triangle is isosceles if and only if two of its sides are equal. No two sides of the triangle are equal. Therefore, triangle is not isosceles."

Solution. Suppose p stands for "The triangle is isosceles" and q for "Two sides of the triangle are equal." The above argument can be written as $(p \Leftrightarrow q) \wedge \sim q \Rightarrow \sim p$.

In symbols of Boolean Algebra, this may be written as

$$\begin{aligned}[(x\,.\,y+x'\,.\,y')\,.\,y']'+x' &= [y'\,.\,(x\,.\,y+x'\,.\,y']+x'\\ &= [y'\,.\,(x\,.\,y)+y'\,.\,(x'\,.\,y')]'+x'\\ &= [(y'\,.\,y)\,.\,x+y'\,.\,(x'\,.\,y')]'+x'\\ &= [0+y'\,.\,(x'\,.\,y')]'+x'\\ &= [y'\,.\,(x'\,.\,y')]'+x'\\ &= y+(x+y)+x'\\ &= y+(x+x')\\ &= y+1=1 \qquad \text{(which is a tautology)}\end{aligned}$$

Therefore, the given argument is valid argument.

CHAPTER 3

GROUPS, RINGS AND FIELDS

1. GROUPS

We recall that by a binary composition on a set S, we mean an operation that joins two elements of S to give a unique element of S. An easy example would be that of the usual addition on the set **N** of natural numbers. For, we know that if $a, b \in \mathbf{N}$ then $a + b$ is a unique natural number suggesting thereby that addition '+' is a binary composition on the set **N** of natural numbers. There can, of course, be any number of binary compositions on a set. We now define a system to be given the name of a group.

Suppose G is a non-empty set and * (star) is a binary composition on G. Then G is said to form a **group** with respect to * if

(*i*) *Associativity.* $a * (b * c) = (a * b) * c, \ \forall\ a, b, c \in G$.

(*ii*) *Existence of Identity.* $\exists\ e \in G$, such that

$$a * e = e * a = a \ \forall\ a \in G.$$

(*iii*) *Existence of Inverse.* For every $a \in G, \exists\ a' \in G$ (depending upon a), such that

$$a * a' = a' * a = e.$$

REMARKS:

(*a*) Since * is a binary composition on G, it is understood that $\forall\ a, b \in G$, $a * b$ is a unique member of G. This property is called the *closure property*.

(*b*) If in addition to the above axioms in the definition of a group

$$a * b = b * a, \forall\ a, b \in G$$

We say that G forms an *abelian group* (or a *commutative group*). Any group, not satisfying this property is called a *non-abelian* or a *non-commutative group*.

(*c*) One can use any symbol for a binary composition but the most commonly used are

*, 0, ⊙, ⊕, ., +, etc.

(*d*) Generally, the binary composition for a group is denoted by (.)

dot as it makes it more convenient to write all the axioms (and they look so natural too). So G forms a group w.r.t. the binary composition, if

(*i*) $a.(b.c) = (a.b).c \;\forall\; a,b,c \in G$

(*ii*) $\exists\; e \in G$, such that $a.e = e.a = a \;\forall\; a \in G$

(*iii*) $\forall\; a \in G$, $\exists\; a' \in G$ (depending upon a) s.t.,

$$a.a' = a'.a = e.$$

In fact, we'll drop (.) dot, too and will write ab in place of $a \,.\, b$.

(*e*) Whenever we say that G is a group, it will mean that there is some binary composition on G and it forms a group w.r.t. that composition [w.r.t. = with respect to].

Definition. A group having finite number of elements is called a *finite group*. If it contains infinite number of elements, it is called *infinite group*.

Order of a group. The number of elements in a group is called the *order* of the group.

Let us now consider a few easy and simple examples.

Example 1. *The set* **Z** *of integers forms an abelian group w.r.t., the usual addition of integers.*

Solution. Let us check all the properties in the definition of a group.

(*i*) *Closure.* If $a, b \in \mathbf{Z}$ be any two integers then we know that $a + b$ is a unique integer $\Rightarrow +$ is a binary composition on **Z**.

(*ii*) *Associativity.* Let $a, b, c \in \mathbf{Z}$ be any three elements, then

$$a + (b + c) = (a + b) + c$$

is known to us

(*iii*) *Existence of Identity.* We know that $\exists\; 0 \in \mathbf{Z}$

s.t., $$a + 0 = 0 + a = a \;\forall\; a \in \mathbf{Z}$$

$\Rightarrow 0$ is identity element in **Z**

(*iv*) *Existence of inverse.* If $a \in \mathbf{Z}$ is any member, then $\exists -a \in \mathbf{Z}$, such that $a + (-a) = (-a) + a = 0$

$\Rightarrow -a$ is inverse of a

Hence each element of **Z** has an inverse.

(*v*) *Commutativity.* $a + b = b + a \;\forall\; a, b \in \mathbf{Z}$ is also known to us.

Hence $< \mathbf{Z}, + >$ forms an abelian group.

Example 2. *The set* **Q** *of rational numbers forms an abelian group w.r.t. the addition of rational numbers.*

Solution. One can easily verify all the axioms as above and thus $< \mathbf{Q}, + >$ forms an abelian group.

Example 3. $<\mathbf{R}, +>$ *where* **R** *is the set of real numbers and* + *is the usual addition forms an abelian group.*

Example 4. *If* Q' *is the set of all non-zero rational numbers and* (.) *denotes the usual multiplication then* $<Q', .>$ *forms an abelian group.*

Solution. It is again easy to verify all the properties. Note 1 will act as identity element and $1/a$ as inverse of any $a \in Q'$ ($a \neq 0$ given).

Example 5. *Let G be the set* $\{1, -1\}$. *Show that it forms an abelian group w.r.t. usual multiplication.*

Solution. We note

$$1 . 1 = 1 \in G$$
$$1 . (-1) = -1 \in G$$
$$(-1) . (-1) = 1 \in G$$

$\Rightarrow$ multiplication is a binary composition on G i.e., closure property holds.

Again $a . (b . c) = (a . b) . c \;\forall\, a, b, c \in G$

is clear by giving any value 1 or – 1 to a, b, c.

Commutativity is also obvious.

Existence of Identity. We observe

$$a . 1 = 1 . a = a \;\forall\; a \in G$$

as
$$1 . 1 = 1 . 1 = 1$$
$$(-1) . 1 = 1 . (-1) = -1$$

$\Rightarrow$ 1 is identity.

Existence of Inverse. Since

$$1 . 1 = 1 . 1 = 1 \text{ (identity)}$$

1 is inverse of 1.

Again as $(-1) . (-1) = (-1) . (-1) = 1$ (identity),

– 1 is inverse of – 1.

Thus each element has an inverse.

Hence $< G, . >$ is an abelian group.

Example 6. *If* $G = \{a\}$ *and* $*$ *is defined on G by* $a * a = a \;\forall\; a \in G$, *then show that* $<G, *>$ *forms an abelian group.*

Solution. Left to the reader as an exercise. Note that a is identity and is its own inverse.

Let us now consider some examples of such systems that do not form a group (although they are very nearly groups).

Example 7. *Does the system* $< \mathbf{Z}, . >$ *form a group? where* **Z** = *set of integers and* '.' *is usual multiplication.*

Solution. It is easy to see that '.' is a binary composition on **Z**. So closure holds.

Again $a \,.\, (b \,.\, c) = (a \,.\, b) \,.\, c$ $\quad \forall\ a, b, c \in \mathbf{Z}$

$$a \,.\, b = b \,.\, a$$

So associativity and commutativity also hold.

Also since $a \,.\, 1 = 1 \,.\, a = a$ $\quad \forall\ a \in \mathbf{Z}$

1 is identity element.

Finally we note that every element of **Z** does not have an inverse. For instance, $\nexists$ any integer a such that

$$2 \,.\, a = a \,.\, 2 = 1 \text{ i.e., 2 has no inverse.}$$

$\Rightarrow$ $< \mathbf{Z}, . >$ is not a group.

Example 8. *If* **Q** = *set of rational nos., and* (.) *is the usual multiplication then show that* $< \mathbf{Q}, . >$ *does not form a group.*

Solution. If we see Example 4 we note all the properties in the definition of a group are satisfied here, except the last one as 0 has no inverse.

Before we take up more examples, let us prove the following properties (that follow in a group from its definition).

2. SOME PROPERTIES

If $< G, . >$ is a group, then

1. Identity element in G is unique.
2. Inverse of each $a \in G$ is unique.
3. $(a^{-1})^{-1} = a, \ \forall\ a \in G$, where a^{-1} stands for inverse of a.
4. $(ab)^{-1} = b^{-1}a^{-1}$ $\quad \forall\ a, b \in G$
5. Cancellation law:

$$ab = ac \ \Rightarrow\ b = c \qquad \forall\ a, b \in G$$
$$ba = ca \ \Rightarrow\ b = c.$$

Proof. (1) Suppose e and e' are two identity elements in G. Then, since e is identity and $e' \in G$

$$e'e = ee' = e' \qquad \text{(definition)}$$

Again since e' is identity and $e \in G$,

$$ee' = e'e = e$$

The two taken together $\Rightarrow e' = e$

Hence identity element is unique.

(2) Let $a \in G$ be some element and let x, y be two inverse elements of a in G.

Then $ax = xa = e$ (definition)

$ay = ya = e$

Now $x = xe = x(ay) = (xa)\,y = ey = y.$

Hence inverse of a is unique.

We shall always denote the inverse of a by a^{-1}.

(3) Since a^{-1} is inverse of a.

$$aa^{-1} = a^{-1}a = e$$

But this also implies that a is inverse of a^{-1}.

$$\Rightarrow \quad a = (a^{-1})^{-1}$$

(4) We have to show that inverse of ab is $b^{-1}a^{-1}$.

i.e., we have to show that

$$(ab)(b^{-1}a^{-1}) = (b^{-1}a^{-1})(ab) = e$$

Now $(ab)(b^{-1}a^{-1}) = [(ab)b^{-1}]a^{-1}$ (Associativity)

$= [a(bb^{-1})]a^{-1}$ (Associativity)

$= (ae)a^{-1} = aa^{-1} = e.$

and $(b^{-1}a^{-1})(ab) = [(b^{-1}a^{-1})a]b$

$= [b^{-1}(a^{-1}a)]b$

$= [b^{-1}e]b = b^{-1}b = e.$

which proves the result.

(5) Suppose $ab = ac$ for some $a, b, c \in G$

we have $b = eb = (a^{-1}a) \,.\, b$

$= a^{-1}(ab) = a^{-1}(ac) = (a^{-1}a)c = ec = c.$

Thus $ab = ac \;\Rightarrow\; b = c$

This is called *left cancellation law.*

We leave it to the reader to prove the *right concellation law i.e.,*

$$ba = ca \;\Rightarrow\; b = c$$

We now consider a few more examples.

Example 9. *Show that the set Q^+ of + ve rational numbers forms an abelian group w.r.t. the composition * defined on it by*

$$a * b = \frac{ab}{2}$$

Solution. *Closure:* Let $a, b \in Q^+$ be any two members,

then $a * b = \dfrac{ab}{2} \in Q^+$

as $\frac{ab}{2}$ will also be a + ve rational number (and it is unique), thus closure holds.

Associativity. For any $a, b, c \in Q^+$

$$(a * b) * c = \left(\frac{ab}{2}\right) * c = \frac{\left(\frac{ab}{2}\right)c}{2} = \frac{abc}{4}$$

$$a * (b * c) = a * \left(\frac{bc}{2}\right) = \frac{a\left(\frac{bc}{2}\right)}{2} = \frac{abc}{4}$$

$$\Rightarrow \quad (a * b) * c = a * (b * c) \qquad \forall\, a, b, c \in Q^+.$$

Commutativity. $a * b = \frac{ab}{2} = \frac{ba}{2} = b * a \qquad \forall\, a, b \in Q^+.$

Existence of identity. Let $a \in Q^+$ be any element

Then $\quad a * 2 = \frac{a \, . 2}{2} = a = \frac{2a}{2} = 2 * a$

$\Rightarrow$ 2 is identity.

Existence of Inverse. Let $a \in Q^+$ be any element.

Now a' will be inverse of a if and only if

$$a * a' = a' * a = 2 \qquad \text{(identity)}$$

$$\Leftrightarrow \quad \frac{aa'}{2} = \frac{a'a}{2} = 2$$

$$\Leftrightarrow \quad aa' = a'a = 4$$

$$\Leftrightarrow \quad a' = \frac{4}{a}.$$

Since $\frac{4}{a} \in Q^+$ whenever $a \in Q^+$, we note that each $a \in Q^+$ has inverse, namely, $\frac{4}{a}$.

Hence $< Q^+, * >$ forms an abelian group.

Example 10. *If* **Z** *is the set of integers and* $*$ *is a composition defined by*

$$a * b = a + b + 1$$

on **Z**, *where + is the usual addition, then show that* $<$ **Z**, $*>$ *is an abelian group.*

Solution. *Closure:* Let $a, b \in$ **Z** be any two members, then

$$a * b = a + b + 1 \text{ also belongs to } \mathbf{Z}.$$

So closure holds.

Associativity. For any $a, b, c \in \mathbf{Z}$,

$$(a * b) * c = (a + b + 1) * c$$
$$= (a + b + 1) + c + 1 = a + b + c + 2$$
$$a * (b * c) = a * (b + c + 1)$$
$$= a + (b + c + 1) + 1 = a + b + c + 2$$
$$(a * b) * c = a * (b * c) \qquad \forall\, a, b, c \in \mathbf{Z}$$

Existence of identity. $e \in \mathbf{Z}$ will be the identity

if $$a * e = e * a = a \qquad \forall\, a \in \mathbf{Z}$$

Let $a \in \mathbf{Z}$ be any element, then

$$a * e = a + e + 1$$

Now $$a + e + 1 = a \Leftrightarrow e + 1 = 0$$
$$\Leftrightarrow e = -1$$

Thus -1 can act as identity. In fact

$$a * -1 = a + (-1) + 1 = a \quad \forall\, a \in \mathbf{Z}$$
$$-1 * a = -1 + a + 1 = a.$$

$\Rightarrow \quad -1$ is the identity.

Existence of inverse. For any $a \in \mathbf{Z}$, a' will be inverse of a, if

$$a * a' = a' * a = -1 \qquad \text{(identity)}$$

i.e., if $a + a' + 1 = a' + a + 1 = -1$

or if $a' = -2 - a$

Since for any $a \in \mathbf{Z}$, $-2 - a \in \mathbf{Z}$, we find that each $a \in \mathbf{Z}$ has inverse, namely, $-2 - a$.

Commutativity. $$a * b = a + b + 1$$
$$= b + a + 1$$
$$= b * a \qquad \forall\, a, b \in \mathbf{Z}$$

Hence $< \mathbf{Z}, * >$ is an abelian group.

Example 11. *Let* $\mathbf{Q}$ *be the set of rational numbers. Define*

$$G = \{(a, b) \mid a, b \in \mathbf{Q}, a \neq 0\}$$

Also define a composition $*$ *on* G *by*

$$(a, b) * (c, d) = (ac, ad + b)$$

Show that $<G, * >$ *forms a non-abelian group.*

Solution. *Closure:* Let $(a, b), (c, d) \in G$ be any two elements. Then $a \neq 0, c \neq 0$.

Now $(a, b) * (c, d) = (ac, ad + b) \in G$

as $a, c \neq 0 \Rightarrow ac \neq 0$.

and also ac and $ad + b$ belong to **Q** whenever, $a, b, c, d \in \mathbf{Q}$.

Hence closure holds.

Associativity. Let $(a, b), (c, d), (e, f)$ be any three members of G. Then

$$[(a, b) * (c, d)] * (e, f) = (ac, ad + b) * (e, f) \qquad a, c, e \neq 0$$
$$= (ace, acf + ad + b)$$
$$(a, b) * [(c, d) * (e, f)] = (a, b) * (ce, cf + d)$$
$$= (ace, a(cf + d) + b)$$
$$= (ace, acf + ad + b)$$

$\Rightarrow$ Associativity holds.

Existence of identity. We observe

$$(a, b) * (1, 0) = (a, a \,.\, 0 + b) = (a, b) = (1, 0) * (a, b)$$
$$\forall\ (a, b) \in \mathbf{Z}$$

$\Rightarrow (1, 0) \in G$ is the identity.

Existence of inverse. If $(a, b) \in G$ be any element then $(c, d) \in G$ will be inverse of (a, b) if

$$(a, b) * (c, d) = (c, d) * (a, b) = (1, 0)$$

Now $(a, b) * (c, d) = (1, 0)$

$\Leftrightarrow \quad (ac, ad + b) = (1, 0)$

$\Leftrightarrow \quad ac = 1$ and $ad + b = 0$

$\Leftrightarrow \quad c = \dfrac{1}{a}$ and $d = -\dfrac{b}{a} \qquad (a \neq 0)$

NOTE. Since $a \neq 0$, we can talk of $\frac{1}{a}$ clearly then $\left(\frac{1}{a}, -\frac{b}{a}\right)$ is the inverse of (a, b).

Hence <G, *> is a group.

To show that it is not abelian, consider the elements $(2, 3), (1, 4) \in G$.

Now $(2, 3) * (1, 4) = (2 \times 1, 8 + 3) = (2, 11)$

and $(1, 4) * (2, 3) = (1 \times 2, 3 + 4) = (2, 7)$

Since $(2, 11) \neq (2, 7)$,

we note that <G, *> is not abelian.

Example 12. *Give an example of a system <G, *> which satisfies all the axioms in the definition of a group, except the associative axiom.*

Solution. Let $G = \{0, 1, 2\}$

Define a composition $*$ on G, by

$$a * b = |a - b|$$

Closure. If $a, b \in G$ are any two elements (*i.e.*, any of the elements 0, 1, 2).

Then $a * b = |a - b| \in G$ is clear.

Thus closure holds and so $*$ is a binary composition defined on G.

Existence of Identity. For any $a \in G$,

$a * 0 = |a - 0| = a = |0 - a| = 0 * a$

$\Rightarrow$ 0 is the identity element.

Existence of inverse. Since for any $a \in G$,

$$a * a = |a - a| = 0. \qquad \text{(identity)}$$

it follows that a is inverse of a for any $a \in G$.

We show now that associativity does not hold in this system.

We note that

$$1 * (1 * 2) = 1 * (|1 - 2|) = 1 * 1 = |1 - 1| = 0$$

$$(1 * 1) * 2 = |1 - 1| * 2 = 0 * 2 = |0 - 2| = 2.$$

$\Rightarrow$ $\quad 1 * (1 * 2) \neq (1 * 1) * 2$

$\Rightarrow$ associativity does not hold.

Example 13. *Show that the set* $G = \{1, -1, i, -i\}$ *forms an abelian group w.r.t. the usual multiplication where* $i = \sqrt{-1}$.

Solution. We draw the composition table

	1	– 1	i	$-i$
1	1	– 1	i	$-i$
– 1	– 1	1	$-i$	i
i	i	$-i$	– 1	1
$-i$	$-i$	i	1	– 1

Suppose we want to find $(i) \cdot (-i)$ then we locate i in the first column and $-i$ in the first row. The product $(i) \cdot (-i)$ is given in the fourth row and fifth column [fourth row is in which i lies and fifth column is in which $-i$ lies].

Closure holds clearly by having a look at the above table.

Associativity and commutativity are also easy to verify. (In fact the above table suggests that these properties hold).

Existence of identity. We observe

$$1 . 1 = 1 . 1 = 1$$
$$-1 . 1 = 1 . (-1) = (-1)$$
$$i . 1 = 1 . i = i$$
$$-i . 1 = 1 . (-i) = -i$$

$\Rightarrow$ 1 is the identity.

Existence of inverse. Since $1 . 1 = 1 . 1 = 1$ (identity)

1 is inverse of 1.

Again $(-1) . (-1) = (-1) . (-1) = 1$ (the identity)

$\Rightarrow$ -1 is the inverse of -1

Also, $i(-i) = (-i).i = 1$

$\Rightarrow$ $-i$ is inverse of i and i is inverse of $-i$

Thus all the elements have inverse in G

$\Rightarrow$ $< G, . >$ is an abelian group.

Example 14. *Let G be the set {e, a, b} and let a composition be defined on G by the following composition table.*

	e	a	b
e	e	a	b
a	a	e	a
b	b	b	e

Does this system <G, ∗> form a group?

Solution. Closure is trivial by having a look at the composition table.

Also since $a * e = e * a = a$

$$b * e = e * b = b$$
$$e * e = e * e = e$$

e is the identity.

Again $a * a = e = a * a \Rightarrow a$ is inverse of a

$b * b = e = b * b \Rightarrow b$ is inverse of b

$e * e = e = e * e \Rightarrow e$ is inverse of e

Let us check associativity.

Now $(a * b) * a = a * a = e$

But $a * (b * a) = a * b = a$

and $a \neq e$

$\Rightarrow$ Associativity does not hold.

Hence $< G, * >$ does not form a group.

Example 15. *Let G = {0, 1, 2, 3, 4}. Define a binary composition ⊕ on G by*

$$a \oplus b = c$$

where c is the least non – ve remainder got by dividing a + b by 5. Show that <G, ⊕> forms an abelian group.

Solution. The composition table would be

⊕	0	1	2	3	4
0	0	1	2	3	4
1	1	2	3	4	0
2	2	3	4	0	1
3	3	4	0	1	2
4	4	0	1	2	3

closure property holds by definition, since $a \oplus b$ can take values 0, 1, 2, 3, 4 only and they belong to G [also, of course, $a \oplus b$ will obviously be unique].

Commutativity is again trivial as the remainder got by dividing $a+b$ by 5 is same as that got by dividing $b+a$ by 5.

Associativity. Let $a, b, c \in G$ be any three members. We show $(a \oplus b) \oplus c = a \oplus (b \oplus c)$

Let $a \oplus b = d$ and $(a \oplus b) \oplus c = d \oplus c = r$

Now $a \oplus b = d \Rightarrow d$ is the least non-negative remainder got by dividing $a \oplus b$ by 5.

i.e., $$a + b = 5k_1 + d$$

[For example, if $a = 3$, $b = 4$, then $a + b = 7$ and here $d = 2$, $k_1 = 1$, so $7 = 5.1 + 2$.]

Again $d \oplus c = r \Rightarrow r$ is the least non-negative remainder got by dividing $d+c$ by 5.

i.e., $d + c = 5k_2 + r$ for some k_2 and, of course $0 \le r < 5$

Thus $$(a + b) + c = d + 5k_1 + c$$
$$= 5k_1 + r + 5k_2$$
$$= r + 5(k_1 + k_2) = 5k + r$$

and $$0 \le r < 5$$

Hence r is the least remainder got by dividing $(a + b) + c$ by 5.

Again if $a \oplus (b \oplus c) = s$

then as above, s will be the remainder (least, non – *ve*) got by dividing $a+(b+c)$ by 5.

But since $(a + b) + c = a + (b + c)$, the two remainders r and s will be equal thereby proving our result.

Identity. The composition table suggests that $a \oplus 0 = 0 \oplus a = a$ $\forall\ a \in G$

$\Rightarrow$ 0 is the identity.

Inverse. We note that $0 \oplus 0 = 0 \oplus 0 = 0$

$\Rightarrow$ 0 is the inverse of 0

Suppose $0 \neq a \in G$ be any element then $5 - a \in G$

Also $(5 - a) \oplus a = 0 = a \oplus (5 - a)$ (definition)

$\Rightarrow$ $5 - a$ is inverse of a $(a \neq 0)$

Hence each element has an inverse.

$\Rightarrow$ $< G, \oplus >$ is an abelian group.

NOTE. The above composition is called addition modulo 5 and is sometimes denoted by $\oplus_5$. Thus $3 \oplus_5 2 = 0$.

One can define this composition in general on the set {0, 1, 2, 3, ..., $(n - 1)$} where it will be called *addition modulo n*.

Example 16. *Let G = {1, 2, 3, 4, 5, 6} and define a binary composition ⊙ on G by a ⊙ b = c, where c is the least non-negative remainder obtained on dividing the product ab by 7. Show that <G, ⊙> forms an abelian group.*

Solution. The composition table will be

⊙	1	2	3	4	5	6
1	1	2	3	4	5	6
2	2	4	6	1	3	5
3	3	6	2	5	1	4
4	4	1	5	2	6	3
5	5	3	1	6	4	2
6	6	5	4	3	2	1

That the closure property holds is clear from the table. Also commutativity and associativity are trivially seen to be true.

Again 1 acts as the identity element

Also $1 \odot 1 = 1 \odot 1 = 1$

$$2 \odot 4 = 4 \odot 2 = 1$$
$$3 \odot 5 = 5 \odot 3 = 1$$
$$6 \odot 6 = 6 \odot 6 = 1.$$

$\Rightarrow$ 1 is inverse of 1

6 is inverse of 6

2 and 4 are inverse of each other and so are 3 and 5.

Hence $<G, \odot>$ is an abelian group.

The above binary composition is called multiplication modulo 7 and is sometimes denoted by $\odot_7$ or X_7.

The following example gives us the general result.

Example 17. (*a*) *Let* $S = \{x \in \mathbf{Z} |\ 1 \le x \le n$, *where* $(x, n) = 1\}$ *and* $\mathbf{Z}$ = *set of integers and by* (x, n) *we mean the Highest Common Factor (HCF) of x and n. Define a composition* $*$ *on S as:*

For all a, b $\in$ *S, a* $*$ *b is the least positive integer obtained as remainder when ab is divided by n. Show that* $<S, *>$ *forms an abelian group.*

Solution. *Closure:* Let $a * b = c$ for any $a, b \in S$.

Then c cannot be zero otherwise n divides ab, which is not possible as $(a, n) = 1$ and $(b, n) = 1$.

So $1 \le c < n$.

Further if $(c, n) \neq 1$ then $\exists$ some prime number p such that it divides both c and n, which means p divides ab as $a * b = c \Rightarrow ab = c + kp$ for some integer k; p being a prime, either p divides a or p divides b.

Thus either p divides *HCF* of a and n or *HCF* of b and n which is impossible as both $(a, n) = 1$ and $(b, n) = 1$.

Thus $(c, n) = 1$

$\Rightarrow$ $c \in S$

$\Rightarrow$ Closure holds.

Associativity. If $a * b = r_1$ and $(a * b) * c = r_2$

We get $r_1 * c = r_2$

i.e., $r_1 c = r_2 + k_2 n$ for some integer k_2

Now $ab = r_1 + k_1 n$ for some integer k_1 and

$$r_1 c = r_2 + k_2 n$$
$$\Rightarrow \quad (ab - k_1 n)c = r_2 + k_1 n$$
$$\Rightarrow \quad (ab)c = r_2 + (k_2 + k_1 c)n$$

which implies that r_2 is the least non-negative remainder got on dividing

$(ab)c$ by n. Similarly if $a * (b * c) = r_3$, then r_3 is the least non-negative integer obtained as remainder when $a(bc)$ is divided by n. But $(ab)c = a(bc)$

$$\Rightarrow \qquad r_2 = r_3$$

$$\Rightarrow \qquad (a * b) * c = a * (b * c)$$

Existence of identity. Clearly $1 \in S$ and

$$1 * a = a * 1 = a \quad \forall\ a \in S$$

$\Rightarrow$ 1 is identity of S.

Existence of inverse. Let $a \in S$, then $(a, n) = 1$

So there exist integers x and t such that

$$ax + ny = 1$$

If $1 \le x < n$ and $(x, n) = 1, x \in S$.

If not, then by division algorithm in integers $\exists$ integers q and r such that

$$x = qn + r, \quad 0 \le r < n$$

Now $\quad ax + ny = 1$

$$\Rightarrow \qquad aqn + ar + ny = 1$$

$$\Rightarrow \qquad ar = 1 + (-aq - y)n$$

So $a * r = 1$. Similarly $r * a = 1$

Again if $(r, n) \neq 1$, let p be a prime number dividing r and n. Then p will divide x.

So p divides 1 as $ax + ny = 1$ which is absurd.

Therefore, $(r, n) = 1$, hence $r \in S$

Thus $<S, *>$ is a group.

It is easy to verify that S is abelian.

Example 17 (*b*) *Does the set A = {0, 1, 2, ..., n – 1} with the operation of multiplication (modulo n) form a group for all positive integral values of n?*

Solution. The answer is no!

We leave it to the reader to reason why? Note 0 has no inverse!

Example 18. *Show that the set G = {1, ω, ω*^{2}*} forms an abelian group under usual multiplication, where 1, ω, ω*^{2} *are cube roots of unity.*

Solution. The composition table will be

	1	ω	ω^2
1	1	ω	ω^2
ω	ω	ω^2	1
ω^2	ω^2	1	ω

closure is easy to see from the above table.

1 will act as the identity element.

as $$1 . 1 = 1 = 1 . 1$$
$$1 . \omega = \omega = \omega . 1$$
$$1 . \omega^2 = \omega^2 = \omega^2 . 1$$

1 is clearly inverse of 1.

Also as $\omega . \omega^2 = \omega^2 . \omega = \omega^3 = 1$ (identity).

We note that ω is inverse of ω^2 and ω^2 is inverse of ω.

Associativity can be verified by the help of the composition table, commutativity being obvious.

Hence the result.

Example 19. *Show that the set of all 2 × 2 matrices over integers forms an abelian group w.r.t. matrix addition.*

Solution. Let $M = \left\{ \begin{bmatrix} a & b \\ c & d \end{bmatrix} \mid a, b, c, d \in \mathbf{Z} \right\}$

Then clearly M is a non-empty set.

Also since for any two matrices $A, B \in M$, $A + B$ is again a 2×2 matrix belonging to M.

We note that closure holds.

Again the fact that matrix addition is both commutative and associative proves the other two axioms in the definition of a group.

The matrix $\begin{bmatrix} 0 & 0 \\ 0 & 0 \end{bmatrix}$ will act as the identity and for any matrix $\begin{bmatrix} a & b \\ c & d \end{bmatrix}$, the matrix $\begin{bmatrix} -a & -b \\ -c & -d \end{bmatrix}$ will act as inverse.

Hence the set M forms an abelian group.

[Reader is referred to the Chapter on Matrices for the proofs of the above results].

Example 20. *Prove that the matrices* $\begin{bmatrix} 1 & 0 \\ 0 & 1 \end{bmatrix}$ *and* $\begin{bmatrix} 0 & 1 \\ 1 & 0 \end{bmatrix}$ *form a group under matrix multiplication.*

Solution. Let G be the set containing the matrices

$I = \begin{bmatrix} 1 & 0 \\ 0 & 1 \end{bmatrix}$ and $A = \begin{bmatrix} 0 & 1 \\ 1 & 0 \end{bmatrix}$. Then we note that

$$IA = \begin{bmatrix} 1 & 0 \\ 0 & 1 \end{bmatrix}\begin{bmatrix} 0 & 1 \\ 1 & 0 \end{bmatrix} = \begin{bmatrix} 0 & 1 \\ 1 & 0 \end{bmatrix} = A$$

$$II = \begin{bmatrix} 1 & 0 \\ 0 & 1 \end{bmatrix}\begin{bmatrix} 1 & 0 \\ 0 & 1 \end{bmatrix} = \begin{bmatrix} 1 & 0 \\ 0 & 1 \end{bmatrix} = I$$

$$AI = \begin{bmatrix} 0 & 1 \\ 1 & 0 \end{bmatrix}\begin{bmatrix} 1 & 0 \\ 0 & 1 \end{bmatrix} = \begin{bmatrix} 0 & 1 \\ 1 & 0 \end{bmatrix} = A$$

$$AA = \begin{bmatrix} 0 & 1 \\ 1 & 0 \end{bmatrix}\begin{bmatrix} 0 & 1 \\ 1 & 0 \end{bmatrix} = \begin{bmatrix} 1 & 0 \\ 0 & 1 \end{bmatrix} = I$$

So closure holds.

I acts as the identity element.

Also A and I act as their own inverse.

Associativity can also be checked easily.

Hence the set G forms a group under matrix multiplication. [It will be an abelian group.]

REMARK: Compare this with Example 5.

3. DEFINITION

If $<G, .>$ is a group and $a \in G$, then we denote $a \,.\, a$ by a^2 which is again a member of G. Similarly by a^3, we mean $a^2 \,.\, a$. This notation can be extended further also. One can show that

$$a^m a^n = a^{m+n}$$
$$(a^m)^n = a^{mn}$$
$$a^{-m} = (a^m)^{-1} \text{ etc.}$$

Example 21. *If G is a group, such that* $(ab)^2 = a^2\, b^2 \;\forall\; a, b \in G$, *show that G is abelian.*

Solution. Let $a, b \in G$ be any two members.

Then $(ab)^2 = a^2b^2$ (given)

$\Rightarrow$ $(ab)(ab) = (aa)(bb)$ (Definition)

$\Rightarrow$ $(aba)b = (aab)b$ (Associativity)

$\Rightarrow \quad aba = aab$ (Cancellation laws)

$\Rightarrow \quad ba = ab$

$\Rightarrow$ G is abelian.

Example 22. *If every element of a group G is its own inverse then G is abelian.*

Solution. Let $a, b \in G$ be any two elements.

$\Rightarrow \quad ab \in G$ (closure)

$\Rightarrow \quad ab = (ab)^{-1}$ (given)

$\Rightarrow \quad ab = b^{-1}a^{-1}$

But as $a, b \in G, a^{-1} = a, b^{-1} = b$

Thus $ab = ba \;\forall\; a, b \in G$

$\Rightarrow$ G is abelian.

Example 23. *A group G having three elements is always abelian.*

Solution. Let G have three elements e, a, b such that $e \neq a \neq b$ [e being the identity].

Now $a, b \in G \;\Rightarrow\; ab \in G$ (closure)

Thus either $ab = e$ or $ab = a$ or $ab = b$

Suppose $ab = a$

$\Rightarrow \quad ab = ae$

$\Rightarrow \quad b = e$

But the is not true. So $ab \neq a$

Suppose $ab = b$

$\Rightarrow \quad ab = eb$

$\Rightarrow \quad a = e$

which is not true. So $ab \neq b$.

Hence $ab = e \Rightarrow b$ is inverse of a

i.e., $b = a^{-1}$

Thus $ab = aa^{-1} = e = a^{-1}a = ba$

Also clearly $ea = ae$, $eb = be$, $ee = ee$ and so each element commutes with all others.

$\Rightarrow$ G is abelian.

Example 24. *Show that for given a, b, in a group G the equations*

$$ax = b$$

$$ya = b$$

have unique solutions for x and y in G.

Solution. We show that the equation $ax = b$ has a unique solution in G, *i.e.*, $\exists$ a unique value of x in G which statisfies this equation.

$$\text{Now } ax = b \quad \Rightarrow \quad a^{-1}(ax) = a^{-1}b$$
$$\Rightarrow \quad (a^{-1}a)x = a^{-1}b$$
$$\Rightarrow \quad ex = a^{-1}b \text{ where } e \text{ is identity element of } G$$
$$\Rightarrow \quad x = a^{-1}b$$

Now $a^{-1}b \in G$ as $a, b \in G$, and this is the value of x that satisfies the equation $ax = b$.

Suppose now $x = x_1$ and $x = x_2$ are two solutions of the equation $ax = b$.

$$\text{Then} \quad ax_1 = b$$
$$ax_2 = b$$
$$\Rightarrow \quad ax_1 = ax_2$$
$$\Rightarrow \quad x_1 = x_2 \qquad \text{(by cancellation laws)}$$

$\Rightarrow$ solution is unique.

Similarly it can be shown that $y = ba^{-1}$ is the unique solution of the equation $ya = b$.

EXERCISES

1. If Q^+ = set of + ve rational numbers and $*$ be a composition defined on Q^+ by
$$a * b = \frac{ab}{3}$$
Show that $\langle Q^+, *\rangle$ forms an abelian group.
2. Let G = set of all real numbers except – 1. Define * on G by $a * b = a + b + ab \ \forall \ a, b \in G$. Show that $\langle G . *\rangle$ is an abelian group.
3. Prove that the set Q of all rational numbers other than 1 with the operation * defined by $a * b = a + b - ab$ constitutes an abelian group.
4. If G is a group in which $a^2 = e, \ \forall \ a \in G$, show that G is abelian [e being the identity of G].
[*Hint.* See Example 22.]
5. Show that a group with
(*i*) one element
(*ii*) two elements
is abelian.
6. Does commutativity hold in Examples 13 and 14?
7. Let $G = \{e, a\}$ be a set on which a composition * is defined by $x * y = e \ \forall \ x, y \in G$.
Show that $\langle G, *\rangle$ does not form a group.
8. If M is the set of all 2 × 2 matrices over the integers then show that it does not form a group w.r.t. matrix multiplication.

9. Let $G = \{1, 2, 3, ..., p - 1\}$ where p is a prime number. Show that G forms an abelian group under multiplication modulo p.
[**Hint.** See Examples 16 and 17]

4. RINGS

A group, we've seen is a system having a non-empty set with one binary composition. We come now to the systems with two binary compositons (the set of integers **Z** being an immediate example with its addition and multiplication as the two binary operations).

Definition. Let R be a non-empty set and let + and '.' be two binary compositions on R. Then R is said to form a ring w.r.t. + and . if

$R-(i)$ $\quad a + b = b + a \quad \forall\ a, b \in R$

$R-(ii)$ $\quad a + (b + c) = (a + b) + c \quad \forall\ a, b, c \in R$

$R-(iii)$ $\quad \exists\ 0 \in R$, such that

$$a + 0 = 0 + a = a \ \ \forall\ a \in R$$

$\mathrm{R}-(iv)$ $\quad$ For every $a \in R$, $\exists\ (-a) \in R$, such that

$$a + (-a) = (-a) + a = 0$$

$R-(v)$ $\quad a\,.\,(b\,.\,c) = (a\,.\,b)\,.\,c \quad \forall\ a, b, c \in R$

$R-(vi)$ $\quad a\,.\,(b + c) = a\,.\,b + a\,.\,c \quad \forall\ a, b, c \in R$

$$(b + c)\,.\,a = b\,.\,a + c\,.\,a$$

REMARKS:

(*a*) Since + and . are binary operations defined on R, the closure properties hold i.e., $\forall\ a, b \in R$, $a + b \in R$ and $a\,.\,b \in R$.

(*b*) We could use any symbols like ⊗, * etc. in place of + and . (but have used them for obvious reasons, after all how natural the axioms look with these symbols). The two are called respectively, addition and multiplication compositions.

(*c*) Axioms *R*—(*i*) to *R*—(*iv*) can also be expressed by saying that $\langle R, +\rangle$ forms an abelian group.

(*d*) Element 0 in *R*—(*iii*) is called *zero* of the ring. It is, of course, unique (we have shown that identity of a group is unique). The zero of R is called the *additive identity* of R.

(*e*) Whenever we say that R is a ring, it will be understood that R is a ring w.r.t. the two operations + (addition) and (multiplication).

5. COMMUTATIVE RING

A ring R, in which

$$ab = ba \ \forall\ a, b \in R$$

is called a *commutative ring*.

6. RING WITH UNITY

An element e of a ring R is called a *unity* of R if $ae = ea = a \ \forall \ a \in R$.

Any ring having unity is called a *ring with unity*.

In general, a ring may or may not have a unity, but if unity exists, it is unique (Prove!)

It is customary to denote the unity of a ring R by 1.

We now take some examples of rings.

Example 25. **<R, +, .>**, *where* **R** *is the set of real numbers and + and . are the usual addition and multiplication forms a commutative ring with unity.*

Solution. It is very easy to verify the axioms *R*—(*i*) to *R*—(*vi*) in the definition of a ring.

The real numbers 0 and 1 act as the zero and unity of this ring.

Example 26. *The system* < **Z**, +, .> *where* **Z** = *set of integers and + and . are the usual addition and multiplication forms a commutative ring with unity.*

Solution. Similar to above example.

Example 27. *Let E be the set of all even integers. Show that E is a commutative ring without unity, under usual addition and multiplication.*

Solution. Since sum and product of any two even integers is again an even integer we note that + and . are well defined binary operations on E.

It is, of course, very easy to prove other properties. Note that since $\nexists$ any even integer e, such that $ex = xe = x$ for all even integers x, E is a ring without unity.

Example 28. *The set M of all 2 × 2 matrices over the integers forms a non-commutative ring w.r.t. matrix addition and multiplication.*

Solution. We have already seen that M forms an abelian group w.r.t. matrix addition.

Again it is known that matrix multiplication is associative and also distributivity holds.

Hence M is a ring.

Note the matrix $\begin{bmatrix} 1 & 0 \\ 0 & 1 \end{bmatrix}$ will act as unity.

So this is a matrix with unity, but it is not commutative as

$$\begin{bmatrix} 1 & 2 \\ 0 & 3 \end{bmatrix}\begin{bmatrix} 1 & 0 \\ 1 & 0 \end{bmatrix} = \begin{bmatrix} 3 & 0 \\ 3 & 0 \end{bmatrix}$$

and $\begin{bmatrix} 1 & 0 \\ 1 & 0 \end{bmatrix}\begin{bmatrix} 1 & 2 \\ 0 & 3 \end{bmatrix} = \begin{bmatrix} 1 & 2 \\ 1 & 2 \end{bmatrix}$

thus $\begin{bmatrix} 1 & 2 \\ 0 & 3 \end{bmatrix}\begin{bmatrix} 1 & 0 \\ 1 & 0 \end{bmatrix} \neq \begin{bmatrix} 1 & 0 \\ 1 & 0 \end{bmatrix}\begin{bmatrix} 1 & 2 \\ 0 & 3 \end{bmatrix}$

Example 29. *Let G be an additive abelian group with at least two elements. Define a binary composition on G by* $x \,.\, y = 0 \;\forall\; x, y \in G$. *Show that* $< G, +, . >$ *is a commutative ring without unity.*

Solution. It is already given that $< G, + >$ is an abelian group. So we need to prove only *R*—(*v*) and *R*—(*vi*)

For any $a, b, c \in G$,

$$a \,.\, (b \,.\, c) = a \,.\, 0 = 0$$

$$(a \,.\, b) \,.\, c = 0 \,.\, c = 0$$

$$\Rightarrow \quad a \,.\, (b \,.\, c) = (a \,.\, b) \,.\, c \quad \forall\; a, b, c \in G$$

Also $\quad a \,.\, (b + c) = 0$

$$a \,.\, b + a \,.\, c = 0 + 0 = 0$$

$$\Rightarrow \quad a \,.\, (b + c) = a \,.\, b + a \,.\, c$$

Similarly $\quad (b + c) \,.\, a = b \,.\, a + c \,.\, a.$

Thus $< G, +, . >$ is a ring

Clearly $\quad a \,.\, b = 0 = b \,.\, a \;\forall\; a, b \in G$

$\Rightarrow$ *G* is commutative.

Again there does not exist any element $e \in G$

such that $\quad a \,.\, e = e \,.\, a = a \quad \forall\; a \in G$

as $\quad a \,.\, e = 0$ for any $a, e \in G$

$\Rightarrow$ *G* is without unity.

Example 30. *Let* $R = \{0, 1, 2, 3, 4, 5, 6\}$ *and let* $\otimes$ *and* $\odot$ *be respectively the addition and multiplication modulo 7. Show that* $<R, \oplus, \odot>$ *forms a ring.*

Solution. We already know that $\oplus$ and $\odot$ are binary operations on *R* [see Groups].

Again it has been proved that $<R, \oplus>$ is an abelian group.

The result $a \odot (b \odot c) = (a \odot b) \odot c$ has also been proved.

Consider

$$2 \odot (3 \oplus 4) = 2 \odot 0 = 0$$

$$2 \odot 3 \oplus 2 \odot 4 = 6 \oplus 1 = 0$$

$$\Rightarrow \quad 2 \odot (3 \oplus 4) = 2 \odot 3 \oplus 2 \odot 4.$$

The result would be true for any $a, b, c \in R$

$\Rightarrow$ $<R, \oplus, \odot>$ is a ring.

Example 31. *Let* $R = \{(a, b) \mid a, b$ *are rational numbers*$\}$. *Define* $\oplus$ *and* $\odot$ *by*

$$(a, b) \oplus (c, d) = (a + c, b + d)$$

$$(a, b) \odot (c, d) = (ac, bd)$$

Show that $<R, \oplus, \odot>$ *forms a commutative ring with unity.*

Solution. Clearly by definition $\oplus$ and $\odot$ are binary operations.

$\oplus$ *is commutative.*

$$(a, b) \oplus (c, d) = (a + c, b + d)$$

$$= (c + a, d + b) = (c, d) \oplus (a, b)$$

$\oplus$ *is associative.*

Similar as above.

Identity. We note $(a, b) \oplus (0, 0) = (a + 0, b + 0) = (a, b)$

$$= (0, 0) \oplus (a, b) \;\forall\; (a, b) \in R$$

$\Rightarrow (0, 0)$ is additive identity.

Inverse. For any $(a, b) \in R$, $(-a, -b) \in R$

such that

$$(a, b) \oplus (-a, -b) = (a - a, b - b) = (0, 0)$$

$\Rightarrow (-a, -b)$ is inverse of (a, b).

Also

$[(a, b) \odot (c, d)] \odot (e, f) = (ac, bd) \odot (e, f) = (ace, bdf)$

$(a, b) \odot [(c, d) \odot (e, f)] = ((a, b) \odot (ce, df) = (ace, bdf))$

$\Rightarrow$ $\odot$ is associative.

Again

$$(a, b) \odot [(c, d) + (e, f)] = (a, b) \odot (c + e, d + f)$$

$$= [a(c + e), b(d + f)]$$

$$= (ac + ae, bd + bf)$$

$$(a, b) \odot (c, d) \oplus (a, b) \odot (e, f) = (ac, bd) \oplus (ae, bf)$$

$$= (ac + ae, bd + bf)$$

$\Rightarrow$ Distributivity holds.

Hence $< R, \oplus, \odot >$ is a ring.

Again $(a, b) \odot (c, d) = (ac, bd) = (ca, db) = (c, d) \odot (a, b)$

$\Rightarrow$ R is commutative.

Also $(a, b) \odot (1, 1) = (a \cdot 1, b \cdot 1) = (a, b) = (1, 1) \odot (a, b)$
$\forall\ (a, b) \in R$

$\Rightarrow$ (1, 1) is unity.

$\Rightarrow$ R is commutative ring with unity.

7. THEOREM

Suppose <R, +, . > is a ring and $a, b, c \in R$ are any members then

(*i*) $a \cdot 0 = 0 \cdot a = 0$

(*ii*) $a \cdot (b - c) = a \cdot b - a \cdot c$

(*iii*) $-(-a) = a$

(*iv*) $a \cdot (-b) = (-a) \cdot b = -a \cdot b$

(*v*) $(-a) \cdot (-b) = a \cdot b$

Where, of course, 0 is the zero (*i.e.*, additive identity) of R and by $-a$ we mean additive inverse of a.

Proof. (*i*) We have

$$a \cdot 0 = a \cdot (0+0)$$
$$= a \cdot 0 + a \cdot 0$$

$$\Rightarrow \quad a \cdot 0 + (-a \cdot 0) = (a \cdot 0 + a \cdot 0) + (-a \cdot 0)$$
$$= a \cdot 0 + [a \cdot 0 + (-a \cdot 0)]$$
$$= a \cdot 0 + 0$$

$\Rightarrow 0 = a \cdot 0 + 0$

$\Rightarrow 0 = a \cdot 0.$

Similarly $0 \cdot a = 0$.

(*ii*) We have $a \cdot (b - c) + a \cdot c \quad = a \cdot [(b - c) + c]$
$= a \cdot [b + (-c + c)]$
$= a \cdot [b + 0] = a \cdot b$

$\Rightarrow a \cdot (b - c) + a \cdot c + (-a \cdot c) = a \cdot b - a \cdot c$

$\Rightarrow a \cdot (b - c) + 0 = a \cdot b - a \cdot c$

$\Rightarrow a \cdot (b - c) = a \cdot b - a \cdot c$

(*iii*) Let b be additive inverse of $-a$,

i.e., $b = -(-a)$

then $\quad b + (-a) = 0$

$\Rightarrow \quad b + (-a) + a = 0 + a$

$\Rightarrow \quad b + 0 = 0 + a$

$\Rightarrow \quad b = a$

$\Rightarrow \quad -(-a) = a$

(*iv*) We have

$$a \,.\, (-b) = a \,.\, (0 - b) = a \,.\, 0 - a \,.\, b$$
$$= 0 - a \,.\, b$$
$$= -a \,.\, b$$

Similarly $(-a) \,.\, b = -a \,.\, b$

(*v*) $(-a) \,.\, (-b) = -[a \,.\, (-b)]$
$$= -[-a \,.\, b] = a \,.\, b$$

Example 32. *Show that a ring $<R, +, .>$ is commutative if and only if $(a + b)^2 = a^2 + 2ab + b^2 \;\forall\; a, b \in R$, where by a^2 we mean $a \,.\, a$.*

Solution. Let R be commutative

Now $(a + b)^2 = (a + b)(a + b)$ $\qquad \forall\; a, b \in R$

$= (a + b)\, a + (a + b) b$ [Distributive law]

$= aa + ba + ab + bb$ [Distributive law]

$= a^2 + ab + ab + b^2$

$= a^2 + 2ab + b^2.$

Conversely, let the given result hold. We show R is commutative. Let $a, b \in R$ be any two elements. Then

$$(a + b)^2 = (a + b)(a + b) = a^2 + ab + ba + b^2.$$

But it is given that $(a + b)^2 = a^2 + 2ab + b^2$.

Thus $a^2 + ab + ba + b^2 = a^2 + 2ab + b^2$

$\Rightarrow \quad ab + ba = 2ab$

$\Rightarrow \quad ab + ba = ab + ab$

$\Rightarrow \quad ba = ab$

$\Rightarrow \quad R$ is commutative.

Example 33. *If $x \in R$ satisfies $x^2 = x$, prove that R must be commutative.*

Solution. Let $a, b \in R$ be any two elements.

$\Rightarrow \quad a + b \in R$ (closure)

$\Rightarrow \quad (a + b)^2 = a + b$ (given)

$\Rightarrow \quad a^2 + b^2 + ab + ba = a + b$

$\Rightarrow \quad a + b + ab + ba = a + b$

$\Rightarrow \quad ab + ba = 0$

$\Rightarrow \quad ab = -\, ba$

$\Rightarrow \quad ab = (-\, b)a$ ...(*i*)

Now $(-\, b)^2 = -\, b$ as $-\, b \in R$

$\Rightarrow \quad (-\, b)(-\, b) = -\, b$

$\Rightarrow \qquad bb = -b$

$\Rightarrow \qquad b^2 = -b$

$\Rightarrow \qquad b = -b$

Thus $(i) \Rightarrow ab = ba$

$\Rightarrow$ R is commutagive.

Example 34. *If $< R, +, . >$ is a system satisfying all axioms of a ring with unity, except that $a + b = b + a$, show that this axiom also holds.*

Solution. It is given that $1 \in R$

$\Rightarrow \qquad 1 + 1 \in R$

Now for any $a, b \in R$

$$(a+b)(1+1) = a(1+1) + b(1+1) = a+a+b+b$$

Also $\qquad (a+b)(1+1) = (a+b)1 + (a+b)1 = a+b+a+b$

Equating the two values

$$a+a+b+b = a+b+a+b$$

$\Rightarrow \qquad a+b = b+a$

8. DEFINITON

If R is a commutative ring, then $0 \neq a \in R$ is said to be a *zero divisor* if $\exists$ some $b \in R$, $b \neq 0$ such that $ab = 0$.

A commutative ring is called an *integral domain* if it has no zero divisors *i.e.*, a commutative ring R is called an integral domain if $ab = 0 \Rightarrow a = 0$ or $b = 0$.

The ring $< \mathbf{Z}, +, . >$ of integers is an integral domain.

Another example of an integral domain will be the ring R of integers mod 5 under addition and multiplication mod 5.

Example 35. *Give an example of a commutative ring, which is not an integral domain.*

Solution. Let $R = \{0, 1, 2, 3, 4, 5\}$ and let $\oplus$ and $\odot$ be respectively addition and multiplication modulo 6.

It is easy to see that this forms a commutative ring [one can proceed as in Example 30].

We note that

$$2 \odot 3 = 0, \quad \text{yet } 2 \neq 0, 3 \neq 0$$

i.e. $\exists\, a, b \in R$, such that $ab = 0$ whereas $a, b \neq 0$

Hence it is not an integral domain.

9. FIELDS

A non empty set F together with two binary operations + and . is said to form a *field* if $\forall\ a, b, c \in F$

(i) $a + (b + c) = (a + b) + c$

(ii) $a + b = b + a$

(iii) $\exists\ 0 \in F$, such that $a + 0 = 0 + a = a$

(iv) For each $a \in F,\ \exists - a \in F,$ such that
$a + (-a) = (-a) + a = 0$

(v) $a\ .\ (b\ .\ c) = (a\ .\ b)\ .\ c$

(vi) $a\ .\ b = b\ .\ a$

(vii) $\exists\ 1 \in F$ such that $a\ .\ 1 = 1\ .\ a = a$

(viii) For any non-zero $a \in F, \exists\ a^{-1} \in F$, such that
$a\ .\ a^{-1} = a^{-1}\ .\ a = 1$

(ix) $a\ .\ (b + c) = a\ .\ b + a\ .\ c$
$(b + c)\ .\ a = b\ .\ a + c\ .\ a$

In short, a field is a commutative ring with unity in which non-zero elements have multiplicative inverse.

10. DEFINITION

A ring with unity is said to be a *division ring* if its non zero elements have multiplicative inverse.

An immediate inference is a *field is a commutative division ring*.

REMARK: One could also say a ring with unity is a division ring if its non-zero elements form a group w.r.t. multiplication.

Example 36. *The set* **R** *of real numbers forms a field under the usual addition and multiplication.*

Solution. It is easy to verify all the axioms in the definition.

Example 37. *The set* **Q** *of all rational numbers forms a field under the usual addition and multiplication.*

Solution. As in the previous example.

Example 38. *The set $R = \{0, 1, 2, 3, 4, 5, 6\}$ under additon $\oplus$ and multiplication $\odot$ mod 7 forms a field.*

Solution. We have already shown that this set forms a commutative ring. Also 1 is unity of this ring.

Again since $1 \odot 1 = 1 = 6 \odot 6$

$2 \odot 3 = 1 = 4 \odot 2$

$3 \odot 5 = 1 = 5 \odot 3$

We note that the non zero elements have multiplicative inverse

1 is inverse of 1

2 is inverse of 4

3 is inverse of 5

Hence R is a field.

Example 39. *Show that the set* $F = \{a + b\sqrt{2} \mid a, b$ *are rational numbers*$\}$ *is a field under usual addition and multiplication.*

Solution. *Closure for addition:*

Let $a + b\sqrt{2}$, $c + d\sqrt{2} \in F$, then a, b, c, d are rationals.

Now $(a + b\sqrt{2}) + (c + d\sqrt{2}) = (a + c) + (b + d)\sqrt{2}$
which also belongs to F as $(a + c)$ and $(b + d)$ are rationals.

Closure for multiplication,

$(a + b\sqrt{2})\,(c + d\sqrt{2}) = (ac + 2bd) + (ad + bc)\sqrt{2} \in F$ as $ac + 2bd$ and $ad + bc$ are rationals.

Associativity for addition.

$$[(a + b\sqrt{2}) + (c + d\sqrt{2})] + (e + f\sqrt{2})$$
$$= (a + c) + (b + d)\sqrt{2} + e + f\sqrt{2}$$
$$= (a + c + e) + (b + d + f)\sqrt{2}$$
$$= (a + b\sqrt{2}) + (c + e) + (d + f)\sqrt{2}$$
$$= (a + b\sqrt{2}) + [(c + d\sqrt{2}) + (e + f\sqrt{2})]$$

Commutativity for addition. Similar as above.

Additive identity.

$0 + 0\sqrt{2} \in F$ and $(a + b\sqrt{2}) + (0 + 0\sqrt{2}) = (a + 0) + (b + 0)\sqrt{2} = a + b\sqrt{2}$

$\Rightarrow$ $0 + 0\sqrt{2}$ is additive identity.

Additive inverse.

For any $a + b\sqrt{2} \in F$,

$-a - b\sqrt{2}$ also belongs to F and

$(a + b\sqrt{2}) + (-a - b\sqrt{2}) = (a - a) + (b - b)\sqrt{2} = 0 + 0\sqrt{2}$

Thus $-a - b\sqrt{2}$ is inverse of $a + b\sqrt{2}$.

Associativity and commutativity for multiplication can also be verified easily.

Distributivity.

$$= (a + b\sqrt{2})[(c + d\sqrt{2}) + (e + f\sqrt{2})]$$
$$= (a + b\sqrt{2})[(c + e) + (d + f)\sqrt{2}]$$
$$= [ac + ae + 2(bd + fb)] + (ad + af + bc + be)\sqrt{2}$$
$$= [(ac + 2bd) + (ad + bc)\sqrt{2}] + [(ae + 2bf) + (af + be)\sqrt{2}]$$
$$= (a + b\sqrt{2})(c + d\sqrt{2}) + (a + b\sqrt{2})(e + f\sqrt{2})$$

Similarly right distributivity can be verified.

Unity.

$1 + 0\sqrt{2} \in F$

and as $\quad (a + b\sqrt{2})\,(1 + 0\sqrt{2}) = a + b\sqrt{2}$

We note that $1 + 0\sqrt{2}$ is the unity.

Multiplicative inverse.

Let $a + b\sqrt{2}$ be any non-zero element of F. Then

$$\frac{1}{a + b\sqrt{2}} = \frac{1}{a + b\sqrt{2}} \times \frac{a - b\sqrt{2}}{a - b\sqrt{2}}$$

$$= \frac{a - b\sqrt{2}}{a^2 - 2b^2} = \frac{a}{a^2 - 2^2} + \frac{(-b)}{a^2 - 2b^2}\sqrt{2}$$

which is again a member of F as

$\dfrac{a}{a^2 - 2b^2}$ and $\dfrac{-b}{a^2 - 2b^2}$ are rationals.

It is easy to verify that this is the required multiplicative inverse of $a + b\sqrt{2}$.

Hence F is a field.

11. THEOREM

A field is an integral domain.

Proof. Let $<F, +, .>$ be a field. We show that F has no zero divisors.

[It is already commutative].

Let, if possible, F have zero divisors.

$\Rightarrow \exists\, 0 \neq a, 0 \neq b \in F$ such that $ab = 0$

$$\Rightarrow a^{-1}(ab) = a^{-1}0$$

where a^{-1} is multiplicative inverse of a (and it exists as $a \neq 0$, by definition of a field)

$$\Rightarrow \quad (a^{-1}a)b = 0$$

$$\Rightarrow \quad b = 0$$

a contradiction as $b \neq 0$

$\Rightarrow$ F has no zero divisors

$\Rightarrow$ F is integral domain.

NOTE: The converse of above is not true.

As the set of integers forms an integral domain but not a field. One can, however, prove that a finite integral domain is a field.

EXERCISES

1. Show that the set Q of rational numbers forms a commutative ring with unity under the usual addition and multiplication. Will it form a field?
2. Does the set of integers form a field under usual addition and multiplication?
3. Let **Q** = set of rational numbers. Define $\oplus$ and $\odot$ on **Q** by

   $a \oplus b = a + b - 1$

   $a \odot b = a + b - ab$

   Show that $\langle \mathbf{Q}, \oplus, \odot \rangle$ forms a field.
4. If in a ring R, $x^2 = x \ \forall \ x \in R$, show that $2x = 0$.
5. If $a, b, c, d \in R$, a ring, evaluate $(a + b)(c + d)$.
6. Given an example of a non-commutative ring with unity which is not a division ring.

   [**Hint.** Set of 2 × 2 matrices over integers.]
7. Show that if R is a ring with unity 1 and $1 = 0$, the zero of R, then $R = \{0\}$.
8. Show that if R is a ring with unity 1 and has at least two elements then $1 \neq 0$.
9. In a ring R, show that

   $(-1)\ a = -a$

   $(-1)(-1) = 1$ where 1 is unity of R
10. In a field, show that

    $a(-b) = -(ab)$

    $(-a)\ (-b) = ab$ for any a, b.
11. Show that cancellation laws hold (w.r.t. the addition operation) in a ring.

ANSWERS

1. Yes 2. No 5. $ac + ad + bc + bd$

CHAPTER 4

REAL NUMBERS AND MATHEMATICAL INDUCTION

1. NATURAL NUMBERS, PEANO'S POSTULATES

"Counting" is one of the greatest achievements of mankind. In the stone age people used to take help of pebbles or dates in counting sheep etc. The discovery of numbers 1, 2, 3, 4, ... made this task so simple and natural that for many centuries no Mathematician took pains to define them formally and in a logical manner. It was towards the end of Nineteenth century that Mathematicians like Peano, Dedekind, Cantor gave serious thoughts to this problem. Peano defined natural numbers in terms of three postulates (called *Peano's Postulates* in his honour).

N is a set with the following properties

P—1: $1 \in \mathbf{N}$ *i.e.*, **N** is a non empty set.

P—2: For each $n \in \mathbf{N}$ there exists a unique $n^* \in \mathbf{N}$

(n^* is called *successor* of n) such that

(*i*) $m^* = n^*$ if and only if $m = n$

(*ii*) There is *no* element $k \in \mathbf{N}$ such that $k^* = 1$.

P—3: Let M be a subset of **N** such that $1 \in M$

and $t \in M \Rightarrow t^* \in M$ for *all* $t \in \mathbf{N}$

then $M = \mathbf{N}$ (*Axiom of Induction*)

The elements of **N** are called *natural numbers.* The successor n^* of n, is nothing but $n + 1$ in the usual sense. Thus $2 = 1^*$, $3 = 2^* = (1^*)^*$, $4 = 3^* = (2^*)^* = [(1^*)^*]^*$ etc. In this way all the natural numbers can be obtained.

REMARK: *P*—3 plays a keyrole in the proofs of many properties of natural numbers. We shall discuss it in details in a later section of this chapter.

2. DEFINITIONS

Addition, multiplication and order in **N** are defined as under:

(*a*) Addition '+'

For any $m \in \mathbf{N}$, $m + 1$ is defined to be m^* and for all $m, n \in \mathbf{N}$, $m + n^*$ is defined as $(m + n)^*$.

(*b*) Multiplication '.'

For any $m \in \mathbf{N}$, $m.1$ is defined to be m and for all $m, n \in \mathbf{N}$. $m. n^*$ is defined to be $mn + m$

(*c*) Order '>'

Let $m, n \in \mathbf{N}$. We write $m > n$ (or $n < m$) if $m = n + p$ for some $p \in \mathbf{N}$. In that case we say that m is greater than n (or n is less than m)

It can be proved with the help of $P - 1$, $P - 2$ and $P - 3$ that addition and multiplication are uniquely defined on **N** *i.e.*, to say that there is just one operation on **N** which has properties similar to those of addition and there is just one operation on **N** which has properties similar to those of multiplication.

In the following we shall deduce some of the properties of addition and multiplication.

3. PROPERTIES OF ADDITION AND MULTIPLICATION

(I) *Addition on N is associative.* Let M be the set of all $p \in \mathbf{N}$ such that $(m + n) + p = m + (n + p)$ holds for all $m, n \in \mathbf{N}$.

Then $1 \in M$ since $(m + n) + 1 = (m + n)^* = m + n^* = m + (n + 1)$.

Also let $k \in M$ *i.e.* $(m + n) + k = m + (n + k)$ for all $m, n \in \mathbf{N}$. We shall show that $k + 1 \in M$ *i.e.*, $(m + n) + (k + 1) = m + (n + k + 1)$ for all $m, n \in \mathbf{N}$.

Now $\quad (m + n) + (k + 1) = (m + n) + k^* = [(m + n) + k)]^* = [m + (n + k)]^*$
$= m + (n + k)^* = m + (n + k + 1)$. This shows that whenever

$k \in M$, then $k + 1 \in M$

By P—3, this means that $M = \mathbf{N}$

Hence $\qquad (m + n) + p = m + (n + p)$ for all $m, n, p \in \mathbf{N}$.

(II) *Addition on* **N** *is commutative.* First of all, we shall prove that $m + 1 = 1 + m$ for all $m \in \mathbf{N}$.

Let $M = \{m \in \mathbf{N} \mid m + 1 = 1 + m\}$ $\quad 1 \in M$ as $1 + 1 = 1 + 1 = 1^*$

Suppose that $k \in M$ $\quad$ *i.e.*, $k + 1 = 1 + k$.

Now $(k + 1) + 1 = (1 + k) + 1 = 1 + (k + 1)$ by Associativity of addition.

Then $(k + 1) + 1 = 1 + (k + 1) \Rightarrow k + 1 \in M$. By $P - 3$, we get $M = \mathbf{N}$

Now let $M' = \{n \in \mathbf{N} \mid m + n = t + m$ for all $m \in \mathbf{N}\}$

$1 \in M'$ by what we have proved above.

Let $t \in M'$ *i.e.*, $m + t = t + m$ for all $m \in \mathbf{N}$

Then $m+(t+1)$

$= m+(1+t)$ as $t+1=1+t$

$= (m+1)+t$

$= t+(m+1)$ as $m+t=t+m$ for all $m \in \mathbf{N}$

$= t+(1+m)$

$= (t+1)+m \Rightarrow t+1 \in M$

P—3, then, yields that $M' = \mathbf{N}$

(III) *Multiplication on* **N** *is left distributive over addition.* *i.e.,* $m(n+p) = mn + mp$

[We omit the sign of '.' just for convenience]

Let $M = \{p \in \mathbf{N} \mid m(n+p) = mn + mp \text{ for all } m, n \in \mathbf{N}\}$

Clearly $1 \in M$ as $m(n+1) = mn^* = mn + m = mn + m1$ by definition of multiplication.

Let $u \in M$ then $nm(n+u) = mn + mu$

Consider $u+1$, $m[n+(u+1)] = m(n+u^*) = m(n+u)^*$

$= m(n+u) + m = (mn+mu) + m = mn + (mu+m)$

$= mn + mu^* = mn + m(u+1)$. Hence $u+1 \in M$.

This forces, in view of P—3, that $M = \mathbf{N}$. With the help of (*I*), (*II*) and (*III*) we can prove the following properties.

(IV) *Multiplication on* **N** *is associative.*

(V) *Multiplication on* **N** *is right distributive over addition i.e.,* $(m+n)p = mp + np$ for all $m, n, p \in \mathbf{N}$.

(VI) *Multiplication on* **N** *is commutative.*

(VII) *Law of Trichotomy* i.e., if $m, n \in \mathbf{N}$ then one and only one of the following holds.

Either $m > n$ or $m = n$ or $n > m$.

Some other properties are proved in solved Examples and stated in exercises

Example 1. *For all* $m, n \in \mathbf{N}$, $m + n \neq m$.

Solution. Let $M = \{m \in \mathbf{N} \mid m + n \neq m \text{ for any } n \in M\}$

$1 \in M$ since $1 + n = n + 1 \neq 1$ by P—2 (*ii*)

Let $t \in M$ *i.e.,* $t + n \neq t$

If possible let $(t+1) + n = t + 1$

i.e., $t^* + n = t^*$

$\Rightarrow$ $n + t^* = t^*$

$\Rightarrow$ $(n+t)^* = t^*$

$\Rightarrow$ $n + t = t$ by P—2 (*i*)

$\Rightarrow \quad t + n = t,$ a contradiction

So $\quad (t+1) + n \neq t + 1$ *i.e.,* $t + 1 \in M$.

Consequently $M = \mathbf{N}$, in other words for no m in $\mathbf{N}$, $m + n$ is equal to m.

Example 2. *Cancellation Law holds for addition i.e., for all m, n,* $p \in \mathbf{N}$, $m + n = m + p \Rightarrow n = p$.

Solution. Let $M = \{m \in \mathbf{N} \mid m + n = m + p \Rightarrow n = p\}$

$1 \in M$ as $1 + n = 1 + p \Rightarrow n + 1 = p + 1 \Rightarrow n^* = p^*$

$\Rightarrow n = p$ by P — 2 (*i*)

Let $k \in M$ *i.e.,* $k + n = k + p \Rightarrow n = p$ for all n, $p \in \mathbf{N}$

Consider $k + 1$.

$(k+1) + n = (k+1) + p$

$\Rightarrow k + n^* = k + p^*$ [+ is Associative and Commutative]

$\Rightarrow n^* = p^*$

$\Rightarrow n = p$ by P—2 (*ii*)

$\Rightarrow k + 1 \in M$

Hence $\quad M = \mathbf{N}$.

Example 3. *Multiplication is Commutative.*

Solution. Firstly we prove that $m \,.\, 1 = 1 \,.\, m$ for all $m \in \mathbf{N}$

Let $\quad M = \{m \in \mathbf{N} \mid m \,.\, 1 = 1 \,.\, m\}$

As $1 \,.\, 1 = 1 \,.\, 1$, $1 \in M$

Let $k \in M$ *i.e.,* $k \,.\, 1 = 1 \,.\, k = k$

Consider $k + 1$,

$1 \,.\, (k+1) = 1 \,.\, k + 1 \,.\, 1 = k + 1$

But $(k+1) \,.\, 1 = k + 1$ by definition of '.'

Hence $1 \,.\, (k+1) = (k+1) \,.\, 1$ *i.e.,* $k + 1 \in M$

So $\quad M = \mathbf{N}$

Now let $M' = \{n \mid m \,.\, n = n \,.\, m$ for all $m \in \mathbf{N}\}$

By what we have proved, $1 \in M'$.

Let $u \in M'$ *i.e.,* $m \,.\, u = u \,.\, m$

Then $m \,.\, (u+1) = m \,.\, u + m \,.\, 1 = u \,.\, m + 1 \,.\, m$

$= (u+1) \,.\, m$ by right distributive law

$\Rightarrow \quad u + 1 \in M'$

So $\quad M' = \mathbf{N}$.

Example 4. *Cancellation law holds for multiplication i.e., for all* $m, n, p \in \mathbf{N}$, $mp = np \Rightarrow m = n$.

Solution. Suppose $mp \Rightarrow np$ but $m \neq n$

Then by Trichotomy law either $m > n$ or $n > m$

In case $m > n$, $\quad m = n + u, u \in \mathbf{N}$

So $mp = np \Rightarrow (n + u)\, p = np$

$$\Rightarrow np + up = np$$

This is absurd (Example 1).

Again if $n > m, n = m + k, k \in \mathbf{N}$

Then $mp = np \Rightarrow mp = (m + k)p = mp + kp$

This is again absurd is view of the result proved in Example 1.

4. INTEGERS

The next job is to extend **N** so as to include the solution of the equations of the type $a + x = b$ with $a, b \in \mathbf{N}$. The extended system **Z**, consists of, ..., $-4, -3, -2, -1, 0, 1, 2, 3, \ldots$ etc. Each member of **Z** is called an *integer*. To construct an *integer* with the help of natural numbers we recall a simple fact that every integer can be written as $m - n$ for some $m, n \in \mathbf{N}$ '–' standing for usual difference sign. But as we have not defined this operation for **N**, we tactfully avoid it and proceed as under :

Consider $\mathbf{N} \times \mathbf{N} = \{(m, n) \mid m, n \in \mathbf{N}\}$ *i.e.*, the elements of $\mathbf{N} \times \mathbf{N}$ are ordered pairs of natural numbers.

We define a relation ~ on **N** as under

$$(m, n) \sim (p, q) \text{ if and only if } m + q = n + p.$$

For instance $(1, 5) \sim (3, 7)$ as $1 + 7 = 5 + 3 = 8$ and $(4, 4) \sim (2, 2)$ as $4 + 2 = 2 + 4 = 6$.

It can be verified that '~' is an equivalence relation on **N**. By $[m, n]$ we mean all ordered pairs (p, q) such that $(m, n) \sim (p, q)$. This $[m, n]$ will be called an *integer.* The set of all $[m, n]$, $m, n \in \mathbf{N}$ is denoted by **Z**.

Addition and multiplication on **Z** are defined as under.

$$[m, n] + [m_1, n_1] = [m + m_1, n + n_1]$$

$$[m, n] . [m_1, n_1] = [mm_1 + nn_1, mn_1 + m_1 n]$$

It can be verified that these operations are well defined *i.e.*, if

$$(m, n) \sim (p, q) \text{ and } (m_1, n_1) \sim (p_1, q_1)$$

Then $\quad [m, n] + [m_1, n_1] = [p, q] + [p_1, q_1]$

and $[m, n]\, [m_1, n_1] = [p, q] . [p_1, q_1]$

We remark that addition and multiplication are motivated by the following observation. Let z and z_1 be two integers $z = m - n$, $z_1 = p - q$ when $m, n, p, q \in \mathbf{N}$.

Then $z + z_1 = (m + p) - (n + q)$ and $zz_1 = mp + nq - (mq + np)$

For numerical instances of addition and multiplication, consider integers [3, 5] and [4, 1]. [3, 5] + [4, 1] =[3 + 4, 5 + 1] = [7, 6]

and $\quad [3, 5] . [4, 1] = [3 . 4 + 5 . 1,\ 3 . 1 + 5 . 4] = [17,\ 23]$

Compare this with the facts that [3, 5] is actually – 2 and [4, 1] is 3 then – 2 + 3 = 1 which is same as 7 – 6 whereas (– 2) (3) = – 6 = 17 – 23.

Following properties hold for integers:

(*i*) Addition is associative and commutative.

(*ii*) Multiplication is associative and commutative.

(*iii*) Multiplication is distributive over addition.

(*iv*) The integer $[n, n]$ is called zero element and is denoted by 0. It can be easily shown that $0 + z = z = z + 0$ for all $z \in \mathbf{Z}$.

(*v*) For each integer $z = [m, n]$, the integer $z' = [n, m]$ is called *negative* of z. It is obvious that $z + z' = z' + z = 0$

REMARK: By $z - z'$ we mean $z + (-z')$ for any $z, z' \in \mathbf{Z}$.

The integer $z = [m, n]$ is called *positive* if $m > n$ and is called *negative* in case $n > m$.

Let $z, z' \in \mathbf{Z}$

We define $z > z'$ if $z = z' + u$, for some positive integer u.

Trichotomy law also holds for integers, i.e.,

(*vi*) Given two integers z and z' one and only one of the following holds. Either $z > z'$ or $z = z'$ or $z' > z$.

Example 5. *Show that addition in* **Z** *is commutative.*

Solution. Let $z = [m, n]$ and $z' = [p, q]$, where $m,\ n,\ p,\ q \in \mathbf{N}$

Now $z + z' = [m + p,\ n + q] = [p + m,\ q + n]$

$\qquad = [p, q] + [m, n] = z' + z.$

Example 6. *Prove that multiplication on* **Z** *is associative.*

Solution. Let $z = [m,\ n], z' = [p,\ q]$ and $z'' = [r,\ s]$ where $m, n, p, q, r, s \in \mathbf{N}$.

$$(zz')\, z'' = [mp + nq,\ mq + np]\,[r, s]$$
$$= [(mp + nq)\, r + (mq + np)\, s, (mp + nq)\, s + (mq + np)\, r)]$$
$$= [mpr + nqr + mqs + nps,\ mps + nqs + mqr + npr] \ldots (1)$$

Further $z\,(z'z'') = [m, n]\,[pr + qs,\ pr + qr]$

$$= [m\,(pr + qs) + n\,(ps + qs), m\,(ps + qr) + n\,(pr + qs)]$$
$$= [(mpn + mqs + nps + nqr,\ mps + mqr + npr + nqs] \quad \ldots(2)$$

Using properties of **N**, one can easily show that the right sides of (1) and (2) are same. As a consequence.

$$(zz')\, z'' = z\,(z'z'')$$

Example 7. *Show that for all* $z \in \mathbf{Z}$, $z.\ 0 = 0$

Solution. Let $z = [m, n], 0 = [p, p]$

$$z \cdot 0 = [mp + np, mp + np] = 0$$

Example 8. *Prove that if* $z > z'$ *then (i) for any* $z'' \in \mathbf{Z}$, $z + z'' > z' + z''$ *(ii) for any + ve integer k*, $zk > z'k$

Solution. (*i*) $z > z' \Rightarrow z = z' + u$, u is a positive integer.

Clearly $z + z'' = z' + u + z''$

$$= z' + z'' + u$$

$$\Rightarrow \quad z + z'' > z' + z''$$

(*ii*) As $zk = (z' + u)\ k = z'k + uk$ it is sufficient to prove that product of two positive integers is a positive integer.

Let $u = [m, n]$ and $k = [p, q]$

Since u is positive, $m > n$. In case $n = 1$ $m > 1$ so there exists a natural number t such that $m = t^*$. So $(m, n) = (t^*, 1)$

If $n \neq 1, n > 1 \Rightarrow n = 1 + k$, for some $k \in \mathbf{N}$.

Then $m > n \quad \Rightarrow m = 1 + k + l$ for some $l \in \mathbf{N}$.

Thus $[m, n] = [1 + k + l, 1 + k] = [1 + l, 1]$

Since $(1 + k + l) + 1 = (1 + k) + (1 + l) \Rightarrow (1 + k + l, 1 + k) \sim (1 + l, 1)$

This implies $[m, n] = [l^*, 1]$

So in each case if $z = [m, n]$ is positive we can write $u = [t^*, 1]$ for some $t \in \mathbf{N}$.

Similarly

$$k = [s^*, 1] \text{ for some } s \in \mathbf{N}$$

Now $uk = [t^*s^* + 1, t^* + s^*]$

But $t^*s^* + 1 = (t + 1)(s + 1) + 1 = (t + 1) + (s + 1) + ts$

$$= (t^* + s^*) + ts \text{ and } ts \in \mathbf{N}$$

So $t^*s^* + 1 > (t^* + s^*) + ts$. In other words uk is + ve. Hence our assertion follows.

REMARKS:

1. It can be shown that $z \in \mathbf{Z}$ is positive if and only if $z > 0$ and negative if and only if $0 > z$.
2. Let z and $z' \in \mathbf{Z}$, then $z > z'$ if and only if $z - z' > 0$
3. By $z \geq z'$ we mean either $z > z'$ or $z = z'$
4. $\mathbf{Z}^+$ denotes the set of all positive integers, $\mathbf{Z}^-$ denotes the set of all negative integers. Law of Trichotomy states that $\mathbf{Z} = Z^+ \cup \mathbf{Z}^- \cup \{0\}$ (disjoint union).
5. As a convention 0 is regarded both positive and negative. When we wish to stress upon a non-zero positive integer, we call it *strictly positive*. Similarly *strictly negative* integer is defined.

5. FACTORIZATION THEORY AND FUNDAMENTAL THEOREM OF ARITHMETIC

Let a, b be two integers such that $a = bc$, b and c are called *factors* of a whereas a is called *multiple* of b. a is also a multiple of c. If b is a factor of a, we say that b divides a and write $b \mid a$. It is easy to prove that ± 1 are factors of a and every non-zero integers is a factors of 0.

For example $6 = (-2)(-3) \Rightarrow -2$ and -3 are factors of 6.

Again $7 = 7.1$, so 7 and 1 are factors of 7.

An integer n different from ± 1 is called a prime integer provided its only factors are ± 1 and $\pm n$.

Thus $2, -3, 7, 11, -13$ are some prime integers, while $-4, 16, 12$ are not prime integers as $-4 = 2(-2)$, $16 = 4.4$, $12 = 6.2$

A positive prime integer is called a prime number.

Properties of Prime Numbers:

I. If a prime number p divides ab then either $p \mid a$ or $p \mid b$.

II. If a prime number p does not divide an integer a then the HCF of p and a is 1 (by convention we take HCF to be a + ve integer).

Fundamental Theorem of Arithmetic

Every integer $n > 1$ can be factorized into a product of finite numbers of prime numbers. This expression is unique except for the order in which the prime factors are written.

For instance $56 = 2.2.2.7 = 2^3.7$

$72 = 2.2.2.3.3 = 2^3.3^2$

6. RATIONAL NUMBERS

We now extend **Z** to a new set **Q** so as to include the solutions of equations of the type $ax = b$, $a, b \in \mathbf{Z}$ and $a \neq 0$.

We know by ordinary arithmetic that $x = b/a$ is a solution of above equation. Also it is easily seen that $\frac{b}{a} = \frac{c}{d}$ with $a \neq 0$, $d \neq 0$ if and only if $bd = ac$. All this motivates the following construction.

We consider $\mathbf{Z} \times \mathbf{Z}^0 = \{(a, b) \mid a, b \in \mathbf{Z}, b \neq 0\}$, where $\mathbf{Z}^0$ is the set of non-zero integers.

Define a relation ~ on $\mathbf{Z} \times \mathbf{Z}^0$ by

$$(a, b) \sim (c, d) \Leftrightarrow ad = bc$$

The set a/b consisting of those pairs (c, d) such that $(a, b) \sim (c, d)$ is called a *rational number*. The set of all rational number is denoted by **Q**.

Now it is the turn of defining addition and multiplication on **Q**. We define them, keeping in mind the arithmetic of fractions. Thus we define

$$\frac{p}{q}+\frac{r}{s}=\frac{ps+qr}{qs}$$

and
$$\frac{p}{q}\cdot\frac{r}{s}=\frac{pr}{qs}$$

It can be easily verified that if $\frac{p}{q}=\frac{p_1}{q_1}$ and $\frac{r}{s}=\frac{r_1}{s_1}$ with q, q_1, s and s_1 non-zero.

then $\frac{p}{q}+\frac{r}{s}=\frac{p_1}{q_1}+\frac{r_1}{s_1}$ and $\frac{p}{q}\cdot\frac{r}{s}=\frac{p_1}{q_1}\cdot\frac{r_1}{s_1}$

Following properties of addition and multiplication on **Q** can be proved easily, using the properties of **Z**.

Q—1. $(x+y)+z = x+(y+z)$ for all $x, y, z \in$ **Q**.

Q—2. $x+y = y+x$ for all $x, y \in$ **Q**

Q—3. There exists a rational number 0 such that $x+0=x$ for all $x \in$ **Q**

Q—4. For each $x \in$ **Q**, there exists a y in **Q** such that $x+y=0$.

Q—5. $(x \cdot y) \cdot z = x \cdot (y \cdot z)$ for all $x, y, z \in$ **Q**.

Q—6. $x \cdot y = y \cdot x$ for all $x, y \in$ **Q**.

Q—7. There exists a rational number 1 ($\neq 0$) such that $x.1 = x$ for all $x \in$ **Q**.

Q—8. For each x ($\neq 0$) there exists $z \in$ **Q** such that $xz = 1$.

Q—9. $x . (y+z) = x \cdot y + x \cdot z$ for all $x, y, z \in$ **Q**

REMARKS:

1. Q—1 and Q—5 are called *associative properties* of addition and multiplication respectively.
2. Q— 2 and Q— 6 are called *commutative properties* of addition and multiplication respectively.
3. Q— 9 is sometimes rephrased as '. is left distributive over +'.
4. Henceforth the sign '.' will be dropped and we shall write xy for $x . y$.
5. The properties Q—1 to Q— 9 are called *Field Properties* and any set satisfying these properties is called a *field*. Thus (**Q**, +, .) is a field.

Following examples will illustrate the method of verifying above properties with the help of those of **Z**.

Example 9. *Prove Q—5.*

Solution. Let $x = \dfrac{p}{q}$, $y = \dfrac{r}{s}$ and $z = \dfrac{u}{v}$

where $p, q, r, s, u, v \in \mathbf{Z}$ and none of q, s, v is zero.

$$(x.y) \, . \, z = \left(\frac{pr}{qs}\right)\left(\frac{u}{v}\right) = \frac{(pr)\, u}{(qs)\, v}$$

$$= \frac{p\,(ru)}{q\,(sv)} = \left(\frac{p}{q}\right)\left(\frac{ru}{sv}\right)$$

$$= \left(\frac{p}{q}\right)\left[\left(\frac{r}{s}\right)\left(\frac{u}{v}\right)\right] = x.\,(y\,.\,z)$$

Example 10. *For each x ($\neq 0$) there exists $z \in \mathbf{Q}$ such that $x\,.z = 1$. Prove.*

Solution. Let $x = \dfrac{p}{q}$, $p, q \in \mathbf{Z}, q \neq 0$.

Since $x \neq 0, p \neq 0$. So $\dfrac{q}{p} \in \mathbf{Q}$

Put $\quad z = \dfrac{q}{p}$

Then $\quad x\,.\,z = \dfrac{p}{q}\,.\,\dfrac{q}{p} = \dfrac{pq}{qp} = 1.$

[Any rational number of type m/m works as unity 1 for multiplication].

7. SIMPLE CONSEQUENCES OF FIELD PROPERTIES

(1) *0 and 1 as defined in* Q—3 *and* Q—7 *are unique.*

Proof. Let $0'$ and $1' \in \mathbf{Q}$ be such that $x + 0' = x$ and $x.1' = x$ for all $x \in \mathbf{Q}$.

Now $0 + 0' = 0$ and $0' + 0 = 0'$. This because of Q—2 forces $0'$ to be equal to 0.

Again $1 1' = 1$ and $1' 1 = 1'$. But multiplication is commutative hence $1 = 1'$

NOTE: 0 is called the zero of Q and 1 is called the unity of **Q**.

(2) (*i*) *For each $x \in \mathbf{Q}$, y defined as in* Q—4 *is unique.*

(*ii*) *For each non-zero $x \in \mathbf{Q}$, z defined as in* Q – 8 *is unique.*

Proof. (*i*) Let $y' \in \mathbf{Q}$ be such that $x + y' = 0$.

Now $y = 0 + y = (x + y') + y = y' + (x + y) = y' + 0 = y'$

(*ii*) Suppose $z' \in \mathbf{Q}$ be such that $xz' = 1$.
Again $z = 1\,z = (x z')\,z = (z' x)\,z = z'(x z) = z'\,1 = z'$.

REMARKS:

1. For each x; $y \in \mathbf{Q}$ satisfying $x + y = 0$ is called the *negative* of x and is denoted by $-x$. Further for each $x\ (\neq 0) \in \mathbf{Q}$; z satisfying $xz = 1$ is called the inverse or reciprocal of x and is denoted by x^{-1}.
2. In the proofs of (1) and (2) above, we have made use of Q—1, Q—2, Q—5, and Q—6.

(3) *Cancellation laws. For all x, y, z* $\in \mathbf{Q}$

(*i*) $x + y = x + z \Rightarrow y = z$.

(*ii*) $x\,y = x\,z,\ x \neq 0 \Rightarrow y = z$.

Proof. (*i*) $x + y = x + z \Rightarrow (-x) + (x + y) = (-x) + (x + z)$

$\Rightarrow (-x + x) + y = (-x + x) + z \Rightarrow 0 + y = 0 + z \Rightarrow y = z$.

(*ii*) $x\,y = x\,z \Rightarrow x^{-1}(x\,y) = x^{-1}(x\,z)$, (as $x \neq 0$, x^{-1} exists)

$\Rightarrow (x^{-1}x)\,y = (x^{-1}x)\,z \Rightarrow 1\,y = 1\,z \Rightarrow y = z$

The proofs of the following properties are left as exercises for the readers.

(I) For all $x, y, z \in \mathbf{Q}$, $(x + y)\,z = x\,z + yz$.

(II) $x0 = 0$ for all $x \in \mathbf{Q}$.

(III) $(-x)\,y = x\,(-y) = -x\,y$ for all $x, y \in \mathbf{Q}$.

(IV) $(-x)\,(-y) = xy$ for all $x, y \in \mathbf{Q}$.

(V) If $x - y$ stands for $x + (-y)$, then

$(x - y)\,z = xz - yz$ for all $x, y, z \in \mathbf{Q}$.

8. ORDER PROPERTIES OF Q

We define > on **Q** as under:

Let $x, y \in \mathbf{Q}$, then $x > y$ if and only if $ps - qr > 0$,

where $x = \dfrac{p}{q}$, $y = \dfrac{r}{s}$, $p, q, r, s \in \mathbf{Z}$ and $q > 0$, $s > 0$.

NOTE: When $x > y$, we read '*x* is greater than *y*'. Also we write $x < y$ for all $x, y \in \mathbf{Q}$ if and only if $y > x$.

The symbol $x < y$ is read as '*x* is less than *y*.

Finally $x \geq y$ if and only if either $x = y$ or $x > y$

Similarly $x \leq y \Leftrightarrow$ either $x = y$ or $x < y$

Following are some of the properties of **Q** with respect to '>'.

(1) *Trichotomy Law.* For all $a, b \in \mathbf{Q}$ *one and only one of the following holds:* $a > b$ *or* $a = b$ *or* $b > a$.

(2) *Transitive Low. For all a, b,* $\in$ **Q**, $a > b$ *and* $b > c \Rightarrow a > c$.

(3) *For all a, b, c* $\in$ **Q**, $a > b \Rightarrow a + c > b + c$.

(4) *For all a, b, c* $\in$ **Q**, $a > b$ *and* $c > 0 \Rightarrow ac > bc$

Because of the properties Q – 1 to Q – 9 and the order properties of **Q** mentioned above, **Q** is called an *ordered field.*

(5) *Archimedean Property. For a, b* $\in$ **Q**, $a > 0, b > 0$ *there exists an* $n \in$ **N** *such that* $nb > a$.

(6) *Dense Property. For every pair of elements a, b in* **Q**, $a > b$, *there exists* $c \in$ **Q** *such that* $a > c > b$.

REMARK: Under identification of any integer z with $\frac{z}{1}$, we can say that every integer is a rational number. Thus $\mathbf{Z} \subset \mathbf{Q}$.

Example 11. *Let* $x, y, z \in$ **Q** *be such that* $x + y > x + z$, *then prove that* $y > z$.

Solution. $x + y > x + z \Rightarrow (-x) + (x + y) > (-x) + (x + z)$

$$\Rightarrow (-x + x) + y > (-x + x) + z \Rightarrow 0 + y > 0 + z \Rightarrow y > z.$$

9. IRRATIONAL NUMBERS

Consider $x^2 = 2$. We claim that no rational number satisfies this equation.

Example 12. $\sqrt{2}$ *is not a rational number.*

Solution. Suppose $\sqrt{2}$ were a rational number. Then $\sqrt{2} = \frac{p}{q}$ where p and q are integers, $q > 0$ and p, q have no common factors except 1.

This would mean that $p^2 = 2q^2$ or p^2 is an even integer. But if the square of an integer is even then that integer must itself be an even integer. Thus $p = 2m$ for some $m \in$ **Z**. Substituting $p = 2m$ in $p^2 = 2q^2$ *we get* $q^2 = 2m^2$. Hence arguing as before we see that q must be an even integer. This implies that 2 is a common factor of p and q. Hence we get a contradiction to the choice of p and q. Consequently $\sqrt{2}$ is not a rational number.

So now one has to extend **Q** to a new system say **R** as to include the solutions of the equations of the type $x^2 = a$ where a is a positive integer (not necessarily a perfect square). This new system will be denoted by **R** and its elements will be called **Real Numbers.** The actual definition of a real number is beyond the scope of this book. We mention an important characterization of **R** namely its representation by points as a line. Let $X'X$ be a line of indefinite length (Fig. 1). Let O be a fixed point on $X'X$. Label O with 0 (zero). O divides this line into two halves *viz.,* OX and OX'.

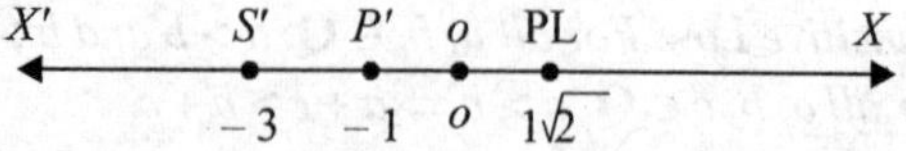

Fig. 1

Take a point *P on OX* such that the length of *OP* is a unit (it may be taken as one centimeter). We label *P* by 1. A point *P*′ on *OX*′ such that *OP*′ = *OP* = 1 will then represent – 1. Now it is easy to plot any point corresponding to a given integer on this line. We note that all positive integers are represented by points on *OX* i.e., the points of line *X′X* on the right side of *O* and negative integers, by the points of *X′X* on the left side of *O*. Thus to represent – 3 on this line, cut a distance *OS′* on *OX′* such that *OS′* = 3*OP.* Then *S′* will represent –3 on this line. For convenience, we shall call this line, the *number line.*

We assert that every rational number can be represented by a point on the number line. In the support of our assertion we give an example and the method indicated therein can easily be extended to any rational number whatsoever.

Example 13. *Represent* $\frac{3}{5}$ *on the number line.*

Solution. Clearly it will be enough to draw a line segment of length $\frac{3}{5}$ units. Take a line *AB* of length 5 cm (Fig. 2). Divide it into five equal parts by $P_1, P_2, P_3,$ and P_4. Through *A* draw *AC* perpendicular to *AB*. From *AC* cut AD of length 3 cm. Again divide *AD* into three equal parts by Q_1 and Q_2. Join *BD* and draw P_1R parallel to *BD* to intersect *AC* at *R.* Then *AR* is of length $\frac{3}{5}$ cm. Since from similar triangles AP_1R and *ABD,* we conclude that

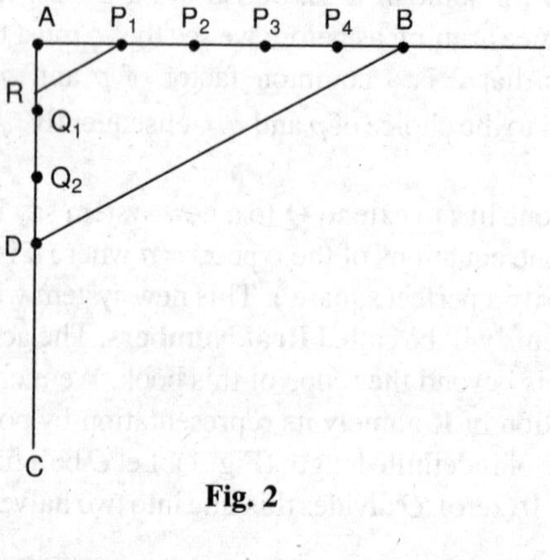

Fig. 2

$$\frac{AP_1}{AR} = \frac{AB}{AD} \text{ i. e., } \frac{AP_1}{AB} = \frac{AR}{AD} \Rightarrow \frac{1}{5} = \frac{AR}{3} \Rightarrow AR = \frac{3}{5}.$$

The above discussion prompts us to describe the following characterization of real numbers,

"To each real number x there is exactly one point P on number line which represents it and conversely for each point P on the number line there is exactly one real number x such that P represents x."

Finally we show that $\sqrt{2}$ is a real number, by using the above characterization of **R.**

Construct a right triangle ABC such that $AB = BC = 1$ and $\angle ABC = \frac{\pi}{2}$ (Fig. 3).

Then $AC = \sqrt{AB^2 + BC^2} = \sqrt{2}$ and so cut a distance $O\,L$ on the portion OX (see Fig. 1 of Chapter 4) of the number line such that $OL = AC = \sqrt{2}$. Thus $\sqrt{2}$ is represented by a point of number line. Hence $\sqrt{2}$ is a real number.

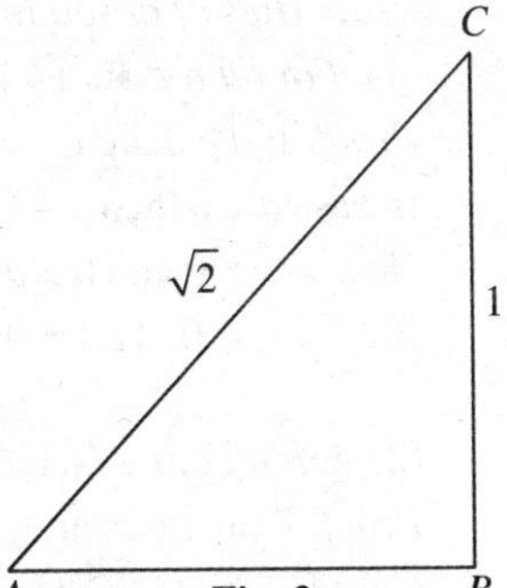

Fig. 3

Earlier we proved that $\sqrt{2}$ is not a rational number. Thus $\sqrt{2}$ is a real number which is not rational number. Real numbers of such type are called *Irrational numbers.* Thus an irrational number is a real number which is not a rational number.

We leave as an exercise for the reader to prove that $\sqrt{5}$ is an irrational number.

10. ORDERED FIELD PROPERTIES OF R

Before proceeding to next section we make a passing remark that under suitably defined addition, multiplication and order, **R** is an ordered field. Further these operations are in conformity with the corresponding operations on **Q**. Note that $\mathbf{Q} \subset \mathbf{R}$ (why ?), so by "Conformity" we mean that these operations agree on **Q.** To understand this point suppose that addition, multiplication and order on **R** are denoted respectively, by $\oplus$,. and *. Then for all $x, y \in \mathbf{Q}$, $x \oplus y = x + y$, $x \odot y = x.\,y$ and $x * y \Leftrightarrow x > y$.

Thus all the propositions which we have deduced as the consequences of the field properties for **Q,** hold good for **R** also.

11. ABSOLUTE VALUE

For any $a \in \mathbf{R}$, we define $|a|$ as under

$$|a| = a \quad \text{if } a \geq 0$$
$$= -a \quad \text{if } a < 0$$

Thus $|-\sqrt{2}| = \sqrt{2}, |0| = 0, |5.7| = 5.7$

Definition. $|a|$ is called *absolute value of a.*

NOTE: It follows from definition that for all $x \in R$, $|x| \geq 0$.

Properties of absolute value function

(1) *For all* $a \in \mathbf{R}$, $|a| \geq a$.

Proof. If $a \geq 0$ then $|a| = a$. As $a \geq a$, we get $|a| \geq a$.

In case $a < 0$ then $a + (-a) < 0 + (-a) \Rightarrow 0 < -a \Rightarrow -a > 0$.

Now $-a > 0$ and $0 > a \Rightarrow -a > a$

But for $a < 0$, $|a| = -a$, hence $|a| > a$. Then by definition of '$\geq$', $|a| \geq a$.

(2) *For all* $a, b \in \mathbf{R}$, $|ab| = |a||b|$.

Proof. Four cases arise

Case I. $a \geq 0$, $b \geq 0$.

By definition $|a| = a$, $|b| = b$. Further $a \geq 0, b \geq 0$ imply $ab \geq 0$. Thus $|ab| = ab = |a||b|$

Case II. $a < 0, b \geq 0$.

In this case $|a| = -a$ and $|b| = b$. But $a < 0$, $b \geq 0$ imply $ab < 0$.

So $|ab| = -ab = |a||b|$.

Case III. $a \geq 0$, $b < 0$.

This is similar to Case II. Just interchange a and b.

Case IV. $a < 0$, $b < 0$.

Here $|a| = -a$, $|b| = -b$ and $ab > 0 \Rightarrow |ab| = ab$.

So $|ab| = (-a)(-b) = |a||b|$.

(3) For all a, b in $\mathbf{R}$, $|a + b| \leq |a| + |b|$.

Proof. For all $a, b \in \mathbf{R}$, $(|a| + |b|)^2 = |a|^2 + 2|a||b| + |b|^2$

$= a^2 + 2|a||b| + b^2$. Since $|a|^2 = a^2$ and $|b|^2 = b^2$

$= a^2 + 2|ab| + b^2$

$\geq a^2 + 2ab + b^2$ by (1) above.

Thus $(|a| + |b|)^2 \geq (a + b)^2 = |a + b|^2$

$\Rightarrow |a| + |b| \geq |a + b|$.

(4) *For* $a, k \in \mathbf{R}$, $|a| < k \Leftrightarrow -k < a < k$.

Proof. Suppose $|a| < k$. In case $a \geq 0$, we get $a < k$

In case $a < 0$, $|a| = -a \Rightarrow -a < k \Rightarrow a > -k$ (Prove!)

$\Rightarrow -k < a$

Hence $|a| < k$ implies $-k < a < k$.

Conversely let $-k < a < k$

If $a \geq 0$ we get $|a| = a < k$.

If $a < 0$ then $|a| = -a$. But $-k < a \Rightarrow k > -a$

or $-a < k$. So $|a| < k$.

12. COMPLEX NUMBERS

It is well known that square of a real number is always positive (or zero). Thus $x^2 = -1$ cannot have a real solution. So we extend **R** to a new set **C** which we shall define as under.

Putting $i = \sqrt{-1}$ we see that $i^2 = -1$ so i satisfies $x^2 = -1$. Any number z of the type $a + bi$ with $a, b \in \mathbf{R}$ is called a *Complex Number.* a is called the *real part* of z [denoted by Re (z)] and b is called the *imaginary part* of z [denoted by Im (z)]. The set of all complex numbers will be denoted by **C**. Since for each $a \in \mathbf{R}$, $a = a + 0i \in \mathbf{C}$, $\mathbf{R} \subset \mathbf{C}$.

In this way $2 + 3i$, $\frac{1}{2} + \sqrt{3}\,i$, 3, $1.789 - 4i$ are all complex numbers.

Let $z_1, z_2 \in \mathbf{C}$, we define $z_1 + z_2$ and $z_1 z_2$ as follows :

Let $z_1 = a + bi$ and $z_2 = c + di$. Then $z_1 + z_2 = (a + c) + (b + d)i$ and $z_1 z_2 = (ac - bd) + (ad + bc)\,i$.

It can be checked that **C** is a field with respect to addition and multiplication defined above.

For any $z = a + bi \neq 0 \in \mathbf{C}$, $a^2 + b^2 \neq 0$ (Prove!), so $\dfrac{1}{a^2 + b^2} \in \mathbf{R}$.

Consequently $u = \dfrac{a}{a^2 + b^2} - \dfrac{b}{a^2 + b^2}\,i \in \mathbf{C}$.

Further $$zu = (a + bi)\left(\frac{a}{a^2 + b^2} - \frac{b}{a^2 + b^2}\,i\right) = \frac{a^2 + b^2}{a^2 + b^2} = 1$$

$\Rightarrow$ $u = z^{-1}$

Definition. (a) For any $z = a + bi \in \mathbf{C}$ we define *complex conjugate* of z (denoted by $\bar{z}$) as the complex number $a - bi$.

(b) For any $z = a + bi \in \mathbf{C}$ we define *modulus* of z (denoted by $|z|$) as the real number $+\sqrt{a^2 + b^2}$.

Properties of conjugates.

For all $z, z_1, z_2 \in \mathbf{C}$

(*i*) $\overline{z_1 + z_2} = \overline{z_1} + \overline{z_2}$

(*ii*) $\overline{z_1 z_2} = \overline{z_1} \cdot \overline{z_2}$

(*iii*) $|z_1 z_2| = |z_1| |z_2|$

(*iv*) $|z_1 + z_2| \le |z_1| + |z_2|$

(*v*) $|z_1| = 0 \Leftrightarrow z_1 = 0$

(*vi*) $|z|^2 = z\bar{z}$

(*vii*) $z = \bar{z} \Leftrightarrow z \in R$

We shall verify a few of above, the rest are left as exercise.

Example 14. *Prove that* (*i*) $|z|^2 = z\bar{z}$

(*ii*) $|z_1 + z_2| \le |z_1| + |z_2|$.

Solution. (*i*) Let $z = x + iy$ then $\bar{z} = x - iy$

and $|z| = \sqrt{x^2 + y^2}$

Clearly $z\bar{z} = (x + iy)(x - iy) = x^2 + y^2$

$= |z|^2$

(*ii*) $|z_1 + z_2|^2 = (z_1 + z_2)\left(\overline{z_1 + z_2}\right)$

$= (z_1 + z_2)\left(\overline{z_1} + \overline{z_2}\right)$

$= z_1\overline{z_1} + z_2\overline{z_2} + z_1\overline{z_2} + z_2\overline{z_1}$

$= |z_1|^2 + |z_2|^2 + z_1\overline{z_2} + \left(\overline{z_1\overline{z_2}}\right)$ by (*ii*) above

$= |z_1|^2 + |z_2|^2 + 2\,\text{Re}\,(z_1 \overline{z_2})$

But $\quad \text{Re}\ z \le |z|$

$\Rightarrow \quad \text{Re}\,(z_1\overline{z_2}) \le |z_1\overline{z_2}| = |z_1|\,|\overline{z_2}| = |z_1|\,|z_2|$

Hence $\quad |z_1 + z_2|^2 \le |z_1|^2 + |z_2|^2 + 2|z_1|.|z_2|$

i.e., $\quad (|z_1| + |z_2|)^2$

$\Rightarrow \quad |z_1 + z_2| \le |z_1| + |z_2|$.

Example 15. *Prove that* $z = \bar{z}$ *if and only if* z *is a real number.*

Solution. Let $z = x + iy$ then $\bar{z} = x - iy$.

In case z is real number, $y = 0$. So $z = x = \bar{z}$.

Supppose $z = \bar{z}$ then $x + iy = x - iy$

$\Rightarrow \quad 2iy = 0$

$\Rightarrow \quad y = 0$

$\Rightarrow \quad z = k$, a real number.

13. PRINCIPLE OF MATHEMATICAL INDUCTION

We have already seen the utility of P—3 in proving properties of natural numbers. This technique is popularly known as *Principle of Mathematical Induction.* Many important formulas in Mathematics owe their proofs to this principle.

We restate this:

"If a result involving natural numbers is true for 1 and its validity for a natural number k implies its validity for $k + 1$, then the formula is true for all natural numbers."

This principle can be easily grasped by a layman, if he follows the reasoning given below:

We have already proved the truth of the result for $n = 1$ and also shown that whenever the result holds for k, it holds for $k + 1$.

As the result holds for $n = 1$, it must hold for $1 + 1$ *i.e.*, $n = 2$. Now it has been proved for $n = 2$, so it must be true for $2 + 1$, *i.e.*, $n = 3$. Following this line of reasoning, one gets that the result must hold for all natural numbers.

Example 16. *Prove that* $1^2 + 2^2 + 3^2 + ... + n^2 = \dfrac{n(n+1)(2n+1)}{6}$ *for all natural numbers.*

Solution. Clearly for $n = 1$, LHS $= 1^2 = 1$

and $$\text{RHS} = \frac{1.2.3}{6} = 1.$$

So the formula is definitely valid for $n = 1$

Suppose that the result is true for $n = k$.

i.e., $$1^2 + 2^2 + 3^2 + ... + k^2 = \frac{k(k+1)(2k+1)}{6} \qquad ...(1)$$

Then $1^2 + 2^2 + 3^2 + ... + k^2 + (k+1)^2$

$$= \frac{k(k+1)(2k+1)}{6} + (k+1)^2 \qquad \text{by (1)}$$

$$= \frac{(k+1)}{6}(2k^2 + k + 6k + 6)$$

$$= \frac{(k+1)}{6}(2k^2 + 7k + 6)$$

$$= \frac{(k+1)}{6}(k+2)(2k+3)$$

$$= \frac{(k+1)[(k+1)+1][2(k+1)+1]}{6}$$

Hence the result is true for $n = k + 1$

Consequently the result is true for all natural numbers n.

Example 17. *By the method of induction, show that*

$10^n + 3.4^{n+2} + 5$ is divisible by 9

Solution. For $n = 1$, $10^n + 3.4^{n+2} + 5 = 10 + 3.4^3 + 5$

$= 10 + 192 + 5 = 207 = 9.23$

$\Rightarrow 10^n + 3.4^{n+2} + 5$ is divisible by 9 in case $n = 1$.

Suppose for $n = k$, $10^k + 3.4^{k+2} + 5$ is divisible by 9.

Consider $10^{k+1} + 3.4^{k+3} + 5$

$$10^{k+1} + 3.4^{k+3} + 5 = 10^k \cdot 10 + 3.4^{k+2} \cdot 4 + 5$$

$$= 10^k(9+1) + 12.4^{k+2} + 5$$

$$= 10^k \cdot (9+1) + (9+3)4^{k+2} + 5$$

$$= (10^k + 3.4^{k+2} + 5) + 9(10^k + 4^{k+2})$$

$\Rightarrow 10^{k+1} + 3.4^{k+3} + 5$ is divisible by 9 as first term in RHS is divisible by 9 by our assumption and second term has 9 as one of its factors.

Consequently $10^n + 3.4^{n+2} + 5$ is divisible by 9 for all natural numbers n.

Example 18. *Prove that*

$$\frac{1}{3.5} + \frac{1}{5.7} + \ldots + \frac{1}{(2n+1)(2n+3)} = \frac{n}{3(2n+3)}$$

Solution. For $n = 1$, $\text{LHS} = \frac{1}{3.5} = \frac{1}{15}$

and $\text{RHS} = \frac{1}{3(2+3)} = \frac{1}{15}$

Hence result is definitely true for $n = 1$

Let it be true for $n = k$

i.e., $$\frac{1}{3.5} + \frac{1}{6.7} + \ldots + \frac{1}{(2k+1)(2k+3)} = \frac{k}{3(2k+3)} \quad \ldots (1)$$

Consider $$\frac{1}{3.5} + \frac{1}{5.7} + \ldots + \frac{1}{(2k+1)(2k+3)} + \frac{1}{(2k+3)(2k+5)}$$

$$= \frac{k}{3(2k+3)} + \frac{1}{(2k+3)(2k+5)} \quad \text{by (1)}$$

$$= \frac{1}{3(2k+3)(2k+5)}[2k^2+5k+3]$$

$$= \frac{1}{3(2k+3)(2k+5)}(k+1)(2k+3)$$

$$= \frac{k+1}{3(2k+5)} = \frac{k+1}{3[2(k+1)+3]}$$

Hence the result holds for $n = k + 1$.

Consequently the result is true for all natural numbers n.

REMARK: Sometimes we apply modified form of Induction Principle. Instead of proving the result for $n = 1$, we prove it for any fixed natural number, say t (*e.g.*, $t = 2$ or 3 or 4 etc.) and then assuming the validity of the formula for k ($k > t$) we try to prove it for $k + 1$. If we are successful then the result holds for all natural numbers $\geq t$.

Example 19. *If n is a positive integer greater than 2, show that* $2^n > 1 + n\sqrt{2^{n-1}}$

Solution. For $n=3$, $\text{LHS} = 2^3 = 8$

and $\text{RHS} = 1 + 3\sqrt{2^2} = 1+6 = 7$

Thus the inequality is satisfied for $n = 3$. Let $k > 3$ and assume the inequality for $n = k$

i.e., $$2^k > 1 + k\sqrt{2^{k-1}} \quad \text{... (1)}$$

Consider 2^{k+1}

$$2^{k+1} = 2^k \cdot 2 > 2(1 + k \cdot 2^{k-1/2}) \text{ by (1)}$$

$$\Rightarrow 2^{k+1} > 2 + k \cdot 2^{k+1/2}$$

$$> 1 + k \cdot 2^{k+1/2} \quad \text{... (2)}$$

Now $k^2\, 2^{k+1} - (k+1)^2\, 2^k = 2^k(2k^2 - k^2 - 2k - 1)$

$$= 2^k(k^2 - 2k - 1)$$

$$= 2^k[(k-1)^2 - 2]$$

Since $k > 3$, $(k-1) > 2 \Rightarrow (k-1)^2 > 4$

$$\Rightarrow (k-1)^2 > 2$$

$$\Rightarrow (k-1)^2 - 2 > 0$$

This, in turn implies that

$$k^2\, 2^{k+1} - (k+1)^2\, 2^k > 0$$

or $k\, 2^{k+1/2} > (k+1)\, 2^{k/2}$

(2) implies that $2^{k+1} > 1 + (k+1)\, 2^{k/2}$

Hence the inequality holds for $n = k + 1$. Consequently, by Principle of Mathematical Induction, the inequality is true for all natural numbers ≥ 3.

Example 20. *Prove that $x^n - y^n$ is divisible by $x - y$ for all natural numbers n.*

Solution. For $n = 1$, $x^n - y^n = x - y$, is clearly divisible by $x - y$.

Let $x^k - y^k$ be divisible by $x - y$.

Consider $x^{k+1} - y^{k+1}$

It can be rewritten as $x^{k+1} - xy^k + xy^k - y^{k+1}$

$$= x\,(x^k - y^k) + y^k\,(x - y)$$

As $x - y$ divides $x^k - y^k$ and also $y^k\,(x - y)$, it must divide $x^{k+1} - y^{k+1}$.

Hence the result follows by Induction Principle.

EXERCISES

Prove by induction (*n stands for a natural number*)

1. $1 + 3 + 5 + ... + (2n - 1) = n^2$
2. $2 + 2^2 + 2^3 + ... + 2^n = 2\,(2^n - 1)$
3. $1^3 + 2^3 + 3^3 + ... + n^3 = \left[\dfrac{n(n+1)}{2}\right]^2$
4. $1.3 + 2.3^2 + 3.3^3 + .. + n.3^n = \dfrac{(2n-1)\,3^{n+1} + 3}{4}$
5. $1 . 2 . 3 + 2 . 3 . 4 + ... + n\,(n + 1)\,(n + 2) = \dfrac{n}{4}(n+1)\,(n+2)\,(n+3)$
6. Prove that $3^n - 2n - 1$ is divisible by 4.
7. Show that $2^{4n} - 1$ is divisible by 15.
8. If $x \neq 0$, prove that $(1 + x)^n > 1 + nx$.
9. Prove by induction that

   $2 + 7 + 12 + ... + (5n - 3) = \dfrac{1}{2}n\,(5n - 1).$
10. Prove that $7^n + 16n - 1$ is divisible by 64.
11. Show that $1 + \dfrac{1}{1+2} + \dfrac{1}{1+2+3} + ... + \dfrac{1}{1+2+3+...+n} = \dfrac{2n}{n+1}$
12. Is $n\,(n - 1)\,(2n - 1)$ divisible by 6? Justify your answer.
13. Prove that $\dfrac{1}{3.8} + \dfrac{1}{8.13} + \dfrac{1}{13.18} + ... + \dfrac{1}{(5n-2)\,(5n+3)} = \dfrac{n}{3(5n+3)}$
14. Prove that $3^{2n} + 7$ is a multiple of 8.
15. Show that $2.7^n + 3.5^n - 5$ is a multiple of 24.

    [**Hint.** Use the fact that $7^n - 5^n$ is an even number].

16. Prove that $\sqrt{3}$, $\sqrt{7}$ and $\sqrt{2}+\sqrt{3}$ are irrational numbers.
17. Let $a \in \mathbf{Q}$ and $b \in \mathbf{R}$ be such that b is not a square of a rational number show that $a+\sqrt{b} = 0 \Rightarrow a = b = 0$.
18. Prove that for all $a, b \in \mathbf{R}$

    (*i*) $a > b > 0 \Rightarrow \dfrac{1}{a} < \dfrac{1}{b}$

    (*ii*) $||a| - |b|| \le |a - b|$

    (*iii*) $\left|\dfrac{a}{b}\right| = \dfrac{|a|}{|b|}$ provided $b \ne 0$
19. Prove that $a + bi = c + di$, $a, b, c, d \in \mathbf{R}$ if and only if $a = c$ and $b = d$.
20. Deduce necessary and sufficient conditions for the equality in

$$|a + b| \le |a| + |b|, \; a, b \in \mathbf{R}$$

ANSWERS

12. Yes, apply Principle of Mathematical Induction.
20. Either $a = 0$ or $b = 0$

    or $a = \lambda b$ for some $\lambda > 0$

CHAPTER 5

LINEAR EQUATIONS AND INEQUALITIES

1. We shall see in Chapter 22 that the equation of a line in a plane is of first degree in x and y and conversely every equation of first degree in x and y represents a line. Thus the set of equations of the type $ax + by + c = 0$ with a, b, c as real numbers and at least one of a and b is not zero, is closely associated with the set of lines in a plane. That is why we call $ax + by + c = 0$, a linear equation.

To discuss this concept more formally, firstly we define a linear expression.

Definition 1. Any expression of the type $ax + by + c$, a, b, c in $\mathbf{R}$ and at least one of a and b is non-zero, is called a *linear expression* (to be more precise, a linear expression in x and y over the reals).

Definition 2. An equation of the type $ax + by + c = 0$, $a, b, c \in \mathbf{R}$ is called a *linear equation.*

In other words a linear equation is obtained by equating to zero a linear expression.

In Chapter 4 we discussed order relation on rational numbers and stated the properties of '>' (greater than). It was further mentioned therein, that real numbers also follow the same laws and the set $\mathbf{R}$ is an ordered field. This prompts us to define

An inequality of the type $ax + by + c > 0$ or $ax + by + c < 0$ is called a *linear inequality* (more precisely a linear inequality in x and y over the reals).

Thus $3x + 5y + 7 = 0$, $2x - 1 = 0$, $\sqrt{3}\,y + 11 = 0$, $x + y - \sqrt{2} = 0$ are some linear equations, while $x > 0$, $4x - 3y + 1 < 0$, $\sqrt{2}x - \sqrt{3}y + 11 > 0$, $x - 1.5y + \frac{1}{2} > 0$, $3.78x - 2\frac{1}{3} < 0$ are some linear inequalities.

2. In this section we explain what we mean by the solution set of a linear equation or a linear inequality or of a system of linear equations and linear inequalities.

Firstly we recall the definition of an ordered pair.

Definition 3. By an ordered pair (a, b) of real numbers a and b we mean a set $\{\{a\}, \{a, b\}\}$.

Thus (a, b) is a set with two elements namely the set $\{a\}$ and the set $\{a, b\}$. With the help of this definition it can be proved that two ordered pairs (a, b) and (c, d) are equal if and only if $a = c$ and $b = d$.

REMARK: Some authors take this property as the defining property for ordered pairs.

Example 1. *The plane of Co-ordinate Geometry (Ref to Chapter 22) is the set of all ordered pairs (x, y) with $x, y \in \mathbf{R}$. For any point P in this plane, its co-ordinates determine an ordered pair (a, b) where a is the abscissa of P and b is the ordinate of P. Also for any ordered pair of real numbers (c, d) there is exactly one point Q in the plane of co-ordinates whose x co-ordinate is c and y co-ordinate is d. We note that the points $(2, 1)$ and $(1, 2)$ are different. In general points (a, b) and (b, a) are different whenever $a \neq b$. This explains why the co-ordinates of a point form an ordered pair.*

Definition 4. Let $ax + by + c = 0$ be a linear relation, then the set of all ordered pairs (x_1, y_1) of real numbers such that $ax_1 + by_1 + c = 0$ is called the *solution set* of the linear equation $ax + by + c = 0$.

Thus $(2, 1)$ is an element of the solution set of the equation $3x - 4y - 2 = 0$ since $3.2 - 4.1 - 2 = 6 - 4 - 2 = 0$. Again $(1, 2)$ is not in the solution set of the same equation as $3.1 - 4.2 - 2 = -7 \neq 0$. Let S be the solution set of $3x - 4y - 2 = 0$ then $S = \{(2, 1), (6, 4), (3\frac{1}{3}, 2), (-2/3, -1), \ldots\}$. Since it is impossible to enumerate all the ordered pairs (x_1, y_1) satisfying $3x_1 - 4y_1 = 2$, the above said notation of S does not convey the actual size of the solution set. Note that $(x_1, y_1) \in S \Leftrightarrow 3x_1 - 4y_1 = 2$

$$\Leftrightarrow \quad x_1 = \frac{2(1+2y_1)}{3}.$$ So we can write

$$S = \left\{(x_1, y_1) \middle| x_1 = \frac{2(1+2y_1)}{3}\right\}$$

or

$$S' = \{(x_1, y_1) \mid 3x_1 - 4y_1 - 2 = 0\}.$$

Similarly we can define solution set of $2x - 1 = 0$ and $4x + y + 1 = 0$ as the set S of ordered pairs (x_1, y_1) such that $2x_1 - 1 = 0$ and $4x_1 + y_1 + 1 = 0$. It can be easily verified that here S consists of only *one* ordered pair, namely $\left(\frac{1}{2}, -3\right)$,

Definition 5. The set of all ordered pairs (x_1, y_1) of real numbers, such that $ax_1 + by_1 + c > 0$ is called the *solution set* of the linear inequality $ax + by + c > 0$.

For example, (5, 1) is the solution set of the inequality $2x - y - 7 > 0$ while (1, 4) is not in its solution set. Similarly (0, 4).

Definitions 4 and 5 can, in an obvious way, be extended to a system consisting of more than one linear equation or linear inequality and also to a system consisting of linear equations and linear inequalities.

NOTE: The word 'linear constraint' is sometimes used in place of 'linear equation' as well as a 'linear inequality'.

3. GRAPHICAL REPRESENTATION OF SOLUTION SETS

As remarked earlier, we can identify an ordered pair (*a*, *b*) of real numbers with a point in the plane of Co-ordinate Geometry. Thus the solution set of any linear equation precisely consists of the points whose co-ordinates satisfy that equation. But every linear equation represents a line, so the solution set consists of points on that line. Thus to draw a graph of the solution set of a linear equation it is sufficient to trace the line represented by that equation on graph paper. For example suppose that we are interested to represent the solution set of the equation $x + y + 1 = 0$ graphically. We trace the line $x + y + 1 = 0$.

We make a table of the following type:

x	0	– 1	2	– 2	– 3	...	...	...	...	...
y	– 1	0	– 3	1	2	...	...	...	...	...

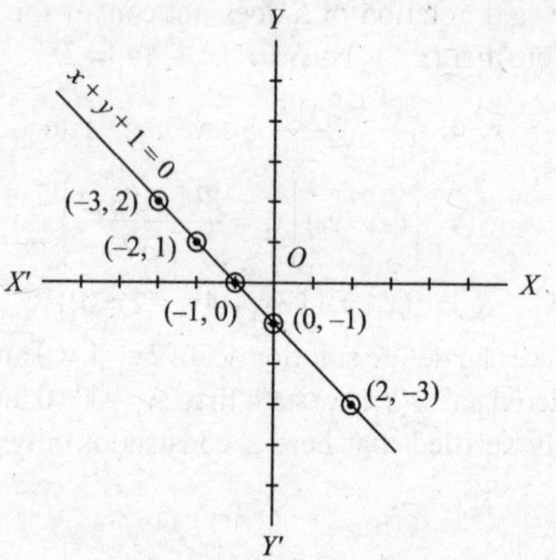

Fig. 1

Now $x + y + 1 = 0 \Rightarrow y = -x - 1$. We give arbitrary values to x and find out the corresponding values of y from $y = -x - 1$.

Suppose we put $x = 0$, then $y = -1$. We write 0 in the row headed by x and put in the column consisting of 0 and the row headed by y. Similarly on putting $x = -1, 2, -2$ we get $y = 0, -3, 1$ respectively. We plot these points on a graph paper and join them. Thus we get a line, every point of which has the co-ordinates satisfying $x + y + 1 = 0$. This line represents the solution set of $x + y + 1 = 0$.

We next consider the solution set of inequality $x - y + 1 > 0$. Again $x - y + 1 > 0 \Rightarrow x + 1 > y \Rightarrow y < x + 1$. Here the solution set S is given by $\{(x_1, y_1) \mid y_1 < x_1 + 1\}$.

Thus if we put $x = 0$ then all points $(0, y)$ with $y < 1$ are in the solution set of $x - y + 1 > 0$. We first plot the graph of equation $x - y + 1 = 0$ following the procedure discussed earlier.

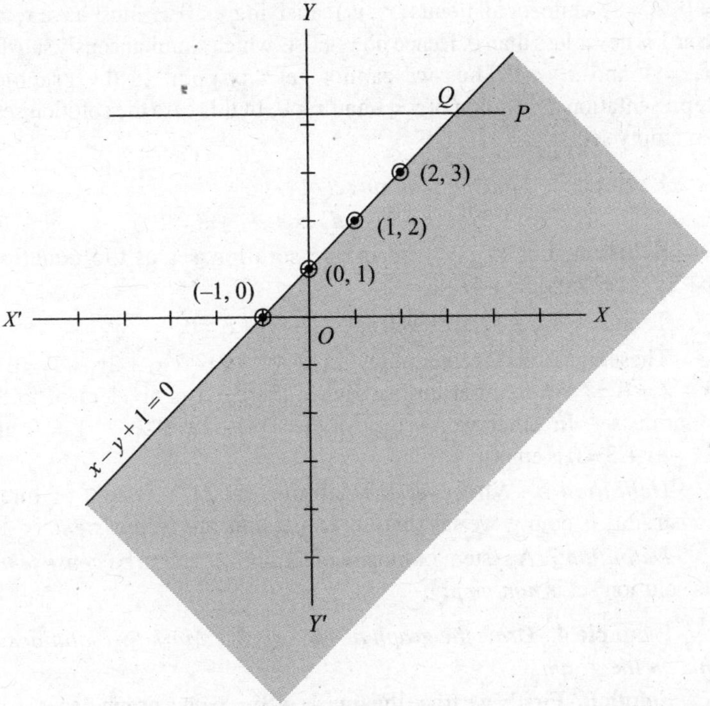

Fig. 2

Let $P(x_1, y_1)$ be any point. Draw PQ parallel to x-axis to meet line $x - y + 1 = 0$ at Q. Let the coordinates of Q be (x_2, y_1). Since $Q(x_2, y_1)$ lies on $x-y+1=0$, we get $x_2-y_1+1=0$. P will lie on right of $x-y+1=0$ if and only if $x_1>x_2 \Leftrightarrow x_1>y_1-1 \Leftrightarrow y_1<x_1+1$. Thus point (x_1, y_1) is in solution set of $x-y+1>0$ if and only if it lies on the right of line $x-y+1=0$. Thus the shaded portion (excluding line $x-y+1=0$) depicts the solution set of $x-y+1>0$. Similarly it can be verified that a point (x_1, y_1) lies on left of $x-y+1=0$ if and only if $x_1<y_1-1 \Leftrightarrow y_1>x_1+1$. So the unshaded portion is the graphical representation of the linear inequality $x-y+1<0$. Note the shaded portion together with the line $x-y+1=0$ represents the solution set of $x-y+1 \geq 0$ or a system of linear constraints $x-y+1=0$ and $x-y+1>0$.

Sometimes a solution set may not exist. Consider the following examples. In such cases no graphical representation is possible.

Example 2. *Find the solution set of* $x-1=0$ *and* $x<0$.

Solution. For all the points (x_1, y_1) lying in the solution set of $x-1=0$, $x_1=1$, while for all points (x_1, y_1) satisfying $x<0$ we must have $x_1<0$. But 1 is never less than 0. Hence no x_1 exists which simultaneously satisfies $x_1=1$ and $x_1<0$. Thus we cannot get any point in the graphical representation of solution of $x=1$ and $x<0$. In this case the solution set is an empty set.

Example 3. *Find the solution set of*

$$x+2y+1=0 \text{ and } 2x+4y+3=0$$

Solution. Let (x_1, y_1) be in the solution set of the equations $x+2y+1=0$ and $2x+4y+3=0$.

Then $x_1+2y_1+1=0$ as well as $2x_1+4y_1+3=0$.

These equations together imply $(2x_1+4y_1+3)-2(x_1+2y_1+1)=0 \Rightarrow 3-2=0 \Rightarrow 1=0$, an absurdity. Hence there exists no element in the solution set. In other words the solution set of $x+2y+1=0$ and $2x+4y+3=0$ is empty.

Definition 6. Whenever the solution set of a system of linear constraints is empty, we say that the constraints are *inconsistent.*

Definition 7. A system of linear constraints is said to be *consistent* if its solution set is *non-empty*.

Example 4. *Draw the graph of* $4x+3y \leq 6$. *Mark two solutions of this on the graph.*

Solution. Firstly we trace the line $4x+3y=6$ on a graph paper.

Now, $4x+3y=6 \quad \Rightarrow \quad 3y=6-4x \Rightarrow y=\dfrac{6-4x}{3}$.

We give values 0, 1, 2, 3, – 1, – 2, – 3, ... to x and find corresponding values of y with the help of $y = \dfrac{6 - 4x}{3}$.

These values we put down in the following table.

x	0	1	2	3	– 1	– 2	– 3	...	...
y	2	2/3	– 2/3	– 2	10/3	14/3	6	...	...

The graph of $4x + 3y = 6$ is shown in figure 3.

Now a point (x_1, y_1) satisfies $4x + 3y < 6$ if and only if $4x_1 + 3y_1 < 6$ $\Leftrightarrow (x_1, y_1)$ lies on left of the line $4x + 3y = 6$. Points of these type lie in the shaded portion of the figure.

Hence the solution set of $3x + 4y \le 6$ consists of the shaded portion including the line $3x + 4y = 6$.

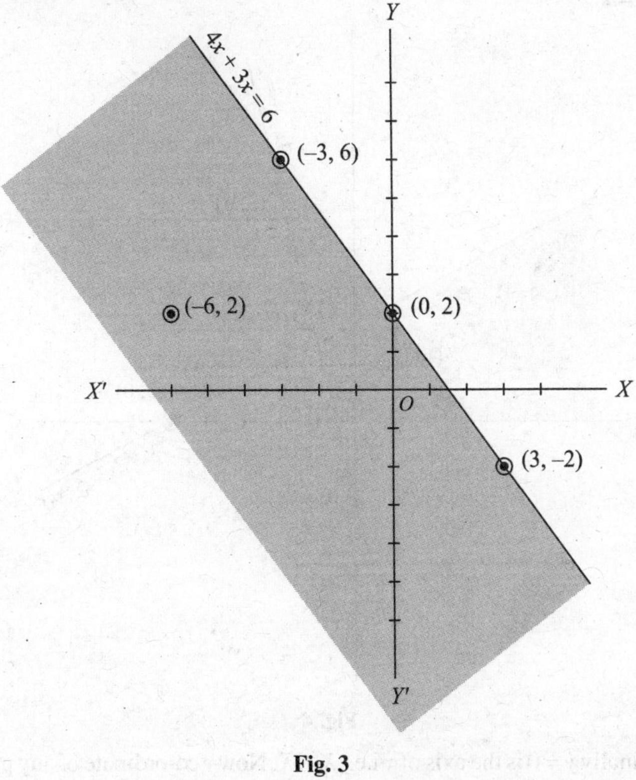

Fig. 3

Clearly the points (– 3, 6) and (– 6, 2) are such that their co-ordinates satisfy $4x + 3y \leq 6$, as $4(-3) + 3(6) = -12 + 18 = 6$ and $4(-6) + 3(2) = -18 < 6$. We mark these points by black dots.

Example 5. *Find the graph of* $x + 2y - 5 < 0$, $4x - y < 2$ *and* $y > 0$. *On the graph mark three points which satisfy these inequalities.*

Solution. Firstly we trace lines $x + 2y - 5 = 0$, $4x - y = 2$ and $y = 0$.

To trace $x + 2y - 5 = 0$, we note that $y = \dfrac{5-x}{2}$. So for $x = 0, 1, 2, 3, \ldots$; $y = \dfrac{5}{2}, 2, \dfrac{3}{2}, 1$ etc. Plot the points $\left(0, \dfrac{5}{2}\right)$, (1, 2), $\left(2, \dfrac{3}{2}\right)$, (3, 1) and join them to obtain the graph of $x + 2y - 5 = 0$.

Again $4x - y = 2 \Rightarrow y = 4x - 2$ so for $x = 0, 1, 2, 3, \ldots$ $y = -2, 2, 6, 10, \ldots$. Plot the points (0, – 2), (1, 2), (2, 6), (3, 10) and join them to get the graph of $4x - y = 2$.

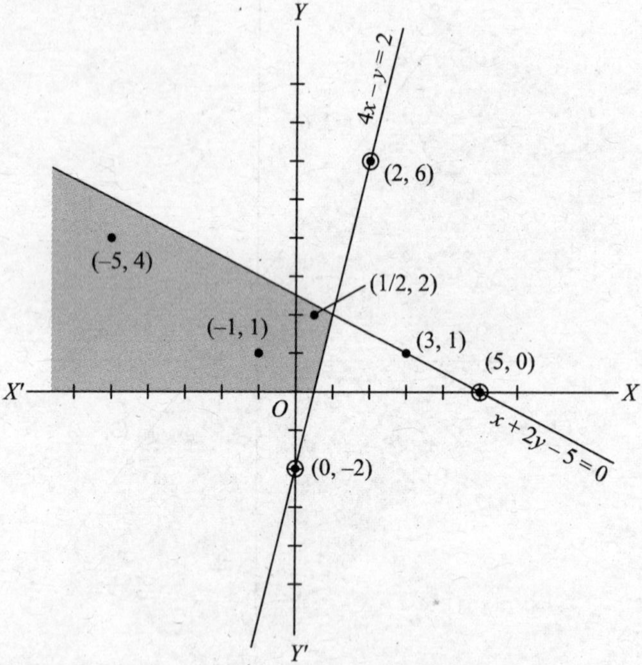

Fig. 4

Finally $y = 0$ is the axis of x i.e., $X'OX$. Now y co-ordinate of any point is positive if and only if that point lies above x-axis. Further (x_1, y_1) satisfies

$x + 2y - 5 = 0$ if and only if it lies on the left of the line $x + 2y - 5 < 0$. Similary (x_1, y_1) satisfies $4x - y < 2$ if and only if the point (x_1, y_1) lies on the left of the line $4x - y - 2 = 0$. Hence the solution set is the shaded portion of the figure excluding the lines $y = 0, x + 2y = 5$ and $4x - y = 2$. The ordered pairs $\left(\frac{1}{2}, 2\right)$, $(-1, 1)$, $(-5, 4)$ are in the solution set of the given system, since $\frac{1}{2} + 2 - 5 = -\frac{5}{2} < 0$, $4.\frac{1}{2} - 2 = 0 < 2$ and $2 > 0$; $-1 + 2.1 - 5 = -4 < 0$, $4(-1) - 1 = -5 < 2$ and $1 > 0$; $-5 + 2.4 - 5 = -2 < 0$, $4(-5) - 4 = -24 < 2$ and $4 > 0$. The points corresponding to these pairs are shown by black dots in the figure.

Example 6. *Find the solution set of the following system of inequalities and represent the solution set by graph.*

$$3x + y < 13, \quad 7y + x > 11, \quad 3y \leq 9 + x.$$

Solution. Firstly we draw lines $3x + y = 13$, $7y + x = 11$ and $3y = 9 + x$.

Now $3x + y < 13$ is represented by the region in the left side of line $3x + y = 13$; $7y + x > 11$ is represented by the portion of plane on right side

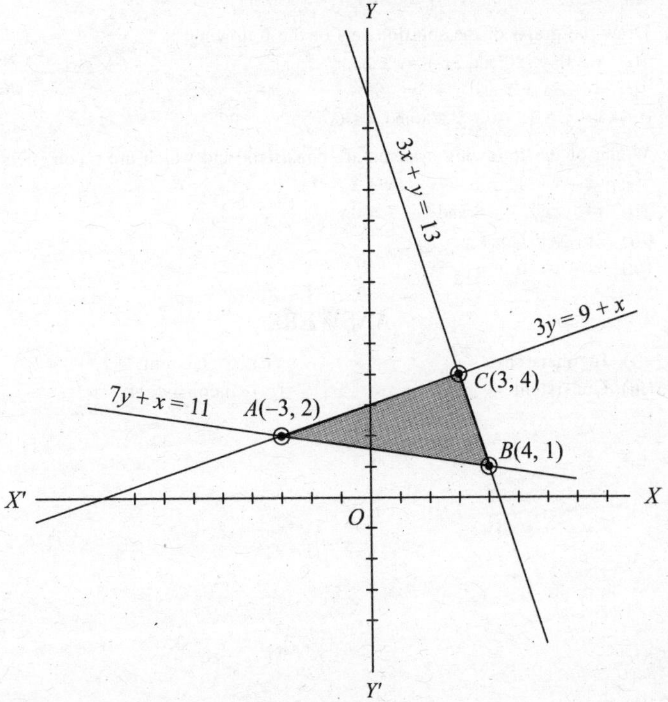

Fig. 5

of line $7y + x = 11$ and $3y \leq 9 + x$ is represented by portion of plane on right of line $3y = 9 + x$ together with the line $3y = 9 + x$. Hence the solution set is the interior of triangle ABC (shown by shaded portion) and the portion of line $3y = 9 + x$ between the points A, C (but excluding A and C). Note that coordinates of A, B, C are respectively equal to $(-3, 2)$, $(4, 1)$, $(3, 4)$. These are obtained by solving the pair of lines $3y = 9 + x$ and $7y + x = 11$, $7y + x = 11$ and $3x + y = 13$; $3x + y = 13$ and $3y = 9 + x$. The point A is not in the solution set of the given system, since $7(2) + (-3) = 11 \ngtr 11$ (where $\ngtr$ stands for *not greater than*). Also C is not in the solution set as $3(3) + 4 = 13 \nless 13$ (where $\nless$ stand for *not less than*).

EXERCISES

1. Draw the graph of following system of linear constraints

   (*i*) $\frac{1}{5}(3x - 4y) = \frac{1}{2}(x - y + 3)$, $\frac{1}{4}(x - y + 7) = \frac{1}{9}(4x - 3y)$

   (*ii*) $2x - y - 3 \leq 0$

   (*iii*) $2x + y > 8$, $4x - 2y \leq 4$

   (*iv*) $3x - 2y + 1 > 0$, $2x + 3y \leq 13$

   (*v*) $x - y - 1 = 0$, $2x - y \geq 0$, $x + y - 3 < 0$.

2. Draw the graph of the solution sets of the following:

   (*i*) $x \geq 0$, $y \geq 0$ and $3x + 4y \leq 2$.

   (*ii*) $3x - 2y = 5$ and $x + 3y \leq 9$

   (*iii*) $x - y \geq 1$, $4x + y \leq 8$ and $y \leq 0$.

3. Which of the following systems are consistent and which are inconsistent?

   (*i*) $4x - y + 11 = 0$, $24x - 6y + 2 = 0$

   (*ii*) $x - y > 1$, $x < 0$ and $y + 7 = 0$

   (*iii*) $2x - y = 1$, $x + y = 2$

   (*iv*) $3x - 1 > 0$, $y = 8$, $5x + 1 = 0$.

ANSWERS

3. (*i*) Inconsistent (*ii*) Consistent
   (*iii*) Consistent (*iv*) Inconsistent.

CHAPTER 6

SOLUTION OF EQUATIONS – QUADRATIC AND SIMULTANEOUS

1. PRELIMINARIES

An expression of the form $a_0x^n + a_1x^{n-1} + ... + a_{n-1}x + a_n$ where $a_0 \neq 0$ and a_i's are constants, real or complex, n is a positive integer and x, a variable (unknown) is called a *polynomial* in x of *degree n*. In this chapter we shall denote a polynomial in x by the symbol $f(x)$.

Thus $x^2 - 3x + 1$, $5x^3 - 7x^2 + 8$, $\sqrt{2}x^4 - x + 3$, $\frac{5}{2}x^3 - ix + \sqrt{7}$ are all polynomials in x.

If $f(x)$ is a polynomial of degree n then the expression $f(x) = 0$ is called an *equation of degree n*. Thus in an equation of degree n, there is *no* term containing x^k with $k \geq n + 1$. For instance $ix^4 - x + 1 = 0$, $\sqrt{2}x^3 - 8x + 9 = 0$, $x^2 + 1 = 0$ are equations of degree 4, 3 and 2 respectively.

An equation of degree 2 is called a *Quadratic Equation*.

NOTE: In this section we shall be mainly dealing with quadratic equations having rational numbers as coefficients.

There are two types of quadratic equations (1) Pure and (2) Affected.

A quadratic equation is called **pure** *if it does not contain single power of x.* In other words in a pure quadratic equation, coefficient of x must be zero. Thus a pure quadratic equation is of the type $ax^2 + b = 0$ with $a \neq 0$.

A quadratic equation which is not *pure* is called an *affected quadratic equation*.

Thus the most general form of an affected quadratic equation is $ax^2 + bx + c = 0$, with $ab \neq 0$. (Recall that $ab \neq 0 \Leftrightarrow a \neq 0$ and $b \neq 0$).

Root. A complex number α is called a *root* of $ax^2 + bx + c$ if $a\alpha^2 + b\alpha + c = 0$.

2. METHOD OF SOLVING PURE QUADRATIC EQUATION

Let $ax^2 + b = 0$ be a pure quadratic equation. This implies

$$ax^2 = -b \Rightarrow x^2 = -\frac{b}{a} \Rightarrow x = \pm\sqrt{\frac{-b}{a}}.$$

It is clear that the roots of $ax^2 + b$ are real if and only if a and b are of opposite signs.

Example 1. *Solve* $9x^2 - 4 = 0$.

Clearly $9x^2 = 4 \Rightarrow x^2 = \frac{4}{9} \quad \Rightarrow \quad x = \pm\frac{2}{3}$.

3. METHODS OF SOLVING AFFECTED QUADRATIC EQUATIONS

REMARK: Since a pure quadratic equation is a particular case of $ax^2 + bx + c = 0$. All these methods are applicable to pure equations also. All that we have to do is to just put $b = 0$ to get the solution of a pure equation.

(I) *Method by Factorisation*

If the expression $ax^2 + bx + c$ can be factored into linear factors then each of the factors, put to zero, provides us with a root of the given quadratic equation.

Thus if $ax^2 + bx + c = a(x - \alpha)(x - \beta)$, then the roots of $ax^2 + bx + c = 0$ are α and β.

Example 2. *Solve* $x^2 - 5x + 6 = 0$.

Solution. Clearly $x^2 - 5x + 6 = 0$

$$\Rightarrow \quad (x-2)(x-3) = 0$$

$$\Rightarrow \quad x-2=0 \text{ or } x-3 = 0$$

$$\Rightarrow \quad x=2 \text{ or } x=3$$

Hence roots of given equation are 2 and 3.

(II) *Method of Perfect Square*

This method is made clear by the following steps. Let $ax^2 + bx + c = 0$ be the given equation.

Step 1. Divide both sides of the equation by a to obtain

$$x^2 + \frac{b}{a}x + \frac{c}{a} = 0$$

(since $a \neq 0$, we are justified in division by a)

Step 2. Transpose the constant term (*i.e.* the term independent of x) on R.H.S., to get

$$x^2 + \frac{b}{a}x = -\frac{c}{a}$$

Step 3. Add $\frac{b^2}{4a^2}$ to both the sides.

Thus we have $x^2 + \frac{b}{a}x + \frac{b^2}{4a^2} = \frac{b^2}{4a^2} - \frac{c}{a}$

or
$$\left(x + \frac{b}{2a}\right)^2 = \frac{b^2 - 4ac}{4a^2}.$$

This is a pure equation in the variable $x + \frac{b}{2a}$.

So the solution is $x + \frac{b}{2a} = \frac{\pm\sqrt{b^2 - 4ac}}{2a}$

or
$$x = \frac{-b \pm \sqrt{b^2 - 4ac}}{2a}$$

REMARK: This method is useful particularly when $ax^2 + bx + c$ cannot be factored into linears factors easily.

Example 3. *Solve* $2x^2 + 3x - 1 = 0$.

Solution. In this case $a = 2, b = 3, c = -1$.

Hence roots are $x = \frac{-3 \pm \sqrt{3^2 - 4(2)(-1)}}{2.2} = \frac{-3 \pm \sqrt{17}}{4}$.

4. NATURE OF ROOTS

The roots of $ax^2 + bx + c = 0$ are given by $\frac{-b \pm \sqrt{b^2 - 4ac}}{2a}$. The expression inside the radical sign *i.e.*, $b^2 - 4ac$ is called *Discriminant.*

Case I. $b^2 - 4ac > 0$ *i.e.*, $b^2 > 4ac$.

In this case $\sqrt{b^2 - 4ac}$ is a real number. Hence the two roots of the given equation are unequal and real.

Case II. $b^2 - 4ac = 0$ *i.e.*, $b^2 = 4ac$.

In this case both the roots are real and equal (each equal to $-b/2a$).

Case III. $b^2 - 4ac < 0$ *i.e.*, $b^2 < 4ac$.

In this case $\sqrt{b^2 - 4ac}$ is an imaginary number and so both the roots are complex and unequal.

Example 4. *Solve* $\dfrac{x+3}{x+2}+\dfrac{x-3}{x-2}=\dfrac{2x-3}{x-1}$.

Solution. Given equation is equivalent to

$$\frac{(x+2)+1}{x+2}+\frac{(x-2)-1}{x-2}=\frac{2(x-1)-1}{x-1}$$

$$\Rightarrow \quad 1+\frac{1}{x+2}+1-\frac{1}{x-2}=2-\frac{1}{x-1}$$

$$\Rightarrow \quad \frac{x-2-x-2}{x^2-4}=-\frac{1}{x-1}$$

$$\Rightarrow \quad \frac{-4}{x^2-4}=-\frac{1}{x-1}$$

$$\Rightarrow \quad 4x-4=x^2-4$$

$$\Rightarrow \quad x^2-4x=0 \Rightarrow x(x-4)=0 \quad \Rightarrow \quad x=0 \text{ or } 4.$$

Hence the roots of the given equation are 0 and 4.

Example 5. *Solve* $x^4-13x^2+36=0$.

Solution. This is not a quadratic equation in x, but on putting $x=t^2$, we get a quadratic in t, namely $t^2-13t+36=0$.

Roots of this equation are given by $(t-4)(t-9)=0$.

Thus $t=4$ or $t=9$. In other words $x^2=4$ or $x^2=9$. Hence $x=\pm 2$ or ± 3.

Consequently roots of given equation are ± 2, ± 3.

Example 6. *Solve* $(x+1)(x+3)(x+4)(x+6)=72$.

Solution. Rearrange the factors on the L.H.S. so as to have the sum of constants in first two factors same as in the case of other two factors.

Since $1+6=3+4$, we get $(x+1)(x+6)(x+3)(x+4)=72$

or $\quad (x^2+7x+6)(x^2+7x+12)=72$

Now put $\quad x^2+7x=t$, to obtain

$$(t+6)(t+12)=72$$

This implies $\quad t^2+18t+72=72$

$$\Rightarrow \quad t(t+18)=0 \quad \Rightarrow \quad t=0 \quad \text{or} \quad t=-18$$

Hence $\quad x^2+7x=0$ or $x^2+7x+18=0$

First quadratic has 0 and – 7 as its roots and the second quadratic has roots given by

$$\frac{-7\pm\sqrt{49-72}}{2} \quad i.e., \quad \frac{-7\pm\sqrt{-23}}{2}$$

Example 7. *Solve* $\sqrt{5x^2-6x+8}-\sqrt{5x^2-6x-7}=1.$

Solution. Consider $(5x^2-6x+8)-(5x^2-6x-7)=15.$

Divide this equation by the given equation.

We get $\sqrt{5x^2-6x+8}+\sqrt{5x^2-6x-7}=15$

Adding this equation to the given equation we obtain

$$2\sqrt{5x^2-6x+8}=16$$

$$\Rightarrow \quad 5x^2-6x+8=64$$

$$\Rightarrow \quad 5x^2-6x-56=0$$

$$\Rightarrow \quad x=\frac{6\pm\sqrt{36+1120}}{10}=\frac{6\pm\sqrt{1156}}{10}$$

$$\Rightarrow \quad x=\frac{6\pm 34}{10} \Rightarrow x=4 \text{ or } -2\frac{4}{5}.$$

Example 8. *Solve* $x^4-5x^3+15x+9=0.$

Solution. Note that in this equation

$$x^4-5x(x^2-3)+9=0$$

$$(x^4-6x^2+9)-5x(x^2-3)+6x^2=0$$

Put $x^2-3=t$.

Thus the given equation is reduced to $t^2-5xt+6x^2=0$

This has the roots $t=2x$ and $t=3x$.

In other words we have two quadratic equations.

$$x^2-3=2x \quad \text{and} \quad x^2-3=3x.$$

The roots of former equation are -1 and 3 and those of the latter are $\frac{3\pm\sqrt{21}}{2}$.

Example 9. *Solve* $5^x+5^{2-x}=26.$

Solution. Multiplying the given equation by 5^x we obtain

$$5^{2x}+25=26.5^{2x}$$

or $$5^{2x}-26.5^{2x}+25=0$$

Put $5^{2x}=t$ to obtain the quadratic equation $t^2-26t+25=0.$

The roots of this equation are $t=1$ or $t=25$.

Then $$5^x=1=5^0 \Rightarrow x=0$$

or $$5^x=25=5^2 \Rightarrow x=2$$

Hence $$x=0 \text{ or } 2.$$

Example 10. *Solve* $3x-4=\sqrt{2x^2-2x+2}$.

Solution. Squaring both sides to eliminate the radical sign, we get

$$9x^2-24x+16 = 2x^2-3x+2$$

or $$7x^2-21x+14 = 0$$

or $$x^2-3x+2 = 0$$

$\Rightarrow$ $$x=1 \quad \text{or} \quad 2$$

Hence the roots of given equation are 1 and 2.

Example 11. Solve $x^4+x^3-4x^2+x+1=0$.

Solution. In equations of such type if the terms are arranged according to descending powers of x, the coefficients of terms equidistant from first and last term are equal or differ in sign. Equations of this type are called *reciprocal equations.*

We collect equidistant terms together.

Thus given equation is equivalent to

$$(x^4+1)+(x^3+x)-4x^2=0$$

Divide by x^2 to obtain

$$\left(x^2+\frac{1}{x^2}\right)+\left(x+\frac{1}{x}\right)-4=0$$

Now put $x+\dfrac{1}{x}=t$. Then $x^2+\dfrac{1}{x^2}=t^2-2$

We get $$t^2-2+t-4 = 0$$

or $$t^2+t-6=0 \Rightarrow \quad t=-3 \text{ or } 2.$$

In other words $$x+\frac{1}{x}=-3 \text{ or } 2$$

i.e. $$x^2+3x+1 = 0 \quad \text{or} \quad x^2-2x+1=0$$

$\Rightarrow$ $$x=\frac{-3\pm\sqrt{5}}{2} \quad \text{or} \quad x = 1, 1.$$

Hence the roots of given equation are

$$1, 1, \frac{-3\pm\sqrt{5}}{2}.$$

Example 12. *Solve the equation*

$$x^2-6x+9 = 4\sqrt{x^2-6x+6}$$

Solution. Putting $x^2-6x+6=t$ in the given equation, we get

$$t+3=4\sqrt{t}$$

or $\quad t^2+6t+9=16t$

or $\quad t^2-10t+9=0$

$\Rightarrow \quad (t-1)(t-9)=0$

$\Rightarrow \quad t=1 \quad \text{or} \quad t=9$

$\Rightarrow \quad x^2-6x+6=1 \quad \text{or} \quad x^2-6x+6=9$

$\Rightarrow \quad x^2-6x+5=0 \quad \text{or} \quad x^2-6x-3=0$

$$\Rightarrow \quad (x-1)(x-5)=0 \quad \text{or} \quad x=\frac{6\pm\sqrt{36-4(-3)}}{2}$$

$$\Rightarrow \quad x=1,5 \quad \text{or} \quad x=\frac{6\pm 4\sqrt{3}}{2}$$

$\Rightarrow \quad x=1,5 \quad \text{or} \quad 3\pm 2\sqrt{3}$.

Example 13. *Solve* $\sqrt{\dfrac{x}{1-x}}+\sqrt{\dfrac{1-x}{x}}=2\dfrac{1}{6}$.

Solution. Put $\dfrac{x}{1-x}=t^2$

We get $t+\dfrac{1}{t}=\dfrac{13}{6}$

$\Rightarrow \quad 6t^2+6=13t$

$\Rightarrow \quad 6t^2-13t+6=0$

$\Rightarrow \quad 6t^2-4t-9t+6=0$

$\Rightarrow \quad (2t-3)(3t-2)=0$

$$\Rightarrow \quad t=\frac{3}{2} \quad \text{or} \quad \frac{2}{3}$$

Now $t=\dfrac{3}{2} \Rightarrow \dfrac{x}{1-x}=\dfrac{9}{4} \Rightarrow 4x=9-9x$

$$\Rightarrow 13x=9 \qquad \Rightarrow x=\frac{9}{13}$$

Whereas $t=\dfrac{2}{3} \Rightarrow \dfrac{x}{1-x}=\dfrac{4}{9} \Rightarrow 9x=4-4x$

$$\Rightarrow 13x=4 \Rightarrow x=\frac{4}{13}$$

So $\quad x=\dfrac{4}{13} \quad \text{or} \quad \dfrac{9}{13}$.

Example 14. *Find the value of* $\sqrt{6+\sqrt{6}+\sqrt{6}+\ldots\infty}$.

Solution. Let $x=\sqrt{6+\sqrt{6}+\sqrt{6}+\ldots\infty}=\sqrt{6+x}$

$\Rightarrow \quad x^2=6+x$

$\Rightarrow \quad x^2-x-6=0$

$\Rightarrow \quad (x-3)(x+2)=0$

$\Rightarrow \quad x=3 \quad \text{or} \quad -2.$

Example 15. *Solve* $\dfrac{x-p}{q}+\dfrac{x-q}{p}=\dfrac{q}{x-p}+\dfrac{p}{x-q}$.

Solution. Given equation can be rewritten as

$$\frac{x-p}{q}-\frac{q}{x-p}=\frac{p}{x-q}-\frac{x-q}{p}.$$

$$\Rightarrow \quad \frac{(x-p)^2-q^2}{q(x-p)}=\frac{p^2-(x-q)^2}{p(x-q)}$$

$$\Rightarrow \quad \frac{(x-p-q)(x-p+q)}{q(x-p)}=\frac{(p+x-q)(p-x+q)}{p(x-q)}$$

Either $x-p-q=0$ *i.e.*, $x=p+q$

or we get

$$\frac{x-p+q}{q(x-p)}=\frac{-(p+x-q)}{p(x-q)}.$$

Simplifying we get $(p+q)x^2-(p^2+q^2)x=0$

$\Rightarrow \quad x=0$ or $x=\dfrac{p^2+q^2}{p+q}$

Hence $x=0$ or $\dfrac{p^2+q^2}{p+q}$ or $p+q$.

Example 16. *Solve* $x+\sqrt{x}=\dfrac{6}{25}$.

Solution. Putting $\sqrt{x}=t$, we get

$$t^2+t=\frac{6}{25}$$

$\Rightarrow \quad 25t^2+25t-6=0$

$$\Rightarrow \quad t=\frac{-25\pm\sqrt{625-4(-6)(25)}}{50}$$

$$= \frac{-25 \pm \sqrt{625+600}}{50}$$

$$= \frac{-25 \pm \sqrt{1225}}{50} = \frac{-25 \pm 35}{50}$$

$$= \frac{10}{50} \quad \text{or} \quad \frac{-60}{50}$$

$$= \frac{1}{5} \quad \text{or} \quad \frac{-6}{5}$$

Then $x = t^2 = \frac{1}{25}$ or $\frac{36}{25}$.

Example 17. *Solve* $x^{2/3} + x^{1/3} - 2 = 0.$

Solution. Put $x^{1/3} = t$, to obtain

$$t^2 + t - 2 = 0$$

$\Rightarrow$ $(t+2)(t-1) = 0$

$\Rightarrow$ $t = 1$ or -2

In case $t = 1$, we get $x^{1/3} = 1 \Rightarrow x = 1$

In case $t = -2$ we get $x^{1/3} = -2 \Rightarrow x = -8$

Hence $x = 1$ or -8.

Example 18. *Solve* $x^2 + x + 10\sqrt{x^2 + 3x + 16} = 2(20 - x).$

Solution. Given equation can be written as

$$x^2 + 3x - 40 + 10\sqrt{x^2 + 3x + 16} = 0$$

Put $\sqrt{x^2 + 3x + 16} = t.$ Then $x^2 + 3x = t^2 - 16.$

So, the given equation simplifies to

$$t^2 - 16 - 40 + 10t = 0$$

or $t^2 + 10t - 56 = 0$

$\Rightarrow$ $(t+14)(t-4) = 0$

$\Rightarrow$ $t = 4$ or -14

Now $t = 4 \Rightarrow x^2 + 3x + 16 = 16$

$\Rightarrow x^2 + 3x = 0 \Rightarrow x = 0$ or -3

While $t = -14 \Rightarrow x^2 + 3x + 16 = 196$

$\Rightarrow x^2 + 3x - 180 = 0$

$$\Rightarrow x = \frac{-3 \pm \sqrt{9+720}}{2}$$

$$= \frac{-3 \pm \sqrt{729}}{2}$$

$$= \frac{-3 \pm 27}{2} = 12 \text{ or } -15$$

Hence $\quad x \Rightarrow 0, -3, 12, -15.$

Example 19. *Solve* $3x^2 - 18 + \sqrt{3x^2 - 4x - 6} = 4x.$

Solution. Putting $\sqrt{3x^2 - 4x - 6} = t$, we get

$$3x^2 - 4x = t^2 + 6$$

So the given equation is reduced to

$$t^2 + 6 - 18 + t = 0$$

$$\Rightarrow \quad t^2 + t - 12 = 0$$

$$\Rightarrow \quad (t+4)(t-3) = 0$$

$$\Rightarrow \quad t = 3 \quad \text{or} \quad -4$$

Now $t = 3 \Rightarrow 3x^2 - 4x - 6 = 9 \Rightarrow 3x^2 - 4x - 15 = 0$

$$\Rightarrow 3x^2 - 9x + 5x - 15 = 0$$

$$\Rightarrow (x-3)(3x+5) = 0$$

$$\Rightarrow x = 3 \text{ or } -\tfrac{5}{3}$$

Also $\quad t = -4 \Rightarrow 3x^2 - 4x - 6 = 16 \Rightarrow 3x^2 - 4x - 22 = 0$

$$\Rightarrow \quad x = \frac{4 \pm \sqrt{16 - 4.3(-22)}}{6}$$

$$= \frac{4 \pm \sqrt{16 + 264}}{6} = \frac{4 \pm \sqrt{280}}{6}$$

$$\Rightarrow \quad x = \frac{2 \pm \sqrt{70}}{3}$$

Hence $\quad x = 3, -\frac{5}{3}, \frac{2 \pm \sqrt{70}}{3}.$

Example 20. *Solve* $\dfrac{\sqrt{1 + x^2} + \sqrt{1 - x^2}}{\sqrt{1 + x^2} - \sqrt{1 - x^2}} = 3.$

Solution. Simplifying given equation, we get

$$\sqrt{1 + x^2} + \sqrt{1 - x^2} = 3\sqrt{1 + x^2} - 3\sqrt{1 - x^2}$$

$$\Rightarrow \quad 2\sqrt{1 + x^2} = 4\sqrt{1 - x^2}$$

$$\Rightarrow \quad \sqrt{1+x^2} = 2\sqrt{1-x^2}$$
$$\Rightarrow \quad 1+x^2 = 4(1-x^2)$$
$$\Rightarrow \quad 5x^2 = 3$$
$$\Rightarrow \quad x^2 = \frac{3}{5}$$
$$\Rightarrow \quad x = \pm\sqrt{\frac{3}{5}}.$$

EXERCISES

Solve the following equations:

1. $x^2 - 8x - 48 = 0.$

2. $3x^2 + 10x + 3 = 0$

3. $\dfrac{77(x-2)}{x+3} - 21x = 7 + \dfrac{7x-49}{x+3}$

4. $\dfrac{21x^2-16}{3x^2-4} - 7x = 5$

5. $(3x - 11)(x - 2) + (2x - 3)(x - 4) + 13x = 10(2x - 1)^2 + 12$

6. $\dfrac{x+2}{x-2} - \dfrac{x-2}{x+2} = \dfrac{5}{6}$

7. $\dfrac{a+2x+\sqrt{a^2-4x^2}}{a+2x-\sqrt{a^2-4x^2}} = \dfrac{5x}{a}$

8. $5 - \sqrt{11x^2 - 3x + 1} = 2x$

9. $\sqrt{2x+7} + \sqrt{3x-18} = \sqrt{7x+1}$

10. $\left(\dfrac{2x+3}{2x-3}\right)^{1/3} + \left(\dfrac{2x-3}{2x-3}\right)^{1/3} = \dfrac{8(4x^2+9)}{13(4x^2-9)}$

11. $(x - 7)(x - 3)(x + 5)(x + 1) = 1680$

12. $(x + 9)(x - 3)(x - 7)(x + 5) = 385$

13. $16x(x + 1)(x + 2)(x + 3) = 9$

14. $(x + 2)(x + 4)(x + 5)(x + 10) = 990x^2$
    [**Hint.** Rearranging, we get $(x + 2)(x + 10)(x + 4)(x + 5) = 990x^2$. Put $x^2 + 20 = t$]

15. $\sqrt{3x^2 - 7x - 30} + \sqrt{2x^2 - 7x - 5} = x + 5$

16. $\sqrt{2x^2 + 5x - 2} - \sqrt{2x^2 + 5x - 9} = 1$

17. $\sqrt{3x^2 - 2x + 9} + \sqrt{3x^2 - 2x + 4} = 13$

18. $\sqrt{x^2 + ax - 1} + \sqrt{x^2 + bx - 1} = \sqrt{a} + \sqrt{b}$

19. $3^{2x} + 9 = 10.3^x$

20. $4^x - 3.2^{x+3} = -128$

21. $\sqrt{3^x} + \dfrac{3}{\sqrt{3^x}} = 4$

22. $5(5^x + 5^{-x}) = 26$

23. $10x^1 - 63x^3 + 52x^2 + 63x + 10 = 0$

24. $x^4 - x^3 + 5/4x^2 - x + 1 = 0$

25. $4x^4 - 16x^3 + 7x^2 + 16x + 4 = 0$

ANSWERS

1. $12, -4$ 2. $-3, -1/3$ 3. $\pm\sqrt{6}$

4. $2, -\frac{2}{15}$ 5. $\frac{3}{5}, \frac{4}{7}$ 6. $10, -\frac{2}{5}$

7. $\pm\frac{2a}{5}$ 8. $1, -3\frac{3}{7}$ 9. $9, -3\frac{3}{5}$

10. $\pm 1\frac{1}{6}, \pm 1\frac{13}{14}$ (Omit imaginary roots, if any)

11. $9, -7, 1\pm\sqrt{-24}$ 12. $2, -4, -1\pm\sqrt{71}$

13. $-1\frac{1}{2}, -1\frac{1}{2}, \frac{3\pm\sqrt{10}}{2}$ 14. $1, 20, -21-\sqrt{421}$

15. $6, -2\frac{1}{2}$ 16. $2, -4\frac{1}{2}$

17. $4, -3\frac{1}{3}$ 18. $1, \frac{(\sqrt{a}+\sqrt{b})^2+4}{(\sqrt{a}-\sqrt{b})^2-4}$

19. $0, 2$ 20. $3, 4$

21. $0, 2$ 22. ± 1

23. $2, 5, -1/2, -1/5$ 24. $\frac{3\pm\sqrt{-7}}{4}, \frac{1\pm\sqrt{-15}}{4}$

25. $2, -\frac{1}{2}, \frac{5\pm\sqrt{41}}{4}$

5. SYMMETRIC EXPRESSIONS OF ROOTS OF A QUADRATIC EQUATION

We first prove that a quadratic equation cannot have more than two roots.

Suppose α, β, γ are three roots of $ax^2 + bx + c = 0$.

Since α is a root of $ax^2 + bx + c = 0$, $x - \alpha$ is a factor of $ax^2 + bx + c$ (by Remainder Theorem). Similarly $x - \beta$ and $x - \gamma$ are factors of $ax^2 + bx + c$.

So $ax^2 + bx + c = k(x - \alpha)(x - \beta)(x - \gamma)$ where k is a non-zero constant. Now left hand side is a polynomial of degree 2, whereas right hand side is a polynomial of degree 3. But two polynomials can be equal only when their degrees are equal and coefficients of equal powers of x are equal. Thus we have a contradiction. Hence a quadratic equation can not have more than two roots.

Definition. An equation $f(x) = 0$ is called an *identity* if it is satisfied by *all* values of x.

For example $(x-2)^2 - x^2 + 4x - 4 = 0$ is an identity while $x^2 - 6x + 5 = 0$ is not an identity as $x = 2$ does not satisfy $x^2 - 6x + 5 = 0$ ($2^2 - 6.2 + 5 = 9 - 12 = -3 \neq 0$).

Notation. An identity is denoted by $\equiv$.

Thus $(x-2)^2 - x^2 + 4x - 4 \equiv 0$.

Theorem. *$ax^2 + bx + c = 0$ is an identity if and only if $a = b = c = 0$.*

Proof.. In case $a = b = c = 0$, given equation reduces to

$$0.x^2 + 0.x + 0 = 0$$

which is clearly satisfied by all values of x.

Conversely let $ax^2 + bx + c = 0$ be satisfied by all values of x. Take three distinct numbers α, β, γ. In particular, the given equation must be satisfied by $x = \alpha, \beta$ and γ.

i.e.,

$$a\alpha^2 + b\alpha + c = 0 \quad ...(1)$$

$$a\beta^2 + b\beta + c = 0 \quad ...(2)$$

$$a\gamma^2 + b\gamma + c = 0 \quad ...(3)$$

(1) and (2) give, on subtraction

$$a(\alpha^2 - \beta^2) + b(\alpha - \beta) = 0$$

$$\Rightarrow \quad a(\alpha + \beta) + b = 0 \text{ as } \alpha \neq \beta. \quad ...(4)$$

Further (2) and (3) yield, on subtraction

$$a(\beta^2 - \gamma^2) + b(\beta - \gamma) = 0$$

$$\Rightarrow \quad a(\beta + \gamma) + b = 0 \text{ as } \beta \neq \gamma. \quad ...(5)$$

Subtract (5) from (4), to get $a(\alpha - \gamma) = 0$

$$\Rightarrow a = 0 \quad \text{as} \quad \alpha \neq \gamma$$

Then (4) $\quad \Rightarrow b = 0$ and (1) $\Rightarrow c = 0$.

Hence the theorem follows.

Coming back to quadratic equation $ax^2 + bx + c = 0$ (*i.e.* $a \neq 0$), we see that if α, β are its roots, then

$$ax^2 + bx + c \equiv a(x - \alpha)(x - \beta)$$

$$(a - a)x^2 + [b + a(\alpha + \beta)]x + c - a\alpha\beta \equiv 0.$$

By previous theorem this means

$$b = -a(\alpha + \beta) \quad \text{or} \quad \alpha + \beta = -\frac{b}{a}$$

and

$$c = a\alpha\beta \quad \text{or} \quad \alpha\beta = \frac{c}{a}.$$

Thus we get the following relation between roots and coefficients

$$\alpha + \beta = -\frac{b}{a}$$

$$\alpha\beta = \frac{c}{a}.$$

Aliter. The above relations can also be found as under.

Take $\alpha = \dfrac{-b + \sqrt{b^2 - 4ac}}{2a}$ and $\beta = \dfrac{-b - \sqrt{b^2 - 4ac}}{2a}$

Then $\alpha + \beta = \dfrac{2b}{2a} = \dfrac{-b}{a}$

and $\alpha\beta = \dfrac{b^2 - (b^2 - 4ac)}{4a^2} = \dfrac{4ac}{4a^2} = \dfrac{c}{a}.$

The above relations imply that

$$ax^2 + bx + c = 0$$

is same as $ax^2 - a(\alpha + \beta)x + a\alpha\beta = 0.$

or $x^2 - (\alpha + \beta)x + \alpha\beta = 0$ as $a \neq 0$

This gives us the method of construction of a quadratic equation whose roots are given.

The required quadratic will be

$$x^2 - (\textit{sum of two roots})x + (\textit{product of two roots}) = 0$$

Definition. Any expression involving α and β is called a *symmetric function* of α and β, if it remains unchanged when α and β are interchanged.

For instance, $\alpha^2 + \beta^2, \alpha\beta, \dfrac{\alpha^3 + \beta^3}{\alpha\beta}, \alpha^2\beta + \alpha\beta^2$

are all symmetric functions of α and β, where $\alpha^3 - \beta$ is not a symmetric function since in general $\alpha^3 - \beta$ need not be equal to $\beta^3 - \alpha$.
[e.g., if $\alpha = 1, \beta = 2$; $\alpha^3 - \beta = 1 - 2 = -1$ while $\beta^3 - \alpha = 8 - 1 = 7$].

With the help of relation $\alpha + \beta = -\dfrac{b}{a}$ and $\alpha\beta = \dfrac{c}{a}$ we can evaluate symmetirc function of α and β. The method will be best illustrated with the help of examples.

Example 21. (*i*) *If α and β are the roots of $x^2 - px + q = 0$, form an equation whose roots are $\alpha\beta + \alpha + \beta$ and $\alpha\beta - \alpha - \beta$.*

(*ii*) *If α and β are the roots of $2x^2 - 4x + 1 = 0$. Form the equation whose roots are $\alpha^2 + \beta$ and $\beta + \alpha$.*

Solution. (*i*) Let $\gamma = \alpha\beta + \alpha + \beta$ and $\delta = \alpha\beta - \alpha - \beta$

The equation whose roots are γ and δ is

$$x^2 - (\gamma + \delta)x + \gamma\delta = 0$$

Now α, β are roots of $x^2 - px + q = 0$

implies that $\alpha + \beta = -\dfrac{(-p)}{1} = p$

and $\alpha\beta = \dfrac{q}{1} = q$

This further yields that

$$\gamma = \alpha\beta + \alpha + \beta = q + p \text{ and } \delta = \alpha\beta - \alpha - \beta = q - p.$$

Hence required equation is

$$x^2 - (q + p + q - p)x + (q + p)(q - p) = 0$$

i.e.,
$$x^2 - 2qx + q^2 - p^2 = 0$$

(*ii*)
$$\alpha + \beta = \frac{4}{2} = 2$$

$$\alpha\beta = \frac{1}{2}$$

Now
$$\begin{aligned} s_1 &= \alpha^2 + \beta + \beta^2 + \alpha \\ &= \alpha^2 + \beta^2 + \alpha + \beta \\ &= (\alpha + \beta)^2 - 2\alpha\beta + \alpha + \beta \\ &= 4 - 1 + 2 = 5 \end{aligned}$$

and
$$\begin{aligned} s_2 &= (\alpha^2 + \beta)(\beta^2 + \alpha) \\ &= \alpha^2\beta^2 + \alpha^3 + \beta^3 + \alpha\beta \\ &= \frac{1}{4} + \frac{1}{2} + (\alpha + \beta)^3 - 3\alpha\beta(\alpha + \beta) \\ &= \frac{3}{4} + 8 - \frac{3}{2}(2) \\ &= 5 + \frac{3}{4} = \frac{23}{4}. \end{aligned}$$

Hence the required equation is

$$x^2 - 5x + \frac{23}{4} = 0$$

or
$$4x^2 - 20x + 23 = 0.$$

Example 22. *α, β are roots of $2x^2 + 3x + 7 = 0$. Find the values of $\frac{\alpha}{\beta} + \frac{\beta}{\alpha}$ and $\alpha^3 + \beta^3$.*

Solution. $\alpha + \beta = -\frac{3}{2}$ and $\alpha\beta = \frac{7}{2}$

Now
$$\frac{\alpha}{\beta} + \frac{\beta}{\alpha} = \frac{\alpha^2 + \beta^2}{\alpha\beta} = \frac{(\alpha + \beta)^2 - 2\alpha\beta}{\alpha\beta}$$

$$= \frac{\frac{9}{4} - 2 \cdot \frac{7}{2}}{\frac{7}{2}} = \frac{\frac{9}{4} - 7}{\frac{7}{2}} = \frac{2}{7}\left(\frac{-19}{4}\right) = \frac{-19}{14}$$

Again $\alpha^3 + \beta^3 = (\alpha + \beta)(\alpha^2 - \alpha\beta + \beta^2)$

$$= (\alpha + \beta)[(\alpha + \beta)^2 - 3\alpha\beta]$$

$$= \left(-\frac{3}{2}\right)\left[\frac{9}{4} - 3 \cdot \frac{7}{2}\right]$$

$$= \left(-\frac{3}{2}\right)\left(\frac{9}{4} - \frac{21}{2}\right)$$

$$= \left(-\frac{3}{2}\right)\left(\frac{-33}{4}\right) = \frac{99}{8}.$$

Example 23. *If α, β are the roots of $ax^2 + bx + c = 0$, find the equation with roots $a\alpha + b\beta$ and $b\alpha + a\beta$.*

Solution. We have

$$(a\alpha + b\beta) + (b\alpha + a\beta) = (a + b)\alpha + (a + b)\beta$$

$$= (a + b)\alpha + (a + b)\beta$$

$$= (a + b)(\alpha + \beta)$$

$$= (a + b)\left(-\frac{b}{a}\right) = -\frac{b}{a}(a + b)$$

Also $(a\alpha + b\beta)(b\alpha + a\beta) = ab\alpha^2 + ab\beta^2 + (a^2 + b^2)\alpha\beta$

$$= ab(\alpha^2 + \beta^2) + (a^2 + b^2)\alpha\beta$$

$$= ab[(\alpha^2 + \beta^2) - 2\alpha\beta] + (a^2 + b^2)\alpha\beta$$

$$= ab\left(\frac{b^2}{a^2} - \frac{2c}{a}\right) + (a^2 + b^2)\frac{c}{a}$$

$$= \frac{b(b^2 - 2ac)}{a} + \frac{(a^2 + b^2)c}{a}$$

$$= \frac{b(b^2 - 2ac) + (a^2 + b^2)c}{a}$$

Hence required equation is

$$x^2 + \frac{b}{a}(a + b)x + \frac{b(b^2 - 2ac) + (a^2 + b^2)c}{a} = 0$$

or $ax^2 + b(a + b)x + b(b^2 - 2ac) + (a^2 + b^2)c = 0$

or $ax^2 + b^2x + abx + b^3 + c(a^2 + b^2 - 2ab) = 0$

or $(ax + b^2)x + b(ax + b^2) + c(a - b)^2 = 0$

$\Rightarrow$ $(ax + b^2)(x + b) + c(a - b)^2 = 0$

Example 24. *If the roots of $ax^2 + bx + c = 0$ are in the ratio $p : q$, prove that $ac(p + q)^2 = b^2pq$.*

Solution. We know that $\alpha+\beta=-\dfrac{b}{a}$ and $\alpha\beta=\dfrac{c}{a}$

By hypothesis $\dfrac{\alpha}{\beta}=\dfrac{p}{q}$

We are to eliminate α, β from these three relations.

$$\alpha\beta=\frac{c}{a} \text{ and } \frac{\alpha}{\beta}=\frac{p}{q} \Rightarrow \alpha^2=\frac{pc}{aq}$$

and
$$\frac{\alpha\beta}{\alpha/\beta}=\left(\frac{c}{a}\right)\bigg/\frac{p}{q} \Rightarrow \beta^2=\frac{cq}{ap}$$

Again $\alpha+\beta=-\dfrac{b}{a} \Rightarrow \alpha^2+\beta^2+2\alpha\beta=\dfrac{b^2}{a^2}$

So we get

$$\frac{pc}{aq}+\frac{cq}{ap}+\frac{2c}{a}=\frac{b^2}{a^2}$$

or
$$\frac{(p^2+q^2)c+2cpq}{apq}=\frac{b^2}{a^2}$$

$\Rightarrow \quad a(p^2+q^2)c+2capq=b^2pq$

$\Rightarrow \quad ac(p^2+q^2+2pq)=b^2pq$

$\Rightarrow \quad ac(p+q)^2=b^2pq.$

Example 25. *If α and β are the roots of $ax^2+bx+c=0$, form the equation whose roots are $\alpha^2+\beta^2$ and $\alpha^{-2}+\beta^{-2}$.*

Solution. Here $\alpha+\beta=-\dfrac{b}{a}$ and $\alpha\beta=\dfrac{c}{a}$

Now $\alpha^2+\beta^2=(\alpha+\beta)^2-2\alpha\beta=\dfrac{b^2}{a^2}-\dfrac{2c}{a}=\dfrac{b^2-2ac}{a^2}$

and
$$\alpha^{-2}+\beta^{-2}=\frac{1}{\alpha^2}+\frac{1}{\beta^2}=\frac{\alpha^2+\beta^2}{\alpha^2\beta^2}=\frac{\dfrac{b^2-2ac}{a^2}}{\dfrac{c^2}{a^2}}=\frac{b^2-2ac}{c^2}$$

So, sum of the new roots $=\dfrac{b^2-2ac}{a^2}+\dfrac{b^2-2ac}{c^2}$

$$=\frac{(b^2-2ac)(c^2+a^2)}{c^2a^2}$$

and product of new roots $=\dfrac{(b^2-2ac)^2}{a^2c^2}$

Hence the required equation is

$$x^2 - \frac{(b^2-2ac)(c^2+a^2)}{c^2a^2}x^2 + \frac{(b^2-2ac)^2}{a^2c^2} = 0$$

or $$a^2c^2x^2 - (b^2-2ac)(c^2+a^2)x^2 + (b^2-2ac)^2 = 0$$

Example 26. *For what values of m will the equation*

$(m + 1)x^2 + 2(m + 3)x + (2m + 3) = 0$ *have equal roots?*

Solution. As shown in previous section, the equation will have equal roots, if and only if

$$[2(m+3)]^2 = 4(m+1)(2m+3)$$

or $$m^2 + 6m + 9 = 2m^2 + 5m + 3$$

or $$m^2 - m - 6 = 0$$

or $$(m-3)(m+2) = 0 \quad \text{or} \quad m = 3 \quad \text{or} \quad -2.$$

Example 27. *Show that* $(x - a)(x - b) = h^2$ *has real roots.*

Solution. Given equation can be simplified to

$$x^2 - (a+b)x + ab - h^2 = 0$$

Discriminant $= (a+b)^2 - 4(ab - h^2)$

$= (a+b)^2 - 4ab + 4h^2$

$= (a-b)^2 + 4h^2$

which is always a +ve quantity.

Hence the roots of given equation are always real.

EXERCISES

If α, β are the roots of $ax^2 + bx + c = 0$ find the value of

1. $\dfrac{\alpha}{\beta} + \dfrac{\beta}{\alpha}$
2. $\alpha^4 + \beta^4$
3. $(\alpha^2 - \beta)^2 + (\beta^2 - \alpha)^2$
4. $\alpha^4\beta^7 + \alpha^7\beta^4$
5. $\left(\dfrac{\alpha}{\beta} - \dfrac{\beta}{\alpha}\right)^2$
6. Find the condition that one root of $ax^2 + bx + c = 0$ shall be n times the other.
7. If the roots of $lx^2 + nx + n = 0$ are in the ratio $p : q$ prove that

$$\sqrt{\frac{p}{q}} + \sqrt{\frac{q}{p}} + \sqrt{\frac{n}{l}} = 0$$

[*Hint.* Let the roots be αp, αq; $\alpha(p + q) = -\dfrac{n}{l}$, $pq\alpha^2 = \dfrac{n}{l} \Rightarrow \alpha = \sqrt{\dfrac{n}{p\alpha l}}$ etc.]

8. If p, q are the roots of $3x^2 + 6x + 2 = 0$, form an equation whose roots are

$$\frac{-p^2}{q} \text{ and } \frac{-q^2}{p}$$

9. Find k if the roots of $2x^2 + 3x + k = 0$ are equal.
10. If r is the ratio of the roots of the equation
$$ax^2 + bx + c = 0 \text{ show that } (r + 1)^2\, ac = b^2 r$$
11. α and β are the roots of $ax^2 + bx - c = 0$, form an equation whose roots are

$$\frac{1}{a\alpha + b}, \frac{1}{a\beta + b}$$

12. Show that the roots of $x^2 - 2ax + a^2 - b^2 - c^2 = 0$ are always real.
13. Prove that the roots of $(a + c - b)x^2 + 2cx + (b + c - a) = 0$ are rational [a, b, c are rational numbers].
14. For what value of m will the equation

$$\frac{x^2 - bx}{ax - c} = \frac{m-1}{m+1}$$

have roots equal in magnitude but opposite in sign.

15. If x is a real number prove that the expression $\frac{x^2 + 2x - 11}{2(x-3)}$ does not lie strictly between 2 and 6.

[*Hint.* Let $y = \frac{x^2 + 2x - 11}{2(x-3)}$ then $x^2 + (2 - 2y)x + 6y - 11 = 0$

$$\Rightarrow \quad x = \frac{(2-2y) \pm \sqrt{(2-2y)^2 - 4(6y-11)}}{2}$$

Since x is real, $(2 - 2y)^2 - 4(6y - 11) > 0$

$\Rightarrow \quad 1 - 2y + y^2 - 6y + 11 > 0$

$\Rightarrow \quad y^2 - 8y + 12 > 0$

$\Rightarrow \quad (y - 2)(y - 6) > 0.$

In case $2 < y < 6$, one of the factors on LHS will be +ve and other will be –ve, so the product can't be +ve.]

16. If x is real prove that $\frac{x}{x^2 - 5x + 9}$ lies between $\frac{-1}{11}$ and 1.

17. If x is real prove that $\frac{x^2 + 34x - 71}{x^2 + 2x - 7}$ cannot lie strictly between 5 and 9.

18. If α, β are the roots of $ax^2 + bx + c = 0$, form equation with roots $\frac{1-\alpha}{1+\alpha}, \frac{1-\beta}{1+\beta}$.

19. If α, β are roots of $x^2 - px + q = 0$, show that

$$\frac{\alpha^2}{\beta^2} + \frac{\beta^2}{\alpha^2} = \frac{p^4}{q^2} - \frac{4p^2}{q} + 2.$$

20. Form an equation whose roots are squares of the roots of $ax^2 + bx + c = 0$.

ANSWERS

1. $\dfrac{b^2 - 2ac}{ac}$ 2. $\dfrac{b^4 - 4ab^2c + 2a^2c^2}{a^4}$

3. $\dfrac{b^4 - 4ab^2c + 2a^2c^2 + a^2b^2 - 2a^3c + 2a^2bc}{a^4}$

4. $\dfrac{bc^4(3ac - b^2)}{a^7}$ 5. $\dfrac{b^2(b^2 - 4ac)}{a^2c^2}$

6. $nb^2 = ac(n + 1)^2$ 8. $3x^2 - 18x + 2 = 0$

9. $k = \dfrac{9}{8}$ 11. $cax^2 - bx + 1 = 0$

14. $m = \dfrac{a - b}{a + b}$ 18. $(a - b + c)x^2 - 2x(a - c) + a + b + c = 0$

20. $a^2x^2 + (2ac - b^2)x + c^2 = 0$

6. SIMULTANEOUS EQUATIONS IN TWO UNKNOWNS

In this section we will consider solutions of linear and non-linear simultaneous equations in two unknowns. There are several techniques for solving such problems and we shall illustrate some of them by means of examples.

Example 28. *Solve* $4x - 3y = 1$, $12xy + 13x^2 = 25$

Solution. From $4x - 3y = 1$, $y = \dfrac{4x - 1}{3}$

Substituting the value of y in $12xy + 13x^2 = 25$, we get

$$12x\left(\frac{4x-1}{3}\right) + 13x^2 = 25$$

$$\Rightarrow \quad 16x^2 - 4x + 13x^2 = 25$$

$$\Rightarrow \quad 29x^2 - 4x - 25 = 0$$

$$\Rightarrow \quad (29x + 25)(x - 1) = 0$$

$$\Rightarrow \quad x = 1 \quad \text{or} \quad -\frac{25}{29}$$

Then $y = \dfrac{4x - 1}{3}$ gives that either $y = 1$ or $-\dfrac{43}{29}$. Hence the required solution is $x = 1, y = 1$

or $\quad x = -\dfrac{25}{29}, y = -1\dfrac{14}{29}$.

Example 29. *Solve* $x^2 + y^2 = 185$, $x - y = 3$.

Solution. Now $\quad (x - y)^2 = x^2 + y^2 - 2xy \Rightarrow 9 = 185 - 2xy$

$$\Rightarrow \quad 2xy = 176 \quad \Rightarrow \quad xy = 88$$

Again $(x+y)^2 = (x-y)^2 + 4xy$ $\Rightarrow (x+y)^2 = 9 + 352 = 361$

$x + y = \pm 19$

Taking +ve sign, we get

$$x - y = 3, x + y = 19 \text{ and so } x = 11, y = 8$$

Taking –ve sign, we get

$$x - y = 3, x + y = -19 \text{ and so } x = -8, y = -11$$

Hence the required solution is $x = 11, y = 8$

or $x = -8, y = -11$

Example 30. *Solve* $2x + 3y = 5, xy = 1$.

Solution. Since $xy = 1$, we get $6xy = 6$, *i.e.*, $2x \cdot 3y = 6$.

Now we have $2x + 3y = 5$ and $2x \cdot 3y = 6$

As $(2x - 3y)^2 = (2x + 3y)^2 - 4.2x.3y$, we get

$$(2x - 3y)^2 = 25 - 24 = 1 \Rightarrow 2x - 3y = \pm 1$$

Taking +ve sign, we obtain $2x + 3y = 5, 2x - 3y = 1$

$$\Rightarrow \qquad x = \frac{3}{2}, \quad y = \frac{2}{3}.$$

Taking –ve sign, we obtain $2x + 3y = 5, 2x - 3y = -1$

$\Rightarrow x = 1, \quad y = 1.$

Hence required solution is $x = 1, \quad y = 1$

$$x = 1\frac{1}{2}, \quad y = \frac{2}{3}.$$

Example 31. *Solve* $x^3 + y^3 = 4914, x + y = 18$.

Solution. We know that $(x + y)^3 = x^3 + y^3 + 3xy(x + y)$

This gives that $(18)^3 = 4914 + 3xy \cdot 18$

or $324 = 273 + 3xy \Rightarrow 180 = 91 + xy \Rightarrow xy = 17.$

Now $x + y = 18, \quad xy = 17$

Solving by the method discussed in previous example, we get

$x = 1, \quad y = 17$

or $x = 17, \quad y = 1$

Example 32. *Solve* $x + y + \sqrt{xy} = 14$

$x^2 + y^2 + xy = 84$

Solution.

$$x^2 + y^2 + xy = (x+y)^2 - xy = (x + y + \sqrt{xy})(x + y - \sqrt{xy})$$

$$\Rightarrow \qquad 84 = 14(x + y - \sqrt{xy}) \quad \Rightarrow \quad x + y - \sqrt{xy} = 6$$

But $\qquad x + y - \sqrt{xy} = 14$

Hence $\qquad x + y = 10, \sqrt{xy} = 4 \quad \text{or} \quad xy = 16.$

By the method of Example 30, $\quad x = 8, \ y = 2$

or $\qquad x = 2, \ y = 8.$

Example 33. (Homogenous Equations)

Solve $x^2 + xy + 4y^2 = 6$

$3x^2 + 8y^2 = 14$

(Note in such equations, sum of powers of x and y in each term is same.)

Solution. Both the equations can be re-written as

$$x^2\left(1 + \frac{y}{x} + \frac{4y^2}{x^2}\right) = 6 \text{ and } x^2\left(3 + \frac{8y^2}{x^2}\right) = 14.$$

Divide first equation by second equation and then put $\frac{y}{x} = m.$

Thus we get $\qquad \dfrac{1 + m + 4m^2}{3 + 8m^2} = \dfrac{3}{7}$

$\Rightarrow \qquad 28m^2 + 7m + 7 = 9 + 24m^2$

$\Rightarrow \qquad 4m^2 + 7m - 2 = 0$

$\Rightarrow \qquad (m + 2)(4m - 1) = 0$

$\Rightarrow \qquad m = -2 \quad \text{or} \quad 1/4.$

In first case $y = -2x$, on substituting this value of y in first of the given equations, we get $x^2 - 2x^2 + 16x^2 = 6.$

or $\qquad 15x^2 = 6 \quad \Rightarrow \quad x = \pm\sqrt{\frac{2}{5}}$

Then $\qquad y = -2x \quad \Rightarrow \quad y = \mp 2\sqrt{\frac{2}{5}}$

In second case $4y = x$; on substituting this value of x in first of the given equations, we get $16y^2 + 4y^2 + 4y^2 = 6.$

or $\qquad 24y^2 = 6 \quad \Rightarrow \quad y = \pm\frac{1}{2}.$ Thus $x = \pm 2.$

Hence the required solutions are

$$x = 2, \ y = \frac{1}{2}; \quad x = -2, \ y = -\frac{1}{2}$$

$$x = \sqrt{\frac{2}{5}}, \ y = -2\sqrt{\frac{2}{5}}; \quad x = -\sqrt{\frac{2}{5}}, \ y = 2\sqrt{\frac{2}{5}}.$$

Example 34. (Symmetrical Equations)

Solve $x^4 + y^4 = 257$

$x + y = 5$

(In such equations if we replace x with y and y with x, the equations are unchanged.)

Solution. Put $x = u + v$ and $y = u - v$.

By second given equation, we get $2u = 5$ or $u = 5/2$.

Hence $x = \frac{5}{2} + v, \quad y = \frac{5}{2} - v$

Substituing these values in first of the given equation and recalling that $(a + b)^4 = a^4 + 4a^3b + 6a^2b^2 + 4ab^3 + b^4$, we get

$$\left(\frac{5}{2} + v\right)^4 + \left(\frac{5}{2} - v\right)^4 = 257$$

$$2\left[\left(\frac{5}{2}\right)^4 + 6\left(\frac{5}{2}\right)^2 v^2 + v^4\right] = 257$$

$\Rightarrow$ $$2\left(\frac{625}{16} + \frac{75}{2}v^2 + v^4\right) = 257$$

$\Rightarrow$ $$625 + 600v^2 + 16v^4 = 2056$$

$\Rightarrow$ $$16v^4 + 600v^2 - 1431 = 0$$

$\Rightarrow$ $$16v^4 + 636v^2 - 36v^2 - 1431 = 0$$

$\Rightarrow$ $$4v^2(4v^2 + 159) - 9(4v^2 + 159) = 0$$

$\Rightarrow$ $$(4v^2 - 9)(4v^2 + 159) = 0$$

$\Rightarrow$ $v^2 = \frac{9}{4}$ or $v^2 = -\frac{159}{4}$

Thus $v^2 = \pm\frac{3}{2}$ or $v = \pm\frac{\sqrt{-159}}{2}$

Hence $x = 4, \quad y = 1; \quad x = 1, \quad y = 4$

$$x = \frac{5 + \sqrt{-159}}{2}, \quad y = \frac{5 - \sqrt{-159}}{2}$$

$$x = \frac{5 - \sqrt{-159}}{2}, \quad y = \frac{5 + \sqrt{-159}}{2}$$

Example 35. *Solve* $x^2 + y^2 = 29, x - y = 3.$

Solution. $(x - y)^2 = x^2 + y^2 - 2xy$

$\Rightarrow$ $9 = 29 - 2xy \Rightarrow 2xy = 20 \Rightarrow xy = 10$

Now $(x + y)^2 = x^2 + y^2 + 2xy = 29 + 20 = 49$

$\Rightarrow$ $x + y = \pm 7$

Taking +ve sign, we get, $2x = 10 \Rightarrow x = 5$

and $y = x - 3 = 2$

Taking –ve sign, we get, $2x = -4 \Rightarrow x = -2$

and $y = x - 3 = -5$

Hence $x = -2, \quad y = -5$

or $x = 5, \quad y = 2$

Example 36. *Solve* $2x^2 + 3xy = 26, \quad 3y^2 + 2xy = 39.$

Solution. $2x^2 + 3xy = 26 \Rightarrow 2x + \frac{3y}{x} = \frac{26}{x^2}$

and $3y^2 + 2xy = 39 \Rightarrow \frac{3y^2}{x^2} + \frac{2y}{x} = \frac{39}{x^2}$

These equations give, on division,

$$\frac{2 + 3m}{3m^2 + 2m} = \frac{26}{39} = \frac{2}{3}, \text{ where } m = \frac{y}{x}$$

$\Rightarrow \quad 6m^2 + 4m = 6 + 9m$

$\Rightarrow \quad 6m^2 - 5m - 6 = 0$

$\Rightarrow \quad 6m^2 - 9m + 4m - 6 = 0$

$\Rightarrow \quad (2m - 3)(3m + 2) = 0$

$\Rightarrow \quad m = \frac{3}{2} \text{ or } -\frac{2}{3}$

In case $m = \frac{3}{2}, \quad y = mx = -\frac{3}{2}x,$

So $2x^2 + 3xy = 26$

$\Rightarrow \quad 2x^2 + \frac{9x^2}{2} = 26$

$\Rightarrow \quad x^2 = 4 \Rightarrow x = \pm 2$

Then $y = \pm 3$

In case $m = -\frac{2}{3}, y = mx = -\frac{2}{3}x$

so $2x^2 + 3xy = 26$

$\Rightarrow \quad 2x^2 - 2x^2 = 26$

$\Rightarrow \quad 0 = 26$ which is absurd.

Hence the only admissible value of m is $\frac{3}{2}$ and then the roots are

$$x = 2, \quad y = 3$$

$$x = -2, \quad y = -3.$$

Example 37. *By selling a table for Rs. 56, gain is as much per cent as its cost in rupees. What is the cost price?*

Solution. Let the cost price be x and gain be y

Then $$x + y = 56$$

Percentage gain $= \dfrac{100y}{x}$

This is equal to x

i.e., $$100y = x^2$$

So we are to solve
$$x + y = 56$$
$$100y = x^2$$

First equation gives $$y = 56 - x$$

Second equation then reduces to
$$x^2 = 5600 - 100x$$

or $$x^2 + 100x - 5600 = 0$$
$$(x + 140)(x - 40) = 0$$

$\Rightarrow$ $$x = 40 \quad \text{or} \quad -140$$

As x is cost, it must be a +ve quantity

Hence $$x = 40$$

Hence cost price of table is Rs. 40.

Example 38. *If the Demand and Supply Laws are respectively given by the equation*

$$4q + 9p = 48 \quad \text{and} \quad p = \frac{q}{9} + 2$$

Find the equilibrium price and quantity.

Solution. In equilibrium, demand = supply *i.e.*, in the above two equations p, q stand for same quantities.

We are to solve $$4q + 9p = 48$$
$$p = \frac{q}{9} + 2$$

First equation, on substitution of
$$p = \frac{q}{9} + 2$$

gives $$4q + q + 18 = 48$$

$\Rightarrow$ $$5q = 30 \Rightarrow q = 6$$

Then $$p = \frac{q}{9} + 2 = \frac{2}{3} + 2 = \frac{8}{3}$$

Hence price is $\frac{8}{3}$ and quantity is 6.

Exmaple 39. *Solve* $\sqrt{\frac{x}{y}}+\sqrt{\frac{y}{x}}=\frac{5}{2}$

$$x+y=10$$

Solution. $\sqrt{\frac{x}{y}}+\sqrt{\frac{y}{x}}=\frac{5}{2}$

$\Rightarrow$ $x+y=\frac{5}{2}\sqrt{xy}$

$\Rightarrow$ $10=\frac{5}{2}\sqrt{xy} \Rightarrow xy=16$

Then $(x-y)^2=(x+y)^2-4xy$

$=100-64=36$

$\Rightarrow$ $x-y=\pm 6$

Taking +ve sign and solving with $x+y=10$

we get $x=8$ and $y=2$

Taking –ve sign and solving with $x+y=10$

We obtain $x=2$ and $y=8$.

Example 40. *As the number of units manufactured increases from 4000 to 6000, the total cost of production increases from Rs. 22,000 to Rs. 30,000. Find the relationship between the cost (y) and the number of units made (x), if the relationship is linear.*

Solution. Let the relationship between x and y be given by

$$ax+by+c=0$$

When $x=4000$, $y=20,000$

So $4000a+22,000\,b+c=0$ ...(1)

Also when, $x=6,000$, $y=30,000$

So $6000a+30000b+c=0$ ...(2)

Multiply (1) by 3 and (2) by 2 to obain

$$12000a+66000b+3c=0$$

$$12000a+60000b+2c=0$$

On subtraction we get $6000\,b+c=0$

or $b=-\frac{c}{6000}$

Then (1) implies $4000a-\frac{11c}{3}+c=0$

or $4000a=\frac{8c}{3}$

$$\Rightarrow \qquad a = \frac{c}{1500}$$

Thus the linear relation is $\dfrac{c}{1500}x - \dfrac{c}{6000}y + c = 0$

or $\qquad 4x - y + 6000 = 0$

or $\qquad y = 4x + 6000.$

EXERCISES

Solve the following equation:

1. $5x - y = 3,\ \ y^2 - 6x^2 = 25$
2. $3x + 4y = 18,\ \dfrac{1}{x} + \dfrac{1}{y} = \dfrac{5}{6}$
3. $3x - 5y = 2,\ \ xy = 8$
4. $x + y = 30,\ xy = 216$
5. $x - y = -18,\ xy = 1363$
6. $5x + 2y = 8,\ \ 9x - 5y = 23$
7. $ax + by = 2,\ abxy = 1$
8. $3x - 2y = 7,\ xy = 20$
9. $x^3 + y^3 = 637,\ x + y = 13$
10. $x^3 - y^3 = 218,\ x - y = 2$
11. $x^4 + x^2y^2 + y^4 = 2613,\ x^2 + xy + y^2 = 67$
12. $x^2 - xy + y^2 = 7,\ x^4 + x^2y^2 + y^4 = 133$
13. $x + y - \sqrt{xy} = 7,\ x^2 + y^2 + xy = 133$
14. $\dfrac{1}{x^2} + \dfrac{1}{y^2} = \dfrac{5}{4},\ \ \dfrac{1}{x} + \dfrac{1}{y} = \dfrac{3}{2}$
15. $3x^2 + xy + y^2 = 15,\ 31xy - 3x^2 - 5y^2 = 45$
16. $x^2 + xy + y^2 = 52,\ xy - x^2 = 8$
17. $3x^2 + 2y^2 = 50,\ xy - 3y^2 = 1$
18. $3x^2 - 4xy + 5y^2 = 33,\ 4x^2 - xy = 10$
19. $x^4 + y^4 = 706,\ x + y = 8.$
20. $x^4 + y^4 = 82,\ x + y = 4.$
21. A horse and a cow were sold for Rs. 3040 marking a profit of 25 per cent on the horse and 10 per cent on the cow. By selling them for Rs. 3070, the profit realised would have been 10 per cent on the horse and 25 per cent on the cow. Find the cost price of each.
22. Demand for goods of an industry is given by the equation $pq = 100$ where p is the price and q is quantity; supply is given by the equation $20 + 3p = q$. What is the equilibrium price and quantity?
23. Demand and supply equations are $2p^2 + q^2 = 11$ and $p + 2q = 7$. Find the equilibrium price and quantity where p stands for price and q for quantity.
24. In a perfect competition, the demand curve of a commodity is $D = 20 - 3p - p^2$, and the supply curve is $S = p - 1$ where p is price, D is demand and S is supply. Find the equilibrium price and the quantity exchanged.
25. A man's income from interest and wages is Rs. 500. He doubles his investment and also gets an increase of 50 per cent in wages and his income increases to Rs. 800. What was his original income separately in terms of interest (I) and wages (W).

ANSWERS

1. $x = 2, y = 7; x = -\frac{8}{19}, y = -\frac{97}{19}$. 2. $x = 2, y = 3; x = 3\frac{3}{5}, y = 1\frac{4}{5}$.

3. $x = 4, y = 2; x = -3\frac{1}{3}, y = -2\frac{2}{5}$. 4. $x = 18, y = 12; x = 12, y = 18$.,

5. $x = 29, y = 47; x = -47, y = -29$. 6. $x = 2, y = -1$.

7. $x = \frac{1}{a},\ y = \frac{1}{b}$

8. $x = 5, y = 4;\ x = -2\frac{2}{3}, y = -7\frac{1}{2}$

9. $x = 5, y = 8; x = 8, y = 5$ 10. $x = 7, y = 5; x = -5, y = -7$

11. $x = 2, y = 7; x = 7, y = 2; x = -2, y = -7; x = -7, y = -2$.

12. $x = 2, y = 3; x = -3, y = 2; x = -2, y = -3; x = -3, y = -2$.

13. $x = 4, y = 9; x = 9, y = 4$. 14. $x = 1, y = 2; x = 2, y = 1$

15. $x = 1, y = 3; x = -1, y = -3; x = 2, y = 1; x = -2, y = -1$.

16. $x = 2, y = 6; x = -2, y = -6: x = \frac{4}{3}\sqrt{3}, y = \frac{10}{3}\sqrt{3}; x = -\frac{4}{3}\sqrt{3}, y = -\frac{10}{3}\sqrt{3}$

17. $x = 4, y = 1; x = -4, y = -1; x = \frac{38\sqrt{87}}{87}, y = \frac{3\sqrt{87}}{87}; x = \frac{-38\sqrt{87}}{87}$,
$y = \frac{-3\sqrt{87}}{87}$.

18. $x = 2, y = 3; x = -2, y = -3; x = 5\sqrt{\frac{5}{67}}, y = \frac{-34}{5}\sqrt{\frac{5}{67}}$;
$x = -5\sqrt{\frac{5}{67}}, y = \frac{34}{5}\sqrt{\frac{5}{67}}$.

19. $x = 3, y = 5; x = 5, y = 3; x = 4+\sqrt{-97}, y = 4-\sqrt{-97}; x = 4-\sqrt{-97}$,
$y = 4+\sqrt{-97}$.

20. $x = 1, y = 3; x = 3, y = 1; x = 2+5\sqrt{-1}, y = 2-5\sqrt{-1}; x = 2-5\sqrt{-1}$,
$y = 2+5\sqrt{-1}$.

21. Horse = Rs. 1200, Cow = Rs. 1400.

22. Price = $\frac{10}{3}$ and quantity exchanged = 30

23. $p = 1, q = 3$; or $p = \frac{5}{9}, q = \frac{29}{9}$

24. $p = 3$ and quantity exchanged = 2

25. $I = 100$ and $W = 400$

7. SIMULTANEOUS EQUATIONS IN THREE OR MORE THAN THREE UNKNOWNS

As in the case of two unkowns, there is no fixed method to solve general non-linear simultaneous equations in three unknowns, however, there are methods for solving particular types of such equations, we shall illustrate some of them by examples.

Example 41. (Cross-multiplication Method)

Solve
$$5x - 4y + z = 0$$
$$2x + 5y - 4z = 0$$
$$x^2 - 2y^2 + z^2 = 0.$$

NOTE: [Cross-multiplication method is applicable only when at least two of the given equations are of the type

$$a_1x + b_1y + c_1z = 0 \quad \ldots(1)$$

and
$$a_2x + b_2y + c_2z = 0 \quad \ldots(2)$$

Multiplying first equation by b_2 and second by b_1 and subtracting the resulting second equation from resulting first equation,

we get $(a_1b_2 - a_2b_1)x = -(c_1b_2 - c_2b_1)z$

or
$$\frac{x}{b_1c_2 - b_2c_1} = \frac{z}{a_1b_2 - a_2b_1}$$

Similarly eliminating x from (1) and (2), we get

$$\frac{y}{c_1a_2 - c_2a_1} = \frac{z}{a_1b_2 - a_2b_1}$$

Thus
$$\frac{x}{b_1c_2 - b_2c_1} = \frac{y}{c_1a_2 - c_2a_1} = \frac{z}{a_1b_2 - a_2b_1}.]$$

Solution. By cross-multiplication,

$$\frac{x}{16-5} = \frac{y}{2-(-20)} = \frac{z}{25-(-8)}$$

$$\Rightarrow \quad \frac{x}{11} = \frac{y}{22} = \frac{z}{33} \quad \Rightarrow \quad x = \frac{y}{2} = \frac{z}{3} = k \quad \text{(say)}$$

Thus $x = k, y = 2k, z = 3k$.

Substitute these values in third equation. We get

$$k^2 - 8k^2 + 9k^2 = 0 \quad \text{or} \quad 2k^2 = 0 \Rightarrow k = 0$$

Hence $\quad x = 0, y = 0, z = 0.$

Example 42. *Solve* $3x + y - 2z = 0, 4x - y - 3z = 0$

and $\quad x^3 + y^3 + z^3 = 467.$

Solution. By cross-multiplication

$$\frac{x}{-3-2}=\frac{y}{-8-(-9)}=\frac{z}{-3-4}$$

or $$\frac{x}{-5}=\frac{y}{1}=\frac{z}{-7}$$

or $$\frac{x}{5}=\frac{y}{-1}=\frac{z}{7}=k \quad \text{(say)}$$

Thus $x=5k,\ y=-k,\ z=7k.$

On substitution of these values in third equation, we obtain

$$125k^3-k^3+343k^3=467$$

$$467k^3=467 \quad \text{or} \quad k^3=1 \Rightarrow k=1$$

Hence $x=5,\ y=-1,\ z=7.$

Example 43. *Solve* $x^2+xy+y^2=13$

$$y^2+yz+z^2=49$$

$$z^2+zx+x^2=31.$$

Solution. Subtract second equation from first to obtain

$$(x^2-z^2)+y(x-z)=-36$$

or $$(x-z)(x+y+z)=-36 \quad ...(1)$$

Similarly subtracting third equation from second equation, we obtain

$$(y-x)(x+y+z)=18 \quad ...(2)$$

Divide (1) by (2), to get $\frac{x-z}{y-x}=-2$

or $$x-z=-2y+2x$$

or $$2y=x+z \Rightarrow y=\frac{x+z}{2}$$

Substitute this value in the given second equation, we get

$$\frac{(x+z)^2}{4}+\frac{z(x+z)}{2}+z^2=49$$

or $$x^2+z^2+2xz+2zx+2z^2+4z^2=196$$

In other words, $x^2+4xz+7z^2=196$

Also we are given that $x^2+xz+z^2=31$

Thus we obtain $$\frac{x^2+4xz+7z^2}{x^2+xz+z^2}=\frac{196}{31}$$

or $$\frac{1+4z/x+7z^2/x^2}{1+z/x+z^2/x^2}=\frac{196}{31}.$$

Put $z/x=m.$

This gives that $31(7m^2+4m+1) = 196(1+m+m^2)$

$$21m^2-72m-165 = 0$$

$\Rightarrow$ $7m^2-24m-55 = 0$

$\Rightarrow$ $(m-5)(7m+11) = 0$

$\Rightarrow$ $m = 5$ or $m = -11/7$.

In case $m=5$, $z=5x$, so $y = \dfrac{z+x}{2} = 3x$.

From first of the given equations we get

$$x^2+3x^2+9x^2 = 13 \Rightarrow 13x^2 = 13 \Rightarrow x = \pm 1$$

So $y = \pm 3$ and $z = \pm 5$.

In case $m = -\dfrac{11}{7}$, $z = -\dfrac{11}{7}x$, and so $y = \dfrac{z+x}{2} = -\dfrac{2}{7}x$.

Again with the help of first of the given equations, we get

$$x^2 - \frac{2x^2}{7} + \frac{4}{49}x^2 = 13$$

or $39x^2 = 637 \Rightarrow x = \pm\dfrac{7}{\sqrt{3}}$

Then $y = \mp\dfrac{2}{\sqrt{3}}$ and $z = \mp\dfrac{11}{\sqrt{3}}$.

Hence the complete solution is $x=1$, $y=3$, $z=5$;

or $x = -1$, $y = -3$, $z = -5$;

or $x = \dfrac{7}{\sqrt{3}}$, $y = \dfrac{-2}{\sqrt{3}}$, $z = \dfrac{-11}{\sqrt{3}}$

or $x = -\dfrac{7}{\sqrt{3}}$, $y = \dfrac{2}{\sqrt{3}}$, $z = \dfrac{11}{\sqrt{3}}$.

Example 44. *Solve* $x^2+xy+xz = 45$

$$y^2+yz+yx = 75$$

$$z^2+zx+zy = 105.$$

Solution. The given equations are equivalent to

$$x(x+y+z) = 45$$

$$y(x+y+z) = 75$$

$$z(x+y+z) = 105$$

Adding, we get $(x+y+z)^2 = 225$

i.e., $x+y+z = \pm 15$

Hence $x = \pm 3$, $y = \pm 5$, $z = \pm 7$.

So the required solutions are $x=3$, $y=5$, $z=7$

or $x=-3, y=-5, z=-7$.

Example 45. *Solve*

$$xyz = 231$$
$$xyu = 420$$
$$xzu = 660$$
$$yzu = 1540.$$

Solution. Multiplying all the given equations, we get

$$x^3y^3z^3u^3 = 231 \times 420 \times 660 \times 1540$$
$$= 3 \times 7 \times 11 \times 2^2 \times 3 \times 5 \times 7 \times 2^2 \times 3 \times 5 \times 11 \times 2^2 \times 5 \times 7 \times 11$$
$$= 2^6 \times 3^3 \times 5^3 \times 7^3 \times 11^3.$$

Thus $xyzu = 2^2 \times 3 \times 5 \times 7 \times 11$
$= 4620.$

Dividing in turn by 1st, 2nd, 3rd and 4th equations, we get

$$u = 20, \quad z = 11, \quad y = 7, \quad x = 3.$$

Hence $x = 3$, $y = 7$, $z = 11$ and $u = 20$.

Example 46. *Solve*

$$x + y + z = 12$$
$$x^2 + y^2 + z^2 = 50$$

and

$$x^3 + y^3 + z^3 = 216.$$

Solution. Now $(x + y + z)^2 = x^2 + y^2 + z^2 + 2(xy + yz + zx)$

$\Rightarrow$ $144 = 50 + 2(xy + yz + zx)$

$\Rightarrow$ $xy + yz + zx = 47$

Further $x^3 + y^3 + z^3 - 3xyz = (x + y + z)(x^2 + y^2 + z^2 - xy - yz - zx)$

gives that $216 - 3xyz = 12(50 - 47) = 36$

$\Rightarrow$ $3xyz = 180$ or $xyz = 60$

Thus we have

$$x + y + z = 12 \quad ...(1)$$
$$xy + yz + zx = 47 \quad ...(2)$$

and

$$xyz = 60 \quad ...(3)$$

From (3), $yz = \dfrac{60}{x}$ and from (1), $y + z = 12 - x$

Substituting these values in (2), we get

$$\frac{60}{x} + x(12 - x) = 47$$
$$60 + 12x^2 - x^3 = 47x$$
$$x^3 - 12x^2 + 47x - 60 = 0$$

i.e.

$$(x - 3)(x^2 - 9x + 20) = 0$$
$$(x - 3)(x - 4)(x - 5) = 0$$

$\therefore$ $x = 3$ or 4 or 5

For $x=3,\ yz=20,\ y+z=9 \ \Rightarrow\ y=5,\ z=4;\ y=4,\ z=5$
For $x=4,\ yz=15,\ y+z=8 \ \Rightarrow\ y=3,\ z=5;\ y=5,\ z=3$
For $x=5,\ yz=12,\ y+z=7 \ \Rightarrow\ y=3,\ z=4;\ y=4,\ z=3$
Hence the complete solution is

$$x=3,\ y=4,\ z=5$$
$$x=3,\ y=5,\ z=4$$
$$x=4,\ y=3,\ z=5$$
$$x=4,\ y=5,\ z=3$$
$$x=5,\ y=3,\ z=4$$

and $\quad x=5,\ y=4,\ z=3$

Example 47. *Solve* $xy + x + y = 23$
$xz + x + z = 41$
$yz + y + z = 27.$

Solution. The given equations are equivalent to

$$xy+x+y+1=24 \quad i.e., \quad (x+1)(y+1)=24 \qquad ..(1)$$
$$xz+x+z+1=42 \quad i.e., \quad (x+1)(z+1)=42 \qquad ...(2)$$
and $$yz+y+z+1=28 \quad i.e., \quad (y+1)(z+1)=28 \qquad ...(3)$$

Multiplying (1), (2) and (3), we obtain

$$(x+1)^2(y+1)^2(z+1)^2 = 24.42.28$$
$$= 6\times4\times6\times7\times4\times7$$
$$\Rightarrow \quad (x+1)(y+1)(z+1) = \pm\, 6\times4\times7 = \pm\, 168$$

Dividing successively by (1), (2) and (3), we get

$$z+1=\pm\,7,\ y+1=\pm\,4 \text{ and } x+1=\pm\,6.$$

In other words $x=5$ or -7, $y=3$ or -5 and $z=6$ or -8.

Thus $\quad x=5,\ \ y=3,\ \ z=6$

or $\quad x=-7,\ \ y=-5,\ \ x=-8.$

EXERCISES

Solve the following equations:

1. $2x + y - 2z = 0,\ 7x + 6y - 9z = 0,\ x^3 + y^3 + z^3 = 1728.$
2. $3x + y - 5z = 0,\ 7x - 3y - 9z = 0,\ x^2 + 2y^2 + 3z^2 = 23.$
3. $9x + y - 8z = 0,\ 4x - 8y + 7z = 0,\ xy + yz + zx = 47.$
4. $x + y + z = 6,\ x^2 + y^2 + z^2 = 14$, and $x + \frac{y}{2} + \frac{z}{3} = 3.$

[*Hint.* First and third equations are equivalent to

$$\left(\frac{x}{1}-1\right)+2\left(\frac{y}{2}-1\right)+3\left(\frac{z}{3}-1\right) = 0, \quad (x-1)+\left(\frac{y}{2}-1\right)+\left(\frac{z}{3}-1\right) = 0$$

Apply cross ratio to equations in $x - 1$, $\frac{y}{2} - 1$, $\frac{z}{3} - 1$]

5. $\frac{1}{x}+\frac{1}{y}+\frac{1}{z} = 9$, $\frac{2}{x}+\frac{3}{y} = 13$, $8x + 3y = 5$
6. $x(y + z) = 5$, $y(z + x) = 8$, $z(x + y) = 9$.
[*Hint.* Add first two and subtract third equation to get $2xy = 4$ or $xy = 2$. Similarly obtain $yz = 6$, and $zx = 3$.]
7. $xy = (x + y)$, $yz = 2(y + z)$, $zx = 3(z + x)$.
8. $x^2 + xy + y^2 = 37$, $y^2 + yz + z^2 = 19$, $z^2 + zx + x^2 = 28$.
9. $x + y + z = 9$, $x^2 + y^2 + z^2 = 29$, $x^3 + y^3 + z^3 = 99$.
10. $(x - y)(y + z) = 22$, $(y + z)(z - x) = 33$, $(z - x)(x - y) = 6$.
11. $x + y + z = 13$, $x^2 + y^2 + z^2 = 65$, $yz = 10$.
12. $x + y + z = 3$, $xy + yz + zx = -1$, $\frac{1}{x}+\frac{1}{y}+\frac{1}{z} = \frac{1}{3}$.
13. $xz + y = 7z$, $yz + x = 8z$, $x + y + z = 12$.
14. $xy^2z^2 = 36$, $x^2yz^2 = 144$, $x^2y^2z = 48$.
15. $xy + x + y = 5$, $yz + y + z = 11$, $zx + z + x = 7$.
16. $2xy - 4x + y = 17$, $3yz + y - 6z = 52$, $6xz + 3z + 2x = 29$.
17. $xy = 6$, $yz = 15$, $zx = 10$.
18. $x + y + z = 13$, $x^2 + y^2 + z^2 = 61$, $x(y + z) = 2yz$.
19. $\frac{1}{29}\left(x+\frac{y}{z}\right) = \frac{1}{34}\left(y+\frac{x}{z}\right) = \frac{1}{6}$, $x + y + z = 15$.
20. $x^2 - yz = 1$, $y^2 - xz = 4$, $z^2 - xy = 9$.

ANSWERS

1. $x = 6, y = 8, z = 10$.
2. $x = 3, y = 1, z = 2; x = -3, y = -1, z = -2$.
3. $x = 3, y = 5, z = 4; x = -3, y = -5, z = -4$.
4. $x = 1, y = 2, z = 3; x = \frac{11}{13}, y = 2\frac{8}{13}, z = 2\frac{7}{13}$.
5. $x = \frac{1}{2}, y = \frac{1}{3}, z = \frac{1}{4}; x = \frac{5}{20}, y = 1\frac{2}{13}, z = \frac{15}{44}$.
6. $x = 1, y = 2, z = 3; x = -1, y = -2, z = -3$.
7. $x = 2\frac{2}{5}, y = 1\frac{5}{7}, z = -12$.
8. $x = 4,\ y = 3,\ z = 2;\ x = -4,\ y = -3,\ z = -2;\ x = \frac{10}{\sqrt{3}}, y = \frac{1}{\sqrt{3}}, z = -\frac{8}{\sqrt{3}}$;
$x = \frac{-10}{\sqrt{3}}, y = \frac{-1}{\sqrt{3}}, z = \frac{8}{\sqrt{3}}$.

9. $x = 2, y = 3, z = 4; x = 2, y = 4, z = 3; x = 3, y = 2, z = 4; x = 3, y = 4, z = 2;$
$x = 4, y = 2, z = 3; x = 4, y = 3, z = 2.$
10. $x = 5, y = 3, z = 8; x = -5, y = -3, z = -8.$
11. $x = 6, y = 5, z = 2; x = 6, y = 2, z = 5; x = 7, y = 3+\sqrt{-1}, z = 3-\sqrt{-1}; x = 7, y = 3-\sqrt{-1}, z = 3+\sqrt{-1}.$
12. $x = 1, y = 3, z = -1; x = 1, y = -1, z = 3; x = -1, y = 1, z = 3; x = -1, y = 3, z = 1; x = 3, y = 1, z = -1; x = 3, y = -1, z = 1.$
13. $x = 4, y = 6, z = 2; x = 8\frac{4}{7}, y = 9\frac{3}{7}, z = -6.$
14. $x = 4, y = 1, z = 3.$
15. $x = 1, y = 2, z = 3; x = -3, y = -4, z = -5.$
16. $x = 1, y = 7, z = 3; x = -2, y = -3, z = -3\frac{2}{3}.$
17. $x = 2, y = 3, z = 5; x = -2, y = -3, z = -5.$
18. $x = 4, y = 3, z = 6; x = 4, y = 6, z = 3; x = 9, y = 2+\sqrt{-14}, z = 2-\sqrt{-14};$
$x = 9, y = 2-\sqrt{-14}, z = 2+\sqrt{-14}.$
19. $x = 4, y = 5, z = 6; x = 8\frac{19}{42}, y = 9\frac{1}{21}, z = -2\frac{1}{2}.$
20. $x = \frac{5}{\sqrt{14}}, y = \frac{1}{\sqrt{14}}, z = -\frac{11}{\sqrt{14}}; x = -\frac{5}{\sqrt{14}}, y = \frac{1}{\sqrt{14}}, z = \frac{11}{\sqrt{14}}.$

CHAPTER 7

PROGRESSIONS (A.P., G.P. and H.P.)

1. ARITHMETICAL PROGRESSION

Quantities $a_1, a_2, a_3, ..., a_n, ...$ are said to be in *Arithmetical Progression* if $a_n - a_{n-1}$ is constant for all integers $n > 1$. The constant quantity $a_n - a_{n-1}$ is called the *common difference* of the arithmetical progression.

Notation. A.P. stands for an arithmetical progression. Consider the following series

$$1, 3, 5, 7, 9, 11, ...$$

$$0, \sqrt{2}, 2\sqrt{2}, 3\sqrt{2}, 4\sqrt{2}, ...$$

$$1, \frac{1}{2}, 0, -\frac{1}{2}, -1, -\frac{3}{2}, ...$$

$$x+y, x, x-y, x-2y, ...$$

$$5{\cdot}3, 5{\cdot}55, 5{\cdot}8, 6{\cdot}05, 6{\cdot}3, ...$$

Each of the above series is an A.P. Common differences are respectively 2, $\sqrt{2}$, $-\frac{1}{2}$, $-y$ and $\cdot 25$.

2. TO FIND THE GENERAL TERM OF A GIVEN ARITHMETICAL PROGRESSION

Let $a_1, a_2, ..., a_n, ...$ be a given A.P. Let d be their common difference. Then $a_n - a_{n-1} = d$ for all n.

$$\Rightarrow \quad a_2 - a_1 = d, \ a_3 - a_2 = d, \ a_4 - a_3 = d \text{ and so on,}$$

$$\Rightarrow \quad a_2 = a_1 + d, \ a_3 = a_2 + d = a_1 + d + d = a_1 + 2d$$

$$a_4 = a_3 + d = a_1 + 2d + d = a_1 + 3d$$

$$... \quad ... \quad ... \quad ... \quad ... \quad ... \quad ... \quad ...$$

$$a_{n-1} = a_1 + (n-2)\, d$$

$$a_n = a_{n-1} + d = a_1 + (n-2)\, d + d$$

$$= a_1 + (n-1)\, d.$$

Thus nth term, a_n of arithmetical progression whose first term is a_1 and common difference d, is given by

$$a_n = a_1 + (n-1)d.$$

Example 1. *Find 16th term of the series 3·75, 3·5, 3·25, ...*

Solution. In this case $a_1 = 3{\cdot}75$, $a_2 = 3{\cdot}5$, $a_3 = 3{\cdot}25$

$$d = a_2 - a_1 = -{\cdot}25$$

$$\begin{aligned} \text{Hence 16th term } &= a_{16} \\ &= 3{\cdot}75 + (16-1)(-{\cdot}25) \\ &= 3{\cdot}75 - 15 \times {\cdot}25 \\ &= 3{\cdot}75 - 3{\cdot}75 = 0. \end{aligned}$$

Example 2. *Which term of the A.P.*

49, 44, 39, ... is 9?

Solution. Let nth term be 9, *i.e.* $a_n = 9$.

Here $\quad a_1 = 49, d = 44 - 49 = -5,$

Thus $\quad a_n = 9 = 49 + (n-1)(-5)$

$\Rightarrow \quad 9 = 49 - 5n + 5$

or $\quad 5n = 54 - 9 = 45$

$$n = 9$$

Thus 9th term of the given A.P. is 9.

Example 3. *If mth term of an A.P. is $\frac{1}{n}$ and nth term is $\frac{1}{m}$, $m \neq n$, show that the first term is equal to the common difference.*

Solution. Let a denote the first term and d the common difference.

Then $$\frac{1}{n} = a + (m-1)d$$

$$\frac{1}{m} = a + (n-1)d$$

Subtracting, we get

$$\frac{m-n}{mn} = (m-n)d$$

So, $$d = \frac{1}{mn}.$$

Also, $$a = \frac{1}{n} - \frac{(m-1)}{mn} = \frac{1}{mn} = d$$

Thus, the first term = common difference.

3. TO FIND THE SUM OF FINITE NUMBER OF QUANTITIES IN A.P.

Let $a_1, a_2, ..., a_n$ be n quantities in A.P., and let the last term a_n be denoted by l. If d is their common difference then

$$a_n = a_1 + (n-1)d = l.$$

Let $S_n = a_1 + a_2 + ... + a_n$

Thus
$$S_n = a_1 + (a_1 + d) + (a_2 + 2d) + ... + [a_1 + (n-1)d]$$
$$= a_1 + (a_1 + d) + (a_1 + 2d) + ... + (l - d) + l \qquad ...(1)$$

Writing, the above series in reverse order, we get

$$S_n = l + (l - d) + (l - 2d) + ... + (a_1 + d) + a_1 \qquad ...(2)$$

Adding (1) and (2), we get

$$2S_n = (a_1 + l) + (a_1 + l) + ... + (a_1 + l), (n \text{ times})$$
$$= n\,(a_1 + l)$$

Therefore $S_n = \frac{n}{2}(a_1 + l) = \frac{n}{2}\{a_1 + [a_1 + (n-1)d]\}$

Consequently $S_n = \frac{n}{2}[2a_1 + (n-1)d].$

Example 4. *Find the sum of* $\frac{3}{4}, \frac{2}{3}, \frac{7}{12}, ...$ *upto 19 terms.*

Solution. Here $a_1 = \frac{3}{4}$, $a_2 = \frac{2}{3}$, $n = 19.$

Thus $d = a_2 - a_1 = \frac{2}{3} - \frac{3}{4} = -\frac{1}{12}$

i.e.,
$$S_{19} = \frac{19}{2}\left[2\times\frac{3}{4} + (19-1)\left(-\frac{1}{12}\right)\right]$$
$$= \frac{19}{2}\left[\frac{3}{2} - \frac{18}{12}\right]$$
$$= \frac{19}{2}\left(\frac{18-18}{12}\right) = \frac{19}{2}\times 0 = 0.$$

Example 5. *How many terms of the following series may be taken so that their sum is 66*

–9, –6, 3, ... ?

Solution. Let $S_n = 66$. Here $a_1 = -9$, $d = -6 + 9 = 3$.

or $$66 = \frac{n}{2}[-18+(n-1)3]$$

$$132 = -18n + 3n^2 - 3n$$

i.e. $$3n^2 - 21n - 132 = 0$$

or $$n^2 - 7n - 44 = 0 \quad \Rightarrow (n-11)(n+4) = 0$$

$$\Rightarrow n = 11 \text{ or } n = -4.$$

As n is positive integer, second value -4 is rejected.

Thus required number of terms = 11.

Example 6. *The sum of first n terms of two A.P. are 3n + 8, 7n + 15.*

Show that the ratio of their 12th term is $\frac{7}{16}$.

Solution: Given $$\frac{2a+(n-1)d}{2a'+(n-1)d'} = \frac{3n+8}{7n+15} \quad \text{...(i)}$$

$$\text{Ratio of 12th term} = \frac{a+11d}{a'+11d'} = \frac{2a+22d}{2a'+22d'}$$

$$= \frac{3\times 23+8}{7\times 23+15} \quad \text{(By taking } n = 23 \text{ in } (i))$$

$$= \frac{77}{176} = \frac{7}{16}$$

4. ARITHMETIC MEANS

If $a_1, a_2, ..., a_n$ are in A.P., then the quantities $a_2, a_3, ..., a_{n-1}$ are called *Arithmetic Means* (written as A. M.) between a_1 and a_n.

Thus in the series, 1, 3, 5, 7, 9, 11, 13, 15, ...

3, 5 are arithmetic means between 1 and 7

9, 11, 13 are arithmetic means between 7 and 15.

5. TO INSERT *n* ARITHMETIC MEANS BETWEEN TWO GIVEN QUANTITIES

Let a and b be two given quantities and $A_1, A_2, ..., A_n$ be the n arithmetic means between them. Then the quantities

$$a, A_1, A_2, ..., A_n, b \text{ are in A. P.}$$

Let d be their common difference.

Now $$b = (n+2)\text{th term}$$

$$= a + (n+1)\,d$$

$$\Rightarrow \quad d = \frac{b-a}{n+1}$$

Further, $A_1 = \text{2nd term}$

$$= a + d = a + \left(\frac{b-a}{n+1}\right) = \frac{na+b}{n+1}$$

$A_2 = \text{3rd term}$

$$= a + 2d = a + 2\left(\frac{b-a}{n+1}\right)$$

$$= \frac{na+2b-a}{n+1}$$

... ...

$$A_n = a + nd = a + n\left(\frac{b-a}{n+1}\right) = \frac{a+nb}{n+1}.$$

Hence $\frac{na+b}{n+1}, \frac{na+2b-a}{n+1}, ..., \frac{a+nb}{n+1}$

are n Arithmetic means between a and b.

Example 7. *Insert 6 Arithmetic means between 1 and 19.*

Solution. Let $A_1, A_2, A_3, A_4, A_5, A_6$, be the required arithmetic means.

Then 1, $A_1, A_2, A_3, A_4, A_5, A_6$, 19 are in A.P.

Let d be their common difference.

Then $19 = \text{8th term}$

$$= 1 + (8-1)d = 1 + 7d$$

Thus $d = \frac{18}{7}$

Hence $A_1 = \text{2nd term} = 1 + \frac{18}{7} = \frac{25}{7}$

$$A_2 = \text{3rd term} = 1 + 2 \times \frac{18}{7} = 1 + \frac{36}{7} = \frac{43}{7}$$

$$A_3 = \text{4th term} = 1 + 3 \times \frac{18}{7} = 1 + \frac{54}{7} = \frac{61}{7}$$

$$A_4 = \text{5th term} = 1 + 4 \times \frac{18}{7} = 1 + \frac{72}{7} = \frac{79}{7}$$

$$A_5 = \text{6th term} = 1 + 5 \times \frac{18}{7} = 1 + \frac{90}{7} = \frac{97}{7}$$

$$A_6 = \text{7th term} = 1 + 6 \times \frac{18}{7} = 1 + \frac{108}{7} = \frac{115}{7}$$

So, the required means are

$$\frac{25}{7}, \frac{43}{7}, \frac{61}{7}, \frac{79}{7}, \frac{97}{7}, \frac{115}{7}.$$

Example 8. *Suppose A.M. of a and b is* $\dfrac{a^{n+1} + b^{n+1}}{a^n + b^n}$. *Find n.*

Solution. Given $\dfrac{a+b}{2} = \dfrac{a^{n+1} + b^{n+1}}{a^n + b^n}$

So, $a\, b^n + a^n\, b = a^{n+1} + b^{n+1}$

$\Rightarrow$ $a^n(a-b) = b^n\,(a-b)$

$\Rightarrow$ $a^n = b^n$, as $a \neq b$

$\Rightarrow$ $(a\, b^{-1})^n = 1$

$\Rightarrow$ $n = 0$

Example 9. *How many terms of the series 4, 2, 0, –2, –4, –6,... may be taken so that their sum is 6?*

Solution. Let n be the required number of terms.

Here $a_1 = 4,\ d = 2 - 4 = -2.$

So $6 = S_n = \dfrac{n}{2}\,[8 + (n-1)(-2)]$

i.e., $12 = 8n - 2n^2 + 2n$

or $2n^2 - 10n + 12 = 0$

or $n^2 - 5n + 6 = 0$

or $(n-3)(n-2) = 0$

Hence $n = 3$ or 2.

We get two answers. As the third term is zero, therefore, sum of the first two terms is same as the sum of first three terms.

Example 10. *If pth, qth, rth terms of an A.P. are a, b, c, respectively, show that*

$$(q-r)\,a + (r-p)b + (p-q)c = 0.$$

Solution. Here pth term $= a = a_1 + (p-1)d$ ...(*i*)

qth term $= b = a_1 + (q-1)d$ ...(*ii*)

rth term $= c = a_1 + (r-1)d$ ...(*iii*)

where a_1 is the first term and d is the common difference of the A.P.

Multiply (*i*) by $q - r$, (*ii*) by $r - p$, (*iii*) by $p - q$ and add to obtain $(q-r)\,a + (r-p)\,b + (p-q)\,c$

$$= a_1(q-r) + a_1(r-p) + a_1(p-q) + d\,[(p-1)(q-r) + (q-1)(r-p) + (r-1)(p-q)]$$

$$= a_1\,[q-r+r-p+p-q] + d\,[pq+r-pr-q + qr-r+p-pq+rp-rq-p+q]$$

$$= 0.$$

Example 11. *The sum of n terms of two A.P's are in the ratio of 7n + 1: 4n + 27. Find the ratio of their 11th terms.*

Solution. Let a_1 and b_1 be the first terms of two A.P.'s and d_1, d_2 be their common difference respectively.

Then $$S_n = \frac{n}{2}[2a_1 + (n-1)\,d_1]$$

$$S'_n = \frac{n}{2}[2b_1 + (n-1)\,d_2]$$

So $$\frac{S_n}{S'_n} = \frac{2a_1 + (n-1)d_1}{2b_1 + (n-1)d_2} = \frac{7n+1}{4n+27}$$

Putting $n = 21$, we get

$$\frac{2a_1 + 20d_1}{2b_1 + 20d_2} = \frac{148}{111}$$

or $$\frac{a_1 + 10d_1}{b_1 + 10d_2} = \frac{148}{111}$$

or $$\frac{a_{11}}{b_{11}} = \frac{148}{111}$$

where a_{11} and b_{11} are 11th terms of two A.P.'s respectively.

$$= \frac{4}{3}.$$

Example 12. *If a^2, b^2, c^2 are in A.P., show that*

$$\frac{1}{b+c}, \frac{1}{c+a}, \frac{1}{a+b} \text{ are also in A.P.}$$

Solution. $\frac{1}{b+c}, \frac{1}{c+a}, \frac{1}{a+b}$ are in A.P.

$$\Leftrightarrow \quad \frac{1}{c+a} - \frac{1}{b+c} = \frac{1}{a+b} - \frac{1}{c+a}$$

$$\Leftrightarrow \quad \frac{b-a}{(c+a)(b+c)} = \frac{c-b}{(a+b)(c+a)}$$

$$\Leftrightarrow \qquad \frac{b-a}{c+b} = \frac{c-b}{b+a}$$

$$\Leftrightarrow \qquad b^2 - a^2 = c^2 - b^2$$

$\Leftrightarrow \qquad a^2, b^2, c^2$ are in A.P.

Hence the result follows.

Example 13. *Sum to n terms of three A.P.'s are s_1, s_2 and s_3. The first term of each of them is 1 and common differences are 1, 2 and 3 respectively. Show that s_1, s_2, s_3 are also in A.P.*

Solution. $$s_1 = \frac{n}{2}[2 + (n-1)] = \frac{n(n+1)}{2}$$

$$s_2 = \frac{n}{2}[2 + (n-1)2] = n^2$$

$$s_3 = \frac{n}{2}[2 + (n-1)3] = \frac{n}{2}(3n-1)$$

or $$s_2 - s_1 = n^2 - \frac{n(n+1)}{2} = \frac{n^2 - n}{2} = \frac{n(n-1)}{2}$$

$$s_3 - s_2 = \frac{n}{2}(3n-1) - n^2 = \frac{3n^2 - n - 2n^2}{2}$$

$$= \frac{n^2 - n}{2} = \frac{n(n-1)}{2}$$

i.e. $\qquad s_2 - s_1 = s_3 - s_2$

Hence s_1, s_2, s_3 are in A.P.

Example 14. *State giving example whether the following statement is true or false.*

In a given A.P. let a be the first term, d the common difference, n the number of terms and s their sum. Given any three of a, d, n and s one can always find a unique value of the fourth quantity.

Solution. The statement is false. Given values of a, d and s there might be two values of n. Consider the series

$$12, 9, 6, 3, 0, -3, -6,$$

It is to find the number of terms from beginning whose sum is 30.

In this case, $\qquad a = 12, d = 9 - 12 = -3, s = 3$

Since $$s = \frac{n}{2}[2a + (n-1)d]$$

we have $$30 = \frac{n}{2}[24 + (n-1)(-3)]$$

or $$60 = 24n - 3n^2 + 3n$$

or $$3n^2 - 27n + 60 = 0$$

$\Rightarrow$ $$n^2 - 9n + 20 = 0$$

$\Rightarrow$ $$(n-4)(n-5) = 0$$

$\Rightarrow$ $$n = 4 \text{ or } 5.$$

Example 15. *Find the sum of all numbers between 200 and 400 which are divisible by 7.*

Solution. Since 4 is left as remainder on division of 200 by 7 the least number greater than 200 divisible by 7 is 203. Again if we divide 400 by 7, 1 is left as remainder. This implies that the greatest number less than 400, which is divisible by 7 is 399.

So we are to find the sum of the series

$203 + 210 + 217 + ... + 399$

Here $$a_1 = 203, d = 7, l = 399$$

Let n be the total number of terms in this series.

Then $$399 = 203 + (n-1)7$$

$\Rightarrow$ $$7n = 399 - 203 + 7$$
$$= 406 - 203 = 203$$

$\Rightarrow$ $$n = 29.$$

Hence required sum $$= \frac{n}{2}(a + l) = \frac{29}{2}(203 + 399)$$
$$= \frac{29}{2}(602)$$
$$= (29)(301)$$
$$= 8729.$$

Example 16. *Mr X arranges to pay off a debt of Rs 9,600 in 48 annual instalments which form an arithmetical series. When 40 of these instalments are paid, Mr X becomes insolvent and his creditor finds that Rs 2,400 still remains unpaid. Find the value of each of the first three instalments of Mr. X. Ignore interest.*

Solution. Let a, $a + d$, $a + 2d$, $a + 3d$ be the annual instalments.

The sum of this series up to $n = 48$ terms is 9600.

i.e., $$9600 = \frac{48}{2}[2a + (48-1)d]$$

$$\Rightarrow \quad 9600 = 24(2a+47d)$$

$$\Rightarrow \quad 2a+47d = 400 \quad \text{...(1)}$$

After 40 instalments are paid, the balance is Rs 2400. In other words in 40 instalments Mr X has paid Rs (9600 – 2400) *i.e.*, Rs 7200.

So the sum of first 40 terms of the above series is 7200.

Thus $$7200 = \frac{40}{2}[2a+(40-1)d]$$

$$\Rightarrow \quad 7200 = 20(2a+39d)$$

$$\Rightarrow \quad 2a+39d = 360 \quad \text{...(2)}$$

Subtracting (2) from (1), we get

$$8d = 40 \quad \Rightarrow \quad d = 5$$

Then (2) $\Rightarrow 2a + 195 = 360$

$$\Rightarrow \quad 2a = 165 \quad \Rightarrow \quad a = 82.50$$

Hence first instalment of Mr X is Rs 82.50, second instalment is Rs (82.50 + 5.00) *i.e.*, Rs 87.50 and third instalment is Rs (87.50 + 5.00) *i.e.*, Rs 92.50.

Example 17. *If* $\frac{1}{b+c}, \frac{1}{c+a}, \frac{1}{a+b}$ *are in A.P., prove that* $a^2, b^2\ c^2$ *are also in A.P.*

Solution. Since $\frac{1}{b+c}, \frac{1}{c+a}, \frac{1}{a+b}$ are in A.P.

We have $$\frac{1}{c+a} - \frac{1}{b+c} = \frac{1}{a+b} - \frac{1}{c+a}$$

$$\Rightarrow \quad \frac{(b+c)-(c+a)}{(b+c)(c+a)} = \frac{(c+a)-(a+b)}{(a+b)(c+a)}$$

$$\Rightarrow \quad \frac{b-a}{b+c} = \frac{c-b}{b+a}$$

$$\Rightarrow \quad b^2 - a^2 = c^2 - b^2$$

$\Rightarrow \quad a^2, b^2, c^2$ are in A.P.

REMARK: This question was also solved implicitly in Example 12.

Example 18. *The monthly salary of a person was Rs 320 for each of the first three years. He next got annual increments of Rs 40 per month for each of the following successive 12 years. His salary remained stationary till retirement when he found that his average monthly salary during the service period was Rs 698. Find the period of his service.*

Solution. Let n be the total number of years of the person's service.

His total salary $= \text{Rs } 12n \times 698$

(As his monthly average is Rs 698)

Total salary in first three years of service

$$= 320 \times 3 \times 12 = \text{Rs } 960 \times 12$$

In the 4th year, his monthly salary was Rs $(320 + 40) =$ Rs 360

5th year his monthly salary was Rs 400 and so on.

Then for next 12 years, his total salary

$$= \text{Rs } 12 \times [360 + 400 + \ldots \text{ up to 12 terms}]$$

$$= \text{Rs } 12 \times \frac{12}{2}[2 \times 360 + (12-1).40]$$

$$= \text{Rs } 12 \times 6(720 + 440)$$

$$= \text{Rs } 12 \times 6 \times 1160$$

$$= \text{Rs } 12 \times 6960$$

At the end of following 12 years, his monthly salary was

$$\text{Rs } [360 + (12-1).40] = \text{Rs } 800$$

This salary he got for the remaining $(n - 15)$ years. So his total salary for the remaining $(n - 15)$ years was $(n - 15)\ 800 \times 12$.

Hence his total salary throughout his service period

$$= 12[960 + 6960 + 800(n - 15)]$$

$$= 12(7920 + 800n - 12000)$$

$$= 12\ (800n - 4080)$$

This must be same as $12n \times 698$

i.e., $\quad 12n \times 698 = 12(800n - 4080)$

$\Rightarrow \quad 102n = 4080 \quad \Rightarrow \quad n = 40$ years.

Example 19. *The sequence of natural numbers is written as*

		1		
	2	*3*	*4*	
5	*6*	*7*	*8*	*9*
...	...	...	...	...
...	...	...	...	...

Find the sum of the numbers in the rth row.

Solution. Let S_r denote the sum of rth row.

$$S_1 = 1, S_2 = 2 + 3 + 4, S_3 = 5 + 6 + 7 + 8 + 9$$

Let initial term of S_k be t_k

and suppose that $\quad M = 1 + 2 + 5 + \ldots + t_k$

be the sum of first terms of $S_1, S_2, ..., S_k$

Now $$M = 1+2+5+10+...+t_k$$

Also $$M = 1+2+5+...+t_{k-1}+t_k$$

Subtracting we get

$$0 = (1+1+3+5+\text{up to } k \text{ terms}) - t_k$$

$$t_k = 1+[1+3+5+... \text{ up to } (k-1) \text{ terms}]$$

$$= 1+\left(\frac{k-1}{2}\right)[2+(k-2).2]$$

$$= 1+(k-1)^2 = k^2-2k+2$$

Also in S_1 there is one term, in S_2 there are 3 terms and so on, in S_k there will be $(2k-1)$ terms.

Hence we are to find the sum of series

$r^2-2r+2, r^2-2r+3, r^2-2r+4,$ up to $(2r-1)$ terms

So $$S_r = \frac{(2r-1)}{2}[2(r^2-2r+2)-(2r-2).1]$$

$$= (2r-1)(r^2-2r+2+r-1)$$

$$= (2r-1)(r^2-r+1)$$

$$= 2r^3-3r^2+3r-1.$$

Example 20. *A lamp lighter has to light 100 gas lamps. He takes 1½ minutes to go from one lamp post to the next. Each lamp post burns 10 c.c. of gas per hour. How many c.c of gas has been burnt by 8.30 P.M. if he lights the first lamp at 6 P.M.*

Solution. Total time from 6 P.M. to 8.30 P.M. is 2.30 hours *i.e.*, 150 minutes.

$$g_1 = \text{Gas burnt in 1st lamp} = \frac{150\times10}{60} = \frac{1}{6}(150) \text{ c.c.}$$

Second lamp burns for $(150-1.5)$ minutes

So the gas burnt in 2nd lamp $= g_2 = \frac{1}{6}(150-1.5)$

Similarly $$g_3 = \frac{1}{6}(150-2\times1.5) \text{ and so on.}$$

We are to calculate

$$S = g_1+g_2+...+g_{100}$$

$$S = \frac{1}{6}[150+(150-1.5)+(150-2\times1.5)+...]$$

The series inside bracket is an A.P. with first term = 150, common difference = –1.5 and number of terms = 100

Hence $$S = \frac{1}{6}.\frac{100}{2}[300+99(-1.5)]$$

$$= \frac{25}{3}(300-1.5\times 99)$$

$$= 25(100-1.5\times 33)$$

$$= 25(100-49.5)$$

$$= 25(50.5)$$

$$= 1265.255 \text{ cc.}$$

Example 21. *Two posts were offered to a man. In one the starting salary was Rs 120 per month and the annual increment was Rs 8; in the other post the salary commenced at Rs 85 per month but the annual increment was Rs 12. The man decided to accept the post which would give him more earnings in the first twenty years of the service. Which post was acceptable to him? Justify your answer.*

Solution. The total earnings of the man in first job

$$= \frac{20}{2}[2\times 120+(20-1)8]\times 12$$

$$= 10(240+152)\times 12$$

$$= 120(392) = 47040 \text{ rupees}$$

His total earnings in second job

$$= \frac{20}{2}[2\times 85+(20-1)12]\times 12$$

$$= 120(170+228)$$

$$= 120(398) = 47760 \text{ rupees}$$

which is greater than Rs 47040. Hence the second job was accepted by the man.

Example 22. *Find the sum of all natural numbers between 500 and 1000 which are divisible by 13.*

Solution. 500 leaves, on division by 13, 6 as remainder, so 507 is the least number greater than 500 which is divisible by 13.

Also the remainder, when 1000 is divided by 13 is 12. So the greatest number less than 1000, divisible by 13 is 988.

We are to find the sum 507 + 520 + ... + 988.

Let n be the number of terms in the series

Then $988 = 507 + (n-1)\,13$

$\Rightarrow$ $76 = 39 + n - 1 = n + 38$

$\Rightarrow$ $n = 76 - 38 = 38.$

Required sum, $S = \frac{n}{2}\,[2a + (n-1)d]$

Here $n = 38, a = 507, d = 13$

Hence $S = \frac{38}{2}\,[2 \times 507 + (38-1)13]$

$= \frac{38}{2}\,(1014 + 37 \times 13)$

$= 19\,(1014 + 481)$

$= 19\,(1495) = 28405.$

Example 23. *A firm produced 1000 sets of TV during its first year. The total sum of the firm's production at the end of 10 years operation is 14,500 sets.*

(i) Estimate by how many units, production increased each year, if the increase in each year is uniform, and

(ii) Forecast, based on the estimate of the annual increment in production, the level of output for the 15th year.

Solution. Here $a = 1000$, $S = 14{,}500$, $n = 10$ and d is to be evaluated.

$$14{,}500 = \frac{10}{2}\,[2 \times 1000 + (10-1)d]$$

$$14500 = 5\,(2000 + 9d)$$

$\Rightarrow$ $2000 + 9d = 2900$

$\Rightarrow$ $9d = 900 \quad \Rightarrow \quad d = 100$

Hence 1000 units is increase per annum

$$a + 14d = 1000 + 14 \times 100$$

$$= 1000 + 1400 = 2400.$$

EXERCISES

1. Find the 7th, 13th and $(n-4)$th terms of each of the following series:

   (*i*) 3, 5, 7, ... (*ii*) 1, 4, 7, 10, ... (*iii*) $\frac{11}{5}, 1, \frac{-1}{5}, \frac{-7}{5}$, ...

   (*iv*) 5, 11, 17, ... (*v*) 8, 3, –2, –7, ...

2. The third and thirteenth terms of an A.P. are respectively equal to –40 and 0. Find the A.P. and its 20th term.

3. Is 203 any term of A.P., 13, 28, 43, 58, 73,...?

4. Find the sum of the following series:
   (*i*) 49, 44, 39,... up to 17 terms.
   (*ii*) 3.75, 3.5, 3.25,... to 16 terms.
   (*iii*) $2a - b, 4a - 3b, 6a - 3b$, ... to n terms.
   (*iv*) $5\frac{1}{2}, 6\frac{3}{4}, 8$, ... to 28 terms.
   (*v*) $\frac{3}{\sqrt{5}}, \frac{4}{\sqrt{5}}, \sqrt{5}$, ... to 25 terms.
5. Insert 9 Arithmetic Means between $\frac{1}{4}$ and $\frac{-39}{4}$.
6. Insert 10 Arithmetic Means between 2 and 24.
7. The 3rd term of an A. P. is 18 and 7th term is 30. Find the sum of 17 terms.
8. The sum of four integers in A.P. is 24 and their product is 945. Find them. [*Hint.* Select the numbers to be $a - 3d$, $a - d$, $a + d$, and $a + 3d$.]
9. Sum of three numbers in A.P. is 15 and sum of the squares of its first and third term is 58. Find the numbers.
10. If x, y, z are in A.P., show that
    (*i*) $\frac{1}{yz}, \frac{1}{zx}, \frac{1}{xy}$ are in A.P. (*ii*) $x^2(y + z), y^2(z + x), z^2(x + y)$ are in A.P.
    (*iii*) $x\left(\frac{1}{y}+\frac{1}{z}\right), y\left(\frac{1}{z}+\frac{1}{x}\right), z\left(\frac{1}{x}+\frac{1}{y}\right)$ are in A.P.
11. There are n Arithmetic Means between 3 and 54. If 8th Arithmetic Mean bears a ratio 3 : 5 to $(n - 2)$th Arithmetic Mean, find n.
12. The interior angles of a polygon of n sides are in A.P., the smallest angle is of 42° and common difference is 33. Find n.
13. The sum of n terms of the series 2, 5, 8,... is 950; find n.
14. Between two numbers whose sum is $2\frac{1}{6}$, an even number of arithmetic means is inserted; the sum of these exceeds their number by unity; how many means are there?
15. The number of n terms of an A.P. is $2n + 3n^2$; find the rth term.
16. The number of terms in an A.P. is even; the sum of the odd terms is 24, of the even terms 30, and the last term exceeds the first by 10½; find the number of terms.
17. Find the relation between x and y in order that the rth mean between x and $2y$, may be the same as the rth mean between $2x$ and y, n means being inserted in each case.
18. Prove that if unity is added to the sum of any number, terms of the A.P. 3, 5, 7, 9,...., the resulting sum is a perfect square.
19. If pth term of an A.P. is $1/q$ and qth term is $1/p$, show that the sum of pq terms is $\frac{1}{2}(pq + 1)$.
20. Find sum of all natural numbers from 100 to 300 which are divisible by 4.

21. If p, q, r, s are any four consecutive terms of an A.P. show that $p^2 - 3q^2 + 3r^2 - s^2 = 0$
[*Hint.* Let $p = \alpha - 3\beta$, $q = \alpha - \beta$, $r = \alpha + \beta$, $s = \alpha + 3\beta$]

22. A piece of equipment costs a certain factory Rs 600,000. If it depreciates in value, 15 per cent the first year, 13½ per cent the next year, 12 per cent the third year and so on, what will be its value at the end of 10 years, all percentages applying to the original cost?

23. The rate of monthly salary of a person is increased annually in A.P. It is known that he was drawing Rs 400 a month during the 11th year of his service, and Rs 760 during the 29th year. Find his starting salary and the rate of annual increment. What should be his salary at the time of retirement just on the completion of 36 years of service.

24. Mr X takes a loan of Rs 2000 from Mr Y and agrees to repay in number of instalments, each instalment (beginning with the second) exceeding the previous one by Rs 10. If the first instalment is Rs 5, find how many instalments will be necessary to wipe out the loan completely.

25. A moneylender lends Rs 1000 and charges an overall interest of Rs 140. He recovers the loan and interest by 12 monthly instalments each less by Rs 10 than the preceding one. Find the amount of the first instalment.

26. To verify cash balances, the auditor of a certain bank, employs his assistant to count cash in hand of Rs 4500. At first he counts quietly at the rate of Rs 150 per minute for 10 minutes only but at the end of that time he begins to count at the rate of Rs 2 less every minute than he could count in the previous minute. Ascertain how much time he will take to count this sum of Rs 4500.

27. Eighty coins are placed in a line on the ground. The distance between any two consecutive coins is 10 metres. How far must a person travel to bring them, one by one, to a basket placed 10 meters behind the first coin.

28. A man saved Rs 16500 in 10 years. In each year after the first he saved Rs 100 more than he did in the preceding year. How much did he save in the first year?

29. An enterprise produced 600 units in the 3rd year of its existence and 700 units in its 7th year, what was the initial production in the first year?

30. A man secures an interest free loan of Rs 14500 from a friend and agrees to repay it in ten instalments. He pays Rs 1000 as first instalment and then increases each instalment by equal amount over the preceding instalment. What will be his last instalment?

ANSWERS

1. (*i*) 15, 27, $2n - 7$, (*ii*) 19, 37, $3n - 14$,
(*iii*) -5, $-12\frac{1}{5}$, $8\frac{1}{5} - \frac{6n}{5}$, (*iv*) 41, 77, $6n - 25$,
(*v*) -22, -52, $33 - 5n$.
2. $-48, -44, -40, \ldots, 28$.
3. No.

4. (*i*) 153; (*ii*) 30; (*iii*) $n(n+1)a - n^2b$;

(*iv*) 626½; (*v*) $75\sqrt{5}$.

5. $-\frac{3}{4}, -\frac{7}{4}, -\frac{11}{4}, -\frac{15}{4}, -\frac{19}{4}, -\frac{23}{4}, -\frac{27}{4}, -\frac{31}{4}, -\frac{35}{4}$.

6. 4, 6, 8, 10, 12, 14, 16, 18, 20, 22. 7. 612.

8. 3, 5, 7, 9. 9. 3, 5, 7.

11. 16. 12. 5. 13. 25.

14. 12. 15. $6r - 1$. 16. 8.

17. $ry = (n + 1 - r)x$. 20. 10200. 22. Rs 105000.

23. Starting salary Rs 200; annual increment Rs 20 and salary at the time of retirement, Rs 900.

24. 20. 25. Rs 150. 26. 34 minutes.

27. 64800 metres. 28. Rs 1200. 29. Rs 550.

30. Rs 1900.

6. GEOMETRICAL PROGRESSION

Non-zero quantities $a_1, a_2, a_3, ..., a_n, ...$, each term of which is equal to the product of preceding term and a constant number are called to form a *Geometrical Progression* (written as G.P.).

Thus all the following quantities are in G.P.

(*i*) 1, 2, 4, 8, 16, ... (*ii*) $3, -1, \frac{1}{3}, \frac{-1}{9}, \frac{1}{27}, ...$

(*iii*) $1, \sqrt{2}, 2, 2\sqrt{2}, ...$ (*iv*) $a, \frac{a}{b}, \frac{a}{b^2}, \frac{a}{b^3}, ...$, where $a \neq 0, b \neq 0$.

(*v*) $1, \frac{1}{5}, \frac{1}{25}, \frac{1}{125}, ...$

The constant number is termed as the *common ratio* of the G.P.

7. TO FIND THE *n*TH TERM OF A G.P.

Let first term be a and r, the common ratio, By definition the G.P. is $a, ar, ar^2, ...$

$$1\text{st term} = a = ar^0 = ar^{1-1}$$
$$2\text{nd term} = ar = ar^1 = ar^{2-1}$$
$$\cdots\cdots\cdots\cdots\cdots\cdots$$

In general, nth term $= ar^{n-1}$.

In examples above, we compute 5th, 7th, 3rd, 11th and 8th term of (*i*), (*ii*), (*iii*), (*iv*) and (*v*) respectively.

In (*i*) Ist term is 1 and common ratio = 2.

Hence 5th term $= ar^4 = 1.2^4 = 16$.

In (*ii*) $a = 3, r = \frac{-1}{3}$, hence 7th term $= ar^6 = 3\left(\frac{-1}{3}\right)^6 = \frac{1}{243}$.

In (*iii*) $a = 1, r = \sqrt{2}$, hence 3rd term $= ar^2 = 2$.

In (*iv*) Ist term $= a, r = \frac{1}{b}$, hence 11th term $= ar^{10} = \frac{a}{b^{10}}$.

In (*v*) $a = 1, r = \frac{1}{5}$, hence 8th term $= ar^2 = \frac{1}{5^7} = \frac{1}{78125}$.

8. TO FIND THE SUM OF FIRST *n* TERMS OF A G.P.

Let $a, ar, ar^2,...$ be a given G.P. and let S_n be the sum of its first n terms.

Then $\quad S_n = a + ar + ar^2 + ... + ar^{n-1}$.

This gives that $\quad rS_n = ar + ar^2 + ... + ar^{n-1} + ar^n$

Subtracting, we get $S_n - r\,S_n = a - ar^n = a\,(1 - r^n)$

In case $r \neq 1$, $S_n = \dfrac{a(1-r^n)}{(1-r)}$

In case $r = 1$, $S_n = a + a + a + ... + a$ (n times)

$= na$.

Thus, sum of n terms of a G.P. is $\dfrac{a(1-r^n)}{1-r}$ provided $r \neq 1$.

In case $r = 1$, sum of G.P. is na.

Example 24. *Find the sum of the first 14 terms of a G.P.*

3, 9, 27, 81, 243, 729,...

Solution. In this case $a = 3, r = 3, n = 14$.

So, $$S_n = \frac{a(1-r^n)}{1-r} = \frac{3(1-3^{14})}{1-3} = \frac{3}{2}\,(3^{14} - 1).$$

Example 25. *Find the sum of first 11 terms of a G.P. given by*

$$1, -\frac{1}{2}, \frac{1}{4}, -\frac{1}{8}, ..., ...$$

Solution. Here $a = 1, r = -\frac{1}{2}, n = 11$.

So, $$S_n = \frac{a(1-r^n)}{1-r} = \frac{1\left[1-\left(-\frac{1}{2}\right)^{11}\right]}{1+\frac{1}{2}} = \frac{2^{11}+1}{3\times 2^{10}} = \frac{683}{1024}.$$

9. TO FIND THE SUM TO INFINITY OF A GEOMETRIC PROGRESSION WHOSE COMMON RATIO IS LESS THAN 1

Let $a, ar, ar^2, \ldots$ be a G.P. with $r<1$.

Now $r<1 \Rightarrow r^2<r, r^3<r^2, \ldots.$

Thus as power of r goes on increasing, the corresponding term in G.P. decreases in value. So, we can assume that as n becomes indefinitely large, r^n becomes indefinitely small i.e., $r^n \to 0$.

Now $$S_n = \frac{a(1-r^n)}{1-r} = \frac{a}{1-r} - \frac{ar^n}{1-r}.$$

So, as $n \to \infty$, $$S_\infty = \frac{a}{1-r}.$$

Example 26. *Find the sum of the following series up to infinity*

$$1 + \frac{3}{7} + \frac{9}{49} + \frac{27}{343} + \frac{81}{2401} + \ldots$$

Solution. Here $a = 1, r = \frac{3}{7} < 1.$

So, $$S_\infty = \frac{a}{1-r} = \frac{1}{1-\frac{3}{7}} = \frac{7}{4}.$$

Example 27. *Evaluate the recurring decimal .17*

Solution. Now $$0.17 = 0.1 + 0.07 + 0.007 + 0.0007 + \ldots$$

$$= \frac{1}{10} + \frac{7}{10^2} + \frac{7}{10^3} + \ldots$$

$$= \frac{1}{10} + \frac{7}{10^2}\left\{1 + \frac{1}{10} + \frac{1}{10^2} + \ldots + \ldots\right\}$$

$$= \frac{1}{10} + \frac{7}{10^2}\frac{1}{1-\frac{1}{10}} = \frac{1}{10} + \frac{7}{100}\frac{10}{9}$$

$$= \frac{1}{10} + \frac{7}{90} = \frac{16}{90} = \frac{8}{45}.$$

10. GEOMETRIC MEAN

If α, β, γ are in G.P. then β is called a *Geometric Mean* between α and γ (written as G.M.).

If $a_1, a_2, \ldots, a_n$ are in G.P., then $a_2, \ldots, a_{n-1}$ are called *Geometric Means* between a_1 and a_n.

Thus 3, 9, 27 are three geometric means between 1 and 81.

11. TO FIND *n* GEOMETRIC MEANS BETWEEN TWO GIVEN NUMBERS *a* AND *b*

Let $G_1, G_2, \ldots G_n$ be n Geometric Means between a and b. Thus $a, G_1, G_2, \ldots G_n, b$ is a G.P., b being $(n+2)$th term $= ar^{n+1}$ where r is the common ratio of G.P.

Thus $\quad b = ar^{n+1} \Rightarrow r = \left(\dfrac{b}{a}\right)^{\frac{1}{n+1}}$

So,
$$G_1 = ar = a\left(\frac{b}{a}\right)^{\frac{1}{n+1}} = \left(a^n b\right)^{\frac{1}{n+1}}$$

$$G_2 = ar^2 = a\left(\frac{b}{a}\right)^{\frac{2}{n+1}} = \left(a^{n-1}b^2\right)^{\frac{1}{n+1}}$$

... .

$$G_n = ar^{n-1} = a\left(\frac{b}{a}\right)^{\frac{n-1}{n+1}} = \left(a^2 b^{n-1}\right)^{\frac{1}{n+1}}$$

Example 28. *Find 7 G.M.'s between 1 and 256.*

Solution. Let $G_1, G_2, \ldots G_7$ be 7 G.M.'s between 1 and 256.

Then 256 = 9th term of G.P.,

$= 1.\, r^8$ where r is the common ratio of the G.P.

This gives that $r^8 = 256 \Rightarrow r = 2$.

Thus
$$G_1 = ar = 1.2 = 2$$
$$G_2 = ar^2 = 1.4 = 4$$
$$G_3 = ar^3 = 1.8 = 8$$
$$G_4 = ar^4 = 1.16 = 16$$
$$G_5 = ar^5 = 1.32 = 32$$
$$G_6 = ar^6 = 1.64 = 64$$
$$G_7 = ar^7 = 1.128 = 128.$$

Hence required G.M.'s are 2, 4, 8, 16, 32, 64, 128.

Example 29. *Sum the series 1 + 3x + 5x² + 7x³ + ... up to n terms, x ≠ 1.*

Solution. Note that *n*th term of this series $= (2n-1)\,x^{n-1}$.

Let $S_n = 1 + 3x + 5x^2 + ... + (2n-1)\,x^{n-1}$.

Then $xS_n = x + 3x^2 + ... + (2n-3)\,x^{n-1} + (2n-1)\,x^n$.

Subtracing, we get

$$S_n(1-x) = 1 + 2x + 2x^2 + ... + 2x^{n-1} + (2n-1)\,x^n$$

$$= 1 + 2x \, . \, \frac{1-x^{n-1}}{1-x} - (2n-1)\,x^n$$

$$= \frac{1 - x + 2\,x - 2x^n - (2n-1)\,x^n\,(1-x)}{1-x}$$

$$= \frac{1 + x - 2\,x^n - (2n-1)\,x^n\,(2n-1)\,x^{n+1}}{1-x}$$

$$= \frac{1 + x - (2n+1)\,x^n + (2n-1)\,x^{n+1}}{1-x}$$

Hence $$S = \frac{1 + x - (2n+1)\,x^n + (2n-1)\,x^{n+1}}{(1-x)^2}$$

Example 30. *If in a G.P, (p + q)th term = m and (p – q)th term = n, then find its pth and qth terms.*

Solution. Suppose that the given G.P. is $a, ar, ar^2, ar^3, \ldots$

By hypothesis, $(p+q)$th term $= m = ar^{p+q-1}$

$(p-q)$th term $= n = ar^{p-q-1}$.

Then $\frac{m}{n} = r^{2q} \Rightarrow r = \left(\frac{m}{n}\right)^{1/2q}$

Hence $m = a\left(\frac{m}{n}\right)^{(p+q-1)/2q} \Rightarrow a = m^{(q-p+1)/2q}\,n^{(p+q-1)/2q}$.

Thus pth term $= ar^{p-1} = m^{1/2}\,n^{1/2} = \sqrt{mn}$

qth term $= ar^{q-1} = m^{\frac{2q-p}{2q}}\,n^{\frac{p}{2q}}$

Example 31. *Sum the series 5 + 55 + 555 + ... up to n terms.*

Solution. Let $S_n = 5 + 55 + 555 + \ldots.$

$S_n = 5\,(1 + 11 + 111 + \ldots.)$

$$= \frac{5}{9}(9+99+999+\ldots)$$

$$= \frac{5}{9}[(10-1)+(100-1)+(1000-1)+\ldots]$$

$$= \frac{5}{9}[(10+10^2+10^3+\ldots+10^n) - (1+1+\ldots.n \text{ terms})]$$

$$= \frac{5}{9}[(10+10^2+10^3+\ldots+10^n)-n]$$

$$= \frac{5}{9}\left[\frac{10(1-10^n)}{1-10} - n\right]$$

$$= \frac{5}{9}\left[\frac{10(10^n-1)}{9} - n\right]$$

$$= \frac{50}{81}(10^n-1) - \frac{5n}{9}.$$

Example 32. *If a, b, c, d are in G.P., prove that a^2-b^2, b^2-c^2 and c^2-d^2 are also in G.P.*

Solution. Since $\frac{b}{a} = \frac{c}{b} = \frac{d}{c} = k$ (say)

we have $b = ak$, $c = bk$, $d = ck$

i.e., $b = ak$, $c = ak^2$, $d = ak^3$.

Now $(b^2-c^2)^2 = (a^2k^2 - a^2k^4)^2$

$= a^4k^4(1-k^2)^2.$

Also $(a^2-b^2)(c^2-d^2) = (a^2 - a^2k^2)(a^2k^4 - a^2k^6)$

$= a^4(1-k^2)(k^4-k^6)$

$= a^4k^2(1-k^2)^2$

Hence $(b^2-c^2) = (a^2-b^2)(c^2-d^2).$

This gives that a^2-b^2, b^2-c^2, c^2-d^2 are in G.P.

Example 33. *Three numbers are in G.P. Their product is 64 and sum is $\frac{124}{5}$. Find them.*

Solution. Let the numbers be $\frac{a}{r}$, a, ar.

Since $\frac{a}{r}+a+a^2=\frac{124}{5}$ and $\frac{a}{r}.a.\,ar=64$,

we have $a^3=64 \Rightarrow a=4$.

This gives that $\frac{4}{r}+4+4r=\frac{124}{5}$

$$\Rightarrow \quad \frac{1}{r}+1+r=\frac{31}{5}$$

$$\Rightarrow \quad \frac{r^2+1}{r}=\frac{26}{5}$$

$$\Rightarrow \quad 5r^2+5=26r$$

$$\Rightarrow \quad r=\frac{1}{5} \text{ or } 5$$

In either case, the numbers are $\frac{4}{5}$, 4 and 20.

Example 34. *If a, b, c are in G.P. and $a^x=b^y=c^z$, prove that*

$$\frac{1}{x}+\frac{1}{z}=\frac{2}{y}$$

Solution. a, b, c are in G.P., $b^2=ac$

But $\quad b^y=a^x \Rightarrow a=b^{y/x}$

and $\quad b^y=c^z \Rightarrow c=b^{y/z}$

So we get $\quad b^2=b^{y/x}.\,b^{y/z}=b^{y\left(\frac{1}{x}+\frac{1}{z}\right)}$

$$\Rightarrow \quad 2=y\left(\frac{1}{x}+\frac{1}{z}\right)$$

$$\Rightarrow \quad \frac{1}{x}+\frac{1}{z}=\frac{2}{y}.$$

Example 35. *Sum to n terms the series*

$$.7+.77+.777+\ldots$$

Solution. Given series

$= .7+.77+.777+\ldots$ up to n terms

$= 7\,(.1+.11+.111+\ldots$ up to n terms)

$= \frac{7}{9}\,(.9+.99+.999+\ldots$ up to n terms)

$$= \frac{7}{9}\left[\left(1-\frac{1}{10}\right)+\left(1-\frac{1}{10^2}\right)+\left(1-\frac{1}{10^3}\right)+\ldots\right]$$

$$= \frac{7}{9}\left[n-\left(\frac{1}{10}+\frac{1}{10^2}+\ldots \text{ up to } n \text{ terms}\right)\right]$$

$$= \frac{7}{9}\left[n-\frac{\frac{1}{10}\left(1-\frac{1}{10^n}\right)}{1-\frac{1}{10}}\right]$$

$$= \frac{7}{9}\left[n-\frac{1}{9}\left(1-\frac{1}{10^n}\right)\right]$$

$$= \frac{7}{9}\left[n-\frac{1}{9}\left(1-\frac{1}{10^n}\right)\right].$$

Example 36. *The sum of three numbers in G.P. is 35 and their product is 1000. Find the numbers.*

Solution. Let the numbers be $\frac{\alpha}{r}$, α, αr

Their product $\alpha^3 = 1000$

$\Rightarrow$ $\alpha = 10$

So the numbers are $\frac{10}{r}$, 10, $10r$

The sum of these numbers = 35

$\Rightarrow$ $\frac{10}{r} + 10 + 10r = 35$

$\Rightarrow$ $\frac{2}{r} + 2r = 5$

$\Rightarrow$ $2r^2 - 5r + 2 = 0$

$\Rightarrow$ $(2r-1)(r-2) = 0$

$\Rightarrow$ $r = 2$ or $\frac{1}{2}$

$r = 2$ gives the numbers as 5, 10, 20

$r = \frac{1}{2}$ gives the numbers as 20, 10, 5, the same as the first set.

Hence the required numbers are 5, 10 and 20.

Example 37. *The sum of the first eight terms of a G.P. (of real terms) is five times the sum of the first four terms. Find the common ratio.*

Solution. Let the G.P. be $a, ar, ar^2, \ldots$

$$S_8 = \text{Sum of first eight terms} = \frac{a(1-r^8)}{1-r}$$

$$S_4 = \text{Sum of first four terms} = \frac{a(1-r^4)}{1-r}$$

By hypothesis $S_8 = 5S_4 \Rightarrow \dfrac{a(1-r^8)}{1-r} = \dfrac{5a(1-r^4)}{1-r}$

$\Rightarrow \quad 1-r^8 = 5(1-r^4)$

$\Rightarrow \quad (1-r^4)(1+r^4) = 5(1-r^4)$

In case $r^4 - 1 = 0$ we get $(r^2-1) = 0 \Rightarrow r = \pm 1$

(Note that $r^2 + 1 = 0 \Rightarrow r$ is imaginary)

Now $r = 1 \Rightarrow$ the given series is $a + a + a + \ldots$

but then $S_8 = 8a$ and $S_4 = 4a$. So $S_8 \neq 4S_4$.

In case $r = -1$, we get $S_8 = 0$ and $S_4 = 0$ hence the hypothesis is satisfied.

Suppose now $r^4 - 1 \neq 0$ then $1 + r^4 = 5$

$\Rightarrow \quad r^4 = 4 \Rightarrow r^2 = 2 \quad (r^2 \neq -2)$

$\Rightarrow r = \pm\sqrt{2}$

Hence $r = -1$ or $\pm\sqrt{2}$

Example 38. *If S is the sum, P the product and R the sum of reciprocals of n terms in G.P., prove that*

$$P^2 R^n = S^n.$$

Solution. Let $a, ar, ar^2, \ldots$ be the given G.P.

Then $S = a + ar + ar^2 + \ldots$ up to n terms

$$= \frac{a(1-r^n)}{1-r} \qquad \ldots(1)$$

$$P = a \cdot ar \cdot ar^2 \ldots\ldots ar^{n-1}$$

$$= a^n \, r^{1+2+3+\ldots+(n-1)}$$

$$= a^n \, r^{\frac{(n-1)}{2}(1+n-1)} = a^n \, r^{\left(\frac{n-1}{2}\right)^n} \qquad \ldots(2)$$

$$R = \frac{1}{a} + \frac{1}{ar} + \frac{1}{ar^2} + \ldots \quad \text{up to } n \text{ terms}$$

$$= \frac{\frac{1}{a}\left(1 - \frac{1}{r^n}\right)}{1 - \frac{1}{r}} = \frac{r}{a}\frac{(r^n - 1)}{(r-1)\,r^n}$$

$$= \frac{(1 - r^n)}{a(1-r)\,r^{n-1}} \qquad \ldots(3)$$

By (2) and (3), $$P^2R^n = a^{2n}\,r^{n(n-1)}\,\frac{(1-r^n)^n}{a^n(1-r)^n\,r^{n(n-1)}}$$

$$= \frac{a^n(1-r^n)^n}{(1-r)^n} = S^n \text{ by (1).}$$

Example 39. *The ratio of the 4th to the 12th term of a G.P. with positive common ratio is* $\frac{1}{256}$. *If the sum of the two terms is 61.68, find the sum of series to 8 terms.*

Solution. Let the series be $a, ar, ar^2, \ldots,$

$$T_4 = \text{4th term} = ar^3$$

$$T_{12} = \text{12th term} = ar^{11}$$

.By hypothesis $$\frac{T_4}{T_{12}} = \frac{1}{256}$$

i.e., $$\frac{ar^3}{ar^{11}} = \frac{1}{256}$$

$$\frac{1}{r^8} = \frac{1}{256}$$

$\Rightarrow$ $$r^8 = 256$$

$\Rightarrow$ $$r = \pm 2$$

Since r is given to be positive, we reject negative sign.

Again it is given that

$$T_4 + T_{12} = 61.68$$

i.e., $$a(r^3 + r^{11}) = 61.68$$

$$a(8 + 2048) = 61.68$$

$$a = \frac{61.68}{2056} = .03$$

Hence S_8 = sum to eight terms

$$= \frac{a(1-r^8)}{1-r} = \frac{a(r^8-1)}{r-1}$$

$$= \frac{(.03)(256-1)}{(2-1)} = .03 \times 255 = 7.65.$$

Example 40. *A manufacturer reckons that the value of a machine which costs him Rs 18750 will depreciate each year by 20%. Find the estimated value at the end of 5 years.*

Solution. At the end of first year the value of machine

$$= 18750 \times \frac{80}{100} = \frac{4}{5}(18750)$$

At the end of 2nd year it is equal to $\left(\frac{4}{5}\right)^2$ (18750); proceeding in this manner, the estimated value of machine at the end of 5 years is $\left(\frac{4}{5}\right)^5$ (18750)

$$= \frac{64 \times 16}{125 \times 25} \times 18750$$

$$= \frac{1024}{125} \times 750$$

$$= (1024) \times 6 = 6144 \text{ rupees}$$

Example 41. *Show that a given sum of money accumulated at 20 per cent per annum more than doubles itself in 4 years at compound interest.*

Solution. Let the given sum be a rupees. After 1 year it becomes $\frac{6a}{5}$ (it is increased by $\frac{a}{5}$).

At the end of two years it becomes $\frac{6}{5}\left(\frac{6a}{5}\right) = \left(\frac{6}{5}\right)^2 a$.

Proceeding in the manner, we get that at the end of 4th year, the amount will be $\left(\frac{6}{5}\right)^4 a = \frac{1296}{625} a$

Now $\frac{1296}{625}a - 2a = \frac{46}{625}a$, a + ve quantity, so the amount after 4 years is more than double the original amount.

Example 42. *If* $x = a + \frac{a}{r} + \frac{a}{r^2} + \ldots\infty$

$$y = b - \frac{b}{r} + \frac{b}{r^2} + \ldots\infty$$

and $$z = c + \frac{c}{r^2} + \frac{c}{r^4} + \ldots\infty$$

Show that $$\frac{xy}{z} = \frac{ab}{c}$$

Solution. Clearly $$x = \frac{a}{1-\frac{1}{r}} = \frac{ar}{r-1},$$

$$y = \frac{b}{1-(-1/r)} = \frac{br}{r+1}$$

and $$z = \frac{c}{1-\frac{1}{r^2}} = \frac{cr^2}{r^2-1}$$

Now $$\frac{xy}{z} = \frac{ab\,r^2}{(r^2-1)} \Big/ \left(\frac{cr^2}{r^2-1}\right) = \frac{ab}{c}.$$

Example 43. *If* $a^2 + b^2$, $ab + bc$ and $b^2 + c^2$ *are in G.P., prove that* a, b, c *are also in G.P.*

Solution. Since $a^2 + b^2$, $ab + bc$ and $b^2 + c^2$ are in G.P., we get

$$(ab+bc)^2 = (a^2+b^2)(b^2+c^2)$$

$$b^2(a^2+2ac+c^2) = a^2b^2 + a^2c^2 + b^4 + b^2c^2$$

$$\Rightarrow \quad 2ab^2c^2 = a^2c^2 + b^4$$

$$\Rightarrow \quad a^2c^2 - 2ab^2c^2 + b^4 = 0$$

$$\Rightarrow \quad (ac-b^2)^2 = 0$$

$$\Rightarrow \quad ac = b^2$$

$\Rightarrow$ a, b, c are in G.P.

EXERCISES

1. Find 6th and 8th terms in each of the following series:

   (*i*) 4, 12, 36, ...   (*ii*) 1, 3, 9, –27, ...

   (*iii*) $-21, 14, -\frac{28}{3}, \ldots \ldots \ldots$ (*iv*) $1, \frac{1}{2}, \frac{1}{2^2}, \frac{1}{2^3}, \ldots\ldots\ldots$

   (*v*) $\frac{1}{\sqrt{2}}, -2, \frac{8}{\sqrt{2}}, \ldots\ldots\ldots$

2. Find the sum of following series:

   (*i*) $\frac{1}{2}+\frac{1}{3}+\frac{2}{9}\ldots\ldots\ldots$ up to 7 terms.

   (*ii*) 16.2 + 5.4 + 1.8 + ... up to 9 terms.

   (*iii*) $-\frac{1}{3}+\frac{1}{2}-\frac{3}{4}+\ldots\ldots\ldots$ up to 10 terms.

   (*iv*) $3 + \sqrt{3} + 1 + \ldots \ldots \ldots$ up to 4 terms and infinity.

   (*v*) 1.665 + (–1.11) + .74 + ... up to infinity.

3. (*i*) Insert 5 geometric means between $\frac{32}{9}$ and $\frac{81}{2}$.

   (*ii*) Insert 3 geometric means between $\frac{9}{4}$ and $\frac{4}{9}$.

4. (*a*) Sum the following series:

   (*i*) $1 + 4x + 7x^2 + 10x^3 + \ldots \ldots \ldots$ up to infinity, $x < 1$.

   (*ii*) 3 + 33 + 333 + ... up to 8 terms.

   (*b*) Evaluate

   (*i*) .132   (*ii*) .178.

5. If *p*th, *q*th, *r*th term of a G.P. are respectively equal to *a*, *b*, *c*, then prove that
$$a^{q-r}\, b^{r-p}\, c^{p-q} = 1.$$

6. If *a*, *b*, *c*, *d* are in G.P., show that

   (*i*) $(a-b)^2$, $(b-c)^2$ and $(c-d)^2$ are in G.P.

   (*ii*) $a^2 + b^2$, $ab + bc$ and $b^2 + c^2$ are in G.P.

   (*iii*) $(b-c)^2 + (c-a)^2 + (d-b)^2 = (a-d)^2$

7. If $a' = 1 + c^a + c^{2a} + c^{3a} + \ldots \ldots \ldots$ up to infinity $(0 < c < 1)$
   and $b' = 1 + c^b + c^{2b} + c^{3b} + \ldots \ldots \ldots$ up to infinity $(0 < c < 1)$

   then prove that $c = \left(\frac{a'-1}{a'}\right)^{1/a} = \left(\frac{b'-1}{b'}\right)^{1/b}$

8. The sum of first six terms of a G.P. is 9 times the sum of first three terms. Find the common ratio.

9. The sum of three numbers in a G.P. is 38 and their product is 1728. Find them.

10. There are *n* terms in G.P., show that *n*th root of their product is equal to the square root of the product of its first and last terms.

11. The sum of an infinite number of terms of a G.P. is 4 and the sum of their cubes is 192, find the series.

12. Prove that the $(n + 1)th$ term of a G.P. of which the first term is a and the third term is b, is equal to the $(2n + 1)th$ term of a G.P. of which the first term is a and the fifth term is b.

13. Find the sum of the infinite series

$$1 + (1 + b)\, r + (1 + b + b^2)r^2 + (1 + b + b^2 + b^3)r^3 \ldots \ldots$$

where $0 < b, r<1$.

14. If the arithmetic mean between a and b $(a>b)$ is twice as great as the geometric mean, show that either $a/b = (2 + \sqrt{3}\,)$ or $(2 - \sqrt{3}\,)$.

15. The sum of $2n$ terms of a G.P. whose first term is a and common ratio r is equal to the sum of n terms of G.P. whose first term is b and common ratio r^2. Prove that b is equal to the sum of the first two terms of the first series.

16. Find the sum of the series.

$$\frac{1}{2}+\frac{1}{3^2}+\frac{1}{2^3}+\frac{1}{3^4}+\frac{1}{2^5}+\frac{1}{3^6}+\ldots \text{ to } \infty$$

17. If $x = 1 + a + a^2 + \ldots \ldots \ldots \infty$, $y = 1 + b + b^2 + \ldots \infty$

prove that if $|a| < 1$ and $|b| < 1$

then $1 + ab + a^2b^2 + \ldots = \dfrac{xy}{x+y-1}$

18. If a, b, c, d are in G.P., prove that

(*i*) $\dfrac{ab-cd}{b^2-c^2}=\dfrac{a+c}{b}$

(*ii*) $(ab + bc + cd)^2 = (a^2 + b^2 + c^2)(b^2 + c^2 + d^2)$

19. At 10 per cent per annum compound interest, a sum of money accumulates to Rs 8650 in 5 years. Find the sum invested initially.

20. If the population of a town increases 25 per thousand per year of the population at the beginning of a year and the present population is 26,24000, what will be the population in three year's time? What was it a year ago?

ANSWERS

1. (*i*) 972, 8748; (*ii*) – 243, –2187; (*iii*) $2\frac{62}{81}, 1\frac{167}{729}$;

(*iv*) $\frac{1}{32}, \frac{1}{128}$ (*v*) –128, –1024.

2. (*i*) $1\frac{601}{1458}$; (*ii*) $242\frac{80}{81}$; (*iii*) $7\frac{853}{1536}$;

(*iv*) $\frac{8}{\sqrt{3}(\sqrt{3}-1)}, \frac{3\sqrt{3}}{\sqrt{3}-1}$, (*iv*) .999

3. (*i*) $5\frac{1}{3}$, 8, 12, 18, 27; (*ii*) $1\frac{1}{3}$, 1, 2/3.

4. (*a*) (*i*) $\frac{1+2x}{(1-x)^2}$, (*ii*) $\frac{10}{27}(108-1)-\frac{8}{3}$

(*b*) (*i*) $\frac{131}{990}$, (*ii*) $\frac{161}{9000}$.

8. 2. 9. 8, 12, 18. 11. 6, – 3, $1\frac{1}{2}$, ...

13. $\frac{1}{(1-r)(1-br)}$ 16. $\frac{19}{24}$

19. Rupees 5908.07 20. 2757840, 2560000.

12. HARMONICAL PROGRESSION

Non-zero quantities whose reciprocals are in A.P. are said to be in *Harmonical Progression* (written as H.P.)

Consider the following examples:

1. $1, \frac{1}{3}, \frac{1}{5}, \frac{1}{7}, \ldots\ldots$
2. $\frac{1}{2}, \frac{1}{5}, \frac{1}{8}, \frac{1}{11}, \ldots\ldots$
3. $2, \frac{5}{2}, \frac{10}{3}, \ldots$
4. $\frac{1}{a}, \frac{1}{a+b}, \frac{1}{a+2b}, \ldots\ldots\ a, b > 0.$
5. $5, \frac{55}{9}, \frac{55}{7}, 11, \ldots\ldots$

It can be easily checked that in each case the series obtained by taking reciprocal of each of the term is an A.P.

13. HARMONIC MEAN

If a, b, c are in H.P., then b is called a *Harmonic Mean* between a and c (written as H.M.)

14. TO INSERT *n* HARMONIC MEANS BETWEEN *a* AND *b*

Let $H_1, H_2, H_3, \ldots, H_n$ be the required Harmonic Means. Then $a, H_1, H_2, \ldots, H_n, b$ are in H.P.

i.e. $\frac{1}{a}, \frac{1}{H_1}, \frac{1}{H_2}, \ldots, \frac{1}{H_n}, \frac{1}{b}$ are in A.P.

Then $\frac{1}{b} = (n+2)$th term of an A.P.

$= \frac{1}{a} + (n+1)d$, where d is the common difference of A.P.

This gives $d = \frac{a-b}{(n+1)ab}$.

Now $\dfrac{1}{H_1} = \dfrac{1}{a} + d = \dfrac{1}{a} + \dfrac{a-b}{(n+1)\,ab}$

$$= \frac{nb+b+a-b}{(n+1)\,ab} = \frac{a+nb}{(n+1)\,ab}$$

So $\dfrac{1}{H_1} = \dfrac{a+nb}{(n+1)\,ab}$

$\Rightarrow$ $H_1 = \dfrac{(n+1)\,ab}{a+nb}$.

Again $\dfrac{1}{H_2} = \dfrac{1}{a} + 2d = \dfrac{1}{a} + \dfrac{2\,(a-b)}{(n+1)\,ab}$

$$= \frac{nb+b+2a-2b}{(n+1)\,ab} = \frac{2a-b+nb}{(n+1)\,ab}$$

$\Rightarrow$ $H_2 = \dfrac{(n+1)\,ab}{2a-b+nb}$

Similarly, $\dfrac{1}{H_3} = \dfrac{1}{a} + 3d = \dfrac{3a-2b+nb}{(n+1)\,ab}$

$\Rightarrow$ $H_3 = \dfrac{(n+1)\,ab}{3a-2b+nb}$

and so on,

$$\frac{1}{H_n} = \frac{1}{a} + nd = \frac{1}{a} + \frac{n\,(a-b)}{(n+1)\,ab}$$

$$= \frac{nb+b+na-nb}{(n+1)\,ab} = \frac{na+b}{(n+1)\,ab}$$

$\Rightarrow$ $H_n = \dfrac{(n+1)\,ab}{na+b}$.

Example 44. *If* $x^2 + 9y^2 + 25z^2 = xyz\left(\dfrac{15}{x} + \dfrac{5}{y} + \dfrac{3}{z}\right)$, *show that x, y and z are in H.P.*

Solution. Given: $x^2 + 9y^2 + 25z^2 = 15yz + 5xz + 3xy$

$\Rightarrow$ $(x-3y)^2 + (3y-5z)^2 + (5z-x)^2 = 0$

$\Rightarrow$ $x - 3y = 3y - 5z = 5z - x = 0$

$\Rightarrow$ $\dfrac{1}{x} + \dfrac{1}{z} = \dfrac{1}{3y} + \dfrac{5}{3y} = \dfrac{2}{y}$

$\Rightarrow$ $\dfrac{1}{x}, \dfrac{1}{y}, \dfrac{1}{z}$ are in *A.P.*

$\Rightarrow$ $x, y, z,$ are in *H.P.*

Example 45. *Find the 5th term of* $2, 2\frac{1}{2}, 3\frac{1}{3}, \ldots\ldots$

Solution. Let 5th term be x. Then $\frac{1}{x}$ is 5th term of corresponding A.P.

$\frac{1}{2}, \frac{2}{5}, \frac{3}{10}, \ldots\ldots$

Then $$\frac{1}{x} = \frac{1}{2} + 4\left(\frac{2}{5} - \frac{1}{2}\right) = \frac{1}{2} + 4\left(\frac{-1}{10}\right)$$

$$\Rightarrow \quad \frac{1}{x} = \frac{1}{2} - \frac{2}{5} = \frac{1}{10} \Rightarrow x = 10.$$

Example 46. *If a, b, c are in H.P., show that* $\frac{1}{b-a} + \frac{1}{b-c} = \frac{2}{b}$.

Solution. Now $$\frac{1}{b-a} + \frac{1}{b-c} = \frac{2b-(a+c)}{b^2 - b(a+c) + ac}$$

$$= \frac{2b - \frac{2ac}{b}}{b^2 - ac} \quad \left(\text{as } a, b, c \text{ are in } H.P. \Rightarrow \frac{1}{a} + \frac{1}{c} = \frac{2}{b}\right)$$

$$= \frac{2}{b}.$$

Example 47. *Insert two Harmonic means between* $\frac{1}{2}$ *and* $\frac{4}{17}$.

Solution. Let H_1, H_2 be two harmonic means between $\frac{1}{2}$ and $\frac{4}{17}$.

Then $2, \frac{1}{H_1}, \frac{1}{H_2}, \frac{17}{4}$ are in A.P. Let d be their common difference.

Then $$\frac{17}{4} = 2 + 3d$$

$$\Rightarrow \quad 3d = \frac{9}{4} \Rightarrow d = \frac{3}{4}.$$

Thus $$\frac{1}{H_1} = 2 + \frac{3}{4} = \frac{11}{4} \Rightarrow H_1 = \frac{4}{11}$$

$$\frac{1}{H_2} = 2 + 2.\frac{3}{4} = \frac{7}{2} \Rightarrow H_2 = \frac{2}{7}.$$

Required Harmonic Means are $\frac{4}{11}, \frac{2}{7}$.

EXERCISES

1. Find 5th and 12th terms of the following series:

   (*i*) $\frac{2}{9}, \frac{4}{17}, \frac{1}{4}, \ldots$ (*ii*) $\frac{1}{3}, \frac{8}{23}, \frac{4}{11}, \ldots$

2. If *a*, *b*, *c* are in *H.P.*, show that $\left(\frac{1}{a}+\frac{1}{b}-\frac{1}{c}\right)\left(\frac{1}{b}+\frac{1}{c}-\frac{1}{a}\right) = \frac{4}{ac}-\frac{3}{b^2}$

3. Insert 4 Harmonic Means between 4 and $\frac{1}{4}$.

4. Insert 7 Harmonic Means between 5 and −11.

5. If *H* is the harmonic mean between *a* and *b*, show that $\frac{H+a}{H-a}+\frac{H+b}{H-b} = 2.$

6. Show that Harmonic mean of the roots of the equation $x^2 - 10x + 11 = 0$ is $\frac{11}{5}$.

7. If $b + c$, $c + a$, $a + b$ are in *H.P*, show that a^2, b^2, c^2 will be in *A.P.*

8. If $\frac{a}{b}, \frac{b}{c}, \frac{c}{a}$ are in *H.P*, show that a^2b, c^2a, b^2c are in *A.P.*

ANSWERS

1. (*i*) $\frac{2}{7}, \frac{4}{7}$ (*ii*) $\frac{2}{5}, \frac{8}{13}$. 3. 1, $\frac{4}{7}, \frac{2}{5}, \frac{4}{13}$.

4. $6\frac{1}{9}, 7\frac{6}{7}, 11, 18\frac{1}{3}, 55, -55, -11\frac{1}{3}$.

15. SUM OF FIRST *n* NATURAL NUMBERS

We wish to find the sum of the series $1 + 2 + 3 + \ldots + n$.

This is an A.P. with first term 1 and common difference 1

Thus $S_n = \frac{n}{2}[2.1 + (n-1).1] = \frac{n(n+1)}{2}$.

Hence sum of first *n* natural numbers is $\frac{n(n+1)}{2}$.

16. SUM OF THE SQUARES OF FIRST *n* NATURAL NUMBERS

Let $S = 1^2 + 2^2 + 3^2 + \ldots + n^2$.

Now $n^3 - (n-1)^3 = 3n^2 - 3n + 1$

Putting successively $n = 1, 2, \ldots, \ldots, \ldots n$, we get

$$1^3 - 0^3 = 3.1^2 - 3.1 + 1$$
$$2^3 - 1^3 = 3.1^2 - 3.2 + 1$$
$$\dots \quad \dots \quad \dots \quad \dots \quad \dots \quad \dots$$
$$n^3 - (n-1)^3 = 3n^2 - 3n + 1$$

Adding, we obtain

$$n^3 = 3(1^2 + 2^2 + \dots + n^2) - 3(1 + 2 + \dots + n) + n$$

Then $3(1^2 + 2^2 + \dots + n^2) = n^3 + 3(1 + 2 + \dots + n) - n$

$$= n^3 + \frac{3n(n+1)}{2} - n$$

$$= \frac{n}{2}[2n^2 + 3n + 3 - 2] = \frac{n}{2}[2n^2 + 3n + 1]$$

i.e., $3S = \frac{n}{2}[(n+1)(2n+1)]$

Hence $S = \frac{n}{6}(n+1)(2n+1).$

17. SUM OF THE CUBES OF FIRST *n* NATURAL NUMBERS

Let $S = 1^3 + 2^3 + 3^3 + \dots + n^3.$

Now $n^4 - (n-1)^4 = 4n^3 - 6n^2 + 4n - 1.$

Putting successively, $n = 1, 2, \dots, n$, we get

$$1^4 - 0^4 = 4.1^3 - 6.1^2 + 4.1 - 1$$
$$2^4 - 1^4 = 4.2^3 - 6.2^2 + 4.2 - 1$$
$$3^4 - 2^4 = 4.3^3 - 6.3^2 + 4.3 - 1$$
$$\dots \quad \dots \quad \dots \quad \dots \quad \dots \quad \dots$$
$$n^4 - (n-1)^4 = 4n^3 - 6n^2 + 4.n - 1.$$

Adding we obtain

$$n^4 = 4(1^3 + 2^3 + \dots + n^3) - 6(1^2 + 2^2 + 3^2 + \dots + n^2) + 4(1 + 2 + 3 + \dots + n) - n$$

Then $4S = n^4 + 6(1^2 + 2^2 + \dots + n^2) - 4(1 + 2 + \dots + n) + n$

$$= n^4 + \frac{6n(2n+1)(n+1)}{6} - \frac{4n(n+1)}{2} + n$$

$$= n^4 + n(2n^2 + 3n + 1) - 2 - 2n^2 - 2n + n$$

$$= n^4 + 2n^3 + 3n^2 + n - 2n^2 - 2n + r$$

$$= n^4 + 2n^3 + n^2 = n^2(n^2 + 2n + 1) = n^2(n+1)^2$$

$$\Rightarrow \quad S = \left[\frac{n(n+1)}{2}\right]^2.$$

Example 48. *a and b are two positive real numbers and A, G, H are their A.M., G.M. and H.M. respectively. If G is to be taken positive, then prove that $A \geq G \geq H$ and they are in G.P.*

Solution. Clearly $A = \dfrac{a+b}{2}$, $G = \sqrt{ab}$ and $H = \dfrac{2ab}{a+b}$

Now $A - G = \dfrac{a+b}{2} - \sqrt{ab} = \dfrac{a+b-2\sqrt{ab}}{2} = \dfrac{\left(\sqrt{a}-\sqrt{b}\right)^2}{2} \geq 0$

$\Rightarrow \quad A \geq G$

Further $G - H = \sqrt{ab} - \dfrac{2ab}{a+b} = \sqrt{ab}\,\dfrac{a+b-2\sqrt{ab}}{a+b}$

$$= \sqrt{ab}\,\frac{\left(\sqrt{a}-\sqrt{b}\right)^2}{a+b} \geq 0$$

$\Rightarrow \quad G \geq H$

Hence $\quad A \geq G \geq H.$

Again $G^2 = ab$ and $AH = \dfrac{a+b}{2} \cdot \dfrac{2ab}{a+b} = ab$ imply that $G^2 = AH$. In other words A, G, H are in G.P.

Example 49. *Find the sum of the series*

$$1 + \frac{2}{5} + \frac{3}{5^2} + \ldots \text{ up to } n \text{ terms.}$$

Solution. Let $S = 1 + \dfrac{2}{5} + \dfrac{3}{5^2} + \dfrac{4}{5^3} + \ldots + t_n$

where t_n = nth term of the series $= \dfrac{3}{5^{n-1}}$. (Note this step)

Thus $\quad S = 1 + \dfrac{2}{5} + \dfrac{3}{5^2} + \ldots + \dfrac{n}{5^{n-1}}$.

Multiplying each side by $\dfrac{1}{5}$ we get

$$\frac{1}{5}S = \frac{1}{5} + \frac{2}{5^2} + \ldots + \frac{n-1}{5^{n-1}} + \frac{n}{5^n}$$

On subtraction, we obtain

$$\frac{4}{5}S = 1 + \frac{1}{5} + \frac{1}{5^2} + \ldots + \frac{1}{5^{n-1}} - \frac{n}{5^n}$$

$$= \frac{1\left(1-\frac{1}{5^n}\right)}{1-\frac{1}{5}} - \frac{n}{5^n} = \frac{5^n-1}{4.5^{n-1}} - \frac{n}{5^n}.$$

$$\Rightarrow \qquad \frac{4}{5}S = \frac{5^{n+1}-5-4n}{4.5^n}.$$

$$\Rightarrow \qquad S = \frac{5^{n+1}-5-4n}{16.5^{n-1}}.$$

Example 50. *The number of terms in an A.P. is even; the sum of the odd terms is 24, of the even terms 30, and the last term exceeds the first term by* $10\frac{1}{2}$. *Find the number of terms.*

Solution. Let a be the first term and d be the common difference of the given A.P., the odd terms are a, $a + 2d$, $a + 4d$, ..., $a + (2n - 2)d$ and the even terms are $a + d$, $a + 3d$, ..., $a + (2n - 1)d$.

By hypothesis

$$24 = a + (a + 2d) + (a + 4d) + \ldots + a + (2n - 2)\,d \qquad \text{...(1)}$$

$$30 = (a + d) + (a + 3d) + (a + 5d) + \ldots + a + (2n - 1)\,d \qquad \text{...(2)}$$

and $$[a + (2n - 1)d] - a = 10\frac{1}{2} = \frac{21}{2} \qquad \text{...(3)}$$

Simplifying (1), (2), and (3) we get

$$24 = \frac{n}{2}[2a + (n - 1)2d]$$

$$\Rightarrow \qquad 24 = n(a + nd - d) \qquad \text{...(4)}$$

$$30 = \frac{n}{2}[2a + 2d + (n - 1)2d]$$

$$\Rightarrow \qquad 30 = n(a + nd) \qquad \text{...(5)}$$

and $$(2n - 1)d = \frac{21}{2}. \qquad \text{...(6)}$$

Subtracting (4) from (5) we obtain $nd = 6$. ...(7)

Then (6) implies $\quad 12 - d = \frac{21}{2} \Rightarrow d = \frac{3}{2}$.

Finally (7) gives that $n = 4$ and so $2n = 8$.

Example 51. *If* $H_1, H_2, \ldots, H_n$ *are n harmonic means between two given numbers then show that*

$$H_1H_2 + H_2H_3 + \ldots + H_{n-1}H_n = (n - 1)H_1H_n.$$

Solution. Let a and b be the two given numbers. Let d be the common difference of the series $\frac{1}{a}, \frac{1}{H_1}, \frac{1}{H_2}, \ldots, \frac{1}{H_n}, \frac{1}{b}$.

Now $\quad \frac{1}{H_2} - \frac{1}{H_1} = d \Rightarrow H_1 - H_2 = d(H_1H_2)$

Similarly $\quad \frac{1}{H_3} - \frac{1}{H_2} = d \Rightarrow H_2 - H_3 = d(H_2H_3)$

... ...

... ...

Finally $\quad \frac{1}{H_n} - \frac{1}{H_{n-1}} = d \Rightarrow H_{n-1} - H_n = d(H_{n-1}H_n)$.

Adding, we get $H_1 - H_n = d(H_1H_2 + H_2H_3 + \ldots + H_{n-1}H_n)$

or $\quad H_1H_2 + H_2H_3 + \ldots + H_{n-1}H_n = \frac{H_1 - H_n}{d}$.

Now $\frac{1}{H_n}$ is nth term of the A.P. with first term as H_1 and common difference d.

So $$\frac{1}{H_n} = \frac{1}{H_n} + (n-1)d$$

$$\Rightarrow \quad \frac{1}{H_n} - \frac{1}{H_1} = (n-1)d$$

$$\Rightarrow \quad H_1 - H_n = (n-1)d(H_1H_n)$$

Hence $H_1H_2 + H_2H_3 + \ldots H_{n-1}H_n = (n-1)H_1H_n$.

Example 52. *A_1, A_2; G_1, G_2 and H_1, H_2 are A.M.'s, G.M.'s and H.M.'s respectively between two given numbers. Prove that*

$$G_1G_2 : H_1H_2 = A_1 + A_2 : H_1 + H_2.$$

Solution. Let the given numbers be x and y.

Then x, A_1, A_2, y; x, G_1, G_2, y; x, H_1, H_2, y are in A.P., G.P., and H.P. respectively.

This implies that $A_1 = \frac{y+2x}{3}, A_2 = \frac{2y+x}{3}$; $\quad G_1 = x^{2/3}y^{1/3}$,

$G_2 = x^{1/3}y^{2/3}$ and $H_1 = \frac{3xy}{x+2y}, H_2 = \frac{3xy}{2x+y}$.

$$\text{Now} \quad \frac{G_1G_2}{H_1H_2} = \frac{(xy)(x+2y)(2x+y)}{9x^2y^2} = \frac{(x+2y)(2x+y)}{9xy} \qquad ...(1)$$

$$\text{while} \quad \frac{A_1+A_2}{H_1+H_2} = \frac{\dfrac{y+2x}{3}+\dfrac{x+2y}{3}}{\dfrac{3xy}{x+2y}+\dfrac{3xy}{2x+y}} = \frac{(x+y)(x+2y)(2x+y)}{3xy(3x+3y)}$$

$$= \frac{(x+2y)(2x+y)}{9xy} \qquad ...(2)$$

(1) and (2) give the required result.

Example 53. *If $a^x = b^y = c^z = ...$ etc. and a, b, c, ... are in G.P., then show that x, y, z, ... are in H.P.*

Solution. Let $a^x = b^y = c^z = ... = k$.

Then $a = k^{1/x}, b = k^{1/y}, c = k^{1/z}, ...,$ etc.

This in turn implies that $\dfrac{b}{a} = k^{1/y-1/x}, \dfrac{c}{b} = k^{1/x-1/y}, ...$

But $a, b, c, ...,$ are in G.P., so $\dfrac{b}{a} = \dfrac{c}{b} = ...$

$$\Rightarrow \quad \frac{1}{y}-\frac{1}{x} = \frac{1}{z}-\frac{1}{y} = ...$$

$$\Rightarrow \quad \frac{1}{x}, \frac{1}{y}, \frac{1}{z}, ... \text{ are in A.P.}$$

$$\Rightarrow \quad x, y, z, ... \text{ are in H.P.}$$

NOTE: See also Example 34.

Example 54. *If the ratio of H.M. and G.M. between two numbers is 12 : 13 then prove that the ratio between the numbers will be 9 : 4.*

Solution. Let the two numbers be *a* and *b*. If G and H stand for the geometric and harmonic means between *a* and *b* respectively, then

$$\frac{H}{G} = \frac{12}{13} \Rightarrow \frac{\dfrac{2ab}{a+b}}{\sqrt{ab}} = \frac{12}{13} \quad \Rightarrow \quad \frac{2\sqrt{ab}}{a+b} = \frac{12}{13}$$

$$\Rightarrow \quad \frac{a+b-2\sqrt{ab}}{a+b+2\sqrt{ab}} = \frac{13-12}{13+12} = \frac{1}{25} \Rightarrow \frac{\sqrt{a}-\sqrt{b}}{\sqrt{a}+\sqrt{b}} = \frac{1}{5} \Rightarrow \frac{\sqrt{a}}{\sqrt{b}} = \frac{6}{4}$$

$$\Rightarrow \quad \frac{\sqrt{a}}{\sqrt{b}} = \frac{3}{2} \Rightarrow \frac{a}{b} = \frac{9}{4}.$$

Example 55. *If 12 and $9\frac{3}{5}$ are the geometric and harmonic means, respectively, between two numbers, find them.*

Solution. Let the two numbers be x and y. Then $\sqrt{xy} = 12$ and $\frac{2xy}{x+y}$ $= \frac{48}{5}$. Since $xy = 144$, we get $x + y = \frac{5}{24}$, $xy = 30$. Solving the two equations, we get $x = 6, y = 24$ or $x = 24, y = 6$. Hence the two numbers are 6 and 24.

Example 56. *Sum to n terms the series*

$$1^2 + (1^2 + 2^2) + (1^2 + 2^2 + 3^2) + \ldots$$

Solution. t_r = rth term of the given series

$$= 1^2 + 2^2 + 3^2 + \ldots + r^2$$

$$= \frac{r(r+1)(2r+1)}{6}$$

$$= \frac{r(2r^2+3r+1)}{6} = \frac{r^3}{3} + \frac{r^2}{2} + \frac{r}{6}$$

So

$$t_1 = \frac{1^3}{3} + \frac{1^2}{2} + \frac{1}{6}$$

$$t_2 = \frac{2^3}{3} + \frac{2^2}{2} + \frac{2}{6}$$

$$t_3 = \frac{3^3}{3} + \frac{3^2}{2} + \frac{3}{6} \text{ and so on}$$

$$t_n = \frac{n^3}{3} + \frac{n^2}{2} + \frac{n}{6}$$

Hence required $= t_1 + t_2 + \ldots + t_n$

$$= \frac{1}{3}(1^3 + 2^3 + \ldots + n^3) + \frac{1}{2}(1^2 + 2^2 + \ldots + n^2) + \frac{1}{6}(1 + 2 + \ldots + n)$$

$$= \frac{1}{3}\frac{n^2(n+1)^2}{4} + \frac{1}{2}\frac{n(n+1)(2n+1)}{6} + \frac{1}{6}\frac{n(n+1)}{2}$$

$$= \frac{n(n+1)}{12}[n(n+1) + 2n + 1 + 1]$$

$$= \frac{n(n+1)}{12}(n^2 + 3n + 2) = \frac{n(n+1)^2(n+2)}{12}.$$

Example 57. *Sum the series*

$$1^2 + 3^2 + 5^2 + 7^2 + \dots \text{ upto } n \text{ terms.}$$

Solution. nth term of the series 1, 3, 5, 7, ... is $2n - 1$

So the nth term t_n of the given series

$$= (2n-1)^2 = 4n^2 - 4n + 1$$

Thus $t_1 = 4.1^2 - 4.1 + 1$

$t_2 = 4.2^2 - 4.2 + 1$

$t_3 = 4.3^2 - 4.3 + 1$

... ... and so on

$t_n = 4.n^2 - 4.n + 1$

Hence $S = t_1 + t_2 + \dots + t_n$

$$= 4(1^2 + 2^2 + \dots + n^2) - 4(1 + 2 + \dots + n) + n$$

$$= 4\frac{n(n+1)(2n+1)}{6} - 4\frac{n(n+1)}{2} + n$$

$$= \frac{2n(n+1)(2n+1)}{3} - 2n(n+1) + n$$

$$= \frac{n(n+1)}{3}(4n + 2 - 6) + n$$

$$= \frac{n(n+1)(4n-4)}{3} + n$$

$$= \frac{n}{3}(4n^2 - 4 + 3) = \frac{n}{3}(4n^2 - 1).$$

Example 58. *Sum the series to n terms*

$$4 + 14 + 30 + 52 + 80 + \dots$$

Solution. Let $S = 4 + 14 + 30 + 52 + 80 + \dots + t_n$ ...(1)

where t_n is the nth term of the given series.

Also $S = 4 + 14 + 30 + 52 + \dots + t_{n-1} + t_n$ ...(2)

Subtracting (2) from (1) we get

$$0 = 4 + 10 + 16 + 22 + 28 + \dots \text{ up to } n \text{ terms} - t_n$$

$\Rightarrow$ $t_n = 4 + 10 + 16 + \dots$ up to n terms

$$= \frac{n}{2}[8 + (n-1)6]$$

$$= n(4 + 3n - 3) = n(3n+1) = 3n^2 + n$$

Hence $S_n = \Sigma t_n = \Sigma\,(3n^2 + n)$

$$= 3\Sigma n^2 + \Sigma n$$

$$= 3\frac{n(n+1)\,(2n+1)}{6} + \frac{n(n+1)}{2}$$

$$= \frac{n(n+1)}{2}(2n+1+1)$$

$$= n\,(n+1)\,(n+1)$$

$$= n\,(n+1)^2.$$

Example 59. *Sum the series to n terms*

$$2.4.6 + 4.6.8 + 6.8.10 + \ldots$$

Solution. Evidently *n*th term of the given series

$$= t_n = 2n\,(2n+2)\,(2n+4)$$

$$= 8n\,(n+1)\,(n+2)$$

$$= 8\,(n^3 + 3n^2 + 2n)$$

Hence $S = \Sigma t_n = 8\Sigma n^3 + 24\Sigma n^2 + 16\Sigma n$

$$= 8\frac{n^2\,(n+1)^2}{4} + 24\frac{n\,(n+1)\,(2n+1)}{6} + 16\frac{n\,(n+1)}{2}$$

$$= 2n^2\,(n+1)^2 + 4n\,(n+1)\,(2n+1) + 8n\,(n+1)$$

$$= 2n\,(n+1)\,[n\,(n+1) + 2\,(2n+1) + 4]$$

$$= 2n\,(n+1)\,(n^2 + 5n + 6)$$

$$= 2n\,(n+1)\,(n+2)\,(n+3).$$

Example 60. *Find the sum of n terms of the series whose nth term is $3(4^n + 2n^2) - 4n^3$.*

Solution. Here $t_n = 3\,(4^n + 2n^2) - 4n^3$

So $S = \Sigma t_n = \Sigma[3\,(4^n + 2n^2 - 4n^3] = 3\Sigma 4^n + 6\Sigma n^2 - 4\Sigma n^3$

$$= 3\frac{4\left(1-4^n\right)}{1-4} + 6\frac{n(n+1)\,(2n+1)}{6} - 4\frac{n^2\,(n+1)^2}{4}$$

$$= 4^{n+1} - 4 + n\,(n+1)\,(2n+1) - n^2\,(n+1)^2$$

$$= 4^{n+1} - 4 + n\,(n+1)\,[2n+1 - n\,(n+1)]$$

$$= 4^{n+1} - 4 + n\,(n+1)\,(-n^2 + n + 1)$$

$$= 4^{n+1} - 4 - n\,(n+1)\,(n^2 - n - 1).$$

EXERCISES

1. Sum the following series :
   (*i*) $2^2 + 4^2 + 6^2 + ...,$ up to n terms.
   (*ii*) $1.2 + 2.3 + 3.4 + 4.5 + ...$ up to n terms.
   (*iii*) $1.3.5 + 3.5.7 + 5.7.9 + ...$ up to n terms.
2. Find the sum of n terms of the series whose rth term is given by
$$2^{r-1} + 8r^3 - 6r^2.$$
3. If pth, qth, rth terms of a H.P. are a, b, c respectively, prove that
$$(q - r)\,bc + (r - p)ca + (p - q)ab = 0.$$
4. If l, m, n are three numbers in G.P., prove that the first term of an A.P. whose lth, mth and nth terms are in H.P. is to the common difference as $m + 1$ to 1.
5. Show that a, b, c are in A.P. or in G.P. or in H.P. according as
$$\frac{a-b}{b-c} = \frac{a}{a} \text{ or } \frac{a}{b} \text{ or } \frac{a}{c} \text{ respectively.}$$
6. If H.M. and G.M. of two numbers are $14\frac{2}{5}$ and 24 respectively, find the numbers.
7. If a, b, c are in A.P., x, y, z in H.P., ax, by, cz are in G.P., prove that
$$\frac{x}{z}+\frac{z}{x} = \frac{a}{c}+\frac{c}{a}.$$
8. If $2(y - a)$ is H.M. between $(y - x)$ and $(y - z)$, then prove that $(x - a)$, $(y - a)$ and $(z - a)$ are in A.P.
9. If a, b, c are in H.P., then prove that
$$\frac{a}{b+c}, \frac{b}{c+a}, \frac{c}{a+b} \text{ are also in H.P.}$$
10. If a, b, c, are in H.P., then prove that
$$a^2 + c^2 > 2b^2.$$
11. Find nth term and the sum to n terms of the following series
    (*i*) $4 + 6 + 9 + 13 + 18 + ...$ (*ii*) $11 + 23 + 59 + 167 + ...$
    (*iii*) $1 + 5 + 12 + 22 + ...$ (*iv*) $1.2.4 + 2.3.5 + 3.4.6 + ...$
12. Find the sum of n terms of the series whose nth term is
    (*i*) $n^3 + \frac{3}{2}n$ (*ii*) $3^n - 2^n$
    (*iii*) $3n^2 - n$

ANSWERS

1. (*i*) $\frac{2}{3}n(n + 1)(2n + 1)$ (*ii*) $\frac{n(n+1)(n+2)}{3}$ (*iii*) $(n + 2)(2n^2 + 4n - 1)$
2. $2^n - 1 + n(n + 1)(2n^2 - 1)$.

6. 8 and 72.

11. (*i*) $\frac{1}{2}(n^2 + n + 6)$, $\frac{n}{6}(n^2 + 3n + 20)$

(*ii*) $2.3^n + 5$, $3^{n+1} + 5n - 3$ (*iii*) $\frac{n}{2}(3n - 1)$, $\frac{n^2}{2}(n + 1)$.

(*iv*) $n(n + 1)(n + 3)$, $\frac{n(n+1)(n+2)(3n+13)}{12}$

12. (*i*) $\frac{n}{4}(n + 1)(n^2 + n + 3)$, (*ii*) $\frac{1}{2}(3^{n+1} + 1) - 2^{n+1}$

(*iii*) $n^2(n + 1)$.

CHAPTER 8

SURDS AND INDICES

1. INDICES

Let n be a positive integer and a any real number. By a^n we mean $a \times a \times \ldots n$ times.

In case $n = 0$, we define $a^0 = 1$. $(a \neq 0)$.

If n is a negative integer and a is any non-zero real number, then by a^n we mean $\frac{1}{a} \times \frac{1}{a} \times \ldots \times (-n)$ times.

Thus if $a \neq 0$, $a^{-1} = \frac{1}{a}$, $a^{-2} = \frac{1}{a^2}$, $a^{-3} = \frac{1}{a^3}$, etc.

Suppose now, $n = \frac{p}{q}$, a rational number. $(q > 0)$

In this case by a^n we shall mean a real number b such that $b^q = a^p$.

We remark that in case n is irrational number then a^n is defined with certain restrictions imposed on a. The rigorous definition of a^n when n is irrational is, however, beyond the scope of this book.

2. DEFINITION

Let a, x and y be real numbers such that $a^x = y$, then y is called the *power* of a, x is called *index* and a is called *base*.

For example in 2^4, $3^{1/2}$, $5^{\sqrt{2}}$ indices are 4, $\frac{1}{2}$ and $\sqrt{2}$ respectively whereas bases are 2, 3 and 5.

NOTE: 0^0 is never defined. It is an indeterminate quantity.

3. LAWS OF INDICES

If m and n are integers, then

(*i*) $a^m \times a^n = a^{m+n}$ (*ii*) $(a^m)^n = a^{mn}$

(*iii*) $\frac{a^m}{a^n} = a^{m-n}$ (*iv*) $(ab)^m = a^m b^m$

Proof (i) Several cases arise

Case I. $m > 0$ and $n > 0$

We have $a^m \times a^n = (a \times a \times \ldots \times m \text{ times}) \times (a \times a \times \ldots n \text{ times})$

$$= a \times a \times a \times \ldots (m + n) \text{ times}$$

$$= a^{m+n}$$

Case II. $m < 0$ and $n < 0$

We can write $m = -k$ and $n = -l$

where $k > 0$ and $l > 0$.

Then $a^m \times a^n = a^{-k} \times a^{-l}$

$$= \frac{1}{a^k} \times \frac{1}{a^l} = \frac{1}{a^k \times a^l}$$

$$= \frac{a}{a^{k+l}} \qquad \text{by first case}$$

$$= a^{-(k+l)} = a^{-k-l} = a^{m+n}$$

Case III. $m > 0$ and $n < 0$

Put $n = -l$ where $l > 0$

Then $a^m \times a^n = a^m \times a^{-l} = a^m \times \frac{1}{a^l}$

If $m = l$, we get $a^m \times a^n = a^m \times \frac{1}{a^m} = 1 = a^0 = a^{m-l} = a^{m+n}$

If $m > l$ then

$$a^m \times \frac{1}{a^l} = \left(a \times \frac{1}{a}\right) \times \left(a \times \frac{1}{a}\right) \times \ldots l \text{ times}$$

$$\times [a \times a \times \ldots (m - l) \text{ times}]$$

$$= (1 \times 1 \times \ldots l \text{ times}) \times a^{m-l}$$

$$= a^{m-l} = a^{m+n}$$

If $m < l$ then $a^m \times \frac{1}{a^l}$

$$= \left(a \times \frac{1}{a}\right) \times \left(a \times \frac{1}{a}\right) \times \ldots m \text{ times}$$

$$\times \left[\frac{1}{a} \times \frac{1}{a} \times \ldots (l - m) \text{ times}\right]$$

$$= (1 \times 1 \times \ldots m \text{ times}) \times \frac{1}{a^{l-m}}$$

$$= \frac{1}{a^{l-m}} = a^{m-l} = a^{m+n}$$

Class IV. $m<0$ and $n>0$

This case is similar to Case III and can be proved by interchanging roles of m and n.

REMARK: The case when one of m and n is zero or both are zero are left for the reader.

(*ii*) Let $m, n>0$ then $(a^m)^n = a^m \times a^m \times \ldots n$ times

$= (a \times a \times \ldots m$ times$) \times (a \times a \times \ldots m$ times$) \times \ldots n$ times

$= a \times a \times \ldots mn$ times

$= a^{mn}$

In case $m>0,\ n<0$ put $n=-l$, where $l>0$

Then $$a(^m)^n = (a^m)^{-l} = \frac{1}{(a^m)^l} = \frac{1}{a^{ml}} = a^{-ml}$$

$$= a^m(^{-l}) - a^{mn}$$

In case $m>0$ and $n=0$, we get $(a^m)^n = (a^m)^0 = 1$ (by definition)

Also $$a^{mn} = a^{m \cdot 0} = a^0 = 1$$

Hence $$(a^m)^n = a^{mn}$$

Other cases can be treated on similar lines.

(*iii*) $$\frac{a^m}{a^n} = a^m \times \frac{1}{a^n} = a^m \times a^{-n} = a^{m+(-n)} = a^{m-n}$$

(*iv*) Let $m>0$ then

$(ab)^m = ab \times ab \times ab \times \ldots m$ times

$= (a \times a \times a \times \ldots m$ times$) \times (b \times b \times .. m$ times$) = a^m b^m$.

If $m=0$ then $(ab)^m = 1 = a^0 b^0 = a^m b^m$

If $m<0$, put $m=-l,\ l>0$

Then $(ab)^m = \frac{1}{(ab)^l} = \frac{1}{a^l b^l} = a^{-l} b^{-l} = a^m b^m$.

The above laws also hold for rational indices. In fact they hold for real indices too. The proof for rational indices is indicated below, while for the proof of the latter case, the reader is referred to any book on advanced real analysis.

Consider a^r and a^s where $r = \frac{p}{q}$ and $s = \frac{m}{n}$ with p, m, q, n integers and $q, n>0$

Let $a^r = b$ and $a^s = c$

Then by definition $b^q = a^p$ and $c^n = a^m$

Now $c^{nq} = a^{mq}$ and $b^{nq} = a^{np}$

$$\Rightarrow \quad b^{nr} \times c^{nq} = a^{mq} \times c^{np} = a^{mq+np}$$

$$\Rightarrow \quad (bc)^{nq} = a^{nq+np}$$

$$\Rightarrow \quad bc = a^{\frac{mq+np}{nq}}$$

$$\Rightarrow \quad a^r \cdot a^s = a^{\left(\frac{m}{n}+\frac{p}{q}\right)} = a^{r+s}$$

In a similar fashion other laws of indices can be proved for rational indices.

Finally, we state another imortant law of indices, which goes like if *a, x, y are real numbers such that* $a \neq 0$ *then* $a^x = a^y$ *implies* either $a = 1$ or $x = y$.

Example 1. *Simplify* $\dfrac{x^{m+2n} \,.\, x^{3m-8n}}{x^{5m-6n}}$.

Solution. $$\frac{x^{m+2n} \,.\, x^{3m-8n}}{x^{5m-6n}} = x^{m+2n+3m-8n-(5m-6n)}$$

$$= x^{4m-6n-5m+6n}$$

$$= x^{-m}$$

$$= \frac{1}{x^m}.$$

Example 2. *Simplify* $\left(\dfrac{81}{256}\right)^{-5/4}$.

Solution. $$\left(\frac{81}{256}\right)^{-5/4} = \left(\frac{3^4}{2^8}\right)^{-5/4}$$

$$= \frac{(3^{4x})^{-5/4}}{(2^8)^{-5/4}} = \frac{3^{-5}}{2^{-10}}$$

$$= \frac{2^{10}}{3^5} = \frac{1024}{243}.$$

Example 3. *If* $a = b^c$, $b = c^a$, *and* $c = a^b$, *show that* $abc = 1$.

Solution. $a = b^c = (c^a)^c = c^{ac} = (a^b)^{ac} = a^{abc}$

Suppose $a \neq 1$ $\quad abc = 1$.

In case $a = 1$ we get $c = a^b = 1, b = c^a = 1$

then $\quad abc = 1.1.1 = 1$

Hence $\quad abc = 1.$

Example 4. *If* $a^x = \left(\frac{a}{k}\right)^y = k^m$ *and* $a \neq 1$*, prove that*

$$\frac{1}{x} - \frac{1}{y} = \frac{1}{m}.$$

Solution.
$$a^x = \frac{a^y}{k^y}$$

$$\Rightarrow \quad a^x k^y = a^y$$

$$\Rightarrow \quad k^y = \frac{a^y}{a^x} = a^{y-x}$$

$$\Rightarrow \quad k = (a^{y-x})^{1/y} = a^{y-x/y}$$

$$\Rightarrow \quad k^m = (a^{y-x/y})^m = a^{m(y-z)/y}$$

$$\Rightarrow \quad a^x = a^{m(1-x/y)}$$

$$\Rightarrow \quad x = m\left(1 - \frac{x}{y}\right) \text{ as } a \neq 1$$

$$\Rightarrow \quad \frac{x}{m} = 1 - \frac{x}{y}$$

$$\Rightarrow \quad \frac{1}{m} = \frac{1}{x} - \frac{1}{y}$$

$$\Rightarrow \quad \frac{1}{x} - \frac{1}{y} = \frac{1}{m}.$$

Example 5. *Obtain the simplest value of*

$[1 - \{1 - (1 - x^3)^{-1}\}^{-1}]^{-1/3}$ *when* $x = 1$.

Solution. Now $[1 - \{1 - (1 - x^3)^{-1}\}^{-1}]^{-1/3}$

$$= \left[1 - \frac{1}{1-(1-x^3)^{-1}}\right]^{-1/3}$$

$$= \left[\frac{1-(1-x^3)^{-1}-1}{1-(1-x^3)^{-1}}\right]^{1/3}$$

$$= \left(\frac{-\frac{1}{1-x^3}}{1-\frac{1}{1-x^3}}\right)^{-1/3} = \left(\frac{1}{x^3}\right)^{-1/3} = (x^3)^{1/3} = x = 1.$$

Example 6. *If* $x = 3^{2/3} + 3^{-2/3}$, *show that*

$$9x^3 - 27x = 82$$

Solution. $x = 3^{2/3} + 3^{-2/3}$

$\Rightarrow$ $x^3 = (3^{2/3} + 3^{-2/3})^3$

$$= (3^{2/3})^3 + (3^{-2/3})^3 + 3(3^{2/3})(3^{-2/3})(3^{2/3} + 3^{-2/3})$$

$$= 3^2 + 3^{-2} + 3x = 9 + \frac{1}{9} + 3x = \frac{82}{9} + 3x$$

$\Rightarrow$ $9x^3 - 27x = 82.$

Example 7. *Obtain the simplest value of*

$$\frac{(2^{2n} - 3.2^{2n-2})(3^n - 2.3^{n-2})}{3^{n-4}(4^{n+3} - 2^{2n})}$$

Solution. Given expression

$$= \frac{2^{2n-2}[2^{2n-(2n-2)} - 3]3^{n-2}[3^{n-(n-2)} - 2]}{3^{n-4}[(2^2)^{n+8} - 2^{2n}]}$$

$$= \frac{2^{2n-2}3^{n-2}(2^2 - 3)(3^2 - 2)}{3^{n-4}(2^{2n+6} - 2^{2n})}$$

$$= \frac{2^{2n-2}3^2 \cdot (1)(7)}{2^{2n}(2^6 - 1)} = \frac{3^2}{2^2}\frac{7}{(64-1)} = \frac{9}{4}\frac{7}{63} = \frac{1}{4}.$$

Example 8. *Find the value of*

$$\frac{(.3)^{1/3}\left(\frac{1}{27}\right)^{1/4}(9)^{1/6}(.81)^{2/3}}{(.9)^{2/3}(3)^{-1/2}\left(\frac{1}{3}\right)^{-2}(243)^{-1/4}}$$

Solution. Given expression

$$= \frac{\left(\frac{3}{10}\right)^{1/3}\left(\frac{1}{3^3}\right)^{1/4}(3^2)^{1/6}\left(\frac{3^4}{10^2}\right)^{2/3}}{\left(\frac{3^2}{10}\right)^{2/3}\left(\frac{1}{3}\right)^{1/2}\left(\frac{1}{3}\right)^{-2}(3^5)^{-1/4}}$$

$$= \frac{3^{\frac{1}{3} - \frac{3}{4} + \frac{1}{3} + \frac{8}{3} - \frac{4}{3} + \frac{1}{2} - 2 + \frac{5}{4}}}{10^{\frac{1}{3} + \frac{4}{3} - \frac{2}{3}}}$$

$$= \frac{3^{\frac{1+1+8-4}{3} + \frac{1}{4}(-3+2+5) - 2}}{10^{\frac{1+4-2}{3}}} = \frac{3^{2+1-2}}{10^1} = \frac{3}{10}.$$

Example 9. *Find x, if* $x^{x\sqrt{x}} = (x\sqrt{x})^x$ *where x is a positive real number.*

Solution. $x^{x \cdot x^{1/2}} = (x \cdot x^{1/2})^x$

$\Rightarrow$ $(x)^{x^{3/2}} = (x^{3/2})^x = x^{3x/2}$

Let $x \neq 1$

then $x^{3/2} = \dfrac{3x}{2}$

$x\,(2x^{1/2} - 3) = 0$

$\Rightarrow$ $x = 0$ or $x^{1/2} = 3/2 \Rightarrow x = 9/4$

Clearly x cannot be zero, otherwise given expressions will be indeterminate.

Hence $x = \dfrac{9}{4}$ or 1.

Example 10. *Show that* $\dfrac{3.2^{n+1} + 2^n}{2^{n+2} - 2^{n-1}} = 2.$

Solution.

$$\text{LHS} = \frac{2^n(3\cdot 2 + 1)}{2^{n-1}[2^{n+2-(n-1)} - 1]}$$

$$= \frac{2^n(7)}{2^{n-1}(2^3 - 1)} = \frac{2\cdot 7}{7} = 2 = \text{RHS}.$$

Example 11. *Show that*

$$\frac{1}{1 + x^{a-b} + x^{a-c}} + \frac{1}{1 + x^{b-c} + x^{b-a}} + \frac{1}{1 + x^{c-a} + x^{a-b}} = 1.$$

Solution.

$$\text{LHS} = \frac{x^{-a}}{x^{-a}(1 + x^{a-b} + x^{a-c})} + \frac{x^{-b}}{x^{-b}(1 + x^{b-c} + x^{b-a})} + \frac{x^{-c}}{x^{-c}(1 + x^{c-a} + x^{c-b})}$$

$$= \frac{x^{-a}}{x^{-a} + x^{-b} + x^{-c}} + \frac{x^{-b}}{x^{-a} + x^{-b} + x^{-c}} + \frac{x^{-c}}{x^{-a} + x^{-b} + x^{-c}}$$

$$= \frac{x^{-a} + x^{-b} + x^{-c}}{x^{-a} + x^{-b} + x^{-c}} = 1.$$

Example 12. *If* $a + b + c = 0$, *simplify* $x^{a^2b^{-1}c^{-1}}\, x^{a^{-1}b^2c^{-1}}\, x^{a^{-1}b^{-1}c^2}$

Solution.

$$\text{LHS} = x^{a^2b^{-1}c^{-1} + a^{-1}b^2c^{-1} + a^{-1}b^{-1}c^2}$$

$$= x^{\frac{a^2}{bc} + \frac{b^2}{ac} + \frac{c^2}{ab}}$$

$$= x^{\frac{a^3+b^3+c^3}{abc}} = x^{\frac{a^3+b^3+c^3-3abc+3abc}{abc}} = x^{\frac{3abc}{abc}}$$

Since $a^3 + b^3 + c^3 - 3abc$

$$= (a + b + c)(a^2 + b^2 + c^2 - ab - bc - ca) = 0,$$

so LHS $= x^3$.

Example 13. *Simplify*

$$\frac{1}{x^b + x^{-c} + 1} + \frac{1}{x^c + x^{-a} + 1} + \frac{1}{x^a + x^{-b} + 1}$$

given that $a + b + c = 0$.

Solution. $\dfrac{1}{x^b + x^{-c} + 1} + \dfrac{1}{x^c + x^{-a} + 1} + \dfrac{1}{x^a + x^{-b} + 1}$

$$= \frac{x^c}{x^{b+c} + 1 + x^c} + \frac{1}{x^c + x^{-a} + 1} + \frac{x^{-a}}{1 + x^{-a-b} + x^{-a}}$$

But $b+c = -a$ and $-a-b = c$

So given expression

$$= \frac{x^c}{x^{-a} + 1 + x^c} + \frac{1}{x^c + x^{-a} + 1} + \frac{x^{-a}}{1 + x^c + x^{-a}}$$

$$= \frac{x^c + 1 + x^{-a}}{x^{-a} + 1 + x^c} = 1.$$

Example 14. *If* $x = \left[a + \sqrt{a^2 + b^3}\right]^{1/3} + \left[a - \sqrt{a^2 + b^3}\right]^{1/3}$ *show that* $x^3 + 3bx - 2a = 0$.

Solution. $x^3 = a + \sqrt{a^2 + b^3} + a - \sqrt{a^2 + b^3} + 3[a^2 - (a^2 + b^3)]^{1/3}x$

$= 2a + 3(-b^3)^{1/3}x = 2a - 3bx$

$\Rightarrow \quad x^3 + 3bx - 2a = 0.$

Example 15. *Solve* $2^{x+y+z} = 8^{x+z-y}$

$5^{3y+2} = (25)^{x+z}$

and $3^{2x+2z+y} = 9^{3x+y}$.

Solution. $2^{x+y+z} = 8^{x+z-y} = (2^3)^{x+z-y} = 2^{3x+3z-3y}$

$\Rightarrow \quad x + y + z = 3x + 3z - 3y$

$\Rightarrow \quad 2x + 2z = 4y \Rightarrow x + z = 2y$ ...(1)

Further $5^{3y+z} = (5^2)^{x+z} = 5^{2x+2z}$

$\Rightarrow \quad 2x + 2z = 3y + 2$

$\Rightarrow \quad 4y = 3y + 2$ by (1)

$\Rightarrow \quad y = 2$ so $x + z = 4$

$$\text{Lastly} \quad 3^{2x+2z+y} = (3^2)^{3x+y} = 3^{6x+2y}$$

$$\Rightarrow \quad 6x+2y = 2x+2z+y$$

$$\Rightarrow \quad 4x+y = 2z \Rightarrow 4x+2=2z$$

$$\Rightarrow \quad 2x-z = 1$$

$$\text{Now} \quad x+z = 4 \quad \text{and} \quad 2x-z=-1$$

$$\Rightarrow \quad 3x = 3 \Rightarrow x=1 \quad \text{and} \quad z=4-x=3$$

$$\text{Hence} \quad x = 1, \quad y=2, \quad z=3.$$

Example 16. *If* $\frac{x}{y} = \frac{z}{w}$, *show that*

$$\frac{x^m + y^m + z^m + w^m}{x^{-m} + y^{-m} + z^{-m} + w^{-m}} = (xyzw)^{m/2}$$

Solution. Let $\frac{x}{y} = \frac{z}{w} = k$, say

Then $x = yk, z = wk,$

Now

$$\frac{x^m + y^m + z^m + w^m}{x^{-m} + y^{-m} + z^{-m} + w^{-m}} = \frac{y^m k^m + y^m + w^m k^m + w^m}{y^{-m}k^{-m} + y^{-m} + w^{-m}k^{-m} + w^{-m}}$$

$$= \frac{(y^m + w^m)(k^m + 1)}{(y^{-m} + w^{-m})(k^{-m} + 1)}$$

$$= \frac{(y^m + w^m)(k^m + 1)}{\left(\frac{1}{y^m} + \frac{1}{w^m}\right)\left(\frac{1}{k^m} + 1\right)} = k^m y^m w^m$$

Also $(xyzw)^{m/2} = (yky\,wkw)^{m/2} = (y^2k^2w^2)^{m/2} = y^m k^m w^m$

Hence the required result follows.

Example 17. *If* $2^x = 4^y = 8^z$ *and* $\frac{1}{2x} + \frac{1}{4y} + \frac{1}{8z} = \frac{22}{7}$, *show that* $x = \frac{7}{16}, y = \frac{7}{32}$ *and* $z = \frac{7}{48}$.

Solution. $2^x = 4^y \Rightarrow 2^x = 2^{2y} \Rightarrow x = 2y \Rightarrow y = \frac{x}{2}$

Also $2^x = 8^z \Rightarrow 2^x = 2^{3z} \Rightarrow x = 3z \Rightarrow z = \frac{x}{3}$

$$\text{Hence} \quad \frac{1}{2x} + \frac{1}{4y} + \frac{1}{8z} = \frac{22}{7}$$

$$\Rightarrow \quad \frac{1}{2x} + \frac{1}{2x} + \frac{1}{\frac{8x}{3}} = \frac{22}{7}$$

$$\Rightarrow \quad \frac{1}{x}+\frac{3}{8x}=\frac{22}{7} \quad \Rightarrow \quad \frac{11}{8x}=\frac{22}{7} \quad \Rightarrow \quad x=\frac{7}{16}$$

Then $\quad y=\frac{x}{2}=\frac{7}{32}$ and $z=\frac{x}{3}=\frac{7}{48}$.

EXERCISES

1. Simplify

(*i*) $(x^{-3/4})8$ (*ii*) $\left(\sqrt[6]{x^9y^{-8}}\right)^3$

(*iii*) $\sqrt[3]{a^6b^{-2}c^{-4}}\times\sqrt[4]{a^{-6}b^4c^3}$ (*iv*) $\left(\frac{a^{-1}b^2}{a^2b^{-4}}\right)^7\div\left(\frac{a^2b^{-5}}{a^{-2}b^3}\right)^{-5}$

(*v*) $\frac{x^{4/7}\cdot\sqrt[5]{x^3}\,\sqrt[7]{x^3}}{\sqrt[8]{x^{-3}}\cdot\sqrt[5]{y^5x^8}}\cdot\frac{y^2}{(x^{1/8})^3}$

2. Evaluate: (*i*) $\frac{35(27)^3\,9^4}{3(81)^4}$ (*ii*) $\frac{\sqrt[3]{(343)^{-2}}}{\sqrt[5]{(32)^{-3}}}$

(*iii*) $\left(\frac{5^{-1}7^2}{5^2\,7^{-4}}\right)^{7/2}\div\left(\frac{5^3\cdot7^{-5}}{5^{-2}\,7^3}\right)^{-5/2}$ (*iv*) $[\sqrt{3\times5^{-3}}\div\sqrt[3]{3^{-1}}\sqrt{5}]\,(\sqrt[6]{3\times5^6})$

(*v*) $\frac{3^{-3}\times6^2\times\sqrt{48}}{5^2\times\sqrt[3]{\frac{1}{25}}\times(15)^{-4/3}\times(3)^{1/3}}$

3. Show that if $\frac{9/3^2(3^{-n})^{-1}-(27)^n}{3^{3m}\cdot2^3}=\frac{1}{27}$ then $m-n=1$.

4. Prove that

(*i*) $\frac{16(32)^m-2^{3m-2}4^{m+1}}{15.2^{m-1}(16)^m}-\frac{5^m}{\sqrt{5^{2m}}}=1$

(*ii*) $\left[\frac{(9^{n+1/4})\sqrt{3\times3^n}}{3\sqrt{3^{-n}}}\right]^{1/n}=27.$

5. Prove $\left(\frac{q+r}{x^{r-p}}\right)^{\frac{1}{p-q}}\times\left(\frac{r+p}{x^{p-q}}\right)^{\frac{1}{q-r}}\times\left(\frac{p+q}{x^{q-r}}\right)^{\frac{1}{r-p}}=1$

6. (*i*) If $x=3^{1/3}+3^{-1/3}$ prove that $3x^3-9x=10$.

(*ii*) If $(2.381)^x=(.2381)^y=10^z$ prove that

$\frac{1}{x}=\frac{1}{y}+\frac{1}{z}$.

7. If $\frac{x^{n+1}}{a^n}=\frac{y^{n+1}}{b^n}=\frac{z^{n+1}}{c^n}=a+b+c$.

Prove that $\left(x^{\frac{n+1}{n}} + y^{\frac{n+1}{n}} + z^{\frac{n+1}{n}}\right)^{\frac{n+1}{n}} = a + b + c.$

8. If $a^x = b^y = c^z = d^w$ and $ab = cd$, show that

$$\frac{1}{x}+\frac{1}{y}=\frac{1}{z}+\frac{1}{w}$$

9. If $x = (\sqrt{2}+1)^{1/3} - (\sqrt{2}-1)^{1/3}$, show that $x^3 + 3x = 2$.

10. If $x = 3^{1/4} + 3^{-1/4}$, $y = 3^{1/4} - 3^{-1/4}$, prove that $3(x^2 + y^2)^2 = 64$.

11. Simplify $[1 - \{1 - (1 - a^2)^{-1}\}^{-1}]^{-1/2}$.

12. If $a = xy^{p-1}$, $b = xy^{q-1}$, $c = xy^{r-1}$.

Prove that $a^{q-r} \times b^{r-p} \times c^{p-q} = 1$.

13. If $2^x = 3^y = 6^{-z}$ show that $\frac{1}{x}+\frac{1}{y}+\frac{1}{z} = 0$.

14. Simplify $(a + b + c)(a^{-1} + b^{-1} + c^{-1}) - a^{-1}b^{-1}c^{-1}(a + b)(b + c)(c + a)$.

15. Solve $a^x a^{y+1} = a^7$ and $a^{2x}a^{3y+5} = 9^z$ (where $a \neq 1, 0$).

16. Solve $a^{x-3}a^{y+2} = a^2a^x$ and $a^x a^y = a^4$ (where $a \neq 0, 1$).

17. Solve $(\sqrt{a})^{x+y} = (\sqrt[3]{a})^{y+z-1}$

$(\sqrt[3]{b})^{x+z-2} = (\sqrt[5]{b})^{y+z}$ and $(\sqrt[4]{c})^{y} = (\sqrt[7]{c})^{x+y+z}$

[It is given that $abc(a - 1)(b - 1)(c - 1) \neq 0$].

18. If $3^x = 5^y = (75)z$ show that $xz = z(2x + y)$.

19. If $pqr = 1$, prove that $\frac{1}{1+p+q^{-1}}+\frac{1}{1+q+r^{-1}}+\frac{1}{1+r+p^{-1}} = 1$.

20. Prove that $\frac{(81)^n 3^5 - 3^{4n-1}(243)}{9^{2n}3^3} - \frac{4.3^n}{3^{n+1}-3^n} = 4$.

21. Solve $4^x 2^y = 128$ and $3^{3x+2y} = 9x^y$.

ANSWERS

1. (*i*) $\frac{1}{x^6}$ (*ii*) $\frac{y^4}{\sqrt{x^9}}$ (*iii*) $a^{1/2}b^{2/3}c^{2/3}$ (*iv*) a^4b^2 (*v*) y

2. (*i*) 243 (*ii*) $\frac{8}{49}$ (*iii*) 175 (*iv*) $\frac{3}{5}$ (*v*) $16\sqrt{3}$

11. a 14. 1 15. $x = 3, y = 3$

16. $x = 1, y = 3$ 17. $x = -1\frac{1}{3}, y = -9\frac{1}{3}, z = -5\frac{2}{3}$

21. $x = 2$ or $\frac{7}{4}$, $y = 3$ or $\frac{41}{7}$.

4. SURDS

Consider the numbers, $\sqrt{2}, \sqrt[3]{3}, \sqrt[4]{16}$. Now $\sqrt{2}, \sqrt[3]{3}$ are not rational numbers whereas $\sqrt[4]{16} = 2$ is a rational number. The numbers of the type such as $\sqrt{2}, \sqrt[3]{3}$ are called *surds*. We now define the concept formally.

5. DEFINITION

A surd is an irrational root of a rational number.

Thus if a is a surd, then $a = \sqrt[n]{b}$ for some rational number b such that a itself is an irrational number.

When $a = \sqrt[n]{b}$ is a surd, n is called *order* of a and b is called *radicand* of a.

Surds of second, third, fourth and higher orders are respectively called *quadratic, cubic, quartic* and *quintic.*

Example of surds are $\sqrt{\frac{2}{3}}, \sqrt[3]{7}, \sqrt[4]{\frac{1}{4}}$ etc. A surd is called *compound surd* if it has coefficient different from ± 1, otherwise it is called a *simple surd*. Thus $5\sqrt{2}, -3\sqrt{7}, 4\sqrt[5]{2}$ are compound surds whereas $\sqrt[11]{\frac{1}{2}}$, $\sqrt[9]{6}$ are simple surds.

REMARK: Every compound surd can be converted into a simple surd.

Let $c\sqrt[n]{b}$ be a compound surd. We can write it as $\sqrt[n]{bc^n}$ which is a simple surd.

6. SIMILAR SURDS

Surds are called *similar* if their reduced (or simplified) forms contain same surds.

For example $\sqrt{45}$ and $\sqrt{80}$ are similar surds; since $\sqrt{45} = 3\sqrt{5}$ and $\sqrt{80} = 4\sqrt{5}$.

Similar surds can be added or subtracted easily, after being reduced to their simplified forms, e.g., $\sqrt{75} + \sqrt{27} = 5\sqrt{3} + 3\sqrt{3} = 8\sqrt{3}$ and $2\sqrt{128} - \sqrt{162} = 16\sqrt{2} - 9\sqrt{2} = 7\sqrt{2}$.

Surds of same order can be multiplied or divided.

Since $\quad \sqrt[n]{a} \times \sqrt[n]{b} = \sqrt[n]{ab}$ and $\sqrt[n]{a} \div \sqrt[n]{b} = \sqrt[n]{\frac{a}{b}}$.

7. RATIONALIZATION

If product of two surds is a rational number and if one of them is multiplied by the other then the process of multiplication is called *Rationalization.*

Thus $\sqrt{3}\times\sqrt{3}=3$, so multiplication by $\sqrt{3}$ is rationalization of $\sqrt{3}$.

Similarly $\sqrt{5}-\sqrt{3}$ when multiplied by $\sqrt{5}+\sqrt{3}$ is ratinalized to 2 as $(\sqrt{5}-\sqrt{3})(\sqrt{5}+\sqrt{3})=5-3=2$.

Example 18. *Express as equivalent fraction with rational denominator* $\dfrac{1}{1+\sqrt{2}-\sqrt{3}}$.

Solution. $$\frac{1}{1+\sqrt{2}-\sqrt{3}}=\frac{1}{(1+\sqrt{2})-\sqrt{3}}\cdot\frac{(1+\sqrt{2})+\sqrt{3}}{(1+\sqrt{2})+\sqrt{3}}$$

$$=\frac{1+\sqrt{2}+\sqrt{3}}{(1+\sqrt{2})^2-\sqrt{3}}$$

$$=\frac{1+\sqrt{2}+\sqrt{3}}{2\sqrt{2}}$$

$$=\frac{\sqrt{2}(1+\sqrt{2}+\sqrt{3})}{4}=\frac{\sqrt{2}+2+\sqrt{6}}{4}.$$

Example 19. *If* $x=\dfrac{2\sqrt{24}}{\sqrt{2}+\sqrt{3}}$, *find the value of*

$$\frac{x+\sqrt{8}}{x-\sqrt{8}}+\frac{x+\sqrt{12}}{x-\sqrt{12}}$$

Solution. We have $$x=\frac{2\sqrt{24}}{\sqrt{2}+\sqrt{3}}$$

$$=\frac{4\sqrt{6}(\sqrt{3}-\sqrt{2})}{(\sqrt{3}+\sqrt{2})(\sqrt{3}-\sqrt{2})}$$

$$=\frac{4\sqrt{6}(\sqrt{3}-\sqrt{2})}{1}$$

$$=4\sqrt{18}-4\sqrt{12}=12\sqrt{2}-8\sqrt{3}$$

Now $$\frac{x+\sqrt{8}}{x-\sqrt{8}}=\frac{x+2\sqrt{2}}{x-2\sqrt{2}}=\frac{12\sqrt{2}-8\sqrt{3}+2\sqrt{2}}{12\sqrt{2}-8\sqrt{3}-2\sqrt{2}}$$

$$=\frac{14\sqrt{2}-8\sqrt{3}}{10\sqrt{2}-8\sqrt{3}}=\frac{7\sqrt{2}-4\sqrt{3}}{5\sqrt{2}-4\sqrt{3}}$$

$$= \frac{(7\sqrt{2} - 4\sqrt{3})(5\sqrt{2} + 4\sqrt{3})}{25 \times 2 - 16 \times 3}$$

$$= \frac{70 - 48 + 18\sqrt{6}}{50 - 48} = \frac{22 + 8\sqrt{6}}{2}$$

$$= 11 + 4\sqrt{6}$$

Again $$\frac{x + \sqrt{12}}{x - \sqrt{12}} = \frac{12\sqrt{2} - 8\sqrt{3} + 2\sqrt{3}}{12\sqrt{2} - 8\sqrt{3} - 2\sqrt{3}}$$

$$= \frac{12\sqrt{2} - 6\sqrt{3}}{12\sqrt{2} - 10\sqrt{3}}$$

$$= \frac{6\sqrt{2} - 3\sqrt{3}}{6\sqrt{2} - 5\sqrt{3}}$$

$$= \frac{(6\sqrt{2} - 3\sqrt{3})(6\sqrt{2} + 5\sqrt{3})}{36 \times 2 - 25 \times 3}$$

$$= \frac{72 - 45 + 12\sqrt{6}}{-3}$$

$$= \frac{27 + 12\sqrt{6}}{-3}$$

$$= -9 - 4\sqrt{6}$$

Hence the required expression $= (11 + 4\sqrt{6}) - (9 + 4\sqrt{6}) = 2.$

Example 20. *If* $x = \frac{\sqrt{3} - \sqrt{2}}{\sqrt{3} + \sqrt{2}}$, $y = \frac{\sqrt{3} + \sqrt{2}}{\sqrt{3} - \sqrt{2}}$, *find the value of* $3x^2 - 5xy + 3y^2$.

Solution. $x = \frac{(\sqrt{3} - \sqrt{2})^2}{1} = 5 - 2\sqrt{6}$

and $y = \frac{(\sqrt{3} + \sqrt{2})^2}{1} = 5 + 2\sqrt{6}$

Then $$3x^2 - 5xy + 3y^2 = 3(x^2 + y^2) - 5xy$$

$$= 3[(5 - 2\sqrt{6})^2 + (5 + 2\sqrt{6})^2] - 5(5 - 2\sqrt{6})(5 + 2\sqrt{6})$$

$$= 6[25 + (2\sqrt{6})^2] - 5 \cdot (25 - 24)$$

$$= 6 \cdot 49 - 5 = 294 - 5 = 289.$$

Example 21. *Simplify* $\frac{7+3\sqrt{5}}{3+\sqrt{5}}+\frac{7-3\sqrt{5}}{3-\sqrt{5}}$.

Solution.

$$\frac{7+3\sqrt{5}}{3+\sqrt{5}}=\frac{(7+3\sqrt{5})(3-\sqrt{5})}{9-5}$$

$$=\frac{21-15+2\sqrt{5}}{4}=\frac{3+\sqrt{5}}{2}$$

Again

$$\frac{7-3\sqrt{5}}{3-\sqrt{5}}=\frac{(7-3\sqrt{5})(3+\sqrt{5})}{9-5}$$

$$=\frac{21-15-2\sqrt{5}}{4}=\frac{3-\sqrt{5}}{2}$$

Hence required expression $=\frac{6}{2}=3$.

Example 22. *If* $x=\sqrt{3}+\frac{1}{\sqrt{3}}$. *Calculate the value of*

$$\left(x-\frac{\sqrt{126}}{\sqrt{42}}\right)\left(x-\frac{1}{x-2\frac{\sqrt{3}}{3}}\right)$$

correct to two places of decimal.

Solution.

$$x=\sqrt{3}+\frac{1}{\sqrt{3}}=\frac{4}{\sqrt{3}}$$

Also

$$x-\frac{\sqrt{126}}{\sqrt{42}}=x-\sqrt{3}=\sqrt{3}+\frac{1}{\sqrt{3}}-\sqrt{3}=\frac{1}{\sqrt{3}}$$

and

$$x-\frac{1}{x-\frac{2}{\sqrt{3}}}=x-\frac{1}{x-\frac{2}{\sqrt{3}}}$$

$$=x-\frac{1}{\frac{2}{\sqrt{3}}}=x-\frac{\sqrt{3}}{2}=\frac{4}{\sqrt{3}}-\frac{\sqrt{3}}{2}=\frac{5}{2\sqrt{3}}$$

Hence given expression

$$=\frac{1}{\sqrt{3}}\cdot\frac{5}{2\sqrt{3}}$$

$$=\frac{5}{6}=.8333$$

$= .83$ correct to two decimal places.

Example 23. *If* $x = \dfrac{5-\sqrt{21}}{2}$ *prove that*

$$\left(x^3+\frac{1}{x^3}\right)-5\left(x^2+\frac{1}{x^2}\right)+\left(x+\frac{1}{x}\right)=0$$

Solution. $\dfrac{1}{x} = \dfrac{2}{5-\sqrt{21}} = \dfrac{2(5+\sqrt{21})}{25-21} = \dfrac{5+\sqrt{21}}{2}$

Thus $\quad x+\dfrac{1}{x} = \dfrac{10}{2} = 5 \qquad$ ...(1)

$$x^2+\frac{1}{x^2} = \left(x+\frac{1}{x}\right)^2 - 2 = 25-2 = 23 \qquad ...(2)$$

Also $\quad x^3+\dfrac{1}{x^3} = \left(x+\dfrac{1}{x}\right)^3 - 3\left(x+\dfrac{1}{x}\right)$

$$= 125-15 = 110 \qquad ...(3)$$

Since $110 - 5.23 + 5 = 0$, the result follows from (1), (2) and (3).

Example 24. *It is given that* $\sqrt{3} = 1.732$ *and*

$\sqrt{5} = 2.236$, *evaluate* $\dfrac{\sqrt{5}+\sqrt{3}}{4+\sqrt{15}}$.

Solution. $\dfrac{\sqrt{5}+\sqrt{3}}{4+\sqrt{15}} = \dfrac{(\sqrt{5}+\sqrt{3})(4-\sqrt{15})}{16-15}$

$$= 4\sqrt{5}+4\sqrt{3}-\sqrt{75}-\sqrt{45}$$

$$= 4\sqrt{5}+4\sqrt{3}-5\sqrt{3}-3\sqrt{5}$$

$$= \sqrt{5}-\sqrt{3} = 2.236-1.732 = 0.504.$$

8. QUADRATIC MIXED SURDS AND THEIR PROPERTIES

By a quadratic mixed surd we mean a surd of the type $a+\sqrt{b}$. Thus $1+\sqrt{5}$, $\sqrt{3}-1$ are quadratic mixed surds.

Property 1. $a+\sqrt{b} = 0$ *if and only if* $a = b = 0$.

Proof. $a+\sqrt{b} = 0 \Rightarrow a = -\sqrt{b} \Rightarrow a^2 = b$.

But b is not a square of a rational number otherwise $\sqrt{b}$ will be no more a surd! (if $b \neq 0$)

So $\qquad b = 0$ and hence $a = 0$.

Property 2. If $a + \sqrt{b} = \sqrt{c}$ *then* $a = 0$ *and* $b = c$.

Proof. $a + \sqrt{b} = \sqrt{c} \Rightarrow a^2 + b + 2a\sqrt{b} = c.$

If $a \neq 0$ then $\sqrt{b} = \dfrac{c - a^2 - b}{2a}$, a rational number which is absurd, so $a = 0$.

Then $\sqrt{b} = \sqrt{c} \Rightarrow b = c.$

Property 3. If $a + \sqrt{b} = c + \sqrt{d}$ *then* $a = c$ *and* $b = d$.

Proof. $a + \sqrt{b} = c + \sqrt{d}$

$\Rightarrow$ $(a - c) + \sqrt{b} = \sqrt{d}$

$\Rightarrow$ $a - c = 0$ and $b = d$ by Property 2

Hence $a = c$ and $b = d$

Property 4. If $\sqrt{(a + \sqrt{b})} = \sqrt{x} + \sqrt{y}$

Then $\sqrt{(a - \sqrt{b})} = \pm(\sqrt{x} - \sqrt{y})$

Proof. Let $\sqrt{(a + \sqrt{b})} = \sqrt{x} + \sqrt{y}$

Then $a + \sqrt{b} = x + y + 2\sqrt{xy}$

$\Rightarrow$ $a = x + y$ and $b = 4xy$ by Property 3.

So $a - \sqrt{b} = x + y - \sqrt{4xy}$

$= x + y - 2\sqrt{xy} = (\sqrt{x} - \sqrt{y})^2$

In other words $\sqrt{(a - \sqrt{b})} = \pm(\sqrt{x} - \sqrt{y})$.

9. TO FIND SQUARE ROOT OF A QUADRATIC MIXED SURD

Let $\sqrt{(a + \sqrt{b})} = \sqrt{x} + \sqrt{y}$

Square to obtain $x + y = a$ and $4xy = b$

Then $(x - y)^2 = (x + y)^2 - 4xy = a^2 - b$

We choose + *ve* sign, Adding to $x + y = a$ we get

$$x = \frac{1}{2}(a + \sqrt{a^2 - b}) \quad \text{and} \quad y = \frac{1}{2}(a + \sqrt{a^2 - b})$$

Hence $\sqrt{(a + \sqrt{b})}$ is determined.

REMARK: If we take –*ve* sign, the value of x and y will be interchanged and we shall get second square root of $a + \sqrt{b}$.

We illustrate the above method by means of examples.

Example 25. *Find the square root of* $31 + 4\sqrt{21}$.

Solution. Let $\sqrt{31+4\sqrt{21}} = \sqrt{x} + \sqrt{y}$

Squaring we get $31 + 4\sqrt{21} = x + y + 2\sqrt{xy}$

Then $x + y = 31, xy = 84$

But $(x-y)^2 = (x+y)^2 - 4xy = 961 - 336 = 625$

$\Rightarrow$ $x - y = \pm 25$

As remarked above, we take only +ve sign.

Thus $x = \frac{1}{2}(31 + 25) = 28$

and $y = \frac{1}{2}(31 - 25) = 3.$

Hence $\sqrt{31+4\sqrt{21}} = \pm(\sqrt{28} + \sqrt{3}) = \pm(2\sqrt{7} + \sqrt{3})$

Example 26. *Evaluate* $\sqrt{(3+\sqrt{5})}$

Solution. Let $\sqrt{3+\sqrt{5}} = \sqrt{x} + \sqrt{y}$

$\Rightarrow$ $3 + \sqrt{5} = x + y + 2\sqrt{xy}$

$\Rightarrow$ $x + y = 3, \quad 4xy = 5$

Now $(x-y)^2 = (x+y)^2 - 4xy = 9 - 5 = 4$

$\Rightarrow$ $x - y = 2$

Hence $x = \frac{5}{2}, \quad y = \frac{1}{2}$

Hence $\sqrt{3+\sqrt{5}} = \pm\frac{1}{\sqrt{2}}\sqrt{(5+1)}$

Example 27. *Find the square root of* $\sqrt{32} - \sqrt{24}$.

Solution. $\sqrt{32} - \sqrt{24} = 4\sqrt{2} - 2\sqrt{6} = \sqrt{2}(4 - 2\sqrt{3})$

Then $\sqrt{\sqrt{32} - \sqrt{24}} = 2^{1/4}\sqrt{4 - 2\sqrt{3}}$

Let $\sqrt{4 - 2\sqrt{3}} = \sqrt{x} - \sqrt{y}$

Then $4 - 2\sqrt{3} = x + y - 2\sqrt{xy}$

$\Rightarrow$ $x + y = 4, \quad 4xy = 12$

Now $(x-y)^2 = (x+y)^2 - 4 + y = 16 - 12 = 4$

$\Rightarrow$ $x - y = 2$

Hence $x = 3, \quad y = 1$

Consequently $\sqrt{\sqrt{32} - \sqrt{24}} = \pm 2^{1/4}(\sqrt{3} - 1).$

10. EVALUATION OF CUBIC ROOT

Before discussing the procedure for evaluation of cubic roots of a quadratic mixed surd, we state and prove a useful theorem.

Theorem. If $\sqrt[3]{(a+\sqrt{b})} = x+\sqrt{y}$

then $\sqrt[3]{(a-\sqrt{b})} = x-\sqrt{y}$

Proof. Now $\sqrt[3]{(a+\sqrt{b})} = x+\sqrt{y}$

$$\Rightarrow \quad a+\sqrt{b} = (x+\sqrt{y})^3$$
$$= x^3 + y\sqrt{y} + 3x\sqrt{y}\,(x+\sqrt{y})$$
$$= x^3 + 3xy + y\sqrt{y} + 3x^2\sqrt{y}$$

So $$a = x^3 + 3xy,\ \sqrt{b} = y\sqrt{y} + 3x^2\sqrt{y}$$

Hence $$a-\sqrt{b} = x^3 + 3xy - y\sqrt{y} - 3x^2\sqrt{y}$$
$$= x^3 - y\sqrt{y} - 3x\sqrt{y}\,(x-\sqrt{y})$$
$$= (x-\sqrt{y})^3$$

$$\Rightarrow \quad \sqrt[3]{(a-\sqrt{b})} = x-\sqrt{y}$$

Procedure. Let $\sqrt[3]{(a+\sqrt{b})} = x+\sqrt{y}$

Then $\sqrt[3]{(a-\sqrt{b})} = x-\sqrt{y}$

Multiplying we get $\sqrt[3]{(a^2-\sqrt{b})} = x^2 - y$ ...(1)

Cubing both sides we get

$$a+\sqrt{b} = x^3 + y\sqrt{y} + 3x\sqrt{y}\,(x+\sqrt{y})$$

Using Property 3, we get

$$a = x^3 + 3xy \qquad ...(2)$$

Solving (1) and (2) we get x and y.

We remark that the above procedure is successful if $x^2 - y$ is rational i.e., $a^2 - b$ is a cube of some rational number and also if we can find a root of the cubic by inspection. Otherwise this procedure will lead to certain complexities which we may not be able to resolve so easily.

Example 28. *Evaluate cube root of* $26 - 15\sqrt{3}$.

Solution. Let $\sqrt[3]{26-15\sqrt{3}} = x-\sqrt{y}$ ...(1)

Then $\sqrt[3]{26+15\sqrt{3}} = x+\sqrt{y}$

Multiplying we get

$$\sqrt[3]{676-675} = x^2 - y \text{ or } x^2 - y = 1 \quad ...(2)$$

Further cubing (1) we get

$$26 - 15\sqrt{3} = x^3 - y\sqrt{y} + 3xy - 3x\sqrt{y}$$

$$\Rightarrow \quad x^3 + 3xy = 26$$

or $$x^3 + 3x(x^2 - 1) = 26 \quad \text{or} \quad 4x^3 - 3x - 26 = 0$$

By inspection $x = 2$ is a root of this equation

[as $4.2^3 - 3.2 - 26 = 32 - 6 - 26 = 0$]

Then $$y = x^2 - 1 = 4 - 1 = 3$$

Hence $$\sqrt[3]{26 - 15\sqrt{3}} = 2 - \sqrt{3}.$$

Example 29. *Evaluate* $\sqrt[3]{(54\sqrt{3} + 41\sqrt{5})}$.

Solution. $$54\sqrt{3} + 41\sqrt{5} = \sqrt{3}\left(54 + 41\sqrt{\frac{5}{3}}\right)$$

Let $$\sqrt[3]{54 + 41\sqrt{\frac{5}{3}}} = x + \sqrt{y} \quad ...(1)$$

Then $$\sqrt[3]{54 - 41\sqrt{\frac{5}{3}}} = x - \sqrt{y} \quad ...(2)$$

Multiplying (1) and (2), we get

$$x^2 - y = \sqrt[3]{2916 - 1681 \cdot \frac{5}{3}}$$

$$= \sqrt[3]{\frac{8748 - 8405}{3}}$$

$$= \sqrt[3]{\frac{343}{3}}$$

$$= \frac{7}{\sqrt[3]{3}}$$

Cubing (1), and equating external parts

We get $x^3 + 3xy = 54$

or $$x^3 + 3x\left(x^2 - \frac{7}{3\sqrt{3}}\right) = 54$$

$$\Rightarrow \quad 4x^3 - 7.3^{2/3}x - 54 = 0$$

Now $x = 2.3^{1/3}$ is a solution of this equation [as $4.8.3 - 7.2.3 - 54 = 96 - 42 - 54 = 0$]

Thus $$y = x^2 - \frac{7}{\sqrt[3]{3}}$$

$$= 4.3^{2/3} - \frac{7}{3^{1/3}} = \frac{12-7}{3^{1/3}} = \frac{5}{3^{1/3}}$$

Hence $$\sqrt[3]{54 + 41\sqrt{\frac{5}{3}}} = 2.3^{1/3} + \frac{\sqrt{5}}{3^{1/6}}$$

Consequently

$$\sqrt[3]{54\sqrt{3} + 41\sqrt{5}} = 3^{1/6}(2.3^{1/3} + \sqrt{5.3^{-1.6}}) = \sqrt[2]{3} + \sqrt{5}.$$

Example 30. *Evaluate* $\sqrt[3]{10 + 6\sqrt{3}}$.

Solution. Let $$\sqrt[3]{10 + 6\sqrt{3}} = x + \sqrt{y}$$

Then $$\sqrt[3]{10 - 6\sqrt{3}} = x - \sqrt{y}$$

We get $$\sqrt[3]{100 - 108} = x^2 - y \quad \text{or} \quad x^2 - y = -2$$

and $$10 + 6\sqrt{3} = x^3 + 3xy + y\sqrt{y} + 3x^2\sqrt{y}$$

$\Rightarrow$ $$x^3 + 3xy = 10$$

Then $$x^3 + 3x(x^2 + 2) = 10$$

or $$4x^3 + 6x - 10 = 0 \quad \text{or} \quad 2x^3 + 3x - 5 = 0$$

Clearly $x = 1$ is a root of this equation

Thus $$y = x^2 + 2 = 3$$

Hence $$\sqrt[3]{10 + 6\sqrt{3}} = 1 + \sqrt{3}.$$

Example 31. *Evaluate fourth root of* $56 - 24\sqrt{5}$.

Solution. Let $$\sqrt{56 - 24\sqrt{5}} = \sqrt{x} - \sqrt{y}$$

Then $$56 - 24\sqrt{5} = x + y - 2\sqrt{xy}$$

$\Rightarrow$ $$x + y = 56 \quad \text{and} \quad 4xy = 2880$$

Now $$(x - y)^2 = (x + y)^2 - 4xy$$

$$= 3136 - 2880 = 256$$

$\Rightarrow$ $$x - y = 16$$

Hence $$x = 36 \text{ and } y = 20$$

In other words

$$\sqrt{56 - 24\sqrt{5}} = 6 - 2\sqrt{5}$$

This implies $\sqrt{56-24\sqrt{5}} = \sqrt{6-2\sqrt{5}} = \sqrt{a}-\sqrt{b}$, say

$$6-2\sqrt{5} = a+b-2\sqrt{ab}$$

$\Rightarrow$ $a+b=6$ and $4ab=20$

Again $(a-b)^2 = (a+b)^2-4ab = 36-20=16$

$\Rightarrow$ $a-b=4$

Solving we get $a=5, b=1$

Hence $\sqrt[4]{56-24\sqrt{5}} = \sqrt{5}-1.$

Example 32. *Find the square root of* $16+4\sqrt{10}-2\sqrt{15}-4\sqrt{6}$.

Solution. Let $\sqrt{16+4\sqrt{10}-2\sqrt{15}-4\sqrt{6}} = \sqrt{x}+\sqrt{y}-\sqrt{z}$

Squaring we get

$$16+4\sqrt{10}-2\sqrt{15}-4\sqrt{6} = x+y+z+2\sqrt{xy}-2\sqrt{yz}-2\sqrt{zx}$$

So $x+y+z=16$ ...(1)

$+2\sqrt{xy} = 4\sqrt{10} \Rightarrow 1\sqrt{xy} = \sqrt{40}$ ...(2)

$-2\sqrt{yz} = -2\sqrt{15} \Rightarrow \sqrt{yz} = \sqrt{15}$ ...(3)

and $-2\sqrt{zx} = -4\sqrt{6} \Rightarrow \sqrt{zx} = \sqrt{24}$ ...(4)

Multiplying, (2) (3), (4), we get $xyz = \sqrt{40.15.24} = \sqrt{144000} = 120$

Hence $\sqrt{xyz} = \pm\sqrt{120}$

$\Rightarrow$ $\sqrt{x} = \sqrt{\frac{120}{15}} = \sqrt{8} = 2\sqrt{2} \Rightarrow x=8$

$\sqrt{y} = \sqrt{\frac{120}{24}} = \sqrt{5} \Rightarrow y=5$

$\sqrt{z} = \sqrt{\frac{120}{40}} = \sqrt{3} \Rightarrow z=3$

These values clearly satisfy (1)

Hence $\sqrt{16+4\sqrt{10}-2\sqrt{15}-4\sqrt{6}} = \pm(2\sqrt{2}+\sqrt{5}-\sqrt{3})$

REMARK: We put $\sqrt{a+\sqrt{b}+\sqrt{c}+\sqrt{d}} = \sqrt{x}+\sqrt{y}+\sqrt{z}$ and in case of two negative terms, like $\sqrt{a-\sqrt{b}+\sqrt{c}-\sqrt{d}}$ we put it equal to $\sqrt{x}-\sqrt{y}+\sqrt{z}$.

Example 33. *If* $x = \sqrt{\frac{7+4\sqrt{3}}{7-4\sqrt{3}}}$ *show that* $x^2(x-14)^2 = 1$.

Solution. We have $x = \sqrt{\frac{7+4\sqrt{3}}{7-4\sqrt{3}}} = \sqrt{\frac{(7+4\sqrt{3})^2}{49-48}} = 7+4\sqrt{3}$

and $\qquad x-14 = 7+4\sqrt{3}-14 = 4\sqrt{3}-7$

So
$$\begin{aligned} x^2(x-14)^2 &= (4\sqrt{3}+7)^2(4\sqrt{3}-7)^2 \\ &= \{(4\sqrt{3}+7)(4\sqrt{3}-7)\}^2 \\ &= (48-49)^2 = 1. \end{aligned}$$

Example 34. *Find the value of x, if*

$$\frac{\sqrt{30+8\sqrt{15}}}{\sqrt{5}+\sqrt{3}} = x^{1/4}$$

Solution. We have, on squaring

$$\begin{aligned} x^{1/2} &= \frac{30+8\sqrt{15}}{8+2\sqrt{15}} = \frac{15+4\sqrt{15}}{4+\sqrt{15}} \\ &= \frac{(15+4\sqrt{15})(4-\sqrt{15})}{16-15} \\ &= 60-60+16\sqrt{15}-15\sqrt{15} = \sqrt{15} \end{aligned}$$

$\Rightarrow \qquad x = 15.$

Example 35. *Convert* $\frac{4}{\sqrt[3]{9}-\sqrt[3]{3}+1}$ *into an equivalent fraction with rational denominator.*

Solution.
$$\begin{aligned} \frac{4}{\sqrt[3]{9}-\sqrt[3]{3}+1} &= \frac{4}{3^{2/3}-3^{1/3}+1} \\ &= \frac{4(3^{1/3}+1)}{(3^{1/3})^3+1} = 3^{1/3}+1 \\ &= \sqrt[3]{3}+1 \end{aligned}$$

Example 36. *Evaluate* $\frac{\sqrt{26-15\sqrt{3}}}{5\sqrt{2}-\sqrt{38+5\sqrt{3}}}$.

Solution. To evaluate the given expression we first determine square roots of $26-15\sqrt{3}$ and $38+5\sqrt{3}$.

Let $\sqrt{26-15\sqrt{3}} = \sqrt{x}+\sqrt{y}$ then

$$26-15\sqrt{3} = x+y-2\sqrt{xy}$$

$\Rightarrow$ $x+y = 26, \quad 4xy = 675$

So $(x-y)^2 = (x+y)^2 - 4xy = 676 - 675 = 1$

$\Rightarrow$ $x - y = 1$

$\Rightarrow$ $x = \frac{25}{2}, \quad y = \frac{25}{2}$

Hence $\sqrt{26-15\sqrt{3}} = \frac{1}{\sqrt{2}}(3\sqrt{3}-5)$

Again let $\sqrt{38+5\sqrt{3}} = \sqrt{a}+\sqrt{b}$ then

$$38+5\sqrt{3} = a+b+2\sqrt{ab}$$

$\Rightarrow$ $a+b = 38$ and $4ab = 75$

So $(a-b)^2 = (a+b)^2 - 4ab = 1444 - 75 = 1369$

$\Rightarrow$ $a - b = 37$

This yields that $a = \frac{75}{2}$ and $b = \frac{1}{2}$

Thus $\sqrt{38+5\sqrt{3}} = 5\sqrt{\frac{3}{2}} + \sqrt{\frac{1}{2}} = \frac{1}{\sqrt{2}}(5\sqrt{3}+1)$

$$\text{Hence given expression} = \frac{\frac{1}{\sqrt{2}}(3\sqrt{3}-5)}{5\sqrt{2} - \frac{1}{\sqrt{2}}(5\sqrt{3}+1)}$$

$$= \frac{3\sqrt{3}-5}{10-5\sqrt{3}-1} = \frac{3\sqrt{3}-5}{9-5\sqrt{3}}$$

$$= \frac{(3\sqrt{3}-5)(9+5\sqrt{3})}{81-75}$$

$$= \frac{27\sqrt{3}-25\sqrt{3}-45+45}{6}$$

$$= \frac{2\sqrt{3}}{6} = \frac{1}{\sqrt{3}}.$$

Example 37. *Evaluate* $\dfrac{\sqrt{x^2-1}}{x-\sqrt{x^2-1}}$ *when* $2x = \sqrt{a} + \dfrac{1}{\sqrt{a}}$.

Solution. $2x = \sqrt{a} + \dfrac{1}{\sqrt{a}} \Rightarrow \dfrac{a+1}{\sqrt{a}} \Rightarrow x = \dfrac{a+1}{2\sqrt{a}}$

$$\Rightarrow \qquad x^2 = \frac{a^2+1+2a}{4a}$$

$$x^2 - 1 = \frac{a^2+1+2a}{4a} - 1 = \frac{(a-1)^2}{4a}$$

Then $$\frac{\sqrt{x^2-1}}{x-\sqrt{x^2-1}} = \frac{\dfrac{a-1}{2\sqrt{a}}}{\dfrac{a+1}{2\sqrt{a}} - \dfrac{a-1}{2\sqrt{a}}} = \frac{a-1}{2}.$$

Example 38. *Evaluate* $\dfrac{(4+\sqrt{15})^{3/2} + (4-\sqrt{15})^{3/2}}{(6+\sqrt{35})^{3/2} - (6-\sqrt{35})^{3/2}}$.

Solution. We first determine the values of

$$(4+\sqrt{15})^{1/2} \text{ and } (6+\sqrt{35})^{1/2}$$

Let $\sqrt{4+\sqrt{15}} = 5x + \sqrt{y}$ then $4+\sqrt{15} = x + y + 2\sqrt{xy}$

This gives $x + y = 4$, $4xy = 15 \Rightarrow (x-y)^2 = 16 - 15 = 1. \Rightarrow x - y = 1.$

Hence $x = \dfrac{5}{2}$, $y = \dfrac{3}{2}$ i.e. $\sqrt{4+\sqrt{15}} = \dfrac{1}{\sqrt{2}}(\sqrt{5}+\sqrt{3})$

Again let $\quad \sqrt{6+\sqrt{35}} = \sqrt{a} + \sqrt{b}$

then $\quad 6+\sqrt{35} = a + b + 2\sqrt{ab}$

$\Rightarrow \quad a + b = 6, \quad 4ab = 35$

$\Rightarrow \quad (a-b)^2 = (a+b)^2 - 4ab = 1$

$\Rightarrow \quad a - b = 1, \quad \text{so} \quad a = \dfrac{7}{2}, b = \dfrac{5}{2}$

i.e. $\quad \sqrt{6+\sqrt{35}} = \dfrac{1}{\sqrt{2}}(\sqrt{7}+\sqrt{5})$

$$\text{Given expression} = \frac{\dfrac{1}{2\sqrt{2}}(\sqrt{5}+\sqrt{3})^3 + \dfrac{1}{2\sqrt{2}}(\sqrt{5}-\sqrt{3})^3}{\dfrac{1}{2\sqrt{2}}(\sqrt{7}+\sqrt{5})^3 + \dfrac{1}{2\sqrt{2}}(\sqrt{7}-\sqrt{5})^3}$$

$$= \frac{2[(\sqrt{5})^3 + 3\sqrt{5}(\sqrt{3})^2]}{2[3(\sqrt{7})^2\sqrt{5} + (\sqrt{5})^3]}$$

$$= \frac{5\sqrt{5}+9\sqrt{5}}{21\sqrt{5}+5\sqrt{5}} = \frac{14\sqrt{5}}{26\sqrt{5}} = \frac{7}{13}.$$

Example 39. *Express* $\dfrac{1}{\sqrt{2}+\sqrt{3}+\sqrt{5}}$ *into an equivalent fraction with rational denominator.*

Solution.
$$\frac{1}{\sqrt{2}+\sqrt{3}+\sqrt{5}} = \frac{(\sqrt{2}+\sqrt{3})-\sqrt{5}}{(\sqrt{2}+\sqrt{3})^2-5}$$
$$= \frac{\sqrt{2}+\sqrt{3}-\sqrt{5}}{2\sqrt{6}}$$
$$= \frac{(\sqrt{2}+\sqrt{3}-\sqrt{5})\sqrt{6}}{12}$$
$$= \frac{\sqrt{12}+\sqrt{18}-\sqrt{30}}{12}$$
$$= \frac{2\sqrt{3}+3\sqrt{2}-\sqrt{30}}{12}$$

EXERCISES

Express as equivalent fractions with rational denominators.

1. $\dfrac{\sqrt{2}}{\sqrt{2}+3\sqrt{-\sqrt{5}}}$ 2. $\dfrac{\sqrt{10}+\sqrt{-5\sqrt{3}}}{\sqrt{3}-\sqrt{10}-\sqrt{5}}$

3. $\dfrac{1}{\sqrt{a}+\sqrt{b}+\sqrt{a+b}}$ 4. $\dfrac{6\sqrt{9}-6\sqrt{8}}{6\sqrt{9}+6\sqrt{8}}$ 5. $\dfrac{\sqrt[3]{3}}{\sqrt{3}+\sqrt[6]{9}}$

Find the square roots of

6. $8+2\sqrt{15}$ 7. $17+12\sqrt{2}$ 8. $37-20\sqrt{3}$

9. $73-12\sqrt{35}$

10. (*i*) $5\sqrt{5}+\sqrt{120}$ (*ii*) $28-5\sqrt{12}$

Find the cubic roots of

11. $38+17\sqrt{15}$ 12. $21\sqrt{6}-23\sqrt{5}$ 13. $19+9\sqrt{6}$

14. $11\sqrt{5}+17\sqrt{2}$ 15. $99\sqrt{2}-59\sqrt{5}$

Find the square roots of

16. $6+\sqrt{12}-\sqrt{24}-\sqrt{8}$

17. $8+2\sqrt{2}+2\sqrt{5}+2\sqrt{10}$ 18. $11+6\sqrt{2}+4\sqrt{3}+2\sqrt{6}$

19. $21-4\sqrt{5}+8\sqrt{3}-4\sqrt{15}$ 20. $10+2\sqrt{6}+2\sqrt{10}+2\sqrt{15}$

21. If $2\sqrt{54}+5\sqrt{294}+\dfrac{19}{30}\sqrt{6}-\sqrt{\dfrac{27}{50}}-\sqrt{\dfrac{2}{3}} = a\sqrt{b}$ find a.

22. If $\dfrac{1+\sqrt{48}}{5\sqrt{3}+4\sqrt{2}-\sqrt{72}-\sqrt{108}+\sqrt{8}+2} = a+b\sqrt{3}$ find a and b.

23. If $x = 3+\sqrt{18}$ show that $x^4 + \dfrac{1}{x^4} = 1154$.

24. If $x = 3 - \sqrt{5}$ prove that $x^4 - x^3 - 20x^2 - 16x + 39 = 15$.

25. Simplify $\dfrac{3+\sqrt{6}}{5\sqrt{3}-2\sqrt{12}-\sqrt{32}+\sqrt{50}}$.

26. Prove that $\dfrac{5}{\sqrt[3]{16}-\sqrt[3]{4}+1} - \dfrac{3}{\sqrt[3]{16}+\sqrt[3]{4}+1} = 2$.

27. If $x = 7-\sqrt{48}$ find the value of

$$\left(x^3+\frac{1}{x^3}\right)-15\left(x^2+\frac{1}{x^2}\right)+20\left(x+\frac{1}{x}\right)-72$$

28. Given $\sqrt{5} = 2.23607$ find the value of

$$\frac{10\sqrt{2}}{\sqrt{18}-\sqrt{3+\sqrt{5}}}-\frac{\sqrt{10}+\sqrt{18}}{\sqrt{8}+\sqrt{3-\sqrt{5}}}$$

29. Evaluate $\sqrt{a+x+\sqrt{2ax+x^2}}$.

30. Evaluate $\dfrac{\sqrt{a+b}+\sqrt{a-b}}{\sqrt{a+b}-\sqrt{a-c}}$ where $b = \dfrac{2ac}{c^2+1}$.

ANSWERS

1. $\dfrac{3+\sqrt{6}+\sqrt{15}}{6}$

2. $\dfrac{3\sqrt{30}+5\sqrt{15}-12-10\sqrt{2}}{7}$

3. $\dfrac{a\sqrt{b}+b\sqrt{a}-\sqrt{ab(a+b)}}{2ab}$

4. $17 - 3^{5/2}.2^{3/2} + 3^{4/3}.2^2 - 3.2^{5/2} + 3^{2/3}.2^3 - 3^{1/3}2^{7/2}$

5. $\dfrac{1}{2}(3^{5/6}-3^{4/6}+3^{3/6}-3^{2/6}+3^{1/6}-1)$

6. $\pm(\sqrt{3}+\sqrt{5})$

7. $\pm(3+2\sqrt{2})$

8. $\pm(5-2\sqrt{3})$

9. $\pm(3\sqrt{5}-2\sqrt{7})$

10. (*i*) $\pm 5^{1/4}(\sqrt{2}+\sqrt{3})$ (*ii*) $\pm(5-\sqrt{3})$

11. $2+\sqrt{5}$

12. $\sqrt{6}-\sqrt{5}$

13. $\sqrt{6}+1$

14. $\sqrt{5}+\sqrt{2}$

15. $3\sqrt{2}-\sqrt{5}$

16. $\pm(1+\sqrt{3}-\sqrt{2})$

17. $\pm(1+\sqrt{2}+\sqrt{5})$

18. $\pm(\sqrt{2}+\sqrt{3}+\sqrt{6})$

19. $\pm(2-\sqrt{5}+2\sqrt{3})$

20. $\pm(\sqrt{2}+\sqrt{3}+\sqrt{5})$

21. $a = 41$.

22. $a = 14, b = 9$

25. $\sqrt{3}$

27. 0

28. $3+\sqrt{5}$ i.e. 5.23607

29. $\pm\left(\sqrt{\dfrac{2a+x}{2}}+\sqrt{\dfrac{x}{2}}\right)$

30. c.

CHAPTER 9

CUBIC AND BIQUADRATIC EQUATIONS

1. An equation in x, in which the highest power of x is 3, is called a *cubic equation,* whereas if the highest power of x is 4, the equation is called a *biquadratic* or *quartic*.

Firstly we find relation between roots and coefficients of a cubic and a biquadratic equation.

Let α, β, γ be the roots of a cubic $a_0x^3 + a_1x^2 + a_2x + a_3 = 0$.

Since α, β, γ are roots; $x - \alpha$, $x - \beta$ and $x - \gamma$ are the factors of $a_0x^3 + a_1x^2 + a_2x + a_3$

i.e.
$$a_0x^3 + a_1x^2 + a_2x + a_3 \equiv a_0(x-\alpha)(x-\beta)(x-\gamma)$$
$$\equiv a_0[x^3 - (\alpha+\beta+\gamma)x^2 + (\alpha\beta+\beta\gamma+\gamma\alpha)x - \alpha\beta\gamma]$$

Because of identity, we get

$$-a_0(\alpha+\beta+\gamma) = a_1 \quad \text{or} \quad \alpha+\beta+\gamma = -\frac{a_1}{a_0}$$

Also
$$a_0(\alpha\beta+\beta\gamma+\gamma\alpha) = a_2 \Rightarrow \alpha\beta+\beta\gamma+\gamma\alpha = \frac{a_2}{a_0}$$

$$-a_0(\alpha\beta\gamma) = a_3 \Rightarrow \alpha\beta\gamma = -\frac{a_3}{a_0}$$

Thus s_1 = sum of the roots taken one at a time

$$= -\frac{\text{coefficient of } x^2}{\text{coefficient of } x^3}$$

and s_2 = sum of the roots taken two at a time

$$= \frac{\text{coefficient of } x}{\text{coefficient of } x^3}$$

and $\qquad s_3$ = product of all the roots

$$= -\frac{\text{constant term}}{\text{coefficient of } x^3}.$$

Next suppose that α, β, γ, δ are the roots of the quartic equation

$$a_0x^4 + a_1x^3 + a_2x^2 + a_3x + a_4 = 0$$

We can write

$$\begin{aligned} a_0x^4 + a_1x^3 + a_2x^2 + a_3x + a_4 &\equiv a_0(x-\alpha)(x-\beta)(x-\gamma)(x-\delta) \\ &\equiv a_0[x^4 - (\alpha+\beta+\gamma+\delta)x^3 \\ &\quad + (\alpha\beta+\beta\gamma+\gamma\delta+\alpha\delta+\beta\delta+\alpha\gamma)x^2 \\ &\quad - (\alpha\beta\gamma+\alpha\beta\delta+\beta\gamma\delta+\alpha\gamma\delta)x + \alpha\beta\gamma\delta] \end{aligned}$$

which in turn implies

$$s_1 = -\frac{a_1}{a_0}, \quad s_2 = \frac{a_2}{a_0}, \quad s_3 = -\frac{a_3}{a_0} \quad \text{and} \quad s_4 = \frac{a_4}{a_0}$$

REMARKS

1. This method can be generalized to give relation between roots and coefficients of an equation of degree *n*.
2. The relations given above are in sufficient for solving the equations in general. But when one more relation between the roots is given, it is possible, in many cases, to solve the equations. How one extra relation helps us in solving the equations, is illustrated by examples.

Example 1. *Solve* $32x^3 - 48x^2 + 21x - 3 = 0$ *the roots being in A.P.*

Solution. Let the roots be α – β, α, α – 1β

As $\qquad s_1 = (\alpha-\beta) + \alpha + (\alpha+\beta) = -\frac{(-48)}{32}$

or $\qquad 3\alpha = \frac{3}{2} \;\Rightarrow\; \alpha = \frac{1}{2}$

So the roots are $\frac{1}{2} - \beta, \; \frac{1}{2}, \; \frac{1}{2} + \beta$

But $\qquad s_3 = \left(\frac{1}{2} - \beta\right)\frac{1}{2}\left(\frac{1}{2} + \beta\right) = -\frac{(-3)}{32}$

$$\frac{1}{4} - \beta^2 = \frac{3}{16}$$

$\Rightarrow \qquad \beta^2 = \frac{1}{4} - \frac{3}{16} = \frac{1}{16}$

$\Rightarrow \qquad \beta = \pm\frac{1}{4}$

$\beta = \frac{1}{4}$ gives the roots as $\frac{1}{2} - \frac{1}{4}, \; \frac{1}{2}, \; \frac{1}{2} + \frac{1}{4}$

i.e. $$\frac{1}{4}, \frac{1}{2}, \frac{3}{4}$$

$\beta = -\frac{1}{4}$ gives the same roots but in different order.

Rule to Choose Roots in A.P.

For a cubic, roots should be taken as $\alpha - \beta, \alpha, \alpha + \beta$; whereas for a quartic equation the roots should be taken as $\alpha - 3\beta, \alpha - \beta, \alpha + \beta$ and $\alpha + 3\beta$.

Example 2. *Solve* $27x^4 - 192x^3 + 494x^2 - 520x + 192 = 0$ *the roots being in G.P.*

Solution. Let the roots be $\frac{\alpha}{\gamma^3}, \frac{\alpha}{\gamma}, \alpha\gamma, \alpha\gamma^3$

Their product $= \alpha^4 = \frac{192}{27} = \frac{64}{9}$

$$\Rightarrow \qquad \alpha^2 = \frac{8}{3}$$

Now $$s_2 = \alpha^2\left(\frac{1}{\gamma^4} + \frac{1}{\gamma^2} + 1 + 1 + \gamma^2 + \gamma^4\right)$$

$$\frac{494}{27} = \frac{8}{3}\left(\gamma^4 + \frac{1}{\gamma^4} + \gamma^2 + \frac{1}{\gamma^2} + 2\right)$$

$$\left(\gamma^4 + \frac{1}{\gamma^4}\right) + \left(\gamma^2 + \frac{1}{\gamma^2}\right) + 2 = \frac{247}{36}$$

$$\left(\gamma^2 + \frac{1}{\gamma^2}\right)^2 + \left(\gamma^2 + \frac{1}{\gamma^2}\right) - \frac{247}{36} = 0$$

$$\gamma^2 + \frac{1}{\gamma^2} = \frac{-1 \pm \sqrt{1 + \frac{247}{9}}}{2} = \frac{-1 \pm \frac{16}{3}}{2}$$

As $$\gamma^2 + \frac{1}{\gamma^2} > 0, \ \gamma^2 + \frac{1}{\gamma^2} = \frac{13}{6}$$

or $$6\gamma^4 - 13\gamma^2 + 6 = 0$$

or $$6\gamma^4 - 9\gamma^2 - 4\gamma^2 + 6 = 0$$

or $$(2\gamma^2 - 3)(3\gamma^2 - 2) = 0$$

$$\Rightarrow \qquad \gamma^2 = \frac{3}{2} \text{ or } \frac{2}{3}$$

$$\gamma^2 = \frac{2}{3} \Rightarrow \frac{\alpha}{\gamma^3} = \frac{2\sqrt{2}}{\sqrt{3}} \cdot \frac{\sqrt{3}}{\sqrt{2}} \frac{3}{2} = 3$$

$$\frac{\alpha}{\gamma} = \frac{2\sqrt{2}}{\sqrt{3}} \cdot \frac{\sqrt{3}}{\sqrt{2}} = 2$$

$$\alpha\gamma = \frac{2\sqrt{2}}{\sqrt{3}} \cdot \frac{\sqrt{2}}{\sqrt{3}} = \frac{4}{3}$$

and $$\alpha\gamma^3 = \frac{4}{3} \cdot \frac{2}{3} = \frac{8}{9}$$

So the roots are $3, 2, \frac{4}{3}, \frac{8}{9}$.

$\gamma^2 = \frac{3}{2}$ gives same roots but in different order.

Hence the roots are $3, 2, \frac{4}{3}, \frac{8}{9}$.

REMARK: *We could have chosen* α *and* γ *such that each of* $\frac{\alpha}{\gamma^3}, \frac{\alpha}{\gamma}, \alpha\gamma, \alpha\gamma^2$ *is – ve, but in that case,* s_1 *would be – ve, whereas we know that* s_1 *is + ve.*

Rule to Choose Roots in G.P.

For a cubic, roots should be chosen as $\frac{\alpha}{\gamma}, \alpha, \alpha\gamma$ and for a quartic roots should be chosen as $\frac{\alpha}{\gamma^3}, \frac{\alpha}{\gamma}, \alpha\gamma, \alpha\gamma^3$.

Example 3. *Solve* $2x^3 + x^2 - 7x - 6 = 0$ *given that the difference of the roots is 3.*

Solution. Let α, $\alpha + 3$ and β be the roots of the given cubic.

$$s_1 = \alpha + \alpha + 3 + \beta = -\frac{1}{2} \Rightarrow 2\alpha + \beta = -\frac{1}{2} - 3 = -\frac{7}{2} \quad ...(1)$$

$$s_2 = \alpha(\alpha + 3) + \alpha\beta + (\alpha + 3)\,\beta = -\frac{7}{2}$$

or $$\alpha(\alpha + 3) + \left(-\frac{7}{2} - 2\alpha\right) + (\alpha + 3)\left(-\frac{7}{2} - 2\alpha\right) = -\frac{7}{2} \quad ...(2)$$

or $$\alpha^2 + 3\alpha - \frac{7}{2}\alpha - 2\alpha^2 - \frac{7}{2}\alpha - \frac{21}{2} - 2\alpha^2 - 6\alpha = -\frac{7}{2}$$

$$\Rightarrow -3\alpha^2 - 10\alpha - 7 = 0$$

$$\Rightarrow \quad \alpha = -1 \quad \text{or} \quad -\frac{7}{3}$$

Now $s_3 = \alpha(\alpha+3)\beta = -\dfrac{(-6)}{2} = 3$ ...(3)

In case $\alpha = -1, \beta = -\dfrac{7}{2} - 2\alpha = -\dfrac{7}{2} + 2 = -\dfrac{3}{2}$.

So the roots are -1, 2, and $-\dfrac{3}{2}$.

Clearly they satisfy (3).

If we take $\alpha = -\dfrac{7}{3}$ then $\beta = -\dfrac{7}{2} - 2\alpha = -\dfrac{7}{2} + \dfrac{14}{3} = \dfrac{7}{6}$

But then these values of α, β do not satisfy (3).

As a consequence this value of α *i.e.*, $-\dfrac{7}{3}$ is rejected.

Hence the roots are -1, 2 and $-\dfrac{3}{2}$.

Example 4. *Solve $2x^3 - x^2 - 22x - 24 = 0$, two of the roots being in the ratio of 3 : 4.*

Solution. Let 3α, 4α and β be the roots of the given cubic.

Then $\quad s_1 = 7\alpha + \beta = \dfrac{1}{2} \quad \Rightarrow \quad \beta = \dfrac{1}{2} - 7\alpha.$

Also $\quad s_2 = 12\alpha^2 + 7\alpha\beta = -\dfrac{22}{2} = -11$

$$\Rightarrow \quad 12\alpha^2 + 7\alpha\left(\frac{1}{2} - 7\alpha\right) = -11 \quad \Rightarrow \quad 74\alpha^2 - 7\alpha - 22 = 0$$

$$\Rightarrow \quad \alpha = -\frac{1}{2} \quad \text{or} \quad \frac{22}{37}.$$

Finally, $\quad s_3 = 12\alpha^2\beta = -\left(\dfrac{-24}{2}\right) = 12$ ...(1)

If $\alpha = \dfrac{22}{37}$ then $\beta = \dfrac{1}{2} - 7\alpha = \dfrac{1}{2} - \dfrac{154}{37} = \dfrac{-271}{74}$.

These values do not satisfy (1), so they are rejected.

When $\quad \alpha = -\dfrac{1}{2}, \beta = \dfrac{1}{2} + \dfrac{7}{2} = 4.$

Evidently $\quad 12 \cdot \dfrac{1}{4} \cdot 4 = 12 \quad$ *i.e.*, (1) is satisfied

Hence the roots are $-\dfrac{3}{2}, -2, 4.$

Example 5. *Solve* $8x^4 - 2x^3 - 27x^2 + 6x + 9 = 0$, *two of the roots being equal but opposite in signs.*

Solution. Let the roots be $\alpha, -\alpha, \beta$ and γ

Now $\quad s_1 = \alpha - \alpha + \beta + \gamma = -\left(\frac{-2}{8}\right) = \frac{1}{4}$

$\Rightarrow \quad \beta + \gamma = \frac{1}{4}$ ...(1)

$s_3 = \alpha\beta\gamma - \alpha\beta\gamma - \alpha^2\beta\alpha^2\gamma = -\frac{6}{8} = -\frac{3}{4}$

$\Rightarrow \quad -\alpha^2(\beta + \gamma) = -\frac{3}{4}$

So by (1), $\quad \alpha^2 = 3 \quad$ *i.e.*, $\alpha = \pm\sqrt{3}$

Without loss of generality we can choose $\alpha = \sqrt{3}$.

Now $\quad s_4 = (-\alpha^2)\beta\gamma = \frac{9}{8}$

$\Rightarrow \quad \beta\gamma = -\frac{9}{8} \cdot \frac{1}{2} = \frac{-3}{8}$

Then $\quad (\beta - \gamma)^2 = (\beta + \gamma)^2 - 4\beta\gamma = \frac{1}{16} + \frac{3}{2} = \frac{25}{16}$

$\Rightarrow \quad \beta - \gamma = \pm\frac{5}{4}$

Taking + *ve* sign, $\quad \beta = \frac{3}{4}, \gamma = -\frac{1}{2}$

[If we choose – ve sign then $\beta = -\frac{1}{2}$ and $\gamma = \frac{3}{4}$]

Hence the roots are $\sqrt{3}, -\sqrt{3}, \frac{3}{4}$ and $-\frac{1}{2}$.

2. We digress for a moment to state two important theorems which will be very useful in the solution of the equations of higher degrees.

Theorem 1. In an equation with real coefficients, roots of the type $\alpha + \beta i$ ($\alpha, \beta \in \mathbf{R}$, $i = \sqrt{-1}$ *and* $\beta \neq 0$) *ocur in pairs. More precisely if* $\alpha + \beta i$ *is a root of such an equation then* $\alpha - \beta i$ *must also be one of its roots.*

Theorem 2. In an equation with rational coefficients, roots of the type $\alpha + \sqrt{\beta}$ ($\alpha, \beta \in \mathbf{Q}, \beta$ *is not a square of a rational number*) *occur in pairs. More exactly if* $\alpha + \sqrt{\beta}$ *is a root of such an equation then* $\alpha - \sqrt{\beta}$ *must also be one of its roots.*

The proofs which are based on Division Algorithm of polynomials in x, are left to the reader.

Example 6. *Solve the equation* $x^4 + 4x^3 + 5x^2 + 2x - 2 = 0$ *when it is given that* $-1 + i$ *is a root.*

Solution. Since $-1 + i$ is a root of the given cubic, $-1 - i$ must also be a root. Let the other roots be α, β

Then $\qquad s_1 = \alpha + \beta + (-1 - i) + (-1 + i) = -4$

$$\alpha + \beta = -4 + 2 = -2$$

Also $\qquad s_4 = \alpha\beta(-1 - i)(-1 + i) = -2$

$\Rightarrow \qquad 2\alpha\beta = -2 \Rightarrow \alpha\beta = -1$

Then $\qquad (\alpha - \beta)^2 = (\alpha + \beta)^2 - 4\alpha\beta = 4 + 4 = 8$

$\Rightarrow \qquad \alpha - \beta = \pm 2\sqrt{2}$

Hence $\qquad \alpha = \sqrt{2} - 1 \quad \text{and} \quad \beta = -\sqrt{2} - 1.$

(Take + ve sign before the radical, since other sign will give same values of α, β, but in reverse order.)

Hence the roots are $-1 \pm i, -1 \pm \sqrt{2}$.

Example 7. *Solve* $x^4 - 8x^3 - 12x^2 + 60x + 63 = 0$*, one root being* $3 + \sqrt{30}$.

Solution. Since one root is $3 + \sqrt{30}$, there must be a root $3 - \sqrt{30}$ also.

Let α, β be other two roots.

Then $\qquad s_1 = \alpha + \beta + 3 + \sqrt{30} + 3 - \sqrt{30} = -(-8) = 8$

$$\alpha + \beta = 2$$

Also $\qquad s_4 = \alpha\beta(3 + \sqrt{30})(3 - \sqrt{30}) = 63$

$$-21\alpha\beta = 63 \Rightarrow \alpha\beta = -3$$

Now $\qquad (\alpha - \beta)^2 = (\alpha + \beta)^2 - 4\alpha\beta = 4 + 12 = 16$

$\Rightarrow \qquad \alpha - \beta = \pm 4$

Hence $\alpha = 3, \beta = -1$ (or $\alpha = -1, \beta = 3$). Consequently the roots are

$$3, -1, 3 \pm \sqrt{30}$$

Example 8. *Solve* $x^3 + 2x^2 - 17x + 42 = 0$ *given that* -6 *is a root.*

Solution. Let α, β be other two roots.

Then $\qquad s_1 = \alpha + \beta - 6 = -2$

$\Rightarrow \qquad \alpha + \beta = 4$

Further $s_3 = \alpha\beta(-6) = -42$

$\Rightarrow$ $\alpha\beta = 7$

Now $(\alpha-\beta)^2 = (\alpha+\beta)^2 - 4\alpha\beta = 16 - 28 = -12$

$\Rightarrow$ $\alpha - \beta = \pm 2\sqrt{3}i$

Hence $\alpha = 2 + i\sqrt{3}, \beta = 2 - i\sqrt{3}$

Consequently the roots are 6, $2 \pm i\sqrt{3}$.

3. CARDAN'S METHOD OF SOLVING THE CUBIC $x^3 + ax + b = 0$

Put $x = p^{1/3} + q^{1/3}$ to obtain

$$x^3 = p + q + 3p^{1/3}q^{1/3}(p^{1/3} + q^{1/3})$$

$$= p + q + 3p^{1/3}q^{1/3}x$$

or $$x^3 - 3p^{1/3}q^{1/3}x - (p+q) = 0$$

So, if x is a root of $x^3 + ax + b = 0$ and if $x = p^{1/3} + q^{1/3}$ then we must have

$$x^3 + ax + b \equiv x^3 - 3p^{1/3}q^{1/3}x - (p+q)$$

This implies that $p + q = -b$ ...(1)

and $-3p^{1/3}q^{1/3} = a$ or $-27pq = a^3$ ...(2)

With the help of (1) and (2) we can evaluate p and q.

Hence x can be determined.

The three values of x are $p^{1/3} + q^{1/3}$,

$p^{1/3}w + q^{1/3}w^2, p^{1/3}w^2 + q^{1/3}w$, where $w = \dfrac{-1+\sqrt{3}i}{2}$

REMARKS

1. w is called imaginary cube root of unity. If $x^3 = 1$, then $(x-1)(x^2+x+1) = 0 \Rightarrow x = 1$ or $x^2 + x + 1 = 0$. If $x^2 + x + 1 = 0$.

   then $x = \dfrac{-1 \pm \sqrt{-3}}{2}$, we take $w = \dfrac{-1+\sqrt{-3}}{2} = \dfrac{-1+\sqrt{3}i}{2}$

   The second root $\dfrac{-1-\sqrt{-3}}{2}$ can be easily verified to be w^2. As w is a root of $x^2 + x + 1 = 0$, $w^2 + w + 1 = 0$.

2. This method is applicable to those cubics in which second term is *missing*. (*i.e.*, coefficient of x^2 is zero).

Example 9. *Solve* $x^3 - 18x - 35 = 0$.

Solution. Here $a = -18$ and $b = -35$

Let $x = p^{1/3} + q^{1/3}$ be a root of the given cubic.

Then $\quad p+q = -b = 35 \quad$ ...(1)

and $\quad pq = -\dfrac{a^3}{27} = 216 \quad$ ...(2)

(1) and (2) imply $p = 27, q = 8$.

Hence the roots are

$$p^{1/3} + q^{1/3}, p^{1/3}w + q^{1/3}w^2, p^{1/3}w^2 + q^{1/3}w$$

i.e., $\quad 3 + 2, 3w + 2w^2, 3w^2 + 2w$

or $\quad 5, 3\left(\dfrac{-1+\sqrt{-3}}{2}\right) + 2\left(\dfrac{-1-\sqrt{-3}}{2}\right), 3\left(\dfrac{-1-\sqrt{-3}}{2}\right) + 2\left(\dfrac{-1+\sqrt{-3}}{2}\right)$

Consequently the roots are $5, \dfrac{-5 \pm \sqrt{-3}}{2}$.

4. ROOTS OF A CUBIC BY INSPECTION

It is sometimes easy to find a root by inspection. Then other roots can be found, with the help of relations between roots and coefficients. We, however, keep in mind that whenever $x = \dfrac{p}{q}$ is a root of $a_n x^n + a_{n-1}x^{n-1} + \ldots + a_0 = 0$ where $\dfrac{p}{q}$ is reduced to its lowest term, (*i.e.*, p, q have no common factor except 1, and $a_0, a_1, a_n, \ldots p, q$ are all integers ($q > 0$) then p divides a_0 and q divides a_n.

Example 10. *Find all the roots of* $x^3 + 9x^2 - x - 9 = 0$.

Solution. The factors of -9 are $\pm 1, \pm 3, \pm 9$.

We substitute $x = 1$ and see that it satisfies the given cubic.

Hence 1 is a root of the given cubic.

Let other roots be α and β.

Then $\quad s_1 = \alpha + \beta + 1 = -9 \Rightarrow \alpha + \beta = -10$

and $\quad s_3 = (\alpha\beta)(1) = (-1)(-9) = 9 \Rightarrow \alpha\beta = 9$

Solving we get $\quad \alpha = -1, \beta = -9$.

Hence the roots are $1, -1$ and -9.

Aliter. $\quad x^3 + 9x^2 - x - 9 = 0$

$\Rightarrow \quad x^2(x+9) - (x+9) = 0$

$\Rightarrow \quad (x^2 - 1)(x+9) = 0$

$\Rightarrow \quad x = 1$ or -1 or -9.

5. FERRARI'S METHOD OF SOLVING A BIQUADRATIC

Let $x^4 + ax^3 + bx^2 + cx + d = 0$ be a given biquadratic.

Add $(\lambda x + \mu)^2$ to both sides, such that the left hand side is of the type $\left(x^2 + \frac{a}{2}x + \beta\right)^2$.

Then $$x^4 + ax^3 + bx^2 + cx + d + (\lambda x + \mu)^2 = (\lambda x + \mu)^2$$

or $$x^4 + ax^3 + (b + \lambda^2)x^2 + (c + 2\lambda\mu)x + d + \mu^2 = (\lambda x + \mu)^2$$

or $$\left(x^2 + \frac{ax}{2} + \beta\right)^2 = (\lambda x + \mu)^2$$

Hence $$x^4 + ax^3 + (b + \lambda^2)x^2 + (c + 2\lambda\mu)x + d + \mu^2 \equiv \left(x^2 + \frac{ax}{2} + \beta\right)^2$$

Comparing coefficients of x^2, x and constant terms, we get

$$b + \lambda^2 = \frac{a^2}{4} + 2\beta$$

$$c + 2\lambda\mu = \alpha\beta \quad \text{and} \quad d + \mu^2 = \beta^2$$

Thus $$\lambda^2 = \frac{a^2}{4} + 2\beta - b$$

$$\mu^2 = \beta^2 - d \quad \text{and} \quad \lambda\mu = \frac{a\beta - c}{2}$$

i.e., $$\lambda^2\mu^2 = \frac{(a\beta - c)^2}{2}$$

As a result of this we get

$$\frac{(a\beta - c)^2}{2} = \left(\frac{a^2}{4} + 2\beta - b\right)(\beta^2 - d)$$

This is a cubic in β. If we can find a single root of this cubic by inspection, we can get λ and μ.

But then $$(\lambda x + \mu)^2 = \left(x^2 + \frac{ax}{2} + \beta\right)^2$$

$$\Rightarrow \quad x^2 + \frac{ax}{2} + \beta = \pm(\lambda x + \mu)$$

and we are left with two quadratic equations whose roots can be easily determined.

Example 11. *Solve* $x^4 - 3x^2 - 42x - 40 = 0.$

Solution. We have $x^4 - 3x^2 - 42x - 40 + (\lambda x + \mu)^2 = (\lambda x + \mu)^2$ ...(1)

where λ and μ are such that the left hand side of (1) is equal to $(x^2 + \beta)^2$

i.e., $x^4 + (\lambda^2 - 3)x^2 + (2\lambda\mu - 42)x + \mu^2 - 40 \equiv x^4 + 2\beta x^2 + \beta^2$

we get on comparison,

$$2\beta = \lambda^2 - 3$$

$$\beta^2 = \mu^2 - 40$$

and $$2\lambda\mu - 42 = 0 \quad \text{i.e.,} \quad \lambda\mu = 21$$

But $$\lambda^2 = 2\beta + 3 \text{ and } \mu^2 = \beta^2 + 40$$

So $$(2\beta + 3)(\beta^2 + 40) = 441 \qquad ...(2)$$

Clearly $$\beta = 3 \text{ satisfies (2)}$$

Hence $$\lambda^2 = 9 \quad \text{or} \quad \lambda = \pm 3$$

and $$\mu^2 = \beta^2 + 40 = 49 \quad \text{or} \quad \mu = \pm 7$$

Since $$\lambda\mu = 21, \text{ we take } \lambda = 3, \mu = 7$$

Hence $$(3x + 7)^2 = (x^2 + 3)^2$$

or $$x^2 + 3 = \pm (3x + 7)$$

i.e., $$x^2 - 3x - 4 = 0 \quad \text{or} \quad x^2 + 3x + 10 = 0$$

Hence $$x = -1, 4 \text{ or } \frac{-3 \pm i\sqrt{31}}{2}$$

EXERCISES

Solve the equations

1. $2x^3 - 15x^2 + 37x - 30 = 0$, roots being in A.P.
2. $x^4 + 15x^3 + 70x^2 + 120x + 64 = 0$ roots being in G.P.
3. $6x^3 - 11x^2 - 3x + 2 = 0$, roots being in H.P.

   [*Hint.* Replace x with $\frac{1}{y}$

   Solve $2y^3 - 3y - 11y^2 + 6 = 0$, roots being in A.P.]
4. $6x^4 - 29x^2 + 40x^2 - 7x - 12 = 0$, product of two roots being 2.
5. $x^4 - 89x^3 + 21x^2 - 20x + 5 = 0$, sum of the roots being equal to sum of other two roots.
6. $8x^3 - 14x^2 + 7x - 1 = 0$, roots being in G.P.
7. $16x^4 - 64x^3 + 56x^2 + 16x - 15 = 0$ roots being in A.P.
8. $x^3 - 9x^2 + 24x + 24 = 0$ roots being in the ratio of 3 : 2.
9. $x^3 - 12x^2 + 15x + 189 = 0$ being given that one of the roots exceeds another by 2.

10. $x^3 - 15x - 126 = 0$ by Cardan's Method.
11. $x^3 + 72x - 1720 = 0$ by Cardan's Method.
12. $x^4 + 8x^3 + 9x^2 - 8x - 10 = 0$ by Ferrari's Method.
13. $x^4 + 2x^3 - 7x^2 - 8x + 12 = 0$ by Ferrari's Method.
14. $6x^4 - 13x^3 - 35x^2 - x + 3 = 0$, one root being $2-\sqrt{3}$.
15. $x^4 + x^3 - 25x^2 + 41x + 66$ one root being $3-i\sqrt{2}$.
16. The roots of $x^4 - 6x^3 + 18x^2 - 30x + 25 = 0$ are of the form $\alpha + i\beta$ and $\beta + i\alpha$ ($\alpha, \beta \in \mathbf{R}$ and non zero). Find all the roots.
17. If the roots of the cubic $x^3 + 3px^2 + 3qx + r = 0$ $(r \neq 0)$ are in (*a*) A.P., (*b*) G.P. and (*c*) H.P. Find a relation between coefficients in each case.
18. Find k if 2 is a root of $x^3 - (k + 1)x + k = 0$. Also, then find the other roots.
19. Solve $24x^3 + 46x^2 + 9x - 9 = 0$ one root being double of another root.
20. Solve by inspection
    (*i*) $x^3 - 28x + 48 = 0$
    (*ii*) $x^3 - 15x^2 - 33x + 847 = 0$
    (*iii*) $x^3 + 63x - 316 = 0$.

ANSWERS

1. $2, \frac{5}{2}, 3$
2. $-1, -2, -4, -8$
3. $-\frac{1}{2}, 2, \frac{1}{3}$
4. $\frac{4}{3}, \frac{3}{2}, 1\pm\sqrt{2}$
5. $\frac{3\pm\sqrt{5}}{2}, \frac{5\pm\sqrt{5}}{2}$
6. $\frac{1}{4}, \frac{1}{2}, 1$
7. $-\frac{1}{2}, \frac{1}{2}, \frac{3}{2}, \frac{5}{2}$
8. $6, 4, -1$
9. $-3, 7, 9$
10. $6, -3\pm 2\sqrt{3}i$
11. $10, -5\pm 7\sqrt{3}i$
12. $\pm 1, -4\pm\sqrt{6}$
13. $1, \pm 2, -3$
14. $-\frac{1}{3}, -\frac{3}{2}, 2\pm\sqrt{3}$
15. $-1, -6, 3 \pm i\sqrt{2}$
16. $2 \pm i, 1 \pm 2i$
17. (*a*) $2p^3 - 3pq + r = 0$ (*b*) $p^3r = q^3$ (*c*) $2q^3 - 3pqr + r^2 = 0$
18. $k = 6$, other roots are 1, 3
19. $-\frac{3}{2}, -\frac{3}{4}, \frac{1}{3}$
20. (*i*) 2, 4, 6 (*ii*) 11, 11, 7 (*iii*) 4, $-2\pm 5\sqrt{3}\,i$

CHAPTER 10

PERMUTATIONS AND COMBINATIONS

1. PERMUTATIONS

Let n be a positive integer and r, a positive integer less than or equal to n. The number of different arrangements of r things taken out of n dissimilar things is denoted by ${}^nP_r$. Each such arrangement is called a *Permutation* of n things taken r at a time.

For example, all the arrangements of two letters chosen out of $\{a, b, c\}$ are given by

ab, ba, ac, ca, bc, cb.

Thus ${}^3P_2 = 6$.

Again all the arrangements of three letters chosen out of $\{a, b, c, d\}$ are given by

abc, bac, acb, bca, cab, cba, abd, adb, bad, bda, dab, dba, acd, adc, cda, cad, dac, dca, bcd, bdc, cdb, cbd, dbc, dcb.

Thus ${}^4P_3 = 24$.

2. SUPPOSE THAT NUMBER OF WAYS OF DOING A WORK IS l AND ONCE THIS WORK IS COMPLETED, THE NUMBER OF WAYS OF DOING SECOND WORK IS m, THEN NUMBER OF PERFORMING BOTH THE WORKS TOGETHER IS $l \times m$

Let A and B be the two works. For each way of performing A; B can be completed in m ways. But A itself can be done in l ways, so that the total number of ways in which A and B can be performed together is $l \times m$.

Similarly if after completing first two works, the number of ways in which a third work can be performed is n, then the total number of different manners in which all the three works can be completed is $l \times m \times n$.

The above result can be understood by the following example.

Let A, B, C be three cities and from A to B there are l different routes while from B to C, the number of different routes is m. What is the number of different paths one can traverse in going from A to C? Suppose a person goes from A to B by route no. 1.

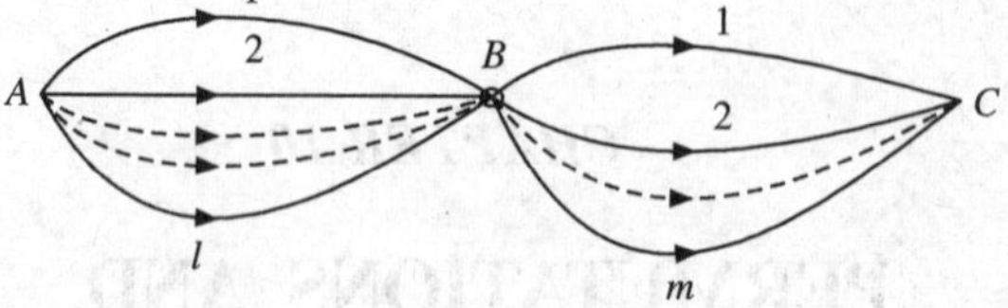

Fig. 1

After reaching *B*, he has at his disposal *m* paths. Thus for every choice of path from *A* to *B*, he has *m* paths at his disposal. So total number of different routes he can undertake is $l \times m$.

3. TO FIND THE NUMBER OF PERMUTATIONS OF *r* THINGS CHOSEN OUT OF *n* DISSIMILAR THINGS

We consider *n* chairs and *r* persons are to be seated in a row, clearly the number of permutations of *r* things chosen out of *n* things is same as that the number of ways in which these *r* persons can occupy these chairs.

We start with one person. He has *n* chairs to sit in. So, he can choose any one of them in *n* ways. Once a chair is occupied by him, only $n-1$ chairs remain unoccupied. So, for the second person, the choice is limited to $n-1$ chairs only. Thus the number of ways second person can occupy any chair is $n-1$. Hence total number of ways in which first two persons selected at random from the group of given *r* persons to occupy chairs is $n(n-1)$. Proceeding in this way, we get that

$$\begin{aligned} {}^nP_r &= n(n-1)(n-2)\ldots(n-\overline{r-1}) \\ &= n(n-1)(n-2)\ldots(n-r+1) \end{aligned}$$

4. FACTORIAL NOTATION

The product of all consecutive integers starting from 1 to *t* is denoted by $t!$ or $\underline{|t}$ and read as *t*-factorial.

Thus $\quad t! = 1 \times 2 \times 3 \times \ldots \times t.$

In this way $\quad 1! = 1,\ 2! = 1 \times 2 = 2,\ 3! = 1 \times 2 \times 3 = 6$

$4! = 1 \times 2 \times 3 \times 4 = 24$ etc.

Note that for $n > 1$, $n! = n(n-1)!$

Now
$$\begin{aligned} {}^nP_r &= n(n-1)(n-2)\ldots(n-r+1) \\ &= \frac{n(n-1)\ldots(n-r+1)(n-r)(n-r-1)\ldots 3.2.1}{(n-r)(n-r-1)\ldots 3.2.1} \\ &= \frac{\underline{|n}}{\underline{|n-r}} \end{aligned}$$

Convention: As a convention we take 0 ! equal to 1.

Example 1. *Find the value of* $^6P_4$.

Solution. $^6P_4 = \dfrac{6!}{(6-4)!} = \dfrac{6!}{2!} = \dfrac{6.5.4.3.2.1}{2.1} = 360.$

Example 2. *If* $^nP_4 = 12\,^nP_2$, *find n.*

Solution. $^nP_4 = \dfrac{n!}{(n-4)!}$ and $^nP_2 = \dfrac{n!}{(n-2)!}$

By hypothesis $\dfrac{n!}{(n-4)!} = 12\dfrac{n!}{(n-2)!}$

$\Rightarrow \quad 12(n-4)! = (n-2)!$

$\Rightarrow \quad 12(n-4)! = (n-2)(n-3)(n-4)!$

$\Rightarrow \quad 12 = n^2 - 5n + 6$

$\Rightarrow \quad n^2 - 5n - 6 = 0$

$\Rightarrow \quad (n-6)(n+1) = 0$

$\Rightarrow \quad n = 6$ or $n = -1$

Since n is positive integer, we reject the second value of n. Thus $n = 6$.

Example 3. *In how many ways 5 passengers can sit in a compartment having 16 vacant seats?*

Solution. Required number of ways $= {}^{16}P_5$

$$= \frac{16!}{(16-5)!} = \frac{16!}{11!}$$

$$= \frac{16.15.14.13.12.\,\underline{|11}}{\underline{|11}}$$

$$= 16\,.\,15\,.\,14\,.\,13\,.\,12 = 524160.$$

5. TO FIND OUT THE NUMBER OF PERMUTATIONS OF *r* THINGS CHOSEN OUT OF *n* DISSIMILAR THINGS, WHEN A PARTICULAR THING IS TO BE ALWAYS INCLUDED IN EACH ARRANGEMENT

Here we have to consider the number of ways in which r places can be filled up when we have n different things such that in each arrangement a particular thing is always to be present.

Suppose $\{a_1, a_2, ..., a_n\}$ are n different things. Let a_i be a particular thing to be included in each arrangement of r things out of n different things given. Now a_i can occupy any of 1st, 2nd, 3rd, ... rth place. Suppose a_i is at the first place. Then remaining $r - 1$ places can be filled up by $n - 1$ things *viz.* $\{a_1, a_2, \ldots a_{i-1}, a_{i+1}, \ldots, a_n\}$ in ${}^{n-1}P_{r-1}$ ways. Similarly, if a_i is at the second place, then the remaining $r - 1$ places can be filled up by $n - 1$ things, again in ${}^{n-1}P_{r-1}$ ways. Thus a_i can occupy r places and each position of a_i, gives rise to ${}^{n-1}P_{r-1}$ arrangements. Hence required number of permutations is $r. {}^{n-1}P_{r-1}$.

6. TO FIND THE NUMBER OF PERMUTATIONS OF *r* THINGS CHOSEN OUT OF *n* DIFFERENT THINGS, WHEN A PARTICULAR THING IS TO BE ALWAYS EXCLUDED IN EACH ARRANGEMENT

Here we have to consider the number of ways in which r places can be filled up when we have n different things such that in each arrangement, a particular thing is always to be missing.

To do so, we exclude that particular thing. Then we are left with $n - 1$ things and r places can be filled up with these $n - 1$ things in ${}^{n-1}P_r$ ways. Hence required number of permutations is ${}^{n-1}P_r$.

7. TO PROVE THAT ${}^nP_r = {}^{n-1}P_r + r. {}^{n-1}P_{r-1}$

Proof. ${}^nP_r$ means that the number of ways in which r places can be filled up by n different things. This can be done as follows.

Consider first those arrangements which contain a particular thing. By § 5 the number of such arrangements $= r. {}^{n-1}P_{r-1}$.

Now, consider these arrangements which donot contain that particular thing. By § 6, the number of such arrangements $= {}^{n-1}P_r$.

Each arrangement of r places, either contains a particular thing or does not. Hence total number of arrangements of r places by n different things $= {}^{n-1}P_r + r. {}^{n-1}P_{r-1}$.

Alternatively. RHS $= {}^{n-1}P_r + r. {}^{n-1}P_{r-1}$

$$= \frac{\lfloor n-1}{\lfloor n-r-1} + r\frac{\lfloor n-1}{\lfloor n-r}$$

$$= \frac{\lfloor n-1}{\lfloor n-r-1} + \frac{r \lfloor n-1}{(n-r) \lfloor n-r-1}$$

$$= \frac{\lfloor n-1}{\lfloor n-r-1}\left[1 + \frac{r}{n-r}\right]$$

$$= \frac{\underline{|n-1}}{\underline{|n-r-1}}\left[\frac{n}{n-r}\right]$$

$$= \frac{n\,\underline{|n-1}}{(n-r)\,\underline{|n-r-1}} = \frac{\underline{|n}}{\underline{|n-r}} = {}^{n}P_{r} = \text{LHS.}$$

8. TO FIND THE NUMBER OF WAYS IN WHICH *n* THINGS MAY BE ARRANGED AMONG THEMSELVES, TAKEN ALL AT A TIME, WHEN *p* THINGS ARE OF ONE KIND, *q* OF SECOND KIND, AND *r* OF THIRD KIND AND REST ALL DIFFERENT

Let x be the required number of permutations. Take any one of these permutations. Replace p like things in this permutation by p unlike things. If we arrange these p unlike things among themselves, we get $\underline{|p}$ permutations (keeping all other things unchanged). So, in all we get $x\,\underline{|p}$ permutations in which now q things are of one kind, r things of second kind and rest of them different. Consider any one of these permutations. Replace q like things by q unlike things. These q unlike things can be arranged among themselves, in $\underline{|q}$ ways. But there are $x\,\underline{|p}$ such permutations. In this way, we get $x\,\underline{|p}\,\underline{|q}$ permutations in which r things are of one kind and rest of them different. Consider any such permutation and replace r like things by r unlike things. These r unlike things can be arranged in $\underline{|r}$ ways. These are $x\,\underline{|p}\,\underline{|q}$ such permutations. This gives rise to $x\,\underline{|p}\,\underline{|q}\,\underline{|r}$ permutations in which all things are different. But, we know n different things can be arranged among themselves in $\underline{|n}$ ways.

Thus $$x\,\underline{|p}\,\underline{|q}\,\underline{|r} = \underline{|n}$$

$$\Rightarrow \qquad x = \frac{\underline{|n}}{\underline{|p}\,\underline{|q}\,\underline{|r}}$$

which is required number of permutations.

Example 4. *How many numbers lying between 10 and 100 can be formed with the help of digits 3, 0, 4, 5, 6?*

Solution. Each number between 10and 100 consists of two digits. Number of permutations of two digits out of given five digits = ${}^{5}P_{2} = 20$.

But these permutations include numbers of type 03, 04, 05, 06 which do not lie between 10 and 100.

Therefore, 16 different numbers can be formed with the help of digits 3, 4, 0, 5, 6 lying between 10 and 100.

Example 5. *How many words can be formed with the help of 3 consonants and 2 vowels, such that no two consonants are adjacent?*

Solution. Let C_1, C_2, C_3 be three consonants and V_1, V_2 be two vowels. Consider any arrangement in which no two consonants are together as shown in the figure.

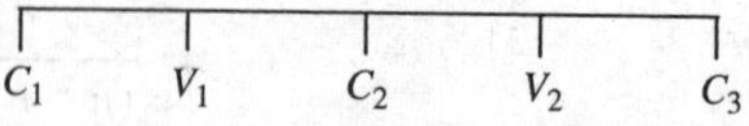

Fig. 2

Now vowels have only two positions to occupy namely, between C_1 and C_2, C_2 and C_3. So, each such arrangement of consonants, gives rise to two arrangements of vowels. But consonants can be arranged in 3 places in 3 ! ways so that total number of arrangements is 2 × 3 ! i.e. 12. Thus the number of different words formed is 12.

Example 6. *How many numbers consisting of 2 digits can be formed with the help of the digits 1, 2, 3, 4 such that*

(i) each number contains 1 *(ii) no number contains 1?*

Solution. (*i*) By § 5 the number of 2-digit numbers containing 1 are $2 \times {}^3P_1 = 2 \times \frac{\underline{|3}}{\underline{|2}} = \underline{|3} = 6.$

(*ii*) By § 6, the number of 2-digit numbers which do not contain 1 are $^3P_2 = \frac{\underline{|3}}{\underline{|1}} = 6.$

Example 7. *How many words can be formed from the letters of VALEDICTORY provided the letters A, E, I, O, Y are not to be separated at all?*

Solution. Put together *A, E, I, O, Y* and count them as one letter. Thus we have *V, L, D, C, T, R,* (AEIOY), these seven letters can be arranged in 7 ! ways. But the group (AEIOY) consisting of five letters can itself be arranged in 5 ! ways.

Hence the required number = 5 ! × 7 ! = 604800.

Example 8. *Out of the letters A, B, C, p, q, r how many arrangements can be made (i) beginning with a capital, (ii) beginning and ending with a capital.*

Solution. (*i*) A capital letter out of given letters can be chosen in 3 ways. Remaining five letters can be arranged among themselves in 5 ! ways. Therefore total number of arrangements beginning with a capital = 5 ! × 3 = 5 × 4 × 3 × 2 × 3 = 360.

(*ii*) Two capitals out of the given letters can be chosen in $^3P_2 = 6$ ways. For each choice of these two letters, remaining four can be arranged in 4 ! ways. Hence the required number of arrangements = $6 \times 4 ! = 6 \times 24 = 144$.

Example 9. *In how many ways 5 girls can be arranged in a circle?*

Solution. Place a girl at any point on the circle. Then the remaining 4 girls can be arranged in $4 \times 3 \times 2 \times 1$ ways. Thus, there are 24 ways to arrange 5 girls in a circle.

Example 10. *The letters of the word ZENITH are written in all possible orders. How many words are possible? If all these words are written as in dictionary, what is the rank of word ZENITH.*

Solution. Total number of letters in ZENITH is 6. So the total number of possible words is 6 ! = 720. Total number of words beginning with *E* is same as the number of possible arrangements of *Z, N, I, T, H.* But total number of arrangements of *Z, N, I, T, H* is 5 ! = 120.

Similarly, total number of letters beginning with *N* is 120; with *I*, is 120; with *T* is 120 and with *H* is 120.

Thus there are 600 words which begin with *E*, or *N* or *I*, or *T*, or *H*. Hence the words beginning with *Z* will have their rank between 601 to 720.

Out of these 120 words, the number of words in which *E* is in second place is equal to 4 ! = 24. (Number of arrangements of *N, I, T, H*).

Thus the rank of words beginning with *ZE* will be between 601 to 624.

Out of these 24 words,

words beginning with *ZEH* are 6, their ranks lie between 601 to 606.

words beginning with *ZEI* are 6, ranks lying between 607 – 612.

words beginning with *ZEN* are 6, rank lying between 613 – 618.

and words beginning with *ZET* are 6, ranks between 619 – 624.

We consider words beginning with *ZEN*.

According to Dictionary order, the words beginning with *ZEN* and containing. *ITH* are

ZEN HIT with rank 613

ZEN HTI with rank 614

ZEN IHT with rank 615

ZEN ITH with rank 616

ZEN THI with rank 617

ZEN TIH with rank 618

Hence rank of *ZENITH* is 616.

Example 11. *Find the number of arrangement that can be made out of the letters of the word ASSASSINATION.*

Solution. There are 13 letters in ASSASSINATION out of which there are 3 *A*'s, 4 *S*'s, 2 *I*'s and two *N*'s.

So the total number of arrangements

$$= \frac{13!}{3!\,4!\,2!\,2!}$$

$$= \frac{13.12.11.10.9.8.7.6.5.4.3.2.1}{(3.2.1).(4.3.2.1)(2.1)(2.1)} = 10810800.$$

Example 12. *Find the number of permutations of the word ACCOUNTANTS.*

Solution. Total number of letters in ACCOUNTANTS is 11 out of which there are two *C*'s, two *A*'s, two *N*'s and two *T*'s. So the required number of permutations

$$= \frac{11!}{2!\,2!\,2!\,2!} = 2494800.$$

Example 13. *Six papers are set in an examination of which two are mathematical. In how many different orders can the papers be arranged so that (i) the two mathematical papers are together (ii) the two mathematical papers are not consecutive.*

Solution. Counting the two mathematical papers as one, total number of arrangements is 5!.

The two mathematical papers can be arranged within themselves in two ways. So required number of arrangements in which the mathematical papers are always together

$$= 2 \times 5! = 2 \times 120 = 240.$$

Again total number of arrangements is 6! = 720.

Hence the number of arrangements in which mathematical papers are not consecutive is

$$= 720 - 240 = 480.$$

Example 14. *How many different words can be formed with the letters of 'HARYANA'? In how many of these H and N are together? How many of these words begin with H and end with N?*

Solution. Total number of letters in HARYANA is 7 with 3 *A*'s. So total number of different words

$$= \frac{7!}{3!} = 840.$$

Counting *HN* as one letter, we are left with 6 letters having 3 *A*'s. *H* and *N* can be put together in two different manners namely *HN* and *NH*.

Required number of words, in which H and N are together

$$= 2 \times \frac{6!}{3!} = 240.$$

Finally the number of words beginning with H and ending with N is same as the number of arrangements of ARYAA, which is equal to

$$\frac{5!}{3!} = 20$$

Example 15. *In how many ways can the letters of the word STRANGE be arranged so that the vowels occupy only the odd places.*

Solution. Number of letters in STRANGE is 7 so there are 4 odd places namely, First, Third, Fifth and Seventh.

Vowels are only 2. The number of ways in which 2 vowels can occupy 4 places is ${}^4P_2$. For each such way, the remaining 5 places are to be occupied by five remaining consonants. This can be achieved in 5! different ways.These vowels can be arranged within themselves in two ways.

Hence the required number is ${}^4P_2 \times 5! \times 2$

$$= 2 \times \frac{4!}{2!} \times 120 = 1440.$$

Example 16. *How many four-digit numbers can be formed with the digits 0, 1, 2, 3, 4, 5, 6, 7, 8, 9, if no two digits are same?*

Solution: Suppose the four-digit number is *abcd*. Since a cannot be 0, a has 9 choices. Again $b \neq a$ implies b has 9 choices as b can be 0. Also, $c \neq b$, $c \neq a$ implies c has 8 choices. Similarly, d has 7 choices. So, there are $9.9.8.7 = 4536$ numbers.

Example 17. *How many four-digit odd numbers can be formed with the digits 0, 1, 2, 3, 4, 5, 6, 7, 8, 9, if no two digits are same?*

Solution. Suppose the four-digit number is *abcd*. Since the number *abcd* is odd, d must be odd. So, d can be chosen in 5 ways. Since $a \neq d$, $a \neq 0$, a has 8 choices. Since $b \neq d$, $b \neq a$, b has 8 choices. Also, $c \neq d$, $c \neq a$, $c \neq b$, c has 7 choices. So, there are $8.8.7.5 = 2240$ four-digit odd numbers such that no two digits are same.

Example 18. *How many four-digit even numbers can be formed with the digits 0, 1, 2, 3, 4, 5, 6, 7, 8, 9, if no two digits are same?*

Solution. Suppose the four-digit number is *abcd*. Since the number *abcd* is even, d must be even. If $d = 0$, then a has 9 choices, b has 8 choices, c has 7 choices. So, there are $9 \times 8 \times 7 \times 1 = 504$ four digit even numbers ending with 0. If $d \neq 0$, then d has 4 choices, a has 8 choices as a

$\neq 0$, $a \neq d$, b has 8 choices, c has 7 choices. So, there are $8 \times 8 \times 7 \times 4 = 1792$ four-digit even numbers not ending with 0. Thus, there are $504 + 1792 = 2296$ four-digit even numbers.

Example 19. *How many 3-digit numbers greater than 300 can be formed with the digits 1, 2, 3, 4, 5, 6, if no digit is repeated in any number.*

Solution. Suppose the 3-digit number is abc. Since the number is greater than 300, a can be 3, 4, 5 or 6. So, a has 4 choices. Since $b \neq a$, b has 5 choices. Since, $c \neq a$, $c \neq b$, c has 4 choices. So, there are $4 \times 5 \times 4 = 80$, three digit number greater than 300.

Example 20. *In how many ways can 3 boys and 5 girls be arranged in a row so that all the 3 boys are together.*

Solution. We count the 3 boys as one boy so that number of persons involved is now 6. They can be arranged in 6 ! ways. But these 3 boys themselves can be arranged in 3 ! ways. Hence required number of arrangements is

$$6! \times 3! = 720 \times 6 = 4320.$$

EXERCISES

1. How many words can be formed from the letters of COURTESY? How many of them will begin with C and end with Y?
2. How many numbers can be formed between 10 and 1000 with the help of digits 2, 3, 4, 0, 8, 9?
3. In how many ways, other arrangements can be made out of the letters of DOGMATIC?
4. How many different words can be formed out of the letters of word TRIANGLE. How many begin with T? How many begin with T and end with E.
5. How many numbers can be formed with the digits 1, 2, 3, 4, 3, 2, 1 so that odd digits always occupy odd places?
6. How many arrangements can be made out of the letters of the word DRAUGHT, the vowels never being separated?
7. There are 5 boys and 3 girls. In how many ways can they stand in a row so that no two girls are together.
8. How many different words can be made out of the letters of the word ALLAHABAD. In how many of these will the vowels occupy the even places?
9. How many numbers less than 1000 and divisible by 5 can be formed with the digits 0, 1, 2, 3, 4, 5, 6, 7, 8, 9, each digit not occurring more than once in each number?
10. A number of four different digits is formed by using the digits 1, 2, 3, 4, 5, 6, 7, in all possible ways, each digit occurring once only. Find (*i*) how many such numbers can be formed and (*ii*) how many of them are greater than 3400.

11. How many three-digit numbers can be formed with the digits 0, 1, 2, 3, 4, 5, 6, 7, 8, 9, if no two digits are same?
12. Find how many words can be formed of the letters of the word 'FAILURE', the four vowels always coming together.
13. How many four digit numbers greater than 3000 can be formed with the digits 2, 3, 4, 5, if repetitions of digits are allowed?
14. Find the number of all possible different words into which the word INTERFERE can be converted by change of place of letters, it is being given that no two consonants are to be together.
15. How many numbers between 1000 and 10000 can be formed with the digits 1, 2, 3, 4, 5, 6, 7, 8, 9? How many of them are odd?
16. In how many ways can a consonant and a vowel be chosen out of the letters of each of the words (*i*) LOGARITHM, (*ii*) EQUATION?
17. How many three-digit odd numbers can the formed with the digits 0, 1, 2, 3, 4, 5, 6, 7, 8, 9, if no two-digits are same?
18. How many three-digit even numbers can be formed with the digits 0, 1, 2, 3, 4, 5, 6, 7, 8, 9, if no two digits are same?
19. Find the number of permutations of the letters of the word SIGNAL such that the vowels may occupy only odd positions?
20. In how many ways n objects can be arranged in a circle?

ANSWERS

1. 40320, 720	2. 125	3. 40319
4. 40320, 5040, 720	5. 18	6. 1440
7. 14400	8. 7560, 60	9. 155
10. 840, 520	11. 648	12. 576
13. 192	14. 240	15. 3024, 1680
16. (*i*) 18 (*ii*) 15	17. 320	18. 328
19. 144	20. $(n - 1)!$	

9. COMBINATIONS

Suppose we are given a number of objects. Each collection of objects which can be made out of the above objects is called a *combination*.

Thus if $\{a, b, c\}$ is a given set of objects and two objects are to be chosen. The different combiantions are given by $\{a, b\}$, $\{b, c\}$ and $\{c, a\}$. Note that permutations are six, namely ab, ba, ca, ac, bc, cb. Although ab, ba are two permutations yet they form a single combination. In combination, the order in which the elements are selected does not matter. Similarly the number of combinations of three objects chosen from $\{a, b, c, d\}$ is 4 namely $\{a, b, c\}$, $\{b, c, d\}$, $\{c, d, a\}$, $\{a, b, d\}$.

Notation: If $0 \leq r \leq n$ then the number of combinations of r objects taken out of n objects is denoted by ${}^nC_r$.

10. TO PROVE THAT $${}^nC_r = \frac{{}^nP_r}{r!} = \frac{n!}{(n-r)!\,r!}$$

Proof. Let ${}^nC_r = x$. So, we get x groups each consisting of r objects chosen out of n given objects. But each of these groups can be re-arranged within itself $r!$ times. Hence the total number of permutations of r objects chosen from n objects is equal to $x \times r!$. In other words ${}^nP_r = x \times r!$

$$\text{i.e.,} \quad x = \frac{{}^nP_r}{r!}. \quad \text{Hence } {}^nC_r = \frac{{}^nP_r}{r!} = \frac{\lfloor n}{\lfloor n-r \; \lfloor r}$$

Cor. ${}^nC_0 = {}^nC_n = 1$

Proof. $${}^nC_0 = \frac{n!}{0!\,n!} = 1 \quad \text{and} \quad {}^nC_n = \frac{n!}{0!\,n!} = 1$$

Example 21. *In how many ways, a party of 4 or more can be selected from 10 persons?*

Solution. We are to calculate

$${}^{10}C_4 + {}^{10}C_5 + {}^{10}C_6 + {}^{10}C_7 + {}^{10}C_8 + {}^{10}C_9 + {}^{10}C_{10}$$

Now $${}^{10}C_4 = \frac{10!}{4!\,6!} = \frac{10.9.8.7}{4.3.2.1} = 210$$

$${}^{10}C_5 = \frac{10!}{5!\,5!} = \frac{10.9.8.7.6}{5.4.3.2.1} = 252$$

$${}^{10}C_6 = \frac{10!}{4!\,6!} = \frac{10.9.8.7}{4.3.2.1} = 210$$

$${}^{10}C_7 = \frac{10!}{3!\,7!} = \frac{10.9.8}{3.2.1} = 120$$

$${}^{10}C_8 = \frac{10!}{2!\,8!} = \frac{10.9}{2.1} = 45$$

$${}^{10}C_9 = \frac{10!}{1!\,9!} = \frac{10}{1} = 10$$

$${}^{10}C_{10} = \frac{10!}{0!\,10!} = \frac{1}{1} = 1$$

Hence required number $= 210 + 252 + 210 + 120 + 45 + 10 + 1 = 848$

Example 22. *If* $^nC_{12} = {}^nC_8$, *find* $^nC_{17}$ *and* $^{22}C_n$.

Solution. $^nC_{12} = {}^nC_8 \Rightarrow \dfrac{n!}{(n-12)!\,12!} = \dfrac{n!}{(n-8)!\,8!}$

$\Rightarrow \quad (n-8)!\,8! = (n-12)!\,12!$

$\Rightarrow \quad (n-8)(n-9)(n-10)(n-11) = 12.11.10.9$

$\Rightarrow \quad (n-8)(n-9)(n-10)(n-11) = 11880$

$\Rightarrow \quad (n^2-19n+88)(n^2-19n+90) = 11880$

$\Rightarrow \quad (x^2+88)(x+90) = 11880$ where $x = n^2 - 19n$

$\Rightarrow \quad x^2+178x+7920 = 11880$

$\Rightarrow \quad x^2+178x-3960 = 0$

$\Rightarrow \quad (x+198)(x-20) = 0$

$\Rightarrow \quad x = -198, x = 20.$

In case $x = 20$, $n^2 - 19n - 20 = 0$

$\Rightarrow \quad (n-20)(n+1) = 0$

$\Rightarrow \quad n = 20, n = -1$

In case $x = -198$, $n^2 - 19n + 198 = 0$

$\Rightarrow \quad n$ is imaginary.

Since n is a positive integer, we get $n = 20$.

Hence $\quad {}^nC_{17} = {}^{20}C_{17} = \dfrac{20.19.18}{3.2.1} = 1140$

$$^{22}C_n = {}^{22}C_{20} = \frac{22.21}{2.1} = 231.$$

11. COMPLEMENTARY COMBINATIONS

Prove that $^nC_r = {}^nC_{n-r}$

Proof.
$$^nC_r = \frac{n!}{(n-r)!\,r!}$$
$$= \frac{n!}{[n-(n-r)]!\,(n-r)!}$$
$$= \frac{n!}{(n-r)!\,[n-(n-r)]!} = {}^nC_{n-r}$$

Two combinations ^nC_x and ^nC_y are said to be *comlementary* if $x + y = n$. Thus ^nC_r and $^nC_{n-r}$ are complementary combinations.

12. TO PROVE THAT ${}^nC_x = {}^nC_y \Rightarrow$ EITHER $x = y$ or $x + y = n$

Proof. $${}^nC_x = {}^nC_y \Rightarrow \frac{n!}{(n-x)!\,x!} = \frac{n!}{(n-y)!\,y!}$$

$$\Rightarrow (n-x)!\,x! = (n-y)!\,y! \quad ...(i)$$

Suppose $x \neq y$ and let $x > y$.

Now (i)

$\Rightarrow (n-x)!\,x(x-1)\ldots(y+1) = (n-y)!$

$\Rightarrow x(x-1)\ldots(y+1) = (n-y)(n-y-1)\ldots(n-x+1)\ ...(ii)$

Suppose further that $x + y \neq n$.

Then either $x + y > n$ or $x + y < n$.

If $x + y > n$, we have $x > n - y$, $x - 1 > n - y - 1, \ldots,$

$$y + 1 = x - (x - y - 1) > n - y - (x - y - 1) = n - x + 1$$

hence the product on LHS $\neq$ product on RHS of (ii)

This is absurd !

If $x + y < n$, we have $x < n - y$, $x - 1 < n - y - 1, \ldots$

$$y + 1 = x - (x - y - 1) < n - y - (x - y - 1) = n - x + 1.$$

Thus LHS < RHS of (ii), which is again absurd.,

Hence if $x > y$, then we must have $x + y = n$.

It can be similarly shown that if $x < y$, then also $x + y = n$.

REMARK: The above result helps us in solving many problems in combination theory. Consider example 22. We are given that ${}^nC_{12} = {}^nC_8$.

Then $12 + 8 = n$ so that $n = 20$ and now rest of the problem can be done by usual calculations.

13. TO PROVE THAT ${}^nC_r + {}^nC_{r-1} = {}^{n+1}C_r$

Proof. $$\text{LHS} = \frac{n!}{(n-r)!\,r!} + \frac{n!}{(n-r)!\,(n-r+1)!}$$

$$= \frac{n!}{(r-1)!\,(n-r)!}\left\{\frac{1}{r} + \frac{1}{n-r+1}\right\}$$

$$= \frac{n!}{(r-1)!\,(n-r)!}\left\{\frac{n-r+1+r}{r(n-r+1)}\right\}$$

$$= \frac{(n+1)\,n!}{r(r-1)!\,(n-r+1)(n-r)!}$$

$$= \frac{(n+1)!}{r!\,(n+1-r)!} = {}^{n+1}C_r$$

14. TO PROVE THAT ${}^nC_0 + {}^nC_1 + {}^nC_2 + \dots\dots + {}^nC_n = 2^n$.

Proof. For $n = 1$, LHS $= {}^1C_0 + {}^1C_1 = 1 + 1 = 2 = 2^1$.

So, our result holds for $n = 1$

Suppose the results is true for $n = k$

i.e., $${}^kC_0 + {}^kC_1 + \dots + {}^kC_k = 2^k \qquad \dots(i)$$

Now put $n = k + 1$

By § 13,
$${}^{k+1}C_1 = {}^kC_1 + {}^kC_0$$
$${}^{k+1}C_2 = {}^kC_2 + {}^kC_1$$
$$\dots \quad \dots \dots \dots$$
$${}^{k+1}C_k = {}^kC_k + {}^kC_{k-1}$$

Adding we get
$${}^{k+1}C_1 + {}^{k+1}C_2 + \dots\dots + {}^{k+1}C_k = {}^kC_0 + 2({}^kC_1 + {}^kC_2 + \dots\dots + {}^kC_{k-1}) + {}^kC_k$$

Thus
$$\begin{aligned} {}^{k+1}C_0 + {}^{k+1}C_1 + \dots + {}^{k+1}C_{k+1} &= {}^{k+1}C_0 + {}^kC_0 + 2({}^kC_1 + {}^kC_2 \\ &\quad + \dots + {}^kC_{k-1}) + {}^kC_k + {}^{k+1}C_{k+1} \\ &= 2({}^kC_0 + {}^kC_1 + \dots\dots + {}^kC_k) \end{aligned}$$

as $\quad {}^{k+1}C_0 = 1 = {}^kC_0$ and ${}^{k+1}C_{k+1} = 1 = {}^kC_k$

Using (i) we get
$${}^{k+1}C_0 + {}^{k+1}C_1 + \dots\dots + {}^{k+1}C_{k+1} = 2.2^k = 2^{k+1}$$

Hence the result holds for $n = k + 1$. Thus, by Principle of Mathematical Induction, result is true for all positive integers.

15. TO FIND THE NUMBER OF WAYS IN WHICH $m + n$ OBJECTS CAN BE DIVIDED INTO TWO GROUPS CONTAINING m AND n OBJECTS RESPECTIVELY

Let the required number of ways be equal to x. This is same as number of combinations of $m + n$ objects taken m at a time, for each combination of m objects gives rise to another combination of n objects.

Thus $$x = {}^{m+1}C_m = \frac{(m+n)!}{n!\,m!}$$

REMARK: In case $m = n$, we shall get $x = \frac{2m!}{(m!)^2}$. But in this counting, all ways are not different. Since it is possible to interchange two groups without obtaining a new distribution.So, in such cases, the number of different combination is $\frac{2m}{2!(m!)^2}$.

Example 23. *Suppose we want to divide the collection {a, b, c, d} into two groups each having two elements.*

Solution. Possible groups are (*ab*), (*cd*); (*cd*), (*ab*); (*ac*), (*bd*); (*bd*), (*ac*); (*ad*), (*bc*); (*bc*), (*ad*).

But if we look carefully, we note that first two groups, second two groups and third two groups are actually the same, placed in different order. So, number of different groups is 3.

i.e. $$\frac{4!}{2!(2!)^2} \text{ and not } \frac{4!}{(2!)^2} = 6.$$

REMARK: The above result can be generalised as under.

The number of ways, $a_1 + a_2 + \dots \dots + a_t$ objects can be divided into groups of $a_1, a_2, \dots \dots, a_t$ objects respectively is equal to

$$\frac{(a_1 + a_2 + \dots \dots + a_t)!}{a_1!\, a_2!\, a_3! \dots \dots a_t!}$$

Further, if $a_1 = a_2 = \dots \dots = a_t$,

the number of different groups obtained $= \dfrac{(a_1 + a_2 + \dots \dots a_t)!}{t!\,(a_1!)^t} = \dfrac{(t \, . a_1)!}{t!\,(a_1!)^t}$.

Example 24. *If* $^{18}C_r = {}^{18}C_{r+2}$, *find* $^{r}C_5$.

Solution. $^{18}C_r = {}^{18}C_{r+2} \Rightarrow r = r + 2$ or $r + r + 2 = 18$

Since $r \neq r + 2$, we get $2r = 16$ i.e. $r = 8$.

Hence $$^{r}C_5 = {}^{8}C_5 = \frac{8\,.\,7\,.\,6}{3\,.\,2\,.\,1} = 56.$$

Example 25. *A boat is to be manned by 8 men, of whom 2 can only row on bow side and 1 can only row on stroke side. In how many ways can the crew be arranged?*

Solution. Let *A, B* be the men on bow side and *C* be on the stroke side. On bow side two more men are to be selected out of remaining 8 – 3 = 5 men. This can be done in $^5C_2$ ways. Once this selection is made, the remaining men are to occupy the stroke side. Further each combination of a side can be made in 4! ways.

So, required number of arrangements $= 4! \times 4! \times {}^5C_2 = 5760$.

Example 26. *How many triangles can be made by joining the vertices of decagon? How many diagonals will it have?*

Solution. A triangle is obtained by joining any three vertices of a decagon. Thus number of triangles obtained from a decagon

$$= {}^{10}C_3 = \frac{10.9.8}{3.2.1} = 120.$$

Now a diagonal is obtained by joining any two vertices which are not adjacent.

Total number of ways in which two vertices of a decagon can be joined $= {}^{10}C_3 = \dfrac{10.9.8}{3.2.1} = 120.$

Now a diagonal is obtained by joining any two vertices which are not adjacent.

Total number of ways in which two vertices of a decagon can be joined $= {}^{10}C_2 = \dfrac{10.9}{2} = 45.$

Number of lines obtained by joining two adjacent vertices

= number of sides of decagon = 10.

Hence number of diagonals = 45 – 10 = 35.

Example 27. *A committee consisting of 5 members is to be formed out of 6 men and 4 women. How many committees can be formed so that at least one woman is always there in the committee?*

Solution. Total number of committees $= {}^{10}C_5 = 252.$

The number of committees in which no woman is there $= {}^{6}C_5 = {}^{6}C_1 =$
6.

Hence the number of committees in which at least one woman is included = 252 – 6 = 246.

Example 28. *In an examination a candidate is required to answer 6 out of 10 questions which are divided into two groups each containing 5 questions and not permitted to attempt more than 4 questions from each group. In how many ways, can he make up his choice?*

Solution. The candidate can have following three choices:

(*i*) 2 questions from group *A* and 4 from group *B*.

(*ii*) 3 questions from group *A* and 3 from group *B*.

(*iii*) 4 questions from group *A* and 2 from group *B*.

Now first choice can be made up in ${}^5C_2 \times {}^5C_4$, *i.e.*, 50 ways. Second choice can be made up in ${}^5C_3 \times {}^5C_3$ ways *i.e.*, 100 ways and third choice can be made up in ${}^5C_4 \times {}^5C_2$ ways *i.e.*, 50 ways.

So, total number of ways, he can make up his choice

$$= 50 + 100 + 50 = 200.$$

Example 29. *Find out the number of ways in which a cricket team consisting of 11 players can be selected from 14 players. Also find out how many of these (a) will include captain, (b) will not include captain?*

Solution. The number of ways in which 11 players can be selected from 14 players is

$$^{14}C_{11} = \frac{14.13.12}{3.2.1} = 14 \times 2 \times 13 = 28 \times 13 = 364.$$

(*a*) Here we have to select 10 players from remaining 13 players as captain is to be included in each solution. Therefore, required number of ways $= {}^{13}C_{10} = \frac{13.12.11}{3.2.1} = 13 \times 2 \times 11 = 26 \times 11 = 286.$

(*b*) Here we have to exclude captain in each selection. In other words, we have to select 11 players from 13 players. This can be done in $^{13}C_{11}$ ways $= \frac{13.12}{2.1} = 78$ ways.

16. TO FIND OUT THE NUMBER OF COMBINATIONS OF *r* THINGS TAKEN OUT OF *n* GIVEN THINGS WHEN THE GIVEN THINGS ARE NOT ALL DIFFERENT

A general formula for such a case may be quite complicated, but a particular case can be solved by methods discussed in following examples.

Example 30. *How many combinations can be made by taking 6 letters out of the word PROPORTION.*

Solution. There are 10 letters in PROPORTION consisting of (*P P*), (*R R*), (*O O O*), *T*, *I*, *N*. Thus two *P*s, two *R*s, and 3 *O*s are similar. In all the required combinations some may contain all dissimilar letters, some may not contain all different letters. Following cases arise:

(*i*) All the letters are different.
(*ii*) 4 letters are different and 2 are similar.
(*iii*) 3 letters are different and 3 are similar.
(*iv*) 2 letters are same, 2 letters are same and remaining 2 letters are different.
(*v*) 3 letters are same, 2 letters are same and one letter different from the others.
(*vi*) 2 letters are same, 2 letters are same and remaining 2 letters are also same.

Case I. There are six different letters. The required number of combinations $= {}^6C_6 = 1$.

Case II. There are three pairs of similar things (*PP*), (*RR*) and two *O*s from (*OOO*). One pair can be chosen in 3 ways. Remaining 4 different letters are to be selected from remaining 5 different letters. This can be done in ${}^5C_4 = 5$ ways. Hence the number of combinations of this type = $3 \times 5 = 15$.

Case III. The only letter which occurs 3 times in 'proportion' is *O*. So three similar letters can be chosen in one way only. Remaining three different letters are to be chosen from the remaining 5 letters. This can be performed in ${}^5C_3$ *i.e.*, 10 ways. Hence the number of combinations of type III is $10 \times 1 = 10$.

Case IV. Two pairs of similar letters can be chosen in ${}^3C_2$ *i.e.*, 3 ways and remaining 2 different letters can be chosen in ${}^4C_2$ *i.e.* 6 ways. Hence the number of combinations in this case is $3 \times 6 = 18$.

Case V. 3 similar letters can be chosen in one way, 2 similar letters can be chosen in 2 ways (either *PP* or *RR*) and the remaining one letter can be chosen in 4 ways. So the required number of combinations is $1 \times 2 \times 4 = 8$.

Case VI. Three pairs of similar letters can be chosen only in one way *i.e.* (*OO*), (*PP*) and (*RR*).

Hence the total number of required combinations

$$= 1 + 15 + 10 + 18 + 8 + 1 = 53$$

Example 31. *There are 10 hockey players including X and Y. A team of 6 players is to be selected out of these 10 players. In how many ways it can be done so that X and Y are not selected together?*

Solution. If *X* and *Y* are not included, then the number of ways team of 6 players may be selected is ${}^8C_6 = \dfrac{8 \times 7}{1 \times 2} = 28$. If one of *X* and *Y* is included, the number of ways team of 6 players may be selected is 2. ${}^8C_5$ = $2 \times \dfrac{8 \times 7 \times 6}{1 \times 2 \times 3} = 112$. So, the required number of ways is $28 + 112 = 140$.

Example 32. *Out of 10 consonants and 4 vowels how many words can be formed each containing 6 consonants and 3 vowels.*

Solution. 6 consonants can be selected out of 10 in ${}^{10}C_6$ ways while 3 vowels can be selected out of 4 in ${}^4C_3$ ways.

Total number of lettters in each choice of 6 consonants and 3 vowels is 9.

So each choice can be arranged in 9! different ways.

Hence total number of words

$$= {}^{10}C_6 \times {}^4C_3 \times 9!$$

$$= \frac{10 \times 9 \times 8 \times 7}{4 \times 3 \times 2 \times 1} \times 4 \times 9! = 304819200.$$

Example 33. *In how many ways can 12 Science students and 9 Commerce students sit in a row so that no two Commerce students may be together?*

Solution. Let the Science students be arranged as

$$- S - S - S - \ldots \ldots S$$

(S standing for position occupied by a science student.) In order that no two Commerce students may be together, they must occupy odd positions which are 13 in number.

Hence we are to select a position out of these 13, which can be done in ${}^{13}C_9$ ways.

But $\quad {}^{13}C_9 = {}^{13}C_4 = \dfrac{13.12.11.10}{4.3.2.1} = 715.$

Consequently required number is 715.

Example 34. *Find the number of combinations if the letters of the word EXAMINATION taken out at a time.*

Solution. There are 11 letters in EXAMINATION consisting of $(AA), (II), (NN), E, X, T, O, M$. Following cases arise:

(*i*) all the four letters are different.

(*ii*) two are different two are alike.

(*iii*) two pairs of alike letters.

Case I. There are 8 different letters, we are to choose 4. Number of combinations formed in this manner $= {}^8C_4 = 70$.

Case *II*. One pair of alike letters can be chosen in three ways and the remaining two different letters are to be chosen from 7.

Number of such combinations $= 3 \times {}^7C_2 = 3 \times 21 = 63$.

Case III. There are three pairs of alike letters:

So the number of combinations having two pairs of alike letters

$$= {}^3C_2 = 3$$

Consequently total number of combinations

$$= 70 + 63 + 2 = 136.$$

Example 35. *From 6 boys and 4 girls, 5 are to be selected to admission for a particular house. In how many ways can this be done if there must be exactly 2 girls.*

Solution. Two girls can be selected out of 4 girls in $^4C_2 = \dfrac{4.3}{2.1} =$ 6 ways.

The remaining three are to be boys. They are to be selected out of 6 boys.

The number of ways in which 3 boys can be chosen out of 6 boys is $^6C_3 = \dfrac{6.5.4}{3.2.1} = 20.$

Required number of ways $= 6 \times 20 = 120.$

Example 36. *How many committees of two or more can be selected from 10 people?*

Solution. The number of subsets from 10 people is 2^{10}. The number of subsets having only one person is 10. There is one empty subset. So, the required number of committees is $2^{10} - 11$.

Example 37. *In how many ways 12 persons may be divided into two groups of 6 persons each?*

Solution. One group of 6 persons can be formed in $^{12}C_6$ ways and the second in one way. So, the total division may be done in $^{12}C_6 =$

$$\frac{12\times11\times10\times9\times8\times7}{6\times5\times4\times3\times2\times1} = 7392 \text{ ways.}$$

EXERCISES

1. If $^{2n}C_r = {}^{2n}C_{r+2}$, prove that $r = n - 1$.
2. If $m = {}^nC_2$, prove that $^mC_2 = {}^{3n+1}C_4$.
3. If $^{28}C_{2r} = {}^{24}C_{2r-4} = 125 : 11$, find r.
4. Find the number of combiantions of 50 things taking 46 at a time.
5. In how many ways can 12 things be divided equally among 4 persons?
6. From 4 officers and 8 privates, in how many ways can 6 be chosen (*i*) to include exactly one officer, (*ii*) to include at least one officer?
7. How many combinations of the letters of the word ALLITERATION can be made if four letters are to be taken at a time?
8. Find the number of combinations of the letters of the word COMMERCE taken four togehter.
9. How many words can be formed by taking three consonants and two vowels from a set of 10 consonants and 4 vowels?
10. How many words formed by taking 6 letters from CENTRIFUGAL will contain *C, T* and *F*?

11. In how many ways committee of one or more persons can be formed from 5 persons?
12. How many words can be formed taking 2 consonants and 2 vowels of the word 'DEVASTATION?'. In how many of them will both *T*'s be together?
13. How many combinations can be formed taking 4 letters at a time from the word SUCCEEDING.
14. There are 8 members of a club. Four members are to be chosen so that it contains *A* or *B* but not both. How many ways it can be done?
15. A question paper contains 6 questions, each having an alternative. In how many ways can an examinee answer one or more questions?
16. In how many ways 12 persons may be divided into three groups of 2, 4 and 6 persons?
17. How many diagonals an octagon has?
18. Two dice can be tossed in 36 ways. In how many ways there sum is equal to 4?
19. How many words can be formed out of the letters of EXAMINATION taken 4 at a time.
20. How many words can be formed from the letters of CIRCUMFERENCE taking 3 consonants and 3 vowels?

ANSWERS

3. 7	4. 230300	5. 369600
6. (*i*) 224, (*ii*) 896	7. 160	8. 26
9. 86400	10. 40320	11. 31
12. 1638, 39	13. 113	14. 40
15. 728	16.. 13,860	17. 20
18. 3	19. 2454	20. 221000

CHAPTER 11

BINOMIAL THEOREM

1. Any expression of the type $x \pm y$ is called a Binomial expression, x is called first term and y, second term. By elementary algebra, we know that $(x+y)^2 = x^2 + 2xy + y^2$; $(x+y)^3 = x^3 + 3x^2y + 3xy^2 + y^3$. In this section, we develop a formula for the nth power of $x + y$, n being a positive integer. We shall make use of Principle of Mathematical Induction in proving the expansion of $(x+y)^n$.

BINOMIAL THEOREM. *If n is a positive integer, then*

$$(x+y)^n = x^n + {}^nC_1 x^{n-1} y + {}^nC_2 x^{n-2} y^2 + \dots + {}^nC_n y^n.$$

Proof. Clearly for $n = 1$, LHS $= x + y$,

and $\quad$ RHS $= x + {}^1C_1 y = x + y$,

so that result is true for $n = 1$.

Let $n + 1 > 1$ and the result be true for n.

i.e. $\quad (x+y)^n = x^n + {}^nC_1 x^{n-1} y + \dots + {}^nC_n y^n$.

Consider

$$\begin{aligned}(x+y)^{n+1} &= (x+y)^n (x+y)\\ &= (x^n + {}^nC_1 x^{n-1} y + \dots + {}^nC_n y^n)(x+y)\\ &= x^{n+1} + ({}^nC_1 x^n y + x^n y)\\ &\quad + ({}^nC_2 x^{n-1} y^2 + {}^nC_1 x^{n-1} y^2) + \dots \dots\\ &\quad + ({}^nC_{n-1} x y^n + {}^nC_n x y^n) + {}^nC_n y^{n+1}\\ &= x^{n+1} + ({}^nC_0 + {}^nC_1) x^n y + ({}^nC_1 + {}^nC_2) x^{n-1} y^2\\ &\quad + ({}^nC_2 + {}^nC_3) x^{n-2} y^3 + \dots\\ &\quad + ({}^nC_{n-1} + {}^nC_n) x y^1 + {}^nC_n y^{n+1}\end{aligned}$$

But $\quad {}^nC_r + {}^nC_{r-1} = {}^{n+1}C_r$ for all $1 \le r \le n$.

Hence we get that

$$(x+y)^{n+1} = x^{n+1} + {}^{n+1}C_1 x^n y + {}^{n+2}C_2 x^{n-1} y^2 + \dots$$
$$\dots + {}^{n+1}C_n x y^n + {}^{n+1}C_{n+1} y^{n+1}.$$

Consequently Binomial Theorem holds for $n + 1$.

Thus by Mathematical Induction, it is true for all positive integers n.

REMARK: The expansion of $(x - y)^n$ is given by

$$(x - y)^n = x^n + {}^nC_1x^{n-1}(-y) + {}^nC_2x^{n-2}(-y)^2 + ... + {}^nC_n(-y)^n$$

$$= x^n - {}^nC_1x^{n-1}y + {}^nC_2x^{n-2}y^2 - {}^nC_3x^{n-3}y^3 + ... + (-1)^n\,{}^nC_n\,y^n.$$

Example 1. *Expand* $(x + y)^5$.

Solution. $(x+y)^5 = x^5 + {}^5C_1x^4y + {}^5C_2x^3y^2 + {}^5C_3x^2y^3 + {}^5C_4xy^4 + {}^5C_5x^0y^5$

Now $${}^5C_1 = {}^5C_4 = 5,\ {}^5C_2 = {}^5C_3 = \frac{5.4}{2.1} = 10$$

Hence $$(x+y)^5 = x^5 + 5x^4y + 10x^3y^2 + 10x^2y^3 + 5xy^4 + y^5.$$

Example 2. *Expand* $(x - 1)^7$.

Solution. By Binomial Theorem

$$(x-1)^7 = x^7 + {}^7C_1x^6(-1) + {}^7C_2x^5(-1)^2 + {}^7C_3x^4(-1)^3$$
$$+ {}^7C_4x^3(-1)^4 + {}^7C_5x^2(-1)^5 - {}^7C_6x(-1)^6 + {}^7C_7(-1)^7$$
$$= x^7 - 7x^6 + 21x^5 - 35x^4 + 35x^3 - 21x^2 + 7x - 1.$$

Example 3. *Expand* $\left(3x - \frac{1}{2}y\right)^4$ *with the help of Binomial theorem. By giving suitable values to x and y obtain the value of* $(29.5)^4$ *correct to fourth decimal place.*

Solution. We have

$$\left(3x - \frac{y}{2}\right)^4 = (3x)^4 + {}^4C_1(3x)^3\left(-\frac{y}{2}\right) + {}^4C_2(3x)^2\left(-\frac{y}{2}\right)^2$$
$$+ {}^4C_3(3x)\left(-\frac{y}{2}\right)^3 + {}^4C_4\left(-\frac{y}{2}\right)^4$$
$$= (3x)^4 - 4(3x)^3\frac{y}{2} + 6(3x)^2\frac{y^2}{4} - 12x\frac{y^3}{8} + \frac{y^4}{16}$$
$$= 81x^4 - 54x^3y + \frac{27}{2}x^2y^2 - \frac{3}{2}xy^3 + \frac{y^4}{16}$$

Now we can write

$$(29\cdot5)^4 = (30 - 0\cdot5)^4 = (3 \times 10 - \frac{1}{2} \times 1)^4$$

Thus if we put $x = 10$ and $y = 1$ in the above expansion, we get

$$(29\cdot5)^4 = 81\times(10)^4 - 54(10)^3 + \frac{27}{2}\cdot(10)^2 - \frac{3}{2}\cdot(10) + \frac{1}{16}.$$

$$= 810000 - 54000 + \frac{27}{2}\times 100 - 15 + \frac{1}{16}$$

$$= 810000 - 54000 + 1350 - 15 + \frac{1}{16}$$

$$= 757335.0625$$

Example 4. *Show that* $\left(\sqrt{3}+\sqrt{2}\right)^3 + \left(\sqrt{3}-\sqrt{2}\right)^3 = 18\sqrt{3}.$

Solution. We have

$$\left(\sqrt{3}+\sqrt{2}\right)^3 = \left(\sqrt{3}\right)^3 + 3\left(\sqrt{3}\right)^2\sqrt{2} + 3\left(\sqrt{3}\right)\left(\sqrt{2}\right)^2 + \left(\sqrt{2}\right)^3$$

$$\left(\sqrt{3}-\sqrt{2}\right)^3 = \left(\sqrt{3}\right)^3 - 3\left(\sqrt{3}\right)^2\sqrt{2} + 3\left(\sqrt{3}\right)\left(\sqrt{2}\right)^2 - \left(\sqrt{2}\right)^3$$

On Addition, we get

$$\left(\sqrt{3}+\sqrt{2}\right)^3 + \left(\sqrt{3}-\sqrt{2}\right)^3 = 2\left(\sqrt{3}\right)^3 + 6\left(\sqrt{3}\right)\left(\sqrt{2}\right)^2$$

$$= 6\sqrt{3} + 12\sqrt{3} = 18\sqrt{3}.$$

2. TO FIND THE GENERAL TERM IN THE EXPANSION OF $(x + y)^n$

Let T_{r+1} be the $(r+1)$th term in the expansion of $(x+y)^n$. Now 1st term $= x^n = n\,C_0 x^{n-0}\,y^0$; second term $= {}^nC_1 x^{n-1}y$; third term $= {}^nC_2 x^{n-2}y^2$. This gives that $(r+1)$th term $= {}^nC_r x^{n-r}y^r$.

Thus $T_{r+1} = {}^nC_r x^{n-r}y^r.$

Also, it can be easily seen that number of terms in the expansion of $(x+y)^n$ is $n+1$.

Example 5. *Find the 9th term in the expansion of* $\left(\sqrt{a} - 2\sqrt{b}\right)^{12}$.

Solution. The general term in the expansion of $(x+y)^n$ *is*

$$T_{r+1} = {}^nC_r x^{n-r}y^r$$

We want to find T_9, *i.e.,* $r = 8$

Now $\quad T_9 = {}^{12}C_8\, x^{12-8}y^8$

$$T_9 = {}^{12}C_8\left(\sqrt{a}\right)^4\left(-2\sqrt{b}\right)^8$$

$$= \frac{12.11.10.9}{4.3.2.1}\,a^2.256.b^4 = 126720\,a^2b^4.$$

Example 6. *Find the coefficient of* x^6 *in* $(x+2)^9$.

Solution. Let x^6 occur in T_{r+1}.

Then $$T_{r+1} = {}^9C_r x^{6-r} 2^r$$

Since x^6 is to occur in this term, $9-r=6$

$$\Rightarrow \quad r=3$$

Hence the term containing x^6 is given by ${}^9C_3 x^6 2^3$. So, the coefficient of x^6 is ${}^9C_3 . 2^3 = \frac{9.8.7}{3.2.1} \times 8 = 672$.

Example 7. *If the coefficients of second, third and fourth terms in the expansion of* $(1+x)^{2n}$ *are in A.P., find n.*

Solution. Let T_2, T_3 and T_4 denote the second, third and fourth terms respectively.

Then, $$T_2 = {}^{2n}C_1 x,\ T_3 = {}^{2n}C_2 x^2,\ T_4 = {}^{2n}C_3 x^3.$$

By hypothesis $$2 . {}^{2n}C_2 = {}^{2n}C_1 + {}^{2n}C_3$$

$$\Rightarrow \quad 2 \cdot \frac{2n(2n-1)}{2} = \frac{2n}{1} + \frac{2n(2n-1)(2n-2)}{6}$$

$$\Rightarrow \quad 2n-1 = 1 + \frac{(2n-1)(2n-2)}{6}$$

$$\Rightarrow \quad 12n-6 = 6 = (2n-1)(2n-2)$$

$$\Rightarrow \quad 12n-12 = 4n^2 - 6n + 2$$

$$\Rightarrow \quad 4n^2 - 18n + 14 = 0$$

$$\Rightarrow \quad 2n^2 - 9n + 7 = 0$$

$$\Rightarrow \quad n = 1 \text{ and } \frac{7}{2}.$$

Example 8. *The first three terms in the expansion of a binomial are 729, 7290, 30375. Find it.*

Solution. Let the binomial be $(x+a)^n$.

Then it is given that

$$x^n = 729$$

$${}^nC_1 x^{n-1} a = 7290$$

$${}^nC_2 x^{n-2} a^2 = 30375$$

i.e.,

$$x^n = 729 \quad \text{...(i)}$$

$$nx^{n-1} a = 7290 \quad \text{...(ii)}$$

$$\frac{n(n-1)}{2} x^{n-2} a^2 = 30375 \quad \text{...(iii)}$$

(*i*) and (*iii*) on multiplication give

$$\frac{n(n-1)}{2}\,x^{2n-2}.a^2 = 729 = 729 \times 30375$$

Also square of (*ii*) is given by

$n^2x^{2n-2}.a^2 = 7290 \times 7290$

Dividing these two results, we get

$$\frac{n\,(n-1)}{2n^2} = \frac{729 \times 30375}{7290 \times 7290}$$

$\Rightarrow \quad n = 6$ (on simplification)

Hence, from (*i*), $x^n = x^6 = 729$

$$\Rightarrow \qquad x = 3$$

Again (*ii*) gives $6.\,(3)^5.a = 7290$

$$\Rightarrow \qquad a = 5$$

The required binomial expansion is, therefore,

$$(3+5)^6$$

Example 9. *If the 21st and 22nd terms in the expansion of $(1 + x)^{44}$ are equal, find the value of x.*

Solution. 21st and 22nd terms in the expansion of $(1 + x)^{44}$ are given by

$$T_{21} = {}^{44}C_{20}x^{20}$$

$$T_{22} = {}^{44}C_{21}x^{21}$$

By the given condition,

$${}^{44}C_{20}x^{20} = {}^{44}C_{21}x^{21}$$

$$\Rightarrow \quad x = \frac{{}^{44}C_{20}}{{}^{44}C_{21}} = \frac{44!}{24!\,20!} \times \frac{23!\,21!}{44!}$$

$$= \frac{23!\,21!}{24!\,20!} = \frac{23!\,20!\,21}{24!\,20!\,24}$$

$$= \frac{21}{24} = \frac{7}{8}$$

which is the required value of x.

Example 10. *If the absolute term in the expansion of $\left(\sqrt{x} - \frac{k}{x^2}\right)^{10}$ is 405, find the value of k.*

Solution. By the absolute term, we mean the term independent of x (also called the constant term).

So suppose T_{r+1} is the absolute term in the expansion of

$$\left(\sqrt{x}-\frac{k}{x^2}\right)^{10}$$

Now $T_{r+1} = {}^{10}C_r\left(\sqrt{x}\right)^{10-r}\left(-\frac{k}{x^2}\right)^r$

$$= {}^{10}C_r x^{(10-r)/2}.x^{-2r}.k^r(-1)^r$$
$$= (-1)^r\,{}^{10}C_r k^r x^{(10-5r)/2}$$

T_{r+1} will be independent of x if $\frac{10-5r}{2}=0$

i.e., if $r=2$

Thus, T_3 is the absolute term.

Now $T_3 = (-1)^2\,{}^{10}C_2k^2$

Also it is given that $T_3 = 405$

$\Rightarrow\quad (-1)^2\,{}^{10}C_2k^2 = 405$

$\Rightarrow\quad k^2 = \frac{405}{45} = 9$

$\Rightarrow\quad k = \pm 3$

These are the required values of k.

Example 11. *Which term in the expansion* $\left(2x^2-\frac{1}{x}\right)^{20}$ *contains* x^7.

Solution. Suppose the required term is $(r+1)$th term T_{r+1}.

Then $\quad T_{r+1} = {}^{20}C_r(2x^2)^{20-r}\left(\frac{-1}{x}\right)^2$

$$= (-1)^r\,{}^{20}C_r\,2^{20-r}x^{40-2r}x^{-r}$$
$$= (-1)^r\,{}^{20}C_r\,2^{20-r}x^{40-3r}$$

So, $\quad x^{40-3r} = x^7$

$\Rightarrow\quad 40-3r = 7$

$\Rightarrow\quad r = 11$

$\Rightarrow$ 12th term contains x^7.

Example 12. *If a is the sum of the odd terms and b the sum of even terms in the expansion of* $(x+a)^n$, *then find* a^2-b^2.

Solution. $(x+a)^n = {}^nC_0x^n + {}^nC_1x^{n-1}a + \ldots + {}^nC_nx^n$

$$= ({}^nC_0x^n + {}^nC_2x^{n-2}a^2 + ...)$$
$$+ ({}^nC_1x^{n-1}a + {}^nC_3x^{n-3}a^3 + ...)$$
$$= a + b$$

$$(x-a)^n = {}^nC_0x^n - {}^nC_1x^{n-1}a + ... + {}^nC_n(-1)^na^n$$
$$= ({}^nC_0x^n + {}^nC_2x^{n-2}a^2 + ...) - ({}^nC_1x^{n-1}a + {}^nC_3x^{n-3}a^3 + ...)$$
$$= a - b$$

So, $(x+a)^n(x-a)^n = a^2 - b^2$

$\Rightarrow$ $a^2 - b^2 = (x^2 - a^2)^n.$

Example 13. *Find the term independent of x in the expansion of* $\left(x - \frac{1}{x}\right)^{10}$.

Solution. Suppose the required term is $(r+1)$th term T_{r+1}.

Then $T_{r+1} = {}^{10}C_r x^{10-r}\left(-\frac{1}{x}\right)^r$

The power of x present in T_{r+1} is $10 - 2r$.

Since there must be no x in T_{r+1}, $10 - 2r = 0 \Rightarrow r = 5$. Hence T_6 is the required term.

Now $T_6 = {}^{10}C_5(-1)^5$

$$= \frac{10.9.8.7.6}{5.4.3.2.1}(-1) = 9.4.7.(-1) = -252.$$

Example 14. *Show that* $(\sqrt{2}+1)^6 + (\sqrt{2}-1)^6 = 198$.

Solution. As seen before

$$(x+a)^n + (x-a)^n = 2(x^n + {}^nC_2x^{n-2}a^2 + {}^nC_4x^{n-4}a^4 + ...)$$

Take $n = 6, x = \sqrt{2}, a = 1$

Then $(\sqrt{2}+1)^6 + (\sqrt{2}-1)^6 = 2[(\sqrt{2})^6 + 15(\sqrt{2})^4 + 15(\sqrt{2})^2 + 1]$

$$= 2[8 + 60 + 30 + 1]$$
$$= 2(99)$$
$$= 198$$

EXERCISES

1. Expand the following:

   (i) $(2x - 3y)^5$ (ii) $(1 - 2x)^{10}$ (iii) $\left(\frac{2x}{3} - \frac{3}{2x}\right)^6$

   (iv) $\left(x + 1 - \frac{1}{x}\right)^6$ (v) $\left(x + \sqrt{x^2 - 1}\right)^7 + \left(x - \sqrt{x^2 - 1}\right)^7$

2. Find the 8th term in the expansion of $(x^{3/2}\, y^{1/2} - x^{1/2}\, y^{3/2})^{10}$.
3. Find the 19th term in the expansion of $(2x^{1/2} - y^{1/2})^{20}$.
4. (i) Determine the coefficient of x^{15} in the expansion of $(x - x^2)^{10}$.

   (ii) Find the coefficient of x^{-6} in the expansion of $\left(x^2 + \frac{1}{x^3}\right)^{12}$.

5. What is the term independent of x in the expansion of $\left(\frac{3}{2}x^2 - \frac{1}{3x}\right)^6$?
6. Find the term independent of x in the expansion of $\left(x^2 + \frac{1}{x}\right)^{12}$.
7. If x^{4r} is present in the expansion of $\left(x - \frac{1}{x^2}\right)^{4n}$, then show that its coefficient is

   $$\frac{4n!}{\left[\frac{4}{3}(n - r)\right]!\left[\frac{4}{3}(2n + r)\right]!}$$

8. If in the expansion of $(x + y)^n$, sum of all odd terms is a and sum of all even terms is b, prove that $(x^2 - y^2)^n = a^2 - b^2$.
9. Use Binomial theorem to evaluate

   (i) $(98)^4$ (ii) $(999)^4$

10. The first three terms in the expansion of a binomial are 32, 240, 720 respectively. Find it.
11. The first three terms in the expansion of a binomial are 1, 10, 40. Find it.
12. If the second, third and fourth terms in the expansion of $(x + a)^n$ are 240, 720 and 1080 respectively. Find x, a, n.
13. In the expansion of $(1 + x)^{11}$, the fifth term is 24 times the third term. Find the value of x.
14. If three successive terms in the expansion of $(1 + x)^n$ are 8064, 13440, 15360, find the values of n and x.
15. If in the expansion of $(1 + x)^n$, the fifth term is four times the fourth term and the fourth term is six times the third term, find the values of n and x.
16. If the absolute term in the expansion of $\left(x^2 + \frac{k}{x}\right)^{12}$ is 495, find the value of k.
17. Find the coefficient of x^4 in the expansion of $\left(x^4 + \frac{1}{x^3}\right)^{15}$.

ANSWERS

1. (*i*) $32x^5 - 240x^4y + 720x^3y^2 - 1080x^2y^3 + 810xy^4 - 243y^5$.

   (*ii*) $1 - 20x + 180x^2 - 960x^3 + 3360x^4 - 8064x^5 + 13440\,x^6 - 15360x^7 + 11520x^8 - 5120\,x^9 + 1024\,x^{10}$.

   (*iii*) $\frac{64}{729}x^6 - \frac{32}{27}x^4 + \frac{20}{3}x^2 - 20 + \frac{135}{4x^2} - \frac{243}{8x^4} + \frac{729}{64x^6}$

   (*iv*) $x^6 + 6x^5 + 9x^4 - 10x^3 - 30x^2 + 6x + 41 - \frac{6}{x} - \frac{30}{x^2} + \frac{10}{x^2} + \frac{9}{x^4} - \frac{6}{x^5} + \frac{1}{x^6}$

   (*v*) $2x(64x^6 - 112x^4 + 56x^2 - 7)$

2. $-120\,x^8y^{12}$ 3. $760\,xy^6$

4. (*i*) -252 (*ii*) 924

5. $\frac{7}{18}$ 6. 495

9. (*i*) 92236816 (*ii*) 996, 0.005, 996, 0.001.

10. $(2 + 3)^5$ 11. $(1 + 2)^5$

12. $x = 2, a = 3, n = 5$. 13. ± 12 14. $n = 10, x = 2$

15. $x = 2, n = 11$ 16. 1 17. ${}^{15}C_8$

3. TO FIND OUT THE MIDDLE TERM IN THE EXPANSION OF $(x + y)^n$

Case I. n is even.

Number of terms in the expansion of $(x + y)^n$ is $n + 1$ *i.e.*, an odd term.

So, the middle term will be $\left(\frac{n}{2}+1\right)$th term *i.e.*, $(T)_{n/2+1}$

Hence middle term $= {}^nC_{n/2}\,x^{n-(n/2)}\,y^{n/2}$

$$= {}^nC_{n/2}\,x^{n/2}\,y^{n/2}$$

$$= \frac{n!}{\left[\left(\frac{n}{2}\right)!\right]^2}\,x^{n/2}\,y^{n/2}$$

Case II. n is odd.

Number of terms in the expansion of $(x + y)^n$ is $n + 1$ *i.e.*, an even number.

In this case there are two middle terms, namely, $\frac{n+1}{2}$ th and $\frac{n+3}{2}$ th terms.

$$\frac{n+1}{2}\text{th term} = T_{(n+1)/2} = T_{\frac{n-1}{2}+1} = {}^nC_{(n-1)/2}\, x^{n-(n-1)/2}\, y^{(n-1)/2}$$

$$= {}^nC_{(n-1)/2}\, x^{(n+1)/2}\, y^{(n-1)/2}$$

and $$\frac{n+3}{2}\text{th term} = T_{(n+3)/2} = T_{\frac{n+1}{2}+1} = {}^nC_{(n+1)/2}\, x^{n-(n+1)/2}\, y^{(n+1)/2}$$

$$= {}^nC_{(n+1)/2}\, x^{(n-1)/2}\, y^{(n+1)/2}$$

Note that coefficients of both the middle terms are same!

4. TO FIND THE GREATEST TERM (NUMERICALLY) IN THE EXPANSION OF $(x + y)^n$

Let rth term be T_r and $(r + 1)$th term be T_{r+1}.

Then $$T_{r+1} = {}^nC_r\, x^{n-r} y^r$$

and $$T_r = {}^nC_{r-1}\, x^{n-r+1}\, y^{r-1}$$

So $$\frac{T_{r+1}}{T_r} = \frac{{}^nC_r y}{{}^nC_{r-1}} \frac{y}{x}$$

$$= \frac{n!}{r!(n-r)!} \frac{(n-r+1)!(r-1)!}{n!} \frac{y}{x} = \frac{(n-r+1)}{r} \frac{x}{y}$$

Thus $$T_{r+1} \gtrless T_r \Leftrightarrow (n-r+1)y \gtrless rx$$

$$\Leftrightarrow \frac{n+1}{r} - 1 \gtrless \frac{x}{y}$$

$$\Leftrightarrow \frac{n+1}{r} \gtrless \left(\frac{x}{y}+1\right)$$

$$\Leftrightarrow \frac{n+1}{\frac{x}{y}+1} \gtrless r$$

$$\Leftrightarrow r \lessgtr \frac{(n+1)\, y}{x+y}$$

(Note that $y > 0$ as we are interested only in numerically greatest term).

Case I. If $\frac{(n+1)\, y}{x+y}$ is a whole integer, say m.

Then for all r varying from 1 to $m-1$, $T_{r+1} > T_r$, *i.e.*, each of $T_1, T_2, ...,$ $T_{m-1}. T_m$ is greater than its preceding term. For $r = m$, $T_{r+1} = T_r$ and for $r > m$, $T_{r+1} < T_r$ *i.e.*, each of $T_{m+2}, T_{m+3}, ..., T_n, T_{n+1}$, is lesser than the preceding value.

Hence T_m and T_{m+1} are equal and are of greatest value among all terms of $(x+y)^n$. In other words mth and $(m+1)$th term are of numerically greatest value.

Case II. If $\dfrac{(n+1)\,y}{x+y}$ is not a whole integer, let m be the integral part of $\dfrac{(n+1)\,y}{x+y}$. For all $r = 1, ..., m$; $T_{r+1} > T_r$ and for all $r = m+1, ..., n+1$, $T_{r+1} < T_r$.

Hence T_{m+1} is of greatest value, *i.e.*, $(m + 1)$th term is of greatest numerical value.

Example 15. *Find the middle term in the expansion of* $(x+y)^{13}$.

Solution. In this case there are two-middle terms *viz.*, T_7, T_8.

Now
$$T_7 = {}^{13}C_6 x^7 y^6 = \frac{13.12.11.10.9.8}{6.5.4.3.2.1}\, x^7 y^6$$
$$= 1716\, x^6 y^7$$
$$T_8 = {}^{13}C_7 x^6 y^7 = {}^{13}C_6 x^6 y^7 = 1716 x^6 y^7.$$

Example 16. *Find out the term of greatest value in the expansion of* $(4 + 3x)^{25}$ *when* $x = 4$.

Solution.
$$\frac{T_{r+1}}{T_r} = \frac{25-r+1}{r}\left(\frac{3x}{4}\right)$$
$$= \frac{25-r+1}{r}\left(\frac{3.4}{4}\right) \quad \text{as } x = 4$$
$$= \frac{78-3r}{r}$$

So,
$$T_{r+1} \gtrless T_r \Leftrightarrow \frac{78-3r}{r} \gtrless 1$$
$$\Leftrightarrow 78 - 3r \gtrless r$$
$$\Leftrightarrow 78 \gtrless 4r$$
$$\Leftrightarrow 39 \gtrless 2r \Leftrightarrow r \gtrless 19\frac{1}{2}.$$

Thus T_{20} is of greatest value.

Example 17. *Show that the middle term in the expansion of* $(1+x)^{2n}$ *is* $\dfrac{1.3.5.\dots(2n-1)}{n!}2^n x^n$.

Solution. In the expansion of $(1+x)^{2n}$ there will be $2n+1$ (*i.e.*, odd number) of terms. The middle term will thus be the $(n+1)$th term.

$$\text{Now } T_{n+1} = {}^{2n}C_n x^n = \frac{(2n)!}{n!\,n!}.x^n$$

$$= \frac{2n(2n-1)(2n-2)(2n-3)\dots 4.3.2.1}{n!\,n!}x^n$$

$$= \frac{[2n(2n-2)(2n-4)\dots 4.2][(2n-1)(2n-3)\dots 3.1]}{n!\,n!}x^n$$

$$= \frac{2^n[n(n-1)(n-2)\dots 2.1][(2n-1)(2n-3)\dots 3.1]}{n!\,n!}x^n$$

$$= \frac{2^n[(2n-1)(2n-3)\dots 3.1]}{n!}x^n$$

$$= \frac{1.3.5.\dots(2n-1)}{n!}2^n x^n$$

Example 18. *Prove that the middle term in the expansion of* $\left(x+\dfrac{1}{2x}\right)^{2n}$ *is* $\dfrac{1.3.5.\dots(2n-1)}{n!}$.

Solution. Here again the middle term is the $(n+1)$th term. We have

$$T_{n+1} = {}^{2n}C_n x^n\left(\frac{1}{2x}\right)^n = {}^{2n}C_n\frac{1}{2^n}$$

$$= \frac{(2n)!}{n!\,n!}.\frac{1}{2^n}$$

$$= \frac{[1.3.5.\dots(2n-1)]\,2^n}{n!}.\frac{1}{2^n} \quad \text{(As in the previous example)}$$

$$= \frac{[1.3.5.\dots(2n-1)]}{n!}$$

5. BINOMIAL COEFFICIENTS

The coefficients ${}^nC_0, {}^nC_1, {}^nC_2, \dots$ in the expansion of a binomial are called *Binomial coefficients.*

We state and prove a few properties of the binomial coefficients.

(1) Sum of the binomial coefficients in the expansion of $(1+x)^n$ is 2^n

i.e., we want to show that

$$^nC_0 + {}^nC_1 + \ldots + {}^nC_n = 2^n$$

We know

$$(1+x)^n = {}^nC_0 + {}^nC_1x + {}^nC_2x^2 + \ldots + {}^nC_nx^n$$

Put $x = 1$ to obtain

$$2^n = {}^nC_0 + {}^nC_1 + {}^nC_2 + \ldots + {}^nC_n$$

which proves the result.

(2) The coefficients of the terms in the expansion of $(1+x)^n$, equidistant from the beginning and end are equal.

The general term T_{r+1} from the beginning is $^nC_rx^r$

$\Rightarrow$ Its coefficient is ^nC_r

Since total number of terms is $n+1$, the $(r+1)$th term from the end has $(n+1)-(r+1) = n-r$ terms before it.

i.e., $(r+1)$th term from the end is $(n-r+1)$th term from the beginning

and $\quad T_{n-r+1} = {}^nC_{n-r}x^{n-r}$

$\Rightarrow$ Its coefficient $= {}^nC_{n-r}$

But $\quad {}^nC_r = {}^nC_{n-r}$

Hence the result follows.

(3) In the expansion of $(1+x)^n$, the sum of the even coefficients is equal to the sum of the odd coefficients.

Put $x = -1$ in the expansion

$$(1+x)^n = {}^nC_0 + {}^nC_1x + {}^nC_2x^2 + \ldots + {}^nC_nx^n$$

We have $\quad 0 = {}^nC_0 - {}^nC_1 + {}^nC_2 - {}^nC_3 + \ldots + (-1)^n\,{}^nC_n$

$\Rightarrow \quad {}^nC_0 + {}^nC_2 + {}^nC_4 + \ldots = {}^nC_1 + {}^nC_3 + {}^nC_5 + \ldots$

which proves our result.

Note that the sum of each $= \dfrac{1}{2}.2^n = 2^{n-1}$

Example 19. *If* $(1+x)^n = C_0 + C_1x + C_2x^2 + \ldots + C_nx^n$, *prove that*

$$C_0C_2 + C_1C_3 + C_2C_4 + \ldots + C_{n-2}C_n = \frac{\lfloor 2n}{\lfloor n-2\;\lfloor n+2}$$

Solution. Since $(1+x)^n = C_0 + C_1x + C_2x^2 + \ldots + C_nx^n$

we get $\left(1+\frac{1}{x}\right)^n = C_0 + \frac{C_1}{x} + \frac{C_2}{x_2} + \ldots + \frac{C_n}{x_n}$

Multiplying these two expansions, we have

$$(1+x)^n\left(1+\frac{1}{x}\right)^n = (C_0 + C_1x + C_2x^2 + \ldots + C_nx^n)$$

$$\times\left(C_0 + \frac{C_1}{x} + \frac{C_2}{x^2} + \ldots + \frac{C_n}{x^n}\right)$$

Clearly $C_0C_2 + C_1C_3 + \ldots + C_{n-2}C_n$ = coefficient of $\frac{1}{x^2}$ in the expansion of RHS.

Thus

$$C_0C_2 + C_1C_3 + \ldots + C_{n-2}C_n = \text{coefficient of } \frac{1}{x^2} \text{ in } (1+x)^n\left(1+\frac{1}{x}\right)^n$$

$$= \text{coefficient of } x^{n-2} \text{ in } (1+x)^{2n}$$

Suppose x^{n-2} occurs in $T_{r+1} = {}^{2n}C_r \cdot x^r$,

Then $r = n-2$

Hence coefficient of x^{n-2} in $(1+x)^{2n}$ is ${}^{2n}C_r = {}^{2n}C_{n-2}$

$$\frac{\underline{|2n}}{\underline{|2n-(n-2)}\ \underline{|n-2}} = \frac{\underline{|2n}}{\underline{|n-2}\ \underline{|n+2}}$$

Consequently $C_0C_2 + C_1C_3 + \ldots + C_{n-2}C_n = \dfrac{\underline{|2n}}{\underline{|n-2}\ \underline{|n+2}}$

Example 20. *If* $(1+x)^n = C_0 + C_1x + C_2x^2 + \ldots + C_nx^n$,

prove that $C_1^2 + 2C_2^2 + 3C_3^2 + \ldots + nC_n^2 = \dfrac{\underline{|2n-1}}{\left(\underline{|n-1}\right)^2}$

Solution. Now $C_1x + 2C_2x^2 + 3C_3x^3 + \ldots + nC_nx^n$

$$= nx\left\{1 + (n-1)x + \frac{(n-1)(n-2)}{1.2}x^2 + \ldots + x^{n-1}\right\}$$

$$= nx(1+x)^{n-1}$$

Changing x into $\frac{1}{x}$, we get

$$\frac{C_1}{x}+\frac{2C_2}{x^2}+\frac{3C_3}{x^3}+...+\frac{nC_n}{x^n}=\frac{n}{x}\left(1+\frac{1}{x}\right)^{n-1}=\frac{n}{x^n}(1+x)^{n-1} \quad ...(1)$$

Also $$C_0+C_1x+C_2x^2+...+C_nx^n=(1+x)^n \quad ...(2)$$

Multiplying the expansion (1) and (2), we note that $C_1^2+2C_2^2+3C_3^2+...+nC_n^2$ is term independent of x in LHS of the product of (1) and (2).

Hence $C_1^2+2C_2^2+3C_3^2+...+nC_n^2$ = term independent of x in $\frac{n}{x^n}(1+x)^{n-1}(1+x)^n$

= coefficient of x^n in $n(1+x)^{2n-1}$

= n times the coefficient of x^n in $(1+x)^{2n-1}$

Suppose x^n occurs in $T_{r+1}={}^{2n-1}C_rx^r$, then $r=n$

As a consequence, coefficient of x^n in $(1+x)^{2n-1}$ is ${}^{2n-1}C_n$.

$$\text{Thus } C_1^2+2C_2^2+3C_3^2+...+nC_n^2=n\cdot\frac{\underline{|2n-1}}{\underline{|2n-1-n}\ \underline{|n}}$$

$$=\frac{\underline{|2n-1}}{\underline{|n-1}\ \underline{|n-1}}$$

$$=\frac{\underline{|2n-1}}{\left(\underline{|n-1}\right)^2}$$

Example 21. *Show that* $1^2C_1+2^2C_2+3^3C_3+...+n^2C_n=n(n+1)\,2^{n-2}$

Solution. Now $(1+x)^n=C_0+C_1x+C_2x^2+...+C_nx^n$

Differentiating *w.r.t.* x,

$$n(1+x)^{n-1}=C_1+2C_2x+3C_3x^2+...nC_nx^{n-1}$$

$$\Rightarrow \quad nx(1+x)^{n-1}=C_1x+2C_2x^2+3C_3x^3+...+nC_nx^n$$

Differentiating *w.r.t.* x

$$n[(1+x)^{n-1}+x(n-1)(1+x)^{n-2}]$$
$$=C_1+4C_2x+9C_3x^2+...+n^2C_nx^{n-1}$$
$$=C_1+2^2C_2x+3^2C_3x^2+...+n^2C_nx^{n-1}$$

Take $x=1$

Then $n[2^{n-1}+(n-1)\,2^{n-2}]=C_1+2^2C_2+3^2C_3+...+n^2C_n$

$$\Rightarrow \quad n2^{n-2}(n+1)=1^2C_1+2^2C_2+3^2C^2+...+n^2C_n$$

Example 22. *Show that* $\frac{C_1}{C_0} + 2\frac{C_2}{C_1} + 3\frac{C_3}{C_2} + ... + n\frac{C_n}{C_{n-1}} = \frac{n(n+1)}{2}$

Solution. $\frac{C_1}{C_0} + 2\frac{C_2}{C_1} + 3\frac{C_3}{C_2} + ... + n\frac{C_n}{C_{n-1}}$

$$= \frac{n}{1} + 2\frac{n(n-1)}{2n} + 3\frac{n(n-1)(n-2)}{6n(n-1)} \cdot 2 + ... + n\frac{1}{n}$$

$$= n + (n-1) + (n-2) + ... + 1$$

$$= \frac{n(n+1)}{2}$$

Example 23. *If a_1, a_2, a_3, a_4 are the coefficients of the second, third, fourth and fifth terms respectively in the binomial expansion of $(1 + x)^n$, prove that*

$$\frac{a_1}{a_1 + a_2} + \frac{a_3}{a_3 + a_4} = \frac{2a_2}{a_2 + a_3}$$

Solution. We know,

$$(1+x)^n = {}^nC_0 + {}^nC_1x + {}^nC_2x^2 + ... + {}^nC_nx^n$$

Thus
$$a_1 = {}^nC_1$$
$$a_2 = {}^nC_2$$
$$a_3 = {}^nC_3$$
$$a_4 = {}^nC_4$$

So
$$\frac{a_1}{a_1 + a_2} + \frac{a_3}{a_3 + a_4} = \frac{{}^nC_1}{{}^nC_1 + {}^nC_2} + \frac{{}^nC_3}{{}^nC_3 + {}^nC_4}$$

$$= \frac{{}^nC_1}{{}^{n+1}C_2} + \frac{{}^nC_3}{{}^{n+1}C_4}$$

$$= \frac{n}{\frac{(n+1)n}{2}} + \frac{\frac{n(n-1)(n-2)}{6}}{\frac{(n+1)n(n-1)(n-2)}{24}}$$

$$= \frac{2}{n+1} + \frac{4}{n+1} = \frac{6}{n+1} \quad ...(i)$$

Again
$$\frac{2a_2}{a_2 + a_3} = \frac{2 . {}^nC_2}{{}^nC_2 + {}^nC_3} = \frac{\frac{2.n(n-1)}{2}}{{}^{n+1}C_3}$$

$$= \frac{n(n-1)}{\frac{(n+1)\,n\,(n-1)}{6}} = \frac{6}{n+1} \qquad \dots (ii)$$

(*i*) and (*ii*) give the result.

Example 24. *Show that* $C_0^2 - C_1^2 + C_2^2 + \dots + (-1)^n (C_n)^2 = 0$ *when n is odd.*

Solution. Now $\quad (1+x)^n = C_0 + C_1 x + \dots + C_n x^n$

$$(x-1)^n = C_0 x^n - C_1 x^{n-1} + C_2 x^{n-2} + \dots + (-1)^n C_n$$

So, $(-1)^n (1-x^2)^n = (C_0 + C_1 x + \dots + C_n x^n)(C_0 x^4 - C_1 x^{n-1} + \dots + (-1)^n C_n)$

Coefficient of x^n in R.H.S. is $C_0^2 - C_1^2 + C_2^2 + \dots + (-1)^n (C_n)^2$

Coefficient of x^n is L.H.S. is 0.

Thus, $C_0^2 - C_1^2 + C_2^2 + \dots + (-1)^n (C_n)^2 = 0$

Example 25. *Show that* $2C_0 + \frac{2^2}{2} C_1 + \frac{2^3}{3} C_2 + \dots + \frac{2^{11}}{11} C_{10} = \frac{3^{11} - 1}{11}$

Solution. $(1+x)^n = C_0 + C_1 x + C_2 x^2 + C_3 x^3 + \dots + C_n x^n$

Integrating *w.r.t. x*

$$\frac{(1+x)^{n+1}}{n+1} = C_0 x + C_1 \frac{x^2}{2} + C_2 \frac{x^3}{3} + \dots + C_n \frac{x^{n+1}}{n+1} + A$$

where *A* is constant.

Take $x = 0$ on both sides.

Then $\qquad \frac{1}{nH} = A$

Take $x = 2$ and $n = 10$.

Then $\qquad \frac{3^{11}}{11} = 2C_0 + \frac{2^2}{2} C_1 + \frac{2^3}{3} C_2 + \dots + \frac{2^{11}}{11} C_{10} + \frac{1}{11}$

$$\Rightarrow \quad 2C_0 + \frac{2^2}{2} C_1 + \frac{2^3}{3} C_2 + \dots + \frac{2^{11}}{11} C_{10} = \frac{3^{11} - 1}{11}$$

Example 26. *If the coefficients of* x^2 *and* x^3 *in the expansion of* $(3 + kx)^9$ *are equal, find the value of k.*

Solution. Coefficient of x^2 in the expansion of $(3 + kx)^9$ is

$${}^9C_2 (3)^7 k^2 = (3)^7\, 36k^2$$

whereas coefficient of x^2 in the expansion of $(3 + kx)^9$ is

$${}^9C_3 (3)^6 k^3 = (3)^6\, 84k^3$$

By hypothesis $\qquad (3)^7\, 36k^2 = (3)^6\, 84k^3$

$$\Rightarrow \qquad k = 0 \text{ or } k = \frac{3.36}{84} = \frac{9}{7}$$

$k = 0$ will imply that $3 + kx$ is no more a binomial expression, so we reject this value of k.

Hence $\qquad k = \dfrac{9}{7}.$

EXERCISES

1. Find out the numerically greatest term in the expansion of

   (*i*) $\left(\dfrac{x}{2} - \dfrac{y}{3}\right)^{15}$ when $x = 8,\ y = 9$.

   (*ii*) $(2 + 3x)^{12}$ when $x = \dfrac{5}{6}$,

   (*iii*) $(3 - 5y)^{11}$ when $y = \dfrac{1}{5}$.

2. Find the middle term in the expansion of $\left(1 - \dfrac{x^2}{2}\right)^{14}$.

3. If $(1 + x)^n = C_0 + C_1x + C_2x^2 + ... + C_n x^n$, find the values of

   $C_0 + 2C_1 + 3C_2 + ... + (n + 1)\, C_n$ and $C_0\, C_1 + C_1\, C_2 + C_2C_3 + C_{n-1}C_n$.

4. If $C_0, C_1, C_2, ..., C_n$ denote the coefficients in the expansion of $(1 + x)^n$, prove that

   (*i*) $C_1 + 2C_2 + 3C_3 + ... + nC_n = n.2^{n-1}$.

   (*ii*) $\dfrac{C_0}{1} + \dfrac{C_1}{2} + ... + \dfrac{C_n}{n+1} = \dfrac{2^{n+1} - 1}{n+1}$.

5. In the expansion of $(1 + x)^{43}$, the coefficients of the $(2r + 1)$th term and the $(r + 2)$th term are equal. Find r.

6. In the expansion of $(1+ x)^{20}$, the coefficient of the rth term is to that of the $(r + 1)$th term in the ratio 1 : 2. Find r.

7. In the expansion of $(1 + x)^{10}$, the coefficient of $(2r + 1)$th term is equal to the coefficient of the $(4r + 5)$ th term. Find r.

8. If three successive coefficients in the expansion of $(1 + x)^n$ are 210, 120 and 45 respectively. Find n.

9. Prove that if x lies between $\dfrac{n}{n+1}$ and $\dfrac{n+1}{n}$, the greatest term in the expansion of $(1 + x)^{2n}$ has the greatest coefficient.

[Hint. Greatest coefficient in the expansion of $(1 + x)^n$ is ${}^nC_{n/2}$, when n is even and it is ${}^nC_r$ where $r = \dfrac{n-1}{2}$ or $\dfrac{n+1}{2}$, when n is odd].

10. Find the middle term/terms in the expansion of

(*i*) $\left(2x^2 - \dfrac{1}{3x^2}\right)^{10}$ (*ii*) $\left(\dfrac{3}{4}x + \dfrac{4}{3}y\right)^{11}$

(*iii*) $\left(3a - \dfrac{a^3}{b}\right)^9$ (*iv*) $\left(2x + \dfrac{3}{x}\right)^{20}$

ANSWERS

1. (*i*) 7th term (*ii*) 8th term (*iii*) 3rd and 4th terms.

2. $\dfrac{429}{16}x^{14}$ 3. $2^{n-1}(n + 2)$; $\dfrac{\underline{|2n}}{\underline{|n-1}\ \underline{|n+1}}$

5. 14 6. 7

7. 1 8. 10

10. (*i*) $\dfrac{-896}{27}$ (*ii*) $\dfrac{693}{2}x^6y^5$, $616\ x^5y^6$

(*iii*) ${}^9C_4\ 3^5 . \dfrac{a^{17}}{b^4}$ (*iv*) $19.17.13.11.3^{10}.\ 2^{12}$.

6. BINOMIAL THEOREM (ANY INDEX)

We have already found out the expansion of $(x + y)^n$, when n is a + ve integer. We now give the expansion of $(1 + x)^n$, where n can be negative integer or fraction.

Binomial theorem for any index:

If $|x| < 1$, *then*

$$(1+x)^n = 1 + nx + \frac{n(n-1)}{\underline{|2}}x^2 + \frac{n(n-1)(n-2)}{\underline{|3}}x^3 + \ldots \infty$$

where n may be negative integer or fraction.

The following examples will illustrate the use of the above expansion.

Example 27. *Expand* $\left(1-\frac{x}{2}\right)^{-\frac{1}{2}}$ *giving the first four terms.*

Solution. We have

$$\left(1-\frac{x}{2}\right)^{-\frac{1}{2}} = 1+\left(-\frac{1}{2}\right)\left(-\frac{x}{2}\right)+\frac{\left(-\frac{1}{2}\right)\left(-\frac{1}{2}-1\right)}{\underline{|2}}\left(-\frac{x}{2}\right)^2$$

$$+\frac{\left(-\frac{1}{2}\right)\left(\frac{-1}{2}-1\right)\left(-\frac{1}{2}-2\right)}{\underline{|3}}\left(-\frac{x}{2}\right)^3 + \ldots \infty$$

$$= 1+\frac{x}{4}+\frac{3x^2}{32}+\frac{5}{128}x^3+\ldots$$

Example 28. *Expand* $(5-x)^{-\frac{1}{2}}$ *upto terms containing* x^3 *, when* $x < 5$.

Solution. We have

$$(5-x)^{-\frac{1}{2}} = (5)^{-\frac{1}{2}}\left(1-\frac{x}{5}\right)^{-\frac{1}{2}}$$

Since $|x| < 5, \left|\frac{x}{5}\right| < 1.$

Thus by Binomial theorem for any index

$$\left(1-\frac{x}{5}\right)^{-\frac{1}{2}} = 1+\left(-\frac{1}{2}\right)\left(-\frac{x}{5}\right)+\frac{\left(-\frac{1}{2}\right)\left(-\frac{1}{2}-1\right)}{\underline{|2}}\left(-\frac{x}{5}\right)^2$$

$$+\frac{\left(-\frac{1}{2}\right)\left(-\frac{1}{2}-1\right)\left(-\frac{1}{2}-2\right)}{\underline{|3}}\left(-\frac{x}{5}\right)^3 + \ldots$$

$$= 1+\frac{1}{2}.\frac{x}{5}+\frac{1.3}{2.4}.\frac{x^2}{25}+\frac{1.3.5}{2.4.6}.\frac{x^3}{125}+\ldots$$

and thus

$$(5-x)^{-1/2} = \frac{1}{\sqrt{5}}\left[1+\frac{1}{2}.\frac{x}{5}+\frac{1.3}{2.4}.\frac{x^2}{25}+\frac{1.3.5}{2.4.6}.\frac{x^3}{125}+\ldots\right]$$

Example 29. *Using Binomial theorem, find the value of* $\sqrt[3]{128}$ *to four decimal places.*

Solution. We have

$$\sqrt[3]{128} = (128)^{1/3} = (125+3)^{1/3}$$

$$= (125)^{\frac{1}{3}}\left[1+\frac{3}{125}\right]^{\frac{1}{3}}$$

$$= 5\,[1+.024]^{1/3}$$

$$= 5\left[1+\frac{1}{3}\times .024+\frac{\frac{1}{3}\left(\frac{1}{3}-1\right)}{2}\times(.024)^2+\ldots\right]$$

$$= 5\,[1+.008-.000064+\ldots]$$

$= 5.0397$ correct up to four places of decimal.

Example 30. *Find the first negative term in the expansion of* $\left(1+\frac{3}{4}x\right)^{\frac{13}{3}}$ *where* $0 < x < \frac{4}{3}$.

Solution. Suppose

$$T_{r+1} = \frac{n(n-1)\,(n-2)\ldots(n-r+1)}{\underline{|r}}\left(\frac{3}{4}x\right)^r$$

is the first negative term. As $\left(\frac{3}{4}x\right)^r$ is positive for $0 < x < \frac{4}{3}$.

T_{r+1} will be the first negative term if r is the least integer satisfying

$$n - r + 1 < 0$$

i.e., $$\frac{13}{3} - r + 1 < 0$$

$\Rightarrow$ $$r > \frac{16}{3}$$

Least r greater than $\frac{16}{3}$ is 6.

Hence value of r is 6.

Thus T_7 is the first negative term.

Now

$$T_7 = \frac{\frac{13}{3}\left(\frac{13}{3}-1\right)\left(\frac{13}{3}-2\right)\left(\frac{13}{3}-3\right)\left(\frac{13}{3}-4\right)\left(\frac{13}{3}-5\right)}{\underline{|6}}\cdot\left(\frac{3}{4}x\right)^6$$

$$= \frac{-91\,x^6}{36864}$$

Example 31. *Find the first three terms of* $\frac{1}{(1+x)^2\sqrt{1+4x}}$ *assuming the validity of the expansion in ascending powers of x.*

Solution. We have

$$\frac{1}{(1+x)^2\sqrt{1+4x}} = (1+x)^{-2}\,(1+4x)^{-1/2}$$

Now $(1+x)^{-2} = 1 + (-2)x + \frac{(-2)(-2-1)}{\underline{|2}}x^2 + \frac{(-2)(-2-1)(-2-2)}{\underline{|3}}x^3 \ldots$

and $(1+4x)^{1/2} = 1 + \left(-\frac{1}{2}\right)4x + \frac{\left(-\frac{1}{2}\right)\left(-\frac{1}{2}-1\right)}{\underline{|2}}(4x)^2 + \ldots$

Hence

$$(1+x)^{-2}\,(1+4x)^{-1/2} = (1 - 2x + 3x^2 + \ldots)\,(1 - 2x + 6x^2 + \ldots)$$

Hence first three terms in the expansion are

$$1 - 4x + 13x^2.$$

Example 32. *Product in thousand kilograms of a certain firm in the first, second, third, etc., weeks is the same as the coefficient of the first, second, third etc., powers of x in the expansion of* $(1+x)(1-x)^{-2}$. *Find the production in the sixth week.*

Solution. The expansion of $(1+x)(1-x)^{-2}$ is given by

$$(1+x)\left[1 + (-2)(-x) + \frac{(-2)(-2-1)}{2}(-x)^2 + \frac{(-2)(-2-1)(-2-2)}{\underline{|3}}(-x)^3 + \frac{(-2)(-2-1)(-2-2)(-2-3)}{\underline{|4}}(-x)^4 + \ldots\right]$$

$$= (1 + 2x)\,[1 + 2x + 3x^2 + 4x^3 + 5x^4 + 6x^5 + 7x^6 + ...]$$
$$= (1 + 2x + 3x^2 + 4x^3 + 5x^4 + 6x^5 + 7x^6 + ...)$$
$$+ (x + 2x^2 + 3x^3 + 4x^4 + 5x^5 + 6x^6 + ...)$$
$$= 1 + 3x + 5x^2 + 7x^3 + 9x^4 + 11x^5 + 13x^6 + ...$$

As the coefficient of the sixth power of x is 13, the required production in the sixth week is 13 thousand kilograms.

EXERCISES

1. Expand the following

   (*i*) $(4 - 3x)^{3/2}$, $|x| < \frac{4}{3}$ (*ii*) $(1 + x)^{-4}$, $|x| < 1$

   (*iii*) $(1 + x)^{-2}$, $|x| < 1$ (*iv*) $(1 - x)^{-1}$, $|x| < 1$

   (*v*) $(1 + 3x)^{1/2}(1 - 2x)^{-1/3}$, $|x| < \min\left(\frac{1}{3}, \frac{1}{2}\right)$.

2. Find

   (*i*) the 8th term of $(1 - 3a^2)^{16/3}$, $|a| < \frac{1}{\sqrt{3}}$

   (*ii*) the 5th term of $(1 - 2x^3)^{11/2}$, $|x| < \frac{1}{3\sqrt{2}}$

   (*iii*) general term of $(2 - 3x)^{3/2}$, $|x| < \frac{2}{3}$

   (*iv*) general term of $(1 - 2x)^{-1/2}$, $|x| < \frac{1}{2}$

3. Find the first negative term in the expansion of

   (*i*) $\left(1+\frac{4}{3}x\right)^{\frac{27}{3}}$ where $0 < x < \frac{3}{4}$

   (*ii*) $(1 + 3x)^{16/3}$ where $0 < x < \frac{1}{3}$

   (*iii*) $\left(1+\frac{4}{3}x\right)^{\frac{19}{4}}$ where $0 < x < \frac{3}{4}$

4. Find $\frac{1}{\sqrt[3]{62}}$, correct to four decimal places.

5. Find $\frac{1}{\sqrt[4]{630}}$, correct to five decimal places.

6. Find the coefficient of x^n in the expansion of $\frac{(1+x)^2}{(1-x)^2}$, $|x|<1$.

7. Find the coefficient of x^n in the expansion of $\frac{x-2}{(x+2)(x-1)^2}$, $|x|<1$.

8. What is the value of n for which the coefficient of x^3 in the expansion of $(1+x^2)(1+x)^n$ is six times the coefficient of x? ($|x|<1$).

9. Use Binomial Theorem to expand $(1+x+x^2)^{-3}$.

$$\left[\textbf{Hint. } 1+x+x^2=\frac{1-x^3}{1-x}\right]$$

10. Expand $(x+y)^n$ when n is not a positive interger.

11. Find the coefficient of x^4 in the expansion of $(1-x+x^2-x^3)^{-1}$

12. Show that

$$x^n-1+n\left(1-\frac{1}{x}\right)+\frac{n(n-1)}{2!}\left(1-\frac{1}{x}\right)^2+\ldots$$

13. Find the value of $(126)^{1/3}$ correct to 4 decimal places, using Binomial theorem.

ANSWERS

1. (*i*) $8-9x+\frac{27}{16}x^2+\ldots$ (*ii*) $1-4x+10x^2-20x^3+\ldots$

   (*iii*) $1-2x+3x^2-4x^3+\ldots$ (*iv*) $1+x+x^2+x^3+\ldots$

   (*v*) $1+\frac{13}{6}x+\frac{55}{72}x^2+\ldots$

2. (*i*) $\frac{208}{9}a^{14}$ (*ii*) $\frac{1155}{8}x^{12}$

   (*iii*) $\frac{2^{3/2}\left[\frac{3}{2}\left(\frac{3}{2}-1\right)\left(\frac{3}{2}-2\right)\ldots\left(\frac{3}{2}-r+1\right)\right]}{\underline{|r}}\cdot\left(-\frac{3}{2}x\right)$

   (*iv*) $(-1)^r\frac{1.3.5\ldots(2r-1)}{\underline{|r}}x^r.|x|<\frac{1}{2}$

3. (*i*) $\frac{-27.23\ldots3}{8!}\left(\frac{3}{4}\right)^8x^8$ (*ii*) $\frac{-208}{9}x^7$ (*iii*) $\frac{-1463}{233}x^6$

4. 0.2527 5. 5.00997 6. $4n$

7. $\frac{(-1)^{n+1}}{9.2^{n-1}}-\frac{n+1}{3}-\frac{4}{9}$ 8. 7 or – 4

9. $1-3x+3x^2+2x^3-9x^4+\ldots$

10. $x^n\left[1+n.\frac{y}{x}+\frac{n(n-1)}{\underline{|2}}\frac{y^2}{x^2}+\frac{n(n-1)(n-2)}{\underline{|3}}.\frac{y^3}{x^3}+...\right]$ when $|x|>|y|$

$y^n\left[1+n.\frac{x}{y}+\frac{n(n-1)}{\underline{|2}}\frac{x^2}{y^3}+\frac{n(n-1)(n-2)}{\underline{|3}}.\frac{x^2}{y^3}+...\right]$ when $|x|<|y|$

11. 1 13. 5.0133.

7. APPLICATION OF BINOMIAL THEOREM

We illustrate below by means of examples how the Binomial Theorem is used in the summation of infinite series and certain other types of problems.

Example 33. *Sum the series*

$$1+\frac{3}{4}+\frac{3.5}{4.8}+\frac{3.5.7}{4.8.12}+...\infty$$

Solution. Comparing the given series with the expansion

$$(1+x)^n=1+nx+\frac{n(n-1)}{\underline{|2}}x^2+\frac{n(n-1)(n-2)}{\underline{|3}}x^3+...$$

we find $$nx=\frac{3}{4} \qquad ...(i)$$

$$\frac{n(n-1)}{2}x^2=\frac{3.5}{4.8} \qquad ...(ii)$$

(*i*) gives $x=\dfrac{3}{4n}$

Putting in (*ii*), we get

$$\frac{n(n-1)}{2}.\frac{9}{16n^2}=\frac{3.5}{4.8}$$

$$\Rightarrow \quad \left(1-\frac{1}{n}\right)9=3.5=15$$

$$\Rightarrow \quad n=-\frac{3}{2}$$

and, therefore, $$x=-\frac{3}{4}\times\frac{2}{3}=-\frac{1}{2}$$

Hence the given series is equal to

$$\left(1-\frac{1}{2}\right)^{-\frac{3}{2}}=\left(\frac{1}{2}\right)^{-\frac{3}{2}}=2^{\frac{3}{2}}=2\sqrt{2}$$

Example 34. *Sum the series*

$$\frac{5}{3.6}+\frac{5.7}{3.6.9}+\frac{5.7.9}{3.6.9.12}+...$$

Solution. The given series can be written as

$$=\frac{1}{3}\left[\frac{3.5}{3.6}+\frac{3.5.7}{3.6.9}+\frac{3.5.7.9}{3.6.9.12}+...\right]$$

$$=\frac{1}{3}\left[2+\frac{3.5}{3.6}+\frac{3.5.7}{3.6.9}+...-2\right]$$

$$=-\frac{2}{3}+\frac{1}{3}\left[1+1+\frac{3.5}{3.6}+\frac{3.5.7}{3.6.9}+...\right]$$

The series inside the bracket will be summed up by means of Binomial Theorem for any index.

Comparing this series with the expansion

$$(1+x)^n = 1+nx+\frac{n(n-1)}{2!}x^2+...$$

we get $$nx = 1 \text{ or } x=\frac{1}{n}$$

and $$\frac{n(n-1)x^2}{2} = \frac{3.5}{3.6} = \frac{5}{6}$$

$$\Rightarrow \quad \frac{n(n-1)}{2}.\frac{1}{n^2} = \frac{5}{6} \quad \Rightarrow \quad n=-\frac{3}{2}$$

This implies that $$x=-\frac{2}{3}$$

Consequently the series inside the bracket

$$=\left(1-\frac{2}{3}\right)^{-3/2}=\left(\frac{1}{3}\right)^{-3/2}=3^{3/2}=3\sqrt{3}$$

Hence the given series $$=-\frac{2}{3}+\frac{1}{3}(3\sqrt{3})=\sqrt{3}-\frac{2}{3}$$

Example 35. *If* $y+\frac{1}{3}+\frac{1.3}{3.6}+\frac{1.3.5}{3.6.9}+...$

prove that $y^2+2y-2=0$

Solution. We have

$$y+1 = 1+\frac{1}{3}+\frac{1.3}{3.6}+\frac{1.3.5}{3.6.9}+\ldots$$

Comparing the series on the RHS with the binomial expansion

$$(1+x)^n = 1+nx+\frac{n(n-1)}{\underline{|2}}x^2+\ldots$$

we get $\qquad nx = \frac{1}{3}$

$$\frac{n(n-1)}{\underline{|2}}x^2 = \frac{1.3}{3.6}$$

giving thereby, $\qquad n = -\frac{1}{2}$ and $x = -\frac{2}{3}$

Thus $\qquad y+1 = \left(1-\frac{2}{3}\right)^{-1/2} = \left(\frac{1}{3}\right)^{-1/2} = 3^{1/2}$

Squaring both sides, we get

$$y^2+1+2y=3$$

$\Rightarrow \qquad y^2+2y-2=0$

Example 36. *If $p = q$ nearly and $n > 1$, show that*

$$\frac{(n+1)p+(n-1)q}{(n-1)p+(n+1)q} = \left(\frac{p}{q}\right)^{1/n}$$

Apply this rule to find approximately the seventh root of $\frac{131}{133}$.

Solution. It is given that $p = q$, nearly,

so let $q = p + h$ where h is very small

Then $\qquad \text{LHS} = \frac{(n+1)\,p+(n-1)\,(p+h)}{(n-1)\,p+(n+1)\,(p+h)}$

$$= \frac{2np+(n-1)\,h}{2np+(n+1)\,h}$$

$$= \frac{2np\left[1+\frac{n-1}{2n}\cdot\frac{h}{p}\right]}{2np\left[1+\frac{n+1}{2n}\cdot\frac{h}{p}\right]}$$

$$= \left(1 + \frac{n-1}{2n} \cdot \frac{h}{p}\right)\left(1 + \frac{n+1}{2n} \cdot \frac{h}{p}\right)^{-1}$$

$$= \left(1 + \frac{n-1}{2n} \cdot \frac{h}{p}\right)\left(1 - \frac{n+1}{2n} \cdot \frac{h}{p}\right), \text{ nearly}$$

$$= 1 + \left(\frac{n-1}{2n} - \frac{n+1}{2n}\right)\frac{h}{p} + \ldots$$

$$= 1 - \frac{h}{np} \text{ approx.}$$

Again $\quad \text{RHS} = \left(\frac{p}{p+h}\right)^{1/n} = \frac{1}{(1 + h/p)^{1/n}}$

$$= \left(1 + \frac{h}{p}\right)^{-1/n} = 1 - \frac{h}{np} \text{ approx.}$$

$\Rightarrow \qquad \text{LHS} = \text{RHS}$

To do the second part, let $p = 131, q = 133, n = 7$

Now $\quad \left(\frac{131}{133}\right)^{1/7} = \left(\frac{p}{q}\right)^{1/7}$

$$= \frac{(7+1)\,131 + (7-1)\,133}{(7-1)\,131 + (7+1)\,133}$$

$$= \frac{1048 + 798}{786 + 1064} = \frac{1846}{1850}$$

$$= \frac{923}{925} = .9978 \text{ nearly.}$$

EXERCISES

1. Sum the series

(*i*) $1 - \frac{3}{4} + \frac{3.5}{4.8} - \frac{3.5.7}{4.8.12} + \ldots \infty$ (*ii*) $1 + \frac{1}{3} + \frac{1.3}{2!}\left(\frac{1}{3}\right)^2 + \frac{1.3.5}{3!}\left(\frac{1}{3}\right)^3 + \ldots \infty$

(*iii*) $1 + \frac{1}{4} + \frac{1.4}{4.8} + \frac{1.4.7}{4.8.12} + \ldots \infty$ (*iv*) $1 + \frac{15}{8} + \frac{15.21}{8.16} + \frac{15.21.27}{8.16.24} + \ldots \infty$

2. Prove that $\frac{1}{4} + \frac{1.3}{4.6} + \frac{1.3.5}{4.6.8} + \ldots = 1$

3. Show that $1+\frac{1}{3}+\frac{2.5}{6.12}+\frac{2.5.8}{6.12.18}+\ldots\infty = 2^{2/3}$

4. Show that $\frac{7}{5}\left(1+\frac{1}{10^2}+\frac{1.3}{1.2}\cdot\frac{1}{10^4}+\frac{1.3.5}{1.2.3}\cdot\frac{1}{10^6}+\ldots\right) = \sqrt{2}$

5. Identify with a binomial expansion and find the sum of the series

$$2+\frac{5}{3\lfloor 2}+\frac{5.7}{3^2\lfloor 3} = \frac{5.7.9}{3^3\lfloor 4}+\ldots$$

6. If x is so small, that its squares and higher powers can be neglected, then show that

(*i*) $\frac{(1-x)^{1/3}+(1-5x)^2}{\sqrt[4]{16-x}} = 1-\frac{989}{192}x$ (*ii*) $\frac{(1+x)^{1/2}+(1-x)^{2/3}}{(1+x)^{2/3}+(1-x)^{1/2}} = 1-\frac{1}{6}x$

(*iii*) $\frac{\left(1+\frac{2x}{3}\right)^{-5}(4+3x)^{1/2}}{(4+x)^{3/2}} = \frac{1}{4}-\left(1-\frac{10x}{3}\right)$

ANSWERS

1. (*i*) $\frac{2\sqrt{2}}{3\sqrt{3}}$ (*ii*) $\sqrt{3}$ (*iii*) $\sqrt[3]{4}$ (*iv*) 32

5. $\left(1-\frac{2}{3}\right)^{-3/2}$; $\sqrt[3]{3}$

CHAPTER 12

SEQUENCES AND INFINITE SERIES

1. SEQUENCE

A *sequence* is an endless succession of numbers placed in a certain order so that there is a first member, a second and so on. Consider, for example, the array

$$1, \frac{1}{2}, \frac{1}{3}, \frac{1}{4}, \ldots, \frac{1}{n}, \ldots$$

This is a sequence where nth member is obtained by taking the reciprocal of n. We can have many more examples, such as

$$1, 2, 3, \ldots, n, \ldots$$

$$\frac{1}{2}, \frac{2}{3}, \frac{3}{4}, \ldots, \frac{n}{n+1}, \ldots$$

$$-1, 1, -1, \ldots (-1)^n, \ldots \text{ etc., etc.}$$

So, in general, a sequence is of the form

$$a_1, a_2, a_3, \ldots, a_n, \ldots$$

where a_is are real numbers (we shall be dealing only with sequences of real numbers) and each a_i has a definite position. This sequence in the notational form, is written as $\langle a_n \rangle$ or $\{a_n\}$ where a_n is the nth (general) term of the sequence. Note that it is not necessary that all the members of the sequence be distinct (as is otherwise clear from the above examples).

2. CONVERGENCE OF A SEQUENCE

Consider the sequence

$$1, \frac{1}{2}, \frac{1}{3}, \ldots, \frac{1}{n}, \ldots$$

In this we see that as we go along the members of the sequence, the members come closer and closer to zero. Thus as n becomes larger, the members come nearer to zero. In such cases we say that the sequence converges to the limit zero.

Consider now the sequence $a_1, a_2, a_3, ..., a_n, ...$ we say that this sequence converges to a number l, if it is possible to make $|a_n - l|$ as small as we like (by making n sufficiently large) which, in other words, would mean something like saying that the sequence $<a_n>$ converges to l if after a certain stage, all the members of the sequence are very near to l. To give a precise shape to the above discussion, we state:

Definition. A sequence $<a_n>$ is said to converge to a number l, if given any $\varepsilon > 0$, there exists a + ve integer m, such that

$$|a_n - l| < \varepsilon, \quad \forall \ n \geq m$$

This number l is called *limit* of the sequence.

Also in this case we write

$$\lim_{n \to \infty} a_n = l$$

It can be easily shown that a sequence cannot converge to more than one limit.

If we use the definition to find limit of the sequence

$$1, \ \frac{1}{2}, \ \frac{1}{3}, \ ..., \ \frac{1}{n}, \ ...$$

we note that here $a_n = \frac{1}{n}$; we claim that l is zero. So if $\varepsilon > 0$, is any given number, then we wish that

$$\left|\frac{1}{n} - 0\right| < \varepsilon,$$

which will be true if $n > \frac{1}{\varepsilon}$.

So if we choose m to be a + ve integer greater than $\frac{1}{\varepsilon}$, we find

$$\left|\frac{1}{n} - 0\right| < \varepsilon \qquad \forall \ n \geq m$$

and thus, zero is the limit of the sequence.

As a particular case, let us suppose that we take $\varepsilon = \frac{1}{1000}$, then if we choose $m = 1001$.

then $$m > \frac{1}{\varepsilon} = 1000$$

and $$\left|\frac{1}{n} - 0\right| < \frac{1}{1000} \quad \forall \ n \geq m.$$

So we find that the value of m depends upon the value of ε, the smaller the value of ε, the larger the value of m.

Divergent Sequences

Let $<a_n>$ be a given sequence and suppose K is any large number. If we find that except for a finite number of elements of the sequence, all members are greater than K, we say that the sequence has $+\infty$ as its limit. In such a case the sequence $<a_n>$ is said to diverge to $+\infty$.

Definition. A sequence $<a_n>$ is said to *diverge* to $+\infty$, if for each positive number K, (however large), it is possible to find a +ve integer m, such that

$$a_n > K \quad \forall\ n \geq m.$$

Similarly, a sequence $<a_n>$ is said to *diverge* to $-\infty$, if for each negative number K (however small), it is possible to find a +ve integer m, such that

$$a_n < K \ \forall\ n \geq m.$$

In the notation, the above two are expressed as

$$\lim_{n \to \infty} a_n = +\infty$$

$$\lim_{n \to \infty} a_n = -\infty$$

As an example the sequence $<1, 2, 3, ..., n, ...>$ diverges to $+\infty$ and the sequence $<-1, -2, -3, ..., -n, ...>$ diverges to $-\infty$.

A sequence is thus convergent if it has a finite limit and is divergent otherwise (*i.e.*, when the limit is infinite or it does not exist).

[Note. Many authors follow the definition thus:

A sequence is convergent if it has finite limit.

It is divergent if it tends to $+\infty$ or $-\infty$ and the sequence is called *oscillatory* if the limit does not exist. Thus the sequences

$< -1, 1, -1, 1, ..., (-1)^n, ...>$

$< -1, 2, -3, 4, ..., (-1)^n\, n, ...>$ are oscillatory.]

3. BOUNDED SEQUENCE

A sequence $<a_n>$ is said to be *bounded* if there exist numbers k and K such that

$$k \leq a_n \leq K, \ \forall\ n$$

e.g., the sequence $<\frac{1}{n}>$ is bounded as

$$0 \leq \frac{1}{n} \leq 1 \ \forall\ n.$$

4. MONOTONIC SEQUENCE

A sequence $<a_n>$ is said be *monotonically increasing* if

$$a_{n+1} \geq a_n \ \forall \ n$$

and it is called *monotonically decreasing* if

$$a_{n+1} \leq a_n \ \forall \ n$$

Also if $a_{n+1} > a_n \ \forall \ n$ we say that the sequence $<a_n>$ is strictly monotonically increasing and if $a_{n+1} < a_n \ \forall \ n$ it is called strictly monotonically decreasing.

The sequence $<\frac{1}{n}>$ is clearly strictly monotonically decreasing, whereas, the sequence $<n>$ is clearly strictly monotonically increasing.

A sequence which is either increasing or decreasing is called a monotonic sequence.

The sequence $<1, -1, 1, ...>$ is not monotonic as it is neither increasing nor decreasing.

5. INFINITE SERIES

We have already considered arithmetic and geometric series etc., which are formed by a certain rule. We shall now consider an infinite series, which has infinite number of terms and there may not be any definite rule to determine its terms. Such a series is denoted by an expression of the form

$$u_1 + u_2 + u_3 + ... + u_n + ... \text{ or } \sum_{n=1}^{\infty} u_n \text{ or } \sum u_n .$$

6. CONVERGENCE OF AN INFINITE SERIES

It might be remarked here that throughout this chapter the word series would mean an infinite series. Suppose we are given the series

$$\sum u_n = u_1 + ... + u_n + ...$$

Let us denote by

$$\begin{aligned} S_1 &= u_1 \\ S_2 &= u_1 + u_2 \\ S_3 &= u_1 + u_2 + u_3 \\ &\ldots \quad \ldots \quad \ldots \\ S_n &= u_1 + u_2 + ... + u_n \\ &\ldots \quad \ldots \quad \ldots \end{aligned}$$

In this manner, we get a sequence $<S_n>$ which we call the sequence of partial sums of the given series $\sum u_n$.

Definition. A series $\sum u_n$ is defined to be *convergent* or *divergent* according as its sequence of partial sums $<S_n>$ is convergent or divergent. If $<S_n>$ converges to s then s is called *sum* of the series $\sum u_n$.

The following two results are direct consequence of the definition:

(*a*) *Addition or omission of a finite number of terms in a series does not affect its convergence or divergence.*

(*b*) *Multiplication of all the terms of a series by a non-zero constant does not affect the convergence or divergence of the series.*

7. POSITIVE TERM SERIES

If all the terms in a series are positive we call it a positive term series. We shall, in major part of the chapter be dealing with series of positive terms. We have defined convergence of a series in terms of its sequence of partial sums. In general practice it is found that it may not be always easy to write down the sequence of partial sums. To avoid this, we have a few tests which can be applied directly to the series to see whether it converges or diverges. Before giving the list of these tests, we give below a few important limits which will be useful in the application of these tests.

8. SOME IMPORTANT LIMITS

(*a*) $\lim_{n \to \infty} \left(1 + \frac{1}{n}\right)^n = e$, where $2 < e < 3$. [See Chapter 13]

(*b*) $\lim_{n \to \infty} n^{1/n} = 1$.

(*c*) $\lim_{n \to \infty} \log_e n = \infty$.

$\lim_{n \to 0} \log_e n = -\infty$.

9. TESTS TO EXAMINE THE NATURE OF A SERIES

Some preliminary tests. Suppose we have a positive term series $\sum u_n$, then the following tests can be applied to determine the nature of the series:

Test 1. If $\lim_{n \to \infty} u_n \neq 0$ then $\sum u_n$ is divergent.

Test 2. $\sum u_n$ is convergent if and only if, there exists a number K, such that $u_1 + u_2 + ... + u_n < K$, for all n.

Test 3. $\sum u_n$ is divergent, if each term after a fixed stage is greater than some fixed positive number.

Test 4. Comparison tests.

Form 1. If $\sum u_n$ and $\sum v_n$ are two positive term series such that, $u_n < kv_n \; \forall \; n$, where k is some fixed positive number, then $\sum u_n$ divergent $\Rightarrow \sum v_n$ is divergent and $\sum v_n$ convergent $\Rightarrow \sum u_n$ is convergent.

Form 2. If $\sum u_n$ and $\sum v_n$ are two positive term series such that, $kv_n < u_n < Kv_n \; \forall \; n$, where k and K are some fixed positive numbers, then $\sum u_n$ and $\sum v_n$ converge or diverge together.

Form 3. If $\sum u_n$ and $\sum v_n$ are two series of positive terms, such that $\lim_{n \to \infty} \frac{u_n}{v_n} = l$, where l is non-zero finite real number then $\sum u_n$ and $\sum v_n$ converge or diverge together.

Example 1. *Show that the series*

$$1 + 1 + 1 + 1 + \ldots$$

is divergent.

If u_n is the nth term of the series then clearly

$$\lim_{n \to \infty} u_n = 1 \qquad (\text{as } u_n = 1)$$

which is non-zero and thus by Test 1, the series is divergent.

Example 2. *Test for convergence, the geometric series*

$$1 + r + r^2 + r^3 + \ldots, \qquad (r > 0).$$

Case I. $0 < r < 1$.

If S_n denotes the sum of the first n terms of the series, then

$$S_n = 1 + r + r^2 + \ldots + r^{n-1}$$

$$= \frac{1 - r^n}{1 - r} < \frac{1}{1 - r} \text{ for all } n.$$

If we write $K = \frac{1}{1 - r}$, we have $S_n < K \; \forall \; n$ and thus by Test 2, the series is convergent.

Case II. $r = 1$. The series becomes

$$1 + 1 + 1 +$$

which by Example, 1, is divergent.

Case III. $r > 1$.

Each term of the series is greater than 1 and so by Test 3, the series is divergent.

Thus we conclude that the above series is convergent, if $0 < r < 1$, and is divergent if $r \geq 1$.

Example 3. *Test for convergence, the series*

$$1+\frac{1}{2^p}+\frac{1}{3^p}+\frac{1}{4^p}+\dots+\frac{1}{n^p}+\dots$$

Solution. Let $S = 1+\frac{1}{2^p}+\frac{1}{3^p}+\frac{1}{4^p}+\dots$

Case I. Let $p > 1$

Then $$S = 1+\frac{1}{2^p}+\frac{1}{3^p}+\dots$$

$$= 1+\left(\frac{1}{2^p}+\frac{1}{3^p}\right)+\left(\frac{1}{4^p}+\frac{1}{5^p}+\frac{1}{6^p}+\frac{1}{7^p}\right)+\dots$$

where we bracket the terms (leaving the first term 1) such that the brackets contain 2, 4, 8, ... terms. Then

$$S < 1+\left(\frac{1}{2^p}+\frac{1}{2^p}\right)+\left(\frac{1}{4^p}+\frac{1}{4^p}+\frac{1}{4^p}+\frac{1}{4^p}\right)+\dots$$

$$= 1+\frac{2}{2^p}+\frac{4}{4^p}+\frac{8}{8^p}+\dots$$

$$= 1+\frac{1}{2^{p-1}}+\frac{1}{4^{p-1}}+\frac{1}{8^{p-1}}+\dots$$

i.e. $$S < 1+\frac{1}{2^{(p-1)}}+\frac{1}{2^{(p-1)}}+\frac{1}{2^{3(p-1)}}+\dots$$

Now RHS is a geometric series with common ratio $\frac{1}{2^{p-1}} < 1$ and is, therefore, convergent by Example 2.

So by comparison test the given series is also convergent (when $p > 1$).

Case II. When $p = 1$, we have

$$S = 1+\frac{1}{2}+\frac{1}{3}+\frac{1}{4}+\dots$$

$$= 1+\frac{1}{2}+\left(\frac{1}{3}+\frac{1}{4}\right)+\left(\frac{1}{5}+\frac{1}{6}+\frac{1}{7}+\frac{1}{8}\right)+\dots$$

where we bracket the terms (leaving the first two terms) such that the brackets contain 2, 4, 8, ... terms.

Thus $$S > 1+\frac{1}{2}+\left(\frac{1}{4}+\frac{1}{4}\right)+\left(\frac{1}{8}+\frac{1}{8}+\frac{1}{8}+\frac{1}{8}\right)+\dots$$

or $$S > 1+\frac{1}{2}+\frac{2}{4}+\frac{4}{8}+\dots = 1+\frac{1}{2}+\frac{1}{2}+\frac{1}{2}+\dots$$

$\Rightarrow$ $$S > \frac{1}{2}+\frac{1}{2}+\frac{1}{2}+\dots$$

But RHS is a divergent series (Test 1).

Hence by comparison test again the given series is divergent.

Case III. When $p < 1$

Here $$\frac{1}{n^p} > \frac{1}{n} \;\forall\, n$$

But $\Sigma \frac{1}{n}$ is divergent by *Case II*

$\Rightarrow \Sigma \frac{1}{n^p}$ *i.e.*, the given series is divergent by comparison test.

We thus conclude that the series $\Sigma \frac{1}{n^p}$ is convergent when $p > 1$ and is divergent when $p \le 1$.

This series is called *Auxiliary Series* and proves very helpful in the solution of many problems.

Example 4. *Test for convergence the series*

$$\frac{1}{1.3.5} + \frac{1}{2.4.6} + \frac{1}{3.5.7} + \frac{1}{4.6.8} + \ldots$$

Clearly the nth term of the series is

$$u_n = \frac{1}{n(n+2)(n+4)} = \frac{1}{n^3\left(1+\frac{2}{n}\right)\left(1+\frac{4}{n}\right)}$$

Take $$v_n = \frac{1}{n^3}$$

then $$\frac{u_n}{v_n} = \frac{1}{\left(1+\frac{2}{n}\right)\left(1+\frac{4}{n}\right)}$$

Now $\lim \frac{u_n}{v_n} = 1$, which is non-zero and finite.

Also since the auxiliary series $\Sigma v_n = \Sigma \frac{1}{n^3}$ is convergent ($p > 1$), it follows by comparison test that the given series is also convergent.

Example 5. *Examine for convergence the series*

$$\sum_{1}^{\infty} \left\{ \sqrt{n^2+1} - n \right\}$$

Solution. Let u_n denote the nth term of the series,

then
$$u_n = \sqrt{n^2+1} - n$$
$$= n\sqrt{1+\frac{1}{n^2}} - n$$
$$= n\left[\left(1+\frac{1}{n^2}\right)^{1/2} - 1\right]$$
$$= n\left[\left(1+\frac{1}{2}\frac{1}{n^2}+\frac{\frac{1}{2}\left(\frac{1}{2}-1\right)}{\underline{|2}}\cdot\frac{1}{n^4}+\ldots\right)-1\right]$$
$$= n\left[\frac{1}{2n^2}-\frac{1}{8n^4}+\ldots\right] = \frac{1}{n}\left[\frac{1}{2}-\frac{1}{8n^2}+\ldots\right]$$

Take
$$v_n = \frac{1}{n}.$$

Then
$$\frac{u_n}{v_n} = \frac{1}{2} - \frac{1}{8n^2} + \text{terms with higher powers of } n$$

$$\Rightarrow \qquad \lim_{n\to\infty}\frac{u_n}{v_n} = \frac{1}{2} \neq 0, \text{ finite}$$

$\Rightarrow \Sigma u_n$ and Σv_n converge or diverge together by comparison test (Form 3).

But Σv_n is divergent (example 3).

Hence Σu_n is divergent.

Aliter. We have

$$u_n = \sqrt{n^2+1} - n$$
$$= \frac{\sqrt{n^2+1}-n}{\sqrt{n^2+1}+n} \times \sqrt{n^2+1}+n$$
$$= \frac{n^2+1-n^2}{\sqrt{n^2+1}+n} = \frac{1}{\left[\sqrt{1+\frac{1}{n^2}}+1\right]}$$

Take
$$v_n = \frac{1}{n} \text{ then}$$

$$\frac{u_n}{v_n} = \frac{1}{\sqrt{1+\frac{1}{n^2}}+1}$$

$$\Rightarrow \qquad \lim_{n\to\infty} \frac{u_n}{v_n} = \frac{1}{1+1} = \frac{1}{2}.$$

$\Rightarrow$ Σu_n is divergent as above.

Example 6. *Test for convergence the series*

$$\sum_{n=1}^{\infty} \frac{1}{(a+n)^p (b+n)^q} \text{. } p.q \text{ being positive.}$$

Solution. We have

$$u_n = \frac{1}{(a+n)^p (b+n)^q} = \frac{1}{n^p\left(\frac{a}{n}+1\right)^p n^q\left(\frac{b}{n}+1\right)^q}$$

$$= \frac{1}{n^{p+q}\left(\frac{a}{n}+1\right)^p \left(\frac{b}{n}+1\right)^q}$$

Take $\qquad \Sigma v_n = \Sigma \frac{1}{n^{p+q}}$

Then $\qquad \frac{u_n}{v_n} = \frac{1}{\left(\frac{a}{n}+1\right)^p \left(\frac{b}{n}+1\right)^q}$

$$\Rightarrow \qquad \lim_{n\to\infty} \frac{u_n}{v_n} = 1 \quad \text{which is non-zero finite}$$

$\Rightarrow$ Σu_n and Σv_n converge or diverge together by comparison test (from 3).

But Σv_n is convergent if $p+q>1$ and divergent if $p+q \le 1$ (auxiliary series).

Hence the given series is convergent when $p+q>1$ and divergent when $p+q \le 1$.

Example 7. *Test for convergence the series whose nth term is*

$$\sqrt[3]{(n^3+1)} - n$$

Solution. We have

$$u_n = (n^3+1)^{1/3} - n$$

$$= n\left(1+\frac{1}{n^3}\right)^{1/3} - n$$

$$= n\left[1+\frac{1}{3n^3}+\frac{\frac{1}{3}\left(\frac{1}{3}-1\right)}{\underline{|2}}\cdot\frac{1}{n^6}+\ldots-1\right]$$

$$= n\left[1+\frac{1}{3n^3}+\frac{\frac{1}{3}\left(\frac{1}{3}-1\right)}{\underline{|2}}\frac{1}{n^6}+\ldots\right]$$

$= \dfrac{1}{3n^2} +$ terms with higher powers of n in the denominator.

Take $\quad v_n = \dfrac{1}{n^2}$

then $\quad \dfrac{u_n}{v_n} = \dfrac{1}{3} +$ terms with higher powers of n in the denominator

$\Rightarrow \quad \lim \dfrac{u_n}{v_n} = \dfrac{1}{3}$ (non-zero finite)

$\Rightarrow \sum u_n$ is convergent (as $\sum v_n$ is convergent).

Example 8. *Show that if $\sum u_n$ is a convergent positive term series, then $\lim u_n = 0$. Does the converse hold?*

Solution. Let $\sum u_n$ be a convergent positive term series. Then $<S_n>$ the sequence of partial sums of $\sum u_n$ is convergent (by definition).

Let $\lim\limits_{n \to \infty} S_n = S$

Now
$$u_n = (u_1 + u_2 + \ldots + u_n) - (u_1 + u_2 + \ldots + u_n - 1)$$
$$= S_n - S_{n-1}$$

$\Rightarrow$
$$\lim u_n = \lim (S_n - S_{n-1})$$
$$= \lim S_n - \lim S_{n-1} = S - S = 0$$

which proves our result.

This is called a **necessary condition** for convergence.

The converse of this does not hold. Consider, for instance, the series

$$1+\frac{1}{2}+\frac{1}{3}+...+\frac{1}{n}+...$$

which, we know by Example 3, is divergent although

$$\lim_{n\to\infty} u_n = \lim_{n\to\infty} \frac{1}{n} = 0$$

See exercise 12 also. In fact the Test 1 follows from this result.

EXERCISES

Test for convergence, the series

1. $\frac{1}{2.3}+\frac{1}{3.4}+\frac{1}{4.5}+...$

2. $\frac{1^2}{1^2+1}+\frac{2^2}{2^2+1}+\frac{3^2}{3^2+1}+...$

3. $\frac{1}{1+1}+\frac{\sqrt{2}}{1+2^2}+\frac{\sqrt{3}}{1+3^2}+...$

4. $\frac{1}{\sqrt{2}+\sqrt{3}}+\frac{1}{\sqrt{3}+\sqrt{4}}+\frac{1}{\sqrt{4}+\sqrt{5}}+...$

5. $\frac{1}{2^2}+\frac{2^2}{3^3}-\frac{3^3}{4^4}+...$ **[Hint.** Take $v_n = \frac{1}{n}$]

Test for convergence the series whose *n*th term is

6. $\sqrt{n^4+1}-\sqrt{n^1-1}$

7. $\sqrt{n^4+1}-n^2$

8. $\sqrt{n+1}-\sqrt{n}$

9. $\sqrt{n^3+1}-\sqrt{n^3}$

10. Show that the series with *n*th term $\sqrt{\frac{n}{n+1}}$ is not convergent.

    [Hint. Find $\lim u_n$]

11. Show that the sequence of partial sums of a positive term series is monotonically increasing.

12. Does the result of Example 8 hold even if the series $\sum u_n$ is *any* convergent series?

ANSWERS

1. Convergent	2. Divergent	3. Convergent
4. Divergent	5. Divergent	6. Convergent
7. Convergent	8. Divergent	9. Convergent

10. SOME MORE TESTS

Test 5. **Cauchy's Root Test.** If $\sum u_n$ is a + ve term series with

$$\lim_{n\to\infty} (u_n)^{1/n} = l, \text{ then}$$

(*i*) if $l < 1$, $\sum u_n$ is convergent,

(*ii*) if $l > 1$, $\sum u_n$ is divergent.

If $l = 1$, the test fails.

Test 6. **D'Alembert's Ratio test.** If Σu_n is a + ve term series with

$$\lim_{n \to \infty} \frac{u_n}{u_{n+1}} = l, \text{ then}$$

(*i*) if $l > 1$, $\sum u_n$ is convergent,

(*ii*) if $l < 1$, $\sum u_n$ is divergent.

If $l = 1$, the test fails.

Test 7. **Raabe's test.** If $\sum u_n$ is a + ve term series with

$$\lim_{n \to \infty} \left[n \left(\frac{u_n}{u_{n+1}} - 1 \right) \right] = l, \text{ then}$$

(*i*) if $l > 1$, $\sum u_n$ is convergent,

(*ii*) if $l < 1$, $\sum u_n$ is divergent.

If $l = 1$, the test fails.

Test 8. **Logarithmic test.** If $\sum u_n$ is a + ve term series with

$$\lim_{n \to \infty} \left(n \log_e \frac{u_n}{u_{n+1}} \right) = l, \text{ then}$$

(*i*) if $l > 1$, $\sum u_n$ is convergent,

(*ii*) if $l < 1$, $\sum u_n$ is divergent.

If $l = 1$, the test fails.

[REMARK: For logarithms and their properties, see next chapter.]

Example 9. *Test for convergence the series* $\Sigma \dfrac{1}{\left(1 + \frac{1}{n}\right)^{n^2}}$.

Solution. Here the *n*th term of the series is

$$u_n = \frac{1}{\left(1 + \frac{1}{n}\right)^{n^2}}.$$

Then $$(u_n)^{1/n} = \frac{1}{\left(1 + \frac{1}{n}\right)^{n}}.$$

$$\Rightarrow \qquad \lim_{n\to\infty} (u_n)^{1/n} = \lim_{n\to\infty} \frac{1}{\left(1+\frac{1}{n}\right)^n} = \frac{1}{e} < 1 \text{ (as } e > 2)$$

So by Root test, the given series is convergent.

Example 10. *Test for convergence the series*

$$x + \frac{x^2}{2} + \frac{x^3}{3} + \frac{x^4}{4} + \ldots \qquad (x > 0)$$

Solution. The nth term of the series is $u_n = \dfrac{x^n}{n}$

then
$$\frac{u_n}{u_{n+1}} = \frac{x^n}{n} \times \frac{n+1}{x^{n+1}} = \left(1+\frac{1}{n}\right)\cdot\frac{1}{x}.$$

Then
$$\lim_{n\to\infty} \frac{u_n}{u_{n+1}} = \lim\left(1+\frac{1}{n}\right)\frac{1}{x} = \frac{1}{x}.$$

So if $\dfrac{1}{x} > 1$ *i.e.*, if $x < 1$, the series is convergent

and if $\dfrac{1}{x} < 1$ *i.e.*, if $x > 1$, the series is divergent by Ratio test.

If $x = 1$, the Ratio test fails, but in that case, we note that the given series reduces to the auxiliary series $1 + \dfrac{1}{2} + \dfrac{1}{3} + \ldots$ which we know is divergent ($p = 1$).

Hence the given series is convergent if $x < 1$

and is divergent if $x \geq 1$.

Example 11. *Test for convergence the series*

$$\sum_{n=1}^{\infty} \frac{1.3.5\ldots(2n-1)}{2.4.6\ldots 2n} . x^n, (x > 0)$$

Solution. If u_n is the nth term of the series then

$$u_n = \frac{1.3.5\ldots(2n-1)}{2.4.6\ldots 2n} . x^n$$

$$u_{n+1} = \frac{1.3.5\ldots(2n-1)\cdot(2n+1)}{2.4.6\ldots 2n.(2n+2)} . x^{n+1}$$

and thus
$$\frac{u_n}{u_{n+1}} = \frac{2n+2}{2n+1}\frac{1}{x} = \frac{\left(1+\frac{1}{n}\right)}{\left(1+\frac{1}{2n}\right)}\cdot\frac{1}{x}.$$

This gives $\lim\limits_{n \to \infty} \dfrac{u_n}{u_{n+1}} = \dfrac{1}{x}$.

So, by Ratio test if $\dfrac{1}{x} > l$ *i.e.*, if $x < 1$, the series is convergent

and if $\dfrac{1}{x} < 1$, *i.e.*, if $x > 1$, the series is divergent.

When $x = 1$, Ratio test fails.

We then use Raabe's test.

By putting $x = 1$, in the given the series, we get

$$\frac{u_n}{u_{n+1}} = \frac{2n+2}{2n+1}$$

i.e., $$n\left(\frac{u_n}{u_{n+1}} - 1\right) = n\left(\frac{2n+2}{2n+1} - 1\right) = \frac{1}{\left(2 + \frac{1}{n}\right)}.$$

So $$\lim_{n \to \infty} n\left(\frac{u_n}{u_{n+1}} - 1\right) = \lim_{n \to \infty} \frac{1}{\left(2 + \frac{1}{n}\right)} = \frac{1}{2} < 1$$

thus by Raabe's test the series is divergent.

Hence the given series is convergent if $x < 1$

and is divergent if $x \geq 1$.

Example 12. *Test for convergence the series*

$$x + \frac{2^2 x^2}{\underline{|2}} + \frac{3^3 x^3}{\underline{|3}} + \frac{4^4 x^4}{\underline{|4}} + \ldots$$

Solution. Let u_n be the nth term of the series then

$$\frac{u_n}{u_{n+1}} = \frac{n^n x^n}{\underline{|n}} \times \frac{\underline{|n+1}}{(n+1)^{n+1} x^{n+1}}$$

$$= \frac{n^n}{(n+1)^{n+1}} \cdot \frac{(n+1)}{x} = \frac{1}{\left(1 + \frac{1}{n}\right)^n} \cdot \frac{1}{x}$$

$$\Rightarrow \qquad \lim \frac{u_n}{u_{n+1}} = \frac{1}{ex} \text{ as } \lim \left(1 + \frac{1}{n}\right)^n = e.$$

So by Ratio test the given series is convergent if $\dfrac{1}{ex} > 1$

i.e. if $x < \dfrac{1}{e}$ and it is divergent if $x > \dfrac{1}{e}$.

If $x = \frac{1}{e}$, Ratio test fails. In this case

$$\frac{u_n}{u_{n+1}} = \frac{e}{\left(1+\frac{1}{n}\right)^n}$$

Now
$$\log_e \frac{u_n}{u_{n+1}} = \log e - n \log\left(1+\frac{1}{n}\right)$$
$$= 1 - n\left(\frac{1}{n} - \frac{1}{2n^2} + \frac{1}{3n^3} + \ldots\right)$$
$$= 1 - 1 + \frac{1}{2n} - \frac{1}{3n^3} + \ldots$$
$$= \frac{1}{2n} - \frac{1}{3n^2} + \ldots$$

$\Rightarrow$
$$n \log_e \frac{u_n}{u_{n+1}} = \frac{1}{2} - \frac{1}{3n} + \text{ other terms with higher powers of } n \text{ in the denominator}$$

thus
$$\lim\left(n \log_e \frac{u_n}{u_{n+1}}\right) = \frac{1}{2} < 1.$$

Hence by logarithmic test the series is divergent.

Example 13. *Prove that the series*

$$\sum_{n=0}^{\infty} \frac{n^3 + a}{2^n + a}$$ *is convergent by using D'A lembert's Ratio test.*

Solution. We have

$$\frac{u_n}{u_n + 1} = \frac{n^3 + a}{2^n + a} \times \frac{2^{n+1} + a}{(n+1)^3 + a} = \frac{n+a}{(n+1)^3 + a} \times \frac{2^{n+1} + a}{2^n + a}$$

$$= \frac{1 + \frac{a}{n^3}}{\left(1+\frac{1}{n}\right)^3 + \frac{a}{n^3}} \times \frac{2 + \frac{a}{2^n}}{1 + \frac{a}{2^n}}$$

$$\Rightarrow \lim_{n\to\infty} \frac{u_n}{u_n + 1} = \frac{1+0}{1+0} \times \frac{2+0}{1+0} = 2 > 1$$

$\Rightarrow$ by Ratio test, that the series is convergent.

Example 14. *Test for convergence the series*

$$\sum_{n=1}^{\infty} \frac{(n+1)}{(n+2)(n+3)} x^n, \quad (x>0)$$

Solution. We have

$$\frac{u_n}{u_{n+1}} = \frac{(n+1)}{(n+2)(n+3)} \cdot x^n \cdot \frac{(n+3)(n+4)}{(n+2)} \cdot \frac{1}{x^{n+1}}$$

$$= \frac{(n+1)(n+4)}{(n+2)^2} \cdot \frac{1}{x} = \frac{\left(1+\frac{1}{n}\right)\left(1+\frac{4}{n}\right)}{\left(1+\frac{2}{n}\right)^2} \cdot \frac{1}{x}$$

$$\Rightarrow \lim_{n \to \infty} \frac{u_n}{u_{n+1}} = \frac{1}{x}.$$

So if $\frac{1}{x} > 1$, *i.e.*, if $x < 1$, the seies is convergent

and if $\frac{1}{x} < 1$, i.e., if $x > 1$, the series is divergent by Ratio test.

If $x = 1$, the Ratio test fails. The series then becomes

$$\sum \frac{n+1}{(n+2)(n+3)}$$

Here $$u_n = \frac{n+1}{(n+2)(n+3)} = \frac{1+1/n}{n\left(1+\frac{2}{n}\right)\left(1+\frac{3}{n}\right)}$$

Take $$v_n = \frac{1}{n}.$$

Thus $$\lim_{n \to \infty} \frac{u_n}{v_n} = \lim \frac{1+1/n}{\left(1+\frac{2}{n}\right)\left(1+\frac{3}{n}\right)} = 1 \text{ (non-zero finite)}$$

So $\sum u_n$ and $\sum v_n$ converge or diverge together. But $\sum v_n$ is divergent (Example 3).

Hence $\sum u_n$ is divergent when $x = 1$.

Example 15. *Show that the series*

$$1 + \frac{1}{2^2} + \frac{1}{3^3} + \frac{1}{4^4} + \ldots$$

is convergent.

Solution. We have $u_n = \dfrac{1}{n^n}$

$$\Rightarrow \quad u_n^{1/n} = \frac{1}{n}$$

$$\Rightarrow \quad \lim_{n \to \infty} u_n^{1/n} = 0 < 1$$

$\Rightarrow \quad \Sigma u_n$ is convergent by Root test.

Example 16. *Test for convergence the series*

$$\frac{\lfloor 1}{3} + \frac{\lfloor 2}{9} + \frac{\lfloor 3}{27} + \frac{\lfloor 4}{81} + \ldots$$

Solution. We have $u_n = \dfrac{\lfloor n}{3^n}$

Thus $$\frac{u_n}{u_{n+1}} = \frac{\lfloor n}{3^n} \times \frac{3^{n+1}}{\lfloor n+1} = \frac{3}{n+1}$$

$$\Rightarrow \quad \lim \frac{u_n}{u_{n+1}} = 0 < 1$$

$\Rightarrow \Sigma u_n$ is divergent. (by Ratio test)

Example 17. *Show by means of examples that the Ratio test fails when* $\lim\limits_{n \to \infty} \dfrac{u_n}{u_{n+1}} = 1.$

Solution. Consider the series

$$1 + \frac{1}{2} + \frac{1}{3} + \ldots + \frac{1}{n} + \ldots$$

Here $$u_n = \frac{1}{n}$$

$$\Rightarrow \quad \frac{u_n}{u_{n+1}} = \frac{1}{n} \times (n+1) = 1 + \frac{1}{n}$$

$$\Rightarrow \quad \lim \frac{u_n}{u_{n+1}} = 1.$$

Also we know that the series is divergent.

Again consider the series

$$1 + \frac{1}{2^2} + \frac{1}{3^2} + \frac{1}{4^2} + \ldots + \frac{1}{n^2} + \ldots$$

Here $$\frac{u_n}{u_{n+1}} = \frac{(n+1)^2}{n^2} = \left(1+\frac{1}{n}\right)^2$$

$$\Rightarrow \qquad \lim \frac{u_n}{u_{n+1}} = 1.$$

But this series, we know is convergent (example 3) and thus $\lim\limits_{n\to\infty} \frac{u_n}{u_{n+1}}$ can be equal to unity in case of convergent as well as divergent series.

Hence the Ratio test is not applicable in this case.

11. ALTERNATING SERIES

A series of the form

$$u_1 - u_2 + u_3 - u_4 + \ldots$$

where $u_n > 0 \ \forall \ n$, is called an *alternating series.*

Leibnitz's Test. The alternating series

$$u_1 - u_2 + u_3 - u_4 + \ldots$$

is convergent if (*i*) $u_{n+1} \le u_n \ \forall \ n$ and (*ii*) $\lim\limits_{n\to\infty} u_n = 0$.

Example 18. *Show that the series*

$$1 - \frac{1}{2} + \frac{1}{3} - \frac{1}{4} + \ldots$$

is convergent.

Clearly $u_{n+1} \le u_n$ for all n. Also $\lim\limits_{n\to\infty} u_n = 0$. Thus by Leibnitz' test the series is convergent.

Example 19. *Show that the series*

$$1 - \frac{1}{2\sqrt{2}} + \frac{1}{3\sqrt{3}} - \frac{1}{4\sqrt{4}} + \ldots$$

is convergent.

The result is evidently true by Leibnitz' test; since here the numerical values of the terms go on decreasing as

$$\frac{1}{(n+1)\sqrt{(n+1)}} \le \frac{1}{n\sqrt{n}} \text{ for all } n$$

and also $\lim\limits_{n\to\infty} u_n = \lim \frac{1}{n\sqrt{n}} = 0.$

Example 20. *Test for convergence the series*

$$\sum_{n=1}^{\infty} (-1)^n \left[\sqrt{n+1} - \sqrt{n}\right].$$

Solution. We have

$$u_n = \sqrt{n+1} - \sqrt{n}$$

$$= \frac{\sqrt{n+1} - \sqrt{n}}{\sqrt{n+1} + \sqrt{n}} \times (\sqrt{n+1} + \sqrt{n})$$

$$= \frac{n+1-n}{\sqrt{n+1} + \sqrt{n}} = \frac{1}{\sqrt{n+1} + \sqrt{n}}$$

Thus

$$u_{n+1} - u_n = \frac{1}{\sqrt{n+2} + \sqrt{n+1}} - \frac{1}{\sqrt{n+1} + \sqrt{n}}$$

$$= \frac{\sqrt{n+1} + \sqrt{n} - \sqrt{n+2} - \sqrt{n+1}}{(\sqrt{n+2} + \sqrt{n+1})(\sqrt{n+1} + \sqrt{n})}$$

$$= \frac{\sqrt{n} - \sqrt{n+2}}{(\sqrt{n+2} + \sqrt{n+1})(\sqrt{n+1} + \sqrt{n})} \times \frac{\sqrt{n} + \sqrt{n+2}}{\sqrt{n} + \sqrt{n+2}}$$

$$= \frac{n - (n+2)}{(\sqrt{n+2} + \sqrt{n+1})(\sqrt{n+1} + \sqrt{n})(\sqrt{n} + \sqrt{n+2})}$$

$$= \frac{-2}{(\sqrt{n+2} + \sqrt{n+1})(\sqrt{n+1} + \sqrt{n})(\sqrt{n} + \sqrt{n+2})}$$

$$< 0, \ \forall\, n$$

as the denominator will always be positive.

Hence $u_{n+1} < u_n \ \forall\, n$

Note that when we check the above property we take the terms u_n and u_{n+1} with the positive sign [see statement of Leibnitz' test].

Again

$$\lim_{n \to \infty} u_n = \lim_{n \to \infty} \frac{1}{\sqrt{n+1} + \sqrt{n}}$$

$$= \lim_{n \to \infty} \frac{1}{\sqrt{n}} \left[\frac{1}{\sqrt{1 + ^{1/n}} + 1}\right] = 0$$

and hence by the Leibnitz' test we observe that the given series is convergent.

EXERCISES

Test for covergence the series

1. $\sum_{n=1}^{\infty} \frac{n^{n^2}}{(1+n)^{n^2}}$

2. $\sum_{1}^{\infty} \left(\frac{n+1}{2n+3}\right)^n$

3. $\frac{2}{3}x + \frac{3}{4}x^2 + \frac{4}{5}x^3 + \ldots \; (x > 0)$

4. $\frac{1}{(\log_e 2)^2} + \frac{1}{(\log_e 3)^3} + \frac{1}{(\log_e 4)^4} + \ldots + \frac{1}{(\log_e n)^n} + \ldots$

5. $\frac{1}{3} + \frac{\lfloor 2}{9} + \frac{\lfloor 3}{27} + \frac{\lfloor 4}{81} + \ldots$

6. $\frac{1}{1+2} + \frac{2}{1+2^2} + \frac{3}{1+2^3} + \ldots$

7. $\frac{2}{1}x + \frac{3}{8}x^2 + \frac{4}{27}x^3 + \frac{5}{64}x^4 + \ldots \; (x > 0)$

8. $\frac{1}{2\sqrt{1}} + \frac{x^2}{3\sqrt{2}} + \frac{x^4}{4\sqrt{3}} + \frac{x^6}{5\sqrt{4}} + \ldots$

9. $\sum_{n=1}^{\infty} \frac{1}{n^n \sqrt{n}}$

10. $1 + \frac{2x}{\lfloor 2} + \frac{3^2 x^2}{\lfloor 3} + \frac{4^3 x^3}{\lfloor 4} + \ldots \; (x > 0)$

11. $\sum \frac{3.6.9\ldots 3n}{7.10.13\ldots 3n+4} x^n \; (x > 0)$

12. $\sum \left[\left(\frac{n+1}{n}\right)^{n+1} - \frac{n+1}{n}\right]^{-n}$

13. $x + \frac{x^3}{\lfloor 3} + \frac{x^5}{\lfloor 5} + \frac{x^7}{\lfloor 7} + \ldots \; (x > 0)$

14. Show that for $a > 0$, the series $\sum \frac{(1+n)^n}{\lfloor n} a^n$

converges or diverges according as $a < \frac{1}{e}$ or $a \geq \frac{1}{e}$.

15. Show that the series $\sum \frac{2^2.4^2.6^2\ldots(2n+2)^2}{3.4.5.6\ldots 2n} x^{2n}, \quad (x > 0)$

is convergent if $x > 1$ and divergent if $x \leq 1$.

Show that the following series are convergent

16. $\sum_{1}^{\infty} \frac{(-1)^{n-1}}{n^2}$

17. $1 - \frac{1}{5} + \frac{1}{9} - \frac{1}{13} + \ldots$

18. $\sum_{n=1}^{\infty} \frac{(-1)n}{\lfloor n}$

19. Test for convergence the series

$$\sum_{1}^{\infty} \frac{\sqrt{n}}{\sqrt{n^2+1}} x^n \text{ for positive values of } x.$$

20. Show that the series

$$\sum \frac{1.3.5\ldots(2n-1)}{2.4.6\ldots 2n} \cdot \frac{1}{n} \text{ is convergent.}$$

21. Test for convergence the series

$$1+\frac{2x}{\lfloor 2}+\frac{3^2x^2}{\lfloor 3}+\frac{4^3x^3}{\lfloor 4}+\ldots\quad (x>0).$$

22. Show by means of examples that the Root test fails when $\lim_{n\to\infty} u_n^{1/n} = 1$.

ANSWERS

1. Convergent
2. Convergent
3. Convergent when $x < 1$
   Divergent when $x \geq 1$
4. Convergent
5. Divergent
6. Convergent
7. Convergent when $x \leq 1$
   Divergent when $x > 1$
8. Convergent when $x^2 \leq 1$
   Divergent when $x^2 > 1$
9. Convergent
10. Convergent when $x \leq 1/e$
    Divergent when $x > 1/e$
11. Convergent when $x < 1$
    Divergent when $x \geq 1$
12. Convergent
13. Convergent
19. Convergent when $x < 1$
    Divergent when $x \geq 1$
21. Convergent when $x \leq 1/e$
    Divergent when $x > 1/e$

CHAPTER 13

LOGARITHMS

1. DEFINITION

If $a^x = N$, then x is called the **logarithm** *of N to the base a and is written as $\log_a N$.*

Thus $a^x = N \Leftrightarrow x = \log_a N$.

For example $8 = 2^3 \Rightarrow \log_2 8 = 3$

$64 = 2^6 \Rightarrow \log_2 64 = 6$

$.01 = 10^{-2} \Rightarrow \log_{10} .01 = -2.$

NOTES: 1. Since $a^0 = 1$, $\log_a 1 = 0$

Thus, logarithm of unity to any base is zero.

2. Since $a^1 = a$, $\log_a a = 1$.

Thus, logarithm of any number to the same base is 1.

3. Logarithm is defined only for positive numbers.

2. PROPERTIES OF LOGARITHMS

(1) *The logarithm of a product is equal to the sum of the logarithms of its factors.*

(In other words, $\log_a mn = \log_a m + \log_a n$)

Proof. Let $\log_a m = x$ and $\log_a n = y$.

Then $a^x = m$ and $a^y = n$.

This gives that $mn = a^x . a^y = a^{x+y}$

Hence $\mathbf{\log_a mn} = x + y = \mathbf{\log_a m + \log_a n}$.

REMARK: $\log_a (m + n) \neq \log_a m + \log_a n$

For, let $m = 1$, $n = 1$, $a = 2$.

We have $\log_a (m + n) = \log_2 (1 + 1) = \log_2 2 = 1$

and $\log_a m + \log_a n = \log_2 1 + \log_2 1 = 0$. (Note 1)

(2) *The logarithm of a fraction is equal to the logarithm of the numerator diminished by the logarithm of the denominator.*

$$\left(\text{In other words, } \log_a\left(\frac{m}{n}\right) = \log_a m - \log_a n\right)$$

Proof. Let $\log_a m = x$ and $\log_a n = y$.

Then, $a^x = m$ and $a^y = n$.

This implies that $\dfrac{m}{n} = \dfrac{a^x}{a^y} = a^{x-y}$

Thus $\mathbf{\log_a\left(\frac{m}{n}\right)} = x - y = \mathbf{\log_a m - \log_a n}$.

REMARK: $\log_a (m - n) \neq \log_a m - \log_a n$.

For, let $m = 2$, $n = 1$, $a = 2$

We have $\log_a (m - n) = \log_2 (2 - 1) = \log_2 1 = 0$

and $\log_a m - \log_a n = \log_2 2 - \log_2 1 = 1 - 0 = 1$.

(3) *The logarithm of the pth power of a number is p times the logarithm of that number.*

(In other words, $\log_a m^p = p \log_a m$.)

Proof. Let $\log_a m = x$. Then $a^x = m \Rightarrow m^p = (a^x)^p = a^{px}$.

Thus $\mathbf{\log_a m^p} = px = \mathbf{p \log_a m}$.

3. TO TRANSFORM A SYSTEM OF LOGARITHMS HAVING GIVEN BASE TO A NEW SYSTEM WITH A DIFFERENT BASE

Let $\log_a N = x$ be given. To find $\log_b N$

Let $y = \log_b N$ so that $b^y = N$

$\Leftrightarrow \quad \log_a (b^y) = \log_a N$

$\Leftrightarrow \quad y \log_a b = \log_a N$

$\Leftrightarrow \quad y = \dfrac{1}{\log_a b} \times \log_a N$.

Hence $\quad \mathbf{\log_b N = \dfrac{1}{\log_a b} \times \log_a N}$.

Thus, to transform a logarithm from base a to base b, we have only to multiply it by $\dfrac{1}{\log_a b}$. This is known as *Base changing formula.*

REMARK: If $N = a$, we get $\log_b a = \dfrac{1}{\log_a b}$.

Example 1. *If $a^2 + b^2 = 7ab$, prove that*

$$\left[\log \frac{1}{3}(a+b)\right] = \frac{1}{2}(\log a + \log b)$$

Solution. $a^2 + b^2 = 7ab$

$$\Rightarrow \quad (a+b)^2 = 9ab \Rightarrow \left(\frac{a+b}{3}\right)^2 = ab$$

$$\Rightarrow \quad 2\log \frac{1}{3}(a+b) = \log a + \log b$$

$$\Rightarrow \quad \log \frac{1}{3}(a+b) = \frac{1}{2}(\log a + \log b).$$

Example 2. *If a, b, c are in G.P., show that $\log_a n$, $\log_b n$, $\log_c n$ are in H.P.*

Solution. $\log_a n, \log_b n, \log_c n$ will be in H.P.

$\Leftrightarrow \quad \dfrac{1}{\log_a n}, \dfrac{1}{\log_b n}, \dfrac{1}{\log_c n}$ are in A.P.

$\Leftrightarrow$ $\log_n a$, $\log_n b$, $\log_n c$ are in A.P.

$\Leftrightarrow 2\log_n b = \log_n a + \log_n c$

$\Leftrightarrow 2\log_n b = \log_n ac$

$\Leftrightarrow \log_n b^2 = \log_n ac.$

Since a, b, c are in G.P. $\Rightarrow b^2 = ac$,

Hence $\log_a n$, $\log_b n$, $\log_c n$ are in H.P.

Example 3. *Show that $\log_{10} \frac{1}{n}$ is negative where $n \geq 2$.*

Solution. Now $\log_{10} \frac{1}{n} = \log_{10} 1 - \log_{10} n = -\log_{10} n$

which is –ve as $\log_{10} x > 0$ for all $x > 1$.

Example 4. *If $\log_a m = n$, show that $\log_{1/a} m = -n$. Hence, find $\log_{1/a} 27\sqrt{3}$.*

Solution. $\log_a m = n \Rightarrow a^n = m$

$$\Rightarrow \left(\frac{1}{a}\right)^n = \frac{1}{m}$$

$$\Rightarrow \left(\frac{1}{a}\right)^{-n} = \left(\frac{1}{m}\right)^{-1}$$

$$\Rightarrow \left(\frac{1}{a}\right)^{-n} = m$$

$$\Rightarrow \log_{1/a} m = -n$$

Let $x = \log_9 27\sqrt{3} \Rightarrow 9^x = 27\sqrt{3}$

$$\Rightarrow 9^x = 9 \times 3\sqrt{3}$$

$$\Rightarrow 9^{x-1} = 3\sqrt{3}$$

$$\Rightarrow 3^{2x-2} = 3^{1+1/2}$$

$$\Rightarrow 2x - 2 = 1 + \frac{1}{2}$$

$$\Rightarrow 2x = \frac{7}{2}$$

$$\Rightarrow x = \frac{7}{4} \Rightarrow \log_9 27\sqrt{3} = \frac{7}{4}$$

Since $\log_9 27\sqrt{3} = \frac{7}{4}$, we have $\log_{\frac{1}{9}} 27\sqrt{3} = -\frac{7}{4}$.

Example 5. *Determine $\log_x 2401$ when $x^3 = 7$.*

Solution. Let $y = \log_x 2401$

$$\Rightarrow x^y = 2401 = 7 \times 343$$

$$\Rightarrow x^y = x^3 \times 343$$

$$\Rightarrow x^{y-3} = 343$$

$$\Rightarrow x^{y-3} = 7^3$$

$$\Rightarrow x^{y-3} = x^9$$

$$\Rightarrow y - 3 = 9$$

$$\Rightarrow y = 12.$$

So, $\log_x 2401 = 12$.

Example 6. *Find the value of the product $\log_2 3 \log_3 4 \log_4 5 \log_5 6 \log_6 7 \log_7 8$.*

Solution. By Base changing formula

$$\log_2 3 \log_3 4 = \log_2 4$$

$$\log_4 5 \log_5 6 = \log_4 6$$

$$\log_6 7 \log_7 8 = \log_6 8$$

So, $\log_2 3 \log_3 4 \log_4 5 \log_5 6 \log_6 7 \log_7 8$

$= \log_2 4 \log_4 6 \log_6 8$

$= \log_2 6 \log_2 8$ (By Base Changing formula)

$= \log_2 8$ (By Base Changing formula)

$= \log_2 2^3$

$= 3 \log_2 2$

$= 3$ (See Note 2, Art. 1)

Example 7. *Find the value of*

$$\frac{\log\sqrt{27} + \log 8 - \log\sqrt{1000}}{\log 1.2}$$

Solution. $\dfrac{\log\sqrt{27} + \log 8 - \log\sqrt{1000}}{\log 1.2}$

$$= \frac{\log 3^{3/2} + \log 2^3 - \log 10^{3/2}}{\log 12 - \log 10}$$

$$= \frac{\frac{3}{2}\log 3 + 3\log 2 - \frac{3}{2}\log 10}{\log(3\times 4) - \log 10}$$

$$= \frac{3\left(\frac{1}{2}\log 3 + \log 2 - \frac{1}{2}\log 10\right)}{\log 3 + \log 4 - \log 10}$$

$$= \frac{3\left(\frac{1}{2}\log 3 + \log 2 - \frac{1}{2}\log 10\right)}{2\left(\frac{1}{2}\log 3 + \log 2 - \frac{1}{2}\log 10\right)} = \frac{3}{2}.$$

Example 8. *Prove that*

$$\log x = \log[1 - \{1 - (1 - x^2)^{-1}\}^{-1}]^{-1/2}$$

Solution. RHS $= -\frac{1}{2}\log[1 - \{1 - (1 - x^2)^{-1}\}^{-1}]$

$$= -\frac{1}{2}\log\left[1 - \left\{1 - \frac{1}{1-x}\right\}^{-1}\right]$$

$$= -\frac{1}{2}\log\left[1-\left\{\frac{1-x^2-1}{1-x^2}\right\}^{-1}\right]$$

$$= -\frac{1}{2}\log\left[1-\left\{\frac{-x^2}{1-x^2}\right\}^{-1}\right]$$

$$= -\frac{1}{2}\log\left[1+\frac{1-x^2}{x^2}\right]$$

$$= -\frac{1}{2}\log\left[\frac{x^2+1-x^2}{x^2}\right]$$

$$= -\frac{1}{2}\log\frac{1}{x^2}$$

$$= -\frac{1}{2}\log(x^2)^{-1}$$

$$= \frac{1}{2}\log x^2 = \log x = \text{LHS}.$$

Example 9. *If* $log_2 x + log_4 x + log_{16} x = \frac{21}{4}$, *find* x.

Solution. LHS $= \log_2 x + \frac{\log_2 x}{\log_2 4} + \frac{\log_2 x}{\log_2 16}$

$$= \log_2 x + \frac{\log_2 x}{2} + \frac{\log_2 x}{4}$$

$$= \frac{7}{4}\log_2 x$$

Therefore, $\frac{7}{4}\log_2 x = \frac{21}{4}$

$\Rightarrow$ $\log_2 x = 3$

$\Rightarrow$ $x = 2^3 \Rightarrow x = 8.$

Example 10. *Find the simplest value of*

$$log_3 \sqrt[4]{729\sqrt[3]{9^{-1}.27^{-4/3}}}$$

Solution. $\log_3 \sqrt[4]{729 \sqrt[3]{9^{-1}.27^{-4/3}}}$

$$= \log_3 \sqrt[4]{3^6 \sqrt[3]{9^{-1}.27^{-4/3}}}$$

$$= \log_3 \sqrt[4]{3^6 \sqrt[3]{3^{-2}\ 3^{-4}}}$$

$$= \log_3 \sqrt[4]{3^6\ 3^{-2}}$$

$$= \log_3 \sqrt[4]{3^4}$$

$$= \log_3 3 = 1.$$

Example 11. *Solve for x, $\log_x (8x-3) - \log_x 4 = 2$.*

Solution. $\log_x (8x-3) - \log_x 4 = 2$

$$\Rightarrow \quad \log_x\left(\frac{8x-3}{4}\right) = 2$$

$$\Rightarrow \quad x^2 = \frac{8x-3}{4}$$

$$\Rightarrow \quad 4x^2 - 8x + 3 = 0$$

$$\Rightarrow \quad x = \frac{8 \pm \sqrt{64-48}}{8}$$

$$= \frac{8 \pm 4}{8} = \frac{1}{2}, \frac{3}{2}.$$

Example 12. (*i*) *Prove that*

$$\log 2 + 16 \log \frac{16}{15} + 12 \log \frac{25}{24} + 7 \log \frac{81}{80} = 1.$$

(assuming that base is 10 in each logarithm)

(*ii*) *If $a^x = b^y = c^z$ and $b^2 = ac$ prove that*

$$y = \frac{2xz}{x+z}$$

Solution. (*i*) LHS $= \log 2 + 16 \log \frac{16}{15} + 12 \log \frac{25}{24} + 7 \log \frac{81}{80}$

$$= \log 2 + 16 \log 16 - 16 \log 15 + 12 \log 25 - 12 \log 24 + 7 \log 81 - 7 \log 80$$

$$= \log 2 + 16 \log 2^4 - 16 \log 3 \times 5 + 12 \log 5^2 - 12 \log 2^3 \times 3 + 7 \log 3^4 - 7 \log 2^4 \times 5$$

$$= \log 2 + 64 \log 2 - 16 \log 3 - 16 \log 5 + 24 \log 5$$
$$-12 \log 3 - 36 \log 2 + 28 \log 3 - 28 \log 2 - 7 \log 5$$
$$= (1 + 64 - 36 - 28) \log 2 + (28 - 12 - 16) \log 3 + (24 - 16 - 7) \log 5$$
$$= \log 2 + \log 5$$
$$= \log 2 \times 5$$
$$= \log 10 = 1.$$

(*ii*) Let $a^x = b^y = c^z = u$ (say)

$$\Rightarrow \quad x = \frac{\log u}{\log a}, \quad y = \frac{\log u}{\log b}, \quad z = \frac{\log u}{\log c}$$

$$\Rightarrow \quad 2xz = 2(\log u)^2/\log a \log c$$

and $$(x+z)y = \log u \frac{(\log ac)}{(\log a)(\log c)} \cdot \frac{\log u}{\log b}$$
$$= (\log u)^2\, 2 \log b/\log a \log b \log c$$

$$\Rightarrow \quad 2xz = y(x+z).$$

Example 13. *Prove that*

$$\frac{1}{\log_a (ab)} + \frac{1}{\log_b (ab)} = 1$$

Solution. Let $x = \log_a (ab)$

$$y = \log_b (ab)$$

Then, by definition

$$a^x = ab, \quad b^y = ab$$

$$\Rightarrow \quad a = (ab)^{1/x}, \quad b = (ab)^{1/y}$$

$$\Rightarrow \quad ab = (ab)^{1/x + 1/y}$$

$$\Rightarrow \quad 1 = \frac{1}{x} + \frac{1}{y}$$

$$\Rightarrow \quad 1 = \frac{1}{\log_a (ab)} + \frac{1}{\log_b (ab)}.$$

Example 14. *Show that, if the logarithm of a^2 to the base b^3 is equal to the logarithm of b^8 to the base a^{12}, then each logarithm must be equal to $\frac{2}{3}$ or $-\frac{2}{3}$.*

Solution. Let $x = \log_{b^3} a^2 = \log_{a^{12}} b^8$

Then, by definition

$$(b^3)^x = a^2 \text{ and } (a^{12})^x = b^8$$

So, $$b^{18x^2} = a^{12x}$$

Therefore, $$b^{18x^2} = b^8$$

$\Rightarrow$ $$18x^2 = 8$$

$\Rightarrow$ $$x^2 = \frac{4}{9}$$

$\Rightarrow$ $$x = \pm\frac{2}{3}.$$

Example 15. *Prove from the definition of logarithm that if m, n, x are positive numbers,*

$$log_{mn} x = \frac{log_n x}{(1+log_n m)}$$

Solution. Let
$$a = \log_{mn} x$$
$$b = \log_n x$$
$$c = \log_n m$$

Then, by definition

$$(mn)^n = x, n^b = x, n^c = m$$

Therefore, $$(mn)^a = n^b$$

$\Rightarrow$ $$n^b = m^a . n^a$$

$\Rightarrow$ $$n^b = n^{ac} . n^a$$

$\Rightarrow$ $$n^b = n^{ac+a}$$

$\Rightarrow$ $$b = ac + a$$

$\Rightarrow$ $$b = a(1+c)$$

$\Rightarrow$ $$a = \frac{b}{1+c}$$

$\Rightarrow$ $$\log_{mn} x = \frac{\log_n x}{(1+\log_n m)}$$

Example 16. *If a, b, c are any three consecutive integers, prove that* $log\,(1 + ac) = 2\,log\,b$.

Solution. RHS $= 2\log b = 2\log(a+1)$
$= \log(a+1)^2 = \log(a^2+1+2a)$
$= \log[1+a(a+2)]$
$= \log[1+ac] = \text{LHS}.$

Example 17. *Simplify* $\log_a b \log_b c \log_c d \log_d a$

Solution. $\log_a b \log_b c \log_c d \log_d a$

$$= \frac{\log_k b}{\log_k a}\frac{\log_k c}{\log_k b}\frac{\log_k d}{\log_k c}\frac{\log_k a}{\log_k d} = 1.$$

Example 18. *Given* $\log 2 = .3010$, $\log 3 = .4771$, *find the value of* $\log \dfrac{(16)^{1/5}(5)^2}{(108)^3}$.

Solution. $\log \dfrac{(16)^{1/5}(5)^2}{(108)^3}$

$$= \log \frac{(2)^{4/5}(5)^2}{(2^2 \times 3^3)^3}$$

$$= \log \frac{2^{4/5}(10)^2(2)^{-2}}{(2^6 \times 3^9)} = \log\left(\frac{2^{4/5} \times 10^2}{2^8 \times 3^9}\right)$$

$$= \log 2^{4/5} + \log 10^2 - \log 2^8 - \log 3^9$$

$$= 4/5 \log 2 + 2 \log 10 - 8 \log 2 - 9 \log 3$$

$$= 4/5 \times .3010 + 2 - 8 \times 0.3010 - 9 \times 0.4771$$

$$= 0.2408 + 2 - 2.4080 - 4.2939 = -4.4611.$$

EXERCISES

1. Express logarithm of $\dfrac{\sqrt{a^2}}{c^5\, b^2}$ in terms of $\log a$, $\log b$, $\log c$.
2. Find x from the equation $a^x c^{-2x} = b^{3x+1}$.
3. Find the value of $\log_8 128$.
4. Express $\log (\sqrt{a^2 b^3})^6$ in terms of $\log a$ and $\log b$.
5. If $\log(x^3 y^3) = a$ and $\log \dfrac{x}{y} = b$ find $\log x$ and $\log y$.
6. If $a^3 + b^3 = 0$, prove that $\log (a + b) = \dfrac{1}{2}(\log a + \log b + \log 3)$ [given $a + b \neq 0$]
7. If a, b, c are G.P., prove that $\log_n a$, $\log_n b$ and $\log_n c$ are in A.P.
8. Prove that $\log_b a \times \log_c b \times \log_a c = 1$.
9. If $\log_{2a} a = x$, $\log_{3a} 2a = y$, $\log_{4a} 3a = z$, show that $xyz + 1 = 2yz$.
10. Prove that $\log_a x \times \log_b y = \log_b x \times \log_a y$.

11. Prove that $\log(1 + 2 + 3) = \log 1 + \log 2 + \log 3$.

12. Prove that $\dfrac{1}{\log_a(abc)} + \dfrac{1}{\log_b(abc)} + \dfrac{1}{\log_c(abc)} = 1$.

13. Show that $\log_2 3 \times \log_3 8 = 1$.

14. Find the value of $\log_4 2 \log_2 6 \log_6 4$.

15. Prove that $\log_b 2a \log_x 2b = \dfrac{1}{4} \log_x a$.

16. Find the value of

$$\frac{1}{6}\sqrt{\frac{3\log 1728}{1+\frac{1}{2}\log 36+\frac{1}{3}\log 8}}$$

17. If the logarithm of 64 is 4, what is the base of the logarithm?

18. The first term of an A.P. is $\log a$ and second term is $\log b$. Show that the sum of first n terms in

$$\frac{1}{6}\log\left[\frac{b^{n(n-1)}}{a^{n(n-3)}}\right]$$

19. Find the logarithms of
    (*i*) 0.25 to the base 0.5
    (*ii*) $243\sqrt[3]{9}$ to the base $3\sqrt{3}$
    (*iii*) $256\sqrt[9]{8}$ to the base $8\sqrt[3]{4}$.

20. Find $\log_8 25$ given that $\log_{10} 2 = 0.3010$

21. If $a = \log_{24}12$, $b = \log_{36}24$, $c = \log_{48} 36$, prove that $1 + abc = 2bc$

22. Find the value of
$\log_2 [\log_2 (\log_3 (\log 27^3)\}]$

23. Find the value of

$$\log_{729}(9^{5/2+7/2}) + \log_{729}(^{279/3+11/3+13/3})$$
$$+ \log_{729}(81^{15/4+17/4+19/4+21/4})$$
$$+ \log_{729}(243^{23/5+25/5+27/5+29/5+31/5})$$

24. Find the value of

$$\log_{243}(3^3) + \log_{243}\left(9^{\frac{5}{2}+\frac{7}{2}}\right) + \log_{243}\left(27^{\frac{9}{3}+\frac{11}{3}+\frac{13}{3}}\right)$$
$$+ \log_{243}\left(81^{\frac{15}{4}+\frac{17}{4}+\frac{19}{4}+\frac{21}{4}}\right)$$

25. Prove that

$$\log_2\left(\frac{75}{16}\right) - 2\log_2\left\{\frac{\sqrt[4]{\left(\frac{25}{81}\right)^3}\,\sqrt[3]{\left(\frac{25}{81}\right)}}{\sqrt[12]{\left(\frac{25}{81}\right)^7}}\right\}$$
$$+ \frac{1}{3}\log_2(2^{15}\cdot 3^{-15}) = 1.$$

26. Evaluate $\log_5 256$ and $\log_2 .015625$.
27. Solve for x, $\log_x 3 + \log_x 9 + \log_x 729 = 9$.
28. Solve for x, $\log_{10}(x - 9) + \log_{10} x = 1$.

ANSWERS

1. $\frac{3}{2} \log a - 5 \log c - 2 \log b$. 2. $\frac{\log b}{\log a - 2\log c - 3\log b}$

3. $\frac{7}{3}$. 4. $6 \log a + 9 \log b$.

5. $\log x = \frac{1}{5}(3b + a)$ and $\log y = \frac{1}{5}(a - 2b)$

14. 1 16. $\frac{1}{2}$ 17. $2^{3/2}$

19. (i) 2 (ii) $\frac{34}{9}$ (iii) $\frac{25}{11}$ 20. 1.5482 22. 0

23. 42 24. 24 26. –8, –6

27. $x = 3$ 28. $x = 10$

4. COMMON LOGARITHMS

The logarithms to the base 10 are called *Common logarithms.* For all numerical computations, the base 10 is used. Now onward, whenever base is omitted, the base 10 is understood.

Consider $10^1 = 10 \quad \Rightarrow \log_{10} 10 = 1$

$10^2 = 100 \quad \Rightarrow \log_{10} 100 = 2$

$10^3 = 1000 \quad \Rightarrow \log_{10} 1000 = 3$ and so on.

We observe from the above that logarithm of a number between 10 and 100 will be between 1 and 2. It is, therefore, equal to $1 + a$ where a is a positive proper fraction. Similarly, logarithm of a number between 100 and 1000 will be between 2 and 3. It is therefore equal to $2 + b$ where b is positive proper fraction.

Again $10^{-1} = 0.1 \quad \Rightarrow \log_{10} 0.1 = -1$

$10^{-2} = 0.01 \quad \Rightarrow \log_{10} 0.01 = -2$ and so on

We observe that logarithm of a number between 0.1 and 0.01 will lie between –1 and –2. It is therefore equal to $-2 + a$ where a is positive proper fraction.

Thus, we have the following

"The logarithm of a number consists of two parts,

(*i*) an integer, positive, negative or zero

(*ii*) a positive proper fraction."

The first part is called *Characteristic* and the second part, *Mantissa*.

Thus, characteristic of logarithm is an integer while mantissa of logarithm is a positive proper fraction.

Example 19. *The logarithm of a number is 5.673. Find the characteristic and mantissa.*

Solution. Let $\log N = 5.673 = 5 + 0.673$.

Here integral part is 5.

So characteristic is 5 and fractional part is 0.673.

Thus mantissa is 0.673.

Example 20. *The logarithm of a number is –3.153. Find the characteristic and mantissa.*

Solution. Let $\log N = -3.153$

$$= -3 - 0.153.$$

Here fractional part is negative. So, we first make the fractional part positive by adding and subtracting 1.

$$\log N = -3 - 1 + 1 - 0.153$$

$$= -4 + 0.847$$

Now characteristic = –4, and mantissa = 0.847.

NOTES: 1. In example (20) above, characteristic is –4. It is also written as $\bar{4}$ (Read 4 bar).

2. $\bar{4}.847$ denotes –4 + 0.847 while –3.153 means –3 – 0.153. Reader is advised to be very careful while making use of these bar notations.

EXERCISES

The logarithm of a number is

(i) 7.123 (ii) –4.356, find the characteristic and mantissa.

ANSWERS

(i) 7 and 0.123 (ii) characteristic is –5 and mantissa is 0.644.

5. RULES FOR FINDING CHARACTERISTIC

(1) *For numbers greater than or equal to one:*

Since $10^0 = 1 \Rightarrow \log_{10} 1 = 0$

and $10^1 = 10 \Rightarrow \log_{10} 10 = 1$, we get that for numbers lying between

1 and 10, the value of logarithm is $0 + a$, where a is positive proper fraction. Thus, characteristic of numbers lying between 1 and 10 is zero.

Again $10^2 = 100 \Rightarrow \log_{10} 100 = 2$.

Therefore, for numbers lying between 10 and 100, the value of logarithm is $1 + a$ where a is positive proper fraction. Thus characteristic of numbers lying between 10 and 100 is one.

Similarly, characteristic of numbers lying between 100 and 1000, is two and so on.

Thus characteristics of log 5, log 12, log 125·5 are respectively equal to 0, 1 and 2.

Thus we have the following rule for finding characteristic of numbers greater than or equal to 1.

"The characteristic of numbers greater than or equal to one, is one less than the number of digits contained in its integral part."

(2) *For numbers less than one:*

Since $10^0 = 1, \log_{10} 1 = 0$

and $10^{-1} = .1, \log_{10} 0.1 = -1$.

Therefore, for numbers lying between 0.1 and 1, the value of logarithm is $-1 + a$, where a is proper positive fraction. Thus, characteristic of numbers lying between 0.1 and 1 is –1.

Again $10^{-2} = 0.01 \Rightarrow \log_{10} 0.01 = -2$.

Therefore, for numbers lying between 0.01 and 0.1, the value of logarithm is $-2 + a$ where a is the positive proper fraction. Thus, characteristic of numbers lying between 0.01 and 0.1 is –2 and so on.

Thus, we note that :

If a number has no cipher immediately after decimal, characteristic of its logarithm is –1, if a number has one cipher immediately after decimal, characteristic of its logarithm is –2 and so on. Hence we have the rule :

"The characteristic of numbers less than unity, is negative and is one more than the number of ciphers immediately after the decimal point before any significant (i.e., non-zero) figure."

Example 21. *Find the characteristic of the logarithms of following numbers:*

(*i*) *196.458* (*ii*) *8.4043*

(*iii*) *0.001203* (*iv*) *0.1002.*

Solution. (*i*) Here, number is greater than unity and its integral part 196 contains 3 digits. Therefore, characteristic $= -3 - 1 = 2$.

(*ii*) Here, number is greater than unity and its integral part 8 contains one digit. Therefore, characteristic = 1 – 1 = 0.

(*iii*) Here, number is less than unity and the number of ciphers immediately after decimal point before significant figure 1 are two.

Thus, characteristic $= -(1+2) = -3$ or $\bar{3}$.

(*iv*) Here, number is less than unity and the number of ciphers immediately after decimal point before significant figure 1 is zero.

Thus, characteristic $= -(1+0) = -1$ or $\bar{1}$.

EXERCISES

Find the characteristic of the logarithms of following numbers:

1. 7.7576 2. 0.0757 3. 0.00102 4. 0.000075.

ANSWERS

1. 0 2. $\bar{2}$ 3. $\bar{3}$ 4. $\bar{5}$.

6. CALCULATION OF MANTISSA

Mantissa is calculated with the help of logarithm tables given at the end of the book. We given below the method of reading logarithm table and rule to calculate the mantissa.

(*i*) Neglect the decimal point of a given number (*e.g.*, Read 43.57 as 4357). If number of digits are not four after neglecting decimal point, then make them four by inserting ciphers to the right of given number accordingly (*e.g.*, Read 10.8 as 1080, similarly, read 5.7 as 5700). If number of digits after neglecting the decimal point are more than four, then neglect the digits after the fourth digit (*e.g.*, Read 56 789 as 5678; similarly read 5048.81 as 5048).

(*ii*) Take first two digits obtained from (*i*) and run the eye down the extreme left hand column and stop at the number consisting of first two digits (*e.g.*, In the number 4357, the first two digits are 43. In the extreme left hand column of the table run the eye down at the number 43).

(*iii*) Take the third digit now. In the example given above, (4357) the third digit is 5. Read the intersection of horizontal row beginning with 43 and vertical column headed by 5, the number in 6385.

(*iv*) Now take the fourth digit which is 7 in the example (4357) and read the intersection of horizontal row beginning with 43 and vertical column headed by 7 in the mean difference column. The number is 7.

(*v*) Add the number obtained in (*iv*) to the number obtained in (*iii*), we get $6385 + 7 = 6392$.

(*vi*) Prefix the decimal to the number obtained in (*v*) and the mantissa of number 43.57 will be .6392.

REMARK: Consider the number 15.83

Let $\log 15.83 = A \cdot B$

Again, consider the number 158.3 (Here the digits and the order of digits are same as the first number 15.83. The only difference is that decimal point is shifted).

$$
\begin{aligned}
\text{Now } \log 158.3 &= \log (15.83 \times 10) \\
&= \log (15.83) + \log 10 \\
&= \log (15.83) + 1 \\
&= A \cdot B + 1 \\
&= A + .B + 1 \\
&= (A + 1) + .B \\
&= (A + 1)\, .B
\end{aligned}
$$

so that mantissa of log 158.3 is $.B$ which is same as that of log 15.83.

So, we make the following observations :

If the position of the decimal point is changed without changing the digits and order of digits, the mantissa of logarithm of a number remains unchanged.

7. TO CALCULATE LOGARITHM OF A NUMBER

Find the characteristic from the rules given before and then calculate mantissa with the help of logarithm table. Then the value of logarithm is (characteristic + mantissa).

Example 22. *Find the values of the following using logarithm table:*
(*1*) *log 513.7* (*2*) *log 2,* (*3*) *log 1367,* (*4*) *log 0.006503.*

Solution. (1) Here, the number 513.7 contains three digits in its integral part 513, therefore, characteristic is $3 - 1 = 2$. Mantissa as calculated from tables is .7107. Thus $\log 513.7 = 2 + .7107 = 2.7107$.

(2) Here, the number 2 contains one digit in its integral part 2, therefore characteristic $= 1 - 1 = 0$. Mantissa is .3010.

Thus $\log 2 = 0 + 0.3010 = 0.3010$.

(3) Here, the number of digits are four in the integral part 1367. Therefore, characteristic $= 4 - 1 = 3$. Mantissa is .1357.

Thus $\log 1367 = 3 + 0.1357 = 3.1357$.

(4) Here, the number is less than unity and the number of ciphers immediately after the decimal point and before significant figure 6, are two. Therefore, characteristic $= -(2 + 1) = -3$.

To find the mantissa, we first shift the decimal point and read the number as 0.6503. Now, mantissa as calculated from the table is .8132.

Then log (0.006503) = −3 + 0.8131 = $\bar{3}$.8131.

8. ANTILOGARITHM

If $\log_a N = x$, then N is called the *antilogarithm* of x to the base a and is written in short as $\text{antilog}_a x$.

At the end of book, a table of antilogarithms is given. To read it, we take following two examples.

Find the numbers whose antilogarithms are (1) 1.6078, (2) $\bar{2}$.5832.

(1) We are given that log N = 1.6078. We want to find the number N using antilogarithm table. Consider the decimal part .6078 and read the tables of antilogarithm in the same manner as we did for finding the mantissa from logarithm tables. Take first two digits 60 and run the eye down at the extreme left hand column. Look for the number .60. Consider the third digit 7 and read the intersection of horizontal row beginning with .60 and vertical column headed by 7 (from left). The intersection number is 4046. Now, consider the fourth digit 8 and again read the intersection of horizontal row beginning with .60 and vertical column headed by 8 (in the mean difference column). The intersection number is 7. Add this to the number obtained above, we get 4046 + 7 = 4053.

Now consider the integral part. If it is greater than or equal to zero, then add 1 to it. In the present example, the integral part is 1. Adding 1 to it we get two. Then prefix the decimal point after two digits in the number obtained above *i.e.* 4053. Thus the required number is 40.53.

(2) Consider the decimal part .5832. Find the number as above with the help of antilog tables. The number is 3830.

Since the integral part is negative, subtract 1 from the number under the bar sign *viz.* two − 1 = 1. Attach one cipher to the left hand side of number 3830 and then prefix the decimal point.

Thus the required number is 0.03830.

MISCELLANEOUS EXAMPLES

Example 23. *Given log 2 = .30103, find the number of digits in* 2^{64}.

Solution. Let $x = 2^{64}$

Then $\qquad \log x = 64 \log 2 = 64 \times {\cdot}30103 = 19{\cdot}26592$

As characteristic of log x is 19, number of digits in 2^{64} is 19 + 1 = 20.

Example 24. *Given log 3 = .4771. Find the position of first significant figure in 3^{-65}.*

Solution. Let $x = 3^{-65}$

Then $\log x = -65 \log 3$

$= -65 \times .4771$

$= -31.0115$

$= -31 - .0115$

$= -31 - 1 + 1 - .0115$

$= -32 + .9885$

$= \overline{32}.9885$

Thus, x has 31 ciphers immediately after decimal point so that first significant figure is 32nd in 3^{-65}.

Example 25. *Find the 7th root of 142.71.*

Solution. Let $x = (142.71)^{1/7}$

Then $\log x = \frac{1}{7} \log (142.71)$

$= \frac{1}{7}(2.1545)$

$= .3078$ nearly.

Thus $x = 2.032$ by using antilog tables.

Example 26. *Find the value of* $\frac{(6.284)^3 \sqrt[3]{624}}{\sqrt[4]{.005}}$

Solution. Let $x = \frac{(6.284)^3 \times (624)^{1/3}}{(.005)^{1/4}}$

Then $\log x = 3 \log 6.284 + \frac{1}{3} \log 624 - \frac{1}{4} \log 0.005$

$= 3 \times (0.7983) + \frac{1}{3} \times (2.7952) - \frac{1}{4} \times (3.6990)$

$= 3 \times (0.7983) + \frac{1}{3} (2.7952) - \frac{1}{4} (-3 + 0.6900)$

$= 2.3949 + 0.9317 + 0.7500 - 0.1748$

$= 4.0766 - 0.1748$

$= 3.9018$

Hence $x = 7979$ using antilog tables.

Example 27. *Solve* $7^x + 7^{x+2} = 250.$

Solution. $\text{LHS} = 7^x + 7^{x+2} = 7^x(1+7^2) = 7^x(1+49) = 7^x \times 50$

Then $7^x \times 50 = 250$

$$\Rightarrow \quad 7^x = 5 \Rightarrow \quad \log 7^x = \log 5$$

$$\Rightarrow \quad x \log 7 = \log 5$$

$$\Rightarrow \quad x(.8451) = 0.6990$$

$$\Rightarrow \quad x = \frac{0.6990}{0.8451} = 0.8271 \text{ nearly.}$$

Example 28. *Solve the equations*

$$2^x + 3^y = 44$$

$$2^{x+2} + 3^{y+2} = 221.$$

Solution. Let $a = 2^x$, $b = 3^y$

Then given equations become

$$a + b = 44$$

$$4a + 9b = 221$$

which imply $a = 35$, $b = 9$.

Now $2^x = 35 \Rightarrow x \log 2 = \log 35$

$$\Rightarrow \quad x = \frac{\log 35}{\log 2}$$

$$= \frac{1.5441}{.3010}$$

$$= 5.1299.$$

Also $3^y = 9 \quad \Rightarrow \quad 3^y = 3^2 \quad \Rightarrow \quad y = 2.$

So, $x = 5{\cdot}1299$ and $y = 2$ is the required solution.

Example 29. *Solve the equation*

$$\log_{10}(x - 14) + \log_{10}(x - 5) = 1$$

Solution. The given equation may be written as

$$\log_{10}(x-14)(x-5) = 1 = \log_{10} 10$$

$$\Rightarrow (x-14)(x-5) = 10$$

$$\Rightarrow x^2 - 19x + 60 = 0$$

$$\Rightarrow x = 4, 15.$$

The value $x = 4$, is not possible for log is not defined for negative numbers. The value $x = 15$ does satisfy the given equation. So, the only solution of the given equation is $x = 15$.

Example 30. *A tree, in a period of 20 years of its growth, is found to grow in any one year to 1.02 times its height in the previous year. If it was 3 ft. high at the end of the third year of the period, how high will it be at the end of the fifteenth year.*

Solution. At the end of 3rd year, the height of the tree = 3 ft.

At the end of 4th year, the height will be = $3 \times (1.02)$ ft.

At the end of 5th year, the height will be = $3 \times (1.02)^2$ ft.

... ...

At the end of 15th year, the height will be = $3 \times (1.02)^{12}$ ft.

Let $\qquad x = 3 \times (1.02)^{12}$

Then,
$$\begin{aligned} \log x &= \log 3 + 12 \log 1.02 \\ &= \log 3 + 12 (\log 102 - \log 100) \\ &= 0.4771 + 12 (2.0086 - 2) \\ &= 0.4771 + 0.1032 \\ &= 0.5803 \end{aligned}$$

Therefore, $\qquad x = \text{antilog } 0.5803 = 3.805.$

So, height of the tree at the end of 15th year will be 3.805 ft.

Example 31. *The first and tenth term of a G.P. are respectively 3 and 65. Find the common ratio.*

Solution. Let $a, ar, ar^2 \ldots ar^9$ be first ten terms of a G.P.

Then $\qquad a = 3$ and $ar^9 = 65$

So, $\qquad r^9 = \dfrac{65}{3}$

$$\begin{aligned} \Rightarrow \quad 9 \log r &= \log 65 - \log 3 \\ &= 1.8129 - .4771 \\ &= 1.3358 \\ \Rightarrow \quad \log r &= 1484 \\ \Rightarrow \quad r &= \text{antilog } .1484 = 1.407. \end{aligned}$$

Example 32. *Evaluate* $\dfrac{24.395 \times (3.16)^3}{8.79}$

Solution. Let $x = \dfrac{24.395 \times (3.16)^3}{8.79}$

Then $\log x = \log 24.395 + 3 \log 3.16 - \log 8.79$

$= 1.3874 + 1.4991 - .9440 = 1.9425$

So, $\qquad x = 87.60.$

Example 33. *Use log tables to find the value of x if x satisfies the equation.*

$$\frac{20}{14\cdot 7} = \left(\frac{.0613}{x}\right)^{1.32}$$

Solution. $$\frac{20}{14.7} = \left(\frac{.0613}{x}\right)^{1.32}$$

$$\Rightarrow \quad \log 20 - \log 14.7 = 1.32\,[\log .0613 - \log x]$$

$$\Rightarrow \quad 1.32 \log x = 1.32 \log .0613 - \log 20 + \log 14.7$$

$$\Rightarrow \quad \log x = \frac{(1.32)\times(\bar{2}.7874) - 1.3010 + 1.1673}{1.32}$$

$$= \frac{(1.32)\times(-2) + (1.32\times.7874) + 1.1673 - 1.3010}{1.32}$$

$$\Rightarrow \qquad x = .049 \text{ (using antilog).}$$

Example 34. *Evaluate*

$$\sqrt[7]{\frac{1}{.8176\times 36.21}}$$

Solution. Let $x = \sqrt[7]{\dfrac{1}{.8176\times 36.21}}$

Then $$\log x = \frac{1}{7}[\log 1 - \log .8176 - \log 36\cdot 21]$$

$$= \frac{1}{7}[0 - (\bar{1}\cdot 9125) - (1\cdot 5588)]$$

$$= \frac{1}{7}[-1\cdot 4713]$$

$$= \frac{-7+7-1\cdot 4713}{7}$$

$$= \frac{-7+5\cdot 5287}{7}$$

$$= -1 + \cdot 7898$$

$$= \bar{1}\cdot 7898$$

So, $x = \cdot 616.$

EXERCISES

1. Find the number of digits in 25^5.
2. Having given that log 3 = ·4771213 find the number of digits in
   (i) 3^{43}, (ii) 3^{27}, (iii) 3^{62}
3. Find the position of first significant figure in
   (i) 3^{-13}, (ii) 3^{-43}, (iii) 3^{-65} given that log 3 = ·4771213.
4. Find the fifth root of ·0011.
5. Find the seventh root of ·00001427.
6. Find the approximate values of

   (*i*) $\sqrt[3]{645{\cdot}3}$ (*ii*) $\sqrt[5]{82360}$

   (*iii*) $\sqrt{\dfrac{\cdot0074\times\cdot0137}{873{\cdot}5}}$ (*iv*) $\dfrac{[3{\cdot}142]^2\times[\cdot078]^{1/3}}{[\cdot005]^{1/4}}$
7. Solve the following equations having given log 2 = ·3010, log 3 = 0·4771 and log 6 = ·8451
   (i) $3^{x-2} = 5$ (ii) $5^x = 10^3$ (iii) $5^{5-3x} = 2^{x+2}$
8. Show that $\left(\dfrac{21}{29}\right)^{100}$ is greater than 100.
9. Solve the equation $3^{2x} - 3^{x+1} = 4$.
10. Show that there is only one real value of x which satisfies the equation $2^{2x} + 6.2^x = 5$ and find it correct to four significant figures.
11. Find the value of x from the equation $18^{4-4x} = (54\sqrt{2})^{3x-2}$
12. Solve the equation
   $$3^x - 2^{y+2} = 10, \quad 2^y - 3^{x-2} = 2$$
13. Solve the equation
   $$\sqrt{2^{x+2}+5}+\sqrt{5{\cdot}2^x-9} = \sqrt{3{\cdot}2^{x+2}+21}$$
14. Find two numbers x and y such that 7, x, y, 100 form a G.P.
15. Solve the equation
   $$\log_3 3 + \log_3 (x+1) - \log_3 (2x-7) = 4.$$
16. If log 2 = ·3010 and log 3 = ·4771, find log (·0005) and log $(405)^{1/2}$.
17. Evaluate $\dfrac{(17{\cdot}5)^{1/2}+(15{\cdot}2)^{1/3}}{(56{\cdot}3)^{3/5}-(12{\cdot}4)^{1/4}}$
18. Evaluate $\dfrac{1}{3}\sqrt[3]{\dfrac{21{\cdot}6\times12{\cdot}6}{562{\cdot}6}}$
19. Evaluate $\dfrac{61{\cdot}92\times\cdot07046}{401{\cdot}535}$
20. Evaluate $\dfrac{2{\cdot}389\times0{\cdot}004679}{0{\cdot}00556\times52{\cdot}14}$

ANSWERS

1. 7. 2. (*i*) 21, (*ii*) 13, (*iii*) 30.
3. (*i*) 7th, (*ii*) 21st, (*iii*) 32nd. 4. 0·2561 nearly.
5. ·2032
6. (*i*) 8·642, (*ii*) 9·618, (*iii*) ·0003408, (*iv*) 49·83.
7. (*i*) 3·467, (*ii*) 4·29, (*iii*) 1·206.
9. 1·262 10. – ·4312
11. 14/17 12. x = 13·166, y = 2·485
13. $x = \log_2 5$ 14. x = 16·98, y = 41·21
15. $3\frac{31}{53}$ 16. $\bar{4}$·6990, $\bar{1}$·8037
17. 0.459 18. 0.2617

9. NATURAL OR NAPERIAN LOGARITHMS

Consider $\left(1+\frac{1}{n}\right)^n$ where n is a natural number.

By Binomial Theorem for positive index,

$$\left(1+\frac{1}{n}\right)^n = 1 + n\frac{1}{n} + \frac{n(n-1)}{2!}\frac{1}{n^2} + \frac{n(n^{-17})(n^{-27})}{3!}\frac{1}{n^3} + \ldots$$

$$= 1 + 1 + \frac{\left(1-\frac{1}{n}\right)}{2!} + \frac{\left(1-\frac{1}{n}\right)\left(1-\frac{2}{n}\right)}{3!} + \ldots$$

Thus $$\lim_{n\to\infty}\left(1+\frac{1}{n}\right)^n = 1 + 1 + \frac{1}{2!} + \frac{1}{3!} + \frac{1}{4!} + \ldots$$

We call $\lim_{n\to\infty}\left(1+\frac{1}{n}\right)^n$, the *Exponential Function* and denote it by e.

Thus $$e = 1 + 1 + \frac{1}{2!} + \frac{1}{3!} + \frac{1}{4!} + \ldots \infty$$

Clearly from definition $e > 2$.

Also $$\frac{1}{4!} + \frac{1}{5!} + \ldots + \frac{1}{n!} = \frac{1}{4.3.2} + \frac{1}{5.4.3.2} + \ldots + \frac{1}{n!}$$

i.e. $$< \frac{1}{2.2.2} + \frac{1}{2.2.2.2} + \ldots < \frac{1}{2^3} + \frac{1}{2^4} + \ldots + \frac{1}{2^{n-1}}$$

This implies $\frac{1}{4!}+\frac{1}{5!}+\frac{1}{6!}+\ldots\infty$

$$\leq \lim_{n\to\infty}\left(\frac{1}{2^3}+\frac{1}{2^4}+\ldots+\frac{1}{2^{n-1}}\right)$$

i.e., $$\leq \frac{1}{2^3}+\frac{1}{2^4}+\ldots+\infty$$

So $$\frac{1}{4!}+\frac{1}{5!}+\frac{1}{6!}+\ldots\infty \leq \frac{\frac{1}{8}}{1-\frac{1}{2}}=\frac{1}{4}$$

$$\Rightarrow\ e\leq 1+1+\frac{1}{2!}+\frac{1}{3!}+\frac{1}{4!}=2\frac{11}{12}$$

This implies that $e<3$

Hence $$2<e<3.$$

10. EXPONENTIAL SERIES

Again for any real x, by binomial theorem for any index and $n\geq 2$, we have

$$\left(1+\frac{1}{n}\right)^{nx}=1+nx\frac{1}{n}+\frac{nx(nx-1)}{2!}\frac{1}{n^2}+\ldots\infty$$

$$=1+x+\frac{x(x-1/n)}{2!}+\frac{x(x-1/n)(x-2/n)}{3!}+\ldots\infty$$

So $$\lim_{n\to\infty}\left(1+\frac{1}{n}\right)^{nx}=1+x+\frac{x^2}{2!}+\frac{x^3}{3!}+\ldots\infty$$

But $$\lim_{n\to\infty}\left(1+\frac{1}{n}\right)^{nx}=\left[\lim_{n\to\infty}\left(1+\frac{1}{n}\right)^{n}\right]^{x}=e^x.$$

Thus for real number x,

$$e^x=1+x+\frac{x^2}{2!}+\frac{x^3}{3!}+\ldots\infty$$

This is called *the Exponential series.*

Let a be any positive real number then $\log_e a$ is called *Natural* or *Naperian Logarithm.*

REMARK: Whenever we write log 2, log 15 etc., and no base is mentioned it is understood that base is 10 and we are talking of common logarithm, whereas when we write log a, log x etc, the base is understood to be e.

11. LOGARITHMIC SERIES

For any positive a and for any real number y, $a^y = e^{y \log a}$ (this can be seen by taking logarithm of both sides with respect to base e).

$$\text{So} \quad a^y = 1 + y \log a + \frac{(y \log a)^2}{2!} + \frac{(y \log a)^3}{3!} + \ldots$$

Putting $a = 1 + x$, we get

$$(1 + x)^y = 1 + y \log (1 + x) + \frac{[y \log(1+x)]^2}{2!} + \ldots$$

$$\text{Suppose} \quad |x| < 1 \text{ then } (1 + x)^y = 1 + yx + \frac{y(y-1)x^2}{2!} + \ldots$$

$$= 1 + y\left(x - \frac{x^2}{2} + \frac{2x^3}{3!} - \frac{3 \cdot 2x^4}{4!} + \ldots\right) + \ldots$$

$$\text{So} \quad 1 + y\left(x - \frac{x^2}{2} + \frac{x^3}{3} - \frac{x^4}{4} + \ldots\right) + \ldots$$

$$= 1 + y \log (1 + x) + \frac{[y \log(1+x)]^2}{2!} + \ldots$$

This equation is valid for each value of y. Hence coefficient of y on both sides must be equal.

Thus for $|x| < 1$,

$$\log (1 + x) = x - \frac{x^2}{2} + \frac{x^3}{3} - \frac{x^4}{4} + \ldots$$

This is called the *Logarithmic Series.*

Replacing x with $-x$ we get

$$\log (1 - x) = -x - \frac{x^2}{2} - \frac{x^3}{3} - \frac{x^4}{4} \ldots$$

$$\text{So} \qquad \log\left(\frac{1+x}{1-x}\right) = \log (1 + x) - \log (1 - x)$$

$$= 2\left(x + \frac{x^3}{3} + \frac{x^5}{5} + \ldots\right).$$

CHAPTER 14

INTEREST AND ANNUITIES

1. When A borrows money from B, then A has to pay certain amount to B for the use of the money. The amount paid by A is called *Interest.*

The amount borrowed by A from B is called *Principal.*

The sum of the interest and principal is usually called the *amount* or *the total amount*. The *rate per cent per annum* is the interest payable on Rs 100 for one year. For example, the rate of interest is 5 per cent per annum means the interest payable on Rs 100 for one year is Rs 5.

When interest is payable on the principal only, it is called *Simple Interest*. For example, simple interest on Rs 100 at 5 per cent per annum will be Rs 5 each year i.e., at the end of one year, total amount will be Rs 105, at the end of second year, it will be Rs 110 and so on.

When interest is calculated on the amount in the previous year, then it is called *Compound Interest*. For example, interest on Rs 100 at 5 per cent per annum compound interest at the end of 1st year will be Rs 5, at the end of second year it will be Rs 5.25, at the end of third year it will be Rs 5.5125 and so on.

When a given amount is due after a specified period of time, its present value is that sum which together with interest for that period produces the given amount. For example, Rs 100 at the rate of 5 per cent per annum compound interest will become Rs 110.25 at the end of 2 years. We say, Rs 100 is the present value of Rs 110.25 in 2 years.

A *sinking fund* is the money accumulated at compound interest by setting aside a fixed amount at regular intervals. For example, a company buys a machine whose life is 25 years. Since it has to buy a new machine after 25 years, the company sets aside every year Rs 100. The sum of money accumulated at the end of 25 years is the sinking fund.

When a loan is repaid in equal instalments, then each instalment consists of interest and repayment of capital. The difference between amount of instalment and interest is called *Amortisation*.

2. TO FIND THE INTEREST AND AMOUNT OF A GIVEN SUM IN A GIVEN TIME AT SIMPLE INTEREST

When money is put out at simple interest, the interest is payable for each year, but is not added to the principal.

Let P be the principal and n, the number of years for which the principal is lent, r the rate of interest per annum.

The amount at the end of one year is

$$= P + P\frac{r}{100} = P\left[1 + \frac{r}{100}\right]$$

In other words, the interest at the end of one year will be $\frac{Pr}{100}$. Since the principal is lent at simple interest, the amount $\frac{Pr}{100}$ will be added to the amount at the end of each year. So that the amount at the end of n years will be

$$\left[P + \frac{Pr}{100}\right] + \frac{Pr}{100} + \ldots + \frac{Pr}{100}$$

$$= P + P\underbrace{\left[\frac{r}{100} + \ldots + \frac{r}{100}\right]}_{n \text{ times}}$$

$$= P\left[1 + \frac{nr}{100}\right]$$

The interest so obtained after n years will be

$$P\left[1 + \frac{nr}{100}\right] - P = P\frac{nr}{100}$$

NOTE. The amounts at the end of each year constitute a series in A.P. with common difference $\frac{Pr}{100}$.

3. TO FIND THE INTEREST AND AMOUNT OF A GIVEN SUM AT COMPOUND INTEREST

If the money is lent at compound interest the interest is added each year to the principal and for the following year the interest is calculated on their sum.

Let P be the principal and n, the number of years for which the principal is lent at r per cent per annum compound interest.

The amount at the end of one year will be

$$= P + P \cdot \frac{r}{100} = P\left[1 + \frac{r}{100}\right] = PR.$$

The amount at the end of two years will be

$$= PR + PR\,\frac{r}{100}$$

$$= PR\left[1 + \frac{r}{100}\right] = PR^2$$

The amount at the end of three years will be

$$= PR^2 + PR^2\,\frac{r}{100}$$

$$= PR^2\left[1 + \frac{r}{100}\right] = PR^3$$

Arguing in this way, the amount at the end of n years will be PR^n.
If A denotes the amount at the end of n years, then

$$A = PR^n$$

Thus $$P = \frac{A}{R^n}$$

This enables us to find the sum of money which will produce amount A in n years.

Also $$R = \sqrt[n]{\frac{A}{P}}$$

from which the rate of interest can be discovered.

Again $$R^n = \frac{A}{P} \Rightarrow n \log R = \log A - \log P$$

$$\Rightarrow \quad n = \frac{\log A - \log P}{\log R}$$

from which the time taken for P to amount A can be found.

NOTE.The amounts in each year constitute terms of a G.P. with 1st term PR and common ratio $R = 1 + \dfrac{r}{100}$.

Example 1. *Prove that in order that a sum of money may double itself in 10 years by investment at compound interest, payable annually, the interest should be approximately 7.2 per cent per annum.*

Solution. Let the amount P be invested. This will become PR^{10} in 10 years where $$R = 1 + \frac{r}{100}$$

We want that this amount should the $2P$. Therefore,

$$2P = PR^{10} \Rightarrow R = 2^{1/10}$$

$$\log R = \frac{1}{10} \log 2$$

$$= \frac{1}{10}(.3010) = .0301$$

$$\Rightarrow \quad R = 1.072$$

$$\Rightarrow \quad 1.072 = 1 + \frac{r}{100}$$

$$\Rightarrow \quad (1.072) \times 100 = 100 + r$$

$$\Rightarrow \quad 107.2 = 100 + r$$

$$\Rightarrow \quad r = 7.2.$$

Example 2. *A man invests Rs 100 at the end of 1971, Rs 200 at the end of 1972, Rs 300 at the end of 1973, Rs 400 at the end of 1974, Rs 500 at the end of 1975. If all interest accumulates at 5 per cent per annum, what do his investments amount to at the end of 1976.*

Solution. Rs 100 is invested for 5 years, Rs 200 for 4 years and so on. The total value at the end of 1976 is

$$100(1.05)^5 + 200(1.05)^4 + 300(1.05)^3 + 400(1.05)^2 + 500(1.05)$$

$$\left[\text{Here } R = 1 + \frac{r}{100} = 1 + \frac{5}{100} = \frac{105}{100} = 1.05\right]$$

$$= 105[(1.05)^4 + 2(1.05)^3 + 3(1.05)^2 + 4(1.05) + 5]$$

Now, let $x = (1.05)^4$

Then $\log x = 4 \log (1.05)$

$$= 4(.0212) = .0848$$

So, $x = 1.215$

Similarly, $(1.05)^3 = 1.158$

$$(1.05)^2 = 1.103$$

$$(1.05) = 1.050$$

Therefore, the total value of at the end of 1976 is

$$= 105\,[1.215 + 2.316 + 3.309 + 4.2 + 5]$$

$$= 105\,[16.04]$$

$$= \text{Rs } 1684.2.$$

Example 3. *Mr Samy invests in a bank Rs x on the 1st day of 1966. In the subsequent years on the Ist of January he deposits money double that of the money deposited in the previous year after withdrawing the interest only on the same day. It was found that balance in his account on January 2, 1975, was Rs 2046. It was requested to find the amount he deposited on 12 January 1966.*

Solution. Let the money invested on 1 January 1966 be x, then

$$x + 2x + 4x + ... + 10 \text{ terms} = 2046$$

$$\Rightarrow \quad x(2^0 + 2^1 + 2^2 + ... + 2^9) = 2046$$

$$\Rightarrow \quad x\frac{(2^{10} - 1)}{2-1} = 2046$$

$$\Rightarrow \quad 1023x = 2046$$

$$\Rightarrow \quad x = 2.$$

Example 4. *Shri V. M. Vardyn's son Varen has just completed 5 years of age. In order to provide a sum of Rs 50,000 when Varen completes 21 years, Shri Varadyn has decided to invest a fixed sum of money every year beginning immediately and the last payment will be when Varen completes 21 years. Find the fixed sum of money assuming money earns interest at the rate of 8 per cent annum.*

Solution. Let the fixed sum be Rs x. After one year, it will be $= \frac{108}{100}x$.

After 2 years, it will be $= \left[\frac{108}{100}\right]^2 x.$

In this way, we get

$$x + \left[\frac{108}{100}\right]x + \left[\frac{108}{100}\right]^2 x + ... + \left[\frac{108}{100}\right]^{16} x = 50000$$

So,
$$x\frac{(1.08)^{17} - 1}{(1.08) - 1} = 50000$$

$$\Rightarrow \quad x = \frac{50000 \times 0.08}{270} \qquad [(1.08)^{17} = 3.70 \text{ using log tables})]$$

$$\Rightarrow \quad x = \text{Rs } 1481 \text{ approx.}$$

Example 5. *Find the interest on Rs 1000 for 10 years at 4 per cent per annum, the interest being paid quarterly.*

Solution. The amount at the end of one quarter of a year will be

$$1000 + 1000 \times \frac{1}{100}$$

$$1000\left[1+\frac{1}{100}\right] = 1000\,R, \text{ where } R = 1+\frac{1}{100} = \frac{101}{100}$$

Similarly, the amount at the end of the first half-year will be

$$= 10000\,R^2$$

Arguing in this way, the amount at the end of 10 years will be

$$= 1000\,R^{40}$$

Let $\quad A = 1000\,R^{40}$

Then $\quad \log A = 3 + 40 \log R$

$$= 3 + 40 \log \frac{101}{100}$$

$$= 3 + 40(\log 101 - \log 100)$$

$$= 3 + 40(0.0043)$$

$$= 3 + .172 = 3.172$$

Therefore, $\quad A = 1486$

So, required interest = 1486 – 1000 = 486

(Note that rate of interest 4 per cent per annum means 1 per cent per quarter of a year.)

Example 6. *A man pays his savings which amount to Rs 25 every six months, into a bank which allows him interest payable quarterly at the rate of 2½ per cent per annum. Find the sum which will stand to his credit at the end of 10 years from his first payment.*

Solution. The first instalment of Rs 25 lies in the bank for 10 years and interest is added quarterly.

Therefore, this will amount to

$$25\left[1+\frac{2\frac{1}{2}}{400}\right]^{40}$$

The second instalment lies in the bank for 9½ years and will amount to

$$25\left[1+\frac{2\frac{1}{2}}{400}\right]^{38}$$

The third instalment lies in the bank for 9 years and will amount to

$$25\left[1+\frac{2\frac{1}{2}}{400}\right]^{36}$$

The last instalment lies in the bank for 1/2 year and will amount to

$$25\left[1+\frac{2\frac{1}{2}}{400}\right]^2$$

Thus, if S denotes the total amount

and $$R = 1+\frac{2\frac{1}{2}}{400},$$

then $$S = 25[R^{40}+R^{38}+...+R^2]$$
$$= 25R^2[1+R^2+...+R^{38}]$$

This is a G. P. whose common ration is R^2, there being 20 terms in the series.

Thus $$S = 25\ R^2\left[\frac{1-R^{40}}{1-R^2}\right]$$
$$= \frac{25R^2}{R^2-1}(R^{40}-1)$$

Now $$R = 1+\frac{2\frac{1}{2}}{400} = 1.00625$$

$\Rightarrow$ $$R^2 = 1.0125$$

Now $$\log R^{40} = 40\log R = 40\times(.0027)$$
$$= .108$$

Therefore $$R^{40} = 1.2823$$

Hence $$S = \frac{25\times 1.0125\times .2823}{.0125}$$
$$= \text{Rs } 572 \text{ approx.}$$

4. ANNUITIES

An *annuity* is a series of equal annual payments extending over a specified number of years.

If P is the amount which produces M in n years at the given rate of interest, then we know

$$M = PR^n \text{ or } P = \frac{M}{R^n}$$

P is called the *present* value of M in n years.

Suppose A is the annual payment and P be its present value, then for the first payment due in 1 year

$$P = \frac{A}{R}.$$

For the second payment

$$P = \frac{A}{R^2} \text{ and so on.}$$

Therefore, the total present value

$$= \frac{A}{R} + \frac{A}{R^2} + \dots + \frac{A}{R^n}$$

$$= A\left\{\frac{1}{R} + \frac{1}{R^2} + \dots + \frac{1}{R^n}\right\}$$

$$= \frac{A\frac{1}{R}\left[1 - \frac{1}{R^n}\right]}{1 - R\frac{1}{R}} = \frac{A\left[1 - \frac{1}{R^n}\right]}{R-1}.$$

This is called *present value of annuity* A in *n* years.

5. PERPETUITY

An annuity which is payable for ever is called *perpetuity*. In this case $n \to \infty$ and so total present value is $\frac{A}{R-1}$.

Example 7. *A man borrows Rs 1000 and repays the loan by yearly instalments of Rs 100, the first instalment being paid one year after the loan. After how many years will he be out of debt, interest being reckoned throughout at 4 per cent annum.*

Solution. Suppose *n* is required number of years.

The present values of the instalments are

$$\frac{100}{1.04}, \frac{100}{(1.04)^2}, \dots, \frac{100}{(1.04)^n}$$

Hence, $$1000 = \frac{100}{1.04} + \dots + \frac{100}{(1.04)^n}$$

$$= \frac{100}{1.04}\left\{1 + \frac{1}{(1.04)} + \dots + \frac{1}{(1.04)^{n-1}}\right\}$$

$$= \frac{100}{1.04} \cdot \frac{1-(1.04)^{-n}}{1-(1.04)^{-1}}$$

Thus $$0.4 = 1 - (1.04)^{-4}$$

i.e., $(1.04)^n = \frac{5}{3}$

Therefore $n = \frac{\log 5 - \log 3}{\log(1.04)}$

$$= \frac{.6990 - .4771}{.0170} = 13.05 \text{ approx.}$$

Thus by slightly increasing the last payment, the debt would be discharged in 13 years.

Alternatively. The first instalment of Rs 100 will amount to (in *n* years) $100 \times (1.04)^{n-1}$.

The second instalment of Rs 100 will amount to $100(1.04)^{n-2}$ and so on.

The last instalment of Rs 100 will amount to 100.

So, total money accumulated at the end of *n* years will be

$$100 \times (1.04)^{n-1} + \ldots + 100$$

$$= 100 \times (1.04)^{n-1}\left[1 + \frac{1}{(1.04)} + \ldots + \frac{1}{(1.04)^{n-1}}\right]$$

Also, the amount Rs 1000 in *n* years will become

$$= 1000 \times (1.04)^n$$

Therefore,

$$1000 \times (1.04)^n = 100 \times (1.04)^{n-1}\left[1 + \ldots + \frac{1}{(1.04)^{n-1}}\right]$$

or $$1000 = \frac{100}{(1.04)}\left[1 + \frac{1}{(1.04)} + \ldots + \frac{1}{(1.04)^{n-1}}\right]$$

which is the same equation as obtained earlier. Now proceed as before.

Example 8. *A man borrows Rs 20,000 and agrees to pay the borrowed amount in 10 equal annual instalments at the rate of 6 per cent per annum. Find the amount of each instalment, the first being paid one year after the money was borrowed.*

Solution. Let *x* be the amount of each instalment. Then as in the previous example.

$$20000 = \frac{x}{(1.06)}\left[1 + \frac{1}{(1.06)} + \ldots + \frac{1}{(1.06)^9}\right]$$

Therefore,

$$20000 = \frac{x}{(1.06)} \frac{1 - \frac{1}{(1.06)^{10}}}{1 - \frac{1}{(1.06)}} = \frac{x}{(0.06)}[1-(1.06)^{-10}]$$

Now $\quad \log 1.06 = .0253$

$$\log (1.06)^{-10} = -.2531 = \bar{1}.7469$$

Thus $\quad (1.06)^{-10} = .5584$

Hence $\quad x = \frac{1200}{.4416}$

$$\log x = 3.0792 - \bar{1}.6450 = 3.4342$$

Therefore, $\quad x = 2718.$

Example 9. *A man puts Rs 10 at the end of every year in the Savings Bank at 2½ per cent compound interest. How much will his savings amount to, in 15 years.*

Solution. At the end of one year he has saved Rs 10.

At the end of second year, the amount of his saving will be (in rupees)

$$= 10 + 10 \times (1.025)$$

At the end of third year, the amount of his savings will be (in rupees)

$$10 + 10(1.025) + 10 \times (1.025)^2$$

Proceedings in this way, the amount of his savings in 15 years will be (in rupees)

$$= 10 + 10(1.025) + 10(1.025)^2 + ... + 10(1.025)^{14}$$

$$= 10 \frac{(1.025)^{15} - 1}{(1.025) - 1}$$

$$= 10 \frac{(1.025)^{15} - 1}{.025} = 400[(1.025)^{15} - 1]$$

Now, $(1.025)^{15} = 1.447$ (using log tables)

Hence, the required amount is $400 \times (.4470) = 178.8$ approx.

Example 10. *A loan of Rs 1000 is to be paid in 5 equal annual instalments, interest being at 6 per cent per annum compound interest and first payment being made after a year. Analyse the payments into those on account of interest and on account of amortization of the principal.*

Solution. Let A be the annual instalment. At the end of 5th year, A will amount to $A\,(1.06)^4$.

When the second annual instalment A is paid, it will amount to $A(1.06)^3$ at the end of 5th year.

The third instalment will amount to $A(1.06)^2$ at the end of 5th year.

The fourth instalment will amount to $A\,(1.06)$ at the end of 5th year.

The fifth instalment will be A. Thus total money accumulated at the end of 5th year will be

$$A(1.06)^4 + A(1.06)^3 + A(1.06)^2 + A(1.06) + A$$
$$= A[1 + (1.06) + (1.06)^2 + (1.06)^3 + (1.06)^4]$$

But total money at the end of 5th year is $1000(1.06)^5$

$$\text{So, } (1000) \times (1.06)^5 = A[1 + \ldots + (1.06)^4] = A\frac{1-(1.06)^5}{1-(1.06)}$$

$$\Rightarrow \quad A = \frac{(1000) \times (.06)}{1-(1.06)^{-5}} = \frac{60}{1-(1.06)^{-5}}$$

$$\text{Now} \quad (1.06)^{-5} = .7473$$

$$\Rightarrow \quad A = \frac{60}{.2527} = 237.44$$

$$\text{Thus} \quad A = \text{Rs } 237.4.$$

At the end of 1st year, the interest will be 6 per cent of Rs 1000 *i.e.*, Rs 60. So, amortization = Rs (237.44 – 60) = Rs 177.44. Therefore, (Rs 1000 – 177.44) = Rs 822.56 is the loan amount at the end of 1st year. At the end of 2nd year, the interest will be 6 per cent of Rs 822.56; *i.e.*, Rs 49.35. So, amortization = Rs (237.44 – 49.35) = Rs 188.09. The loan amount at the end of 2nd year is Rs (822.56 – 188.09) = Rs 634.47. At the end of third year the interest will be 6 per cent of Rs 634.47, *i.e.*, Rs 38.07 and amortization = Rs (237.44 – 38.07) = Rs 199.37. The loan amount at the end of 3rd year will be Rs (634.47 – 199.37) = Rs 435.10. At the end of 4th year, the interest will be 6 per cent of Rs 435.10, *i.e.*, Rs 26.10 and amortization = Rs (237.44 – 26.10) = Rs 211.34. The loan amount at the end of 4th year will be Rs (435.10 – 211.34) = Rs 223.76. At the end of 5th year, the interest will be 6 per cent of Rs 223.76 *i.e.* Rs 13.43 and amortization = Rs (237.44 – 13.43) = Rs 224.01).

Example 11. *A company sets aside a sum of Rs 20,000 annually to enable it to pay off a debenture issue of Rs 230,000 at the end of 10 years Assuming that the sum accumulates at 4 per cent per annum compound, find the surplus after paying off the debenture stock.*

Solution. Rs 20,000 will amount to (at the end of 10 years) as

$$\text{Rs}\,[20{,}000 \times (1.04)^{10}]$$

The second sum of Rs 20,000 will amount to Rs $[20{,}000 \times 1.04)^9]$

In this way, total money at the end of 10th year will be

$$= 20{,}000[1 + (1.04) \quad + \ldots + (1.04)^9] \times (1.04)$$

$$= 20{,}000\left[\frac{1-(1.04)^{10}}{1-(1.04)}\right] \times (1.04)$$

$$= \frac{20{,}000 \times (1.04)}{.04}[(1.04)^{10} - 1]$$

$$= \frac{20{,}000 \times 1.04}{.04} \times (1.4790 - 1)$$

$$= \frac{20{,}000 \times 1.04}{.04} \times (.4790)$$

$$= \text{Rs}\ 249{,}080$$

Thus, the required surplus

$$= \text{Rs}\ (249{,}080 - 230{,}000)$$

$$= \text{Rs}\ 19{,}080.$$

Example 12. *A machine costs a company Rs 52,000 and its effective life is estimated to be 25 years. A sinking fund is created for replacing the machine by new model at the end of its left time, when its scrap realizes a sum of Rs 2500 only. The price for new model is estimated to be 25 per cent higher than the present one. Find what amount should be set aside every year, out of profits for the sinking fund, it accumulates at* $3\frac{1}{2}$ *per cent per annum compound.*

Solution. The cost of new machine at the end of 25 years will be

$$52{,}000 + 52{,}000 \times \frac{25}{100} = 65{,}000$$

Since scrap of old machine realizes a sum of Rs 2,500, the amount of sinking found is = 65,000 + 2,500 = Rs 62,500. If A is the amount set aside every year, then A set aside at the end of 1st year will amount to (in 25 years) is $A(1.035)^{24}$.

Similarly A set aside at the end of 2nd year will amount to $(1.035)^{23}$. In this way, total money at the end of 25th year will be

$$A(1.035)^{24} + A(1.035)^{23} + \ldots + A.$$

This should be 62.500

So, $62.500 = A[1+(1.035)+...+(1.035)^{24}]$

$$= A\frac{(1.035)^{25}-1}{.035}$$

$\Rightarrow$ $A = \text{Rs } 1610.82.$

Example 13. *A lends B Rs 320. B is to pay interest on whatever amount he has not paid back at the rate of 5 per cent per annum for the first year, 6 per cent for the second year and 7 per cent for the third year. B pays A Rs 100 at the end of first year, Rs 100 at the end of second year and enough to pay off completely the debt and interest at the end of the third year. How much is the last payment.*

Solution. Rs 320 will amount to (at the end of 1st year)

$$= 320\,(1.05) = \text{Rs } 336.$$

Since *B* pays Rs 100 at the end of 1st year, the amount outstanding at the end of 1st year = 336 – 100 = Rs 226. Rs 226 at the end of 2nd year will amount to 226 × (1.06) = Rs 239.56. Since B pays Rs 100 at the end of 2nd year, the amount outstanding at the end of 2nd year = 239.56 – 100 = Rs 139.56.

Now, Rs 139.56 will amount to (at the end of third year)

$$= 139.56(1.07) = \text{Rs } 149.33$$

Thus, the last payment is Rs 149.33.

Example 14. *A man buys a car for Rs 16,000. He estimates that its value will depreciate each year by 20 per cent of its value at the beginning of a year. Find the depreciated value (Rs x, correct to the nearest rupee) of the car at the end of five years. If the man sets aside at the end of each of the five years a certain fixed sum (Rs y) to accumulate at 4 per cent compound interest in order to be able to buy at the end of the five years another car costing Rs 22,000 (after allowing the above depreciated value Rs x for the old car in past exchange), find to nearest paisa the value Rs y of each payment.*

Solution. At the end of 1st year, the depreciated value of car

$$= \frac{80}{100}\times 16000 = \frac{4}{5}\times 16000$$

At the end of 2nd year, the depreciated value of car $= \left(\frac{4}{5}\right)^2 \times 16000$.

In this way, at the end of 5th year the depreciated value of car

$$= \left(\frac{4}{5}\right)^5 \times 16000$$

So $$x = \left(\frac{4}{5}\right)^5 \times 16000$$

$$\log x = 5 \log \frac{4}{5} + \log 16000$$

$$= 3.7196$$

$$\Rightarrow \quad x = 52.47$$

Now y invested at the end of 1st year will amount in 5 years to $y\,(1.04)^4$

In this way, total amount accumulated at the end of 5th year

$$= y\,(1.04)^4 + y\,(1.04)^3 + y\,(1.04)^2 + y\,(1.04) + y$$

$$= y\,[1 + (1.04) + ... + (1.04)^4] = y\frac{(1.04)^5 - 1}{:04}$$

Therefore $$22000 - x = y\left[\frac{(1.04)^5 - 1}{.04}\right]$$

$$\Rightarrow \quad 16753 = y\left[\frac{1.2168 - 1}{.04}\right]$$

$$\Rightarrow \quad 16753 = y\left(\frac{.2168}{.04}\right)$$

$$\Rightarrow \quad 16753 = 5.4y$$

$$\Rightarrow \quad y = \frac{16753}{5.4} = 3102.41$$

$$\Rightarrow \quad y = \text{Rs } 3102.41.$$

Example 15. *A person desires to create an endowment fund to provide for a prize of Rs 300 every year. If the fund can be invested at 10 per cent annum compound interest, find the amount of the endownment.*

Solution. Let P be endowment fund. At the end of one year, interest on P at the rate of 10 per cent per annum should be Rs 300.

Therefore, $$P \times 1 \times \frac{1}{10} = 300$$

$$\Rightarrow \quad P = 3000$$

Thus, endowment fund should be Rs 3000.

Example 16. *A person is entitled to receive an annual payment which for each year is less by* $\frac{1}{10}$ *th of what it was for the year before. If the first payment is Rs 100, show that he cannot receive more than Rs 1000 however long he may live.*

Solution. The first payment = Rs 100

The second payment $= 100 - \frac{1}{10} \times 100$

$$= 90 = \frac{9}{10} \times (100)$$

The third payment $= 90 - \frac{1}{10} \times 90$

$$= 81 = \left(\frac{9}{10}\right)^2 \times 100$$

In this way, nth payment $= \left(\frac{9}{10}\right)^{n-1} \times 100$

Let $S = 100 + \frac{9}{10} \times 100 + \left(\frac{9}{10}\right)^2 \times 100 + \ldots$

$$= 100\left[1 + \frac{9}{10} + \left(\frac{9}{10}\right)^2 + \ldots\right]$$

$$= \frac{100}{1 - \frac{9}{10}} = 1000.$$

In other words, he cannot receive more than Rs 1000 however long he may live.

6. DISCOUNTS

Suppose P is the sum which is due after n years at the simple interest r per cent per annum. Let A be the amount which will become P after n years. Then

$$P = A\left(1 + \frac{nr}{100}\right)$$

and so, $A = \dfrac{P}{1 + \frac{nr}{100}}$

Let $$D = P - A$$

$$= P - \frac{P}{1+\frac{nr}{100}}$$

$$= \frac{P\left(\frac{nr}{100}\right)}{1+\frac{nr}{100}} = \frac{Anr}{100}$$

$$= \text{Interest on } A \text{ for } n \text{ years.}$$

D is called *True Discount.*

(Note that interest can also be compound interest)

If a sum of money P is due after n years, then the interest (simple or compound) on P for n years is called *Banker's Discount.*

If the interest is simple interest, the Banker's Discount $= Pn\,\frac{r}{100}$.

Banker's Gain is defined to be the difference between Banker's discount and true discount.

$$\text{Clearly, Banker's Gain} = \frac{P\left(\frac{nr}{100}\right)^2}{1+\frac{nr}{100}} = A\left(\frac{nr}{100}\right)^2$$

$$= \text{Interest on True Discount.}$$

When a bill is presented to a banker for payment and the banker makes payment before it is due, then he deducts the banker's discount from the face value of bill. The value so payable is called *discounted value of the bill.*

To the due date of bill, banker generally adds 3 days (called *grace period*) *i.e.* if bill is due on 10th August, then it is considered to be actually due on 13th August.

Example 17. *If a bill of Rs 1000 is due after 10 years at simple interest 5 per cent annum, what is true discount, banker's discount?*

Solution. We first calculate interest on Rs 100.

$$\text{Interest} = 100 \times 10 \times \frac{5}{100} = 50.$$

So, Rs 100 will become Rs 150 in 10 years.

Therefore, true discount on Rs 150 = interest on Rs 100 for 10 years = Rs 50

Thus, when bill value is Rs 1000, true discount

$$= \frac{50}{100} \times 1000 = \text{Rs } 333.33$$

Banker's discount = Interest on Rs 1000 for 10 years

$$= 1000 \times 10 \times \frac{5}{100} = \text{Rs } 500.$$

Example 18. *Establish the formula:*

$$BG = \frac{BV \times (ni)^2}{1 + ni}$$

where BV = *Bill value (i.e. face of the bill)*
BG = *Banker's Gain*
n = *number of years between the date of discounting and date of maturity of the bill*
i = *simple interest of Re 1 for 1 year.*

Solution. Let P denote the bill value. Now i = simple interest of Re 1 for 1 year

$\Rightarrow$ rate of interest = $100i$

Therefore interest on Rs P for n years

$$= P \times n \times \frac{100i}{100} = Pni$$

So, for a bill of Rs $P + Pni$, the true discount = Pni

$$\text{Banker's discount} = (P + Pni) \times n \times \frac{100i}{100} = P(1 + ni)ni$$

Thus, $$BG = Pni[1 + ni - 1] = P(ni)^2$$

when bill value is $P + Pni$.

Therefore, when bill value is P,

$$BG = \frac{P(ni)^2}{P + Pni} \times P$$

$$= \frac{P \times (ni)^2}{1 + ni} = \frac{BV \times (ni)^2}{1 + ni}$$

Example 19. *A bill for Rs X was drawn on 1 April 1970 at six months and discounted on 23 July 1970 at 2½ per cent per annum. If the Banker's discount was Rs 80, find the value of X. How much more would the bill owner obtain if it were discounted on 24 July 1970?*

Solution. The bill is actually due on 4 October 1970 (including grace period of 3 days). It is discounted on 23 July *i.e.*, $8+31+30+4=73$ days $=\frac{1}{5}$ year, before it is due.

Banker's discount = Interest on X for $\frac{1}{5}$ year at 2.5 per cent per annum

$$= \frac{X}{5} \cdot \frac{25}{1000} = .005\,X$$

So, $\quad 80 = .005\,X$

$\Rightarrow \quad X = 16000.$

If the bill is discounted on 24 July then it is discounted 72 days before its due.

So, $\quad$ Banker's discount $= \frac{X}{365} \cdot (72) \cdot \frac{(25)}{1000}$

$$= \frac{18\,X}{3650}$$

$$= \frac{18 \times 16000}{3650}$$

$$= \frac{28800}{365} = 78.90$$

Thus, the additional amount bill owner would obtain

$$= \text{Rs}\,(80 - 78.90) = \text{Rs}\,1.10$$

Example 20. *The Banker's gain on a certain bill due 6 months hence, is Rs 10, the rate of interest being 10 per cent per annum. Find the face value of the bill.*

Solution. Interest on Rs 100 for 6 months at the rate of 10 per cent simple interest

$$= 100 \times \frac{1}{2} \times \frac{10}{100} = \text{Rs}\,5$$

So, when the bill is Rs 105, the true discount is Rs 5

Banker's discount on Rs 105

$$= 105 \times \frac{1}{2} \times \frac{10}{100}$$

$$= \text{Rs}\,5.25$$

So, Banker's gain on Rs 105 = Rs (5.25 – 5) = Rs .25

Therefore, when Banker's gain is Rs .25, the face value of bill

$$= \text{Rs } 105$$

Thus, when Banker's gain is Rs 10, the face value of bill

$$= \frac{105}{25} \times 100 \times 10 = \text{Rs } 4200$$

Hence, Rs 4200 is the required face value of bill.

Example 21. *A bill was drawn on 14 April 1970 at 8 months after date and was discounted on 24 July 1970 at 5 per cent per annum. If the Banker's gain on the basis of simple interest is Rs 2 for what sum the bill was drawn.*

Solution. The bill is due on 17, December (including the grace period of 3 days). The bill is discounted on 24 July *i.e.,* 7 + 31 + 30 + 31 + 30 + 17 = 146 days before it is due.

Interest on Rs 100 for 146 days at simple interest

$$= 100 \times \frac{146}{365} \times \frac{5}{100}$$

$$= 2$$

Thus for a bill amount of Rs 102, the true discount = Rs 2.

$$\text{Banker's discount} = 102 \times \frac{146}{365} \times \frac{5}{100} = 2.04$$

So, when the bill amount is Rs 102, the banker's gain

$$= \text{Rs } (2.04 - 2) = \text{Rs } 0.04.$$

Therefore, when Banker's gain is Rs 2, the bill amount is

$$= \frac{2 \times 102}{0.04} = \frac{20400}{4} = 5100$$

Thus Rs 5100 is the required sum.

7. DEPRECIATION

Various assets like vehicles, machines, tools, residential structures are such that their value goes down with time. This decrease can be because of the wearing out of the asset physically or the asset becoming obsolete. Indeed, we cannot use a machine forever. Productive capacity of any machine will decline with constant use leading to a fall in its value. On the other hand, some assets become obsolete with the introduction of new improved versions. Such decrease in value is referred to as depreciation. Thus **depreciation is the decline in an asset's economic value over time.**

The quantum and rate of this decline can vary from asset to asset. The value at which the asset is finally sold off is called its *scrap value*.

We use the following method to calculate the depreciated value of any asset.

Suppose there is an asset whose original value is Rs C and suppose $r\%$ per year is the rate at which the value falls. Then at the end of one year, the value of the asset will be

$$C - \frac{Cr}{100} = C\left(1 - \frac{r}{100}\right) = C' \text{ (say)}$$

The value of the asset at the end of the second year will be

$$C' - \frac{C'r}{100} = C\left(1 - \frac{r}{100}\right)^2$$

and so on. The value after n years will, thus, be

$$C\left(1 - \frac{r}{100}\right)^n.$$

This, assuming that the rate of decline in value is same every year.

Suppose, now the rate of depreciation varies every few years say, it is $r_1\%$ in the first n_1 years, $r_2\%$ in the next n_2 years and so on and is $r_t\%$ in the last n_t years. The depreciated value of the asset at the end of $n_1 + n_2 + ... + n_t$ years will be given by

$$C\left(1 - \frac{r_1}{100}\right)^{n_1}\left(1 - \frac{r_2}{100}\right)^{n_2} ... \left(1 - \frac{r_t}{100}\right)^{n_t}.$$

Example 22. *Suppose the value of a machine depreciates every year at the rate of 5% of its original cost. If the value of the machine is Rs 10,000 at the end of 6 years, then what is its original cost?*

Solution. Suppose the original cost is Rs C. The value of the machine at the end of 6 years is given by

$$C\left(1 - \frac{5}{100}\right)^6$$

Hence $$10{,}000 = C\left(1 - \frac{5}{100}\right)^6 = C\left(\frac{95}{100}\right)^6$$

$\Rightarrow$ $$\log 10{,}000 = \log C + 6\,(\log 95 - \log 100)$$

$$4 = \log C + 6\,(1.9777 - 2) = \log C - 0.1338$$

$\Rightarrow$ $$\log C = 4.1338$$

$\Rightarrow$ $$C = \text{antilog}\,(4.1338) = 13{,}608.$$

Example 23. *The cost of a new car is Rs 3 lakhs. Suppose its value depreciates at the rate of 6% per year. What would be its value after 3 years? What would be its depreciated value for the 4th year? If the car becomes obsolete after 15 years, then what is its scrap value?*

Solution. The value of the car after 3 years will be

$$3,00,000\left(1-\frac{6}{100}\right)^3 = 3,00,000\times\left(\frac{94}{100}\right)^3 = 2,49,175.2$$

Value of car after 4 years will be

$$3,00,000\left(1-\frac{6}{100}\right)^4 = 2,34,224$$

Thus depreciation charge for 4th year is

$$2,49,175.2 - 2,34,224.5 = 14,950.7$$

The scrap value of the car (after 15 years) will be

$$S = 3,00,000\times\left(1-\frac{6}{100}\right)^{15}$$

$$= 3,00,000\times\left(\frac{94}{100}\right)^{15}$$

Taking log, we get $\log S = 5+\log 3+15\,(\log 94-\log 100)$

$$= 5+0.4771+15\,(1.9731-2)$$

$$= 5.0736$$

Hence $S = \text{antilog}\,(5.0736) = 1,18,450.$

Example 24. *A car costs Rs 2 lakhs. Suppose it depreciates at 5% per annum for first 7 years and 6% per annum for next 8 years, depreciation being calculated on diminishing value. What would be its cost after 15 years?*

Solution. The value of the car after 15 years is given by

$$V = 2,00,000\left(1-\frac{5}{100}\right)^7\left(1-\frac{6}{100}\right)^8$$

$$= 2,00,000\times\left(\frac{95}{100}\right)^7\left(\frac{94}{100}\right)^8$$

$$\Rightarrow \quad \log V = \log 2,00,000 + 7\,(\log 95-\log 100) + 8\,(\log 94-\log 100)$$

$$= 5+\log 2+7\,(1.9777-2)+8\,(1.9731-2)$$

$$= 5.3010-0.1561-0.2152 = 4.9279$$

Hence, $V = \text{antilog}\,(4.9279) = 96,835.$

EXERCISES

1. Find in what time a sum of money trebles itself at 5 per cent per annum compound interest.
2. The sum of Rs 20,000 is borrowed at 4 per cent per annum compound interest. Principal and interest are to be repaid in 25 equal annual instalments beginning one year hence. Find the yearly payment.
3. If Re 1 was deposited in the Post Office Savings Bank on 1 April 1903, what would it amount to on 1 April 1933 if compound interest at 3 per cent per annum was allowed?
4. An Officer drawing a salary of Rs 1500 per month in pay scale of Rs 1300 – 100 – 1800 borrowed from his employer on 1 January 1964, a sum of Rs 15,000 for the purchase of a car. The money is to be recovered by making a deduction of 20 per cent from his salary every month. If the interest is calculated at the rate of 5 per cent on 31 December, each year on the highest amount due on any day in the preceding year and added to the balance due, when will the Officer receive his full salary? Note that first deduction is made from the salary of January paid on 1 February 1964 and his increment falls due on 1 July.
5. A sum of money invested at compound interest amounts to Rs 21,632 at the end of 2nd year and to Rs 22,497.28 at the end of the third year. Find the rate of interest and sum invested.
6. To accumulate a fund for his son's higher education, a person invests a sum of Rs 100 on the son's first birthday and an equal amount on each of his subsequent birthdays. If the interest is compounded half-yearly after the investment has been made on the 18th birthday.
7. Calculate the present value of an annuity of Rs 5000 per annum for 12 years, the interest being 4 per cent annum compounded annually.
8. The accumulations in a Provident Fund are invested at the end of every years to earn 10 per cent per annum. A person contributes $12\frac{1}{2}$ per cent of his salary to which the employer adds 10 per cent every month. Find how much the accumulations will amount to at the end of 30 years of his service, for every 100 rupees of his monthly salary.
9. A machine costs a company Rs 100,000 and its effective life is estimated to be 20 years. If the scrap is expected to realise Rs 5000 only. Find the sum to be invested every year at 5 per cent per annum compound interest for 20 years, to replace the machine which is expected to cost them 25 per cent more over its present cost. Assume that the sale of scrap would be utilised for meeting the cost of the machine.
10. A machine depreciates in value each year at the rate of 120 per cent of its value at the beginning of a year. The machine was purchased for Rs 10,000. Obtain its value at the end of 10th year.
11. A sinking fund was formed by setting aside Rs 1,000 at the end of 1st year and then at the end of each of the following years an amount 10 per cent more than that set aside at the end of the immediately previous year. Find the total amount of the fund at the end of 10 years reckoning interest, at 5 per cent per annum compound.

12. The difference between the true and the Banker's discount on a certain bill due 4 months hence is 5 paise. If the rate of interest is 6 per cent, find the amount of the bill.
13. What is the face value of bill discounted at 5 per cent per annum 73 days earlier than the date of maturity, the banker's gain being Rs 10 only.
14. A banker's discounts a bill, which has to run 73 days before it is legally due, at 5 per cent and the banker's gain is Rs 15. For what sum the bill was drawn?
15. A man holds a bill for Rs 12,000 which is due for payment after 8 months. After 3 months, however he sells the bill to a broker who charges 5 per cent per annum. The man then invests the discounted suffer any loss on discounting the bill. Find the rate of interest per annum of the security.
16. Calculate Banker's Gain a bill of Rs 37,500 due in 8 months at 8 per cent per annum.
17. A bill for Rs 3,225 was drawn on 3rd February 1965 at 6 months date and discounted on 13 March 1965 at the rate of 8 per cent per annum. For what sum the bill was discounted and how much did the banker gain in this?
18. The difference between true discount and banker's discount on a bill of Rs 1500 legally due in 4 month's time is Rs 0.50, on the basis of simple interest. Find the rate of interest.
19. A bill drawn on the 10th May at two months after sight was accepted on the 14th May and was discounted on 2nd July at $8^1/_9$ per cent. If the banker's gain be 6 paise, for what sum was the bill drawn?
20. A fixed royalty of Rs 1500 per annum for 20 years in guaranteed to the author of some textbooks by a publisher. The right of receiving the royalty is put up for action after 12 years have already passed. Find the price at which it may be sold, assuming the money is worth 8 per cent per annum compounded annually.
21. A machine costs Rs 10,000. Suppose it has scrap value of Rs 500 at the end of 20 years. What is the rate of depreciation?
22. A machine depreciates at the rate of 5%, of its value at the beginning of a year. It was originally bought for Rs 50,000 and fetched a scrap value of Rs 8,000. Find the number of years the machine was used.
23. An asset costs Rs 70,000 and suppose it depreciates at the rate of 6% p.a. Assuming it will last for 20 years find its scrap value.

ANSWERS

1. 22.52 years	2. Rs 1271	3. Rs 2.421
4. 1 April 1968	5. 4 per cent, Rs 20,000	6. Rs 3112.46
7. Rs 46,926.25	8. Rs 44,407	9. Rs 3630
10. Rs 3487	11. Rs 19,288	12. Rs 127.50
13. Rs 101,000	14. Rs 151,500	
15. $5\frac{5}{47}$ per cent per annum		16. Rs 104
17. Rs 3121.80	18. 5.53 per cent per annum.	
19. Rs 10,067	20. 8626	

CHAPTER 15

MEASUREMENT OF ANGLES

1. INTRODUCTION

Trigonometry is that branch of Mathematics which deals with measurement of angles. It is derived from two Greek words '*Trigonon*' (a triangle) and '*metron*' (a measure), meaning thereby measurement of triangles. But now this definition has been modified to include measurement of angles in gneneral, whether the angles are of a triangle or not. The plane trigonometry which we are going to study, is restricted to measurement of angles in a plane.

2. ANGLES

An angle is defined as the rotation of a line about one of its extremities in a plane from one position to another. Two lines are said to be at *right angles*, if a revolving line starting from one position to another describes one-quarter of a circle. If the revolving line moves in anti-clockwise direction, the angle described by it, is said to be *positive*. It is called *negative* otherwise. There is no limitation to the size of angles in trigonometry.

Consider the coplanar lines $X'OX$ and YOY' at right angles to each other. If the revolving line starts from OX and reaches the position OA, in the anticlockwise direction, it has described a positive angle less than a right angle. If it continues to move in the same direction, then in the position OB, it has described an angle XOB, more than a right angle. In the position OC, it has described an angle XOC more than two right angles but less than three right angles. Similarly in the position OD, it has described

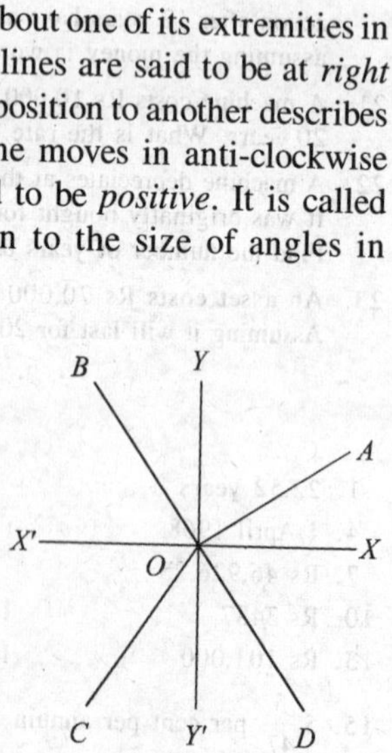

Fig. 1

an angle XOD less than four right angles but more than three right angles. Now, if it continues to revolve in the same direction, then in the position OA, it has described an angle equal to four right angles + $\angle XOA$. In this way, angle of any size can be described. Thus, there is no limitation to the size of angles in trigonometry.

3. QUADRANTS

The four portions XOY, $X'OY$, $X'OY'$ and XOY' into which a plane is divided as in §.2 are called *first, second, third* and *fourth quadrants* respectively.

4. MEASUREMENT OF ANGLES

To measure angles, a particular angle is fixed and is taken as a unit of measurement so that any other angle is measured by the number of times it contains the unit. For example, if we call $\angle XOY$ one right angle, as a unit of measurement, then $\angle XOX'$ is equal to two right angles, as it contains two units.

We study the following three systems of measurement:

1. Sexagesimal System (English System)
2. Centesimal System (French System)
3. Circular System.

1. Sexagesimal System. In this system, a right angle is divided into 90 equal parts called *degrees*. Each degree is divided into 60 equal parts called *minutes* and each minute is further, subdivided into 60 equal parts called *seconds*.

Thus 1 right angle = 90 degrees
1 degree = 60 minutes
1 minute = 60 seconds.

In symbols, a degree, a minute and a second are respectively written as 1°; $1'$, $1''$. Thus, $40^\circ\, 15'\, 20''$ denotes the angle which contains 40 degrees 15 minutes and 20 seconds. The unit of measurement in this system is degree. The system is called *Sexagesimal* because each unit is divided into 60 parts (*Sexagesimus* means sixtieth) so that number 60 comes in marking the divisions.

2. Centesimal System. In this system, a right angle is divided into 100 equal parts called *grades*. Each grade is divided into 100 equal parts called *minutes* and each minute is divided into 100 equal parts called *seconds*.

Thus 1 right angle = 100 grades
1 grade = 100 minutes
1 minute = 100 seconds

The symbols 1^g, $1^`$, $1^{``}$ stand for a grade, a minute and a second respectively in this system. Thus $20^g\ 12^`\ 85^{``}$ denotes the angle which contains 20 grades 12 minutes and 85 seconds. The unit of measurement here is grade. This system is called *Centesimal system* because the number 100 comes in marking the divisions (*centesimus* means hundredth).

[NOTE. The reader should observe the difference in notations of minutes and seconds in the Sexagesimal and Centesimal systems.]

3. Circular System. In this system, the unit of measurement is *Radian*. It is defined as the angle subtended at the centre of a circle by an arc equal to radius of the circle.

Consider a circle with centre O. Take any point A on it and cut off an arc AB of length equal to the radius of the circle. Then $\angle AOB$ is called a *radian*.

The symbol 1^c denotes a radian.

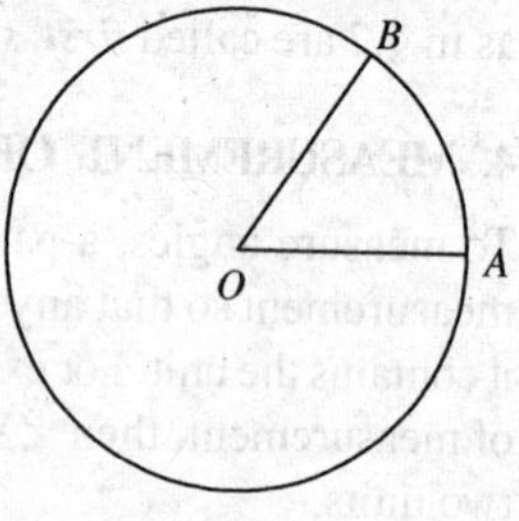

Fig. 2

5. IT IS WELL KNOWN THAT

"The circumference of a circle bears a constant ratio to its diameter."

This constant ratio is denoted by Greek letter π (pronounced as "pie").

The value of π correct upto two places of decimal is $\dfrac{22}{7}$ and upto six places of decimal is $\dfrac{355}{113}$.

6. RADIAN IS A CONSTANT ANGLE

Consider a circle with centre O. Let A be any point on it. Let AB be an arc equal to radius OA. Then

$$\frac{\angle AOB}{\text{Arc } AB} = \frac{\angle AOA'}{\text{Arc } AA'}$$

i.e.

$$\frac{\angle AOB}{\angle AOA'} = \frac{\text{Arc } AB}{\text{Arc } AA'}$$

$$= \frac{\text{Radius}}{\frac{1}{2}\text{ Circumference}}$$

$$= \frac{\text{Diameter}}{\text{Circumference}} = \frac{1}{\pi}$$

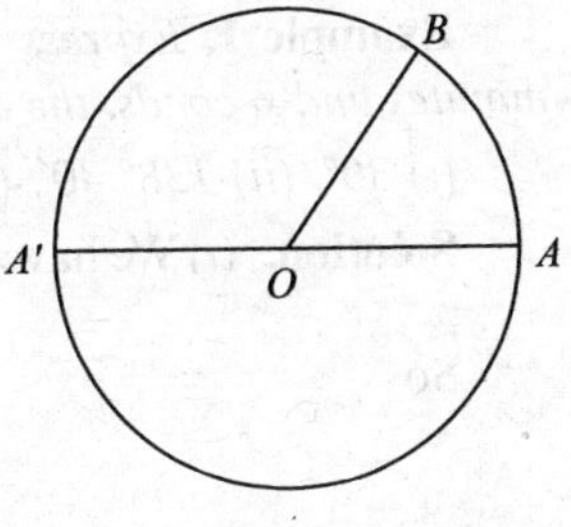

Fig. 3.

Therefore $\angle AOB = \dfrac{1}{\pi} \angle AOA'$

$= \dfrac{1}{\pi} \times 2$ right angles

$= \dfrac{180^\circ}{\pi}$,

which is constant as π is a constant.

Thus a radian $= \dfrac{180^\circ}{\pi}$.

Hence π radians $= 180^\circ$.

7. RELATIONS BETWEEN THE THREE SYSTEMS OF MEASUREMENTS

Since 1 rt. angle $= 90^\circ$ and $100^g = 1$ rt. angle

we have $90^\circ = 100^g$ so that $180^\circ = 200^g$

But $180^\circ = \pi$ radians (§.6)

Hence $180^\circ = 200^g = \pi^c$.

[NOTE: Sometimes the superscript 'c' is omitted while writing the angles, so that angle θ means, an angle of magnitude θ radians. Therefore, we shall be writing π both for an angle as well as number so that angle π stands for π radians and number π stands for ratio of circumference of a circle to its diameter.]

8. TO PROVE THAT THE NUMBER OF RADIANS IN AN ANGLE SUBTENDED BY AN ARC OF A CIRCLE AT THE CENTRE IS EQUAL TO $\dfrac{\text{ARC}}{\text{RADIUS}}$

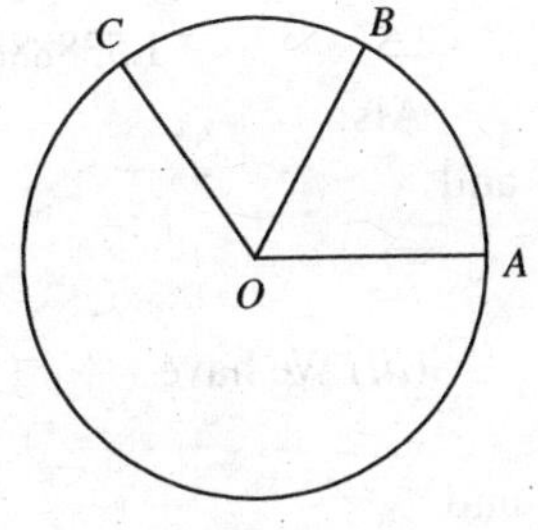

Fig. 4

Proof. Consider a circle with centre O. Let A be any point on it. Let arc AB = radius OA. Let C be any point on the circle. Then

$\angle AOB = 1$ radian

Now $\dfrac{\angle AOC}{\angle AOB} = \dfrac{\text{Arc } AC}{\text{Arc } AB}$

$\Rightarrow \angle AOC = \dfrac{\text{Arc } AC}{\text{Arc } AB} \times 1$ Radian

So the no. of radians in $\angle AOC = \dfrac{\text{arc } AC}{\text{radius}}$

[**NOTE.** If θ is number of radians in an angle; l, the length of arc of the circle subtending the angle θ at the centre of the circle and r, the radius of circle, then $\theta = \dfrac{l}{r}$.]

Example 1. *Express in terms of right angles and also in grades, minutes and seconds, the angles*

(i) 30°, (ii) 138° 30′, (iii) 35° 47′ 15″.

Solution. (*i*) We have $90^\circ = 100^g$, Also $90^\circ = 1$ rt. angle

So $1^\circ = \frac{10}{9}g$ so $30^\circ = \frac{1}{3}$ rt. angle

$= 0.33$ rt. angles

so that $30^\circ = \frac{300}{9}g = 33\frac{1}{3}g.$

Now $1^g = 100^`$

$\Rightarrow \frac{1}{3}^g = \frac{100^`}{3} = 33\frac{1^`}{3}$

Also $1^` = 100^{``}$

$\Rightarrow \frac{1^`}{3} = \frac{100^{``}}{3} = 33.3^{``}$

$\Rightarrow 30^\circ = 300^g 33^` 33.3^{``}.$

(*ii*) We have $30^` = \frac{1^\circ}{2} = .5^\circ$

$\Rightarrow 138^\circ 30^` = 138.5^\circ$

Now $90^\circ = 1$ rt. angle

$\Rightarrow 1^\circ = \frac{1}{90}$ rt. angle

$\Rightarrow 138.5^\circ = \frac{138.5}{90}$ rt. angle $= 1.5388888$ rt. angle.

Now 1 rt. angle $= 100^g$

$\Rightarrow$ 1.5388888 rt. angle $= 153.88888^g$.

Also $.88888^g = 88.888^`$.

and $.888^` = (.888 \times 100)^{``} = 88.88^{``}$

$\Rightarrow 138.5 = 153^g 88^` 88.88^{``}$.

(*iii*) We have $15^{``} = \frac{15^`}{60} = \frac{1^`}{4} = .25^`$

and $47^` 15^{``} = 47.25^` = \frac{47.25^\circ}{60} = .7875^\circ$.

$\Rightarrow 35^\circ 47^` 15^{``} = 35.7875^\circ$

$= \frac{35.7875}{90}$ rt. angle

$= .3976388$ rt. angle $= 39.76388^g$.

Now $$0.76388^g = 76.388'$$

$$0.388' = 38.88''.$$

$\Rightarrow$ $$35^\circ 47' 15'' = 39^g 76' 38.88''.$$

Example 2. *Express in terms of right angles and also in degrees, minutes and seconds, the angles.*

(i) 120^g (ii) $45^g\ 35'\ 24''$.

Solution. (*i*) We have $1^g = \frac{9^\circ}{10}$. Also $100^g = 1$ rt. angle.

So $$120^g = 108^\circ = \frac{6}{5} \text{ rt. angles.}$$

(*ii*) $$24'' = .24'$$

$\Rightarrow$ $$35'\ 24'' = 35.24' = .3524^g$$

Thus $$45^g\ 35'\ 24'' = 45.3524^g$$

$$= .453524 \text{ rt. angle}$$

$$= (.453524 \times 90)^\circ = 40.81716^\circ$$

Now $$.81716^\circ = (.81716 \times 60)' = 49.0296'$$

and $$.0296' = (.0296 \times 60)'' = 1.776''.$$

Hence $$45^g\ 35'\ 24'' = 40^\circ 49'\ 1.776''$$

Example 3. *Convert $5^\circ\ 37'\ 30''$ into radians.*

Solution. We have $30'' = \frac{1'}{2}$

$\Rightarrow$ $$37'\ 30'' = 37\frac{1'}{2} = \frac{75'}{2} = \left(\frac{75}{2 \times 60}\right)^\circ = \frac{5^\circ}{8}$$

Then $$5^\circ 37'\ 30'' = 5\frac{5^\circ}{8} = \frac{45^\circ}{8}.$$

Now $$1^\circ = \frac{\pi^c}{180} \Rightarrow \frac{45^\circ}{8} = \left(\frac{\pi}{180} \times \frac{45}{8}\right)^c = \frac{\pi^c}{32}.$$

Example 4. *Convert $1^g\ 1'$ into radians.*

Solution. We have $1' = \frac{1^g}{100}$

$\Rightarrow$ $$1^g\ 1' = 1\frac{1^g}{100} = \frac{101^g}{100}.$$

Now $$1^g = \frac{\pi^c}{200}$$

$\Rightarrow$ $$\frac{101^g}{100} = \left(\frac{\pi \times 101}{20000}\right)^c = .00505\,\pi^c.$$

Example 5. *If D, G, C are respectively, the number of degrees, grades and radians in an angle, prove that*

$$\frac{D}{90} = \frac{G}{100} = \frac{2C}{\pi}.$$

Solution. The given angle = D degrees = $\frac{D}{90}$ of a rt. angle.

Also, the given angle = G grades = $\frac{G}{100}$ of a rt. angle, further, the given angle = C radians = $\frac{2C}{\pi}$ of a rt. angle.

Hence $$\frac{D}{90} = \frac{G}{100} = \frac{2C}{\pi}.$$

Example 6. *The number of degrees in a certain angle added to the number of grades in the angle is 152. Find the angle.*

Solution. Let x be the no. of degrees in the angle.

Then no. of grades in the angle will be $\frac{10}{9}x$.

So $$x + \frac{10}{9}x = 152$$

or $$\frac{19}{9}x = 152 \text{ i.e. } x = \frac{152 \times 9}{19} = 72.$$

Example 7. *The angles of a triangle are in A.P., the number of grades in the least to the number of radians in the greatest is 40 to π, find the angles in degrees.*

Solution. Let the angles of a triangle in A.P. be

$$(a-d)^\circ, a^\circ, (a+d)^\circ.$$

Since the sum of angles of a triangle is 180°.

$$\Rightarrow \quad (a-d) + a + (a+d) = 180^\circ.$$

$$\Rightarrow \quad a = 60.$$

So the angles are $(60-d)^\circ, 60^\circ, (60+d)^\circ$

$$\text{The least angle} = (60-d)^\circ = \left(\frac{(60-d)\times 10}{9}\right)^g$$

$$\text{The greatest angle} = (60+d)^\circ = \left((60+d)\times\frac{\pi}{180}\right)^c$$

Hence $$\frac{(60-d)\times\frac{10}{9}}{(60+d)\times\frac{\pi}{180}} = \frac{40}{\pi}$$

$$\text{Hence} \quad \frac{(60-d)\times 200}{60+d} = 40 \Rightarrow (60-d)\times 5 = 60+d$$

$$\Rightarrow \quad 300-5d = 60+d$$

$$\Rightarrow \quad 6d = 240 \Rightarrow d = 40.$$

Hence the angles are $(60-40)^\circ, 60^\circ, (60+40)^\circ$ or $20^\circ, 60^\circ, 100^\circ$.

Example 8. *The angles of a pentagon are in A.P. and greatest is three times the least, find the angles in grades.*

Solution. Let the angles of the pentagon in A.P. be $(a-2d)^\circ, (a-d)^\circ, a^\circ, (a+d)^\circ, (a+2d)^\circ$.

Now, sum of the angles of polygon of n sides is

$$= (2n-4) \text{ right angles.}$$

$\Rightarrow$ sum of angles of pentagon is 6 right angles $= 540^\circ$.

$\Rightarrow (a-2d)+(a-d)+a+(a+d)+(a+2d) = 540^\circ$

$\Rightarrow 5a = 540^\circ$ or $a = 108^\circ$.

Hence the angles are

$$(108-2d)^\circ, (108-d)^\circ, 108^\circ (108+d), (108+2d)^\circ.$$

The greatest angle $= (108+2d)^\circ$

The least angle $= (108-2d)^\circ$.

By hypothesis,

$$(180+2d) = 3(108-2d) \quad \text{or} \quad 108+2d = 324-6d$$

or $$8d = 216 \quad \text{or} \quad d = 27.$$

Hence angles are $54^\circ, 81^\circ, 108^\circ, 135^\circ, 162^\circ$,

or $60^g, 90^g, 120^g, 150^g, 180^g$.

Example 9. *A cow is tied to a post by a rope. If the cow moves along a circular path always keeping the rope tight and describes 44 ft. when it has traced out 72° at the centre, find the length of the rope.*

Solution. The cow starts from A and describes an arc of length

$$l = 44 \text{ ft.} = AB.$$

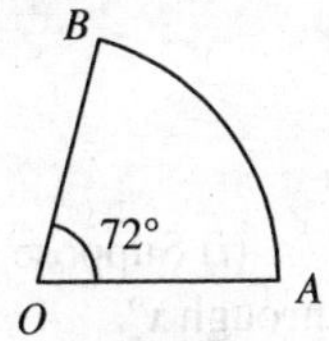

Fig. 5

$$\text{Also} \quad \angle AOB = 72^\circ = \left(72 \times \frac{\pi}{180}\right)^c = \left(\frac{2\pi}{5}\right)^c$$

If length of rope be r, then by § 8, we know that

$$\theta = \frac{l}{r} \Rightarrow \frac{2\pi}{5} = \frac{44}{r}$$

$$\Rightarrow r = \frac{44\times 5}{2\pi} = \frac{44\times 5\times 7}{2\times 22} = 35 \text{ ft.}, \left(\pi = \frac{22}{7}\right)$$

Example 10. *The large hand of a big clock is 3 feet long. How many inches does its extremity move in 10 minutes time?*

Solution. The large hand of a clock starts from A and describes an arc of length $l = AB$ in 10 minutes.

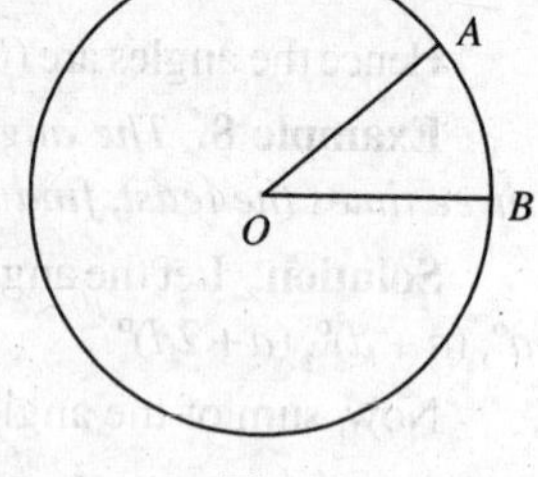

Fig. 6

Now 60 minutes = 360°

$\Rightarrow$ 10 minutes = 36°.

Thus $\angle AOB = 36° = \frac{\pi^c}{5}$.

Also $OA = 3$ feet $= r$.

So $\theta = \frac{l}{r} \Rightarrow \frac{\pi}{5} = \frac{l}{3}$

$$\Rightarrow l = \frac{3\pi}{5} = \frac{3 \times 22}{5 \times 7} = \frac{66}{35} \text{ feet}$$

$$\Rightarrow l = \frac{66}{35} \times 12 \text{ inches} = 22.63 \text{ inches.}$$

Example 11. *Find the times between 6 o'clock and 7 o'clock when the angle betwen the minute hand and hour hand is 29°.*

Solution. There are two possibilities (*i*) when the minute hand has not crossed the hour hand (*ii*) when the minute hand has crossed the hour hand.

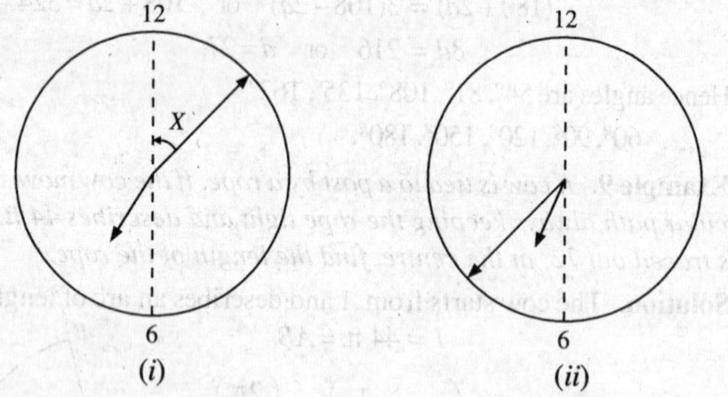

Fig. 7

(*i*) Suppose after the time is 6 o'clock the minute hand has moved through $x°$.

Now, when minute hand moves through 360°, the hour hand moves through 30°.

So, in this case the minute hand has moved through

$$\left(\frac{1}{12}\times x\right)^{o} = \left(\frac{x}{12}\right)^{o}$$

with respect to hour hand.

$$\text{Therefore, } 29^{o} - \left(\frac{x}{12}\right)^{o} + x^{o} = 180^{o}$$

$$\Rightarrow \quad x = \left(\frac{151\times 12}{11}\right)^{o}$$

$$\Rightarrow x = \frac{151\times 12}{11}\times\frac{1}{6} \text{ minutes}$$

$$= \frac{302}{11} \text{ minutes} = 27\frac{5}{11} \text{ minutes}$$

$\Rightarrow$ Time is $27\frac{5}{11}$ minutes past 6.

(*ii*) Proceeding as above

$$180^{o} + \left(\frac{x}{12}\right)^{o} + 29 = x$$

$$\Rightarrow \quad x = (12\times 19)^{o} = 38 \text{ minutes}$$

$\Rightarrow$ Time is 38 minutes past 6.

EXERCISES

1. Convert the following into Centesimal System:
   (*i*) 146° 42`` (*ii*) 30° 46` 48`` (*iii*) 15° 28` 48``.
2. Convert the following into Sexagesimal System
   (*i*) 64^g 12` 32`` (*ii*) $79^g$ 32` 15`` (*iii*) 56^g 87` 50``.
3. Convert 18° 33` 45`` in terms of radians.
4. Convert 66^g 36`` to radians.
5. If *G*, *D*, *C* are the number of grades, degrees and radians in any angle, prove that
   $G - D = \frac{20C}{\pi}$.
6. The sum of two angles is 80 grades and their difference is 18°. Find the angles in degrees.
7. Find in grades, the vertical angle of an isosceles triangle, each of whose base angles is two and half times the vertical angle.
8. The number of grades in one acute angle of a right triangle is ten times the number of degrees in the other. Show that the difference between these two angles is 80^g.

9. If the angles of a triangle are in A.P. and one of them is 95°, find all the angles in radians.
10. The angles of a triangle are in A.P., the number of degrees in the least is to the circular measure of the greatest as 60 to π. Find the angles in degrees.
11. The angles of a quadrilateral are in A.P. and the greatest is double the least. Express the least angle in radians.
12. The angles of a hexagon are in A.P. and the greatest is double the least, find all the anlges in degrees.
13. A wire 121 inches long is bent so as to lie along the arc of a circle of 180 inches radius. Find in degrees the angle subtended by the arc at the centre.
14. A railway train is travelling on a curve of half-a-mile radius at the rate of 20 miles per hour, through what angle has it turned in 10 seconds?
15. Find the times between the 4 o'clock and 5 o'clock when the anlge between the minute hand and hour hand is 78°.
16. Find the times between 7 o'clock and 8 o'clock when the angle beween the minute hand and hour hand is 54°.

ANSWERS

1. (*i*) $162^g\ 23'\ 52''$, (*ii*) $34^g\ 20'$, (*iii*) $17^g\ 20'$.

2. (*i*) 57° 42′ 39.168″, (*ii*) 71° 23′ 21.66″, (*iii*) 51° 11′ 15″.

3. $\frac{33\pi}{320}$ radians.

4. .330018π radians.

6. 45° and 27°.

7. $\left(33\frac{1}{3}\right)^g$

9. $\frac{5\pi}{36}, \frac{\pi}{3}, \frac{19\pi}{36}$.

10. 30°, 60°, 90°.

11. $\frac{\pi}{3}$ radians.

12. 80°, 96°, 112°, 128°, 144°, 160°.

13. 38° 30′.

14. $\left(6\frac{4}{11}\right)^\circ$ nearly.

15. At $7\frac{7}{11}$ and 36 minutes past 4.

16. At $28\frac{4}{11}$ and 48 minutes past 7.

CHAPTER 16

TRIGONOMETRICAL RATIOS

1. Let a revolving line OP start from OX in the anticlockwise direction and trace out an angle XOP. From P draw $PM \perp OX$ (Produce OX, if necessary). Let $\angle XOP = \theta$.

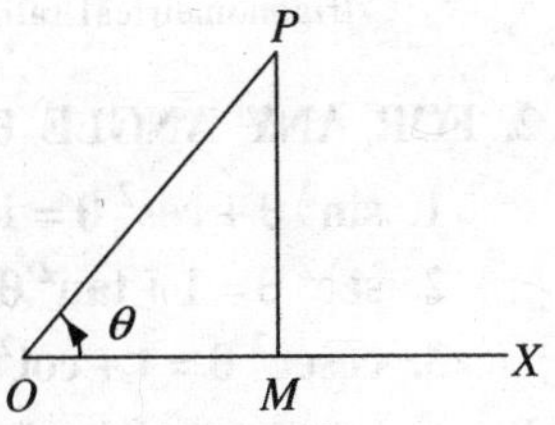

Fig. 1

Then (1) $\dfrac{MP}{OP}$ is called sine of angle θ and is written as $\sin\theta$.

(2) $\dfrac{OM}{OP}$ is called *cosine* of angle θ and is written as $\cos\theta$.

(3) $\dfrac{MP}{OM}$ is called *tangent* of angle θ and is written as $\tan\theta$.

(4) $\dfrac{OM}{MP}$ is called *cotangent* of angle θ and is written as $\cot\theta$.

(5) $\dfrac{OP}{OM}$ is called *secant* of angle θ and is written as $\sec\theta$.

(6) $\dfrac{OP}{MP}$ is called *cosecant* of angle θ and is written as $\operatorname{cosec}\theta$.

These ratios are called *Trigonometrical Ratios* of the angle θ.

REMARKS:

1. It follows from the definition that

$$\sec\theta = \frac{1}{\cos\theta},\quad \operatorname{cosec}\theta = \frac{1}{\sin\theta},\quad \cot\theta = \frac{1}{\tan\theta},$$

$$\tan\theta = \frac{\sin\theta}{\cos\theta},\quad \cot\theta = \frac{\cos\theta}{\sin\theta}.$$

2. Trigonometrical ratios are same for the same angle. For, let P' be any point on the revolving line OP. Draw $P'M' \perp OX$. Then triangles OPM and $OP'M'$ are similar, so $\dfrac{MP}{OP} = \dfrac{M'P'}{OP'}$ *i.e.*, each of these ratios is $\sin\theta$.

   Therefore, whatever be the triangle of reference (*i.e.*, ΔOPM or $\Delta OP'M'$) might be, we find that $\sin\theta$ remains the same for a particular angle θ.

It can be similarly shown that no trigonometrical ratio depends on the size of triangle of reference.

3. $(\sin\theta)^n$ is written as $\sin^n\theta$, where n is positive. Similar notation holds good for other trigonometrical ratios.
4. $\sin^{-1}\theta$ denotes that angle whose sine is θ. Note that $\sin^{-1}\theta$ does not stand for $\frac{1}{\sin\theta}$. Similar notation holds good for other trigonometrical ratios.

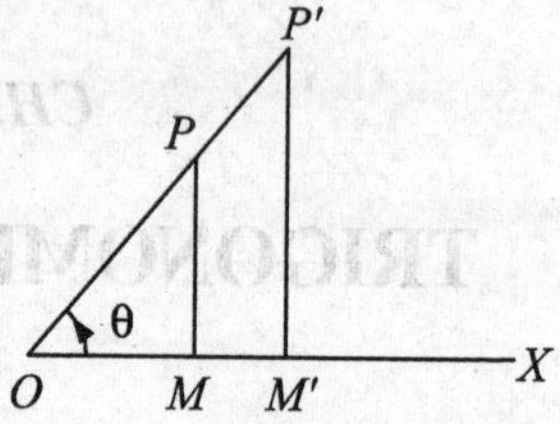

Fig. 2

2. FOR ANY ANGLE θ,

1. $\sin^2\theta + \cos^2\theta = 1$
2. $\sec^2\theta = 1 + \tan^2\theta$
3. $\operatorname{cosec}^2\theta = 1 + \cot^2\theta$

Proof. Let the revolving line OP start from OX and trace out an angle θ in the anti-clockwise direction. From P draw $PM \perp OX$. (Produce OX, if necessary.) (See Fig. 1).

Then $\angle XOP = \theta$.

(1) $\sin\theta = \dfrac{MP}{OP}$, $\cos\theta = \dfrac{OM}{OP}$

Then $\sin^2\theta + \cos^2\theta = \dfrac{(MP)^2 + (OM)^2}{(OP)^2} = \dfrac{(OP)^2}{(OP)^2} = 1.$

(2) $\sec\theta = \dfrac{OP}{OM}$, $\tan\theta = \dfrac{MP}{OM}$

Then $$1 + \tan^2\theta = 1 + \frac{(MP)^2}{(OM)^2} = \frac{(OM)^2 + (MP)^2}{(OM)^2}$$

$$= \frac{(OP)^2}{(OM)^2} = \left(\frac{OP}{OM}\right)^2 = (\sec\theta)^2 = \sec^2\theta$$

(3) $\cot\theta = \dfrac{OM}{MP}$, $\operatorname{cosec}\theta = \dfrac{OP}{MP}$.

Then $$1 + \cot^2\theta = 1 + \left(\frac{OM}{MP}\right)^2 = \frac{(MP)^2 + (OM)^2}{(MP)^2}$$

$$= \frac{(OP)^2}{(MP)^2} = \left(\frac{OP}{MP}\right)^2 = (\operatorname{cosec}\theta)^2 = \operatorname{cosec}^2\theta.$$

3. SIGNS OF TRIGONOMETRICAL RATIOS

Consider four lines OX, OX', OY, OY' at right angles to each other. Let a revolving line OP start from OX in the anticlockwise direction. From P draw $PM \perp OX$ or OX'. We have the following convention of signs regarding the sides of ΔOPM.

1. OM is positive, if it is along OX.
2. OM is negative, if it is along OX'.
3. MP is negative, if it is along OY'.
4. MP is positive, if it is along OY.
5. OP is regarded always positive.

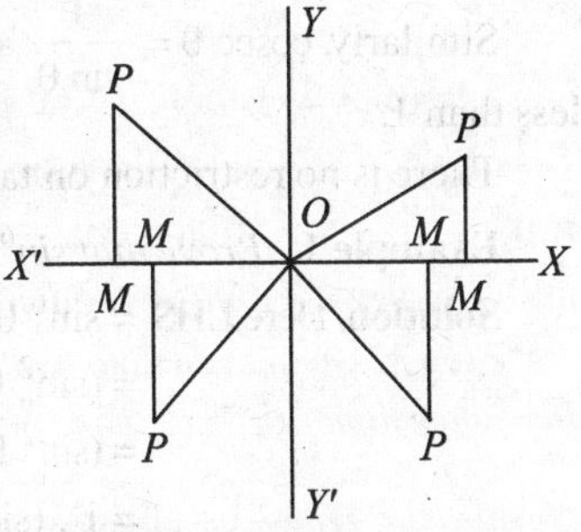

Fig. 3

First Quadrant. If the revolving line OP is in the first quadrant, then all the sides of the triangle OPM are positive. Therefore, all the trigonometrical ratios are positive in the first quadrant.

Second Quadrant. If the revolving line OP is in the second quadrant, then OM is negative and the other two sides of ΔOPM are positive. Therefore, ratios involving OM will be negative. So, cosine, secant, tangent, cotangent of an angle in the second quadrant are negative while sine and cosecant of anlge in the second quadrant are positive.

Third Quadrant. If the revolving line is in the third quadrant, then sides OM and MP both are negative. Since OP is always positive, therefore, ratios involving each one of OM and MP alone will be negative. So, sine, cosine, cosecant and secant of an angle in the third quadrant are negative. Since tangent or cotangent of any angle involve both OM and MP, therefore, these will be positive. So, tangent and cotangent of an angle in the third quadrant are positive.

Fourth Quadrant. If the revolving line OP is in the fourth quadrant, then MP is negative and the other two sides of ΔOPM are positive. Therefore, ratios involving MP will be negative and others positive. So, sine, cosecant, tangent and cotangent of an angle in the fourth quadrant are negative while cosine and secant of an angle in the fourth quadrant are positive.

4. LIMITS TO THE VALUE OF TRIGONOMETRICAL RATIOS

We know that $\sin^2 \theta + \cos^2 \theta = 1$ for any angle θ. $\sin^2 \theta$ and $\cos^2 \theta$ being perfect squares, will be positive. Again neither of them can be greater than 1 because then the other will have to be negative.

Thus $\sin^2 \theta \leq 1, \cos^2 \theta \leq 1.$

$\Rightarrow$ sin θ and cos θ cannot be numerically greater than 1.

Similarly, $\text{cosec}\,\theta = \dfrac{1}{\sin\theta}$ and $\sec\theta = \dfrac{1}{\cos\theta}$ cannot be numerically less than 1.

There is no restriction on tan θ and cot θ. They can have any value.

Example 1. *Prove that* $\sin^6\theta + \cos^6\theta = 1 - 3\sin^2\theta\cos^2\theta$.

Solution. Here

$$\begin{aligned}\text{LHS} &= \sin^6\theta + \cos^6\theta\\ &= (\sin^2\theta)^3 + (\cos^2\theta)^3\\ &= (\sin^2\theta + \cos^2\theta)(\sin^4\theta - \sin^2\theta\cos^2\theta + \cos^4\theta)\\ &= 1\,.\,(\sin^4\theta - \sin^2\theta\cos^2\theta + \cos^4\theta)\\ &= [(\sin^2\theta + \cos^2\theta)^2 - 3\sin^2\theta\cos^2\theta]\\ &= 1 - 3\sin^2\theta\cos^2\theta = \text{RHS}.\end{aligned}$$

Example 2. *Prove that* $\sqrt{\dfrac{1+\cos\theta}{1-\cos\theta}} = \text{cosec}\,\theta + \cot\theta$. *Provided* $\cos\theta \neq 1$.

Solution.

$$\begin{aligned}\text{LHS} &= \sqrt{\frac{1+\cos\theta}{1-\cos\theta}}\\ &= \sqrt{\frac{(1+\cos\theta)(1+\cos\theta)}{(1-\cos\theta)(1+\cos\theta)}} = \frac{1+\cos\theta}{\sqrt{1-\cos^2\theta}}\\ &= \frac{1+\cos\theta}{\sin\theta} = \frac{1}{\sin\theta} + \frac{\cos\theta}{\sin\theta} = \text{cosec}\,\theta + \cot\theta.\end{aligned}$$

Example 3. *Prove that* $(1 + \cot\theta - \text{cosec}\,\theta)(1 + \tan\theta + \sec\theta) = 2$.

Solution.

$$\begin{aligned}\text{LHS} &= (1 + \cot\theta - \text{cosec}\,\theta)(1 + \tan\theta + \sec\theta)\\ &= \left(1 + \frac{\cos\theta}{\sin\theta} - \frac{1}{\sin\theta}\right)\left(1 + \frac{\sin\theta}{\cos\theta} + \frac{1}{\cos\theta}\right)\end{aligned}$$

$$\begin{aligned}\text{LHS} &= \frac{(\sin\theta + \cos\theta - 1)(\cos\theta + \sin\theta + 1)}{\sin\theta\cos\theta}\\ &= \frac{(\sin\theta + \cos\theta)^2 - 1}{\sin\theta\cos\theta}\\ &= \frac{\sin^2\theta + \cos^2\theta + 2\sin\theta\cos\theta - 1}{\sin\theta\cos\theta}\\ &= \frac{1 + 2\sin\theta\cos\theta - 1}{\sin\theta\cos\theta} = \frac{2\sin\theta\cos\theta}{\sin\theta\cos\theta} = 2 = \text{RHS}.\end{aligned}$$

Example 4. *Prove that* $\frac{\tan\theta}{1-\cot\theta}+\frac{\cot\theta}{1-\tan\theta}=1+\operatorname{cosec}\theta\sec\theta$, *if* $\cot\theta\neq 1, 0$ *and* $\tan\theta\neq 1, 0$.

Solution.

$$\text{LHS} = \frac{\tan\theta}{1-\cot\theta}+\frac{\cot\theta}{1-\tan\theta}$$

$$= \frac{\tan\theta}{1-\frac{1}{\tan\theta}}+\frac{\frac{1}{\tan\theta}}{1-\tan\theta}$$

$$= \frac{\tan^2\theta}{\tan\theta-1}+\frac{1}{\tan\theta(1-\tan\theta)}$$

$$= \frac{\tan^2\theta}{\tan\theta-1}-\frac{1}{\tan\theta(\tan\theta-1)}$$

$$= \frac{\tan^3\theta-1}{\tan\theta(\tan\theta-1)}$$

$$= \frac{(\tan\theta-1)(\tan^2\theta+\tan\theta+1)}{\tan\theta(\tan\theta-1)}$$

$$= \frac{\tan^2\theta+\tan\theta+1}{\tan\theta} \quad \text{since } \tan\theta\neq 1$$

$$= \frac{\sec^2\theta+\tan\theta}{\tan\theta}$$

$$= \frac{\sec^2\theta}{\tan\theta}+1 = \sec\theta\operatorname{cosec}\theta+1 = \text{RHS}.$$

Example 5. *Which of the six trigonometrical ratios are positive for (i) 960° (ii) – 560°?*

Solution. (*i*) 960° = 720° + 240°.

Therefore, the revolving line starting from *OX* will make two complete revolutions in the anticlockwise direction and further trace out an angle of 240° in the same direction. Thus, it will be in the third quadrant. So, the tangent and cotangent are positive and rest of trigonometrical ratios will be negative.

(*ii*) – 560° = – 360° – 200°.

Therefore, the revolving line after making one complete revolution in the clockwise direciton, will trace out further an angle of 200° in the same direction. Thus, it will be in the second quadrant. So, only sine and cosecant are positive.

Example 6. *In what quadrants can* θ *lie if sec* $\theta = \frac{-7}{6}$ *?*

Solution. As sec θ is negative in second and third quadrants, θ can lie in second or third quadrant only.

Example 7. *If sin* $\theta = \frac{-12}{13}$, *determine other trigonometrical ratios of* θ.

Solution. $\cos^2\theta = 1 - \sin^2\theta$

$$= 1 - \frac{144}{169} = \frac{169-144}{169} = \frac{25}{169}.$$

$\Rightarrow$ $$\cos\theta = \pm\frac{5}{13}.$$

So $$\tan\theta = \frac{\sin\theta}{\cos\theta} = \mp\frac{12}{5}$$

$$\operatorname{cosec}\theta = \frac{-13}{12},\ \sec\theta = \pm\frac{13}{5},\ \cot\theta = \mp\frac{5}{12}.$$

Example 8. *Express all the trigonometrical ratios of* θ *in terms of the sin* θ.

Solution. Let $\sin\theta = k$.

Then $$\cos^2\theta = 1 - \sin^2\theta = 1 - k^2 \Rightarrow \cos\theta = \pm\sqrt{1-k^2}$$

$$\tan\theta = \frac{\sin\theta}{\cos\theta} = \pm\frac{k}{\sqrt{1-k^2}}$$

$$\cot\theta = \frac{\cos\theta}{\sin\theta} = \pm\frac{\sqrt{1-k^2}}{k}$$

$$\sec\theta = \frac{1}{\cos\theta} = \pm\frac{1}{\sqrt{1-k^2}}$$

$$\operatorname{cosec}\theta = \frac{1}{\sin\theta} = \frac{1}{k}.$$

Example 9. *Prove that sin* $\theta = a + \frac{1}{a}$ *is impossible, if a is real.*

Solution. $$\sin\theta = a + \frac{1}{a} \Rightarrow \sin\theta = \frac{a^2+1}{a}$$

$$\Rightarrow a^2 - a\sin\theta + 1 = 0$$

$$\Rightarrow a = \frac{\sin\theta \pm \sqrt{\sin^2\theta - 4}}{2}$$

For a to be real, the expression under the radical sign, must be positive or zero.

i.e. $\sin^2\theta - 4 \geq 0$

or $\sin^2\theta \geq 4 \Rightarrow$ sin θ is numerically greater than or equal to 2 which is impossible.

Thus, if a is real, $\sin\theta = a + \frac{1}{a}$ is impossible.

Example 10. *Determine the quadrant in which θ must lie if cot θ is positive and cosec θ is negative.*

Solution. cot θ is positive ⇒ θ lies in first or third quadrant.

cosec θ is negative ⇒ θ lies in third or fourth quadrant.

In order that cot θ is positive and cosec θ is negatie, we see that θ must lie in third quadrant.

Example 11. *Prove that*

$$\frac{1}{\operatorname{cosec}\theta + \cot\theta} - \frac{1}{\sin\theta} = \frac{1}{\sin\theta} - \frac{1}{\operatorname{cosec}\theta - \cot\theta}$$

Solution.

$$\text{LHS} = \frac{1}{\operatorname{cosec}\theta + \cot\theta} - \frac{1}{\sin\theta}$$

$$= \frac{\sin\theta}{1+\cos\theta} - \frac{1}{\sin\theta}$$

$$= \frac{\sin^2\theta - (1+\cos\theta)}{(1+\cos\theta)\sin\theta}$$

$$= \frac{-(1-\sin^2\theta) - \cos\theta}{(1+\cos\theta)\sin\theta}$$

$$= \frac{-\cos^2\theta - \cos\theta}{(1+\cos\theta)\sin\theta}$$

$$= \frac{-\cos\theta\,(1+\cos\theta)}{(1+\cos\theta)\sin\theta} = -\cot\theta$$

$$\text{RHS} = \frac{1}{\sin\theta} - \frac{1}{\operatorname{cosec}\theta - \cot\theta}$$

$$= \frac{1}{\sin\theta} - \frac{\sin\theta}{1-\cos\theta}$$

$$= \frac{1-\cos\theta-\sin^2\theta}{\sin\theta(1-\cos\theta)}$$

$$= \frac{\cos^2\theta-\cos\theta}{\sin\theta\,(1-\cos\theta)}$$

$$= \frac{-\cos\theta\,(1-\cos\theta)}{\sin\theta\,(1-\cos\theta)} = -\cot\theta$$

Therefore, LHS = RHS.

Example 12. *Prove that*

sin θ*(1 + tan* θ*) + cos* θ *(1 + cot* θ*) = sec* θ *+ cosec* θ*.*

Solution. $\text{LHS} = \sin\theta\,(1+\tan\theta)+\cos\theta\,(1+\cot\theta)$

$$= \sin\theta\left(1+\frac{\sin\theta}{\cos\theta}\right)+\cos\theta\left(1+\frac{\cos\theta}{\sin\theta}\right)$$

$$= \sin\theta+\frac{\sin^2\theta}{\cos\theta}+\cos\theta+\frac{\cos^2\theta}{\sin\theta}$$

$$= \frac{\sin^2\theta\cos\theta+\sin^3\theta+\cos^2\theta\sin\theta+\cos^3\theta}{\sin\theta\cos\theta}$$

$$= \frac{\sin^2\theta(\sin\theta+\cos\theta)+\cos^2\theta\,(\sin\theta+\cos\theta)}{\sin\theta\cos\theta}$$

$$= \frac{(\sin^2\theta+\cos^2\theta)\,(\sin\theta+\cos\theta)}{\sin\theta\cos\theta}$$

$$= \frac{\sin\theta+\cos\theta}{\sin\theta\cos\theta}$$

$$= \frac{1}{\cos\theta}+\frac{1}{\sin\theta} = \sec\theta+\text{cosec}\,\theta = \text{RHS}.$$

Example 13. *If tan* $\theta = \frac{4}{3}$*, find the value of*

$$\frac{2\sin\theta+3\cos\theta}{4\cos\theta+3\sin\theta}.$$

Solution. $\dfrac{2\sin\theta+3\cos\theta}{4\cos\theta+3\sin\theta} = \dfrac{2\tan\theta+3}{4+3\tan\theta} = \dfrac{\frac{8}{5}+3}{4+\frac{12}{5}} = \dfrac{23}{32}.$

Example 14. *State giving the reason whether the following equation is possible.*

$$2\sin^2\theta - 3\cos\theta - 6 = 0$$

Solution. $2\sin^2\theta - 3\cos\theta - 6 = 0$

$\Rightarrow \quad 2(1-\cos^2\theta) - 3\cos\theta - 6 = 0$

$\Rightarrow \quad -2\cos^2\theta - 3\cos\theta - 4 = 0$

$\Rightarrow \quad 2\cos^2\theta + 3\cos\theta + 4 = 0$

$$\Rightarrow \quad \cos\theta = \frac{-3 \pm \sqrt{9-32}}{4} = \frac{-3 \pm \sqrt{-23}}{4}$$

$\Rightarrow \quad \cos\theta$ is imaginary, which is not true.

Example 15. *Prove that*

$$\frac{1-\sin\theta}{1+\sec\theta} - \frac{1+\sin\theta}{1-\sec\theta} = 2\cos\theta\,(\cot\theta + \text{cosec}^2\,\theta)$$

Solution.

$$\text{LHS} = \frac{(1-\sin\theta)\cos\theta}{1+\cos\theta} - \frac{(1+\sin\theta)\cos\theta}{\cos\theta - 1}$$

$$= \cos\theta\left[\frac{(1-\sin\theta)}{(1+\cos\theta)} + \frac{(1+\sin\theta)}{(1-\cos\theta)}\right]$$

$$= \cos\theta\left[\frac{(1-\sin\theta)(1-\cos\theta) + (1+\sin\theta)(1+\cos\theta)}{1-\cos^2\theta}\right]$$

$$= \cos\theta\left[\frac{1-\sin\theta-\cos\theta+\sin\theta\cos\theta + 1+\sin\theta+\cos\theta+\sin\theta\cos\theta}{\sin^2\theta}\right]$$

$$= \cos\theta\left[\frac{2+2\sin\theta\cos\theta}{\sin^2\theta}\right]$$

$$= 2\cos\theta\,[\text{cosec}^2\,\theta + \cos\theta] = \text{RHS}.$$

Example 16. *If* $\tan x = \dfrac{\sin\theta - \cos\theta}{\sin\theta + \cos\theta}$ *where* θ *and* x *are both positive and acute angles, prove that*

$$\sin x = \frac{1}{\sqrt{2}}(\sin\theta - \cos\theta)$$

Solution. $1+\tan^2 x = 1+\dfrac{\sin^2\theta+\cos^2\theta-2\sin\theta\cos\theta}{\sin^2\theta+\cos^2\theta+2\sin\theta\cos\theta}$

$$= 1+\frac{(1-2\sin\theta\cos\theta)}{(1+2\sin\theta\cos\theta)} = \frac{2}{1+2\sin\theta\cos\theta}$$

Therefore, $\sec^2 x = \dfrac{2}{1+2\sin\theta\cos\theta}$

$$\Rightarrow \quad \cos^2 x = \frac{1+2\sin\theta\cos\theta}{2}$$

$$\Rightarrow \quad 1-\cos^2 x = \frac{2-(1+2\sin\theta\cos\theta)}{2}$$

$$= \frac{1-2\sin\theta\cos\theta}{2} = \frac{(\sin\theta-\cos\theta)^2}{2}$$

$$\Rightarrow \quad \sin^2 x = \frac{(\sin\theta-\cos\theta)^2}{2}$$

$$\Rightarrow \quad \sin x = \pm\frac{(\sin\theta-\cos\theta)}{\sqrt{2}}.$$

Since θ is acute and $\tan x \geq 0$, $\sin\theta \geq \cos\theta$

$\Rightarrow \quad \sin\theta-\cos\theta \geq 0$

Also x is acute $\Rightarrow \sin x \geq 0$

$$\Rightarrow \quad \sin x = +\frac{(\sin\theta-\cos\theta)}{\sqrt{2}}.$$

Example 17. *Exhibit*

$$(\sin\theta-3)(\sin\theta-1)(\sin\theta+1)(\sin\theta+3)+16$$

as a perfect square and examine if there is any suitable value of θ *for which the above expression can vanish.*

Solution. Now $(\sin\theta-3)(\sin\theta-1)(\sin\theta+1)(\sin\theta+3)+16$

$$= (\sin^2\theta-1)(\sin^2\theta-9)+16$$

$$= \sin^4\theta-10\sin^2\theta+25$$

$$= (\sin^2\theta-5)^2.$$

This is 0 only when $\sin^2\theta-5=0$ *i.e.*, only when $\sin^2\theta=5$ which is not possible as the maximum value of $\sin^2\theta$ is 1.

Thus, there is no value of θ for which the given expression can vanish.

Example 18. *Find the value in terms of p and q of*

$$\frac{p\cos\theta + q\sin\theta}{p\cos\theta - q\sin\theta} \text{ where } \cot\theta = \frac{p}{q}.$$

Here use of any figure not allowed.

Solution. $\dfrac{p\cos\theta + q\sin\theta}{p\cos\theta - q\sin\theta} = \dfrac{p\dfrac{\cos\theta}{\sin\theta} + q}{p\dfrac{\cos\theta}{\sin\theta} - q}$

$$= \frac{p\cot\theta + q}{p\cot\theta - q} = \frac{\dfrac{p^2}{q} + q}{\dfrac{p^2}{q} - q} = \frac{p^2 + q^2}{p^2 - q^2}.$$

Example 19. *Show that*

$$\frac{\tan\theta}{\sec\theta - 1} + \frac{\tan\theta}{\sec\theta + 1} = 2\operatorname{cosec}\theta.$$

Solution. LHS $= \dfrac{\tan\theta}{\sec\theta - 1} + \dfrac{\tan\theta}{\sec\theta + 1}$

$$= \tan\theta\left[\frac{1}{\sec\theta - 1} + \frac{1}{\sec\theta + 1}\right]$$

$$= \tan\theta\left[\frac{2\sec\theta}{\sec^2\theta - 1}\right]$$

$$= \tan\theta\left[\frac{2\sec\theta}{\tan^2\theta}\right]$$

$$= \frac{2\sec\theta}{\tan\theta} = \frac{2}{\sin\theta} = 2\operatorname{cosec}\theta = \text{RHS}.$$

EXERCISES

1. Prove that $\sqrt{\sec^2\theta + \operatorname{cosec}^2\theta} = \tan\theta + \cot\theta$.
2. $(\operatorname{cosec}\theta - \sin\theta)(\sec\theta - \cos\theta)(\tan\theta + \cot\theta) = 1$.
3. $\cos^4\theta - \sin^4\theta + 1 = 2\cos^2\theta$.
4. $\sec^6\theta - \tan^6\theta = 1 + 3\tan^2\theta + 3\tan^4\theta$.
5. $\sqrt{\dfrac{1 - \sin\theta}{1 + \sin\theta}} = \sec\theta - \tan\theta$, provided $\sin\theta \neq -1$.

6. $\sqrt{\dfrac{1-\cos\theta}{1+\cos\theta}} = \text{cosec}\,\theta - \cot\theta$, provided $\cos\theta \neq -1$.

7. $\dfrac{1}{\sec\theta+\tan\theta} = \sec\theta + \tan\theta$, if $\sec\theta \neq \tan\theta$.

8. $\dfrac{\cos\theta}{1-\tan\theta}+\dfrac{\sin\theta}{1-\cot\theta} = \sin\theta + \cos\theta$, if $\tan\theta \neq 1$ and $\cot\theta \neq 1$.

9. Express all the trigonometrical ratios in terms of the cotangent.

10. If $\cos\theta = \dfrac{3}{5}$, find the values of other ratios.

11. The sine of a certain angle is $\dfrac{1}{4}$, find the numerical values of the other trigonometrical ratios.

12. If $2\sin\theta = 2 - \cos\theta$, find $\sin\theta$.

13. If $\cot\theta + \sec\theta = 5$, find $\cos\theta$.

14. If $3\sec^4\theta + 8 = 10\sec^2\theta$, find $\tan\theta$.

15. Which of the six trigonometrical ratios are positive for
(*i*) 452° (*ii*) – 1200°

16. Prove that $\cos\theta = a+\dfrac{1}{a}$ is not possible for real values of a.

17. Find the values of $\cos\theta$ for which the equation, $2\cos\theta = a+\dfrac{1}{a}$ is possible, a being real.

18. For what relations between a and b is the equation $\sin\theta = \dfrac{a+b}{2\sqrt{ab}}$ possible.

19. Prove that $\dfrac{\tan\theta+\sec\theta-1}{\tan\theta-\sec\theta+1} = \dfrac{1+\sin\theta}{\cos\theta}$.

20. If $\tan\theta + \cot\theta = 2$ show that $\sin\theta = \cos\theta$.

21. Prove that $\dfrac{\sin\theta}{1-\cos\theta}+\dfrac{\cos\theta}{1-\tan\theta} = \sin\theta + \cos\theta$.

22. Prove that $\dfrac{1}{\text{cosec}\,\theta-\cot\theta}+\dfrac{1}{\text{cosec}\,\theta+\cot\theta} = 2\,\text{cosec}\,\theta$.

23. If $7\sin^2\theta + 3\cos^2\theta = 4$, show that $\cot\theta = \pm\sqrt{3}$.

24. Prove that if $\cos\theta + \sin\theta = \sqrt{2}\cos\theta$ then $\cos\theta - \sin\theta = \sqrt{2}\cos\theta$.

ANSWERS

10. $\sin\theta = \dfrac{4}{5}$, $\tan\theta = \dfrac{4}{3}$, $\cot\theta = \dfrac{3}{4}$, $\text{cosec}\,\theta = \dfrac{5}{4}$, $\sec\theta = \dfrac{5}{3}$.

11. $\frac{\sqrt{15}}{4}, \frac{1}{\sqrt{15}}$ etc.

12. 1 or $\frac{3}{5}$.

13. $\frac{12}{13}$.

14. $\frac{1}{\sqrt{3}}$ or 1.

15. (*i*) sine and cosecant. (*ii*) tangent and cotangent.

17. 1 and – 1.

18. $a = \pm b$.

TRIGONOMETRICAL RATIOS OF SOME STANDARD ANGLES

5. ANGLE OF 45°, 60°, 30°

Angle of 45°. Let the revolving line OR starting from OX trace out an angle of 45° in the anti-clockwise direction. Take any point P on OR. From P draw $PM \perp OX$.

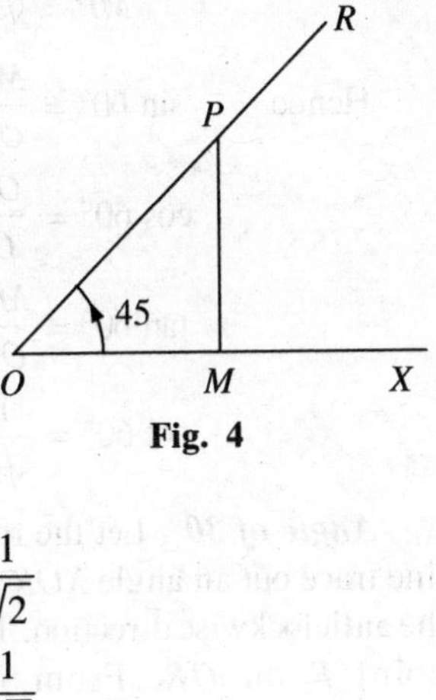

Fig. 4

Then in ΔOMP,

$$\angle MOP = 45°,$$
$$\angle OMP = 90°$$
$$\Rightarrow \quad \angle OPM = 45°.$$

Then $\quad OM = MP = a$ (say)

Also $\quad (OP)^2 = (OM)^2 + (MP)^2$
$$= a^2 + a^2 = 2a^2$$
$$\Rightarrow \quad OP = \sqrt{2}a$$

Now
$$\sin 45° = \frac{MP}{OP} = \frac{a}{\sqrt{2}a} = \frac{1}{\sqrt{2}}$$
$$\cos 45° = \frac{OM}{OP} = \frac{a}{\sqrt{2}a} = \frac{1}{\sqrt{2}}$$
$$\tan 45° = \frac{MP}{OM} = \frac{a}{a} = 1$$
$$\cot 45° = \frac{1}{\tan 45°} = 1$$
$$\text{cosec } 45° = \frac{1}{\sin 45°} = \sqrt{2}$$
$$\sec 45° = \frac{1}{\cos 45°} = \sqrt{2}.$$

Angle of 60°. Let the revolving line OR starting from OX trace out an angle of 60° in the anti-clockwise direction. Take any point P on OR. From P draw $PM \perp OX$. Take a point M' on OX such that $MM' = OM = a$ (say)

Then $\angle MOP = 60°$,

$\angle OPM = 30°$.

The two Δs OMP and $MM'P$ are congruent.

So $\quad OP = M'P$

and $\angle MOP = \angle OM'P$.

So that $\Delta OM'P$ is an equilateral triangle.

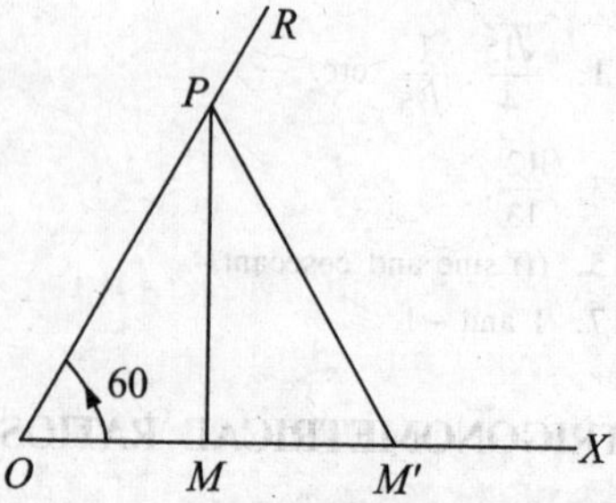

Fig. 5

Then $OP = 2OM = 2a$

and $\quad (MP)^2 = (OP)^2 - (OM)^2 = 4a^2 - a^2 = 3a^2$

$$MP = \sqrt{3}\,a.$$

Hence $\quad \sin 60° = \dfrac{MP}{OP} = \dfrac{\sqrt{3}a}{2a} = \dfrac{\sqrt{3}}{2}.$

$$\cos 60° = \frac{OM}{OP} = \frac{a}{2a} = \frac{1}{2}.$$

$$\tan 60° = \frac{MP}{OP} = \sqrt{3}$$

$$\cot 60° = \frac{1}{\sqrt{3}},\ \text{cosec}\ 60° = \frac{2}{\sqrt{3}},\ \sec 60° = 2.$$

Angle of 30°. Let the revolving line trace out an angle $XOR = 30°$ in the anticlockwise direction. Take any point P on OR. From P draw $PM \perp OX$. Produce PM *to* P' making $MP' = PM$.

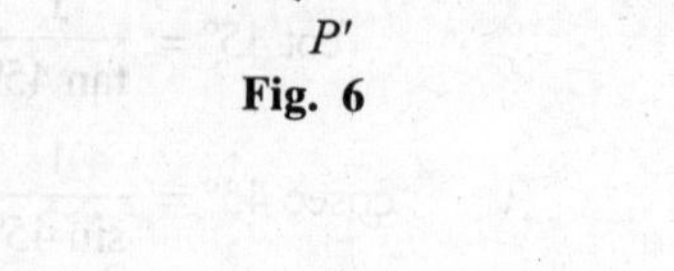

Fig. 6

Then $\angle MOP = 30°$,

$\angle OPM = 60°$.

The two Δs OPM and $OP'M$ are congruent as two sides are equal and the included angles are equal.

Then $\angle OPM = \angle OP'M = 60°$

so that $\Delta OPP'$ is equilateral.

Let $\quad MP = MP' = a$ (say)

Then $\quad OP = 2a$ and $OM = \sqrt{3}a.$

Hence $\quad \sin 30° = \dfrac{MP}{OP} = \dfrac{a}{2a} = \dfrac{1}{2}.$

$$\cos 30^\circ = \frac{OM}{OP} = \frac{\sqrt{3}a}{2a} = \frac{\sqrt{3}}{2}.$$

$$\tan 30^\circ = \frac{MP}{OM} = \frac{a}{\sqrt{3}a} = \frac{1}{\sqrt{3}}.$$

$$\cot 30^\circ = \sqrt{3},\ \sec 30^\circ = \frac{2}{\sqrt{3}},\ \text{cosec } 30^\circ = 2.$$

6. WHAT IS INFINITY

Consider the fraction a/n, where a is a fixed positie number and n is any positive number. As we give smaller values to n, the fraction a/n becomes larger and larger, and so a/n can be made as large as we like by giving sufficiently small values to n. This fact is expressed by saying "a/n approaches infinity as n approaches zero" and is written in symbols as

$$\lim_{n \to 0} \frac{a}{n} = \infty.$$

If a is a negative quantity then as n approaches zero, a/n is said to approach $-\infty$.

Angle of 0°. Let the revolving line OR starting from OX in the anti-clockwise direction trace out a very small angle $XOR = \theta$. Take any point P on OR. Let $PM \perp OX$.

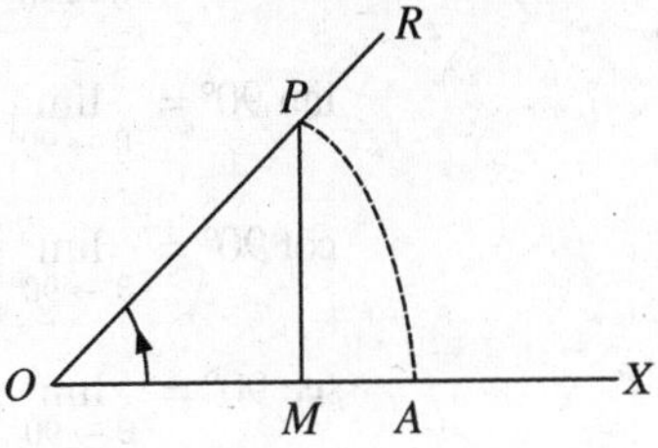

Fig. 7

Draw an arc of circle with centre O and radius OP, cutting OX at A. Then as θ tends to zero, OM tends to OA and MP tends to zero.

Then $$\sin 0^\circ = \lim_{\theta \to 0^\circ} \sin\theta = \lim_{\theta \to 0^\circ} \frac{MP}{OP} = \frac{0}{OA} = 0.$$

$$\cos 0^\circ = \lim_{\theta \to 0^\circ} \cos\theta = \lim_{\theta \to 0^\circ} \frac{OM}{OP} = \frac{OA}{OA} = 1.$$

$$\tan 0^\circ = \lim_{\theta \to 0^\circ} \tan\theta = \lim_{\theta \to 0^\circ} \frac{MP}{OM} = \frac{0}{OA} = 0.$$

$$\cot 0^\circ = \lim_{\theta \to 0^\circ} \cot\theta = \lim_{\theta \to 0^\circ} \frac{OM}{MP} = \infty.$$

$$\sec 0^\circ = \lim_{\theta \to 0^\circ} \sec\theta = \lim_{\theta \to 0^\circ} \frac{OP}{OM} = \frac{OA}{OA} = 1.$$

$$\text{cosec } 0^\circ = \lim_{\theta \to 0^\circ} \text{cosec }\theta = \lim_{\theta \to 0^\circ} \frac{OP}{MP} = \infty.$$

Angle of 90°. Let the revolving line OR starting from OX trace out an angle θ in the anticlockwise direction, very nearly equal to 90°. Take any point P on OR.

Let $PM \perp OX$ and $OY \perp OX$. With O as centre and OP as radius, draw an arc of a circle cutting OY at B and OX at A.

Then as θ tends to 90°, OP approaches OB, PM approaches OB and OM tends to zero.

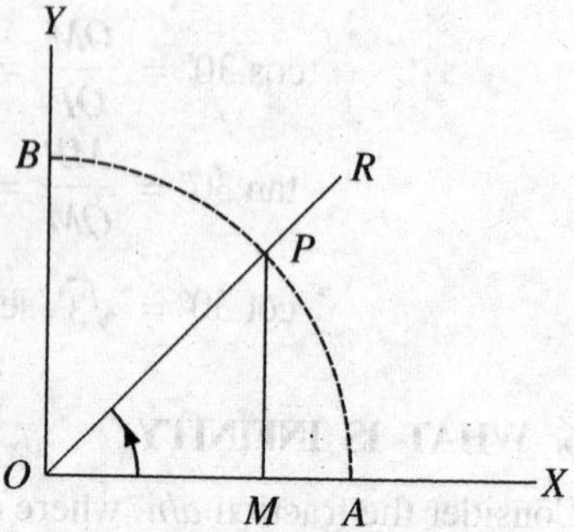

Fig. 8

Then
$$\sin 90^\circ = \lim_{\theta \to 90^\circ} \sin\theta = \lim_{\theta \to 90^\circ} \frac{MP}{OP} = \frac{OB}{OB} = 1.$$

$$\cos 90^\circ = \lim_{\theta \to 90^\circ} \cos\theta = \lim_{\theta \to 90^\circ} \frac{OM}{OP} = \frac{0}{OB} = 0.$$

$$\tan 90^\circ = \lim_{\theta \to 90^\circ} \tan\theta = \lim_{\theta \to 90^\circ} \frac{MP}{OM} = \infty.$$

$$\cot 90^\circ = \lim_{\theta \to 90^\circ} \cot\theta = \lim_{\theta \to 90^\circ} \frac{OM}{MP} = \frac{0}{OB} = 0.$$

$$\sec 90^\circ = \lim_{\theta \to 90^\circ} \sec\theta = \lim_{\theta \to 90^\circ} \frac{OP}{OM} = \infty.$$

$$\text{cosec } 90^\circ = \lim_{\theta \to 90^\circ} \text{cosec } \theta = \lim_{\theta \to 90^\circ} \frac{OP}{MP} = \frac{OB}{OB} = 1.$$

We summarize the results of this section in the following table. The student is advised to make himself familiar with it.

Angle	*0°*	*30°*	*45°*	*60°*	*90°*
sine	0	$\frac{1}{2}$	$\frac{1}{\sqrt{2}}$	$\frac{\sqrt{3}}{2}$	1
cosine	1	$\frac{\sqrt{3}}{2}$	$\frac{1}{\sqrt{2}}$	$\frac{1}{2}$	0
tangent	0	1	1	$\sqrt{3}$	∞
cotangent	∞	$\sqrt{3}$	1	$\frac{1}{\sqrt{3}}$	0
cosecant	∞	2	$\sqrt{2}$	$\frac{2}{\sqrt{3}}$	1
secant	1	$\frac{2}{\sqrt{3}}$	$\sqrt{2}$	2	∞

Example 20. *Find the value of cot 60° tan 30° + sec² 45°.*

Solution. $\cot 60° \tan 30° + \sec^2 45° = \frac{1}{\sqrt{3}}\frac{1}{\sqrt{3}} + 2 = \frac{1}{3} + 2 = \frac{7}{3}$.

Example 21. *Find x if $\tan^2 45° - \cos^2 60° = x \sin 45° \cos 45° \tan 60°$.*

Solution. $\text{LHS} = 1 - \frac{1}{4} = \frac{3}{4}$.

$\text{RHS} = x\frac{1}{\sqrt{2}}\frac{1}{\sqrt{2}}\sqrt{3} = \frac{\sqrt{3}x}{2}$.

Then $\frac{3}{4} = \frac{\sqrt{3}x}{2} \Rightarrow x = \frac{\sqrt{3}}{2}$.

Example 22. *If θ = 30°, verify that*

(*i*) $\sin 3\theta = 3\sin\theta - 4\sin^3\theta$

(*ii*) $\cos 3\theta = 4\cos^3\theta - 3\cos\theta$.

Solution. (*i*) $\sin 3\theta = \sin 90° = 1$

and $3\sin\theta - 4\sin^3\theta = 3\sin 30° - 4\sin^3 30°$

$$= \frac{3}{2} - \frac{4}{8} = \frac{3}{2} - \frac{1}{2} = 1.$$

This proves (*i*).

(*ii*) $\cos 3\theta = \cos 90° = 0$

and $4\cos^3\theta - 3\cos\theta = 4\cos^3\theta - 3\cos 30°$

$$= 4\frac{3\sqrt{3}}{8} - 3\frac{\sqrt{3}}{2} = 0.$$

Example 23. *Find a solution of the following equation:*

$$\cot\theta + \tan\theta = 2\,\text{cosec}\,\theta.$$

Solution. $\cot\theta + \tan\theta = \frac{1}{\tan\theta} + \tan\theta = \frac{1+\tan^2\theta}{\tan\theta} = \frac{\sec^2\theta}{\tan\theta}$.

Then $\frac{\sec^2\theta}{\tan\theta} = 2\,\text{cosec}\,\theta$

$\Rightarrow$ $\sec^2\theta = 2\,\text{cosec}\,\theta\tan\theta = 2\sec\theta$

$\Rightarrow$ $\sec\theta(\sec\theta - 2) = 0$

$\Rightarrow$ $\sec\theta = 0$ or 2.

As $\sec\theta = 0$ is impossible.

we get $\sec\theta = 2 \Rightarrow$ one value of $\theta = \pi/3$.

Thus a solution of given equation is $\theta = \pi/3$.

Example 24. *If θ is an acute angle, find its value from tan θ = 2 sin θ.*

Solution.
$$\tan\theta = 2\sin\theta \Rightarrow \sin\theta = 2\sin\theta\cos\theta$$
$$\Rightarrow \sin\theta(1-2\cos\theta)=0$$
$$\Rightarrow \sin\theta=0 \quad \text{or} \quad 1-2\cos\theta=0$$
$$\sin\theta = 0 \Rightarrow \theta = 0° \text{ as } \theta \text{ is acute.}$$
$$1-2\cos\theta = 0 \Rightarrow \cos\theta = \frac{1}{2} \Rightarrow \theta = 60° = \pi/3.$$

Example 25. *Prove that cot 30º, cot 45º, cot 60º, are in G.P.*

Solution. Now
$$\cot 30° = \sqrt{3} = a \text{ (say)}$$
$$\cot 45° = 1 = b \text{ (say)}$$
$$\cot 60° = \frac{1}{\sqrt{3}} = c \text{ (say)}$$

Then $b^2 = 1 = ac$.

Thus a, b, c are in G.P.

i.e., cot 30°, cot 45°, cot 60° are in G.P.

Example 26. *Find the value of θ from the equation,*

$$cot^2\theta - (1+\sqrt{3})\cot\theta + \sqrt{3} = 0, \text{ for } 0 < \theta < \frac{\pi}{2}.$$

Solution. Now
$$\cot\theta = \frac{(1+\sqrt{3}) \pm \sqrt{1+3+2\sqrt{3}-4\sqrt{3}}}{2}$$
$$= \frac{(1+\sqrt{3}) \pm (1-\sqrt{3})}{2} = 1, \sqrt{3}$$

$$\cot\theta = 1 \Rightarrow \theta = \frac{\pi}{4}$$
$$\cot\theta = \sqrt{3} \Rightarrow \theta = \frac{\pi}{3}.$$

Therefore, there are two values of θ, namely $\frac{\pi}{4}$ and $\frac{\pi}{3}$ which satisfy the given equation.

Example 27. *ABC is a right-angled triangle in which the angle C is a right angle and BC =* $\frac{1}{2}$ *AB. The line AD bisecting the angle A meets BC at D. Obtain the value of tan 15º from this figure.*

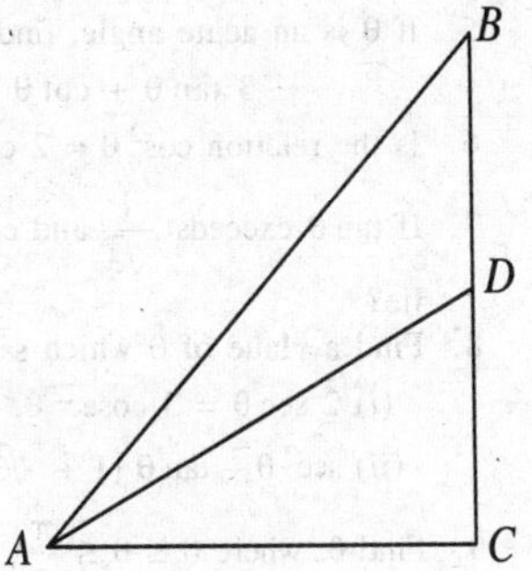

Fig. 9

Solution. Let $AB = 2x$.

Then $BC = x$.

Let $\angle CAB = 2\theta$

Then $\sin 2\theta = \dfrac{BC}{AB} = \dfrac{1}{2}$

$\Rightarrow 2\theta = 30^\circ \quad \Rightarrow \quad \theta = 15^\circ$.

Now $\quad \dfrac{AC}{AB} = \dfrac{CD}{BD}$

and $\quad AC = \sqrt{4x^2 - x^2} = \sqrt{3}x$

$$\Rightarrow \quad \frac{\sqrt{3}x}{2x} = \frac{CD}{BD}$$

$$\Rightarrow \quad CD = \frac{\sqrt{3}}{2} BD$$

Now $\quad BD + CD = x$

$$\Rightarrow \quad \frac{2}{\sqrt{3}} CD + CD = x$$

$$\Rightarrow \quad CD = \frac{x\sqrt{3}}{(2+\sqrt{3})}.$$

Now from ΔACD

$$\tan 15^\circ = \frac{CD}{AC}$$

$$= \frac{x\sqrt{3}}{(2+\sqrt{3})} \cdot \frac{1}{\sqrt{3}x} = \frac{1}{2+\sqrt{3}} = 2 - \sqrt{3}.$$

EXERCISES

1. Find the values of the following:
   (*i*) $\sin^2 30^\circ + \sin^2 45^\circ + \sin^2 60^\circ$,
   (*ii*) $\cos 45^\circ \cos 60^\circ - \sin 45^\circ \sin 60^\circ$,
   (*iii*) $4 \cot^2 45^\circ - \sec^2 60^\circ + \sin^2 30^\circ$.
2. If $\theta = 30^\circ$, verify that $\tan 3\theta = \dfrac{3 \tan \theta - \tan^3 \theta}{1 - 3 \tan^2 \theta}$.
3. Show that $2 \sin^2 45^\circ - 6 \tan^2 30^\circ + \text{cosec } 30^\circ = \sec 60^\circ - \sin^2 90^\circ$.
4. If $\theta = 60^\circ$, $\phi = 30^\circ$, verify

$$\tan(\theta - \phi) = \frac{\tan \theta - \tan \phi}{1 + \tan \theta \tan \phi}.$$

5. If θ is an acute angle, find its value from the equation

$$3 \tan \theta + \cot \theta = 5 \operatorname{cosec} \theta.$$

6. Is the relation $\cos^2 \theta = 2 \cos \theta - 1$ true, where $\theta = 0°$?

7. If tan θ exceeds $\frac{1}{\sqrt{3}}$ and cot θ exceeds 1, between what limits does the angle θ lie?

8. Find a vlaue of θ which satisfies the equation

(*i*) $2 \sec \theta = 3 \operatorname{cosec}^2 \theta$,

(*ii*) $\sec^2 \theta - \tan \theta (1 + \sqrt{3}) + \sqrt{3} - 1 = 0$.

9. Find θ, where $0 \le \theta \le \frac{\pi}{2}$, satisfying

$$2 \cos^2 \theta + 3 \sin \theta = 3.$$

10. Prove that $2 \sin^2 30° + 2 \sin^2 45° + 2 \sin^2 60° - 3 = 0$.

11. Prove that $2\sqrt{2} \cos 45° \cos 60° - 2\sqrt{2} \sin 45° \sin 60° + \sqrt{3} = 1$.

12. Prove that $3 \tan^2 30° + 3 \tan^2 45° + 3 \tan^2 60° - 13 = 0$.

13. If $\tan^2 45° - \cos^2 60° - x \sin 45° \cos 45° \tan 60° = 0$ find x.

14. Find θ which satisfies the equation $\sin \theta + \cos \theta = \sqrt{2}$.

15. If $(1 + 2 \sin 60°) (\sin \theta - \cos \theta) = (1 - 2 \sin 60°)(\sin \theta + \cos \theta)$ find θ, $0 \le \theta \le \frac{\pi}{2}$.

ANSWERS

1. (*i*) $\frac{3}{2}$, (*ii*) $\frac{\sqrt{3}-1}{2\sqrt{2}}$, (*iii*) $\frac{1}{8}$.
5. $\theta = 60°$.
6. Yes.
7. Between 30° and 45°.
8. (*i*) 60, (*ii*) 45° or 60°.
9. 30°, 90°.
13. $\frac{\sqrt{3}}{2}$
14. 45°.
15. 30°.

TRIGONOMETRICAL RATIOS OF ALLIED ANGLES

7. The figures in this section are so drawn that revolving line lies in the first quadrant. The figures when revolving line lies in second, third or fourth quadrant can be similarly drawn. The same proofs hold good in all other cases too.

Angle (– θ). Let the revolving line *OR* starting from *OX*, move in anticlockwise direction and trace out an angle *XOR* = θ. Let another revolving line *OR′* starting from *OX*, move in clockwise direction and trace out an angle *XOR′* = – θ.

Take a point *P* on *OR*.

Draw $PM \perp OX$ and produce it to meed OR' at P'.

Δs OPM and $OP'M$ are congruent.

By convention of signs

$$MP = -MP'$$

$$OP = OP'$$

So $$\sin(-\theta) = \frac{MP'}{OP'} = \frac{-MP}{OP} = -\sin\theta.$$

$$\cos(-\theta) = \frac{OM}{OP'} = \frac{OM}{OP} = \cos\theta.$$

$$\tan(-\theta) = \frac{MP'}{OM} = \frac{-MP}{OM} = -\tan\theta.$$

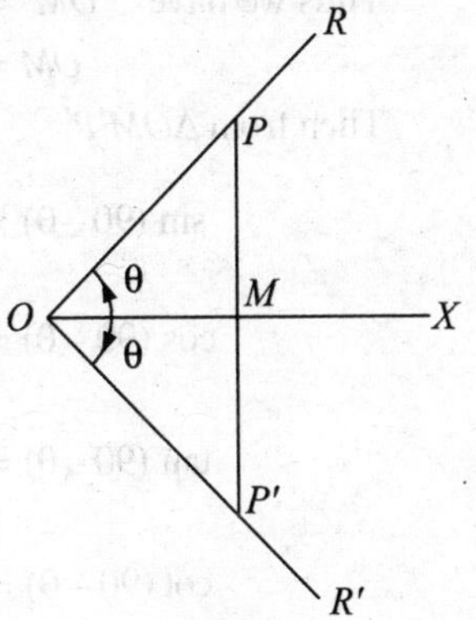

Fig. 10

$$\cot(-\theta) = \frac{OM}{MP'} = \frac{-OM}{MP} = -\cot\theta.$$

$$\sec(-\theta) = \frac{OP'}{OM} = \frac{OP}{OM} = \sec\theta.$$

$$\operatorname{cosec}(-\theta) = \frac{OP'}{MP'} = \frac{-OP}{MP} = -\operatorname{cosec}\theta.$$

Thus, when θ is changed to $-\theta$, $\cos\theta$ and $\sec\theta$ remain unaltered both in magnitude and sign. All other trigonometrical ratios remain unaltered in magnitude but the sign is changed.

Angle $(90 - \theta)$. Let a revolving line OR starting from OX, move in anticlockwise direction and trace an angle $XOR = \theta$.

Let OR' be another revolving line starting from OX in anticlockwise direction, trace out an angle of 90° and then revolve back through angle θ. Thus OR' has traced an angle

$$XOR' = 90 - \theta.$$

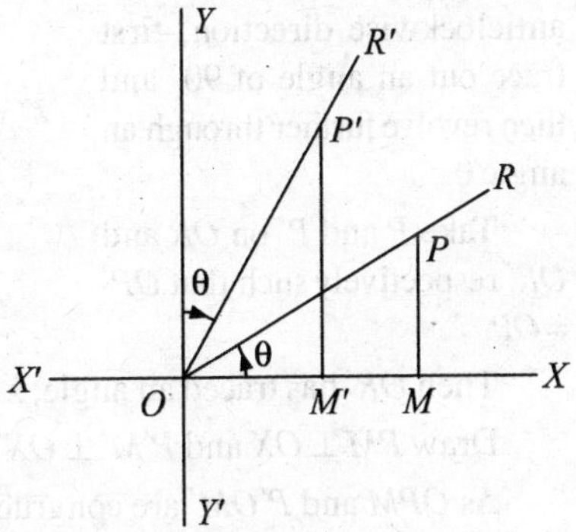

Fig. 11

Take P and P' on OR and OR' respectively such that $OP = OP'$. From P and P' draw $PM \perp OX$ and $P'M' \perp OX$.

Then Δs OPM and $P'OM'$ are congruent.

Thus we have $OM' = MP$

$OM = M'P'$.

Then from $\Delta OM'P'$

$$\sin(90-\theta) = \frac{M'P'}{OP'} = \frac{OM}{OP} = \cos\theta.$$

$$\cos(90-\theta) = \frac{OM'}{OP'} = \frac{MP}{OP} = \sin\theta.$$

$$\tan(90-\theta) = \frac{M'P'}{OM'} = \frac{OM}{MP} = \cot\theta.$$

$$\cot(90-\theta) = \frac{OM'}{M'P'} = \frac{MP}{OM} = \tan\theta.$$

$$\sec(90-\theta) = \frac{OP'}{OM'} = \frac{OP}{MP} = \text{cosec}\,\theta.$$

$$\text{cosec}(90-\theta) = \frac{OP'}{M'P'} = \frac{OP}{OM} = \sec\theta.$$

Angle $(90+\theta)$. Let a revolving line OR starting from OX in anticlockwise direction, trace out an angle $XOR = \theta$. Let another revolving line OR' starting from OX in anticlockwise direction, first trace out an angle of 90° and then revolve further through an angle θ.

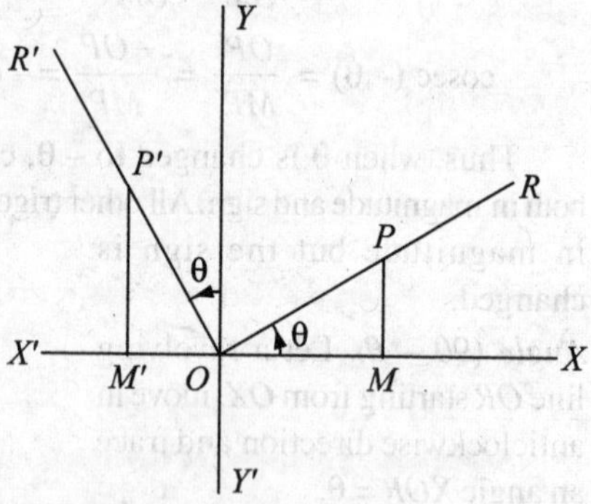

Fig. 12

Take P and P' on OR and OR' respectively such that $OP' = OP$.

Then OR' has traced an angle, $XOR' = 90° + \theta$.

Draw $PM \perp OX$ and $P'M' \perp OX'$.

Δs OPM and $P'OM'$ are congruent.

We have $OM = M'P' - OM' = MP$ by convention of signs,

Then $$\sin(90+\theta) = \frac{M'P'}{OP} = \frac{OM}{OP} = \cos\theta.$$

$$\cos(90+\theta) = \frac{OM'}{OP'} = \frac{-MP}{OP} = -\sin\theta.$$

$$\tan(90+\theta) = \frac{M'P'}{OM'} = \frac{OM}{-MP} = -\cot\theta.$$

$$\cot(90+\theta) = \frac{OM'}{M'P'} = \frac{-MP}{OM} = -\tan\theta.$$

$$\sec(90+\theta) = \frac{OP'}{OM'} = \frac{OP}{-MP} = -\operatorname{cosec}\theta.$$

$$\operatorname{cosec}(90+\theta) = \frac{OP'}{M'P'} = \frac{OP}{OM} = \sec\theta.$$

Angle (180 – θ). Let a revolving line OR starting from OX in anticlockwise direction, trace out an angle $XOR = \theta$. Let another revolving OR' starting from OX in anti-clockwise direction trace out an angle of 180° and then revolve back through an angle θ. Thus OR' has traced an angle

$$XOR' = 180 - \theta.$$

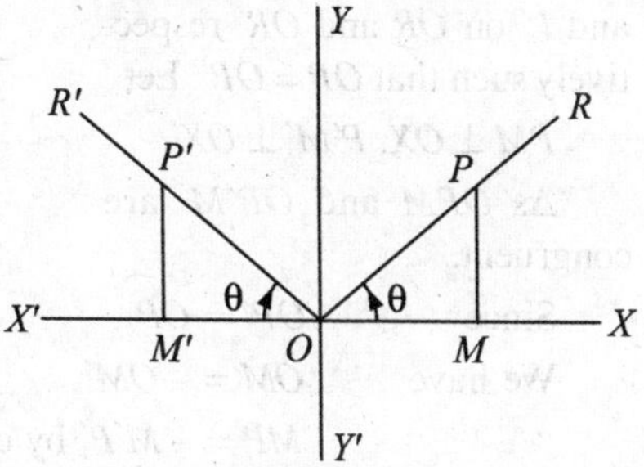

Fig. 13

Take P and P' on OR and OR' respectively such that $OP = OP'$. Draw $PM \perp OX$, $P'M' \perp OX'$.

Δs OPM and $OP'M'$ are congruent.

When have $OM' = -OM$ by convention of signs.

$M'P' = MP$

Then from $\Delta OM'P'$,

$$\sin(180-\theta) = \frac{M'P'}{OP'} = \frac{MP}{OP} = \sin\theta.$$

$$\cos(180-\theta) = \frac{OM'}{OP'} = \frac{-OM}{OP} = -\cos\theta.$$

$$\tan(180-\theta) = \frac{M'P'}{OM'} = \frac{MP}{-OM} = -\tan\theta.$$

$$\cot(180-\theta) = \frac{OM'}{M'P'} = \frac{-OM}{MP} = -\cot\theta.$$

$$\sec(180-\theta) = \frac{OP'}{OM'} = \frac{OP}{-OM} = -\sec\theta.$$

$$\text{cosec}(180-\theta) = \frac{OP'}{M'O'} = \frac{OP}{MP} = \text{cosec}\,\theta.$$

Angle (180 + θ). Let a revolving line *OR* starting from *OX* in anticlockwise direction trace an angle *XOR* = θ. Let another revolving line starting from *OX* in anticlockwise direction first trace out an angle of 180° and revolve further through an angle θ in the same direction. Take *P* and *P′* on *OR* and *OR′* respectively such that *OP* = *OP′*. Let

$PM \perp OX$, $P'M' \perp OX'$.

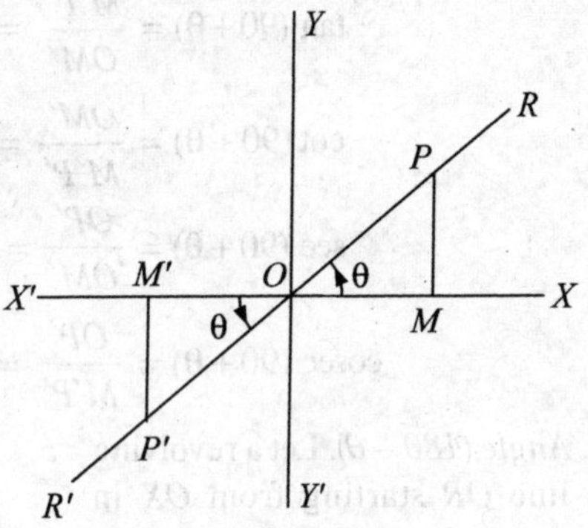

Fig. 14

Δs *OPM* and *OP′M′* are congruent.

Since $OP' = OP$

We have $OM = -OM'$

$MP = -M'P'$ by convention of signs.

Then $\sin(180+\theta) = \dfrac{M'P'}{OP'} = \dfrac{-MP}{OP} = -\sin\theta.$

$$\cos(180+\theta) = \frac{OM'}{OP'} = \frac{-OM}{OP} = -\cos\theta.$$

$$\tan(180+\theta) = \frac{M'P'}{OM'} = \frac{-MP}{-OM} = \frac{MP}{OM} = \tan\theta.$$

$$\cot(180+\theta) = \frac{OM'}{M'P'} = \frac{-OM}{-MP} = \frac{OM}{MP} = \cot\theta.$$

$$\sec(180+\theta) = \frac{OP'}{OM'} = \frac{OP}{-OM} = -\sec\theta.$$

$$\text{cosec}(180+\theta) = \frac{OP'}{MP'} = \frac{OP}{-MP} = -\text{cosec}\,\theta.$$

Angle (360° – θ). As before let ∠*XOR* = θ. Let another revolving line *OR′* starting from *OX* in anticlockwise direction, first trace out an angle of 360° and then revolve back through an angle θ. Thus *OR′* has turned through an angle $XOR' = 360 - \theta$. Take P and P' on OR and OR' respectively such that $OP = OP'$.

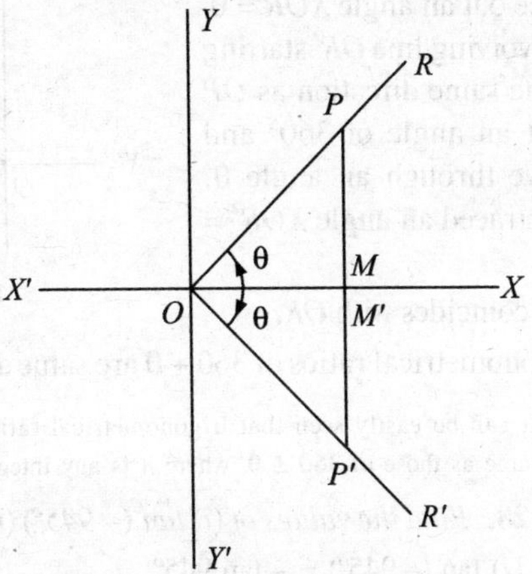

Fig. 15

Let $PM \perp OX$, $P'M' \perp OX$.

Δs OPM, $OP'M'$ are congruent.

Now $\qquad OP' = OP$

we have $\qquad OM = OM'$

$M'P' = -MP$, by convention of signs.

Then $$\sin(360-\theta) = \frac{M'P'}{OP'} = \frac{-MP}{OP} = -\sin\theta.$$

$$\cos(360-\theta) = \frac{OM'}{OP'} = \frac{-OM}{OP} = \cos\theta.$$

$$\tan(360-\theta) = \frac{M'P'}{OM'} = \frac{-MP}{OM} = -\tan\theta.$$

$$\cot(360-\theta) = \frac{OM'}{M'P'} = \frac{OM}{-MP} = -\cot\theta.$$

$$\text{cosec}(360-\theta) = \frac{OP'}{M'P'} = \frac{OP}{-MP} = -\text{cosec}\,\theta.$$

$$\sec(360-\theta) = \frac{OP'}{OM'} = \frac{OP}{OM} = \sec\theta.$$

Angle ($360° + \theta$). Let a revolving line OR starting from OX in anti-clockwise direction, trace out an angle $XOR = \theta$. Let another revolving line OR' starting from OX in the same direction as OP first trace out an angle of 360° and further revolve through an angle θ. Thus OR' has traced an angle $XOR' = 360° + \theta$.

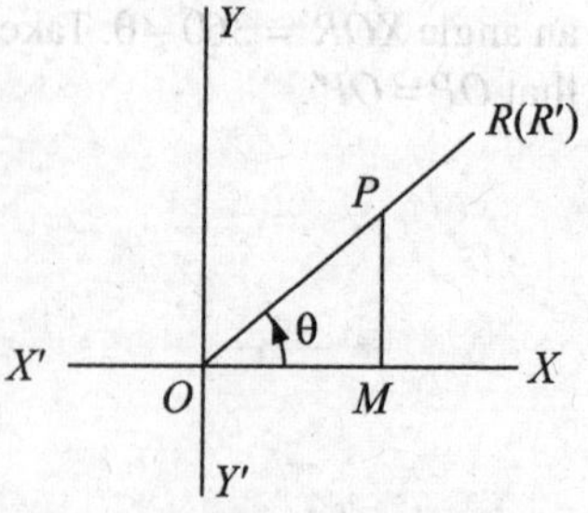

Fig. 16

Here OR' coincides with OR.

Thus trigonometrical ratios of $360 + \theta$ are same as those of θ.

[NOTE: It can be easily seen that trigonometrical ratios of ($n \times 360 \pm \theta$) are same as those of $360 \pm \theta$, where n is any integer.]

Example 28. *Find the values of (i) tan (– 945°) (ii) sec (225°).*

Solution. (*i*) $\tan(-945°) = -\tan 945°$

$$= -\tan(3 \times 360 - 135°)$$
$$= -\tan(360° - 135°)$$
$$= -[-\tan 135°] = \tan 135°$$
$$= \tan(90° + 45°) = -\cot 45° = -1.$$

(*ii*) $\sec 225° = \sec(180° + 45°) = -\sec 45° = -\sqrt{2}$.

Example 29. *If* $\cos\theta = a$, *find the values of cosec* $\left(\frac{\pi}{2} + \theta\right)$ *and* $sin\left(\frac{3\pi}{2} - \theta\right)$.

Solution. Now $\text{cosec}\left(\frac{\pi}{2} + \theta\right) = \sec\theta = \frac{1}{\cos\theta} = \frac{1}{a}$

and $\sin\left(\frac{3\pi}{2} - \theta\right) = \sin\left(\pi + \frac{\pi}{2} - \theta\right)$

$$= -\sin\left(\frac{\pi}{2} - \theta\right) = -\cos\theta = -a.$$

Example 30. *Find the trigonometrical ratios of* $270° - \theta$ *in terms of those of* θ *for all vlaues of* θ.

Solution. $\sin(270° - \theta) = \sin\left(180° + \overline{90° - \theta}\right)$

$$= -\sin(90° - \theta) = -\cos\theta.$$

$$\cos(270^\circ - \theta) = \cos\left(180^\circ + \overline{90^\circ - \theta}\right)$$
$$= -\cos(90^\circ - \theta) = -\sin\theta.$$
$$\tan(270^\circ - \theta) = \tan\left(180^\circ + \overline{90^\circ - \theta}\right)$$
$$= \tan(90^\circ - \theta) = \cot\theta.$$
$$\cot(270^\circ - \theta) = \cot\left(180^\circ + \overline{90^\circ - \theta}\right)$$
$$= \cot(90^\circ - \theta) = \tan\theta.$$
$$\sec(270^\circ - \theta) = \sec\left(180^\circ + \overline{90^\circ - \theta}\right)$$
$$= -\sec(90^\circ - \theta) = -\operatorname{cosec}\theta.$$
$$\operatorname{cosec}(270^\circ - \theta) = \operatorname{cosec}\left(180^\circ + \overline{90^\circ - \theta}\right)$$
$$= -\operatorname{cosec}(90^\circ - \theta) = -\sec\theta.$$

Example 31. *If A, B, C are angles of a triangle, prove that*

$$\cot(A + B) + \cot C = 0.$$

Solution. Since $A + B + C = 180^\circ$

$$A + B = 180^\circ - C.$$

$$\Rightarrow \quad \cot(A + B) + \cot C = \cot(180^\circ - C) + \cot C$$
$$= -\cot C + \cot C = 0.$$

Example 32. *What value of x between 0° and 90° will satisfy the equation tan 2x tan 4x = 1?*

Solution. $\tan 2x \tan 4x = 1$

$$\Rightarrow \quad \tan 2x = \frac{1}{\tan 4x} = \cot 4x$$

$$\Rightarrow \quad \tan 2x = \tan\left(\frac{\pi}{2} - 4x\right)$$

$$\Rightarrow \quad 2x = \frac{\pi}{2} - 4x, \quad \text{or} \quad 2x = \pi + \left(\frac{\pi}{2} - 4x\right),$$

or

$$2x = 2\pi + \left(\frac{\pi}{2} - 4x\right)$$

$$\Rightarrow \quad x = 15^\circ, 45^\circ, 75^\circ.$$

Example 33. *Find the value of tan 5° tan 25° tan 45° tan 65° tan 85°.*

Solution. Now $\tan 85^\circ = \tan(90^\circ - 5^\circ) = \cot 5^\circ$

and $\tan 65^\circ = \tan(90^\circ - 25^\circ) = \cot 25^\circ$

So, tan 5° tan 25° tan 45° tan 65° tan 85°

$$= (\tan 5^\circ \cot 5^\circ)(\tan 25^\circ \cot 25^\circ) \tan 45^\circ$$
$$= \tan 45^\circ = 1.$$

Example 34. *Show that*

$$\frac{\sin(270^\circ + \theta)\cos^3(720^\circ - \theta) - \sin(270^\circ - \theta)\sin^3(540^\circ + \theta)}{\sin(90^\circ + \theta)\sin(-\theta) - \cos^2(280^\circ - \theta)}$$
$$+ \frac{\cot(270^\circ - \theta)}{\operatorname{cosec}^2(450^\circ + \theta)} = 1.$$

where θ is taken such that the denominator appearing in any fraction in the expression does not vanish.

Solution. Now $\cos^3(720^\circ - \theta) = \cos^3\theta$

$$\sin^3(540^\circ + \theta) = -\sin^3\theta$$
$$\operatorname{cosec}^2(450^\circ + \theta) = \sec^2\theta$$
$$\sin(270^\circ + \theta) = -\cos\theta$$
$$\sin(270^\circ - \theta) = -\cos\theta$$
$$\cot(270^\circ - \theta) = \tan\theta$$

So, the given expression is equal to

$$= \frac{-\cos\theta\cos^3\theta - \sin^3\theta\cos\theta}{-\cos\theta\sin\theta - \cos^2\theta} + \frac{\tan\theta}{\sec^2\theta}$$
$$= \frac{-\cos\theta(\sin^3\theta + \cos^3\theta)}{-\cos\theta(\sin\theta + \cos\theta)} + \frac{\sin\theta\cos\theta}{1}$$
$$= \frac{-(\sin\theta + \cos\theta)(\sin^2\theta + \cos^2\theta - \sin\theta\cos\theta)}{-(\sin\theta + \cos\theta)} + \frac{\sin\theta\cos\theta}{1}$$
$$= 1 - \sin\theta\cos\theta + \sin\theta\cos\theta = 1.$$

Example 35. *If θ is the angle in the fourth quadrant satisfying the equation $\cot^2\theta = 4$, find the vlaue of $\frac{1}{\sqrt{5}}(\sec\theta - \operatorname{cosec}\theta)$.*

Solution. $\cot^2\theta = \operatorname{cosec}^2\theta - 1$

$\Rightarrow$ $4 = \operatorname{cosec}^2\theta - 1$

$\Rightarrow$ $\operatorname{cosec}^2\theta = 5$

$\Rightarrow$ $\operatorname{cosec}\theta = -\sqrt{5}$ (as θ lies in fourth quadrant)

Also $\cot^2\theta = 4 \Rightarrow \tan^2\theta = \frac{1}{4}$

So, $\tan^2\theta = \sec^2\theta - 1$

$$\Rightarrow \quad \frac{1}{4} = \sec^2\theta - 1 \Rightarrow \sec^2\theta = \frac{5}{4}$$

$$\Rightarrow \quad \sec\theta = \frac{\sqrt{5}}{2}$$

Therefore, $\frac{1}{\sqrt{5}}(\sec\theta - \operatorname{cosec}\theta) = \frac{1}{\sqrt{5}}\left(\frac{\sqrt{5}}{2} + \sqrt{5}\right) = \frac{3}{2}$.

Example 36. *In any triangle ABC, $2\sin A + \sqrt{3}\sin B = \frac{5}{2}$ and $\sqrt{3}\sin A + 2\sin B = \frac{3\sqrt{3}}{2}$. Find the angle C.*

Solution. Solving given equations for $\sin A$ and $\sin B$, we get $\sin A = \frac{1}{2}$ and $\sin B = \frac{\sqrt{3}}{2}$

$\Rightarrow \quad A = 30^\circ$ or 150°, $\quad B = 60^\circ$ or 120°

$\Rightarrow \quad A = 30^\circ$ and $B = 60^\circ$ or 120°

If $A = 30^\circ$ and $B = 60^\circ$, then $C = 90^\circ$ and if $A = 30^\circ$ and $B = 120^\circ$, then $C = 30^\circ$.

Example 37. *Given that θ is an angle between 180° and 270° find the value of θ if it satisfies the equation $3\cos^2\theta - \sin^2\theta = 1$.*

Solution. $3\cos^2\theta - \sin^2\theta = 1$

$\Rightarrow \quad 3\cos^2\theta - (1 - \cos^2\theta) = 1$

$\Rightarrow \quad 4\cos^2\theta = 2$

$\Rightarrow \quad \cos^2\theta = \frac{1}{2}$

$\Rightarrow \quad \cos\theta = \pm\frac{1}{\sqrt{2}}$

Since $180^\circ \le \theta \le 270^\circ \Rightarrow \cos\theta = \frac{-1}{\sqrt{2}} \Rightarrow \theta = 225^\circ$.

EXERCISES

1. Find the values of $\sin 4620^\circ$ and $\cot 510^\circ$.
2. Find x from the equation
   $\operatorname{cosec}(90^\circ + A) + x\cos A\cot(90^\circ + A) = \sin(90^\circ + A)$.

3. Simplify $\dfrac{\tan 120° + \tan 240°}{1 - \tan 120° \tan 240°}$.

4. Find all the positive values of x less than 2π which satisfy the equation $\cos^2 x = \dfrac{1}{4}$.

5. Find all the angles between 0° and 360° each of which has sine equal to $\dfrac{1}{\sqrt{2}}$.

6. Find θ between 0° and 360° such that

$$\sin\theta = \frac{1}{2} \text{ and } \tan\theta = -\frac{1}{\sqrt{3}}.$$

7. Find the trigonometrical ratios of 270° + θ in terms of θ.

8. If A, B, C are angles of a triangle, prove that $\tan(A + B) + \tan C = 0$.

9. Prove that $\cot A + \tan(180° + A) + \tan(90° + A) + \tan(360° - A) = 0$.

10. Prove that

$$\sin(270° + A) - \sin(270° - A) + \cos(180° + A) + \cos A = 0.$$

11. Simplify $\dfrac{\cot(450° + A)\sin(180° + 2A)\cos(720° - A)}{\cos(180° + A)\sin(360° - A)\cos(630 + A)}$.

12. Find the value of
$\sin 480° \cos 690° + \cos 780° \sin 1050°$.

13. Prove that $\sin 690° \cos 390° - \cos 570° \sin 870° = 0$.

14. Find the vlaue of $\sin(-330°)\cos(-300°) + \cos 390° \sin 420°$.

15. Prove that $1 + \tan 765° \cot 675° + \tan 225° \cot 405° = 1$.

16. Find the value of θ (0° ≤ θ ≤ 360°) when
(*i*) $\cot\theta + \tan 2\theta = 2\sec\theta$ (*ii*) $\cos\theta + \sqrt{3}\sin\theta = 2$.

ANSWERS

1. $-\dfrac{\sqrt{3}}{2}$ and -1. 2. $\tan A$. 3. 0.

4. $\dfrac{\pi}{3}, \dfrac{2\pi}{3}, \dfrac{4\pi}{3}, \dfrac{5\pi}{3}$. 5. 45°, 135° 6. 150°.

11. 2. 12. $\dfrac{1}{2}$. 14. 1.

16. (*i*) 30°, 150° (*ii*) 60°.

CHAPTER 17

TRIGONOMETRICAL RATIOS OF SUMS AND DIFFERENCES OF TWO ANGLES

1. TO PROVE THAT FOR ANY ANGLES A AND B

(1) $\sin(A+B) = \sin A \cos B + \cos A \sin B$

(2) $\cos(A+B) = \cos A \cos B - \sin A \sin B$

(3) $\tan(A+B) = \dfrac{\tan A + \tan B}{1 - \tan A \tan B}$

Proof. Let the revolving line start from *OX* and trace out the angle *XOY* = *A* in the anticlockwise direction. Let the revolving line further trace out the angle *YOZ* = *B* in the same direction.

From any point *P* on *OZ*, draw $PM \perp OX$ and $PN \perp OY$. Through *N* draw $NR \parallel OX$ to meet *MP* in *R*.

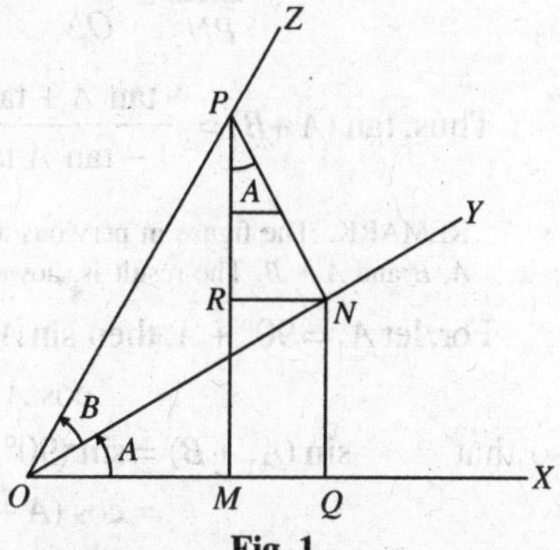

Fig. 1

Then $\angle RPN = 90° - \angle PNR = \angle RNO = A$

(1) $\sin(A+B) = \dfrac{MP}{OP} = \dfrac{MR + RP}{OP}$

$= \dfrac{MR}{OP} + \dfrac{RP}{OP} = \dfrac{QN}{OP} + \dfrac{RP}{OP}$ (where $NQ \perp OX$)

$= \dfrac{QN}{ON} \cdot \dfrac{ON}{OP} + \dfrac{RP}{NP} \cdot \dfrac{NP}{OP}$ (Note this step)

$= \sin A \cos B + \cos A \sin B.$

(2) $$\cos(A+B) = \frac{OM}{OP} = \frac{OQ - MQ}{OP}$$

$$= \frac{OQ}{OP} - \frac{MQ}{OP} = \frac{OQ}{OP} - \frac{RN}{OP}$$

$$= \frac{OQ}{ON} \cdot \frac{ON}{OP} - \frac{RN}{NP} \cdot \frac{NP}{OP} \quad \text{(Note this step)}$$

$$= \cos A \cos B - \sin A \sin B.$$

(3) $$\tan(A+B) = \frac{MP}{OM} = \frac{QN + RP}{OQ - RN}$$

$$= \frac{\dfrac{QN}{OQ} + \dfrac{RP}{OQ}}{1 - \dfrac{RN}{OQ}} = \frac{\tan A + \dfrac{RP}{OQ}}{1 - \dfrac{RN}{RP} \cdot \dfrac{RP}{OQ}}.$$

Since the angles *RPN* and *QON* are equal, the triangles *RPN* and *QON* are similar, so that

$$\frac{RP}{PN} = \frac{OQ}{ON} \quad \textit{i.e.} \quad \frac{RP}{OQ} = \frac{PN}{ON} = \tan B.$$

Thus, $$\tan(A+B) = \frac{\tan A + \tan B}{1 - \tan A \tan B}.$$

REMARK. The figure in pervious article has been drawn for acute angles A, B and $A + B$. The result is, however, true for all angles A and B.

For, let $A_1 = 90° + A$, then $\sin A_1 = \cos A$,

$$\cos A_1 = -\sin A$$

so that $$\sin(A_1 + B) = \sin(90° + A + B)$$

$$= \cos(A+B)$$

$$= \cos A \cos B - \sin A \sin B$$

$$= \sin A_1 \cos B + \cos A_1 \sin B.$$

Similarly, if B is increased by 90°, the result is again true and so on.

2. TO PROVE THAT FOR ANY ANGLES A AND B

(1) $\sin(A - B) = \sin A \cos B - \cos A \sin B$

(2) $\cos(A - B) = \cos A \cos B + \sin A \sin B$

(3) $\tan(A - B) = \dfrac{\tan A - \tan B}{1 + \tan A \tan B}$.

Proof. Let the revolving line starting from OX in anticlockwise direction trace out the angle $YOX = A$ and then revolving back in clockwise direction, trace out angle $YOZ = B$. The revolving line thus traced out the angle $XOZ = A - B$.

From any point P on OZ, draw $PM \perp OX$, $PN \perp OY$, $NQ \perp OX$. Through N draw $NR \parallel OX$ to meet MP produced at R.

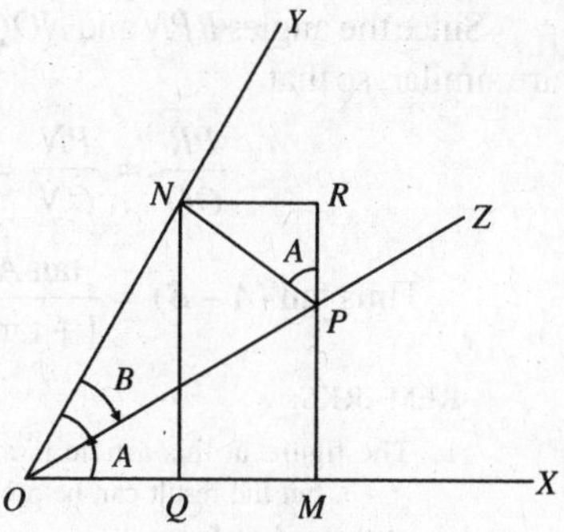

Fig. 2

Then $\angle RPN = 90° - \angle PNR = \angle RNY = A.$

(1) $\sin(A - B) = \sin XOZ$

$$= \frac{MP}{OP} = \frac{MR - PR}{OP}$$

$$= \frac{MR}{OP} - \frac{PR}{OP} = \frac{QN}{OP} - \frac{PR}{OP}$$

$$= \frac{QN}{ON} \cdot \frac{ON}{OP} - \frac{PR}{NP} \cdot \frac{NP}{OP} \qquad \text{(Note this step)}$$

$$= \sin A \cos B - \cos A \sin B.$$

(2) $\cos(A - B) = \cos XOZ$

$$= \frac{OM}{OP} = \frac{OQ + QM}{OP} = \frac{OQ}{OP} + \frac{QM}{OP}$$

$$= \frac{OQ}{OP} + \frac{NR}{OP}$$

$$= \frac{OQ}{ON} \cdot \frac{ON}{OP} + \frac{NR}{NP} \cdot \frac{NP}{OP} \qquad \text{(Note this step)}$$

$$= \cos A \cos B + \sin A \sin B.$$

(3) $\tan(A - B) = \tan XOZ$

$$= \frac{MP}{OM} = \frac{MR - PR}{OQ + QM} = \frac{QN - PR}{OQ + NR}$$

$$= \frac{\dfrac{QN}{OQ} - \dfrac{PR}{OQ}}{1 + \dfrac{NR}{OQ}} = \frac{\tan A - \dfrac{PR}{OQ}}{1 + \dfrac{NR}{PR} \cdot \dfrac{PR}{OQ}}$$

Since the angles *RPN* and *NOQ* are equal, the triangles *RPN* and *NOQ* are similar, so that

$$\frac{PR}{OQ} = \frac{PN}{ON} = \tan B.$$

$$\text{Thus } \tan(A-B) = \frac{\tan A - \tan B}{1 + \tan A \tan B}.$$

REMARKS:

1. The figure in this article is again drawn for acute angles *A*, *B* and *A* +*B*, but the result can be proved for all angles *A* and *B*. See Remark at the end of § 1.
2. The results of § 2 can also be deduced from § 1 by putting *B* – *B* in § 1 and keeping *A* unchanged.

3. TRIGONOMETRICAL RATIOS OF MULTIPLE AND SUB MULTIPLE ANGLES TO PROVE THAT

(1) (*i*) $\sin 2A = 2 \sin A \cos A$

(*ii*) $\cos 2A = 2\cos^2 A - 1 = 1 - 2\sin^2 A = \cos^2 A - \sin^2 A$

(*iii*) $\tan 2A = \dfrac{2 \tan A}{1 - \tan^2 A}$

Proof. By § 1, $\sin(A+B) = \sin A \cos B + \cos A \sin B$.

Put $A = B$

we have $\sin 2A = \sin A \cos A + \cos A \sin A$

$= 2 \sin A \cos A$.

(*ii*) Again by § 1, $\cos(A+B) = \cos A \cos B - \sin A \sin B$

Put $A = B$

we have $\cos 2A = \cos A \cos A - \sin A \sin A$

$= \cos^2 A - \sin^2 A$.

Also $\cos^2 A - \sin^2 A = (1 - \sin^2 A) - \sin^2 A$

$= 1 - 2\sin^2 A$.

and $\cos^2 A - \sin^2 A - \cos^2 A - (1 - \cos^2 A) = 2\cos^2 A - 1$.

(*iii*) Also by § 1, $\tan(A+B) = \dfrac{\tan A + \tan B}{1 - \tan A \tan B}$.

Put $A = B$

we have $\tan 2A = \dfrac{\tan A + \tan A}{1 - \tan A \tan A} = \dfrac{2 \tan A}{1 - \tan^2 A}$.

(2) (*i*) $\mathbf{\sin 3A = 3 \sin A - 4 \sin^3 A}$

(*ii*) $\mathbf{\cos 3A = 4 \cos^3 A - 3 \cos A}$

(*iii*) $\mathbf{\tan 3A = \dfrac{3 \tan A - \tan^3 A}{1 - 3 \tan^2 A}}$

Proof. (*i*)

$$
\begin{aligned}
\sin 3A &= \sin (A + 2A) \\
&= \sin A \cos 2A + \cos A \sin 2A \\
&= \sin A (1 - 2 \sin^2 A) + \cos A (2 \sin A \cos A) \\
&= \sin A - 2 \sin^3 A + 2 \sin A (1 - \sin^2 A) \\
&= 3 \sin A - 4 \sin^3 A.
\end{aligned}
$$

(*ii*)

$$
\begin{aligned}
\cos 3A &= \cos (A + 2A) \\
&= \cos A \cos 2A - \sin A \sin 2A \\
&= \cos A (2 \cos^2 A - 1) - \sin A (2 \sin A \cos A) \\
&= 2 \cos^3 A - \cos A - 2 \cos A (1 - \cos^2 A) \\
&= 4 \cos^3 A - 3 \cos A.
\end{aligned}
$$

(*iii*)

$$
\begin{aligned}
\tan 3A &= \tan (A + 2A) \\
&= \frac{\tan A + \tan 2A}{1 - \tan A \tan 2A} = \frac{\tan A + \dfrac{2 \tan A}{1 - \tan^2 A}}{1 - \tan A \dfrac{2 \tan A}{1 - \tan^2 A}} \\
&= \frac{\tan A (1 - \tan^2 A) + 2 \tan A}{(1 - \tan^2 A) - 2 \tan^2 A} \\
&= \frac{3 \tan A - \tan^3 A}{1 - 3 \tan^2 A}.
\end{aligned}
$$

(3) (*i*) $\mathbf{\sin A = 2 \sin \dfrac{A}{2} \cos \dfrac{A}{2}}$

(*ii*) $\mathbf{\cos A = \cos^2 \dfrac{A}{2} - \sin^2 \dfrac{A}{2}}$

$\mathbf{= 2 \cos^2 \dfrac{A}{2} - 1 = 1 - 2 \sin^2 \dfrac{A}{2}}$

(*iii*) $\mathbf{\tan A = \dfrac{2 \tan \dfrac{A}{2}}{1 - \tan^2 \dfrac{A}{2}}}$

Proof. Replace A by $\frac{A}{2}$ in (1) of this article. All relations in (3), will immediately follow.

(4) **(*i*)** $\sin \frac{A}{2} = \pm\sqrt{\frac{1 - \cos A}{2}}$

(*ii*) $\cos \frac{A}{2} = \pm\sqrt{\frac{1 + \cos A}{2}}$

(*iii*) $\tan \frac{A}{2} = \pm\sqrt{\frac{1 - \cos A}{1 + \cos A}}$

Proof. We have $\cos A = 1 - 2\sin^2 \frac{A}{2}$, form (3)

Then $2\sin^2 \frac{A}{2} = 1 - \cos A$

so that $\sin^2 \frac{A}{2} = \frac{1 - \cos A}{2} \Rightarrow \sin \frac{A}{2} = \pm\sqrt{\frac{1 - \cos A}{2}}$.

Similarly, $\cos A = 2\cos^2 \frac{A}{2} - 1.$

$\Rightarrow \quad 2\cos^2 \frac{A}{2} = 1 + \cos A$

$\Rightarrow \quad 2\cos^2 \frac{A}{2} = \frac{1 + \cos A}{2}$

$\Rightarrow \quad \cos \frac{A}{2} = \pm\sqrt{\frac{1 + \cos A}{2}}$

Hence $\tan \frac{A}{2} = \frac{\sin \frac{A}{2}}{\cos \frac{A}{2}} = \pm\sqrt{\frac{1 - \cos A}{1 + \cos A}}$.

Example 1. *If* $\sin \alpha = \frac{3}{5}$ *and* $\cos \beta = \frac{9}{41}$, *find the value of* $\sin (\alpha - \beta)$, α, β *being acute angles.*

Solution. $\cos^2 \alpha = 1 - \sin^2 \alpha = 1 - \frac{9}{25} = \frac{16}{25}$

$\Rightarrow \quad \cos^2 \alpha = \pm\frac{4}{5}$

Since α is acute angle, $\cos\alpha = \frac{4}{5}$

Also $\sin^2\beta = 1 - \cos^2\beta$

$$= 1 - \frac{81}{1681} = \frac{1600}{1681}$$

$\Rightarrow$ $\sin\beta = \pm\frac{40}{41}$

β is acute angle $\Rightarrow \sin\beta = \frac{40}{41}$

Therefore, $\sin(\alpha - \beta) = \sin\alpha\cos\beta - \sin\beta\cos\alpha$

$$= 1 - \frac{27}{205} - \frac{150}{205} = -\frac{133}{205}.$$

Example 2. *Find the value of sin 18° and cos 18°.*

Solution. Put $18° = x$ so that $90° = 5x$

Then $2x = 90° - 3x$

$\Rightarrow$ $\sin 2x = \sin(90° - 3x) = \cos 3x$

or $2\sin x\cos x = 4\cos^3 x - 3\cos x$

or $4\cos^3 x - 2\sin x\cos x - 3\cos x = 0$

or $\cos x(4\cos^2 x - 2\sin x - 3) = 0$

or $4\cos^2 x - 2\sin x - 3 = 0$ since $\cos x \neq 0$

or $4(1 - \sin^2 x) - 2\sin x - 3 = 0$

or $4\sin^2 x + 2\sin x - 1 = 0$

$\Rightarrow$ $\sin x = \frac{-2 \pm \sqrt{20}}{8} = \frac{-1+\sqrt{5}}{4}$ or $\frac{-1-\sqrt{5}}{4}$.

Since $x = 18°$. $\sin x$ is positive so that the value $\frac{-1-\sqrt{5}}{4}$ is rejected.

Hence $\sin x = \frac{-1+\sqrt{5}}{4}$ *i.e.* $\sin 18° = \frac{-1+\sqrt{5}}{4}$

Also $\cos 18° = \sqrt{1 - \sin^2 18°} = \sqrt{1 - \left(\frac{5+1-2\sqrt{5}}{16}\right)}$

$$= \sqrt{1 - \frac{16-6+2\sqrt{5}}{16}} = \sqrt{\frac{10+2\sqrt{5}}{4}}.$$

Example 3. *Prove that sin 105° + cos 105° = cos 45°.*

Solution. LHS = sin 105° + cos 105°

$$= \sin(60° + 45°) + \cos(60° + 45°)$$

$$= (\sin 60° \cos 45° + \cos 60° \sin 45°) + (\cos 60° \cos 45° - \sin 60° \sin 45°)$$

$$= \left(\frac{\sqrt{3}}{2}\frac{1}{\sqrt{2}} + \frac{1}{2}\frac{1}{\sqrt{2}}\right) + \left(\frac{1}{2}\frac{1}{\sqrt{2}} - \frac{\sqrt{3}}{2}\frac{1}{\sqrt{2}}\right) = \frac{1}{\sqrt{2}}$$

$$\text{RHS} = \cos 45° = \frac{1}{\sqrt{2}}.$$

Hance the result follows.

Example 4. *Find the value of tan 75° and hence prove that tan 75° + cot 75° = 4.*

Solution. tan 75° = tan (45° + 30°)

$$= \frac{\tan 45° + \tan 30°}{1 - \tan 45° \tan 30°} = \frac{1 + \frac{1}{\sqrt{3}}}{1 - \frac{1}{\sqrt{3}}}$$

$$= \frac{\sqrt{3}+1}{\sqrt{3}-1} = \frac{\left(\sqrt{3}+1\right)^2}{2}$$

$$= \frac{4 + 2\sqrt{3}}{2} = 2 + \sqrt{3}$$

Now $\tan 75° + \cot 75° = 2 + \sqrt{3} + \frac{1}{2+\sqrt{3}}$

$$= (2+\sqrt{3}) + \frac{(2-\sqrt{3})}{(2+\sqrt{3})(2-\sqrt{3})}$$

$$= (2+\sqrt{3}) + \frac{(2-\sqrt{3})}{4-3}$$

$$= 2 + \sqrt{3} + (2 - \sqrt{3}) = 4.$$

Example 5. *If* $\tan\theta = \frac{12}{5}$ *and θ is in third quadrant, find the value of* $2\sin\frac{\theta}{2} - 3\cos\frac{\theta}{2}$

Solution. θ lies in third quadrant

$\Rightarrow$ θ lies between 180° and 270°

$\Rightarrow$ $\frac{\theta}{2}$ lies between 90° and 135°

$\Rightarrow$ $\sin\frac{\theta}{2}$ is positive and $\cos\frac{\theta}{2}$ is negative.

Now $\tan\theta = \frac{12}{5} \Rightarrow \sin\theta = \frac{-12}{13}$ and $\cos\theta = \frac{-5}{13}$

(as θ lies in 3rd quadrant)

Therefore $\cos\frac{\theta}{2} = -\sqrt{\frac{1+\cos\theta}{2}} = -\sqrt{\frac{8}{26}}$

and $\sin\frac{\theta}{2} = \sqrt{\frac{1-\cos\theta}{2}} = \sqrt{\frac{18}{26}}$

So $2\sin\frac{\theta}{2} - 3\cos\frac{\theta}{2} = 2\sqrt{\frac{18}{26}} + 3\sqrt{\frac{8}{26}} = 2\sqrt{\frac{9}{13}} + 3\sqrt{\frac{4}{13}}$

$= \frac{1}{\sqrt{13}}[6+6] = \frac{12}{\sqrt{13}}.$

Example 6. *Prove that* $\sin 5\theta = 5\sin\theta - 20\sin^3\theta + 16\sin^5\theta$

Solution. LHS $= \sin 5\theta$

$= \sin(2\theta + 3\theta)$

$= \sin 2\theta\cos 3\theta + \cos 2\theta\sin 3\theta$

$= 2\sin\theta\cos\theta(4\cos^3\theta - 3\cos\theta)$
$+ (3\sin\theta - 4\sin^3\theta)(1 - 2\sin^2\theta)$

$= 2\sin\theta\cos^2\theta(4\cos^2\theta - 3)$
$+ \sin\theta(3 - 4\sin^2\theta)(1 - 2\sin^2\theta)$

$= \sin\theta[2(1-\sin^2\theta)(1 - 4\sin^2\theta)$
$+ (3 - 4\sin^2\theta)(1 - 2\sin^2\theta)$

$= \sin\theta[2 - 10\sin^2\theta + 8\sin^4\theta + 3$
$- 10\sin^2\theta + 8\sin^2\theta]$

$= 5\sin\theta - 20\sin^3\theta + 16\sin^5\theta.$

Example 7. *Prove that* $\frac{\sin A + \sin 3A}{\cos A + \cos 3A} = \tan 2A.$

Solution. LHS $= \frac{\sin A + \sin 3A}{\cos A + \cos 3A} = \frac{\sin A + 3\sin A - 4\sin^3 A}{\cos A + 4\cos^3 A - 3\cos A}$

$$= \frac{4 \sin A (1 - \sin^2 A)}{2 \cos A (2 \cos^2 A - 1)}$$

$$= \frac{2 \sin A \cos 2A}{\cos A \cos^2 A} = \frac{2 \sin A \cos A}{\cos 2A}$$

$$= \frac{\sin 2A}{\cos 2A} = \tan 2A.$$

Example 8. *Prove that $1 + \cos^2 2\theta = 2 (\cos^4 \theta + \sin^4 \theta)$.*

Solution. RHS $= 2 (\cos^4 \theta + \sin^4 \theta)$

$$= 2 [(\cos^2 \theta - \sin^2 \theta)^2 + 2 \sin^2 \theta \cos^2 \theta]$$
$$= 2 [(\cos 2\theta)^2 + 2 \sin^2 \theta \cos^2 \theta]$$
$$= 2 (\cos 2\theta)^2 + 4 \sin^2 \theta \cos^2 \theta$$
$$= 2 (\cos 2\theta)^2 + (\sin 2\theta)^2$$
$$= (\cos 2\theta)^2 + [(\cos 2\theta)^2 + (\sin 2\theta)^2]$$
$$= (\cos 2\theta)^2 + 1 = \text{LHS}.$$

Example 9. *If $\sin \theta + \sin \phi = a$, $\cos \theta + \cos \phi = b$, find the value of $\tan \frac{\theta - \phi}{2}$.*

Solution. $\sin \theta + \sin \phi = a$

$\cos \theta + \cos \phi = b.$

Squaring and adding, we get

$(\sin^2 \theta + \cos^2 \theta) + (\sin^2 \phi + \cos^2 \phi) + 2 (\sin \theta \sin \phi + \cos \theta \cos \phi) = a^2 + b^2$

$$\Rightarrow \quad 2 \{1 + \cos (\theta - \phi)\} = a^2 + b^2$$

$$\Rightarrow \quad 1 + \cos (\theta - \phi) = \frac{a^2 + b^2}{2}$$

Also $\quad 1 - \cos (\theta - \phi) = 1 - \left(\frac{a^2 + b^2}{2} - 1\right)$

$$= 2 - \frac{a^2 + b^2}{2} = \frac{4 - a^2 - b^2}{2}$$

$$\Rightarrow \quad \tan \frac{\theta - \phi}{2} = \pm \sqrt{\frac{1 - \cos (\theta - \phi)}{1 + \cos (\theta - \phi)}} = \pm \sqrt{\frac{4 - a^2 - b^2}{a^2 + b^2}}.$$

Example 10. *Find the value of sin 9° and cos 9°.*

Solution. Now $\cos 2\theta = 1 - 2\sin^2\theta$

Put $\theta = 9°$, we get

$$\cos 18° = 1 - 2\sin^2 9°.$$

By Example 2, $\cos 18° = \dfrac{\sqrt{10+2\sqrt{5}}}{4}$

So $$\frac{\sqrt{10+2\sqrt{5}}}{4} = 1 - 2\sin^2 9°$$

or $$2\sin^2 9° = 1 - \frac{\sqrt{10+2\sqrt{5}}}{4} = \frac{4-\sqrt{10+2\sqrt{5}}}{4}$$

or $$\sin^2 9° = \frac{4-\sqrt{10+2\sqrt{5}}}{8}$$

or $$\sin 9° = \pm\sqrt{\frac{4-\sqrt{10+2\sqrt{5}}}{8}}.$$

Sin 9° is positive, so that the negative value is rejected.

Hence $$\sin 9° = +\sqrt{\frac{4-\sqrt{10+2\sqrt{5}}}{8}}$$

Also $$\cos 9° = \sqrt{1-\sin^2 9°} = \sqrt{1-\left(\frac{4-\sqrt{10+2\sqrt{5}}}{8}\right)}$$

$$= \sqrt{\frac{8-4+\sqrt{10+2\sqrt{5}}}{8}} = \sqrt{\frac{4+\sqrt{10+2\sqrt{5}}}{8}}.$$

Example 11. *Prove that* $\dfrac{\tan A + \sec A - 1}{\tan A - \sec A + 1} = \dfrac{1+\sin A}{\cos A}$.

Solution. $$\text{LHS} = \frac{\tan A + \sec A - 1}{\tan A - \sec A + 1} = \frac{\dfrac{\sin A}{\cos A} + \dfrac{1}{\cos A} - 1}{\dfrac{\sin A}{\cos A} - \dfrac{1}{\cos A} + 1}$$

$$= \frac{\sin A + 1 - \cos A}{\sin A - 1 + \cos A} = \frac{\sin A + 2\sin^2\dfrac{A}{2}}{\sin A - 2\sin^2\dfrac{A}{2}}$$

$$= \frac{2\sin\frac{A}{2}\cos\frac{A}{2} + 2\sin^2\frac{A}{2}}{2\sin\frac{A}{2}\cos\frac{A}{2} - 2\sin^2\frac{A}{2}}$$

$$= \frac{\cos\frac{A}{2} + \sin\frac{A}{2}}{\cos\frac{A}{2} - \sin\frac{A}{2}}$$

$$= \frac{\left(\cos\frac{A}{2} + \sin\frac{A}{2}\right)\left(\cos\frac{A}{2} + \sin\frac{A}{2}\right)}{\left(\cos\frac{A}{2} - \sin\frac{A}{2}\right)\left(\cos\frac{A}{2} + \sin\frac{A}{2}\right)}$$

$$= \frac{\cos^2\frac{A}{2} + \sin^2\frac{A}{2} + 2\sin\frac{A}{2}\cos\frac{A}{2}}{\cos^2\frac{A}{2} - \sin^2\frac{A}{2}}$$

$$= \frac{1 + \sin A}{\cos A} = \text{RHS.}$$

Example 12. *Prove that* $\frac{\cos 13° + \sin 13°}{\cos 13° - \sin 13°} = \tan 58°$.

Solution. $\text{LHS} = \frac{\cos 13° + \sin 13°}{\cos 13° - \sin 13°}$

$$= \frac{1 + \frac{\sin 13°}{\cos 13°}}{1 - \frac{\sin 13°}{\cos 13°}} = \frac{1 + \tan 13°}{1 - \tan 13°}$$

$$= \frac{\tan 45° + \tan 13°}{1 - \tan 45° \tan 13°} \qquad (\text{as } \tan 45° = 1)$$

$$= \tan(45° + 13°) = \tan 58° = \text{RHS.}$$

Example 13. *Prove that*

$$\tan\left(45° + \frac{\theta}{2}\right) = \sqrt{\frac{1 + \sin\theta}{1 - \sin\theta}}, \text{ where } 0 < \theta < 90°.$$

Solution. $\text{LHS} = \tan\left(45° + \frac{\theta}{2}\right)$

$$= \frac{\tan 45° + \tan\frac{\theta}{2}}{1 - \tan 45° \tan\frac{\theta}{2}} = \frac{1 + \tan\frac{\theta}{2}}{1 - \tan\frac{\theta}{2}}$$

$$= \frac{\cos\frac{\theta}{2} + \sin\frac{\theta}{2}}{\cos\frac{\theta}{2} - \sin\frac{\theta}{2}} = \frac{\left(\cos\frac{\theta}{2} + \sin\frac{\theta}{2}\right)^2}{\cos^2\frac{\theta}{2} - \sin^2\frac{\theta}{2}}$$

$$= \frac{1 + 2\sin\frac{\theta}{2}\cos\frac{\theta}{2}}{\cos\theta} = \frac{1 + \sin\theta}{\pm\sqrt{1 - \sin^2\theta}}$$

$$= \frac{1 + \sin\theta}{\pm\sqrt{(1 - \sin\theta)(1 + \sin\theta)}} = \pm\sqrt{\frac{1 + \sin\theta}{1 - \sin\theta}}$$

Since $0 < \theta < 90°$, we have $\frac{\theta}{2} < 45°$, so that $\tan\left(45° + \frac{\theta}{2}\right)$ is positive.

Thus $\tan\left(45° + \frac{\theta}{2}\right) = \sqrt{\frac{1 + \sin\theta}{1 - \sin\theta}}$ = RHS.

Example 14. *Prove that*

$$\frac{\cos 15° + \sin 15°}{\cos 15° - \sin 15°} = \sqrt{3}.$$

Solution. LHS $= \frac{1 + \tan 15°}{1 - \tan 15°} = \frac{\tan 45 + \tan 15}{1 - \tan 45 \tan 15}$

$$= \tan(45 + 15) = \tan 60° = \sqrt{3} = \text{RHS}.$$

Example 15. *Prove that*

$$\tan 2A - \tan A = \frac{2\sin A}{\cos A + \cos 3A}.$$

Solution. LHS $= \frac{\sin 2A}{\cos 2A} - \frac{\sin A}{\cos A}$

$$= \frac{\sin 2A\cos A - \sin A\cos 2A}{\cos 2A\cos A}$$

$$= \frac{\sin(2A - A)}{\cos 2A\cos A} = \frac{\sin A}{\cos 2A\cos A}$$

Also $$\text{RHS} = \frac{2\sin A}{\cos A + 4\cos^3 A + 3\cos A}$$

$$= \frac{2\sin A}{2\cos A\,(2\cos^2 A + 1)} = \frac{\sin A}{\cos 2A \cos A}.$$

Hence the result follows.

Example 16. *Prove that*

$$\cot\alpha = \tan\alpha + 2\tan 2\alpha + 4\tan 4\alpha + 8\cot 8\alpha.$$

Solution. Consider $\cot\alpha - \tan\alpha - 2\tan 2\alpha - 4\tan 4\alpha - 8\cot 8\alpha$

$$= \left(\frac{\cos\alpha}{\sin\alpha} - \frac{\sin\alpha}{\cos\alpha}\right) - 2\tan 2\alpha - 4\tan 4\alpha - 8\cot 8\alpha$$

$$= \frac{\cos 2\alpha}{\sin\alpha\cos\alpha} - 2\tan 2\alpha - 4\tan 4\alpha - 8\cot 8\alpha$$

$$= \frac{2\cos 2\alpha}{\sin 2\alpha} - 2\frac{\sin 2\alpha}{\cos 2\alpha} - 4\tan 4\alpha - 8\cot 8\alpha$$

$$= 2\left(\frac{\cos^2 2\alpha - \sin^2 2\alpha}{\sin 2\alpha\cos 2\alpha}\right) - 4\tan 4\alpha - 8\cot 8\alpha$$

$$= 2\times 2\frac{\cos 4\alpha}{\sin 4\alpha} - 4\frac{\sin 4\alpha}{\cos 4\alpha} - 8\cot 8\alpha$$

$$= 4\left(\frac{\cos^2 4\alpha - \sin^2 4\alpha}{\sin 4\alpha\cos 4\alpha}\right) - 8\cot 8\alpha$$

$$= 4\times 2\frac{\cos 8\alpha}{\sin 8\alpha} - 8\cot 8\alpha = 8\cot 8\alpha - 8\cot 8\alpha = 0$$

This proves the result.

Example 17. *Given that*

$$\tan A + \tan B = p \text{ and } \tan A\tan B = q$$

find $\sin^2(A+B)$ *and* $\cos 2(A+B)$.

Solution. $$\sin^2(A+B) = \frac{1}{\operatorname{cosec}^2(A+B)} = \frac{1}{1+\cot^2(A+B)}$$

$$= \frac{1}{1+\dfrac{1}{\tan^2(A+B)}} = \frac{\tan^2(A+B)}{1+\tan^2(A+B)}$$

$$= \frac{\dfrac{p^2}{(1-q)^2}}{1+\dfrac{p^2}{(1-q)^2}} = \frac{p^2}{p^2+(1-q)^2}$$

and $$\cos 2(A+B) = \cos^2(A+B) - \sin^2(A+B)$$

$$= \frac{\cos^2(A+B) - \sin^2(A+B)}{\cos^2(A+B) + \sin^2(A+B)}$$

$$= \frac{1 - \tan^2(A+B)}{1 + \tan^2(A+B)} = \frac{1 - \dfrac{p^2}{(1-q)^2}}{1 + \dfrac{p^2}{(1-q)^2}}$$

$$= \frac{(1-q)^2 - p^2}{(1-q)^2 + p^2}.$$

Example 18. *If* $\sec^2 A - 2\tan^2 B = 2$, *prove that*

$$2\cos 2A - \cos 2B + 1 = 0.$$

Solution. $\sec^2 A - 2\tan^2 B = 2$

$$\Rightarrow \quad \frac{1}{\cos^2 A} - \frac{2\sin^2 B}{\cos^2 B} = 2$$

$$\Rightarrow \quad \cos^2 B - 2\sin^2 B\cos^2 A = 2\cos^2 A\cos^2 B$$

$$\Rightarrow \quad \cos^2 B = 2\cos^2 A(\cos^2 B + \sin^2 B) = 2\cos^2 A$$

Now $2\cos 2A - \cos 2B + 1$

$$= 2(2\cos^2 A - 1) - (2\cos^2 B - 1) + 1$$

$$= 2(\cos^2 B - 1) - (2\cos^2 B - 1) + 1$$

$$= 2\cos^2 B - 2 - 2\cos^2 B + 1 + 1$$

$$= 0.$$

This proves the result.

Example 19. *Given that*

$$\cos 45° = \frac{1}{\sqrt{2}} \text{ show that}$$

$$\sin\left(292\frac{1}{2}\right)^\circ = -\frac{1}{2}\sqrt{2+\sqrt{2}}.$$

Solution. $\sin\left(292\frac{1}{2}\right)^\circ = \sin\left(270° + 22\frac{1}{2}^\circ\right) = -\cos 22\frac{1}{2}^\circ$

Now $$\cos 45° = 2\cos^2\left(22\frac{1}{2}\right)^\circ - 1$$

$$\Rightarrow \quad \frac{1}{\sqrt{2}} = 2\cos^2\left(22\frac{1}{2}\right)^\circ - 1$$

$$\Rightarrow \quad 2\cos^2\left(22\frac{1}{2}\right)^\circ = 1 + \frac{1}{\sqrt{2}} = \frac{\sqrt{2}+1}{\sqrt{2}}$$

$$\Rightarrow \quad \cos\left(22\frac{1}{2}\right)^\circ = \sqrt{\frac{\sqrt{2}+1}{2\sqrt{2}}} = \frac{1}{2}\sqrt{2+\sqrt{2}}$$

$$\Rightarrow \quad \sin\left(292\frac{1}{2}\right)^\circ = -\frac{1}{2}\sqrt{2+\sqrt{2}}.$$

This proves the result.

Example 20. *ABC is an acute-angled triangle inscribed in a circle of centre O and radius OA (= 10 cm). If* $\cos \angle BOC = \frac{4}{5}$, *calculate*

(*i*) *sin* $\angle BAC$

(*ii*) *the length of BC*

(*iii*) *cos* $\angle OBC$

Solution.

(*i*) $\qquad 2\angle BAC = \angle BOC$

$$\Rightarrow \quad \cos 2\angle BAC = \cos \angle BOC = \frac{4}{5}$$

$$\Rightarrow 2\cos^2 \angle BAC - 1 = \frac{4}{5}$$

$$\Rightarrow \quad 2\cos^2 \angle BAC = \frac{9}{5}$$

$$\Rightarrow \quad \cos^2 \angle BAC = \frac{9}{10}$$

$$\Rightarrow \quad \sin^2\angle BAC = 1 - \frac{9}{10} = \frac{1}{10}$$

$$\Rightarrow \quad \sin \angle BAC = \frac{1}{\sqrt{10}}$$

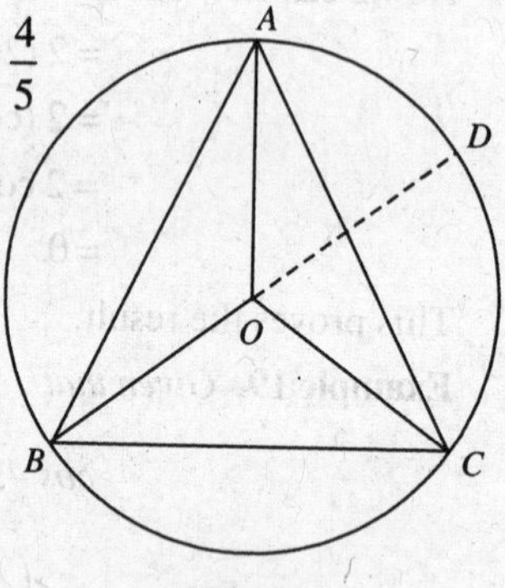

Fig. 3

(as BAC is acute angle).

(*ii*) Produce BO to meet the circle at D.

Then BCD is a right angle (angle in a semi- circle). Also $\angle BDC = \angle BAC$ (angles in same segment).

So, $\sin \angle BDC = \dfrac{BC}{BD} = \dfrac{BC}{20}$

$\Rightarrow \sin \angle BAC = \dfrac{BC}{20}$

$\Rightarrow \dfrac{1}{\sqrt{10}} = \dfrac{BC}{20} \Rightarrow BC = 2\sqrt{10}$.

(*iii*) $\cos \angle OBC = \cos (90° - \angle BDC) = \cos (90° - \angle BAC$

$= \sin \angle BAC = \dfrac{1}{\sqrt{10}}$.

Example 21. *If tan A tan 2A ≠ – 1 prove that*
tan 3A tan 2A tan A = tan 3A – tan 2A – tan A.

Solution. Now $\tan 3A \tan 2A \tan A - \tan 3A$

$$= \tan 3A (\tan 2A \tan A - 1)$$
$$= \tan (2A + A) (\tan 2A \tan A - 1)$$
$$= \frac{\tan 2A + \tan A}{1 - \tan A \tan 2A} (\tan A \tan 2A - 1)$$
$$= -(\tan 2A + \tan A).$$

This proves the result.

Example 22. *Prove that* $\cot 22\frac{1}{2}^\circ - \tan 22\frac{1}{2}^\circ = 2$

Solution. LHS $= \cot 22\frac{1}{2}^\circ - \tan 22\frac{1}{2}^\circ$

$$= \frac{\cos^2\left(22\frac{1}{2}\right)^\circ - \sin^2\left(22\frac{1}{2}\right)^\circ}{\sin 22\frac{1}{2}^\circ \cos 22\frac{1}{2}^\circ}$$

$$= \frac{2\cos 45°}{2\sin 22\frac{1}{2}^\circ \cos 22\frac{1}{2}^\circ} = \frac{2\cos 45°}{\sin 45°}$$

$$= 2\cot 45° = 2 = \text{RHS}.$$

Example 23. *Prove that*

$$\frac{1 + \sin A - \cos A}{1 + \sin A + \cos A} = \tan\frac{A}{2}.$$

Solution. $$\text{LHS} = \frac{(1-\cos A)+\sin A}{(1+\cos A)+\sin A}$$

$$= \frac{2\sin^2\frac{A}{2} + 2\sin\frac{A}{2}\cos\frac{A}{2}}{2\cos^2\frac{A}{2} + 2\sin\frac{A}{2}\cos\frac{A}{2}}$$

$$= \frac{2\sin\frac{A}{2}\left(\sin\frac{A}{2}+\cos\frac{A}{2}\right)}{2\cos\frac{A}{2}\left(\sin\frac{A}{2}+\cos\frac{A}{2}\right)} = \tan\frac{A}{2}.$$

Example 24. *If* $\tan x = \dfrac{1-\cos y}{\sin y}$ *then prove that one of the solutions will be* $y = 2x$. *Use this result to prove that* $\tan 7\frac{1}{2}^\circ = \sqrt{6}-\sqrt{3}+\sqrt{2}-2$.

Solution. Now $\dfrac{1-\cos y}{\sin y} = \dfrac{1-\cos 2x}{\sin 2x} = \dfrac{2\sin^2 x}{2\sin x\cos x} = \tan x$

$\Rightarrow y = 2x$ is one of the solution.

Thus $$\tan 7\frac{1}{2}^\circ = \frac{1-\cos 15^\circ}{\sin 15^\circ}$$

But $$\cos 15^\circ = \cos(45-30) = \frac{\sqrt{3}}{2}\frac{1}{\sqrt{2}} + \frac{1}{\sqrt{2}}\frac{1}{2} = \frac{\sqrt{3}+1}{2\sqrt{2}}$$

and $$\sin 15^\circ = \sin(45-30) = \frac{1}{\sqrt{2}}\frac{\sqrt{3}}{2} - \frac{1}{2}\frac{1}{\sqrt{2}} = \frac{\sqrt{3}-1}{2\sqrt{2}}$$

$$\Rightarrow \quad \tan 7\frac{1}{2}^\circ = \frac{1-\frac{\sqrt{3}+1}{2\sqrt{2}}}{\frac{\sqrt{3}-1}{2\sqrt{2}}} = \frac{2\sqrt{2}-\sqrt{3}-1}{\sqrt{3}-1}$$

$$= \frac{(2\sqrt{2}-\sqrt{3}-1)(\sqrt{3}+1)}{2}$$

$$= \frac{2\sqrt{6}-2\sqrt{3}+2\sqrt{2}-4}{2} = \sqrt{6}-\sqrt{3}+\sqrt{2}-2.$$

Example 25. *Prove that*

$$\left(1+\cos\frac{\pi}{8}\right)\left(1+\cos\frac{3\pi}{8}\right)\left(1+\cos\frac{5\pi}{8}\right)\left(1+\cos\frac{7\pi}{8}\right)=\frac{1}{8}.$$

Solution. Now $\cos\frac{3\pi}{8}=\cos\left(\frac{\pi}{2}-\frac{\pi}{8}\right)=-\sin\frac{\pi}{8}$

$$\cos\frac{5\pi}{8}=\cos\left(\frac{\pi}{2}+\frac{\pi}{8}\right)=-\sin\frac{\pi}{8}$$

$$\cos\frac{7\pi}{8}=\cos\left(\pi-\frac{\pi}{8}\right)=-\cos\frac{\pi}{8}$$

$$\text{LHS}=\left(1+\cos\frac{\pi}{8}\right)\left(1+\sin\frac{\pi}{8}\right)\left(1-\sin\frac{\pi}{8}\right)\left(1-\cos\frac{\pi}{8}\right)$$

$$=\left(1-\cos^2\frac{\pi}{8}\right)\left(1-\sin^2\frac{\pi}{8}\right)$$

$$=\sin^2\frac{\pi}{8}\cos^2\frac{\pi}{8}$$

$$=\frac{1}{4}\left(2\sin\frac{\pi}{8}\cos\frac{\pi}{8}\right)^2=\frac{1}{4}\left(\sin\frac{\pi}{4}\right)^2$$

$$=\frac{1}{4}\left[\frac{1}{\sqrt{2}}\right]^2=\frac{1}{8}=\text{RHS}.$$

Example 26. *Prove that*

$$\text{cosec}^6\alpha-\cot^6\alpha=3\,\text{cosec}^2\alpha\cot^2\alpha+1.$$

Solution. $\text{LHS}=\text{cosec}^6\alpha-\cot^6\alpha$

$$=(\text{cosec}^2\alpha-\cot^2\alpha)(\text{cosec}^4\alpha+\text{cosec}^2\alpha\cot^2\alpha+\cot^4\alpha)$$

$$=(\text{cosec}^4\alpha+\text{cosec}^2\alpha\cot^2\alpha+\cot^4\alpha)$$

$$=(\text{cosec}^2\alpha-\cot^2\alpha)^2+3\,\text{cosec}^2\alpha\cot^2\alpha$$

$$=1+3\,\text{cosec}^2\alpha\cot^2\alpha.$$

Example 27. *If $A = 580°$, prove that*

$$2\sin\frac{A}{2}=-\sqrt{1+\sin A}-\sqrt{1-\sin A}.$$

Solution. $A=580°\Rightarrow\frac{A}{2}=290°$

Now $\sin\frac{A}{2} + \cos\frac{A}{2} = \sin 290° + \cos 290°$

$= \sin(270° + 20°) + \cos(270° + 20°)$

$= -\cos 20° + \sin 20° = -\text{ve}$ (as $\cos 20° > \sin 20°$)

Again $\sin\frac{A}{2} - \cos\frac{A}{2} = -\cos 20° - \sin 20° = -\text{ve}$

Now $\left[\sin\frac{A}{2} + \cos\frac{A}{2}\right]^2 = 1 + \sin A \Rightarrow \sin\frac{A}{2} + \cos\frac{A}{2} = -\sqrt{1 + \sin A}$

Similarly $\left[\sin\frac{A}{2} - \cos\frac{A}{2}\right] = -\sqrt{1 - \sin A}$

Therefore $2\sin\frac{A}{2} = -\sqrt{1 + \sin A} - \sqrt{1 - \sin A}$

This proves the result.

Example 28. *Prove that* $\dfrac{\cos A + \sin A}{\sqrt{1 + \sin 2A}} = 1.$

Solution. LHS $= \dfrac{\cos A + \sin A}{\sqrt{1 + \sin 2A}}$

$$= \frac{\cos A + \sin A}{\sqrt{\cos^2 A + \sin^2 A + 2\sin A\cos A}}$$

$$= \frac{\cos A + \sin A}{\sqrt{(\cos A + \sin A)^2}} = \frac{\cos A + \sin A}{\cos A + \sin A} = 1.$$

Example 29. *$\tan A \tan(60° + A) \tan(120° + A) = -\tan 3A$.*

Solution. LHS $= \tan A \tan(60° + A) \tan(120° + A)$

$$= \tan A\left(\frac{\tan 60° + \tan A}{1 - \tan A\tan 60°}\right)\left(\frac{\tan 120° + \tan A}{1 - \tan A\tan 120°}\right)$$

$$= \tan A\left(\frac{\sqrt{3} + \tan A}{1 - \sqrt{3}\tan A}\right)\left(\frac{-\sqrt{3} + \tan A}{1 + \sqrt{3}\tan A}\right)$$

$$= \tan A\left(\frac{\tan^2 A - 3}{1 - 3\tan^2 A}\right) = \frac{\tan^3 A - 3\tan A}{1 - 3\tan^2 A}$$

$$= -\left(\frac{3\tan A - \tan^3 A}{1 - 3\tan^2 A}\right) = -\tan 3A.$$

Example 30. *Express $\sqrt{3}\cos\theta + \sin\theta$ as cosine of an angle. Hence find their greatest and least values.*

Solution. $\sqrt{3}\cos\theta + \sin\theta$

$$= 2\left(\frac{\sqrt{3}}{2}\cos\theta + \frac{1}{2}\sin\theta\right)$$

$$= 2\left(\cos\frac{\pi}{6}\cos\theta + \sin\frac{\pi}{6}\sin\theta\right) = 2\cos\left(\theta - \frac{\pi}{6}\right).$$

Since the greatest value of $\cos\alpha = 1$ and least value is -1, the greatest and least values of $\sqrt{3}\cos\theta + \sin\theta$ are 2 and -2 respectively.

Example 31. *If $A + B = \frac{\pi}{4}$, prove that $(1 + \tan A)(1 + \tan B) = 2$.*

Solution. $\text{LHS} = (1 + \tan A)(1 + \tan B)$

$$= 1 + \tan A + \tan B + \tan A \tan B$$

Now $\tan(A + B) = \tan\frac{\pi}{4}$

$$\Rightarrow \frac{\tan A + \tan B}{1 - \tan A \tan B} = 1$$

$$\Rightarrow \tan A + \tan B = 1 - \tan A \tan B$$

Therefore, $\text{LHS} = 1 + 1 - \tan A \tan B + \tan A \tan B = 2 = \text{RHS}.$

Example 32. *Prove that*

$$\frac{1 - \sin 36^\circ + \cos 36^\circ}{1 + \sin 36^\circ + \cos 36^\circ} = \frac{3\tan 9^\circ - \tan^3 9^\circ}{1 - 3\tan^2 9^\circ}.$$

Solution. $\text{LHS} = \dfrac{(2\cos^2 18^\circ) - \sin 36^\circ}{(2\cos^2 18^\circ) + \sin 36^\circ}$

$$= \frac{2\cos^2 18^\circ - 2\sin 18^\circ \cos 18^\circ}{2\cos^2 18^\circ + 2\sin 18^\circ \cos 18^\circ}$$

$$= \frac{2\cos 18^\circ(\cos 18^\circ - \sin 18^\circ)}{2\cos 18^\circ(\cos 18^\circ + \sin 18^\circ)}$$

$$= \frac{1 - \tan 18^\circ}{1 + \tan 18^\circ} = \tan\left(\frac{\pi}{4} - 18^\circ\right)$$

$$= \tan(45^\circ - 18^\circ) = \tan(27^\circ)$$

$\text{RHS} = \tan 3(9^\circ) = \tan 27^\circ.$

Thus $\text{LHS} = \text{RHS}.$

Example 33. *Prove that*

$$\cos^4\frac{\pi}{8}+\cos^4\frac{3\pi}{8}+\cos^4\frac{5\pi}{8}+\cos^4\frac{7\pi}{8}=\frac{3}{2}.$$

Solution.

$$\text{LHS}=\cos^4 22\frac{1}{2}^\circ+\cos^4 67\frac{1}{2}^\circ+\cos^4 112\frac{1}{2}^\circ+\cos^4 157\frac{1}{2}^\circ$$

$$=\left(\frac{1+\cos 45^\circ}{2}\right)^2+\left(\frac{1+\cos 135^\circ}{2}\right)^2+\left(\frac{1+\cos 225^\circ}{2}\right)^2+\left(\frac{1+\cos 315^\circ}{2}\right)^2$$

$$=\left(\frac{1+\frac{1}{\sqrt{2}}}{2}\right)^2+\left(\frac{1-\frac{1}{\sqrt{2}}}{2}\right)^2+\left(\frac{1-\frac{1}{\sqrt{2}}}{2}\right)^2+\left(\frac{1+\frac{1}{\sqrt{2}}}{2}\right)^2$$

$$=\frac{1+\frac{1}{2}+\sqrt{2}+1+\frac{1}{2}-\sqrt{2}}{2}=\frac{3}{2}=\text{RHS}.$$

Example 34. *Prove that* $\sin\theta\tan\theta$ *is greater than* $2(1-\cos\theta)$*, if* θ *is an acute angle. Indicate the step where you have used the fact that* θ *should be an acute angle.*

Solution. Now $\sin\theta\tan\theta-2(1-\cos\theta)$

$$=\frac{2\tan\frac{\theta}{2}}{1+\tan^2\frac{\theta}{2}}\,\frac{2\tan\frac{\theta}{2}}{1-\tan^2\frac{\theta}{2}}-2\left(2\sin^2\frac{\theta}{2}\right)$$

$$\left(\text{because }\sin\theta=2\sin\frac{\theta}{2}\cos\frac{\theta}{2}=\frac{2\sin\frac{\theta}{2}\cos\frac{\theta}{2}}{\sin^2\frac{\theta}{2}+\cos^2\frac{\theta}{2}}=\frac{2\tan\frac{\theta}{2}}{1+\tan^2\frac{\theta}{2}}\right)$$

$$=\frac{4\tan^2\frac{\theta}{2}}{\sec^2\frac{\theta}{2}}\,\frac{1}{1-\tan^2\frac{\theta}{2}}-4\sin^2\frac{\theta}{2}$$

$$=4\left[\frac{\sin^2\frac{\theta}{2}-\cos^2\frac{\theta}{2}}{\cos^2\frac{\theta}{2}-\sin^2\frac{\theta}{2}}-\sin^2\frac{\theta}{2}\right]$$

$$= 4\sin^2\frac{\theta}{2}\left[\frac{\cos^2\frac{\theta}{2}}{\cos^2\frac{\theta}{2}-\sin^2\frac{\theta}{2}}-1\right]$$

$$= 4\sin^2\frac{\theta}{2}\left[\frac{\sin^2\frac{\theta}{2}}{\cos^2\frac{\theta}{2}-\sin^2\frac{\theta}{2}}\right]$$

$$= 4\sin^2\frac{\theta}{2}\left[\frac{\sin^2\frac{\theta}{2}}{\cos\theta}\right] \geq 0 \qquad \text{[since } \theta \text{ is acute angle, } \cos\theta > 0]$$

$$\Rightarrow \sin\theta\tan\theta > 2(1-\cos\theta).$$

EXERCISES

1. Find the values of (*i*) $\sin 36°$ and $\cos 36°$, (*ii*) $\sin 15°$ and $\cos 15°$.

2. If $\sin A = \frac{1}{\sqrt{10}}$, $\sin B = \frac{1}{\sqrt{5}}$, show that $A + B = 45°$.

3. Prove that $\tan A + \tan B = \frac{\sin(A+B)}{\cos A\cos B}$.

4. If $\tan\theta = \frac{a}{b}$, $\tan\phi = \frac{c}{d}$ prove that $\tan(\theta+\phi) = \frac{ad+dc}{bd-ac}$.

5. Prove that $\cos(A+B) + \sin(A-B) = 2\sin\left(\frac{\pi}{4}+A\right)\cos\left(\frac{\pi}{4}+B\right)$.

6. Express $\cos\theta - \sin\theta$ as sine or cosine of an angle and find the greatest and least values of $(\cos\theta - \sin\theta)$.

7. If $A + B = \frac{\pi}{4}$, prove that $(\cot A - 1)(\cot B - 1) = 2$.

8. Prove that $\frac{\sec 8A - 1}{\sec 4A - 1} = \frac{\tan 8A}{\tan 2A}$.

9. If $2\tan\alpha = 3\tan\beta$, show that $\tan(\alpha-\beta) = \frac{\sin 2\beta}{5-\cos 2\beta}$

10. If $\cos\alpha = \frac{3}{5}$ and $\cos\beta = \frac{5}{13}$, find the values of $\sin^2\frac{(\alpha-\beta)}{2}$ and $\cos^2\left(\frac{\alpha-\beta}{2}\right)$.

11. Prove that

    (*i*) $\cos 5\theta = 16\cos^5\theta - 20\cos^3\theta + 5\cos\theta$

    (*ii*) $\cos 4\theta = 1 - 8\cos^2\theta + 8\cos^4\theta$.

12. Prove that $\tan(60° + A) + \tan(120° + A) + \tan A = 3\tan^3 A$.

13. Prove that $\dfrac{1+\sin 2\theta}{1-\sin 2\theta} = \tan^2\left(\dfrac{\pi}{4}+\theta\right)$.

14. Prove that $\dfrac{\sin 16A\cos 2A - \cos 6A\sin 12A}{\cos 4A\cos^2 A - \sin 6A\sin 8A} = \tan 4A$.

15. If $\sin\theta = \dfrac{5}{13}$ and θ lies in third quadrant, prove that the value of $2\cos\dfrac{\theta}{2} - 3\sin\dfrac{\theta}{2}$ $= -\dfrac{17}{\sqrt{26}}$

16. Prove that

(*i*) $\cot 7\dfrac{1}{2}° = \dfrac{1+\cos 15°}{\sin 15°}$

(*ii*) $\tan 7\dfrac{1}{2}° = \dfrac{1-\cos 15°}{\sin 15°}$.

17. Prove that $\cot 7\dfrac{1}{2}° = \sqrt{2}+\sqrt{3}+\sqrt{4}+\sqrt{6}$.

18. Prove that $\cos^3\left(A-\dfrac{2\pi}{3}\right)+\cos^3 A+\cos^3\left(A+\dfrac{2\pi}{3}\right)=\dfrac{3}{4}\cos^3 A$.

19. Prove that $\dfrac{\cos^3 x - \cos^3 x}{\cos x} + \dfrac{\sin^3 x + \sin^3 x}{\sin x} = 3$.

20. Prove that $\dfrac{1-\cos A+\cos B+\cos C}{1-\cos C+\cos A+\cos B} = \dfrac{\tan\dfrac{A}{2}}{\tan\dfrac{B}{2}}$ if $A + B + C = 180°$.

21. Prove that $\sin 3A + \sin 2A - \sin A = 4\sin A\cos\dfrac{A}{2}\cos\dfrac{3A}{2}$.

22. Prove that $16\cos\dfrac{2\pi}{15}\cos\dfrac{4\pi}{15}\cos\dfrac{8\pi}{15}\cos\dfrac{14\pi}{15}=1$.

23. Prove that $\sin 3A = 4\sin A\sin(60° + A)\sin(60° - A)$.

24. Prove that $\dfrac{1+\sin^2\theta-\cos^2\theta}{1+\sin^2\theta+\cos^2\theta} = \tan\theta$.

ANSWERS

1. (*i*) $\dfrac{\sqrt{5}+1}{4}, \dfrac{\sqrt{10-2\sqrt{5}}}{4}$ (*ii*) $\dfrac{\sqrt{3}-1}{2\sqrt{2}}, \dfrac{\sqrt{2+\sqrt{3}}}{2}$

9. $\sqrt{2}, -\sqrt{2}$

10. $\dfrac{1}{65}, \dfrac{64}{65}$

4. TRANSFORMATION OF PRODUCTS INTO SUMS OR DIFFERENCES

We know that

$$\sin A \cos B + \sin B \cos A = \sin (A + B) \quad ...(1)$$

and $$\sin A \cos B - \sin B \cos A = \sin (A - B) \quad ...(2)$$

Adding (1) and (2), we get

$$2 \sin A \cos B = \sin (A + B) + \sin (A - B)$$

subtracting (1) and (2), we get

$$2 \cos A \sin B = \sin (A + B) - \sin (A - B)$$

Again,

$$\cos A \cos B + \sin A \sin B = \cos (A - B) \quad ...(3)$$

$$\cos A \cos B - \sin A \sin B = \cos (A + B) \quad ...(4)$$

Adding (3) and (4), we'll have

$$2 \cos A \cos B = \cos (A - B) + \cos (A + B)$$

and subtracting (3) and (4), we'll have

$$2 \sin A \sin B = \cos (A - B) - \cos (A + B)$$

Thus, we have the following formulas

(1) $2 \sin A \cos B = \sin (A + B) + \sin (A - B)$

(2) $2 \cos A \sin B = \sin (A + B) - \sin (A - B)$

(3) $2 \cos A \cos B = \cos (A + B) + \cos (A - B)$

(4) $2 \sin A \sin B = \cos (A - B) - \cos (A + B)$

5. TRANSFORMATION OF SUMS OR DIFFERENCES INTO PRODUCTS TO PROVE THAT FOR ALL ANGLES C AND D,

(i) $\sin C + \sin D = 2 \sin \frac{C + D}{2} \cos \frac{C - D}{2}$

(ii) $\sin C - \sin D = 2 \cos \frac{C + D}{2} \sin \frac{C - D}{2}$

(iii) $\cos C + \cos D = 2 \cos \frac{C + D}{2} \cos \frac{C - D}{2}$

(iv) $\cos C - \cos D = 2 \sin \frac{C + D}{2} \sin \frac{D - C}{2}$

Proof. We know that for all values of A and B

$$\sin (A + B) = \sin A \cos B + \cos A \sin B$$

$$\sin (A - B) = \sin A \cos B - \cos A \sin B$$

By addition and subtraction, we have

$$\sin(A+B)+\sin(A-B)=2\sin A\cos B$$

$$\sin(A+B)-\sin(A-B)=2\sin A\cos B.$$

Put $A+B=C$ and $A-B=D$

we get $A=\dfrac{C+D}{2},\quad B=\dfrac{C-D}{2}.$

Then $\sin C+\sin D=2\sin\dfrac{C+D}{2}\cos\dfrac{C-D}{2}$

$$\sin C-\sin D=2\cos\frac{C+D}{2}\sin\frac{C-D}{2}.$$

Similarly, by adding and subtracting the relations

$$\cos(A+B)=\cos A\cos B-\sin A\sin B$$

$$\cos(A-B)=\cos A\cos B+\sin A\sin B.$$

we have

$$\cos(A+B)+\cos(A-B)=2\cos A\cos B$$

$$\cos(A+B)-\cos(A-B)=-2\sin A\sin B.$$

Put $A+B=C,\quad A-B=D$

so that $A=\dfrac{C+D}{2},\quad B=\dfrac{C-D}{2}.$

Hence $\cos C+\cos D=2\cos\dfrac{C+D}{2}\cos\dfrac{C-D}{2}$

$$\cos C-\cos D=-2\sin\frac{C+D}{2}\sin\frac{C-D}{2}$$

$$=2\sin\frac{C+D}{2}\sin\frac{D-C}{2}.$$

[NOTE. It should be noted carefully that the second factor on RHS of equation (*iv*) is $\sin\dfrac{D-C}{2}$ and not $\sin\dfrac{C-D}{2}$].

6. TO PROVE THAT

(i) $\sin(A+B)\sin(A-B)=\sin^2 A-\sin^2 B$

(ii) $\cos(A+B)\cos(A-B)=\cos^2 A-\sin^2 B=\cos^2 B-\sin^2 A$

Proof. (*i*) $\sin(A+B)\sin(A-B)$

$$=(\sin A\cos B+\cos A\sin B)(\sin A\cos B-\cos A\sin B)$$

$$=\sin^2 A\cos^2 B-\cos^2 A\sin^2 B$$

$= \sin^2 A\,(1 - \sin^2 B) - (1 - \sin^2 A)\sin^2 B$
$= \sin^2 A - \sin^2 A \sin^2 B - \sin^2 B + \sin^2 A \sin^2 B$
$= \sin^2 A - \sin^2 B.$

(*i*) $\cos(A + B)\cos(A - B)$.
$= (\cos A \cos B - \sin A \sin B)(\cos A \cos B + \sin A \sin B)$
$= \cos^2 A \cos^2 B - \sin^2 A \sin^2 B$
$= \cos^2 A\,(1 - \sin^2 B) - (1 - \cos^2 A)\sin^2 B$
$= \cos^2 A - \cos^2 A \sin^2 B - \sin^2 B + \cos^2 A \sin^2 B$
$= \cos^2 A - \sin^2 B$
$= (1 - \sin^2 A) - (1 - \cos^2 B)$
$= \cos^2 B - \sin^2 A$

Example 35. *If the angles A, B, C, of a triangle are in A.P, show that*

$$\frac{\cos C - \cos A}{\sin A - \sin C} = \tan B.$$

Solution. LHS $= \dfrac{-\cos(A + B) - \cos A}{\sin A - \sin(A + B)}$

$$= \frac{-2\cos\left(A + \frac{B}{2}\right)\cos\frac{B}{2}}{-2\cos\left(A + \frac{B}{2}\right)\sin\frac{B}{2}}$$

$$= \cot\frac{B}{2} = \cot\left(\frac{\pi}{2} - \left[\frac{A + C}{2}\right]\right)$$

$$= \tan\left[\frac{A + C}{2}\right] = \tan B$$

$$\left(\text{as } A, B, C \text{ are in A.P.} \Rightarrow \frac{A + C}{2} = B\right)$$

Example 36. *Prove that*

$$\frac{\sin^2 A - \sin^2 B}{\sin A \cos A - \sin B \cos B} = \tan(A + B).$$

Solution. LHS $= \dfrac{2\sin(A + B)\sin(A - B)}{\sin^2 A - \sin^2 B}$

$$= \frac{2\sin(A + B)\sin(A - B)}{2\cos(A + B)\sin(A - B)} = \tan(A + B) = \text{RHS}.$$

Example 37. *Prove that* $4(\cos^3 10^\circ + \sin^3 20^\circ) = 3(\cos 10^\circ + \sin 20^\circ)$.

Solution.

$$\begin{aligned}\text{LHS} &= 4(\cos 10^\circ + \sin 20^\circ)(\cos^2 10^\circ + \sin^2 20^\circ + \cos 10^\circ \sin 20^\circ)\\ &= 4(\cos 10^\circ + \sin 20^\circ)(1 - \sin^2 10^\circ + \sin^2 20^\circ + \cos 10^\circ \sin 20^\circ)\\ &= 4(\cos 10^\circ + \sin 20^\circ)(1 + \sin 30^\circ \sin 10^\circ - \cos 10^\circ \sin 20^\circ)\\ &= 4(\cos 10^\circ + \sin 20^\circ)\left[1 + \frac{\sin 10^\circ}{2} - \frac{(\sin 30^\circ + \sin 10^\circ)}{2}\right].\\ &= 2(\cos 10^\circ + \sin 20^\circ)\left[2 + \sin 10^\circ - \frac{1}{2} - \sin 10^\circ\right]\\ &= 2(\cos 10^\circ + \sin 20^\circ)\left[\frac{3}{2}\right]\\ &= 3(\cos 10^\circ + \sin 20^\circ) = \text{RHS}.\end{aligned}$$

Example 38. *Given* $x = \cos 55^\circ$, $y = \cos 65^\circ$, $z = \cos 175^\circ$ *prove that*

$$x + y + z = 0 \text{ and } xy + yz + zx = -\frac{3}{4}.$$

Solution.

$$\begin{aligned}x + y + z &= \cos 55^\circ + \cos 65^\circ + \cos 175^\circ\\ &= 2\cos 60^\circ \cos 5^\circ + \cos(180^\circ - 5^\circ)\\ &= \cos 5^\circ - \cos 5^\circ = 0.\end{aligned}$$

$$\begin{aligned}xy + yz + zx &= \cos 55^\circ \cos 65^\circ + \cos 65^\circ \cos 175^\circ + \cos 175^\circ \cos 55^\circ\\ &= \frac{1}{2}(\cos 120^\circ + \cos 10^\circ) + \frac{1}{2}(\cos 240^\circ + \cos 110^\circ) + \frac{1}{2}(\cos 230^\circ + \cos 120^\circ)\\ &= -\frac{1}{4} + \frac{1}{2}\cos 10^\circ - \frac{1}{4} + \frac{1}{2}\cos 110^\circ + \frac{1}{2}\cos 230^\circ - \frac{1}{4}\end{aligned}$$

$$= -\frac{3}{4} + \frac{1}{2}\,[\cos 10° + \cos 110° + \cos 230°]$$

$$= -\frac{3}{4} + \frac{1}{2}\,[2\cos 60° \cos 50° - \cos 50°]$$

$$= -\frac{3}{4} + \frac{1}{2}\,[\cos 50° - \cos 50°] = -\frac{3}{4}.$$

Example 39. *Prove that*

$$\sin^2 B = \sin^2 A + \sin^2 (A - B) - 2\sin A \cos B \sin (A - B).$$

Solution. RHS $= \sin^2 A + \sin^2 (A - B) - (2\sin A \cos B)\sin (A - B)$

$$= \sin^2 A + \sin^2 (A - B) - [\sin (A + B) + \sin (A - B)] - \sin (A - B)$$

$$= \sin^2 A + \sin^2 (A - B) - \sin (A + B) \sin (A - B) \sin^2 (A - B)$$

$$= \sin^2 A - \sin (A + B) \sin (A - B)$$

$$= \sin^2 A - (\sin^2 A - \sin^2 B)$$

$$= \sin^2 B = \text{LHS}.$$

Example 40. *If* $y \sin \alpha = x \sin (2\beta + \alpha)$ *show that* $(x + y) \cot (\alpha + \beta) = (y - x) \cot \beta$.

Solution. $y \sin \alpha = x \sin (2\beta + \alpha)$

$$\Rightarrow \frac{y}{x} = \frac{\sin (2\beta + \alpha)}{\sin \alpha} \Rightarrow \frac{y + x}{y - x} = \frac{\sin (2\beta + \alpha) + \sin \alpha}{\sin (2\beta + \alpha) - \sin \alpha}$$

$$\Rightarrow \frac{y + x}{y - x} = \frac{2\sin (\alpha + \beta) \cos \beta}{2\cos (\alpha + \beta) \sin \beta} \Rightarrow \frac{y + x}{y - x} = \tan (\alpha + \beta) \cot \beta$$

$$\Rightarrow (y + x) \cot (\alpha + \beta) = (y - x) \cot \beta$$

This proves the result.

Example 41. *Prove that*

$$\left[\frac{\cos A + \cos B}{\sin A - \sin B}\right]^n + \left[\frac{\sin A + \sin B}{\cos A - \cos B}\right]^n$$

$$= 2\cot^n \left[\frac{A - B}{2}\right] \textit{ or 0 according as n is even or odd.}$$

Solution. $\left[\dfrac{\cos A + \cos B}{\sin A - \sin B}\right]^n + \left[\dfrac{\sin A + \sin B}{\cos A - \cos B}\right]^n$

$$= \left[\frac{2\cos\frac{A+B}{2}\cos\frac{A-B}{2}}{2\sin\frac{A-B}{2}\cos\frac{A+B}{2}}\right]^n + \left[\frac{2\sin\frac{A+B}{2}\cos\frac{A-B}{2}}{2\sin\frac{A+B}{2}\sin\frac{B+A}{2}}\right]^n$$

$$= \left[\cot\frac{(A-B)}{2}\right]^n + \left[-\cot\frac{(A-B)}{2}\right]^n$$

So, LHS = $2\cot^n\left[\frac{A-B}{2}\right]$ if n is even and is 0 is n is odd.

Example 42. *If $\sin x + \sin y = a$ and $\cos x + \cos y = b$ show that*

$$\cos(x+y) = \frac{b^2 - a^2}{b^2 + a^2}$$

Solution. Now $\sin x + \sin y = a$

$$\Rightarrow \quad 2\sin\frac{x+y}{2}\cos\frac{x-y}{2} = a$$

and $\cos x + \cos y = b$

$$\Rightarrow \quad 2\cos\frac{x+y}{2}\cos\frac{x-y}{2} = b$$

Therefore, $\tan\left[\frac{x+y}{2}\right] = \frac{a}{b}$

Now $\cos(x+y) = \dfrac{1-\tan^2\left[\frac{x+y}{2}\right]}{1+\tan^2\left[\frac{x+y}{2}\right]} = \dfrac{1-\frac{a^2}{b^2}}{1+\frac{a^2}{b^2}} = \dfrac{b^2-a^2}{b^2+a^2}.$

Example 43. *Prove that in a triangle ABC*

$$\frac{\sin(A-B)}{\sin A\sin B} + \frac{\sin(B-C)}{\sin B\sin C} + \frac{\sin(C-A)}{\sin C\sin A} = 0.$$

Solution. LHS

$$= \frac{\sin C\sin(A-B) + \sin A\sin(B-C) + \sin B\sin(C-A)}{\sin A\sin B\sin C}$$

$$= \frac{\sin(A+B)\sin(A-B)\sin(B+C)\sin(B-C) + \sin(C+A)\sin(C-A)}{\sin A\sin B\sin C}$$

(Using $A+B+C=\pi$)

$$= \frac{(\sin^2 A - \sin^2 B) + (\sin^2 B - \sin^2 C) + (\sin^2 C - \sin^2 A)}{\sin A \sin B \sin C}$$

$= 0 = \text{RHS}.$

Example 44. *Prove that* $1 + \cos 56° + \cos 58° - \cos 66°$

$$= 4 \cos 28° \cos 29° \sin 33°$$

Solution. Now $1 - \cos 66° = 2 \sin^2 33°$.

Therefore,

$$\begin{aligned}\text{LHS} &= 2 \sin^2 33° + (\cos 56° + \cos 58°)\\ &= 2 \sin^2 33° + 2 \cos 57° \cos 1°\\ &= 2 \sin^2 33° + 2 \cos (90° - 33°) \cos 1°\\ &= 2 \sin^2 33° + 2 \sin 33° \cos 1°\\ &= 2 \sin 33° (\sin 33° + \cos 1°)\\ &= 2 \sin 33° (\cos 57° + \cos 1°)\\ &= 2 \sin 33° (2 \cos 29° + \cos 28°)\\ &= 4 \cos 28° \cos 29° \sin 33° = \text{RHS}.\end{aligned}$$

Example 45. *Prove that* $\sin^2 12° + \sin^2 21° + \sin^2 39° + \sin^2 48°$

$$= 1 + \sin^2 9° + \sin^2 18°.$$

Solution. Consider $(\sin^2 12° - \sin^2 18°) + (\sin^2 21° - \sin 9°)$

$$\begin{aligned}&= (-\sin 30° \sin 6°) + (\sin 30° \sin 12°)\\ &= \sin 30° (\sin 12° - \sin 6°)\\ &= \frac{1}{2} (2 \sin 3° \cos 9°) = \sin 3° \cos 9°\end{aligned}$$

Also, $1 - \sin^2 39° - \sin^2 48° = \cos^2 39° - \sin^2 48°$

$$= \cos 87° \cos 9° = \sin 3° \cos 9°$$

Therefore $(\sin^2 12° - \sin^2 18°) + (\sin^2 21° - \sin^2 9°)$

$$= 1 - \sin^2 39° - \sin^2 48°.$$

The proves the result.

Example 46. *Prove that* $\cos 10° \cos 50° \cos 70° = \dfrac{\sqrt{3}}{8}$.

Solution. $\text{LHS} = \cos 10° \cos 50° \cos 70°$

$$= \cos 10° \left[\frac{1}{2}(\cos 120° + \cos 20°)\right]$$

$$= \frac{1}{2} \cos 10° \left(-\frac{1}{2} + \cos 20°\right)$$

$$= \frac{1}{2}\cos 10^\circ\left(-\frac{1}{2} + 2\cos^2 10^\circ - 1\right)$$

$$= \frac{1}{2}\cos 10^\circ\left(-\frac{3}{2} + 2\cos^2 10^\circ\right)$$

$$= \frac{1}{4}\cos 10^\circ\,(4\cos^2 10^\circ - 3)$$

$$= \frac{1}{4}(4\cos^3 10^\circ - 3\cos 10^\circ)$$

$$= \frac{1}{4}\cos 3\times 10^\circ = \frac{1}{4}\cos 30^\circ$$

$$= \frac{1}{4}\frac{\sqrt{3}}{2} = \frac{\sqrt{3}}{8} = \text{RHS.}$$

Example 47. *If $A + B + C = \pi$, prove that*

$\tan A + \tan B + \tan C = \tan A \tan B \tan C$.

Solution. $A + B + C = \pi$

$\Rightarrow \quad A + B = \pi - C$

$\Rightarrow \quad \tan(A + B) = -\tan C$

$$\Rightarrow \quad \frac{\tan A + \tan B}{1 - \tan A \tan B} = -\tan C$$

$\Rightarrow \quad \tan A + \tan B + \tan C = \tan A \tan B \tan C$

This proves the result.

Example 48. *If $A + B + C = \pi$, prove that*

$$\sin^2\frac{A}{2} + \sin^2\frac{B}{2} + \sin^2\frac{C}{2} = 1 - 2\sin\frac{A}{2}\sin\frac{B}{2}\sin\frac{C}{2}.$$

Solution. Consider

$$1 - \sin^2\frac{A}{2} - \sin^2\frac{B}{2} - \sin^2\frac{C}{2} = \cos^2\frac{A}{2} - \sin^2\frac{B}{2} - \sin^2\frac{C}{2}$$

$$= \cos\left[\frac{A+B}{2}\right]\cos\left[\frac{A-B}{2}\right] - \sin^2\frac{C}{2}$$

$$= \cos\left[\frac{A+B}{2}\right]\cos\left[\frac{A-B}{2}\right] - \cos^2\left(\frac{A+B}{2}\right)$$

$$\text{as } \frac{C}{2} = \frac{\pi}{2} - \left(\frac{A+B}{2}\right)$$

$$= \cos\left(\frac{A+B}{2}\right)\left[\cos\left(\frac{A-B}{2}\right) - \cos\left(\frac{A+B}{2}\right)\right]$$

$$= \cos\left(\frac{A+B}{2}\right)\left[2\sin\frac{A}{2}\sin\frac{B}{2}\right]$$

$$= 2\sin\frac{A}{2}\sin\frac{B}{2}\sin\frac{C}{2}$$

Hence $\sin^2\frac{A}{2} + \sin^2\frac{B}{2} + \sin^2\frac{C}{2} = 1 - 2\sin\frac{A}{2}\sin\frac{B}{2}\sin\frac{C}{2}$.

Example 49. *If $A + B + C = \pi$, prove that*

$$\cos^2 A + \cos^2 B + \cos^2 C = 1 - 2\cos A\cos B\cos C.$$

Solution. Consider $1 - (\cos^2 A + \cos^2 B + \cos^2 C)$

$$= (1 - \cos^2 A) - \cos^2 B - \cos^2 C$$
$$= \sin^2 A - \cos^2 B - \cos^2 C$$
$$= -\cos(A+B)\cos(A-B) - \cos^2 C$$
$$= -\cos(\pi - C)\cos(A-B) - \cos^2 C$$
$$= \cos C\cos(A-B) - \cos^2 C$$
$$= \cos C[\cos(A-B) - \cos C]$$
$$= \cos C[\cos(A-B) - \cos(\pi - (A+B))]$$
$$= \cos C[\cos(A-B) + \cos(A+B)]$$
$$= \cos C[2\cos A\cos B]$$
$$= 2\cos A\cos B\cos C$$

This proves the result.

Example 50. *If $A + B + C = \pi$, show that*

$$\sin 2A + \sin 2B - \sin 2C = 4\cos A\cos B\sin C.$$

Solution. LHS $= 2\sin(A+B)\cos(A-B) - \sin 2C$

$$= 2\sin C\cos(A-B) - 2\sin C\cos C$$
$$= 2\sin C[\cos(A-B) - \cos C]$$
$$= 2\sin C[\cos(A-B) + \cos(A+B)]$$
$$= 2\sin C[2\cos A\cos B] = 4\cos A\cos B\cos C.$$

Example 51. *In a ΔABC, prove that*

$$\sin 2A + \sin 2B + \sin 2C = 4\sin A\sin B\sin C.$$

Solution.
$$\begin{aligned}
\text{LHS} &= \sin 2A + \sin 2B + \sin 2C \\
&= 2 \sin (A+B) \cos (A-B) + \sin 2C \\
&= 2 \sin (A+B) \cos (A-B) + \sin [2\pi - 2(A+B)] \\
&\qquad\qquad \text{as } A + B + C = \pi \\
&= 2 \sin (A+B) \cos (A-B) - \sin 2(A+B) \\
&= 2 \sin (A+B) [\cos (A-B) - \cos (A+B)] \\
&= 2 \sin (A+B) [2 \sin A \sin B] \\
&= 2 \sin (\pi - C) [2 \sin A \sin B] \\
&= 4 \sin A \sin B \sin C = \text{RHS}.
\end{aligned}$$

EXERCISES

1. If $A + B + C = \pi$, prove that $\dfrac{\cos A}{\sin B \sin C} + \dfrac{\cos B}{\sin C \sin A} + \dfrac{\cos C}{\sin A \sin B} = 2$.
2. If $A + B + C = \pi$, prove that $\cot A \cot B + \cot B \cot C + \cot C \cot A = 1$.
3. If $A + B + C = \pi$, prove that $\cos^2 \dfrac{A}{2} + \cos^2 \dfrac{B}{2} - \cos^2 \dfrac{C}{2} = 2 \cos \dfrac{A}{2} \cos \dfrac{B}{2} \sin \dfrac{C}{2}$.
4. If $\alpha + \beta = \gamma$, show that $\cos^2 \alpha + \cos^2 \beta + \cos^2 \gamma = 1 + 2 \cos \alpha \cos \beta \cos \gamma$.
5. If $\sin x + \sin y = a$

   $\cos x + \cos y = b$

   show that $\sin (x + y) = \dfrac{2ab}{a^2 + b^2}$.
6. If α, β are distinct roots of the equation $a \tan \theta + b \sec \theta = c$, prove that $\tan (\alpha + \beta) = \dfrac{2ac}{a^2 - c^2}$.
7. Prove that $\cos^2 A + \cos^2 \left(A + \dfrac{\pi}{3}\right) + \cos^2 \left(A - \dfrac{\pi}{3}\right) = \dfrac{3}{2}$.
8. Prove that $\tan 2A - \tan A = \dfrac{2 \sin A}{\cos A + \cos 3A}$.
9. If $\theta = \dfrac{\pi}{9}$, prove that $\sec^4 \theta \sec^2 \theta \sec \theta = \operatorname{cosec}^3 \dfrac{\pi}{6}$.
10. Show that an acute angle θ which satisfies the equation $\cos \theta + \sin \theta = \cos 2\theta + \sin 2\theta$ is 30°.
11. If A, B, C are the angles of a triangle prove that

    $$a \sin \frac{A}{2} \sin \left(\frac{B-C}{2}\right) + b \sin \frac{B}{2} \sin \left(\frac{C-A}{2}\right) + c \sin \frac{C}{2} \sin \left(\frac{A-B}{2}\right) = 0.$$

    If $A + B + C = \pi$, prove that,
12. $\cos 2A + \cos 2B + \cos 2C = -1 - 4 \cos A \cos B \cos C$.

13. $\sin A + \sin B + \sin C = 4 \cos\frac{A}{2}\cos\frac{B}{2}\cos\frac{C}{2}$.

14. $\sin^2 A + \sin^2 B + \sin^2 C = 2 + 2 \cos A \cos B \cos C$.

15. $\cos^2\frac{A}{2} + \cos^2\frac{B}{2} - \cos^2\frac{C}{2} = 2\cos\frac{A}{2}\cos\frac{B}{2}\sin\frac{C}{2}$.

16. $\sin (B + C - A) + \sin (C + A - B) + \sin (A + B - C) = 4 \sin A \sin B \sin C$.

17. Prove that $\sin^2 72° - \sin^2 60° = \frac{\sqrt{5}-1}{8}$

18. Find the value of $\tan 22\frac{1}{2}^{\circ}$.

19. Prove that $\sin\frac{\pi}{10} + \sin\frac{13\pi}{10} = -\frac{1}{2}$.

20. If $2 \cos \theta = x + \frac{1}{x}$, show that (i) $2 \cos 2\theta = x^2 + \frac{1}{x^2}$,

(ii) $2 \cos 3\theta = x^3 + \frac{1}{x^3}$.

21. Prove that $\cos 20° \cos 40° \cos 60° \cos 80° = \frac{1}{16}$.

22. Prove that $\sin 20° \sin 40° \sin 60° \sin 80° = \frac{3}{16}$.

23. Prove that $\sin 10° \sin 30° \sin 50° \sin 70° = \frac{1}{16}$.

24. Prove that $\cos 20° \cos 30° \cos 40° \cos 80° = \frac{\sqrt{3}}{16}$.

25. Prove that $\tan 70° - \tan 20° = 2 \tan 50°$.

26. Prove that $\sin 36° \sin 72° \sin 108° \sin 144° = \frac{5}{16}$.

27. Prove that $\sin 10° + \sin 20° + \sin 40° + \sin 50° = \sin 70° + \sin 80°$.

CHAPTER 18

PROPERTIES OF TRIANGLES

1. INTRODUCTION

In this chapter, we shall first study the relation between the sides and angles of a triangle. We shall make use of these relations in studying the properties of triangles later on.

The capital letters A, B, C will denote the angles of triangle ABC and the sides opposite to the angles A, B, C will be denoted by a, b, c respectively. The sum of the three sides of a triangle, called perimeter will be denoted by $2s$.

i.e., $$2s = a + b + c.$$

2. SINE FORMULA

In any triangle ABC

$$\frac{a}{\sin A} = \frac{b}{\sin B} = \frac{c}{\sin C}.$$

Proof. In any triangle, two angles must be acute. Let B and C be the two acute angles.

From A draw $AD \perp BC$.

Then from ΔABD

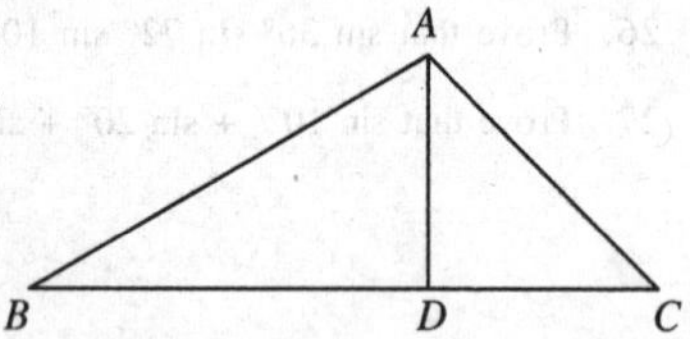

Fig. 1

$$\frac{AD}{AB} = \sin B \Rightarrow AD = c \sin B$$

and from ΔADC

$$\frac{AD}{AC} = \sin C \Rightarrow AD = b \sin C$$

Then $c \sin B = b \sin C$

$$\Rightarrow \qquad \frac{b}{\sin B} = \frac{c}{\sin C} = k \text{ (say)}.$$

Now $\quad BC = BD + DC$

So
$$
\begin{aligned}
a &= AB\cos B + AC\cos C\\
&= c\cos B + b\cos C\\
&= k\sin C\cos B + k\sin B\cos C\\
&= k\,[\sin C\cos B + \sin B\cos C]\\
&= k\sin(B+C)\\
&= k\sin(\pi - A) = k\sin A.
\end{aligned}
$$

$\Rightarrow$
$$\frac{a}{\sin A} = k.$$

Thus
$$\frac{\mathbf{a}}{\mathbf{\sin A}} = \frac{\mathbf{b}}{\mathbf{\sin B}} = \frac{\mathbf{c}}{\mathbf{\sin C}}.$$

3. COSINE FORMULA

In any triangle ABC

$$\cos A = \frac{b^2 + c^2 - a^2}{2bc}$$

$$\cos B = \frac{c^2 + a^2 - b^2}{2ca}$$

$$\cos C = \frac{a^2 + b^2 - c^2}{2ab}$$

Proof. Let B and C be the two acute angles of triangle ABC. From A,draw $AD \perp BC$ (see Fig. 1).

Then from triangle ADC,

$$\left.\begin{aligned}
&\frac{AD}{AC} = \sin C \Rightarrow AD = b\sin C\\
\text{Also}\quad &\frac{CD}{AC} = \cos C \Rightarrow CD = b\cos C
\end{aligned}\right\} \quad ...(i)$$

Similarly from triangle ABD,

$$\left.\begin{aligned}
&\frac{AD}{AB} = \sin B \Rightarrow AD = c\sin B\\
\text{and}\quad &\frac{BD}{AB} = \cos B \Rightarrow BD = C\cos B
\end{aligned}\right\} \quad ...(ii)$$

Since $\quad AB^2 = AD^2 + BD^2$

we get
$$
\begin{aligned}
c^2 &= b^2\sin^2 C + (BC - CD)^2 \qquad \text{Using } (i)\\
&= b^2\sin^2 C + (a - b\cos c)^2
\end{aligned}
$$

$$= b^2 \sin^2 C + a^2 + b^2 \cos^2 C - 2ab \cos C$$
$$= a^2 + b^2 - 2ab \cos c.$$

$$\Rightarrow \quad \cos C = \frac{a^2 + b^2 - c^2}{2ab}.$$

Similarly, $AC^2 = AD^2 + DC^2$

gives $b^2 = c^2 \sin^2 B + (BC - BD)^2$ from (*ii*)

$$= c^2 \sin^2 B + (a - c \cos B)^2$$
$$= c^2 \sin^2 B + a^2 + c^2 \cos^2 B - 2ac \cos B$$
$$= a^2 + c^2 - 2ac \cos B$$

$$\Rightarrow \quad \cos B = \frac{a^2 + c^2 - b^2}{2ac}.$$

Since $A + B + C = \pi$

$$C = \pi - (A + B)$$

or $\sin C = \sin [\pi - (A + B)]$

$$= \sin (A + B)$$
$$= \sin A \cos B + \cos A \sin B$$

i.e. $c = a \cos B + b \cos A$ (Using sine formula)

$$= a\left(\frac{a^2 + c^2 - b^2}{2ac}\right) + b \cos A$$

$$\Rightarrow \quad b \cos A = c - \left(\frac{a^2 + c^2 - b^2}{2c}\right)$$

$$= \frac{2c^2 - a^2 - c^2 + b^2}{2c}$$

$$\Rightarrow \quad \cos A = \frac{c^2 + b^2 - a^2}{2bc}.$$

4. NAPIER'S FORMULA

In any triangle *ABC*

(*i*) $\tan \dfrac{B - C}{2} = \dfrac{b - c}{b + c} \cot \dfrac{A}{2}$

(*ii*) $\tan \dfrac{C - A}{2} = \dfrac{c - a}{c + a} \cot \dfrac{B}{2}$

(*iii*) $\tan \dfrac{A - B}{2} = \dfrac{a - b}{a + b} \cot \dfrac{C}{2}$

Proof. Since $\dfrac{a}{\sin A} = \dfrac{b}{\sin B} = \dfrac{c}{\sin C} = k \text{ (say)}$

We have
$$\frac{b-c}{b+c} = \frac{k \sin B - k \sin C}{k \sin B + k \sin C}$$
$$= \frac{\sin B - \sin C}{\sin B + \sin C}$$
$$= \frac{2 \cos \frac{B+C}{2} \sin \frac{B-C}{2}}{2 \sin \frac{B+C}{2} \cos \frac{B-C}{2}}$$
$$= \tan \frac{B-C}{2} \cot \frac{B+C}{2}$$
$$= \tan \frac{B-C}{2} \cot \left(90° - \frac{A}{2}\right)$$
$$= \tan \frac{B-C}{2} \tan \frac{A}{2}$$

Hance $\tan \dfrac{B-C}{2} = \dfrac{b-c}{b+c} \cot \dfrac{A}{2}$.

Similarly, we can prove the other relations.

5. PROJECTION FORMULA

In any triangle ABC

(*i*) $a = b \cos C + c \cos B$

(*ii*) $b = c \cos A + a \cos C$

(*iii*) $c = b \cos A + a \cos B$

Proof. (*i*) Consider $b \cos C + c \cos B$

$= k \sin B \cos C + k \sin C \cos B$

$$\left(\text{Using sine formula } \frac{a}{\sin A} = \frac{b}{\sin B} = \frac{c}{\sin C} = k\right)$$

$= k (\sin B \cos C + \sin C \cos B)$

$= k \sin (B + C)$

$= k \sin (\pi - A) = k \sin A = a$

Similarly, we can prove the other relations.

6. TO EXPRESS THE SINE, COSINE AND TANGENTS OF HALF THE ANGLES IN TERMS OF SIDES

(*i*) $\sin \dfrac{A}{2} = \sqrt{\dfrac{(s-b)(s-c)}{bc}}$

$\sin \dfrac{B}{2} = \sqrt{\dfrac{(s-c)(s-a)}{ca}}$

$\sin \dfrac{C}{2} = \sqrt{\dfrac{(s-a)(s-b)}{ab}}$.

Proof. Here $2s = a+b+c.$

Now $\cos A = 1 - 2\sin^2 \dfrac{A}{2}$

$$\Rightarrow \quad \frac{b^2+c^2-a^2}{2bc} = 1 - 2\sin^2 \frac{A}{2}$$

$$\Rightarrow \quad 2\sin^2 \frac{A}{2} = 1 - \left(\frac{b^2+c^2-a^2}{2bc}\right)$$

$$= \frac{(2bc-b^2-c^2)+a^2}{2bc}$$

$$= \frac{a^2-(b-c)^2}{2bc}$$

$$\Rightarrow \quad \sin^2 \frac{A}{2} = \frac{[a-(b-c)][a+(b-c)]}{4bc}$$

$$= \frac{(a+b+c-2b)(a+b+c-2c)}{4bc}$$

$$= \frac{(2s-2b)(2s-2c)}{4bc} = \frac{(s-b)(s-c)}{bc}$$

$$\Rightarrow \quad \sin \frac{A}{2} = \pm\sqrt{\frac{(s-b)(s-c)}{bc}}$$

Since $0 < A < 180° \Rightarrow 0 < \dfrac{A}{2} < 90°$

$$\Rightarrow \quad \sin \frac{A}{2} = +\sqrt{\frac{(s-b)(s-c)}{bc}}.$$

Similarly, we can prove the other relations.

(*ii*) $\cos\frac{A}{2} = \sqrt{\frac{s(s-a)}{bc}}$

$\cos\frac{B}{2} = \sqrt{\frac{s(s-b)}{ca}}$

$\cos\frac{C}{2} = \sqrt{\frac{s(s-c)}{ab}}$

Proof. $\cos A = 2\cos^2\frac{A}{2} - 1 \Rightarrow \frac{b^2+c^2-a^2}{2bc} = 2\cos^2\frac{A}{2} - 1$

$$\Rightarrow \quad 2\cos^2\frac{A}{2} = 1 + \left(\frac{b^2+c^2-a^2}{2bc}\right)$$

$$= \frac{2bc + b^2 + c^2 - a^2}{2bc} = \frac{(b+c)^2 - a^2}{2bc}$$

$$= \frac{(b+c-a)(b+c+a)}{2bc}$$

$$= \frac{(a+b+c-2a)(a+b+c)}{2bc}$$

$$= \frac{(2s-2a)(2s)}{2bc} = \frac{(s-a)2s}{bc}$$

$$\Rightarrow \quad \cos^2\frac{A}{2} = \frac{2s(s-a)}{2bc}$$

$$\cos\frac{A}{2} = \pm\sqrt{\frac{s(s-a)}{bc}}$$

Since $0 < A < 180° \Rightarrow 0 < \frac{A}{2} < 90° \Rightarrow \cos\frac{A}{2} = +\sqrt{\frac{s(s-a)}{bc}}$

Similarly, we can prove the other relations.

(*iii*) $\tan\frac{A}{2} = \sqrt{\frac{(s-b)(s-c)}{s(s-a)}}$

$\tan\frac{B}{2} = \sqrt{\frac{(s-c)(s-a)}{s(s-b)}}$

$\tan\frac{C}{2} = \sqrt{\frac{(s-a)(s-b)}{s(s-c)}}$.

Proof. Since $\sin\frac{A}{2}=\sqrt{\frac{(s-b)(s-c)}{bc}}$ and $\cos\frac{A}{2}=\sqrt{\frac{s(s-a)}{bc}}$ dividing, we have $\tan\frac{A}{2}=\sqrt{\frac{(s-b)(s-c)}{s(s-a)}}$.

Similarly, we can prove the other relations.

7. TO EXPRESS THE SINES OF ANGLES IN TERMS OF SIDES

(*i*) $\sin A=\frac{2}{bc}\sqrt{s(s-a)(s-b)(s-c)}$

(*ii*) $\sin B=\frac{2}{ca}\sqrt{s(s-a)(s-b)(s-c)}$

(*iii*) $\sin C=\frac{2}{ab}\sqrt{s(s-a)(s-b)(s-c)}$.

Proof. $\sin A=2\sin\frac{A}{2}\cos\frac{A}{2}=2\sqrt{\frac{(s-b)(s-c)}{bc}}\sqrt{\frac{s(s-a)}{bc}}$

$$=\frac{2}{bc}\sqrt{s(s-a)(s-b)(s-c)}$$

Similarly, we can prove the other relations.

Example 1. *In any* ΔABC, *show that*

$$\frac{\sin(B-C)}{\sin(B+C)}=\frac{b^2-c^2}{a^2}.$$

Solution. RHS $=\frac{b^2-c^2}{a^2}$

$$=\frac{\sin^2 B-\sin^2 C}{\sin^2 A} \quad \text{(Using Sine formula)}$$

$$=\frac{\sin(B-C)\sin(B+C)}{\sin^2 A}$$

$$=\frac{\sin(B-C)\sin A}{\sin^2 A}$$

$$=\frac{\sin(B-C)}{\sin A}=\frac{\sin(B-C)}{\sin(B+C)}=\text{LHS}.$$

Example 2. *If in a* ΔABC, $\dfrac{\cos B}{b} = \dfrac{\cos C}{c}$, *prove that the triangle is isosceles.*

Solution. $\dfrac{\cos B}{b} = \dfrac{\cos C}{c} \Rightarrow \dfrac{a^2+c^2-b^2}{b.2ac} = \dfrac{a^2+b^2-c^2}{c.2ab}$

$$\Rightarrow \frac{a^2+c^2-b^2}{bc} = \frac{a^2+b^2-c^2}{bc}$$

$$\Rightarrow a^2+c^2-b^2 = a^2+b^2-c^2$$

$$\Rightarrow 2c^2 = 2b^2$$

$\Rightarrow$ $c = b$. Thus the triangle is isosceles.

Example 3. *In any triangle ABC, prove that*

$$\sin\frac{A-B}{2} = \frac{a-b}{c}\cos\frac{C}{2}.$$

Solution. We have $\dfrac{a}{\sin A} = \dfrac{b}{\sin B} = \dfrac{c}{\sin C} = k$ (say)

$$\Rightarrow \quad \frac{a-b}{c} = \frac{\sin A - \sin B}{\sin C}$$

$$= \frac{2\cos\frac{A+B}{2}\sin\frac{A-B}{2}}{2\sin\frac{C}{2}\cos\frac{C}{2}}$$

$$= \frac{2\sin\frac{C}{2}\sin\frac{A-B}{2}}{2\sin\frac{C}{2}\cos\frac{C}{2}} \quad \text{as } \frac{A+B}{2} = 90° - \frac{C}{2}$$

$$= \frac{\sin\frac{A-B}{2}}{\cos\frac{C}{2}}$$

$$\Rightarrow \quad \sin\frac{A-B}{2} = \frac{a-b}{c}\cos\frac{C}{2}.$$

Example 4. *In any* ΔABC

$$2\left(a\sin^2\frac{C}{2} + c\sin^2\frac{A}{2}\right) = c + a - b.$$

Solution $$\text{LHS} = a\left(2\sin^2\frac{C}{2}\right) + c\left(2\sin^2\frac{A}{2}\right)$$
$$= a(1 - \cos C) + c(1 - \cos A)$$
$$= a + c - (a\cos C + c\cos A)$$
$$= a + c - b \qquad \text{(From Projection formula)}$$
$$= \text{RHS}.$$

Example 5. *In any triangle ABC, prove that*
$$a^3 \sin(B - C) + b^3 \sin(C - A) + c^3 \sin(A - B) = 0.$$
Solution.

Since $$\frac{a}{\sin A} = \frac{b}{\sin B} = \frac{c}{\sin C} = k.$$
$$a^3 \sin(B - C) = k^3 \sin^3 A \sin(B - C)$$
$$= k^3 \sin^2 A \sin A \sin(B - C)$$
$$= k^3 \sin^2 A \sin(B + C)\sin(B - C)$$
$$= k^3 \sin^2 A(\sin^2 B - \sin^2 C)$$
Therefore, $$\text{LHS} = k^3[\sin^2 A(\sin^2 B - \sin^2 C)$$
$$+ \sin^2 B(\sin^2 C - \sin^2 A) + \sin^2 C(\sin^2 A - \sin^2 B)]$$
$$= 0 = \text{RHS}.$$

Example 6. $2(bc\cos A + ca\cos B + ab\cos C) = a^2 + b^2 + c^2$.

Solution. $$\text{LHS} = [b^2 + c^2 - a^2 + c^2 + a^2 - b^2 + a^2 + b^2 - c^2]$$
$$= a^2 + b^2 + c^2$$
$$= \text{RHS}.$$

Example 7. *The sides of a triangle are $x^2 + x + 1$, $2x + 1$ and $x^2 - 1$. Prove that its greatest angle = 120°.*

Solution. Let $$a = x^2 + x + 1, b = 2x + 1, c = x^2 - 1$$

Then $$s = x^2 + \frac{3x}{2} + \frac{1}{2}$$
$$s - b = x^2 - \frac{x}{2} - \frac{1}{2}$$
$$s - c = \frac{3}{2}(x + 1)$$
$$bc = (x + 1)(x - 1)(2x + 1)$$

So, $$\sin\frac{A}{2} = \sqrt{\frac{(s-b)(s-c)}{bc}}$$

$$= \sqrt{\frac{3}{4}\frac{(2x^2-x-1)}{(x-1)(2x+1)}}$$

$$= \sqrt{\frac{3}{4}\frac{(x-1)(2x+1)}{(x-1)(2x+1)}}$$

$$= \frac{\sqrt{3}}{2} \Rightarrow \frac{A}{2} = 60° \Rightarrow A = 120°$$

which is required greatest angle.

Example 8. *If the sides of a triangle are in AP, prove that so also are the cotangents of half the angles.*

Solution. Now $$\cot\frac{A}{2} = \sqrt{\frac{s(s-a)}{(s-b)(s-c)}}$$

$$\cot\frac{B}{2} = \sqrt{\frac{s(s-b)}{(s-a)(s-c)}}$$

Therefore $\cot\frac{B}{2} - \cot\frac{A}{2}$

$$= \sqrt{\frac{s}{(s-c)}}\left[\sqrt{\frac{(s-b)}{(s-a)}} - \sqrt{\frac{(s-a)}{(s-b)}}\right]$$

$$= \sqrt{\frac{s}{(s-c)}}\left[\frac{(s-b)-(s-a)}{\sqrt{(s-a)}\sqrt{(s-b)}}\right]$$

$$= \frac{\sqrt{s}\,(a-b)}{\sqrt{(s-a)(s-b)(s-c)}}$$

Similarly, $$\cot\frac{C}{2} - \cot\frac{B}{2} = \frac{\sqrt{s}\,(b-c)}{\sqrt{(s-a)(s-b)(s-c)}}$$

$$= \frac{\sqrt{s}\,(a-b)}{\sqrt{(s-a)(s-b)(s-c)}}$$

(as a, b, c are in AP $\Rightarrow a-b = b-c$)

Thus, $\cot\frac{A}{2}, \cot\frac{B}{2}, \cot\frac{C}{2}$ are also in AP.

Example 9. *Prove that in* ΔABC

$$\frac{a^2 \sin(B-C)}{\sin B+\sin C}+\frac{b^2 \sin(C-A)}{\sin C+\sin A}+\frac{c^2 \sin(A-B)}{\sin A+\sin B}=0.$$

Solution. $\dfrac{a^2 \sin(B-C)}{\sin B+\sin C}=\dfrac{ak \sin A \, 2\sin\dfrac{B-C}{2}\cos\dfrac{B-C}{2}}{2\sin\dfrac{B+C}{2}\cos\dfrac{B-C}{2}}$

$$=\frac{ak \sin(B+C)\sin\dfrac{B-C}{2}}{\sin\dfrac{B+C}{2}}$$

$$=\frac{ak\, 2\sin\dfrac{B+C}{2}\cos\dfrac{B+C}{2}\sin\dfrac{B-C}{2}}{\sin\dfrac{B+C}{2}}$$

$$= ak\, 2\sin\frac{B-C}{2}\cos\frac{B+C}{2}$$

$$= ak(\sin B-\sin C)$$

$$= ak\left(\frac{b}{k}-\frac{c}{k}\right)=a(b-c)$$

Similarly, $\dfrac{b^2 \sin(C-A)}{\sin C+\sin A}=b(c-a)$

$\dfrac{c^2 \sin(A-B)}{\sin A+\sin B}=c(a-b)$

Therefore, $\quad \text{LHS} = a(b-c)+b(c-a)+c(a-b)=0$

Example 10. *In a* ΔABS*, prove that*

$$a^3 \cos(B-C)+b^3\cos(C-A)+c^3\cos(A-B)=3abc$$

Solution. $\text{LHS} = a^3\cos(B-C)+b^3\cos(C-A)+c^2\cos(A-B)$

$$= a^3k\sin A\cos(B-C)+b^3k\sin B\cos(C-A)$$
$$+c^3k\sin C\cos(A-B)$$

$$= \frac{ka^2}{2}[\sin(A+B-C)+\sin(A-B+C)]$$
$$+\frac{kb^2}{2}[\sin(B+C-A)+\sin(B-C+A)]$$
$$+\frac{kc^2}{2}[\sin(C+A-B)+\sin(C-A+B)]$$

$$= \frac{ka^2}{2}[\sin(\pi-2C)+\sin(\pi-2B)]$$
$$+\frac{kb^2}{2}[\sin(\pi-2A)+\sin(\pi-2C)]$$
$$+\frac{kc^2}{2}[\sin(\pi-2B)+\sin(\pi-2A)]$$

$$= \frac{ka^2}{2}[\sin 2C+\sin 2B]+\frac{kb^2}{2}[\sin 2A+\sin 2C]$$
$$+\frac{kc^2}{2}[\sin 2B+\sin 2A]$$

$$= \frac{k}{2}\sin 2A\,(b^2+c^2)+\frac{k}{2}\sin 2B\,(c^2+a^2)+\frac{k}{2}\sin 2C\,(a^2+b^2)$$

$$= k\sin A\cos A\,(b^2+c^2)+k\sin B\cos B\,(c^2+a^2)$$
$$+k\sin A\cos A\,(b^2+c^2)$$

$$= a\cos A\,(b^2+c^2)+b\cos B\,(c^2+a^2)+c\cos C\,(a^2+b^2)$$

$$= \frac{a(b^2+c^2)(b^2+c^2-a^2)}{2bc}+\frac{b(c^2+a^2)(c^2+a^2-b^2)}{2ca}$$
$$+\frac{c(a^2+b^2)(a^2+b^2-c^2)}{2ab}$$

$$= \frac{a^2[(b^2+c^2)^2-a^2b^2-a^2c^2]+b^2[(c^2+a^2)^2-b^2c^2-a^2b^2)+c^2[(a^2+b^2)^2-c^2a^2-b^2c^2]}{2abc}$$

$$= \frac{2a^2b^2c^2+2a^2b^2c^2+2a^2b^2c^2}{2abc}$$

$= 3abc =$ RHS.

Example 11. *In a ΔABC, prove that*

$$\frac{b-c}{a}\cos^2\frac{A}{2}+\frac{c-a}{b}\cos^2\frac{B}{2}+\frac{a-b}{c}\cos^2\frac{C}{2}=0$$

Solution. LHS $= \dfrac{b-c}{a}\dfrac{s(s-a)}{bc}+\dfrac{c-a}{b}\dfrac{s(s-b)}{ca}+\dfrac{a-b}{c}\dfrac{s(s-c)}{ab}$

$$=\frac{s}{abc}[(b-c)(s-a)+(c-a)(s-b)+(a-b)(s-c)]$$

$$=\frac{s}{abc}[s(b-c)-ab+ac+s(c-a)-bc+ab+s(a-b)-ac+bc]$$

$$=\frac{s}{abc}[s(b-c+c-a+a-b)]$$

$= 0 =$ RHS.

Example 12. *If in ΔABC, $a\cos^2\frac{C}{2}+c\cos^2\frac{A}{2}=\frac{3b}{2}$ prove that a, b, c are in AP.*

Solution. Now $a\cos^2\dfrac{C}{2}+c\cos^2\dfrac{A}{2}=\dfrac{3b}{2}$

$$\Rightarrow \frac{as(s-c)}{ab}+\frac{cs(s-a)}{bc}=\frac{3b}{2}$$

$$\Rightarrow \frac{s(-s-c)}{b}+\frac{s(s-a)}{b}=\frac{3b}{2}$$

$$\Rightarrow \frac{s}{b}[s-c+s-a]=\frac{3b}{2}$$

$$\Rightarrow 2s[a+b+c-c-a]=3b^2 \qquad (\text{as } 2s=a+b+c)$$

$$\Rightarrow 2s[b]=3b^2$$

$$\Rightarrow 2s=3b$$

$$\Rightarrow a+b+c=3b$$

$$\Rightarrow a+c=2b$$

$\Rightarrow$ a, b, c are in AP.

Example 13. *In a ΔABC, prove that*

$$\sin(B-C)=\frac{b^2-c^2}{a^2}\sin A.$$

Solution. RHS $=\dfrac{b^2-c^2}{a^2}\sin A$

$$= \frac{k^2 (\sin^2 B - \sin^2 C)}{k^2 \sin^2 A} \sin A$$

$$= \frac{(\sin B + \sin C)(\sin B - \sin C)}{\sin A}$$

$$= \frac{4 \sin \frac{B+C}{2} \cos \frac{B-C}{2} \sin \frac{B-C}{2} \cos \frac{B+C}{2}}{\sin A}$$

$$= \frac{\sin (B+C) \sin (B-C)}{\sin A}$$

$$= \frac{\sin A \sin (B-C)}{\sin A} = \sin (B-C) = \text{LHS}.$$

EXERCISES

In any *ABC*, prove that

1. $c \cos \frac{A-B}{2} = (a+b) \sin \frac{C}{2}$.
2. $a \sin \left(\frac{B-C}{2}\right) = (b-c) \cos \frac{A}{2}$.
3. $a \cos A + b \cos B + c \cos C = 2a \sin B \sin C$.
4. $\frac{(b+c)}{(b-c)} \tan \frac{A}{2} - \frac{(b-c)}{(b+c)} \cot \frac{A}{2} = 2 \cot (B-C)$.
5. $c^2 = (a-b)^2 \cos^2 \frac{C}{2} + (a+b)^2 \sin^2 \frac{C}{2}$.
6. $\frac{\cot A}{b^2 + c^2 - a^2} = \frac{\cot B}{c^2 + a^2 - b^2} = \frac{\cot C}{a^2 + b^2 - c^2}$.
7. $(b+c) \cos A + (c+a) \cos B + (a+b) \cos C = a + b + c$.
8. $\frac{b^2 - c^2}{a^2} \sin 2A + \frac{c^2 - a^2}{b^2} \sin 2B + \frac{a^2 - b^2}{c^2} \sin 2C = 0$.
9. $(a^2 - b^2 + c) \tan B = (a^2 + b^2 - c^2) \tan C$.
10. $a^2 \sin 2B + b^2 \sin 2A = 2ab \sin C$.
11. $b^2 \cos 2A - a^2 \cos 2B = b^2 - a^2$.
12. $\cot \frac{A}{2} + \cot \frac{B}{2} + \cot \frac{C}{2} = \frac{a+b+c}{a+b-c} \cot \frac{C}{2}$.
13. $c^2 = (a-b)^2 \cos^2 \frac{C}{2} + (a+b)^2 \sin^2 \frac{C}{2}$.

14. If $a \cos^2 \frac{C}{2} + c \cos^2 \frac{A}{2} = \frac{3b}{2}$, then show that a, b, c are in AP.
15. If a^2, b^2, c^2 are in AP, prove that cot A, cot B, cot C are in AP.
16. In a ΔABC, AD is a median, prove that cot BAD – cot B = 2 cot A.

8. PROPERTIES OF TRIANGLES

We shall now study some of the simple properties of triangles. In what follows, Δ denotes the area of triangle, R, the circum-radius; r, the inradius (*i.e.*, the radius of circle inscribed in a triangle).

Area of a triangle.

In any triangle ABC,

$$\Delta = \frac{1}{2} bc \sin A = \frac{1}{2} ca \sin B = \frac{1}{2} ab \sin C.$$

Also $$\Delta = \sqrt{s(s-a)(s-b)(s-c)} \quad \textit{(Heron's formula)}$$

Proof. Let B and C be the two acute angles of a triangle ABC. From A draw $AD \perp BC$. (See Fig. 1)

Then $$\Delta = \frac{1}{2} \text{(base)} \times \text{(perp.)}$$

$$= \frac{1}{2} (BC) \times (AD) = \frac{1}{2} a \times c \sin B.$$

Since $$\frac{a}{\sin A} = \frac{b}{\sin B} = \frac{c}{\sin C} \Rightarrow a \sin B = b \sin C$$

We get $$\Delta = \frac{1}{2} bc \sin A$$

Also $c \sin A = a \sin C \Rightarrow \Delta = \frac{1}{2} ab \sin C.$

In other words, area of a triangle

$$= \frac{1}{2} \text{(product of two sides)} \times \text{(sine of the included angle)}$$

Again $\sin A = \frac{2}{bc} \sqrt{s(s-a)(s-b)(s-c)}$, §7

$$\Rightarrow \quad \Delta = \frac{1}{2} bc \frac{2}{bc} \sqrt{s(s-a)(s-b)(s-c)}$$

$$= \sqrt{s(s-a)(s-b)(s-c)}$$

Circumradius of a triangle

In any triangle ABC,

$$\frac{a}{\sin A} = \frac{b}{\sin B} = \frac{c}{\sin C} = 2R$$

Proof. Let O be the circumcentre of a triangle ABC. It is the point of intersection of right bisectors of three sides of triangle. Join BO and produce it to meet the circumcircle in D. Join CD.

(*i*) When O lies inside the ΔABC

Let $OE \perp BC$

ΔBOC is isosceles triangle

OE bisects $\angle BOC$

So $\quad \angle BOE = \frac{1}{2} \angle BOC$

$$= \frac{1}{2} \times 2 \angle BAC = \angle A$$

$\Rightarrow \quad \angle BDC = \angle BOE = \angle A$

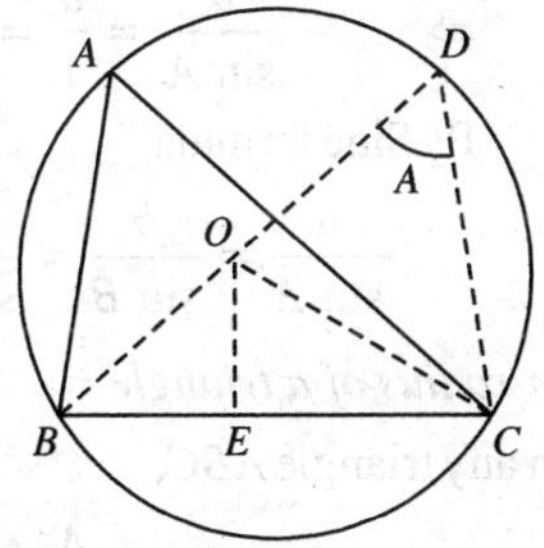

Fig. 2

As $\angle BCD = 90°$ (angle in a semi-circle)

So triangle BCD is a right triangle

Thus $\quad \sin A = \frac{BC}{BD} = \frac{a}{2R}$ where R is radius of the circle

$\Rightarrow \quad \frac{a}{\sin A} = 2R$

By Sine formula

$$\frac{a}{\sin A} = \frac{b}{\sin B} = \frac{c}{\sin C} = 2R.$$

(*ii*) When O lies outside the ΔABC.

Again $\angle BCD = 90°$ (angle in a semi-circle)

$\angle BDC = \pi - A$ (opposite angles of cyclic quadrilateral are supplementary)

Then from right angled ΔBDC,

$$\sin(\pi - A) = \frac{BC}{BD} \Rightarrow \sin A = \frac{a}{2R}$$

and so $\quad \frac{a}{\sin A} = 2R.$

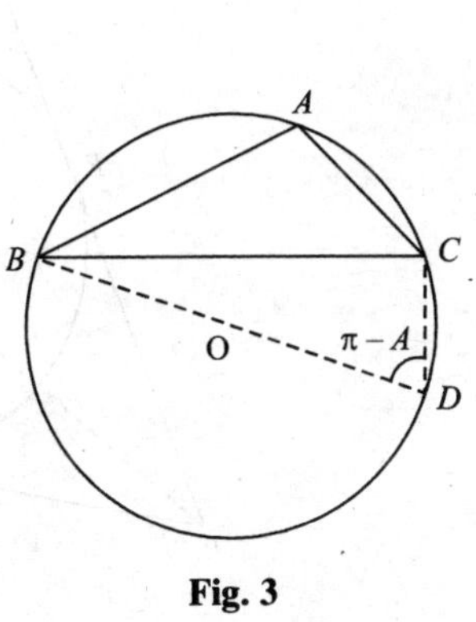

Fig. 3

By Sine formula

$$\frac{a}{\sin A} = \frac{b}{\sin B} = \frac{c}{\sin C} = 2R.$$

(*iii*) When O lies on one side of the ΔABC.

Here, $\angle BAC$ is a right angle, being angle in a semi-circle.

Also $2R = BD = BC = a$

and $\sin A = \sin 90° = 1$

$$\Rightarrow \quad \frac{a}{\sin A} = \frac{a}{1} = 2R$$

By Sine formula

$$\frac{a}{\sin A} = \frac{b}{\sin B} = \frac{c}{\sin C} = 2R.$$

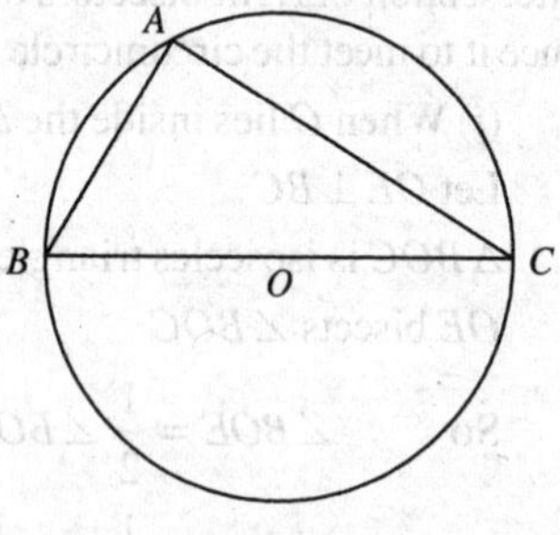

Fig. 4

In-radius of a triangle

In any triangle ABC,

$$r = \frac{\Delta}{s}$$

where r is the radius of the circle inscribed in the ΔABC and s is semi-perimeter of the ΔABC.

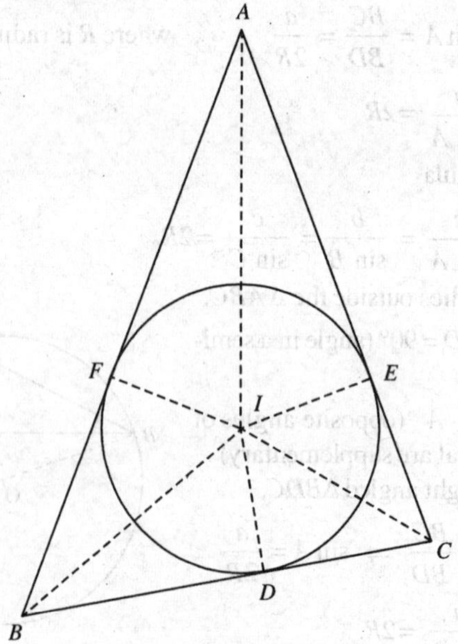

Fig. 5

Proof. Let I be the incentre of ΔABC. It is the point of intersection of internal bisectors of the angles of the triangle.

Let D, E, F be the points where the circle touches the sides of the triangle ABC.

Join ID, IE, IF and IA, IB, IC

Here $ID \perp BC, IE \perp CA, IF \perp AB$

Now Area of ΔABC

$$= \text{Area of } \Delta BCI + \text{Area of } \Delta CAI + \text{Area of } \Delta ABI$$

$$= \frac{1}{2}(a \times ID) + \frac{1}{2}(b \times IE) + \frac{1}{2}(c \times IF)$$

$$= \frac{1}{2}(a \times r) + \frac{1}{2}(b \times r) + \frac{1}{2}(c \times r) \quad \text{where } r \text{ is the radius}$$

$$= \frac{1}{2}r(a+b+c) = \frac{1}{2}r(2s) = rs$$

i.e., $\Delta = rs$

Thus $r = \dfrac{\Delta}{s}$.

Example 14. *If $B = 45°$, $C = 60°$ and $a = 2(\sqrt{3}+1)$ cm, find the area of ΔABC.*

Solution. Since $\dfrac{a}{\sin A} = \dfrac{b}{\sin B} = \dfrac{c}{\sin C}$

we have $b = \dfrac{a \sin B}{\sin A}, c = \dfrac{\sin C}{\sin A}$

$$\Delta = \frac{1}{2}bc \sin A = \frac{1}{2}\frac{a \sin B}{\sin A}\frac{a \sin C}{\sin A}\sin A$$

$$= \frac{1}{2}\frac{a^2 \sin B \sin C}{\sin A} = \frac{1}{2}\frac{a^2 \sin B \sin C}{\sin (B+C)}$$

$$= \frac{1}{2}\frac{4(\sqrt{3}+1)^2 \frac{1}{\sqrt{2}}\frac{\sqrt{3}}{2}}{\frac{1}{\sqrt{2}}\frac{1}{2} + \frac{1}{\sqrt{2}}\frac{\sqrt{3}}{2}} = \frac{1}{2}\frac{4(\sqrt{3}+1)^2 \times \sqrt{3}}{1+\sqrt{3}}$$

$$= \frac{2(\sqrt{3}+1)^2\sqrt{3}}{\sqrt{3}+1} = 2\sqrt{3}(\sqrt{3}+1)$$

$$= 2(3+\sqrt{3}) \text{ sq. cm.}$$

Example 15. *Prove that* $\Delta = s(s-a)\tan\dfrac{A}{2}$.

Solution. Now $\tan\dfrac{A}{2} = \sqrt{\dfrac{(s-b)(s-c)}{s(s-a)}}$

$$\Rightarrow \qquad \text{RHS} = \sqrt{s(s-a)(s-b)(s-c)} = \Delta = \text{LHS}.$$

Example 16. *Prove that*

$$a\cos A + b\cos B + c\cos C = 4R\sin A\sin B\sin C.$$

Solution. Since $\dfrac{a}{\sin A} = \dfrac{b}{\sin B} = \dfrac{c}{\sin C} = 2R,$

$$\left.\begin{aligned} a &= 2R\sin A \\ b &= 2R\sin B \\ c &= 2R\sin C \end{aligned}\right\}$$

Now

$$\begin{aligned} \text{LHS} &= a\cos A + b\cos B + c\cos C \\ &= 2R\sin A\cos A + 2R\sin B\cos B + 2R\sin C\cos C \\ &= R[\sin 2A + \sin 2B + \sin 2C] \\ &= R[2\sin(A+B)\cos(A-B) + \sin 360° - 2(A+B)] \\ &= R[2\sin(A+B)\cos(A-B) - \sin 2(A+B)] \\ &= R[2\sin(A+B)\cos(A-B) - 2\sin(A+B)\cos(A+B)] \\ &= 2R\sin(A+B)[\cos(A-B) - \cos(A+B)] \\ &= 2R\sin(A+B)\,2\sin A\sin B = 2R\sin C\,2\sin A\sin B \\ &= 4R\sin A\sin B\sin C = \text{RHS}. \end{aligned}$$

Example 17. *Prove that* $\sin A + \sin B + \sin C = \dfrac{s}{R}$.

Solution.

$$\begin{aligned} \text{LHS} = \sin A + \sin B + \sin C &= \frac{a}{2R} + \frac{b}{2R} + \frac{c}{2R} \\ &= \frac{a+b+c}{2R} = \frac{2s}{2R} = \frac{s}{R}. \end{aligned}$$

Example 18. *Prove* $r = (s-b)\tan\dfrac{B}{2}$.

Solution. Now $\tan\dfrac{B}{2} = \sqrt{\dfrac{(s-a)(s-c)}{s(s-b)}}$

$$\Rightarrow \qquad \text{RHS} = \sqrt{\frac{(s-a)(s-b)(s-c)}{s^2}} = \frac{\Delta}{s} = r = \text{LHS}.$$

Example 19. *Prove that Rr (sin A + sin B + sin C) = Δ.*

Solution. $\text{LHS} = Rr\left(\frac{a}{2R}+\frac{b}{2R}+\frac{c}{2R}\right) = \frac{(a+b+c)}{2}r$

$$= rs = \frac{\Delta}{s}s = \Delta = \text{RHS}.$$

EXERCISES

1. The sides of a triangle are 13, 14, 15 cm. Calculate its area.
2. Find the area of triangle ABC, when $b = 5$, $c = 6$, $A = 45°$.

Prove that, in any triangle ABC.

3. $abcs \sin\frac{A}{2}\sin\frac{B}{2}\sin\frac{C}{2} = \Delta^2$.
4. $4\Delta \cot A = b^2 + c^2 - a^2$.
5. $R = \frac{abc}{4\Delta}$.
6. $s = 4R\cos\frac{A}{2}\cos\frac{B}{2}\cos\frac{C}{2}$.
7. $\Delta = 2R^2 \sin A \sin B \sin C$.
8. $\frac{1}{4}(b^2 \sin 2C + c^2 \sin 2B) = \Delta$.
9. $a\cos^2\frac{A}{2}+b\cos^2\frac{B}{2}+c\cos^2\frac{C}{2} = s+\frac{\Delta}{R}$.
10. $\frac{1}{s-a}+\frac{1}{s-b}+\frac{1}{s-c}-\frac{1}{s} = \frac{4R}{\Delta}$.
11. $\frac{1}{ab}+\frac{1}{bc}+\frac{1}{ca} = \frac{1}{2Rr}$.
12. $4Rr\cos\frac{A}{2}\cos\frac{B}{2}\cos\frac{C}{2} = \Delta$
13. $a\cot A + b\cot B + c\cot C = 2(R + r)$.
14. $4Rrs = abc$.

ANSWERS

1. 84 sq. cm. 2. $\frac{15}{\sqrt{2}}$.

CHAPTER 19

VARIATION OF TRIGONOMETRICAL RATIOS AND THEIR INVERSES

1. TO TRACE THE VARIATION OF TRIGONOMETRICAL RATIOS OF AN ANGLE, AS THE ANGLE INCREASES FROM 0° TO 360° AND TO DRAW THEIR GRAPHS

Let the revolving line *OP* be of constant length *a* and let it, starting from *OX*, move in anticlockwise direction and trace out an angle $XOP = \theta$. There are four possibilities. The revolving line can be in first, second, third or fourth quadrant. We discuss each possibility separately. From *P*, draw $PM \perp OX$ or OX' where XOX', YOY' are two lines at right angles to each other.

By convention of signs, *OP* is always regarded as positive. *OM* is positive if the revolving line is in first and fourth quadrants, and negative, if the revolving line is in second and third quadrants. Similarly, *MP* is positive if the revolving line is in first and second quadrants, and negative if the revolving line is in third and fourth quadrants.

Sine Curve

$$\sin\theta = \frac{MP}{OP}, \; OP \text{ is of fixed length } a.$$

First Quadrant. When $\theta = 0°$, *MP* is zero so that $\sin\theta$ is zero. As θ increases further, *MP* also increases so that $\sin\theta$ increases. When $\theta = 90°$, $MP = OP$. Then $\sin\theta = 1$.

Thus, $\sin\theta$ increases from 0 to 1 in first quadrant.

Second Quadrant. When θ increases from 90°, *MP* decreases so that $\sin\theta$ also decreases. When $\theta = 180°$, *MP* is zero. So $\sin\theta = 0$.

Thus, $\sin\theta$ decreases from 1 to 0 in second quadrant.

Third Quadrant. When θ increases from 180°, *MP* becomes negative and decreases. Therefore, $\sin\theta$ also decreases. When $\theta = 270°$, $MP = -OP$. Then $\sin\theta = -1$.

Thus, sin θ decreases from 0 to – 1 in third quadrant.

Fourth Quadrant. As θ increases further form 270°, *MP* increases from – *a* to zero when θ = 360°.

Thus, sin θ increases from – 1 to 0 in fourth quadrant.

To sum up:

As θ increases from	*sin θ*
0° to 90°	increases from 0 to 1
90° to 180°	decreases from 1 to 0
180° to 270°	decreases from 0 to –1
270° to 360°	increases from – 1 to 0

Graph of sin θ. Let *OX* and *OY* be two lines at right angles to each other. Along *OX*, measure the angle θ from 0° to 360° and along *OY*, Measure the corresponding values of sin θ. Measure the positive values of sin θ above *OX* and negative values, below *OX*. Draw a table of values of sin θ corresponding to θ = 0°, 30°, 60° , 90° and so on upto 360°. The greatest value of sin θ is 1 and the, least value is – 1.

θ	0°	30°	60°	90°	120°	150°	180°	210°	240°	270°	300°	330°	360°
sin θ	0	.5	.87	1	.87	.5	0	– .5	–.87	– 1	– .87	– .5	0

Now plot the values of sin θ corresponding to the different values of θ as shown in the table. Then the continuous curve as shown in the figure is the graph of sin θ.

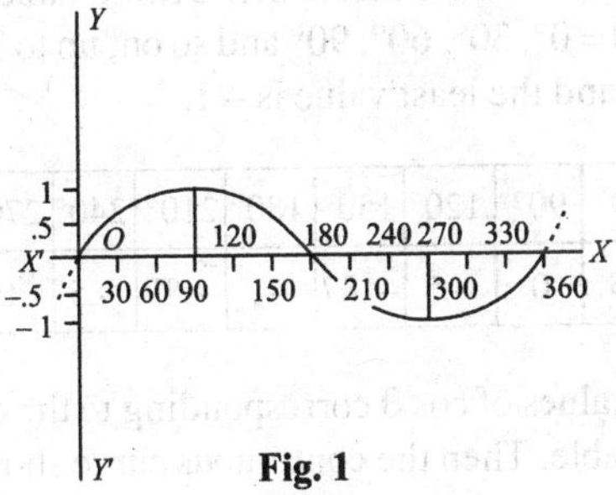

Fig. 1

Cosine Curve

$\cos\theta = \dfrac{OM}{OP}$, *OP* is of fixed length *a*.

First Quadrant. When $\theta = 0°$, $OM = OP$ so that $\cos\theta$ is 1. As θ increases further, OM decreases so that $\cos\theta$ also decreases. When $\theta = 90°$, OM is zero, so $\cos\theta = 0$.

Thus, $\cos\theta$ decreases from 1 to 0 in first quadrant.

Second Quadrant. When θ increases from 90°, OM becomes negative and decreases from 0 to $-a$. When $\theta = 180°$, $\cos\theta = -1$.

Thus, $\cos\theta$ decreases from 0 to -1 in second quadrant.

Third Quadrant. When θ increases further from 180°, OM increases from $-a$ to 0. When $\theta = 270°$, $\cos\theta = 0$.

Thus, $\cos\theta$ increases from -1 to 0 in third quadrant.

Fourth Quadrant. As θ increases from 270°, OM becomes positive and increases from 0 to a. When $\theta = 360°$, $\cos\theta = 1$.

Thus, $\cos\theta$ increases from 0 to 1 in fourth quadrant.

To sum up:

As θ increases from	*cos θ*
0° to 90°	decreases from 1 to 0
90° to 180°	decreases from 0 to – 1
180° to 270°	increases from – 1 to 0
270° to 360°	increases from 0 to 1

Graph of $\cos\theta$. Let OX and OY be two lines at right angles to each other. Along OX, measure the angle θ from 0° to 360° and along OY, measure the corresponding values of $\cos\theta$. Measure the positive values of $\cos\theta$ above OX and negative values below OX. Draw a table of values of $\cos\theta$ corresponding to $\theta = 0°, 30°, 60°, 90°$ and so on, up to 360°. The greatest value of $\cos\theta$ is 1 and the least value is -1.

θ	0°	30°	60°	90°	120°	150°	180°	210°	240°	270°	300°	330°	360°
cos θ	1	.87	.5	0	–.5	–.87	–1	–.87	–.5	0	.5	.87	1

Now plot the values of $\cos\theta$ corresponding to the different values of θ as shown in the table. Then the continuous curve shown in Fig. 2 is the graph of $\cos\theta$.

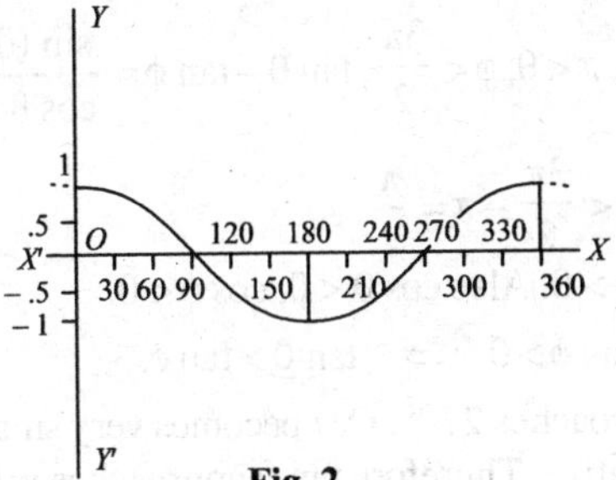

Fig. 2

Tangent Curve

$$\tan \theta = \frac{MP}{OM}.$$

First Quadrant. When $\theta = 0°$, MP is zero and $OM = OP$ so that $\tan \theta = 0$. We claim that as θ increases further, $\tan \theta$ also increases. For, let $\theta > \phi$ and $0 < \theta, \phi < \pi/2$, we have

$$\tan \theta - \tan \phi = \frac{\sin \theta}{\cos \theta} - \frac{\sin \varphi}{\cos \varphi} = \frac{\sin (\theta - \varphi)}{\cos \theta \cos \varphi} > 0.$$

$$\Rightarrow \quad \tan \theta - \tan \phi > 0$$

so that $\theta > \tan \phi$. When θ is slightly less than $90°$, MP becomes large compared to OM so that $\tan \theta$ approaches infinity.

Thus, $\tan \theta$ increases from 0 to infinity in first quadrant.

Second Quadrant. When θ just crosses $90°$, OM becomes negative and is very small compared to MP so that $\tan \theta$ approaches $-\infty$. As θ increases further, $\tan \theta$ also increases. For let $\theta > \phi$ and $\frac{\pi}{2} < \theta, \phi < \pi$, we have

$$\tan \theta - \tan \phi = \frac{\sin (\theta - \varphi)}{\cos \theta \cos \varphi}$$

Since $\theta < \pi, \phi > \frac{\pi}{2}, 0 < \theta - \phi < \frac{\pi}{2}$ so that

$\sin (\theta - \phi) > 0$ and $\cos \theta < 0, \cos \phi < 0$.

Therefore, $\tan \theta - \tan \phi > 0 \Rightarrow \tan \theta > \tan \phi$.

When $\theta = 180°$, MP is zero so that $\tan \theta$ is zero.

Thus, $\tan \theta$ increases from $-\infty$ to 0 in second quadrant.

Third Quadrant. When θ increases from $180°$, $\tan \theta$ also increases.

For, let $\theta > \phi, \pi < \theta, \phi < \frac{3\pi}{2}$, $\tan\theta - \tan\phi = \frac{\sin(\theta - \varphi)}{\cos\theta \cos\varphi}$.

Clearly $\theta - \phi < \frac{3\pi}{2} - \pi = \frac{\pi}{2}$.

so that $\sin(\theta - \phi) > 0$. Also $\cos\theta < 0$, $\cos\phi < 0$.

$\Rightarrow \quad \tan\theta - \tan\phi > 0 \quad \Rightarrow \quad \tan\theta > \tan\phi.$

When θ approaches 270°, *OM* becomes very small compared to *MP* and both are negative. Therefore $\tan\theta$ approaches infinity.

Thus, $\tan\theta$ increases from 0 to ∞ in third quadrant.

Fourth Quadrant. When θ just crosses 270°, *OM* becomes positive and is very small compared to *MP* so that $\tan\theta$ approaches $-\infty$ (as *MP* is negative). As θ increases further, $\tan\theta$ also increases. For, let $\theta > \phi$,

$$\tan\theta - \tan\phi = \frac{\sin(\theta - \varphi)}{\cos\theta \cos\varphi}, \quad \frac{3\pi}{2} < \theta, \phi < 2\pi$$

As before $\quad \theta - \phi < \pi/2$ so that $\sin(\theta - \phi) > 0$.

Also $\quad \cos\theta > 0$ and $\cos\phi > 0$.

So $\tan\theta - \tan\phi > 0 \quad \Rightarrow \quad \tan\theta > \tan\phi.$

When $\theta = 360°$, *MP* is zero so that $\tan\theta = 0$.

Thus, $\tan\theta$ increases from $-\infty$ to 0 in fourth quadrant.

To sum up:

As θ increases from	$\tan\theta$
0° to 90°	increases from 0 to ∞
90° to 180°	increases from $-\infty$ to 0
180° to 270°	increases from 0 to ∞
270° to 360°	increases from $-\infty$ to 0

Graph of $\tan\theta$. Let *OX* and *OY*, be two lines at right angles to each other. Along *OX*, measure θ and along *OY* measure the corresponding values of $\tan\theta$. The positive values are measured above *OX* and negative values below *OX*. Draw a table of values of $\tan\theta$ corresponding to the different values of θ as shown:

θ	0°	30°	60°	90°–	90°+	120°	150°	180°	210°	240°	270°–	270°+	300°	330°	360°
$\tan\theta$	0	.58	1.73	∞	$-\infty$	–1.73	–.58	0	.58	1.73	∞	$-\infty$	–1.73	–.58	0

Now plot the values of tan θ corresponding to the different values of θ as given in the table. Since tan (180° + θ) = tan θ, that complete graph of tan θ is determined by the values of tan θ from θ = 0° to θ = 180° (see Fig. 3).

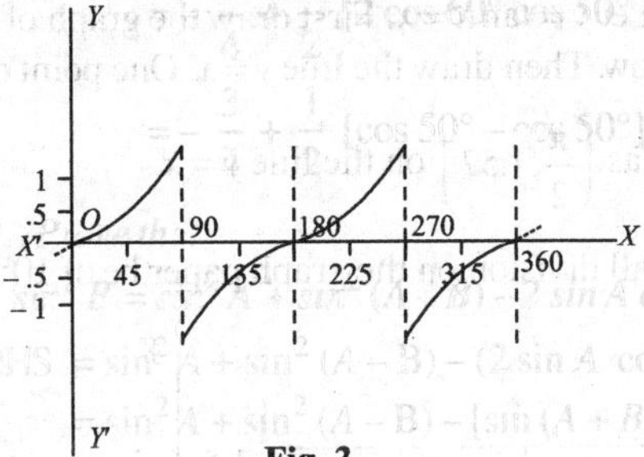

Fig. 3

Example 1. *Solve graphically the equation* $\sin x = \frac{1}{2}$ *between* $x = 0$ *and* $x = \pi$.

Solution. Let $y = \sin x = \frac{1}{2}$.

First draw the graph of $y = \sin x$ from $x = 0$ to $x = \pi$. Then draw the graph of $y = \frac{1}{2}$ which is a line parallel to x-axis.

To draw the graph of sin x, we first find the values of sin x corresponding to the different values of x and write them in a table.

x	0°	30°	60°	90°	120°	150°	180°
sin x	0	.5	.87	1	.87	.5	0

Now plot the values of sin x corresponding to the different values of x on a graph paper.

Draw the line $y = \frac{1}{2}$ and let it cut the graph of $y = \sin x$ at P and Q. The points P and Q are at $x = 30°$ and $x = 150°$ respectively.

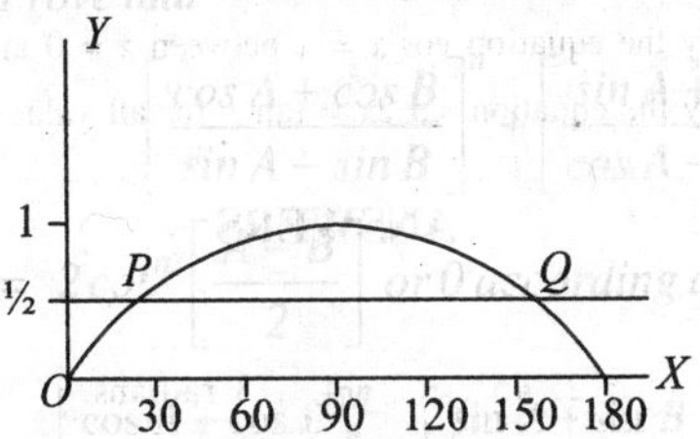

Fig. 4

Thus required solution is $x = 30°$ and $x = 150°$.

Example 2. *Solve graphically, the equation tan x = x between x = 0 and x = $\frac{\pi}{2}$.*

Solution. Let $y = \tan x = x$. First draw the graph of $y = \tan x$ from the tables given below. Then draw the line $y = x$. One point can be taken (0, 0) and other point as $\left(\frac{\pi}{2}, 1.57\right)$ on the line $y = x$.

Let one small division on the graph paper be of 10° or $\frac{\pi}{18}$ radians.

x	0°	30°	60°	90°
tan x	0	.58	1.73	∞

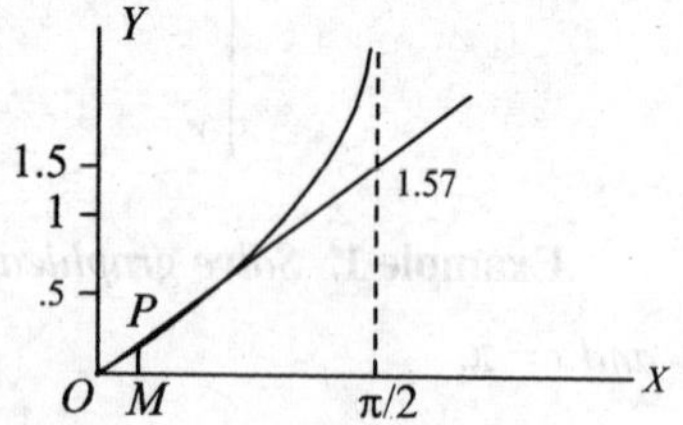

Fig. 5

The points of intersection O and P are at distances of 0 and 1.5 divisions from 0 respectively. From P draw PM perpendicular to OX.

So $\quad OM = 1.5$ divisions

$= 15° = .26$ radians.

Hence $x = .26$ radians is one solution and the other solution is $x = 0$.

EXERCISES

1. Solve graphically the equation $\cos x = \frac{1}{2}$ between $x = -\frac{\pi}{2}$ and $x = \frac{\pi}{2}$.
2. Solve graphically $\tan x = 1$ between $x = 0$ and $x = \frac{\pi}{2}$.
3. Trace the variation of trigonometrical ratios: cot θ, cosec θ, sec θ as θ varies from 0° to 360°. Draw their graphs.
4. Solve graphically the equation $\cos x = x$ between $x = 0$ and $x = 2\pi$.
5. Solve graphically the equation $\sin 2x = \tan x$ for all values of x between 0 and π.

ANSWERS

1. − 60° and 60°. 2. 45°. 4. .73 radians. 5. $\frac{\pi}{4}, \frac{3\pi}{4}, \pi$.

2. INVERSE CIRCULAR FUNCTIONS

Consider $y = \sin x$. This means x is that angle whose sine is y. This relation may also be expressed as $x = \sin^{-1} y$.

Note that y is uniquely determined, if $\frac{-\pi}{2} \le x \le \frac{\pi}{2}$. Thus $x = \sin^{-1} y$ means x is that angle (*i*) whose sine is y (*ii*) x lies between $-\frac{\pi}{2}$ and $\frac{\pi}{2}$.

Similarly, we say $x = \cos^{-1} y$ if

(*i*) $\cos x = y$ (*ii*) $0 \le x \le \pi$

$x = \tan^{-1} y$, if

(*i*) $y = \tan x$ (*ii*) $\frac{-\pi}{2} \le x \le \frac{\pi}{2}, x \ne \pm\frac{\pi}{2}$

$x = \cot^{-1} y$ if,

(*i*) $y = \cot x$ (*ii*) $\frac{-\pi}{2} \le x \le \frac{\pi}{2}, x \ne 0$

$x = \sec^{-1} y$, if,

(*i*) $y = \sec x$ (*ii*) $0 \le x \le \pi, x \ne \frac{\pi}{2}$

$x = \text{cosec}^{-1} y$, if

(*i*) $y = \text{cosec}\, x$, (*ii*) $\frac{-\pi}{2} \le x \le \frac{\pi}{2}, x \ne 0$

The expressions $\sin^{-1} x$, $\cos^{-1} x$, $\tan^{-1} x$, $\cot^{-1} x$, $\text{cosec}^{-1} x$, $\sec^{-1} y$ are called inverse circular functions.

REMARK: Since $-1 \le \sin x \le 1$ and $-1 \le \cos x \le 1$, $\sin^{-1} y$ and $\cos^{-1} y$ are real numbers only when $-1 \le y \le 1$.

Example 3. *Prove that* (*i*) $\sin^{-1} x = \text{cosec}^{-1} \frac{1}{x}$

(*ii*) $\cos^{-1} x = \sec^{-1} \frac{1}{x}$

(*iii*) $\tan^{-1} x = \cot^{-1} \frac{1}{x}$.

Solution. (*i*) Let $y = \sin^{-1} x$

Then $\sin y = x$ or $\text{cosec}\, y = \frac{1}{x}$

Therefore $y = \text{cosec}^{-1} \frac{1}{x}$

Thus $\sin^{-1} x = \text{cosec}^{-1} \frac{1}{x}$

(*ii*) Let $y = \cos^{-1} x$

Then $\cos y = x$ or $\sec y = \frac{1}{x}$

Therefore $y = \sec^{-1} \frac{1}{x}$

Thus $\cos^{-1} x = \sec^{-1} \frac{1}{x}$

(*iii*) Let $y = \tan^{-1} x$

Then $\tan y = x$ or $\cot y = \frac{1}{x}$

Therefore, $y = \cot^{-1} \frac{1}{x}$

Thus $\tan^{-1} x = \cot^{-1} \frac{1}{x}$

Example 4. *Prove that* (*i*) $sin^{-1} (-x) = - sin^{-1} x$

(*ii*) $cos^{-1} (x) = - cos^{-1} x$

(*iii*) $tan^{-1}(-x) = - tan^{-1} x.$

Solution. (*i*) Let $y = \sin^{-1} (-x)$

Then $-x = \sin y$

or $x = \sin (-y)$

or $\sin^{-1} x = -y = -\sin^{-1} (-x)$

Thus $\sin^{-1} (-x) = -\sin^{-1} (x)$

(*ii*) Let $y = \cos^{-1} (x)$

Then $x = \cos y$

or $x = \cos (-y)$

or $\cos^{-1} x = -y = -\cos^{-1} x$

(*iii*) Let $y = \tan^{-1} (-x)$

Then $\tan y = -x$

or $x = -\tan y = \tan (-y)$

Therefore, $\tan^{-1} x = -y$

or $y = -\tan^{-1} x$

Thus $\tan^{-1} (-x) = -\tan^{-1} x.$

Example 5. *Prove that* (*i*) $\sin^{-1} x + \cos^{-1} x = \frac{\pi}{2}$

(*ii*) $\tan^{-1} x + \cot^{-1} x = \frac{\pi}{2}$

(*iii*) $\sec^{-1} x + \operatorname{cosec}^{-1} x = \frac{\pi}{2}$.

Solution. (*i*) Let $y = \sin^{-1} x$

Then $x = \sin y = \cos\left(\frac{\pi}{2} - y\right)$

So, $\cos^{-1} x = \frac{\pi}{2} - y = \frac{\pi}{2} - \sin^{-1} x$

$\Rightarrow \sin^{-1} x + \cos^{-1} x = \frac{\pi}{2}$

(*ii*) Let $y = \tan^{-1} x$

Then $x = \tan y = \cot\left(\frac{\pi}{2} - y\right)$

So, $\cot^{-1} x = \frac{\pi}{2} - y = \frac{\pi}{2} - \tan^{-1} x$

$\Rightarrow \tan^{-1} x + \cot^{-1} x = \frac{\pi}{2}$

(*iii*) Let $y = \sec^{-1} x$

Then $\sec y = x$

or $\operatorname{cosec}\left(\frac{\pi}{2} - y\right) = x$

So, $\operatorname{cosec}^{-1} x = \frac{\pi}{2} - y = \frac{\pi}{2} - \frac{\pi}{2} \sec^{-1} x$

$\Rightarrow \sec^{-1} x + \operatorname{cosec}^{-1} x = \frac{\pi}{2}$.

Example 6. *Prove that* $\tan^{-1} x \tan^{-1} y = \tan^{-1}\left(\frac{x+y}{1-xy}\right)$.

Solution. Let $\alpha = \tan^{-1} x,\ \beta = \tan^{-1} y$

Then $\tan \alpha = x,\ \tan \beta = y$

So, $\tan(\alpha + \beta) = \frac{\tan \alpha + \tan \beta}{1 - \tan \alpha \tan \beta} = \frac{x + y}{1 - xy}$

Therefore, $\alpha+\beta = \tan^{-1}\left(\frac{x+y}{1-xy}\right)$

Thus $\tan^{-1} x + \tan^{-1} y = \tan^{-1}\left(\frac{x+y}{1-xy}\right)$.

Example 7. *Prove that* $2\tan^{-1}x = \sin^{-1}\frac{2x}{1+x^2}$.

Solution. Let $\tan^{-1} x = y$

Then $x = \tan y$

or $\frac{\sin y}{\cos y} = \frac{x}{1}$

or $\frac{\sin y}{x} = \frac{\cos y}{1} = \frac{\sqrt{\sin^2 y + \cos^2 y}}{\sqrt{x^2+1}} = \frac{1}{\sqrt{1+x^2}}$

Therefore, $\sin y = \frac{x}{\sqrt{1+x^2}}, \cos y = \frac{1}{\sqrt{1+x^2}}$

Thus $\sin 2y = 2\sin y\cos y$

$$= 2\frac{x}{\sqrt{1+x^2}}\frac{1}{\sqrt{1+x^2}} = \frac{2x}{1+x^2}$$

$$\Rightarrow \quad 2y = \sin^{-1}\left(\frac{2x}{1+x^2}\right)$$

$$\Rightarrow \quad 2\tan^{-1} x = \sin^{-1}\left(\frac{2x}{1+x^2}\right).$$

Example 8. *Prove that* (*i*) $2\tan^{-1} x = \cos^{-1}\left(\frac{1-x^2}{1+x^2}\right)$

(*ii*) $2\tan^{-1} x = \tan^{-1}\left(\frac{x^2}{1-x^2}\right)$.

Solution. (*i*) Now $\cos 2y = \cos^2 y - \sin^2 y$

$$= \frac{1}{1+x^2} - \frac{x^2}{1+x^2} \qquad \text{(From Example 7)}$$

$$= \frac{1-x^2}{1+x^2}$$

$$2y = \cos^{-1}\left(\frac{1-x^2}{1+x^2}\right)$$

$$2\tan^{-1} x = \cos^{-1}\left(\frac{1-x^2}{1+x^2}\right)$$

(*ii*) Now $\tan 2y = \dfrac{2\tan y}{1-\tan^2 y} = \dfrac{2x}{1-x^2}$ (From Example 7)

$\Rightarrow$ $$2y = \tan^{-1}\frac{2x}{1-x^2}$$

$\Rightarrow$ $$2\tan^{-1} x = \tan^{-1}\frac{2x}{1-x^2}.$$

Example 9. *Prove that* $\sin\left(2\tan^{-1}\frac{1}{4} + \cot^{-1}\frac{23}{7}\right) = \frac{1}{\sqrt{2}}$.

Solution. Now $\sin\left(2\tan^{-1}\dfrac{1}{4} + \cot^{-1}\dfrac{23}{7}\right)$

$$= \sin\left(\tan^{-1}\frac{2\times\frac{1}{4}}{1-\left(\frac{1}{4}\right)^2} + \tan^{-1}\frac{7}{23}\right)$$

$$= \sin\left(\tan^{-1}\frac{16}{30} + \tan^{-1}\frac{7}{23}\right)$$

$$= \sin\left(\tan^{-1}\frac{\frac{16}{30}+\frac{7}{23}}{1-\frac{16}{30}\times\frac{7}{23}}\right)$$

$$= \sin\left(\tan^{-1}\frac{289}{289}\right) = \sin(\tan^{-1} 1)$$

$$= \sin 45^\circ = \frac{1}{\sqrt{2}}.$$

Example 10. *If $-1 \leq x \leq 1$, prove that $\cos(\sin^{-1} x) = \sin(\cos^{-1} x)$.*

Solution. Let $y = \sin^{-1} x$

Then $\sin y = x$ or $\cos y = \sqrt{1-x^2}$

or $y = \cos^{-1} \sqrt{1-x^2}$

Thus $\cos(\sin^{-1} x) = \cos(\cos^{-1} \sqrt{1-x^2}) = \sqrt{1-x^2}$

Again, let $z = \cos^{-1} x$. Then $\cos z = x$

or $\sin z = \sqrt{1-x^2}$ or $z = \sin^{-1} \sqrt{1-x^2}$

Thus $\sin(\cos^{-1} x) = \sin(\sin^{-1} \sqrt{1-x^2}) = \sqrt{1-x^2}$

Hence $\sin(\cos^{-1} x) = \cos(\sin^{-1} x)$.

Example 11. *If $-1 \leq x \leq 1$, prove that $\cos^{-1} x + \cos^{-1}(1-x) = 180°$.*

Solution. Let $\alpha = \cos^{-1} x,\ \beta = \cos^{-1}(-x)$

Then $\cos\alpha = x,\ \cos\beta = -x$

So, $\cos\alpha + \cos\beta = 0$.

or $\cos\alpha = -\cos\beta = \cos(\pi - \beta)$

$\Rightarrow$ $\alpha = \pi - \beta$

$\Rightarrow$ $\alpha + \beta = 180°$

$\Rightarrow$ $\cos^{-1} x + \cos^{-1}(-x) = 180°$.

Example 12. *Find the value of*

$$\sin\left[\left(\cos^{-1}\left(-\frac{1}{2}\right)\right) + \tan^{-1}\left(\frac{1}{\sqrt{3}}\right)\right].$$

Solution. Let $\alpha = \cos^{-1}\left(-\frac{1}{2}\right),\quad \beta = \tan^{-1}\left(\frac{1}{\sqrt{3}}\right)$

Then $\cos\alpha = -\frac{1}{2},\quad \tan\beta = \frac{1}{\sqrt{3}}$

$\Rightarrow$ $\alpha = 120°,\quad \beta = 30°$

Therefore, $\sin\left[\left(\cos^{-1}\left(-\frac{1}{2}\right)\right) + \tan^{-1}\left(\frac{1}{\sqrt{3}}\right)\right]$

$= \sin(\alpha + \beta) = \sin(120° + 30°)$

$= \sin(150°) = \frac{1}{2}$.

Example 13. *Prove that*

$$2\tan^{-1}\left(\frac{1}{3}\right)+\tan^{-1}\left(\frac{1}{7}\right)=\frac{\pi}{4}.$$

Solution. $\text{LHS} = \tan^{-1}\dfrac{2\times\frac{1}{3}}{1-\left(\frac{1}{3}\right)^2}+\tan^{-1}\dfrac{1}{7}$

$$= \tan^{-1}\frac{2}{3}\times\frac{9}{8}+\tan^{-1}\frac{1}{7}$$

$$= \tan^{-1}\frac{3}{4}+\tan^{-1}\frac{1}{7}$$

$$= \tan^{-1}\frac{\frac{3}{4}+\frac{1}{7}}{1-\frac{3}{28}} = \tan^{-1}\frac{25}{25}$$

$$= \tan^{-1}1 = \frac{\pi}{4}.$$

EXERCISES

1. Prove that $2\sec^{-1}x = \sec^{-1}\dfrac{x^2}{2-x^2}$.
2. Prove that $3\cot^{-1}x = \cot^{-1}\dfrac{x(x^2-3)}{3x^2-1}$.
3. Prove that $\tan^{-1}\dfrac{1}{2}+\tan^{-1}\dfrac{1}{3} = \dfrac{\pi}{4}$.
4. Prove that $\tan^{-1}1+\tan^{-1}2+\tan^{-1}3 = \pi$.
5. Prove that $\tan^{-1}\sqrt{x} = \dfrac{1}{2}\cos^{-1}\dfrac{1-x}{1+x}$.
6. If $\cot^{-1}\left[\dfrac{1}{a}\right]+\cot^{-1}\left[\dfrac{1}{b}\right]+\cot^{-1}\left[\dfrac{1}{c}\right] = \dfrac{\pi}{2}$, Prove that $bc+ca+ab=1$.
7. If $\cos^{-1}(a)+\cos^{-1}(b)+\cos^{-1}(c)=\pi$, show that $a^2+b^2+c^2+2abc=1$.
8. If $\sin^{-1}(a)+\sin^{-1}(b)+\sin^{-1}(c)=\pi$, show that

   $$a\sqrt{1-a^2}+b\sqrt{1-b^2}+c\sqrt{1-c^2} = 2abc.$$
9. Find the value of $\tan(\tan^{-1}x+\cot^{-1}x)$.

10. Find the value of $\sin^{-1} 2x + \sin^{-1} x$ for $x = \dfrac{1}{2}$ and $x = \dfrac{\sqrt{21}}{14}$.

11. Find the value of

$$\cot^{-1}\frac{\frac{1}{\sqrt{2}}-2}{\frac{1}{\sqrt{2}}-1}+\cot^{-1}\frac{\frac{1}{\sqrt{2}}+2}{\frac{1}{\sqrt{2}}+1}.$$

ANSWERS

9. $\tan\dfrac{\pi}{2}$ 10. $\dfrac{\pi}{3}$ 11. $\dfrac{\pi}{4}$.

CHAPTER 20

HEIGHTS AND DISTANCES

One of the important applications of trigonometry is finding the distances between points and heights of objects without actually measuring them. The examples given below will illustrate how with the help of trigonometry we find the heights and distances. For this, we require the following two definitions.

Angle of Elevation. Let P and A be two points. Through A draw a horizontal line AB. Then the angle PAB is called the angle of elevation of the point P as seen from A.

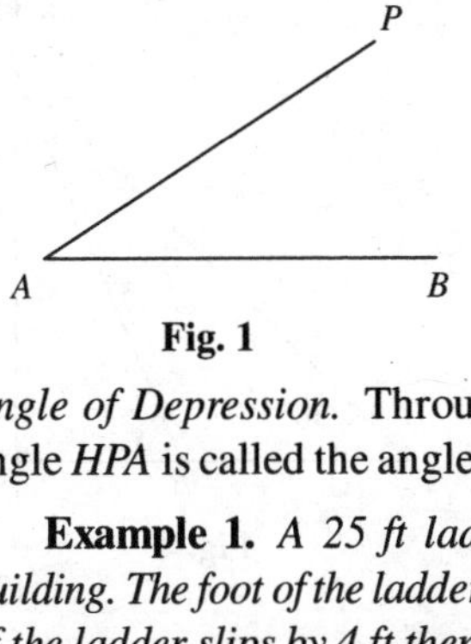

Fig. 1

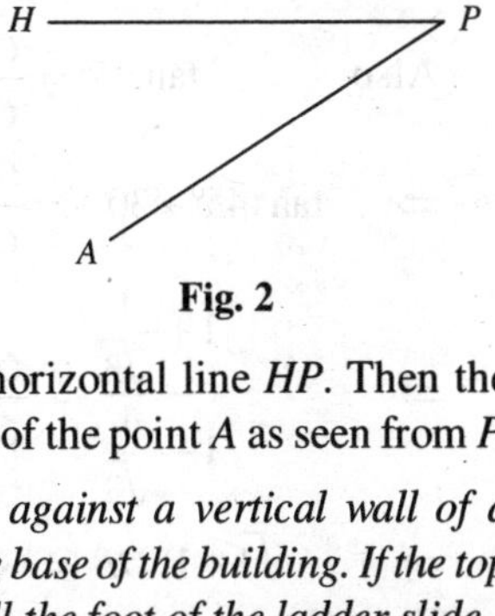

Fig. 2

Angle of Depression. Through P draw a horizontal line HP. Then the angle HPA is called the angle of depression of the point A as seen from P.

Example 1. *A 25 ft ladder is placed against a vertical wall of a building. The foot of the ladder is 7 ft from the base of the building. If the top of the ladder slips by 4 ft then how much will the foot of the ladder slide.*

Solution. AB is the initial position of ladder.

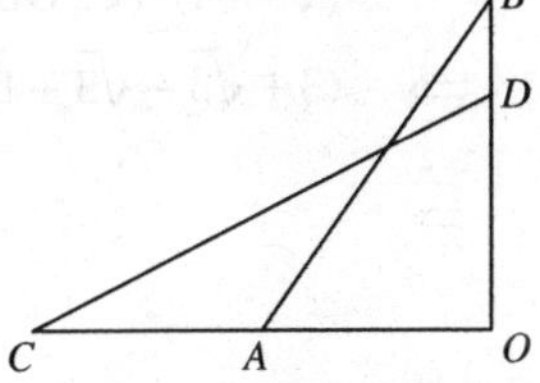

Fig. 3

$$OA = 7 \text{ ft}$$
$$AB = 25 \text{ ft}$$
$$BD = 4 \text{ ft}$$
$$AC = ?$$

Now $\quad (AB)^2 = (OA)^2 + (OB)^2$

$\Rightarrow \quad 625 = 49 + (OB)^2$

$\Rightarrow \quad (OB)^2 = 625 - 49 = 576 = (24)^2$

$\Rightarrow \quad OB = 24 \text{ ft}$

$\Rightarrow \quad OD = OB - BD = 20 \text{ ft}$

Again, $\quad (OC)^2 + (OD)^2 = (CD)^2$

$\Rightarrow \quad (7 + AC)^2 + 400 = 625$

$\Rightarrow \quad 49 + (AC)^2 + 14AC = 225$

$\Rightarrow \quad (AC)^2 + 14AC - 176 = 0$

$$\Rightarrow \quad AC = \frac{-14 \pm \sqrt{196 + 704}}{2} = \frac{-14 \pm 30}{2} = 8 \text{ ft.}$$

Example 2. *A person walking along a straight road observes that at two consecutive kilometre stones the angles of elevation of a hill in front of him are 30° and 75° respectively. Find the height of the hill.*

Solution. OC is the height of hill and A, B are two consecutive kilometre stones so that $AB = 1$ kilometre

Now $\quad \tan 30° = \dfrac{OC}{OA} = \dfrac{OC}{AB + OB}$

$$\Rightarrow \quad 1 + OB = \sqrt{3}\, OC \qquad \text{... (1)}$$

Also $\quad \tan 75° = \dfrac{OC}{OB}$

$$\Rightarrow \quad \tan (45° + 30°) = \frac{OC}{OB}$$

$$\Rightarrow \quad \frac{1 + \frac{1}{\sqrt{3}}}{1 - \frac{1}{\sqrt{3}}} = \frac{OC}{OB}$$

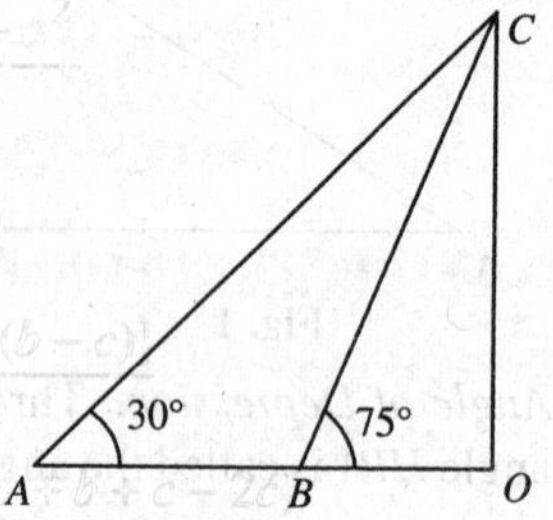

Fig. 4

$$\Rightarrow \quad (\sqrt{3} + 1)\, OB = (\sqrt{3} - 1)\, OC \qquad \text{... (2)}$$

From (1) and (2), we have

$$(\sqrt{3} + 1)\ (\sqrt{3}\, OC - 1) = (\sqrt{3} + 1)\, OC$$

$$\Rightarrow \quad (3 + \sqrt{3} - \sqrt{3} + 1)\, OC = (\sqrt{3} + 1)$$

$$\Rightarrow \quad OC = \frac{(\sqrt{3} + 1)}{4}$$

$$= \frac{1.732 + 1}{4} = \frac{2.732}{4}$$

$= .683$ kilometre $= 683$ metres.

Example 3. *A telegraph post stands on the top of a vertical tower, the elevation of the top of post from a certain place on the same horizontal level with the base of the town is found to be α. Advancing a distance d towards the tower on the same horizontal plane, the elevation of the top of the electric post is found to be β and that of the top of the tower is observed to be δ. If h is the height of the top of the post from the base of the tower and x is the height of the tower, prove that*

$$h \tan \delta = x \tan \beta$$

and $$h (\cot \alpha - \cot \beta) = d.$$

Solution. $AC = h$

$AB = x$

Now $\tan \beta = \dfrac{AC}{AP} = \dfrac{h}{AP}$

and $\tan \delta = \dfrac{AB}{AP} = \dfrac{x}{AP}$

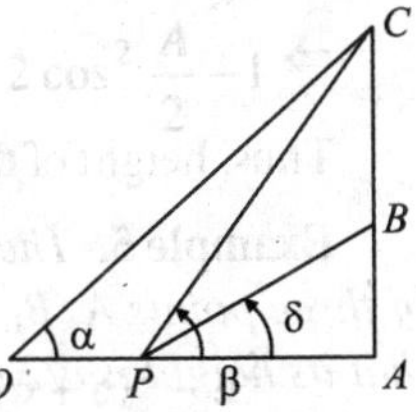

Fig. 5

So, $\dfrac{h}{\tan \beta} = \dfrac{x}{\tan \delta}$

$\Rightarrow$ $h \tan \delta = x \tan \beta$

Also, $\cot \alpha = \dfrac{OA}{AC} = \dfrac{d + AP}{h}$

Therefore, $\cot \alpha - \cot \beta = \dfrac{d + AP - AP}{h} = \dfrac{d}{h}$

$\Rightarrow$ $h (\cot \alpha - \cot \beta) = d.$

Example 4. *From the deck of a ship, the angle of elevation of the top of a tower on the shore is observed to be 30° and the angle of depression of the reflection of the top in water to be 45°. If the height of the deck above the water level is 15 metres find the height of the tower.*

Solution. Let O be the observer, 15 metres above the water. BD = height of the tower.

Let $CD = x$. Let E be the reflection of the top of the tower.

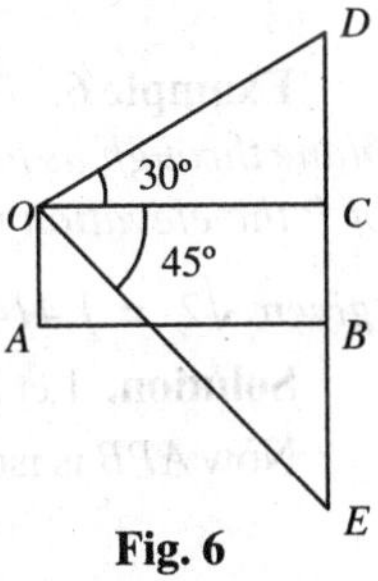

Fig. 6

Now $\tan 30° = \dfrac{x}{OC}$

Again, $BE = BD = 15 + x$

Therefore, $OC = CE \cot 45° = CE$

$\Rightarrow$ $OC = BC + BE = 30 + x$

$$\Rightarrow \qquad \tan 30^\circ = \frac{x}{30+x}$$

$$\Rightarrow \qquad \frac{1}{\sqrt{3}} = \frac{x}{30+x}$$

$$\Rightarrow \qquad 30+x = \sqrt{3}x = (1.732)\,x$$

$$\Rightarrow \qquad 30 = (.732)\,x$$

$$\Rightarrow \qquad x = \frac{30}{.732} = \frac{30000}{732} = 40.98$$

Thus, height of the tower = $15 + x = 55.98$ metres.

Example 5. *The altitude of the top of a mountain observed from each of three points A, B, C forming a triangle ABC on the plane is α. Show that its height is a/2 tan α cosec A where ∠BAC = A and BC = a.*

Solution. Let MO be the mountain of height h.

$$\angle MAO = \angle MBO = \angle MCO = \alpha$$

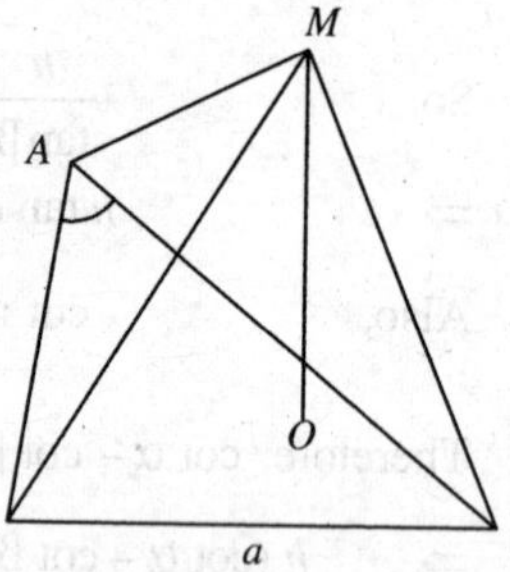

Fig. 7

Now $\tan\alpha = \dfrac{h}{AO} = \dfrac{h}{BO} = \dfrac{h}{CO}$

$\Rightarrow \qquad AO = BO = CO = R$ (say)

$\Rightarrow O$ is the centre of the circumscribed circle of the $\Delta\, ABC$

Again $\angle BAC = A \Rightarrow \angle BOC = 2A$

Therefore in $\Delta\, OBC$,

$$OB^2 + OC^2 - 2OB\,.\,OC\cos 2A = BC^2$$

$$\Rightarrow \qquad a^2 = R^2 + R^2 - 2R^2\cos 2A$$

$$= 2R^2\,(1-\cos 2A) = 4R^2\sin^2 A$$

$$\Rightarrow \qquad a = 2R\sin A$$

Now $\qquad h = R\tan\alpha = \dfrac{a}{2}\operatorname{cosec} A\tan\alpha.$

Example 6. *The elevation of a hill from a place P on the horizontal plane through its foot and due East of it is 45° and at a place Q due South of P the elevation is 30°. If PQ = 200 metres, find the height of the hill (given $\sqrt{2}$ = 1.4142.)*

Solution. Let AB be the hill of height x.

Now APB is isosceles triangle in which

$$PA = PB = x \qquad (\text{as } \angle APB = \angle PBA = 45^\circ)$$

Also, $AQ^2 = PQ^2 + AP^2$

$= (200)^2 + x^2$

Now $\tan 30° = \frac{AB}{AQ} = \frac{x}{\sqrt{40000 + x^2}}$

$\Rightarrow \quad \sqrt{3}x = \sqrt{40000 + x^2}$

$\Rightarrow \quad 3x^2 = 40000 + x^2$

$\Rightarrow \quad 2x^2 = 40000$

$\Rightarrow \quad x^2 = 20000$

$\Rightarrow \quad x = 100\sqrt{2}$

$\Rightarrow \quad x = 100 \times 1.4142$

$\Rightarrow \quad x = 141.42$ metres.

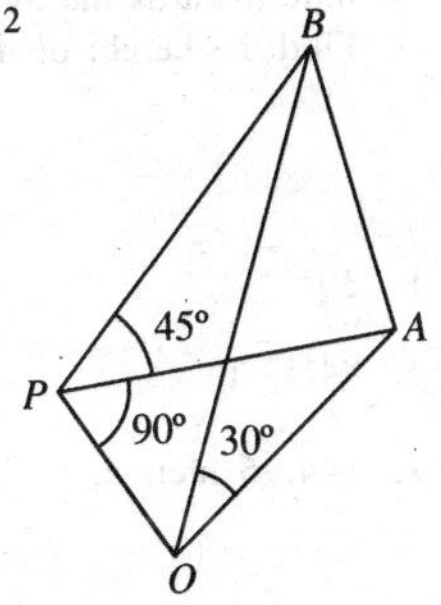

Fig. 8

EXERCISES

1. The top of a pole across a canal 40 ft wide is tied to a rope 80 ft long to a point on the other bank opposite the foot of the pole. Find the angle made by the rope with the pole and the ground.
2. From the top of a tower 100 ft high the angles of depression of the top and the bottom of a mansion, standing on the other side of the road are 30° and 60° respectively. What is the width of the road and the height of the mansion?
3. A flower bed is to be laid in the form of a right angled triangle of which one of the other two angles is 30° and hypotenuse is 20 cm. Find the other sides.
4. From the top of a lighthouse, the angles of depression of two ships are found to be 45° and 60°. If the line joining the ships passes through foot of the lighthouse and if the height of lighthouse is 200 ft, find the distance between the ships.
5. A tower subtends an angle α at a point A on the same level as the foot of the tower. B is a point vertically above A and $AB = h$ ft. The angle of depression of the foot of the tower, measured from B is β. Find the height of the tower.
6. From a lighthouse, the angles of depression of two ships on opposite sides of a lighthouse are 300 metres, find the distance between the ships if the line joining them passes through the foot of the lighthouse.
7. A man observes that the angle of elevation of the top of a Gopuram of a temple due east of him is 60°. After he walked 240 metres towards the north he observed that the angle of elevation has been reduced to 30°. If the Gopuram is standing on a horizontal plane, find its height.
8. AB is a straight rod leading to P, the foot of the tower. A being at a distance of 512 metres from P, and B 320 metres nearer. If the angle of elevation of tower at B be the double of the angle of elevation at A, find the height of the tower.
9. An object is observed from three points A, B, C lying in a horizontal line which passes directly underneath the object; the angular elevation at B is twice that at A and at C is three times that at A. If $AB = a$, $BC = b$ and A, B, C are all on one

side of the foot of perpendicular dropped from the object to the line AB produced, show that the object is at a height $\frac{a}{ab}\sqrt{(a+3b)(3b-a)}$ above AB.

10. At the foot of a mountain the elevation of its summit is 45°. After ascending one mile towards the mountain up an incline of 30°, the elevation changes to 60°. Find the height of mountain to its nearest foot.

ANSWERS

1. 30°.	2. 57.73 ft, 66.67 ft.	3. 10 cm, 17.32 cm.
4. 84.53 ft.	5. $h\frac{\tan\alpha}{\tan\beta}$.	6. 219 metres.
7. 144.96 metres.	8. 256 metres.	10. 7213 ft.

CHAPTER 21

CO-ORDINATES AND LOCI

1. Coordinate Geometry or Analytical Geometry is that branch of Mathematics in which we make use of algebra to solve the geometrical problems. This is made possible by the use of a co-ordinate system which represents points in a plane by means of a pair of real numbers called co-ordinates. This representation is based on the assumption that there exists a one-to-one correspondence between the real numbers and points on a line.

2. CARTESIAN CO-ORDINATE SYSTEM

Let $X'OX$ and $Y'OY$ be two perpendicular lines in the plane of the paper intersecting at O. Let P be any point in the plane of the paper and let PM be perpendicular on OX. The lengths OM and PM are called the rectangular cartesian co-ordinates, or briefly, the cordinates of P and are usually denoted by the letters x and y respectively. The line $X'OX$ is called the x-axis and the line YOY' is called the y-axis. The point O is called the origin. The two axes divide the plane, called the co-ordinate plane, into four quadrants XOY, YOX', $X'OY'$ and $Y'OX$ which are respectively referred to as the first, second, third and fourth quadrants.

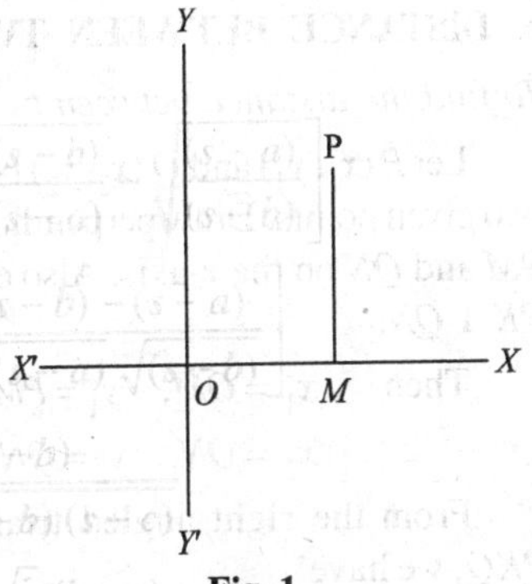

Fig. 1

The length OM is called *abscissa* or the x-co-ordinate of the point P, and MP is called the *ordinate* or the y-co-ordinate of P. This is expressed, in the notational form, by writing $P(x, y)$, which indicates that the point P has abscissa x and ordinate y.

In Analytical Geometry (Co-ordinate Geometry) we have the same rule as regards the signs that the reader has already met with in

Trigonometry. Thus lengths measured along OX are regarded as positive whilst those measured along OX' are taken as negative. Similarly distances measured along OY are positive and those along OY' are negative. Suppose Q is any point in the second quadrant $X'OY$. Drop $QK \perp OX'$. If numerical values of OK and QK be a and b respectively the co-ordinates of Q are $(-a, b)$ as the distance measured along OX' is negative.

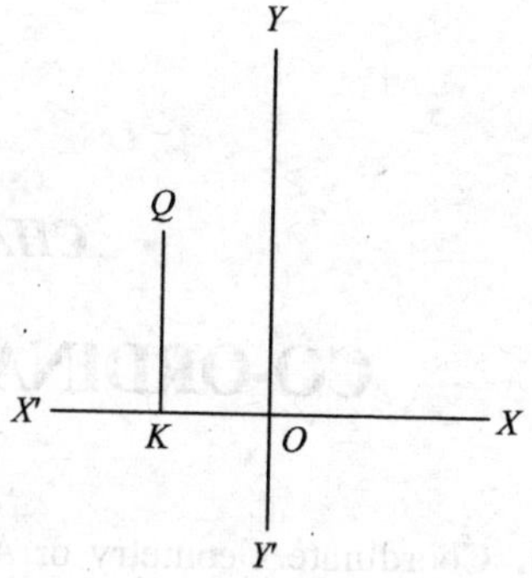

Fig. 2

In general we find that in first quadrant, both abscissa and ordinate are +ve, in second quadrant abscissa is –ve, ordinate is +ve, in third quadrant both abscissa and ordinate are –ve, and in the fourth quadrant abscissa is +ve whereas the ordinate is –ve.

Clearly, the co-ordinates of the origin are (0, 0).

[Note. Throughout our study of Co-ordinate Geometry we shall be dealing with lines and curves in a plane only (*i.e.*, we shall be dealing with only two dimensional problems).]

3. DISTANCE BETWEEN TWO POINTS

To find the distance between two points whose co-ordinates are given.

Let $P(x_1, y_1)$ and $Q(x_2, y_2)$ be the two given points. Draw perpendicular PM and QN on the x-axis. Also draw $PK \perp QN$.

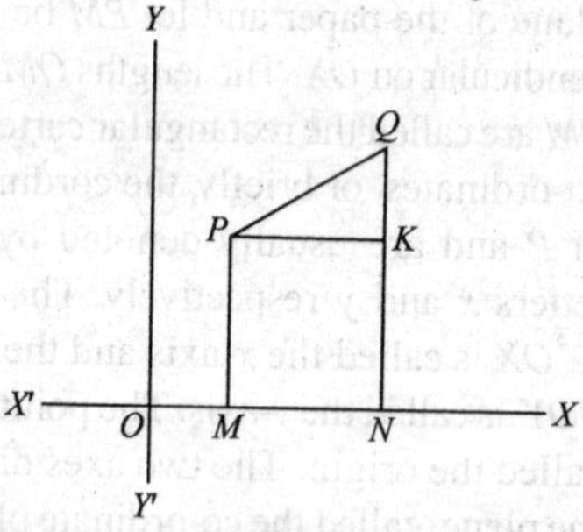

Fig. 3

Then $\quad x_1 = OM, \quad y_1 = PM$

$\quad x_2 = ON, \quad y_2 = QN$

From the right angled triangle PKQ, we have

$$PQ^2 = PK^2 + QK^2$$

or $$PQ^2 = MN^2 + (QN - KN)^2$$

$$= (ON - OM)^2 + (QN - PM)^2$$

$$= (x_2 - x_1)^2 + (y_2 - y_1)^2$$

Giving the required distance between P and Q by

$$PQ = \sqrt{(x_2 - x_1)^2 + (y_2 - y_1)^2}$$

Note. (*i*) Positive sign is taken with the square root sign, as the distance between two points is by definition positive.

(*ii*) If the points P and Q are in different quadrants, the result still holds, provided proper sign is taken with the co-ordinates.

Corollary. Distance of any point $P(x_1, y_1)$ from the origin is $\sqrt{x_1^2 + y_1^2}$.

4. SECTION FORMULAS

To find the co-ordinates of the point which divides the joins of two given points (x_1, y_1) and (x_2, y_2) in the ratio $m_1 : m_2$.

Case I. Internal division. Let P and Q be the two given points with co-ordinates (x_1, y_1) and (x_2, y_2) respectively and let $R(x, y)$ be the point which divides the join of P, Q in the ratio $m_1 : m_2$ internally. Draw perpendiculars PL, RM, QN on the x-axis and take RT parallel to x-axis meeting QN in T and LP produced in K.

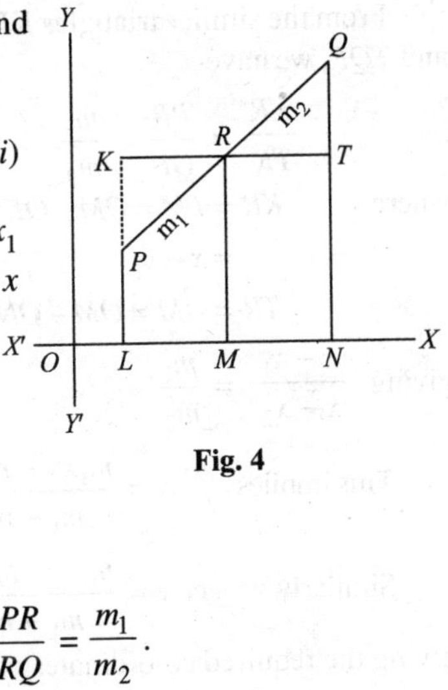

Fig. 4

Then from similar triangles KPR and TQR, we have

$$\frac{KR}{RT} = \frac{PR}{RQ} = \frac{m_1}{m_2} \quad \text{... (i)}$$

Now, $KR = LM = OM - OL = x - x_1$

$RT = MN = ON - OM = x_2 - x$

Thus (*i*) gives

$$\frac{x - x_1}{x_2 - x} = \frac{m_1}{m_2}$$

$$\Rightarrow \qquad x = \frac{m_1 x_2 + m_2 x_1}{m_1 + m_2}$$

Similarly by considering, $\dfrac{PK}{TQ} = \dfrac{PR}{RQ} = \dfrac{m_1}{m_2}$.

we get $$y = \frac{m_1 y_2 + m_2 y_1}{m_1 + m_2}$$

Hence the co-ordinates of R are

$$\left(\mathbf{\frac{m_1 x_2 + m_2 x_1}{m_1 + m_2}, \frac{m_1 y_2 + m_2 y_1}{m_1 + m_2}}\right)$$

Corollary. If R is the middle point of PQ, we have

$$\mathbf{x} = \frac{\mathbf{x_1 + x_2}}{\mathbf{2}}$$

$$\mathbf{y} = \frac{\mathbf{y_1 + y_2}}{\mathbf{2}}$$

Thus the co-ordinates of the *middle point* of the line joining the points (x_1, y_1) and (x_2, y_2) are

$$\left(\frac{x_1 + x_2}{2}, \frac{y_1 + y_2}{2}\right).$$

Case II. External division. Let now R divide PQ, externally, in the ratio $m_1 : m_2$. Drop perpendiculars PL, QN, RM on the x-axis and complete the figure as shown.

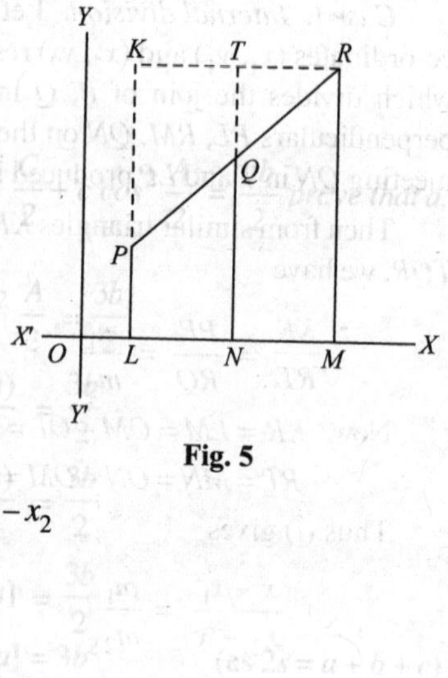

Fig. 5

From the similar triangles KPR and TQR, we have

$$\frac{KR}{TR} = \frac{PR}{QR} = \frac{m_1}{m_2}$$

where $KR = LM = OM - OL$

$= x - x_1$

$TR = NM = OM - ON = x - x_2$

giving $$\frac{x - x_1}{x - x_2} = \frac{m_1}{m_2}$$

This implies $$x = \frac{m_1 x_2 - m_2 x_1}{m_1 - m_2}$$

Similarly, we get $$y = \frac{m_1 y_2 - m_2 y_1}{m_1 - m_2}$$

giving the required co-ordinates of the point R.

REMARKS:

1. The co-ordinates for external division are obtained from those for internal division by changing m_2 to $-m_2$.
2. In external division if K lies towards P *i.e.*, on QP produced, we shall get the co-ordinates of K by putting $-m_1$ for m_1 in the formula for internal division.

Example 1. *Find the distance between the points (4, – 7) and (–1, 5).*

Solution. Using the distance formula, the required distance between the two given points will be $\sqrt{[4-(-1)]^2+[(-7)-5]^2}$,

$$= \sqrt{(4+1)^2+(-7-5)^2} = \sqrt{169} = 13.$$

Example 2. *Find the point which divides the join of (2, 1) and (3, 5) externally in the ratio 2 : 3, the point lying towards the point (3, 5).*

Solution. Let $R\ (x, y)$ be the required point, then we have

$$m_1 = 2, m_2 = 3$$

Using the formula for external division, we have

$$x = \frac{m_1x_2 - m_2x_1}{m_1 - m_2} = \frac{2.3-3.2}{2-3} = 0$$

$$y = \frac{m_1y_2 - m_2y_1}{m_1 - m_2} = \frac{2.5-3.1}{2-3} = \frac{10-3}{-1} = -7.$$

So R is the point $(0, -7)$.

Example 3. *Show that the medians of a triangle are concurrent.*

Solution. Let the co-ordinates of the vertices A, B, C of a triangle be (x_1, y_1), (x_2, y_2) and (x_3, y_3). If D is the middle point of BC then D has co-ordinates $\left(\frac{x_2+x_3}{2}, \frac{y_2+y_3}{2}\right)$.

Let G be the point which divides AD, internally in the ratio 2 : 1, then if (x, y) are the co-ordinates of G, we have

$$x = \frac{2\times\frac{x_2+x_3}{2} + 1\times x_1}{2+1} = \frac{x_1+x_2+x_3}{3}$$

Similarly $$y = \frac{y_1+y_2+y_3}{3}.$$

Now if E and F are middle points of AC and AB, then by the same process, we can show that the above are the co-ordinates of the points that divide BE and CF in the ratio 2 : 1 (which is also seen to be true by symmetry).

Hence the point $\left(\frac{x_1+x_2+x_3}{3}, \frac{y_1+y_2+y_3}{3}\right)$ lies on each of the lines AD, BE and CF and therefore, these three lines meet in a point. This point is called the *centroid* of the triangle.

Example 4. *Show that the points (6, 6), (2, 3), (4, 7) are the vertices of a right angled triangle.*

Solution. Let A (6, 6), B (2, 3), C (4, 7) be the three points.

Then
$$AB = \sqrt{(6-2)^2 + (6-3)^2} = \sqrt{16+9} = 5$$
$$BC = \sqrt{(2-4)^2 + (3-7)^2} = \sqrt{4+16} = \sqrt{20}$$
$$CA = \sqrt{(4-6)^2 + (7-6)^2} = \sqrt{4+1} = \sqrt{5}$$

Hence
$$25 = AB^2 = 20 + 5 = BC^2 + CA^2$$

$\Rightarrow$ ABC is a right triangle, right angled at C.

Example 5. *Show that the points (2, 6), (5, 1), (0, – 2) and (– 3, 3) are the vertices of a square.*

Solution. Let the four given points be A (2, 6), B (5, 1), C (0, – 2), D (–3, 3).

Then
$$AB = \sqrt{(2-5)^2 + (6-1)^2} = \sqrt{3^3 + 5^2} = \sqrt{34}$$
$$BC = \sqrt{(5-0)^2 + (1+2)^2} = \sqrt{5^2 + 3^2} = \sqrt{34}$$
$$CD = \sqrt{(0+3)^2 + (-2-3)^2} = \sqrt{3^2 + 5^2} = \sqrt{34}$$
$$DA = \sqrt{(-3-2)^2 + (3-6)^2} = \sqrt{5^2 + 3^2} = \sqrt{34}$$

$\Rightarrow$
$$AB = BC = CD = DA.$$

Again $AC^2 = (2-0)^2 + (6+2)^2 = 4 + 64 = 68.$

Thus
$$AC^2 = 34 + 34 = AB^2 + BC^2$$

$\Rightarrow$ ABC is a right triangle, right angled at B.

Hence $ABCD$ is a square.

5. AREA OF A TRIANGLE

To find the area of a triangle, co-ordinates of the vertices being given.

Let ABC be the given triangle, the vertices A, B, C having co-oridinates (x_1, y_1), (x_2, y_2) and (x_3, y_3). Draw perpendiculars AL, BM, CN on the x-axis If Δ denotes the area of the triangle ABC, we have

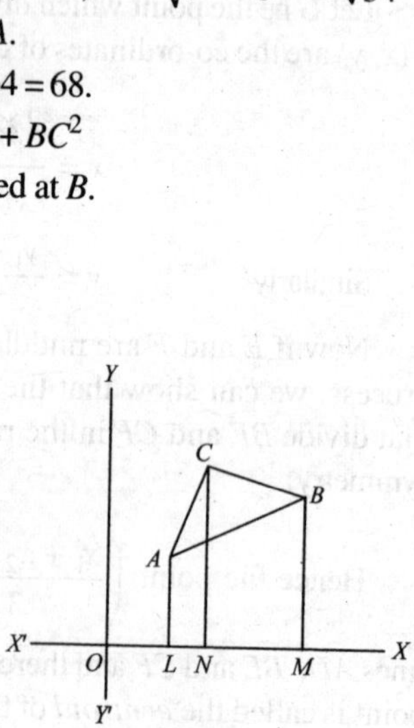

Fig. 6

Δ = trapezium *ALNC* + trap. *CNMB* – trap. *ALMB*.

Since the area of a trapezium is given by

$\frac{1}{2}$ (sum of parallel sides) × (distance between them)

The required area is

$$= \frac{1}{2} LN (LA + NC) + \frac{1}{2} NM (NC + MB) - \frac{1}{2} LM (LA + MB)$$

$$= \frac{1}{2} (x_3 - x_1)(y_1 + y_3) + \frac{1}{2} (x_2 - x_3)(y_2 + y_3) - \frac{1}{2} (x_2 - x_1)(y_1 + y_2)$$

which on simplification reduces to

$$\frac{1}{2} [x_1 (y_2 - y_3) + x_2 (y_3 - y_1) + x_3 (y_1 - y_2)]$$

The result can also be expressed in the determinant form

$$\Delta = \frac{1}{2} \begin{vmatrix} x_1 & y_1 & 1 \\ x_2 & y_2 & 1 \\ x_3 & y_3 & 1 \end{vmatrix}$$

REMARK: It may be noted that the above expression for the area of a triangle is positive if the order of the angular points such that in going round the triangle, the area is always on the left hand, *i.e.*, the order of description of the circuit *ABCA* is anticlockwise. Otherwise the area is found to be negative. The sign may, however, be disregarded whenever numerical value of the area is required.

Corollary. The points *A*, *B*, *C* are collinear, if and only if the area of the triangle *ABC* is zero. Thus a necessary and sufficient condition for three points (x_1, y_1), (x_2, y_2) and (x_3, y_3) to be collinear is that

$$x_1 (y_2 - y_3) + x_2 (y_3 - y_1) + x_3 (y_1 - y_2) = 0.$$

Example 6. *Find the area of the triangle whose vertices are* $(at_i^2, 2at_i)$, $i = 1, 2, 3$. *Also show that these points can never be collinear.*

Solution. The required area of the triangle is given by

$$\frac{1}{2} [at_1^2 (2at_2 - 2at_3) + at_2^2 (2at_3 - 2at_1) + at_3^2 (2at_1 - 2at_2)]$$

$$= a^2 [t_1^2 (t_1 - t_3) + t_2^2 (t_3 - t_1) + t_3^2 (t_1 - t_2)]$$

$$= -a^2 (t_1 - t_2)(t_2 - t_3)(t_3 - t_1).$$

Now the three points will be collinear if the area of the triangle determined by them is zero. But area can be zero if either $t_1 = t_2$ or $t_2 = t_3$ or

$t_3 = t_1$. *i.e.*, only if at least two of the three points coincide. Thus if all the three points are distinct, the area cannot be zero and so the points can never be collinear. (Note *a* cannot be zero.)

Example 7. *Show that the three points (1, 4), (3, – 2) and (– 3, 16) are collinear.*

Solution. The three points will be collinear if the area of the triangle formed by these three is zero.

Area is given by

$$\frac{1}{2}[1(-2-16)+3(16-4)-3(4+2)] = \frac{1}{2}[-18+36-18]=0$$

Hence the three points are collinear.

Example 8. *If A* (x_1, y_1), *B* (x_2, y_2), *C* (x_3, y_3), *and D* (x_4, y_4) *are the vertices of a quadrilateral, taken in order; find its area.*

Solution. Join AC, then the required area of the quadrilateral is given by

$$\Delta ABC + \Delta ACD$$

Thus the required area is

$$\frac{1}{2}[x_1(y_2-y_3)+x_2(y_3-y_1)+x_3(y_1-y_2)]$$

$$+\frac{1}{2}[x_1(y_3-y_4)+x_3(y_4-y_1)+x_4(y_1-y_3)]$$

$$=\frac{1}{2}[(x_1y_2-x_2y_1)+(x_2y_3-x_3y_2)+(x_3y_4-x_4y_3)+(x_4y_1-x_1y_4)]$$

EXERCISES

1. Find the distance between the points.
   (*i*) (1, 2), (– 1, – 2)
   (*ii*) (2, 1), (3, 4)
   (*iii*) (– 1, 0), (0, 3).
2. In what ratio is the line joining the points (4, 4) and (7, 7) divided by (–1, –1)?
3. Find the point that divides the join of (1, 2), (3, 4) in the ratio 2 : 5.
4. Show that the points (8, –10), (7, – 3) and (0, – 4) are the vertices of a right triangle.
5. Show that the points (1, 1), (– 1, – 1) and $(-\sqrt{3}, \sqrt{3})$ are the angular points of an equilateral triangle.
6. The middle point of a line is (2, 3) and one end of the line is (3, 4). What are the co-ordinates of the other end?

7. In what ratio is the line joining the points (1, 2) and (4, 5) divided by the x-axis?
8. Find the centroid of the triangle whose vertices are the points
   (3, – 5), (– 7, 4) and (10, – 2).
9. If A, B, C are any three points on the x-axis, show that
   $AB + BC + CA = 0$.
10. Show that the following points are collinear
    (*i*) (3, – 2), (– 1, 1), (– 5, 4)
    (*ii*) (2, – 1), (5, 3) (– 4, – 9)
    (*iii*) (5, 1), (1, – 1), (3, 0).
11. Are the following points collinear?
    (*i*) (1, 3), (3, – 1), (– 2, 9)
    (*ii*) (– 1, 0), (3, 0), (1, 2)
    (*iii*) (1, 1), (– 1, – 1), $(-\sqrt{3}, -\sqrt{3})$.
12. Show that the points (3, 3), (0, – 1), (– 2, 3) are the vertices of an isosceles triangle.
13. From two perpendicular roads X and Y, a building A is at a distance of 100 yards and 150 yards respectively, a building B is at a distance of 150 yards and 100 yards respectively and a building C is at a distance of 200 yards and 175 yards respectively. Find the distance between A and B and examine if all the buildings are in a straight line or not.
14. Find the area of the triangle, the co-ordinates of whose vertices are
    (*i*) (1, 1), (0, 0), (– 1, 2)
    (*ii*) (1, 3), (1, 2), (– 1, 1).
15. Show that the points (2, – 2), (8, 4), (5, 7) and (– 1, 1) are the vertices of a triangle.
16. If $A(x_1, y_1)$, $B(x_2, y_2)$ and $C(x_3, y_3)$ be the co-ordinates of the vertices of a triangle, find the co-ordinates of its in-centre.
17. Find the area of the triangle, the co-ordinates of whose vertices are
    $(a, c + a)$, (a, c) and $(-a, c - a)$.
18. In any triangle ABC prove that
    $AB^2 + AC^2 = 2(AD^2 + DC^2)$
    Where D is the middle point of BC.
    [*Hint.* Take origin at B and select BC as x-axis.]
19. Show that the area of a triangle is four times the area of the triangle formed by joining the middle points of its sides.
20. Find the co-ordinates of the in-centre of the triangle whose vertices are the points (1, – 2), (– 2, 4) and (3, – 6).
21. Show that the distance between the points which divide the join of (4, 3) and (5, 7) internally and externally in the ratio 2 : 3 is $\dfrac{12\sqrt{17}}{5}$.

22. Find the area of the quadrilateral whose angular points taken in order are (3, 2), (– 3, 4), (– 2, – 3) and (2, – 2).

23. The vertices of a triangle ABC are A (3, 0), B (0, 6) and C (6, 9). A line DE divides AB and AC in the ratio 1 : 2 meeting AB in D and AC at E. Prove that $\Delta ABC = 9 \Delta ADE$.

24. Find the area of the pentagon, the co-ordinates of whose vertices are (– 5, – 2), (– 2, 5), (2, 7), (5, 1) and (2, – 4).

25. Show that the points (4, 3), (7, – 1) and (9, 3) are the vertices of an isosceles triangle.

ANSWERS

1. (*i*) $\sqrt{20}$ (*ii*) $\sqrt{10}$ (*iii*) $\sqrt{10}$.
2. – 5 : 6.
3. $\left(\frac{11}{7}, \frac{18}{7}\right)$.
6. (1, 2).
7. 2 : – 5.
8. (2, – 1).
11. (*i*) Yes (*ii*) No (*iii*) No.
13. $\sqrt{5000}$, No .
14. (*i*) 3 (*ii*) 1
16. $\left(\frac{ax_1 + bx_2 + cx_3}{a+b+c}, \frac{ay_1 + by_2 + cy_3}{a+b+c}\right)$, where $AB = c$, $BC = a$, $CA = b$.
17. a^2.
20. (1, – 2).
22. $\frac{55}{2}$.
24. 66.

LOCUS AND ITS EQUATION

6. DEFINITION

When a point moves under a certain condition, or conditions, the path it traces out is called its *Locus* under these conditions.

Consider, for example, a point P which moves in such a way that its distance from a fixed point O remains always the same, say equal to a. Then we know that it traces out a circle of radius a. Thus the locus of P is a circle of radius a.

Again, let A and B be two fixed points in the plane of the paper. Let a point P move in the plane of the paper such that its distance remains same from both A and B. Then clearly this point P lies on the right bisector of AB. Also there is no other point, which is equidistant from A and B and which does not lie on the right bisector of AB. So locus of P is nothing but the right bisector of AB.

When a point moves so as to satisfy any given condition or conditions it describes some definite curve, (or locus) and a relation can always be found between the co-ordinates of any point on the path. This relation is called the equation of the curve or the locus. Thus the equation to a curve is the relation which exists between the co-ordinates of any point on the curve, and which holds for no other points except those lying on the curve.

In the definition of locus we have considered a point which can occupy different positions. Sometimes the various positions are regarded as different points and the locus is the join of all such points. Consider, for example, that we are given a set of parallel lines under certain condition (say a set of parallel chords of a circle). We wish to find the locus of middle points of these chords. Then the required locus will be nothing but the join of all the middle points of all such chords.

We consider below a few examples on the formation of the equation to a locus.

Example 9. *Find the locus of a point which is equidistant from the points (1, 2) and (3, 5).*

Solution. Let $P(x, y)$ be any point on the locus. It is given that the distance of P from $A(1, 2)$ and $B(3, 5)$ is always same, *i.e.*, $PA = PB$

Now $$PA = \sqrt{(x-1)^2 + (y-2)^2}$$

$$PB = \sqrt{(x-3)^2 + (y-5)^2}$$

Thus $$PA = PB \Rightarrow (x-1)^2 + (y-2)^2 = (x-3)^2 + (y-5)^2$$

or $$4x + 6y = 29$$

which is the required locus.

Example 10. *Find the equation to the locus of a point which moves so that its distance from the x-axis is three times its distance from the axis of y.*

Solution. Let $P(x, y)$ be any point on the locus, then its distance from the x-axis is y and its distance from the y-axis is x, so by the given condition $y = 3x$ which is the required locus.

In working out problems, the co-ordinate axes, if not specified, should always be chosen such that lengthy calculations are avoided. For instance, consider

Example 11. *Find the locus of a point which moves so that the sum of the squares of its distances from two fixed points is constant.*

Solution. Let A and B be the two fixed points. Take the line joining A, B as the axis of x and the line through middle point of AB and perpendicular to it as y-axis. Let O be the middle point of AB.

Also let $$OA = OB = a$$

Then co-ordinates of A and B are respectively, $(-a, 0)$ and $(a, 0)$

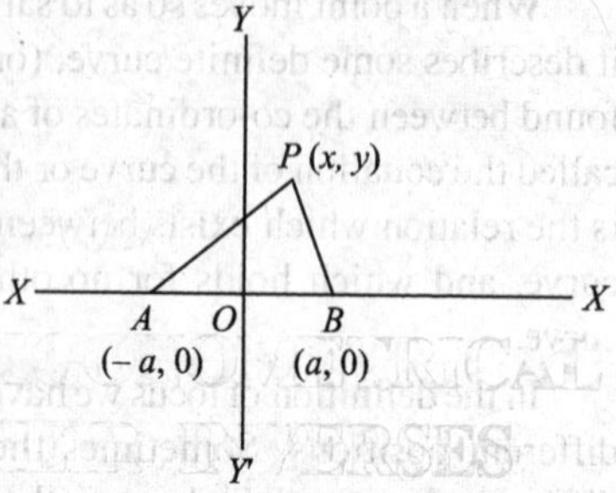

Fig. 7

Let $P(x, y)$ be any point on the locus. Then it is given that

$$PA^2 + PB^2 = \text{constant} = 2k^2 \text{ (say)}$$

Since $$PA^2 = (x+a)^2 + y^2$$
$$PB^2 = (x-a)^2 + y^2$$

we have $$(x+a)^2 + y^2 + (x-a)^2 + y^2 = 2k^2$$

or $$x^2 + y^2 = k^2 - a^2$$

which is the required locus.

EXERCISES

1. Find the equation to the locus of a point which is always equidistant from the points $(a + b, a - b)$ and $(a - b, a + b)$.
2. Let A and B be two fixed points having co-ordinates $(a, 0)$ and $(-a, 0)$. Find locus of a point P which moves in such a way that
$$PA^2 - PB^2 = \text{a constant} = 2k^2.$$
3. A stick of length l rests against the floor and a wall of a room. If the stick begins to slide on the floor, find the locus of its middle point.
4. A point moves so that its distance from the points $(ae, 0)$ and $(-ae, 0)$ is $2a$; prove that its locus is
$$\frac{x^2}{a^2} + \frac{y^2}{a^2(1-e^2)} = 1.$$
5. If the join of points (2, 3) and (– 1, 5) subtends a right angle at the point P, find the locus of P.

ANSWERS

1. $y = x$.
2. $2ax + k^2 = 0$.
3. $4(x^2 + y^2) = l^2$.
5. $x^2 + y^2 - x - 8y + 13 = 0$.

CHAPTER 22

THE STRAIGHT LINE

1. EQUATION OF A STRAIGHT LINE

We shall start by finding the equation of a straight line in different forms. The equation of a straight line, we know, is the (linear) relation between x and y which is satisfied by the co-ordinates of each and every point on the line and by those of no other point.

REMARK: Henceforth we shall be using the word line in place of straight line in accordance with the modern terminology.

2. EQUATION OF LINE PARALLEL TO THE AXES

Let AB be a line parallel to the axis of y, at a distance a from it. Also let AB be on the right of y-axis. Then abscissa of any point on the line AB will be a, and so $x = a$ for all points on the line AB and for no other points.

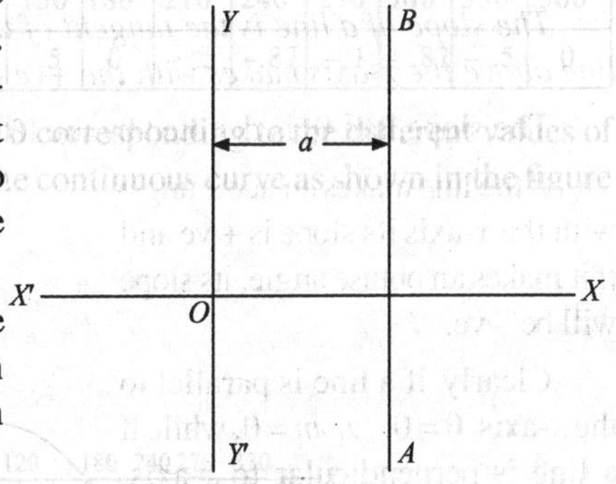

Fig. 1

Hence equation of the line AB is $x = a$. If the line was on the left of y-axis, its equation would have been $x = -a$.

Similarly, the equation of a line parallel to the axis of x (at a distance b) is $y = b$ (if the line is above the x-axis) and $y = -b$ (if it is below the x-axis).

It may be noted here that the equation of a curve does not necessarily contain both x and y.

Corollary. The equation to the x-axis is $y = 0$.

The equation to the y-axis is $x = 0$.

3. SLOPE A LINE

When we say that a line makes an angle θ with the x-axis, it means that θ is the angle through which a ray coincident with the positive direction of the x-axis is to revolve in the anticlockwise direction to coincide with the line. So this angle θ is a +ve angle lying between 0° and 180°.

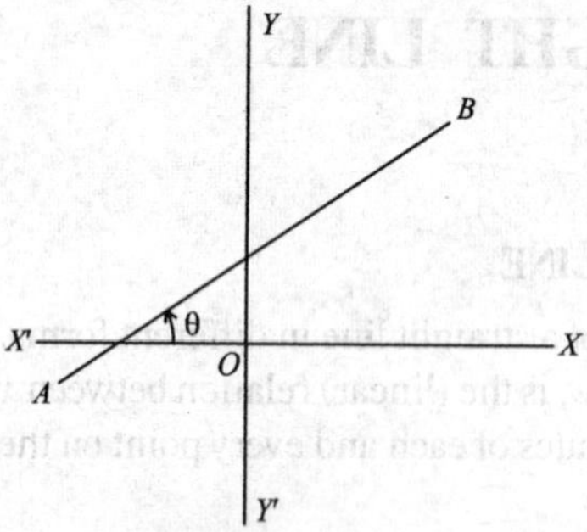

Fig. 2

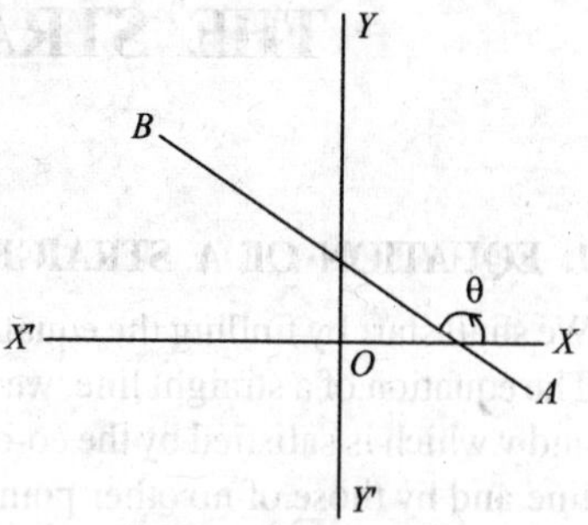

Fig. 3

Let, now a line AB make an angle θ with the axis of x (in the sense explained above) then tan θ is defined to be the *slope* (or *gradient*) of the line. So summing up, we can say that

The slope of a line is the tangent of the angle which the part of the line above the x-axis makes with the +ve direction of the x-axis.

The slope, tan θ, is denoted by the letter m.

If the line makes an acute angle with the x-axis its slope is + ve and if it makes an obtuse angle, its slope will be – ve.

Clearly, if a line is parallel to the x-axis, $\theta = 0$. $\therefore$ $m = 0$, while if a line is perpendicular to x-axis, $1/m = 0$.

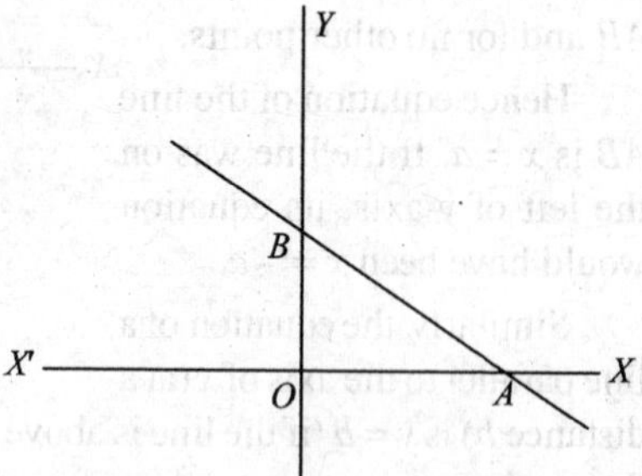

Fig. 4

4. INTERCEPTS

Let a line AB cut the co-ordinate axes in points A and B (on x and y axes respectively). Then OA is defined to be the intercept of the line on x-axis and OB is the intercept of the line on y-axis.

5. EQUATION OF A LINE IN THE SLOPE FORM

To find the equation of a line which cuts off a given intercept on the y-axis and is inclined at a given angle to the x-axis.

Let AB be the line meeting the y-axis at K. Let $OK = c$, be the given intercept on the y-axis, and let the line make an angle θ with the x-axis. Take any point $P(x, y)$ on the line. Draw PN perpendicular to x-axis to meet a line through K parallel to x-axis, in M. Then

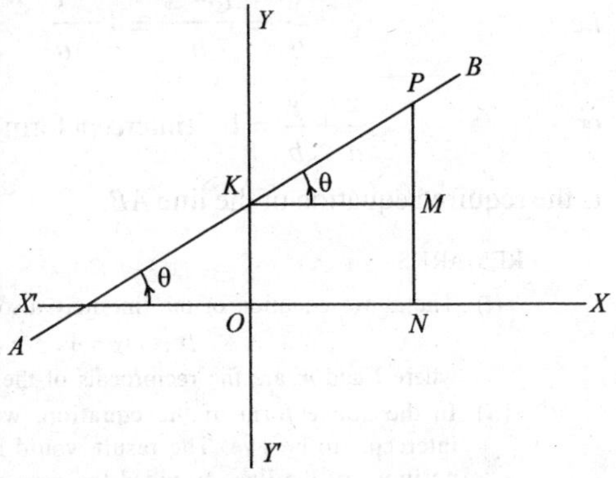

Fig. 5

$$PN = PM + MN$$
$$= KM \tan\theta + OK = x\tan\theta + c$$

Since $PN = y$, $\tan\theta = m$ = slope of the line AB, we have the required equation of the line as

$$y = mx + c.$$

[Note. In the equation $y = mx + c$, c is + ve if the point K lies above the x-axis, and –ve otherwise.]

By giving suitable values to m and c we can make the equation $y = mx + c$ represent any line except those which are parallel to the y-axis.

Cor. Equation of a line passing through the origin and making an angle θ with the x-axis is

$$y = mx, \quad \text{where } m = \tan\theta$$

6. EQUATION OF A LINE IN THE INTERCEPT FORM

To find the equation of a line which cuts off given intercepts from the axes.

Let the line AB make intercepts $OA = a$, $OB = b$ on the axes.

Take $P(x, y)$ any point on the line. Draw PN perpendicular on x-axis. Then from similar triangles PNA and BOA, we have

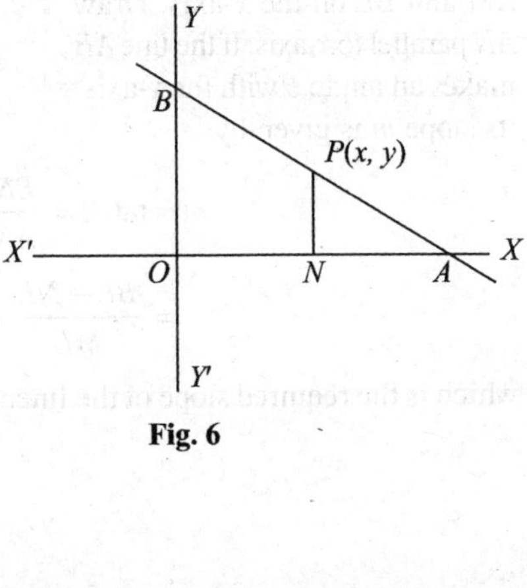

Fig. 6

$$\frac{NP}{OB} = \frac{NA}{OA} = \frac{OA - ON}{OA}$$

i.e., $\frac{y}{b} = \frac{a - x}{a} = 1 - \frac{x}{a}$

or $\frac{x}{a} + \frac{y}{b} = 1$ (intercept form)

is the required equation of the line AB.

REMARKS:

(*i*) The above equation of the line may also be written in the form

$$lx + my = 1$$

where l and m are the reciprocals of the intercepts on the axis.

(*ii*) In the above form of the equation, we have taken both the intercepts to be +ve. The result would however be true for all positions of the line, provided the proper sign is taken with the intercepts. For instance, a line which makes intercepts 2 and – 4 on the x and y axis respectively will have the equation

$$\frac{x}{2} - \frac{y}{4} = 1$$

In this case it cuts the x-axis on the +ve side and the y-axis on the –ve side at distance 2 and 4 respectively.

Example 1. *Find the slope of the line passing through two given points* (x_1, y_1) *and* (x_2, y_2), *where* $x_2 \neq x_1$.

Solution. Let the two given points on the line be $A(x_1, y_1)$ and $B(x_2, y_2)$. Draw perpendiculars AM and BL on the x-axis. Draw AN parallel to x-axis. If the line AB makes an angle θ with the x-axis, its slope m is given by

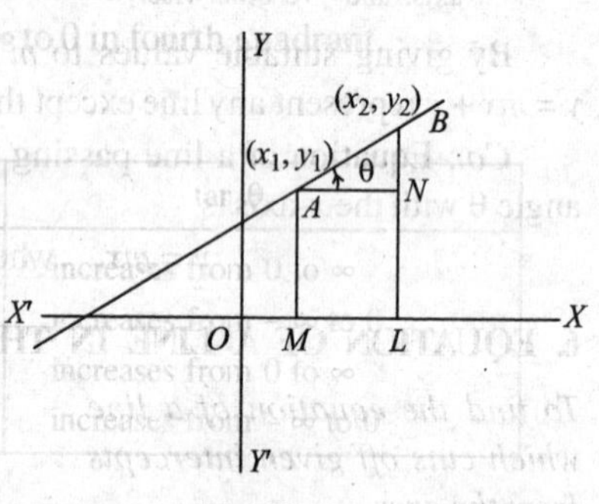

Fig. 7

$$m = \tan\theta = \frac{BN}{AN}, \quad \text{(from the rt. angled } \Delta\, ANB)$$

$$= \frac{BL - NL}{ML} = \frac{y_2 - y_1}{OL - OM} = \frac{y_2 - y_1}{x_2 - x_1}$$

which is the required slope of the line.

Notes: 1. The above should be remembered as a formula.

2. When $x_1 = x_2$, the line is perpendicular to x-axis.

Example 2. *Show that a line which is equally inclined to the axes has slope +1 or –1.*

Solution. There are two possible positions of a line AB which is equally inclined to the axes. Equally inclined means $\angle OBA = \angle OAB$ and each is 45° as $\angle AOB$ is a right triangle.

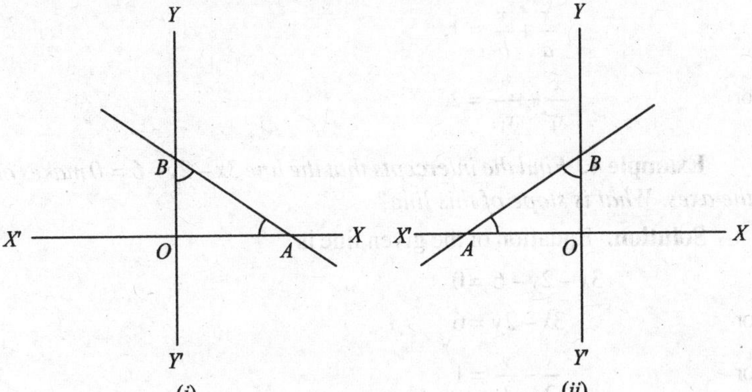

Fig. 8

In Fig. (*i*) $m = \tan XAB = \tan 135° = -1$

In Fig. (*ii*) $m = \tan XAB = \tan 45° = 1$.

Thus the slope can either be 1 or – 1.

Example 3. *Prove that the equation to a line which passes through the given point (x_1, y_1) and is such that the given point bisects the part intercepted between the axis, is* $\frac{x}{x_1} + \frac{y}{y_1} = 2$.

Solution. Let AB be the required line passing through $P(x_1, y_1)$. Let the line cut off intercepts a and b from the axis. Then $OA = a$, $OB = b$.

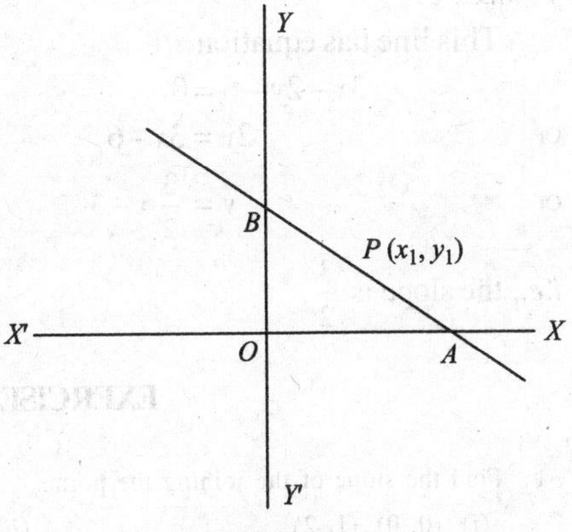

Fig. 9

So the co-ordinates of the points A and B are $(a, 0)$ and $(0, b)$.

Since it is given that the point (x_1, y_1) bisects the portion intercepted between the axes, we have

$$x_1 = \frac{a+0}{2}, \qquad y_1 = \frac{0+b}{2}$$

or $$a = 2x_1, \qquad b = 2y_1.$$

Hence equation of AB (in the intercept form) is

$$\frac{x}{a} + \frac{y}{b} = 1,$$

or $$\frac{x}{x_1} + \frac{y}{y_1} = 2.$$

Example 4. *Find the intercepts that the line $3x - 2y - 6 = 0$ makes on the axes. What is slope of this line?*

Solution. Equation of the given line is

$$3x - 2y - 6 = 0$$

or $$3x - 2y = 6$$

or $$\frac{x}{2} - \frac{y}{3} = 1$$

or $$\frac{x}{2} + \frac{y}{-3} = 1$$

which is the intercept form. Hence, the intercepts made on the axes are 2 and – 3.

To find slope of this line, we write the equation of the line in the form $y = mx + c$.

This line has equation

$$3x - 2y - 6 = 0$$

or $$2y = 3x - 6$$

or $$y = \frac{3}{2}x - 3$$

i.e., the slope is $\frac{3}{2}$.

EXERCISES

1. Find the slope of the joining the points

   (*i*) (0, 0), (1, 2) (*ii*)(– 1, 3), (2, 5)

   (*iii*) (– 2, – 1), (1, 3).

   [**Hint.** Use result of Example 1 as formula.]

2. Find the equation of the line making intercepts 1, – 1 on the x- and y-axes respectively.
3. Find the equation of the line passing through the point (0, 2) and making an angle of 45° with the x-axis.
4. Find the slope of the line $\sqrt{3}y = x - 2\sqrt{3}$.
5. Find the equation of a line, which makes an intercept of 5 on x-axis and 7 on y-axis. Find the angle it makes with y-axis.
6. Prove that the line which makes an angle $\tan^{-1} 5$ with the axis of x, and which cuts the axis of y in the point (0, – 5), passes through the point (1, 0).
7. Find the equation of the line which passes through the point (–5, 4) and is such that the portion of it between the axes is divided by the point in the ratio 1 : 2.
8. Find slope of the line passing through the point (– 1, 2) and the origin.
9. Find the intercepts that the line $3x - 4y + 12 = 0$ makes on the axes. What is slope of this line?
10. Find the intercepts that the line $x - 2y = 2$ makes on the axes. Find also the slope of the line.

ANSWERS

1. (*i*) 2. (*ii*) $\frac{2}{3}$. (*iii*) $\frac{4}{3}$.

2. $x - y = 1$. 3. $y = x + 2$. 4. $\frac{1}{\sqrt{3}}$.

5. $\frac{x}{5} + \frac{y}{7} = 1$; $\tan^{-1} \frac{5}{7}$. 7. $5x - 8y = 60$.

8. – 2. 9. – 4, 3 ; $\frac{3}{4}$. 10. 2, – 1 ; $\frac{1}{2}$.

7. LINE THROUGH GIVEN POINTS

To find the equation of a line passing through a given point (x_1, y_1) and having slope m.

Let AB be the line passing through the given point $A (x_1, y_1)$ and having slope $m = \tan \theta$.

Let $P (x, y)$ be any point on the line and complete the figure as shown, then

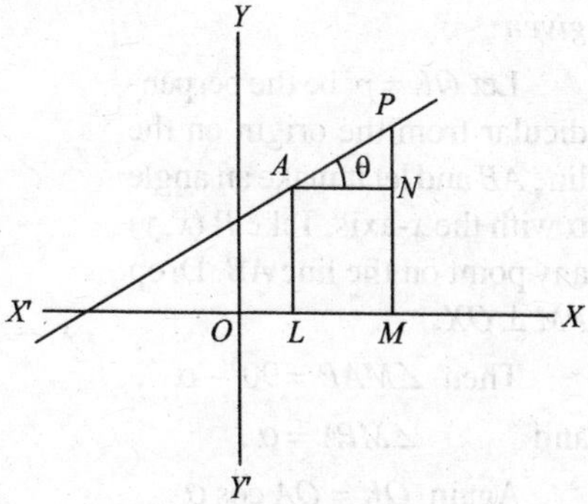

Fig. 10

$$m = \tan\theta = \frac{PN}{AN} = \frac{PM - NM}{LM}$$

$$= \frac{PM - NM}{OM - OL}$$

or $$m = \frac{y - y_1}{x - x_1}$$

or $$y - y_1 = m(x - x_1).$$

This is the required equation of the line.

8. TO FIND THE EQUATION OF THE LINE PASSING THROUGH TWO GIVEN POINTS (x_1, y_1) AND (x_2, y_2)

Since the line passes through the points (x_1, y_1) and (x_2, y_2), its slope m is given by

$$m = \frac{y_2 - y_1}{x_2 - x_1}. \qquad \text{(See Example 1)}$$

Hence by above article, we have the required equation of the line as

$$\mathbf{y - y_1 = \frac{y_2 - y_1}{x_2 - x_1}(x - x_1)} \qquad ...(1)$$

[Note. If $x_2 = x_1$, the expression $\frac{y_2 - y_1}{x_2 - x_1}$ becomes meaningless but in this case the line is parallel to the y-axis and its equation will be $x = x_1$.]

9. PERPENDICULAR FORM

To find the equation of a line when the length of the perpendicular on it from the origin and the inclination of this perpendicular to the x-axis are given.

Let $OK = p$, be the perpendicular from the origin on the line AB and let it make an angle α with the x-axis. Take $P(x, y)$ any point on the line AB. Drop $PM \perp OX$.

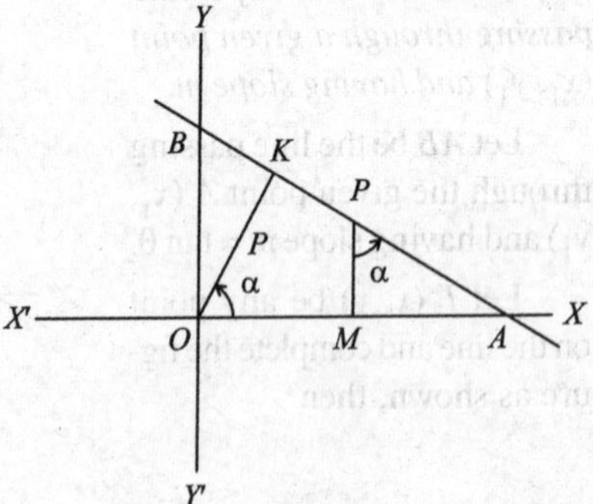

Fig. 11

Then $\angle MAP = 90° - \alpha$

and $\angle MPA = \alpha$.

Again $OK = OA \cos\alpha$ (from ΔOKA)

$$= (OM + MA) \cos \alpha = (x + PM \tan \alpha) \cos \alpha \quad (\text{from } \Delta PMA)$$
$$= x \cos \alpha + y \tan \alpha \, . \cos \alpha$$
$$= x \cos \alpha + y \sin \alpha.$$

Hence the required equation of the line AB is

$$x \cos \alpha + y \sin \alpha = p.$$

10. LINEAR EQUATION

We observe that the various forms of the equation of a line obtained so far have all been linear, *i.e.*, equations of first degree in x and y. This leads us to examine the validity of the result.

The equation of a line is of first degree in x and y.

Clearly, a line can either be parallel to the y-axis or meet it in some point. In the first case the equation of the line is of the form $x = a$, and in the second case, the equation can be put in the form $y = mx + c$, (by giving suitable values to m and c). Since both the forms are linear, the above result is a reality.

A very natural question arising at this stage would be "Is the converse true?" The answer to which is

Every equation of the first degree in x and y represents a line.

To prove this result, we consider the most general equation of first degree in x and y, namely

$$ax + by + c = 0 \qquad \text{...(1)}$$

Case (1) $b \neq 0$. Solve Equation (1) for y and write it as

$$y = -\frac{a}{b}x - \frac{c}{b}.$$

Now this is clearly of the form $y = mx + c$ and thus (I) represents a line having slope $-\frac{a}{b}$ and intercept on y-axis as $-\frac{c}{b}$.

Case (II) $b = 0$. In this case $a \neq 0$, because if it were so, the equation will reduce to $c = 0$, which has no meaning.

Dividing the Equation (1) by a and transposing, we see that it can be written as $x = -\frac{c}{a}$.

which is of the form $x = a$ (*i.e.*, in this case Equation (1) represents a line parallel to y-axis) and hence the result is established.

REMARKS.

(*i*) From above we see that slope of the line

$$ax + by + c = 0 \text{ is given by } - a/b$$

i.e., $$\text{slope} = -\frac{\text{coefficient of } x}{\text{coefficient of } y}$$

Provided, of course, that b, the coeff. of y is not zero. If $b = 0$ the line is parallel to y-axis.

(*ii*) Number of arbitrary constants in the equation of a line is at most 2. If a line is parallel to y-axis, its equation is of the form $x = a$, so it contains an arbitrary constant a. If the line is not parallel to y-axis, its equation will be of the form $y = mx + c$. So it contains at most two arbitrary constants m and c.

11. COMPARISON OF COEFFICIENTS

If the equations

$$ax + by + c = 0$$
$$a'x + b'y + c' = 0$$

represent the same line, then $\frac{a}{a'} = \frac{b}{b'} = \frac{c}{c'}$.

Writing the two equations in the form $y = mx + c$, we have

$$y = -\frac{a}{b}x - \frac{c}{b}$$

$$y = -\frac{a'}{b'}x - \frac{c'}{b'}.$$

Since these two represent the same line, equating the slopes, we have

$$\frac{-a}{b} = \frac{-a'}{b'} \quad \text{or} \quad \frac{a}{a'} = \frac{b}{b'}$$

again equating the intercepts on y-axis, we have

$$\frac{-c}{b} = \frac{-c'}{b'} \quad \text{or} \quad \frac{b}{b'} = \frac{c}{c'}$$

Hence $$\frac{a}{a'} = \frac{b}{b'} = \frac{c}{c'}.$$

(In above, we have, of course, been assuming the coeffs. to be non-zero.)

Example 5. *In what ratio is the line joining (–1, 1) and (5, 7) divided by the line $x + y - 4 = 0$.*

Solution. Let the ratio be a : 1, thus the co-ordinates of the point of division are $\left(\frac{5a-1}{a+1}, \frac{7a+1}{a+1}\right)$.

Since this point lies on the line $x + y - 4 = 0$, we have

$$\frac{5a-1}{a+1} + \frac{7a+1}{a+1} = 4 \text{ giving } a = \frac{1}{2}.$$

Hence the required ratio is $\frac{1}{2} : 1$ or $1:2$.

Example 6. *Show that the three points (1, 4), (3, – 2) and (– 3, 16) are collinear.*

Solution. Equation of the line passing through (1, 4) and (3, – 2) is

$$y - 4 = \frac{-2-4}{3-1}(x-1)$$

or $$3x + y - 7 = 0.$$

Since the third point (– 3, 16) lies on this line, the result follows.

Example 7. *Find the equation of a line which passes through the point (1, – 2) and makes intercepts on the axes equal in magnitude and opposite in sign.*

Solution. Suppose the intercepts made by the line on the axes are a and $-a$, then equation of the line will be

$$\frac{x}{a} + \frac{y}{-a} = 1$$

Hence a is to be determined, by the other given condition since the line passes through (1, –2), we have

$$\frac{1}{a} + \frac{-2}{-a} = 1 \text{ i.e., } a = 3.$$

So the required equation of the line is

$$\frac{x}{3} + \frac{y}{-3} = 1 \text{ or } x - y = 3.$$

Example 8. *As the number of units manufactured increases from 4,000 to 6,000, the total cost of production increases from Rs. 22,000 to Rs. 30,000. Find the relationship between the cost (y) and the number of units (x), if the relationship is linear.*

Solution. It is given that

when $x = 4{,}000$, $y = 22{,}000$

and when $x = 6{,}000$, $y = 30{,}000$

Let us write $(x_1, y_1) = (4{,}000, 22{,}000)$

$(x_2, y_2) = (6{,}000, 30{,}000)$

Now a linear relationship between x and y is given by

$$y - y_1 = \frac{y_2 - y_1}{x_2 - x_1}(x - x_1)$$

[The equation of the line through two points (x_1, y_1), (x_2, y_2)]

i.e., the required relationship is

$$y - 22{,}000 = \frac{30{,}000 - 22{,}000}{6{,}000 - 4{,}000}(x - 4{,}000)$$

or $\quad y - 22{,}000 = 4\,(x - 4{,}000)$

or $\quad 4x - y + 6{,}000 = 0$

EXERCISES

1. Find the equation of the line joining the points

   (*i*) (1, 2), (2, 1) (*ii*) (a, b), $(-a, -b)$ (*iii*) (3, – 1), (– 2, 0)

   Write their slopes also.

2. Find the equation of the line passing through the point (– 1, 3) with slope $\frac{1}{3}$.
3. Prove that the line joining (3, 5) and (– 2, 7) bisects the line joining (7, 2) and (9, 4).
4. Find the equations to the diagonals of the rectangle, the equations of whose sides are $x = 2$, $x = -1$, $y = 6$ and $y = -2$.
5. In what ratio is the line joining (1, 3) and (2, 7) divided by the line $3x + y = 9$.
6. Find the equation of the line which passes through the point (1, 4) and makes equal intercepts on the axes.
7. Find the equation of the line through (2, 5) and making equal intercepts of opposite sign on the axes.
8. Find the equation of the line which cuts off an intercept of length a on the x-axis, and is inclined at an angle α to that axis.
9. Show that the points with co-ordinates (2, –1), (5, 3) and (–4, –9) are collinear.
10. Reduce $x \cos \alpha + y \sin \alpha = p$ to the slope form. What is slope of this line?
11. A firm invested Rs. 10 million in a new factory that has a net return of 5,00,000 per year. An investment of Rs. 20 million would yield net income of Rs. 2 million per year. What is the linear relationship between investment and annual income? What would be the annual return on an investment of Rs. 15 million?

ANSWERS

1. (*i*) $x + y = 3$; -1 (*ii*) $a(y - b) = b(x - a)$; $\frac{b}{a}$ (iii) $x + 5y - 2 = 0$; $\frac{-1}{5}$.
2. $x - 3y + 10 = 0$.

4. $8x - 3y + 2 = 0$; $8x + 3y - 10 = 0$. 5. 3 : 4.
6. $x + y = 5$. 7. $x - y + 3 = 0$.
8. $y = (x - a)\tan\alpha$. 10. $-\cot\alpha$.
11. $3x - 2y = 20{,}000{,}000$; Rs. 12,500,000.

12. ANGLE BETWEEN TWO LINES

To find the angle between the two lines $y = m_1x + c_1$ and $y = m_2x + c_2$.

Let the two given lines *AB* and *CD* make angles θ_1 and θ_2 with the *x*-axis. Let them meet in the point *E*.

We have $m_1 = \tan\theta_1$

$m_2 = \tan\theta_2$

We wish to find the angle $BED = \theta$, say

Now, $\theta = \angle CEA = \theta_1 - \theta_2$

thus $$\tan\theta = \tan(\theta_1 - \theta_2) = \frac{\tan\theta_1 - \tan\theta_2}{1 + \tan\theta_1\tan\theta_2} = \frac{m_1 - m_2}{1 + m_1m_2}.$$

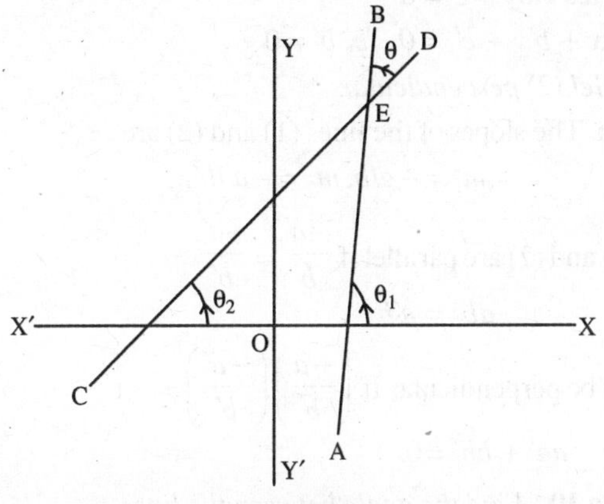

Fig. 12

Hence the angle between the lines $y = m_1x_1 + c_1$ and $y = m_2x_2 + c_2$ is

$$\tan^{-1}\frac{m_1 - m_2}{1 + m_1m_2}.$$

REMARK: If we wish to find the angle *AED*, then since
$\tan AED = \tan(\pi - \theta) = -\tan\theta$

$$= \frac{\tan\theta_2 - \tan\theta_1}{1 + \tan\theta_1\tan\theta_2} = \frac{m_2 - m_1}{1 + m_1m_2}.$$

We get the angle *AED* to be $\tan^{-1}\dfrac{m_2 - m_1}{1 + m_1m_2}$.

We may generalize the result by taking the angle as

$$\tan^{-1} \frac{m_1 \sim m_2}{1 + m_1 m_2},$$

though it is normally the acute angle that is considered.

Corollary 1. If the two lines are *parallel*, $\theta = 0$,

thus, $\tan \theta = 0 \Rightarrow m_1 = m_2$

and conversely if $m_1 = m_2$ then $\theta = 0$.

Hence, we observe that *two lines are parallel if and only if they have the same slope.*

Corollary 2. If the two lines are *perpendicular*, $\theta = \frac{\pi}{2}$,

thus, $\cot \theta = 0 \Rightarrow 1 + m_1 m_2 = 0 \Rightarrow m_1 m_2 = -1$ and conversely.

Thus we conclude that *two lines are perpendicular if and only if the product of their slopes equals –1.*

Example 9. *Find the conditions under which the lines*

$$ax + by + c = 0 \quad \text{...(1)}$$

$$a'x + b'y + c' = 0 \quad b, b' \neq 0 \quad \text{...(2)}$$

are (1) *parallel* (2) *perpendicular.*

Solution. The slopes of the lines (1) and (2) are

$$m_1 = -a/b, m_2 = -a'/b'.$$

Thus (1) and (2) are parallel if $\frac{-a}{b} = \frac{-a'}{b'}$

or if $ab' = a'b$

and they will be perpendicular if $\left(\frac{-a}{b}\right)\left(\frac{-a'}{b'}\right) = -1$

or $aa' + bb' = 0$.

Example 10. *Find the angle between the lines*

$$x \cos \alpha + y \sin \alpha = p$$

$$x \cos \beta + y \sin \beta = q.$$

Solution. Since the angle between the lines is same as the angle between their perpendiculars, it follows that the required angle is $\alpha \sim \beta$.

13. LINES PARALLEL TO THE LINE $ax + by + c = 0$

Two lines are parallel if they have the same slope. Now slope of the given line $ax + by + c = 0$ is $\frac{-a}{b}$.

Another line having slope $\frac{-a}{b}$ will be of the type

$$y = \left(\frac{-a}{b}\right)x + c'$$

or $$by = -ax + c'b$$

or $$ax + by + \lambda = 0 \qquad \text{where } \lambda = -bc', \text{ a constant.}$$

So we have a line $ax + by + \lambda = 0$ which has the same slope as the given line $ax + by + c = 0$ and therefore is parallel to it. Here λ is a constant and by giving different values to λ, we will get different lines, all parallel, to the given line. In problems, value of λ is found by using the other given condition.

14. LINES PERPENDICULAR TO THE LINE $ax + by + c = 0$

Two lines are perpendicular if the product of their slopes is – 1. Since slope of the given line is $-a/b$. Therefore, slope of a line perpendicular to the given line is

$$\frac{(-1)}{\left(\frac{-a}{b}\right)} = \frac{b}{a}.$$

Thus a line perpendicular to the given line is of the form

$$y = \left(\frac{b}{a}\right)x + c'$$

which can be written as

$$ay - bx + \lambda = 0$$

where $\lambda = -ac'$ is a constant, to be found by the other given condition. For different values of λ, we get different lines perpendicular to the given line.

We have a simple rule: *To obtain the equation of a line perpendicular to another line whose equation is given, interchange the co-efficients of x and y, change the sign of one of them and suitably change the constant term.*

Example 11. *Find the equation of line passing through the point (1, 1) and parallel to the line 4x + 4y + 7 = 0.*

Solution. Any line parallel to $4x + 4y + 7 = 0$ is

$$4x + 4y + \lambda = 0.$$

Since this is to pass through (1, 1), we have

$$41 + 41 + \lambda = 0 \quad \text{or} \quad \lambda = -8$$

thus the required line is $4x+4y-8=0$

or $$x+y-2=0.$$

Example 12. *Find the equation of the line passing through the point (3, 1) and perpendicular to the line 2x + 7y – 5 = 0.*

Solution. Any line perpendicular to $2x+7y-5=0$ is

$$7x-2y+\lambda=0.$$

Since this is to pass through (3, 1), we have

$$7\,.\,3-2\,.\,1+\lambda=0$$

or $$\lambda=-19$$

thus the required line is $7x-2y-19=0$.

Example 13. *The vertices of a triangle ABC are A (0, 0), B (1, 5) and C (– 2, 2). Find the equation of altitude through A.*

Solution. Equation of the side BC is

$$y-5=\frac{2-5}{-2-1}(x+2)$$

or $$x-y+7=0$$

Any line perpendicular to this has equation

$$x+y+\lambda=0$$

It will pass through A (0, 0) if

$$0+0+\lambda=0$$

i.e., $$\lambda=0$$

Hence the required equation of the altitude through A is $x+y=0$.

15. INTERSECTION OF TWO LINES

To find the co-ordinates of the point of intersection of two lines.

Let the two lines be

$$ax+by+c=0 \quad \text{...(1)}$$

$$a'x+b'y+c'=0 \quad \text{...(2)}$$

Since the point of intersection lies on both the lines, its co-ordinates satisfy both the equations (1) and (2).

If (x_1, y_1) are the co-ordinates of the point of intersection, then we have

$$ax_1+by_1+c=0$$

$$a'x_1+b'y_1+c'=0.$$

Solving these two equations, we get

$$\frac{x_1}{bc' - cb'} = \frac{y_1}{ca' - ac'} = \frac{1}{ab' - a'b}.$$

Giving $$x_1 = \frac{bc' - cb'}{ab' - ba'}$$

$$y_1 = \frac{ca' - ac'}{ab' - ba'}$$

as the required co-ordinates.

[Note. If $ab' - ba' = 0$, then the expressions for the co-ordinates (x_1, y_1) become meaningless, for then the denominators become zero, but then in this case, we have

$$ab' = ba' \quad \text{or} \quad \frac{-a}{b} = \frac{-a'}{b'}$$

i.e., slopes of the two lines (1) and (2) are equal and thus the lines are parallel and do not, therefore, intersect.]

16. LINES THROUGH THE INTERSECTION OF TWO GIVEN LINES

To find the general equation of the lines passing through the point of intersection of two given lines.

Let the two given intersecting lines be

$$ax + by + c = 0 \qquad \text{...(1)}$$

$$a'x + b'y + c' = 0 \qquad \text{...(2)}$$

and let them meet at the point (x_1, y_1). Since this point lies on both (1) and (2), we have

$$\left.\begin{aligned} ax_1 + by_1 + c &= 0 \\ a'x_1 + b'y_1 + c' &= 0 \end{aligned}\right\} \qquad \text{...(3)}$$

Consider now the equation

$$(ax + by + c) + \lambda\,(a'x + b'y + c') = 0 \qquad \text{...(4)}$$

where λ is an arbitrary constant.

As Equation (4) is linear, it represents a line. Again in view of condition (3), it is clear that the point (x_1, y_1) lies on (4), whatever λ may be. Consequently (4) represents a line passing through the point of intersection of (1) and (2), whatever value λ may take. By giving different values to λ, we can write down equations of different lines passing through (x_1, y_1).

If, in short, we write Equations (1) and (2) as

$$P \equiv ax + by + c = 0$$

$$P' \equiv a'x + b'y + c' = 0$$

then equation of any line passing through the point of intersection of the lines $P=0$ and $P'=0$ is given by $P+\lambda P'=0$, where λ is an arbitrary constant.

17. CONDITION FOR CONCURRENCE OF THE THREE LINES

To find the condition that the three lines

$$a_1x + b_1y + c_1 = 0 \quad \text{... (1)}$$

$$a_2x + b_2y + c_2 = 0 \quad \text{... (2)}$$

$$a_3x + b_3y + c_3 = 0 \quad \text{... (3)}$$

may be concurrent.

Any three lines are concurrent if the point of intersection of any two of them lies on the third. The point of intersection of (1) and (2) is given by

$$x = \frac{b_1c_2 - b_2c_1}{a_1b_2 - a_2b_1}, y = \frac{c_1a_2 - c_2a_1}{a_1b_2 - a_2b_1}$$

For concurrency this point has to lie on (3) which gives the condition

$$a_3\left(\frac{b_1c_2 - b_2c_1}{a_1b_2 - a_2b_1}\right) + b_2\left(\frac{c_1a_2 - c_2a_1}{a_1b_2 - a_2b_1}\right) + c_3 = 0$$

which simplifies to

$$a_1(b_2c_3 - b_3c_2) + b_1(c_2a_3 - c_3a_2) + c_1(a_2b_3 - a_3b_2) = 0$$

which is the required condition.

This condition can be written in the determinant form as

$$\begin{vmatrix} a_1 & b_1 & c_1 \\ a_2 & b_2 & c_2 \\ a_3 & b_3 & c_3 \end{vmatrix} = 0.$$

Example 14. *Find the co-ordinates of the foot of the perpendicular from the point* (2, 3) *on the line* $y - 3x - 4 = 0$.

Solution. First we find equation of the line through (2, 3) and perpendicular to $y-3x-4=0$. The point of intersection of this line with the given line will be the required foot of the perpendicular.

Now any line perpendicular to $y-3x-4=0$ is

$$3y + x + \lambda = 0.$$

Since it passes through (2, 3), we have $3 \cdot 3 + 2 + \lambda = 0$

$$\Rightarrow \qquad \lambda = -11$$

The required perpendicular line is $3y + x - 11 = 0$.

To find the point of intersection, we solve the two equations,

$$y-3x-4=0$$
$$3y+x-11=0$$

and get $\qquad x=-\frac{1}{10}, y=\frac{37}{10}.$

Thus the required foot of perpendicular is $\left(-\frac{1}{10}, \frac{37}{10}\right).$

Example 15. *Show that the three lines given by the equations*

$$4y-3x+22=0,\ x-y-6=0 \text{ and } 6x+5y-8=0$$

are concurrent. Find their point of intersection.

Solution. Solving the first two equations simultaneously, we get

$$x=2, y=-4.$$

Since $6 \cdot 2+5(-4)+8=0$, we find that the point of intersection of the first two lines, lies on the third and thus the three lines are concurrent. Also the point of intersection is $(2, -4)$.

Example 16. *Find the equations of the lines passing through the point of intersection of the lines $4x-3y-1=0$ and $2x=5y-3$, and equally inclined to the axes.*

Solution. Any line passing through the point of intersection of the given two line is

$$(4x-3y-1)+\lambda(2x-5y+3)=0 \qquad \text{...(1)}$$

where λ is some constant.

Slope of this line is $\qquad -\frac{4+2\lambda}{-3-5\lambda}$

Now a line is equally inclined to the axes if its slope is ± 1.

Thus line (1) would be equally inclined to the axes if

$$-\frac{4+2\lambda}{-3-5\lambda}=\pm 1 \Rightarrow \lambda=-1 \text{ or } \frac{1}{3}.$$

Hence the required lines are obtained by putting $\lambda=-1$ and $\frac{1}{3}$ in (1), which gives the required two lines as

$$x+y=2 \quad \text{and} \quad x-y=0$$

Example 17. *Find the area of the triangle formed by the lines*

$$y=m_1x+c_1 \qquad \text{...(1)}$$
$$y=m_2x+c_2 \qquad \text{...(2)}$$
$$x=0 \qquad \text{...(3)}$$

Solution. Solving Equations (1) and (2), we get their point of intersection as

$$\left(\frac{c_1 - c_2}{m_2 - m_1}, \frac{m_2 c_1 - m_1 c_2}{m_2 - m_1}\right).$$

Similarly points of intersection of (2) and (3) and (3) and (1) are $(0, c_2)$ and $(0, c_1)$ respectively.

Thus area of the triangle is given by

$$\frac{1}{2}\left(\frac{c_1 - c_2}{m_2 - m_1}(c_1 - c_2) + 0 + 0\right) = \frac{1}{2}\frac{(c_1 - c_2)^2}{(m_2 - m_1)}$$

Example 18. *Find the equations of the two lines through the point (2, – 1) making an angle of 45° with the line 6x + 5y = 1. Show also that these two lines are perpendicular to each other.*

Solution. Equation of any line with slope m and passing through (2, – 1) is

$$y + 1 = m(x - 2) \qquad \text{... (1)}$$

This line is to make an angle of 45° with $6x + 5y = 1$. If m' is the slope of the given line, then $m' = -6/5$. So we have

$$\tan 45° = \frac{m \sim m'}{1 + mm'} = \pm\frac{m - (-6/5)}{1 + m(-6/5)}.$$

Since tan 45° = 1, we get from above $m = 11, -\frac{1}{11}$. Putting these values of m in (1) we get the two required lines as

$$x + 11y + 9 = 0$$

and
$$11x - y - 23 = 0.$$

Again slopes of these two lines are $-\frac{1}{11}$ and 11, so we find that they are perpendicular to each other (as product of their slopes equals – 1).

EXERCISES

1. Find the angle between the lines

   (*i*) $x - 4y = 3$ and $6x - y = 11$

   (*ii*) $y = x\sqrt{3} + 1$ and $x - \sqrt{3}y + 2 = 0$.

2. Find the angle between the lines $ax + by + c = 0$ and $a'x + b'y + c' = 0$.

3. Show that the line joining the middle points of two sides of a triangle is parallel to the third side, and equal to half of its length.

4. Find the equation of the line passing through the point $(-1, 2)$ and parallel to the line $2x + 3y + 1 = 0$.
5. Find the equation of the line passing through the point $(0, 1)$ and parallel to the line $x + y + 1 = 0$.
6. Find the equation of the line through $(-1, 2)$ and perpendicular to the line $2x + 3y + 1 = 0$.
7. Find the equation of the line through the origin and parallel to $y = mx + c$.
8. Show that the lines $y = 2x - 3$ and $2y + x + 1 = 0$ are perpendicular to each other.
9. Find the equation of the line passing through the point $(3, -1)$ and perpendicular to the line $2x - 3y = 1$.
10. Find the equation to the line which passes through the point (x_1, y_1) and is perpendicular to the line $yy_1 = 2a(x + x_1)$.
11. Find the condition that the lines $t_1 y = x + at_1^2$ and $t_2 y = x + at_2^2$ may be at right angles to each other.
12. Show that the three lines $5x + 3y - 7 = 0$, $3x - 4y - 10 = 0$ and $x + 2y = 0$ meet in a point.
13. Find the equation to the lines which pass through the origin and are inclined at 75° to the line $x + y + \sqrt{3}(y - x) = a$.
14. Find the equation of the line joining the origin to the point of intersection of $2x + 5y - 4 = 0$ and $3x - 2y + 2 = 0$.
15. Find the area of the triangle formed by the lines $y - x = 0$, $y + x = 0$, $x - c = 0$.
16. Find the equation to the line which bisects, and is perpendicular to, the line joining the points (a, b) and (a', b').
17. Find the equation of the line that passes through the point of intersection of the lines $2x + y - 3 = 0$, $x - 2y + 1 = 0$ and is parallel to the line $y - x + 2 = 0$.
18. The vertices of a triangle ABC are $A(6, 2)$, $B(-3, 8)$ and $C(-5, -3)$. Find the equation of the altitude through A.
19. Find the equation of a line through the point of intersection of the lines $x - y + 1 = 0$ and $x + y + 1 = 0$ and parallel to the line $2x + 3y + 4 = 0$.
20. Find the value of k so that the three lines $3x + y - 2 = 0$, $kx + 2y - 1 = 0$ and $2x - y - 3 = 0$ meet in a point.
21. Find the value of k so that the three lines $4y - 3x + 22 = 0$, $kx - y - 6 = 0$ and $6x + 5y - 8 = 0$ are concurrent.
22. Find the area of the triangle formed by the lines

    $y = x + 1 \qquad y = 2x - 3 \qquad x = 0.$
23. Find the orthocentre of the triangle formed by the lines $x - y = 5$, $2x - y = 8$, $3x - y = 9$.
24. Find the co-ordinates of the foot of the perpendicular from the point $(2, 3)$ on the line $x + y - 11 = 0$.
25. Show that the three lines given by the equations $4x + 5y = 45$, $3x - 4y + 5 = 0$, $7x - 8y + 5 = 0$ are concurrent.

ANSWERS

1. (*i*) $\tan^{-1}\frac{23}{10}$, (*ii*) 30°. 2. $\tan^{-1}\left(\frac{a'b - ab'}{aa' + bb'}\right)$. 4. $2x + 3y = 4$.

5. $x + y = 1$. 6. $3x - 2y + 7 = 0$. 7. $y = mx$.

9. $2y + 3x + 7 = 0$. 10. $2a(y - y_1) + y_1(x - x_1) = 0$.

11. $t_1 t_2 = -1$. 13. $y = \pm\sqrt{3}x$. 14. $8x + y = 0$.

15. c^2. 16. $2x(a - a') + 2y(b - b') = a^2 - a'^2 + b^2 - b'^2$.

17. $y - z = 0$. 18. $2x + 11y = 34$. 19. $2x + 3y + 2 = 0$.

20. 3. 21. 1. 22. 8.

23. (– 6, 1). 24. (5, 6).

18. LENGTH OF PERPENDICULAR

To find the length of the perpendicular from a given point on a given line.

Let the given line *AB* have equation

$$x \cos \alpha + y \sin \alpha = p \qquad ...(1)$$

and let the given point *P* have co-ordinates (x_1, y_1). Draw $PN \perp AB$. Then we wish to find the length *PN*. Draw a line *PK* through *P* parallel to *AB* and from *O*, the origin, draw a perpendicular on the lines. *AB* and *PK*, meeting them at *L* and *K* respectively.

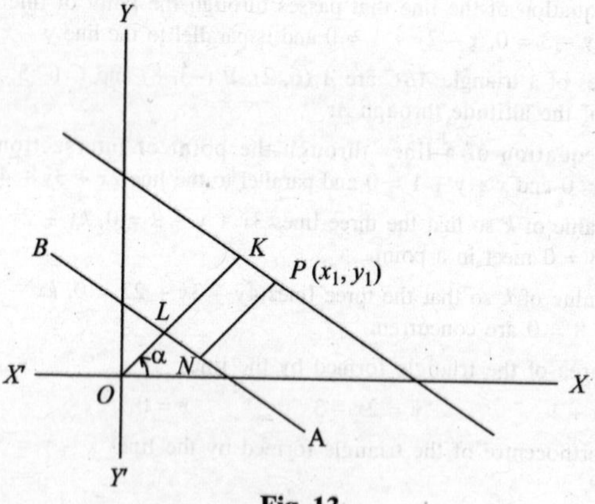

Fig. 13

Then $OL = p$, $\angle LOX = \alpha$ and let $OK = q$.

Equation of the line *PK* will then be

$$x \cos \alpha + y \sin \alpha = q$$

Since this passes through $P(x_1, y_1)$, we have

$$x_1 \cos \alpha + y_1 \sin \alpha = q \qquad ...(2)$$

Now $\quad PN = KL = OK - OL = q - p$

$$= x_1 \cos \alpha + y_1 \sin \alpha - p \qquad \text{by (2)}$$

which gives us the required length.

Hence the length of the perpendicular from (x_1, y_1) on the line

$x \cos \alpha + y \sin \alpha = p$ is $\mathbf{x_1 \cos \alpha + y_1 \sin \alpha - p}$.

Corollary. Suppose equation of the line is given in the form

$$ax + by + c = 0$$

We write this equation as

$$\frac{a}{\sqrt{a^2 + b^2}} x + \frac{b}{\sqrt{a^2 + b^2}} y + \frac{c}{\sqrt{a^2 + b^2}} = 0$$

which is of the form (1) where

$$\cos \alpha = \frac{a}{\sqrt{a^2 + b^2}}, \sin \alpha = \frac{b}{\sqrt{a^2 + b^2}} \text{ and } -p = \frac{c}{\sqrt{a^2 + b^2}}$$

So applying the result obtained above, we have the required length of perpendicular from (x_1, y_1) on the line $ax + by + c = 0$ to be

$$\frac{\mathbf{ax_1 + by_1 + c}}{\sqrt{\mathbf{a^2 + b^2}}}.$$

REMARK. The equations $ax + by + c = 0$ and $-ax - by - c = 0$ represent the same line, but the perpendicular distances obtained by above formula will have opposite signs in the two cases. Keeping in mind the distances are +ve, we shall neglect the –ve sign, if any.

19. TWO SIDES OF A LINE

To show that a point $P(x_1, y_1)$ is on one side or the other of the line $ax + by + c = 0$ according as the quantity $ax_1 + by_1 + c$ is +ve or –ve.

Let AB be the given line having equation

$$ax + by + c = 0.$$

Let P be the given point (x_1, y_1). We have two possibilities (excluding, of course, the case when P lies on the line). Either P lies 'above' the line AB as in Fig. 14 (*i*) or it lies 'below' the line AB as in Fig. 14 (*ii*).

In both the cases draw a line through P parallel to the y-axis meeting AB in Q. Let co-ordinates of Q be (x_2, y_2). Since the point Q lies on AB, we have

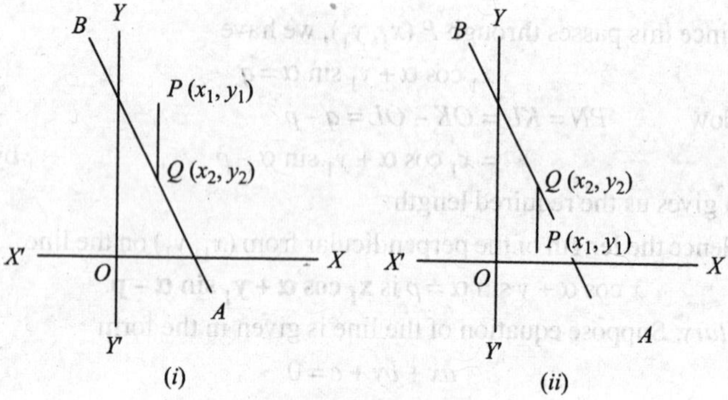

Fig. 14

$$ax_1 + by_2 + c = 0$$

or $$by_2 = -(ax_1 + c).$$

This gives $$b(y_1 - y_2) = ax_1 + by_1 + c. \quad ...(1)$$

Now $y_1 - y_2$ is +ve or –ve according as the point P lies on one side or the other of the line AB, and therefore the LHS of Equation (1), *i.e.*, $b(y_1 - y_2)$ is +ve or –ve according as the point P lies on one side or the other of the line AB. Hence the RHS of Equation (1) *i.e.*, $ax_1 + by_1 + c$ is +ve or –ve according as the point P lies on one side or the other of the line AB. And so the result follows.

Corollary 1. Two points (x_1, y_1) and (x_2, y_2) lie on the same side of the line $ax + by + c = 0$, if the expressions $ax_1 + by_1 + c$ and $ax_2 + by_2 + c$ have the same sign. If they have apposite signs, the two points lie on the opposite sides of the line.

Corollary 2. The point (x_1, y_1) lies on the same side of the line $ax + by + c = 0$ as the origin, if $ax_1 + by_1 + c$ has the same sign as $a \cdot 0 + b \cdot 0 + c = c$.

Example 19. *Show that the points (2, – 1) and (1, 1) are on opposite sides of the line 3x + 4y – 6 = 0.*

Solution. Since $3 \cdot 2 + 4 \cdot (-1) - 6 = 6 - 4 - 6 = -4$

and $$3 \cdot 1 + 4 \cdot 1 - 6 = 1$$

are of opposite sign, the result follows by Corollary 1.

20. BISECTORS OF ANGLES

To find the equation of the bisectors of the angles between the line

$$a_1x + b_1y + c_1 = 0$$

and line $$a_2x + b_2y + c_2 = 0.$$

Let AB and CD be the two given lines intersecting at K. Let EF and GH be the bisectors of the angles between AB and CD. Take a point $P(x_1, y_1)$ on one of the bisectors, say EF, and draw perpendiculars PQ_1 and PQ_2 on AB and CD respectively.

Then as P lies on the bisector, $PQ_1 = PQ_2$

i.e.,
$$\frac{a_1x_1+b_1y_1+c_1}{\sqrt{a_1^2+b_1^2}}$$

and
$$\frac{a_2x_1+b_2y_1+c_2}{\sqrt{a_2^2+b_2^2}}$$

are equal in magnitude, *i.e.*, co-ordinates of P satisfy

$$\frac{a_1x_1+b_1y_1+c_1}{\sqrt{a_1^2+b_1^2}} = \pm\frac{a_2x_1+b_2y_1+c_2}{\sqrt{a_2^2+b_2^2}}$$

Thus the equations of the bisectors are

$$\frac{\mathbf{a_1x+b_1y+c_1}}{\sqrt{\mathbf{a_1}^2+\mathbf{b_1}^2}} = \pm\frac{\mathbf{a_2x+b_2y+c_2}}{\sqrt{\mathbf{a_2}^2+\mathbf{b_2}^2}}.$$

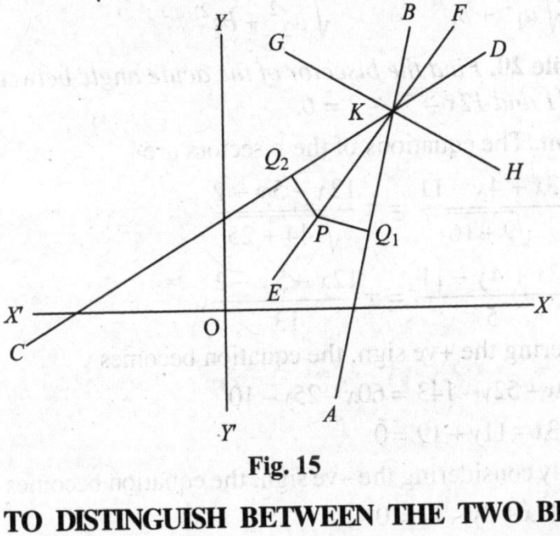

Fig. 15

21. HOW TO DISTINGUISH BETWEEN THE TWO BISECTORS

First write down the equations of the two lines such that the constant terms c_1 and c_2 are +ve (multiplying by –1, if necessary). Also take +ve sign with the square roots. Consider the bisector of the angle which contains the origin (EF in Fig. 15). Then a point on this bisector lies on the same side of each of the two lines in which the origin lies. Thus $P(x_1, y_1)$ and (0, 0) are on the same side of the line $a_1x + b_1y + c_1 = 0$.

Therefore $a_1x + b_1y + c_1$ and $a_1 . 0 + b_1 . 0 + c_1$, have the same sign. Since we took c_1 to be +ve $a_1x_1 + b_1y_1 + c_1$ is also +ve.

Thus $\dfrac{a_1x_1 + b_1y_1 + c_1}{\sqrt{a_1^2 + b_1^2}}$ is +ve.

Similarly as (x_1, y_1) and (0, 0) lie on the same side of the line $a_2x + b_2y + c_2 = 0$.

$\dfrac{a_2x_1 + b_2y_1 + c_2}{\sqrt{a_2^2 + b_2^2}}$ is also +ve.

Hence the required equation of the bisector of the angle which contains the origin is

$$\frac{a_1x + b_1y + c_1}{\sqrt{a_1^2 + b_1^2}} = \frac{a_2x + b_2y + c_2}{\sqrt{a_2^2 + b_2^2}}.$$

Similarly the equation of the bisector of the angle in which the origin does not lie is

$$\frac{a_1x + b_1y + c_1}{\sqrt{a_1^2 + b_1^2}} = -\frac{a_2x + b_2y + c_2}{\sqrt{a_2^2 + b_2^2}}.$$

Example 20. *Find the bisector of the acute angle between the lines 3x + 4y = 11 and 12x – 5y – 2 = 0.*

Solution. The equations of the bisectors are

$$\frac{3x + 4y - 11}{\sqrt{9 + 16}} = \pm\frac{12x - 5y - 2}{\sqrt{144 + 25}}$$

i.e.,
$$\frac{3x + 4y - 11}{5} = \pm\frac{12x - 5y - 2}{13}.$$

Considering the +ve sign, the equation becomes

$$39x + 52y - 143 = 60x - 25y - 10$$

or
$$3x - 11y + 19 = 0 \quad ...(1)$$

Similarly considering the –ve sign, the equation becomes

$$11x + 3y - 17 = 0 \quad ...(2)$$

Now we wish to find the equation of the bisector of the acute angle. The angle between the lines being acute (*i.e.*, < 90°), the angle between one of the lines and the bisector of the acute angle is $< \frac{1}{2}.90°$ *i.e.*, <45°.

If θ is the angle between one of the lines say $3x + 4y = 11$ and one of the bisectors say (1), then

$$\tan\theta = \frac{m_1 - m_2}{1 + m_1 m_2} = \frac{\left(-\frac{3}{4}\right) - (3/11)}{1 + \left(-\frac{3}{4}\right)(3/11)} = -\frac{9}{7}$$

which is numerically greater than 1 $\Rightarrow \theta$ is greater then 45°.

Thus (1) is not the bisector of the acute angle.

Hence $11x + 3y - 17 = 0$ is the required bisector of the acute angle.

Example 21. *Find the bisectors of the angles between the lines $4x - 3y + 1 = 0$ and $12x + 5y + 13 = 0$. Distinguish between the two.*

Solution. The equations of the bisectors are

$$\frac{4x - 3y + 1}{\sqrt{16 + 9}} = \pm \frac{12x + 5y + 13}{\sqrt{144 + 25}}$$

or
$$\frac{4x - 3y + 1}{5} = \pm \frac{12x + 5y + 13}{13}.$$

Since the constant terms in the equations of the lines are both +ve, the equation of the bisector of the angle in which the origin lies, is with +ve sign.

EXERCISES

1. Find the length of the perpendicular from the point (3, 4) on the line $2x - 3y - 7 = 0$. Show that the point (3, 4) lies on the same side of the line on which the origin lies.
2. Find the lengths of the perpendiculars drawn from the origin on the sides of the triangle, the co-ordinates of whose angular points are (2,1), (3, 2) and (– 1, – 1).
3. Find the bisectors of the acute angle between the lines

   $5x - 12y - 24 = 0$ and $12x - 5y - 10 = 0$.
4. Find the equations of the bisectors of the angles between the lines

   $4x + 3y - 7 = 0$ and $24x + 7y - 31 = 0$.

   Distinguish between the two bisectors.
5. Find the equations of the bisectors of the angles between the lines

   $3x - 4y + 1 =$ and $5x + 12y - 3 = 0$.

   Distinguish between the two bisectors.

ANSWERS

1. $\sqrt{13}$. 2. $\frac{1}{5}, \frac{1}{\sqrt{13}}, \frac{1}{\sqrt{2}}$ 3. $x - y - 2 = 0$.
4. $x - 2y + 1 = 0$ (bisector of the angle containing the origin) $2x + y - 3 = 0$.
5. $32x + 4y - 1 = 0$ (bisector of the angle in which the origin lies) $7x - 56y + 14 = 0$.

MISCELLANEOUS EXERCISES

1. Find the co-ordinates of the orthocentre of the triangle whose angular points are (0, 0), (2, – 1) and (– 1, 3).
2. Show that the altitudes of a triangle are concurrent.
3. Show that the medians of a triangle are concurrent.
4. The vertices of a triangle are A (10, 4), B (–4, 9) and C (–2, –1). Find the equation of the altitude through A.
5. Show that the equation of the line through the origin making an angle ϕ with the line $y = mx + b$ is $y/x = (m + \tan \phi)/(1 - m \tan \phi)$.
6. Find the equation of the two lines passing through the point (1, – 1) and inclined at the angle of 45° to the line $2x - 5y + 7 = 0$.
7. If p is the distance of the origin from the line $\frac{x}{a}+\frac{y}{b} = 1$, show that
$$\frac{1}{p^2} = \frac{1}{a^2}+\frac{1}{b^2}.$$
8. Find the equation of the line through (4, 5) parallel to $2x - 3y - 5 = 0$.
9. Show that the line joining (1, 2) and (4, 3) is bisected by the line joining (2, 3) and (4, 1).
10. Show that the perpendicular from the origin upon the line joining the points $(c \cos \alpha, c \sin \alpha)$ and $(c \cos \beta, c \sin \beta)$ bisects the distance between them.
11. Find the co-ordinates of the foot of the perpendicular from $(a, 0)$ on the line
$$y = mx + \frac{a}{m}.$$
12. Find the equation of the line through the intersection of $(2x - 3y + 4 = 0$ and $3x + 4y - 5 = 0$, parallel to the y-axis.
13. The points (1, 2) and (3, 8) are a pair of opposite vertices of a square. Find the equation of the sides and diagonals of the square.
14. Show that the lines $\frac{x}{a}+\frac{y}{b} = 1$, $\frac{x}{b}+\frac{y}{a} = 1$ and $y = x$ meet in a point.
15. Show that the bisector of the angle between the lines $x \cos \alpha + y \sin \alpha = p$ and $x \cos \beta + y \sin \beta = q$ $(p > 0, q > 0)$ which contains the origin is $x \cos \alpha + y \sin \alpha - p = x \cos \beta + y \sin \beta - q$.

16. The line $x \cos \alpha - y \sin \alpha = p$ forms a triangle with the axes. Find the co-ordinates of the in-centre of the triangle.

17. Find the equation to the line which passes through the intersection of the lines,
$$2x - 3y + 4 = 0 \quad \text{and} \quad 3x + 4y - 5 = 0$$
and is perpendicular to the line
$$6x - 7y + 8 = 0.$$

18. Find the co-ordinates of the orthocentre of the triangle formed by the lines
$$2x + y - 5 = 0$$
$$x + 2y - 4 = 0$$
$$x + y - 6 = 0.$$

19. Two lines drawn through the point (0, 1) are such that the length of the perpendicular dropped from the point (2, 2) on each is one unit of length. Find their equations.

20. The total cost of printing 1000 books is Rs. 12000 and the cost for printing 2000 books is Rs. 18000. If the cost curve is a line, find the relation between the cost y and number of books x. Deduce the cost of printing 500 books.

ANSWERS

1. $(-4, -3)$.

4. $5y - x - 10 = 0$.

6. $y + 1 = -\frac{3}{7}(x-1)$; $3x + 7y + 4 = 0$.

8. $2x - 3y + 7 = 0$.

11. $\left(0, \frac{a}{m}\right)$.

12. $17x + 1 = 0$.

13. Sides: $2x + y - 4 = 0$, $2x + y - 14 = 0$, $x - 2y + 3 = 0$, $x - 2y + 13 = 0$.
Diagonals: $3x - y - 1 = 0$, $x + 3y - 17 = 0$.

16. $\left(\frac{1}{1 + \sin\alpha + \cos\alpha}, \frac{1}{1 + \sin\alpha + \cos\alpha}\right)$.

17. $119x + 102t - 125 = 0$.

18. $(-10, -11)$.

19. $y = 1$, $3y - 4x = 3$.

20. $6x - y + 6000 = 0$; Rs. 9000.

CHAPTER 23

THE CIRCLE

1. DEFINITIONS

A circle is the locus of a point which moves (in a plane) in such a way that its distance from a fixed point (in the plane) always remains constant.

The fixed point is called the *centre* of the circle and the constant distance is termed as the *radius* of the circle.

2. EQUATION TO A CIRCLE

To find the equation of a circle, the centre and radius being given.

Let $C\ (h, k)$ be the given centre of the circle and let a be the given radius. Take any point $P(x, y)$ on the circle. Then

$$CP = \text{radius} = a$$

Also $CP^2 = (x-h)^2 + (y-k)^2$ (distance between two points)

Equating the two values of CP^2, we get the required equation of the circle as $\mathbf{(x-h)^2 + (y-k)^2 = a^2}$.

Corollary. Equation of the circle with radius a and centre at origin is

$$x^2 + y^2 = a^2.$$

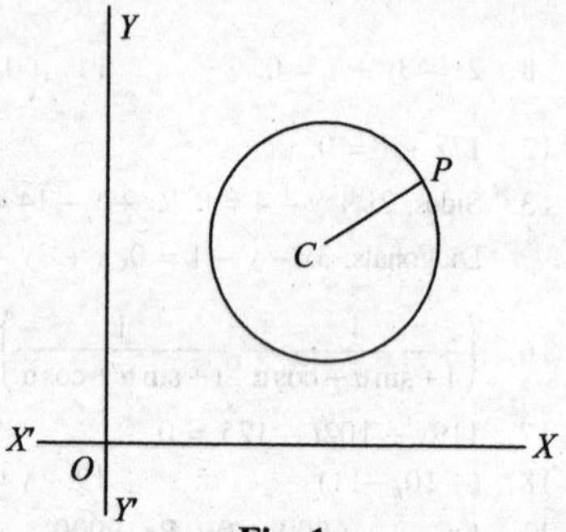

Fig. 1

3. GENERAL FORM OF THE EQUATION OF A CIRCLE

We have found the equation of a circle in the form

$$(x-h)^2 + (y-k)^2 = a^2$$

which can be written as

$$x^2 + y^2 - 2hx - 2ky + (h^2 + k^2 - a^2) = 0.$$

If we put $-h = g,\ -k = f,\ c = h^2 + k^2 - a^2$, the equation becomes

$$x^2 + y^2 + 2gx + 2fy + c = 0$$

which is referred to as the general form of the equation to a circle.

Conversely, any equation of the form $x^2 + y^2 + 2gx + 2fy + c = 0$ represents a circle, as we can write this equation in the form

$$(x^2 + 2gx) + (y^2 + 2fy) = -c$$

or
$$(x+g)^2 + (y+f)^2 = g^2 + f^2 - c$$

or
$$[x-(-g)]^2 + [y-(-f)]^2 = \sqrt{(g^2 + f^2 - c^2)^2}$$

which is of the form

$$(x-h)^2 + (y-k)^2 = a^2.$$

Comparing the two equations, we find that the equation $x^2 + y^2 + 2gx + 2fy + c = 0$, represents a circle with

centre $(-\mathbf{g}, -\mathbf{f})$

and radius $\sqrt{\mathbf{g}^2 + \mathbf{f}^2 - \mathbf{c}}$.

REMARK: If the quantity $g^2 + f^2 - c$ is +ve, the circle is real, if it is zero, the circle is a point circle (*i.e.*, a circle with radius zero) and if it is –ve, the circle is imaginary.

Again, multiplying the equation $x^2 + y^2 + 2gx + 2fy + c = 0$ by a and comparing it with the general equation of second degree, *i.e.*, $ax^2 + 2hxy + by^2 + 2gx + 2fy + c = 0$. We arrive at the conclusion that *an equation of second degree in x and y represents a circle if (i) co-efficients of x^2 and y^2 are same and (ii) co-efficient of xy is zero, i.e., there is no term involving xy.*

We further observe that the general equation of the circle, namely, $x^2 + y^2 + 2gx + 2fy + c = 0$ contains three constants. These three constants g, f and c correspond to the geometrical fact that a circle can be found to satisfy three independent geometrical conditions and no more.

Example 1. *Find the radius and the centre of the circle*

$$2x^2 + 2y^2 - x + 3y + 1 = 0.$$

Solution. Equation of the circle can be written as

$$x^2 + y^2 - \frac{1}{2}x + \frac{3}{2}y + \frac{1}{2} = 0$$

Thus here
$$g = -\frac{1}{4}, f = +\frac{3}{4}, c = \frac{1}{2}.$$

Hence the co-ordinates of the centre are $\left(\frac{1}{4}, -\frac{3}{4}\right)$ and radius is

$$\sqrt{\frac{1}{16} + \frac{9}{16} - \frac{1}{4}} = \sqrt{\frac{3}{8}}.$$

Example 2. *Find the equation of the circle which passes through the points (1, 3), (2, – 1) and (– 1, 1).*

Solution. Let equation of the circle be $x^2 + y^2 + 2gx + 2fy + 2fy + c = 0$.

Since it passes through (1, 3), (2, – 1) and (– 1, 1), we have

$$1^2 + 3^2 + 2g \,.\, 1 + 2f \,.\, 3 + c = 0$$
$$2^2 + 1^2 + 2g \,.\, 2 + 2f \,.\, (-1) + c = 0$$
$$1^2 + 1^2 + 2g \,.\, (-1) + 2f \,.\, 1 + c = 0$$

or

$$2g + 6f + c + 10 = 0$$
$$4g - 2f + c + 5 = 0$$
$$-2g + 2f + c + 2 = 0.$$

Solving these three equations, we get

$$g = -\frac{11}{10}, f = -\frac{9}{10}, a = -\frac{12}{5}$$

Hence the required equation of the circle is

$$x^2 + y^2 - \frac{11}{5}x - \frac{9}{5}y - \frac{12}{5} = 0$$

or

$$5x^2 + 5y^2 - 11x - 9y - 12 = 0$$

Example 3. *Find the equation of the line joining the centres of the two circles.*

$$x^2 + y^2 - 2x + 4y - 1 = 0$$
$$x^2 + y^2 + 2x - 4y + 1 = 0.$$

Solution. The centres of the two circles have co-ordinates (1, – 2) and (– 1, 2).

Equation of the line joining these is

$$y + 2 = \frac{2+2}{-1-1}(x - 1)$$

or

$$y + 2x = 0.$$

4. DIAMETER FORM

To find the equation of the circle having (x_1, y_1) and (x_2, y_2) as the ends of a diameter.

Let the two given points be $A\ (x_1, y_1)$ and $B(x_2, y_2)$. Take any other point $P\ (x, y)$ on the circle. Join AP and BP. Since AB is diameter of the circle, the angle APB is a right angle as it is the angle in a semicircle. Thus, the two lines AP and BP are perpendicular to each other. So if m_1 and m_2 are the slopes of AP and BP respectively, then $m_1 m_2 = -1$.

Now $m_1 = \dfrac{y - y_1}{x - x_1}$

$m_2 = \dfrac{y - y_2}{x - x_2}$

$\Rightarrow \left(\dfrac{y - y_1}{x - x_1}\right)\left(\dfrac{y - y_2}{x - x_2}\right) = -1$

or $\mathbf{(x - x_1)(x - x_2) + (y - y_1)(y - y_2) = 0}$

is the required equation of the circle.

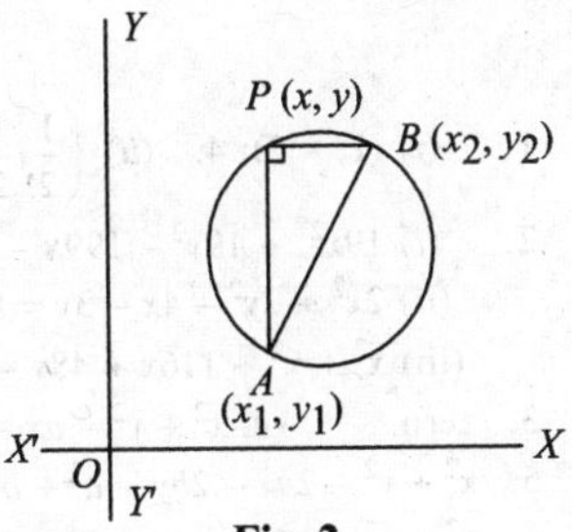

Fig. 2

EXERCISES

1. Find the centre and radius of the circles
   (*i*) $x^2 + y^2 - 2x + 4y - 11 = 0$
   (*ii*) $x^2 + y^2 + x + y - 1 = 0$
   (*iii*) $x^2 + y^2 + 2x + 2y + 3 = 0$.
2. Find the equation of the circle passing through the points
   (*i*) (1, 2), (5, 7), (8, 6)
   (*ii*) (0, 0), (1, 2), (2, 0)
   (*iii*) (5, – 8), (– 2, 9), (2, 1).
3. What should be the value of k so that the equation
   $$x^2 + y^2 + 2kxy + 2x + y + 1 = 0$$
   will represent a circle.
4. Find the equation of the circle passing through the origin and making intercepts a and b on the axes.
5. Derive the equation of the circle which has centre (a, b) and diameter c.
6. Find the equation of the circle circumscribing the triangle formed by the lines $x + y = 6$, $x + 2y = 5$ and $2x + y = 4$.
7. Find the equation of a circle passing through the points (4, 1) and (6, 5) and having its centre on the line $4x + y = 16$.
8. Find the equation of a circle which passes through the centre of the circle $x^2 + y^2 + 8x + 10y - 7 = 0$ and is concentric with the circle $x^2 + y^2 - 4x - 6y = 0$.
9. If $y = mx$ is the equation of a chord of the circle $x^2 + y^2 - 2ax = 0$ prove that the equation of the circle of which this chord is the diameter, is
   $$(1 + m^2)(x^2 + y^2) - 2a(x + my) = 0.$$
10. Find the equation of the line joining the centre of the circle
    $$x^2 + y^2 - 2x + 4y - 11 = 0$$
    to the origin.

ANSWERS

1. (*i*) (1, – 2); 4. (*ii*) $\left(\frac{1}{2}, \frac{1}{2}\right); \sqrt{\frac{3}{2}}$. (*iii*) (1, 1); $\sqrt{-7}$.
2. (*i*) $19x^2 + 19y^2 - 199x - 103y + 310 = 0$.
   (*ii*) $2x^2 + 2y^2 - 4x - 3y = 0$.
   (iii) $x^2 + y^2 + 116x + 48y - 285 = 0$.
3. zero. 4. $x^2 + y^2 - ax - by = 0$.
5. $x^2 + y^2 - 2ax - 2by + a^2 + b^2 - c^2/4 = 0$.
6. $x^2 + y^2 - 17x - 19y + 50 = 0$.
7. $x^2 + y^2 - 6x - 8y + 15 = 0$.
8. $x^2 + y^2 - 4x - 6y - 87 = 0$.
10. $y + 2x = 0$.

5. A LINE AND A CIRCLE

We now show that a line cuts a circle in two points. Let the equation of a circle be

$$x^2 + y^2 = a^2 \quad \text{... (1)}$$

and let $\quad y = mx + c \quad$ ...(2)

be the equation of any line.

(1) and (2) will intersect each other, if and only if they have same point (or points) in common. Solving the two equations, we get

$x^2 + (mx + c)^2 = a^2$

or $(1 + m^2)\, x^2 + 2mcx$

$$+ (c^2 - a^2) = 0 \quad \text{...(3)}$$

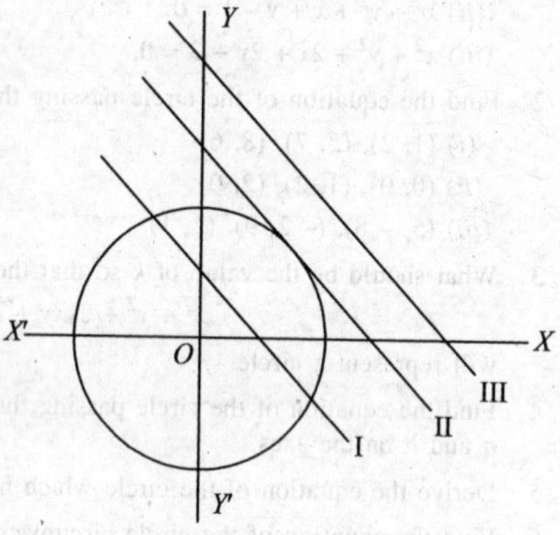

Fig. 3

This, being an equation of second degree, will have two roots and so there are two points of intersection of (1) and (2).

We have the following cases:

Case I. Equation (3) has real and distinct roots, for this the condition is

$$(2mc)^2 - 4\,(1 + m^2)\,(c^2 - a^2) > 0$$

or
$$a^2\,(1 + m^2) - c^2 > 0$$

or
$$a^3\,(1 + m^2) > c^2.$$

Thus whenever $a^2(1 + m^2) > c^2$, (3) has real and distinct roots and therefore the line cuts the circle in two real and distinct points.

Case II. (3) has coincident roots.

The condition for this will be $a^2(1+m^2)=c^2$. In this case the two points of intersection are coincident and we say that the line (2) is a tangent to the circle (1) (*see* 'definition of tangent').

Case III. (3) has imaginary roots.

The condition for this will be $a^2(1+m^2)<c^2$ under this case the two points of intersection are said to be imaginary (See figure).

6. TANGENT TO A CURVE

Let P be a given point on a curve and let Q be any other point on the curve, very near to P. As Q tends to P along the curve, the line PQ tends to a definite line PT, which is called the *tangent* to the curve at P. Thus when Q coincides with P, the position of the line PQ is the position of the tangent at P. This fact is sometimes expressed by saying that a line is a tangent to a curve if it cuts the curve in two coincident points.

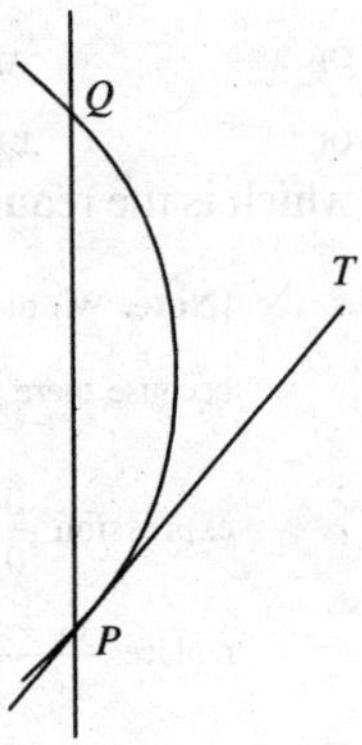

Fig. 4

7. EQUATION OF TANGENT

To find the equation of tangent at any point (x_1, y_1) *on the circle* $x^2+y^2=a^2$.

Let the given point be $P(x_1, y_1)$. Take another point $Q\ (x_2, y_2)$ on the circle. Since both P and Q lie on the circle, we have

$$x_1^2+y_1^2=a^2 \qquad ...(1)$$

$$x_2^2+y_2^2=a^2 \qquad ...(2)$$

Also equation of the line PQ is

$$y-y_1=\frac{y_2-y_1}{x_2-x_1}(x-x_1) \qquad ...(3)$$

(1) and (2) on subtraction give

$$(y_2^2-y_1^2)+(x_2^2-x_1^2)=0$$

or $$(y_2-y_1)(y_2+y_1)+(x_2-x_1)(x_2+x_1)=0$$

or $$\frac{y_2-y_1}{x_2-x_1}=-\frac{x_2+x_1}{y_2+y_1}$$

Putting this value of $\frac{y_2 - y_1}{x_2 - x_1}$ in (3), we get the equation of *PQ* as

$$y - y_1 = -\frac{x_2 + x_1}{y_2 + y_1}(x - x_1).$$

Now this line will become a tangent to the circle, at *P*, as $Q \to P$ (*Q* tends to *P*).

Now $Q \to P$ implies $x_2 \to x_1$ and $y_2 \to y_1$ so the equation becomes

$$y - y_1 = -\frac{2x_1}{2y_1}(x - x_1).$$

or $$xx_1 + yy_1 = x_1^2 + y_1^2$$

or $$\mathbf{xx_1 + yy_1 = a^2} \qquad \text{by (1)}$$

which is the required equation of tangent.

[**Note.** We did not take the limits $x_2 \to x_1$ and $y_2 \to y_1$ in (3) directly, because there the quantity $\frac{y_2 - y_1}{x_2 - x_1}$ would have approached a meaningless expression $\frac{0}{0}$. To avoid this we used given conditions (1) and (2) to replace $\frac{y_2 - y_1}{x_2 - x_1}$ by $-\frac{x_2 + x_1}{y_2 + y_1}$ the limit of which can be evaluated easily.]

8. TANGENT TO THE GENERAL CIRCLE

To find the equation of tangent at any point (x_1, y_1) on the circle

$$x^2 + y^2 + 2gx + 2fy + c = 0$$

Let $P(x_1, y_1)$ be the given point and take $Q(x_2, y_2)$ any other point on the circle, then we have

$$x_1^2 + y_1^2 + 2gx_1 + 2fy_1 + c = 0 \qquad \text{...(1)}$$

$$x_2^2 + y_2^2 + 2gx_2 + 2fy_2 + c = 0 \qquad \text{...(2)}$$

(1) and (2) on subtraction give

$$(x_2^2 - x_1^2) + (y_2^2 - y_1^2) + 2g(x_2 - x_1) + 2f(y_2 - y_1) = 0$$

or $$\frac{y_2 - y_1}{x_2 - x_1} = -\frac{x_1 + x_2 + 2g}{y_1 + y_2 + 2f}$$

Equation of *PQ* is

$$y - y_1 = \frac{y_2 - y_1}{x_2 - x_1}(x - x_1) \quad \text{or} \quad y - y_1 = -\frac{x_1 + x_2 + 2g}{y_1 + y_2 + 2f}(x - x_1).$$

This would become tangent to the circle at P, when $Q \to P$ *i.e.*, $x_2 \to x_1$ and $y_2 \to y_1$.

Hence the tangent to the circle at (x_1, y_1) is

$$y - y_1 = -\frac{x_1 + g'}{y_1 + f}(x - x_1)$$

or $$(x_1 + g)\, x + (y_1 + f)\, y - (x_1^2 + gx_1 + y_1^2 + fy_1) = 0$$

or $$(x_1 + g)\, x + (y_1 + f)\, y + (gx_1 + fy_1 + c) = 0 \quad \text{by (1)}$$

Thus the required equation of the tangent is

$$\mathbf{xx_1 + yy_1 + g\,(x + x_1) + f\,(y + y_1) + c = 0.}$$

9. TANGENT IN THE SLOPE FORM

We have already seen (Article 5) that the condition for the line $y = mx + c$ to meet the circle $x^2 + y^2 = a^2$ in two coincident point is $a^2 (1 + m^2) = c^2$.

i.e., $$c = \pm a \sqrt{1 + m^2}$$

and so this is *the condition for the line $y = mx + c$, to be a tangent to the circle $x^2 + y^2 = a^2$*. Also then the lines $y = mx \pm a\sqrt{1 + m^2}$ are tanents to the circle $x^2 + y^2 = a^2$, whatever be the value of m. This form of the equation of tangent is sometimes referred to as the tangent in the slope form.

Corollary. Since the lines $y = mx + c$, $y = mx \pm a\sqrt{1 + m^2}$ have the same slope, it follows that *two tangents can be drawn to a circle, parallel to any given line.*

10. NORMAL

Definition. *The normal to a curve at any point is the line in the plane of circle passing through that point and perpendicular to the tangent thereat.*

To find the equation of the normal at any point (x_1, y_1) on the circle $x^2 + y^2 = a^2$.

Let P be the point (x_1, y_1).

Equation of tangent at P is

$$xx_1 + yy_1 = a^2.$$

Now slope of tangent $= -\dfrac{x_1}{y_1}$ and slope of normal $\dfrac{y_1}{x_1}$.

Hence equation of normal at (x_1, y_1) is

$$y - y_1 = \frac{y_1}{x_1}(x - x_1)$$

or $\quad yx_1 - xy_1 = 0.$

If equation of the circle is given to be

$$x^2 + y^2 + 2gx + 2fy + c = 0.$$

the equation of normal at any point (x_1, y_1) on the circle will be

$$y(x_1 + g) - x(y_1 + f) + fx_1 - gy_1 = 0$$

which can be proved easily by proceeding as in the previous case.

REMARK: It is clear from the equation of the normal that it passes through the centre of the circle. So it is always along the radius of the circle through that point.

Example 4. *Find the condition under which the tangents at (x_1, y_1) and (x_2, y_2) to the circle $x^2 + y^2 + 2gx + 2fy + c = 0$ will be perpendicular.*

Solution. The tangents at (x_1, y_1) and (x_2, y_2) are

$$xx_1 + yy_1 + g(x + x_1) + f(y + y_1) + c = 0$$

$$xx_2 + yy_2 + g(x + x_2) + f(y + y_2) + c = 0.$$

These will be perpendicular if the product of their slopes is – 1.

i.e., if $\quad \left(-\dfrac{x_1 + g}{y_1 + f}\right)\left(-\dfrac{x_2 + g}{y_2 + f}\right) = -1$

or if $\quad (x_1 + g)(x_2 + g) + (y_1 + f)(y_2 + f) = 0$

which is the required condition.

Example 5. *Find the co-ordinates of the point where the line $y = 2x + 1$ cuts the circle $x^2 + y^2 = 2$.*

Solution. The points of intersection of the line with the circle are got by solving their equations, thus solving the two equations $x^2 + y^2 = 2$ and $y = 2x + 1$, we find

$$x^2 + (2x + 1)^2 = 2$$

or $\quad 5x^2 + 4x - 1 = 0$

$\Rightarrow \quad x = -1, \dfrac{1}{5}$

When $\quad x = -1, y = 2(-1) + 1 = -1$ and

when $\quad x = \dfrac{1}{5}, y = 2\left(\dfrac{1}{5}\right) + 1 = \dfrac{7}{5}.$

Thus the two points of intersection are $(-1, -1)$ and $\left(\dfrac{1}{5}, \dfrac{7}{5}\right)$.

Example 6. *Find the condition that the line $ax + by + c = 0$ may touch the circle $(x - h)^2 + (y - k)^2 = r^2$.*

Solution. The line $ax + by + c = 0$ will touch the given circle, if the radius of the circle is equal to the perpendicular distance of the line from the centre of the circle.

Now radius of the given circle = r.

Centre of the given circle is (h, k).

Also perpendicular distance of (h, k) from $ax + by + c = 0$ is

$$\frac{ah + bk + c}{\sqrt{a^2 + b^2}}.$$

Hence the required condition is

$$r = \frac{ah + bk + c}{\sqrt{a^2 + b^2}}$$

or $$(ah + bk + c)^2 = (a^2 + b^2)\, r^2.$$

Example 7. *Find the equations of the tangents to the circle $x^2 + y^2 = 4$, which are parallel to the line $x + 2y + 3 = 0$.*

Solution. Tangents to the circle $x^2 + y^2 = 4$, in the slope form are

$$y = mx \pm 2\sqrt{1 + m^2}.$$

These will be parallel to the line $x + 2y + 3 = 0$, if

$$m = -\frac{1}{2} = \text{slope of the line.}$$

Hence the required tangents are

$$y = -\frac{1}{2}x \pm 2\sqrt{1 + \frac{1}{4}}$$

or $$2y + x = \pm\sqrt{5}$$

Example 8. *Show that the circles*

$$x^2 + y^2 = 2 \text{ and } x^2 + y^2 - 6x - 6y + 10 = 0$$

touch one another at the point (1, 1).

Solution. Since $1^2 + 1^2 = 2$

$$1^2 + 1^2 - 6 - 6 + 10 = 0$$

It is clear that the point (1, 1) lies on both the circles. Again tangent at (1, 1) to the circle $x^2 + y^2 = 2$ is

$$x \,.\, 1 + y \,.\, 1 = 2$$

or $$x + y = 2.$$

Tangent at (1, 1) to the circle $x^2 + y^2 - 6x - 6y + 10 = 0$ is

$$x \,.\, 1 + y \,.\, 1 - 3\,(x + 1) - 3\,(y + 1) + 10 = 0$$

or $$x+y-3x-3-3y-3+10=0$$

or $$x+y=2.$$

Thus, we find that the two circles pass through the point (1, 1) and also have the same tangent at (1, 1), implying thereby that the circles touch each other at (1, 1).

EXERCISES

1. Find the equations of tangent and normal at the point (2, 1) on the circle $$x^2+y^2+116x+48y-285=0.$$
2. Find the equations of the tangents to the circle $x^2+y^2=4$,
   (*i*) which are inclined at an angle of 45° to x-axis.
   (*ii*) which are parallel to the line $2x-y+4=0$
   (*iii*) which are perpendicular to the line $3x+2y-5=0$.
3. Find the points where the line $x-y=0$ meets the circle $$x^2+y^2+2x+y+1=0.$$
4. Find the condition that the line $lx+my+n=0$, may touch the circle $$x^2+y^2+2gx+2fy+c=0.$$
5. Find the equation of the circle which has its centre at the point (3, 4) and touches the line $5x+12y=1$.
6. Find where the line $3x+4y+7=0$ cuts the circle $x^2+y^2-4x-6y-12=0$.
7. Find the equation of the tangents to the circle $x^2+y^2=9$ which are perpendicular to the line $x-y-1=0$.
8. Find the equation to the circle which touches both the axes and passes through the point (– 2, – 3).
9. Find the equation of the normal to the circle $x^2+y^2-2ax=0$ at the point $$(a(1+\cos\alpha),\ a\sin\alpha).$$
10. Show that the line $x+y\sqrt{3}=4$ touches the circles $x^2+y^2=4$ and $x^2+y^2-4x-4\sqrt{3}y+12=0$ at the same point.
11. Find the length of the chord joining the points in which the line $$\frac{x}{a}+\frac{y}{b}=1,\text{ cuts the circle } x^2+y^2=r^2.$$
12. Find the points of intersection of the line $y-5x-2=0$ and the circle $x^2+y^2-13x-4y=0$.

ANSWERS

1. $12x+5y-29=0$; $12x-5y-2=0$.
2. (*i*) $y=x\pm5\sqrt{2}$ (*ii*) $2x-y=\pm5\sqrt{5}$ (*iii*) $2x-3y\pm5\sqrt{13}=0$.
3. (–1, –1), (–2, –2).
4. $(gl+fm-n)^2=(l^2+m^2)(g^2+f^2-c)$.

5. $x^2 + y^2 - 6x - 8y + \dfrac{381}{169} = 0.$

6. Touches at (– 1, – 1).

7. $x + y - 3\sqrt{2} = 0$

$x + y + 3\sqrt{2} = 0.$

8. $x^2 + y^2 + 2(5 \pm \sqrt{12})(x + y) + 37 \pm 10\sqrt{12} = 0.$

9. $y = (x - a) \tan \alpha.$

11. $2\sqrt{\dfrac{r^2(a^2+b^2) - a^2b^2}{a^2+b^2}}.$

12. (1, 7) and $\left(-\frac{1}{2}, -\frac{1}{2}\right).$

11. A POINT AND A CIRCLE

Suppose we are given the circle

$$x^2 + y^2 + 2gx + 2fy + c = 0 \qquad \text{...(1)}$$

and a point $P(x_1, y_1)$. We wish to find whether the point P lies outside or inside the circle. If C is the centre of the circle then C has co-ordinates $(-g, -f)$. Now P will lie outside the circle if the distance PC is greater than the radius of the circle and the point P will lie inside the circle if the distance PC is less than the radius.

Thus P lies outside, on, or inside the circle (1), according as

$$\sqrt{(x_1 + g)^2 + (y_1 + f)^2} \text{ is } >, =, \text{ or } < \sqrt{g^2 + f^2 - c}$$

which on squaring and transposing gives

$$x_1^2 + y_1^2 + 2gx_1 + 2fy_1 + c \text{ is } >, =, \text{ or } < 0.$$

Similarly $P(x_1, y_1)$ lies outside, on or inside the circle $x^2 + y^2 = a^2$, according as $x_1^2 + y_1^2 - a^2$, is $> =$, or < 0.

12. TANGENTS FROM A POINT

We now show that two tangents can be drawn to a circle from any point.

Let equation of the circle be $x^2 + y^2 = a^2$ and let (x_1, y_1) be any given point.

Any tangent to the circle is given by the equation

$$y = mx + a\sqrt{1 + m^2} \qquad \text{...(1)}$$

This will pass through (x_1, y_1) if

$$y_1 = mx_1 + a\sqrt{1 + m^2}$$

or $$(y_1 - mx_1)^2 = a^2(1 + m^2)$$

or $m^2\left(x_1^2 - a^2\right) - 2mx_1y_1 + y_1^2 - a^2 = 0$ ... (2)

which is a quadratic in m, giving two values of m. Corresponding to each value of m, Equation (1) gives a tangent through (x_1, y_1).

Case I. Equation (2) has real and distinct roots, condition for which is

$$x_1^2\, y_1^2 - \left(x_1^2 - a^2\right)\left(y_1^2 - a^2\right) > 0$$

or $$x_1^2 + y_1^2 > a^2$$

or that (x_1, y_1) lies outside the circle

Thus if (x_1, y_1) lies outside the circle, two real and distinct tangents can be drawn to the circle from the point (x_1, y_1)

Cass II. (2) has coincident roots, condition for which is $x_1^2 + y_1^2 = a^2$

or that (x_1, y_1) lies on the circle.

Thus if (x_1, y_1) lies on the circle, two coincident tangents can be drawn to the circle through (x_1, y_1).

Case III. (2) has imaginary roots, condition for which is

$$x_1^2 + y_1^2 < a^2$$

or that (x_1, y_1) lies inside the circle.

Thus if (x_1, y_1) lies inside the circle, two imaginary tangents can be drawn to the circle through (x_1, y_1).

Hence we conclude that *two tangents can be drawn to a circle from any point, and these tangents are real, coincident, or imaginary according as the point lies outside, on, or inside the circle.*

13. LENGTH OF THE TANGENT

Suppose we have the circle

$$x^2 + y^2 + 2gx + 2fy + c = 0$$

and let $P\ (x_1, y_1)$ be a point lying outside the circle. Draw a tangent to the circle from P. Let T be the point of contact. Then by the length of the tangent we mean the length PT. If C is the centre of the circle, then from the right angled triangle PTC we have

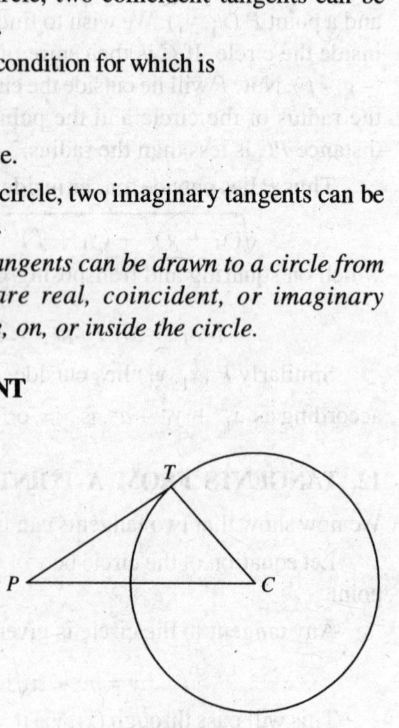

Fig. 5

$$PC^2 = PT^2 + TC^2.$$

$$\Rightarrow \quad PT^2 = PC^2 - TC^2$$
$$= [x_1 - (-g)]^2 + [y_1 - (-f)]^2 - [g^2 + f^2 - c]$$
$$= \mathbf{x_1^2 + y_1^2 + 2gx_1 + 2fy_1 + c}$$

which gives the square of the length of the tangent.

Example 9. *Find the length of the tangent drawn from the point (2, – 1) to the circle $3x^2 + 3y^2 + 4x + 2y + 6 = 0$.*

Solution. Equation of circle is

$$3x^2 + 2y^2 + 4x + 2y + 6 = 0$$

or
$$x^2 + y^2 + \frac{4}{3}x + \frac{2}{3}y + 2 = 0$$

Length of tangent from (2, – 1) to this circle is

$$\sqrt{2^2 + 1^2 + \frac{4}{3}.2 + \frac{2}{3}.(-1) + 2} = \sqrt{4 + 1 + \frac{8}{3} - \frac{2}{3} + 2} = 3.$$

Example 10. *Find the tangents to the circle $x^2 + y^2 = 25$ from the point (11, 2).*

Solution. Any line through the point (11, –2) with slope m is

$$y + 2 = m(x - 11)$$

or $\quad mx - y - (2 + 11m) = 0$ ...(1)

This will be a tangent to the circle $x^2 + y^2 = 25$, if radius of the circle is equal to the length of the perpendicular from the centre (0, 0) on the line (1)

i.e., if
$$\pm 5 = \frac{2 + 11m}{\sqrt{m^2 + 1}}$$

or
$$25(m^2 + 1) = (2 + 11m)^2$$

or
$$96m^2 + 44m - 21 = 0.$$

This gives
$$m = -\frac{3}{4}, \frac{7}{24}$$

Hence the two tangents are

$$y + 2 = -\frac{3}{4}(x - 11) \quad \text{or} \quad 3x + 4y - 25 = 0$$

$$y + 2 = \frac{7}{24}(x - 11) \quad \text{or} \quad 7x - 24y - 125 = 0.$$

14. CIRCLE THROUGH THE INTERSECTION OF A LINE AND A CIRCLE

Suppose we are given a circle

$$x^2+y^2+2gx+2fy+c=0 \qquad \text{...(1)}$$

and a line
$$ax+by+d=0 \qquad \text{...(2)}$$

intersecting in two points. We wish to find the equation of the circle passing through the points of intersection of (1) and (2). Let one of these points be (x_1, y_1), then since it lies on both (1) and (2).

we have

$$\left.\begin{aligned} x_1^2+y_1^2+2gx_1+2fy_1+c&=0 \\ ax_1+by_1+d&=0 \end{aligned}\right] \qquad \text{...(3)}$$

Consider now the equation

$$(x^2+y^2+2gx+2fy+c)+\lambda\,(ax+by+d)=0 \qquad \text{...(4)}$$

when λ is an arbitrary constant.

Equation (4) is a second degree equation in which coefficients of x^2 and y^2 are same and there is no term involving xy and thus it represents a circle. Again, in view of conditions (3) it is clear that the point (x_1, y_1) lies on (4), whatever λ may be. If (x_2, y_2) is the other point of intersection of (1) and (2), then by the above argument, this point also lies on (4) and hence equation (4) represents the required equation of a circle passing through the points of intersection of (1) and (2), for all values of λ.

NOTE. Value of λ can be found from the other given condition.

15. CIRCLE THROUGH THE INTERSECTION OF TWO CIRCLES

Proceeding exactly in the above manner, we can write down the equation of a circle passing through points of intersection of the two circles

$$x^2+y^2+2gx+2fy+c=0$$
$$x^2+y^2+2g'x+2f'y+c'=0$$

as $(x^2+y^2+2gx+2fy+c)+\lambda\,(x^2+y^2+2g'x+2f'y+c')=0$
where λ is some constant.

Example 11. *Find the equation of the circle passing through $(-1, 1)$ and the points of intersection of*

$$x^2+y^2=5 \text{ and } x^2+y^2-3x-y=0.$$

Solution. Any circle through the points of intersection of the given circles is

$$x^2+y^2-3x-y+\lambda\,(x^2+y^2-5)=0.$$

If it passes through $(-1, 1)$, we will have

$$1+1+3-1+\lambda(1+1-5)=0$$

or
$$\lambda=4/3.$$

Hence the equation of the required circle is

$$x^2+y^2-3x-y+\frac{4}{3}(x^2+y^2-5)=0$$

or $$7x^2+7y^2-9x-3y-20=0.$$

Example 12. *Find the equation of the circle passing through the points of intersection of the circles*

$$x^2+y^2=2ax \quad \textit{and} \quad x^2+y^2=2by$$

and having its centre on the line $\frac{x}{a}-\frac{y}{b}=2.$

Solution. Any circle through the points of intersection of the given circles is

$$(x^2+y^2-2ax)+\lambda(x^2+y^2-2by)=0 \qquad ...(1)$$

or $$(1+\lambda)x^2+(1+\lambda)y^2-2ax-2by\lambda=0$$

or $$x^2+y^2-\frac{2ax}{1+\lambda}-\frac{2b\lambda}{1+\lambda}y=0.$$

Centre of this circle is $\left(\frac{a}{1+\lambda},\frac{b\lambda}{1+\lambda}\right)$

This will lie on the line $\frac{x}{a}-\frac{y}{b}=2$ if

$$\frac{a}{(1+\lambda)b}-\frac{b\lambda}{(1+\lambda)b}=2 \text{ or } \lambda=-\frac{1}{3}$$

Thus, the equation of the required circle is

$$x^2+y^2-\frac{2ax}{1-\frac{1}{3}}-\frac{2bx}{1-\frac{1}{3}}\times\left(-\frac{1}{3}\right)=0$$

or $$x^2+y^2-3ax+by=0.$$

[NOTE. In the above example, we divided the equation by $1+\lambda$, assuming that $\lambda\neq-1$. It may be noted that if $\lambda=-1$, the Equation (1) will no more represent a circle.]

Example 13. *Find the equation of the circle drawn on the line segment joining the points of intersection of the circle* $x^2+y^2=a^2$ *and the line* $x\cos\alpha+y\sin\alpha=p$ *as a diameter.*

Solution. Equation of any circle through the points of intersection of the given circle and the given line is

$$(x^2+y^2-a^2)+\lambda(x\cos\alpha+y\sin\alpha-p)=0$$

Centre of this circle is $\left(-\frac{\lambda}{2}\cos\alpha, -\frac{\lambda}{2}\sin\alpha\right)$

It is given that the given chord is a diameter of this circle and so the centre lies on it.

i.e., $$-\frac{\lambda}{2}\cos\alpha.\cos\alpha - \frac{\lambda}{2}\sin\alpha.\sin\alpha = p$$

$$\Rightarrow \quad -\frac{\lambda}{2}(\cos^2\alpha + \sin^2\alpha) = p$$

$$\Rightarrow \quad \lambda = -2p.$$

Hence the required equation of the circle is

$$(x^2 + y^2 - a^2) - 2p\,(x\cos\alpha + y\sin\alpha - p) = 0.$$

16. CHORD WITH GIVEN MIDDLE POINT

To find the equation of chord of the circle $x^2 + y^2 = a^2$ *having* (x_1, y_1) *as its middle point.*

Let AB be a chord with its middle point at (x_1, y_1). Also let co-ordinates of A and B be (x', y') and (x'', y''). Now equation of AB is

$$y - y_1 = m(x - x_1) \qquad ...(1)$$

where m, the slope of AB, is to be found out.

Since A and B both lie on the circle, we have

$$x'^2 + y'^2 = a^2$$
$$x''^2 + y''^2 = a^2$$

Subtraction gives $(y''^2 - y'^2) + (x''^2 - x'^2) = 0$

or $$(y'' - y')(y'' + y') + (x'' - x')(x'' + x') = 0$$

or $$\frac{y'' - y'}{x'' - x'} = -\frac{x'' + x'}{y'' + y'}. \qquad ...(2)$$

Again since (x_1, y_1) is middle point of AB,

$$x_1 = \frac{x' + x''}{2} \text{ and } y_1 = \frac{y' + y''}{2}$$

and so (2) gives

$$\frac{y'' - y'}{x'' - x'} = \text{slope of } AB = m = -\frac{2x_1}{2y_1} = -\frac{x_1}{y_1}.$$

Putting this value of m in (1), we get the required equation of AB as

$$y - y_1 = -\frac{x_1}{y_1}(x - x_1)$$

or $$xx_1 + yy_1 = x_1^2 + y_1^2.$$

[**Note.** This formula fails in case the middle point happens to be the centre of the circle (why?).]

17. LOCUS OF MIDDLE POINTS OF A SYSTEM OF PARALLEL CHORDS

Let equation of the circle be $x^2 + y^2 = a^2$, and suppose we are given a system of parallel chords of this circle. Let m be the slope of this system of chords. If (x_1, y_1) is the middle point of any one chord of the system then equation of this chord is

$$xx_1 + yy_1 = x_1^2 + y_1^2.$$

Its slope is $-\dfrac{x_1}{y_1}$.

But slope of the system is given to be m

so $$m = -\frac{x_1}{y_1}$$

or $$x_1 + my_1 = 0.$$

Hence locus of (x_1, y_1) is

$$x + my = 0$$

which is a line passing through (0, 0) and perpendicular to the given system of chords.

Hence *the locus of middle points of a system of parallel chords of a circle is the diameter perpendicular to the chords.*

18. CHORD OF CONTACT

Let PT and PT' be two tangents drawn from a point to a circle. The line TT' (join of the points of contact) is called *chord of contact* of the tangents drawn from P. To find the equation of the chord of contact.

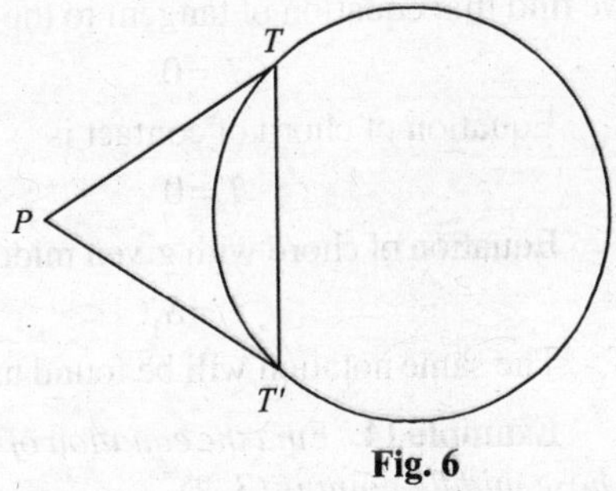

Fig. 6

Let $x^2 + y^2 = a^2$ be the equation of the circle and let P (x_1, y_1) be the point from which the tangents PT and PT' are drawn. Let the co-ordinates of T and T' be (x', y') and (x'', y''). Then the equation of PT is

$$xx' + yy' = a^2$$

and equation of PT' is

$$xx'' + yy'' = a^2.$$

Since both PT and PT' pass through (x_1, y_1), we have

$$x_1x' + y_1y' = a^2$$

and $$x_1x'' + y_1y'' = a^2.$$

This shows that the points (x', y') and (x'', y'') lie on

$$xx_1 + yy_1 = a^2.$$

Since this is a linear equation in x and y, it represents a line and hence is the required equation of TT'.

[NOTE. If the point P lies on the circle, the chord of contact becomes the tangent at P.]

19. PARAMETRIC CO-ORDINATES

It is clear that the point with co-ordinates $(a \cos \theta, a \sin \theta)$ always lies on the circle $x^2 + y^2 = a^2$, whatever θ may be. Here θ is called the *parameter* and the co-ordinates are referred to as the parametric co-ordinates. The point $(a \cos \theta, a \sin \theta)$ is also sometimes written in short as 'the point θ'.

Equation of tangent at 'the point θ' will be

$$xa \cos \theta + ya \sin \theta = a^2$$

or $$x \cos \theta + y \sin \theta = a.$$

20. NOTATION

If we write $$S_1 \equiv x_1^2 + y_1^2 - a^2,$$

$$T \equiv xx_1 + yy_1 - a^2,$$

$$S \equiv x^2 + y^2 - a^2,$$

we find that equation of tangent to the circle $S = 0$ is

$$T = 0.$$

Equation of chord of contact is

$$T = 0$$

Equation of chord with given middle point (x_1, y_1) is

$$T = S_1.$$

The same notation will be found useful in the next chapter also.

Example 14. *Find the equation of the chord of the circle $x^2 + y^2 = 16$ whose middle point is (3, 2).*

Solution. Equation of the chord with given middle point (x_1, y_1) is given by

$$xx_1 + yy_1 = x_1^2 + y_1^2 .$$

Thus the required equation of the chord is

$$x \cdot 3 + y \cdot 2 = 9 + 4$$

i.e., $$3x + 2y = 13.$$

Example 15. *Find the equation of normal at the point 'θ' on the circle $x^2 + y^2 = a^2$.*

Solution. Equation of tangent at the point 'θ' is

$$xa \cos \theta + ya \sin \theta = a^2$$

or $$x \cos \theta + y \sin \theta = a.$$

$$\text{Slope of tangent} = -\frac{\cos \theta}{\sin \theta}$$

$$\text{Thus, slope of normal} = \frac{\sin \theta}{\cos \theta} = \tan \theta.$$

Hence equation of normal is

$$y - a \sin \theta = \tan \theta \, (x - a \cos \theta)$$

or $$y \cos \theta - a \sin \theta \cos \theta = x \sin \theta - a \sin \theta \cos \theta$$

or $$y \cos \theta - x \sin \theta = 0.$$

MISCELLANEOUS EXERCISES

1. Find the equation of a circle whose centre is (4, 5) and which passes through the centre of the circle $x^2 + y^2 + 4x - 6y - 12 = 0$.
2. Show that the centres of the circles $x^2 + y^2 = 1$, $x^2 + y^2 + 6x - 2y = 1$, $x^2 - y^2 - 12x + 4y = 1$ lie on a line.
3. Find the equation of a circle passing through the points (1, 0), (0, – 6) and (3, 4).
4. Find the equations to a circle passing through (2, 3) and (4, 5) and having its centre on the line $y - 4x + 3 = 0$.
5. Find the equations of the tangents to the circle $x^2 + y^2 = 25$, which are inclined at an angle of 30° to the *x*-axis.
6. Find the equations of the circles which touch the lines $x = 0$, $y = 0$ and $x = k$.
7. Show that the line $3x - 4y = 10$ touches the circle $x^2 + y^2 + 2x - 6y = 15$. Find the point of contact.
8. Tangents are drawn from the point (4, – 2) to the circle $x^2 + y^2 = 10$. Find their equations.
9. Show that the condition that the line joining the points $(-a, 0)$ and $(a, 0)$ subtends an angle θ at the point (x_1, y_1) is $x^2 + y^2 - a^2 \pm 2ay_1 \cot \theta = 0$.

10. Tangents are drawn from the point (x_1, y_1) to the circle $x^2 + y^2 = a^2$. Prove that the area of the triangle formed by them and the chord of contact is

$$\frac{a(x_1^2 + y_1^2 - a^2)^{3/2}}{x_1^2 + y_1^2}.$$

11. Find the locus of the middle points of chords of the circle $x^2 + y^2 = a^2$ which pass through the fixed point (h, k).

12. Find the equation of the diameter of the circle $x^2 + y^2 - 6x + 2y - 8 = 0$ which contains the origin.

13. Find the equation of a circle circumscribing the triangle formed by the lines $x = 6$, $x + 2y = 0$ and $x - 2y = 8$.

14. Find the equation of the circle described on the intersection of the circle $x^2 + y^2 = 2$ and the line $y - 2x - 1 = 0$ as diameter.

ANSWERS

1. $x^2 + y^2 - 8x - 10y + 1 = 0$.
3. $4x^2 + 4y^2 - 142x + 47y + 138 = 0$.
4. $x^2 + y^2 - 4x - 10y + 25 = 0$.
5. $x - \sqrt{3}y + 10 = 0$, $x - \sqrt{3}y - 10 = 0$.
6. $4x^2 + 4y^2 - 4kx \pm 4ky + k^2 = 0$.
7. $(2, -1)$.
8. $x - 3y - 10 = 0$, $3x + y - 10 = 0$.
11. $x^2 + y^2 - hx - ky = 0$.
12. $x + 3y = 0$.
13. $2x^2 + 2y^2 - 21x + 8y + 60 = 0$.
14. $5x^2 + 5y^2 + 4x - 2y - 8 = 0$.

CHAPTER 24

CONIC SECTIONS

1. DEFINITIONS

A *conic section* or a *conic* is the locus of a point which moves in such a way that its distance from a fixed point bears a constant ratio to its distance from a fixed line (not passing through the fixed point).

The fixed point is called a *focus*; the fixed line, a *directrix* and the constant ratio is called the *eccentricity*. The eccentricity is usually denoted by the letter e.

The line passing through the focus and perpendicular to the directrix is called the *axis* of the conic and each of the points where the axis meets the conic is called *vertex* of the conic.

We have the following three situations

(*a*) If $e = 1$, the conic is called a **parabola**.

(*b*) If $0 < e < 1$, the conic is called an **ellipse.**

(*c*) If $e > 1$, the conic is called a **hyperbola.**

We shall deal with the three curves separately under different sections.

REMARK: Conic sections are plane sections of a cone.

SECTION A
THE PARABOLA

2. DEFINITION

A parabola is the locus of a point which moves in such a way that its distance from a fixed point (the focus) is equal to its distance from a fixed line (the directrix), not passing through the focus.

3. EQUATION OF PARABOLA IN THE STANDARD FORM

Let S be the focus and ZK be the directrix of the parabola. Through S, draw a line SZ, perpendicular to ZK. Take a point A on SZ, such that

$$ZA = AS = a, \text{ say.}$$

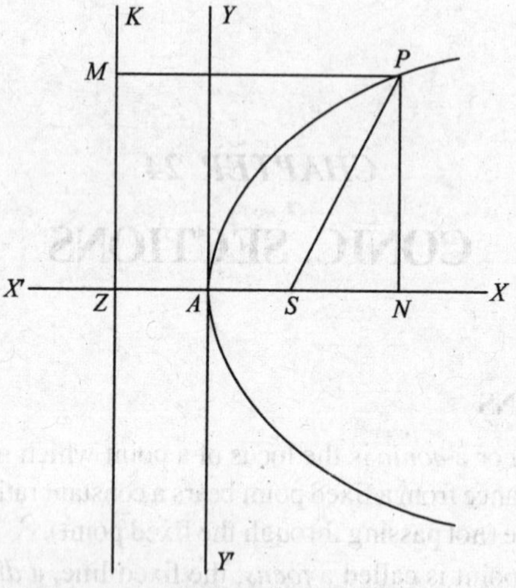

Fig. 1

Then by definition, A lies on the curve. Take the origin at A, the x-axis along AS and the y-axis along the perpendicular to AS at A.

The focus S will then have co-ordinates $(a, 0)$.

Let (x, y) be the co-ordinates of the moving point P at any position. Drop $PM \perp ZK$ and $PN \perp AX$.

By definition,

$$PM = PS$$

or $$ZA + AN = PS$$

or $$a + x = \sqrt{(x-a)^2 + (y-0)^2}$$

or $$y^2 = 4ax.$$

which is the required equation of the parabola in the standard form.

The point A is called the *vertex* of the parabola and has co-ordinates (0, 0). The line AS is called *axis* of the parabola and has equation $y = 0$.

The equation of the directrix ZK (a line parallel to y-axis) is clearly $x = -a$.

4. SHAPE OF THE PARABOLA

From the equation $y^2 = 4ax$ of the parabola, we find that the curve is symmetrical about the x-axis (axis of the parabola). The curve passes through the origin (0, 0). In fact when $x = 0$, two values of y are zero and therefore the y axis is a tangent to the curve at the vertex. Also y is imaginary for negative values of x and thus no part of the curve lies on the left of y-axis.

If x tends to infinity (*i.e.*, becomes very large) then so does y. The parabola thus extends to infinity on either side of the axis. The final shape of the curve is as shown in the figure above.

It might be noted that the equations

$$(i)\ y^2 = -4ax \qquad (ii)\ x^2 = 4ay \qquad (iii)\ x^2 = -4ay$$

also represent equal parabolas (see Latus Rectum). We give below the relevant details about these along with their diagrams.

Equation of the curve

$y^2 = -4ax$

Focus	$(-a, 0)$
Directrix	$x = a$
Axis	$y = 0$
Vertex	$(0, 0)$
Tangent at vertex	$x = 0$

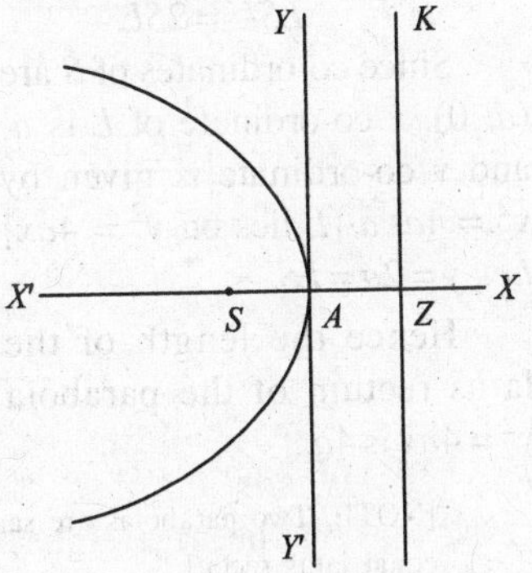

Fig. 2

Equation of the curve $x^2 = 4ay$

Focus	$(0, a)$
Directrix	$y = -a$
Axis	$x = 0$
Vertex	$(0, 0)$
Tangent at vertex	$y = 0$

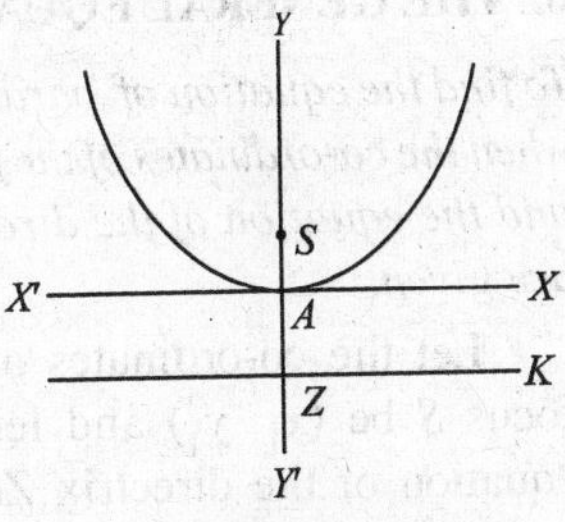

Fig. 3

Equation of the curve

$x^2 = -4ay$.

Focus	$(0, -a)$
Directrix	$y = a$
Axis	$x = 0$
Vertex	$(0, 0)$
Tangent at a vertex	$y = 0$

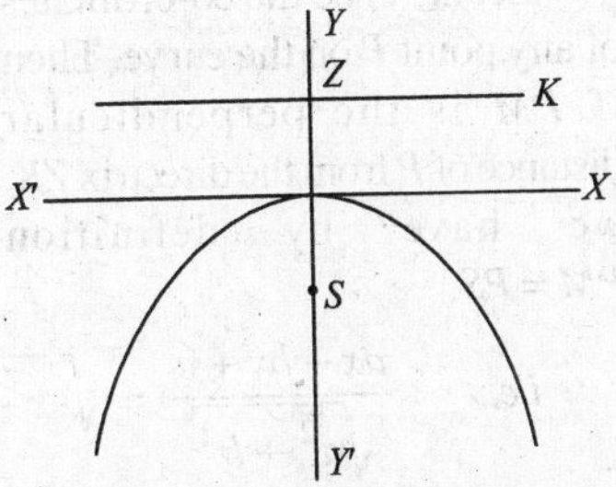

Fig. 4

5. LATUS RECTUM

The chord of the parabola which passes through the focus and is perpendicular to the axis of the parabola is called *latus rectum* of the parabola. In the figure, LSL' is the latus rectum. Due to symmetry of the curve,

$$LSL' = 2SL.$$

Since co-ordinates of S are $(a, 0)$, x co-ordinate of L is a, and y co-ordinate is given by $y^2 = 4a.\ a$ [L lies on $y^2 = 4ax$] *i.e.*, $y = 2a = LS$.

Hence the length of the latus rectum of the parabola $y^2 = 4ax$ is $4a$.

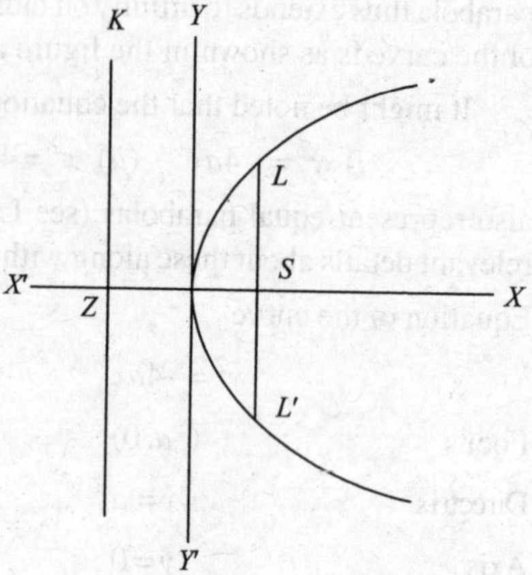

Fig. 5

[NOTE. Two parabolas are said to be equal in magnitude if they have equal latus recta.]

6. THE GENERAL EQUATION OF A PARABOLA

To find the equation of parabola, when the co-ordinates of the focus and the equation of the directrix are given.

Let the co-ordinates of the focus S be (x_1, y_1) and let the equation of the directrix ZK be $ax + by + c = 0$.

Let (x, y) be the co-ordinates of any point P on the curve. Then if PM is the perpendicular distance of P from the directrix ZK, we have by definition $PM = PS$.

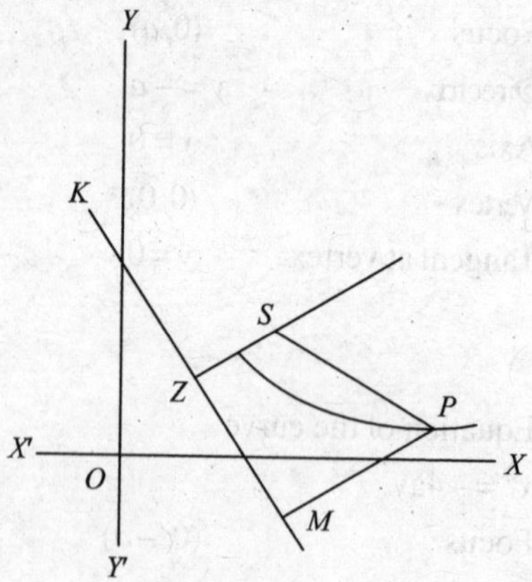

Fig. 6

i.e., $$\frac{ax + by + c}{\sqrt{a^2 + b^2}} = \sqrt{(x - x_1)^2 + (y - y_1)^2}$$

or $$(ax + by + c)^2 = (a^2 + b^2)\,[(x - x_1)^2 + (y - y_1)^2]$$

which on simplification, can be put in the form

$$(bx - ay)^2 + 2gx + 2fy + k = 0$$

and is the required equation of the parabola. It is clear from the equation that the second degree terms in the equation of parabola form a perfect square.

Example 1. *Find equation of a parabola whose focus is the point (–1, 1) and the directrix is the line x + y + 1 = 0*

Solution. Let S (–1, 1) be the focus. Take (x, y) any point on the curve. If PM is the perpendicular distance of P from the directrix, then by definition

$$PM = PS \Rightarrow \frac{x + y + 1}{\sqrt{1+1}} = \sqrt{(x+1)^2 + (y-1)^2}$$

or $(x + y + 1)^2 = 2[(x + 1)^2 + (y - 1)^2]$ which on simplification reduces to $(x - y)^2 + 2x - 6y + 3 = 0$.

This is the required equation of the parabola.

Example 2. *Find equation of a parabola whose focus is the point (– 2, 3) and the focus at (– 7, 3).*

Solution. Let A (–2, 3) be the vertex and S (– 7, 3) be the focus. If SZ is the perpendicular from the focus S on the directrix, then it is known to us that A is the middle point of SZ.

Thus if Z had co-ordinates (x_1, y_1),

then $$-2 = \frac{x_1 + (-7)}{2} \text{ and } 3 = \frac{y_1 + 3}{2}$$

$\Rightarrow$ $$x_1 = 3, y_1 = 3$$

i.e., directrix is the line passing through (3, 3) and perpendicular to SZ (the axis of the parabola)

Now slope of $SZ = 0$.

$\Rightarrow$ it is a line parallel to x-axis

and so directrix is the line through (3, 3) and perpendicular to the x-axis.

$\Rightarrow$ equation of directrix is $x = 3$.

Now if P (x, y) is any point on the parabola, then, by definition, $PM = PS$, where M is the foot of perpendicular from P on the directrix.

So $$PM = PS$$

$\Rightarrow$ $$x - 3 = \sqrt{(x+7)^2 + (y-3)^2}$$

$\Rightarrow$ $$(x - 3)^2 = (x + 7)^2 + (y - 3)^2$$

which reduces to

$$y^2 - 6y + 20x + 49 = 0$$

the required equation to the parabola.

7. A POINT AND A PARABOLA

Let equation of parabola be $y^2 = 4ax$. Let $P(x_1, y_1)$ be a point in first or fourth quadrant lying outside the curve. Draw $PM \perp AX$, the axis of the parabola and let PM meet the curve in N. Since P lies outside the curve

$$PM > NM.$$

Now $PM = y_1$. Also as x co-ordinate of N is x_1, its y co-ordinate is given by

$y^2 = 4ax_1$ [as N lies on $y^2 = 4ax$]

So $PM^2 = y_1^2$. $NM^2 = 4ax_1$

The condition $PM > NM$, reduces to $PM^2 - NM^2 > 0$

or $y_1^2 - 4ax_1 > 0$.

Similarly, we can show that the point $P(x_1, y_1)$ lies inside the parabola $y^2 = 4ax$ if $y_1^2 - 4ax_1 < 0$. In case the point $P(x_1, y_1)$ lies in the second or third quadrant, x_1 is –ve and so $y_1^2 - 4ax_1$ is necessarily positive, and in this case the point P is clearly lying outside the parabola.

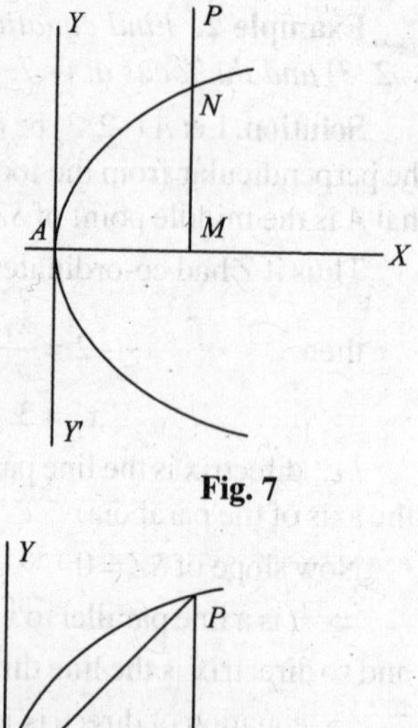

Fig. 7

Hence we conclude that the *point (x_1, y_1) lies outside, on or inside the parabola $y^2 = 4ax_1$, according as*

$y_1^2 - 4ax_1$ is >, =, or < zero.

Example 3. *A double ordinate of the curve $y^2 = 4ax$ is of length 8a. Prove that the lines through the vertex to its two ends are at right angles.*

Solution. Let PNP' be the double ordinate of length $8a$. By symmetry $PN = NP' = 4a$.

Now y co-ordinate of P is $4a$, and x co-ordinate will be given by the equation $(4a)^2 = 4ax$ [P lies on

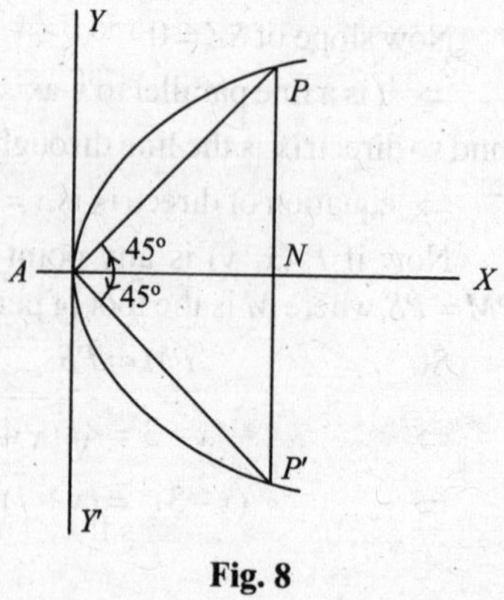

Fig. 8

$y^2 = 4ax$] *i.e.*, x co-ordinate $= 4a$ Thus $PN = AN = 4a = NP'$ [AN is x co-ordinate of P]

$$\Rightarrow \quad \angle PAN = \angle APN = 45^\circ \text{ as } \angle ANP = 90^\circ$$

also $$\angle NAP' = \angle AP'N = 45^\circ.$$

Hence $$\angle PAP' = 90^\circ.$$

Example 4. *Prove that the area of the triangle inscribed in parabola $y^2 = 4ax$ is*

$$\frac{1}{8a}(y_1 \sim y_2)(y_2 \sim y_3)(y_3 \sim y_1)$$

where $y_1, y_2\ y_3$ are the ordinates of the vertices of the triangle.

Solution. Let (x_1, y_1) be one vertex of the triangle. Then $y_1^2 - 4ax_1 = 0$

$$\Rightarrow \quad x_1 = \frac{y_1^2}{4a} \quad \Rightarrow \quad \text{one vertex is } \left(\frac{y_1^2}{4a}, y_1\right)$$

Similarly the other vertices are $\left(\frac{y_2^2}{4a}, y_2\right)$ and $\left(\frac{y_3^2}{4a}, y_3\right)$.

Hence the required area of the triangle is

$$= \frac{1}{2}\left[\frac{y_1^2}{4a}(y_2 - y_3) + \frac{y_2^2}{4a}(y_3 - y_1) + \frac{y_3^2}{4a}(y_1 - y_2)\right]$$

$$= \frac{1}{8a}[y_1^2(y_2 - y_3) + y_2^2(y_3 - y_1) + y_3^2(y_1 - y_2)]$$

$$= \frac{1}{8a}(y_1 \sim y_2)(y_2 \sim y_3)(y_3 \sim y_1)$$

8. A LINE AND A PARABOLA

We now consider the intersection of a parabola with a line. Let the equation of parabola be $$y^2 = 4ax \quad \text{...(1)}$$
and let $$y = mx + c \quad \text{...(2)}$$
be the equation of any line.

(1) and (2) will intersect each other, if and only if they have some point (or points) in common. Solving the two equations, we get

$$(mx + c)^2 = 4ax$$

or $$m^2x^2 + 2(mc - 2a)x + c^2 = 0 \quad \text{...(3)}$$

This being a quadratic in x, has two roots and thus we see that the line (2) cuts the parabola (1) in two points, which may be real and distinct, coincident, or imaginary.

Condition for (3) to have coincident roots is that

$$(mc-2a)^2 - m^2c^2 = 0$$

or
$$c = \frac{a}{m}.$$

Hence *the condition that the line y = mx + c be a tangent to the parabola $y^2 = 4ax$ is that $c = \frac{a}{m}$.*

9. TANGENT IN SLOPE FORM

The condition for the line $y = mx + c$ to be a tangent to the parabola $y^2 = 4ax$ is that $c = \frac{a}{m}$ and hence the equation of tangent to the parabola, in the slope form is

$$y = mx + \frac{a}{m}.$$

Also putting value of c in equation (3), we get

$$m^2x^2 + 2(a-2a)x + \frac{a^2}{m^2} = 0$$

$\Rightarrow$
$$x = \frac{a}{m^2}$$

and so
$$y = m\frac{a}{m^2} + \frac{a}{m} = \frac{2a}{m}.$$

Hence the point of contact of the tangent $y = mx + \frac{a}{m}$ is $\left(\frac{a}{m^2}, \frac{2a}{m}\right)$

REMARK: Since the two lines $y = mx + c$ and $y = mx + \frac{a}{m}$ are parallel, we see that one tangent can be drawn to a parabola parallel to any given line.

10. TANGENT AT ANY POINT (x_1, y_1)

To find the equation of tangent at any point (x_1, y_1) on the parabola $y^2 = 4ax$.

Let the given point be $P(x_1, y_1)$. Take another point $Q(x_2, y_2)$ on the parabola. Since both P and Q lie on the curve, we have

$$y_1^2 = 4ax_1 \quad ...(1)$$
$$y_2^2 = 4ax_2 \quad ...(2)$$

Also equation of the line PQ is

$$y-y_1=\frac{y_2-y_1}{x_2-x_1}(x-x_1) \quad ...(3)$$

(1) and (2) on subtraction give

$$y_2^2-y_1^2=4a(x_2-x_1) \quad \text{or} \quad \frac{y_2-y_1}{x_2-x_1}=\frac{4a}{y_1+y_2}$$

Thus, equation of PQ becomes

$$y-y_1=\frac{4a}{y_1+y_2}(x-x_1)$$

Taking limits as Q tends to P (*i.e.*, $x_2 \to x_1$ and $y_2 \to y_1$). we get

$$y-y_1=\frac{4a}{2y_1}(x-x_1)$$

or $$yy_1-y_1^2=2ax-2ax_1$$

or $$\mathbf{yy_1=2a(x+x_1)} \quad \text{by (1)}$$

which is the required equation of the tangent to the parabola $y^2 = 4ax$ at the point (x_1, y_1).

11. NORMAL AT ANY POINT (x_1, y_1)

To find the equation of normal at any point (x_1, y_1) on the parabola $y^2 = 4ax$.

Equation of tangent at (x_1, y_1) is

$$yy_1=2a(x+x_1).$$

Slope of tangent $=\frac{2a}{y_1}$.

Thus, slope of normal $=-\frac{y_1}{2a}$

Since the normal must pass through (x_1, y_1), we have the required equation of the normal as

$$\mathbf{y-y_1=\frac{-y_1}{2a}(x-x_1)} \qquad [y-y_1=m(x-x_1)\text{ form}]$$

12. EQUATION OF NORMAL IN THE SLOPE FORM

If in the above equation of normal, we put,

slope of the normal $=\frac{-y_1}{2a}=m,$

we get $y_1 = -2am$

and, therefore, $x_1 = \frac{y_1^2}{4a} = am^2.$

Thus on substituting for x_1 and y_1, the equation of the normal reduces to $y + 2am = m(x - am^2)$

or $\mathbf{y = mx - 2am - am^3}$

which is the equation of the normal at the point $(am^2, -2am)$ on the parabola $y^2 = 4ax$.

Example 5. *Find the equations of the tangents and the normals to the parabola $y^2 = 4ax$ at the ends of its latus rectum.*

Solution. The extremities of the latus rectum are $(a, 2a)$ and $(a, -2a)$.

Equation of tangent at $(a, 2a)$ is

$$y.2a = 2a(x + a)$$

or $y = x + a$

Equation of normal at $(a, 2a)$ is

$$y - 2a = -\frac{2a}{2a}(x - a)$$

or $y = -x + 3a$

or $y + x = 3a$

Similarly, equations of tangent and normal at the point $(a, -2a)$ will be

$$y = -(x + a)$$

and $y - x + 3a = 0$

Example 6. *Show that the line $3y - 6x - 2 = 0$ touches the parabola $3y^2 = 16x$ and find the co-ordinates of its point of contact.*

Solution. Solving the two equations, we see that

$$3\left(\frac{6x+2}{3}\right)^2 = 16x$$

or $9x^2 - 6x + 1 = 0$

i.e., $x = \frac{1}{3}, \frac{1}{3}$

So $y = \frac{6 \times \frac{1}{3} + 2}{3} = \frac{4}{3}$

Since the two points of intersection are coincident, the line touches the curve and the point of contact is $\left(\frac{1}{3}, \frac{1}{3}\right)$.

Example 7. *Find the condition that the line $lx + my + n = 0$ may touch the parabola $y^2 = 4ax$.*

Solution. Suppose the line $lx + my + n = 0$ touches the parabola $y^2 = 4ax$ at the point (x_1, y_1). Then equation of tangent at (x_1, y_1) is

$$yy_1 = 2a\,(x + x_1)$$

or $$2ax - y_1 y + 2\,ax_1 = 0$$

Comparing co-efficients of the two equations

$$lx + my + n = 0$$

and $$2ax - y_1 y + 2ax_1 = 0$$

which represent the same line, we get

$$\frac{2a}{l} = -\frac{y_1}{m} = \frac{2ax_1}{n}$$

$\Rightarrow$ $$x_1 = \frac{n}{l}$$

and $$y_1 = -\frac{2am}{l}$$

Since (x_1, y_1) lies on the parabola $y^2 = 4ax$

$$y_1^{\,2} = 4ax_1$$

or $$\frac{4a^2\, m^2}{l^2} = 4a.\,\frac{n}{l}$$

or $$am^2 = nl$$

which is the required condition for the line $lx + my + n = 0$ to touch the parabola $y^2 = 4ax$.

Also, then the point of contact is

$$\left(\frac{n}{l}, -2\sqrt{\frac{na}{l}}\right).$$

13. TANGENTS FROM A POINT

Let equation of parabola be $y^2 = 4ax$ and let (x_1, y_1) be any given point.

Any tangent to the parabola is given by

$$y = mx + \frac{a}{m} \qquad ...(1)$$

If this passes through the given point (x_1, y_1) we have

$$y_1 = mx_1 + \frac{a}{m}$$

or $$m^2 x_1 - my_1 + a = 0 \qquad ...(2)$$

which is a quadratic in m, giving two values of m. Corresponding to each value of m, equation (1) gives a tangent through (x_1, y_1).

The roots of equation (2) are real and distinct, real and coincident or imaginary according as

$$y_1^2 - 4ax_1 >, =, \text{or} < 0$$

i.e., according as the point (x_1, y_1) lies outside, on, or inside the parabola.

Hence, we conclude that *two tangents can be drawn from a point to a parabola, and these tangents are real and distinct, real and coincident, or imaginary according as the point lies outside, on or inside the parabola.*

14. CHORD WITH GIVEN MIDDLE POINT

To find the equation of a chord of the parabola $y^2 = 4ax$ having (x_1, y_1) as its middle point.

Let AB be a chord with its middle point at (x_1, y_1). Also let co-ordinates of A and B be (x', y') and (x'', y''). Now equation of AB is

$$y - y_1 = m(x - x_1) \quad \text{...(1)}$$

where m, the slope of AB, is to be found out,

since A and B both lie on the parabola, we have

$$y'^2 = 4ax'$$
$$y''^2 = 4ax''$$

Subtraction gives $y''^2 - y'^2 = 4a(x'' - x')$

or
$$\frac{y'' - y'}{x'' - x'} = \frac{4a}{y' + y''}$$

Again since (x_1, y_1) is middle point of AB,

$$x_1 = \frac{x' + x''}{2}, \; y_1 = \frac{y' + y''}{2},$$

and thus m, the slope of AB is given by

$$m = \frac{y'' - y'}{x'' - x'} = \frac{4a}{y' + y''} = \frac{4a}{2y_1} = \frac{2a}{y_1}$$

Putting this value of m in (1), we get the required equation of the chord AB as

$$y - y_1 = \frac{2a}{y_1}(x - x_1)$$

or
$$yy_1 - y_1^2 = 2ax - 2ax_1$$

or $\quad yy_1 - 2a(x + x_1) = y_1^2 - 4ax_1$

or $\quad T = S_1,$

where $T \equiv yy_1 - 2a(x + x_1)$ and $S_1 \equiv y_1^2 - 4ax_1$.

15. LOCUS OF MIDDLE POINTS OF A SYSTEM OF PARALLEL CHORDS

Let equation of the parabola be $y^2 = 4ax$ and suppose we are given a system of parallel chords of this parabola, having slope m. If (x_1, y_1) is the middle point of any one chord of this system, then we wish to find the locus of (x_1, y_1).

Now equation of the chord with middle point (x_1, y_1), is

$$yy_1 - 2a(x + x_1) = y_1^2 - 4ax_1$$

$$\text{Slope of this chord} = \frac{2a}{y_1}$$

But since slope is given to be m,

$$m = \frac{2a}{y_1} \quad \text{or} \quad y_1 = \frac{2a}{m}$$

Hence locus of (x_1, y_1) is

$$y = \frac{2a}{m}$$

which is clearly a line, parallel to the axis of the parabola.

Such a line is defined to be a *diameter* of the parabola.

REMARK: Evidently the diameter $y = \frac{2a}{m}$, meets the parabola $y^2 = 4ax$ in the point $\left(\frac{a}{m^2}, \frac{2a}{m}\right)$. The tangent to parabola at this point is,

$$y.\frac{2a}{m} = 2a\left(x + \frac{a}{m^2}\right)$$

or

$$y = mx + \frac{a}{m}$$

which has slope m and is therefore parallel to the given chords.

We thus conclude that *the tangent to a parabola at the point where the diameter cuts the curve is parallel to the chords bisected by the diameter.*

16. PARAMETRIC CO-ORDINATES

We note that the point with co-ordinates $(at^2, 2at)$ lies on the parabola

$y^2 = 4ax$, whatever be the value of t. We thus say that the parametric equations of the parabola are

$$x = at^2, y = 2at$$

In short, the point $(at^2, 2at)$ is usually referred to as the point 't'.

It can be easily seen that the equation of tangent to the parabola $y^2 = 4ax$ at the point 't' *is*

$$ty = x + at^2$$

and the equation of the normal at the normal at the point 't' is

$$y + tx = 2at + at^3$$

Parametric representation of a point is sometimes very helpful. It will be seen in the later part of the chapter.

17. CHORD OF CONTACT

To find the equation of the chord of contact of tangents drawn to the parabola $y^2 = 4ax$ from a point $P(x_1, y_1)$ outside it.

Let PT and PT' be the tangents drawn through P. Let T and T' have co-ordinates (x', y') and (x'', y'').

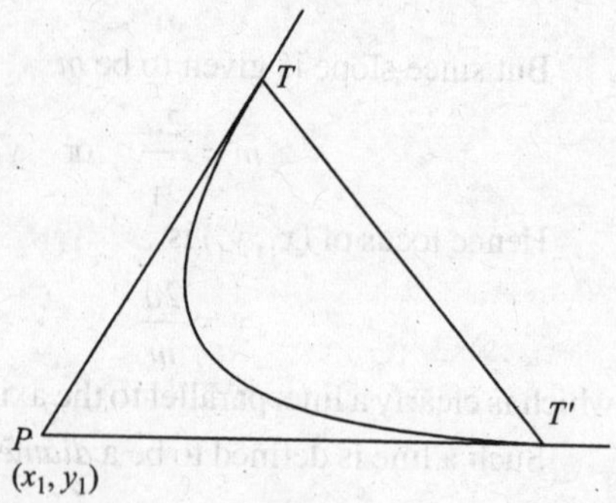

Fig. 9

The equation of PT is

$$yy' = 2a(x + x')$$

and equation of PT' is

$$yy'' = 2a(x + x'').$$

Since both PT and PT' pass through $P(x_1, y_1)$

we get

$$y_1y' = 2a(x_1 + x')$$

$$y_1y'' = 2a(x_1 + x'').$$

The two equations show that the points (x', y') and (x'', y'') lie on

$$\mathbf{yy_1 = 2a(x + x_1)}.$$

Since this is a linear equation in x and y, it represents a line and hence is the required equation of the chord of contact TT'.

[NOTE. If the point $P(x_1, y_1)$ lies on the parabola, the chord of contact becomes the tangent at P.]

18. DEFINITIONS

Let the tangent and normal at any point P on the parabola cut the axis of the parabola in the points T and N respectively.

Draw PM perpendicular to the axis of the parabola. Then TM is defined to be the **sub-tangent** and MN is called **sub-normal** at the point P.

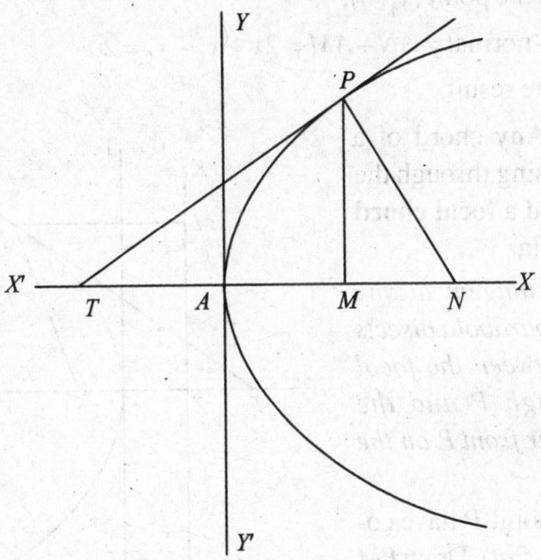

Fig. 10

19. PROPOSITIONS ON THE PARABOLA

(1) *The sub-tangent at a point on a parabola is bisected at the vertex.*

Let $P(x_1, y_1)$ be any point on the parabola $y^2 = 4ax$. Let TM be the sub-tangent at the point P (See the above Fig.) Equation of tangent at P is

$$yy_1 = 2a(x + x_1)$$

Co-ordinates of the point T, which is the point of intersection of the tangent and the x-axis are given by solving the equations

$$yy_1 = 2a(x + x_1) \text{ and } y = 0$$

This gives $\quad x = -x_1, y = 0.$

Hence T has co-ordinates $(-x_1, 0)$.

Their middle point is $(0, 0)$ *i.e.*, the vertex A. Hence the result.

(2) *Sub-normal at a point on a parabola is of constant length and equals half the latus rectum.*

Let $P(x_1, y_1)$ be any point on the parabola and let PN be the normal. (See the above Fig.)

Equation of the normal PN is

$$y - y_1 = -\frac{y_1}{2a}(x - x_1)$$

Put $y = 0$ in this to get co-ordinates of N, which come out to be $(2a + x_1, 0)$.

But M is the point $(x_1, 0)$,

so MN = Sub-normal $= AN - AM = 2x + x_1 - x_1 = 2a$

Hence the result.

Definition. Any chord of a parabola passing through the focus is called a **focal chord** of the parabola.

(3) *The tangent at any point P on a parabola bisects the angle between the focal chord through P and the perpendicular from P on the directrix.*

Let the point P have co-ordinates $(at^2, 2at)$. Draw PM perpendicular on the directrix and let PT be tangent at P.

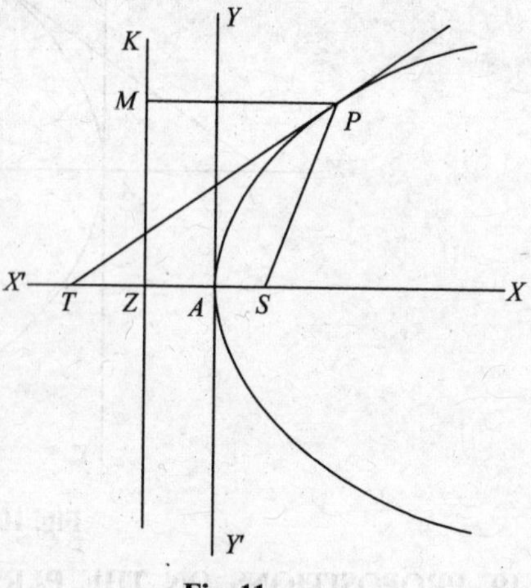

Fig. 11

Equation of tangent at P is

$$ty = x + at^2$$

Now slope of the focal chord

$$PS \text{ is } \frac{2at - 0}{at^2 - a} = \frac{2t}{t^2 - 1} = m_1, \text{ say.}$$

Also slope of the tangent

$$PT = \frac{1}{t} = m_2, \text{ say.}$$

Thus $$\tan SPT = \frac{m_1 - m_2}{1 + m_1 m_2} = \frac{\frac{2t}{t^2 - 1} - \frac{1}{t}}{1 + \frac{2t}{t^2 - 1} \times \frac{1}{t}} = 1/t \qquad \text{...(1)}$$

Now $\frac{1}{t} = m_2$ = slope of tangent $PT = \tan PTS = \tan TPM$ and hence (1) gives $\angle SPT = \angle TPM$.

This proves the result.

Corollary. The normal at any point of a parabola bisects the angle between the focal chord and the diameter through that point.

(4) *The tangents at the extremities of a focal chord of a parabola intersect at right angles on the directrix.*

Let $P(at_1^2, 2at_1)$ and $Q(at_2^2, 2at_2)$ be the extremities of a focal chord of the parabola $y^2 = 4ax$.

The equations of tangents at P and Q are

$$t_1 y = x + at_1^2$$

$$t_2 y = x + at_2^2.$$

Solving these two equations, we get the point of intersection of the two tangents as $\{at_1t_2, a(t_1 + t_2)\}$.

Again equation of the chord PQ is

$$y - 2at_1 = \frac{2at_2 - 2at_1}{at_2^2 - at_1^2}(x - at_1^2).$$

or $$(t_1 + t_2)y = 2(x + at_1t_2)$$

Since PQ is a focal chord, it passes through the focus $S(a, 0)$, and therefore we have

$$(t_1 + t_2).0 = 2(a + at_1t_2)$$

or $$t_1t_2 = -1.$$

and thus we see that the x co-ordinate of the point of intersection of the tangents is $-a$, and therefore the tangents intersect on the directrix (Equation of directrix is $x = -a$).

Again slopes of the two tangents at P and Q are

$$\frac{1}{t_1} \text{ and } \frac{1}{t_2}, \text{ but since } t_1 t_2 = -1,$$

product of the slopes of the two tangents is equal to -1 implying thereby that they intersect at right angles.

Hence the proposition.

Corollary1. The extremities of a focal chord of the parabola $y^2 = 4ax$ have co-ordinates $(at^2, 2at)$ and $\left(\frac{a}{t^2}, -\frac{2a}{t}\right)$ i.e., they are the points t and $-\frac{1}{t}$.

Corollary 2. The tangent at one extremity of a focal chord of a parabola is parallel to the normal at the other extremity.

(5) *The portion of a tangent to a prabola cut off between the directrix and the curve subtends a right angle at the focus.*

Let $P(x_1, y_1)$ be any point on the parabola $y^2 = 4ax$.

Then equation of tangent at P is

$$yy_1 = 2a(x + x_1). \quad ...(1)$$

Also equation of directrix is $x = -a$. ...(2)

If the tangent at P cuts the directrix in K then co-ordinates of K are $\left\{-a, \frac{2a(x_1 - a)}{y_1}\right\}$ which we get by solving the equations (1) and (2)

Let $S(a, 0)$ be the focus.

$$\text{Then slope of } SK = \frac{\frac{2a(x_1 - a)}{y_1}}{-a - a} = -\frac{x_1 - a}{y_1}$$

$$\text{Slope of } PS = \frac{y_1 - 0}{x_1 - a} = \frac{y_1}{x_1 - a}$$

Since the product of the slopes of SK and PS is, -1, it follows that PK subtends a right angle at the focus.

(6) *If SV is the perpendicular to the tangent at any point P on the parabola whose focus is S and vertex A, prove that V lies on the tangent at vertex (i.e., y-axis) and also*

$$SV^2 = AS \cdot SP.$$

Let the point P have co-ordinates $(at^2, 2at)$.

Equation of the tangent at P is then $ty = x + at^2$. ...(1)

Now SV is a line which passes through $S(a, 0)$ and is perpendicular to the tangent at P.

$$\text{Slope of tangent} = \frac{1}{t}$$

$$\text{So slope of } SV = -\frac{1}{t}$$

Hence equation of SV is

$$y - 0 = -t(x - a)$$

or $\quad y + tx = at \quad ...(2)$

If we solve (1) and (2) to find their point of intersection, we see

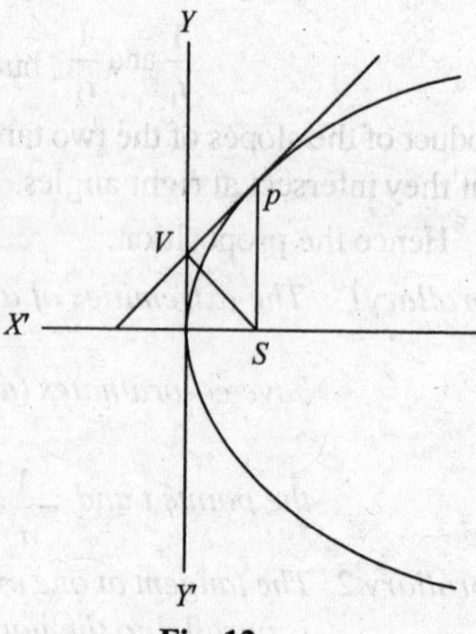

Fig. 12

that the x co-ordinate is zero and thus the point of intersection V lies on the y-axis, or the tangent at the vertex.

To prove the second part, consider the points

$$S(a, 0), V(0, at), P(at^2, 2at), A(0, 0)$$

$$SV^2 = (a-0)^2 + (0-at)^2 = a^2 + a^2t^2 = a^2(1+t^2)$$

$$AS = a, SP = \sqrt{(a-at^2)^2 + (0-2at)^2} = a(t^2+1)$$

And hence $\quad SV^2 = AS \,.\, SP.$

(7) *The ortho-centre of the triangle formed by three tangents to a parabola lies on the directrix.*

Suppose the triangle is formed by the tangents

$$t_1 y = x + at_1^2 \qquad ...(1)$$

$$t_2 y = x + at_2^2 \qquad ...(2)$$

$$t_3 y = x + at_3^2 \qquad ...(3)$$

to the parabola $y^2 = 4ax$ at the three points 't_1', 't_2' and 't_3'.

Point of intersection of (1) and (2) is

$\{at_1 t_2, a(t_1 + t_2)\}$ (See Proposition 4)

The line through this point and perpendicular to (3) is given by

$$y - a(t_1 + t_2) = -t_3(x - at_1t_2) \qquad \left[\text{Slope of (3) is } \frac{1}{t_3}\right]$$

or $$y + xt_3 = a(t_1 + t_2 + t_1t_2t_3) \qquad ...(4)$$

Similarly equation of the line through the point of intersection of (2) and (3) and perpendicular to (1) will be

$$y + xt_1 = a(t_2 + t_3 + t_1t_2t_3) \qquad ...(5)$$

The ortho-centre is the point where the lines (4) and (5) meet. On solving these equations, we see that the x co-ordinate of the orthocentre is $-a$ and hence the ortho-centre lies on the directrix.

Example 8. *Prove that the locus of middle points of the focal chords of the parabola $y^2 = 4ax$ is another parabola.*

Solution. Let (x_1, y_1) be the middle point of a focal chord of the parabola.

Then its equation is

$$yy_1 - 2a(x + x_1) = y_1^2 - 4ax_1.$$

Since this passes through the focus $(a, 0)$.

$$-2a(a + x_1) = y_1^2 - 4ax_1 \quad \text{or} \quad y_1^2 = 2a\,x_1 - 2a^2$$

or $$y_1^2 = 2a(x_1 - a)$$

Hence locus of (x_1, y_1) is $y^2 = 2a(x-a)$

which is a parabola.

Example 9. *Find the locus of the point of intersection of two tangents to the parabola $y^2 = 4ax$, which are at right angles to each other.*

Solution. Let equations of the two tangents be

$$y = mx + \frac{a}{m}$$

and $$y = m'x + \frac{a}{m'}$$

Since the two are at right angles to one another.

$$mm' = -1$$

or $$m' = -\frac{1}{m}.$$

Thus the two tangents will have equations

$$y = mx + \frac{a}{m}$$

and $$y = -\frac{1}{m}x - am.$$

To get the locus of the point of intersection, we solve the two equations.

Subtraction gives

$$0 = \left(m + \frac{1}{m}\right)x + \frac{a}{m} + am$$

or $$x\left(m + \frac{1}{m}\right) + a\left(m + \frac{1}{m}\right) = 0$$

or $$x + a = 0.$$

which is the required locus. Note that the locus is the equation of the directix.

20. CHANGE OF ORIGIN

Suppose we have the co-ordinate axes OX, OY and wish to shift the origin O to another position O'. Let co-ordinates of the point O' be (h, k) with respect to the co-ordinate system OXY.

Take $O'X'$, $O'Y'$ lines through O' parallel respectively to OX and OY.

Let P be any point having co-ordinates (x, y) with respect to the old system OXY and suppose it has co-ordinates (x', y') referred to the new axes $O'X'Y'$.

Drop perpendiculars PN and PK on the axes OX and OY respectively. Suppose PN meets $O'X'$ in M and PK meets $O'Y'$ in L.

Then $x = ON$
$= KP$
$= KL + LP$
$= h + x'$

and $y = PN = PM + MN$
$= y' + k.$

Hence an equation in x, y is transformed to an equation in x' and y' by replacing x by $x' + h$ and y by $y' + k$.

The use of the above change in origin would be clear in the following example.

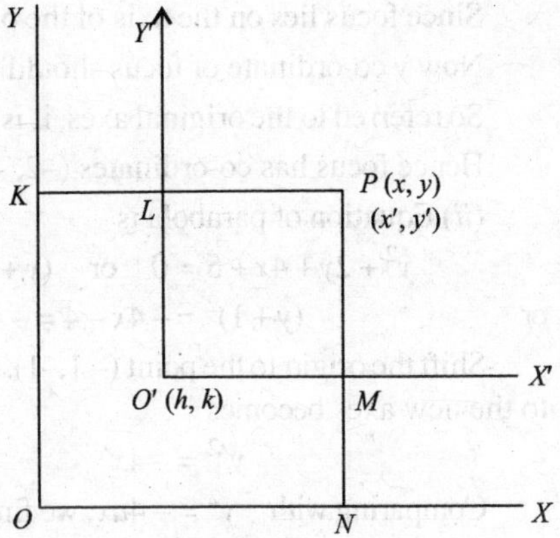

Fig. 13

Example 10. *Find the co-ordinates of the vertex, focus and the equations of the directrix and the axis of the parabola*

(i) $x^2 + 20y + 4x = 56$

(ii) $y^2 + 2y + 4x + 5 = 0$

Solution. (*i*) The equation of parabola is

$$x^2 + 4x + 20y - 56 = 0 \quad \text{or} \quad x^2 + 4x = 56 - 20y$$

or $$(x+2)^2 = 4 + 56 - 20y$$

or $$(x+2)^2 = -20(y-3)$$

Shift the origin to the point (– 2, 3).

The equation of the given parabola becomes (referred to the new system of axes).

$$x'^2 = -20y' \qquad \text{[It is of the form } x^2 = -4ay]$$

New equation of axis of the parabola is $x' = 0$

i.e., $$x + 2 = 0 \qquad \text{[referred to the original axes]}$$

Again comparing the equations

$$x'^2 = -20y'$$

and $$x^2 = -4ay$$

We find, here $a = 5$

Thus equations of directrix is $y' = a$.

or $$y - 3 = 5$$

or $$y = 8$$

Also clearly the vertex is the new origin *i.e.*, the point (–2, 3) [referred to old system of axes]

Since focus lies on the axis of the parabola, its x co-ordinate is -2.

Now y co-ordinate of focus should be $-a$ i.e., -5

So referred to the original axes, it is $-5+3=-2$

Hence focus has co-ordinates $(-2, -2)$

(*ii*) Equation of parabola is

$$y^2+2y+4x+5=0 \quad \text{or} \quad (y+1)^2=-4x-5+1$$

or $$(y+1)^2=-4x-4=-4(x+1)$$

Shift the origin to the point $(-1,-1)$. The equation of parabola referred to the new axes becomes

$$y'^2=-4x'$$

Comparing with $y^2=-4ax$, we find $a=1$.

Now equation of axis is $y'=0$

i.e., $$y+1=0$$

Equation of directrix is $x'=a$

i.e., $$x+1=1$$

i.e., $$x=0$$

Co-ordinates of the vertxex are, of course, $(-1,-1)$, the new origin

Again focus has co-ordinates $(-a, 0)$ *i.e.,* $(-1, 0)$ referred to the new axes.

These referred to the old (original) axes will be $(-1-1, 0-1)$ *i.e.,* $(-2,-1)$.

EXERCISES

1. Find equation of the parabola whose focus is the point (a, b) and the directrix is the line $\frac{x}{a}+\frac{y}{b}=1$.
2. A point moves in such a way that its distance from the point (2, 5) is equal to the distance from the line $2x+4y-3=0$. Find the equation of its path. What is the name of this curve?

   [Hint. (2, 5) is the focus and $2x+4y-3=0$ is the directrix.]
3. A point moves in such a way that its distance form the point (2, 3) is equal to the distance from the line $4x+3y=5$. Find the equation of its path.
4. Find the equation of the parabola whose focus is the point (5, 1) and whose directrix is the line $3x-4y+5=0$.
5. Find the equation of parabola with its vertex at (3, 2) and focus at (5, 2).
6. Find the equation of parabola whose focus is (1, – 1) and vertex (2, 1).
7. Show that the line $y-x=2$ touches the parabola $y^2=8x$. Find the co-ordinate of the point of contact.

8. Find the equations of the tangent and normal at the point (4, 6) to the parabola $y^2 = 9x$.
9. Find the equation of normal to $y^2 = 8x$, perpendicular to the line $2x + 6y - 5 = 0$. Find foot of the normal also.
10. Find the equation of the tangent to the parabola $y^2 = 8x$ which makes an angle of 45° with the x-axis.
11. If the point $(at^2, 2at)$ is one end of a focal chord of the parabola $y^2 = 4ax$, find the co-ordinates of the other end, and show that the length of the chord is $a\left(t+\frac{1}{t}\right)^2$.
12. Prove that the line $y = mx + c$ touches the parabola $y^2 = 4a(x + a)$ if
$$c = ma + \frac{a}{m}.$$
13. Find the length of the side of an equilateral triangle inscribed in the parabola $y^2 = 4ax$ so that one angular point is at the vertex.
14. Prove that the locus of the middle point of all chords of the parabola $y^2 = 4ax$ passing through the vertex is the parabola $y^2 = 2ax$.
15. Find the equation of the chord of the parabola $y^2 = 4ax$, joining the points $(at_1^2, 2at_1)$ and $(at_2^2, 2at_2)$. Hence deduce the equation to the tangent at $(at_1^2, 2at)$.
16. Find the co-ordinates of the vertex, focus and the equation of the directrix and the axes of the parabola

(*i*) $y^2 + 2y + 4x + 5 = 0$ (*ii*) $5x^2 + 30x + 2y + 59 = 0$

(*iii*) $y^2 - 4y - 8x + 28 = 0$ (*iv*) $y2 - 6y + 20x + 49 = 0$

ANSWERS

1. $(ax - by)^2 - 2a^3x - 2b^3y + a^4 + a^2b^2 + b^4 = 0$
2. $4x^2 + y^2 - 4xy - 17x + 44y + \frac{571}{4} = 0$, parabola
3. $9x^2 + 16y^2 + 24xy - 60x - 120y + 300 = 0$
4. $16x^2 + 9y^2 + 24xy - 280x - 10y + 625 = 0$
5. $y^2 - 4y - 8x + 28 = 0$ 6. $4x^2 + y^2 - 4xy + 8x + 46y + 91 = 0$
7. (2, 4) 8. $4y - 3x = 12$; $4x + 3y = 34$
9. $y = 3x - 66$, (18, – 12). 10. $x - y + 2 = 0$
11. $\left(\frac{a}{t^2}, -\frac{2a}{t}\right)$ 13. $8a\sqrt{3}$
15. $(t_1 + t_2)y = 2(x + at_1t_2)$; $ty = x + at^2$
16. (*i*) (– 1, – 1), (– 2, – 1), $x = 0$, $y + 1 = 0$.

(*ii*) (– 3, – 7), $\left(-3, -\frac{71}{10}\right)$, $10y + 69 = 0$, $x + 3 = 0$.

(*iii*) (3, 2), (5, 2), $x = 1$, $y = 2$ (*iv*) (– 2, 3), (– 7, 3), $x = 3$, $y - 3 = 0$

SECTION B
THE ELLIPSE

21. DEFINITION

An *ellipse* is the locus of a point which moves in such a way that its distance from a fixed point (focus) bears a constant ratio e $(0 < e < 1)$ to its distance from a fixed line (the directrix, not passing through the focus).

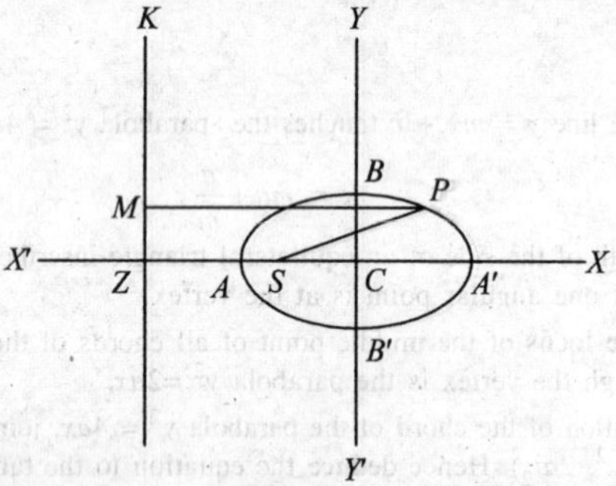

Fig. 14

22. EQUATION OF ELLIPSE IN THE STANDARD FORM

Let S be the focus, ZK be the directrix and e the eccentricity of the ellipse. Draw SZ perpendicular to the directix ZK. Since $0 < e < 1$, we can divide ZS both internally and externally in the ratio $1 : e$, and the two points will be on the same side of ZK. Let the points of division be A and A'.

Then we have $\quad AS = e.\,ZA \quad$ ...(1)

$SA' = e.\,ZA' \quad$ ...(2)

By definition, the points A and A' lie on the ellipse.

Let C be the middle point of AA' and let $AC = CA' = a$.

Now (1) and (2) can be written as

$$AC - SC = e\,(CZ - CA)$$

$$SC + CA' = e\,(CZ + CA') \quad \text{or} \quad a - SC = e\,(CZ - a)$$

$$SC + a = e\,(CZ + a)$$

Addition gives $\quad 2a = 2e\,.CZ \quad$ or $\quad CZ = a/e$

and subtraction gives $2SC = 2ea \quad$ or $\quad SC = ae.$

Now take the origin at C, the x-axis along CA' and the y-axis along the perpendicular to CA' at C.

Then co-ordinates of the focus S are $(-ae, 0)$ and the equation of the directrix ZK is $x = -a/e$.

Take $P(x, y)$ any point on the ellipse. Draw $PM \perp ZK$ and join P and S. Then by definition

$$PS = e\,PM$$
$$PS = e^2\,PM^2$$

or $$(x + ae)^2 + (y - 0)^2 = e^2 . \frac{(x + a/e)^2}{1}$$

or $$x^2(1 - e^2) + y^2 = a^2(1 - e^2)$$

or $$\frac{x^2}{a^2} + \frac{y^2}{a^2(1 - e^2)} = 1$$

Put $a^2(1 - e^2) = b^2$ [Note. $1 - e^2 > 0$ as $e < 1$]

We get the required equation of ellipse as

$$\boldsymbol{\frac{x^2}{a^2} + \frac{y^2}{b^2} = 1}$$

If we put $x = 0$ in the equation of the ellipse, we get $y = \pm b$, which gives the intercept CB and CB' on the y-axis.

23. DEFINITIONS

AA' is called the **major axis** of the ellipse and its length is $2a$.

BB' is called the **minor axis** of the ellipse and its length is $2b$.

The points A and A' are called **vertices** of the ellipse.

The eccentricity of the curve is given by the relation

$$\boldsymbol{a^2(1 - e^2) = b^2 \text{ or } e^2 = 1 - b^2/a^2}$$

24. SHAPE OF THE ELLIPSE

From the equation $\frac{x^2}{a^2} + \frac{y^2}{b^2} = 1$ of the ellipse, we find that the curve is symmetrical about both the axes and passes through the points $(\pm a, 0)$ and $(0, \pm b)$. It is a closed curve and looks like a circle when elongated along one diameter and flattened along the perpendicular diameter. The complete shape is as shown in the figure.

From the symmetrical nature of the curve, it follows that there is a second focus S' $(ae, 0)$ and a corresponding directrix $Z'K'$ with equation $x = a/e$ so that the same ellipse is described if a point moves in such a way that its distance from S' is e times its distance from the directrix $x = a/e$.

We observe that if a point (x_1, y_1) lies on the ellipse then so does the point $(-x_1, -y_1)$, implying thereby that any chord of the ellipse passing through the point C (0, 0) is bisected at C. If in a curve, there is a point, such that all the chords passing through it are bisected there at, we call such a curve a *central curve* and the point is called the *centre* of the curve. In case of the ellipse, therefore, C is the centre of the ellipse.

25. LATUS RECTUM

The chord of the ellipse passing through the focus and perpendicular to the major axis is defined to be the *latus rectum* of the ellipse.

If LSL' is the latus rectum, then by symmetry $LSL' = 2LS$.

Since co-ordinate of S are $(-ae, 0)$, x co-ordinate of L is $-ae$ and y co-ordinate is given by

$$\frac{a^2e^2}{a^2}+\frac{y^2}{b^2}=1. \qquad \left[L \text{ lies on } \frac{x^2}{a^2}+\frac{y^2}{b^2}=1\right]$$

or $$y = b\sqrt{1-e^2} = \pm\frac{b^2}{a} \quad \text{as } e^2 = 1-\frac{b^2}{a^2}$$

Hence semi-latus rectum $LS = \dfrac{b^2}{a}$

or that the length of the latus rectum of the ellipse

$$\frac{x^2}{a^2}+\frac{y^2}{b^2}=1 \text{ is } \frac{2b^2}{a}$$

26. THE GENERAL EQUATION OF AN ELLIPSE

To find the equation of ellipse, when the co-ordinates of the focus and the equation of the directrix are given.

Let the focus S have co-ordinates (x_1, y_1) and let equation of the directrix ZK be $ax + by + c = 0$. If (x, y) are the co-ordinates of any point P on the curve, we have by definition

$$PS^2 = e^2\, PM^2 \qquad \text{...(1)}$$

where PM is the perpendicular distance of P from the directrix.

(1) then gives $$(x-x_1)^2+(y-y_1)^2 = e^2\left[\frac{(ax+by+c)^2}{a^2+b^2}\right]$$

as the required equation of the ellipse.

27. A POINT AND AN ELLIPSE

The point (x_1, y_1) lies outside, on, or inside the ellipse

$$\frac{x^2}{a^2}+\frac{y^2}{b^2}=1,$$

according as $\frac{x^2}{a^2}+\frac{y_1^2}{b^2}-1$ is >, = or < 0.

The proof of this is similar to what we did in parabola.

28. A LINE AND AN ELLIPSE

We show that a line cuts the ellipse

$$\frac{x^2}{a^2}+\frac{y^2}{b^2}=1 \qquad ...(1)$$

in two points.

Let $$y = mx + c \qquad ...(2)$$

be the equation of any line. If we solve the equations (1) and (2), we get

$$\frac{x^2}{a^2}+\frac{(mx+c)^2}{b^2}=1$$

or $$x^2(b^2+a^2m^2)+2a^2cmx+a^2(c^2-b^2)=0$$

This is a quadratic in x and therefore has two roots, giving two points of intersection of the line (2) with the ellipse (1). The two points will be real and distinct, real and coincident or imaginary according as

$$(a^2cm)^2-(b^2+a^2m^2)a^2(c^2-b^2) \text{ is } >, =, \text{ or } < 0.$$

The two roots are coincident if

$$(a^2cm)^2-(b^2+a^2m^2)a^2(c^2-b^2)=0$$

or if $$c=\pm\sqrt{a^2m^2+b^2}$$

Hence *the condition that the line* $y = mx + c$ *be a tangent to the ellipse* $\frac{x^2}{a^2}+\frac{y^2}{b^2}=1$ *is that* $c=\pm\sqrt{a^2m^2+b^2}$

29. TANGENT IN SLOPE FORM

It follows from above, that the lines

$$y=mx\pm\sqrt{a^2m^2+b^2}$$

are tangents to the ellipse $\frac{x^2}{a^2}+\frac{y^2}{b^2}=1$, whatever be the value of m.

REMARK: Since the lines $y = mx + c$ and $y = mx \pm \sqrt{a^2m^2 + b^2}$ are parallel, we see that *two tangents can be drawn to an ellipse parallel to any given line.*

30. TANGENT AT ANY POINT (x_1, y_1)

Proceeding exactly as in case of parabola, it can be shown that the line

$$\frac{xx_1}{a^2} + \frac{yy_1}{b^2} = 1$$

represents the equation of tangent at the point (x_1, y_1) on the ellipse

$$\frac{x^2}{a^2} + \frac{y^2}{b^2} = 1.$$

The reader should attempt this as an exercise.

31. NORMAL AT THE POINT (x_1, y_1)

Slope of the tangent at any point (x_1, y_1) is

$$-\frac{x_1}{a^2} \cdot \frac{b^2}{y_1}$$

So the slope of the normal $= \dfrac{a^2}{x_1} \cdot \dfrac{y_1}{b^2}$

Hence equation of normal at (x_1, y_1) is

$$y - y_1 = \frac{a^2}{b^2} \cdot \frac{y_1}{x_1}(x - x_1).$$

This is generally written in the form

$$\frac{x - x_1}{x_1/a^2} = \frac{y - y_1}{y_1/b^2}$$

32. PARAMETRIC CO-ORDINATES

We note that the point with co-ordinates $(a \cos \phi, b \sin \phi)$ lies on the ellipse $\dfrac{x^2}{a^2} + \dfrac{y^2}{b^2} = 1$, whatever be the value of ϕ. These are called the parametric co-ordinates of any point on the ellipse, the parameter being ϕ.

In short the point $(a \cos \phi, b \sin \phi)$ is usually referred to as the point 'ϕ'.

The equation of tangent at the point 'ϕ' is

$$\frac{xa\cos\phi}{a^2}+\frac{yb\sin\phi}{b^2}=1 \quad \text{or} \quad \frac{x}{a}\cos\phi+\frac{y}{b}\sin\phi=1.$$

Also equation of normal at the point 'ϕ' is

$$ax\sec\phi - by\operatorname{cosec}\phi = a^2 - b^2$$

ϕ is called *eccentric angle* of the point.

33. PROPOSITIONS ON THE ELLIPSE

(1) *The sub-tangent and sub-normal of a point* (x_1, y_1) *on the ellipse* $\frac{x^2}{a^2}+\frac{y^2}{b^2}=1$ *are* $\left(\frac{a^2}{x_1}\right)-x_1$ *and* $\frac{b^2x_1}{a^2}$ *respectively.*

Let P be the point (x_1, y_1) on the ellipse. Let the tangent and normal at P cut the x-axis in T and N respectively. Then MT is the sub-tangent and NM is the sub-normal of the point P.

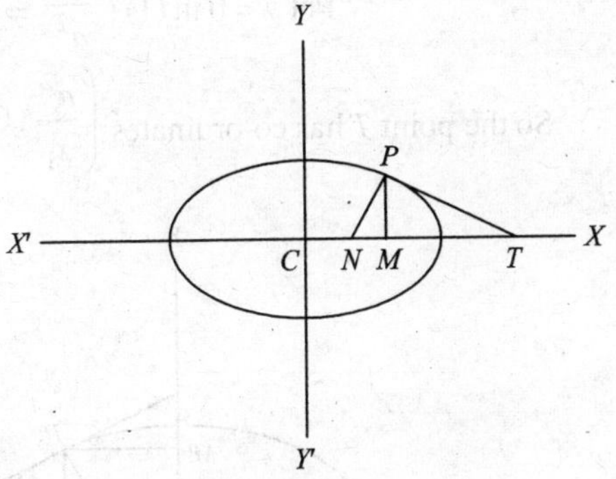

Fig. 15

Now T is the point of intersection of the lines

$$\frac{xx_1}{a^2}+\frac{yy_1}{b^2}=1 \text{ and } y=0.$$

Solving the two equations, we get the co-ordinates of T as $\left(\frac{a^2}{x_1}, 0\right)$

Again N is the point of intersection of the lines

$$\frac{x-x_1}{x_1/a^2}=\frac{y-y_1}{y_1/b^2} \text{ and } y=0.$$

Solving these we get the co-ordinates of N as $\left(x_1-\frac{x_1b^2}{a^2}, 0\right)$.

Hence $$MT = CT - CM = \frac{a^2}{x_1} - x_1$$

$$CN = CM - NM = x_1 - \left(x_1 - \frac{x_1b^2}{a^2}\right) = \frac{x_1b^2}{a^2}$$

are the lengths of the sub-tangent and sub-normal.

(2) *If the tangent at any point P on the ellipse* $\frac{x^2}{a^2}+\frac{y^2}{b^2}=1$ *meets the major axis in T and the minor axis in T′ and PM and PM′ are the perpendiculars from P on the major and minor axes respectively, then*

(i) $CM \,.\, CT = a^2$ *(ii)* $CM' \,.\, CT' = b^2$

where C is the centre of the ellipse.

Let co-ordinates of P be (x_1, y_1).

Equation of tangent at P is $\frac{xx_1}{a^2}+\frac{yy_1}{b^2}=1$ ...(1)

Equation of x- axis is $y = 0$. ...(2)

Co-ordinates of T are obtained by solving these two equations.

$$\text{Put } y = 0 \text{ in (1)}; \ \frac{xx_1}{a^2} = 1 \text{ or } x = \frac{a^2}{x_1}$$

So the point T has co-ordinates $\left(\frac{a^2}{x_1}, 0\right)$.

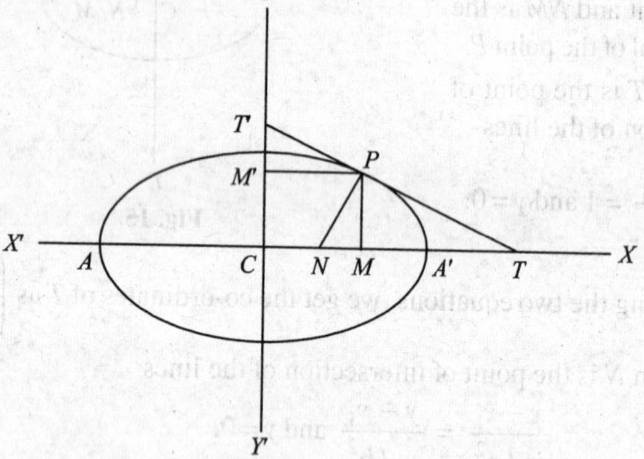

Fig. 16

Similarly putting $x = 0$ in (1), we get the co-ordinates of T' as $\left(0, \frac{b^2}{y_1}\right)$.

Now $CM = x_1,\ CT = \frac{a^2}{x_1}. \Rightarrow CM \,.\, CT = x_1 . \frac{a^2}{x_1} = a^2,$

also $CM' = y_1$ and $CT' = b^2/y_1 \Rightarrow CM' \,.\, CT' = b^2.$

Hence the result.

(3) *If the normal to the ellipse* $\frac{x^2}{a^2}+\frac{y^2}{b^2}=1$ *at any point P, meets the major axis in N, then CN =* e^2*. CM where C is the centre of the ellipse and M is the foot of the ordinate through P.*

Let co-ordinates of the point P be (x_1, y_1). Then equation of normal PN is

$$\frac{x-x_1}{x_1/a^2}=\frac{y-y_1}{y_1/b^2}$$ [See Fig. of Prop. 2]

To get co-ordinates of N put $y = 0$ in the above, thus

$$\frac{x-x_1}{x_1/a^2}=-b^2 \quad \text{or} \quad x=\frac{a^2-b^2}{a^2}x_1=e^2x_1.$$

Thus $$CN=e^2x_1=e^2CM.$$

(4) *The product of the perpendiculars from the foci on any tangent to an ellipse is equal to the square of the semi-minor axis.*

Let $S\,(-ae, 0)$ and $S'\,(ae, 0)$ be the foci of the ellipse $\frac{x^2}{a^2}+\frac{y^2}{b^2}=1$, and let SY and $S'Y'$ be the perpendiculars from S and S' on any tangent to the ellipse.

Any tangent to the ellipse is given by the equation

$$y=mx+\sqrt{a^2m^2+b^2} \quad \text{or} \quad mx-y+\sqrt{a^2m^2+b^2}=0$$

Now $$SY=\frac{-aem+\sqrt{a^2m^2+b^2}}{\sqrt{1+m^2}}$$

$$S'Y'=\frac{aem+\sqrt{a^2m^2+b^2}}{\sqrt{1+m^2}}$$

Hence $$SY.\,S'Y'=\frac{a^2m^2+b^2-a^2e^2m^2}{1+m^2}=\frac{b^2+m^2a^2(1-e^2)}{1+m^2}$$

$$=\frac{b^2(1+m^2)}{1+m^2}=b^2.$$

Hence the result.

(5) *The sum of the focal distances of any point on the ellipse is equal to the length of the major axis.*

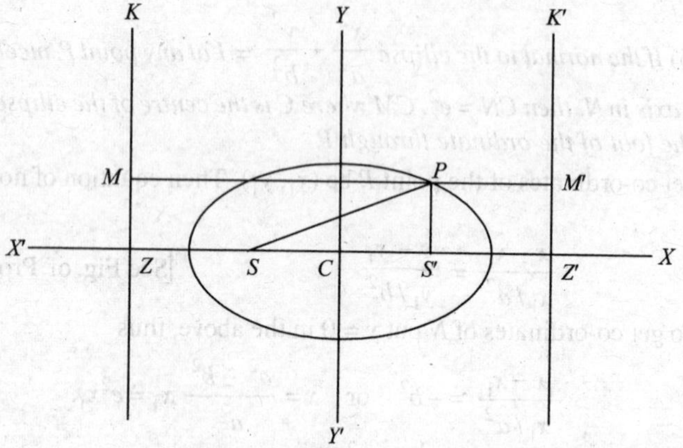

Fig. 17

Let $P(x_1, y_1)$ be any point on the ellipse, with foci at S and S'. Drop perpendiculars PM and PM' on the directrices ZK and $Z'K'$.

Then $$SP = ePM$$

and $$S'P = ePM'$$

$\Rightarrow$ $$SP + S'P = e(PM + PM')$$

$$= eMM' = eZZ' = 2e.\ CZ = 2a.$$

Example 11. *Find the equation of the ellipse whose focus is (1, 2) and eccentricity is $\frac{1}{2}$. Equation of directrix being 3x + 4y =5.*

Solution. Let $S(1,2)$ be the focus

$$e = \frac{1}{2}, \text{ the eccentricity}$$

and let $P(x, y)$ be any point on the curve.

then by definition

$$PS = e\,PM$$

where M is the foot of the perpendicular drawn form P on the directirx.

We thus have,

$$\sqrt{(x-1)^2 + (y-2)^2} = \frac{1}{2}\frac{3x + 4y - 5}{\sqrt{9+16}}$$

which on squaring and simplifying reduces to

$$91x^2 + 84y^2 - 24xy - 170x - 360y + 475 = 0$$

This is the required equation of the ellipse.

Example 12. *Show that the length of perpendicular from the centre of the ellipse* $\frac{x^2}{a^2}+\frac{y^2}{b^2} = 1$ *to the tangent at the point 'ϕ' is*

$$\frac{ab}{\sqrt{a^2 \sin^2\phi + b^2 \cos^2\phi}}.$$

Solution. Equation of tangent at the point 'ϕ' is

$$\frac{x}{a}\cos\phi + \frac{y}{b}\sin\phi = 1.$$

Then the required perpendicular distance from (0, 0) is

$$\frac{1}{\sqrt{\frac{\cos^2\phi}{a^2}+\frac{\sin^2\phi}{b^2}}} = \frac{ab}{\sqrt{b^2\cos^2\phi + a^2\sin^2\phi}}.$$

Example 13. *Find the condition that the line* $lx + my + n = 0$ *be a normal to the ellipse* $\frac{x^2}{a^2}+\frac{y^2}{b^2} = 1.$

Solution. Suppose that the given line is a normal to the ellipse at the point 'ϕ'.

Equation of normal at 'ϕ' is $ax \sec\phi - by \operatorname{cosec}\phi = a^2 - b^2$.

Since this equation and the equation $lx + my = -n$ represent the same line, we have

$$\frac{l}{a\sec\phi} = \frac{m}{-b\operatorname{cosec}\phi} = \frac{-n}{a^2-b^2}$$

$$\frac{l\cos\phi}{a} = \frac{-m\sin\phi}{b} = \frac{-n}{a^2-b^2}$$

This implies $\cos\phi = \frac{-an}{l(a^2-b^2)}, \sin\phi = \frac{bn}{m(a^2-b^2)}.$

Squaring and adding, we get

$$1 = \cos^2\phi + \sin^2\phi = \frac{a^2n^2}{l^2(a^2-b^2)^2} + \frac{b^2n^2}{m^2(a^2-b^2)^2}$$

$$= n^2\left[\frac{a^2m^2 + b^2l^2}{l^2m^2(a^2-b^2)^2}\right]$$

or $$\frac{a^2}{l^2} + \frac{b^2}{m^2} = \frac{(a^2 - b^2)^2}{n^2}$$

which is the required condition.

Example 14. *Find the equations of the tangents to the ellipse* $\frac{x^2}{16} + y^2$ *= 1 which make with the x-axis an angle of 60°.*

Solution. Equation of the ellipse is $\frac{x^2}{16} + \frac{y^2}{1} = 1$.

Any tangent is given by

$$y = mx \pm \sqrt{a^2m^2 + b^2}$$

Here $a^2 = 16, b^2 = 1, m = \tan 60° = \sqrt{3}$

Hence the required equations of tangents are

$$y = \sqrt{3}x \pm \sqrt{16.3 + 1}$$

i.e., $$y = \sqrt{3}x \pm 7.$$

Example 15. *Find the locus of the point of intersection of two perpendicular tangents to the ellipse.*

Solution. If m is the slope of one tangent then slope of the other tangent will be $-\frac{1}{m}$.

Equations of the two perpendicular tangents are

$$y = mx + \sqrt{a^2m^2 + b^2} \quad \text{and} \quad y = -\frac{1}{m}x + \sqrt{\frac{a^2}{m^2} + b^2},$$

which can also be written as

$$y - mx = \sqrt{a^2m^2 + b^2}$$

$$my + x = \sqrt{a^2 + b^2m^2}$$

To get the locus of the point of intersection, square and add the two equations and obtain

$$(1 + m^2)\,y^2 + (1 + m^2)\,x^2 = a^2(1 + m^2) + b^2(1 + m^2)$$

or $$x^2 + y^2 = a^2 + b^2,$$

which is the required locus. Note that this is a circle with its centre at the centre of the ellipse, *i.e.*, (0, 0). This is called the **Director circle** of the ellipse.

Example 16. *The tangent and the normal at a point P on an ellipse meet the minor axis in T and N. Prove that TN subtends a right angle at each of the foci.*

Solution. Let co-ordinates of P be (x_1, y_1). The equations of tangent and normal are

$$\frac{xx_1}{a^2}+\frac{yy_1}{b^2}=1 \text{ and } \frac{x-x_1}{x_1/a^2}=\frac{y-y_1}{y_1/b^2}.$$

Also equation of minor axis is $x = 0$. By solving these equations we get the co-ordinates of T and N as

$$\left(0, \frac{b^2}{y_1}\right) \text{ and } \left(0, y_1-\frac{a^2 y_1}{b^2}\right).$$

Now equation of the circle on TN as diameter is

$$x^2+\left(y-\frac{b^2}{y_1}\right)\left[y-y_1\left(1-\frac{a^2}{b^2}\right)\right]=0.$$

Since it passes through the foci $(\pm ae, 0)$, it follows that TN subtends a right angle at each of the foci, because the angle in a semi-circle is a right angle.

Aliter. Show that the product of the slopes of the lines TS and NS is -1, where S is the focus.

EXERCISES

1. Find the equation of the ellipse whose focus is the point $(-1, 1)$, directrix is the line $x - y + 3 = 0$ and whose eccentricity is $\frac{1}{2}$.
2. Find the eccentricity, foci and the latus rectum of the ellipse $2x^2 + 5y^2 = 20$.
3. Show that the line $y = x+\sqrt{5/6}$ touches the ellipse $2x^2 + 3y^2 = 1$.
4. Find the equations of the tangent and the normal at the point $\left(1, \frac{4}{3}\right)$ of the ellipse $4x^2 + 9y^2 = 20$.
5. Show that the triangle whose vertices are $(1, 2)$, $(-2, 1)$ and $(3, -1)$, lies wholly inside the ellipse $x^2 + 2y^2 = 13$.
6. Find the tangents to the ellipse $4x^2 + 3y^2 = 1$, which are perpendicular to the line $3x - 4y + 5 = 0$.
7. Find the equation of a chord of the ellipse $\frac{x^2}{a^2}+\frac{y^2}{b^2} = 1$ with given middle point (x_1, y_1).

8. Find the locus of middle points of a system of parallel chords with slope m, of the ellipse $\frac{x^2}{a^2}+\frac{y^2}{b^2}=1$.

9. Show that two tangents can be drawn to the ellipse $\frac{x^2}{a^2}+\frac{y^2}{b^2}=1$, from any point (x_1, y_1).

10. Find the condition that line $lx+my+n=0$ be a tangent to the ellipse $\frac{x^2}{a^2}+\frac{y^2}{b^2}=1$.

11. Find the equation of the chord of contact of tangents drawn to the ellipse $\frac{x^2}{a^2}+\frac{y^2}{b^2}=1$ from a point (x_1, y_1), outside it.

12. Any tangent to an ellipse is cut by the tangents at the ends of the major axis in the points T, T'. Prove that the circle whose diameter is TT' passes through the foci.

13. Show that the tangents at the ends of the latus recta of the ellipse pass through the intersections of the axes and the directrices.

14. Find the angle between the tangents to the ellipse $\frac{x^2}{4}+\frac{y^2}{9}=1$ and the circle $\frac{x^2}{6}+\frac{y^2}{6}=1$ at their point of intersection.

15. Show that locus of the middle point of the portion of a tangent to the ellipse $\frac{x^2}{a^2}+\frac{y^2}{b^2}=1$ included between the axes is $\frac{a^2}{x^2}+\frac{b^2}{y^2}=4$.

16. Show that the locus of middle points of normal chords of the ellipse $\frac{x^2}{a^2}+\frac{y^2}{b^2}=1$ is given by $\left[\frac{x^2}{a^2}+\frac{y^2}{b^2}\right]^2\left[\frac{a^2}{x^2}+\frac{b^2}{y^2}\right]=(a^2-b^2)^2$

ANSWERS

1. $7x^2+2xy+7y^2+10y+7=0$. 2. $\sqrt{\frac{3}{5}}$, $(\pm\sqrt{6}, 0)$, $\frac{4\sqrt{10}}{5}$.

4. $x+3y-5=0$, $9x-3y-5=0$. 6. $4x+3y=\pm\sqrt{7}$.

7. $\frac{xx_1}{a^2}+\frac{yy_1}{b^2}=\frac{x_1^2}{a^2}+\frac{y_1^2}{b^2}$. 8. $y=-\frac{b^2}{a^2m}x$.

10. $a^4l^2+b^4m^2=n^2$. 11. $\frac{xx_1}{a^2}+\frac{yy_1}{b^2}=1$,

14. $\tan^{-1}\frac{1}{\sqrt{6}}$.

SECTION C
THE HYPERBOLA

34. DEFINITION

A *hyperbola* is the locus of a point which moves in such a way that its distance from a fixed point (*focus*) bears a finite constant ration $e > 1$ to its distance from a fixed line (the *directrix,* not passing through the focus).

35. EQUATION OF HYPERBOLA IN STANDARD FORM

Let S be the focus, ZK be the directrix and e the eccentricity of the hyperbola. Draw SZ perpendicular to ZK, the directrix. Since $e > 1$, we can divide SZ internally and externally in the ratio $e : 1$ and these points will be on the opposite sides of ZK. Let the points of division be A and A'.

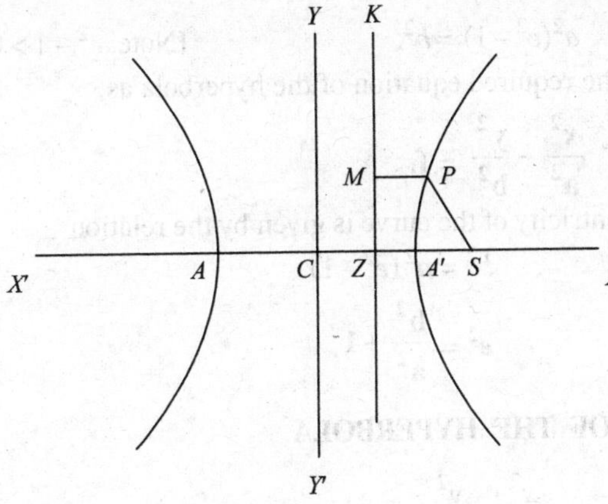

Fig. 18

Then we have

$$SA = e.AZ \quad ...(1)$$

$$SA' = e.ZA' \quad ...(2)$$

By definition the points A and A' lie on the hyperbola.

Let C be the middle point of AA', and take

$$AC = CA' = a.$$

Now (1) and (2) can be written as

$$CS + CA = e\,(AC + CZ)$$

$$CS - A'C = e\,(-ZC + A'C),$$

addition gives $\quad 2CS = 2ae$ or $CS = ae$, while

subtraction gives $\quad ZC = a/e$.

Now take the origin at C, the x-axis along CS and the y-axis along the perpendicular line CY.

Then co-ordinates of the focus S are $(ae, 0)$ and equation of the directrix ZK is $x = a/e$.

Take $P(x, y)$ any point on the hyperbola. Draw $PM \perp ZK$. Then by definition

$$PS = ePM$$

or $$PS^2 = e\,PM^2$$

or $$(x-ae)^2 + (y-0)^2 = e^2.\left(x - \frac{a}{e}\right)^2$$

or $$\frac{x^2}{a^2} - \frac{y^2}{a^2(e^2-1)} = 1.$$

Put $a^2(e^2-1) = b^2$. [Note. $e^2 - 1 > 0$ as $e > 1$]

We get the required equation of the hyperbola as

$$\mathbf{\frac{x^2}{a^2} - \frac{y^2}{b^2} = 1.}$$

The eccentricity of the curve is given by the relation

$$b^2 = a^2(e^2 - 1)$$

or $$e^2 = \frac{\mathbf{b^2}}{\mathbf{a^2}} + \mathbf{1}.$$

36. SHAPE OF THE HYPERBOLA

From the equation $\frac{x^2}{a^2} - \frac{y^2}{b^2} = 1$ of the hyperbola, we find that the curve is symmetrical about both the axes. Also if $x = 0$ or the value of x lies between 0 and a, the corresponding value of y is imaginary. Thus no part of the curve lies between the lines $x = 0$ and $x = a$.

At $x = a$, $y = 0$ and as x gets larger, y also increases. The final shape of the curve is as shown in the figure.

From the symmetrical nature of the curve it follows that there is a second focus S' $(-ae, 0)$ and a corresponding directrix with equation $x = -a/e$ so that the same hyperbola is described if a point moves in such a way that its distance from S is e (> 1) times its distance from the directrix $x = -a/e$.

Just as in case of ellipse, we observe that if a point (x_1, y_1) lies on the hyperbola then so does $(-x_1, -y_1)$, implying thereby that any chord of the hyperbola passing through the point $C(0, 0)$ is bisected by C. Thus the hyperbola is a central curve and the point C is the centre of the hyperbola.

37. DEFINITIONS

The points A and A' (where the line joining the two foci cuts the hyperbola) are called *vertices* of the hyperbola.

The line joining the vertices is called the *transverse axis* of the hyperbola. The length of the transverse axis is $2a$.

We know that the hyperbola does not cut the y-axis. But if we take two points B and B' on the y-axis such that $BC = B'C = b$, the line BB' is called the *conjugate axis* of the hyperbola.

38. LATUS RECTUM

The chord of the hyperbola passing through the focus and perpendicular to the transverse axis is defined to be the *latus rectum* of the hyperbola. Its length can easily be seen to be $\mathbf{2b^2/a}$.

39. SOME RESULTS ABOUT THE HYPERBOLA

In view of what we have done earlier, the following results can easily be established for the hyperbola $\frac{x^2}{a^2} - \frac{y^2}{b^2} = 1$.

(1) The equation of *tangent at* any point $(x_1\ y_1)$ on the curve is

$$\frac{xx_1}{a^2} - \frac{yy_1}{b^2} = 1.$$

(2) The equation of *normal* at any point (x_1, y_1) on the curve is

$$\frac{x - x_1}{x_1 / a^2} = \frac{y - y_1}{-y_1 / b^2}.$$

(3) The lines $y = mx \pm \sqrt{a^2m^2 - b^2}$ are tangents to the curve for all values of m.

(4) The line $y = mx + c$ is a tangent to the hyperbola if

$$c = \pm\sqrt{a^2m^2 - b^2}.$$

(5) Two tangents can be drawn from a point to the hyperbola.

(6) The equation of chord of contact of the tangents from any point $P(x_1, y_1)$ is

$$\frac{xx_1}{a^2} - \frac{yy_1}{b^2} = 1.$$

(7) The equation of chord of the hyperbola with given middle point (x_1, y_1) is

$$\frac{xx_1}{a^2} - \frac{yy_1}{b^2} = \frac{x_1^2}{a^2} - \frac{y_1^2}{b^2}.$$

(8) The locus of middle points of a system of parallel chords with slope m is

$$y = \frac{b^2}{a^2 m} x.$$

(9) The line $lx + my + n = 0$ is a tangent to the curve if

$$a^2l^2 - b^2m^2 = n^2.$$

The reader is advised to prove all thc above results.

Example 17. *If S and S′ are the foci of the hyperbola* $\frac{x^2}{a^2} - \frac{y^2}{b^2} = 1$ *and P (x, y) is any point on the curve, prove that S′P – SP = 2a.*

Solution. The co-ordinates of S and S' are respectively $(ae, 0)$ and $(-ae, 0)$.

Draw a line through P parallel to x-axis, meeting the directrices in M and M' (see figure),

By definition

$$SP = e.PM$$
$$= e(x - a/e) = ex - a \quad [\text{Equation of } ZK \text{ is } x = a/e].$$

Similarly $\quad S'P = e\,PM' = e(x + a/e) = ex + a,$

Subtraction gives $S'P - SP = 2a$.

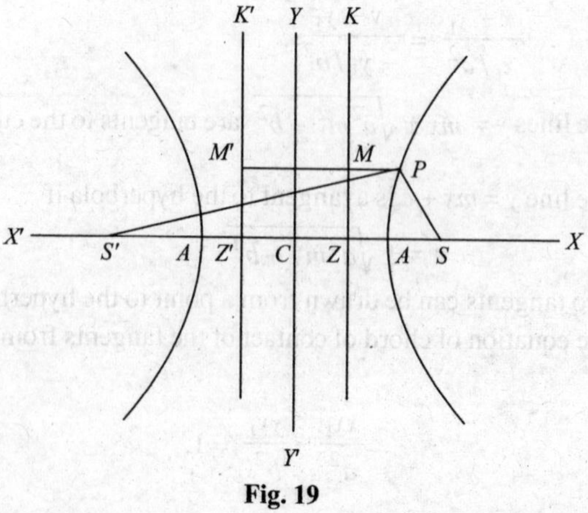

Fig. 19

REMARK: The distances SP and $S'P$ are called the *focal distances* of the point P on the hyperbola and thus we have proved that *the difference of the focal distances of any point on the hyperbola is constant and equals the length of the transverse axis.*

Example 18. *Find the equation of the hyperbola whose directrix is the line $2x + y = 1$, focus is (1, 1) and eccentricity is $\sqrt{3}$.*

Solution. Let $P(x, y)$ be any point on the hyperbola. Draw PM perpendicular on the directrix.

Then by definition

$$SP = ePM \quad \text{where } S(1, 1) \text{ is the focus,}$$

i.e.,
$$SP^2 = e^2 PM^2$$

or
$$(x-1)^2 + (y-1)^2 = \frac{3(2x + y - 1)^2}{5}$$

or
$$7x^2 + 12xy - 2y^2 - 2x + 4y - 7 = 0$$

is the required equation of the hyperbola.

40. PARAMETRIC REPRESENTATION

It is easy to see that the point whose co-ordinates are $(a \sec \theta, b \tan \theta)$ lies on the hyperbola $\frac{x^2}{a^2} - \frac{y^2}{b^2} = 1$.

These are called the *parametric co-ordinates* of a point on the hyperbola. In short this point may be referred to as the point 'θ'.

Clearly equation of tangent at the point 'θ' is

$$\frac{xa \sec \theta}{a^2} - \frac{yb \tan \theta}{b^2} = 1$$

or
$$\frac{x}{a} \sec \theta - \frac{y}{b} \tan \theta = 1.$$

Similarly, equation of normal at the point 'θ' is

$$by \cot \theta + ax \cos \theta = a^2 + b^2.$$

41. ASYMPTOTES

A line which touches a curve at infinity but does not lie wholly at infinity is called as *asymptote* of the curve.

To find the equations of the asymptotes to the hyperbola

$$\frac{x^2}{a^2} - \frac{y^2}{b^2} = 1 \qquad \text{...(1)}$$

Suppose the line $y = mx + c$ is an asymptote to the hyperbola (1).

Now points of intersection of (1) and the line $y = mx + c$ are given by the equation

$$\frac{x^2}{a^2} - \frac{(mx+c)^2}{b^2} = 1$$

or $$x^2(a^2m^2 - b^2) + 2a^2mcx + a^2(c^2 + b^2) = 0$$

The two roots of this equation will be coincident, each equal to infinity if

$$a^2m^2 - b^2 = 0$$

and $2a^2mc = 0$. This in turn gives that

$$m = \pm b/a \text{ and } c = 0$$

Hence the equations of the asymptotes are

$$y = \frac{b}{a}x \quad \text{and} \quad y = -\frac{b}{a}x$$

or $$\frac{x}{a} - \frac{y}{b} = 0 \text{ and } \frac{x}{a} + \frac{y}{b} = 0.$$

Clearly both the asymptotes pass through the centre of the hyperbola and since only two tangents can be drawn to the hyperbola from any point, if follows that the asymptotes to the hyperbola are the tangents to the curve drawn from its centre.

42. RECTANGULAR HYPERBOLA

A hyperbola in which $b = a$ is called a *rectangular* or *equilateral* hyperbola. Thus the equation of rectangular hyperbola becomes

$$\frac{x^2}{a^2} - \frac{y^2}{a^2} = 1$$

or $$x^2 - y^2 = a^2$$

Also since we have the relation $b^2 = a^2(e^2 - 1)$,

For rectangular hyperbola, it follows that

$$a^2 = a^2(e^2 - 1)$$

or $$e^2 - 1 = 1 \quad \text{or} \quad e = \sqrt{2}$$

Hence the eccentricity of a rectangular hyperbola is $\sqrt{2}$.

A hyperbola is rectangular if and only if its two asymptotes are at right angles to each other.

If the hyperbola is rectangular, then by definition $b = a$ and therefore equations of the asymptotes become

$$x - y = 0 \text{ and } x + y = 0$$

which are clearly perpendicular to each other.

Conversely if the asymptotes $\frac{x}{a} - \frac{y}{b} = 0$ and $\frac{x}{a} + \frac{y}{b} = 0$ are at right angles to each other, the product of their slopes is -1.

i.e., $\frac{b}{a} \times \frac{-b}{a} = 1$ or $b = a$

$\Rightarrow$ The hyperbola is rectangular.

43. RECTANGULAR HYPERBOLA REFERRED TO ITS ASYMPTOTES AS AXES

Let the equation of a rectangular hyperbola referred to its transverse and conjugate axis be

$$x^2 - y^2 = a^2 \quad ...(1)$$

We now obtain equation of this hyperbola when its asymptotes DD' and EE' are at right angles to each other, and their equations are

$$x - y = 0$$

and

$$x + y = 0.$$

Clearly the angle $D'CX$ is 45° as slope of DD' is 1.

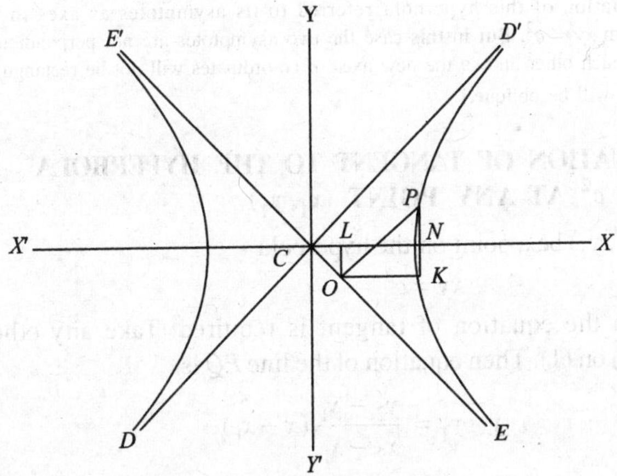

Fig. 20

Let (x, y) be the co-ordinates of any point P on the hyperbola (1) referred to old axes CX and CY. Let (x', y') be the co-ordinates of the same point when the equation of the curve is referred to its asymptotes as the axes.

Draw PQ parallel to CD' to meet EE' in Q. Also draw PN perpendicular to CX and produce it to meet a line through Q parallel to CX in the point K. Drop $QL \perp CX$.

Then $\qquad CQ = x', PQ = y'$

Now $\qquad x = CN = CL + LN = CL + QK$

$$= x' \cos 45° + y' \cos 45° = \frac{x'}{\sqrt{2}} + \frac{y'}{\sqrt{2}}$$

and $\qquad y = PN = PK - NK = PK - LQ = y' \sin 45° - x' \sin 45°$

$$= \frac{y'}{\sqrt{2}} - \frac{x'}{\sqrt{2}}$$

Substituting these values of x and y in (1) we get

$$\frac{(x'+y')^2}{2} - \frac{(y'-x')^2}{2} = a^2 \quad \text{or} \quad x'y' = \frac{a^2}{2} = c^2 \quad \text{(say)}.$$

Changing to current co-ordinates we get the required equation of the rectangular hyperbola as $\mathbf{xy = c^2}$.

[NOTE: If we have the hyperbola $\frac{x^2}{a^2} - \frac{y^2}{b^2} = 1$, with asymptotes $\frac{x}{a} \pm \frac{y}{b} = 0$, then also by proceeding as in the above case we can find equation of this hyperbola referred to its asymptotes as axes in the form $xy = c^2$. But in this case the two asymptotes are not perpendicular to each other and so the new axes of co-ordinates will not be rectangular, but will be oblique.]

44. EQUATION OF TANGENT TO THE HYPERBOLA $xy = c^2$ AT ANY POINT (x_1, y_1)

Let $P(x_1, y_1)$ be a point on the hyperbola

$$xy = c^2 \qquad \text{...(1)}$$

at which the equation of tangent is required. Take any other point $Q(x_2, y_2)$ on (1). Then equation of the line PQ is

$$y - y_1 = \frac{y_2 - y_1}{x_2 - x_1}(x - x_1) \qquad \text{...(2)}$$

Since both P and Q lie on (1), we have

$$x_1y_1 = c^2$$
$$x_2y_2 = c^2.$$

These give $y_2 - y_1 = \dfrac{c^2}{x_2} - \dfrac{c^2}{x_1} = c^2\left[\dfrac{x_1 - x_2}{x_1\, x_2}\right]$

or $$\frac{y_2 - y_1}{x_2 - x_1} = -\frac{c^2}{x_1x_2}.$$

Putting in (3), we get the equation of PQ as

$$y - y_1 = -\frac{c^2}{x_1x_2}(x - x_1)$$

This line becomes a tangent to (1) at P when $Q \to P$ *i.e.*, $x_2 \to x_1$.
So taking the limit we get

$$y - y_1 = -\frac{c^2}{x_1^{\,2}}(x - x_1) = -\frac{y_1}{x_1}(x - x_1) \text{ as } y_1 = \frac{c^2}{x_1}$$

or $$xy_1 + yx_1 = 2x_1y_1$$

or $$\frac{\mathbf{x}}{\mathbf{x_1}} + \frac{\mathbf{y}}{\mathbf{y_1}} = \mathbf{2.}$$

This is the required equation of the tangent at (x_1, y_1).

[NOTE: The above equation of the tangent is also sometimes written as $xy_1 + yx_1 = 2c^2$.]

45. EQUATION OF NORMAL TO THE HYPERBOLA $xy = c^2$ AT (x_1, y_1)

Equation of tangent at (x_1, y_1) is

$$xy_1 + yx_1 = 2c^2.$$

The slope of tangent $= -\dfrac{y_1}{x_1}$

giving slope of normal to be $\dfrac{x_1}{y_1}$.

Hence equation of the noraml at (x_1, y_1) is

$$y - y_1 = \frac{x_1}{y_1}(x - x_1)$$

or $$\mathbf{xx_1 - yy_1 = x_1^{\,2} - y_1^{\,2}.}$$

46. PARAMETRIC REPRESENTATION

It is clear that the point with co-ordinates $\left(ct, \frac{c}{t}\right)$ always lies on $xy = c^2$, whatever be the non-zero value of the parameter t. These are called the parametric co-ordinates of a point on the hyperbola $xy = c^2$.

Equation of tangent at the point 't' will be

$$x.\frac{c}{t} + y.ct = 2c^2 \quad \text{or} \quad \frac{x}{t} + yt = 2c.$$

Equation of normal at the point 't' on the rectangular hyperbola $xy = c^2$ is $x \cdot ct - y\frac{c}{t} = c^2t^2 - \frac{c^2}{t^2}$ or $xt^3 - yt = ct^4 - c$.

47. GEOMETRICAL PROPERTIES OF THE HYPERBOLA

(1) *If the tangent at any point P on the hyperbola*

$$\frac{x^2}{a^2} - \frac{y^2}{b^2} = 1$$

meets the transverse axis in T and the conjugate axis in T′ then

$$CN.\, CT = a^2$$

$$CN'.CT' = -b^2$$

where N and N′ are the feet of the perpendiculars from P on the axes and C is the centre of the curve.

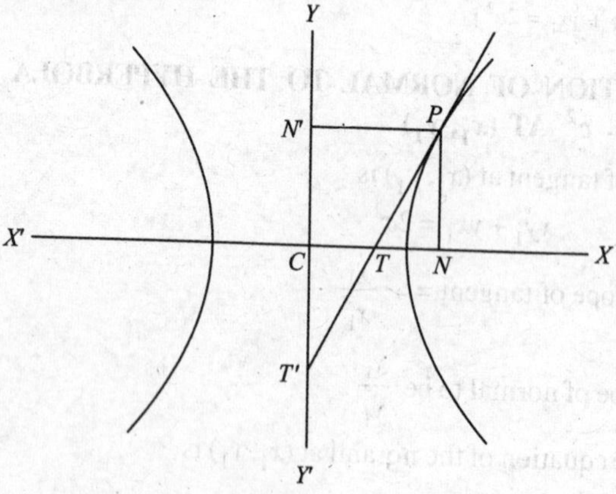

Fig. 21

Let the point P have co-ordinates (x_1, y_1), then equation of tangent at P is

$$\frac{xx_1}{a^2} - \frac{yy_1}{b^2} = 1.$$

Put $y = 0$ to get co-ordinates of T, which come out to be $\left(\frac{a^2}{x_1}, 0\right)$.

Similarly co-ordinates of T' are $\left(0, -\frac{b^2}{y_1}\right)$.

Thus $\quad CN.\, CT = x_1 . \frac{a^2}{x_1} = a^2$

$$CN'.\, CT' = y_1 . \frac{-b^2}{y_1} = -b^2$$

which proves the result.

(2) *If the normal at any point P on the hyperbola* $\frac{x^2}{a^2} - \frac{y^2}{b^2} = 1$ *meets the transverse axis in G, then*

$$CG = e^2.\, CN$$

where C is the centre of the hyperbola and N is the foot of the ordinate through P.

The equation of normal at any point P is

$$\frac{x - x_1}{x_1 / a^2} + \frac{y - y_1}{y_1 / b^2} = 0.$$

To find co-ordinates of G, put $y = 0$ in this to get

$$\frac{x - x_1}{x_1 / a^2} - b^2 = 0 \quad \text{or} \quad x = x_1\left(\frac{b^2}{a^2} + 1\right) = CG.$$

Now $\quad e^2\, CN = e^2\, x_1$

$$= \left(\frac{b^2}{a^2} + 1\right) x_1$$

Hence $\quad CG = e^2.\, CN.$

(3) *The normal at any point P on a hyperbola meets the transverse axis in G and the conjugate axis in g. F is the foot of the perpendicular from the centre C on the normal. Prove that*

$$PF.\, PG = b^2$$

$$PF.\, Pg = a^2.$$

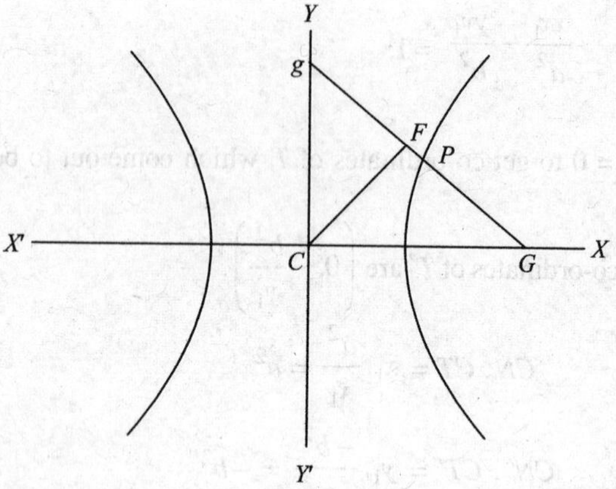

Fig. 22

Let the point P have co-ordinates ($a \sec \theta, b \tan \theta$). Then the equation of the normal at P is

$$by \cot \theta + ax \cos \theta = a^2 + b^2 \quad ...(1)$$

To get co-ordinates of G, put $y = 0$ in this,

we get $\quad ax \cos \theta = a^2 + b^2$

or $$x = \frac{a^2 + b^2}{a \cos \theta}$$

Thus the point G has co-ordinates $\left(\frac{a^2 + b^2}{a \cos \theta}, 0\right)$.

Hence $$PG = \sqrt{\left(\frac{a^2 + b^2}{a \cos \theta} - a \sec \theta\right)^2 + b^2 \tan^2 \theta}$$

$$= \sqrt{\frac{b^4}{a^2 \cos^2 \theta} + b^2 \frac{\sin^2 \theta}{\cos^2 \theta}}$$

$$= \frac{b}{a \cos \theta} \sqrt{b^2 + a^2 \sin^2 \theta} \quad ...(2)$$

Similarly by putting $x = 0$ in the equation we can find co-ordinates of g and then

$$Pg = \frac{a}{b \cos \theta} \sqrt{b^2 + a^2 \sin^2 \theta} \quad ...(3)$$

Now PF = perpendicular distance of C from the tangent at P.

Equation of tangent at P is

$$\frac{x}{a}\sec\theta - \frac{y}{b}\tan\theta = 1$$

thus
$$PF = \frac{1}{\sqrt{\dfrac{1}{a^2\cos^2\theta} + \dfrac{\sin^2\theta}{b^2\cos^2\theta}}}$$

$$= \frac{ab\cos\theta}{\sqrt{b^2 + a^2\sin^2\theta}} \qquad ...(4)$$

Hence from (2), (3) and (4)

$$PF \, . \, PG = b^2$$
$$PF \, . \, Pg = a^2$$

which proves the result.

Example 19. *Show that the portion of any tangent to a rectangular hyperbola intercepted by the asymptotes is bisected at the point of contact.*

Solution. Let equation of the hyperbola, referred to asymptotes as the axes be $xy = c^2$. Take P $(ct, c/t)$ any point on it. Then equation of tangent at P is

$$x + t^2 y = 2ct.$$

It meets the asymptote $x = 0$ at $y = \dfrac{2c}{t}$ and the asymptote $y = 0$ at $x = 2ct$.

Thus the points where the tangent meets the asymptotes have co-ordinates $(2ct, 0)$ and $(0, 2c/t)$.

Co-ordinates of the middle point of these are $(ct, c/t)$, which is the point of contact P.

Hence the result follows.

Example 20. *If a triangle is inscribed in a rectangular hyperbola, prove that the ortho-centre of the triangle lies on the curve.*

Solution. Let equation of the rectangular hyperbola be $xy = c^2$ (referred to asymptotes as axes).

Let $P\left(ct_1, \dfrac{c}{t_1}\right)$, $Q\left(ct_2, \dfrac{c}{t_2}\right)$ and $R\left(ct_3, \dfrac{c}{t_3}\right)$ be the vertices of the triangle.

Then slope of the side QR is

$$\frac{\dfrac{c}{t_3} - \dfrac{c}{t_2}}{ct_3 - ct_2} \quad \text{or} \quad -\frac{1}{t_2 t_3}$$

Hence equation of the line passing through P and perpendicular to QR is

$$y - \frac{c}{t_1} = t_2 t_3 (x - ct_1) \quad \text{or} \quad y + ct_1 t_2 t_3 = t_2 t_3 \left(x + \frac{c}{t_1 t_2 t_3} \right) \qquad ...(1)$$

Similarly equation of the line passing through Q and perpendicular to RP is

$$y + ct_1 t_2 t_3 = t_3 t_1 \left(x + \frac{c}{t_1 t_2 t_3} \right) \qquad ...(2)$$

Solving (1) and (2), we get

$$t_2 t_3 x + \frac{c}{t_1} = t_3 t_1 x + \frac{c}{t_2}$$

This gives $\quad x = -\dfrac{c}{t_1 t_2 t_3}$

Putting in (1), we get $y = -ct_1 t_2 t_3$.

Hence co-ordinates of the ortho-centre are $\left(-\dfrac{c}{t_1 t_2 t_3}, -ct_1 t_2 t_3 \right)$

Substituting in $xy = c^2$ we find that they satisfy the equation, implying thereby that the ortho centre lies on the curve.

Example 21. *Show that the locus of the middle points of normal chords of the rectangular hyperbola* $x^2 - y^2 = a^2$ is

$$(y^2 - x^2)^3 = 4a^2 x^2 y^2.$$

Solution. Let (x_1, y_1) be the middle point of one of the normal chords. Then equation of this chord is

$$xx_1 - yy_1 = x_1^2 - y_1^2 \qquad ...(1)$$

Suppose this chord is normal to the hyperbola at the point (a sec θ, b tan θ). Then equation of the normal is

$$x \cos \theta + y \cot \theta = 2a. \qquad ...(2)$$

Since (1) and (2) represent the same line, comparing coefficients, we get

$$\frac{\cos \theta}{x_1} = \frac{\cot \theta}{-y_1} = \frac{2a}{x_1^2 - y_1^2}.$$

which give $\quad \cos \theta = \dfrac{2ax_1}{x_1^2 - y_1^2}$

$$\sin \theta = -\frac{x_1}{y_1}$$

Eliminating θ, we get

$$\frac{4a^2x_1^2}{(x_1^2-y_1^2)^2}+\frac{x_1^2}{y_1^2}=1 \quad \text{or} \quad \frac{4a^2x_1^2}{(x_1^2-y_1^2)^2}=1-\frac{x_1^2}{y_1^2}=\frac{y_1^2-x_1^2}{y_1^2}$$

or $\quad (y_1^2-x_1^2)^3=4a^2x_1^2y_1^2.$

Hence the required locus of (x_1, y_1) is $(y^2-x^2)^3=4a^2x^2y^2$.

EXERCISES

1. Find the equation of the hyperbola whose focus is (2, 2), the corresponding directrix is $x + y = 2$ and eccentricity is $\sqrt{2}$.
2. Show that the product of the perpendicular distances of a point on a hyperbola from the asymptotes is constant.
3. If S and S' are the foci of a rectangular hyperbola and P is any point on it, prove that $SP.\ S'P = CP^2$ where C is the centre of the hyperbola.
4. A line cuts a hyperbola in the points Q, Q' and its asymptotes in the points R, R'. Prove that QQ' and RR' have the same middle point.
5. Show that the normal to the rectangular hyperbola $xy = c^2$ at the point t meets the curve again at the point t', such that $t^3t' = -1$.
6. Find the equation of the tangents to the hyperbola $3x^2 - y^2 = 3$ which are

   (*i*) parallel to the line $y = 2x + 4$

   (*ii*) perpendicular to the line $x + 3y - 2 = 0$.
7. Find the condition that the line $x \cos \alpha + y \sin \alpha = p$ should touch the hyperbola $\frac{x^2}{a^2}-\frac{y^2}{b^2}=1$.
8. Show that the tangent at any point of a hyperbola cuts off a triangle of constant area from the asymptotes.
9. Show that the line $5x + 12y = 9$ touches the hyperbola $x^2 - 9y^2 = 9$. Find the point of contact.
10. A tangent to the hyperbola $\frac{x^2}{a^2}-\frac{y^2}{b^2}=1$ cuts the ellipse $\frac{x^2}{a^2}+\frac{y^2}{b^2}=1$ in A and B. Find the locus of the middle point of AB.

ANSWERS

1. $xy = 2$
6. $2x - y \pm 1 = 0;\ 3x - y \pm \sqrt{6} = 0$
7. $a^2 \cos^2 \alpha - b^2 \sin^2 \alpha = p^2$
9. $\left(5, -\frac{4}{3}\right)$
10. $\left(\frac{x^2}{a^2}+\frac{y^2}{b^2}\right)^2=\frac{x^2}{a^2}-\frac{y^2}{b^2}.$

CHAPTER 25

DIFFERENTIATION

1. FUNCTIONS AND THEIR LIMITS

In Mathematics we usually deal with two kinds of quantities namely constants and variables. A quantity which is liable to vary is called a *variable quantity* or simply a *variable*. Temperature, pressure, distance of a moving train from a station are all variable quantities. On the other hand, a quantity that retains its value through all mathematical operations is termed as a *constant quantity* or a *constant.* Numbers like 4, 5, 2.5, π etc., are all constants.

Suppose now that x is a real variable (*i.e.*, x takes up different values that are real numbers). We explain what we mean by a **function** of x (a concept that we have already talked about in the chapter on sets). We shall discuss it here in a little different way. Consider the quantities $\log x$, $\sin x$, x^2 etc. In these log, sin, square are the functions.

Let us write $y = x^2$.

Then if $x = 2$, y is 4, if x is 3, y is 9 etc.

Thus for each value of x, y gets a unique corresponding value and this value is assigned each time by a certain *rule* (namely, square). This rule is what we call a function.

So in general, by a function of x, we mean a **rule** that gives us a unique value corresponding to each value of x.

So if $y = \sin x$ then when we give different values to x we get, each time, a corresponding unique value for y [with the *assistance* of the function sine].

Above are some examples of certain well-known functions. When we are dealing with any function, we simply write

$$y = f(x)$$

and say that y is a function of x although to be very correct we should say that y is the value assigned by the function f corresponding to a value of x. And we call x as the *independent* variable and y the *dependent* variable.

We remark here that the above definition of a function is equivalent to the definition given in the chapter on Sets.

Functions play important role in Mathematics and its applications to Physical and Social Seiences.

A function which assigns a *fixed* value for every value of x is called a *constant function.* For example, $f(x) = 3$ is a constant function, since for any value of x, $f(x)$ remains equal to 3.

The next important notion is that of the limit of a function. It is quite possible that $f(x)$ may not be defined for all values of x. As an illustration consider $f(x) = \dfrac{x^2 - 25}{x - 5}$. This is a function of x, provided x takes all real values except 5. If it were defined at $x = 5$, we would have got $f(5) = \dfrac{25 - 25}{5 - 5} = \dfrac{0}{0}$; a meaningless quantity. $\dfrac{0}{0}$ can take any finite value whatsoever, like $\dfrac{0}{0} = 5$. $\dfrac{0}{0} = \pi$ etc., since $0 \times 5 = 0, 0 \times \pi = 0$. One could perhaps say here that why don't we cancel $x - 5$ first and then put $x = 5$ to get $f(5)$ equal to 10. There is a lapse in this argument as $x - 5$ is zero when $x = 5$ and cancellation of zero factor is not allowed in Mathematics, because we would get very absurd results like $1 = 2$ and $3 = 15$ etc., since $0 \times 1 = 0 \times 2$ and $0 \times 3 = 0 \times 15$. As a consequence we cannot determine $f(5)$, the value of $f(x)$ at $x = 5$. But we do not leave the problem here. Instead we try to evaluate the value of $f(x)$ when x is *very* near to 5 (and this will finally lead us to a value that would *almost* be the value of $f(5)$).

Thus we can evaluate $f(x)$ at $x = 4.9998$ or $x = 5.00001$. The technique is quite simple. Cancel $x - 5$ first (This step is perfectly legitimate as x is *not* equal to 5); then substitute the value of x. For example $f(4.9998) = 4.9998 + 5 = 9.9998$ and $f(5.00001) = 5.00001 + 5 = 10.00001$.

We now write down some of the values given to x and the corresponding values acquired by $f(x)$ in the following tables. In first table values of x are *increasing up to* 5 (being always less than 5) and in second table values of x are *decreasing down* to 5 (being always greater than 5).

Table 1

Value of x	*Value of f (x)*
4	9
4.235	9.235
4.976	9.976
4.99998	9.99998
4.9999999	9.9999999
↓	↓

Table 2

Value of x	*Value of f (x)*
7	12
6.31	11.31
5.7984	10.7984
5.2175	10.2175
5.0039	10.0039
5.0000001	10.0000001
↓	↓

The above is expressed mathematically as: x tends to 5 from the left [In the Table 1] and x tends to 5 from the right [in the Table 2]. In the first case we write $x \to 5-$ and in the second case we write $x \to 5+$.

Observe the pattern of change in the second column of each table. One could, after slight concentration see that in the first situation $f(x) \to 10-$ while in the second case $f(x) \to 10+$. Thus we are *tempted* to assert that $f(x)$ approaches 10 (both from left and from right) as x approaches 5. This number 10, we call *limit* of $f(x)$ as x approaches 5.

This fact is denoted by $\lim_{x \to 5} f(x) = 10$.

Consider now any small positive number, say, .01. When $|x-5| < .01$

i.e., $-.01 < x-5 < .01$

or $4.99 < x < 5.01$ then $-.01 < f(x) - 10 < .01$

or $|f(x) - 10| < .01$

[$4.99 < x < 5.01$ and $x \neq 5 \Rightarrow f(x) = x + 5$

This yields in turn $f(x) - 10 = x - 5$

so $-.01 < f(x) - 10 < .01$]

One can repeat the above experiment by starting with another small positive number say .00002 and note that whenever $|x-5| < .00002$, then $|f(x) - 10| < .00002$.

The expected conclusion will be that however small a positive number ε we may start with, we shall always be able to find a $\delta > 0$ such that whenever $|x-5| < \delta$ then $|f(x) - 10| < \varepsilon$. In the above illustration $\delta = \varepsilon$ will suffice.

Thus we are led to the following definition of limit.

We say that $\lim_{x \to a} f(x) = l$ if corresponding to any $\varepsilon > 0$, we can find $\delta > 0$, such that $|f(x) - l| < \varepsilon$ whenever $|x - a| < \delta$.

We shall evaluate some limits using this definition. Later on we'll give other convenient methods too.

NOTE. The reader is reminded that we have already talked of the limit concept for a sequence in chapter (on Sequences).

Example 1. *Evaluate* $\lim_{x \to a} x$.

Solution. Let $\varepsilon > 0$ be any number.

Take $\delta = \varepsilon$. Evidently $\delta > 0$.

Now $|x - a| < \delta \Rightarrow |f(x) - a| < \varepsilon$

Since $f(x) = x$.

Hence $\lim_{x \to a} x = a$.

Example 2. *Evaluate* $\lim_{x \to a} x^2$.

Solution. Let $\varepsilon > 0$ be any number.

Take $\delta = -2 + \sqrt{4 + \varepsilon}$. Clearly $\delta > 0$

Now $|x + 2| = |x - 2 + 4| \le |x - 2| + 4 < \delta + 4$

So $|x - 2| < \delta \Rightarrow |x^2 - 4| = |x + 2|\, |x - 2| < \delta^2 + 4\delta = \varepsilon$

Hence $\lim_{x \to 2} x^2 = 4$.

Example 3. *Determine* $\lim_{x \to 3} \frac{1}{x}$.

Solution. Let $\varepsilon > 0$.

Put $$\delta = \frac{9\varepsilon}{1 + \varepsilon}$$

Now $|x - 3| < \delta \Rightarrow |x - 3| < \dfrac{9\varepsilon}{1 + 3\varepsilon}$ ...(1)

Also $|x - 3| < \delta \Rightarrow -\delta < x - 3$

$$\Rightarrow x > 3 - \delta = 3 - \frac{9\varepsilon}{1 + 3\varepsilon} = \frac{3}{1 + 3\varepsilon}$$

$$\Rightarrow \frac{1}{x} < \frac{1 + 3\varepsilon}{3}$$ ...(2)

(1) and (2) imply

$$\left|\frac{1}{x}-\frac{1}{3}\right| = \left|\frac{x-3}{3x}\right| < \frac{9\varepsilon}{1+3\varepsilon}\ \frac{1+3\varepsilon}{3}\cdot\frac{1}{3} = \varepsilon$$

Consequently $\lim\limits_{x\to 3}\frac{1}{x} = \frac{1}{3}$.

Example 4. *Find out the limit of* $\frac{x^2-1}{x-1}$ *as* $x \to 1$.

Solution. Let $\varepsilon > 0$ be any number.

Take $\delta = \varepsilon$.

Now $|x-1| < \delta \Rightarrow |x-1| < \varepsilon$

$$\Rightarrow |x+1-2| < \varepsilon$$

$$\Rightarrow \left|\frac{x^2-1}{x-1} - 2\right| < \varepsilon$$

$$\Rightarrow \lim_{x\to 1}\frac{x^2-1}{x-1} = 2.$$

2. *h*-METHOD FOR DETERMINING LIMITS

We put $a + h$ in place of x and simplify such that h gets cancelled from denominator and numerator. Putting $h = 0$, we get limit of $f(x)$ as $x \to a$.

Example 5. *Evalute* $\lim\limits_{x\to 1}\frac{x^3-1}{x^2-1}$.

Solution.
$$\lim_{x\to 1}\frac{x^3-1}{x^2-1} = \lim_{h\to 0}\frac{(1+h)^3-1}{(1+h)^2-1}$$

$$= \lim_{h\to 0}\frac{3h+3h^2+h^3}{2h+h^2}$$

$$= \lim_{h\to 0}\frac{3+3h+h^2}{2h+h}$$

$$= \frac{3}{2}.$$

3. EXPANSION METHOD FOR EVALUATING LIMITS

This method is applicable to the functions which can be expanded in series. Following expansions are often utilized.

(1) $(1+x)^n = 1 + nx + \dfrac{n(n-1)x^2}{2!} + \dfrac{n(n-1)(n-1)x^3}{3!} + \ldots$ provided $|x| < 1$ and n is any real number.

NOTE: If n is a positive integer, the expansion on RHS has finite number of terms only.]

(2) $\log(1+x) = x - \dfrac{x^2}{2} + \dfrac{x^3}{3} - \dfrac{x^4}{4} + \ldots \infty$

provided $|x| < 1$.

(3) $e^x = 1 + x + \dfrac{x^2}{2!} + \dfrac{x^3}{3!} + \ldots \infty$

(4) $\sin x = x - \dfrac{x^3}{3!} + \dfrac{x^5}{5!} \ldots \infty$

(5) $\cos x = 1 - \dfrac{x^2}{2!} + \dfrac{x^4}{4!} \ldots \infty$

The method will be illustrated by means of the following examples.

Example 6. *Show that* $\lim\limits_{x\to 0} \dfrac{\sin x}{x} = 1.$

Solution. $$\lim_{x\to 0} \frac{\sin x}{x} = \lim_{x\to 0} \frac{x - \dfrac{x^3}{3!} + \dfrac{x^5}{5!} \ldots}{x}$$

$$= \lim_{x\to 0} \left(1 - \frac{x^2}{3!} + \frac{x^4}{5!} \ldots\right) = 1.$$

REMARK: The result of Example 6 shall be frequently used later on.

Example 7. *Evaluate* $\lim\limits_{x\to 0} \dfrac{e^x - e^{-x}}{x}.$

Solution. $$\lim_{x\to 0} \frac{e^x - e^{-x}}{x}$$

$$= \lim_{x\to 0} \frac{\left(1 + x + \dfrac{x^2}{2!} + \dfrac{x^3}{3!} \ldots\right) - \left(1 - x + \dfrac{x^2}{2!} - \dfrac{x^3}{3!} \ldots\right)}{x}$$

$$= \lim_{x\to 0} \frac{2\left(x+\frac{x^3}{3!}+\frac{x^5}{5!}\ldots\right)}{x}$$

$$= \lim_{x\to 0} 2\left(1+\frac{x^2}{3!}+\frac{x^4}{5!}+\ldots\right)$$

$$= 2.$$

REMARKS 1. $\lim_{x\to a} f(x) = l$ if and only if

$\lim_{x\to a-} f(x) = l = \lim_{x\to a+} f(x)$.

[$\lim_{x\to a-} f(x)$ and $\lim_{x\to a+} f(x)$ are called left and right limits of $f(x)$]

If one of the two equalities fails to hold we asy that limit of $f(x)$ as $x \to a$ does not exist.

Consider $\lim_{x\to 0} \frac{1}{x}$. It can be easily seen that if $x \to 0-$, $\frac{1}{x} \to -\infty$ while if $x \to 0+$, then $\frac{1}{x} \to \infty$. So $\lim_{x\to 0} \frac{1}{x}$ does not exist.

2. If $\lim_{x\to a} f(x)$ exists then it must be *unique*.

Example 8. *f(x) is defined as under*

$$f(x) = 0 \qquad \text{for } x \le 0$$

$$= \frac{1}{2} - x \qquad \text{for } x > 0.$$

Show that $\lim_{x\to 0} f(x)$ *does not exist.*

Solution. $\lim_{x\to 0-} f(x) = \lim_{h\to 0} f(0-h) = 0.$

Also $\lim_{x\to 0+} f(x) = \lim_{h\to 0} f(0+h) = \lim_{h\to 0} f\left(\frac{1}{2}-h\right)$

$$= \frac{1}{2}$$

Since $\lim_{x\to 0-} f(x) \ne \lim_{x\to 0+} f(x)$,

$\lim_{x\to 0} f(x)$ does not exist.

We can also evaluate the limits as follows:

$$\lim_{x\to 0-} f(x) = \lim_{x\to 0}(0) = 0 \quad (\text{as } f(x) = 0 \text{ when } x < 0)$$

$$\lim_{x\to 0+} f(x) = \lim_{x\to 0}\left(\frac{1}{2} - x\right) = \frac{1}{2} \quad (\text{as } f(x) = \frac{1}{2} - x \text{ when } x < 0)$$

Proofs of following results on limits are beyond the scope of this book and so they are omitted.

(*A*) If $\lim_{x\to a} f(x) = l$ and $\lim_{x\to a} g(x) = m$

then (1) $\lim_{x\to a} [f(x) \pm g(x)] = l \pm m$

(2) $\lim_{x\to a} [f(x)\, g(x)] = lm$

(3) $\lim_{x\to a} \dfrac{f(x)}{g(x)} = \dfrac{l}{m}$ provided $m \neq 0$

(4) $\lim_{x\to a} [f(x)]^{g(x)} = l^m$, provided l^m is defined.

(*B*) If $f(x) < g(x)$ for all x

then $\lim_{x\to a} f(x) \le \lim_{x\to a} g(x)$.

4. CONTINUOUS FUNCTIONS

We have seen in Example 2 that $\lim_{x\to 2} x^2 = 4$ which is same as value of x^2 at $x = 2$. Whereas in Example 4, $\lim_{x\to 1} \dfrac{x^2 - 1}{x - 1} = 2$ but the function itself is not defined at $x = 1$.

Again consider

$$f(x) = \frac{x^2 - 9}{x - 3}, x \neq 3.$$
$$= 1 \qquad x = 3.$$

In this case $\lim_{x\to 3} \dfrac{x^2 - 9}{x - 3} = 6$, and $f(3) = 1$.

Thus a function may possess a limit as $x \to a$ but it may or may not be defined at $x = a$. Even if it is defined at $x = a$, its value may not be equal to its limit. This prompts us to define the following type of functions.

A function $f(x)$ is said to be continuous at $x = a$ if $\lim_{x\to a} f(x) = f(a)$.

In other words, $f(x)$ is said to be continuous at $x = a$ if given $\varepsilon > 0$ there exists $\delta > 0$ such that $|f(x) - f(a)| < \varepsilon$, whenever $|x - a| < \delta$.

Example 9. *Check for continuity at x = 0, the function f (x) = | x |.*

Solution. By definition of absolute value, we can write

$$f(x) = x \text{ for all } x \geq 0$$
$$= -x \text{ for all } x < 0.$$

We note that $f(0) = 0$

$$\lim_{x \to 0-} f(x) = \lim_{x \to 0} (-x) = 0 \quad [\text{as } f(x) = -x, \text{ when } x < 0]$$

$$\lim_{x \to 0+} f(x) = \lim_{x \to 0} (x) = 0 \quad [\text{as } f(x) = x, \text{ when } x > 0]$$

Thus $\lim_{x \to 0-} f(x) = \lim_{x \to 0+} f(x) = f(0)$

Hence $f(x)$ is continuous at $x = 0$.

Example 10. *A function f is defined as*

$$f(x) = \frac{x^2 - 4x + 3}{x^2 - 1} \quad \text{when } x \neq 1$$
$$= 2 \quad \text{when } x = 1$$

Test the continuity of the function at $x = 1$.

Solution. $$\lim_{x \to 1+} f(x) = \lim_{x \to 1+} \frac{(x-1)(x-3)}{(x-1)(x+1)}$$

$$= \lim_{x \to 1+} \frac{x-3}{x+1} = \lim_{h \to 0} \frac{1+h-3}{1+h+1}$$

$$= \lim_{h \to 0} \frac{h-2}{h+2} = -1$$

But $f(1) = 2$

So, f is not continuous at $x = 1$.

Example 11. *Check for continuity the function*

$$f(x) = 2x - 1 \qquad 0 \leq x \leq 1$$
$$2x + 1 \qquad 1 < x \leq 2$$

at $x = 0, 1, 2.$

Solution. We consider the point $x = 1$ first.

$$\lim_{x \to 1+} f(x) = \lim_{x \to 1} (2x + 1) = 2 + 1 = 3$$

$$\lim_{x \to 1-} f(x) = \lim_{x \to 1} (2x - 1) = 2 - 1 = 1$$

thus as $\lim_{x \to 1+} f(x) \neq \lim_{x \to 1-} f(x)$, $\lim_{x \to 1} f(x)$ does not exist.

Hence f is not continuous at $x = 1$.

At $x = 0$ we have $\lim_{x \to 0+} f(x) = \lim_{x \to 0} (2x - 1) = -1$.

Also $f(0) = -1$

thus $\lim_{x \to 0+} f(x) = f(0) = -1$

$\Rightarrow$ $f(x)$ is continuous from the right at $x = 0$

Again $\lim_{x \to 2-} f(x) = \lim_{x \to 2} (2x + 1) = 4 + 1 = 5$

$f(2) = 4 + 1 = 5$

$\Rightarrow$ $\lim_{x \to 2-} f(x) = f(2) = 5$

$\Rightarrow$ $f(x)$ is continuous (from the left) at $x = 2$.

REMARK: As the value of the function is not given from $x < 0$ and $x > 2$, we consider only one-sided continuity at these points.

EXERCISES

1. Evaluate the following limits:

$$\lim_{x \to 3} \left(\frac{x^3 - 27}{x - 3} \right), \ \lim_{x \to 1} (x^2 + 1), \ \lim_{x \to 0} \left(\frac{\tan x}{x} \right).$$

$$\lim_{x \to 0} (1 + x)^{1/x}, \ \lim_{x \to 0} \left(\frac{\sin ax}{\sin bx} \right) \text{ where } b \neq 0.$$

2. Show that $\lim_{x \to 0} \dfrac{x^n - a^n}{x - a} = na^{n-1}$.

3. Evaluate $\lim_{x \to 0} \dfrac{xe^x - \log(1 + x)}{x^2}$.

4. Prove that if $\lim_{x \to a} f(x)$ exists, it must be unique.

5. Show that the function defined by

$$\phi(x) = \begin{cases} 0 & \text{for } x \leq 0 \\ \frac{1}{2} - x & \text{for } 0 < x < \frac{1}{2} \\ \frac{1}{2} & \text{for } x = \frac{1}{2} \\ \frac{3}{2} - x & \text{for } \frac{1}{2} < x < 1 \\ 1 & \text{for } x \geq 1 \end{cases}$$

is not continuous at $x = 0, \frac{1}{2}$ and 1.

6. Show that $f(x) = x \sin \frac{1}{x}, x \neq 0$ and $f(0) = 0$ is continuous for all values of x.

7. Evaluate $\lim_{x \to 0} \left[\frac{\log (1+x)}{x} \right]$.

8. Prove that if $f(x)$, $g(x)$ are continuous functions of x at $x = a$ then $f(x) \pm g(x)$, $f(x)\, g(x)$ and $\frac{f(x)}{g(x)}$ [provided $g(a) \neq 0$] are continuous, at $x = a$.

9. Evaluate $\lim_{x \to 0} \frac{\left(\sin^{-1} \frac{4}{3} x\right)}{x}$.

10. Prove that the function $f(x)$ defined as under

$$f(x) = x \sin \frac{1}{x}, \quad x \neq 0$$
$$= 0, \quad x = 0$$

is continuous at $x = 0$.

ANSWERS

1. 27, 2, 1, e, $\frac{a}{b}$. 3. 0 7. 1 9. $\frac{4}{3}$

5. DIFFERENTIATION

Let y be a function of x. We call x an *independent variable* and y *dependent variable.*

REMARK: There is no sanctity about x being independent and y dependent. This depends upon which variable we allow to take any value and then corresponding to that value determine the value, of other variable. Thus in $y = x^2$, x is independent variable and y dependent whereas the same function can be re-written as $x = \sqrt{y}$. Now y is independent variable, and x is dependent variable. Such an 'inversion' is not always possible. For example in $y = \sin x + x^3 + \log x + x^{1/2}$ it is rather impossible to find x in terms of y.

DIFFERENTIAL COEFFICIENT OF $f(x)$ WITH RESPECT TO x

Let $$y = f(x) \qquad ...(1)$$

and let x be changed to $x + \delta x$ then if the corresponding change in y is δy, then

$$y + \delta y = f(x + \delta x) \qquad ...(2)$$

(1) and (2) imply that

$$\delta y = f(x + \delta x) - f(x)$$

$$\Rightarrow \quad \frac{\delta y}{\delta x} = \frac{f(x + \delta x) - f(x)}{\delta x}$$

$\lim\limits_{\delta x \to 0} \dfrac{f(x + \delta x) - f(x)}{\delta x}$, if it exists, is called *differential coefficient* of y with respect to x and is written as $\dfrac{dy}{dx}$.

Thus $$\frac{dy}{dx} = \lim_{\delta x \to 0} \frac{\delta y}{\delta x} = \lim_{\delta x \to 0} \frac{f(x + \delta x) - f(x)}{\delta x}.$$

Let $f(x)$ be defined at $x = a$. The derivative of $f(x)$ at $x = a$ is defined as $\lim\limits_{h \to 0} \dfrac{f(a + h) - f(a)}{h}$ provided the limit exists and then it is written as $f'(a)$, or $\left(\dfrac{dy}{dx}\right)_{x=a}$. We sometimes write the definition in the form

$$f'(a) = \lim_{x \to a} \frac{f(x) - f(a)}{x - a}.$$

NOTE. $f'(a)$ can also be evaluated by first finding out $\dfrac{dy}{dx}$ and then putting in it, $x = a$.

Notation. $\dfrac{dy}{dx}$ is also denoted by y' or y_1

or dy or $f'(x)$ in case $y = f(x)$.

REMARK: We define right and left derivatives of $f(x)$ at $x = a$ by

$$Rf'(a) = \lim_{x \to a+} \frac{f(x) - f(a)}{x - a} \quad \text{and} \quad Lf'(a) = \lim_{x \to a-} \frac{f(x) - f(a)}{x - a}$$

It is clear that $f'(a)$ exists iff $Rf'(a)$ and $Lf'(a)$ exist and are equal.

Example 12. *Find* $\frac{dy}{dx}$ *and* $\left(\frac{dy}{dx}\right)_{x=3}$ *for* $y = x^3$.

Solution. We have $y = x^3$

Let δx be the change in x and let the corresponding change in y be δy

Then $\quad y + \delta y = (x + \delta x)^3$

$$\Rightarrow \quad \delta y = (x+\delta x)^3 - y = (x+\delta x)^3 - x^3$$

$$= 3x^2(\delta x) + 3x(\delta x)^2 + (dx)^3$$

$$\Rightarrow \quad \frac{\delta y}{\delta x} = 3x^2 + 3x(\delta x) + (\delta x)^2$$

Consequently $\quad \frac{dy}{dx} = \lim_{\delta x \to 0} \frac{\delta y}{\delta x} = 3x^2.$

Also $\left(\frac{dy}{dx}\right)_{x=3} = 3 \,.\, 3^2 = 27.$

Example 13. *Show that for* $y = |x|$, $\frac{dy}{dx}$ *does not exist at* $x = 0$.

Solution. Let $f(x) = |x|$

then $\quad f(x) = x \quad$ if $x \geq 0$

$\quad = -x \quad$ if $x < 0$

Now $\quad Rf'(0) = \lim_{x \to 0+} \frac{f(x) - f(0)}{x - 0} = \lim_{x \to 0} \frac{x - 0}{x - 0} = 1$

$$Lf'(0) = \lim_{x \to 0-} \frac{f(x) - f(0)}{x - 0} = \lim_{x \to 0} \frac{(-x) - 0}{x - 0} = -1$$

thus $\quad Rf'(0) \neq Lf'(0).$

$\Rightarrow \quad f(x)$ is not differentiable at $x = 0$.

REMARKS: 1. A function $f(x)$ is said to be *derivable* or *differentiable* at $x = a$ if its derivative exists at $x = a$.

2. A differentiable function is necessarily continuous.

Proof. Let $f(x)$ be differentiable at $x = a$

$\Rightarrow \quad f'(a) = \lim_{x \to a} \frac{f(x) - f(a)}{x - a}$ exists

Now $f(x) - f(a) = \frac{f(x) - f(a)}{x - a} \times (x - a), \; (x \neq a)$

$$\Rightarrow \quad \lim [f(x) - f(a)] = \lim_{x \to a} \frac{f(x) - f(a)}{x - a} \times \lim_{x \to a} (x - a) = f'(a) \times 0 = 0$$

$\Rightarrow \quad \lim_{x \to a} f(x) = f(a) \quad \Rightarrow \quad f(x)$ is continuous at $x = a$

3. Converse of the statement in Remark 2 is *not true* in general.

We have seen in Example 9 that $|x|$ is continuous at $x = 0$, whereas in Example 13 we have proved that it is not differentiable at $x = 0$.

Example 14. *Show that* $f(x) = x^2 \sin \frac{1}{x}, \; x \neq 0$

$$= 0, \qquad x = 0$$

is differentiable at $x = 0$.

Solution. $$\lim_{h \to 0} \frac{f(h) - f(0)}{h} = \lim_{h \to 0} \frac{\left(h^2 \sin \frac{1}{h} - 0\right)}{h}$$

$$= \lim_{h \to 0} \left(h \sin \frac{1}{h}\right)$$

Now $\left|\sin \frac{1}{h}\right| < 1$ and so $\left|h \sin \frac{1}{h}\right| < |h|$

$$\Rightarrow \lim_{h \to 0} \left|h \sin \frac{1}{h}\right| \leq \lim_{h \to 0} |h| = 0$$

Hence $\lim_{h \to 0} \frac{f(h) - f(0)}{h} = 0.$

i.e. $f(x)$ is differentiable at $x = 0$

and $f'(0) = 0$.

6. ALGEBRA OF DIFFERENTIABLE FUNCTIONS

We now prove the following results for two differentiable functions $f(x)$ and $g(x)$

(1) $\frac{d}{dx}[f(x) \pm g(x)] = f'(x) + g'(x)$

(2) $\frac{d}{dx}[f(x) \cdot g(x)] = f'(x)\, g(x) + f(x)\, g'(x)$

(3) $\frac{d}{dx}\left[\frac{f(x)}{g(x)}\right] = \frac{f'(x)\, g(x) - f(x)\, g'(x)}{[g(x)]^2}$

(4) $\frac{d}{dx}[cf(x)] = cf'(x)$ where c is a constant

where, of course, by $f'(x)$ we mean $\frac{d}{dx} f(x)$.

Proof. (1) $\frac{d}{dx}[f(x) + g(x)]$

$$= \lim_{\delta x \to 0} \frac{[f(x+\delta x) + g(x+\delta x)] - [f(x) + g(x)]}{\delta x}$$

$$= \lim_{\delta x \to 0} \left[\frac{f(x+\delta x) - f(x)}{\delta x} + \frac{g(x+\delta x) - g(x)}{\delta x} \right]$$

$$= \lim_{\delta x \to 0} \frac{f(x+\delta x) - f(x)}{\delta x} + \lim_{\delta x \to 0} \frac{g(x+\delta x) - g(x)}{\delta x}$$

$$= f'(x) + g'(x).$$

Similarly it can be shown that

$$\frac{d}{dx}[f(x) - g(x)] = f'(x) - g'(x).$$

Thus we have the following rule:

The derivative of sum (or difference) of two functions is equal to sum (or difference) of their derivatives.

(2) $\frac{d}{dx}[f(x)\, g(x)]$

$$= \lim_{\delta x \to 0} \frac{f(x+\delta x)\, g(x+\delta x) - f(x)\, g(x)}{\delta x}$$

$$= \lim_{\delta x \to 0} \frac{g(x+\delta x)[f(x+\delta x) - f(x)] + f(x)[g(x+\delta x) - g(x)]}{\delta x}$$

$$= \lim_{\delta x \to 0} \left\{ g(x+\delta x). \left[\frac{f(x+\delta x) - f(x)}{\delta x} \right] + f(x) \left[\frac{g(x+\delta x) - g(x)}{\delta x} \right] \right\}$$

$$= [\lim_{\delta x \to 0} g(x+\delta x)] \lim_{\delta x \to 0} \left[\frac{f(x+\delta x) - f(x)}{\delta x} \right]$$

$$+ [\lim_{\delta x \to 0} f(x)] [\lim_{\delta x \to 0} \frac{g(x+\delta x) - g(x)}{\delta x}]$$

$$= g(x) f'(x) + f(x) g'(x).$$

Thus we have the following rule for the derivative of a product of two functions.

The derivative of a product of two functions = (the derivative of first fuction × second function) + (first function × derivative of second functions).

(3) $\frac{d}{dx}\left[\frac{f(x)}{g(x)}\right]$

$$= \lim_{\delta x \to 0} \frac{\frac{f(x+\delta x)}{g(x+\delta x)} - \frac{f(x)}{g(x)}}{\delta x}$$

$$= \lim_{\delta x \to 0} \frac{f(x+\delta x)\, g(x) - f(x)\, g(x+\delta x)}{\delta x . g\,(x+\delta x)\, g(x)}$$

$$= \lim_{\delta x \to 0} \frac{g(x)[f(x+\delta x) - f(x)] - f(x)[g(x+\delta x) - g(x)]}{\delta x . g(x+\delta x) g(x)}$$

$$= [\lim_{\delta_x \to 0} \frac{1}{g(x+\delta x)} \cdot \frac{1}{g(x)}] \left\{ \lim_{\delta x \to 0} \frac{g(x)[f(x+\delta x) - f(x)]}{\delta x} - \lim_{\delta x \to 0} \frac{f(x)[g(x+\delta x) - g(x)]}{\delta x} \right\}$$

$$= \frac{1}{[g(x)]^2} \cdot [g(x) f'(x) - f(x) g'(x)]$$

$$= \frac{f'(x) g(x) - f(x) g'(x)}{[g(x)]^2}.$$

The corresponding rule is stated as under:

The derivative of quotient of two functons

$$= \frac{\text{(Derivative of Numerator} \times \text{Denominator)} - \text{(Numerator} \times \text{Derivative of Denominator)}}{\text{(Denominator)}^2}$$

(4) $\frac{d}{dx}[cf(x)] = \lim_{\delta x \to 0} \frac{cf(x+\delta x) - cf(x)}{\delta x}$

$$= c \lim_{\delta x \to 0} \left[\frac{f(x+\delta x) - f(x)}{\delta x}\right] = cf'(x).$$

So the derivative of a constant function is equal to the constant × derivative of the function.

7. DIFFERENTIAL CO-EFFICIENTS OF STANDARD FUNCTIONS

I. $\frac{d}{dx}(x^n) = nx^{n-1}$.

Proof. Let $y = x^n$

Then $(y + \delta y) = (x + \delta x)^n$

$$\Rightarrow \quad \delta y = (y + \delta y) - y = (x + \delta x)^n - x^n$$

$$= x^n\left[\left(1+\frac{\delta x}{x}\right)^n - 1\right]$$

$$= x^n\left[1+n\left(\frac{\delta x}{x}\right)+\frac{n(n-1)}{2!}\left(\frac{\delta x}{x}\right)^2+\ldots-1\right]$$

$$= nx^{n-1}(\delta x)+\frac{n(n-1)}{2!}x^{n-2}(\delta x)^2+\ldots$$

$$\frac{\delta y}{\delta x} = nx^{n-1} + \text{terms containing powers of } \delta x$$

$$\Rightarrow \lim_{\delta x \to 0}\frac{\delta y}{\delta x} = nx^{n-1}$$

Hence $\frac{dy}{dx} = nx^{n-1}$.

II. (i) $\frac{d}{dx}(a^x) = a^x \log_e a$

(ii) $\frac{d}{dx}(e^x) = e^x$.

Proof. Let $y = a^x$

then $y + \delta y = a^{x+\delta x}$

$$\Rightarrow \quad \delta y = a^{x+\delta x} - a^x = a^x(a^{\delta x} - 1)$$

$$\Rightarrow \quad \frac{\delta y}{\delta x} = \frac{a^x(a^{\delta x}-1)}{\delta x}$$

$$\Rightarrow \quad \frac{dy}{dx} = \lim_{\delta x \to 0}\frac{\delta y}{\delta x} = a^x \lim_{\delta x \to 0}\left(\frac{a^{\delta x}-1}{\delta x}\right)$$

$$= a^x \lim_{\delta x \to 0}\frac{\left[1+\delta x(\log a)+\frac{(\delta x)^2(\log a)^2}{2}+\ldots-1\right]}{\delta x}$$

$$= a^x \lim_{\delta x \to 0} [\log a + \text{terms containing } \delta x]$$

$$= a^x \log a = a^x \log_e a$$

proving the first part.

Since $\log_e e = 1$, it follows from result (*i*) that $\frac{d}{dx} e^x = e^x$.

III. $\mathbf{\frac{d}{dx} \log_e x = \frac{1}{x}}$.

Let $\quad y = \log x$

$\Rightarrow \quad y + \delta y = \log (x + \delta x)$

$$\Rightarrow \quad \delta y = \log (x + \delta x) - \log x = \log\left(\frac{x + \delta x}{x}\right)$$

$$\Rightarrow \frac{\delta y}{\delta x} = \frac{\log\left(1 + \frac{\delta x}{x}\right)}{\delta x}$$

$$= \frac{1}{x} \cdot \frac{x}{\delta x} \log\left(1 + \frac{\delta x}{x}\right) = \frac{1}{x} \log\left(1 + \frac{\delta x}{x}\right)^{x/\delta x}$$

$$\Rightarrow \lim_{\delta x \to 0} \frac{\delta y}{\delta x} = \frac{1}{x} \lim_{\delta x \to 0} \log_e \left(1 + \frac{\delta x}{x}\right)^{x/\delta x}$$

$$= \frac{1}{x} \log_e e = \frac{1}{x} \text{ as } \lim_{n \to \infty} \left(1 + \frac{1}{n}\right)^n = e \text{ and } \log_e e = 1$$

Hence $\quad \frac{dy}{dx} = \frac{1}{x}$.

IV. $\mathbf{\frac{d}{dx} (\sin x) = (\cos x)}$

Proof. Now $y = \sin x \Rightarrow y + \delta y = \sin (x + \delta x)$

$$\Rightarrow \quad \delta y = \sin (x + \delta x) - \sin x = 2 \cos\left(x + \frac{\delta x}{2}\right) \sin \frac{\delta x}{2}$$

$$\Rightarrow \quad \frac{\delta y}{\delta x} = \frac{2 \cos\left[x + \frac{\delta x}{2}\right] \sin \frac{\delta x}{2}}{\delta x} = \cos\left(x + \frac{\delta x}{2}\right) \cdot \left(\frac{\sin \frac{\delta x}{2}}{\frac{\delta x}{2}}\right)$$

$$\Rightarrow \lim_{\delta x \to 0} \frac{\delta y}{\delta x} = \left[\lim_{\delta x \to 0} \cos\left(x + \frac{\delta x}{2}\right)\right]\left\{\lim_{\delta_x \to 0} \frac{\sin \frac{\delta x}{2}}{\frac{\delta x}{2}}\right\}$$

$$= [\cos x]\left\{\lim_{\frac{\delta x}{2} \to 0} \frac{\sin \frac{\delta x}{2}}{\frac{\delta x}{2}}\right\} = (\cos x)(1) = \cos x$$

$$\Rightarrow \quad \frac{dy}{dx} = \cos x.$$

V. $\frac{d}{dx}(\cos x) = -\sin x.$ [The proof is similar to that of (IV).]

REMARKS:

1. The technique employed in the proofs of (1) to (IV) above is known an "ab initio" technique. Since we have utilized (apart from simple formulas of Algebra and Trigonometry) definition of differential coefficient only. We have no-where used the algebra of differentiable functions.
2. In (VI) to (XII) we shall utilize the algebra of differentiable functions.

VI. $\frac{d}{dx}(c) = 0,$ **c is a constant.**

Proof. Let $\quad y = c = cx^0.$

Then $\quad \frac{dy}{dx} = c\left(\frac{dx^0}{dx}\right) = c(0.x^{0-1}) = 0.$

VII. $\frac{d}{dx}(\tan x) = \sec^2 x.$

Proof. Let $\quad y = \tan x = \frac{\sin x}{\cos x}$

$$\frac{dy}{dx} = \frac{\frac{d}{dx}(\sin x)\cos x - \sin x \frac{d}{dx}(\cos x)}{(\cos x)^2}$$

$$= \frac{(\cos x)(\cos x) - \sin x(-\sin x)}{(\cos x)^2}$$

$$= \frac{\cos^2 x + \sin^2 x}{\cos^2 x} = \frac{1}{\cos^2 x} = \sec^2 x.$$

VIII. $\mathbf{\frac{d}{dx}(sec\ x) = sec\ x\ tan\ x.}$

Proof. Let $y = \sec x = \dfrac{1}{\cos x}$

Then $$\frac{dy}{dx} = \frac{\frac{d}{dx}(1)\cos x - (1)\frac{d}{dx}(\cos x)}{(\cos x)^2}$$

$$= \frac{(0)(\cos x) - (-\sin x)}{\cos^2 x}$$

$$= \frac{\sin x}{\cos^2 x} = \frac{\sin x}{\cos x}\cdot\frac{1}{\cos x} = \tan x \sec x.$$

Before we proceed further, we introduce hyperbolic functions.

We define hyperbolic sine of x as $\dfrac{e^x - e^{-x}}{2}$ and write it as $\sinh x = \dfrac{e^x - e^{-z}}{2}$.

Hyperbolic cosine of x is defined to be $\dfrac{e^x + e^{-x}}{2}$ and is denoted by $\cosh x$. It can be easily verified that

$$\cosh^2 x - \sinh^2 x = 1$$

Since $(\cosh \theta, \sinh \theta)$ satisfies the equation $x^2 - y^2 = 1$ of a hyperbola, these functions are called hyperbolic functions.

In analogy with circular functions (*i.e.*, $\sin x$, $\cos x$ etc.) we define $\tanh x$, $\coth x$, $\text{sech } x$ and $\text{cosech } x$.

Thus by definition, $\tanh x = \dfrac{\sinh x}{\cosh x}$, $\coth x = \dfrac{1}{\tanh x}$,

$\text{sech } x = \dfrac{1}{\cosh x}$ and $\text{cosech } x = \dfrac{1}{\sinh x}$.

IX. $\mathbf{\frac{d}{dx}(sinh\ x) = cosh\ x.}$

Proof. Before proving this result, we remark that

$\dfrac{d}{dx}(e^{-x}) = -e^{-x}$, because

$e^{-x} = (e^{-1})^x$

$$\Rightarrow \quad \frac{d(e^{-x})}{dx} = (e^{-1})^x \log_e (e^{-1}) = e^{-x}(-1) = -e^{-x}$$

Now let $y = \sinh x = \frac{1}{2}(e^x - e^{-x})$

Then $$\frac{dy}{dx} = \frac{1}{2}\left(\frac{d}{dx}(e^x) - \frac{d}{dx}(e^{-x})\right)$$

$$= \frac{1}{2}[e^x - (-e^{-x})] = \frac{1}{2}(e^x + e^{-x}) = \cosh x.$$

X. $\frac{\mathbf{d}}{\mathbf{dx}}(\mathbf{\cosh x}) = \mathbf{\sinh x}$**.**

Proof is similar to that of (IX).

XI. $\frac{d}{dx}(\tanh x) = \text{sech}^2 x.$

Proof. Let $$y = \tanh x = \frac{\sinh x}{\cosh x}$$

$$\frac{dy}{dx} = \frac{\frac{d}{dx}(\sinh x)\cosh x - \sinh x \frac{d}{dx}(\cosh x)}{(\cosh x)^2}$$

$$= \frac{(\cosh x)(\cosh x) - (\sinh x)(\sinh x)}{\cosh^2 x}$$

$$= \frac{\cosh^2 x - \sinh^2 x}{\cosh^2 x} = \frac{1}{\cosh^2 x} = \text{sech}^2 x.$$

XII. $\frac{d}{dx}(\text{sech}\, x) = -\text{sech}\, x \tanh x.$

Proof. Let $$y = \text{sech}\, x = \frac{1}{\cosh x}$$

$$\frac{dy}{dx} = \frac{\frac{d}{dx}(1)\cosh x - (1)\frac{d}{dx}(\cosh x)}{\cosh^2 x}$$

$$= \frac{(0)(\cosh x) - \sinh x}{\cosh^2 x}$$

$$= -\left(\frac{\sinh x}{\cosh x}\right)\left(\frac{1}{\cosh x}\right) = -\tanh x \ \text{sech}\, x.$$

Example 15 (*a*). *If* $y = x^2 \sin x$, *find* $\dfrac{dy}{dx}$.

Solution. This is a problem of the type $\dfrac{d}{dx}(uv)$.

So we apply formula (2) of Section 6.

$$\frac{dy}{dx} = \frac{d}{dx}(x^2)\sin x + x^2\frac{d}{dx}(\sin x)$$
$$= 2x \sin x + x^2 \cos x.$$

Example 15 (*b*). *If* $y = x^2$ *cosec x find* $\dfrac{dy}{dx}$.

Solution. We can write y as $\dfrac{x^2}{\sin x}$

Now formula (3) of Section 6 can be applied

$$y = \frac{x^2}{\sin x}$$

$$\Rightarrow \quad \frac{dy}{dx} = \frac{\frac{d}{dx}(x^2)\sin x - x^2\frac{d}{dx}(\sin x)}{\sin^2 x}$$

$$= \frac{2x \sin x - x^2 \cos x}{\sin^2 x}.$$

8. CHAIN RULE OF DIFFERENTIATION

This is the most important and widely used rule for differentiation.

The rule states that

"If y is a differentiable function of z and z is a differentiable function of x, then y is a differentiable function of x and

$$\frac{dy}{dx} = \frac{dy}{dz} \cdot \frac{dz}{dx}."$$

Proof. Let $y = F(z)$ and $z = f(x)$.

If δx is change in x and corresponding changes in y and z are δy, δz respectively, then $y + \delta y = F(z + \delta z)$ and $z + \delta z = f(x + \delta x)$.

Thus $\quad \delta y = F(z + \delta z) - F(z)$ and $\delta z = f(x + \delta x) - f(x)$

Now $\quad \dfrac{\delta y}{\delta x} = \dfrac{\delta y}{\delta z} \cdot \dfrac{\delta z}{\delta x}$

$$\Rightarrow \lim_{\delta x \to 0} \frac{\delta y}{\delta x} = \lim_{\delta x \to 0} \frac{\delta y}{\delta z} \lim_{\delta x \to 0} \frac{\delta z}{\delta x}$$

$$\Rightarrow \quad \frac{dy}{dx} = \left(\lim_{\delta z \to 0} \frac{\delta y}{\delta z} \right) \frac{dz}{dx}, \text{ since } \delta x \to 0 \text{ implies that } \delta z \to 0$$

$$= \frac{dy}{dz} \cdot \frac{dz}{dx}.$$

Corollary. If y is a differentiable function of x_1, x_1 is a differentiable function of x_2, ..., x_{n-1} is a differentiable function of x, then y is a differentiable function of x

and $$\frac{dy}{dx} = \frac{dy}{dx_1} \frac{dx_1}{dx_2} \cdots \frac{dx_{n-1}}{dx}.$$

Proof. Apply induction on n.

Example 16. *Find differential coefficient of sin log x with respect to x.*

Solution. Put $z = \log x$, then $y = \sin z$

Now $$\frac{dy}{dx} = \frac{dy}{dz} \cdot \frac{dz}{dx} = \cos z \cdot \frac{1}{x} = \frac{1}{x} \cos (\log x).$$

Example 17. *Find differential coefficient of (i) $e^{\sin x^2}$ (ii) log sin x^2 with respect to x.*

Solution. (*i*) Put $x^2 = y$, $\sin x^2 = z$ and $u = e^{\sin x^2}$

Then $u = e^z$, $z = \sin y$ and $y = x^2$

By chain rule

$$\frac{du}{dx} = \frac{du}{dz} \frac{dz}{dy} \frac{dy}{dx}$$

$$= e^z \cos y \, 2x = e^{\sin y} \cos y \, 2x = 2xe^{\sin x^2} \cos x^2.$$

(*ii*) Let $u = x^2$

$v = \sin x^2 = \sin u$

Then $y = \log \sin x^2 = \log \sin u = \log v$

So $$\frac{du}{dx} = 2x, \quad \frac{dv}{du} = \cos u \text{ and } \frac{dy}{dv} = \frac{1}{v}$$

Then $$\frac{dy}{dx} = \frac{dy}{dv} \cdot \frac{dv}{du} \cdot \frac{du}{dx} = \frac{1}{v} \cdot \cos u \cdot 2x$$

$$= \frac{1}{\sin u} \cos u \cdot 2x = 2x \cot u = 2x \cot x^2.$$

REMARK: After some practice we can use the chain rule, without actually going through the substitutions. For example

if $y = \log(\sin x^2)$ then $\frac{dy}{dx} = \frac{1}{\sin x^2}\cos x^2 \cdot 2x = 2x\cot x^2$.

Note that we have first differentiated log function according to the formula $\frac{d}{dt}(\log t) = \frac{1}{t}$. Since here we have $\log(\sin x^2)$, so the first term on differentiation is $\frac{1}{\sin x^2}$.

Now consider $\sin x^2$ and differentiate it according to the formula $\frac{d}{du}(\sin u) = \cos u$. Thus second term is $\cos x^2$.

Finally we differentiate x^2 with respect to x so the third term is $2x$.

Then we multiply all these three terms to get the answer $2x\cot x^2$. We illustrate this *quick method* by a few more examples.

Example 18. *Find* $\frac{dy}{dx}$ *when* $y = e^{(2x+3)^3}$.

Solution. Since $\frac{d(e^t)}{dt} = e^t$ and $\frac{du^3}{du} = 3u^2$

and $\frac{d(2v)}{dv} = 2$ we get

$$\frac{dy}{dx} = e^{(2x+3)^3} \cdot 3(2x+3)^2 \cdot (2.1+0) = 6(2x+3)^3 e^{(2x+3)^2}$$

Example 19. *Differentiate* $y = \log[\sin(3x^2+5)]$ *with respect to x.*

Solution. $\frac{dy}{dx} = \frac{1}{\sin(3x^2+5)}\cos(3x^2+5)\,6x = 6x\cot(3x^2+5)$.

Example 20. *Diffferentiate* $y = \tan^2(\sqrt{x}+3)$.

Solution.
$$\frac{dy}{dx} = 2\tan(\sqrt{x}+3)\cdot\sec^2(\sqrt{x}+3)\cdot\frac{1}{2\sqrt{x}}$$

$$= \frac{\tan(\sqrt{x}+3)\sec^2(\sqrt{x}+3)}{\sqrt{x}}.$$

EXERCISES

Differentiate with respect to x, the functions

1. $\cot x$, $\operatorname{cosec} x$.
2. $\coth x$, $\operatorname{cosech} x$.
3. $3x^2 - 6x + 1, (2x^2 + 5x - 7)^{5/2}$.
4. $\dfrac{x-1}{x+1}, \dfrac{ax^2+hx+g}{hx^2+bx+f}$.
5. $e^{\sin x}$, $\log^{\tan x}$, $\log \sin^2 x^3$, $\log a^x$.
6. $\sqrt{1-x^2}$, $\sin x \cos x$, $\tan x \log x$.
7. $\dfrac{(3x-4)^3(2-x)}{5x^2+1}$.
8. $\sqrt{1-3\tan^2 x}$.
9. $\sin\left(\dfrac{\pi}{4}-x\right)$.
10. $\sqrt{\cos\sqrt{x}}$.
11. $\log(\sqrt{x-a}+\sqrt{x-b})$.
12. $\sqrt{1+\log x \log \sin x}$.
13. $\sin x°$, $\tan x°$.
14. $\sin \log (1 + x^2)$.
15. $\dfrac{e^x \log x}{\sin x}$.
16. $e^{3x} \log x \sin x$.
17. $\sin x \cos x \sin 2x$.
18. $\dfrac{3x^2+6x+7}{\sqrt{x+3}}$.
19. $\dfrac{(x^2-1)\sin x}{\log x}$.
20. Prove that $\dfrac{dy}{dx}\dfrac{dx}{dy} = 1$.

ANSWERS

1. $-\operatorname{cosec}^2 x$, $-\operatorname{cosec} x \cot x$.
2. $-\operatorname{cosech}^2 x$, $-\operatorname{cosech} x \coth x$.
3. $6x - 6$, $\dfrac{5}{2}(4x+5)(2x^2+5x-7)^{3/2}$.
4. $\dfrac{2}{(x+1)^2}, \dfrac{(ab-h^2)x^2+2(af-gh)x+fh-bg}{(hx^2+bx+f)^2}$.
5. $e^{\sin x}\cos x$, $2 \operatorname{cosec} 2x$, $6x^2 \cot x^3$, $\dfrac{1}{x}\log_a e$.
6. $\dfrac{-x}{\sqrt{1-x^2}}, \cos 2x \cdot \sec^2 x \log x + \dfrac{\tan x}{x}$.
7. $\dfrac{2(11+34x+5x^2-15x^3)(3x-4)^2}{(5x^2+1)^2}$.
8. $-3\tan x \sec^2 x (1 - 3\tan^2 x)^{-1/2}$.
9. $-\cos\left(\dfrac{\pi}{4}-x\right)$.
10. $-\dfrac{1}{4\sqrt{\cos\sqrt{x}}}\left(\dfrac{\sin\sqrt{x}}{\sqrt{x}}\right)$.

11. $\dfrac{1}{2\sqrt{(x-a)(x-b)}}$.

12. $\dfrac{1}{2(1+\log\log\sin x)}\left[\cot x\log x+\dfrac{1}{x}\log\sin x\right]$.

13. $\dfrac{\pi}{180}\cos x°, \dfrac{\pi}{180}\sec^2 x°$.

14. $\dfrac{2x\cos[\log(1+x^2)]}{1+x^2}$.

15. $e^x\dfrac{(\sin x\log x+x^{-1}\sin x-\cos x)}{\sin^2 x}$.

16. $e^{3x}(3\log x\sin x+x^{-1}\sin x+\cos x\log x)$.

17. $\sin 4x$.

18. $\dfrac{15x^2+54x+43}{2(x+3)^{3/2}}$.

19. $\dfrac{[2x^2\sin x+(x^3-x)\cos x]\log x-(x^2-1)\sin x}{x(\log x)^2}$.

9. INVERSE TRIGONOMETRIC FUNCTIONS AND THEIR DERIVATIVES

Definition. If $\sin\theta = a$ then θ is defined to be $\sin^{-1} a$.

In other words θ is that angle whose sine is equal to a.

In similar manner we can define $\cos^{-1} a$, $\tan^{-1} a$, $\sec^{-1} a$, and $\text{cosec}^{-1} a$, $\sinh^{-1} a$, $\cosh^{-1} a$, $\tanh^{-1} a$ etc.

We remind the reader that $\sin^{-1} a$ is not single-valued since there are infinitely many angles whose sine is equal to a. All such angles are given by $n\pi+(-1)^n\theta$ where n is any integer.

So according to our definition of a function $\sin^{-1} a$ is not a function of a. To make it single valued we restrict θ to be between $\dfrac{-\pi}{2}$ and $\dfrac{\pi}{2}$. In this manner $\sin^{-1} a$ is single valued. Thus we shall confine to the case $\dfrac{-\pi}{2}\le\sin^{-1} a\le\dfrac{\pi}{2}$. Similarly we shall always assume that $0\le\cos^{-1} x\le\pi$ and $-\dfrac{\pi}{2}\le\tan^{-1} x\le\dfrac{\pi}{2}$.

Note, $\sin^{-1}a \neq \dfrac{1}{\sin a}$

(I) $\dfrac{d}{dx}(\sin^{-1} x) = \dfrac{1}{\sqrt{1-x^2}}$.

Proof. Let $\quad y=\sin^{-1} x$.

Then $\quad \sin y = x$

$$\Rightarrow \qquad \frac{dx}{dy} = \cos y = \sqrt{1-\sin^2 y} = \sqrt{1-x^2}$$

We take only +ve sign under radical as cos y is always positive for $-\frac{\pi}{2} \le y \le \frac{\pi}{2}$.

Now $\qquad \frac{\delta y}{\delta x} \times \frac{\delta x}{\delta y} = 1$

$$\Rightarrow \qquad \frac{dy}{dx}\frac{dx}{dy} = 1 \Rightarrow \frac{dy}{dx} = \frac{1}{\left(\frac{dx}{dy}\right)} = \frac{1}{\sqrt{1-x^2}}.$$

(II) $\frac{d}{dx}(\cos^{-1} x) = \frac{1}{\sqrt{1-x^2}}$.

Proof. Let $\qquad y = \cos^{-1} x$

Then $\qquad x = \cos y$

$$\Rightarrow \qquad \frac{dx}{dy} = -\sin y = -\sqrt{1-\cos^2 y} = -\sqrt{1-x^2}$$

Again sin y is +ve since $0 \le y \le \pi$, so $\sin y = \sqrt{1-x^2}$.
This in turn implies that

$$\frac{dy}{dx} = -\frac{1}{\sqrt{1-x^2}}.$$

(III) $\frac{d}{dx}(\tan^{-1} x) = \frac{1}{\sqrt{1+x^2}}$.

Proof. $\qquad y = \tan^{-1} x$

$$\Rightarrow \qquad x = \tan y \Rightarrow \frac{dx}{dy} = \sec^2 y = 1 + \tan^2 y = 1 + x^2.$$

So $\qquad \frac{dy}{dx} = \frac{1}{1+x^2}$.

10. PARAMETRIC DIFFERENTIATION

When x and y are separately given as functions of a single variable t (called a *parameter*) then we first evaluate $\frac{dx}{dt}$ and $\frac{dy}{dt}$ and then use chain formula $\frac{dy}{dt} = \frac{dy}{dx}\frac{dx}{dt}$, to obtain

$$\frac{dy}{dx} = \frac{dy/dt}{dx/dt}.$$

The equations $x = F(t)$ and $y = G(t)$ are called *parametric equations.*

Example 21. *Let* $x = a\left(\cot t + \log \tan \frac{t}{2}\right)$ *and* $y = a \sin t$, *find* $\frac{dy}{dx}$.

Solution.

$$\frac{dx}{dt} = a\left(-\sin t + \frac{1}{\tan t/2} \sec^2 \frac{t}{2} \cdot \frac{1}{2}\right)$$

$$= a\left(-\sin t + \frac{1}{2 \sin t/2 \cos t/2}\right)$$

$$= a\left(-\sin t + \frac{1}{\sin t}\right)$$

$$= \frac{a(1 - \sin^2 t)}{\sin t} = \frac{a \cdot \cos^2 t}{\sin t}$$

and

$$\frac{dy}{dt} = a \cos t$$

Hence

$$\frac{dy}{dx} = \frac{\frac{dy}{dt}}{\frac{dx}{dt}} = \frac{a \cos t}{(a \cos^2 t/\sin t)} = \frac{\sin t}{\cos t} = \tan\ t.$$

Example 22. *Determine* $\frac{dy}{dx}$ *where* $x = a(1 + \sin \theta)$ *and* $y = a(1 - \cos \theta)$.

Solution.

$$\frac{dx}{d\theta} = a(1 + \cos \theta) = 2a \cos^2 \frac{\theta}{2}$$

Also

$$\frac{dy}{d\theta} = a \sin \theta = 2a \sin \frac{\theta}{2} \cos \frac{\theta}{2}$$

So

$$\frac{dy}{dx} = \frac{\frac{dy}{d\theta}}{\frac{dx}{d\theta}} = \frac{\sin \theta/2}{\cos \theta/2} = \tan \frac{\theta}{2}.$$

11. LOGARITHMIC DIFFERENTIATION

Whenever we have a function which is a product or quotient of functions whose differential coefficients are known or a function in which variables occur in powers, we take help of logarithms. This makes the task of finding differential coefficients much easier than by the usual methods. The technique is illustrated below with the help of examples.

Example 23. *Prove that* $\frac{d}{dx}(x^x) = x^x(1 + \log x)$

Solution. Let $y = x^x$

Then $\log y = x \log x$

$$\Rightarrow \frac{d}{dx}(\log y) = (1) \log x + x\left(\frac{1}{x}\right) = 1 + \log x$$

$$\Rightarrow \frac{d}{dy}(\log y)\frac{dy}{dx} = 1 + \log x$$

$$\Rightarrow \frac{1}{y}\frac{dy}{dx} = 1 + \log x$$

$$\Rightarrow \frac{dy}{dx} = y(1 + \log x) = x^x(1 + \log x)$$

REMARK: Since $\log e = 1$, the above result can also be written as

$$\frac{d}{dx}(x^x) = x^x(\log ex).$$

Example 24. (i) *Differentiate* $y = x^2(x + 1)(x^3 + 3x + 1)$ *with respect to x.*

(ii) If $x^m y^n = (x + y)^{m+n}$, *prove that* $\frac{dy}{dx} = \frac{y}{x}$.

Solution. *(i)* $y = x^2(x + 1)(x^3 + 3x + 1)$

$$\Rightarrow \log y = 2 \log x + \log(x + 1) + \log(x^3 + 3x + 1)$$

$$\Rightarrow \frac{1}{y}\frac{dy}{dx} = \frac{2}{x} + \frac{1}{x+1} + \frac{3x^2 + 3}{x^3 + 3x + 1}$$

$$\Rightarrow \frac{dy}{dx} = y\left(\frac{2}{x} + \frac{1}{x+1} + \frac{3x^2 + 3}{x^3 + 3x + 1}\right)$$

$$= x^2(x + 1)(x^3 + 3x + 1)\left[\frac{2}{x} + \frac{1}{x+1} + \frac{3(x^2 + 1)}{x^3 + 3x + 1}\right]$$

(ii) $x^m y^n = (x + y)^{m+n}$

$$\Rightarrow m \log x + n \log y = (m + n) \log(x + y)$$

$$\Rightarrow \frac{m}{x} + \frac{n}{y}\frac{dy}{dx} = \left(\frac{m+n}{x+y}\right)\cdot\left(1 + \frac{dy}{dx}\right)$$

$$\Rightarrow \left(-\frac{m+n}{x+y}+\frac{n}{y}\right)\frac{dy}{dx} = \frac{m+n}{x+y}-\frac{m}{x}$$

$$\Rightarrow \left[\frac{-my-ny+nx+ny}{y(x+y)}\right]\frac{dy}{dx} = \frac{mx+nx-mx-my}{x(x+y)}$$

$$\Rightarrow \left[\frac{(-my+nx)}{y(x+y)}\right]\frac{dy}{dx} = \frac{nx-my}{x(x+y)}$$

$$\Rightarrow \frac{dy}{dx} = \frac{y}{x}.$$

Example 25. *(i) If* $x^y = e^{x-y}$, *show that*

$$\frac{dy}{dx} = \frac{log\ x}{(1+log\ x)^2}$$

(ii) Find $\frac{dy}{dx}$ *if* $y = x^{e^x}$.

Solution. *(i)* $x^y = e^{x-y}$

$$\Rightarrow y\log x = (x-y)\log e = x-y$$

$$\Rightarrow y(1+\log x) = x$$

$$\Rightarrow y = \frac{x}{1+\log x}$$

$$\Rightarrow \frac{dy}{dx} = \frac{(1)(1+\log x)-x\left(\frac{1}{x}\right)}{(1+\log x)^2}$$

$$= \frac{1+\log x-1}{(1+\log x)^2} = \frac{\log x}{(1+\log x)^2}$$

(ii) Let $y = x^{e^x}$

$$\log y = e^x \log x$$

$$\Rightarrow \frac{1}{y}\frac{dy}{dx} = e^x\log x + e^x\frac{1}{x}$$

$$\Rightarrow \frac{dy}{dx} = y\left(e^x\ \log x+\frac{e^x}{x}\right) = x^{e^x}\left(e^x\ \log x+\frac{e^x}{x}\right)$$

$$= x^{e^x}e^x\ \log x + e^x e^{x^{-1}}.$$

12. DIFFERENTIATION OF ONE FUNCTION WITH RESPECT TO ANOTHER FUNCTION AND THE SUBSTITUTION METHOD

Parametric differentiation is also applied in differentiating one function with respect to another function, x being treated as a parameter. Sometimes a proper substitution makes the solution of such problems quite easy.

Example 26. (*i*) *Differentiate x with respect to* x^3.

(*ii*) *Differentiate* $\tan^{-1}\dfrac{2x}{1-x^2}$ *with respect to x.*

Solution. (*i*) Let $y = x$ and $z = x^3$

We are to evaluate $\dfrac{dy}{dz}$

Now $\quad \dfrac{dy}{dx} = 1$ and $\dfrac{dz}{dx} = 3x^2$

So $\quad \dfrac{dy}{dz} = \dfrac{dy/dx}{dz/dx} = \dfrac{1}{3x^2}$.

(*ii*) Let $\quad y = \tan^{-1}\left(\dfrac{2x}{1-x^2}\right)$

Putting $\quad x = \tan\theta$, we see that

$$y = \tan^{-1}\left(\frac{2\tan\theta}{1-\tan^2\theta}\right)$$

$$= \tan^{-1}(\tan 2\theta) = 2\theta = 2\tan^{-1} x$$

So $\quad \dfrac{dy}{dx} = 2\dfrac{1}{1+x^2} = \dfrac{2}{1+x^2}$.

Example 27. *Differentiate sin x with respect to log x.*

Solution. Let $y = \sin x$ and $z = \log x$

then $\quad \dfrac{dy}{dx} = \cos x$ and $\dfrac{dz}{dx} = \dfrac{1}{x}$

imply that $\quad \dfrac{dy}{dz} = \dfrac{dy/dx}{dz/dx} = \dfrac{\cos x}{\frac{1}{x}} = x\cos x$.

Example 28. *Differentiate* $\tan^{-1}\left(\dfrac{\sqrt{1+x^2}-1}{x}\right)$ *with respect to* $\tan^{-1} x$.

Solution. (*i*) Let $y = \tan^{-1}\left(\dfrac{\sqrt{1+x^2}-1}{x}\right)$ and $z = \tan^{-1} x$

Then

$$\frac{dy}{dx} = \frac{1}{1+\left(\dfrac{\sqrt{1+x^2}-1}{x}\right)^2}\cdot\frac{\left(\dfrac{1}{2\sqrt{1+x^2}}\,2x\right)x-(\sqrt{1+x^2}-1)}{x^2}$$

$$= \frac{x^2}{x^2+1+x^2+1-2\sqrt{1+x^2}}\cdot\frac{x^2-(1+x^2-\sqrt{1+x^2})}{x^2\sqrt{1+x^2}}$$

$$= \frac{1}{2(1+x^2-\sqrt{1+x^2})}\,\frac{\sqrt{1+x^2}-1}{\sqrt{1+x^2}}$$

$$= \frac{1}{2\sqrt{1+x^2}\,(\sqrt{1+x^2}-1)}\,\frac{\sqrt{1+x^2}-1}{\sqrt{1+x^2}} = \frac{1}{2(1+x^2)}$$

and $\dfrac{dz}{dx} = \dfrac{1}{1+x^2}$

So $\dfrac{dy}{dz} = \dfrac{dy/dx}{dz/dx} = \dfrac{1}{2}$.

Solution. (*ii*) $z = \tan^{-1} x \Rightarrow x = \tan z$

So $\quad y = \tan^{-1}\left(\dfrac{\sqrt{1+\tan^2 z}-1}{\tan z}\right)$

$$= \tan^{-1}\left[\frac{\sec z-1}{\tan z}\right] = \tan^{-1}\left[\frac{1-\cos z}{\sin z}\right]$$

$$= \tan^{-1}\left[\frac{2\sin^2 z/2}{2\sin z/2\cos z/2}\right] = \tan^{-1}(\tan z/2) = z/2$$

So $\dfrac{dy}{dz} = \dfrac{1}{2}$.

13. DIFFERENTIATION "*ab initio*" OR BY FIRST PRINCIPLES

Earlier we discussed how to differentiate some standard functions starting from the definition. We give more examples to illustrate the techniques.

Example 29. *Differentiate* $\sqrt{\cos x}$ *with respect to x by first principles.*

Solution. Let $y = \sqrt{\cos x}$.

If δx is change in x then the corresponding change δy in y is given by

$$y + \delta y = \sqrt{\cos(x + \delta x)}$$

So $$\delta y = \sqrt{\cos(x + \delta x)} - \sqrt{\cos x}$$

or
$$\frac{\delta y}{\delta x} = \frac{\sqrt{\cos(x + \delta x)} - \sqrt{\cos x}}{\delta x}$$

$$= \frac{\cos(x + \delta x) - \cos x}{\delta x\left[\sqrt{\cos(x + \delta x)} + \sqrt{\cos x}\right]}$$

$$= \frac{2 \sin\left(\frac{-\delta x}{2}\right) \sin\left(x + \frac{\delta x}{2}\right)}{\delta x\left[\sqrt{\cos(x + \delta x)} + \sqrt{\cos x}\right]}$$

Thus
$$\frac{dy}{dx} = \lim_{\delta x \to 0} \frac{\delta y}{\delta x} = \lim_{\delta x \to 0}\left(\frac{-2 \sin \frac{\delta x}{2}}{\delta x}\right) \cdot \frac{\sin x}{\sqrt{\cos x} + \sqrt{\cos x}}$$

$$= -\frac{\sin x}{2\sqrt{\cos x}} \lim_{\delta x \to 0}\left(\frac{\sin \frac{\delta x}{2}}{\frac{\delta x}{2}}\right)$$

$$= -\frac{\sin x}{2\sqrt{\cos x}} \quad \text{as} \lim_{\delta x \to 0}\left(\frac{\sin \frac{\delta x}{2}}{\frac{\delta x}{2}}\right) = 1.$$

Example 30. *Differentiate* $e^{\sqrt{x}}$ *ab initio.*

Solution. Let $y = e^{\sqrt{x}}$ and let δx be change in x, corresponding to which δy is change in y

Then $$y + \delta y = e^{\sqrt{x + \delta x}}$$

$$\Rightarrow \qquad \delta y = e^{\sqrt{x+\delta x}} - e^{\sqrt{x}}$$

$$\Rightarrow \qquad \frac{\delta y}{\delta x} = \frac{e^{\sqrt{x}}\,(e^{\sqrt{x+\delta x}-\sqrt{x}} - 1)}{\delta x}$$

$$= e^{\sqrt{x}}\left(\frac{e^{\sqrt{x+\delta x}-\sqrt{x}} - 1}{\sqrt{x+\delta x}-\sqrt{x}}\right)\left(\frac{\sqrt{x+\partial x}-\sqrt{x}}{\delta x}\right)$$

$$= e^{\sqrt{x}}\,\frac{\left[1+(\sqrt{x+\delta x}-\sqrt{x})+\dfrac{(\sqrt{x+\delta x}-\sqrt{x})^2}{2!}+\ldots-1\right]}{\sqrt{x+\delta x}-\sqrt{x}}\left[\frac{\sqrt{x+\delta x}-\sqrt{x}}{\delta x}\right]$$

$$= e^{\sqrt{x}}\left[1+\frac{(\sqrt{x+\delta x}-\sqrt{x})}{2!}+\ldots\right]\frac{\sqrt{x}\left[\left(1+\dfrac{\delta x}{x}\right)^{1/2}-1\right]}{\delta x}$$

$$\Rightarrow \lim_{\delta x\to 0}\frac{\delta y}{\delta x} = (e^{\sqrt{x}}\sqrt{x})\lim_{\delta x\to 0}\left\{\frac{1+\dfrac{1}{2}\dfrac{\delta x}{x}+\dfrac{\frac{1}{2}\left(\frac{1}{2}-1\right)}{2!}\left(\dfrac{\delta x}{x}\right)^2+\ldots-1}{\delta x}\right\}$$

$$= (e^{\sqrt{x}}\sqrt{x})\lim_{\delta x\to 0}\left(\frac{1}{2}\frac{1}{x}-\frac{1}{8}\frac{\delta x}{x^2}+\ldots\right)$$

$$= \frac{e^{\sqrt{x}}\sqrt{x}}{2x} = \frac{1}{2}\frac{e^{\sqrt{x}}}{\sqrt{x}}.$$

Example 31. *Starting from definition find the derivative of*

tan (2x + 3).

Solution. Let $y = \tan(2x+3)$

then $\quad y+\delta y = \tan(2x+2\delta x+3)$

$$\Rightarrow \qquad \delta y = \tan(2x+2\delta x+3) - \tan(2x+3)$$

$$= \frac{\sin(2x+2\delta x+3)}{\cos(2x+2\delta x+3)} \cdot \frac{\sin(2x+3)}{\cos(2x+3)}$$

$$= \frac{\sin(2x+2\delta x+3)\cos(2x+3) - \sin(2x+3)\cos(2x+2\delta x+3)}{\cos(2x+2\delta x+3)\cos(2x+3)}$$

$$= \frac{\sin(2\delta x)}{\cos(2x+2\delta x+3)\cos(2x+3)}$$

$$\Rightarrow \quad \frac{\delta y}{\delta x} = \frac{\sin(2\delta x)}{\delta x} \cdot \frac{1}{\cos(2x+3)\cos(2x+2\delta x+3)}$$

$$\Rightarrow \quad \frac{\delta y}{\delta x} = 2\left[\lim_{\delta x \to 0} \frac{\sin(2\delta x)}{2\delta x}\right] \frac{1}{\cos^2(2x+3)}$$

$$= 2\sec^2(2x+3) \qquad \text{as } \lim_{\delta x \to 0} \frac{\sin(2\delta x)}{2\delta x} = 1.$$

EXERCISES

Differentiate with respect to x.

1. $\sec^{-1} x$, $\cot^{-1} x$, $\operatorname{cosec}^{-1} x$.
2. $\sinh^{-1} x$, $\cosh^{-1} x$, $\tanh^{-1} x$.
3. $\operatorname{sech}^{-1} x$, $\operatorname{cosech}^{-1} x$, $\coth^{-1} x$.
4. $(\sin x)^{\log x} + (\log x)^{\cos x}$.
5. $x = \tan^{-1} t$, $y = t \sin 2t$.
6. $\cos^{-1}\left(\frac{1-x^2}{1+x^2}\right)$. **[Hint.** Put $x = \tan\theta$.]
7. $y = \tan^{-1}\left[\frac{x}{1+\sqrt{1-x^2}}\right]$.
8. $y = \cos^{-1}(4x^3 - 3x)$. **[Hint.** Put $x = \cos\theta$.]
9. $x = \frac{3at}{1+t^3}$, $y = \frac{3at^2}{1+t^3}$.
10. $y = (\sin x)^x + x^{\sin x}$.
11. $y = x^{x^{x^x}}$.
12. Differentiate from first principles

    (*i*) x^2 (*ii*) $x \sin x$ (*iii*) $\log \sec x$ (*iv*) e^{x^2} (*v*) $\sin\sqrt{x}$

    (*vi*) $\log\cos x$ (*vii*) $\sec x$ (*viii*) $x^{5/2}$ (*ix*) $\tan x^2$ (*x*) $\log(3x+1)$.
13. Differentiate

    (*i*) $\tan^{-1}\frac{2x}{1-x^2}$ with respect to $\sin^{-1}\frac{2x}{1+x^2}$. **[Hint.** Put $x = \tan\theta$.]

(*ii*) $\sin^2 x$ with respect to $(\log x)^2$.

(*iii*) $\tan^{-1}\left(\dfrac{\sqrt{1+x}-\sqrt{1-x}}{\sqrt{1+x}+\sqrt{1-x}}\right)$ with respect to $\cos^{-1} x$. [**Hint.** Put $x = \cos\phi$.]

14. $y = x^{x^{x^{\cdot^{\cdot^{\infty}}}}}$. [**Hint.** $y = xy$.]

15. $y = \sqrt{x+\sqrt{x+\sqrt{x+\ldots \textit{ad inf}}}}$.

16. If $y = (1-x)^{1/2}(\sin x)\, e^x$,

prove that $\dfrac{dy}{dx} = (1-x)^{1/2}(\sin x)\, e^x \left[1+\cot x - \dfrac{1}{2}(1-x)^{-1}\right]^x$.

17. If $\sqrt{1-x^4}+\sqrt{1-y^4} = k(x^2-y^2)$,

prove that $\dfrac{dy}{dx} = \dfrac{x}{y}\dfrac{\sqrt{1-y^4}}{\sqrt{1-x^4}}$. [**Hint.** Put $x^2 = \sin\theta$, $y^2 = \sin\phi$.]

18. If $x\sqrt{1+y}+y\sqrt{1+x} = 0$, prove that

$$\frac{dy}{dx} = -\frac{1}{(1+x)^2}.$$

19. Differentiate with respect to x

(*i*) $(x+1)(x+2)(x-1)$ (*ii*) $\dfrac{x^{\sin x}}{\tan x}$.

20. Given that $\cos\dfrac{x}{2}\cos\dfrac{x}{2^2}\cos\dfrac{x}{2^3}\ldots \textit{ad inf} = \dfrac{\sin x}{2}$,

prove that $\dfrac{1}{2}\tan\dfrac{x}{2}+\dfrac{1}{2^2}\tan\dfrac{x}{2^2}+\dfrac{1}{2^3}\tan\dfrac{x}{2^3}+\ldots \textit{ad inf} = \dfrac{1}{x}-\cot x$.

ANSWERS

1. $\dfrac{1}{x\sqrt{x^2-1}},\ -\dfrac{1}{1+x^2},\ -\dfrac{1}{x\sqrt{x^2-1}}$. 2. $\dfrac{1}{\sqrt{x^2+1}},\ \dfrac{1}{\sqrt{x^2-1}},\ \dfrac{1}{1-x^2}$.

3. $-\dfrac{1}{x(1-x^2)},\ -\dfrac{1}{x(1+x^2)},\ \dfrac{1}{1-x^2}$.

4. $(\sin x)^{\log x}(x^{-1}\log\sin x + x\cos^{-1} x) + (\log x)^{\cos x}[-\sin x\log x + (x\log x)^{-1}\cos x]$.

5. $(1+t^2)(\sin 2t + 2t\cos 2t)$. 6. $\dfrac{2}{1+x^2}$.

7. $\dfrac{1}{\sqrt[2]{1-x^2}}$. 8. $-\dfrac{3}{\sqrt{1-x^2}}.\dfrac{3a}{a^2+x^2}$.

9. $\dfrac{t(2-t^3)}{(1-2t^3)}$.

10. $(\sin x)^x$ [log sin x + x cos x] + $x^{\sin x}$ [(log x)(cos x) + x^{-1} sin x].

11. $x^{x^x} \cdot x^{x \log x}\left[1+\log x+\dfrac{1}{x\log x}\right]$.

12. (*i*) $2x$ (*ii*) $\sin x + x\cos x$ (*iii*) $\tan x$ (*iv*) $2xe^{x^2}$ (*v*) $\dfrac{1}{2\sqrt{x}}\cos\sqrt{x}$

(*vi*) $-\tan x$ (*vii*) $\sec x \tan x$ (*viii*) $\dfrac{5}{2}x^{3/2}$ (*ix*) $2x\sec^2 x^2$

(*x*) $\dfrac{3}{3x+1}$.

13. (*i*) 1 (*ii*) $\dfrac{x\sin x\cos x}{\log x}$ (*iii*) $-\dfrac{1}{2}$.

14. $\dfrac{y^2}{x(1-y\log x)}$.

15. $\dfrac{1}{1-2y}$.

16. (*i*) $(x+1)(x+2)(2x-1)\left[\dfrac{1}{x+1}+\dfrac{1}{x+2}+\dfrac{2}{2x-1}\right]$.

(*ii*) $\dfrac{x^{\sin x}}{\tan x}(x^{-1}\sin x+(\cos x)\log x-2\operatorname{cosec} 2x)$.

14. SUCCESSIVE DIFFERENTIATION

Let **$y = f(x)$** then $\dfrac{dy}{dx}$ is again a function, say, **$g(x)$** of **x**.

We can find $\dfrac{dg(x)}{dx}$. This is called *second deriative* of y with respect to x and is denoted by $\dfrac{d^2y}{dx^2}$ or by y_2.

In similar fashion we can define $\dfrac{d^3y}{dx^3}, \dfrac{d^4y}{dx^4}, \ldots, \dfrac{d^ny}{dx^n}$ for any positive integer *n*.

REMARK: Sometimes $y^{(n)}$ or $D^n(y)$ are also used in place of $\dfrac{d^ny}{dx^n}$ or y_n.

The process of differentiating a function more than once is called *successive differentiation.*

Example 32. *Differentiate* $x^3 + 5x^2 - 7x + 2$ *four times.*

Solution. Let $y = x^3 + 5x^2 - 7x + 2$

then $y_1 = 3x^2 + 10x - 7$

$y_2 = 6x + 10$

$y_3 = 6$ and $y_4 = 0.$

SOME STANDARD FORMULAS FOR THE *nTH* DERIVATIVE

I. $y = (ax + b)^m$

Here $y_1 = m\,(ax + b)^{m-1} a = ma(ax + b)^{m-1}$

$y_2 = ma\,(m-1)(ax + b)^{m-2} a$

So $y_2 = m(m-1)a^2(ax + b)^{m-2}$

Thus $y_3 = m(m-1)a^2(m-2)(ax + b)^{m-3} a$

$= m(m-1)(m-2)a^3(ax - b)^{m-3}$

Proceeding in this manner, we see that

$$y_n = m(m-1)(m-2)\ldots(m-n+1)a^n(ax + b)^{m-n}$$

Aliter. The above result can also be obtained by principle of Mathematical Induction. The result has already been proved true for $n = 1$.

Suppose it is rue for $n = k$.

i.e., $y_k = m(m-1)(m-2)\ldots(m-k+1)\,a^k(ax + b)^{m-k}$

Differentiating once more with respect to x, we get

$y_{k+1} = m(m-1)(m-2)\ldots(m-k+1)\,a^k\,(m-k)(ax + b)^{m-k-1} a$

$= m(m-1)(m-2)\ldots(m-k+1)\,[m-(k+1)+1]a^{k+1}$

$(ax + b)^{m-(k+1)}$

Hence the result is true for $n = k + 1$ also. Consequently the formula holds true for all positive integral values of n.

Corollary 1. If $y = x^m$ then

$$y_n = m(m-1)\ldots(m-n+1)x^{m-n}.$$

Corollary 2. If $y = x^m$ and m is a positive integer then

$$y_m = m(m-1)\ldots(m-m+1)x^0 = m!$$

and $y_{m+1} = 0,\quad y_n = 0 \;\forall\; n > m.$

Corollary 3. If $y = (ax + b)^{-1}$ then

$y_n = (-1)(-2)\ldots(-1-n+1)\,a^n(ax + b)^{-1-n}$

$\Rightarrow$ $y_n = (-1)^n\,n!\,a^n(ax + b)^{-(n+1)}.$

II. $y = \sin(ax+b)$

Here $y_1 = a\cos(ax+b)$

$$= a\sin\left(ax+b+\frac{\pi}{2}\right) \quad \left[\text{since } \sin\left(\theta+\frac{\pi}{2}\right) = \cos\theta\right]$$

$$y_2 = a^2\cos\left(ax+b+\frac{\pi}{2}\right)$$

$$= a^2\sin\left(ax+b+\frac{\pi}{2}+\frac{\pi}{2}\right) = a^2\sin\left(ax+b+2\frac{\pi}{2}\right)$$

$$y_3 = a^3\cos\left(ax+b+\frac{2\pi}{2}\right)$$

$$= a^3\sin\left(ax+b+\frac{2\pi}{2}+\frac{\pi}{2}\right) = a^3\sin\left(ax+b+\frac{3\pi}{2}\right)$$

Proceeding in this manner, we get

$$y_n = a^n\sin\left(ax+b+\frac{n\pi}{2}\right).$$

NOTE. All the formulas discussed above can be proved by using principle of Mathematical Induction. We have illustrated the technique in alternative method of formula (I).

Corollary. For $y = \cos(ax+b)$

$$y_n = a^n\cos\left(ax+b+\frac{n\pi}{2}\right)$$

Proof. $y = \cos(ax+b) = \sin\left(ax+b+\frac{\pi}{2}\right)$

So $y_n = a^n\sin\left(ax+b+\frac{\pi}{2}+\frac{n\pi}{2}\right) = a^n\cos\left(ax+b+\frac{n\pi}{2}\right)$.

III. $y = e^{ax}$

Clearly $y_1 = ae^{ax}$

$y_2 = a^2e^{ax}$

$y_3 = a^3e^{ax}$ ... and so on, till we get

$y_n = a^ne^{ax}$.

IV. $y = \log(ax+b)$

Here $y_1 = \dfrac{a}{ax+b} = a(ax+b)^{-1}$

$$y_n = \frac{d^{n-1}}{dx^{n-1}}(y_1)$$
$$= a(-1)^{n-1}(n-1)!a^{n-1}(ax+b)^{-1-(n-1)}$$

by Cor. 3 to (I)

$$= (-1)^{n-1}(n-1)!\,a^n(ax+b)^{-n}$$
$$= \frac{(-1)^{n-1}(n-1)!a^n}{(ax+b)^n}.$$

V. $y = e^{ax}\cos(bx+c)$

In this case

$$y_1 = ae^{ax}\cos(bx+c) - be^{ax}\sin(bx+c)$$
$$= e^{ax}[\gamma\cos\varphi\cos(bx+c) - \gamma\sin\varphi\sin(bx+c)]$$

where $a = \gamma\cos\varphi$ and $b = \gamma\sin\varphi$

so $y_1 = \gamma e^{ax}\cos(bx+c+\varphi)$

Again $y_2 = \gamma[ae^{ax}\cos(bx+c+\varphi) - be^{ax}\sin(bx+c+\varphi)]$

$$= \gamma^2 e^{ax}[\cos\phi\cos(bx+c+\varphi) - \sin\varphi\sin(bx+c+\varphi)]$$
$$= \gamma^2 e^{ax}\cos(bx+c+2\varphi)$$

Proceeding in this manner, we get

$$y_n = \gamma^n e^{ax}\cos(bx+c+n\varphi)$$

where $\tan\varphi = \frac{b}{a}$ and $\gamma = (a^2+b^2)^{1/2}$

[since $a = \gamma\cos\gamma$, $b = \gamma\sin\varphi \Rightarrow \frac{b}{a} = \tan\varphi$ and $a^2+b^2 = \gamma^2$]

Corollary. For $y = e^{ax}\sin(bx+c)$

$$y_n = \gamma^n e^{ax}\sin(bx+c+n\varphi)$$

where $\varphi = \tan^{-1}\frac{b}{a}$ and $\gamma = (a^2+b^2)^{1/2}$

Proof is left as an exercise.

VI. $y = \tan^{-1}\left(\frac{x}{a}\right)$

Now $y_1 = \frac{1}{1+\frac{x^2}{a^2}} \cdot \frac{1}{a} = \frac{a}{a^2+x^2}$

$$= \frac{a}{(x+ia)(x-ia)} \quad \text{where } i = \sqrt{-1}$$

$$= \frac{1}{2i}\left[\frac{1}{x-ia} - \frac{1}{x+ia}\right]$$

$$= \frac{1}{2i}[(x-ia)^{-1} - (x+ia)^{-1}]$$

$$\Rightarrow \quad y_n = D^{n-1}(y_1)$$

$$= \frac{1}{2i}\Big[(n-1)!(-1)^{n-1}(x-ia)^{-1-(n-1)}$$

$$-(n-1)!(-1)^{n-1}(x+ia)^{-1-(n-1)}\Big]$$

$$= \frac{(-1)^{n-1}(n-1)!}{2i}[(x-ia)^{-n} - (x+ia)^{-n}]$$

Put $\quad x = \gamma\cos\theta$ and $a = \gamma\sin\theta$

then $\quad \tan\theta = \dfrac{a}{x}$ and $\gamma = \dfrac{a}{\sin\theta}$

$$\text{Thus } y_n = \frac{(-1)^{n-1}(n-1)!}{2i}[\gamma^{-n}(\cos\theta - i\sin\theta)^{-n}$$

$$-\gamma^{-n}(\cos\theta - i\sin\theta)^{-n}]$$

$$= \frac{(-1)^{n-1}(n-1)!}{2i\gamma^n}[\cos n\theta + i\sin n\theta - (\cos n\theta - i\sin n\theta)$$

[By De Moivre's theorem $(\cos\theta + i\sin\theta)^n = \cos n\theta + i\sin n\theta$ for an integer n.]

$$= \frac{(-1)^{n-1}(n-1)!\,2i\sin n\theta}{2i\gamma^n}$$

$$= \frac{(-1)^{n-1}(n-1)!\sin n\theta}{a^n/\sin n\theta}$$

$$= \frac{(-1)^{n-1}(n-1)!\sin n\theta \cdot \sin n\theta}{a^n}$$

where $\quad \theta = \tan^{-1}\left(\dfrac{a}{x}\right).$

REMARK: Since $\tan\theta = \frac{a}{x} \Rightarrow \frac{x}{a} = \cot\theta = \tan y$

we get $\theta = \frac{\pi}{2} - y$, so the above formula can also be put in the form

$$y_n = \frac{(-1)^{n-1}(n-1)!\sin n\left(\frac{\pi}{2}-y\right)\sin^n\left(\frac{\pi}{2}-y\right)}{a^n}$$

To prove De Moivre's theorem for an integer we proceed as:

For $n = 1$, $(\cos\theta + i\sin\theta)^1 = \cos\theta + i\sin\theta = \cos 1\theta + i\sin 1\theta$

For $n = 2$, $(\cos\theta + i\sin\theta)^2 = \cos^2\theta - \sin^2\theta + 2i\sin\theta\cos\theta$

$$= \cos 2\theta + i\sin 2\theta$$

Proceeding in this manner $(\cos\theta + i\sin\theta)^n = \cos n\theta + i\sin n\theta$

In case n is negative integer, put $n = -m$, $m > 0$

$$(\cos\theta + i\sin\theta)^n = \frac{1}{(\cos\theta + i\sin\theta)^m} = \frac{1}{\cos m\theta + i\sin m\theta}$$

$$= \frac{\cos m\theta - i\sin m\theta}{\cos^2 m\theta + \sin^2 m\theta} = \cos m\theta - i\sin m\theta$$

$$= \cos(-m)\theta + i\sin(-m)\theta = \cos n\theta + i\sin n\theta.$$

Notation. By $y_n(a)$ we shall mean the value of y_n at $x = a$.

Thus for example if $y = \sin 3x$

$$y_n\left(\frac{\pi}{3}\right) = \left(3^4\sin\left(3x + \frac{4\pi}{2}\right)\right) \text{ at } x = \frac{\pi}{3}$$

$$= 81\sin(3x + 2\pi) \quad \text{at} \quad x = \frac{\pi}{3}$$

$$= 81\sin 3x \quad \text{at } x = \frac{\pi}{3}$$

$$= 0.$$

15. LEIBNITZ THEOREM

If u and v are two functions of x possessing derivatives of every order, then

$$(uv)_r = u_n v + {}^nC_1 u_{n-1} v_1 + {}^nC_2 u_{n-2} v_2 + \ldots$$

This is called *Leibnitz theorem.*

Proof. For $n = 1$, LHS $= (uv)_1 = u_1 v + u v_1$ by product formula and RHS $= u_1 v + u v_1$, so the theorem is true for $n = 1$.

Let the theorem be true for $n = k$, *i.e.*,

$$(uv)_k = u_k v + {}^kC_1 u_{k-1} v_1 + {}^kC_2 u_{k-2} v_2 + \dots$$
$$+ \dots + {}^kC_r u_{k-r} v_r + {}^kC_{r+1} u_{k-r-1} v_{r+1} + \dots + \dots + uv_k$$

Differentiating with respect to x, we get

$$(uv)_{k+1} = (u_{k+1} v + u_k v_1) + {}^kC_1 (u_k v_1 + u_{k-1} v_2)$$
$$+ {}^kC_2 (u_{k-1} v_2 + u_{k-2} v_3) + \dots + \dots + {}^kC_r (u_{k-r+1} v_r + u_{k-r} v_{r+1})$$
$${}^kC_{r+1} (u_{k-r} v_{r+1} + u_{k-r-1} v_{r+2}) + \dots + (u_1 v_k + uv_{k+1})$$
$$= u_{k+1} v + ({}^kC_0 + {}^kC_1) u_k v_1 + ({}^kC_1 + {}^kC_2) u_{k-1} v_2$$
$$+ \dots + ({}^kC_r + {}^kC_{r+1}) u_{k-r} v_{r+1} + \dots + \dots + uv_{k+1}, \text{ as } {}^kC_0 = 1$$
$$= u_{k+1} v + {}^{k+1}C_1 u_k v_1 + {}^{k+1}C_2 u_{k-1} v_2 + \dots + {}^{k+1}C_{r+1} u_{k-r} v_{r+1}$$
$$+ \dots + uv_{k+1}$$

Since ${}^kC_r + {}^kC_{r+1} = {}^{k+1}C_{r+1}$ for all $r + 1 \le k$.

Hence $(uv)_{k+1} = u_{k+1} v + {}^{k+1}C_1 u_k v_1 + {}^{k+2}C_2 u_{k+1} v_2 + \dots$
$$+ \dots + {}^{k+1}C_{r+1} u_{(k+1)-(r+1)} v_{r+1} + \dots + \dots + uv_{k+1}.$$

In other words the theorem holds for $n = k + 1$.

Consequently Leibnitz theorem is true for all positive integral values of n.

Example 33. (*i*) *If* $y = \dfrac{ax + b}{cx + d}$, *show that* $2y_1 y_3 = 3y_2^2$.

(*ii*) *If* $y = \dfrac{1}{2} (\sin^{-1} x)^2$ *show that* $(1 - x_2) y_2 - xy_1 = 1$.

Solution. (*i*) $y_1 = \dfrac{ax + b}{cx + d} \Rightarrow y_1 = \dfrac{a(cx + d) - (ax + b)c}{(cx + d)^2}$

$$\Rightarrow \quad y_1 = \frac{ad - bc}{(cx + d)^2}$$

$$\Rightarrow \quad y_2 = \frac{-2c(ad - bc)}{(cx + d)^3}$$

$$\Rightarrow \quad y_3 = \frac{6c^2 (ad - bc)}{(cx + d)^4}$$

So $$2y_1 y_3 = 2\frac{ad-bc}{(cx+d)^2}\cdot\frac{6c^2(ad-bc)}{(cx+d)^4}$$

$$= \frac{12c^2(ad-bc)^2}{(cx+d)^6},$$

whereas $$3y_2^2 = 3\cdot\frac{4c^2(ad-bc)^2}{(cx+d)^6} = \frac{12c^2(ad-bc)^2}{(cx+d)^6}$$

Hence $2y_1y_3 = 3y_2^2$.

(*ii*) $$y = \frac{1}{2}(\sin^{-1}x)^2 \qquad ...(1)$$

$$y_1 = \frac{1}{2}2(\sin^{-1}x)\frac{1}{\sqrt{1-x^2}}$$

$$\sqrt{1-x^2}\,y_1 = \sin^{-1}x$$

$$(1-x^2)y_1^2 = (\sin^{-1}x)^2 = 2y \text{ by}(1)$$

Differentiate again with respect to x, to obtain

$$-2xy_1^2 + (1-x^2)2y_1y_2 = 2y_1$$

Cancelling out the common factor $2y_1$, we get

$$-xy_1 + (1-x^2)y_2 = 1 \text{ or } (1-x^2)y_2 - xy_1 = 1.$$

Example 34. *If* $y = \left(\frac{1}{x}\right)^x$, *prove that* $\frac{d^2y}{dx^2}$ *at* $x = 1$ *is equal to zero.*

Solution. $y = \left(\frac{1}{x}\right)^x \Rightarrow \log y = -x\log x$

$$\Rightarrow \frac{1}{y}\frac{dy}{dx} = -\log x - x\frac{1}{x} = -\log x - 1$$

$$\Rightarrow y_1 = \frac{dy}{dx} = -y(1+\log x)$$

Now at $x = 1$, $y = 1$ so

$$y_1 = -(1+0) = -1$$

Further $$y_2 = -y_1(1+\log x) - y\frac{1}{x}$$

So at $x = 1$, $y_2 = 1(1+0) - 1 = 0.$

Hence $y_2(1) = 0.$

Example 35. *If* $y = a\cos(\log x) + b\sin(\log x)$

prove that $x^2\dfrac{d^2y}{dx^2} + x\dfrac{dy}{dx} + y = 0.$

Hence deduce that $x^2y_{n+2} + (2n+1)xy_{n+1} + (n^2+1)y_n = 0.$

Solution. $y = a\cos(\log x) + b\sin(\log x)$

$$\Rightarrow \quad y_1 = -\frac{a\sin(\log x)}{x} + \frac{b\cos(\log x)}{x}$$

$$\Rightarrow \quad xy_1 = -a\sin(\log x) + b\cos(\log x)$$

Differentiating with respect to x, we get

$$y_1 + xy_2 = -\frac{a\cos(\log x)}{x} - \frac{b\sin(\log x)}{x}$$

or $$xy_1 + x^2y_2 = -a\cos(\log x) - b\sin(\log x) = -y$$

$$\Rightarrow \quad x^2\frac{d^2y}{dx^2} + x\frac{dy}{dx} + y = 0.$$

That proves first part.

Now differentiate n times termwise, using Leibnitz theorem for each product, and we get

$$y_{n+2}x^2 + {}^nC_1y_{n+1}(2x) + {}^nC_2y_n(2) + y_{n+1}x + {}^nC_1y_n(1) + y_n = 0$$

or $$x^2y_{n+2} + 2n \times y_{n+1} + n(n-1)y_n + x\,y_{n+1} + ny_n + y_n = 0$$

or $$x^2y_{n+2} + (2n+1)xy_{n+1} + (n^2+1)y_n = 0.$$

Example 36. If $y = \sin ax + \cos ax$ *prove that*

$$y_n = a^n[1 + (-1)^n\sin 2ax]^{1/2}$$

Solution. $$y_n = a^n\sin\left(ax + \frac{n\pi}{2}\right) + a^n\cos\left(ax + \frac{n\pi}{2}\right)$$

[By Formula II and its corollary]

$$= a^n\left\{\left[\sin\left(ax + \frac{n\pi}{2}\right) + \cos\left(ax + \frac{n\pi}{2}\right)\right]^2\right\}^{1/2}$$

$$= a^n\left[\sin^2\left(ax + \frac{n\pi}{2}\right) + \cos^2\left(ax + \frac{n\pi}{2}\right)\right.$$

$$\left. + 2\sin\left(ax + \frac{n\pi}{2}\right)\cos\left(ax + \frac{n\pi}{2}\right)\right]^{1/2}$$

$$= a^n[1 + \sin(2ax + n\pi)]^{1/2} = a^n[1 + (-1)^n\sin 2ax]^{1/2}.$$

EXERCISES

Differentiate n times with respect to x,

1. $\sin^2 x \sin 2x$, $\cos^4 x$, $\cos^2 x \sin^3 x$.

2. $e^x \log x$, $x^3 \log x$.
3. $\dfrac{x}{(x-a)(x-b)(x-c)}$.

4. $x^{n-1} \log x$.
5. $x^3 \cos x$.

6. If $y = x^2 e^x$, show that

$$y_n = \frac{n(n-1)}{2} y_2 - n(n-2)n\, y_1 + \frac{1}{2}(n-1)(n-2)\, y.$$

7. If $y = \sin(m \sin^{-1} x)$ prove that
$(1 - x^2)y_2 - xy_1 + m^2 y = 0$.
Deduce that $(1 - x^2)y_{n+2} - (2n + 1)xy_{n+1} - (n^2 - m^2)y_n = 0$.

8. If $y = \sin(\sin x)$ prove that $y_2 + y_1 \tan x + y \cos^2 x = 0$.

9. If $y_n = \dfrac{d^n}{dx^n}(x^n \log x)$ prove that $y_n = ny_{n-1} + (n-1)!$

10. Prove that $2^{n/2} \sin\dfrac{n\pi}{4} = {}^nC_1 - {}^nC_3 + {}^nC_5 \ldots$

[**Hint.** Use $\dfrac{d^n}{dx^n}(e^{ax} \sin bx) = (a^2 + b^2)^{n/2} e^{ax} \sin(bx + n\varphi)$

where $\tan\varphi = \dfrac{b}{a}$. Apply Leibnitz theorem to LHS and then compare

the two results after putting $a = b = 1$ and $x = 0$.]

11. If $y = e^{e^x}$ prove that

$$e^{-x}\frac{d^3y}{dx^3} = \frac{d^2y}{dx^2} + \frac{2dy}{dx} + y.$$

12. If $y = \dfrac{1}{x}\sin x$ show that

$$\frac{d^2y}{dx^2} + \frac{2}{x}\frac{dy}{dx} + y = 0.$$

13. If $y = e^{\sin^2 x}$ prove that

$$y_2 = \frac{y}{2}(1 + 4\cos 2x + \cos 4x).$$

14. Determine the values of constants A and B such that if $y = e^x(A\cos x + B\sin x)$ then for all values of x

$$\frac{d^2y}{dx^2} - 3\frac{dy}{dx} + 4y = e^x \sin x.$$

15. Given that $y = e^{ax} \sin x$, prove that

$$\frac{d^2y}{dx^2} - 2a\frac{dy}{dx} + (a^2+1)\,y = 0.$$

Hence or otherwise calculate

$y_1(0)$, $y_2(0)$, $y_3(0)$, $y_4(0)$, and $y_5(0)$.

16. If $\cos^{-1}\left(\frac{y}{b}\right) = \log\left(\frac{x}{n}\right)^n$

show that $x^2y_{n+2} + (2n+1)xy_{n+1} + 2n^2y_n = 0$.

17. If $y = e^m \sin^{-1} x$

show that $(1 - x^2)y_2 - xy_1 - m^2y = 0$ and deduce that

$(1 - x^2)y_{n+2} - (2n+1)xy_{n+1} - (n^2 + m^2)y_n = 0$.

ANSWERS

1. $2^{n-1}\sin\left(2x+\frac{n\pi}{2}\right) - 4^{n-1}\sin\left(4x+\frac{n\pi}{2}\right)$

$2^{n-1}\cos\left(2x+\frac{n\pi}{2}\right) + \frac{4^{n-1}}{2}\cos\left(4x+\frac{n\pi}{2}\right)$

$\frac{3}{8}\sin\left(x+\frac{n\pi}{2}\right) + \frac{2^n}{8}\sin\left(2x+\frac{n\pi}{2}\right) - \frac{3^n}{8}\sin\left(3x+\frac{n\pi}{2}\right) - \frac{4^n}{16}\sin\left(4x+\frac{\pi n}{2}\right)$.

2. $e^x\left[\frac{1}{x} - \frac{n}{x^2} + \frac{n(n-1)}{x^3} + \frac{n(n-1)(n-2)}{x^4} + \ldots + \frac{(-1)^{n-1}(n-1)!}{x^n}\right]$.

3. $(-1)^n n! \sum \frac{a}{(a-b)(a-c)(x-a)^{n+1}}$.

4. $\frac{(-1)^{n-1}(n-1)!}{x}[1 - {}^nC_1 + {}^nC_2 - {}^nC_3 + \ldots + (-1)^{n-2}\,{}^nC_{n-1}]$.

5. $[x^3 - 3n(n-1)x]\cos\left(x+\frac{n\pi}{2}\right) + \left[3nx^2 - \frac{n(n-1)(n-2)}{2}\right]\sin\left(x+\frac{n\pi}{2}\right)$.

14. $A = B = \frac{1}{2}$.

15. $1, 2a, 3a^2 - 1, 4a^3 - 4a, 5a^4 - 10a^2 + 1$.

16. PARTIAL DIFFERENTIATON

Till now we've been talking about functions of one variable. But there may be functions of more than one variable. For example

$$z = \frac{xy}{x+y},\quad u = x^2 + y^2 + z^2$$

are functions of two variables and three variables respectively. As another example demand for any good depends not only on the price of the goods, but also on the income of the individuals and on the price of related goods.

Let $z = f(x, y)$ be function of two variables x and y. x and y can take any value independently of each other. If we allot a fixed value to one variable say x, and second variable y is allowed to vary, $f(x, y)$ can be regarded as a function of single variable y. So we can talk of its derivative with respect to y, in the usual sense. We call this partial derivative of z with respect to y, and denote it by the symbol $\frac{\partial z}{\partial y}$.

Thus we have

$$\frac{\partial z}{\partial y} = \lim_{\delta y \to 0} \frac{f(x, y + \delta y) - f(x, y)}{\delta y}$$

Similarly we define partial derivative of z with respect to x, as the derivative of z, regarded as a function of x alone. Thus here y is kept constant and x is allowed to vary.

So $$\frac{\partial z}{\partial x} = \lim_{\delta x \to 0} \frac{f(x + \delta x, y) - f(x, y)}{\delta x}.$$

REMARK. $\frac{\partial z}{\partial x}$ is also denoted by z_x and

$\frac{\partial z}{\partial y}$, by z_y.

In similar manner we can define $\frac{\partial^2 z}{\partial x^2}, \frac{\partial^2 z}{\partial x \partial y}, \frac{\partial^2 z}{\partial y \partial x}, \frac{\partial^2 z}{\partial y^2}$. Thus $\frac{\partial^2 z}{\partial x^2}$ is nothing but $\frac{\partial}{\partial x}\left(\frac{\partial z}{\partial x}\right)$; $\frac{\partial^2 z}{\partial x \partial y}$ is same as $\frac{\partial}{\partial x}\left(\frac{\partial z}{\partial y}\right)$, $\frac{\partial^2 z}{\partial y \partial x} = \frac{\partial}{\partial y}\left(\frac{\partial z}{\partial x}\right)$ and $\frac{\partial^2 z}{\partial y^2} = \frac{\partial}{\partial y}\left(\frac{\partial z}{\partial y}\right)$. In this manner one can define partial derivatives of higher orders.

CAUTION. In general $\frac{\partial^2 z}{\partial x \partial y} \neq \frac{\partial^2 z}{\partial y \partial x}$, i.e., change of order of differentiation does not always yield the same answer. There are famous theorems like Young's theorem and Schwarz theorem which give sufficient conditions for two derivatives to be equal. But as far as we are concerned all the *functions that we deal with in this book are supposed to satisfy the relation* $\frac{\partial^2 z}{\partial x\, \partial y} = \frac{\partial^2 z}{\partial y\, \partial x}$.

Example 37. *Evaluate* $\frac{\partial z}{\partial x}$ *and* $\frac{\partial z}{\partial y}$ *when* $z = \frac{x^2}{x-y+1}$.

Solution.
$$z = \frac{x^2}{x-y+1}$$

$$\frac{\partial z}{x\partial} = \frac{2x(x-y+1) - x^2 \frac{\partial}{\partial x}(x-y+1)}{(x-y+1)^2}$$

$$= \frac{2x^2 - 2xy + 2x - x^2(1)}{(x-y+1)^2}$$

$$= \frac{x^2 - 2xy + 2x}{(x-y+1)^2} = \frac{x(x-2y+2)}{(x-y+1)^2}$$

Again
$$\frac{\partial z}{\partial y} = \frac{\partial}{\partial y}\left(\frac{x^2}{x-y+1}\right)$$

$$= x^2 \frac{\partial}{\partial y}[(x-y+1)^{-1}]$$

$$= x^2\left\{-(x-y+1)^{-2}\frac{\partial}{\partial y}(-y)\right\}$$

$$= -x^2(x-y+1)^{-2}(-1) = \frac{x^2}{(x-y+1)^2}.$$

Example 38. *Verify that for* $z = \log(x^2 - y^2)$

$$\frac{\partial^2 z}{\partial x \partial y} = \frac{\partial^2 z}{\partial y \partial x}.$$

Solution.
$$\frac{\partial z}{\partial x} = \frac{\partial}{\partial x}[\log(x^2 - y^2)] = \frac{2x}{x^2 - y^2}$$

$$\frac{\partial^2 z}{\partial y \partial x} = \frac{\partial}{\partial y}\left(\frac{2x}{x^2 - y^2}\right) = 2x\frac{\partial}{\partial y}[(x^2 - y^2)^{-1}]$$

$$= 2x\left\{-(x^2 - y^2)^{-2}\frac{\partial}{\partial y}(-y^2)\right\}$$

$$= +\,2x(x^2 - y^2)^{-2}(-\,2y) = \frac{+4xy}{(x^2 - y^2)^2}$$

further $$\frac{\partial z}{\partial y} = \frac{\partial}{\partial y}[\log(x^2 - y^2)] = \frac{-2y}{x^2 - y^2}$$

$$\frac{\partial^2 z}{\partial x\,\partial y} = \frac{\partial}{\partial x}\left[-\frac{2y}{x^2 - y^2}\right] = (-2y)\frac{\partial}{\partial x}[(x^2 - y^2)^{-1}]$$

$$= (-2y)\left[-(x^2 - y^2)^{-2}\frac{\partial}{\partial x}(x^2)\right] = \frac{4xy}{(x^2 - y^2)^2}.$$

Hence the result follows.

Example 39. *Show that* $\dfrac{\partial^2}{\partial x\partial y}[(x + y)e^{x+y}] = (x + y + 2)e^{x+y}$.

Solution. $$\frac{\partial}{\partial y}\{(x + y)e^{x+y}\} = \frac{\partial}{\partial y}\{e^x e^y (x + y)\}$$

$$= e^x\{e^y(x + y) + e^y\}$$

$$= e^x e^y(x + y + 1)$$

$$\frac{\partial^2}{\partial x\,\partial y}\{(x + y)e^{x+y}\} = \frac{\partial}{\partial x}\{e^x e^y(x + y + 1)\}$$

$$= e^y\frac{\partial}{\partial x}\{e^x(x + y + 1)\}$$

$$= e^y\{e^x(x + y + 1) + e^x\}$$

$$= e^x e^y(x + y + 1 + 1)$$

$$= e^{x+y}(x + y + 2)$$

$$= (x + y + 2)\,e^{x+y}.$$

Example 40. *If* $u = \log(x^2 + y^2 + z^2)$, *prove that*

$$x\frac{\partial^2 u}{\partial y\,\partial z} = y\frac{\partial^2 u}{\partial z\,\partial x} = z\frac{\partial^2 u}{\partial x\,\partial y}.$$

Solution. $u = \log(x^2 + y^2 + z^2)$

$$\Rightarrow \quad \frac{\partial u}{\partial x} = \frac{d}{d(x^2 + y^2 + z^2)}[\log(x^2 + y^2 + z^2)]\,\frac{\partial(x^2 + y^2 + z^2)}{\partial x}$$

$$= \frac{1}{x^2 + y^2 + z^2} \cdot 2x = \frac{2x}{x^2 + y^2 + z^2}$$

$$\Rightarrow \quad \frac{\partial^2 u}{\partial z \partial x} = \frac{\partial}{\partial z}\left(\frac{\partial u}{\partial x}\right)$$

$$= -\frac{2x}{(x^2 + y^2 + z^2)^2}.(2z) = \frac{-4xz}{(x^2 + y^2 + z^2)^2}$$

$$\Rightarrow \quad y\frac{\partial^2 u}{\partial z \partial x} = \frac{-4xyz}{(x^2 + y^2 + z^2)^2} \quad ...(1)$$

Again $\dfrac{\partial^2 u}{\partial x \partial y} = \dfrac{\partial^2 u}{\partial y \partial x} = \dfrac{\partial}{\partial y}\left[\dfrac{\partial u}{\partial x}\right]$

$$= -\frac{2x}{(x^2 + y^2 + z^2)^2}(2y) = \frac{-4xy}{(x^2 + y^2 + z^2)^2}$$

$$\Rightarrow \quad z\frac{\partial^2 u}{\partial x \partial y} = -\frac{4xyz}{(x^2 + y^2 + z^2)^2} \quad ...(2)$$

Similarly it can be shown that

$$x\frac{\partial^2 u}{\partial y \partial z} = -\frac{4xyz}{(x^2 + y^2 + z^2)^2} \quad ...(3)$$

(1), (2) and (3) give the required result.

Example 41. *If* $u = f(r)$ *where* $r = \sqrt{x^2 + y^2}$

prove that $\dfrac{\partial^2 u}{\partial x^2} + \dfrac{\partial^2 u}{\partial y^2} = f''(r) + \dfrac{1}{r} f'(r)$.

Solution. $r = (x^2 + y^2)^{1/2}$

$$\Rightarrow \quad \frac{\partial r}{\partial x} = \frac{1}{2}\cdot(x^2 + y^2)^{-1/2} \cdot 2x = \frac{x}{\sqrt{x^2 + y^2}} = \frac{x}{r}$$

Similarly $\dfrac{\partial r}{\partial y} = \dfrac{y}{r}$.

Now $u = f(r)$

$$\Rightarrow \quad \frac{\partial u}{\partial x} = \frac{d}{dr}(u)\frac{\partial r}{\partial x}$$

$$\Rightarrow \quad = \frac{u'x}{r} \text{ where } u' = \frac{du}{dr} = f'(r)$$

$$\Rightarrow \quad \frac{\partial^2 u}{\partial x^2} = \frac{u'}{r} + \frac{x}{r}\frac{\partial u'}{\partial x} + u'\, x \frac{\partial}{\partial x}\left(\frac{1}{r}\right)$$

$$= \frac{u'}{r} + \frac{x}{r}\frac{d}{dr}(u')\frac{\partial r}{\partial x} + xu'\frac{d}{dx}\left(\frac{1}{r}\right)\frac{\partial r}{\partial x}$$

$$= \frac{u'}{r} + \frac{x^2}{r^2}u'' - \frac{xu'}{r^2}\frac{x}{r} \text{ where } u'' = \frac{d^2 u}{dr^2} = f''(r)$$

$$= \frac{u'}{r} + \frac{x^2 u''}{r^2} - \frac{x^2}{r^3}u'.$$

In a similar manner it can be proved that

$$\frac{\partial^2 u}{\partial y^2} = \frac{u'}{r} + \frac{y^2 u''}{r^2} - \frac{y^2}{r^3}u'$$

So
$$\frac{\partial^2 u}{\partial x^2} + \frac{\partial^2 u}{\partial y^2} = \frac{2u'}{r} + \frac{u''}{r^2}(x^2 + y^2) - \frac{u'}{r^3}(x^2 + y^2)$$

$$= \frac{2u'}{r} + \frac{u''}{r^2}\cdot r^2 - \frac{u'}{r^3}\cdot r^2 = \frac{2u'}{r} + u'' - \frac{u'}{r}$$

$$= u'' + \frac{u''}{r} = f''(r) + \frac{1}{r}f'(r).$$

EXERCISES

1. Compute $\dfrac{\partial z}{\partial x}$ and $\dfrac{\partial z}{\partial y}$ for the functions

   (i) $z = (x + y)^2$ (ii) $z = \log(x + y)$

   (iii) $z = \dfrac{x}{x^2 + y^2}$ (iv) $z = e^{x^y}$

   (v) $z = e^{ax} \sin by$ (vi) $z = \log(x^2 + y^2)$.

2. If $z = \tan(y + ax) + (y - ax)^{3/2}$.

   Find the value of $\dfrac{\partial^2 z}{\partial x^2} - a^2\dfrac{\partial^2 z}{\partial y^2}$.

3. If $\theta = t^n e^{-r^2/ut}$, find the value of n which will make

   $$\frac{1}{r^2}\frac{\partial}{\partial r}\left(r^2\frac{\partial \theta}{\partial r}\right) \text{ equal to } \frac{\partial \theta}{\partial t}.$$

4. If $v = r^m$ where $r^2 = x^2 + y^2 + z^2$, show that

   $$\frac{\partial^2 v}{\partial x^2} + \frac{\partial^2 v}{\partial y^2} + \frac{\partial^2 v}{\partial z^2} = m(m + 1)\, r^{m-2}.$$

5. If $u = f(ax^2 + 2hxy + by^2)$, $v = \phi(ax^2 + 2hxy + by^2)$

prove that $\frac{\partial}{\partial y}\left(u\frac{\partial u}{\partial x}\right) = \frac{\partial}{\partial x}\left(u\frac{\partial v}{\partial y}\right)$.

6. If $u = (1 - 2xv + y^2)^{-1/2}$ prove that

$$\frac{\partial}{\partial x}\left[(1-x^2)\frac{\partial u}{\partial x}\right] + \frac{\partial}{\partial x}\left(y^2\frac{\partial u}{\partial y}\right) = 0.$$

7. If $\frac{\partial^2 v}{\partial x^2} = 2k\frac{\partial v}{\partial t}$ has a solution of the form $Ae^{-ax}\sin(wt - bv)$ prove that $a = b$

$= \left(\frac{1}{2}rwk\right)^{1/2}$.

8. If $u = \frac{1}{\sqrt{x^2 + y^2 + x^2}}$, show that

$$\frac{\partial^2 u}{\partial x^2} + \frac{\partial^2 u}{\partial y^2} + \frac{\partial^2 u}{\partial z^2} = 0.$$

9. If $z(x + y) = x^2 + y^2$, prove that

$$\left(\frac{\partial z}{\partial x} - \frac{\partial z}{\partial y}\right)^2 = 4\left(1 - \frac{\partial z}{\partial x} - \frac{\partial z}{\partial y}\right).$$

10. Find the value of $\frac{1}{a^2}\frac{\partial^2 z}{\partial x^2} + \frac{1}{b^2}\frac{\partial^2 z}{\partial y^2}$ when $a^2x^2 + b^2y^2 - c^2z^2 = 0$.

ANSWERS

1. (*i*) $2(x + y)$ (*ii*) $\frac{1}{x+y}$ (*iii*) $\frac{y^2 - x^2}{(x^2+y^2)^2}, \frac{-2xy}{(x^2+y^2)^2}$

(*iv*) $ye^{xy}x^{y-1}$, $x^y e^{xy}\log x$ (*v*) $ae^{ax}\sin by$, $be^{ax}\cos by$

(*vi*) $\frac{2x}{x^2+y^2}, \frac{2y}{x^2+y^2}$.

2. 0. 3. $n = -3/2$. 10. $\frac{1}{c^2 z}$.

17. HOMOGENEOUS FUNCTIONS

A function $f(x, y)$ is called homogeneous function of degree n in x and y if for all λ

$$f(\lambda x, \lambda y) = \lambda^n f(x, y)$$

For instance $x^3 + 3x^2y - xy^2 - y^3$ and $\frac{x^3 + y^3}{x^2 + y^2}$ are homogeneous functions of degree 3 and 1 respectively. Since it is easy to see that

$$(\lambda x)^3 + 3(\lambda x)^2(\lambda y) - \lambda x(\lambda y)^2 - (\lambda y)^3 = \lambda^3(x^3 + 3x^2y - xy^2 - y^3)$$

and
$$\frac{(\lambda x)^3 + (\lambda y)^3}{(\lambda x)^2 + (\lambda y)^2} = \lambda \frac{x^3 + y^3}{x^2 + y^2}.$$

As an example of a non-homogeneous function consider $x^2 + y$.

Then $$(\lambda x)^2 + \lambda y = \lambda^2 x^2 + \lambda y$$

Since $\lambda^2 = \lambda$ may not hold for all λ, $x^2 + y$ is not a homogeneous function of x, y.

18. EULER'S THEOREM

If $f(x, y)$ is a homogeneous function in x and y of degree n then

$$x\frac{\partial f}{\partial x} + y\frac{\partial f}{\partial y} = nf. \quad ...(1)$$

Proof. Since

$$f(\lambda x, \lambda y) = \lambda^n f(x, y) \text{ for all } \lambda,$$

$$f\left(1, \frac{y}{x}\right) = \frac{1}{x^n} f(x, y) \qquad \left[\text{Put } \lambda = \frac{1}{x}\right]$$

or $$f(x, y) = x^n f(1, y/x)$$

i.e., $$f = x^n \phi(y/x)$$

where $f(1, y/x)$, being a function of y/x above is put equal to $\varphi(y/x)$.

Now $$\frac{\partial f}{\partial x} = nx^{n-1}\varphi(y/x) + x^n \frac{\partial}{\partial x}\left(\frac{y}{x}\right)$$

$$= nx^{n-1}\varphi\left(\frac{y}{x}\right) + x^n \frac{d}{d(y/x)} \phi \left(\frac{y}{x}\right) \frac{\partial}{\partial x}\left(\frac{y}{x}\right).$$

[Note the step: If z is a function of u where u is a function of x and y then

$$\frac{\partial z}{\partial x} = \frac{dz}{du}\frac{\partial u}{\partial x} \text{ and } \frac{\partial z}{\partial y} = \frac{dz}{du}\frac{\partial u}{\partial y}\Bigg]$$

Then $$\frac{\partial f}{\partial x} = nx^{n-1}\varphi\left(\frac{y}{x}\right) + x^n \varphi'\left(\frac{y}{x}\right)\left(-\frac{y}{x^2}\right)$$

where $$\frac{d}{d(y/x)}\phi\left(\frac{y}{x}\right) = \varphi'\left(\frac{y}{x}\right)$$

$$\Rightarrow \quad \frac{\partial f}{\partial x} = nx^{n-1}\varphi\left(\frac{y}{x}\right) - yx^{n-2}\varphi'\left(\frac{y}{x}\right) \quad ...(2)$$

also
$$\frac{\partial f}{\partial y} = x^n \frac{\partial}{\partial y} \varphi\left(\frac{y}{x}\right)$$
$$= x^n \frac{d}{d(y/x)} \varphi\left(\frac{y}{x}\right) \frac{\partial}{\partial y}\left(\frac{y}{x}\right)$$
$$= x^n \varphi'\left(\frac{y}{x}\right)\frac{1}{x} = x^{n-1}\varphi'\left(\frac{y}{x}\right) \quad \text{...(3)}$$

(2) and (3) imply
$$x\frac{\partial f}{\partial x} + y\frac{\partial f}{\partial y} = nx^n\varphi\left(\frac{y}{x}\right) - yx^{n-1}\varphi'\left(\frac{y}{x}\right) + x^{n-1}y\varphi'\left(\frac{y}{x}\right)$$
$$= nx^n\varphi\left(\frac{y}{x}\right) = f \quad \text{by (1)}$$

Hence Euler's theorem is proved.

Example 42. *Verify Euler's theorem for*

(*i*) $ax^2 + 2hxy + by^2$. (*ii*) $\dfrac{x^4 + y^4}{x + y}$.

Solution. (*i*) Here $f = ax^2 + 2hxy + by^2$

$$\Rightarrow \frac{\partial f}{\partial x} = 2ax + 2hy \quad \text{and} \quad \frac{\partial f}{\partial y} = 2hx + 2by$$

So
$$x\frac{\partial f}{\partial x} + y\frac{\partial f}{\partial y} = (2ax^2 + 2hxy) + (2hxy + 2by^2)$$
$$= 2(ax^2 + 2hxy + by^2) = 2f.$$

Also $a(\lambda x)^2 + 2h(\lambda x)(\lambda y) + b(\lambda y)^2 = \lambda^2(ax^2 + 2hxy + by^2) \;\forall\; \lambda$

$\Rightarrow f$ is a homogeneous function of degree 2. Hence Euler's theorem is verified.

(*ii*) In this case $\dfrac{(\lambda x)^4 + (\lambda y)^4}{(\lambda x) + (\lambda y)} = \lambda^3 \dfrac{x^4 + y^4}{x + y}$ for all λ

implies that the given function is homogeneous of degree 3.

Let
$$f = \frac{x^4 + y^4}{x + y}$$

$$\Rightarrow \quad \frac{\partial f}{\partial x} = \frac{4x^3(x + y) - (x^4 + y^4)}{(x + y)^2} = \frac{3x^4 + 4x^3y - y^4}{(x + y)^2}.$$

As f is symmetric function of x and y (*i.e.*, if we interchange x and y, f is unaltered)

$$\frac{\partial f}{\partial y} = \frac{3y^4 + 4xy^3 - x^4}{(x+y)^2}$$

Thus $$x\frac{\partial f}{\partial x} + y\frac{\partial f}{xy} = \frac{3x^5 + 4x^4y - xy^4 + 3y^5 + 4xy^4 - x^4y}{(x+y)^2}$$

$$= \frac{3x^5 + 3x^4y + 3xy^4 + 3y^5}{(x+y)^2}$$

$$= \frac{3[x^4(x+y) + y^4(x+y)]}{(x+y)^2}$$

$$= \frac{3(x^4 + y^4)(x+y)}{(x+y)^2} = 3\left(\frac{x^4 + y^4}{x+y}\right) = 3f.$$

Hence Euler's theorem is verified.

Example 43. *If* $z = xy\,f(x/y)$, *show that*

$$x\frac{\partial z}{\partial x} + y\frac{\partial z}{\partial y} = 2z.$$

Solution. $$z = F(x, y) = xy\,f(x/y)$$

$$F(\lambda x, \lambda y) = \lambda x\,\lambda y\,f\left(\frac{\lambda x}{\lambda y}\right) = \lambda^2 xy\,f(x/y) = \lambda^2 F(x, y)$$

Hence z is a homogeneous function in x and y, of degree 2.

By Euler's theorem therefore,

$$x\frac{\partial z}{\partial x} + y\frac{\partial z}{\partial y} = 2z.$$

Example 44. *If* $u = \log\dfrac{x^2 + y^2}{x+y}$ *prove that* $x\dfrac{\partial u}{\partial x} + y\dfrac{\partial u}{\partial y} = 1.$

Solution. Here $u(x, y) = \log\dfrac{x^2 + y^2}{x+y}$

$$\Rightarrow \qquad u(\lambda x, \lambda y) = \log\left(\frac{\lambda^2x^2 + \lambda^2y^2}{\lambda x + \lambda y}\right) = \log\frac{\lambda(x^2 + y^2)}{(x+y)}.$$

This shows that $u(x, y)$ is not a homogeneous function of x and y.

However, if we put $z = e^u = \dfrac{x^2 + y^2}{x+y}$

then clearly z is a homogeneous function of x and y, of degree 1.

So by Euler's theorem

$$x\frac{\partial z}{\partial x}+y\frac{\partial z}{\partial y}=z \quad \text{or} \quad x\frac{\partial u}{\partial x}\frac{dz}{du}+y\frac{\partial u}{\partial y}\frac{dz}{du}=z$$

But $$\frac{dz}{du}=e^u=z$$

So we get $$zx\frac{\partial u}{\partial x}+zy\frac{\partial u}{\partial y}=z \quad \text{or} \quad x\frac{\partial u}{\partial x}+y\frac{\partial u}{\partial y}=1.$$

EXERCISES

1. Verify Euler's theorem for the functions

   (*i*) $z=(x^2+xy+y^2)^{-1}$ (*ii*) $z=\sin^{-1}\frac{x}{y}+\tan^{-1}\frac{y}{x}$

   (*iii*) $z=\dfrac{x^{3/4}+y^{3/4}}{x^{3/5}+y^{3/5}}$ (*iv*) $z=x^{-3}\log\frac{y}{x}$.

2. If $u=\sin^{-1}\dfrac{x^2+y^2}{x+y}$ show that $x\dfrac{\partial u}{\partial x}+y\dfrac{\partial u}{\partial y}=\tan u$.

3. If $u=\sin^{-1}\dfrac{\sqrt{x}-\sqrt{y}}{\sqrt{x}+\sqrt{y}}$ show that $x\dfrac{\partial u}{\partial x}+y\dfrac{\partial u}{\partial y}=0$.

4. Find the value of $x\dfrac{\partial u}{\partial x}+y\dfrac{\partial u}{\partial y}$ where $u=f(y/x)$.

5. If $u=\tan^{-1}\dfrac{x^3+y^3}{x-y}$, prove that $x\dfrac{\partial u}{\partial x}+y\dfrac{\partial u}{\partial y}=\sin 2u$.

6. Let $z=f(x+y)+(x+y)\varphi(y/x)$

   Show that $x\left(\dfrac{\partial^2 z}{\partial x^2}-\dfrac{\partial^2 z}{\partial y\partial x}\right)=y\left(\dfrac{\partial^2 z}{\partial y^2}-\dfrac{\partial^2 z}{\partial x\partial y}\right)$.

7. Prove that $z=xf(y/x)+g(y/x)$

   satisfies the relation $x^2\dfrac{\partial^2 z}{\partial x^2}+2xy\dfrac{\partial^2 z}{\partial x\partial y}+y^2\dfrac{\partial^2 z}{\partial y^2}=0$.

8. If u is a homogeneous function of degree n in x and y, prove that

   $$x^2\frac{\partial^2 z}{\partial x^2}+2xy\frac{\partial^2 z}{\partial x\partial y}+y^2\frac{\partial^2 z}{\partial y^2}=n(n-1)z.$$

9. If $u = \tan^{-1}\dfrac{x^3 + y^3}{x + y}$ find the value of $x^2\dfrac{\partial^2 u}{\partial x^2} + 2xy\dfrac{\partial^2 u}{\partial x\,\partial y} + y^2\dfrac{\partial^2 u}{\partial y^2}$.

10. If $u = \sin^{-1}\dfrac{x + y}{\sqrt{x} + \sqrt{y}}$, prove that

$$x^2\frac{\partial^2 u}{\partial x^2} + 2xy\frac{\partial^2 u}{\partial x\,\partial y} + y^2\frac{\partial^2 u}{\partial y^2} = -\frac{\sin u \cos u^2}{4\cos^2 u}.$$

ANSWERS

4. 0.
9. $(1 - 4\sin^2 u)\sin^2 u$.

CHAPTER 26

APPLICATIONS OF DIFFERENTIATION

SECTION A
TANGENTS AND NORMALS

1. GEOMETRICAL INTERPRETATION OF $\frac{dy}{dx}$

We recall that the tangent at any point P of a curve is the limiting position of a secant (*i.e.* a line intersecting the curve at two points) through P such that other point of intersection approaches P. We shall show that $\frac{dy}{dx}$ at any point of a curve is the slope of the tangent there at.

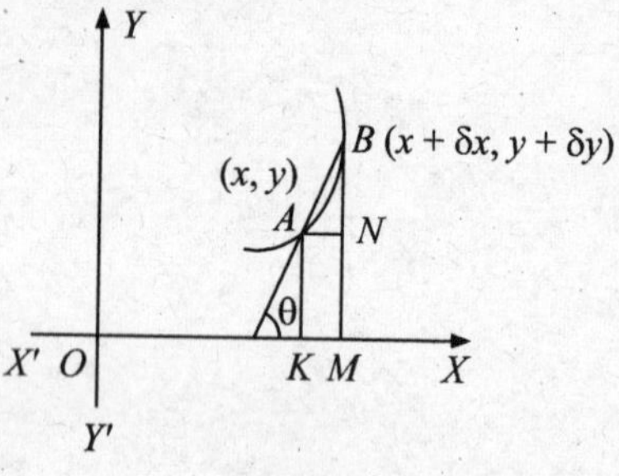

Fig. 1

Let A, B be two points on a plane curve $y = f(x)$ with co-ordinates (x, y) and $(x + \delta x, y + \delta y)$ respectively.

Let θ be the angle that secant AB makes with the +ve direction of x-axis.

As $\delta x \to 0$ and $\delta y \to 0$, the point B approaches A and conversely if $B \to A$ then $\delta x \to 0$ $\delta y \to 0$. So in limiting position, secant AB coincides with the tangent to $y = f(x)$ at A.

If ψ is the angle that tangent at A makes with +ve direction of x-axis, then

$$\lim_{\substack{\delta x \to 0 \\ \delta y \to 0}} \theta = \psi$$

$\Rightarrow$ $$\lim_{\delta x \to 0} \tan \theta = \tan \psi \qquad \text{[Note that } \delta x \to 0 \Rightarrow \delta y \to 0\text{]}$$

But $\tan\theta = \dfrac{BN}{AN}$ where AN is perpendicular from A on BM, (BM being perpendicular from B on x-axis).

Let AK be perpendicular from A to x-axis, then

$$BN = BM - NM = BM - AK = (y + \delta y) - y = \delta y$$

Also $$AN = KM = OM - OK = (x + dx) - x = dx.$$

Thus $$\tan\theta = \frac{\delta y}{\delta x}$$

and so $$\tan\psi = \lim_{\delta x \to 0} \frac{\delta y}{\delta x} = \frac{dy}{dx}.$$

Hence our assertion follows.

2. TANGENT AND NORMAL

Let $P(x', y')$ be any point on a curve $y = f(x)$

Equation of any line through (x', y') is

$$y - y' = m(x - x')$$

In case this line is tangent at P, its slope must be equal to the value of $\dfrac{dy}{dx}$ at (x', y')

Let us denote the value of $\dfrac{dy}{dx}$ at (x', y') by $\left(\dfrac{dy}{dx}\right)'$

Thus $$m = \left(\frac{dy}{dx}\right)'.$$

Hence equation of tangent at (x', y') of $y = f(x)$ is given by

$$y - y' = \left(\frac{dy}{dx}\right)'(x - x')$$

REMARK: Sometimes this formula is written as

$$Y - y = \left(\frac{dy}{dx}\right)(X - x)$$

where now X and Y are current co-ordinates and (x, y) is the given point (*i.e.*, the point of contact).

A normal at a point P of a plane curve $y = f(x)$ is a line through P in the plane of curve, perpendicular to the tangent there at.

So if PT is tangent to a curve $y = f(x)$ at a point P and if PN is perpendicular to PT then PN is normal to the curve at P.

Equation of normal at $P(x', y')$ is therefore

$$y - y' = -\frac{1}{\left(\frac{dy}{dx}\right)'}(x - x')$$

or $$(y - y')\left(\frac{dy}{dx}\right)' + (x - x') = 0$$

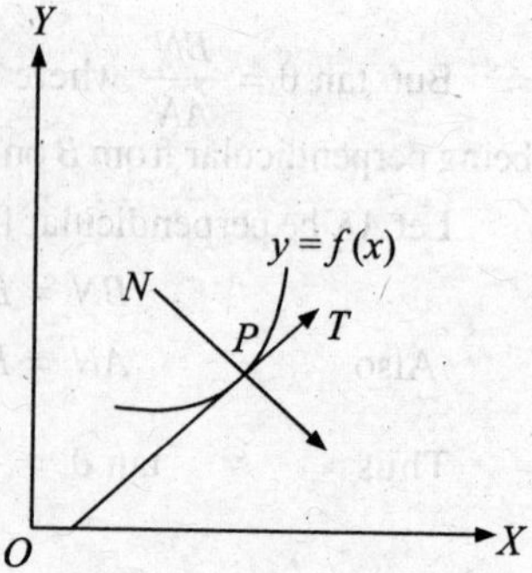

Fig. 2

REMARK: As, in the case of tangent, if we take X and Y to be current co-ordinates and P as the point (x, y) the equation of normal at P can be written as

or $$(Y - y)\left(\frac{dy}{dx}\right) + (X - x) = 0$$

Example 1. *Find the equation of tangent at (x', y') on the ellipse*

$$\frac{x^2}{a^2} + \frac{y^2}{b^2} = 1.$$

Solution. $$\frac{x^2}{a^2} + \frac{y^2}{b^2} = 1 \Rightarrow \frac{2x}{a^2} + \frac{2y}{b^2} \cdot \frac{dy}{dx} = 0$$

$$\Rightarrow \quad \frac{dy}{dx} = -\frac{b^2 x}{a^2 y}$$

$$\Rightarrow \quad \left(\frac{dy}{dx}\right)' = -\frac{b^2 x'}{a^2 y'}$$

The equation of tangent at (x', y') is therefore

$$y - y' = -\left(\frac{dy}{dx}\right)' \cdot (x - x')$$

or $$y - y' = -\frac{b^2 x'}{a^2 y'}(x - x')$$

$$\Rightarrow \quad a^2 yy' - a^2 y'^2 = -b^2 xx' + b^2 x'^2$$

$$\Rightarrow \quad b^2 xx' + a^2 yy' = b^2 x'^2 + a^2 y'^2$$

$$\Rightarrow \quad \frac{xx'}{a^2} + \frac{yy'}{b^2} = \frac{x'^2}{a^2} + \frac{y'^2}{b^2}$$

$= 1$ since (x', y') lies on the ellipse.

Example 2. *Find the equation of normal at a point (x', y') on the curve $y = a \log \sin x$.*

Solution. Here $\dfrac{dy}{dx} = a\dfrac{1}{\sin x}\cos x = a\cot x$

$$\Rightarrow \quad \left(\frac{dy}{dx}\right)' = a\cot x'$$

So the normal has equation

$$(y - y')\, a\cot x' + (x - x') = 0$$

i.e., $$a(y - y')\cos x' + (x - x')\sin x' = 0.$$

Example 3. *Find the equation of tangent at a point (2, 2) on the curve $y^2 = 2x$.*

Solution. Differentiating $y^2 = 2x$ with respect to x, we get

$$2y\frac{dy}{dx} = 2$$

$$\Rightarrow \quad \frac{dy}{dx} = \frac{1}{y}$$

So $\dfrac{dy}{dx}$ at the point (2, 2) is equal to $\dfrac{1}{2}$.

i.e., $$\left(\frac{dy}{dx}\right)' = \frac{1}{2}$$

Hence equation of tangent to $y^2 = 2x$ at (2, 2) is

$$y - y' = \left(\frac{dy}{dx}\right)'(x - x')$$

i.e., $$y - 2 = \frac{1}{2}(x - 2)$$

or $$2y - 4 = x - 2$$

$$\Rightarrow \quad x - 2y + 2 = 0.$$

Example 4. *Find the equation of normal at a point $\left(3, \dfrac{4}{3}\right)$ on $xy = 4$.*

Solution. Differentiating $xy = 4$ with respect to x, we get

$$y + x\frac{dy}{dx} = 0$$

$$\Rightarrow \quad \frac{dy}{dx} = -\frac{y}{x}$$

So $\dfrac{dy}{dx}$ at $\left(3, \dfrac{4}{3}\right)$ is equal to $= \dfrac{-\frac{4}{3}}{3} = -\dfrac{4}{9}$

Hence equation of normal at $\left(3, \dfrac{4}{3}\right)$ is

$$\left(y - \frac{4}{3}\right)\left(-\frac{4}{9}\right) + (x-3) = 0$$

or $$\left(-4y + \frac{16}{3}\right) + 9(x-3) = 0$$

or $$-12y + 16 + 27x - 81 = 0$$

or $$27x - 12y - 65 = 0.$$

3. SUBTANGENT AND SUBNORMAL

Let *PT* and *PN* respectively be the tangent and the normal at a point *P* of a curve $y = f(x)$.

PM is perpendicular from *P* on *x*-axis. Let the tangent and normal at *P* meet *x*-axis at *K* and *L* respectively.

Length *PK* is called, the *length of tangent* at *P* and length *PL* is called the *length of normal* at *P*.

Further *KM i.e.*, the projection of *KP* on *x*-axis is called subtangent at *P* and *LM*, the projection of *PL* on *x*-axis is called the *subnormal* at *P*.

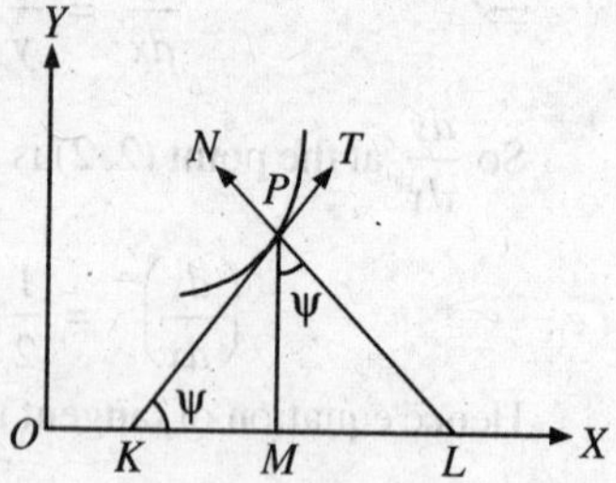

Fig. 3

Suppose that (x', y') are the co-ordinates of *P* then if ψ is the angle *TKL*, $\left(\dfrac{dy}{dx}\right)' = \tan\psi$

$$\angle MPL = \frac{\pi}{2} - \angle KAM = \frac{\pi}{2} - \left(\frac{\pi}{2} - \psi\right) = \psi$$

So subtangent at $P = KM = PM\dfrac{KM}{PM} = y' \cot\psi$

$$= y' \frac{1}{\left(\frac{dy}{dx}\right)'} = \frac{y'}{\left(\frac{dy}{dx}\right)'}$$

whereas subnormal at $P = LM = PM \cdot \dfrac{LM}{PM} = y' \tan \psi$

$$= y' \left(\frac{dy}{dx}\right)'$$

Length of tangent at $P = PK = \sqrt{PM^2 + KM^2}$

$$= \sqrt{y'^2 + \left[\frac{y'}{\left(\frac{dy}{dx}\right)'}\right]^2}$$

$$= \frac{y'}{\left(\frac{dy}{dx}\right)'} \sqrt{\left[\left(\frac{dy}{dx}\right)'\right]^2 + 1}$$

$$= \frac{y'}{\left(\frac{dy}{dx}\right)'} \sqrt{1 + \left[\left(\frac{dy}{dx}\right)'\right]^2}$$

Also length of normal at $P = PL = \sqrt{PM^2 + LM^2}$

$$= \sqrt{y'^2 + \left[y'\left(\frac{dy}{dx}\right)'\right]^2}$$

$$= y' \sqrt{1 + \left[\left(\frac{dy}{dx}\right)'\right]^2}.$$

Example 5. *Prove that for the parabola $y^2 = 4ax$, subtangent at any point is twice its abscissa and subnormal is constant.*

Solution. Let (x', y') be any point on $y^2 = 4ax$

So $$y'^2 = 4ax' \qquad ...(1)$$

Differentiating we get

$$2y\frac{dy}{dx} = 4a \quad \Rightarrow \quad \frac{dy}{dx} = \frac{2a}{y} \quad \Rightarrow \left(\frac{dy}{dx}\right)' = \frac{2a}{y'}$$

Hence the subtangent at (x', y') is

$$\frac{y'}{\left(\frac{dy}{dx}\right)'} = \frac{y'}{\left(\frac{2a}{y'}\right)} = \frac{y'^2}{2a} = \frac{4ax'}{2a}, \text{ by (1)} = 2x'$$

$$= \text{twice abscissa of the point } P.$$

Also subnormal at P is equal to $y'\left(\frac{dy}{dx}\right)'$

$$= y'.\frac{2a}{y'} = 2a, \text{ a constant.}$$

Example 6. *Find the lengths of tangent and normal at any point (x', y') of the curve $y = \frac{a}{2}(e^{x/a} + e^{-x/a})$*

Solution. $$y = \frac{a}{2}\left(e^{x/a} + e^{-x/a}\right) = a\cosh\frac{x}{a}$$

$$\Rightarrow \quad \frac{dy}{dx} = a\left(\sin h\frac{x}{a}\right)\frac{1}{a} = \sinh\frac{x}{a}$$

This gives that $\left(\frac{dy}{dx}\right)' = \sinh\frac{x'}{a}$

Then the length of tangent at (x', y') is

$$\frac{y'}{\left(\frac{dy}{dx}\right)'}\sqrt{1+\left[\left(\frac{dy}{dx}\right)'\right]^2} = \frac{a\cosh\frac{x'}{a}}{\sinh\frac{x'}{a}}\sqrt{1+\sinh^2\frac{x'}{a}}$$

as (x', y') lies on the given curve,

$$= \frac{a\cosh\frac{x'}{a}}{\sinh\frac{x'}{a}}\cosh\frac{x'}{a} = a\cosh\frac{x'}{a}\coth\frac{x'}{a}.$$

Also the length of normal at (x', y') is

$$y'\sqrt{1+\left[\left(\frac{dy}{dx}\right)'\right]^2} = \left\{a\cosh\frac{x'}{a}\right\}\sqrt{1+\sinh^2\frac{x'}{a}}$$

$$= a\cosh^2\frac{x'}{a}.$$

4. INTERSECTION OF TWO CURVES

Definition. The angle of intersection between two curves is the angle between the tangents to the two curves at the point of intersection.

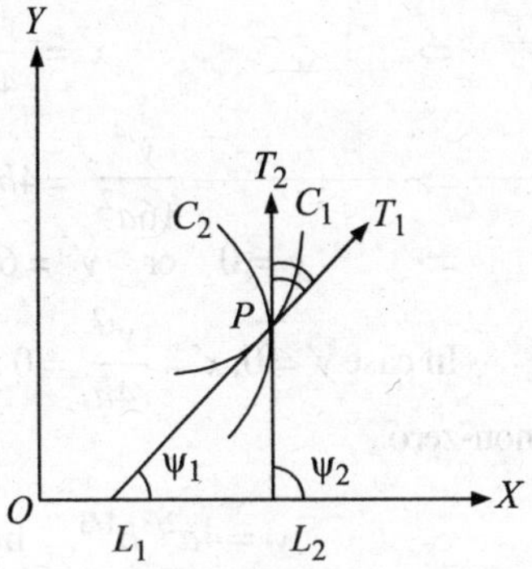

Fig. 4

Let C_1 and C_2 be two plane curves intersecting each other at P and let PT_1 and PT_2 be tangents to C_1 and C_2 respectively at P.

$\angle T_1PT_2$ is the angle of intersection of the curves C_1 and C_2.

Suppose that PT_1 and PT_2 intersect OX at L_1 and L_2 respectively.

If $\quad \angle T_1L_1X = \psi_1 \quad$ and $\quad \angle T_2L_2X = \psi_2$

then $\quad \angle T_1PT_2 = \theta$ say

is given by $\psi_2 - \psi_1$

Now tan ψ_1 = slope of tangent at P to curve $C_1 = m_1$, say

and tan ψ_2 = slope of tangent at P to curve $C_2 = m_2$, say

$$\text{Then } \tan\theta = \tan(\psi_2 - \psi_1) = \frac{m_2 - m_1}{1 + m_1 m_2}$$

NOTE. $m_1 = \left(\dfrac{dy}{dx}\right)'$ for the curve C_1

while $m_2 = \left(\dfrac{dy}{dx}\right)'$ for the curve C_2.

In case $\psi_2 - \psi_1 = \pm\dfrac{\pi}{2}$, we say that C_1 and C_2 are *orthogonal curves* or C_1 and C_2 *cut orthogonally.*

Thus C_1 and C_2 are orthogonal if and only if $m_1m_2 = -1$.

Example 7. *Find the angle of intersection of*

(*i*) $y^2 = 4ax$ *and* $x^2 = 4by$ *at a point different from* (0, 0).

(*ii*) $x^2 + y^2 = 8$ *and* $x^2 = 2y$ *at* (2, 2)

Solution. (*i*) Let $P(x', y')$ be the point of intersection different from (0, 0).

So at least one of x', y' is non-zero.

Now as P lies on $y^2 = 4ax$ and $x^2 = 4by$,

we get $$y'^2 = 4ax' \text{ and } x'^2 = 4by'$$

$$\Rightarrow \quad x' = \frac{y'^2}{4a} \text{ and } x'^2 = 4by'$$

$$\Rightarrow \quad \frac{y'^4}{16a^2} = 4by'$$

$$\Rightarrow \quad y' = 0 \quad \text{or} \quad y'^3 = 64a^2b \quad i.e., \quad y' = 4a^{2/3}b^{1/3}.$$

In case $y' = 0$, $x' = \frac{y'^2}{4a} = 0$ which is absurd as one of x' or y' must be non-zero.

$$\therefore \quad y' = 4a^{2/3}b^{1/3}, \quad \text{hence } x' = \frac{y'^2}{4a} = 4a^{1/3}b^{2/3}.$$

Thus P is $(4a^{1/3}b^{2/3}, 4a^{2/3}b^{1/3})$

$$m_1 = \left(\frac{dy}{dx}\right)' \quad \text{for} \quad y^2 = 4ax$$

$$= \frac{2a}{y'} = \frac{2a}{4a^{2/3}b^{1/3}} = \frac{a^{1/3}}{2b^{1/3}}$$

Also $$m_2 = \left(\frac{dy}{dx}\right)' \quad \text{for} \quad x^2 = 4by$$

$$= \frac{x'}{2b} = \frac{2a^{1/3}}{b^{1/3}}.$$

Hence if θ is the angle of intersection between given curves,

$$\tan\theta = \frac{m_2 - m_1}{1 + m_1 m_2} = \frac{\frac{2a^{1/3}}{b^{1/3}} - \frac{a^{1/3}}{2b^{1/3}}}{1 + \frac{2a^{1/3}}{b^{1/3}} \cdot \frac{a^{1/3}}{2b^{1/3}}}$$

$$= \frac{3a^{1/3}b^{1/3}}{a^{2/3} + b^{2/3}}$$

Hence $\theta = \tan^{-1}\left(\frac{3a^{1/3}b^{1/3}}{a^{2/3} + b^{2/3}}\right)$.

Solution. (*ii*) $$x^2 + y^2 = 8$$

$$\Rightarrow \quad 2x + 2y\frac{dy}{dx} = 0$$

$$\Rightarrow \qquad \frac{dy}{dx} = -\frac{x}{y}$$

At (2, 2), $\qquad m_1 = \frac{dy}{dx} = -\frac{2}{2} = -1$

For second curve $x^2 = 2y$

$$2x = 2\frac{dy}{dx} \Rightarrow \frac{dy}{dx} = x$$

So at (2, 2), $\qquad m_2 = \frac{dy}{dx} = 2.$

Hence if θ is the angle of intersection,

$$\tan\theta = \frac{m_1 - m_2}{1 + m_1 m_2} = \frac{-1-2}{1+(-1)2} = 3$$

Consequently $\qquad \theta = \tan^{-1} 3.$

Example 8. *Show that the curves* $\frac{x^2}{a^2} + \frac{y^2}{b^2} = 1$ *and* $\frac{x^2}{a'^2} + \frac{y^2}{b'^2} = 1$ *will intersect orthogonally if* $a^2 - b^2 = a'^2 - b'^2$.

Solution. Let $P(x', y')$ be the point of intersection

Then $\qquad \frac{x'^2}{a^2} + \frac{y'^2}{b^2} = 1 = \frac{x'^2}{a'^2} + \frac{y'^2}{b'^2}$

$$\Rightarrow \qquad x'^2\,\frac{a'^2 - a^2}{a^2 a'^2} = y'^2\,\frac{b^2 - b'^2}{b^2 b'^2}$$

$$\Rightarrow \qquad x' = \frac{y'aa'}{bb'}\sqrt{\frac{b^2 - b'^2}{a'^2 - a^2}}. \qquad ...(1)$$

[We take +ve sign under radical since the two curves are symmetrical in four quadrants.]

Now $\frac{dy}{dx}$ for any point on first curve is given by

$$\frac{2x}{a^2} + \frac{2y}{b^2}\frac{dy}{dx} = 0 \Rightarrow \frac{dy}{dx} = \frac{-b^2 x}{a^2 y}$$

So $\qquad m_1 = \left(\frac{dy}{dx}\right)'$ for first curve

$$= -\frac{b^2 x'}{a^2 y'} = -\frac{b^2}{a^2}\frac{aa'}{bb'}\sqrt{\frac{b^2 - b'^2}{a'^2 - a^2}}, \text{ by (1)}$$

$$= -\frac{ba'}{ab'}\sqrt{\frac{b^2 - b'^2}{a'^2 - a^2}}.$$

For second curve, we have, in similar manner

$$m_2 = -\frac{b'^2}{a'^2}\frac{x'}{y'} = -\frac{ab'}{a'b}\sqrt{\frac{b^2 - b'^2}{a'^2 - a^2}}$$

The two curves C_1 and C_2 are orthogonal in case $m_1 m_2 = -1$

i.e., if $$\frac{b^2 - b'^2}{a'^2 - a^2} = -1$$

if $$b^2 - b'^2 = -a'^2 + a^2$$

if $$a^2 - b^2 = a'^2 - b'^2.$$

Hence the result follows.

EXERCISES

1. Find the equation of tangent and normal to each of the following curves at the given point

   (*i*) $y = x^3 - 3x + 2$ at (2, 4) (*ii*) $x = a \sin^3 t$, $y = b \cos^3 t$ at $t = \frac{\pi}{4}$

   (*iii*) $y^2 = 4ax$ at (x', y') (*iv*) $x^2 + y^2 = a^2$ at (x', y')

   (*v*) $x^3 = y^2$ at $(4am^2, 8am^3)$.

2. Find the point on $y^2 = 4ax$ at which tangent is parallel to y-axis.

   [**Hint.** Tangent at (x', y') will be parallel to y-axis if and only if $\frac{1}{\left(\frac{dy}{dx}\right)'} = 0.$]

3. Find the points on $\frac{x^2}{a^2} + \frac{y^2}{b^2} = 1$ at which tangents are parallel to x-axis.

   [**Hint.** Tangent at a point (x', y') will be parallel to x-axis if and only if $\left(\frac{dy}{dx}\right)' = 0.$]

4. Find the angle of intersection of two curves $2y^2 = x^3$ and $y^2 = 32x$, at a point of intersection different from origin.

5. Prove that the two curves $x^2 + y^2 + 4x + 3 = 0$ and $x^2 + y^2 + y - 3 = 0$ cut each other orthogonally.

6. Show that for any point on the curve $y = a \log (x^2 - a^2)$ the sum of the subtangent and tangent; varies as the product of the co-ordinates of the point.
7. For the curve $x^{m+n} = a^{m+n} y^2$, prove that the *m*th power of the subtangent at any point varies as the *n*th power of subnormal there at.
8. If the normal to the curve $x^{2/3} + y^{2/3} = a^{2/3}$ makes as angle ϕ with the axis of *x*, show that its equation is $y \cos \phi - x \sin \phi = a \cos 2\phi$.
9. Show that the curves $xy = a^2$ and $x^2 + y^2 = 2a^2$ touch each other.

   [**Hint.** Prove that the angle of Intersection between the given curves is zero.]
10. What should be the value of *n* in the equation to the curve $y = a^{1-n} x^n$ in order that the subnormal may be of constant length.

ANSWERS

1. (*i*) $9x - y = 14, \quad x + 9y = 38$

   (*ii*) $\dfrac{x}{a}+\dfrac{y}{b} = \dfrac{1}{\sqrt{2}}, \quad xa + yb = \dfrac{a^2+b^2}{2\sqrt{2}}$

   (*iii*) $xx' + yy' = a^2, \quad x'y = xy'$

   (*iv*) $y = 3mx - 4am^3, \quad x + 3my = 4am^2 + 64\, am^4.$

2. (0, 0). 3. (0, *b*), (0, –*b*). 4. $\tan^{-1}\left(\dfrac{1}{2}\right)$. 5. $n = \dfrac{1}{2}$.

SECTION B

MAXIMA AND MINIMA

5. DEFINITION 1

A point $(c, f(c))$ is called a *maximum point* of $y = f(x)$

if (*i*) $f(c+h) \le f(c)$

and (*ii*) $f(c-h) \le f(c)$ for small $h \ge 0$.

$f(c)$ itself is called a *maximum value* of $f(x)$.

6. DEFINITION 2

A point $(d, f(d))$ is called a *minimum point* of $y = f(x)$ if

(*i*) $f(d+h) \ge f(d)$

and (*ii*) $f(d-h) \ge f(d)$

for all small $h \ge 0$.

$f(d)$ itself is called a *minimum value* of $f(x)$.

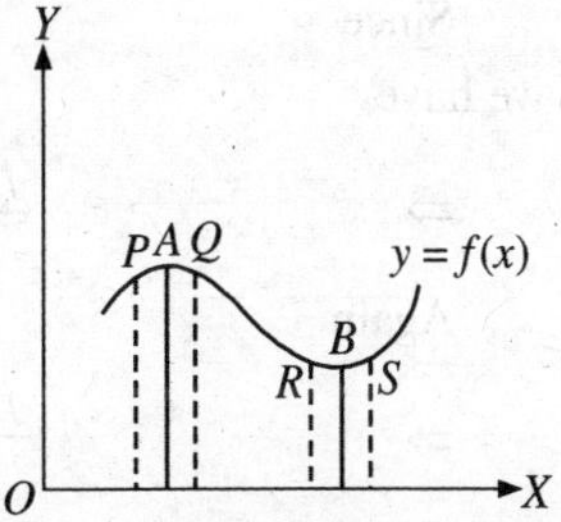

Fig. 5

Thus we observe that points $P(c-h, f(c-h))$ and $Q(c+h, f(c+h))$, which are very *near* to A, have ordinates less than that of A, whereas the points

$$R(d-h,\ f(d-h)),\quad \text{and}\quad S(d+h,\ f(d+h))$$

which are very *close* to B have ordinates greater than that of B.

We now prove that at a maximum or minimum point, first differential coefficient with respect to x must vanish (in other words tangent at a maximum or minimum point is parallel to x-axis, which is otherwise evident from the figure).

Let $(c, f(c))$ be a maximum point and let $h \geq 0$ be a small number.

Since $$f(c-h) \leq f(c)$$

we have $$f(c-h) - f(c) \leq 0$$

$$\Rightarrow \quad \frac{f(c-h)-f(c)}{-h} \geq 0. \qquad ...(1)$$

Again $$f(c+h) \leq f(c) \;\Rightarrow\; f(c+h) - f(c) \leq 0$$

$$\Rightarrow \quad \frac{f(c+h)-f(c)}{h} \leq 0. \qquad ...(2)$$

(1) implies that $$\lim_{k \to 0} \frac{f(c+k)-f(c)}{k} \geq 0, \qquad [\text{put } k = -h]$$

and (2) gives that $$\lim_{k \to 0} \frac{f(c+h)-f(c)}{k} \leq 0 \qquad [\text{put } k = h]$$

Thus $$0 \leq \lim_{k \to 0} \frac{f(c+k)-f(c)}{k} \leq 0$$

$\Rightarrow \left(\dfrac{dy}{dx}\right)$ at $x = c$ is equal is to zero.

i.e., $$f'(c) = 0.$$

Again let $(d, f(d))$ be a minimum point and let $h \geq 0$ be a small number

Since $$f(d-h) \geq f(d)$$

we have $$f(d-h) - f(d) \geq 0$$

$$\Rightarrow \quad \frac{f(d-h)-f(d)}{-h} \leq 0. \qquad ...(3)$$

Again $$f(d+h) \geq f(d)$$

$$\Rightarrow \quad \frac{f(d+h)-f(d)}{h} \geq 0. \qquad ...(4)$$

(3) and (4) imply $$\lim_{k \to 0} \frac{f(d+k)-f(d)}{k} = 0$$

i.e., $f'(d) = 0.$

Hence our assertion follows.

Before we proceed to find out the criterion for determining whether a point is maximum or minimum we discuss increasing and decreasing functions of x.

A function $f(x)$ is said to be *increasing* (decreasing) if

$$f(x+c) \geq f(x) \geq f(x-c) [f(x+c) \leq f(x) \leq f(x-c)] \text{ for all } c \geq 0.$$

7. THEOREM

If $f'(x) \geq 0$ then $f(x)$ is increasing function of x and if $f'(x) \leq 0$ then $f(x)$ is decreasing function of x.

Proof. $f'(x) \geq 0 \Rightarrow \lim_{\delta x \to 0} \dfrac{f(x+\delta x) - f(x)}{\delta x} \geq 0$ ...(I)

In case $\delta x > 0$, put $c = \delta x$, then (I) yields that

$$f(x+c) \geq f(x).$$

In case $\delta x < 0$, put $c = -\delta x$, then (I) gives that

$$\frac{f(x-c) - f(x)}{-c} \geq 0$$

$$\Rightarrow \quad f(x-c) - f(x) \leq 0$$

$$\Rightarrow \quad f(x) \geq f(x-c)$$

Hence $\quad f(x+c) \geq f(x) \geq f(x-c).$

In other words $f(x)$ is increasing function of x.

Suppose that $f'(x) \leq 0$

Then $\quad \lim_{\delta x \to 0} \dfrac{f(x+\delta x) - f(x)}{\delta x} \leq 0$ ...(II)

In case $\delta x > 0$, putting $c = \delta x$, we see

that $\quad f(x+c) - f(c) \leq 0$

i.e., $\quad f(x+c) \leq f(x).$

If $\delta x < 0$, putting $c = -\delta x$, we get

$$\frac{f(x-c) - f(x)}{-c} \leq 0$$

$$\Rightarrow \quad f(x-c) - f(x) \geq 0$$

$$\Rightarrow \quad f(x) \leq f(x-c)$$

So $\quad f(x+c) \leq f(x) \leq f(x-c).$

This means that $f(x)$ is a decreasing function of x.

REMARKS:

1. A function $f(x)$ is said to be *strictly increasing* (*strictly decreasing*) if $f(x + c) > f(x) > f(x - c)$ $[f(x + c) < f(x) < f(x - c)]$ for all $c > 0$.
2. It can be seen easily that $f(x)$ is increasing if $f(x) > f(y)$ whenever $x > y$ and $f(x)$ is decreasing if $x > y \Rightarrow f(x) < f(y)$ and conversely.
3. It can be proved as above that a function $f(x)$ is strictly increasing or strictly decreasing according as $f'(x) > 0$ or $f'(x) < 0$.

8. Geometrically the above theorem means that for an increasing function, tangent at any point makes acute angle with OX whereas for a decreasing function, tangent at any point makes an obtuse angle with x-axis.

Let A be a maximum point $(c, (f(c))$ of a curve $y = f(x)$.

Let $P(c - h,\ f(c - h))$ and $Q(c + h,\ f(c + h))$ be two points in the vicinity of A [*i.e.*, h is very small].

If ψ_1 and ψ_2 are inclinations of tangents at P and Q respectively, it is quite obvious from the figure that ψ_1 is acute and ψ_2 is obtuse.

Analytically it is apparent from the fact that function is increasing from P to A and decreasing from A to Q. So $\tan \psi$ decreases as we pass through A [$\tan \psi$ is +ve when ψ is acute and is –ve when ψ is obtuse].

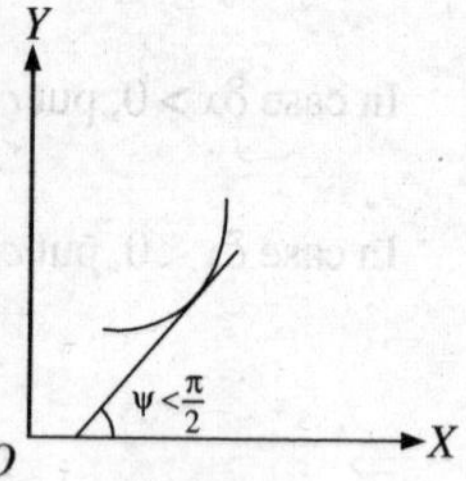

Fig. 6

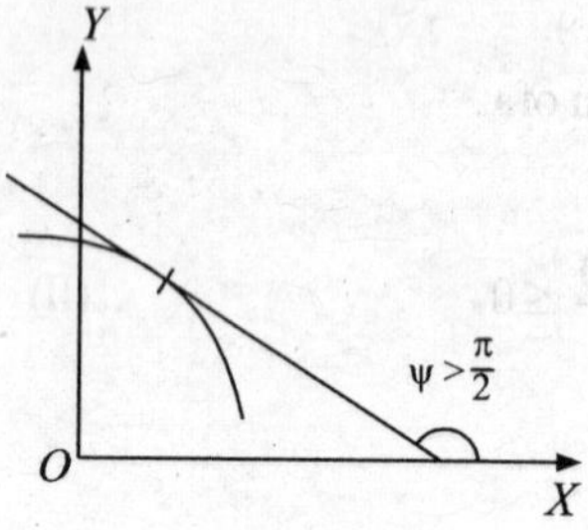

Fig. 7

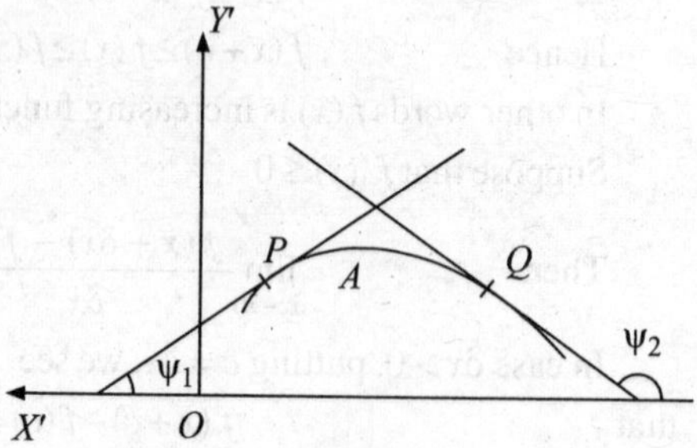

Fig. 8

Thus $\dfrac{dy}{dx} = \tan \psi$ is a decreasing function of x. In other words $\dfrac{d^2 y}{dx^2} \leq 0$.

Since ψ is strictly decreasing function of x, ($f(x)$ is not a constant function), so $\dfrac{d^2 y}{dx^2} < 0$. Consequently at a maximum point $(c, f(c))$

$$f''(c) < 0.$$

Similarly it can be easily seen that if $R(d-h, f(d-h))$ and $S(d+h, f(d+h))$ are two points in the neighbourhood of a minimum point $B(d, f(d))$, slopes of tangents as we pass through B increase. (Here ψ_1 is obtuse so $\tan\psi_1 < 0$ and ψ_2 is acute so $\tan\psi_2 > 0$.)

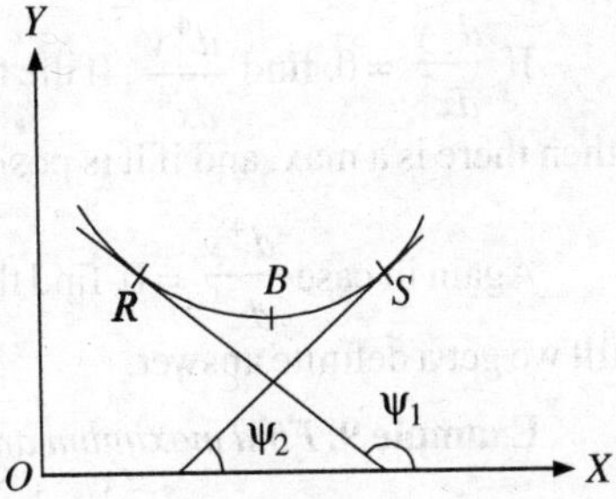

Fig. 9

Therefore for a minimum point

$(d, f(d)),\ \dfrac{d^2y}{dx^2} > 0$

i.e., $\quad f''(d) > 0.$

REMARKS:

1. A point (α, β) such that $f'(\alpha) = 0, f''(\alpha) = 0$ but $f'''(\alpha) \neq 0$ is called a *point of inflection.*
2. Any point at which $\dfrac{dy}{dx} = 0$ is called a *stationary point*, thus maxima and minima are stationary points while a stationary point need not be a maximum or a minimum point (it could be a point of inflexion). Value of $f(x)$ at a stationary point is called *stationary value.*

We have the following rule for the determination of maxima and minima, if they exist, of a function $y = f(x)$.

Step I. Putting $\dfrac{dy}{dx} = 0$, calculate the stationary points.

Step II. Compute $\dfrac{d^2y}{dx^2}$ at these stationary points.

In case $\dfrac{d^2y}{dx^2} > 0$, the stationary point is a minimum point.

In case $\dfrac{d^2y}{dx^2} < 0$, the stationary point is a maximum point.

If $\dfrac{d^2y}{dx^2} = 0$, then compute $\dfrac{d^3y}{dx^3}$.

If $\dfrac{d^3y}{dx^3} \neq 0$ for a stationary point it is neither a max. nor a min. at the point.

If $\frac{d^3y}{dx^3}=0$, find $\frac{d^4y}{dx^4}$. If the fourth derivative is negative at the point then there is a max. and if it is positive then there is a min.

Again in case $\frac{d^4y}{dx^4}=0$, find the fifth derivative and proceed as above till we get a definite answer.

Example 9. *Find maximum and minimum values of the expression*

$$x^3-3x^2-9x+27.$$

Solution. Let $y=x^3-3x^2-9x+27$

$$\frac{dy}{dx}=3x^2-6x-9$$

For maxima and minima, $\frac{dy}{dx}=0$

$\Rightarrow$ $3x^2-6x-9=0$

$\Rightarrow$ $(x-3)(x+1)=0$

$\Rightarrow$ $x=-1, 3$

Now $\frac{d^2y}{dx^2}=6x-6$

At $x=-1$, $\frac{d^2y}{dx^2}=-12<0$, so $x=-1$ gives a maximum point of y.

Again at $x=3$, $\frac{d^2y}{dx^2}=12>0$, so $x=3$ gives a minimum point of y.

Hence maximum value of y is $(-1)^3-3(-1)^2-9(-1)+27$

$$=36+1-3=34$$

While minimum value of y is $3^3-3(3)^2-9(3)+27$

$$=54-27-27=0.$$

Example 10. *Find the maximum and minimum values of the function*

$$8x^5-15x^4+10x^2.$$

Solution. Let $f(x)=8x^5-15x^4+10x^2$.

$\Rightarrow$ $f'(x)=40x^4-60x^3+20x$

$$f'(x)=0 \Rightarrow x=0, 1, -\frac{1}{2}$$

So these are the points where there can be a max. or a min.

Now $f''(x) = 160x^3 - 180x^2 + 20$

Thus $f''(0) = 20 > 0 \Rightarrow$ There is a min. at $x = 0$

Again $f''\left(-\frac{1}{2}\right) = 160\left(-\frac{1}{2}\right)^3 - 180\left(-\frac{1}{2}\right)^2 + 20 = -45 < 0$

$\Rightarrow$ there is a max. at $x = -\frac{1}{2}$.

Since $f''(1) = 160 - 180 + 20 = 0$, we cannot say anything regarding a max. or a min. at $x = 1$ at this stage. So we find $f'''(x)$.

Now $f'''(x) = 480x^2 - 360x$

But $f'''(1) = 480 - 360 \neq 0$

$\Rightarrow$ There is neither a maximum nor a minimum at $x = 1$

Hence $f\left(-\frac{1}{2}\right) = \frac{21}{16}$ is maximum value

and $f(0) = 0$ is minimum value.

Example 11. *Prove that the minimal value of* $\frac{(a+x)(b+x)}{(c+x)}$, $c + x > 0$ *is* $\left[\sqrt{a-c} + \sqrt{b-c}\right]^2$.

Solution. Let $y = c + x$.

Then
$$z = \frac{(a+x)(b+x)}{(c+x)}$$
$$= \frac{(a-c+y)(b-c+y)}{y}$$
$$= \frac{(a-c)(b-c)}{y} + y + (a-c) + (b-c)$$

$$\therefore \quad \frac{dz}{dx} = \frac{-(a-c)(b-c)}{y^2} + 1 \text{ as } \frac{dy}{dx} = 1$$

$$\Rightarrow \quad \frac{d^2z}{dx^2} = \frac{2}{y^3}(a-c)(b-c)$$

$$\frac{dz}{dx} = 0 \Rightarrow y^2 = (a-c)(b-c)$$

So,
$$\frac{d^2z}{dx^2} = \frac{2}{y} \text{ when } y^2 = (a-c)(b-c)$$

$$= \frac{2}{c+x} > 0$$

$\therefore$ z is minimum when $y = \sqrt{(a-c)(b-c)}$

and minimum values of z is

$$z = (a-c) + (b-c) + 2\sqrt{(a-c)(b-c)}$$

$$= \left[\sqrt{a-c} + \sqrt{b-c}\right]^2$$

Example 12. *Find out maxima and minima of sin x + cos x, when x lies between 0 and 2π.*

Solution. Let $y = \sin x + \cos x$ $\qquad 0 \le x \le 2\pi$

For maxima and minima $\frac{dy}{dx} = 0$

$\Rightarrow \quad \cos x - \sin x = 0$

$\Rightarrow \quad \tan x = 1$

$\Rightarrow \quad x = \frac{\pi}{4}$ or $\frac{3\pi}{4}$.

Now $\quad \frac{d^2y}{dx^2} = -\sin x - \cos x$

At $x = \frac{\pi}{4}$, $\frac{d^2y}{dx^2} = -\frac{1}{\sqrt{2}} - \frac{1}{\sqrt{2}} = -\sqrt{2} < 0$

and at $x = \frac{3\pi}{4}$, $\frac{d^2y}{dx^2} = \frac{1}{\sqrt{2}} + \frac{1}{\sqrt{2}} = \sqrt{2} > 0.$

So $x = \frac{\pi}{4}$ gives a maximum and $x = \frac{3\pi}{4}$ gives a minimum point of given function.

Example 13. *Find maxima and minima of*

sin x + cos 2x for 0 ≤ x ≤ π/2.

Solution. Let $y = \sin x + \cos 2x$

for maxima and minima $\frac{dy}{dx} = 0$

$\Rightarrow \quad \cos x - 2\sin x = 0$

$\Rightarrow \quad \cos x(1 - 4\sin x) = 0$

$\Rightarrow \quad \cos x = 0$ or $\sin x = \frac{1}{4}$

$\Rightarrow \quad x = \dfrac{\pi}{4} \quad \text{or} \quad x = \sin^{-1}\dfrac{1}{4}$

Now

$$\frac{d^2y}{dx^2} = -\sin x - 4\cos 2x$$
$$= -\sin x - 4(1 - 2\sin^2 x)$$
$$= 8\sin^2 x - \sin x - 4$$

At $x = \pi/2$,

$$\frac{d^2y}{dx^2} = 8 - 1 - 4 = 3 > 0$$

So $x = \dfrac{\pi}{2}$ gives a minimum point of $\sin x + \cos 2x$

At $x = \sin^{-1}\dfrac{1}{4}$,

$$\frac{d^2y}{dx^2} = 8\left(\frac{1}{16}\right) - \frac{1}{4} - 4$$
$$= \frac{1}{2} - \frac{1}{4} - 4$$
$$= \frac{1}{2} - \frac{17}{4} = -\frac{15}{4} < 0.$$

Consequently $x = \sin^{-1}\dfrac{1}{4}$ gives a maximum point of $\sin x + \cos 2x$.

Example 14. *For all real x, show that the minimum value of* $\dfrac{1 - x + x^2}{1 + x + x^2}$ *is* $\dfrac{1}{3}$.

Solution. Let

$$y = \frac{x^2 + x + 1}{x^2 - x + 1} = \frac{x^2 - x + 1 + 2x}{x^2 - x + 1}$$
$$= 1 + 2\frac{x}{x^2 - x + 1}$$
$$= 1 + \frac{2}{x - 1 + \dfrac{1}{x}}$$
$$= 1 + \frac{2}{z}, \text{ where } z = x - 1 + \frac{1}{x}$$

y is maximum or minimum when z is minimum or maximum.

But

$$z = x - 1 + \frac{1}{x}$$

$$\Rightarrow \qquad \frac{dz}{dx} = 1 - \frac{1}{x^2} = 0$$

$$\Rightarrow \qquad x = 1 \text{ or } -1$$

Now $$\frac{d^2z}{dx^2} = \frac{2}{x^3} < 0 \text{ when } x = -1$$

$$> 0 \text{ when } x = 1.$$

So, z is minimum when $x = 1$

or, y is maximum when $x = 1$

or, $\frac{1}{y}$ is minimum when $x = 1$.

Thus $\frac{1 - x + x^2}{1 + x + x^2} = \frac{1}{y}$ is minimum when $x = 1$.

$\therefore$ The minimum value of $\frac{1 - x + x^2}{1 + x + x^2}$ is $\frac{1}{3}$.

Example 15. *The sum of two numbers is 24. Find the numbers if the sum of their squares is to be minimum.*

Solution. Let x and y be two number such that

$$x + y = 24$$

Let $$s = x^2 + y^2 = x^2 + (24 - x)^2$$

For maxima and minima, $\frac{ds}{dx} = 0$

$$\Rightarrow \qquad 2x - 2(24 - x) = 0$$

$$\Rightarrow \qquad 2x = 24 \Rightarrow x = 12$$

Further $\frac{d^2s}{dx^2} = 4 > 0$

So $\qquad x = 12, y = 12$ give minimum value.

Hence the required numbers are 12 and 12.

Example 16. *Show that right circular cylinder of given surface and maximum volume is such that its height is equal to the diameter of its base.*

Solution. Let h be the height and r be the radius of the cylinder. Let its surface be denoted by S.

Then $$S = 2\pi rh + 2\pi r^2 \qquad ...(1)$$

If V is the volume of the cylinder,

$$V = \pi r^2 h = \pi r^2 \frac{S - 2\pi r^2}{2\pi r} \text{ by (1)}$$

$$= \frac{r}{2}(S - 2\pi r^2).$$

$$= \frac{Sr}{2} - \pi r^3$$

For maxima and minima $\frac{dV}{dr} = 0$

$$\Rightarrow \quad \frac{S}{2} - 3\pi r^2 = 0 \Rightarrow S = 6\pi r^2$$

$$\Rightarrow \quad 2\pi rh + 2\pi r^2 = 6\pi r^2, \text{ by (1)}$$

$$\Rightarrow \quad 2\pi rh = 4\pi r^2 \Rightarrow h = 2r$$

Also $$\frac{d^2V}{dr^2} = -6\pi r < 0 \text{ (as } r \text{ is always +ve)}$$

Hence $h = 2r$ gives maximum volume.

Example 17. *A wire of given length is cut into two portions which are bent into the shape of a circle and a square respectively. Show that the sum of the areas of the circle and the square will be least when the side of the square is equal to the diameter of the circle.*

Solution. Let L be the length of the wire and x, y be the lengths of two portions

Thus $$x + y = L \qquad ...(1)$$

Suppose that wire of length x is bent into the form of a circle and that of length y, into a square.

So radius of the circle is $\frac{x}{2\pi}$ whereas the side of the square is $\frac{y}{4}$.

$$\text{Area of circle} = \pi\,(\text{radius})^2 = \frac{x^2}{4\pi}$$

$$\text{Area of square} = (\text{side})^2 = \frac{y^2}{16}$$

Let $$K = \frac{x^2}{4\pi} + \frac{y^2}{16} = \frac{x^2}{4\pi} + \frac{(L-x)^2}{16} \text{ by (1)}$$

for maxima and minima, $\frac{dK}{dx} = 0$

$$\Rightarrow \quad \frac{x}{2\pi} - \frac{L-x}{8} = 0$$

$$\Rightarrow \quad 4x - \pi L + \pi x = 0$$

$$\Rightarrow \quad x = \frac{\pi L}{\pi + 4}$$

Also $\frac{d^2K}{dx^2} = \frac{1}{2\pi} + \frac{1}{8} > 0$, so $x = \frac{\pi L}{\pi + 4}$

gives minimum value of K.

Now side of the square is $\frac{y}{4} = \frac{1}{4}(L - x) = \frac{1}{4}\left[L - \frac{\pi L}{\pi + 4}\right] = \frac{L}{\pi + 4}$

Whereas radius of the circle $= \frac{x}{2\pi} = \frac{L}{2(\pi + 4)}$

Hence our assertion follows.

EXERCISES

Discuss the maxima and minima of

1. $x^5 - 5x^4 + 5x^3 - 10$.
2. (*i*) $x^3 - 3x^2 - 9$ (*ii*) $x + \frac{1}{x+1}$
3. $x + \sin 2x \quad (0 \le x \le \pi)$.
4. $\frac{(x+3)^2}{x^2+1}$.
5. (*i*) $\cos x + \cos 3x \ (0 \le x \le \pi)$
   (*ii*) Show that there is a min. at $x = 0$ for the function
   $$f(x) = x^4\left(x - \frac{\pi}{2}\right)^2 + \sin^4 x$$
6. Show that the maximum rectangle inscribed in a circle is square.
7. The three sides of a trapezium are equal, each being 6 cm long. Find the maximum possible area of the trapezium.
8. Show that the semi-vertical angle of the cone of maximum volume and given slant height is $\tan^{-1}\sqrt{2}$.
9. A quantity of metal is to be cast into a half cylinder (*i.e.*, with rectangular base and semi-circular ends). Show that in order that the total surface may be minimum, the ratio of the length of the cylinder to the diameter of its semi-circular end is $(\pi + 2) : \pi$.

10. Show that the triangle of maximum area that can be inscribed in a given circle is an equilateral triangle.
11. The fuel charges for running a train with uniform speed over a given distance of 80 kilometres vary as the square of its speed and at 16 km/hour they are found to be Rs. 48 per hour. The fixed charges, salaries etc., amount to Rs. 300 for every hour of run. What should be the most economical speed?
12. If the sum of the lengths of the hypotenuse and another side of a right angled triangle is given, show that the area of the triangle is maximum when the angle between the above two sides is $\frac{\pi}{3}$.
13. Product of two numbers is 16. Find the numbers if their sum is to be minimum.
14. Prove that if the sum of the radii of two circles remain constant, the sum of their areas will be least when the circles are equal.
15. A rectangle is inscribed in a quadrant of a circle of radius 5 cm, two of the sides being along the bounding radii. Find the maximum value of the area of the rectangle.
16. A lane runs at right angles to a road a cm wide. Find how many metres wide the lane must be if it is just possible to carry a pole b cm long $(b > a)$ from the road into the lane, keeping it horizontal.

ANSWERS

1. Max. at $x = 1$, Min. at $x = 3$
2. (*i*) Max. at $x = 0$, Min. at $x = 2$
   (*ii*) Max. at $x = -2$
   Min. at $x = 0$.
3. Max. at $x = \frac{\pi}{3}$, Min. at $x = \frac{2\pi}{3}$.
4. Max. at $x = \frac{1}{3}$, Min. at $x = -3$.
5. Max. at $x = 0$, Min. at $x = \sin^{-1}\sqrt{\frac{5}{6}}$, π.
7. $27\sqrt{3}$ sq. cm.
11. 40 km/hour.
13. 4, 4.
15. 12.5 sq. cm.
16. $(b^{2/3} - a^{2/3})^{3/2}$ metres.

9. MAXIMUM AND MINIMUM VALUES OF A FUNCTION OF TWO VARIABLES

We have the following rule for determination of maxima or minima, if it exists, of a function $z = f(x, y)$

$z = f(x, y)$ has a max. or min. if

(*i*) $\frac{\partial z}{\partial x} = 0 = \frac{\partial z}{\partial y}$.

$$(ii) \quad \left(\frac{\partial^2 z}{\partial x^2}\right)\left(\frac{\partial^2 z}{\partial y^2}\right) > \left(\frac{\partial^2 z}{\partial x \partial y}\right)^2$$

and if $\dfrac{\partial^2 z}{\partial x^2} < 0$, there is a max.,

if $\dfrac{\partial^2 z}{\partial x^2} > 0$, there is a min.

In case $\left(\dfrac{\partial^2 z}{\partial x^2}\right)\left(\dfrac{\partial^2 z}{\partial y^2}\right) < \left(\dfrac{\partial^2 z}{\partial x \partial y}\right)^2$

There is neither a max. nor a min. and we call such a point, a *saddle point.*

REMARK: If $\left(\dfrac{\partial^2 z}{\partial x^2}\right)\left(\dfrac{\partial^2 z}{\partial y^2}\right) = \left(\dfrac{\partial^2 z}{\partial x \partial y}\right)^2$, we cannot say any thing definite.

In view of condition *(ii)* we observe that

$$\text{if } \frac{\partial^2 z}{\partial x^2} \gtrless 0 \text{ then so is } \frac{\partial^2 z}{\partial y^2}.$$

The procedure is made clear in the following examples:

Example 18. *Find the points of max. min. for the function*

$$z = 3x^2 + 2y^2 - xy - 4x - 7y + 12.$$

Solution. We have,

$$\frac{\partial z}{\partial y} = 6x - y - 4.$$

$$\frac{\partial z}{\partial y} = 4y - x - 7.$$

Solving $\quad \dfrac{\partial z}{\partial x} = 0 = \dfrac{\partial z}{\partial y}$

we obtain, $\quad x = 1, y = 2.$

Thus, (1, 2) is a *critical point, i.e.*, a point where there is a possibility of max. or a min.

Now, $\quad \dfrac{\partial^2 z}{\partial x^2} = 6, \quad \dfrac{\partial^2 z}{\partial y^2} = 4, \quad \dfrac{\partial^2 z}{\partial x \partial y} = -1.$

Thus, $\quad \left(\dfrac{\partial^2 z}{\partial x^2}\right)\left(\dfrac{\partial^2 z}{\partial y^2}\right) > \left(\dfrac{\partial^2 z}{\partial x \partial y}\right)^2$

and since $\frac{\partial^2 z}{\partial x^2} > 0$, there is a min. at the point (1, 2).

Also at (1, 2) we notice

$$z = 3(1)^2 + 2(2)^2 - (1)(2) - 4(1) - 7(2) + 12 = 3.$$

i.e., $z = 3$ is a point of minimum.

Example 19. *Check for max. or min. for the function*

$$z = 4x^2 - xy + y^2 - x^3.$$

Solution. We have,

$$\frac{\partial z}{\partial x} = 8x - y - 3x^2.$$

$$\frac{\partial z}{\partial y} = -x + 2y.$$

Solving $\frac{\partial z}{\partial x} = 0 = \frac{\partial z}{\partial y}$

we get, $x = 0;\ y = 0$ or $x = \frac{5}{2};\ y = \frac{5}{4}.$

Again

$$\frac{\partial^2 z}{\partial x^2} = 8 - 6x$$

$$\frac{\partial^2 z}{\partial y} = 2$$

$$\frac{\partial^2 z}{\partial x \partial y} = -1.$$

At (0, 0) $\frac{\partial^2 z}{\partial x^2} = 8,\ \frac{\partial^2 z}{\partial y^2} = 2,\ \frac{\partial^2 z}{\partial x \partial y} = -1.$

and thus $\left(\frac{\partial^2 z}{\partial x^2}\right)\left(\frac{\partial^2 z}{\partial y^2}\right) > \left(\frac{\partial^2 z}{\partial x \partial y}\right)^2$

and as $\frac{\partial^2 z}{\partial x^2} > 0$, there is a min. at (0, 0).

Again at $\left(\frac{5}{2}, \frac{5}{4}\right)$

$$\frac{\partial^2 z}{\partial x^2} = -7,\ \frac{\partial^2 z}{\partial y^2} = 2,\ \frac{\partial^2 z}{\partial x \partial y} = -1$$

and so $\left(\frac{\partial^2 z}{\partial x^2}\right)\left(\frac{\partial^2 z}{\partial y^2}\right) < \left(\frac{\partial^2 z}{\partial x \partial y}\right)^2$

$\Rightarrow$ there is neither a max. nor a min. at

$\left(\frac{5}{2}, \frac{5}{4}\right)$ *i.e.*, it is a saddle point.

Since for (0, 0), $z = 0$

and for $\left(\frac{5}{2}, \frac{5}{4}\right)$, $z = \frac{125}{16}$

we observe at $z = 0$, there is a min.

and at $z = \frac{125}{16}$, there is a saddle point.

Example 20. *Check for max. or min. the function*

$$z = x^3 - y^3 + 3x^2 + 3y^2 - 9x$$

Solution: We have,

$$\frac{\partial z}{\partial x} = 3x^2 + 6x - 9$$

$$\frac{\partial z}{\partial y} = -3y^2 + 6y.$$

Solving $\frac{\partial z}{\partial x} = 0 = \frac{\partial z}{\partial y}$

we find, $x = -3, 1, \ y = 0, 2$

Thus, critical points are

(–3, 0), (–3, 2), (1, 0) and (1, 2).

Also $\frac{\partial^2 z}{\partial x^2} = 6x + 6; \quad \frac{\partial^2 z}{\partial y^2} = -6y + 6; \quad \frac{\partial^2 z}{\partial x \partial y} = 0.$

At the point (–3, 0)

$$\frac{\partial^2 z}{\partial x^2} = -12, \quad \frac{\partial^2 z}{\partial y^2} = 6, \quad \frac{\partial^2 z}{\partial x \partial y} = 0$$

Thus there is neither a max. nor a min. at (–3, 0) *i.e.*, (–3, 0) is a saddle point. Similarly, it is easily seen that (1, 2) is also a saddle point.

Again at (1, 0)

$$\frac{\partial^2 z}{\partial x^2} = 12, \quad \frac{\partial^2 z}{\partial y^2} = 6, \quad \frac{\partial^2 z}{\partial x \partial y} = 0$$

Hence, there is a min. at (1, 0).

Finally, at the point (–3, 2)

$$\frac{\partial^2 z}{\partial x^2} = -12, \quad \frac{\partial^2 z}{\partial y^2} = -6, \quad \frac{\partial^2 z}{\partial x \partial y} = 0$$

implying that there is a max. at (–3, 2).

EXERCISES

Examine for maximum or minimum the following functions:

1. $x^3y^3(12 - 3x - 4y)$.
2. $6x^2 - 9x - 3xy - 7y + 5y^2$.
3. $2x + y - x^2 + xy - y^2$
4. $5x^2 - 30x + 4xy - 3y^2 + 7y$.
5. $y^2 + 4xy + 3x^2 + x^3$.

ANSWERS

1. Max. at (2, 1)
2. Max. at (1, 1)
3. Max. at $\left(\frac{5}{3}, \frac{4}{3}\right)$.
4. Saddle point at $\left(2, \frac{5}{2}\right)$
5. Min. at $\left(\frac{2}{3}, -\frac{4}{3}\right)$.

SECTION C

10. DERIVATIVE AS RATE MEASURER AND APPROXIMATIONS

Let $y = f(x)$. Suppose when x is changed to $x + \delta x$ then y is changed to $y + \delta y$. Supposing that change in y is uniform when x is changing from x to $x + \delta x$, the average change in y compared to the change δx in x is given by $\frac{\delta y}{\delta x}$. But in fact y is continuously changing from y to $y + \delta y$ so we cannot assume that rate of change in y is uniform throughout the period x changes from x to $x + \delta x$. So the ratio $\frac{\delta y}{\delta x}$ at $(x + \delta x, y + \delta y)$ will definitely differ from the ratio at the point (x, y). But as $\delta x \to 0$, this difference becomes smaller and smaller. So we are justified in saying that $\frac{dy}{dx}$ is *rate of change* of y with respect to x *at the point* (x, y).

Till now we evaluated $\frac{dy}{dx}$ by first finding out $\frac{\delta y}{\delta x}$ and then taking its limit as $\delta x \to 0$. Now the converse problem arises. Suppose that y is a function of x for which $\frac{dy}{dx}$ is known. From $\frac{dy}{dx} = \lim_{\delta x \to 0} \frac{\delta y}{\delta x}$, it follows that if δx and δy are negligibly small, $\frac{\delta y}{\delta x} = \frac{dy}{dx}$ *i.e.*, $\frac{\delta y}{\delta x}$ is approximately equal to $\frac{dy}{dx}$.

Let δx be error committed in determining a certain quantity x. δx is called *Absolute Error* while its ratio with x *i.e.*, $\frac{\delta x}{x}$ is called *Relative Error*. Percentage error is given by $100 \times \frac{\delta x}{x}$.

Example 21. *The side of an equilateral triangle is increasing at the rate of 2 cm/sec. At what rate is its area increasing when the side is 20 cm.*

Solution. Let A = Area of an equilateral triangle of side a at time t.

$$A = \frac{\sqrt{3}a^2}{4}$$

$$\frac{dA}{da} = \frac{\sqrt{3}a}{2}$$

$$\frac{dA}{dt}\frac{dt}{da} = \frac{\sqrt{3}a}{2}$$

$$\Rightarrow \frac{dA}{dt} = \frac{\sqrt{3}a}{2}\frac{da}{dt} = \frac{\sqrt{3}a}{2} \cdot 2 = \sqrt{3}\, a \text{ sq. cm/sec.}$$

[As $= \frac{da}{dt}$, by hypothesis is 2 cm/sec.]

When $a = 20$, $\frac{dA}{dt} = 20\sqrt{3}$ sq. cm/sec.

Example 22. *If the radius of a spherical balloon increases by 1%, find approximately the percentage increase in volume.*

Solution. Let r be the radius of balloon and V, its volume,

$$V = \frac{4}{3}\pi r^3 \Rightarrow \frac{dV}{dr} = 4\pi r^2$$

Then $\frac{\delta V}{\delta r} = 4\pi r^2$ (approximately)

$$\delta V = 4\pi r^2\, \delta r.$$

Now $\quad 100\dfrac{\delta r}{r}=.1 \Rightarrow dr=(.001)\,r$

Hence $\quad \delta V=4\pi r^2(.001)\,r=4\pi r^3(.001)$

$$=3V(.001)=V(.003)$$

$\Rightarrow \quad \dfrac{\delta V}{V}=.003.$

Hence percentage increase in volume

$$=100\frac{\delta V}{V}=.3.$$

Example 23. *A cubical block of metal when heated expands slightly, remaining cubical. If its volume increases by x per cent, show that the length of each edge increases by $\frac{x}{3}$ per cent approximately. By what approximate percentage is the surface area increased?*

Solution. Let a be a side of the cube and V its volume.

$$V=a^3 \Rightarrow \frac{dV}{da}=3a^2$$

$$\Rightarrow \frac{\delta r}{\delta a}=3a^2 \qquad \text{(approx.)}$$

Now $\quad x=100\dfrac{\delta V}{V}, \Rightarrow \dfrac{Vx}{100\delta a}=3a^2$

$$\frac{xa^3}{100\,\delta a}=3a^2$$

$$\frac{x}{3}=\frac{100\delta a}{a}$$

Hence percentage error in a is $\frac{x}{3}$.

Further, surface of cube $= S = 6a^2$

$\Rightarrow \quad \delta S=12a\,\delta a \qquad$ (approx.)

$$=12a\frac{ax}{300}=\frac{a^2x}{25}=\frac{\delta x}{150}$$

$\Rightarrow \quad \dfrac{100\,\delta S}{S}=100\dfrac{x}{150}=\dfrac{2x}{3}.$

Example 24. *Find approximate value of* $\frac{1}{x^4}$ *when* $x = 2.04$.

Solution. Let $y = \frac{1}{x^4}$

$$\Rightarrow \qquad \delta y = -\frac{4}{x^5}\,\delta x \qquad \text{(approx.)}$$

We know that when $x = 2$

$$y = \frac{1}{16}$$

If $\delta x = .04$ then $\delta y = -\frac{4}{32}(.04) = -.005.$

Hence if $x = 2.04$, approximate value of $\frac{1}{x^4}$ is

$$\frac{1}{16} - .005 = \frac{.92}{16} = .0575.$$

EXERCISES

1. A balloon which always remains spherical has a variable radius. Find the rate at which its volume is increasing with radius when the latter is 10 cm.
2. Vander Waal's equation for a gas is $\left(p + \frac{a}{V^2}\right)(V - b) = k$ where p is the pressure, V is the volume and a, b, k are constants. What is the change in volume per unit increase in pressure.
3. The time of oscillation of a pendulum clock is given by $T = 2\pi\sqrt{\frac{l}{g}}$, where l is the length of the pendulum and g, the acceleration due to gravity. Prove that if a pendulum clock l centimetres long is shortened by one millimetre, the clock will go faster by 43.2 seconds every day.
   [**Hint.** $l = 100$ cm for a correct pendulum clock.]
4. Find approximate value of $x^3 - 3x^2 + 4x - 2$ when $x = 1.03$.
5. The side of a square of side 6 cm is incorrectly measured as 6.11 cm. Find to one decimal place the resulting error in the calculation of the area of the square.
6. The formula $v = 8\sqrt{x}$ gives the velocity v of a particle when it has travelled a distance x from rest. Prove that if δv and δx denote the corresponding small increases in v and x respectively, $\delta x = \frac{32\,\delta x}{v}$.

Hence find the approximate increase in the velocity of the particle when x increases from 36 to 37.

7. If a point moves in a line $2y - 7x - 5 = 0$ so that its ordinate decreases at the rate of 3 units/sec. At what rate is the point moving in the direction of x-axis?
8. The pressure p and the volume v of a gas are connected by the relation $pv^{1.4} =$ constant. Find the percentage increases in the pressure corresponding to a diminution of $\frac{1}{2}$ per cent in volume.
9. Given $\log_e 10 = 2.3026$, find the value of $\log_e (10.02)$.
10. A spherical balloon is being inflated so that at the time when the radius is 5 cm, the radius is increasing at the rate of 15 cm/sec. Find the rate of increase of the volume at this time.

    If the rate of increase of the volume thereafter remains constant, find the rate at which the radius is increasing when the balloon has a diameter of 12 cm.

ANSWERS

1. 400 πcu. cm/unit.
2. $\dfrac{V^3(b-V)}{PV^3 - aV + 2ab}$.
4. 4.003.
5. 1.3 sq cm.
6. $\dfrac{2}{3}$.
7. $-\dfrac{6}{7}$ units/sec.
8. .7
9. 2.3046.
10. 15 π cu cm/sec, .104 cm/sec.

SECTIOND

EXPANSIONS, TAYLOR'S AND MACLAURIN'S THEOREMS

11. We know that $1 + \gamma + \gamma^2 + \gamma^3 + \ldots + \gamma^{n-1} = \dfrac{1-\gamma^n}{1-\gamma}$ (*see* Geometric Progression) and if $|\gamma| < 1$ and $n \to \infty$ then

$$1 + \gamma + \gamma^2 + \ldots + \infty \to \frac{1}{1-\gamma}$$

since $\gamma^n \to 0$ as $n \to \infty$.

Coming to the converse problem, we consider $\dfrac{1}{1-\gamma}$. Apply the following process of division. (This process is called Long Division Method.)

$$
\begin{array}{r l}
 & 1+\gamma+\gamma^2 \\
1+\gamma) & 1 \\
 & 1-\gamma \\
\hline
 & \gamma \\
 & \gamma-\gamma^2 \\
\hline
 & \gamma^2 \\
 & \gamma^2-\gamma^3 \\
\hline
 & \gamma^3 \\
 & \ldots
\end{array}
$$

We observe that $\dfrac{1}{1-\gamma} = 1+\gamma+\gamma^2+\dfrac{\gamma^3}{1-\gamma}$

$$= 1+\gamma+\gamma^2+\gamma^3+\frac{\gamma^4}{1-\gamma}$$

....

$$= 1+\gamma+\gamma^2+\ldots+\gamma^{n-1}+\frac{\gamma^n}{1-\gamma}.$$

When $|\gamma|<1$ and n becomes indefinitely large, γ^n becomes very small and ultimately in the limit as $n \to \infty$ $\gamma^n \to 0$, so

$$\frac{1}{1-\gamma} = 1+\gamma+\gamma^2+\gamma^3+\ldots \text{ up to } \infty.$$

The process by means of which a given function can be expressed in terms of a series is called *Expansion*. We have, in the above example shown that when r is numerically less than 1, $(1-\gamma)^{-1}$ can be expanded. A series of type $\sum_{n=0}^{\infty} x^n$ is called a *power series*. In a power series powers of *x ascend*. Thus $(1-\gamma)^{-1}$ can be expanded into a power series if $|\gamma|<1$.

This problem can be generalized. Suppose $f(x)$ is a function. "Can we find a suitable power series (convergent, of course) whose sum is equal to $f(x)$?"

A complete answer to this problem is beyond the scope of this book. But a partial answer to this problem is 'yes', if $f(x)$ has derivatives of each order.

We tackle the problem in a different manner. Suppose $f(x)$ has derivatives of each order and its expansion in a power series is possible, *i.e.*,

$$f(x) = \alpha_0 + \alpha_1 x + \alpha_2 x^2 + \ldots \text{ upto infinity}$$

We shall determine $\alpha_0, \alpha_1, \alpha_2, \ldots$ etc. If we can do so, then certainly we shall be able to complete our job *i.e.*, to expand $f(x)$ into a power series.

Firstly we take the case of *finite expansions*.

Let $\quad f(x) = \alpha_0 + \alpha_1 x + \alpha_2 x^2 + \ldots + \alpha_k x^k$

This immediately implies that $\alpha_0 = f(0)$.

Also $\quad f'(x) = \alpha_1 + 2\alpha_2 x + 3\alpha_3 x^2 + \ldots k\alpha_k x^{k-1}$

$\Rightarrow \quad \alpha_1 = f'(0).$

Again $\quad f''(x) = 2\alpha_2 + (3.2)\,\alpha_3 x + \ldots + k(k-1)\alpha_k x^{k-2}$

$\Rightarrow \quad 2\alpha_2 = f''(0) \quad \text{or} \quad \alpha_2 = \frac{1}{2} f''(0).$

Further $\quad f'''(x) = (3!)\,\alpha_3 + (4.3.2)\alpha_4 x + \ldots + k(k-1)\,(k-2)\alpha_k x^{k-3}$

$\Rightarrow \quad (3!)\alpha_3 = f'''(0)$

$\Rightarrow \quad \alpha_3 = \frac{1}{3!} f'''(0)$

Proceeding in this manner, we get at the end,

$$\alpha_k = \frac{1}{k!} f^{(k)}(0)$$

Hence $f(x) = f(0) + xf'(0) + \frac{x^2}{2!} f''(0) + \ldots +$

$$\frac{x^r}{r!} f^{(r)}(0) + \ldots + \frac{x^k}{k!} f^k(0)$$

where $f^{(r)}(0)$ stands for the value of rth derivative of $f(x)$ at $x = 0$.

The next question, which arises, is "Can this method be used for infinite expansions?"

The reply would be "not always". It can be done, of course, when series is uniformly convergent, a concept for a student of Advanced Real Analysis. Omitting the niceties and subtleties of such concepts to aficionados, we now assume that whatever functions we are dealing in, can be expanded into a power series which can be differentiated termwise.

The above process, now, can be repeated to given

$$f(x) = f(0) + xf'(0) + \frac{x^2}{2!} f''(0) + \ldots \text{ upto } \infty$$

$$= \sum_{r=0}^{\infty} \frac{x^r}{r!} f^{(r)}(0)$$

This is called *Maclaurin's Expansion*.

Example 25. *Expand sin x into a power series.*

Solution. Let $f(x) = \sin x$, then $f(0) = 0$

Also
$$f'(x) = \cos(x) \Rightarrow f'(0) = 1$$
$$f''(x) = -\sin x \Rightarrow f''(0) = 0$$
$$f'''(x) = -\cos x \Rightarrow f'''(0) = -1$$

etc.

Hence $f(x) = \sin x = x - \dfrac{x^3}{3!} + \dfrac{x^5}{5!} - \dfrac{x^7}{7!} + \ldots \infty$

REMARK: One can proceed by first evaluating rth derivative at $x = 0$ and then put $r = 0, 1, 2, \ldots$ etc.

For instance, here $f^r(x) = \sin\left(x + \dfrac{r\pi}{2}\right)$

So
$$f^r(0) = \sin\frac{r\pi}{2} = 0 \text{ if } r \text{ is even}$$
$$= (-1)^{\frac{r-1}{2}} \text{ if } r \text{ is odd}$$

Hence $\sin x = \sum\limits_{r=0}^{\infty} \dfrac{r^r}{r!} f^r(0) = \dfrac{(-1)^0}{1!} x + \dfrac{(-1)}{3!} x^3 + \dfrac{(-1)^2}{5!} x^5 + \ldots$

$$= x - \frac{x^3}{3!} + \frac{x^5}{5!} \ldots \infty.$$

Example 26. *Show that*

(i) $e^x = 1 + x + \dfrac{x^2}{\underline{|2}} + \dfrac{x^3}{\underline{|3}} + \ldots$ *(ii)* $e^{-x} = 1 - x + \dfrac{x^2}{\underline{|2}} - \dfrac{x^3}{\underline{|3}} + \ldots$

(iii) Coefficient of x^n *in the expansion of*

$$(1 + ax + bx^2)e^{-x} \text{ is } (-1)^n \left[\frac{1}{\underline{|n}} - \frac{a}{\underline{|n-1}} + \frac{b}{\underline{|n-2}}\right]$$

(iv) $e^{\sin x} = 1 + \dfrac{x}{1} + \dfrac{x^2}{2} - \dfrac{x^4}{8} + \ldots$

Solution. *(i)* Let $f(x) = e^x$

Then $f'(x) = f''(x) = f'''(x) = \ldots f^n(x) = e^x$

Thus $f(0) = 1 = f'(0) = f''(0) = \ldots$

So by Maclaurin's expansion

$f(x) = f(0) + xf'(0) + \dfrac{x^2}{\underline{|2}} f''(0) + \ldots$ we get

$$e^x = 1 + x + \frac{x^2}{\lfloor 2} + \frac{x^3}{\lfloor 3} + \ldots + \frac{x^n}{\lfloor n} + \ldots$$

(*ii*) Put $x = -x$ in result of (*i*) and we get the required expansion.

(*iii*) We have

$$(1 + ax + bx^2)\, e^{-x} = (1 + ax + bx^2)\left(1 - x + \frac{x^2}{\lfloor 2} - \frac{x^3}{\lfloor 3} + \ldots\right)$$

and hence coefficient of x^n is

$$\frac{bx^2 \cdot x^{(n-2)}}{\lfloor n-2} - ax\frac{x^{n-1}}{\lfloor n-1} + \frac{x}{\lfloor n} \text{ if n is even}$$

and $\dfrac{-bx^2 \cdot x^{n-2}}{\lfloor n-2} + ax \cdot \dfrac{x^{n-1}}{\lfloor n-1} - \dfrac{x^n}{\lfloor n}$ if n is odd and thus the coefficient is

$$\pm\left[\frac{1}{\lfloor n} - \frac{a}{\lfloor n-1} + \frac{b}{\lfloor n-2}\right] \quad \text{or} \quad (-1)^n\left[\frac{1}{\lfloor n} - \frac{a}{\lfloor n-1} + \frac{b}{\lfloor n-2}\right]$$

(*iv*) Let $y = e^{\sin x}$ then $y(0) = e^{\sin 0} = 1$

Also $y_1 = e^{\sin x} \cos x = y \cos x$

$\Rightarrow \qquad y_1(0) = y\,(0) \cos 0 = 1.1 = 1$

Again $y_2 = y_1 \cos x - y \sin x \;\Rightarrow\; y_2(0) = y_1(0) \cos 0 - y(0) \cdot \sin 0 = 1.$

Further $\qquad y_3 = y_2 \cos x - 2y_1 \sin x - y \cos x$

$\Rightarrow \qquad y_3(0) = y_2(0) - y(0) = 1 - 1 = 0$

Lastly $\qquad y_4 = y_3 \cos x - 3y_2 \sin x - 3y_1 \cos x + y \sin x$

$\Rightarrow \qquad y_4(0) = y_3(0) - 3y_1(0) = 0 - 3 = -3$

Hence $\qquad e^{\sin x} = f(0) + xf'(0) + \dfrac{x^2}{2} f''(0) + \ldots.$

$$= 1 + x + \frac{x^2}{2!} + \frac{x^3}{3!}(0) + \frac{x^4}{4!}(-3) + \ldots$$

$$= 1 + x + \frac{x^2}{2} - \frac{x^4}{8} \ldots$$

Example 27. *Prove that*

$$e^x \sin^2 x = x^2 + x^3 + \frac{x^4}{6}.$$

Solution. Ley $y = e^x \sin^2 x$

Then $\qquad y(0) = 0.$

Also $y_1 = e^x\sin^2 x + 2e^x \sin x \cos x$

$= e^x(\sin^2 x + 2\sin x \cos x)$

$\Rightarrow \quad y_1(0) = 0$

Again $y_2 = e^x(\sin^2 x + 2 \sin x \cos x)$

$+ e^x(2 \sin x \cos x + 2\cos^2 x - 2\sin^2 x)$

$= e^x(\sin^2 x + 4 \sin x \cos x - 2 \sin^2 x + 2 \cos^2 x)$

$\Rightarrow \quad y_2(0) = 2$

Further $y_3 = e^x(\sin^2 x + 4 \sin x \cos x - 2 \sin^2 x + 2 \cos^2 x)$

$+ e^x(2 \sin x \cos x + 4 \cos^2 x - 4 \sin^2 x - 4 \sin x \cos x$

$- 4 \cos x \sin x)$

$= e^x(\sin^2 x - 2 \sin x \cos x - 6 \sin^2 x + 6 \cos^2 x)$

$\Rightarrow \quad y_3(0) = 6.$

Lastly $y_4 = e^x(\sin^2 x - 12 \sin x \cos x - 6 \sin^2 x + 6 \cos^2 x)$

$+ e^x(2 \sin x \cos x - 2 \cos^2 x + 2 \sin^2 x - 12 \sin x \cos x$

$- 12 \sin x \cos x)$

$= e^x (\sin^2 x - 24 \sin x \cos x - 4 \sin^2 x + 4 \cos^2 x)$

$\Rightarrow \quad y_4(0) = 4$

Hence $e^x \sin^2 x = y(0) + x\, y_1(0) + \dfrac{x^2}{2!} y_2(0) + \ldots \infty$

$= 0 + 0 + \dfrac{x^3}{2!}(2) + \dfrac{x^3}{3!}(6) + \dfrac{x^4}{4!}(4) \ldots$

$= x^2 + x^3 + \dfrac{x^4}{6}.$

Example 28. *Show by using Maclaurin's expansion that*

$$\log(1 + x) = x - \frac{x^2}{2} + \frac{x^3}{3} - \frac{x^4}{4} + \ldots$$

Solution. Let $f(x) = \log(1 + x)$

Then $f'(x) = \dfrac{1}{1 + x} \quad \Rightarrow \quad f'(0) = 1$

$f''(x) = -\dfrac{1}{(1 + x)^2} \quad \Rightarrow \quad f''(0) = -1$

$f'''(x) = \dfrac{(-1)(-2)}{(1 + x)^3} \quad \Rightarrow \quad f'''(0) = \underline{|2}$

$$f^{iv}(x) = \frac{(-1)(-2)(-3)}{(1+x)^4} \Rightarrow f^{iv}(0) = -\underline{|3}$$

and so on.

Thus by Maclaurin's expansion,

$$f(x) = f(0) + xf'(0) + \frac{x^2}{\underline{|2}} f''(0) + \ldots$$

We get

$$\log(1+x) = \log 1 + x.1 + \frac{x^2}{\underline{|2}}(-1) + \frac{x^2}{\underline{|3}}.\underline{|2} - \frac{x^4}{4}.\underline{|3} + \ldots$$

$$= x - \frac{x^2}{2} + \frac{x^3}{3} - \frac{x^4}{4} + \ldots$$

12. TAYLOR'S EXPANSION

Let $f(x+h)$ be expandable into a power series in the variable h. Again the flat assumption is that this series can be differentiated term by term.

Taylor's theorem states that, under the conditions laid down as above,

$$f(a+h) = f(a) + hf'(a) + \frac{h^2}{2!} f''(a) + \ldots \infty$$

Proof. Let $f(a+h) = \alpha_0 + \alpha_1 h + \alpha_2 h^2 + \alpha_3 h^3 + \ldots \infty$

Put $h = 0$ to get $\alpha_0 = f(a)$.

Differentiating each side with respect to h, we obtain

$$\frac{d}{dh}[f(a+h)] = \alpha_1 + 2\alpha_2 h + 3\alpha_3 h^2 + \ldots \infty$$

But $$\frac{d}{dh}[f(a+h)] = \frac{d[f(a+h)]}{d(a+h)} \cdot \frac{d(a+h)}{d(h)}$$

$$= f'(a+h) \,.\, 1 = f'(a+h)$$

This in turn yields that

$$\alpha_1 = f'(a)$$

[*Observe that* $f'(a+h)$ *is first derivative of* $f(a+h)$ *with respect to* $a+h$.]

Again, differentiate both sides with respect to h.

Thus $$f''(a+h) = 2\alpha_2 + (3.2)\alpha_3 h + \ldots \infty$$

$$\Rightarrow \quad 2\alpha_2 = f''(a) \quad \text{or} \quad \alpha_2 = \frac{f''(a)}{2!}$$

Proceeding in this manner, we get

$$\alpha_r = \frac{1}{r!} f^{(r)}(a)$$

Hence $$f(a+h) = \sum_{r=0}^{\infty} \frac{h^r}{r!} f^{(r)}(a).$$

Example 29. *Show that*

$$\log (n+1) = \log n + \left(\frac{1}{n} - \frac{1}{2n^2} + \frac{1}{3n^3} - \frac{1}{4n^4} + \ldots\right).$$

Solution. We expand log $(n+h)$ in terms of h and then put $h = 1$.

$$f(n+h) = \log (n+h) \Rightarrow f(n) = \log n$$

Also $$f'(n+h) = \frac{d}{d(n+h)}[\log (n+h)] = \frac{1}{n+h}$$

$$\Rightarrow \quad f'(n) = \frac{1}{n}.$$

Further $$f''(n+h) = -\frac{1}{(n+h)^2} \Rightarrow f''(n) = -\frac{1}{n^2}$$

ans so on.

In general $$f^{(r)}(n+h) = \frac{(-1)^{r-1}(r-1)^r}{(n+h)^r}$$

$$\Rightarrow \quad f^{(r)}(n) = \frac{(-1)^{r-1}(r-1)}{n^r}.$$

Consequently by Taylor's Expansion

$$\log (n+h) = f(n) + hf'(n) + \frac{h^2}{2!} f''(n) + \ldots + \frac{h^r}{r!} f^{(r)}(n) + \ldots$$

$$= \log n + \frac{h}{n} - \frac{h^2}{2n^2} + \frac{2!}{3!}\frac{h^3}{n^3} + \ldots$$

$$+ \frac{(-1)^{r-1} hr\,(r-1)!}{(r!)\,nr} + \ldots$$

Put $h = 1$, to obtain

$$\log (n+1) = \log n + \left[\frac{1}{n} - \frac{1}{2n^2} + \frac{1}{3n^3} - \frac{1}{4n^4} + \ldots\right].$$

Example 30. *Prove that*

$$\tan^{-1}(x+2) = \tan^{-1} x + 2 \sin z \frac{\sin z}{1} - \frac{(2 \sin z)^2}{2} \sin^2 z + \frac{(2 \sin z)^3 \sin 3z}{3} - \ldots$$

where $\cot z = x$.

Solution. We expand $\tan^{-1}(x+h)$ by Taylor's Expansion and then put $h = 2$.

Here $f(x+h) = \tan^{-1}(x+h) \Rightarrow f(x) = \tan^{-1} x$

In this case $f^{(r)}(x+h) = (-1)^{r-1}(r-1)! \sin^n \theta \sin n\theta$

where $\cos \theta = x + h$

Thus $f^{(r)}_{(x)} = (-1)^{r-1}(r-1)! \sin^n z \sin nz$

since by definition value of $\cot \theta$ at $h = 0$

is $\cot z$ *i.e.*, $\theta = z$

$$\text{Hence } \tan^{-1}(x+h) = \tan^{-1} x + h \sin z \sin z + \frac{h^2}{2!}(-\sin^2 z \sin 2z) + \frac{h^3}{3!}(2! \sin^3 z \sin 3z) \ldots$$

$$= \tan^{-1} x + h \sin z \frac{\sin z}{1} - \frac{h^2 \sin^2 z}{2} \sin 2z + \frac{h^3}{3} \sin^3 z \sin 3z \ldots$$

Put $h = 2$, to get the required result.

Example 31. *Show that if x is numerically less than 1*

$$\frac{1}{(1-x)^2} = 1 + 2x + 3x^2 + 4x^3 +$$

Solution. Here $\quad f(a+h) = \dfrac{1}{(a+h)^2}$

$$\Rightarrow \quad f(a) = \frac{1}{a^2}$$

$$f'(a+h) = -\frac{2}{(a+h)^3}$$

$$\Rightarrow \qquad f'(a) = -\frac{2}{a^3}$$

Again $$f''(a+h) = \frac{6}{(a+h)^4}$$

$$\Rightarrow \qquad f''(a) = \frac{6}{a^4}.$$

and so on.

By Taylor's Expansion

$$\frac{1}{(a+h)^2} = \frac{1}{a^2} - \frac{2}{a^3}h + \frac{6}{a^4}\frac{1}{2!}h^2 \ldots$$

Put $a = -1$, $h = x$ to get

$$\frac{1}{(-1+x)^2} = 1 + 2x + 3x^2 + \ldots$$

or $$\frac{1}{(1-x)^2} = 1 + 2x + 3x^2 + \ldots$$

NOTE. That series on RHS is convergent only when x is numerically less than 1.

REMARK: One might think that in the proof of $\frac{d}{dx}\left(\frac{1}{x^2}\right)$ (by definition), we use the series $(1-x)^{-2} = 1 + 2x + 3x^2 + \ldots$. We could avoid this circular argument by finding out derivative of x^{-n}, n is any integer by following technique

$$\frac{d}{dx}\left(\frac{1}{x^n}\right) = \frac{\frac{d}{dx}(1)x^n - 1.nx^{n-1}}{x^{2n}}$$

$$= \frac{0.x^n - nx^{n-1}}{x^{2n}}$$

$$= \frac{-nx^{n-1}}{x^{2n}} = -\frac{n}{x^{n+1}} = -nx^{-n-1}$$

Now put $n = 1, 2, 3, \ldots$, to get derivative of reciprocal of any integral power of x.

Example 32. *Prove that*

$$\log \tan\left(\frac{\pi}{4} + x\right) = 2x + \frac{4}{3}x^3 + \frac{9}{3}x^5 \ldots$$

Solution. Put $f(a+h) = \log \tan\left(\frac{\pi}{4} + x\right)$, $a = \frac{\pi}{4}$, $h = x$

$$f(a) = \log \tan \frac{\pi}{4} = \log 1 = 0$$

$$f'(a+h) = \tan(\pi/4 + x)\sec^2(\pi/4 + x)$$

$$= \frac{1}{\sin(\pi/4 + x)\cos(\pi/4 + x)}$$

$$= \frac{2}{2\sin(\pi/4 + x)\cos(\pi/4 + x)} = \frac{2}{\sin(\pi/2 + 2x)}$$

$$= \frac{2}{\cos 2x} = 2\sec 2x$$

$$\Rightarrow \quad f'(a) = 2\sec 0 = 2$$

$$f''(a+h) = 4\sec 2x \tan 2x$$

$$\Rightarrow \quad f''(a) = 0$$

$$f'''(a+h) = 4[2\sec 2x \tan^2 2x + 2\sec^3 2x]$$

$$= 8(\sec 2x \tan^2 2x + \sec^3 2x)$$

$$\Rightarrow \quad f'''(a) = 8$$

$$f^{(4)}(a+h) = 8[2\sec^2 2x \tan^3 2x + 4\sec^3 2x \tan 2x + 6\sec^3 2x \tan 2x]$$

$$= 8[2\sec^2 x \tan^3 2x + 10\sec^3 2x \tan 2x]$$

$$\Rightarrow \quad f^{(4)}(a) = 0$$

Finally

$$f^{(5)}(a+h) = 8[4\sec 2x \tan^4 2x + 18\sec^3 x \tan^2 2x + 60\sec^3 2x \tan^2 2x + 20\sec^5 2x]$$

$$\Rightarrow \quad f^{(5)}(a) = 8.20 = 160.$$

Hence by Taylor's Expansion

$$\log \sin\left(\frac{\pi}{4} + x\right) = f(a) + f'(a)x + \frac{f''(a)x^2}{2!} + \ldots$$

$$= .0 + 2x + 0 + 8\frac{x^3}{3!} + 0 + \frac{160x^5}{5!} + \ldots$$

$$= 2x + \frac{4x^3}{3} + \frac{4}{3}x^5 + \ldots$$

Example 33. *Prove that*

$$\sin^{-1} x = x + \frac{1}{2}.\frac{x^3}{3} + \frac{1}{2}.\frac{3}{4}.\frac{x^5}{5} + \ldots$$

Solution. Here $f(x) = \sin^{-1} x \Rightarrow f(0) = 0$

$$f'(x) = \frac{1}{\sqrt{1-x^2}} = (1-x^2)^{-1/2} \Rightarrow f'(0) = 1$$

$$f''(x) = -\frac{1}{2}(1-x^2)^{-3/2}(-2x)$$

$$= x(1-x^2)^{-3/2} \Rightarrow f''(0) = 0$$

$$f'''(x) = (1-x^2)^{-3/2} - \frac{3x}{2}(1-x^2)^{-5/2}(-2x)$$

$$= (1-x^2)^{-3/2} + 3x^2(1-x^2)^{-5/2}$$

$$\Rightarrow \quad f'''(0) = 1$$

$$f^{(4)}(x) = -\frac{3}{2}(1-x^2)^{-5/2}(-2x) + 6x(1-x^2)^{-5/2}$$

$$+ 3x^2\left[-\frac{5}{2}(1-x^2)^{-7/2}(-2x)\right]$$

$$= 9x(1-x^2)^{-5/2} + 15x^3(1-x^2)^{-7/2}$$

$$\Rightarrow \quad f^{(4)}(a) = 0$$

Finally

$$f^{(5)}(x) = 9(1-x^2)^{-5/2} + 9x\left(-\frac{5}{2}\right)(1-x^2)^{-7/2}(-2x)$$

$$+ 45x^2(1-x^2)^{-7/2} + 15x^3(-7/2)(1-x^2)^{-9/2}(-2x)$$

$$= 9(1-x^2)^{-5/2} + 90x^2(1-x^2)^{-7/2} + 105x^4(1-x^2)^{-9/2}$$

$$\Rightarrow f^{(5)}(0) = 9.$$

Hence by Maclaurin's Expansion

$$f(x) = f(0) + xf'(0) + \frac{x^2}{2!}f''(0) + \ldots$$

$$\Rightarrow \quad \sin^{-1} x = 0 + x + 0 + \frac{x^3}{3!} + 0 + \frac{9x^5}{5!} + \ldots$$

$$= x + \frac{1}{2}\cdot\frac{x^3}{3} + \frac{1}{2}\cdot\frac{3}{4}\cdot\frac{x^5}{5} + \ldots$$

EXERCISES

Prove the following Expansions:

1. $\cos^2 x = 1 - x^2 + \frac{x^4}{3} - \frac{2}{45}x^6 + \ldots$

2. $\log \sec x = \frac{1}{2}x^2 + \frac{1}{12}x^4 + \frac{1}{45}x^6 + \ldots$ 3. $(\sin^{-1} x)^2 = 2\frac{x^2}{2!} + \frac{2.2^2}{4!}x^4 + \ldots$

4. $e^{ax} \cos bx = 1 + ax + \frac{a^2 - b^2}{2!}x^2 + \ldots$ 5. $e^m \sin^{-1} x = 1 + mx + \frac{m^2}{2!}x^2 + \ldots$

6. $\tan x = x + \frac{1}{3}x^2 + \frac{2}{15}x^5 + \ldots$ 7. $\cos x = 1 - \frac{x^2}{\lfloor 2} + \frac{x^4}{\lfloor 4} - \frac{x^6}{\lfloor 6} + \ldots$

8. $\log \sin (x + h) = \log \sin x + h \cot x - \frac{h^2}{2!} \operatorname{cosec}^2 x + \ldots$

9. $\log (1 + \tan x) = x - \frac{x^2}{2} + \frac{2}{3}x^3$.

10. Expand $\log \sin x$ in powers of $x - 1$.

[**Hint.** $\log \sin x = \log \sin (1 + x - 1)$. Now apply Taylor's theorem to $\log \sin (a + h)$, $a = 1$, $h = x - 1$.]

11. Expand $\cos x$ in powers of $x + 2$.

ANSWERS

10. $\log \sin 1 + (x - 1) \cot 1 - \frac{(x-1)^2}{2} \operatorname{cosec}^2 1 + \frac{(x-1)^3}{3} \cot 1 \operatorname{cosec}^2 1 + \ldots$

11. $\cos 2 - (x - 2) \sin 2 - \frac{(x-2)^2}{2!} \cos 2 + \frac{(x-2)^3}{3!} \sin 2 \ldots$.

SECTIONE

APPLICATIONS TO COMMERCE AND ECONOMICS

13. SUPPLY AND DEMAND CURVES

Let p be the price and x be quantity demanded. The curve $x = f(p)$ is called a *demand curve*. It usually slopes downwards as demand decreases when prices are increased.

Once again let p be the price and x the quantity supplied. The curve $x = g(p)$ is called a *supply curve*. It is often noted that when supply is increased, the profiteers increase prices, so a supply curve frequently slopes upwards.

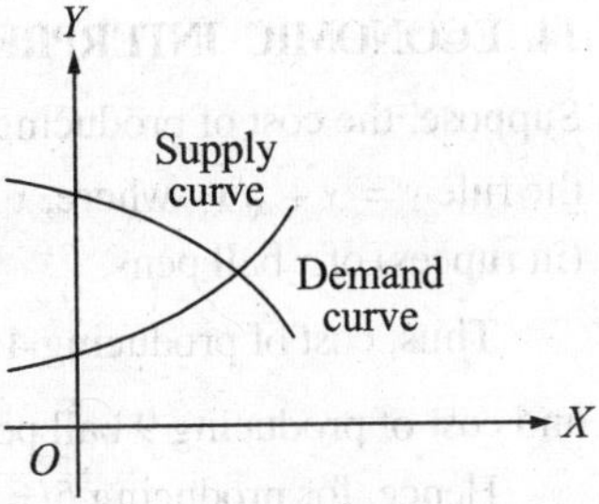

Fig. 10

Let us plot the two curves on a graph paper.

If the two curves intersect, we say that an *economic equilibrium* is attained (at the point of intersection).

It is also possible that the two curves may not intersect *i.e.*, economic equilibrium need not always be obtained.

Revenue Curve: If $x = f(p)$ is demand curve and if it is possible to express p as a function of x say $p = g(x)$ then function g is called inverse of f. In the problems we deal in this book, each demand function f always possesses inverse. So we can write,

$$x = f(p) \text{ as well as } p = g(x).$$

The product R of x and p is called the *total revenue*.

Thus, $R = xp$ where, x is demand and p is price. We can write $R = pf(p) = x\,g(x)$.

The *total revenue* function is defined as $R = x\,g(x)$ and if we measure x along x-axis and R along y-axis, we can plot the curve $y = xg(x)$.

This curve is called *total revenue curve*.

Cost Function: The cost c is composed of two parts, namely, the fixed cost and variable cost. Fixed costs are those which are not affected by the change in the amount of production. Suppose, there is a publishing firm, then the rent of the building in which the firm is situated is fixed cost (whether the number of books published increases or decreases). Similarly, the salaries of people employed is also fixed cost (even when the production is zero).

On the other hand, cost of printing paper is variable cost, as the more books they publish the more paper is required, etc.

Thus, $\qquad C = VC + FC$

where, C is total cost, VC, variable cost and FC is fixed cost.

14. ECONOMIC INTERPRETATION OF DERIVATIVE

Suppose, the cost of producing a certain type of ball pens is governed by the rule $y = x + \sqrt{x}$, where, x is the number of ball pens and y is the cost (in rupees) of x ball pens.

Thus, cost of producing 4 ball pens is $4 + \sqrt{4} = 6$

and cost of producing 9 ball pens is $9 + \sqrt{9} = 12$.

Hence, for producing $5 (= 9 - 4)$ more ball pens, the cost goes up by $12 - 6 = 6$ rupees.

So, each extra pen produced (from 4 to 9) costs $\frac{6}{5}$ = Rs 1.20.

This we call the average rate of change in cost. Again cost of producing 25 pens will be $25 + \sqrt{25} = 30$ and thus if the production is increased form 4 to 25 the average cost for each pen is given by

$$\frac{30-6}{25-4} = \frac{24}{21} = \text{Rs } 1.14.$$

In other wards, the average rate of change in cost is Rs 1.14 if production is increased form 4 to 25.

Again, if production is increased from 9 to 25 pens, the average rate

$$= \frac{30-12}{25-9} = \frac{18}{16} = \text{Rs } 1.12.$$

We, thus, notice that the average rate of change (in cost) depends upon '*where we start* and *where we finish*'. We have, of course, assumed here that the cost depends upon only the number of units produced.

We generalise the above concept as follows:

Let the governing rule be $y = f(x)$.

If x is increased form x_1 to x_2, y changes from $f(x_1)$ to $f(x_2)$.

The average rate of change is given by

$$\frac{f(x_2) - f(x_1)}{x_2 - x_1}$$

Which we write as $\frac{\delta y}{\delta x}$ and which clearly depends upon the value of x from which we start and on the amount of increase (change) allotted to x.

We now extend this idea of average rate of change, a little further.

Suppose, we fix the starting value of x (although it may be any value) and make a change in it say x to $x + \delta x$.

Then the average rate of change (in $f(x)$, per unit change in x) is

$$\frac{f(x+\delta x) - f(x)}{x + \delta x - x} = \frac{f(x+\delta x) - f(x)}{\delta x}$$

Now, if we make δx approach zero (*i.e.*, the change in x is almost nil), we get, what is called the *instantaneous rate of change* of the function at the point x.

i.e., by definition,

$$\text{Instantaneous rate of change} = \lim_{\delta x \to 0} \frac{f(x+\delta x) - f(x)}{\delta x} = \lim_{\delta x \to 0} \frac{\delta y}{\delta x}.$$

Consider as an example, the function $y = f(x) = x^2$.

If x changes from x_1 to x_2

average rate of change is

$$\frac{f(x+\delta x)-f(x)}{\delta x}=\frac{(x+\delta x)^2-x^2}{\delta x}=\delta x+2x$$

and instantaneous rate of change at x will be

$$\lim_{\delta x\to 0}\frac{f(x+\delta x)-f(x)}{\delta x}=\lim_{\delta x\to 0}(\delta x+2x)=2x.$$

It is clear that we can determine the instantaneous rate of change of $y=f(x)$ at any value of x, *e.g.*, for $y=x^2$.

At $x=2$ it is $2\times 2=4$

at $x=2$ it is $2\times 3=6$

at $x=4$ it is $2\times 4=8$ etc.

(It is being given by $2x$).

Example 34. *Find the average rate of change for the function $y = 2x + 1$, when x changes from 2 to 6.*

Solution. Here, $\delta x=6-2=4$.

To calculate δy, we notice,

$$f(6)=12+1=13$$

$$f(2)=4+1=5$$

$$\Rightarrow \quad \delta y=f(6)-f(2)=13-5=8.$$

Thus, average rate of change in y is 2 when x changes from 2 to 6.

REMARKS:

(*a*) Recalling the definition of derivative, we notice, that $\frac{dy}{dx}$, the derivative of y with respect to x is the instantaneous rate of change of y at a point x.

(*b*) The average rate of change is over a certain interval (say over a certain time period) or from a certain number of units to some other number of units, whereas the instantaneous rate of change is at a particular instance.

15. TOTAL AND MARGINAL CONCEPTS

In economics, we know that marginal cost at a certain level of output is the change in cost that results when output is increased by a very small unit amount for this level, *i.e*, if total cost is known then the extra cost of producing one additional unit is called marginal cost, which will be the instantaneous change in cost at the point where total cost is known and, thus, we can say that

$$MC=\frac{d}{dx}TC$$

where TC is a function of x, the level of output.

Similarly, marginal revenue is defined as the change in total revenue brought about by the sale of an extra good.

i.e., mathematically, $MR = \frac{d}{dx} TR$

where x is level of output.

Thus, in general, we notice that the marginal concepts of an economic function are the derivatives of the total functions.

Since, total revenue TR is given by $TR = px$ where p is the price and x the quantity demanded, we find

$$\text{Marginal revenue } MR = \frac{d}{dx} TR = \frac{d}{dx}(px) = p + x\frac{dp}{dx}.$$

16. RELATION BETWEEN AVERAGE AND MARGINAL COSTS

Let TC denote total cost, x denote quantity demanded then average cost

$AC = \frac{TC}{x}$ and marginal cost $MC = \frac{d}{dx} TC$.

Slope of the average cost curve is given by

$$\frac{d}{dx} AC = \frac{d}{dx}\left[\frac{TC}{x}\right]$$

$$= \frac{x\frac{d}{dx}TC - TC\frac{dx}{dx}}{x^2}$$

$$= \frac{xMC - TC}{x^2} = \frac{1}{x}(MC - AC).$$

If cost curve is u-shaped and if AC has a curve sloping downward

then $\frac{d}{dx}\left(\frac{TC}{x}\right) < 0.$

So, $MC < AC$.

Thus, when AC decreases, $MC < AC$. On the lowest point of AC curve, the tangent will be horizontal,

so $\frac{d}{dx}\left(\frac{TC}{x}\right) = 0$, *i.e.*, $MC = AC$.

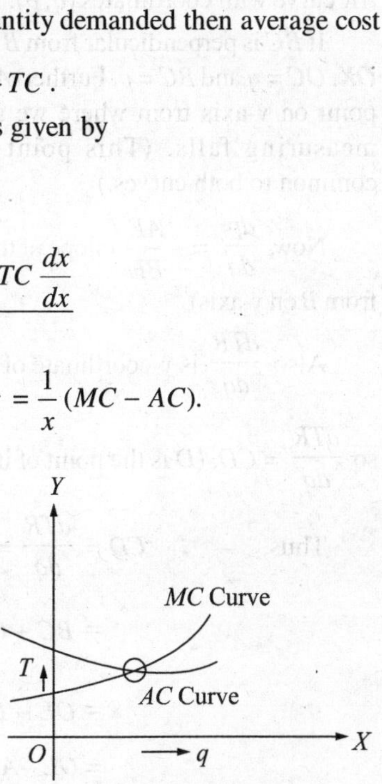

Fig. 11

Hence, for a u-shaped curve, at the lowest point $MC = AC$.

If AC curve is rising then $MC > AC$, since in this situation

$\frac{d}{dx}\left(\frac{TC}{x}\right) > 0$.

17. RELATIONSHIP BETWEEN AVERAGE AND MARGINAL REVENUES

Theorem: *Rate of fall of MR curve is twice the rate of fall of the average revenue (AR) curve.*

Proof: Since, $TR = pq$,

$$\frac{dTR}{dq} = p + q\frac{dp}{dq}.$$

Let us assume that B is a point of AR curve with coordinates (q, p).

If BC is perpendicular from B on OX, $OC = q$ and $BC = p$. Further, A is point on y-axis from where we are measuring falls. (This point is common to both curves.)

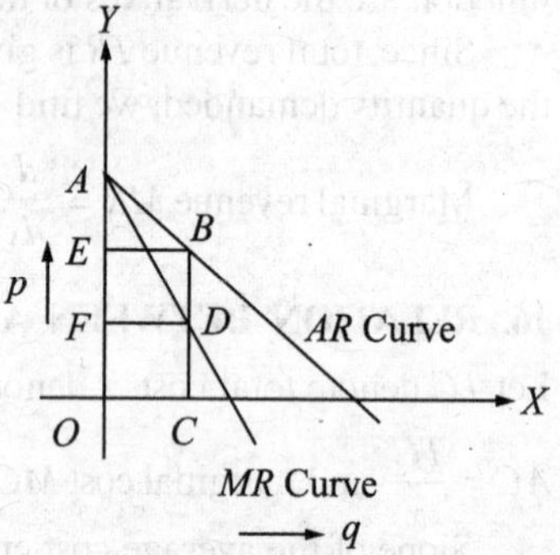

Fig. 12

Now, $\frac{dp}{dq} = -\frac{AE}{BE}$ (slope of the AB, E being the foot of perpendicular from B on y-axis)

Also $\frac{dTR}{dq}$ is y-coordinate of a point on MR curve with abscissa q,

so $\frac{dTR}{dq} = CD$, (D is the point of intersection of MR curve with BC).

Thus,
$$CD = \frac{dTR}{dq} = p + q\frac{dp}{dq}$$
$$= BC + OC\left(-\frac{AE}{BE}\right)$$
$$= OE - BE\left(-\frac{AE}{BE}\right)$$
$$= OE - AE$$

Also, $CD = BC - BD = OE - EF$

where, F is the foot of perpendicular form D on y-axis.

Thus, $OE - AE = OE - EF$

$\Rightarrow \qquad AE = EF$

i.e, $\qquad AF = AE + EF = 2AE.$

So, the rate of fall of *MR* curve is twice that of *AR* curve.

Example 35. *Show that if* $TC = aq^b + k$ $(a > 0, b > 0, k \geq 0)$ *then* $MC = abq^{b-1}$ *and marginal average cost* $= a(b-1)q^{b-2} - \dfrac{k}{q^2}$.

Solution. $MC = \dfrac{dTC}{dq} = abq^{b-1}$

$$\text{Average cost} = \frac{TC}{q} = aq^{b-1} + \frac{k}{q}.$$

So marginal average cost

$$= \frac{d}{dq}\left(\frac{TC}{q}\right) = a(b-1)q^{b-2} - \frac{k}{q^2}.$$

Example 36. *Find average cost and marginal cost, if* $TC = 1000 + 100q - 10q^2 + q^3$.

Solution. $AC = \dfrac{TC}{q} = \dfrac{1000}{q} + 100 - 10q + q^2$

$$MC = \frac{dTC}{dq} = 100 - 20q + 3q^2.$$

Example 37. *Show that if* $TC = ae^{bq}$, *then marginal cost is equal to average cost, provided* $q = b^{-1}$.

Solution: $AC = \dfrac{TC}{q}$ and $MC = \dfrac{dTC}{dq} = \dfrac{d}{dq}(ae^{bq}) = abe^{bq}$

So, $\qquad AC = MC$

$\Rightarrow \qquad \dfrac{TC}{q} = abe^{bq}$

$\Rightarrow \qquad \dfrac{a}{q}e^{bq} = abe^{bq}$

$\Rightarrow \qquad 1 = qb$ as $e^{bq} \neq 0$

$\Rightarrow \qquad q = b^{-1}.$

Example 38. *The total cost function of a firm is*

$$c = \frac{1}{3}x^3 - 5x^2 + 28x + 10$$

where c is total cost and x is output. A tax at the rate of Rs 2 per unit of output is imposed and the producer adds it to his cost. If the market demand function is given by

$$p = 2530 - 5x$$

where Rs p is the price per unit of output, find the profit maximising output and price.

Solution. The total cost TC after the producer adds tax is

$$TC = \frac{1}{3}x^3 - 5x^2 + 28x + 10 + 2x$$

$$= \frac{x^3}{3} - 5x^2 + 30x + 10$$

Total revenue $TR = px = 2530x - 5x^2$.

Profit $\pi = TR - TC$

$$= -\frac{x^3}{3} + 2500x - 10.$$

For max. or min. profit, $\frac{d\pi}{dx} = 0$

i.e., $-x^2 + 2500 = 0$

$\Rightarrow$ $x = \pm 50.$

Now, $\frac{d^2\pi}{dx^2} = -2x$ which is – ve for $x = 50$.

Hence, $x = 50$ gives maximum profit.

Corresponding price is given by $p = 2530 - 5 \times 50 = 2280$.

Hence, the profit maximizing output is 50 and price is Rs 2280.

Example 39. *A firm's demand function is $3p + x = 48$. Find the level of output where total revenue is maximised. Also if the average cost function is given by $AC = x^2 - 2x + 10$, find the level of output which minimises marginal costs.*

Solution. We have,

$$3p + x = 48$$

$\Rightarrow$ $$p = 16 - \frac{x}{3}.$$

Since, $$TR = p \times x = 16x - \frac{x^2}{3}.$$

For max. or min., $$\frac{d}{dx}R = 0$$

$$\Rightarrow \quad 16 - \frac{2x}{3} = 0 \Rightarrow x = 24.$$

Again as $$\frac{d^2}{dx^2}TR = -\frac{2}{3} < 0$$

We find that TR is maximum at $x = 24$.

Again since, $$AC = x^2 - 2x + 10$$

$$TC = AC \times x = x^3 - 2x^2 + 10x.$$

Hence, $$MC = \frac{d}{dx}TC = 3x^2 - 4x + 10.$$

For max. or min., $$\frac{d}{dx}MC = 0$$

i.e, $$6x - 4 = 0$$

i.e, $$x = \frac{2}{3}$$

again $$\frac{d^2}{dx^2}MC = 6 > 0.$$

i.e, at $x = \frac{2}{3}$, marginal cost is minimum.

Example 40. *If demand function is $p = 30 - 2x$, find the marginal revenue when level of output x is 4.*

Solution. We know,

$$TR = p \times x = 30x - 2x^2$$

thus, $$MR = \frac{d}{dx}TR = 30 - 4x$$

Hence when $x = 4$,

$$MR = 30 - 16 = 14.$$

Example 41. *A certain machine sells for Rs p hundred and the demand of x hundred machines per year is given by*

$$x = \frac{90}{p+5} - 3.$$

Determine at which price and output, the total revenue is maximum.

Solution. Let the total revenue be R hundred rupees. Then

$$R = xp \times 100 = 100\left(\frac{90p}{p+5} - 3p\right).$$

For max. or min., $\quad \frac{dR}{dp} = 0$

$$\Rightarrow \quad \frac{90(p+5) - 90p}{(p+5)^2} - 3 = 0$$

$$\Rightarrow \quad 150 = (d+5)^2$$

or, $\quad p + 5 = \pm 5\sqrt{6}$

or, $\quad p = -5 \pm 5\sqrt{6}.$

Since, p cannot be – ve

we have, $\quad p = 5(\sqrt{6} - 1)$

Again $\quad \frac{d^2R}{dp^2} = -\frac{900}{(p+5)^3}$ which will be – ve

for $\quad p = 5(\sqrt{6} - 1).$

Hence, at $p = 5(\sqrt{6} - 1)$, R is maximum.

Also then, the output $= \frac{90}{5(\sqrt{6}-1)+5} - 3$

$= 3(\sqrt{6} - 1)$ hundred.

Hence, for maximum revenue, the price of the machine must be $5(\sqrt{6} - 1)$ hundred rupees, *i.e.*, Rs 618 and the output per annum should be $300(\sqrt{6} - 1)$ *i.e.*, 371.

Example 42. *A firm has the following total revenue and total cost functions.*

$$TR = 100x - x^2$$

$$TC = x^3 - \frac{57}{2}x^2 \text{ where } x \text{ is level of output.}$$

Find maximum profit.

Solution. Profit $\quad \pi = TR - TC$

$$= (100x - x^2) - \left(x^3 - \frac{57}{2}x^2\right)$$

$$= 100x + \frac{55}{2}x^2 - x^3$$

For max. or min., $\frac{d\pi}{dx} = 0$

$\Rightarrow \quad 100 - 55x + 3x^2 = 0$

$\Rightarrow \quad x = 20, -\frac{5}{3},$

Again, $\frac{d^2\pi}{dx^2} = 55 - 6x$

which is –ve at $x = 20$.

Hence, at $x = 20$, the profit is maximum.

Also then maximum value of profit is

$$100 \times 20 + \frac{55}{3}(20)^2 - (20)^2 = 5000.$$

Example 43. *The relationship between sales and advertising x is given by* $s = \frac{400x}{1+x}$. *If the gross profit is 25% of sales revenue, find net profit π as a function of s and x. Find x so as to maximize net profit.*

Solution. Net profit π is given by

$$\pi = \frac{25s}{100} - x$$

i.e., $\pi = \frac{s}{4} - x$

Thus, $\pi = \frac{400x}{(1+x)4} - x = \frac{100x}{1+x} - x$

For max. or min.,

$$\frac{d\pi}{dx} = 0 \Rightarrow \frac{(1+x)100 - 100x}{(1+x)^2} - 1 = 0$$

$\Rightarrow \quad (1+x)^2 = 100$

$\Rightarrow \quad x = 9$ (neglecting –ve value)

Again $\frac{d^2\pi}{dx^2} = -\frac{200}{(1+x)^3} < 0$ when $x = 9$

Hence at $x = 9$, π is maximum.

Example 44. *A firm's total costs C are related to total output x over a five year period by the function* $C = ax^3 - bx^2 + cx$, *where a, b and c are positive constants.*

(i) *What is the average cost function?*
(ii) *At what output is average cost a minimum?*
(iii) *What is the marginal cost function?*
(iv) *At what output does average cost equal marginal cost?*

Solution. (*i*) Average cost function $= \frac{C}{x} = ax^2 - bx + c.$

(*ii*) $\frac{C}{x}$ will be minimum or maximum if $\frac{d}{dx}\left(\frac{C}{x}\right) = 0$, *i.e.*, if $2ax - b = 0$.

$$\Rightarrow \qquad x = \frac{b}{2a}$$

Since, $\frac{d^2}{dx^2}\left(\frac{C}{x}\right) = 2a > 0,$

so, $x = \frac{b}{2a}$ gives minimum average cost.

(*iii*) Marginal cost function $= \frac{dC}{dx} = 3ax^2 - 2bx + c.$

(*iv*) $AC = MC$

$$\Rightarrow \qquad ax^2 - bx + c = 3ax^2 - 2bx + c$$

$$\Rightarrow \qquad 2ax^2 = bx$$

$\Rightarrow$ either $x = 0$ or $x = \frac{b}{2a}$.

Example 45. *The demand function for a particular commodity is* $y = 15e^{-x/3}$ *for* $0 \le x \le 8$, *where y is the price per unit and x is the number of units demanded. Determine the price and the quantity for which the revenue is maximum.*

Solution. Total Revenue = Total amount returned when all the units are sold

$$= xy.$$

Let $R = xy$, we are to calculate maximum R.

$$R = xy = 15xe^{-x/3}$$

For maximum or minimum, $\frac{dR}{dx} = 0$

$$\Rightarrow \qquad 15\left[e^{-x/3} - \frac{x}{3}e^{-x/3}\right] = 0.$$

$$\Rightarrow \qquad x = 3 \text{ as } e^{-x/3} \neq 0$$

Further at $x = 3$,

$$\frac{d^2R}{dx^2} = 15\left[-\frac{1}{3}e^{-x/3} - \frac{1}{3}e^{-x/3} + \frac{x}{9}e^{-x/3}\right]$$

$$= 15e^{-x/3}\left(-\frac{2}{3} + \frac{x}{9}\right)$$

$$= \frac{15}{e}\left(-\frac{2}{3} + \frac{1}{3}\right) = -\frac{5}{e} < 0$$

implies that $x = 3$ gives maximum revenue.

Now at $x = 3$, price per unit $= y = \dfrac{15}{e}$

$\Rightarrow$ total price $= xy = \dfrac{45}{e}$.

Hence, number of units demanded is 3 and total price is $\dfrac{45}{e}$, in order that total revenue is maximum.

Example 46. *(i) If the supply function for a good is $x = S(p) = p - 10$ and the demand function is $x = D(p) = 20 - \dfrac{p}{2}$, what are the equilibrium price and quantity?*

(ii) If a monopolist takes over this market what are his total and average revenues expressed as functions of quantity sold?

(iii) The monopolist takes over all plants in the industry so that his marginal cost function is the same as the old supply relation when this relation is expressed as a function of x. How much will he produce for maximum profit and what price will he charge?

(iv) The monopolist introduces more efficient plants so that his marginal cost function changes to $\dfrac{dc}{dx} = 11 + \dfrac{x}{4}$. How much will he, now, produce and what price will he charge?

Solution. (*i*) Equilibrium will be obtained, when $p - 10 = 20 - \dfrac{p}{2}$

or, $\dfrac{3p}{2} = 30 \Rightarrow p = 20.$

So, $x = p - 10 = 10.$

Hence, quantity for equilibrium is 10 and price is 20.

(*ii*) Let R be the total revenue.

Then $\frac{R}{x}$ = price = p, where x is the quantity sold.

But, $$x = 0 - \frac{p}{2} = 20 - \frac{R}{2x}$$

$\Rightarrow$ $$2x^2 = 40x - R \Rightarrow R = 40x - 2x^2.$$

Also average revenue = $\frac{R}{x} = 40 - 2x$.

(*iii*) Old supply relation is $x = p - 10$

where p is given by $x = 20 - \frac{p}{2}$ *i.e.*, $p = 40 - 2x$.

So marginal cost function is $p - 10 = 40 - 2x - 10$.

$$= 30 - 2x$$

i.e., $$\frac{dC}{dx} = 30 - 2x. \quad \text{... (1)}$$

Total revenue $R = 40x - 2x^2$.

The total profit $N = R - C$.

It will be maximum or minimum, if

$$\frac{dN}{dx} = 0$$

i.e., $$\frac{dR}{dx} = \frac{dC}{dx}$$

$\Rightarrow$ $$40 - 4x = 30 - 2x$$

$\Rightarrow$ $$2x = 10$$

$\Rightarrow$ $$x = 5.$$

Also $$\frac{d^2N}{dx^2} = \frac{d^2R}{dx^2} - \frac{d^2C}{dx^2}$$

$$= -4 - (-2) = -2$$

So, $x = 5$ gives maximum profit.

Thus, $p = 40 - 2x = 30$.

Hence, for maximum profit, the monopolist should produce 5 units and price per unit is 30.

(*iv*) Now, $$\frac{dC}{dx} = 11 + \frac{x}{4}.$$

In this case for maximum or minimum profit

$$\frac{dR}{dx} = \frac{dC}{dx} \Rightarrow 40 - 4x = 11 + \frac{x}{4}$$

$$\Rightarrow \quad \frac{17x}{4} = 29$$

$$\Rightarrow \quad x = \frac{116}{17} = 6.83.$$

Also $\dfrac{d^2N}{dx^2} = \dfrac{d^2R}{dx^2} - \dfrac{d^2C}{dx^2} = (-4) - \left(\dfrac{1}{4}\right) = -\dfrac{17}{4} < 0.$

So, $x = 6.83$ gives maximum value of profit.

Also $p = 40 - 2x = 40 - 13.66 = 26.34.$

18. PRODUCTION FUNCTION

Production of a good depends upon various productive factors like price of raw material, cost of labour, etc. A production function is generally written in the form

$$Q = f(L, K)$$

where Q is the output and L, K are the inputs (say, labour and capital).

A production function of the form

$$Q = AK^{\alpha} L^{\beta},$$

where A is a positive constant, K and L are inputs of capital and labour respectively, is called a *Cobb-Douglas production function.*

Here, $0 \le \alpha, \beta \le 1$

If $\alpha + \beta = 1$, it is called *strict* Cobb-Douglas function.

If $\alpha + b \gtrless 1$, it is termed as a *generalized* Cobb-Duuglas function.

If $\quad f(L, K) = Q = AK^{\alpha} L^{\beta}$

then as $\quad f(tL, tK) = A(tK)^{\alpha}(tL)^{\beta}$

$$= t^{\alpha+\beta} AK^{\alpha} L^{\beta} = t^{\alpha+\beta} f(L, K),$$

we notice that it is a homogeneous function of degree $\alpha + \beta$.

Hence, by Euler's theorem, we have

$$K\frac{\partial Q}{\partial K} + L\frac{\partial Q}{\partial L} = (\alpha + \beta)Q.$$

In case $\alpha + \beta = 1$, *i.e*, function is strict Cobb-Douglas function, we have,

$$K\frac{\partial Q}{\partial K} + L\frac{\partial Q}{\partial L} = Q.$$

REMARK: $\frac{\partial Q}{\partial L}$ and $\frac{\partial Q}{\partial K}$ are called *marginal productivity* of *labour* and *capital* respectively.

Example 47. *The production function of a firm is given by* $Q = 4L^{3/4} K^{1/4}, L > 0, K > 0$. *Find the marginal productivity of labour (L) and capital (K). Also show that*

$$L\frac{\partial Q}{\partial L} + K\frac{\partial Q}{\partial K} = Q.$$

Solution. We have,

$$Q = 4L^{3/4} K^{1/4}$$

thus,
$$\frac{\partial Q}{\partial L} = 4 \times \frac{3}{4} L^{\frac{3}{4}-1} K^{1/4} = 3L^{-1/4} K^{1/4}$$

and
$$\frac{\partial Q}{\partial K} = 4L^{3/4} \cdot \frac{1}{4} K^{\frac{1}{4}-1} = L^{3/4} K^{-3/4}$$

The second part follows by Euler's theorem, as the given function $Q = 4L^{3/4} K^{1/4}$ is a homogeneous function of degree one.

Example 48. *The cost of manufacturing a certain product P is given by C = 20x + 12y + 50, where x is the cost (in rupees) of raw material and y is the cost of labour with 50 as the fixed cost. Find the marginal cost of raw material as well as that of labour.*

Solution. We have, $C(x, y) = 20x + 12y + 50$

$$\frac{\partial C}{\partial x} = 20$$

$$\frac{\partial C}{\partial y} = 12$$

$\frac{\partial C}{\partial x}$ represents the marginal cost, when y, the cost of labour is kept constant, thus $\frac{\partial C}{\partial x}$ represents the marginal cost of raw material.

Similarly, $\frac{\partial C}{\partial y}$ represents the marginal cost of labour (now cost of raw material is kept fixed).

In other words, we can say that if cost of labour is kept constant, an increase of Re 1 in cost of raw material results in an increase of Rs 20 in the total cost of production.

Similarly, if cost of raw material is kept fixed, an increase of Re 1 in cost of labour causes an increase of Rs 12 in the total cost of production.

Tax Revenue. The problem of how large the tax should be on any commodity, so as to fetch maximum revenue is vital for any government. As soon as a commodity is put under tax, its demand decreases. In fact a very large tax might result into zero demand of the product (and thus no revenue). On the other hand, if no tax is imposed then evidently there will be no revenue: thus the problem is to find the tax rate which optimises tax revenue (*TR*).

Tax revenue is defined as the product of tax per unit times the actual market quantity consumed.

Example 49. *For a certain product, it is found that the relationship between tax rate t and the quantity consumed x, is given by* $t + 3x^2 = 18$*.*

Find the optimal tax rate and the revenue generated by this tax rate.

Solution. We have, $t + 3x^2 = 18$

or, $$t = 18 - 3x^2.$$

Let R be the total tax revenue generated by tax rate t.

Then, $$R = tx = 18x - 3x^3.$$

For max. or min., $$\frac{dR}{dx} = 0$$

i.e., $$18 - 9x^2 = 0 \Rightarrow x = \sqrt{2} = 1.41$$

Again, $$\frac{d^2R}{dx^2} = -18x \text{ which is } - \text{ ve when } x = \sqrt{2}$$

Hence, R is maximum when $x = \sqrt{2}$

and maximum value of $R = 18\sqrt{2} - 3(\sqrt{2})^3 = 18\sqrt{2} - 6\sqrt{2}$

$= \text{Rs } 16.92.$

Inventory Control: Sometimes a manufacturer has to keep his products in storage in order to meet smooth running of his trade. This is also done to avoid sudden shortage in the supply of raw material etc. The cost of keeping the stock is called *inventory cost*, and the goods kept in storage are termed as *inventory*. The management of inventory is known as inventory control.

Example 50. *A store sells 50 lawnmowers per year. It costs the owner Rs 10 to store each lawnmower. For each order he places for lawnmowers,* *he incurs a charge of Rs 20 for handling and delivery. How many orders should he place to minimize the cost of storing and ordering?*

Solution. Let x be the number of lawnmowers ordered at any time.

The storage cost for x lawnmowers is Rs $10x$. Since, the store sells 50 lawnmowers every year, the number of orders required per year will be $\frac{50}{x}$ (Note that $\frac{50}{x}$ may not be an integer and in that case we approximate by choosing the integer nearest to $\frac{50}{x}$).

Again cost for each order placed is Rs 20.

Thus, cost for $\frac{50}{x}$ orders placed is $c_1 = 20 \times \frac{50}{x} = \frac{1000}{x}$

The cost function is, thus, given by

$$c = \text{storage cost} + c_1$$

$$= 10x + \frac{1000}{x}.$$

For max. or min., $\frac{dc}{dx} = 0$

i.e., $10 - \frac{1000}{x^2} = 0$

$$x^2 = 100 \Rightarrow x = \pm 10.$$

But x cannot be – ve.

Again, $\frac{d^2c}{dx^2} = \frac{2000}{x^3}$ which is +ve for $x = 10$.

Hence, $x = 10$ gives minimum c.

19. ELASTICITIES

Elasticity of Demand. Let $x = f(p)$ be a demand law. The average price elasticity of demand is the proportionate response of quantity demanded to the change in price. If δp is small change in price p and δx is small change in quantity demanded x, then we define,

$$\textit{average price elasticity of demand} = \frac{\frac{\delta x}{x}}{\frac{\delta p}{p}} = \frac{p}{x} \cdot \frac{\delta x}{\delta p}.$$

The price elasticity of demand ε_d is defined to be the limiting value of average price elasticity. Hence,

$$\varepsilon_d = \frac{p}{x} \cdot \frac{dx}{dp}.$$

Since, the demand curve $x = f(p)$ slopes downwards, $\frac{dx}{dp}$ will be –ve and, thus, a –ve sign is added to the value $\frac{dx}{dp}$ so as to get the value of elasticity as positive, *i.e.*, we write,

$$\varepsilon_d = -\frac{p}{x}\frac{dx}{dp} \quad \text{or} \quad \varepsilon_d = \left|\frac{p}{x}\frac{dx}{dp}\right|$$

REMARKS:

1. Elasticity of demand is also sometimes written without the –ve sign. (The addition of minus sigh to make ε_d +ve is due to *A*. Marshall, (1920).
2. *Elasticity of price with respect to demand* is defined to be the quantity $-\frac{x}{p} \cdot \frac{dp}{dx}$ *i.e.*, it is reciprocal of elasticity of demand and is also sometimes called *flexibility of price.*
3. We can also express

$$\varepsilon_d = \frac{\dfrac{dx}{dp}}{\dfrac{x}{p}} = \frac{\text{marginal function}}{\text{average function}}.$$

Elasticity of supply ε_s is the elasticity of quantity supplied in response to change in price and is given by

$$\varepsilon_s = \frac{p}{x}\frac{dx}{dp}$$

where x is quantity supplied and p is the price.

Example 51. *Find the price elasticity of demand for the demand law* $x = 20 - 3p$ *at* $p = 2$.

Solution. We have, $x = 20 - 3p$

$$\Rightarrow \qquad \frac{dx}{dp} = -3$$

Also at $p = 2$, $\qquad x = 20 - 6 = 14.$

Thus, $\qquad \varepsilon_d = -\frac{2}{14} \cdot (-3) = \frac{3}{7}.$

Example 52. *Show that for the demand curve $x = f(p)$,*

$$\varepsilon_d = \left|\frac{d(\log x)}{d(\log p)}\right|.$$

Solution. We have $x = f(p)$

Now, $$\frac{d}{dp}(\log x) = \frac{d}{dx}(\log x)\frac{dx}{dp} = \frac{1}{x}\frac{dx}{dp}.$$

Also $$\frac{d}{dp}(\log p) = \frac{1}{p}$$

Hence, $$\varepsilon_d = \left|\frac{p}{x}\frac{dx}{dp}\right| = \left|\frac{\frac{1}{x}\cdot\frac{dx}{dp}}{1/p}\right|$$

$$= \left|\frac{\frac{d}{dp}(\log x)}{\frac{d}{dp}(\log p)}\right| = \left|\frac{d(\log x)}{d(\log p)}\right|.$$

Example 53. *The demand function $x_1 = 50 - p_1$ intersects another linear demand function x_2 at $p = 10$. The elasticity of demand for x_2 is six times larger than that of x_1 at that point. Find the demand function for x_2.*

Solution. We have, $x_1 = 50 - p_1$

$$\Rightarrow \quad \frac{dx_1}{dp_1} = -1.$$

Also at $p = 10$, $\quad x_1 = 50 - 10 = 40$.

If ε_1 is elasticity of demand for x_1

then, $$\varepsilon_1 = -\frac{p_1}{x_1}\frac{dx_1}{dp_1} = -\frac{10}{40}(-1) = \frac{1}{4}.$$

Again if ε_2 is elasticity of demand for x_2.

then, $$\varepsilon_2 = 6\times\frac{1}{4} = \frac{3}{2}$$

i.e., $$-\frac{p_2}{x_2}\frac{dx}{dp_2} = \frac{3}{2}.$$

But at the point of intersection

$$p_2 = 10, \quad x_2 = 40$$

Thus, $$-\frac{10}{40}\frac{dx_2}{dp_2} = \frac{3}{2}$$

$$\Rightarrow \quad \frac{dx_2}{dp_2} = -6$$

$$\Rightarrow \quad x_2 = -6p_2 + c$$ (See chapter on Integration)

Since, $x_2 = 40$ when $p_2 = 10$

$$40 = -60 + c \Rightarrow c = 100.$$

Hence, $x_2 = 100 - 6p_2$ is the required second demand function.

Example 54. *Show that* $MR = AR\left(1 - \frac{1}{\varepsilon}\right)$ *where* ε *is the price elasticity of demand.*

Solution. We know by definition, that

$$\varepsilon = -\frac{p}{x}\cdot\frac{dx}{dp}$$

Again $$AR = \frac{TR}{x}$$

and $$MR = \frac{d}{dx}TR = \frac{d}{dx}(x\,AR)$$

$$= x\frac{d}{dx}AR + AR\frac{d}{dx}x$$

$$= AR + x\frac{d}{dx}AR$$

Again $$TR = px \Rightarrow p = \frac{TR}{x} = AR.$$

Thus, $$MR = AR + x\frac{d}{dx}p$$

$$= AR + \frac{x}{p}\cdot\frac{dp}{dx}.p = AR - \frac{1}{\varepsilon}p$$

$$= AR\left(1 - \frac{1}{\varepsilon}\right).$$

Hence the result.

Constant Elasticity Curves. A constant elasticity curve is defined by $xp^n = c$ where, n and c are constants, p is price and x is quantity demanded. For such curve e_d is constant, so the reason for nomenclature.

Now, $$e_d = \frac{-p}{x}\frac{dx}{dp}$$

But, $$xp^n = c \Rightarrow \log x + n \log p = 0$$

$$\Rightarrow \quad \frac{1}{x}\frac{dx}{dp} + \frac{n}{p} = 0$$

$$\Rightarrow \quad \frac{dx}{dp} = -\frac{nx}{p}$$

$$\Rightarrow \quad e_d = -\frac{p}{x}\frac{dx}{dp} = n, \text{ a constant.}$$

Example 55. *If ε_1 and ε_2 are price elasticities of demand for the demand laws $x = e^{-p}$ and $x = \frac{e^{-p}}{p}$, show that $\varepsilon_2 = 1 + \varepsilon_1$.*

Solution. We have,

$$\varepsilon_1 = -\frac{p}{x}\frac{dx}{dp} \qquad \text{where, } x = \varepsilon^{-p}$$

Thus, $$\varepsilon_1 = -\frac{p}{x}.-\varepsilon^{-p} = p\frac{e^{-p}}{e^{-p}} = p.$$

Again $$\varepsilon_2 = -\frac{p}{x}\cdot\frac{dx}{dp} \qquad \text{where, } x = \frac{e^{-p}}{p}$$

Thus, $$\varepsilon_2 = -\frac{p}{x}\left[-\frac{e^{-p}(p+1)}{p^2}\right]$$

$$= \frac{p}{e^{-p}}, \frac{e^{-p}(p+1)}{p}$$

$$= p + 1 = 1 + \varepsilon_1.$$

Hence the result.

Example 56. *If the demand laws for two goods are given by $x_1 = p_1^{-a_{11}} e^{a_{12}p_2 + a_1}$ and $x_2 = p_2^{a_{22}} e^{a_{21}p_i + a_2}$ where, x_i is the quantity and p_i is the price for good i (i = 1, 2) and a_1, a_2, a_{11}, a_{12}, a_{21}, a_{22} are constants, show that the direct price elasticities of demand are independent of the price while the cross price elasticities are determined in sign by the constants a_{12} and a_{21}.*

Solution. If demand functions for two related goods x_1 and x_2 with their respective prices p_1 and p_2 are $x_1 = f(p_1, p_2)$ and $x_2 = g(p_1, p_2)$

then, by *direct elasticities* of demand we mean the quantities η_{rr} given by

$-\dfrac{p_r \partial x_r}{r_r \partial p_r}$ $(r = 1, 2)$ and by *cross elasticities* of demand we mean the

quantities η_{rs} given by $-\dfrac{p_r \partial x_r}{x_r \partial p_s}$ when $r, s = 1, 2$ but $r \neq s$ and all these are called *partial elasticities* of demand. Actually speaking the cross elasticities are the partial elasticities of demand for one good with respect to the price of other.

Now,

$$\eta_{11} = -\frac{p_1}{x_1}\frac{\partial x_1}{\partial p_1}$$

$$= -\frac{p_1}{p_1^{-a_{11}} e^{a_{12} p_2 + a_1}} \cdot (-a_{11}) p_1^{-a_{11}-1} e^{a_{12} p_2 + a_1}$$

$$= a_{11}, \text{ independent of } p_1 \text{ and } p_2.$$

and

$$\eta_{22} = -\frac{p_2}{x_2}\frac{\partial x_2}{\partial p_2}$$

$$= -\frac{p_2}{p_2^{a_{22}} e^{a_{21} p_1 + a_2}} \cdot a_{22} p_2^{a_{22}-1} e^{a_{21} p_1 + a_2}$$

$$= -a_{22}, \text{ independent of } p_1 \text{ and } p_2.$$

Further,

$$\eta_{12} = -\frac{p_2}{x_1}\frac{\partial x_1}{\partial p_2}$$

$$= \frac{-p_1}{p_1^{-a_{11}} e^{a_{12} p_2 + a_1}} \cdot p_1^{-a_{11}} (a_{12}) e^{a_{12} p_2 + a_1}$$

$$= -p_2 a_{12}$$

and

$$\eta_{21} = -\frac{p_1}{x_2}\frac{\partial x_2}{\partial p_1}$$

$$= -\frac{p_1}{p_2^{a_{22}} e^{a_{21} p_1 + a_2}} \cdot p_2^{a_{22}} (a_{21}) e^{a_{21} p_1 + a_2}$$

$$= -p_1 a_{21}.$$

Hence, signs of η_{12} and η_{21} are determined by the constants a_{12} and a_{21} since p_1 and p_2 are always positive.

20. UTILITY FUNCTION AND INDIFFERENCE CURVES

let X and Y be two goods that a consumer wishes to buy. He has a choice in respect of these goods and distributes his expenditure on these according to his preferences. There are different combinations according to which he can make his purchases. For example, he can buy x_1 (quantity) of goods X and y_1 (quantity) of goods Y. Or he can buy x_2 of X and y_2 of Y and so on.

Let us plot the quantity x of X purchased along x-axis and quantity y of Y purchased along y-axis. Then anyone set of purchases can be represented by a point (x, y).

Let us now start with anyone given set of purchases represented by a point $A(x_0, y_0)$ then all other purchases can be divided into three categories.

(*i*) Those purchases which he (consumer) would prefer more in comparison to (x_0, y_0).

(*ii*) Those which he would prefer less in comparison to (x_0, y_0).

(*iii*) Those purchases to which he is indifferent *i.e.*, any such purchase, say, (x_1, y_1) such that he does not care whether it is (x_0, y_0) or (x_1, y_1). In other words, he derives the same satisfaction in making the purchase (x_0, y_0) or (x_1, y_1).

Let us collect all purchases of the third type and plot the points representing them and join these points. The curve so got is called an *indifference curve* corresponding to the level of preference associated with (x_0, y_0).

Similarly, if we start with any purchase (x', y') not included in the above indifference curve, we get another indifference curve at the level of preference of (x', y'). Note that such purchase [of the type (x', y')] can be picked up from (*i*) or (*ii*).

We can, thus, get various indifference curves by considering different sets of purchases. We, therefore, get a system of indifference curves, each consisting of points at one level of indifference. This system is said to constitute an *indifference map*. Also, clearly the indifference curve can be put in an ascending order of preference of the consumer.

Let the indifference map be represented by the equation

$$\phi(x, y) = \text{constant.}$$

Then, $u = \phi(x, y)$ takes a constant value on anyone of the indifference curves and increases as we move from lower to higher indifference curves.

Hence, as the purchases of the individual change, the value of u increases, remains constant or decreases according as the change leaves the consumer '*better off*', indifferent or '*worse off*'. Thus, the value of u indicates the level of preference or the utility of the purchases x and y to the individual consumer.

u is called *utility function* of that individual. In short, we can say that $u(x, y)$ is called utility function if it represents the satisfaction of the consumer when he buys x (quantity) of X and y (quantity) of Y.

The above can be generalised for n items $x_1, x_2, ..., x_n$.

If $\phi(x_1, x_2, ..., x_n) = \text{constant}$

is their indifference map, then

$$u = \phi(x_1, x_2, ..., x_n)$$

is utility function.

Each of $\frac{\partial u}{\partial x_1}, \frac{\partial u}{\partial x_2}, ..., \frac{\partial u}{\partial x_n}$ is called *marginal utility*.

Example 57. *Find the marginal utilities with respect to two commodities x_1 and x_2 when $X_1 = 1$ and $X_2 = 2$ units of the two commodities are consumed and if the utility function X_1 and X_2 is given by*

$$u = (x_1 + 3)(x_2 + 5)$$

Solution. We have,

$$u = (x_1 + 3)(x_2 + 5)$$

$$\Rightarrow \quad \frac{\partial u}{\partial x_1} = x_2 + 5$$

and $\frac{\partial u}{\partial x_2} = x_1 + 3.$

So at $x_1 = 1$ and $x_2 = 2$

$$\frac{\partial u}{\partial x_1} = 7, \quad \frac{\partial u}{\partial x_2} = 4$$

which are the required marginal utilities.

EXERCISES

1. If the total cost is given by $TC = (3 + 2x^2)^2$, where x is level of output, find marginal cost.
2. Find the maximum average cost if cost function is given by

$$TC = 36x - 10x^2 + 2x^3.$$

Also obtain MC at $x = \frac{5}{2}$.

3. A demand function for a commodity is given by $p = 12e^{-\infty/4}$ where p is the price per unit and x is the number of units demanded. Determine the price and the quantity for which revenue is maximum.
4. A firm has the revenue function $R = 200x - .01x^2$ and cost function $T = 50x + 20000$. Obtain maximum profit.
5. Find the minimum average cost for $T = (2e^x + e^{-x})x$.
6. A company has for x items produced, the total cost C and the total revenue R given by equations $R = 3x$ and $C = 100 + 0.015x^2$. Find how many items be produced to maximise profit. What is this profit?
7. Find ε for the demand function $x = 7 - 2p$, when $p = 2$.
8. Find ε for the supply function $x = 2p^2 + 5$ when $p = 3$.
9. Find the elasticity of demand for the demand law $p = (a - bx)^2$. For what value of x, it becomes unity?
10. Show that the elasticity of demand at all points on the curve $xy = \alpha^2$ will be numberically equal to one.
11. If ε_1 and ε_2 are the price elasticities of demand for the demand laws

$$x = 1 - p$$

and $\quad x = p - p^2,$

show that $\quad \varepsilon_2 = \varepsilon_1 - 1.$

12. A firm produces an output of x tons of a certain product at a total variable cost given by

$$c = x^3 - 4x^2 + 7x$$

Find the output at which the average cost is least. Also find the corresponding value of AC.

13. Show that average cost is minimum where it equals marginal cost whereas average revenue is maximum when it equals marginal revenue.
14. A refrigerator manufacturer produces x units in a production run at a total cost of manufacturing and stocking given by

$$c = 25x + 1000\frac{s}{x}$$

where s is the total annual sales.

For a fixed values of s, find the rate of change of c w.r.t. x. Also find the value of x at which $\dfrac{dc}{dx} = 0$ for $s = 100{,}000$ units.

15. If q is the number of workers employed, the average cost of production is given by

$$c = \frac{3}{2(q-4)} + 24q$$

Show that $q = 4.25$ will make the expression minimum. In the interest of the management will you then advice to employ four or five workers? Give reasons for your answer.

16. If the demand law is $x = ae^{-bp}$, express demand elasticity ε and total average and marginal revenue as functions of x. At what output is total revenue maximum?

17. Determine the equation of a curve which has price elasticity of demand as unity throughout.

18. If AR and MR denote the average and marginal revenues at any output, show that the elasticity of demand ε is equal to $\frac{AR}{AR-MR}$, verify this for the linear demand law

$$p = a - bx.$$

19. If ε_1 and ε_2 are the price elasticities of demand for the demand laws $p = e^x$ and $p = \frac{e^x}{x}$, show that $\varepsilon_2 = \frac{\varepsilon_1}{\varepsilon_1 - 1}$.

20. The demand y for a commodity when its price x is given by

$$y = \frac{x+2}{x-1}.$$

Find the elasticity of demand when the price is 3 units.

21. For the demand functions

$$x_1 = \frac{4}{p_1^2 p_2} \text{ and } x_2 = \frac{16}{p_1 p_2^2}.$$

Find the four partial elasticities of demand.

22. The production function of a commodity is given by

$$Q = 40F + 3F^2 - \frac{F^3}{3}$$

where Q is the total output and F is the unit of input. Find (*i*) the number of units input required to given maximum output, (*ii*) the maximum value of marginal product. Verify that when the average product is maximum it is equal to marginal product.

23. The revenue R due to the tax rate t is the product of tax rate per unit by the market quantity consumed. Related tax t is given by $t = \sqrt{27 - 3x^2}$. Find t for maximum tax revenue.

24. Given the production function $Q = 110\ K^{0.7}\ L^{0.8}$, find marginal productivity of labour and capital.

25. If $Q = 1.01\ L^{0.75}\ K^{0.25}$, where Q is output, L is labour and K is capital, show that

$$L\frac{\partial Q}{\partial L} + K\frac{\partial Q}{\partial K} = Q.$$

26. Find the ratio of the marginal utility of the good X_1 to the marginal utility of good X_2. If the utility function of the goods X_1 and X_2 is given by

(*i*) $u = \log\left(ax_1 + bx_2 + c\sqrt{x_1 x_2}\right)$ (*ii*) $u = ax_1 + bx_2 + c\sqrt{x_1 x_2}$

where a, b and c are constants.

27. Let $u = axy$ be utility function. Show that

(*a*) $\frac{\partial^2 u}{\partial x^2} = 0$. (*b*) If $U = \sqrt{u}$ then $\frac{\partial^2 u}{\partial x^2} < 0$. (*c*) If $U = e^u$ then $\frac{\partial^2 u}{\partial x^2} > 0$.

28. A monopolist faces the demand function $x = 500 - 5p$.

(*i*) What is the relation between total revenue and quantity sold?

(*ii*) Writing revenue as a function of x, $R = R(x)$, find $R(11) - R(10)$ and $R(10) - R(9)$.

(*iii*) What is the relation between marginal revenue and quantity sold?

(*iv*) What is the marginal revenue at the point when $x = 10$?

[Hint. (*i*) Total revenue = xp].

29. A firm has the demand function $p = 12 - 3q$ and cost function $T = q^2 + 2q$. Find AC, AR, MC, MR and profit for the firm at the point of equilibrium. What is the condition for profit maximization?

[Hint. Profit = $pq - T$].

30. A firm has the revenue function $R = 14q - q^2$ and cost function $T = q(q^2 - 2)$. Find AC, AR, MC, MR and profit for the them at the point of equilibrium. What is the condition for maximum profit?

31. If a monopolist has a total cost $T = \alpha x^2 + bx + c$ and if the demand law is $p = \beta - \alpha x^2$, show that output for maximum revenue is

$$x = \frac{\sqrt{a^2 + 3\alpha(\beta - b)} - a}{3\alpha}$$

[Hint. Revenue = $px - T$].

32. A sugar refinery has total cost equal to Rs $\frac{x^2}{10} + 5x + 40$ when x quintals of sugar are produced per week. The fixed market price is Rs p per quintal. What is the lowest price to cover total costs?

[Hint. Total revenue = $px = \frac{x^2}{10} + 5x + 40$. Minimise p].

ANSWERS

1. $8x(3 + 2x^2)$
2. 23.5, 23.5.
3. $x - 4$, Revenue = $\frac{48}{e}$
4. 10487500.
5. $2\sqrt{2}$
6. Max. at $x = 100$, profit 50.
7. $\frac{4}{3}$
8. $\frac{36}{23}$,
9. $\frac{a - bx}{2ax}, \frac{a}{3b}$
12. 2, 6
14. rate of change = $25 - \frac{1000s}{x^2}$; 2000
15. 5
16. $\log\frac{a}{x}$, $\frac{x}{b}\log\frac{a}{x}$, $\frac{1}{b}\log\frac{a}{x}$, $\frac{1}{b}\left[\log\frac{a}{x} - 1\right]$, $x = \frac{a}{c}$.
17. xp = constant.
20. 9/10.
21. 2, 1, 1, 2.
22. 10, 3.
23. 3.67.
24. $77k^{-.3}L^{.8}$, $88k^{.7}L^{-.2}$.

26. $\dfrac{24\sqrt{x_1x_2}+cx_2}{2b\sqrt{x_1x_2}+cx_1}$ is the common answer for both the parts (*i*) and (*ii*).

28. (*i*) $R = 100\ x - \dfrac{x^2}{5}$ (*ii*) 95.8, 96.2

    (*iii*) $\dfrac{dR}{dx} = 100 - \dfrac{2x}{5}$ (*iv*) 96.

29. $AC = q + 2$; $MC = 2q + 2$; $AR = 12 - 3q$, $MR = 126 - q$

    Max. profit = $\dfrac{25}{4}$ at $q = \dfrac{5}{4}$.

30. $AC = q^2 - 2$, $MC = 3q^2 - 2$, $AR = 14 - q$, $MR = 14 - 2q$,

    Max. profit = 20 at $q = 2$.

32. Rs 9 per quintal.

CHAPTER 27

INTEGRATION–DIFFERENT METHODS

1. After having learnt what is meant by differentiation, we come to the 'reverse' process of it, namely, integration. To give a precise shape to the definition of integration, we observe: If $g(x)$ is a function of x such that

$$\frac{d}{dx} g(x) = f(x)$$

then we define integral of $f(x)$, w.r.t. x to be the function $g(x)$. This is put in the notational form as

$$\int f(x)\, dx = g(x)$$

The function $f(x)$ is called the Integrand. Presence of dx is there just to remind us that integration is being done w.r.t. x.

As an example we note the since $\frac{d}{dx} \sin x = \cos x$

$$\int \cos x\, dx = \sin x$$

We get many such results as a direct consequence of the definition of integration, and can treat them as 'formulas'. A list of such standard results could be given:

(1) $\int 1\, dx = x$ because $\frac{d}{dx}(x) = 1$

(2) $\int x^n\, dx = \frac{x^{n+1}}{n+1}\ (n \neq -1)$ because $\frac{d}{dx}\left(\frac{x^{n+1}}{n+1}\right) = x^n,\ n \neq -1$

(3) $\int \frac{1}{x}\, dx = \log x$ because $\frac{d}{dx}(\log x) = \frac{1}{x}$

(4) $\int e^x dx = e^x$ because $\frac{d}{dx}(e^x) = e^x$

(5) $\int \sin x\, dx = -\cos x$ because $\frac{d}{dx}(-\cos x) = \sin x$

(6) $\int \cos x\, dx = \sin x$ because $\frac{d}{dx}(\sin x) = \cos x$

(7) $\int \sec^2 x dx = \tan x$ because $\frac{d}{dx}(\tan x) = \sec^2 x$

(8) $\int \text{cosec}^2 x\, dx = -\cot x$ because $\frac{d}{dx}(-\cot x) = \text{cosec}^2 x$

(9) $\int \sec x \tan x\, dx = \sec x$ because $\frac{d}{dx}(\sec x) = \sec x \tan x$

(10) $\int \text{cosec}\, x \cot x\, dx = -\text{cosec}\, x$ because $\frac{d}{dx}(-\text{cosec}\, x) = \text{cosec}\, x \cot x$

(11) $\int \frac{1}{\sqrt{1-x^2}} dx = \sin^{-1} x$ because $\frac{d}{dx}(\sin^{-1} x) = \frac{1}{\sqrt{1-x^2}}$

(12) $\int \frac{1}{1+x^2} dx = \tan^{-1} x$ because $\frac{d}{dx}(\tan^{-1} x) = \frac{1}{1+x^2}$

(13) $\int \frac{1}{x\sqrt{x^2-1}} dx = \sec^{-1} x$ because $\frac{d}{dx}(\sec^{-1} x) = \frac{1}{x\sqrt{1+x^2}}$

(14) $\int \frac{1}{ax+b} dx = \frac{\log(ax+b)}{a}$ because $\frac{d}{dx}\left[\frac{\log(ax+b)}{a}\right] = \frac{1}{ax+b}$

(15) $\int (ax+b)^n\, dx = \frac{(ax+b)^{n+1}}{n+1} \cdot \frac{1}{a} \quad (n \neq -1)$

because $\frac{d}{dx}\frac{(ax+b)^{n+1}}{a(n+1)} = (ax+b)^n, n \neq -1$

(16) $\int a^x\, dx = \frac{a^x}{\log a}$ because $\frac{d}{dx} a^x = a^x \log a$

One might wonder at this stage that since

$$\frac{d}{dx}(\sin x + 4) = \cos x$$

then by definition, why $\int \cos x\, dx$ is not $(\sin x + 4)$? In fact there is nothing very sacred about number 4 and it could very well have been any constant. This suggests perhaps a small alteration in the definition.

We now define integration as:

If $\frac{d}{dx} g(x) = f(x)$

then $\int f(x)\, dx = g(x) + c$

where c is *some* constant, called the *constant of integration.* Obviously, c could have *any* value and thus integral of a function is not unique! But we could say one thing here that *any two integrals of the same function differ by a constant.* Since c could also have the value zero, $g(x)$ is one of the values of $\int f(x)dx$. By convention, we will not write the constant of integration (although it is there), and thus $\int f(x)dx = g(x)$ and our definition stands.

The above is also referred to as **Indefinite Integral** (indefinite, because we are not really giving a *definite* value to the integral by not writing the constant of integration). Very soon we'll define a definite integral also.

2. SOME PROPERTIES OF INTEGRATION

(*i*) *Differentiation and integration cancel each other.*

The result is clear by definition of integration.

or, let $\frac{d}{dx} g(x) = f(x)$

then $\int f(x)\, dx = g(x)$ [by definition]

$$\Rightarrow \frac{d}{dx}\left[\int f(x)\, dx\right] = \frac{d}{dx}[g(x)] = f(x)$$

which proves the result.

(*ii*) *For any constant a,* $\int a\, f(x)\, dx = a \int f(x)\, dx$

Since $\frac{d}{dx}\left(a \int f(x) dx\right) = a \frac{d}{dx} \int f(x)\, dx = a f(x)$

By definition, $\int a\, f(x)\, dx = a \int f(x)\, dx$.

(*iii*) *For any two functions* $f(x)$ and $g(x)$

$$\int [f(x) \pm g(x)]\, dx = \int f(x)\, dx \pm \int g(x)\, dx$$

As $\frac{d}{dx}\left[\int f(x)\, dx \pm \int g(x) dx\right] = \frac{d}{dx} \int f(x)\, dx \pm \frac{d}{dx} \int g(x)\, dx$

$= f(x) \pm g(x)$

it follows by definition that

$$\int [f(x) \pm g(x)]dx = \int f(x)\,dx \pm \int g(x)dx$$

This result could be extended to a finite number of functions, *i.e.*, in general,

$$\int [f_1(x) \pm f_2(x) \pm \ldots \pm f_n(x)]dx = \int f_1(x)\,dx \pm \int f_2(x)dx \pm \ldots \pm \int f_n(x)\,dx$$

Let us now solve some problems to illustrate the use of these results.

Example 1. *Find* $\int (2x-3)^2\,dx$.

Solution. We have

$$\int (2x-3)^2\,dx = \int (4x^2+9-12x)\,dx$$

$$= \int 4x^2\,dx + \int 9\,dx - \int 12x\,dx$$

$$= 4\int x^2 dx + 9\int dx - 12\int xdx$$

$$= 4\frac{x^3}{3} + 9x - \frac{12x^2}{2} = \frac{4}{3}x^3 - 6x^2 + 9x.$$

Example 2. *Find* $\int (2x+1)^{1/3}\,dx$.

Solution. We have $\int (2x+1)^{1/3}\,dx = \dfrac{(2x+1)^{1/3+1}}{\frac{1}{3}+1} \times \dfrac{1}{2}$

$$= \frac{3}{8}(2x+1)^{4/3}.$$

Example 3. *Solve* $\int \dfrac{x^3}{x+1}\,dx$.

Solution. By division, we note

$$\frac{x^3}{x+1} = (x^2 - x + 1) - \frac{1}{x+1}$$

Thus $\int \dfrac{x^3}{x+1}\,dx = \int (x^2 - x + 1)\,dx - \int \dfrac{1}{x+1}\,dx$

$$= \int x^2 dx - \int xdx + \int dx - \int \frac{1}{x+1}\,dx$$

$$= \frac{x^3}{3} - \frac{x^2}{2} + x - \log(x+1).$$

Example 4. *Find* $\int \sqrt{1+\cos 2x}\, dx$

Solution. We observe

$$\int \sqrt{1+\cos 2x}\, dx = \int \sqrt{2\cos^2 x}\, dx = \sqrt{2} \int \cos x\, dx$$

$$= \sqrt{2} \sin x.$$

Example 5. *Evaluate* $\int \left[\sqrt{x} - \frac{1}{\sqrt{x}}\right] dx.$

Solution. $\int \left[\sqrt{x} - \frac{1}{\sqrt{x}}\right] dx = \int \sqrt{x dx} - \int \frac{1}{\sqrt{x}}\, dx$

$$= \frac{x^{1/2+1}}{\frac{1}{2}+1} - \frac{x^{-1/2+1}}{-\frac{1}{2}+1}$$

$$= \frac{2}{3} x^{3/2} - 2\sqrt{x}$$

Example 6. *Evaluate*

(*i*) $\int \left(\frac{ax^3 + bx^2 + cx + d}{x}\right) dx$ (*ii*) $\int \sin^3 x dx.$

Solution. We have

(*i*) $\int \left(\frac{ax^3 + bx^2 + cx + d}{x}\right) dx = \int \left(ax^2 + bx + c + \frac{d}{x}\right) dx$

$$= a \int x^2\, dx + b \int x\, dx + c \int dx + d \int \frac{1}{x}\, dx$$

$$= a \frac{x^3}{3} + \frac{bx^2}{2} + cx + d \log x$$

(*ii*) We have

$$\int \sin^3 x\, dx = \frac{1}{4} \int (3 \sin x - \sin 3x)\, dx$$

$$= \frac{3}{4} \int \sin x\, dx - \frac{1}{4} \int \sin 3\, x\, dx$$

$$= -\frac{3}{4} \cos x + 9 \frac{\cos 3x}{12}$$

$$= \frac{1}{12}(\cos 3x - 9 \cos x)$$

REMARK: Note that as $\frac{1}{a}\frac{d}{dx}$ cos ax = – sin ax

$$\int \sin ax\,dx = -\frac{\cos ax}{a}$$

Similarly $$\int \cos ax\,dx = \frac{\sin ax}{a}$$

and $$\int e^{bx}\,dx = \frac{e^{bx}}{b}.$$

EXERCISES

Integrate the following functions w.r.t. x

1. (*i*) $\frac{1}{\sqrt{x}}$ (*ii*) $\frac{1}{x^{3,2}}$ (*iii*) $\sqrt{x}(1+x)$

(*iv*) $\frac{ax^3+bx}{2}$

2. (*i*) e^{2x} (*ii*) e^{2x-3} (*iii*) $\frac{1}{e^x}$

3. (*i*) $\left(\sqrt{x}-\frac{1}{\sqrt{x}}\right)^2$ (*ii*) $\frac{1}{\sqrt{1+x}+\sqrt{x}}$ (iii) $\frac{1}{\sqrt{x-1}-\sqrt{x+1}}$

[Hint: Rationalise**]**

4. (*i*) $(\sin x - \cos x)^2$ (*ii*) $\sin^2 x$ (*iii*) $\cos^3 x$

(*iv*) $\frac{1}{1+\sin x}$ (*v*) $\sin(4x+3)$ (*vi*) $\frac{\sin 2x}{\sin x}$

5. (*i*) $\frac{1}{x^2+4}$ (*ii*) $\frac{1-x}{1-x^2}$ (*iii*) $\frac{x^4+x^2+1}{2(x^2+1)}$

(*iv*) $2^x-\frac{1}{\sqrt[3]{x}}$ (*v*) $\frac{\left(\sqrt{x}+\sqrt[3]{x^2}\right)^2}{x}$

ANSWERS

1. (*i*) $2\sqrt{x}$ (*ii*) $-\frac{2}{\sqrt{x}}$ (*iii*) $\frac{2x^{3/2}}{3}+\frac{2x^{5/2}}{5}$

(*iv*) $\frac{ax^4}{8}+\frac{bx^2}{4}$

2. (*i*) $\frac{e^{2x}}{2}$ (*ii*) $\frac{e^{2x-3}}{2}$ (*iii*) $-e^{-x}$

3. (*i*) $\frac{x^2}{2}-2x+\log x$ (*ii*) $\frac{2}{3}(1+x)^{3/2}-\frac{2x^{2/3}}{3}$

(*iii*) $-(\frac{1}{3}x-1)^{3/2}-(x+1)^{3/2}]$

4. (*i*) $x + \frac{\cos 2x}{2}$ (*ii*) $\frac{1}{2}(x - \sin x \cos x)]$

(*iii*) $\frac{1}{12}$ [9 sin x + sin 3x] (*iv*) tan x − sec x

(*v*) $-\frac{\cos(4x+3)}{4}$ (*vi*) 2 sin x

5. (*i*) $\frac{1}{2}\tan^{-1}\frac{x}{2}$ (*ii*) log (1 + x) (*iii*) $\frac{1}{2}\left[\frac{x^3}{3} + \tan^{-1} x\right]$

(*iv*) $\frac{2^x}{\log 2} - \frac{3}{2}x^{2/3}$ (*v*) $x + \frac{3}{4}x^{4/3} + \frac{12}{7}x^{7/6}$

3. DEFINITE INTEGRAL

Suppose $f(x)$ is a function such that

$$\int f(x)\,dx = g(x)$$

The definite integral $\int_a^b f(x)\,dx$ is defined by

$$\int_a^b f(x)\,dx = \{g(x)\}_a^b = g(b) - g(a)$$

where a and b are two real numbers, and are called, respectively, the *lower* and the *upper* limits of the integral.

Example 7. *Evaluate* $\int_0^{\frac{\pi}{2}} \cos x\,dx$

Solution. We know that $\int \cos x\,dx = \sin x$

$$\int_0^{\frac{\pi}{2}} \cos x\,dx = \{\sin x\}_0^{\frac{\pi}{2}} = \sin\frac{\pi}{2} - \sin 0 = 1 - 0 = 1$$

Example 8. *Evaluate* $\int_a^b 1\,dx$.

Solution. $\int_a^b 1\,dx = \{x\}_a^b = b - a.$

REMARK: It might be noticed that in case of a definite integral, there is no constant of integration. For, suppose

$$\int f(x)dx = g(x) + c$$

then $\int_a^b (f(x))\,dx = \{g(x) + c\}_a^b = [g(b) + c] - [g(a) + c] = g(b) - g(a)$

So when we talk of a definite integral, we note it has a unique definite value.

We will study in details the properties of definite integrals again at the end.

EXERCISES

Evaluate the following integrals:

1. $\int_0^{\pi/2} \sin x \, dx$

2. $\int_0^{\pi/4} \sin^2 x \, dx$

3. $\int_2^3 \frac{1}{x} dx$

4. $\int_0^1 (x+1)^2 \, dx$

5. $\int_0^1 \frac{1}{1+x^2} dx$

6. $\int_a^b x^2 \, dx$

ANSWERS

1. 1
2. 1
3. log 3–log 2
4. $\frac{11}{6}$
5. $\frac{\pi}{4}$
6. $\frac{b^3 - a^3}{3}$

4. METHODS OF INTEGRATION

In the previous section we have seen that many integrals can be evaluated by using definition of integration. Still a good number of problems cannot be solved in this manner. We, in the rest of this section of the book, will try to list a few methods by which integration is made possible. The very first (and perhaps the most useful) of them is the

5. METHOD OF SUBSTITUTION

In this method, we express the given integral $\int f(x)\, dx$ in terms of another integral in which the independent variable x is changed to another variable t through some suitable relation $x = \phi(t)$.

Let $$I = \int f(x)\, dx$$

$$\Rightarrow \quad \frac{dI}{dx} = f(x)$$

Now $$\frac{dI}{dt} = \frac{dI}{dx} \cdot \frac{dx}{dt} = f(x) \frac{dx}{dt}$$

Thus $$I = \int f(x) \frac{dx}{dt} \cdot dt = \int f[\varphi(t)]\, \varphi'(t)\, dt$$

Note that we replace dx by $\varphi'(t)\, dt$, which we get from the relation $\frac{dx}{dt} = \varphi'(t)$ by *assuming* that dx and dt can be separated.

In fact this is done only for convenience.

The following example will make the process clear:

Example 9. *Integrate* $x(x^2 + 1)^3$.

Solution. Put $x^2 + 1 = t \Rightarrow 2x\frac{dx}{dt} = 1$

Thus $\Rightarrow 2xdx = dt$

$$\int x(x^2+1)^3\, dx = \int \frac{1}{2} t^3\, dt = \frac{1}{2}\int t^3\, dt = \frac{1}{2}\frac{t^4}{4} = \frac{t^4}{8} = \frac{(x^2+1)^4}{8}$$

Example 10. *Find* $\int e^{\tan\theta} \sec^2 \theta d\theta.$

Solution. Put $\tan\theta = t$, then $\sec^2\theta\, d\theta = dt$

Thus $\int e^{\tan\theta} \sec^2\theta d\theta = \int e^t\, dt = e^t = e^{\tan\theta}$

Example 11. *Integrate* $\frac{\cos x}{1+\sin^2 x}$.

Solution. Put $\sin x = t$, then $\cos x\, dx = dt$

Thus $\int \frac{\cos x}{1+\sin^2 x}\, dx = \int \frac{dt}{1+t^2} = \tan^{-1} t = \tan^{-1}(\sin x)$.

Example 12. *Integrate* $\frac{4x^2}{\sqrt{1-x^6}}$.

Solutin. Put $x^3 = t$, then $3x^2\, dx = dt$

Thus $\int \frac{4x^2}{\sqrt{1-x^6}}\, dx = \frac{4}{3}\int \frac{dt}{\sqrt{1-t^2}} = \frac{4}{3}\sin^{-1} t = \frac{4}{3}\sin^{-1}(x^3)$

Example 13. *Find* $\int_0^1 \frac{(\tan^{-1} x)^2}{1+x^2}\, dx$

Solution. Put $\tan^{-1} x = t$, then $\frac{1}{1+x^2}dx = dt$

Also $x = \tan t$

thus when $x = 0$, $\tan t = 0 \Rightarrow t = 0$

when $x = 1$, $\tan t = 1 \Rightarrow t = \pi/4$

Hence

$$\int_0^1 \frac{(\tan^{-1} x)^2}{1+x^2}\, dx = \int_0^{\pi/4} t^2\, dt = \left\{\frac{t^3}{3}\right\}_0^{\pi/4} = \frac{1}{3}\left(\frac{\pi}{4}\right)^3 - 0$$

$$= \frac{\pi^3}{192}$$

Note. In the above method, when we make the substitution, we also change the limits accordingly, the new limits being the values of the new variable which correspond to the values 0 and 1 of x. Alternatively we could attempt the problem in the following way:

We first consider the integral $\int \frac{(\tan^{-1} x)^2}{1+x^2}\, dx$

i.e., we do not take limits. Then as before, by the same substitution

$$\int \frac{(\tan^{-1} x)^2}{1+x^2}\, dx = \frac{t^3}{3} = \frac{(\tan^{-1} x)^3}{3}$$

and thus

$$\int_1^0 \frac{(\tan^{-1} x)^2}{1+x^2}\, dx = \left\{\frac{(\tan^{-1} x)^3}{3}\right\}_0^1 = \frac{(\tan^{-1} 1)^3}{3} - \frac{(\tan^{-1} 0)^3}{3}$$

$$= \frac{(\pi/4)^3}{3} - 0 = \frac{\pi^3}{192}$$

It might be remarked here that although both the methods are correct, the first will prove very helpful in certain cases.

EXERCISES

1. Integrate the following functions

(*i*) $\frac{\sin^{-1} x}{\sqrt{1-x^2}}$ (*ii*) $\frac{\cos(\log x)}{x}$ (*iii*) $\frac{1}{3^x + e^{-x}}$

2. (*i*) $\frac{\sin\sqrt{x}}{\sqrt{x}}$ (*ii*) $\sqrt{\tan\theta}\,\sec^2\theta$ (*iii*) $e^{\cos x}\sin x$

3. (*i*) $\sec x \log(\sec x + \tan x)$ (*ii*) $\tan x$ (*iii*) $\frac{\log x}{x}$ (*iv*) $\tan^2 x$

4. (*i*) $\sin^6 x \cos x$ (*ii*) $\cos^6 x \sin x$ (*iii*) $\frac{e^{2x}}{e^{4x}+1}$

5. (*i*) $\frac{x^2}{1+x^6}$ (*ii*) $\sqrt{\frac{1+x}{1-x}}$ (*iii*) $\frac{2x+3}{x^2+3x+7}$

[**Hint.** Put $x = \cos\theta$]

6. Evaluate

(i) $\displaystyle\int_0^{\pi/2} \frac{\cos x}{1+\sin^2 x}\,dx$ (ii) $\displaystyle\int_0^{\pi/2} \sin^6 x \cos x\,dx$ (iii) $\displaystyle\int_0^{\pi/2} \cos^6 x \sin x\,dx$

(iv) $\displaystyle\int_0^{a} \frac{x\,dx}{\sqrt{2ax - x^2}}$ (v) $\displaystyle\int_0^{1} x\sqrt{\frac{1-x^2}{1+x^2}}\,dx$

7. Evaluate $\displaystyle\int \frac{1}{x^2\sqrt{1-x^2}}\,dx.$

ANSWERS

1. (i) $\frac{1}{2}(\sin^{-1} x)^2$ (ii) $\sin(\log x)$ (iii) $\tan^{-1} e^x$

2. (i) $-2\cos\sqrt{x}$ (ii) $\frac{2}{3}(\tan\theta)^{3/2}$ (iii) $-e^{\cos x}$

3. (i) $\frac{1}{2}[\log(\sec x + \tan x)]^2$ (ii) $\log \sec x$ (iii) $\frac{(\log x)^2}{2}$

(iv) $\frac{\tan^2 x}{2} - \log \sec x$

4. (i) $\frac{\sin^7 x}{7}$ (ii) $-\frac{\cos^7 x}{x}$ (iii) $\frac{1}{2}\tan^{-1}\left(e^{2x}\right)$

5. (i) $\frac{1}{3}\tan^{-1} x^3$ (ii) $-\left[\cos^{-1} x + \sqrt{1-x^2}\right]$ (iii) $\log(x^2 + 3x + 7)$

6. (i) $\frac{\pi}{4}$ (ii) $\frac{1}{7}$ (iii) $\frac{1}{7}$ (iv) $\frac{a}{2}(\pi - 2)$ (v) $\frac{\pi-2}{4}$

7. $\frac{-\sqrt{1-x^2}}{x}$.

6. TO EVALUATE $\displaystyle\int \frac{f'(x)}{f(x)}\,dx$ WHERE $f'(x)$ IS THE DERIVATIVE OF $f(x)$

Put $f(x) = t$, then $f'(x)dx = dt$

Thus $$\int \frac{f'(x)}{f(x)}\,dx = \int \frac{dt}{t} = \log t = \log f(x)$$

7. TO EVALUATE $\displaystyle\int [f(x)]^n f'(x)dx,\ n \neq -1$

Put $f(x) = t$, then $f'(x)dx = dt$

Thus $$\int [f(x)]^n f'(x)dx = \int t^n\,dt = \frac{t^{n+1}}{n+1} = \frac{[f(x)]^{n+1}}{n+1}$$

8. TO EVALUATE $\int f'(ax+b)dx$

Put $ax + b = t$, then $adx = dt$

$$\int f'(ax+b)dx = \int f'(t)\frac{dt}{a} = \frac{1}{a}\int f'(t)\,dt = \frac{f(t)}{a} = \frac{f(ax+b)}{a}$$

Example 14. *Evaluate* (*i*) $\int \tan x\,dx$ (*ii*) $\int \sec x\,dx$

Solution. (*i*) $\int \tan x dx = \int \frac{\sin x}{\cos x}dx = \int \frac{\sec x \tan x}{\sec x}dx = \log \sec x$

(*ii*) $\int \sec x dx = \int \frac{\sec x(\sec x + \tan x)}{\sec x + \tan x}dx = \log(\sec x + \tan x)$

Example 15. *Find* $\int x\sqrt{x^2+1}dx$.

Solution. We have

$$\int x\sqrt{x^2+1}\,dx = \frac{1}{2}\int (2x)(x^2+1)^{\frac{1}{2}}\,dx$$

$$= \frac{1}{2}\frac{(x^2+1)^{\frac{1}{2}+1}}{\frac{1}{2}+1} \quad \text{[using 7]}$$

$$= \frac{1}{2}(x^2+1)^{3/2}$$

Example 16. *Evaluate* $\int \frac{x+1}{x^2+2x+3}\,dx.$

Solution. We have $\int \frac{x+1}{x^2+2x+3}\,dx = \frac{1}{2}\int \frac{2x+2}{x^2+2x+3}\,dx$

$$= \frac{1}{2}\log(x^2+2x+3)$$

$$= \frac{-\cos 6x}{12} - \frac{\cos 2x}{4}$$

$$= -\frac{1}{4}\left[\frac{\cos 6x}{3} + \cos 2x\right]$$

Example 17. *Evaluate* (*i*) $\int \cos x \cos 2x\,dx$

(*ii*) $\int \sin 4x \cos 2x\,dx$

Solution. (*i*) $\int \cos x \cos 2x dx = \frac{1}{2}\int 2 \cos x \cos 2x \, dx$

$$= \frac{1}{2}\int (\cos 3x + \cos x) \, dx$$

$$= \frac{1}{2}\int \cos 3x \, dx + \frac{1}{2}\int \cos x \, dx$$

$$= \frac{1}{2}\frac{\sin 3x}{3} + \frac{1}{2}\sin x$$

(*ii*) We have

$$\sin 4x \cos 2x = \frac{1}{2} 2 \sin 4x \cos 2x$$

$$= \frac{1}{2}[\sin (4x+2x) + \sin (4x-2x)]$$

$$= \frac{1}{2}[\sin 6x + \sin 2x]$$

Thus

$$\int \sin 4x \cos 2x \, dx = \frac{1}{2}\int (\sin 6x + \sin 2x) dx$$

$$= \frac{1}{2}\int \sin 6x \, dx + \frac{1}{2}\int \sin 2x \, dx$$

$$= \frac{-\cos 6x}{12} - \frac{\cos 2x}{4}$$

$$= -\frac{1}{4}\left[\frac{\cos 6x}{3} + \cos 2x\right]$$

EXERCISES

Integrate the following:

1. (*i*) $\cot x$ (*ii*) $\operatorname{cosec} x$ (*iii*) $\frac{1}{x \log x}$ (*iv*) $\frac{1}{x(1+\log x)}$

2. (*i*) $\frac{2x+3}{x^2+3x+7}$ (*ii*) $\frac{x^5}{1+x^6}$ (*iii*) $\frac{\cos x}{a + b \sin x}$ $(b \neq 0)$

3. (*i*) $\tan^3 x \cdot \sec^2 x$ (*ii*) $x\sqrt{a^2 - x^2}$ (*iii*) $\frac{(\sin^{-1} x)^4}{\sqrt{1-x^2}}$

   (*iv*) $x^4(1+x^5)^{\frac{1}{2}}$

4. (*i*) $\frac{1-\tan x}{1+\tan x}$ (*ii*) $\frac{1}{\sqrt{x}+x}$ (*iii*) $\frac{\sec x \operatorname{cosec} x}{\log \tan x}$

5. (*i*) $e^x\sqrt{1+e^x}$ (*ii*) $(e^x + e^{-x})(e^x - e^{-x})$

   (*iii*) $e^x(a + be^x)^n$ $(b \neq 0)$

6. (*i*) $\cos^3 x$ (*ii*) $\sin^3 x$ (*iii*) $\sin 2x \cos 3x$

   (*iv*) $\sqrt{1+\sin x}$ (*v*) $\sqrt{1-\cos x}$

ANSWERS

1. (*i*) $\log \sin x$ (*ii*) $\log (\text{cosec } x - \cot x)$
   (*iii*) $\log (\log x)$ (*iv*) $\log (1 + \log x)$

2. (*i*) $\log (x^2 + 3x + 7)$ (*ii*) $\frac{1}{6} \log (1 + x^6)$ (*iii*) $\frac{1}{b} \log (a + b \sin x)$

3. (*i*) $\frac{\tan^4 x}{4}$ (*ii*) $-\frac{1}{3} (a^2 - x^2)^{3/2}$ (*iii*) $\frac{1}{5} (\sin^{-1} x)^5$

   (*iv*) $\frac{3}{20} (1 + x^5)^{4/3}$

4. (*i*) $\log (\sin x + \cos x)$ (*ii*) $2 \log (1+\sqrt{x})$ (*iii*) $\log (\log \tan x)$

5. $\frac{2}{3} (1 + e^x)^{3/2}$ (*ii*) $\frac{1}{2} (e^x - e^{-x})^2$ (*iii*) $\frac{(a+be^x)^{n+1}}{b(n+1)}$

6. (*i*) $\frac{1}{12} (9 \sin x + \sin 3x)$ (*ii*) $\frac{1}{12} (\cos 3x - 9 \cos x)$

   (*iii*) $\frac{1}{2}\left(\cos x - \frac{\cos 5x}{5}\right)$ (*iv*) $2 \left(\sin \frac{x}{2} - \cos \frac{x}{2}\right)$

   (*v*) $-2\sqrt{2} \cos \frac{x}{2}$

9. SIX IMPORTANT INTEGRALS

We now evaluate the following six integrals

(*i*) $\int \frac{1}{\sqrt{a^2 - x^2}} dx$ (*ii*) $\int \frac{1}{\sqrt{a^2 + x^2}} dx$ (*iii*) $\int \frac{1}{\sqrt{x^2 - a^2}} dx$

(*iv*) $\int \sqrt{a^2 - x^2}\, dx$ (*v*) $\int \sqrt{a^2 + x^2}\, dx$ (*vi*) $\int \sqrt{x^2 - a^2}\, dx$

(*i*) To evaluate $\int \frac{1}{\sqrt{a^2 - x^2}} dx$

Put $x = a \sin \theta$, then $dx = a \cos \theta\, d\theta$

Thus

$$\int \frac{1}{\sqrt{a^2 - x^2}} dx = \int \frac{a \cos \theta\, d\theta}{\sqrt{a^2 - a^2 \sin^2 \theta}} = \int \frac{a \cos \theta}{a \cos \theta} d\theta$$

$$= \int 1 . d\theta = \theta$$

$$= \sin^{-1}\left(\frac{x}{a}\right)$$

(*ii*) To evaluate $\int \frac{1}{\sqrt{a^2 + x^2}} dx$

Put $x = a \sinh \theta$. then $dx = a \cosh d\theta$

Thus

$$\int \frac{1}{\sqrt{a^2 + x^2}} = dx = \int \frac{a \cosh \theta \, d\theta}{\sqrt{a^2 + a^2 \sinh^2 \theta}} = \int \frac{a \cosh \theta}{a \cosh \theta} d\theta$$

as $\cosh^2 \theta - \sinh^2 \theta = 1$

$$= \int d\theta = \theta = \sin^{-1}\left(\frac{x}{a}\right)$$

Aliter. Put $x = a \tan \theta$, then $dx = a \sec^2 \theta \, d\theta$

Thus

$$\int \frac{1}{\sqrt{a^2 + x^2}} dx = \int \frac{a \sec^2 \theta \, d\theta}{\sqrt{a^2 + a^2 \tan^2 \theta}} = \int \frac{\sec^2 \theta \, d\theta}{\sec \theta} = \int \sec \theta \, d\theta$$

$$= \log (\sec \theta + \tan \theta)$$

$$= \log \left[\frac{\sqrt{x^2 + a^2}}{a} + \frac{x}{a}\right]$$

$$= \log \left[\frac{x + \sqrt{x^2 + a^2}}{a}\right]$$

(*iii*) To evaluate $\int \frac{1}{\sqrt{x^2 - a^2}} dx.$

Put $x = a \cosh \theta$ then $dx = a \sinh \theta d\theta$.

Thus

$$\int \frac{1}{\sqrt{x^2 - a^2}} dx = \int \frac{a \sinh \theta \, d\theta}{\sqrt{a^2 \sinh^2 \theta - a^2}} = \int \frac{a \sinh \theta}{a \sinh \theta} d\theta = \int d\theta$$

$$= \theta = \cosh^{-1} \frac{x}{a}.$$

Aliter. Put $x = a \sec \theta$, then $dx = a \sec \theta \tan \theta d\theta$

Thus

$$\int \frac{1}{\sqrt{x^2 - a^2}} dx = \int \frac{a \sec \theta \tan \theta \, d\theta}{\sqrt{a^2 \sec^2 \theta - a^2}} = \int \sec \theta \, d\theta$$

$$= \log (\sec \theta + \tan \theta)$$

$$= \log\left[\frac{x}{a}+\frac{\sqrt{x^2-a^2}}{a}\right]$$

$$= \log\left[\frac{x+\sqrt{x^2-a^2}}{a}\right]$$

(*iv*) To evaluate $\int\sqrt{a^2-x^2}\ dx.$

Put $x = a\sin\theta$, then $dx = a\cos\theta\, d\theta.$

Thus

$$\int\sqrt{a^2-x^2}\ dx = \int\sqrt{a^2-a^2\sin^2\theta}\ .\ a\cos\theta\, d\theta = \int a^2\cos^2\theta\, d\theta$$

$$= a^2\int\left(\frac{1+\cos 2\theta}{2}\right)d\theta$$

$$= \frac{a^2}{2}\left(\theta+\frac{\sin 2\theta}{2}\right)$$

$$= \frac{a^2}{2}(\theta+\sin\theta\cos\theta)$$

$$= \frac{a^2}{2}\left(\theta+\sin\theta\sqrt{1-\sin^2\theta}\right)$$

$$= \frac{a^2}{2}\left[\sin^{-1}\frac{x}{a}+\frac{x}{a}\sqrt{1-\frac{x^2}{a^2}}\right]$$

and hence

$$\int\sqrt{a^2-x^2}\ dx = x\frac{\sqrt{a^2-x^2}}{2}+\frac{a^2}{2}\sin^{-1}\frac{x}{a}.$$

(*v*) To evaluate $\int\sqrt{a^2+x^2}\ dx.$

Put $x = a\sinh\theta$ then $dx = a\cosh\theta\, d\theta$

Thus

$$\int\sqrt{a^2+x^2}\ dx = \int\sqrt{a^2+x^2\sinh^2\theta}\ .\ a\cosh\theta\, d\theta$$

$$= \int a^2\cosh^2\theta\, d\theta$$

$$= a^2\int\frac{(\cosh 2\theta+1)}{2}\, d\theta \quad \text{as } 2\cosh^2\theta = 1+\cosh 2\theta$$

$$= \frac{a^2}{2}\left(\frac{\sinh 2\theta}{2} + \theta\right)$$

$$= \frac{a^2}{2}[\sinh\theta\cosh\theta + \theta]$$

as $\sinh 2\theta = 2\sinh\theta\cosh\theta$

$$= \frac{a^2}{2}\left[\sinh\theta\sqrt{1+\sinh^2\theta} + \theta\right]$$

$$= \frac{a^2}{2}\left[\frac{x}{a}\sqrt{1+\frac{x^2}{a^2}} + \sin^{-1}\frac{x}{a}\right]$$

and hence

$$\int\sqrt{a^2+x^2}\;dx = \frac{x}{2}\sqrt{a^2+x^2} + \frac{a^2}{2}\sin^{-1}\frac{x}{a}.$$

Aliter. Put $x = a\tan\theta$, then $dx = a\sec^2\theta d\theta$

Thus

$$\int\sqrt{a^2+x^2}\;dx = \int\sqrt{a^2+a^2\tan^2\theta}\;.\;a\sec^2\theta d\theta$$

$$= \int a^2\sec^2\theta\,d\theta$$

$$= \frac{a^2}{2}[\sec\theta\tan\theta + \log(\sec\theta + \tan\theta)]$$

[See Example 26]

$$= \frac{a^2}{2}\sqrt{1+\frac{x^2}{a^2}}\,.\,\frac{x}{a} + \frac{a^2}{2}\log\left[\sqrt{1+\frac{x^2}{a^2}} + \frac{x}{a}\right]$$

$$= \frac{x}{2}\sqrt{x^2+a^2} + \frac{a^2}{2}\log\left[\frac{x+\sqrt{x^2+a^2}}{a}\right]$$

(*vi*) To evaluate $\int\sqrt{x^2-a^2}\;dx$

Put $x = a\cosh\theta$, then $dx = a\sinh\theta d\theta$

Thus

$$\int\sqrt{x^2-a^2}\;dx = \int\sqrt{a^2\cosh^2\theta - a^2}\;a\sinh\theta d\theta$$

$$= a^2\int\sinh^2\theta\,d\theta$$

$$= a^2\int\frac{(\cosh 2\theta - 1)}{2}d\theta$$

$$= \frac{a^2}{2}\left(\frac{\sinh 2\theta}{2} - \theta\right)$$

$$= \frac{a^2}{2}(\sinh\theta\cosh\theta - \theta)$$

$$= \frac{a^2}{2}[\sqrt{\cosh^2\theta - 1}\,.\cosh\theta - \theta]$$

$$= \frac{a^2}{2}\left[\sqrt{\frac{x^2}{a^2} - 1}.\frac{x}{a}\cosh^{-1} x/a\right]$$

and hence

$$\int\sqrt{x^2 - a^2}\,dx = \frac{x}{2}\sqrt{x^2 - a^2} - \frac{a^2}{2}\cosh^{-1} x/a.$$

Aliter. Put $x = a\sec\theta$, then $dx = a\sec\theta\tan\theta\, d\theta$

Thus

$$\int\sqrt{x^2 - a^2}\,dx = \int\sqrt{a^2\sec^2\theta - a^2}\;a\sec\theta\tan\theta\,d\theta$$

$$= \int a^2\sec\theta\,.\tan^2\theta\,d\theta$$

$$= a^2\int\sec\theta\,(\sec^2\theta - 1)\,d\theta$$

$$= a^2\int\sec^3\theta\,d\theta - a^2\int\sec\theta\,d\theta$$

$$= \frac{a^2}{2}[\sec\theta\tan\theta + \log(\sec\theta + \tan\theta)]$$

$$-a^2\log(\sec\theta + \tan\theta) \text{ [as in previous case]}$$

$$= \frac{a^2}{2}\sec\theta\tan\theta - \frac{a^2}{2}\log(\sec\theta + \tan\theta)$$

$$= \frac{a^2}{2}\frac{x}{a}\sqrt{\frac{x^2}{a^2} - 1} - \frac{a^2}{2}\log\left[\frac{x}{a} + \sqrt{\frac{x^2}{a^2} - 1}\right]$$

$$= \frac{x}{2}\sqrt{x^2 - a^2} - \frac{a^2}{2}\log\left[\frac{x + \sqrt{x^2 - a^2}}{a}\right]$$

We thus get six results to remember

$$\int\frac{1}{\sqrt{a^2 - x^2}}\,dx = \sin^{-1}\frac{x}{a}$$

$$\int \frac{1}{\sqrt{a^2 + x^2}} dx = \sinh^{-1}\frac{x}{a} = \log\left[\frac{x + \sqrt{x^2 + a^2}}{a}\right]$$

$$\int \frac{1}{\sqrt{x^2 - a^2}} dx = \cosh^{-1}\frac{x}{a} = \log\left[\frac{x + \sqrt{x^2 - a^2}}{a}\right]$$

$$\int \sqrt{a^2 - x^2}\, dx = \frac{x}{2}\sqrt{a^2 - x^2} + \frac{a^2}{2}\sin^{-1}\frac{x}{a}$$

$$\int \sqrt{a^2 + x^2}\, dx = \frac{x}{2}\sqrt{a^2 + x^2} + \frac{a^2}{2}\sinh^{-1}\frac{x}{a}$$

$$= \frac{x}{2}\sqrt{a^2 + x^2} + \frac{a^2}{2}\log\left[\frac{x + \sqrt{a^2 + x^2}}{a}\right]$$

$$\int \sqrt{x^2 - a^2}\, dx = \frac{x}{2}\sqrt{x^2 - a^2} - \frac{a^2}{2}\cosh^{-1}\frac{x}{a}$$

$$= \frac{x}{2}\sqrt{x^2 - a^2} - \frac{a^2}{2}\log\left[\frac{x + \sqrt{x^2 - a^2}}{a}\right]$$

Example 18. *Solve* $\int \frac{1}{\sqrt{x^2 + x + 1}} dx.$

We have

$$I = \int \frac{1}{\sqrt{x^2 + x + 1}} dx = \int \frac{1}{\sqrt{\left(x + \frac{1}{2}\right)^2 + \left(\frac{\sqrt{3}}{2}\right)^2}} dx$$

Put $x + \frac{1}{2} = t$, then $dx = dt$

thus

$$I = \int \frac{dt}{\sqrt{t^2 + \left(\frac{\sqrt{3}}{2}\right)^2}} = \sinh^{-1}\frac{t}{\sqrt{3/2}}$$

(by the second integral evaluated above)

$$= \sinh^{-1}\frac{x + 1/2}{\sqrt{3}/2} = \sinh^{-1}\frac{2x + 1}{\sqrt{3}}$$

The above result could, of course, be written directly without actually making the substitution $x + \frac{1}{2} = t$ by taking x be $x + \frac{1}{2}$ in the formula.

Example 19. *Evaluate* $\int \sqrt{-3x^2 + x + 2}\, dx.$

Solution. $\int \sqrt{-3x^2 + x + 2}\, dx = \int \sqrt{3}\sqrt{-x^2 + \frac{x}{3} + \frac{2}{3}}\, dx$

$$= \sqrt{3}\int \sqrt{\frac{2}{3} - \left(x^2 - \frac{x}{3}\right)}\, dx$$

$$= \sqrt{3}\int \sqrt{\left(\frac{2}{3} + \frac{1}{36}\right) - \left(x - \frac{1}{6}\right)^2}\, dx$$

$$= \sqrt{3}\int \sqrt{\left(\frac{5}{6}\right)^2 - \left(x - \frac{1}{6}\right)^2}\, dx$$

$$= \sqrt{3}\left[\frac{x - \frac{1}{6}}{2}\sqrt{\left(\frac{5}{6}\right)^2 - \left(x - \frac{1}{6}\right)^2} + \frac{\left(\frac{5}{6}\right)^2}{2}\sin^{-1}\frac{x - \frac{1}{6}}{5/6}\right]$$

$$= \frac{1}{12}(6x - 1)\sqrt{-3x^2 + x + 2} + \frac{25}{72}\sqrt{3}\sin^{-1}\left(\frac{6x - 1}{5}\right).$$

Example 20. *Evaluate* $\int \frac{4x - 3}{\sqrt{x^2 + 1}}\, dx.$

Solution. We have

$$\int \frac{4x - 3}{\sqrt{x^2 + 1}}\, dx = \int \frac{4x}{\sqrt{x^2 + 1}}\, dx - 3\int \frac{1}{\sqrt{x^2 + 1}}\, dx$$

$$= 4\int x(x^2 + 1)^{-1/2}\, dx - 3\sinh^{-1} x$$

$$= 2\int (2x)\,(x^2 + 1)^{-1/2}\, dx - 3\sinh^{-1} x$$

$$= 2\,\frac{(x^2 + 1)^{-1/2+1}}{-\frac{1}{2} + 1} - 3\sinh^{-1} x$$

$$= 4\sqrt{x^2 + 1} - 3\sinh^{-1} x.$$

Example 21. *Evaluate* $\int (4x + 5)\sqrt{x^2 + 4x + 9}\, dx$

Solution. We have $\int (4x+5)\sqrt{x^2+4x+9dx}$

$$= \int 4x\sqrt{x^2+4x+9dx} + 5\int \sqrt{x^2+4x+9dx}$$

$$= 2\int (2x+4-4)\int \sqrt{x^2+4x+9}\,dx + 5\int \sqrt{x^2+4x+9}\,dx$$

$$= 2\int (2x+4)\int \sqrt{x^2+4x+9}\,dx - 3\int \sqrt{x^2+4x+9}\,dx$$

$$= 2\int (2x+4)\,(x^2+4x+9)^{1/2}\,dx - 3\int \sqrt{(x+2)^2+5}\,dx$$

$$= 2\,\frac{(x^2+4x+9)^{1/2+1}}{\frac{1}{2}+1} - 3\left[\frac{x+2}{2}\sqrt{x^2+4x+9} + \frac{5}{2}\sinh^{-1}\frac{x+2}{\sqrt{5}}\right]$$

$$= \frac{4}{3}(x^2+4x+9)^{3/2} - 3\left[\frac{x+2}{2}\sqrt{x^2+4x+9} + \frac{5}{2}\sinh^{-1}\frac{x+2}{\sqrt{5}}\right]$$

Example 22. *Evaluate* $\int \frac{x^2+2x+3}{\sqrt{x^2+x+1}}\,dx$.

Let us determine three constants λ, μ, ν, such that

$$x^2+2x+3 = \lambda(x^2+x+1) + \mu(2x+1) + \nu$$

where $2x+1$ = derivative of x^2+x+1.

Comparing coefficients of x^2, x and constant terms

we get $\lambda = 1$, $\lambda + 2\mu = 2$, $\lambda + \mu + \nu = 3$ $\Rightarrow$ $\lambda = 1$, $\mu = \frac{1}{2}$, $\nu = \frac{3}{2}$

Thus

$$x^2+2x+3 = (x^2+x+1) + \frac{1}{2}(2x+1) + \frac{3}{2}$$

$$\Rightarrow \frac{x^2+2x+3}{\sqrt{x^2+x+1}}\,dx = \frac{x^2+x+1}{\sqrt{x^2+x+1}} + \frac{1}{2}\,\frac{(2x+1)}{\sqrt{x^2+x+1}} + \frac{3}{2}\,\frac{1}{\sqrt{x^2+x+1}}$$

$$\Rightarrow \int \frac{x^2+2x+3}{\sqrt{x^2+x+1}}\,dx = \int \sqrt{x^2+x+1}\,dx + \frac{1}{2}\int \frac{2x+1}{\sqrt{x^2+x+1}}\,dx + \frac{3}{2}\int \frac{dx}{\sqrt{x^2+x+1}}$$

$$= \int\sqrt{\left(x+\frac{1}{2}\right)^2+\left(\frac{\sqrt{3}}{2}\right)^2}\,dx + \tfrac{1}{2}\int(2x+1)\,(x^2+x+1)^{-1/2}dx$$

$$+\frac{3}{2}\int\frac{1}{\sqrt{\left(x+\frac{1}{2}\right)^2+\left(\frac{\sqrt{3}}{2}\right)^2}}dx$$

$$= \tfrac{1}{2}(x+\tfrac{1}{2})\sqrt{x^2+x+1}+\tfrac{3}{2}\sinh^{-1}\frac{x+\frac{1}{2}}{\sqrt{3}/2}+\tfrac{1}{2}\frac{(x^2+x+1)^{-1/2+1}}{-\frac{1}{2}+1}+$$

$$\tfrac{3}{2}\sinh^{-1}\frac{x+\frac{1}{2}}{\sqrt{3}/2}$$

$$= \frac{2x+5}{4}\sqrt{x^2+x+1}+\frac{15}{8}\sinh^{-1}\frac{2x+1}{\sqrt{3}}$$

EXERCISES

Integrate the following:

1. (*i*) $\dfrac{1}{\sqrt{x^2+2x+2}}$ (*ii*) $\dfrac{1}{\sqrt{1+12x-9x^2}}$ (*iii*) $\dfrac{1}{\sqrt{2a^2-x^2/2}}$

2. (*i*) $\sqrt{-2x^2+3x+4}$ (*ii*) $\sqrt{2-3x^2}$ (*iii*) $\sqrt{9-4x^2}$

3. (*i*) $\dfrac{x^2}{\sqrt{x^2-1}}$ (*ii*) $\dfrac{x^3}{\sqrt{x^8+1}}$ (*iii*) $\dfrac{1}{(\sqrt{a^2-x^2})^3}$

4. (*i*) $\sqrt{3-2x-x^2}$ (*ii*) $\sqrt{3x^2+5}$ (*iii*) $x^3\sqrt{x^8+16}$ [Put $x^4 = t$]

   (*iv*) $\cos x\sqrt{4-\sin^2 x}$

5. (*i*) Show that $\displaystyle\int\frac{x^2+2x+3}{\sqrt{x^2+1}}\,dx = \frac{5}{2}\left[\sqrt{x^2+1}+\sinh^{-1}x\right]$

6. Prove that $\displaystyle\int(2x+3)\sqrt{x^2+2x+3}\,dx$

$$= \tfrac{1}{2}(x+1)\sqrt{x^2+2x+3}+\tfrac{2}{3}(x^2+2x+3)^{3/2}+\sinh^{-1}\frac{x+1}{\sqrt{2}}$$

ANSWERS

1. (*i*) $\sinh^{-1}(x+1)$ (*ii*) $\tfrac{1}{3}\sinh^{-1}\dfrac{3x-2}{\sqrt{5}}$ (*iii*) $\sqrt{2}\sin^{-1}\dfrac{x}{2a}$

2. (i) $\frac{1}{8}(4x-3)\sqrt{-2x^2+3x+4} + \frac{41}{32}\sqrt{2}\sin^{-1}\left[\frac{4x-3}{\sqrt{41}}\right]$

(ii) $\frac{x}{2}\sqrt{2-3x^2}+\frac{\sqrt{3}}{3}\sin^{-1}\left[\frac{x\sqrt{3}}{\sqrt{2}}\right]$

(iii) $\frac{x}{2}\sqrt{9-4x^2}+\frac{9}{4}\sin^{-1}\frac{2x}{3}$

3. (i) $\frac{x}{2}\sqrt{x^2-1}+\frac{1}{2}\cosh^{-1}x$ (ii) $\frac{1}{4}\sinh^{-1}x^4$

(iii) $\frac{1}{a^2}\frac{x}{\sqrt{a^2-x^2}}$

4. (i) $\frac{x+1}{2}\sqrt{3-2x-x^2}+2\sin^{-1}\left[\frac{x+1}{2}\right]$

(ii) $\frac{x}{2}\sqrt{3x^2+5}+\frac{5}{2\sqrt{3}}\sinh^{-1}\left[\frac{x\sqrt{3}}{\sqrt{5}}\right]$

(iii) $\frac{x^4}{8}\sqrt{x^3+16}+2\sinh^{-1}\left[\frac{x^4}{4}\right]$

(iv) $\frac{\sin x}{2}\sqrt{4-\sin^2 x}+2\sin^{-1}\left[\frac{\sin x}{2}\right]$

10. INTEGRATION BY PARTS

We now develop a formula which will help us in finding the integral of a product of two functions.

We know that if u and v are two functions of x.

then $$\frac{d}{dx}(uv) = u\frac{dv}{dx} + v\frac{du}{dx}$$

$\Rightarrow$ $$u\frac{dv}{dx} = \frac{d}{dx}(uv) - v\frac{du}{dx}$$

Integrating both sides with respect to x, we get

$$\int u\frac{dv}{dx}\,dx = \int\frac{d}{dx}(uv)\,dx - \int v\frac{du}{dx}\,dx$$

or $$\int u\frac{dv}{dx}\,dx = uv - \int v.\frac{du}{dx}\,dx$$

Put $u = f(x)$, $\frac{dv}{dx} = g(x)$, then $v = \int g(x)dx$

The above reduces to

$$\int f(x)\,g(x)\,dx = f(x)\int g(x)\,dx - \int[f'(x)\int g(x)\,dx]$$

where $f'(x)$ denotes the derivative of $f(x)$. This is the required formula. In words, Integral of the product of two functions

= first function × Integral of the second — Integral of (differential of first × integral of the second function)

It is clear from the formula that it is helpful only when we know (or can easily evaluate) integral of at least one of the two given functions. The following examples will illustrate how to apply this rule.

Example 23. *Find* $\int x^2 e^x dx$.

Solution. Taking x^2 as the first function and e^x as the second function, we note

$$\int x^2 e^x dx = x^2 e^x - \int (2x)e^x dx.$$

$$= x^2 e^x - 2\int x\, e^x dx$$

$$= x^2 e^x - 2\left[xe^x - \int e^x\, dx\right] \text{ (integrating by parts again)}$$

$$= x^2 e^x - 2[xe^x - e^x]$$

Note. If we had taken e^x as the first function and x^2 as the second function, we would not have got the answer. The reader would do well to try it and reason why?

Example 24. *Evaluate* (*i*) $\int \log x\, dx$, (*ii*) $\int x^n \log x\, dx$ $(n \neq -1)$

Solution. (*i*) We have $\int \log x\, dx = \int 1.\log x\, dx$

$$= (\log x).\, x - \int x.\frac{1}{x}\, dx$$

$$= x\log x - x$$

(*ii*) We have $\int x^n \log x\, dx = (\log x)\dfrac{x^{n+1}}{n+1} - \int \dfrac{x^{n+1}}{n+1} \times \dfrac{1}{x}\, dx$

$$= \frac{x^{n+1}}{n+1}\log x - \frac{1}{n+1}\int x^n\, dx$$

$$= \frac{x^{n+1}}{n+1}\log x - \frac{1}{n+1}\cdot\frac{x^{n+1}}{n+1}$$

$$= \frac{x^{n+1}}{n+1}\left[\log x - \frac{1}{n+1}\right]$$

Example 25. *Evaluate* $\int \frac{x\,dx}{1+\cos x}$.

Solution. We have

$$\int \frac{x\,dx}{1+\cos x}\,dx = \int \frac{x}{2\cos^2 \frac{x}{2}}\,dx = \frac{1}{2}\int x \sec^2 \frac{x}{2}\,dx$$

$$= \frac{1}{2}\left[2x \tan\frac{x}{2} - \int 2\tan\frac{x}{2}\,dx\right]$$

$$= x\tan\frac{x}{2} - \int \tan\frac{x}{2}\,dx$$

$$= x\tan\frac{x}{2} - \left(-2\log\cos\frac{x}{2}\right)$$

$$= x\tan\frac{x}{2} + 2\log\cos\frac{x}{2}.$$

Example 26. *Evaluate* $\int \sec^3\theta\, d\theta$.

Solution. We have

$$I = \int \sec^3\theta\, d\theta = \int \sec\theta.\sec^2\theta\, d\theta$$

$$= \sec\theta\tan\theta - \int (\sec\theta.\tan\theta)\tan\theta\, d\theta$$

$$= \sec\theta\tan\theta - \int \sec\theta.\tan^2\theta\, d\theta$$

$$= \sec\theta\tan\theta - \int \sec\theta(\sec^2\theta - 1)\,d\theta$$

$$= \sec\theta\tan\theta - I + \int \sec\theta\, d\theta$$

$$\Rightarrow\ 2I = \sec\theta\tan\theta + \log(\sec\theta + \tan\theta)$$

$$\Rightarrow\ I = \tfrac{1}{2}[\sec\theta\tan\theta + \log(\sec\theta + \tan\theta)]$$

Example 27. *Evaluate* $\int x\cos 2x\, dx$

Solution. We have $\int x\cos 2x\,dx = \frac{x\sin 2x}{2} - \int \frac{\sin 2x}{2}\,dx$ [By parts]

$$= \frac{x}{2}\sin 2x + \tfrac{1}{2}\,\frac{\cos 2x}{2}$$

$$= \tfrac{1}{4}[2x\sin 2x + \cos 2x].$$

EXERCISES

Integrate the following functions:

1. (*i*) $e^x \sin x$ (*ii*) $e^x \cos x$ (*iii*) $x\, e^x$
2. (*i*) $x \log x$ (*iii*) $x^2 \log x$
3. (*i*) $\tan^{-1} x$ (*ii*) $\sin^{-1} x$
4. (*i*) $x \sin^{-1} x$ (*ii*) $x \tan^{-1} x$ (*iii*) $x^2 \tan^{-1} x$
   (*iv*) $x \sin x \sec^3 x$
5. (*i*) $\dfrac{x+\sin x}{1+\cos x}$ (*ii*) $\dfrac{x-\sin x}{1-\cos x}$
6. $x \log (1 + x^2)$
7. $x^n e^x$
8. $\log \{x+\sqrt{a^2+x^2}\}$
9. $\cos x. \log \sin x$

ANSWERS

1. (*i*) $\dfrac{e^x}{2}(\sin x - \cos x)$ (*ii*) $\dfrac{e^x}{2}(\sin x + \cos x)$ (*iii*) $e^x (x - 1)$
2. (*i*) $\frac{1}{4}x^2 \log \left[\dfrac{x^2}{e}\right]$ (*ii*) $\frac{1}{9}\, x^2 \log \left[\dfrac{x^2}{e}\right]$
3. (*i*) $x \tan^{-1} x - \frac{1}{2} \log (1 + x^2)$
   (*ii*) $x \sin^{-1} x + \sqrt{1-x^2}$
4. (*i*) $\frac{1}{4}(2x^2 - 1)\sin^{-1} x + \frac{1}{4}\, x\, \sqrt{1-x^2}$
   (*ii*) $\dfrac{x^2}{2} \tan^{-1} x - \frac{1}{2}\, [x - \tan^{-1} x]$
   (*iii*) $\dfrac{x^3}{3} \tan^{-1} x - \dfrac{x^2}{6} + \dfrac{1}{6} \log (1 + x^2)$
   (*iv*) $\frac{1}{2}[x - \tan x + x \tan^2 x]$
5. (*i*) $x \tan \dfrac{x}{2}$ (*ii*) $-x \cot \dfrac{x}{2}$
6. (*i*) $\dfrac{x^2}{2} \log (1 + x^2) - \dfrac{x^2}{2} + \frac{1}{2} \log (1 + x^2)$
7. (*i*) $\{x^n - n\, x^{n-1} + n(n - 1)\, x^{n-2} ... + (-1)^n \underline{\lfloor n} \}\, e^x$
8. $x \log \{ x + \sqrt{a^2+x^2} \} - \sqrt{a^2+x^2}$
9. $\sin x \log \sin x - \sin x.$

11. TO EVALUATE THE INTEGRALS

(*i*) $\int e^x [f(x)+f'(x)]\,dx$ (*ii*) $I_1 = \int e^{ax} \sin(bx+c)\,dx$

(*iii*) $I_2 = \int e^{ax} \cos(bx+c)\,dx$

(*i*) Consider $\int e^x f(x)\,dx$

Integration by parts yields

$$\int e^x f(x)\,dx = f(x)e^x - \int f'(x)\,e^x\,dx$$

$$\Rightarrow \int e^x f(x)\,dx + \int e^x f'(x)\,dx = f(x)\,e^x$$

i.e., $\int e^x [f(x)+f'(x)]\,dx = f(x)\,e^x$

(*ii*) Using integration by parts, we find

$$I_1 = \int e^{ax} \sin(bx+c)\,dx$$

$$= \frac{e^{ax}}{a}\sin(bx+c) - \int \frac{e^{ax}}{a}.\cos(bx+c).\,b\,dx$$

$$= \frac{e^{ax}}{a}\sin(bx+c) - \frac{b}{a}I_2$$

Again, similarly,

$$I_2 = \int e^{ax} \cos(bx+c)\,dx$$

$$= \frac{e^{ax}}{a}\cos(bx+c) - \int \frac{-e^{ax}}{a}\sin(bx+c)\,b\,dx$$

$$= \int \frac{e^{ax}}{a}\cos(bx+c) + \frac{b}{a}I_1$$

and thus

$$I_1 = \frac{e^{ax}}{a}\sin(bx+c) - \frac{b}{a}\left[\frac{e^{ax}}{a}\cos(bx+c) + \frac{b}{a}I_1\right]$$

$$\Rightarrow \left(1+\frac{b^2}{a^2}\right)I_1 = \frac{e^{ax}}{a}\sin(bx+c) - \frac{b}{a^2}e^{ax}\cos(bx+c)$$

$$\Rightarrow \left(\frac{a^2+b^2}{a^2}\right)I_1 = e^{ax}\left[\frac{a\sin(bx+c) - b\cos(bx+c)}{a^2}\right]$$

$$\Rightarrow I_1 = \int e^{ax}\sin(bx+c)\,dx = e^{ax}\left[\frac{a\sin(bx+c) - b\cos(bx+c)}{a^2+b^2}\right]$$

Similiarly,

$$I_2 = e^{ax}\left[\frac{a\cos(bx+c)+b\sin(bx+c)}{a^2+b^2}\right]$$

The above two integrals could be put into another form by the substitution $a = r\cos\theta$, $b = r\sin\theta$

$$I_1 = e^{ax}\left[\frac{r\cos\theta.\sin(bx+c) - r\sin\theta\cos(bx+c)}{a^2+b^2}\right]$$

$$= e^{ax}\frac{r\sin(bx+c-\theta)}{a^2+b^2}$$

$$\Rightarrow \quad \int e^{ax}\sin(bx+c)\,dx = e^{ax}\frac{\sin(bx+c-\tan^{-1}b/a)}{\sqrt{a^2+b^2}}$$

as $r^2 = a^2 + b^2$ and $\tan\theta = \frac{b}{a}$

Similarly,

$$\int e^{ax}\cos(bx+c)\,dx = e^{ax}\frac{\cos(bx+c-\tan^{-1}b/a)}{\sqrt{a^2+b^2}}$$

Example 28. *Find* $\int e^x\,[\sin x + \cos x]\,dx$.

Solution. Since $\frac{d}{dx}(\sin x) = \cos x$.

$$\int e^x(\sin x + \cos x)\,dx = e^x\sin x.$$

Example 29. *Find* $\int \frac{xe^x}{(x+1)^2}dx$.

Solution. We have $\int \frac{xe^x}{(x+1)^2}dx = \int e^x\left[\frac{1}{x+1} - \frac{1}{(x+1)^2}\right]dx$

$$= e^x.\frac{1}{x+1} \text{ as } \frac{d}{dx}\left(\frac{1}{x+1}\right) = -\frac{1}{(x+1)^2}$$

Example 30. *Evaluate* $\int e^{2x}\cos(3x+4)\,dx$.

Solution. We have by the formula proved in Art. 11

$$\int e^{2x}\cos(3x+4)\,dx = e^{2x}\frac{\cos 3x + 4 - \tan^{-1}\frac{3}{2}}{\sqrt{13}}$$

Example 31. *Evaluate* $\int x\, e^{2x} \cos x\, dx.$

Solution. We know that $\int e^{2x} \cos x\, dx = e^{2x} \dfrac{\cos (x - \tan^{-1} \frac{1}{2})}{\sqrt{5}}$

Thus using integration by parts and taking x as the first function and $e^{2x} \cos x$ as the second function we find

$$\int x e^{2x} \cos x\, dx = x . e^{2x} \frac{\cos (x - \tan^{-1} \frac{1}{2})}{\sqrt{5}}$$

$$- \int \frac{1 . e^{2x} \cos (x - \tan^{-1} \frac{1}{2})}{\sqrt{5}} dx$$

$$= x . \frac{e^{2x}}{\sqrt{5}} \cos (x - \tan^{-1} \tfrac{1}{2}) - \frac{1}{\sqrt{5}} \left[\frac{e^{2x}}{5} \cos (x - 2 \tan^{-1} \tfrac{1}{2}) \right]$$

$$= e^{2x} \left[\frac{x}{\sqrt{5}} \cos (x - \tan^{-1} \tfrac{1}{2}) - \tfrac{1}{2} \cos (x - 2 \tan^{-1} \tfrac{1}{2}) \right]$$

Example 32. *Find (i)* $\int e^x . \dfrac{1 + \sin x}{1 + \cos x} dx$, *(ii)* $\int x e^x\, dx$

Solution. (*i*) We have $\int e^x \left(\dfrac{1 + \sin x}{1 + \cos x} \right) dx$

$$= \int e^x \left(\frac{1 + 2 \sin x/2 \cos x/2}{2 \cos^2 x/2} \right) dx$$

$$= \int e^x \left[\tfrac{1}{2} \sec^2 \frac{x}{2} + \tan \frac{x}{2} \right] dx$$

$$= e^x \tan \frac{x}{2} \qquad \text{as } \frac{d}{dx} \left(\tan \frac{x}{2} \right) = \tfrac{1}{2} \sec^2 \frac{x}{2}$$

(*ii*) We have $\int x e^x\, dx = \int e^x (x - 1 + 1)\, dx$

$$= e^x (x - 1)$$

as $\qquad \dfrac{d}{dx} (x - 1) = 1$

One could, of course, solve the problem directly, using integration by parts.

EXERCISES

Evaluate the integrals

1. $\int e^x \left[\log x + \frac{1}{x}\right] dx$ 2. $\int e^x [\tan x + \sec^2 x] dx$

3. $\int e^x \left[\frac{1-x}{1+x^2}\right]^2 dx$ 4. $\int e^x \left(\frac{1+\sin x \cos x}{\cos^2 x}\right) dx$

5. (*i*) $\int e^{3x} \cos 4x\, dx$ (*ii*) $\int e^x \sin x$

(*iii*) $\int e^{2x} \sin (3x+4)\, dx$

6. $\int x^2 e^x \sin x\, dx$ 7. $\int e^x \cos^2 x\, dx$

ANSWERS

1. $e^x \log x$ 2. $e^x \tan x$ 3. $\frac{e^x}{1+x^2}$

4. $e^x \tan x$

5. (*i*) $e^{3x} \frac{\cos(4x - \tan^{-1} \frac{4}{3})}{5}$ (*ii*) $e^x \frac{\sin (x - \tan^{-1} 1)}{\sqrt{2}}$ (*iii*) $e^{2x} \frac{\sin (3x + 4 - \tan^{-1} 3/2)}{\sqrt{13}}$

6. $\frac{e^x}{\sqrt{2}}\left[x^2 \sin\left(x - \frac{\pi}{4}\right) + \sin\left(x - \frac{3\pi}{4}\right)\right] + xe^x \cos x$

7. $\frac{1}{2} e^x + \frac{1}{2\sqrt{5}} (2x - \tan^{-1} 2)$

12. SOME MORE EXAMPLES

We give below a few more examples, where both substitution and integration by parts is used.

Example 33. *Find* $\int \frac{e^{m \tan^{-1} x}}{(1+x^2)^{3/2}} dx$

Solution. Put $\tan^{-1} x = t$ then $x = \tan t$

Also $\frac{1}{1+x^2} dx = dt$ and $1 + x^2 = 1 + \tan^2 t = \sec^2 t$

Thus

$$\int \frac{e^{m \tan^{-1} x}}{(1+x^2)^{3/2}} dx = \int \frac{e^{mt}}{\sec t} dt = \int e^{mt} \cos t\, dt$$

$$= e^{mt} \frac{\cos\left(t - \tan^{-1}\frac{1}{m}\right)}{\sqrt{1+m^2}}$$

where $t = \tan^{-1} x.$

Example 34. *Evaluate* $\int x^2 \sin^{-1} x\, dx$.

Solution. We have, by integration by parts,

$$\int x^2 \sin^{-1} x dx = (\sin^{-1} x)\frac{x^3}{3} - \int \frac{x^3}{3} \cdot \frac{1}{\sqrt{1-x^2}} dx$$

$$= \frac{x^3}{3} \sin^{-1} x - \tfrac{1}{3} \int \frac{x^3}{\sqrt{1-x^2}} dx \qquad \ldots(1)$$

To evaluate $\int \frac{x^3}{\sqrt{1-x^2}} dx$, put $\sqrt{1-x^2} = t$

$$1 - x^2 = t^2$$

$\Rightarrow$ $-2x\, dx = 2t\, dt$

$\Rightarrow$ $x\, dx = -t\, dt$

Also $x^2 = 1 - t^2$

thus $$\int \frac{x^3 dx}{\sqrt{1-x^2}} = -\int \frac{(1-t^2)\, tdt}{t} = \int (t^2 - 1)\, dt = \frac{t^3}{3} - t$$

$$= \frac{(1-x^2)^{3/2}}{3} - \sqrt{1-x^2}$$

Hence the required value is [from (1)]

$$\int x^2 \sin^{-1} x dx = \frac{x^3}{3} \sin^{-1} x - \tfrac{1}{3}\left[\frac{(1-x^2)^{3/2}}{3} - \sqrt{1-x^2}\right]$$

EXERCISES

Evaluate the integrals

1. (*i*) $\int \frac{x \sin^{-1} x}{\sqrt{1-x^2}} dx$ (*ii*) $\int \frac{x e^{a \sin^{-1} x}}{\sqrt{1-x^2}} dx$

2. (*i*) $\int \tan^{-1} \sqrt{\frac{1-x}{1+x}} dx$ (*ii*) $\int \sin^{-1} \sqrt{\frac{x}{a+x}} dx$

3. $\int x^5 \tan^{-1} x^2\, dx$

4. $\int \dfrac{x^2 dx}{(x \sin x + \cos x)^2}$

5. $\int_0^{1/\sqrt{2}} \dfrac{\sin^{-1} x dx}{(1-x^2)^{3/2}}$

6. $\int_0^1 (\sin^{-1} x)^4\, dx$

7. $\int \sqrt{x} \tan^{-1} \sqrt{x}\, dx$.

ANSWERS

1. (*i*) $x - \sqrt{1-x^2} \sin^{-1} x$ (*ii*) $\dfrac{e^{at} \sin(t - \tan^{-1} 1/a)}{\sqrt{1+a^3}}$

where $t = \sin^{-1} x$

2. (*i*) $\frac{1}{2} \left[x \cos^{-1} x - \sqrt{1-x^2} \right]$

(*ii*) $a \left[\dfrac{x}{a} \tan^{-1} \sqrt{\dfrac{x}{a}} - \sqrt{\dfrac{x}{a}} + \tan^{-1} \sqrt{\dfrac{x}{a}} \right]$

3. $\frac{1}{6}$ $[(x^6 + 1) \tan^{n-1} x^3 - x^3]$ 4. $\tan x - \dfrac{x}{\cos x(x \sin x + \cos x)}$

5. $\dfrac{\pi}{4} - \dfrac{1}{2} \log 2$ 6. $\dfrac{\pi^4}{16} - 3\pi^2 + 24$

7. $\frac{2}{3} x^{3/2} \tan^{-1} \sqrt{x} - \dfrac{x}{3} + \dfrac{1}{2} \log (x + 1)$.

13. INTEGRATION OF RATIONAL FUNCTIONS

A function of the type $\dfrac{f(x)}{g(x)}$, where $f(x)$ and $g(x)$ are polynomials in x, is called a *rational function.* We now give a few methods by which integration of such functions is done. we shall be making an extensive use of partial fractions here.

Let us first establish the integrals

(1) $\displaystyle\int \frac{dx}{ax+b} = \frac{1}{a} \log (ax+b)$

(2) $\displaystyle\int \frac{1}{x^2 + a^2} dx = \frac{1}{a} \tan^{-1} \frac{x}{a}$

(3) $\displaystyle\int \frac{1}{x^2 - a^2} dx = \frac{1}{2a} \log \frac{x-a}{x+a}$ $(x > a)$

(4) $\displaystyle\int \frac{1}{a^2 - x^2} dx = \frac{1}{2a} \log \frac{a+x}{a-x}$ $(a > x)$

it being assumed that $(a \neq 0)$

Integrals (1) and (2) follow easily from definition.

To evaluate integral (3), we note

$$\frac{1}{x^2 - a^2} \equiv \frac{1}{(x-a)(x+a)} \equiv \frac{A}{x-a} + \frac{B}{x+a} \quad \text{(say)}$$

$\Rightarrow \quad I \equiv A\,(x+a) + B\,(x-a)$

Putting $x = -a$ and $x = a$, we get

$$A = \frac{1}{2a} \text{ and } B = -\frac{1}{2a}$$

Thus

$$\frac{1}{x^2 - a^2} = \frac{1}{2a}\left[\frac{1}{x-a} - \frac{1}{x+a}\right]$$

and hence

$$\int \frac{1}{x^2 - a^2}\,dx = \frac{1}{2a}\int \frac{1}{x-a}\,dx - \frac{1}{2a}\int \frac{1}{x+a}\,dx$$

$$= \frac{1}{2a}\log(x-a) - \frac{1}{2a}\log(x+a)$$

$$= \frac{1}{2a}\log\frac{x-a}{x+a}.$$

Integral (4) can be evaluated similarly, keeping in mind that

$$\int \frac{1}{a-x}\,dx = -\log(a-x)$$

Let us now study some examples that will illustrate the use of the above formulas.

Example 35. *Integrate* (*i*) $\dfrac{1}{4x^2 + 4x + 10}$.

(*ii*) $\dfrac{1}{x^2 + x + 1}$

Solution. (*i*) We have $\displaystyle\int \frac{1}{4x^2 + 4x + 10}\,dx$

$$= \frac{1}{4}\int \frac{1}{(x + \frac{1}{2})^2 + \left(\frac{3}{2}\right)^2}\,dx$$

$$= \frac{1}{4}.\frac{2}{3}\tan^{-1}\left(\frac{x+\frac{1}{2}}{\frac{3}{2}}\right) = \tfrac{1}{6}\tan^{-1}\left(\frac{2x+1}{3}\right)$$

(*ii*) Also $\displaystyle\int\frac{1}{x^2+x+1}\,dx = \int\frac{1}{(x+\frac{1}{2})^2+\left(\frac{\sqrt{3}}{2}\right)^2}\,dx$

$$= \frac{2}{\sqrt{3}}.\tan^{-1}\left(\frac{x+\frac{1}{2}}{\frac{\sqrt{3}}{2}}\right)$$

$$= \frac{2}{\sqrt{3}}\tan^{-1}\left(\frac{2x+1}{\sqrt{3}}\right)$$

Example 36. *Integrate* $\dfrac{1}{1-6x-9x^2}$.

Solution. We have $\displaystyle\int\frac{1}{1-6x-9x^2}\,dx$

$$= \tfrac{1}{9}\int\frac{1}{\frac{1}{9}-(x^2+\frac{2}{3}x)}\,dx$$

$$= \tfrac{1}{9}\int\frac{1}{\left(\frac{\sqrt{2}}{3}\right)^2-(x+\frac{1}{3})^2}\,dx$$

$$= \frac{1}{9}\;\frac{1}{2\left(\frac{\sqrt{2}}{3}\right)}\log\frac{\frac{\sqrt{2}}{3}+x+\frac{1}{3}}{\frac{\sqrt{2}}{3}-x-\frac{1}{3}}$$

$$= \frac{\sqrt{2}}{12}\log\left(\frac{\sqrt{2}+3x+1}{\sqrt{2}-3x-1}\right).$$

Example 37. *Evaluate* $\displaystyle\int\frac{x^3}{x^2+8x+12}\,dx$

Solution. We have

$$\frac{x^3}{x^2+8x+12} = x-8+\frac{52x+96}{x^2+8x+12} \quad \text{(by division)}$$

Again $$\frac{52x+96}{x^2+8x+12} = \frac{52x+96}{(x+2)(x+6)}.$$

If $$\frac{52x+96}{(x+2)(x+6)} \equiv \frac{A}{x+2} + \frac{B}{x+6}$$

then $52x+96 \equiv A(x+6)+B(x+2)$

Putting $x=-6$ and $x=-2$, we get

$A=-2, B=54$

Hence

$$\int \frac{x^3}{x^2+8x+12}\,dx = \int \left(x-8+\frac{54x}{x+6} - \frac{2}{x+2} \right) dx$$

$$= \frac{x^2}{2} - 8x + 54\log(x+6) - 2\log(x+2).$$

Example 38. *Evaluate* $\int \frac{x}{(x-1)(2x+1)}\,dx$.

Solution. We write $$\frac{x}{(x-1)(2x+1)} \equiv \frac{A}{x-1} + \frac{B}{2x+1}$$

$\Rightarrow$ $x \equiv A(2x+1)+B(x-1)$

Putting $x=1$ and $x=-\frac{1}{2}$, we get

$A=\frac{1}{3}, B=\frac{1}{3}$

Thus

$$\int \frac{x}{(x-1)(2x+1)}\,dx = \frac{1}{3}\int \frac{1}{x-1}\,dx + \frac{1}{3}\int \frac{1}{2x+1}\,dx$$

$$= \frac{1}{3}\log(x-1) + \frac{1}{3}\,\frac{\log(2x+1)}{2}$$

$$= \frac{1}{3}\left[\log(x-1) + \frac{1}{6}\log(2x+1)\right].$$

Example 39. *Evaluate* $\int \frac{x+5}{(x+1)(x+2)^2}\,dx$.

Solution. We write $$\frac{x+5}{(x+1)(x+2)^2} \equiv \frac{A}{x+1} + \frac{B}{x+2} + \frac{C}{(x+2)^2}$$

$\Rightarrow$ $x+5 \equiv A(x+2)^2 + B(x+1)(x+2) + C(x+1)$

Putting $x=-1, -2$, we get $A=4$, $C=-3$

Again comparing coefficients of x^2 on both sides

We get $0 = A + B \Rightarrow B = -A = -4$

Hence

$$\int \frac{x+5}{(x+1)(x+2)^2}\,dx = \int \left[\frac{4}{x+1} - \frac{4}{x+2} - \frac{3}{(x+2)^2}\right] dx$$

$$= 4\int \frac{1}{x+1}\,dx - 4\int \frac{1}{x+2}\,dx - 3\int \frac{1}{(x+2)^2}\,dx$$

$$= 4\log(x+1) - 4\log(x+2) - 3\,\frac{(x+2)^{-2+1}}{-2+1}$$

$$= 4\log\left(\frac{x+1}{x+2}\right) + \frac{3}{x+2}.$$

Example 40. *Evaluate* $\int \frac{1}{(x-1)(x-1)^2}\,dx$.

Solution. We write $\frac{1}{(x-1)(x-1)^2} \equiv \frac{A}{x+1} + \frac{B}{x-1} + \frac{C}{(x-1)^2}$

$\Rightarrow \quad 1 \equiv A(x-1)^2 + B(x-1)(x+1) + C(x+1)$

Putting $x = 1$ and -1, we get $C = \frac{1}{2}, A = \frac{1}{4}$

Again comparing coefficients of x^2, we get

$$0 = A + B \Rightarrow B = -\frac{1}{4}$$

Hence

$$\int \frac{1}{(x+1)(x-1)^2}\,dx = \frac{1}{4}\int \frac{dx}{x+1} - \frac{1}{4}\int \frac{dx}{x-1} + \frac{1}{2}\int \frac{1}{(x-1)^2}\,dx$$

$$= \frac{1}{4}\log(x+1) - \frac{1}{4}\log(x-1) + \frac{1}{2}\,\frac{(x-1)^{-2+1}}{-2+1}$$

$$= \frac{1}{4}\log\frac{x+1}{x-1} - \frac{1}{2(x-1)}$$

Example 41. *Find* $\int \frac{1}{x^3+1}\,dx$.

Solution. We write $\frac{1}{x^3+1} \equiv \frac{1}{(x+1)(x^2-x+1)}$

$$\equiv \frac{A}{x+1} + \frac{Bx+C}{x^2-x+1}$$

$$\Rightarrow \quad 1 \equiv A(x^2 - x + 1) + (Bx + C)(x + 1)$$

Putting $x = -1, 0, 1$, we find

$$A = \tfrac{1}{3}, C = \tfrac{2}{3}, B = -\tfrac{1}{3}$$

Thus

$$\int \frac{1}{x^3 + 1} dx = \tfrac{1}{3} \int \frac{1}{x+1} dx - \tfrac{1}{3} \int \frac{x-2}{x^2 - x + 1} dx$$

$$= \tfrac{1}{3} \log(x+1) - \tfrac{1}{3} \int \frac{x-2}{x^2 - x + 1} dx \qquad \ldots (1)$$

Let us now consider $\int \frac{x-2}{x^2 - x + 1} dx$

We have $\int \frac{x-2}{x^2 - x + 1} dx = \tfrac{1}{2} \int \frac{(2x-4)}{x^2 - x + 1} dx = \tfrac{1}{2} \int \frac{(2x-1) - 3}{x^2 - x + 1} dx$

$$= \tfrac{1}{2} \int \frac{(2x-1)\, dx}{x^2 - x + 1} - \tfrac{3}{2} \int \frac{1}{x^2 - x + 1} dx$$

$$= \tfrac{1}{2} \log(x^2 - x + 1) - \tfrac{3}{2} \int \frac{1}{x^2 - x + 1} dx$$

as $\frac{d}{dx}(x^2 - x + 1) = 2x - 1$

$$= \tfrac{1}{2} \log(x^2 - x + 1) - \tfrac{3}{2} \int \frac{1}{(x - \tfrac{1}{2})^2 + \left(\frac{\sqrt{3}}{2}\right)^2} dx$$

$$= \tfrac{1}{2} \log(x^2 - x + 1) - \frac{3}{2} \cdot \frac{2}{\sqrt{3}} \tan^{-1} \frac{x - \tfrac{1}{2}}{\frac{\sqrt{3}}{2}}$$

$$= \tfrac{1}{2} \log(x^2 - x + 1) - \sqrt{3} \tan^{-1} \frac{2x-1}{\sqrt{3}}$$

Putting in (1) we get the required result

$$= \tfrac{1}{3} \log(x+1) - \tfrac{1}{6} \log(x^2 - x + 1) + \frac{1}{\sqrt{3}} \tan^{-1} \frac{2x-1}{\sqrt{3}}$$

Example 42. *Evaluate* $\int \frac{3x+1}{2x^2 - 2x + 3} dx$.

Solution. Let us find two constants λ and μ such that

Numerator = $\lambda \times$ differential of denominator + μ

i.e., $3x+1=\lambda(4x-2)+\mu$

On comparison we get $3=4\lambda$

$$1=-2\lambda+\mu$$

$$\Rightarrow \quad \lambda=\tfrac{3}{4},\ \mu=\tfrac{5}{2}$$

thus

$$3x+1=\tfrac{3}{4}(4x-2)+\tfrac{5}{2}$$

$$\Rightarrow \frac{3x+1}{2x^2-2x+3}=\frac{3}{4}\frac{(4x-2)}{(2x^2-2x+3)}+\frac{5}{2}\frac{(4x-2)}{(2x^2-2x+3)}$$

$$\Rightarrow \int\frac{3x+1}{2x^2-2x+3}\,dx=\frac{3}{4}\int\frac{4x-2}{2x^2-2x+3}\,dx+\frac{5}{2}\int\frac{1}{2x^2-2x+3}\,dx$$

$$=\tfrac{3}{4}\log(2x^2-2x+3)+\tfrac{5}{4}\cdot\tfrac{1}{2}\int\frac{1}{x^2-x+\frac{3}{2}}\,dx$$

$$=\tfrac{3}{4}\log(2x^2-2x+3)+\tfrac{5}{4}\int\frac{1}{(x-\frac{1}{2})^2+\left(\frac{\sqrt{5}}{2}\right)^2}\,dx$$

$$=\tfrac{3}{4}\log(2x^2-2x+3)+\tfrac{5}{4}\cdot\frac{2}{\sqrt{5}}\tan^{-1}\frac{x-\frac{1}{2}}{\frac{\sqrt{5}}{2}}$$

$$=\tfrac{3}{4}\log(2x^2-2x+3)+\frac{\sqrt{5}}{2}\tan^{-1}\left(\frac{2x-1}{\sqrt{5}}\right).$$

EXERCISES

Integrate

1. (*i*) $\dfrac{1}{2x-3}$ (*ii*) $\dfrac{1}{3-2x}$ (*iii*) $\dfrac{4}{3(3-x)}$

2. (*i*) $\dfrac{1}{2x^2+x+3}$ (*ii*) $\dfrac{1}{x^2+x+1}$ (*iii*) $\dfrac{1}{2x^2+x-1}$

3. (*i*) $\dfrac{x^2+5x+41}{(x+3)(x-1)(2x-1)}$ (*ii*) $\dfrac{x^3}{(x-1)(x-2)(x-3)}$ (*iii*) $\dfrac{x-1}{(x-2)(x-3)}$

4. (*i*) $\dfrac{x^2}{(x-1)^3(x+1)}$ (*ii*) $\dfrac{x^2+x+1}{(x-1)^2(x+2)}$ (*iii*) $\dfrac{1}{x^2(1+x)}$

5. (*i*) $\dfrac{3x+1}{2x^2+x+1}$ (*ii*) $\dfrac{3x+4}{x^2+2x+5}$

6. (*i*) $\dfrac{1}{(x-1)^2(x-2)(x^2+4)}$ (*ii*) $\dfrac{x^2}{x^3+1}$ (*iii*) $\dfrac{1}{x^3+x^2+x+1}$

7. (*i*) $\dfrac{1}{(x-1)^2(1+x^2)}$ (*ii*) $\dfrac{x^2}{(x-1)^2(1+x^2)}$

8. (*i*) Show that

$$\int \frac{dx}{(x^3-1)^2} = \frac{1}{9}\log\frac{x^2+x+1}{(x-1)^2} - \frac{1}{3(x^3-1)} + \frac{2\sqrt{3}}{9}\tan^{-1}\frac{2x+1}{\sqrt{3}}$$

ANSWERS

1. (*i*) $\frac{1}{2}\log(2x-3)$ (*ii*) $-\frac{1}{2}\log(3-2x)$ (*iii*) $-\frac{4}{3}\log(3-x)$

2. (*i*) $\frac{1}{2}\tan^{-1}\dfrac{4x+1}{\sqrt{23}}$ (*ii*) $\dfrac{2}{\sqrt{3}}\tan^{-1}\left(\dfrac{2x+1}{\sqrt{3}}\right)$ (*iii*) $\frac{1}{3}\log\dfrac{2x-1}{2(x+1)}$

3. (*i*) $\dfrac{5}{4}\log(x+3) + \dfrac{47}{4}\log(x-1) - \dfrac{25}{2}\log(2x-1)$

(*ii*) $x + \frac{1}{2}\log(x-1) - 8\log(x-2) + \dfrac{27}{2}\log(x-3)$

(*iii*) $\log\dfrac{(x-3)^2}{x-2}$

4. (*i*) $-\dfrac{1}{4}\left[\dfrac{3}{x-1} + \dfrac{1}{(x-2)^2}\right]$ (*ii*) $\log\dfrac{(x+2)^3}{(x+1)^2} - \dfrac{1}{x+1}$

5. (*i*) $\dfrac{3}{4}\log(2x^2+x+1) + \dfrac{1}{2\sqrt{15}}\tan^{-1}\dfrac{4x+1}{\sqrt{15}}$

(*ii*) $\dfrac{3}{2}\log(x^2+2x+5) + \frac{1}{2}\tan^{-1}\left(\dfrac{x+1}{2}\right)$

6. (*i*) $\dfrac{1}{5(x-1)} - \dfrac{3}{25}\log(x-1) + \dfrac{1}{8}\log(x-2) - \dfrac{1}{400}\log(x^2+4) + \dfrac{7}{200}\tan^{-1}\dfrac{x}{2}$

(*ii*) $\dfrac{x^2}{2} - \dfrac{1}{6}\log\dfrac{x^2-x+1}{(x+1)^2} - \dfrac{1}{\sqrt{3}}\tan^{-1}\dfrac{2x-1}{\sqrt{3}}$

(*iii*) $\frac{1}{2}\log(1+x) - \frac{1}{4}\log(x^2+1) + \frac{1}{2}\tan^{-1}x$

7. (*i*) $\frac{1}{4}\log(x^2+1) - \frac{1}{2}\left[\dfrac{1}{x-1} + \log(x-1)\right]$

(*ii*) $\frac{1}{2}\log(x-1) - \frac{1}{2}\left[\dfrac{1}{x-1} + \dfrac{1}{2}\log(x^2+1)\right]$

14. SOME MORE METHODS

If the integrand consists of even powers of x only, then the substitution $x^2 = t$ while resolving into partial fractions is helpful.

[Note the substitution is not to be made in the integral].

Example 43. *Evaluate* $\int \frac{x^2 dx}{(x^2+1)(3x^2+1)}$

Solution. Put $x^2 = t$ in $\frac{x^2}{(x^2+1)(3x^2+1)}$

Then $\frac{t}{(t+1)(3t+1)} \equiv \frac{A}{t+1} + \frac{B}{3t+1}$

$\Rightarrow t \equiv A\,(3t+1) + B\,(t+1)$

Putting $t = -1$ and $-\frac{1}{3}$, we get

$A = \frac{1}{2}, B = -\frac{1}{2}$

$$\Rightarrow \frac{t}{(t+1)(3t+1)} = \frac{1}{2(t+1)} - \frac{1}{2(3t+1)}$$

Thus

$$\frac{x^2}{(x^2+1)(3x^2+1)} = \frac{1}{2(x^2+1)} - \frac{1}{2(3x^2+1)}$$

$$\Rightarrow \int \frac{x^2}{(x^2+1)(3x^2+1)}\,dx = \frac{1}{2}\int \frac{dx}{x^2+1} - \frac{1}{2}\int \frac{dx}{3x^2+1}$$

$$= \frac{1}{2}\tan^{-1} x - \frac{1}{6}\int \frac{dx}{x^2+\frac{1}{3}} = \frac{1}{2}\tan^{-1} x - \frac{1}{6}\cdot\frac{1}{1/\sqrt{3}}\tan^{-1}\frac{x}{1/\sqrt{3}}$$

$$= \frac{1}{2}\tan^{-1} x - \frac{x}{2\sqrt{3}}\tan^{-1}(x\sqrt{3})$$

We give two more examples that would help us in solving many other problems.

Example 44. *Solve* $\int \frac{x^2+1}{x^4+1}\,dx$.

Solution. We have $I = \int \frac{x^2+1}{x^4+1}\,dx = \int \frac{1+1/x^2}{x^2+1/x^2}\,dx$

Put $x - \frac{1}{x} = t$

then $\left(1+\frac{1}{x^2}\right) dx = dt$

Also $x^2 + \frac{1}{x^2} - 2 = t^2$

So $I = \int \frac{dt}{t^2+2} = \frac{t}{\sqrt{2}} \tan^{-1} \frac{t}{\sqrt{2}} = \frac{1}{\sqrt{2}} \tan^{-1} \left[\frac{1}{\sqrt{2}}\left(x - \frac{1}{x}\right)\right]$

Example 45. *Evaluate* $\int \frac{x^2-1}{x^4+1} dx.$

Solution. We have $I = \int \frac{x^2-1}{x^4+1} dx = \int \frac{1-1/x^2}{x^2+1/x^2} dx$

Put $x + \frac{1}{x} = t$

then $\left(1-\frac{1}{x^2}\right) dx = dt$

Also $x^2 + \frac{1}{x^2} + 2 = t^2$

Thus
$$I = \int \frac{dt}{t^2-2} = \frac{1}{2\sqrt{2}} \log \frac{t-\sqrt{2}}{t+\sqrt{2}}$$
$$= \frac{1}{2\sqrt{2}} \log \frac{x+1/x-\sqrt{2}}{x+1/x+\sqrt{2}}$$
$$= \frac{1}{2\sqrt{2}} \log \frac{x^2-\sqrt{2}\,x+1}{x^2+\sqrt{2}x+1}.$$

EXERCISES

Integrate

1. (*i*) $\frac{(x^2+1)(x^2+2)}{(x^2+3)(x^2+4)}$ (*ii*) $\frac{x^2+1}{(x^2+2)(2x^2+1)}$

(*iii*) $\frac{x^2}{(x^2-1)(x^2+2)}$

2. (*i*) $\frac{1}{x^4+1}$ (*ii*) $\frac{x^2}{x+1}$

(*iii*) $\frac{\sqrt{x^4}}{x^4+x^2+1}$ (*iv*) $\frac{x^2-1}{x^4+x^2+1}$

ANSWERS

1. (*i*) $x+\frac{2}{\sqrt{3}}\tan^{-1}\frac{x}{\sqrt{3}}-3\tan^{-1}\frac{x}{2}$ (*ii*) $\frac{1}{3\sqrt{2}}\tan^{-1}\left[\frac{3x}{(1-x^2)\sqrt{2}}\right]$

(*iii*) $\frac{1}{6}\log\frac{x-1}{x+1}+\frac{\sqrt{2}}{3}\tan^{-1}\frac{x}{2}$

2. (*i*) $\frac{1}{4}\sqrt{2}\tan^{-1}\frac{x^2-1}{x\sqrt{2}}-\frac{1}{8}\sqrt{2}\log\left(\frac{x^2-x\sqrt{2}+1}{x^2+x\sqrt{2}+1}\right)$

(*ii*) $\frac{1}{8}\sqrt{2}\log\left(\frac{x^2-x\sqrt{2}+1}{x^2+x\sqrt{2}+1}\right)+\frac{1}{4}\sqrt{2}\tan^{-1}\left(\frac{x^2-1}{x\sqrt{2}}\right)$

(*iii*) $\frac{1}{4}\log\left(\frac{x^2-x+1}{x^2+x+1}\right)+\frac{\sqrt{3}}{6}\tan^{-1}\left(\frac{x^2-1}{x\sqrt{2}}\right)$

(*iv*) $\frac{1}{2}\log\left(\frac{x^2-x+1}{x^2+x+1}\right)$

15. SUBSTITUTION BEFORE RESOLVING INTO PARTIAL FRACTIONS

The integration process is sometimes greatly simplified by a substitution as is seen in the following examples:

Example 46. *Solve* $\int\frac{dx}{x(x^4-1)}$.

Solution. Put $x^4=t$ then $4x^3\,dx=dt$

Thus $\int\frac{dx}{x(x^4-1)}=\int\frac{x^3\,dx}{x^4(x^4-1)}=\frac{1}{4}\int\frac{dt}{t(t-1)}$

Now $\int\frac{1}{t(t-1)}dt=\int\frac{1}{t-1}-\frac{1}{t}$

and hence the given integral

$$=\frac{1}{4}\int\left(\frac{1}{t-1}-\frac{1}{t}\right)dt=\frac{1}{4}[\log(t-1)-\log t]$$

$$=\frac{1}{4}\log\left(\frac{t-1}{t}\right)$$

$$=\frac{1}{4}\log\left(\frac{x^4-1}{x^4}\right)$$

Example 47. *Solve* $\int_0^{\pi/4}\sqrt{\tan x}\,dx$.

Solution. Put $\sqrt{\tan x} = t$ then $\tan x = t^2$

and $\sec^2 x\, dx = 2\, t\, dt$

$$\Rightarrow \quad dx = \frac{2t}{1+\tan^2 x}\, dt = \frac{2t\, dt}{1+t^4}$$

Also when $x = 0,\ t = \sqrt{\tan 0} = 0$

when $x = \dfrac{\pi}{4},\ t = \sqrt{\tan \dfrac{\pi}{4}} = 1$

Hence the given integral becomes

$$\int_0^1 \frac{t.2t\, dt}{1+t^4} = 2\int_0^1 \frac{t^2}{1+t^4}$$

$$= 2\left[\frac{\sqrt{2}}{8}\log\frac{t^2-\sqrt{2}t+1}{t^2+\sqrt{2}t+1} + \tfrac{1}{4}\sqrt{2}\tan^{-1}\frac{t^2-1}{t\sqrt{2}}\right]_0^1$$

By using Q. 2 (*ii*) of previous exercise

$$= 2\left[\left\{\frac{\sqrt{2}}{8}\log\frac{2-\sqrt{2}}{2+\sqrt{2}} + \frac{\sqrt{2}}{4}\tan^{-1}0\right\} - \left\{\frac{\sqrt{2}}{8}\log 1 - \frac{\sqrt{2}}{4}\tan^{-1}\infty\right\}\right]$$

$$= 2\left[\frac{\sqrt{2}}{8}\log\frac{2-\sqrt{2}}{2+\sqrt{2}} + \frac{\sqrt{2}}{4}\frac{\pi}{2}\right]$$

$$= \frac{\sqrt{2}}{4}\log\frac{2-\sqrt{2}}{2+\sqrt{2}} + \frac{\sqrt{2}}{4}\pi = \frac{1}{2\sqrt{2}}\log\frac{2-\sqrt{2}}{2+\sqrt{2}} + \frac{1}{2\sqrt{2}}\pi.$$

EXERCISES

Integrate

1. (*i*) $\dfrac{1}{x(x^2+1)^3}$ (*ii*) $\dfrac{1}{x(x^5+1)}$ (*iii*) $\dfrac{1}{x(x^n+1)}$

2. (*i*) $\dfrac{1}{e^{-x}-1}$ (*ii*) $\dfrac{1}{(e^x-1)^2}$ (*iii*) $\dfrac{1}{1+3e^x+2e^{2x}}$

3. (*i*) $\dfrac{1+\sin x}{\sin x\,(1+\cos x)}$ (*ii*) $\dfrac{\cos x}{(1+\sin x)(2+\sin x)(3+\sin x)}$

   (*iii*) $\sqrt{\cot x}$ under the limits 0 to $\dfrac{\pi}{4}$

   (*iv*) $\dfrac{1}{\sin x + \sin 2x}$ (*v*) $\dfrac{\sin x}{\sin 4x}$

ANSWERS

1\. (i) $\dfrac{1}{x^2+1} - \log(x^2+1) + \dfrac{1}{2(x^2+1)} + \log x^2$

(ii) $\dfrac{1}{5}\log\dfrac{x^5}{x^5+1}$ (iii) $\dfrac{1}{n}\log\dfrac{x^n}{x^n+1}$

2\. (i) $\log(e^x-1) - x$ (ii) $\log\dfrac{e^x}{e^x-1} - \dfrac{1}{e^x-1}$

(iii) $\log\dfrac{e^x(e^x+1)}{(2e^x+1)^2}$

3\. (i) $\dfrac{1}{2}\log\tan\dfrac{x}{2} + \dfrac{1}{4}\tan^2\dfrac{x}{2} + \tan\dfrac{x}{2}$

(ii) $\dfrac{5}{2}\log 2 - \dfrac{3}{2}\log 3$

(iii) $\dfrac{\sqrt{2}}{2}\log(\sqrt{2}+1) + \dfrac{\sqrt{2}}{4}\pi$ (iv) $\dfrac{1}{6}\log\dfrac{(1-\cos x)(3+2\cos x)^4}{(1+\cos x)^3}$

(v) $\dfrac{1}{8}\log\dfrac{\sin x-1}{\sin x+1} - \dfrac{1}{4\sqrt{2}}\log\dfrac{\sqrt{2}\sin x-1}{\sqrt{2}\sin x+1}$

16. INTEGRALS OF THE TYPE

$$\int\frac{dx}{a+b\cos x+c\sin x},\ b^2+c^2\neq 0$$

The substitution $\tan\dfrac{x}{2} = t$ converts every rational function of $\sin x$ and $\cos x$ into a rational function of t and we can then evaluate the integral by using the previous methods.

Example 48. *Evaluate* (i) $\displaystyle\int_0^{\pi/2}\frac{dx}{4+5\cos x}$ (ii) $\displaystyle\int_0^{\pi}\frac{dx}{5+3\cos x}$

Solution. Put $\tan\dfrac{x}{2} = t$, then $\frac{1}{2}\sec^2\dfrac{x}{2}\,dx = dt$

$$\Rightarrow \qquad dx = \frac{2\,dt}{1+\tan^2 x/2} = \frac{2\,dt}{1+t^2}$$

Also as $\cos x = \dfrac{1-\tan^2 x/2}{1+\tan^2 x/2} = \dfrac{1-t^2}{1+t^2}$

the given integral reduces to

$$\int_0^1 \frac{2\,dt}{(1+t^2)\left[4+\frac{5-5t^2}{1+t^2}\right]}$$

$$\left[\begin{array}{ll}\text{Note when} & x=0 \\ & t=\tan 0=0 \\ \text{When} & x=\pi/2 \\ & t=\tan \pi/4=1\end{array}\right]$$

$$=2\int_0^1 \frac{dt}{4+4t^2+5-5t^2}=2\int_0^1 \frac{dt}{9-t^2}$$

$$=2.\frac{1}{2\times 3}\left[\log\frac{3+t}{3-t}\right]_0^1$$

$$=\tfrac{1}{3}\log\frac{3+1}{3-1}-\tfrac{1}{3}\log\frac{3}{3}$$

$$=\tfrac{1}{3}\log 2$$

(*ii*) Put $\tan\frac{x}{2}=t$, then $\frac{1}{2}\sec^2\frac{x}{2}\,dx=dt$

$$\Rightarrow \qquad dx=\frac{2\,dt}{1+\tan^2 x/2}=\frac{2dt}{1+t^2}$$

Also as $\cos x=\dfrac{1-\tan^2 x/2}{1+\tan^2 x/2}=\dfrac{1-t^2}{1+t^2}$

the given integral reduces to

$$\int_0^\infty \frac{2\,dt}{(1+t^2)\left[5+3\frac{(1-t^2)}{1+t^2}\right]}$$

$$\left[\begin{array}{l}\textit{Note when } x=0,\ t=\tan 0=0 \\ \textit{When } x=\pi,\ t=\tan\frac{\pi}{2}=\infty\end{array}\right]$$

$$=2\int_0^\infty \frac{dt}{5+5t^2+3-3t^2}=2\int_0^\infty \frac{dt}{2t^2+8}=\int_0^\infty \frac{dt}{t^2+4}$$

$$=\left\{\tfrac{1}{2}\tan^{-1}\frac{t}{2}\right\}_0^\infty=\tfrac{1}{2}\tan^{-1}\infty-\tfrac{1}{2}\tan^{-1}0=\frac{\pi}{2}-0=\frac{\pi}{2}$$

Example 49. *Evaluate* $\displaystyle\int\frac{dx}{1+\sin x+\cos x}$

Solution. Put $\tan\frac{x}{2}=t$ then $dx=\dfrac{2\,dt}{1+t^2}$

$$\sin x = \frac{2\tan x/2}{1+\tan^2 x/2} = \frac{2t}{1+t^2}$$

$$\cos x = \frac{1-t^2}{1+t^2}$$

Thus

$$\int \frac{dx}{1+\sin x+\cos x} = \int \frac{2\,dt}{(1+t^2)\left[1+\dfrac{2t}{1+t^2}+\dfrac{1-t^2}{1+t^2}\right]}$$

$$= 2\int \frac{dt}{2t+2} = \log(t+1)$$

$$= \log\left(1+\tan\frac{x}{2}\right).$$

Although the above substitution is very useful. Sometimes other substitutions like $\tan x = t$, $\sin x = t$ or $\cos x = t$ also prove helpful like in the following examples:

Example 50. *Solve* $\displaystyle\int_0^{\pi/2} \frac{\cos x\,dx}{(1+\sin x)(2+\sin x)}$

Solution. Put $\sin x = t$, then $\cos x\,dx = dt$

and when $x=0$

$\sin x = 0 \Rightarrow t = 0$

When $x = \pi/2$

$$\sin\frac{\pi}{2} = 1 \Rightarrow t = 1$$

$$\text{The given integral} = \int_0^1 \frac{dt}{(1+t)(2+t)}$$

$$= \int_0^1 \left(\frac{1}{t+1} - \frac{1}{2+t}\right) dt$$

$$= \{\log(t+1) - \log(t+2)$$

$$= \left\{\log\frac{t+1}{t+2}\right\}_0^1$$

$$= \log\tfrac{2}{3} - \log\tfrac{1}{2} = \log\tfrac{4}{3}$$

Example 51. *Evaluate* $\int \frac{dx}{3 + 2\cos^2 x}$

Solution. Put $\tan x = t$, then $\sec^2 x\, dx = dt$

Now $$\int \frac{dx}{3+2\cos^2 x} = \int \frac{\sec^2 x\, dx}{3\sec^2 x + 2} = \int \frac{dt}{3(1+t^2)+2}$$

$$= \int \frac{dt}{3t^2+5} = \frac{1}{3}\int \frac{dt}{t^2+\frac{5}{3}}$$

$$= \frac{1}{3} \times \frac{\sqrt{3}}{\sqrt{5}} \tan^{-1} \frac{t\sqrt{3}}{\sqrt{5}}$$

$$= \frac{1}{\sqrt{15}} \tan^{-1}\left(\sqrt{\frac{3}{5}} \tan x\right)$$

17. INTEGRATION OF $\frac{a\cos x + b\sin x}{c\cos x + d\sin x}$, $(a^2+b^2)(c^2+d^2) \neq 0$

We determine two constants λ and μ such that,

$$a\cos x + b\sin x = \lambda(-c\sin x + d\cos x) + \mu(c\cos x + d\sin x)$$

where $-c\sin x + d\cos x = \frac{d}{dx}(c\cos x + d\sin x)$

Comparing coefficients of $\cos x$ and $\sin x$, we get

$$a = \lambda d + \mu c$$
$$b = -\lambda c + \mu d$$

$$\Rightarrow \lambda = \frac{ad - bc}{d^2 + c^2},\ \mu = \frac{ac - bd}{d^2 + c^2}$$

Hence

$$\int \frac{a\cos x + b\sin x}{c\cos x + d\sin x}\, dx = \lambda \int \frac{-c\sin x + d\cos x}{c\cos x + d\sin x}\, dx + \mu \int 1.dx$$

$$= \lambda \log(c\cos x + d\sin x) + \mu x$$

18. INTEGRATION OF $\frac{a\cos x + b\sin x + c}{d\cos x + e\sin x + f}$

In this case we determine three constants λ, μ, ν, such that $a\cos x + b\sin x + c = \lambda(d\cos x + e\sin x + f) + \mu(-d\sin x + e\cos x) + \nu$ and proceed as in the earlier case.

Example 52. *Find* $\int \frac{4 \sin x + 2 \cos x + 3}{2 \sin x + \cos x + 3} dx.$

Solution. We determine λ, μ, ν such that

$4 \sin x + 2 \cos x + 3 = \lambda (2 \sin x + \cos x + 3) + \mu (2 \cos x - \sin x) + \nu$

Comparing coefficients of sin *x*, cos *x* and the constant terms, we get

$$4 = 2\lambda - \mu,$$
$$2 = \lambda + 2\mu$$
$$3 = 3\lambda + \nu$$
$$\Rightarrow \quad \lambda = 2, \mu = 0, \nu = -3$$

Thus

$4 \sin x + 2 \cos x + 3 = 2(2 \sin x + \cos x + 3) + 0\,(2 \cos x - 1) - 3$

$$\Rightarrow \int \frac{4 \sin x + 2 \cos x + 3}{2 \sin x + \cos x + 3} dx = 2 \int 1.\, dx - 3 \int \frac{1}{2 \sin x + \cos x + 3} dx$$

$$= 2x - 3 \int \frac{1}{2 \sin x + \cos x + 3} dx$$

To solve $\int \frac{1}{2 \sin x + \cos x + 3}$

We put $\tan \frac{x}{2} = t$ then $dx = \frac{2\,dt}{1 + t^2}$

and the integral

$$= \int \frac{2dt}{(1 + t^2)\left[\frac{2.2t}{t^2 + 1} + \frac{1 - t^2}{1 + t^2} + 3\right]}$$

$$= \int \frac{2\,dt}{4t + 1 - t^2 + 3 + 3t^2} = \int \frac{dt}{t^2 + 2t + 2} = \int \frac{dt}{(t + 1)^2 + 1}$$

$$= \tan^{-1}(t + 1) = \tan^{-1}\left(1 + \tan \frac{x}{2}\right)$$

Hence the required result is

$$2x - 3 \tan^{-1}\left(1 + \tan \frac{x}{2}\right)$$

EXERCISES

Evaluate the following integrals

1. (i) $\int_0^{\pi/2} \frac{dx}{4+5\sin x}$ (ii) $\int_0^{\pi/2} \frac{dx}{1+2\cos x}$

   (iii) $\int \frac{dx}{\cos\alpha + \cos x}$ (iv) $\int \frac{dx}{3\sin x + 4\cos x}$

2. (i) $\int \frac{dx}{1+\cos^2 x}$ (ii) $\int \frac{dx}{1-\cos^4 x}$ (iii) $\int \frac{dx}{1+3\sin^2 x}$

   (iv) $\int \frac{\sin x \cos x}{a^2\cos^2 x + b^2 \sin^2 x}\, dx$

3. (i) $\int_0^{\pi/2} \frac{dx}{1+\cot x}$ (ii) $\int \frac{2\sin x + 3\cos x}{3\sin x + 4\cos x}\, dx$

   (iii) $\int \frac{5\cos x + 6}{2\cos x + \sin x + 3}\, dx$ (iv) $\int_0^{\pi} \frac{3+4\sin x + 2\cos x}{3+2\sin x + \cos x}\, dx$

4. (i) $\int \frac{dx}{3\sin x + \sin^2 x}$ (ii) $\int \frac{\sin x}{\sin 4x}\, dx.$

ANSWERS

1. (i) $\frac{1}{3}\log 2$ (ii) $\frac{1}{\sqrt{3}}\log(2+\sqrt{3})$

   (iii) $\operatorname{cosec}\alpha.\log \frac{\cos\frac{1}{2}(x-\alpha)}{\cos\frac{1}{2}(x+\alpha)}$ (iv) $\frac{1}{5}\log\frac{1+2\tan x/2}{4-2\tan x/2}$

2. (i) $\frac{1}{\sqrt{2}}\tan^{-1}\left(\frac{1}{\sqrt{2}}\tan x\right)$ (ii) $-\frac{1}{2}\cot x + \frac{1}{2\sqrt{2}}\tan^{-1}\left(\sqrt{\tfrac{1}{2}}\tan x\right)$

   (iii) $\frac{1}{2}\tan^{-1}(2\tan x)$ (iv) $-\frac{1}{2(a^2-b^2)}\log(a^2\cos^2 x + b^2\sin^2 x)$

3. (i) $\frac{\pi}{4}$ (ii) $\frac{18}{25}x + \frac{1}{25}\log(3x + 4\cos x)$

   (iii) $2x + \log(2\cos x + \sin x + 3)$ (iv) $\frac{5\pi}{4}$

4. (i) $\frac{1}{12}\left[2\log\frac{\cos x - 1}{\cos x + 1} + \log\frac{\cos x + 2}{2-\cos x}\right]$

   (ii) $\frac{1}{8}\log\frac{\sin x - 1}{\sin x + 1} - \frac{1}{4\sqrt{2}}\log\frac{\sqrt{2}\sin x - 1}{\sqrt{2}\sin x + 1}.$

CHAPTER 28

REDUCTION FORMULAS, DEFINITE INTEGRALS AND APPLICATIONS

1. REDUCTION FORMULAS

A formula that connects a given integral with another simpler integral (of the same type) is called a ***reduction formula***. Reduction formulas are generally useful when we have integrals involving higher powers. Integration by parts is very helpful in finding the reduction formulas. We obtain below a few of these formulas and explain the method to use them.

2. REDUCTION FORMULA FOR $\int \sin^n x\, dx$ WHERE n IS A + ve INTEGER

We have $\int \sin^n x\, dx = \int \sin^{n-1} x \,.\, \sin x\, dx$

$= (\sin^{n-1} x)(-\cos x) - \int (n-1)\sin^{n-2} x \cos x\,(-\cos x)\, dx$

[Using integration by parts]

$$= -\cos x \sin^{n-1} x + (n-1)\int \sin^{n-2} x \cos^2 x\, dx$$

$$= -\cos x \sin^{n-1} x + (n-1)\int \sin^{n-2} x\,(1-\sin^2 x)\, dx$$

$$= -\cos x \sin^{n-1} x + (n-1)\int \sin^{n-2} x - (n-1)\int \sin^{n-2} x\, dx$$

$$\Rightarrow\quad [1+(n-1)]\int \sin^n x\, dx = -\cos x \sin^{n-1} x + (n-1)\int \sin^{n-2} x\, dx$$

$$\Rightarrow\quad \int \sin^n x dx = -\frac{\cos x \sin^{n-1} x}{n} + \frac{n-1}{n}\int \sin^{n-2} x\, dx$$

which is the required reduction formula.

Example 1. *Use the above reduction formula to evaluate* $\int sin^7 x\, dx$.

Solution. We have

$$\int \sin^7 x dx = -\frac{\cos x \sin^6 x}{7} + \frac{6}{7}\int \sin^5 x\, dx$$

$$\int \sin^5 x\,dx = -\frac{\cos x \sin^4 x}{5} + \frac{4}{5}\int \sin^3 x\,dx$$

$$\int \sin^3 x\,dx = -\frac{\cos x \sin^2 x}{3} + \frac{2}{3}\int \sin x\,dx$$

$$= -\frac{\cos x \sin^2 x}{3} - \frac{2}{3}\cos x$$

Hence $\int \sin^7 x\,dx$

$$= -\frac{\cos x \sin^6 x}{3} + \frac{6}{7}\left[-\frac{\cos x \sin^4 x}{5} + \frac{4}{5}\left\{-\frac{\cos x \sin^2 x}{3} - \frac{2}{3}\cos x\right\}\right]$$

$$= -\frac{\cos x \sin^6 x}{7} - \frac{6\cos x \sin^4 x}{35} - \frac{8\cos x \sin^2 x}{35} - \frac{16}{35}\cos x.$$

Similarly, it can be proved that

$$\int \cos^n x\,dx = \frac{\sin x \cos^{n-1} x}{n} + \frac{n-1}{n}\int \cos^{n-2} x dx$$

NOTE. If the power n is odd in the integral $\int \sin^n x\,dx$ then we can solve the integral by the following method also.

Consider $\int \sin^5 x dx = \int \sin^4 x \sin x\,dx$

$$= \int (\sin^2 x)^2 \sin x\,dx$$

$$= \int (1 - \cos^2 x)^2 \sin x dx$$

Put $\cos x = t$ then $-\sin x dx = dt$

Thus $\int \sin^5 x dx = -\int (1 - t^2)^2\,dt$

$$= -\int (1 + t^4 - 2t^2)\,dt$$

$$= -t - \frac{t^5}{5} + \frac{2t^3}{3}$$

$$= -\frac{\cos^5 x}{5} + \frac{2}{3}\cos^3 x - \cos x$$

But this method is not helpful when the power n is an even number. A similar method holds for $\int \cos^n x\,dx$ too.

3. REDUCTION FORMULA FOR $\int \tan^n x\, dx$

We have $\int \tan^n x\, dx = \int \tan^{n-2} x \tan^2 x\, dx$

$$= \int \tan^{n-2} x\, (\sec^2 x - 1)\, dx$$

$$= \int \tan^{n-2} x \sec^2 x\, dx - \int \tan^{n-2} x\, dx$$

$$= \frac{\tan^{n-1} x}{n-1} - \int \tan^{n-2} x\, dx \text{ as } \frac{d}{dx}(\tan x) = \sec^2 x$$

Hence, the required reduction formula is

$$\int \tan^n x dx = \frac{\tan^{n-1} x}{n-1} - \int \tan^{n-2} x\, dx$$

Similarly, it can be shown that reduction formula for $\int \cot^n x\, dx$ is

$$\int \cot^n x\, dx = -\frac{\cot^{n-1} x}{n-1} - \int \cot^{n-2} x\, dx\, .$$

4. REDUCTION FORMULA FOR $\int \sec^n x dx$.

We have $\int \sec^n x dx = \int \sec^{n-2} x \,.\, \sec^2 x\, dx$

$= \sec^{n-2} x.\, \tan x - \int (n-2) \sec^{n-2} x.\, \sec x \tan x.\, \tan x\, dx$

[using integration by parts]

$= \sec^{n-2} x \tan x - (n-2) \int \sec^{n-2} x.\, \tan^2 x dx$

$= \sec^{n-2} x \tan x - (n-2) \int \sec^{n-2} x\, (\sec^2 x - 1)\, dx$

$= \sec^{n-2} x \tan x - (n-2) \int \sec^n x dx + (n-2) \int \sec^{n-2} x\, dx$

$\Rightarrow\ [1 + (n-2)] \int \sec^n x dx = \sec^{n-2} x \tan x + (n-2) \int \sec^{n-2} x\, dx$

$$\Rightarrow\ \int \sec^n x dx = \frac{\sec^{n-2} x \tan x}{n-1} + \frac{n-2}{n-1} \int \sec^{n-2} x dx$$

which is the required reduction formula.

Similarly it can be proved that

$$\int \operatorname{cosec}^n x dx = -\frac{\cot x \operatorname{cosec}^{n-2} x}{n-1} + \frac{n-2}{n-1} \int \operatorname{cosec}^{n-2} x\, dx$$

REMARK: We have taken n to be a + ve integer in the above six reduction formulas, but since – ve integral powers of sin x, cos x, tan x, cot x, sec x, cosec x, are respectively the + ve integral powers of cosec x, sec x, cot x, tan x, cos x, and sin x, we note that both positive and negative integral powers of these six functions can be integrated.

5. REDUCTION FORMULA FOR $\int \sin^m x \cos^n x\, dx$

We have $\int \sin^m x \cos^n x\, dx = \int \sin^{m-1} x\, (\sin x \cos^n x)\, dx$

Using integration by parts and taking $\sin^{m-1} x$ as the function to be differentiated, we get

$$= -\sin^{m-1} x \frac{\cos^{n+1} x}{n+1} - \int (m-1)\sin^{m-2} x \cos x \left(-\frac{\cos^{n+1} x}{n+1}\right) dx$$

$$= -\frac{\sin^{m-1} x \cos^{n+1} x}{n+1} + \frac{m-1}{n+1}\int \sin^{m-2} x \cos^{n+2} x\, dx$$

$$= -\frac{\sin^{m-1} x \cos^{n+1} x}{n+1} + \frac{m-1}{n+1}\int \sin^{m-2} x \cos^{n} x (1-\sin^2 x)\, dx$$

$$= -\frac{\sin^{m-1} x \cos^{n+1} x}{n+1} + \frac{m-1}{n+1}\int \sin^{m-2} x \cos^{n} x\, dx$$

$$- \frac{m-1}{n+1}\int \sin^{m} x \cos^{n} x dx$$

$$\Rightarrow \left(1+\frac{m-1}{n+1}\right)\int \sin^m x \cos^n x\, dx = -\frac{\sin^{m-1} x \cos^{n+1} x}{n+1}$$

$$+ \frac{m-1}{n+1}\int \sin^{m-2} x \cos^n x\, dx$$

$$\Rightarrow \int \sin^m x \cos^n x dx = -\frac{\sin^{m-1} x \cos^{n+1} x}{n+m}$$

$$+ \frac{m-1}{n+1}\int \sin^{m-2} x \cos^n x\, dx$$

NOTE. If we had started by writing

$$\int \sin^m x \cos^n x\, dx = \int (\sin^m x \cos x)\cos^{n-1} x\, dx$$

We would have reached the formula

$$\int \sin^m x \cos^n x dx = \frac{\sin^{m+1} x \cos^{n-1} x}{m+n} + \frac{n-1}{m+n}\int \sin^m x \cos^{n-2} x dx.$$

Example 2. *Solve* $\int (1+x^2)^{3/2}\, dx.$

Solution. Put $x = \tan\theta$, then $dx = \sec^2\theta\, d\theta$

Thus

$$\int (1+x^2)^{3/2} dx = \int (1+\tan^2\theta)^{3/2} . \sec^2\theta\, d\theta$$

$$= \int \sec^3\theta . \sec^2\theta\, d\theta = \int \sec^5\theta\, d\theta$$

Now using reduction formula

$$\int \sec^5\theta\, d\theta = \frac{\sec^3\theta\tan\theta}{4} + \frac{3}{4}\int \sec^3\theta\, d\theta$$

$$\int \sec^3\theta\, d\theta = \frac{\sec\theta\tan\theta}{2} + \frac{1}{2}\int \sec\theta\, d\theta$$

$$= \frac{\sec\theta\tan\theta}{2} + \frac{1}{2}\log(\sec\theta + \tan\theta)$$

Thus required result

$$= \frac{\sec^3\theta\tan\theta}{4} + \frac{3}{4}\left[\frac{\sec\theta\tan\theta}{2} + \frac{1}{2}\log(\sec\theta + \tan\theta)\right]$$

where $\theta = \tan^{-1}x$.

Example 3. *Evaluate* $\int \cot^4 x\, dx$.

Solution. We have by the reduction formula

$$\int \cot^4 x\, dx = \frac{-\cot^3 x}{3} - \int \cot^2 x dx$$

Also

$$\int \cot^2 x dx = \frac{-\cot x}{1} - \int dx = -\cot x - x$$

Thus

$$\int \cot^4 x dx = \frac{-\cot^3 x}{3} + \cot x + x.$$

Example 4. *If* $U_n = \int_0^{\pi/4} \tan^n x\, dx$, *show that*

$$U_n + U_{n-2} = \frac{1}{n-1}$$

and deduce the value of U_5.

Solution. We have shown that

$$\int \tan^n x\,dx = \frac{\tan^{n-1} x}{n-1} - \int \tan^{n-2} x\,dx$$

$$\text{So, } U_n = \int_0^{\pi/4} \tan^n x\,dx = \left[\frac{\tan^{n-1} x}{n-1}\right]_0^{\pi/4} - \int_0^{\pi/4} \tan^{n-2} x\,dx$$

$$= \frac{1}{n-1} - 0 - U_{n-2}$$

$$= \frac{1}{n-1} - U_{n-2} \Rightarrow U_n + U_{n-2} = \frac{1}{n-1} \quad \ldots(1)$$

Now if we put $n = 5$, in this equation, we find

$$U_5 + U_3 = \tfrac{1}{4} \quad \ldots(2)$$

Put $n = 3$ in (1) and we get

$$U_3 + U_1 = \tfrac{1}{2} \quad \ldots(3)$$

(2) and (3) $\Rightarrow$

$$U_5 = \tfrac{1}{4} - U_3 = \tfrac{1}{4} - (\tfrac{1}{2} - U_1) = \tfrac{1}{4} - \tfrac{1}{2} + U_1$$

$$\text{But } U_1 = \int_0^{\pi/4} \tan x\,dx = [\log \sec x]_0^{\pi/4} = \log \sec \frac{\pi}{4} - \log \sec 0$$

$$= \log \sqrt{2} - \log 1 = \log \sqrt{2}$$

Thus

$$U_5 = \tfrac{1}{4} - \tfrac{1}{2} + \log \sqrt{2} = \log \sqrt{2} - \tfrac{1}{4}.$$

Example 5. *Prove that* $\dfrac{22}{7} - \pi = \displaystyle\int_0^1 \frac{x^4(1-x)^4}{1+x^2}\,dx.$

Solution. Put $x = \tan\theta$ in the integral

$$I = \int_0^1 \frac{x^4(1-x)^4}{1+x^2}\,dx.$$

when $x = 0$, $\tan\theta = 0 \Rightarrow \theta = 0$ when $x = 1$, $\tan\theta = 1 \Rightarrow \theta = \pi/4$

$$\text{we get } I = \int_0^{\pi/4} \frac{\tan^4\theta(1-\tan\theta)^4}{1+\tan^2\theta} . \sec^2\theta\,d\theta$$

$$= \int_0^{\pi/4} \tan^4\theta\,(1-\tan\theta)^4\,d\theta$$

$$= \int_0^{\pi/4} \tan^4\theta\,(1+\tan^4\theta+6\tan^2\theta-4\tan^3\theta-4\tan\theta)\,d\theta$$

$$= \int_0^{\pi/4} \tan^8\theta\,d\theta + 6\int_0^{\pi/4} \tan^5\theta\,d\theta - 4\int_0^{\pi/4} \tan^7\theta\,d\theta - 4\int_0^{\pi/4} \tan^5\theta\,d\theta + \int_0^{\pi/4} \tan^4\theta\,d\theta$$

Using reduction formula for $\int \tan^n\theta\,d\theta$, we get

$$I = \left\{\frac{\tan^7\theta}{7}\right\}_0^{\pi/4} - \int_0^{\pi/4} \tan^6\theta\,d\theta + 6\int_0^{\pi/4} \tan^6\theta\,d\theta - 4\left[\left\{\frac{\tan^6\theta}{6}\right\}_0^{\pi/4} - \int_0^{\pi/4} \tan^5\theta\,d\theta\right] - 4\int_0^{\pi/4} \tan^5\theta\,d\theta + \int_0^{\pi/4} \tan^4\theta\,d\theta$$

$$= \left\{\tan^7\theta\right\}_0^{\pi/4} - \frac{2}{3}\left\{\tan^6\theta\right\}_0^{\pi/4} + 5\int_0^{\pi/4} \tan^6\theta\,d\theta + \int_0^{\pi/4} \tan^4\theta\,d\theta$$

$$= \frac{1}{7} - \frac{2}{3} + 5\left[\left\{\tan^5\frac{\theta}{2}\right\}_0^{\pi/4} - \int_0^{\pi/4} \tan^4\theta\,d\theta\right] + \int_0^{\pi/4} \tan^4\theta\,d\theta$$

$$= \frac{1}{7} - \frac{2}{3} + \left\{\tan^5\theta\right\}_0^{\pi/4} - 4\int_0^{\pi/4} \tan^4\theta\,d\theta$$

$$= \frac{1}{7} - \frac{2}{3} + 1 - 4\left[\left\{\frac{\tan^3\theta}{3}\right\}_0^{\pi/4} - \int_0^{\pi/4} \tan^2\theta\,d\theta\right]$$

$$= \frac{1}{7} - \frac{2}{3} + 1 - \frac{4}{3} + 4\int_0^{\pi/4} (\sec^2\theta - 1)\,d\theta = \frac{1}{7} - \frac{2}{3} + 1 + \frac{4}{3} + 4\left[\tan\theta - \theta\right]_0^{\pi/4}$$

$$= \frac{1}{7} - \frac{2}{3} + 1 - \frac{4}{3} + 4 - 4\frac{\pi}{4} = \frac{22}{7} - \pi.$$

EXERCISES

1. Obtain the reduction formulas for $\cos^n x$, $\cot^n x$, $\operatorname{cosec}^n x$.

2. Show that $\int \sin^6 x\,dx = -\frac{1}{6}\sin^5 x\cos x - \frac{5}{24}\sin^3 x\cos x - \frac{5}{16}\sin x\cos x + \frac{5}{16}x$

3. Show that

$$\int \sin^m x\cos^n x\,dx = \frac{\sin^{m+1} x\cos^{n-1} x}{m+n} + \frac{n-1}{m+n}\int \sin^m x\cos^{n-2} x\,dx$$

4. If $U_n = \int_0^{\pi/4} \tan^n x\,dx$, prove that

$$n(U_{n-1} + U_{n+1}) = 1$$

Hence or otherwise show that

$$\int_0^a x^5 (2a^2 - x^2)^{-3}\,dx = \log\sqrt{2} - \frac{1}{4}$$

[Hint. Use substitution $x = \sqrt{2}\,a\sin\theta$ for the second part.]

5. Evaluate $\int_0^a (a^2 + x^2)^{3/2}\,dx$.

6. Show that

$$\int \sin^m x\cos^n x\,dx = \frac{\sin^{m+1} x\cos^{n+1} x}{m+1} + \frac{m+n+2}{m+1}\int \sin^{m+2}\cos^n x\,dx$$

6. REDUCTION FORMULA FOR $\int_0^{\pi/2} \sin^n x\,dx$.

Let $$I_n = \int_0^{\pi/2} \sin^n x\,dx \qquad \ldots(1)$$

The sub-suffix n corresponds to the power of $\sin x$.

We have already proved that

$$\int \sin^n x\,dx = -\frac{\cos x\sin^{n-1} x}{n} + \frac{n-1}{n}\int \sin^{n-2} x\,dx$$

$$\Rightarrow \int_0^{\pi/2} \sin^n x\,dx = \left\{-\frac{\cos x\sin^{n-1} x}{n}\right\}_0^{\pi/2} + \frac{n-1}{n}\int_0^{\pi/2} \sin^{n-2} x\,dx$$

$$= \frac{n-1}{n}\int_0^{\pi/2} \sin^{n-2} x\,dx$$

which in the notational form (as of (1)) reads as

$$I_n = \frac{n-1}{n} I_{n-2}$$

Put $$n = n-2, n-4, \ldots$$

$$I_{n-2} = \frac{n-3}{n-2} I_{n-4}$$

$$I_{n-4} = \frac{n-5}{n-4} I_{n-6}$$

... ...

... ...

(If n is odd) $I_3 = \frac{3-1}{3} I_1 = \frac{2}{3} \int_0^{\pi/2} \sin x \, dx = \frac{2}{3} [-\cos x]_0^{\pi/2} = \frac{2}{3}$

(If n is even) $I_2 = \frac{2-1}{2} I_0 = \frac{1}{2} \int_0^{\pi/2} (\sin x)^0 \, dx = \frac{1}{2}\frac{\pi}{2}$

and thus we finally get

$$I_n = \frac{n-1}{n} \frac{n-3}{n-2} \frac{n-5}{n-4} \cdots \frac{2}{3}, \quad \text{if } n \text{ is odd}$$

$$= \frac{n-1}{n} \frac{n-3}{n-2} \frac{n-5}{n-4} \cdots \frac{1}{2} \cdot \frac{\pi}{2}, \quad \text{if } n \text{ is even}$$

Example 6. *Evaluate (i)* $\int_0^{\pi/2} \sin^7 x dx$ *and (ii)* $\int_0^{\pi/2} \sin^8 x dx$.

Solution. (*i*) We have by the reduction formula

$$\int_0^{\pi/2} \sin^7 x dx = \frac{6}{7} \cdot \frac{4}{5} \cdot \frac{2}{3} = \frac{16}{35}$$

(*ii*) Also]

$$\int_0^{\pi/2} \sin^8 x dx = \frac{7}{8} \cdot \frac{5}{6} \cdot \frac{3}{4} \cdot \frac{1}{2} \cdot \frac{\pi}{2}$$

$$= \frac{35}{128} \cdot \frac{\pi}{2}$$

Similarly it can be shown that the reduction formula for

$\int_0^{\pi/2} \cos^n x dx$ is same as that for $\int_0^{\pi/2} \sin^n x dx$.

7. REDUCTION FORMULA FOR $\int_0^{\pi/2} \sin^m x \cos^n x\, dx$, m, n BEING +ve INTEGERS

Let us write $I_{m,\,n} = \int_0^{\pi/2} \sin^m x \cos^n x dx$

where the first subscript corresponds to the power of sin x and the second subscript corresponds to the power of cos x in the integral.

We have already proved that

$$\int \sin^m x \cos^n x dx = -\frac{\sin^{m-1} x \cos^{n+1} x}{n+m} + \frac{m-1}{n+m} \int \sin^{m-2} x \cos^n x dx$$

$$\Rightarrow \int_0^{\pi/2} \sin^m x \cos^n x dx = \left\{-\frac{\sin^{m-1} x \cos^{n+1} x}{n+m}\right\}_0^{\pi/2} + \frac{m-1}{n+m} \int_0^{\pi/2} \sin^{m-2} x \cos^n x dx$$

$$= \frac{m-1}{n+m} \int_0^{\pi/2} \sin^{m-2} x \cos^n x dx$$

which in our notation reads as

$$I_{m,\,n} = \frac{m-1}{n+m} I_{m-2,\,n}$$

Put $m = m-2, m-4, \ldots$, we get

$$I_{m-2,\,n} = \frac{m-3}{m+n-2} I_{m-4,\,n}$$

$$I_{m-4,\,n} = \frac{m-5}{n+m-4} I_{m-6,\,n}$$

....

....

$$I_{3,\,r} = \frac{2}{n+3} \qquad I_{1,\,n} \text{ (when } m \text{ is odd)}$$

$$I_{2,\,n} = \frac{1}{n+2} \qquad I_{0,\,n} \text{ (when } m \text{ is even)}$$

Thus we get

$$I_{m,n} = \frac{m-1}{m+n} \cdot \frac{m-3}{m+n-2} \cdot \frac{m-5}{m+n-4} \cdots \frac{2}{n+3} I_{1,n}$$

(when m is odd)

$$= \frac{m-1}{m+n} \cdot \frac{m-3}{m+n-2} \cdot \frac{m-5}{m+n-4} \cdots \frac{1}{n+2} I_{0,n}$$

(when m is even)

Now

$$I_{1,n} = \int_0^{\pi/2} \sin x \cos^n x dx = -\left\{\frac{\cos^{n+1} x}{n+1}\right\}_0^{\pi/2} = -0 + \frac{1}{n+1} = \frac{1}{n+1}$$

and

$$I_{0,n} = \int_0^{\pi/2} \sin^0 x \cos^n x dx = \int_0^{\pi/2} \cos^n x\, dx$$

$$= \frac{n-1}{n} \cdot \frac{n-3}{n-2} \cdots \frac{2}{3} \quad \text{if } n \text{ is odd}$$

$$= \frac{n-1}{n} \cdot \frac{n-3}{n-2} \cdot \frac{1}{2} \cdot \frac{\pi}{2} \quad \text{if } n \text{ is even}$$

Hence putting these values we finally arrive at

$$\frac{m-1}{m+n} \cdot \frac{m-3}{m+n-2} \cdots \frac{2}{n+3} \cdot \frac{1}{n+1}, \text{ when } m \text{ is odd, } n \text{ is odd or even}$$

$$I_{m,n} = \frac{m-1}{m+n} \cdot \frac{m-3}{m+n-2} \cdots \frac{1}{n+2} \cdot \frac{n-1}{n} \cdot \frac{n-3}{n-2} \cdots \frac{2}{3}$$

when m is even and n is odd

$$= \frac{m-1}{m+n} \cdot \frac{m-3}{m+n-2} \cdots \frac{1}{n+2} \cdot \frac{n-1}{n} \cdot \frac{n-3}{n-2} \cdots \frac{1}{2} \cdot \frac{\pi}{2}$$

when both m and n are even

Example 7. *Evaluate* $\int_0^{\pi/2} \sin^6 x \cos^5 x\, dx$.

Solution. Here m is even, n is odd, so

$$\int_0^{\pi/2} \sin^6 x \cos^5 x dx = \frac{5}{11} \cdot \frac{3}{9} \cdot \frac{1}{7} \cdot \frac{4}{5} \cdot \frac{2}{3} = \frac{6}{693}.$$

REMARK: Note that when m is odd, $I_{m,n} = \dfrac{(m-1)(m-3)...}{(m+n)(m+n-2)}$

$\dfrac{1}{n+1} \dfrac{(n-1)}{(n-1)} \dfrac{(n-3)}{(n-3)}$, so we have a simple rule to apply the formula to the integral.

$\int_0^{\pi/2} \sin^m x \cos^n x dx$ is to write the value of this integral

$$= \frac{(m-1)(m-3)...(n-1)(n-3)...}{(m-n)(m+n-2).(m+n-4)...}$$

the products to be continued till we reach 1 or 2. Again multiply by $\dfrac{\pi}{2}$ only when both m and n are even.

EXERCISES

Evaluate

1. (*i*) $\int_0^{\pi/2} \sin^2 x dx$ (*ii*) $\int_0^{\pi/2} \sin^{10} x dx$ (*iii*) $\int_0^{\pi/2} \sin^5 x dx$

2. (*i*) $\int_0^{\pi/2} \cos^3 x\, dx$ (*ii*) $\int_0^{\pi/2} \cos^{10} x\, dx$ (*iii*) $\int_0^{\pi/2} \cos^5 x\, dx$

3. (*i*) $\int_0^{\pi/2} \sin^2 x \cos^3 x\, dx$ (*ii*) $\int_0^{\pi/2} \sin^6 x \cos^6 x dx$

   (*iii*) $\int_0^{\pi/2} \sin^5 x \cos^7 x dx$ (*iv*) $\int_0^{\pi/2} \sin^6 x \cos^8 x dx$

   (*v*) $\int_0^{\pi/2} \sin x \cos x dx$

4. (*i*) $\int_0^{\pi/4} \sin^2 x \cos^4 x dx$ (*ii*) $\int_0^{\pi} \cos^7 \dfrac{x}{2} dx$

ANSWERS

1. (*i*) $\dfrac{1}{3}$ (*ii*) $\dfrac{315}{2560}\pi$ (*iii*) $\dfrac{8}{15}$

2. (*i*) $\dfrac{1}{3}$ (*ii*) $\dfrac{315\pi}{2560}$ (*iii*) $\dfrac{8}{15}$

3. (i) $\frac{2}{15}$ (ii) $\frac{8}{693}$ (iii) $\frac{1}{120}$

(iv) $\frac{35}{14336}\frac{\pi}{2}$ (v) $\frac{1}{2}$

4. (i) $\frac{1}{192}(4+3\pi)$ (ii) $\frac{95}{105}$

We give some more examples to explain the use of the above reduction formulas:

Example 8. *Evaluate* $\int_0^1 x^4(1-x^2)^{5/2}\,dx$

Solution. Put $x = \sin\theta$, then $dx = \cos\theta\, d\theta$

Also when $x = 0$, $\sin\theta = 0 \Rightarrow \theta = 0$

when $x = 1$, $\sin\theta = 1, \Rightarrow \theta = \pi/2.$

Thus

$$\int_0^1 x^4(1-x^2)^{5/2}\,dx = \int_0^{\pi/2}\sin^4\theta\,(1-\sin^2\theta)^{5/2}.\cos\theta\, d\theta$$

$$= \int_0^{\pi/2}\sin^4\theta.\cos^6\theta d\theta$$

$$= \frac{3.1.5.3.1}{10.8.6.4.2}.\frac{\pi}{2} = \frac{3\pi}{512}.$$

Example 9. *Evaluate* $\int_0^1 x^m(1-x)^n\,dx$ *, m, n are + ve integers.*

Solution. Put $x = \sin^2\theta$, then $dx = 2\sin\theta\cos\theta\, d\theta$

Also when $x = 0, \theta = 0$ when $x = 1, \theta = \frac{\pi}{2}$

thus

$$\int_0^1 x^m(1-x)^n\,dx = \int_0^{\pi/2}\sin^{2m}\theta(1-\sin^2\theta)^n.2\sin\theta\cos\theta\, d\theta$$

$$= 2\int_0^{\pi/2}\sin^{2m+1}\theta.\cos^{2n+1} q\, dq$$

$$= 2\int_0^{\pi/2}\sin^p\theta.\cos^q q\, dq$$

where p, q are odd integers.

$$= 2.\ \frac{p-1}{p+q} \cdot \frac{p-3}{p+q-2} \cdots \frac{2}{q+3} \cdot \frac{1}{q+1}$$

EXERCISES

Evaluate

1. $\int_0^a x^2(a^3 - x^2)^{3/2}\, dx$
2. $\int x^2(1-x^2)^{3/2}\, dx$
3. $\int_0^{\pi/2} \frac{\sin^2\theta}{(1+\cos\theta)^2}\, d\theta$
4. $\int_0^2 x^3\sqrt{2x - x^2}\, dx$
5. $\int_0^1 x^{3/2}(1-x)^{3/2}\, dx$

ANSWERS

1. $\frac{1}{32}\pi a^6$
2. $\frac{\pi}{32}$
3. $2 - \frac{\pi}{2}$
4. $\frac{7\pi}{8}$
5. $\frac{3\pi}{128}$

8. SOME MORE REDUCTION FORMULAS

To find a reduction formula for $\int x^m \sin nx\, dx$.

Using integration by parts, we get

$$\int x^m \sin nx\, dx = -\frac{x^m \cos nx}{n} - \int \frac{(-\cos nx)}{n} mx^{m-1}\, dx$$

$$= -\frac{x^m \cos nx}{n} \frac{m}{n} \int x^{m-1} \cos nx\, dx$$

$$= -\frac{x^m \cos nx}{n} + \frac{m}{n}\left[x^{m-1}\frac{\sin nx}{n} - \int \frac{\sin nx}{n}(m-1)x^{m-2}\, dx\right]$$

$$= -\frac{x^m \cos nx}{n} + \frac{m}{n^2}x^{m-1}\sin nx - \frac{m(m-1)}{n^2}\int x^{m-2}\sin nx\, dx$$

which is the required reduction formula.

To find a reduction formula for $\int \cos^m x \cos nx\, dx$

Using integration by parts, we get

$$I = \int \cos^m x \cos nx\, dx = \frac{\cos^m x \sin nx}{n} + \int \frac{\sin nx}{n} m \cos^{m-1} x \sin x dx$$

$$= \frac{\cos^m x \sin nx}{n} + \frac{m}{n} \int \cos^{m-1} x. \sin nx \sin x dx$$

Now $\cos (n-1) x = \cos (nx - x)$

$$= \cos nx \cos x + \sin nx \sin x$$

$\Rightarrow \quad \sin nx \sin x = \cos (n-1) x - \cos nx \cos x$

Thus

$$I = \frac{\cos^m x \sin nx}{n} + \frac{m}{n} \int \cos^{m-1} x \{\cos (n-1) x - \cos nx \cos x\} dx$$

$$= \frac{\cos^m x \sin nx}{n} + \frac{m}{n} \int \cos^{m-1} x \cos (n-1) x dx - \frac{m}{n} \int \cos^m x \cos nx\, dx$$

$$\Rightarrow \left(1 + \frac{m}{n}\right) I = \frac{\cos^m x \sin nx}{n} + \frac{m}{n} \int \cos^{m-1} x \cos (n-1) x dx$$

$$\Rightarrow \int \cos^m x \cos nx dx = \frac{\cos^m x \sin nx}{n} + \frac{m}{m+n} \int \cos^{m-1} x \cos (n-1) x dx$$

To find a reduction formula for $\int x \sin^n x dx$

$$I = \int x \sin^n x dx = \int x \sin^{n-2} x \sin^2 x dx$$

$$= \int x \sin^{n-2} x (1 - \cos^2 x)\, dx$$

$$= \int x \sin^{n-2} x dx - \int x \sin^{n-2} x \cos^2 x\, dx \qquad ...(1)$$

Consider

$$\int x \sin^{n-2} x \cos^2 x dx = \int x \cos x (\sin^{n-2} x \cos x)\, dx$$

$$= \frac{(x \cos x) \sin^{n-1} x}{n-1} - \int \frac{\sin^{n-1} x}{n-1} \{\cos x - x \sin x)\, dx$$

[using integration by parts]

$$= \frac{x \cos x. \sin^{n-1} x}{n-1} - \frac{1}{n-1} \int \sin^{n-1} x \cos x dx + \frac{1}{n-1} \int x \sin^n dx$$

$$= \frac{x \cos x. \sin^{n-1} x}{n-1} - \frac{1}{n-1} \frac{\sin^n x}{n} + \frac{1}{n+1} I$$

Putting in (1) we get

$$I = \int x \sin^{n-2} x dx - \frac{x \cos x \sin^{n-1} x}{n-1} + \frac{\sin^n x}{n(n-1)} - \frac{1}{n-1}$$

$$\Rightarrow \quad I = \frac{\sin^n x}{n^2} - \frac{x \cos x \sin^{n-1} x}{n} + \frac{n-1}{n} x \sin^{n-2} x dx$$

which is the required reduction formula.

To find a reduction formula for $\int e^{ax} \sin^n x dx$

Using integration by parts, we have

$$I = \int e^{ax} \sin^n x dx = \frac{e^{ax}}{a} \sin^n x - \int \frac{e^{ax}}{a} n \sin^{n-1} x \cos x dx$$

$$= \frac{e^{ax} \sin^n x}{a} - \frac{n}{a} e^{ax} \sin^{n-1} x \cos x dx$$

$$= \frac{e^{ax} \sin^n x}{a} - \frac{n}{a} \left[\frac{e^{ax}}{a} \sin^{n-1} x \cos x \right.$$

$$\left. - \int \frac{e^{ax}}{a} \{(n-1) \sin^{n-2} x \cos^2 x - \sin^{n-1} x \sin x\} dx \right]$$

$$= \frac{e^{ax} \sin^n x}{a} - \frac{n}{a^2} e^{ax} \sin^{n-1} x \cos x +$$

$$\frac{n(n-1)}{a^2} \int e^{ax} \sin^{n-2} x \cos^2 x dx - \frac{n}{a^2} \int e^{ax} \sin^n x dx$$

$$\Rightarrow \quad \left(1 + \frac{n}{a^2}\right) I = \frac{e^{ax} \sin^n x}{a} - \frac{n}{a^2} e^{ax} \sin^{n-1} x \cos x +$$

$$\frac{n(n-1)}{a^2} \int e^{ax} \sin^{n-2} x (1 - \sin^2 x) dx$$

$$= \frac{e^{ax} \sin^n x}{a} - \frac{n}{a^2} e^{ax} \sin^{n-1} x \cos x + \frac{n(n-1)}{a^2} \int e^{ax} \sin^{n-2} x dx$$

$$- \frac{n(n-1)}{a^2} I$$

$$\Rightarrow \left[1 + \frac{n}{a^2} + \frac{n(n-1)}{a^2}\right] I = \frac{e^{ax} \sin^n x}{a} - \frac{n}{a^2} e^{ax} \sin^{n-1} x \cos x$$

$$+ \frac{n(n-1)}{a^2} \int e^{ax} \sin^{n-2} x dx$$

$$\Rightarrow I = \frac{ae^{ax}\sin^n x}{(a^2+n^2)} - \frac{ne^{ax}\sin^{n-1} x\cos x}{a^2+n^2} + \frac{n(n-1)}{(a^2+n^2)}\int e^{ax}\sin^{n-2} x dx$$

$$\text{or } \int e^{ax}\sin^n x dx = \frac{e^{ax}\sin^{n-1} x}{a^2+n^2}(a\sin x - n\cos x) +$$

$$\frac{n(n-1)}{a^2+n^2}\int e^{ax}\sin^{n-2} x dx$$

To find a reduction formula for $\int (a^2+x^2)^{n/2}\,dx$

We have

$$I = \int (a^2+x^2)^{n/2}\,dx = \int 1.\,(a^2+x^2)^{n/2}\,dx$$

$$= x(a^2+x^2)^{n/2} - \int x\frac{n}{2}(a^2+x^2)^{n/2-1}\,2x dx$$

$$= x(a^2+x^2)^{n/2} - n\int x^2(a^2+x^2)^{n/2-1}\,dx$$

$$= x(a^2+x^2)^{n/2} - n\int (a^2+x^2-a^2)(a^2+x^2)^{n/2-1}\,dx$$

$$= x(a^2+x^2)^{n/2} - n\int (a^2+x^2)^{n/2}\,dx + n\int a^2(a^2+x^2)^{n/2-1}\,dx$$

$$\Rightarrow (1+n)\int (a^2+x^2)^{n/2}\,dx = x(a^2+x^2)^{n/2} + na^2\int (a^2+x^2)^{n/2-1}\,dx$$

$$\Rightarrow \int (a^2+x^2)^{n/2}\,dx = \frac{x(a^2+x^2)^{n/2}}{n+1} + \frac{na^2}{n+1}\int (a^2+x^2)^{n/2-1}\,dx$$

the required reduction formula.

EXERCISES

Establish the following reduction formulas

1. $\int e^{ax}x^n dx = \frac{x^n e^{ax}}{a} - \frac{n}{a}\int x^{n-1}e^{ax}dx$
2. $\int x^m \cos nx dx = x^{m-1}\frac{n\sin nx + m\cos nx}{n^2} - \frac{m(m-1)}{n^2}\int x^{m-2}\cos nx\, dx$
3. $\int x^m (\log x)^n\, dx = \frac{x^{m+1}}{m+1}(\log x)^n - \frac{n}{m+1}\int x^m(\log x)^{n-1}\, dx$
4. $\int e^{ax}\cos^n x dx = e^{ax}\cos^{n-1}x\left(\frac{a\cos x + n\sin x}{a^2+n^2}\right) + \frac{n(n-1)}{a^2+n^2}\int e^{ax}\cos^{n-2} x dx$
5. $\int \cos^m x\sin nx dx = -\frac{\cos^m x\cos nx}{m+n} + \frac{m}{m+n}\int \cos^{m-1} x\sin(n-1)x dx$

6. $\int \sin^m x \sin nx dx = \frac{n \sin^m x \cos nx}{n^2 + m^2} - \frac{m \sin^{m-1} x \cos x \sin nx}{n^2 - m^2}$

$$+ \frac{m(m-1)}{n^2 - m^2} \int \sin^{m-2} x \sin nx dx, \; m \neq n$$

7. $\int \frac{1}{(x^2 + a^2)^n} dx = \frac{x}{2(n-1)a^2(x^2 + a^2)^{n-1}} + \frac{2n-3}{2(n-1)a^2} \frac{dx}{(x^2 + a^2)^{n-1}}$

8. If $I_n = \int_0^{\pi/2} x^n \sin nx dx \; (n > 1)$ show that

$$I_n + n(n-1) I_{n-2} = n \left(\frac{\pi}{2}\right)^{n-1}$$

9. If m, n are positive integers, and

$$f(m, n) = \int_0^1 x^{n-1} (\log x)^m \, dx$$

prove that $f(m, n) = -\frac{m}{n} f(m-1, n)$.

Deduce that $f(m, n) = (-1)^m = \frac{m!}{n^{m+1}}$

10. Prove that $\int_0^{\pi/2} \cos^n x \cos nx \, dx = \frac{\pi}{2^{n+1}}$

11. If $I_n = \int_0^{\pi/2} x \sin^n x \, dx \; (n > 1)$, show that

$$I_n = \frac{n-1}{n} I_{n-2} + \frac{1}{n^2}$$

Hence deduce that $I_5 = \frac{149}{225}$

9. DEFINITE INTEGRALS

We give below some properties of the definite integral

$\int_a^b f(x) dx$. It will be assumed that $\int f(x) dx = g(x)$

(1) $\int_a^b f(x) dx = - \int_b^a f(x) dx$

$$\text{L.H.S.} = \int_a^b f(x) dx = \{g(x)\}_a^b = g(b) - g(a)$$

$$\text{R.H.S.} = -\int_b^a f(x)dx = \{-g(x)\}_b^a = -g(a) + g(b) = g(b) - g(a)$$

which proves the result.

(2) $$\int_a^b f(x)dx = \int_a^b f(t)dt$$

$$\text{L.H.S.} = \{g(x)\}_a^b = g(b) - g(a)$$

$$\text{R.H.S.} = \{g(t)\}_a^b = g(b) - g(a).$$

(3) $$\int_a^b f(x)dx = \int_a^c f(x)dx + \int_c^b f(x)dx \qquad (a < c < b)$$

$$\text{L.H.S.} = \int_a^b f(x)dx = g(b) - g(a)$$

$$\text{R.H.S.} = \int_a^c f(x)dx + \int_c^b f(x)dx = [g(c) - g(a)] + [g(b) - g(c)]$$

$$= g(b) - g(a).$$

(4) $$\int_0^a f(x)dx = \int_0^a f(a-x)dx$$

Put $a - x = t$ in the RHS, then $dx = -dt$

Also when $x = 0, t = a \quad x = a, t = 0$

$$\text{RHS} = -\int_a^0 f(t)dt = \int_0^a f(t)dt = \int_0^a f(x)dx = \text{LHS}.$$

(5) $$\int_0^a f(x)dx = 2\int_0^{a/2} f(x)dx \quad \text{if } f(a-x) = f(x)$$

$$= 0 \quad \text{if } f(a-x) = -f(x)$$

We have

$$\int_0^a f(x)dx = \int_0^{a/2} f(x)dx + \int_{a/2}^a f(x)dx \qquad \ldots(i)$$

Let us consider $\int_{a/2}^a f(x)dx$

Put $a - x = t$, then $-dx = dt$, also when $x = \frac{a}{2}$, $t = \frac{a}{2}$

when $x = a$, $t = 0$

Thus $\int_{a/2}^{a} f(x)dx = -\int_{a/2}^{0} f(a-t)dt = \int_{0}^{a/2} f(a-t)dt = \int_{0}^{a/2} f(a-x)dx$

So (*i*) gives

$$\int_0^a f(x)dx = \int_0^{a/2} f(x)dx + \int_0^{a/2} f(a-x)dx$$

Clearly if $f(a-x) = f(x)$, RHS $= 2\int_0^{a/2} f(x)dx$

and if $f(a-x) = -f(x)$, RHS $= 0$

and that establishes what we wanted to prove.

Before giving the last property, we define **odd function**. A function $f(x)$ is said to be an odd function if $f(-x) = -f(x)$.

Example 10. *sin x is an odd function as*

$$\sin(-x) = -\sin x$$

Even function. A function $f(x)$ is said to be an even function if $f(-x) = f(x)$.

Example 11. *cos x is an even function as* $\cos(-x) = \cos x$

The function $\sin x + \cos x$ is neither even nor odd.

We now prove

(6) $\int_{-a}^{a} f(x)dx = 0$ if $f(x)$ is an odd function

$= \int_0^a f(x)dx$ if $f(x)$ is an even function

We know $\int_{-a}^{a} f(x)dx = \int_{-a}^{0} f(x)dx + \int_0^a f(x)dx$ ...(*i*)

Consider the integral $\int_{-a}^{0} f(x)dx$

Put $x = -t$, then $dx = -dt$

Also when $x = -a$, $t = a$

when $x = 0$, $t = 0$

Thus $\int_{-a}^{0} f(x)dx = -\int_{a}^{0} f(-t)dt = \int_{0}^{a} f(-t)dt = \int_{0}^{a} f(-x)dx$

So by (*i*) we get

$$\int_{-a}^{a} f(x)dx \; dx = \int_{0}^{a} f(-x)dx + \int_{0}^{a} f(x)dx$$

Clearly if $f(x)$ is an odd function

$$\text{RHS} = -\int_{0}^{a} f(x)\, dx + \int_{0}^{a} f(x)dx = 0$$

and if $f(x)$ is an even function

$$\text{RHS} = \int_{0}^{a} f(x)\, dx + \int_{0}^{a} f(x)\, dx = 2\int_{0}^{a} f(x)\, dx$$

thereby proving the result.

Example 12. *Verify property (1) for the integral* $\int_{0}^{\pi/2} \cos x\, dx$.

Solution. We have to show that $\int_{0}^{\pi/2} \cos x\, dx = -\int_{\pi/2}^{0} \cos x\, dx$

$$\text{Now LHS} = \{\sin x\}_0^{\pi/2} = \sin\frac{\pi}{2} - \sin 0 = 1 - 0 = 1$$

$$\text{RHS} = -\{\sin x\}_{\pi/2}^{0} = -\sin 0 - \left(-\sin\frac{\pi}{2}\right) = 0 + 1 = 1.$$

Example 13. *Show that* $\int_{0}^{2\pi} \sin^8 x \cos^7 x\, dx = 0.$

Solution. If $f(x) = \sin^8 x \cos^7 x$

then $f(\pi - x) = \sin^8(\pi - x)\cos^7(\pi - x) = (-1)^7 \sin^8 x \cos^7 x$

$= -\sin^8 x \cos^7 x = -f(x)$

By property (5), the given integral = 0.

Example 14. *Evaluate* $\int_{0}^{2\pi} \sin^6 x \cos^8 x\, dx$.

Solution. If $f(x) = \sin^6 x \cos^8 x$

then $f(2\pi - x) = \sin^6(2\pi - x)\cos^8(2\pi - x)$

$= \sin^6 x \cos^8 x = f(x)$

$$\text{thus} \int_0^{2\pi} \sin^6 x \cos^8 x \, dx = 2\int_0^{\pi} \sin^6 x \cos^8 x \, dx$$

Again if $\varphi(x) = \sin^6 x \cos^8 x$

then $\varphi(\pi - x) = \sin^6(\pi - x)\cos^8(\pi - x)$

$= \sin^6 x \cos^8 x = \varphi(x)$

$$\text{Hence} \int_0^{\pi} \sin^6 x \cos^8 x \, dx = 2\int_0^{\pi/2} \sin^6 x \cos^8 x \, dx$$

and so finally

$$\int_0^{2\pi} \sin^6 x \cos^8 x dx = 4\int_0^{\pi/2} \sin^6 x \cos^8 x dx$$

$$= 4 \frac{5.3.1.7.5.3.1}{14.12.10.8.6.4.2} \frac{\pi}{2} = \frac{5\pi}{1024}.$$

Example 15. *Evaluate* $\int_0^{\pi/2} \frac{\sqrt{\sin x}}{\sqrt{\sin x} + \sqrt{\cos x}} dx.$

Solution. Let $I = \int_0^{\pi/2} \frac{\sqrt{\sin x}}{\sqrt{\sin x} + \sqrt{\cos x}} dx$ ...(*i*)

$$= \int_0^{\pi/2} \frac{\sqrt{\sin\left(\frac{\pi}{2} - x\right)}}{\sqrt{\sin\left(\frac{\pi}{2} - x\right)} + \sqrt{\cos\left(\frac{\pi}{2} - x\right)}} dx \text{ (by property 4)}$$

$\Rightarrow$ $I = \int_0^{\pi/2} \frac{\sqrt{\cos x}}{\sqrt{\cos x} + \sqrt{\sin x}} dx$ ...(*ii*)

Adding (*i*) and (*ii*) we get

$$2I = \int_0^{\pi/2} \frac{\sqrt{\sin x} + \sqrt{\cos x}}{\sqrt{\sin x} + \sqrt{\cos x}} dx = \int_0^{\pi/2} 1 \, dx = \frac{\pi}{2} \Rightarrow I = \frac{\pi}{4}.$$

Example 16. *Evaluate* $\int_0^{\pi} \frac{x \sin x}{1 + \cos^2 x} dx.$

Solution. We have

$$I = \int_0^{\pi} \frac{x \sin x}{1 + \cos^2 x} dx = \int_0^{\pi} \frac{(\pi - x)\sin(\pi - x)}{1 + \cos^2(\pi - x)} dx \quad \text{(by Prop. 4)}$$

$$= \int_0^{\pi} \frac{(\pi - x)\sin x}{1+\cos^2 x} dx$$

$$= \pi \int_0^{\pi} \frac{\sin x}{1+\cos^2 x} dx - I \Rightarrow 2I = \pi \int_0^{\pi} \frac{\sin x}{1+\cos^2 x} dx$$

Put $\cos x = t$, then $\sin x\, dx = dt$ also when $x = 0, t = 1$ and $x = \pi, t - 1$

Thus $2I = \pi \int_1^{-1} \frac{-dt}{1+t^2} = \pi \int_{-1}^{1} \frac{dt}{1+t^2} = \pi\{\tan^{-1} t\}_{-1}^{1}$

$$= \pi[\tan^{-1} 1 - \tan^{-1}(-1)]$$

$$= \pi\left[\frac{\pi}{4} + \frac{\pi}{4}\right] = \frac{\pi^2}{2}$$

Hence $I = \frac{\pi^2}{4}$.

Example 17. *Evaluate* $\int_0^{\pi/2} \log \sin x\, dx$.

Solution. We have

$$I = \int_0^{\pi/2} \log \sin x\, dx = \int_0^{\pi/2} \log \sin\left(\frac{\pi}{2} - x\right) dx$$

$$\Rightarrow \quad I = \int_0^{\pi/2} \log \cos x\, dx$$

Adding the two values of I, we get

$$2I = \int_0^{\pi/2} (\log \sin x + \log \cos x) dx = \int_0^{\pi/2} (\log (\sin x \cos x) dx$$

$$= \int_0^{\pi/2} \left(\frac{2 \sin x \cos x}{2}\right) dx = \int_0^{\pi/2} (\log \sin 2x - \log 2)\, dx$$

$$= \int_0^{\pi/2} \log \sin 2x\, dx - \int_0^{\pi/2} \log 2\, dx$$

$$= \int_0^{\pi/2} \log \sin 2x\, dx - \frac{\pi}{2} \log 2 \qquad \ldots(1)$$

Consider now $J = \int_0^{\pi/2} \log \sin 2x \, dx$

Put $2x = t$, then $dx = \dfrac{dt}{2}$

Also when $x = 0,\ t = 0$

$x = \dfrac{\pi}{2},\ t = \pi$

Thus $J = \frac{1}{2} \int_0^{\pi} \log \sin t \, dt = \frac{1}{2} \cdot \int_0^{\pi} \log \sin x \, dx$

$= \frac{1}{2} . 2 \int_0^{\pi/2} \log \sin x \, dx$ (by Property 5)

as $\log \sin (\pi - x) = \log \sin x$

So $J = I$

(1), therefore, gives

$$2I = I - \frac{\pi}{2} \log 2 \quad \Rightarrow \quad I = -\frac{\pi}{2} \log 2.$$

Example 18. *Evaluate* $\int_0^{\pi/4} \log (1 + \tan\theta) \, d\theta$.

Solution. We have $I = \int_0^{\pi/4} \log (1 + \tan \theta) \, d\theta$

$$= \int_0^{\pi/4} \log \left[1 + \tan\left(\frac{\pi}{4} - \theta\right)\right] d\theta$$

$$= \int_0^{\pi/4} \log \left(1 + \frac{1 - \tan\theta}{1 + \tan\theta}\right) d\theta$$

$$= \int_0^{\pi/4} \log \left(\frac{2}{1 + \tan\theta}\right) d\theta$$

$$= \int_0^{\pi/4} [\log 2 - \log (1 + \tan\theta)] \, d\theta = \int_0^{\pi/4} \log 2 \, d\theta - I$$

Thus $2I = \log 2 \int_0^{\pi/4} d\theta = \frac{\pi}{4} . \log 2 \quad \Rightarrow \quad I = \frac{\pi}{8} \log 2.$

EXERCISES

Evaluate the following integrals:

1. (*i*) $\int_0^{\pi} \sin^4 x \cos^5 x\, dx$ (*ii*) $\int_0^{2\pi} \sin^4 x \cos^6 x\, dx$

(*iii*) $\int_0^{\pi/2} \sin^4 3x \cos^2 6x\, dx$ (*iv*) $\int_0^{\pi} \cos^{11} x\, dx$

Prove that

2. $\int_0^{\pi/2} \log(\tan x)\, dx = 0$

3. $\int_0^{\pi/2} \log \cos x\, dx = \pi/2 \log\left(\frac{1}{2}\right)$

4. $\int_0^{\pi} x \log \sin x\, dx = -\frac{\pi^2}{2} \log 2$

5. $\int_0^{2} \log \sin\left(\frac{\pi}{2} x\right) dx = 2 \log\left(\frac{1}{2}\right)$

6. $\int_0^{\pi} \frac{x \sin x}{1 + \sin x}\, dx = \pi(\pi/2 - 1)$

7. $\int_0^{\pi/2} x \cot x\, dx = \pi/2 \log 2$

8. $\int_0^{\pi/2} \left(\frac{\theta}{\sin \theta}\right)^2 d\theta = \pi \log 2$

9. $\int_0^{\infty} \log\left(x + \frac{1}{x}\right) \frac{dx}{1 + x^2} = \pi \log 2$

10. $\int_0^{\pi/2} \frac{dx}{1 + \tan x} = \frac{\pi}{4}$

11. $\int_0^{\pi} \frac{x \tan x}{\sec x + \cos x}\, dx = \frac{\pi^2}{4}$

12. $\int_0^{\pi/2} \log \operatorname{cosec} x\, dx = \pi/2 \log 2$

13. $\int_0^{1} \frac{\log x}{\sqrt{1 - x^2}}\, dx = \frac{\pi}{2} \log \frac{1}{2}$

14. $\int_{-\pi/4}^{\pi/4} \log(\sin x + \cos x)\, dx = -\pi/4 \log 2$

15. $\int_0^{\pi/2} \frac{\sin x}{\cos x + \sin x}\, dx = \frac{\pi}{4}$

ANSWERS

1. (*i*) 0 (*ii*) $\frac{3\pi}{128}$ (*iii*) $\frac{5\pi}{96}$ (*iv*) 0.

10. INTEGRALS AS AREAS

One can show that the integral $\int_a^b f(x)\, dx$ represents the area enclosed by the curve $y = f(x)$, the x-axis and the two ordinates $x = a$ and $x = b$.

If in the figure, AB is the curve $y = f(x)$

$$ON = a, \quad OM = b$$

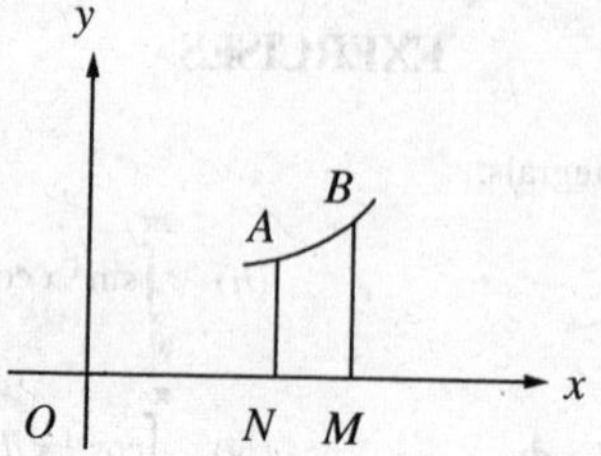

Fig. 1

then area *ANMBA* is represented by $\int_a^b f(x)\,dx$

Example 19. *Find the area enclosed by the line y = x, the x-axis and the ordinate x = 3.*

Solution. We know the required area is represented by the integral $\int_a^b f(x)\,dx$.

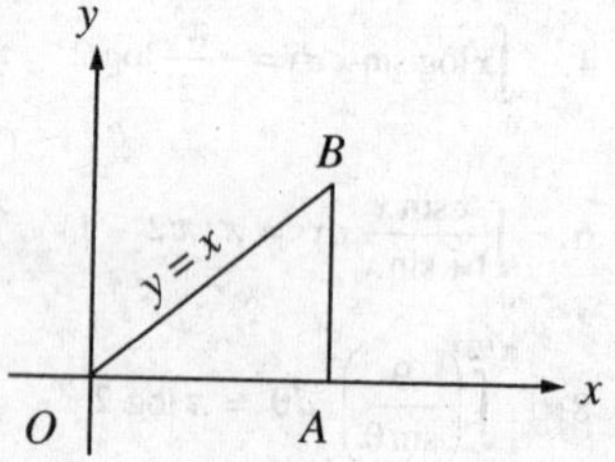

Fig. 2

Here, $a = 0, b = 3, \ f(x) = x$

Thus, required area is $\int_0^3 x\,dx = \left\{\frac{x^2}{2}\right\}_0^3$

$$= \frac{9}{2}$$

Example 20. *Find the area of the region bounded by the parabola $y^2 = 4ax$, and the line x = a.*

Solution. Let *AB* be the line $x = a$. Since the parabola is symmetrical about the *x*-axis, we find the area *OSA* and twice of that will be required area.

Area $OSA = \int_0^a \sqrt{4x}\,dx = 2\cdot\left\{\frac{2}{3}x^{3/2}\right\}_0^a$

$$= \frac{4}{3}a^{3/2}$$

Hence, the required area is $\frac{8}{3}a^{3/2}$.

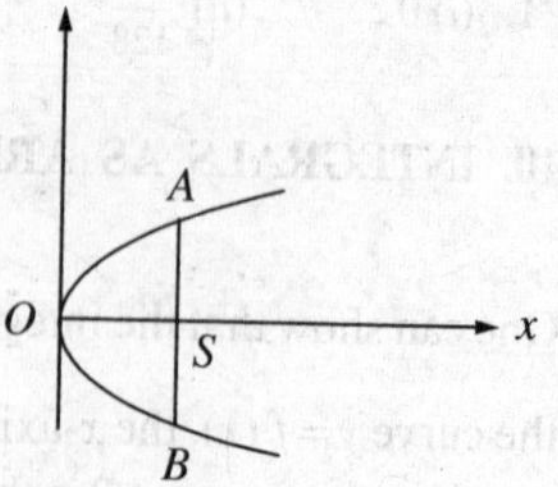

Fig. 3

11. IMPROPER INTEGRALS

A definite integral with one (or both) of its limits as ∞ is called an *improper integral*. Consider, for example, the integral

$$I = \int_1^{\infty} \frac{1}{x^3}\, dx.$$

We evaluate such integrals as follows:

$$I = \lim_{\in \to \infty} \int_1^{\in} \frac{1}{x^3}\, dx = \lim_{\in \to \infty} \left(-\frac{1}{2x^2} \right)_1^{\in}$$

$$= \lim_{\in \to \infty} \left[1 - \frac{1}{2\in^2} + \frac{1}{2} \right] = \frac{1}{2}.$$

If in such cases (as above) the limit exists, we say the improper integral is convergent (and the integral has a definite value). If the limit does not exist, we say the integral is divergent.

Sometimes, integrals with finite limits can also be improper, if within the interval of integration the integrand becomes infinite.

Consider as an example, the integral

$$I = \int_{-1}^{0} \frac{1}{x^{1/3}}\, dx.$$

We evaluate the integral as follows:

$$I = \lim_{\in \to 0} \int_{-1}^{\in} \frac{1}{x^{1/3}}\, dx = \lim_{\in \to 0} \left(\frac{3}{2} x^{2/3} \right)_{-1}^{\in}$$

$$= \lim_{\in \to 0} \left[\frac{3}{2} \in^{2/3} + \frac{3}{2} \right] = \frac{3}{2}.$$

Example 21. *Evaluate* $\int_0^{\infty} x^3 e^{-x^2}\, dx$.

Solution. We put, $x^2 = t$

$\Rightarrow$ $2x\,dx = dt$.

Also when $x = 0, t = 0$

and when $x = \infty, t = \infty$.

Thus, $$\int_0^{\infty} x^3 e^{-x^2}\, dx = \frac{1}{2} \int_0^{\infty} t e^{-t}\, dt.$$

Now, $I = \int_0^{\infty} te^{-t}\,dt = \lim_{\epsilon \to \infty} \int_0^{\epsilon} te^{-t}\,dt.$

Integration by parts, yields

$$I = \lim_{\epsilon \to \infty} \left[\left\{ -te^{-t} \right\}_0^{\epsilon} + \int_0^{\epsilon} e^{-t}\,dt \right] = \lim_{\epsilon \to \infty} \left[-\frac{t}{e^t} - \frac{1}{e^t} \right]_0^{\epsilon}$$

$$= \lim_{\epsilon \to \infty} \left[-\frac{\epsilon}{e^{\epsilon}} - \frac{1}{e^{\epsilon}+1} \right] = 1.$$

Hence, the required integral $\int_0^{\infty} x^3 e^{-x^2}\,dx = \frac{1}{2}.$

EXERCISES

1. Verify that (*i*) $\int_1^3 x^2 dx = \int_1^2 x^2 dx + \int_2^3 x^2 dx.$

   (*ii*) $\int_2^3 \log x\,dx = \int_2^3 \log t\,dt.$

2. Evaluate $\int_{-2}^{2} (4x^2 + 3x)dx.$
3. Find the area enclosed by axes and line $x + y = 1$.
4. Find the area enclosed by the curve $y = e^x$ and the two ordinates $x = -1, x = 1$.
5. Find the area enclosed by the hyperbola $xy = c^2$, the axis of x and the ordinates $x = a, x = b$.
6. Evaluate the following integrals

   (*i*) $\int_1^{\infty} \frac{2x}{(x^2+1)^2}$ (*ii*) $\int_1^{\infty} 3x^{-2} dx$

7. Are the following integrals convergent?

   (*i*) $\int_{-1}^{1} \frac{1}{x^3} dx$ (*ii*) $\int_{-\infty}^{0} (5-x)^{-2} dx$

8. Find the area above the x-axis bounded by $x = 4x - x^2 - 3, x = 1, x = 3$.
9. Find the area bounded by the parabola $x^2 = 4by$, the x-axis and the ordinate $x = 3$.

ANSWERS

2. $\frac{64}{3}$ 3. a^2. 4. $\frac{(e^2-1)}{e}$ **5.** c^2 log

6. (*i*) $\frac{1}{2}$ (*ii*) 3. 7. (*i*) No. (*ii*) Yes, $\frac{1}{5}$. 8. $\frac{4}{3}$. **9.** $\frac{9}{4b}$.

12. APPLICATIONS OF INTEGRATION

In this section, we take up various examples to illustrate how integration proves helpful in different problems relating to Commerce and Economics.

Example 22. *Suppose the marginal cost of a product is given by $25 + 30x - 9x^2$ and fixed cost is known to be 55. Find the total cost and average cost functions.*

Solution. We know that

$$MC = \frac{d}{dx}(TC).$$

Thus, $$TC = \int MC\,dx + k$$

$\Rightarrow$ $$TC = \int (25 + 30x - 9x^2)\,dx + k$$

$\Rightarrow$ $$TC = 25x + 15x^2 - 3x^3 + k.$$

Since, fixed cost is 55 and $TC = FC$ when $x = 0$,

(total cost is the fixed cost or initial cost when number of units produced is zero),

we find that $55 = k$.

Thus, $$TC = 25x + 15x^2 - 3x^3 + 55$$

AC by definition is $\frac{TC}{x} = 25 + 15x - 3x^2 + \frac{55}{x}$.

Example 23. *If the marginal revenue is given by $15 - 2x - x^2$, find the total revenue and demand function. Find also the maximum revenue.*

Solution. We know that,

$$MR = \frac{d}{dx}(TR)$$

$\Rightarrow$ $$TR = \int MR\,dx + k$$

Thus, $$TR = \int (15 - 2x - x^2)\,dx + k = 15x - x^2 - \frac{x^3}{3} + k.$$

At $x = 0$, $TR = 0$, and thus $k = 0$.

Hence, $TR = 15x - x^2 - \dfrac{x^3}{3}$.

If p is the demand function, then

$$TR = px \text{ (definition)}$$

$$\Rightarrow \quad p = \frac{TR}{x} = 15 - x - \frac{x^2}{3}.$$

Again, for maximum revenue

$$\frac{d}{dx}(TR) = 0 \Rightarrow 15 - 2x - x^2 = 0$$

$$\Rightarrow \quad x = -5, 3.$$

Since, $x = -5$ is not possible, we take $x = 3$.

Now, $$\frac{d^2(TR)}{dx^2} = -2 - 2x$$

$$\therefore \quad \left(\frac{d^2}{dx^2}(TR)\right)_{x=3} = -2 - 6 = -8 < 0$$

$\Rightarrow$ there is a max. at $x = 3$.

i.e., revenue is max. when $x = 3$.

Also then, maximum revenue $= 15 \times 3 - 9 - \dfrac{27}{3} = 27$.

Example 24. *ABC Co. Ltd. has approximated the marginal revenue function for one of its products by $MR = 20x - 2x^2$. The marginal cost function is approximated by $MC = 81 - 16x + x^2$.*

Determine the profit maximizing output and the total profit at the optimal output.

Solution. Profit π is maximum if $MR = MC$

i.e., if $\quad 20x - 2x^2 = 81 - 16x + x^2$

or, $\quad 3x^2 - 36x + 81 = 0$

or, $\quad x^2 - 12x + 27 = 0$

or, $\quad (x-3)(x-9) = 0$

$$x = 3, 9.$$

For max. profit, we should have, $\dfrac{d^2\pi}{dx^2} < 0$

i.e., $$\frac{d^2R}{dx^2} < \frac{d^2C}{dx^2}$$

$$\Rightarrow \qquad \frac{d}{dx}(MR) < \frac{d}{dx}(MC)$$

i.e., $\qquad 20 - 4x < -16 + 2x$

or, $\qquad 6x - 36 > 0$

or, $\qquad x > 6.$

Thus, we take $x = 9$ (out of the two values of x) for maximum profit.

Now, profit $\pi = R - C$

$$\text{So, at } x = 9, \text{ profit} = \int_0^9 \frac{d}{dx}(R - C)dx = \int_0^9 \left(\frac{dR}{dx} - \frac{dc}{dx}\right)dx$$

$$= \int_0^9 (MR - MC)dx$$

$$= \int_0^9 (20x - 2x^2 - 81 + 16x - x^2)dx$$

$$= \int_0^9 (-3x^2 + 36x + 81)dx$$

$$= \left[-x^3 + 18x^2 - 81x\right]_0^9$$

$$= -729 + 1458 - 729 = 0.$$

Thus, profit maximizing value is 9 and the total profit is zero.

REMARK: We have used the definite integral idea above. We could also proceed as:

$$\pi = TR - TC = \int MR - \int MC$$

$$= \int (20x - 2x^2)dx - \int (81 - 16x + x^2)dx$$

$$= \int (-3x^2 + 36x + 81)dx$$

$$\Rightarrow \qquad \text{Profit} = -x^3 + 18x^2 - 81x$$

and thus profit at the optimal output 9, is

$$-9^3 + 18.9^2 - 18.9 = -729 + 1458 - 729 = 0.$$

Example 25. *The marginal cost of production is given by MC = 3x + 4. If the initial cost is Rs 10, find total cost function. If the price is fixed at Rs 40 per unit, find the revenue function and maximum profit.*

Solution. We have, $MC = 3x + 4$

Thus, $\qquad TC = \int MC dx + k = \frac{3x^2}{2} + 4x + k$

Since, initial cost is 10, we have,

when $x = 0$

$$10 = 0 + 0 + k \Rightarrow k = 10.$$

Thus, $$TC = \frac{3x^2}{2} + 4x + 10.$$

Again it is given that $MR = 40$

therefore, $$TR = \int 40dx + c$$

$$TR = 40x + c$$

But when $x = 0,\ TR = 0,\ \Rightarrow c = 0$

So, $$TR = 40x$$

which is the required revenue function.

Again, profit $$\pi = TR - TC$$

$$= 40x - \frac{3x^2}{2} - 4x - 10$$

$$= -\frac{3x^2}{2} + 36x - 10$$

For max. or min.

$$\frac{d\pi}{dx} = 0$$

$\Rightarrow$ $$-3x + 36 = 0$$

$\Rightarrow$ $$x = 12$$

Also $$\frac{d^2\pi}{dx^2} = -3 < 0$$

hence when $x = 12$, profit is maximum.

Also then maximum profit is

$$-\frac{3}{2}(12)^2 + 36(12) - 10 = 206.$$

REMARK: For the last part, we can also use the fact that maximum profit occurs when marginal cost equals marginal revenue. We leave it as an exercise for the reader to try.

Example 26. *The marginal cost function of manufacturing x pairs of shoes is $6 + 10x - 6x^2$. The total cost of producing a pair of shoes is Rs 12. Find the total average cost function.*

Solution. We have,

$$MC = 6 + 10x - 6x^2$$

$$\Rightarrow \quad TC = \int (6 + 10x - 6x^2)dx + k$$

$$= 6x + 5x^2 - 2x^3 + k.$$

For one pair of shoes $TC = 12$

i.e., for $\quad x = 1, \; TC = 12$

Thus, $\quad 12 = 6 + 5 - 2 + k \Rightarrow k = 3.$

Hence, $\quad TC = 6x + 5x^2 - 2x^3 + 3$

Again $\quad AC = \dfrac{TC}{x} = 6 + 5x - 2x^2 + \dfrac{3}{x}$

which gives the average cost function.

Example 27. *If π is the total cost of an output x, and it is known that marginal cost equals average cost $\frac{\pi}{x}$. Show that π is a fixed multiple of x, i.e., the average cost is constant.*

Solution. Given,

$$\frac{d\pi}{dx} = \frac{\pi}{x}$$

$$\Rightarrow \quad \frac{1}{\pi}\frac{d\pi}{dx} = \frac{1}{x}$$

$$\Rightarrow \quad \int \frac{1}{\pi}\frac{d\pi}{dx}\,dx = \int \frac{1}{x}\,dx + k$$

$$\Rightarrow \quad \log \pi = \log x + k$$

$$\Rightarrow \quad \log \frac{\pi}{x} = k$$

or, $\quad \dfrac{\pi}{x} = e^k = c \text{ (say)}$

Hence, $\pi = cx$, *i.e.*, a fixed multiple of x.

Definition. Net investment I is defined as the rate of change in capital stock formation K over time t (assuming that capital formation is continuous over time).

Example 28. *The rate of net investment is given by $I(t) = 120t^{2/3}$ and initial stock of capital at time $t = 0$ is 90. Find the capital function K.*

Solution. We have,

$$K = \int I(t)\, dt + c$$

$$\Rightarrow \qquad K = \int 120t^{2/3} dt + c$$

$$= \frac{120t^{5/3}}{5/3} + c$$

$$\Rightarrow \qquad K = 72t^{5/3} + c.$$

Since, at $t = 0$, $K = 90$, we get $c = 90$

Hence, $K = 72t^{5/3} + 90$.

Example 29. *A firm has 100 employees and its production rate is 700 units per hour. It is observed that addition of one extra employee makes an increase of 8 units per hour. What is the relation between the production rate and the number of employees?*

Solution. Let y be production rate per hour and x be number of employees.

Then by the given condition

$$\frac{dy}{dx} = 8.$$

Integrating, we get, $y = 8x + c$, where c is a constant.

Initially, when $x = 100$, $y = 700$

Thus, $700 = 800 + c \Rightarrow c = -100$

Hence, $y = 8x - 100$ is the required relation.

Note the above equation is valid for $x > 12$.

13. CONSUMER AND PRODUCER SURPLUS

Suppose, p is the price that a consumer is willing to pay for a quantity x of a certain commodity, then p and x are related to each other through the demand function and we express this by saying that $p = f(x)$. The graph of this is generally sloping downwards as demand decreases when price is increased (with increase in price, the consumer is inclined to buy less).

Again, suppose now that p is the price that a producer wishes to charge for selling a quantity x of a particular commodity. Then, p and x are related to each other through what is called the *supply curve* $p = g(x)$. This is generally sloping upwards as when the price increases, the producer is inclined to supply more.

If the two curves (supply and demand) intersect, we say *economic equilibrium* is attained. The point of intersection is then called the *equilibrium point*. It is, of course, not essential that the two curves intersect (*i.e.*, economic equilibrium is achieved).

If the point of intersection N has coordinates (x_0, p_0) then p_0 (the market price) is the price which both the consumer and the producer are ready to pay and accept respectively for the quantity x_0 of the commodity. The total revenue in that case is $p_0 \times x_0$.

Sometimes, it happens that a consumer is ready to pay, say, Rs 50 for a certain commodity but gets it for, say, Rs 40 in the market and thus earns (saves) Rs 10. This gain to the consumer is termed as the *consumer surplus*. It is shown by the shaded portion in Figure 4 and is given by the formula

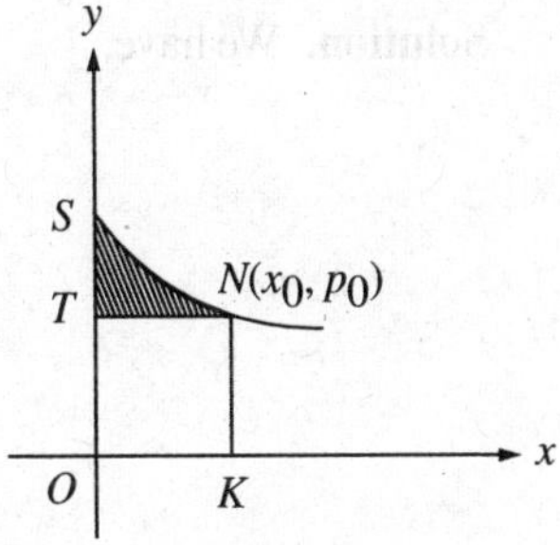

Fig. 4

$$CS = \int_0^{x_0} f(x)dx - (p_0 \times x_0)$$

where, of course, we know the integral $\int_0^{x_0} f(x)dx$ represents the area enclosed by the curve $p = f(x)$, the x-axis and the ordinate NK $(x = x_0)$ *i.e*, the area $STOKNS$ in the figure. This is, in fact, total revenue that would have been generated because of the willingness of some consumers to pay more.

Again $p_0 \times x_0$ is the area of the rectangle $TOKN$ and represents the actual revenue achieved. The difference is thus the surplus.

Similarly, sometimes there are producers who are willing to charge less than the market price (to increase sales) which the consumer actually pays. The gain of this to the producer is called Producer Surplus (PS). It is shown by the shaded portion in the Figure 5 and is given by the formula.

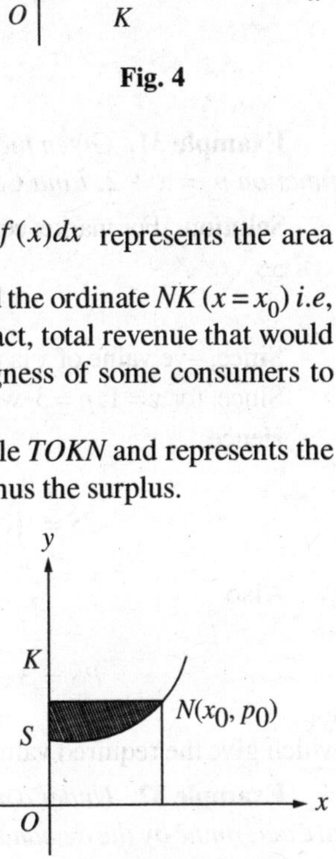

Fig. 5

$$PS = (p_0 \times x_0) - \int_0^{x_0} g(x)dx$$

where, $p = g(x)$ is the supply curve.

It is the difference of the total revenue actually achieved and the revenue that would have been generated by the willingness of some producers to charge less.

Example 30. *Given the demand function* $p = 45 - \frac{x}{2}$ *find consumer surplus when* $p_0 = 32.5$, $x_0 = 25$.

Solution. We have,

$$CS = \int_0^{25}\left(45 - \frac{x}{2}\right)dx - (32.5)\times 25$$

$$= \left\{45x - \frac{x^2}{4}\right\}_0^{25} - 812.5$$

$$= 45\times 25 - \frac{25\times 25}{4} - 812.5$$

$$= 156.25$$

Example 31. *Given the demand function* $p_d = 4 - x^2$ *and the supply function* $p_s = x + 2$. *Find CS and PS (assuming pure competition).*

Solution. For market equilibrium, $p_s = p_d$

$$\Rightarrow \quad x + 2 = 4 - x^2$$

$$\Rightarrow \quad x = -2, 1$$

Since, –ve value of x is not possible, we have, $x = 1$.

Since, for $x = 1$, $p = 3$, we have, $x_0 = 1$, $p_0 = 1$.

Hence,

$$CS = \int_0^1 (4 - x^2)dx - 3 = \left\{4x - \frac{x^3}{3}\right\}_0^1 - 3 = \frac{2}{3}.$$

Also

$$PS = 3 - \int_0^1 (x+2)dx = 3 - \left\{\frac{x^2}{2} + 2x\right\}_0^1 = \frac{1}{2}.$$

which give the required values.

Example 32. *Under a monopoly, the quantity sold and market price are determine by the demand function. If the demand function for a profit maximizing monopolist is* $p = 274 - x^2$ *and* $MC = 4 + 3x$, *find CS.*

Solution. We are given that $p = 274 - x^2$.

$$\Rightarrow \quad TR = p\times x = 274x - x^3$$

$$\Rightarrow \quad MR = \frac{d}{dx}(TR) = 274 - 3x^2$$

Now, the monopolist maximizes profit at

$$MR = MC.$$

$$i.e., \quad 274 - 3x^2 = 4 + 3x$$

$$\Rightarrow \quad 3(x^2 + x - 90) = 0$$

$$\Rightarrow \quad x = 9, -10$$

Since, $x = -10$ is not possible, we have,

$x_0 = 9$, also then $p_0 = 193$.

Hence,

$$CS = \int_0^9 (274 - x^2)dx - 193 \times 9 = 486.$$

Example 33. *Find the consumer surplus at equilibrium price, if the demand function is* $D = \frac{25}{4} - \frac{p}{8}$ *and supply function is* $p = 5 + D$.

Solution. We have, $p = 5 + D$

$$= 5 + \left(\frac{25}{4} - \frac{p}{8}\right)$$

$$\Rightarrow \quad p = 10$$

and thus $\quad D = 5.$

So the equilibrium price $p = 10$, and $D = 5$.

Hence, $CS = \int_0^5 (50 - 8D)dD - 10 \times 5, \quad \left[D = \frac{25}{4} - \frac{p}{8} \Rightarrow p = 50 - 8D\right]$

$$= \left\{50D - \frac{8D^2}{2}\right\}_0^5 - 50$$

$$= 250 - 150 - 50 = 100$$

which is the required value.

14. ECONOMIC LOT SIZE FORMULA

In an earlier chapter we discussed inventory control problems assuming that amount of inventory remains same throughout the production run. But in actual practice, since goods are being sold all through, the amount of inventory goes on decreasing and so the cost of keeping it also decreases, We discuss now this type of situation.

Suppose, a contractor has an order of supplying goods at a uniform rate R per unit of time. His one production run takes t units of time where t is supposed to be fixed for each production. We assume that production time is negligible and so there is no delay in fulfilling the demand as long as a new run is started whenever inventory is zero. The zero inventory, in fact, is a signal for the *start* of next production run. The cost of holding inventory is proportional to the amount of inventory and the time for which it is kept. Suppose time is measured along x-axis and inventory along y-axis.

In the beginning, the inventory is Rt and at the end of a production run it is zero. Let B be the point $(0, Rt)$ and A be $(t, 0)$.

Suppose at any instant x, inventory is y.

We can safely assume that for small change in time, say, dx, it remains same.

The cost of holding y units of inventory for dx units of time will be equal to $c_1\, y\, dx$, where, c_1 is the fixed cost of holding one unit of inventory for one unit of time.

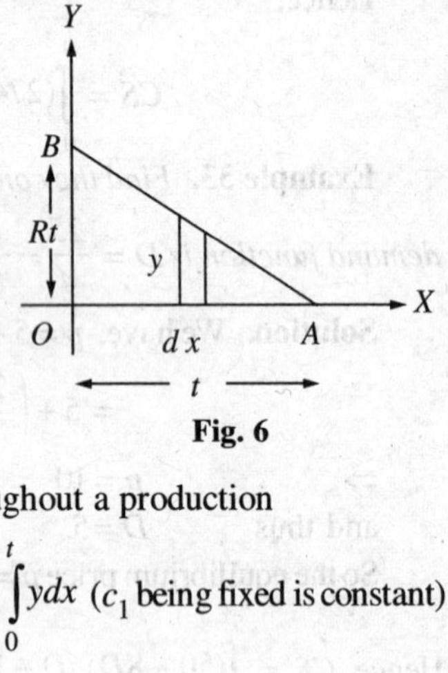

Fig. 6

The cost of holding inventory throughout a production

$$= \int_0^t c_1 y\, dx = c_1 \int_0^t y dx \quad (c_1 \text{ being fixed is constant})$$

Equation of line AB is $\dfrac{x}{t} + \dfrac{y}{Rt} = 1$

or, $\qquad y = Rt - xR$

Thus, cost of holding inventory Rt

$$= c_1 \int_0^t (Rt - xR) dx$$

$$= c_1 \left[Rtx - \frac{x^2}{2} R \right]_0^t$$

$$= \frac{1}{2} c_1 Rt^2.$$

Suppose, now that c_2 is the cost of step-up per production run, then total cost

$$c = \frac{1}{2} c_1 Rt^2 + c_2$$

Hence, average cost $AC = \frac{1}{2} c_1 Rt + \frac{c_2}{t}$.

For AC to be max. or min.

$$\frac{dA}{dt} = 0.$$

or, $\frac{1}{2} c_1 R - \frac{c_2}{t_2} = 0$

or, $t = \sqrt{\frac{2c_2}{c_1 R}}$

Since, for this value of t, $\frac{d^2 A}{dt^2} = \frac{2c_2}{t^3} > 0$.

The value gives a min.

Hence, $t = \sqrt{\frac{2c_2}{c_1 R}}$ gives minimum cost.

The quantity produced q, in one production run is Rt.

Hence, $q = Rt$

$\Rightarrow$ $q = \sqrt{\frac{2c_2}{c_1} R}$

for minimum cost.

This quantity produced, *i.e.*, $\sqrt{\frac{2c_2}{c_1} R}$ is called optimum run size and the equation.

$$q = \sqrt{\frac{2c_2}{c_1} R}$$

is called *Economic Lot Size Formula.*

The minimal average cost

$$= \frac{1}{2} c_1 R \sqrt{\frac{2c_2}{c_1 R}} + c_2 \sqrt{\frac{c_1 R}{2c_2}} = \sqrt{2c_1 c_2 R}$$

Example 34. *A radio manufacturing company uses a particular kind of resistance at an approximately constant rate of 5000 per year. Each resistance costs Rs 2 and the company personnel estimate that it costs*

Rs 20 to place an order and that the carrying cost of inventory is 10% per year. How frequently should orders for the resistance be placed and what quantity should be ordered?

Solution. Here, $R = 5000, c_1 = 10\%$ of $2 = .2, c_2 = 20$

$$\text{Required time} = \sqrt{\frac{2c_2}{c_1 R}} = \sqrt{\frac{2 \times 20}{.2 \times 5000}} = .2$$

or $\frac{1}{5}$ years.

Example 35. *If in the above example the actual costs are Rs 50 to place an order and 15% for carrying cost, the optimal policy will change. How much will the company be losing per year because of the imperfect cost information.*

Solution. Here, $c_2 = 50, c_1 = 15\%$ of $2 = .3$.

In this case, required time

$$= \sqrt{\frac{2c_2}{c_1 R}} = \sqrt{\frac{2 \times 50}{.3 \times 5000}} = \sqrt{\frac{1}{15}}$$

$$\text{Average cost} = \sqrt{2c_1 c_2 R}$$

$$= \sqrt{2 \times 50 \times .3 \times 5000}$$

$$= 100\sqrt{15} = 387.30$$

The average cost in 1st case is $\sqrt{2 \times 20 \times .2 \times 5000}$

$$= 200$$

Hence, the company loses Rs (387.30 – 200)

i.e., Rs 187.30 per year.

EXERCISES

1. If the marginal cost of a product is given by $36 - 20x + 6x^2$ and the initial cost is Rs 20, find the total cost and average cost functions.
2. Let the marginal cost function of a firm be $100 - 10x + 0.1x^2$ where x is the output. Obtain the total cost function of the firm under the assumption that its fixed cost is Rs 500.
3. If the marginal revenue function for output x is given by $\frac{6}{(x+2)^2} + 5$, find the total revenue function and the demand law.
4. If the marginal revenue of output is $p_m = a - bx$, find the total revenue function by integration and deduce the demand function.

5. The marginal cost function for a product is $1 + 2x + 6x^2$, where x is the output. Find the total cost function if the fixed cost is Rs 100 when the output is zero.
6. Find the total cost function if it is known that the cost of zero output is c and that marginal cost of output x is $x_m = ax + b$.
7. It is known that the elasticity of a demand law $x = \varphi(p)$ is of the form $bp - a$ where a and b are given constants. Show that the demand law is $x = p^a e^{-b(p+c)}$, c being an arbitrary constant.
8. If the marginal revenue function is $p_m = \dfrac{ab}{(x+b)^2} - c$, show that $p = \dfrac{a}{x+b} - c$ is the demand law.
9. If $\pi_m = \dfrac{a}{\sqrt{ax+b}}$ is the marginal cost function and if cost of zero output is zero, find total cost as a function of x.
10. Given the demand function $p = 20 - 3x$, find consumer surplus assuming that market equilibrium is attained at $x_0 = 5$, $p_0 = 6$.
11. Under pure competition for a commodity the demand and supply laws are $p_d = \dfrac{8}{x+1} - 2$ and $p_s = \dfrac{1}{2}(x+3)$ respectively. Determine the consumer surplus and the producer surplus.
12. The demand law for a commodity is $p = 20 - 2D - D^2$. Find the consumer surplus when demand is 3.
13. The demand function for a commodity is $p = 20 - 3D$. The supply function on this market is $p = 2D$. Find consumer surplus.
14. If the supply function is given by $p = x^2 + 1$ and market equilibrium occurs at $x_0 = 2$, $p_0 = 3$, find the producer surplus.
15. If the demand and supply functions are given by $p_d = 7 - x^2$, $p_8 = x + 1$, find consumer surplus and producer surplus, assuming pure competition.
16. In a perfect competition, the demand and supply curves of a commodity are given by $p_d = 20 - 3x - x^2$ and $p_s = x - 1$. Find the point of equilibrium and deduce the consumer surplus and producer surplus.
17. The marginal cost of production is given by $MC = 1000 - 20x + x^2$, where x is the number of units produced. The fixed cost is Rs 9000. Find the cost function. If the price per unit is fixed at Rs 3400, find the revenue and profit functions and the sales volume that yields maximum profit.
18. A manufacturer has to supply his customer with 600 units of his product per year. Shortages are not allowed and shortage cost amounts to Rs 60 per unit per year. The set up cost per run is Rs 80. Find the optimum run size and the minimum average yearly cost.
19. For an item, the production is instantaneous. The shortage cost of one item is Re 1 per month and the set up cost is Rs 25 per run. If the demand is 200 units per month, find the optimum quantity to be produced per set up.
20. The demand for a particular item is 18000 units per year. The holding cost per unit is Re 1.20 per year and the cost of one procurement is Rs 400. No shortages are allowed and the replacement rate is instantaneous. Determine.
    (*a*) Optimum order quantity, (*b*) Number of orders per year,
    (*c*) Time between orders.

ANSWERS

1. $TC = 36x - 10x^2 + 2x^3 + 20$, $AC = 36 - 10x + 2x^2 + \dfrac{20}{x}$
2. $TC = 100x - 5x^2 + \dfrac{x^3}{30} + 500$
3. $TR = 3 - \dfrac{6}{x+2} + 5x$; $p = \dfrac{3}{x+2} + 5$.
4. $TR = a.x - \dfrac{bx^2}{2}$; $p = a - \dfrac{bx}{2}$
5. $TC = 2x^3 + \dfrac{x^2}{2} + x + 100$
6. $\dfrac{ax^2}{2} + bx + c$
9. $2(\sqrt{ax+b} - \sqrt{b})$
10. 65
11. $CS = 8 \log 2 - 4$, $PS = \dfrac{3}{4}$
12. 27.
13. 24.
14. 5, 33
15. $\dfrac{16}{3}, 2$
16. $\dfrac{63}{2}, \dfrac{3}{2}$
17. $TC = 9000 + 1000x - 10x^2 + \dfrac{x^3}{3}$, $TR = 3100\,x$,

    $\pi = 2400 + 10x^2 - \dfrac{x^3}{3} - 9000$, Max. profit at $x = 60$.
18. $q = 400$, $AC = 240$
19. 100.
20. (*a*) 3465 (*b*) 52 orders per year (*c*) 1925 years

CHAPTER 29

MATRICES AND DETERMINANTS

1. DEFINITION OF A MATRIX

Let F be a field and n, m be two integers ≥ 1. An array of elements in F, of the type

$$\begin{bmatrix} a_{11} & a_{12} & a_{13} & \cdots & a_{1n} \\ a_{21} & a_{22} & a_{23} & \cdots & a_{2n} \\ \vdots & \vdots & \vdots & \vdots & \vdots \\ a_{m1} & a_{m2} & a_{m3} & \cdots & a_{mn} \end{bmatrix}$$

is called a matrix in F. We denote this matrix by (a_{ij}), $i = 1, \ldots, m$ and $j = 1, \ldots, n$. We say that it is an $m \times n$ matrix (or matrix of order $m \times n$). It has m rows and n columns. For example, the first row is $(a_{11}, a_{12}, \ldots, a_{1n})$ and first column is

$$\begin{bmatrix} a_{11} \\ a_{21} \\ \vdots \\ a_{m1} \end{bmatrix}$$

Also, a_{ij} denotes the element of the matrix (a_{ij}) lying in ith row and jth column and we call this element as the (i, j)th element of the matrix.

For example, in the matrix

$$\begin{bmatrix} 1 & 2 & 3 \\ 4 & 5 & 6 \\ 7 & 8 & 9 \end{bmatrix}$$

$a_{11} = 1, a_{12} = 2, a_{32} = 8.$ *i.e.* (1, 1)th element is 1

(1, 2)th element is 2.

(3, 2)th element is 8.

REMARKS:

1. Unless otherwise stated, we shall consider matrices over the field **C** of complex numbers only.
(Note the field of real numbers is contained in **C**.)
2. A matrix is simply an arrangement of elements and has no numerical value.

2. DIFFERENT TYPES OF MATRICES

1. *Row Matrix*. A matrix which has exactly one row is called a *row matrix.*
For example (1, 2, 3, 4) is a row matrix.
2. *Column Matrix*. A matrix which has exactly one column is called a *column matrix*.
For example $\begin{bmatrix} 5 \\ 6 \\ 7 \end{bmatrix}$ is a column matrix.
3. *Square Matrix*. A matrix in which the number of rows is equal to the number of columns is called a *square matrix*.
For example $\begin{bmatrix} 1 & 2 \\ 3 & 4 \end{bmatrix}$ is a 2×2 square matrix.
4. *Null* or *Zero Matrix*. A matrix each of whose elements is zero is called a *Null Matrix* or *Zero Matrix*.
For example, $\begin{bmatrix} 0 & 0 & 0 \\ 0 & 0 & 0 \end{bmatrix}$ is a 2×3 Null matrix.
5. *Diagonal Matrix*. The elements a_{ij} are called diagonal elements of a square matrix (a_{ij}). For example, in

$$\begin{bmatrix} 1 & 2 & 3 \\ 4 & 5 & 6 \\ 7 & 8 & 9 \end{bmatrix}$$

the diagonal elements are $a_{11} = 1, a_{22} = 5, a_{33} = 9$

A square matrix whose every element other than diagonal elements is zero, is called a *Diagonal Matrix*. For example,

$$\begin{bmatrix} 1 & 0 & 0 \\ 0 & 2 & 0 \\ 0 & 0 & 3 \end{bmatrix} \text{ is a diagonal matrix.}$$

Note that, the diagonal elements in a diagonal matrix may also be zero. For example

$\begin{bmatrix} 0 & 0 \\ 0 & 2 \end{bmatrix}$ and $\begin{bmatrix} 0 & 0 \\ 0 & 0 \end{bmatrix}$ are also diagonal matrices.

6. *Scalar Matrix.* A diagonal matrix whose diagonal elements are equal, is called a *Scalar Matrix*. For example

$$\begin{bmatrix} 5 & 0 \\ 0 & 5 \end{bmatrix}, \begin{bmatrix} 1 & 0 & 0 \\ 0 & 1 & 0 \\ 0 & 0 & 1 \end{bmatrix}, \begin{bmatrix} 0 & 0 & 0 \\ 0 & 0 & 0 \\ 0 & 0 & 0 \end{bmatrix}$$ are scalar matrices.

7. *Identity Matrix.* A diagonal matrix whose diagonal elements are all equal to 1 (unity) is called **Identity Matrix** or **(Unit Matrix).** For example,

$$\begin{bmatrix} 1 & 0 \\ 0 & 1 \end{bmatrix}$$ is an identity matrix.

8. *Triangular Matrix.* A square matrix (a_{ij}) whose elements $a_{ij} = 0$ wherever $i < j$ is called a *Lower Triangular Matrix.*
Similarly, a square matrix (a_{ij}) whose elements $a_{ij} = 0$ whenever $i > j$ is called an *Upper Triangular Matrix.*
For example,

$$\begin{bmatrix} 1 & 0 & 0 \\ 4 & 5 & 0 \\ 7 & 8 & 9 \end{bmatrix}, \begin{bmatrix} 1 & 0 \\ 2 & 0 \end{bmatrix}$$ are lower triangular matrices

and $$\begin{bmatrix} 1 & 2 & 3 \\ 0 & 4 & 5 \\ 0 & 0 & 6 \end{bmatrix}, \begin{bmatrix} 1 & 2 \\ 0 & 3 \end{bmatrix}$$ are upper triangular matrices.

3. ALGEBRA OF MATRICES

Equality of Matrices. Two matrices *A* and *B* are said to be equal if

(*i*) *A* and *B* are of same order.

(*ii*) Corresponding elements in *A* and *B* are same. For example, the following two matrices are equal

$$\begin{bmatrix} 3 & 4 & 9 \\ 16 & 25 & 64 \end{bmatrix} = \begin{bmatrix} 3 & 4 & 9 \\ 16 & 25 & 64 \end{bmatrix}$$

But the following two matrices are not equal.

$$\begin{bmatrix} 1 & 2 & 3 \\ 4 & 5 & 6 \end{bmatrix} \begin{bmatrix} 1 & 2 & 3 \\ 4 & 5 & 6 \\ 7 & 8 & 9 \end{bmatrix}$$

as matrix on left is of order 2×3, while on right it is of order 3×3.

The following two matrices are also not equal

$$\begin{bmatrix} 1 & 2 & 3 \\ 7 & 8 & 9 \end{bmatrix} \begin{bmatrix} 1 & 2 & 3 \\ 4 & 8 & 9 \end{bmatrix}$$

as (2, 1)th element in 1st matrix is 7 while in 2nd matrix it is 4.

Addition of Matrices. If A and B are two matrices of the same order then addtion of A and B is defined to be the matrix obtained by adding the corresponding elements of A and B.

For example, if

$$A = \begin{bmatrix} 1 & 2 & 3 \\ 4 & 5 & 6 \end{bmatrix}, B = \begin{bmatrix} 2 & 3 & 4 \\ 5 & 6 & 7 \end{bmatrix}$$

Then $\quad A + B = \begin{bmatrix} 1+2 & 2+3 & 3+4 \\ 4+5 & 5+6 & 6+7 \end{bmatrix} = \begin{bmatrix} 3 & 5 & 7 \\ 9 & 11 & 3 \end{bmatrix}$

Also $\quad A - B = \begin{bmatrix} 1-2 & 2-3 & 3-4 \\ 4-5 & 5-6 & 6-7 \end{bmatrix} = \begin{bmatrix} -1 & -1 & -1 \\ -1 & -1 & -1 \end{bmatrix}$

Note that addition (or subtraction) of two matrices is defined only when A and B are of the same order.

Properties of Matrix Addition.

(*i*) Matrix addition is commutative

i.e., $\quad A + B = B + A$

For, (i, j)th element of $A + B$ is $(a_{ij} + b_{ij})$ and of $B + A$ is $(b_{ij} + a_{ij})$, and they are same as a_{ij}, and b_{ij} are complex numbers.

(*ii*) Matrix addition is associative

i.e., $\quad A + (B + C) = (A + B) + C$

For, (i, j)th element of $A + (B + C)$ is $a_{ij} + (b_{ij} + c_{ij})$ and of $(A + B) + C$ is $(a_{ij} + b_{ij}) + c_{ij}$ which are same.

(*iii*) If O denotes null matrix of the same order as that of A then

$A + O = A = O + A$

For (i, j)th element of $A + O$ is $a_{ij} + 0 = a_{ij}$, which is same as (i, j)th element of A.

(*iv*) To each matrix A there corresponds a matrix B such that $A + B = O = B + A$.

For, let (i, j)th element of B be $- a_{ij}$. Then (i, j)th element of $A + B$ is $a_{ij} - a_{ij} = 0$.

Thus, the set of $m \times n$ matrices forms an abelian group under the composition of matrix addition.

Multiplication of Matrix by a Scalar. If k is any complex number and A, a given matrix, then kA is the matrix obtained from A by multiplying each element of A by k. The number k is called a *Scalar*.

For example, if

$$A = \begin{bmatrix} 1 & 2 & 3 \\ 4 & 5 & 6 \end{bmatrix} \text{ and } k = 2$$

then
$$kA = \begin{bmatrix} 2 & 4 & 6 \\ 8 & 10 & 12 \end{bmatrix}$$

It can be easily shown that

(*i*) $k(A+B) = kA + kB$ (*ii*) $(k_1 + k_2)A = k_1A + k_2A$

(*iii*) $1A = A$ (*iv*) $(k_1k_2)A = k_1(k_2A)$.

Example 1. *If* $A = \begin{bmatrix} 1 & 2 & 3 \\ 4 & 5 & 6 \end{bmatrix}$ *and* $B = \begin{bmatrix} 0 & 1 & 2 \\ 3 & 4 & 5 \end{bmatrix}$

Verify $A + B = B + A$.

Solution. $$A + B = \begin{bmatrix} 1+0 & 2+1 & 3+2 \\ 4+3 & 5+4 & 6+5 \end{bmatrix} = \begin{bmatrix} 1 & 3 & 5 \\ 7 & 9 & 11 \end{bmatrix}$$

$$B + A = \begin{bmatrix} 0+1 & 1+2 & 2+3 \\ 3+4 & 4+5 & 5+6 \end{bmatrix} = \begin{bmatrix} 1 & 3 & 5 \\ 7 & 9 & 11 \end{bmatrix}$$

So, $A + B = B + A$.

Example 2. *If A and B are matrices as in Example 1*

and $C = \begin{bmatrix} -1 & 0 & 1 \\ 1 & 2 & 3 \end{bmatrix}$, *verify* $(A + B) + C = A + (B + C)$

Solution. Now $A + B = \begin{bmatrix} 1 & 3 & 5 \\ 7 & 9 & 11 \end{bmatrix}$

So, $$(A+B) + C = \begin{bmatrix} 1-1 & 3+0 & 5+1 \\ 7+1 & 9+2 & 11+3 \end{bmatrix} = \begin{bmatrix} 0 & 3 & 6 \\ 8 & 11 & 14 \end{bmatrix}$$

Again $$B + C = \begin{bmatrix} 0-1 & 1+0 & 2+1 \\ 3+1 & 4+2 & 5+3 \end{bmatrix} = \begin{bmatrix} -1 & 1 & 3 \\ 4 & 6 & 8 \end{bmatrix}$$

So, $$A + (B + C) = \begin{bmatrix} 1-1 & 2+1 & 3+3 \\ 4+4 & 5+6 & 6+8 \end{bmatrix} = \begin{bmatrix} 0 & 3 & 6 \\ 8 & 11 & 14 \end{bmatrix}$$

Therefore, $(A + B) + C = A + (B + C)$.

Example 3. *If* $A = \begin{bmatrix} 1 & 2 \\ 3 & 4 \\ 5 & 6 \end{bmatrix}$*, find a matrix B such that A + B = 0.*

Solution. Let $B = \begin{bmatrix} b_{11} & b_{12} \\ b_{21} & b_{22} \\ b_{31} & b_{32} \end{bmatrix}$

Then $$A + B = \begin{bmatrix} 1+b_{11} & 2+b_{12} \\ 3+b_{21} & 4+b_{22} \\ 5+b_{31} & 6+b_{32} \end{bmatrix} = \begin{bmatrix} 0 & 0 \\ 0 & 0 \\ 0 & 0 \end{bmatrix}$$

implies, $b_{11} = -1, b_{12} = -2, b_{21} = -3, b_{22} = -4,$
$b_{31} = -5, b_{32} = -6.$

Therefore, required $B = \begin{bmatrix} -1 & -2 \\ -3 & -4 \\ -5 & -6 \end{bmatrix}$.

Example 4. (*i*) *If* $A = \begin{bmatrix} 0 & 1 & 2 \\ 2 & 3 & 4 \\ 4 & 5 & 6 \end{bmatrix}$ *and* $k_1 = i,\ k_2 = 2$*, verify* $(k_1 + k_2) A = k_1A + k_2A$.

(*ii*) *If* $A = \begin{bmatrix} 0 & 2 & 3 \\ 2 & 1 & 4 \end{bmatrix}, B = \begin{bmatrix} 7 & 6 & 3 \\ 1 & 4 & 5 \end{bmatrix}$ *find the value of 2A + 3B.*

Solution. (*i*) Now $k_1A = \begin{bmatrix} 0 & i & 2i \\ 2i & 3i & 4i \\ 4i & 5i & 6i \end{bmatrix}$ and $k_2A = \begin{bmatrix} 0 & 2 & 4 \\ 4 & 6 & 8 \\ 8 & 10 & 12 \end{bmatrix}$

So, $$k_1A + k_2A = \begin{bmatrix} 0 & 2+i & 4+2i \\ 4+2i & 6+3i & 8+4i \\ 8+4i & 10+5i & 12+6i \end{bmatrix}$$

Also, $$(k_1 + k_2) A = \begin{bmatrix} 0 & 2+i & 4+2i \\ 4+2i & 6+3i & 8+4i \\ 8+4i & 10+5i & 12+6i \end{bmatrix}$$

Therefore $(k_1 + k_2)A = k_1A + k_2A$.

(ii) $2A = \begin{bmatrix} 0 & 4 & 6 \\ 4 & 1 & 8 \end{bmatrix}$

$3B = \begin{bmatrix} 21 & 18 & 9 \\ 3 & 12 & 15 \end{bmatrix}$

So, $2A + 3B = \begin{bmatrix} 21 & 22 & 15 \\ 7 & 13 & 23 \end{bmatrix}.$

Example 5. *If* $A = \begin{bmatrix} 1 & 2 & 3 \\ 4 & 5 & 6 \\ 7 & 8 & 9 \\ 0 & 1 & 2 \end{bmatrix}$ *find* $a_{11}, a_{22}, a_{33}, a_{31}, a_{41}$.

Solution. a_{11} = element of A in first row and first column = 1

a_{22} = element of A in second row and second column = 5

a_{33} = element of A in third row and thrid column = 9

a_{31} = element of A in third row and first column = 7

a_{41} = element of A in fourth row and first column = 0

Example 6. *In an examination of Mathematics, 20 students from college A, 30 students from college B and 40 students from college C appeared. Only 15 students from each college could get through the examination. Out of them 10 students from college A and 5 students from college B and 10 students from college C secured full marks. Write down the above data in matrix form.*

Solution. Consider the matrix

$$\begin{bmatrix} 20 & 30 & 40 \\ 15 & 15 & 15 \\ 10 & 5 & 10 \end{bmatrix}$$

First row represents the number of students in college A, college B, college C respectively.

Second row represents the number of students who got through the examination in three colleges respectively.

Third row represents the number of students who got full marks in the three colleges respectively.

Example 7. *A publishing house has two branches. In each branch, there are three offices. In each office, there are 3 peons, 4 clerks and 5 typists. In one office of a branch, 6 salesmen are also working. In each office of other branch 2 head-clerks are also working. Using matrix* *notation find (i) the total number of posts of each kind in all the offices taken together in each branch, (ii) the total number of posts of each kind in all the offices taken together from both the branches.*

Solution. (*i*) Consider the following row matrices

$$A_1 = [3\ 4\ 5\ 6\ 0],\quad A_2 = [3\ 4\ 5\ 0\ 0],\quad A_3 = [3\ 4\ 5\ 0\ 0]$$

These matrices represent the three offices of the branch (say A) where elements appearing in the row represent the number of peons, clerks, typists, salesmen and head-clerks taken in that order working in the three offices.

Then $A_1 + A_2 + A_3 = [3+3+3\ \ 4+4+4\ \ 5+5+5\ \ 6+0+0\ \ 0+0+0]$
$= [9\ \ 12\ \ 15\ \ 6\ \ 0]$

Thus, total number of posts of each kind in all the offices of branch A are the elements of matrix $A_1 + A_2 + A_3 = [9\ \ 12\ \ 15\ \ 6\ \ 0]$

Now consider the following row matrices

$$B_1 = [3\ 4\ 5\ 0\ 2],\quad B_2 = [3\ 4\ 5\ 0\ 2],\quad B_3 = [3\ 4\ 5\ 0\ 2]$$

Then B_1, B_2, B_3 represent three offices of other branch (say B) where the elements in the row represent number of peons, clerks, typists, salesmen and head-clerks respectively.

Thus, total number of posts of each kind in all the offices of branch B are the elements of the matrix $B_1 + B_2 + B_3 = [9\ \ 12\ \ 15\ \ 0\ \ 6]$

(*ii*) The total number of posts of each kind in all the offices taken together from both branches are the elements of matrix

$$[A_1 + A_2 + A_3] + [B_1 + B_2 + B_3] = [18\ \ 24\ \ 30\ \ 6\ \ 6]$$

Example 8. *Let* $A = \begin{bmatrix} 10 & 20 \\ 30 & 40 \end{bmatrix}$

where first row represents the number of table fans and second row represents the number of ceiling fans which two manufacturing units A and B make in one day. The first and second column represent the manufacturing units A and B. Compute 5A and state what it represents.

Solution. $5A = \begin{bmatrix} 50 & 100 \\ 150 & 200 \end{bmatrix}$

It represents the number of table fans and ceiling fans that the manufacturing units A and B produce in five days.

Example 9. *Let* $A = \begin{bmatrix} 2 & 3 & 4 & 5 \\ 3 & 4 & 5 & 6 \\ 4 & 5 & 6 & 7 \end{bmatrix}$

where rows represent the number of items of type I, II, III, respectively. The four columns represents the four shops A_1, A_2, A_3, A_4 respectively.

$$\text{Let}\quad B = \begin{bmatrix} 1 & 2 & 3 & 4 \\ 2 & 1 & 2 & 3 \\ 3 & 2 & 1 & 2 \end{bmatrix},\quad C = \begin{bmatrix} 1 & 2 & 2 & 3 \\ 1 & 2 & 3 & 4 \\ 2 & 3 & 4 & 4 \end{bmatrix}$$

where elements in B represent the number of items of different types delivered at the beginning of a week and matrix C represents the sales during that week. Find

(i) the number of items immediately after delivery of items.
(ii) the number of items at the end of the week.
(iii) the number of items needed to bring stocks of all items in all shops to 6.

Solution. (*i*) $A + B = \begin{bmatrix} 3 & 5 & 7 & 9 \\ 5 & 5 & 7 & 9 \\ 7 & 7 & 7 & 9 \end{bmatrix}$

represents the number of items immediately after delivery of items.

(*ii*) $(A + B) - C = \begin{bmatrix} 2 & 3 & 5 & 6 \\ 4 & 3 & 4 & 5 \\ 5 & 4 & 3 & 5 \end{bmatrix}$

represents the number of items at the end of the week.

(*iii*) We want that all elements in $(A + B) - C$ should be 6.

$$\text{Let } D = \begin{bmatrix} 4 & 3 & 1 & 0 \\ 2 & 3 & 2 & 1 \\ 1 & 2 & 3 & 1 \end{bmatrix}$$

Then $(A + B) - C + D$ is a matrix in which all elements are 6. So, D represents the number of items needed to bring stocks of all items of all shops to 6.

Example 10. *The following matrix represents the results of the examination of B. Com. class:*

$$\begin{bmatrix} 1 & 2 & 3 & 4 \\ 5 & 6 & 7 & 8 \\ 9 & 10 & 11 & 12 \end{bmatrix}$$

The rows represent the three sections of the class. The first three columns represent the number of students securing 1st, 2nd, 3rd divisions respectively in that order and fourth column represents the number of students who failed in the examination.

(*a*) *How many students passed in three sections respectively?*
(*b*) *How many students failed in three sections respectively?*
(*c*) *Write down the matrix in which number of successful students is shown.*
(*d*) *Write down the column matrix where only failed students are shown.*
(*e*) *Write down the column matrix showing students in 1st division from three sections.*

Solution. (*a*) The number of students who passed in three sections respectively are $1+2+3=6$, $5+6+7=18$, $9+10+11=30$.

(*b*) The number of students who failed from three sections respectively are 4, 8, 12.

(*c*) $\begin{bmatrix} 1 & 2 & 3 \\ 5 & 6 & 7 \\ 9 & 10 & 11 \end{bmatrix}$

(*d*) $\begin{bmatrix} 4 \\ 8 \\ 12 \end{bmatrix}$ represents column matrix where only failed students are shown.

(*e*) $\begin{bmatrix} 1 \\ 5 \\ 9 \end{bmatrix}$ represents column matrix of students securing 1st division.

EXERCISES

1. If $A = \begin{bmatrix} 2 & 1 & 0 \\ 0 & 1 & 3 \\ 4 & 2 & 1 \end{bmatrix}$ find $a_{11}, a_{12}, a_{13}, a_{21}, a_{22}, a_{23}, a_{31}, a_{32}, a_{33}$.

2. What is the order of the following matrices?

(*i*) $\begin{bmatrix} 1 & 2 \\ 3 & 4 \end{bmatrix}$ (*ii*) $\begin{bmatrix} 1 & 2 & 3 \\ 4 & 5 & 6 \end{bmatrix}$ (*iii*) $\begin{bmatrix} 0 & 0 \\ 1 & 2 \\ 1 & 3 \end{bmatrix}$ (*iv*) (0)

3. What are the diagonal elements of the following matrices?

(*i*) $\begin{bmatrix} 1 & 0 & 3 \\ 0 & 4 & 5 \\ 7 & 0 & 6 \end{bmatrix}$ (*ii*) $\begin{bmatrix} 1 & 3 & 5 \\ 7 & 9 & 1 \\ 3 & 5 & 7 \end{bmatrix}$ (*iii*) $\begin{bmatrix} 0 & 0 & 0 \\ 0 & 0 & 0 \\ 0 & 0 & 0 \end{bmatrix}$

4. Which of the following matrices are diagonal matrices?

(i) $\begin{bmatrix} 1 & 2 \\ 0 & 0 \end{bmatrix}$ (ii) $\begin{bmatrix} 0 & 1 \\ 2 & 0 \end{bmatrix}$ (iii) $\begin{bmatrix} 0 & 0 \\ 0 & 0 \end{bmatrix}$ (iv) $\begin{bmatrix} 1 & 0 & 0 \\ 0 & 1 & 0 \\ 0 & 0 & 1 \end{bmatrix}$

5. Which of the following matrices are scalar matrices?

(i) $\begin{bmatrix} 1 & 0 \\ 0 & 1 \end{bmatrix}$ (ii) $\begin{bmatrix} 5 & 1 \\ 0 & 5 \end{bmatrix}$ (iii) $\begin{bmatrix} 2 & 0 & 0 \\ 0 & 2 & 0 \\ 0 & 0 & 2 \end{bmatrix}$ (iv) $\begin{bmatrix} 0 & 0 & 0 \\ 0 & 0 & 0 \\ 0 & 0 & 0 \end{bmatrix}$

6. Which of the following matrices are triangular matrices?

(i) $\begin{bmatrix} 1 & 0 & 0 \\ 5 & 1 & 0 \\ 6 & 2 & 0 \end{bmatrix}$ (ii) $\begin{bmatrix} 1 & 2 & 3 \\ 0 & 0 & 4 \\ 0 & 0 & 5 \end{bmatrix}$ (iii) $\begin{bmatrix} 0 & 1 & 2 \\ 0 & 0 & 1 \\ 1 & 2 & 0 \end{bmatrix}$ (iv) $\begin{bmatrix} 0 & 0 \\ 0 & 0 \end{bmatrix}$

7. Compute $A + B$ for the following matrices:

(i) $A = \begin{bmatrix} 1 & 0 & 0 \\ 2 & 3 & 4 \end{bmatrix}$, $B = \begin{bmatrix} 2 & 1 & 3 \\ 1 & 3 & 2 \end{bmatrix}$

(ii) $A = \begin{bmatrix} 1 & 4 & 7 \\ 2 & 5 & 8 \end{bmatrix}$, $B = \begin{bmatrix} -1 & -4 & -7 \\ -2 & -5 & -8 \end{bmatrix}$

(iii) $A = \begin{bmatrix} 1 & 2 & 3 \\ 4 & 5 & 6 \end{bmatrix}$, $B = \begin{bmatrix} 0 & 0 & 0 \\ 0 & 0 & 0 \end{bmatrix}$

(iv) $A = \begin{bmatrix} 1 & 4 \\ 5 & 6 \end{bmatrix}$, $B = \begin{bmatrix} 1 & 4 \\ 5 & 6 \end{bmatrix}$

(v) $A = (1)$, $B = (-1)$

8. Compute kA, if

(i) $A = \begin{bmatrix} 1 & 3 & 5 \\ 7 & 5 & 3 \end{bmatrix}$, $k = i$ (ii) $A = \begin{bmatrix} i & 1 & -i \\ 1+i & 0 & i \end{bmatrix}$, $k = -1$

9. If $A = \begin{bmatrix} 1 & 3 & 4 \\ 1 & 2 & 3 \end{bmatrix}$, find a matrix B such that $A + B$ is zero matrix.

10. Find a matrix A such that

$$4A = \begin{bmatrix} 4 & 8 & 12 \\ 16 & 20 & 24 \\ 28 & 32 & 36 \end{bmatrix}$$

11. Find x and y, if

(i) $[x + 2 \quad 5] + [6 \quad y + 3] = (0 \; 0)$ (ii) $[2 \; 3] + [-2 \quad -3] = [x \quad y]$

12. If $A = \begin{bmatrix} 0 & 1 & 2 \\ 2 & 3 & 4 \end{bmatrix}$, $B = \begin{bmatrix} 1 & 2 & 3 \\ 3 & 4 & 5 \end{bmatrix}$, $C = \begin{bmatrix} 2 & 3 & 4 \\ 4 & 5 & 6 \end{bmatrix}$

Compute the following:

(i) $(A + B) + C$ (ii) $(A - B) + C$ (iii) $A - B - C$

(iv) $2A + 3B$ (v) $A + 2B + 3C$

13. If $A = \begin{bmatrix} 1 & 2 \\ 3 & 4 \end{bmatrix}$, $B = \begin{bmatrix} 4 & 5 \\ 6 & 7 \end{bmatrix}$, find a matrix C such that (*i*) $(A + B) + C = 0$ (*ii*) $A + B = 2C$

14. If $A = \begin{bmatrix} 1 & 0 & 2 \\ 2 & 3 & 4 \\ 3 & 1 & 2 \end{bmatrix}$, find a matrix B such that $A + B$ is a diagonal matrix.

15. If $A = \begin{bmatrix} 0 & 1 & 1 \\ 1 & 2 & 2 \end{bmatrix}$ and $B = \begin{bmatrix} 1 & 0 & 0 \\ 2 & 3 & 4 \end{bmatrix}$ find k_1 and k_2 such that $k_1 A k_2 B$ is zero matrix.

16. Suppose that Brown, Jones, and Smith go to the grocery store and purchase the following items:
Brown: two apples, six lemons and five mangoes.
Jones: two dozen eggs, two lemons and two dozen oranges,
Smith ;ten apples, one dozen eggs, two dozen oranges and a half dozen mangoes.
Construct the 3 × 5 matrix whose rows give the various purchases of Brown, Jones and Smith.

17. In Problem 16, write down five column matrices each of order 3 × 1 giving the number of items of different kinds purchased by Brown, Jones and Smith. By means of matrix addition, find the total amount of their purchases as a column matrix.

18. Suppose that there are three industries which we call as coal, electricity and steel and three consumers 1, 2, 3. Suppose that consumer 1 uses 3 units of coal, 2 units of electricity and 5 units of steel, consumer 2 uses 17 units of electricity and 1 unit of steel and consumer 3 uses 4 units of coal, 6 units of electricity and 12 units of steel. Assume that coal industry uses 1 unit of electricity and 4 units of steel, electricity industry uses 20 units of coal and 8 units of steel and steel industry uses 30 units of coal and 5 units of electricity. Using matrix algebra, find the total over all demand of three products.

19. Suppose that matrices A and B represent the number of items of different kind produced by two manufacturing units in one day.

$$A = \begin{bmatrix} 4 \\ 5 \\ 6 \end{bmatrix}, \quad B = \begin{bmatrix} 3 \\ 4 \\ 5 \end{bmatrix}. \quad \text{Compute } 2A + 3B.$$

What does the matrix $2A + 3B$ represent?

20. $$A = \begin{matrix} & \begin{matrix} A_1 & A_2 & A_3 \end{matrix} \\ \begin{matrix} I \\ II \\ III \end{matrix} & \begin{bmatrix} 1 & 2 & 3 \\ 4 & 5 & 6 \\ 7 & 8 & 9 \end{bmatrix} \end{matrix}, \quad B = \begin{bmatrix} 2 & 3 & 4 \\ 5 & 6 & 7 \\ 8 & 9 & 10 \end{bmatrix}, \quad C = \begin{bmatrix} 3 & 5 & 7 \\ 9 & 11 & 13 \\ 15 & 17 & 19 \end{bmatrix}$$

Matrix A shows the stock of 3 types of items *I*, *II*, *III* in three shops A_1, A_2, A_3. Matrix B shows the number of items delivered to three shops at the beginning of a week. Matrix C shows the number of items sold during that week. Using matrix algebra, find

(*i*) the number of items immediately after the delivery.

(*ii*) the number of items at the end of the week.

ANSWERS

1. $a_{11} = 2, a_{12} = 1, a_{13} = 0, a_{21} = 0, a_{22} = 1, a_{23} = 3, a_{31} = 4, a_{32} = 2, a_{33} = 1.$
2. (*i*) 2×2 (*ii*) 2×3 (*iii*) 3×2 (*iv*) 1×1
3. (*i*) 1, 4, 6 (*ii*) 1, 9, 7 (*iii*) 0, 0, 0
4. (*i*) Not diagonal (*ii*), (*iii*) and (*iv*) are diagonal
5. (*i*), (*iii*) and (*iv*) are scalar matrices
6. (*i*), (*ii*) and (*iv*) are triangular matrices
7. (*i*) $\begin{bmatrix} 2 & 1 & 3 \\ 3 & 6 & 6 \end{bmatrix}$ (*ii*) $\begin{bmatrix} 0 & 0 & 0 \\ 0 & 0 & 0 \end{bmatrix}$ (*iii*) $\begin{bmatrix} 1 & 2 & 3 \\ 4 & 5 & 6 \end{bmatrix}$

   (*iv*) $\begin{bmatrix} 2 & 8 \\ 10 & 12 \end{bmatrix}$ (*v*) (0)
8. (*i*) $\begin{bmatrix} i & 3i & 5i \\ 7i & 5i & 3i \end{bmatrix}$ (*ii*) $\begin{bmatrix} 1 & -i & -1 \\ -i+1 & 0 & 1 \end{bmatrix}$
9. $B = \begin{bmatrix} -2 & -3 & -4 \\ -1 & -2 & -3 \end{bmatrix}$ 10. $A = \begin{bmatrix} 1 & 2 & 3 \\ 4 & 5 & 6 \\ 7 & 8 & 9 \end{bmatrix}$
11. (*i*) $x = -8, y = -8$ (*ii*) $x = 0, y = 0$
12. (*i*) $\begin{bmatrix} 3 & 6 & 9 \\ 9 & 12 & 15 \end{bmatrix}$ (*ii*) $\begin{bmatrix} 1 & 2 & 3 \\ 3 & 4 & 5 \end{bmatrix}$ (*iii*) $\begin{bmatrix} -3 & -4 & -5 \\ -5 & -6 & -7 \end{bmatrix}$

    (*iv*) $\begin{bmatrix} 3 & 8 & 13 \\ 13 & 18 & 23 \end{bmatrix}$ (*v*) $\begin{bmatrix} 8 & 14 & 18 \\ 20 & 26 & 32 \end{bmatrix}$
13. (*i*) $C = \begin{bmatrix} -5 & -7 \\ -9 & -11 \end{bmatrix}$ (*ii*) $C = \begin{bmatrix} \frac{5}{2} & \frac{7}{2} \\ \frac{9}{2} & \frac{11}{2} \end{bmatrix}$
14. $B = \begin{bmatrix} 1 & 0 & -2 \\ -2 & 3 & -4 \\ -3 & -1 & 2 \end{bmatrix}$ 15. $k_1 = 0 = k_2$
16. $\begin{bmatrix} 2 & 6 & 5 & 0 & 0 \\ 0 & 24 & 0 & 2 & 24 \\ 10 & 0 & 6 & 12 & 24 \end{bmatrix}$ 17. $\begin{bmatrix} 13 \\ 28 \\ 52 \end{bmatrix}$
18. 57 units of coal, 31 units of electricity and 30 units of steel.
19. $2A + 3B$ represents the total number of items of three types produced by two units if one unit works for 2 days and other unit works for 3 days.
20. (*i*) $\begin{bmatrix} 3 & 5 & 7 \\ 9 & 11 & 13 \\ 15 & 17 & 19 \end{bmatrix}$ (*ii*) $\begin{bmatrix} 0 & 0 & 0 \\ 0 & 0 & 0 \\ 0 & 0 & 0 \end{bmatrix}$

4. MULTIPLICATION OF MATRICES

The product AB of two matrices A and B is defined only when the number of columns of A is same as the number of rows in B and by definition the product AB is a matrix C of order $m \times p$ if A and B are of order $m \times n$ and $n \times p$ respectively. The following example will give the rule to multiply two matrices:

Let $A = \begin{bmatrix} a_1 & b_1 & c_1 \\ a_2 & b_2 & c_2 \end{bmatrix}$ $B = \begin{bmatrix} d_1 & e_1 \\ d_2 & e_2 \\ d_3 & e_3 \end{bmatrix}$

order of $A = 2 \times 3$, order of $B = 3 \times 2$

So, AB is defined and is the matrix

$$G = AB = \begin{bmatrix} a_1d_1 + b_1d_2 + c_1d_3 & a_1e_1 + b_1e_2 + c_1e_3 \\ a_2d_1 + b_2d_2 + c_2d_3 & a_2e_1 + b_2e_2 + c_2e_3 \end{bmatrix}$$

$$= \begin{bmatrix} g_{11} & g_{12} \\ g_{21} & g_{22} \end{bmatrix} \text{ where to get}$$

g_{11} : Multiply elements of the first row of A with corresponding elements of the first column of B and add.

g_{12} : Multiply elements of the first row of A with corresponding elements of the second column of B and add.

g_{21} : Multiply elements of the second row of A with corresponding elements of the first column of B and add.

g_{22} : Multiply elements of the second row of A with corresponding elements of the second column of B and add.

NOTES:

1. In general, if A and B are two matrices then AB may not be equal to BA. For example, if

$$A = \begin{bmatrix} 1 & 1 \\ 0 & 0 \end{bmatrix}, \; B = \begin{bmatrix} 1 & 0 \\ 0 & 0 \end{bmatrix} \quad \text{then } AB = \begin{bmatrix} 1 & 0 \\ 0 & 0 \end{bmatrix}$$

and $\quad BA = \begin{bmatrix} 1 & 1 \\ 0 & 0 \end{bmatrix}$. So, $AB \neq BA$.

2. If product AB is defined, then it is not necessary that BA must also be defined. For example, if A is of order 2×3 and B is of order 3×1, then clearly AB is defined but BA is not defined (as the number of columns of $B \neq$ the number of rows of A).

It can be easily verified that (whenever products are defined).

(*i*) $A(BC) = (AB)C$

(*ii*) $A(B + C) = AB + AC$

$(A + B)C = AC + BC$.

Example 11. *If* $A = \begin{bmatrix} 2 & -1 \\ 0 & 3 \end{bmatrix}$ *and* $B = \begin{bmatrix} 7 & 0 \\ -2 & -3 \end{bmatrix}$ *write down AB.*

Solution. $$AB = \begin{bmatrix} 2\times7+(-1)\times(-2) & 2\times0+(-1)\times(-3) \\ 0\times7+3\times(-2) & 0\times0+3\times(-3) \end{bmatrix}$$

$$= \begin{bmatrix} 16 & 3 \\ -6 & 9 \end{bmatrix}.$$

Example 12. *Verify the associative law A(BC) = (AB)C for the following* matrices.

$$A = \begin{bmatrix} -1 & 0 & 5 \\ 7 & -2 & 0 \end{bmatrix}, \quad B = \begin{bmatrix} -1 & 0 & 5 \\ 7 & -2 & 0 \end{bmatrix}, \quad C = \begin{bmatrix} -1 & -1 \\ 2 & 0 \\ 0 & 4 \end{bmatrix}$$

Solution. $$AB = \begin{bmatrix} 4 & -7 & 25 \\ 13 & 51 & 0 \end{bmatrix}$$

So, $$(AB)C = \begin{bmatrix} -18 & 96 \\ 89 & -13 \end{bmatrix}$$

Again, $$BC = \begin{bmatrix} 13 & -1 \\ 1 & 3 \\ -1 & 19 \end{bmatrix}$$

So, $$A(BC) = \begin{bmatrix} -18 & 96 \\ 89 & -13 \end{bmatrix}$$

Therefore, $A(BC) = (AB)C$.

Example 13. *If A is a square matrix, then A can be multiplied by itself. Define* $A^2 = A.\,A$ *(called power of a matrix). Compute* A^2 *for the following matrix:*

$$A = \begin{bmatrix} 1 & 0 \\ 3 & 4 \end{bmatrix}$$

Solution. $$A^2 = \begin{bmatrix} 1 & 0 \\ 3 & 4 \end{bmatrix}\begin{bmatrix} 1 & 0 \\ 3 & 4 \end{bmatrix} = \begin{bmatrix} 1 & 0 \\ 15 & 16 \end{bmatrix}$$

(Similarly, we can define $A^3, A^4, A^5, \ldots$ for any square matrix A.)

Example 14. *If* $A = \begin{bmatrix} 1 & 2 \\ -3 & 0 \end{bmatrix}$ *find* $A^2 + 3A + 5I$ *where I is unit matrix of order 2.*

Solution. $A^2 = \begin{bmatrix} 1 & 2 \\ -3 & 0 \end{bmatrix}\begin{bmatrix} 1 & 2 \\ -3 & 0 \end{bmatrix} = \begin{bmatrix} -5 & 2 \\ -3 & -6 \end{bmatrix}$

$$3A = \begin{bmatrix} 3 & 6 \\ -9 & 0 \end{bmatrix}$$

$$I = \begin{bmatrix} 1 & 0 \\ 0 & 1 \end{bmatrix}$$

So, $A^2 + 3A + I = \begin{bmatrix} 5 & 2 \\ -3 & -6 \end{bmatrix} + \begin{bmatrix} 3 & 7 \\ -9 & 0 \end{bmatrix} + \begin{bmatrix} 1 & 0 \\ 0 & 1 \end{bmatrix}$

$$= \begin{bmatrix} -1 & 8 \\ -12 & -5 \end{bmatrix}$$

Example 15. *If* $A = \begin{bmatrix} 0 & 1 \\ 1 & 0 \end{bmatrix}, B = \begin{bmatrix} 0 & -i \\ i & 0 \end{bmatrix}$

show that $AB = -BA$ *and* $A^2 = B^2 = I.$

Solution. Now $AB = \begin{bmatrix} 0 & 1 \\ 1 & 0 \end{bmatrix}\begin{bmatrix} 0 & -i \\ i & 0 \end{bmatrix} = \begin{bmatrix} i & 0 \\ 0 & -i \end{bmatrix}$

$$BA = \begin{bmatrix} 0 & -i \\ i & 0 \end{bmatrix}\begin{bmatrix} 0 & 1 \\ 1 & 0 \end{bmatrix} = \begin{bmatrix} -i & 0 \\ 0 & i \end{bmatrix}$$

So, $AB = -BA$

Also $A^2 = \begin{bmatrix} 0 & 1 \\ 1 & 0 \end{bmatrix}\begin{bmatrix} 0 & 1 \\ 1 & 0 \end{bmatrix} = \begin{bmatrix} 1 & 0 \\ 0 & 1 \end{bmatrix} = I$

$$B^2 = \begin{bmatrix} 0 & -i \\ i & 0 \end{bmatrix}\begin{bmatrix} 0 & -i \\ i & 0 \end{bmatrix} = \begin{bmatrix} 1 & 0 \\ 0 & 1 \end{bmatrix} = I$$

This proves the result.

Example 16. *In South Delhi there are 20 colleges and 50 schools. Each school and college has 1 peon, 5 clerks, 1 cashier. Each college, in addition has 1 accountant and 1 head-clerk. The monthly salary of each of them is as follows. Peon Rs. 150, clerk Rs. 250, cashier Rs. 300, accountant Rs. 350, head-clerk Rs. 400 using matrix notation find*

(i) *the total number of posts of each kind in schools and colleges taken together.*

(ii) *the total monthly salary bill of each school and college separately.*

(iii) *the total monthly salary bill of all the schools and colleges taken together.*

Solution. (*i*) Consider the row matrix of order 1×2

$$A = [20 \quad 50]$$

This represents number of colleges and schools in that order.

Let $$B = \begin{bmatrix} 1 & 5 & 1 & 1 & 1 \\ 1 & 5 & 1 & 0 & 0 \end{bmatrix}$$

where columns represent number of peons, clerks, cashiers, accountants, head-clerks while rows represent colleges and schools in that order.

Then $$AB = [70 \quad 350 \quad 70 \quad 20 \quad 20]$$

where first element represents total number of peons, second represents total number of clerks, third represents total number of cashiers, fourth represents total number of accountants and fifth element represents total number of head-clerks.

(*ii*) Let $$C = \begin{bmatrix} 150 \\ 250 \\ 300 \\ 350 \\ 400 \end{bmatrix}$$

where column matrixe represents monthly salary of peon, clerk, cashier, accountant and head-clerk in that order.

Then $$BC = \begin{bmatrix} 150 + 1250 + 300 + 350 + 400 \\ 150 + 1250 + 300 + 0 + 0 \end{bmatrix} = \begin{bmatrix} 2450 \\ 1700 \end{bmatrix}$$

Thus, total monthly salary bill of each college is Rs. 2450 and of each school is Rs. 1700.

(*iii*) Consider $$A(BC) = [2450 \times 20 + 50 \times 1700]$$
$$= [49000 + 85000] = [134000]$$

which gives the total monthly salary bill of schools and colleges.

Example 17. *A manufacturing unit produces three types of television sets A, B, C. The following matrix shows the sale of television sets in two different cities*:

$$\begin{matrix} A & B & C \end{matrix}$$
$$\begin{bmatrix} 400 & 300 & 200 \\ 300 & 200 & 100 \end{bmatrix}$$

If cost price of each set A, B, C is Rs. 1000, Rs. 2000, Rs. 3000 respectivley and selling price Rs. 1500, Rs. 3000, Rs. 4000 respectively, find the total profit using matrix algebra only.

Solution. Consider the product

$$[1000\ \ 2000\ \ 3000]\begin{bmatrix}400 & 300\\ 300 & 200\\ 200 & 100\end{bmatrix}$$

$$=[400\times1000+300\times2000+200\times3000\quad 300\times1000+200\times2000+100\times3000]$$

$$=[400000+600000+600000\quad 300000+400000+300000]$$

$$=[1600000+1000000]$$

Thus total money spent in producing the television sets is Rs. (1600000 1000000) is 2600000. Consider the product.

$$[1500\ \ 3000\ \ 4000]\begin{bmatrix}400 & 300\\ 300 & 200\\ 200 & 100\end{bmatrix}$$

$$=[600000+900000+800000\quad 450000+600000+400000]$$

$$=[2300000\quad 14500000]$$

Hence the total money obtained after selling the sets is Rs. [23,00,000, 14,50,000] *i.e.*, 37,50,000 and the total profit is Rs. 11,50,000.

Example 18. *The cost of manufacturing three types of motor cars is given below:*

Car	*Labour hrs.*	*Material used*	*Subcontracted work*
A	*40*	*100 units*	*50 units*
B	*80*	*150 units*	*80 units*
C	*100*	*250 units*	*100 units*

Labour cost £ 2 per hour, per unit material cost is 10 \$ and one unit of subcontracted work costs £ 1. Find the total cost of manufacturing 3000, 2000 and 1000 vehicles of type A, B, C respectively.

Solution. Consider the following matrices,

$$M=\begin{bmatrix}40 & 100 & 50\\ 80 & 150 & 80\\ 100 & 250 & 100\end{bmatrix}, N=\begin{bmatrix}2\\ 1/2\\ 1\end{bmatrix}$$

M represents labour hours, material used, subcontracted work for three types of cars *A*, *B*, *C* respectively.

Column matrix *N* represents labour cost per unit material cost and cost of subcontracted work

Then $MN = \begin{bmatrix} 180 \\ 315 \\ 425 \end{bmatrix}$

The column matrix represents cost of each car *A*, *B*, *C* in that order.

Let $\quad P = [3000 \quad 2000 \quad 1000]$

This row matrix *P* represents number of cars *A*, *B*, *C* to be manufactured in that order.

Consider $P(MN) = [15,95,000]$

Thus total cost of manufacturing three cars *A*, *B*, *C* is £ 15,95,000.

Example 19. *The following matrix shows the sale of cold drinks in a shop during one week from Monday to Sunday.*

$$A = \begin{array}{c} \begin{matrix} C & F & L \end{matrix} \\ \begin{bmatrix} 20 & 25 & 30 \\ 25 & 30 & 40 \\ 30 & 25 & 20 \\ 40 & 30 & 50 \\ 45 & 40 & 20 \\ 50 & 20 & 30 \\ 60 & 40 & 60 \end{bmatrix} \end{array}$$

where C = Coca-Cola, F = Fanta, L = Limca. The cost of each bottle of C, F, L is Re 1; Rs. 2, Rs. 3 respectively. Using matrix algebra only

(*i*) *find the total sale of C, F, L separately during one week,*

(*ii*) *find the total earning during one week.*

(*iii*) *find total sale of C, F, L taken together each day from Monday to Sunday.*

(*iv*) *find the total sale of C, F, L taken together during one week.*

Solution. Consider the product

$[1 \ 1 \ 1 \ 1 \ 1 \ 1 \ 1] \ A = [270 \quad 210 \quad 250]$

This represents the total sale of *C*, *F*, *L* separately during one week.

(*ii*) Consder the product

$$[270 \quad 210 \quad 250] \begin{bmatrix} 1 \\ 2 \\ 3 \end{bmatrix} \quad [270 + 420 + 750] = [1440].$$

Thus total earning during one week is Rs. 1440.

(*iii*) Consider the product

$$A\begin{bmatrix}1\\1\\1\end{bmatrix}=[75\ \ 95\ \ 75\ \ 120\ \ 105\ \ 100\ \ 160]$$

This gives the total sale of *C*, *F*, *L* taken together each day from Monday to Sunday.

(*iv*) Consider the product

$$[1\ \ 1\ \ 1\ \ 1\ \ 1\ \ 1\ \ 1]\,A\begin{bmatrix}1\\1\\1\end{bmatrix}=[270\ \ 210\ \ 250]\begin{bmatrix}1\\1\\1\end{bmatrix}$$
$$=[730]$$

Thus total sale of *C*, *F*, *L* taken together during one week is 730 bottles.

5. TRANSPOSE OF A MATRIX

Let *A* be a matrix. The matrix obtained from *A* by interchange of its rows and columns, is called the *transpose* of *A*. For example,

if $A=\begin{bmatrix}1 & 0 & 2\\2 & 1 & 0\end{bmatrix}$ then transpose of $A=\begin{bmatrix}1 & 2\\0 & 1\\2 & 0\end{bmatrix}$

Transpose of *A* is denoted by A'.

It can be easily verified that

(*i*) $(A')'=A$ (*ii*) $(A+B)'=A'+B'$ (*iii*) $(AB)'=B'A'$.

Example 20. *For the following matrices A and B verify* $(A+B)'=A'+B'$.

$$A=\begin{bmatrix}1 & 2 & 3\\4 & 5 & 6\end{bmatrix},\quad B=\begin{bmatrix}2 & 3 & 4\\1 & 8 & 6\end{bmatrix}$$

Solution. $A'=\begin{bmatrix}1 & 4\\2 & 5\\3 & 6\end{bmatrix}$ $B'=\begin{bmatrix}2 & 1\\3 & 8\\4 & 6\end{bmatrix}$

So, $A'+B'=\begin{bmatrix}3 & 5\\5 & 13\\7 & 12\end{bmatrix}$

Again $A+B=\begin{bmatrix}3 & 5 & 7\\ 5 & 13 & 12\end{bmatrix}$

So, $(A+B)'=\begin{bmatrix}3 & 5\\ 5 & 13\\ 7 & 12\end{bmatrix}$

Therefore $(A+B)'=A'+B'$.

EXERCISES

Find the product AB when

1. (*i*) $A=\begin{bmatrix}1 & 0 & 0\\ 0 & 1 & 0\\ 0 & 0 & 1\end{bmatrix}$, $B=\begin{bmatrix}1 & 1 & 2\\ 0 & 2 & 3\\ 4 & 5 & 6\end{bmatrix}$

   (*ii*) $A=\begin{bmatrix}2 & 0 & 0\\ 0 & 3 & 0\\ 0 & 0 & 4\end{bmatrix}$, $B=\begin{bmatrix}0 & 1 & 2\\ 1 & 0 & 2\\ 2 & 3 & 0\end{bmatrix}$

   (*iii*) $A=\begin{bmatrix}1 & 2 & 3\\ 4 & 5 & 6\end{bmatrix}$, $B=\begin{bmatrix}0 & 0 & 0\\ 0 & 0 & 0\\ 0 & 0 & 0\end{bmatrix}$

   (*iv*) $A=\begin{bmatrix}1 & i\\ -i & 1\end{bmatrix}$, $B=\begin{bmatrix}1 & i\\ -i & 1\end{bmatrix}$

2. If $A=\begin{bmatrix}1 & 0 & 0\\ 0 & 1 & 0\\ 0 & 0 & 1\end{bmatrix}$, show that $AA=A$.

3. If $A=\begin{bmatrix}-2 & 3 & -1\\ -1 & 2 & -1\\ -6 & 9 & -4\end{bmatrix}$, $B=\begin{bmatrix}1 & 3 & -1\\ 2 & 2 & -1\\ 3 & 0 & -1\end{bmatrix}$.

   show that $AB=BA$.

4. If $A=\begin{bmatrix}\cos\alpha & \sin\alpha\\ -\sin\alpha & \cos\alpha\end{bmatrix}$, $B=\begin{bmatrix}\cos\alpha & -\sin\alpha\\ \sin\alpha & \cos\alpha\end{bmatrix}$.

   show that $AB=\begin{bmatrix}1 & 0\\ 0 & 1\end{bmatrix}=BA$.

5. Find matrices A and B such that A and B are both non-zero matrices but the product AB is a zero matrix.
6. Is it necessary that if two matrices A and B are such that AB and BA are both defined and $AB=0$ then BA must also be a zero matrix?
7. If $A=\begin{bmatrix}2 & 5\\ 1 & 3\end{bmatrix}$ and $B=\begin{bmatrix}1 & -1\\ -3 & 2\end{bmatrix}$, find AB and BA. Is $AB=BA$?

8. Let $A = \begin{bmatrix} 1 & 1 \\ 0 & 1 \end{bmatrix}$

(*a*) Find a matrix B such that $AB = \begin{bmatrix} 1 & 0 \\ 0 & 1 \end{bmatrix}$.

(*b*) Find a matrix D such that $AD = \begin{bmatrix} 2 & 0 \\ 4 & 3 \end{bmatrix}$.

9. Consider the matrices

$$A = \begin{bmatrix} 0 & 1 & 0 \\ 0 & 0 & 1 \\ 1 & 0 & 0 \end{bmatrix}, \quad B = \begin{bmatrix} 0 & 0 & 1 \\ 1 & 0 & 0 \\ 0 & 1 & 0 \end{bmatrix}.$$

(*a*) Show that $A^2 = B$ and $A^3 = I$. What is A^4?

(*b*) Show that $B^2 = I$

(*c*) Show that $A^3 = BA = AB = B^3 = I$, hence A and B commute.

10. Show that the product of the matrices.

$$\begin{bmatrix} 0 & 2 & -3 \\ -3 & 0 & 4 \\ 3 & -4 & 0 \end{bmatrix} \quad \text{and} \quad \begin{bmatrix} 16 & 12 & 8 \\ 12 & 9 & 6 \\ 8 & 6 & 4 \end{bmatrix}$$

is the zero matrix.

11. Consider the matrices

$$A = \begin{bmatrix} 1 & 0 \\ 0 & 4 \end{bmatrix}, \quad B = \begin{bmatrix} 3 & 0 \\ 0 & 2 \end{bmatrix}$$

(*a*) Show that A and B commute.

(*b*) Show that any pair of diagonal matrices of the same order commute when multiplied together.

12. For the matrix

$$A = \begin{bmatrix} 0 & 1 & 0 & 0 \\ 0 & 0 & 1 & 0 \\ 0 & 0 & 0 & 1 \\ 1 & 0 & 0 & 0 \end{bmatrix}$$

What is the smallest positive integer k such that $A^k = I$.

13. Verify the associative law $A(BC) = (AB)C$ for the following matrices:

$$A = \begin{bmatrix} 1 & 1 & 1 \\ 2 & 2 & 2 \\ 3 & 3 & 3 \\ 0 & 0 & 0 \end{bmatrix}, \quad B = \begin{bmatrix} 1 & 0 & -1 \\ 0 & -1 & 1 \\ -1 & 1 & 0 \end{bmatrix}, \quad C = \begin{bmatrix} -1 & -1 \\ 2 & 2 \\ 1 & 1 \end{bmatrix}.$$

14. Verify the distributive law $A(B + C) = AB + AC$ and $(A + B)C = AC + BC$ for the matrices in Exercise 13.

15. Compute the transpose of the following matrices

(*i*) $\begin{bmatrix} 1 & 0 & 0 \\ 0 & 1 & 0 \\ 0 & 0 & 1 \end{bmatrix}$ (*ii*) $[1]$ (*iii*) $\begin{bmatrix} 1 \\ 2 \\ 3 \end{bmatrix}$ (*iv*) $[1 \quad 2 \quad 3]$

16. For each of the following matrices, show that $A + A' = 0$

$$(i)\ \begin{bmatrix} 0 & 1 & 4 \\ -1 & 0 & 7 \\ -4 & -7 & 0 \end{bmatrix} \quad (ii)\ \begin{bmatrix} 0 & 6 & -4 \\ -6 & 0 & 8 \\ 4 & -8 & 0 \end{bmatrix} \quad (iii)\ \begin{bmatrix} 0 & -1 & 2 \\ 1 & 0 & 5 \\ -2 & -5 & 0 \end{bmatrix}.$$

17. If $A = \begin{bmatrix} \cos\alpha & -\sin\alpha \\ \sin\alpha & \cos\alpha \end{bmatrix}$, show that $AA' = A'A = \begin{bmatrix} 1 & 0 \\ 0 & 1 \end{bmatrix}$.

18. If $A = \begin{pmatrix} 1 & 2 & 3 \end{pmatrix}$, $B = \begin{bmatrix} 4 \\ 5 \\ 6 \end{bmatrix}$.

verify $(AB)' = B'A'$.

19. If $A = \begin{bmatrix} 1 & 1 & 2 \\ 2 & 1 & 3 \end{bmatrix}$, $B = \begin{bmatrix} 1 & 3 & 4 \\ 5 & 6 & 7 \end{bmatrix}$

verify $(A + B)' = A' + B'$.

20. If $A = \begin{bmatrix} \cos\alpha & -\sin\alpha \\ \sin\alpha & \cos\alpha \end{bmatrix}$

verify $(A')' = A$.

21. Suppose a man named Smith goes into a grocery store to buy a dozen each of eggs and oranges, a half dozen each of apples and mangoes and three lemons. Suppose the apples are one rupee each, eggs are 40 paise each, lemons are 30 paise each, oranges are 50 paise each and mangoes are 70 paise each. What is the total amount that Smith must pay for his purchases? Use only matrix algebra.

22. The production of a book involves several steps: first it must be set in type, then it must be printed and finally it must be supplied with covers and bound. Suppose that typesetter charges Rs. 6 per hour, paper costs 1/4 paisa per sheet, that the printer charges 11 paise for each minute that his press runs, that the cover costs 28 paise, and the binder charges 15 paise to bind each book. Suppose now that a publisher wishes to print a book that requires 300 hours of work by the typesetter, 220 sheets of paper per book and five minutes of press time per book.

(*i*)Using matrix multiplication, find the cost of publishing one copy of the book.

(*ii*)Using matrix addition and multiplication find the cost of printing a first edition run of 5000 copies.

23. Suppose that a building contractor has accepted orders for five houses of type *I*, seven houses of type *II* and twelve houses of type *III*. The matrix below gives the amount of each raw material to be used in each type of house, expressed in convenient units.

$$R = \begin{array}{r} \\ \text{Type I} \\ \text{Type II} \\ \text{Type III} \end{array}\!\!\begin{array}{c} \begin{array}{ccccc} \text{Steel} & \text{Wood} & \text{Glass} & \text{Paint} & \text{Labour} \end{array} \\ \begin{bmatrix} 5 & 20 & 16 & 7 & 17 \\ 7 & 18 & 12 & 9 & 21 \\ 6 & 25 & 8 & 5 & 13 \end{bmatrix} \end{array}$$

Using matrix multiplication, find how much of each raw material the contractor should order.

24. In Exercise 23, if steel costs Rs. 15 per unit, wood costs Rs. 8 per unit, glass costs Rs. 5 per unit, paint costs Rs. 91 per unit and labour costs Rs. 10 per unit, find (using matrix algebra only)

    (*i*) the cost of materials for each type of house,

    (*ii*) the total cost of raw materials for all the houses he will build.

25. The following matrix gives the vitamin content of food items, in conveniently chosen units

    Vitamins:

$$\begin{array}{l} \\ \text{Food I} \\ \text{Food II} \\ \text{Food III} \end{array} \begin{array}{c} \begin{array}{cccc} \text{A} & \text{B} & \text{C} & \text{D} \end{array} \\ \begin{bmatrix} .5 & .5 & 0 & 0 \\ .3 & 0 & .2 & .1 \\ .1 & .1 & .2 & .5 \end{bmatrix} \end{array}$$

If we eat 5 units of food *I*, 10 units of food *II*, and 8 units of food *III*, how much of each type of vitamin we have consumed? If we pay only for the vitamin content of each food, paying 10 paise, 20 paise, 25 paise, 50 paise respectively for units of the four vitamins, how much does a unit of each type of food costs? Compute the total cost of the food eaten.

26. A company is considering which of three methods of production it should use in producing three goods *A*, *B* and *C*. The amount of each good produced by each method is shown in the matrix

$$R = \begin{array}{c} \begin{array}{ccc} A & B & C \end{array} \\ \begin{bmatrix} 2 & 3 & 1 \\ 1 & 2 & 3 \\ 2 & 4 & 1 \end{bmatrix} \end{array} \begin{array}{l} \\ \text{Method I} \\ \text{Method II} \\ \text{Method III} \end{array}$$

Let *P* be a 3 × 1 matrix whose components represent the profit per unit for each of the goods. What does the matrix *RP* represent? Find two different matrices *P* under which method 2 and method 3 are most profitable.

ANSWERS

1. (*i*) $\begin{bmatrix} 1 & 1 & 2 \\ 0 & 2 & 3 \\ 4 & 5 & 6 \end{bmatrix}$ (*ii*) $\begin{bmatrix} 0 & 2 & 4 \\ 3 & 0 & 6 \\ 8 & 12 & 0 \end{bmatrix}$ (*iii*) $\begin{bmatrix} 0 & 0 & 0 \\ 0 & 0 & 0 \end{bmatrix}$

   (*iv*) $\begin{bmatrix} 0 & 0 \\ 0 & 0 \end{bmatrix}$

5. $A = \begin{bmatrix} 0 & 0 \\ 0 & 1 \end{bmatrix}$ $B = \begin{bmatrix} 1 & 0 \\ 0 & 0 \end{bmatrix}$

6. No, $A = \begin{bmatrix} 0 & 1 \\ 0 & 1 \end{bmatrix}$, $B = \begin{bmatrix} 1 & 0 \\ 0 & 0 \end{bmatrix}$, $AB = O$, $BA \neq O$.

7. No

8. (*a*) $\begin{bmatrix} 1 & -1 \\ 0 & 1 \end{bmatrix}$ (*b*) $\begin{bmatrix} -2 & -3 \\ 4 & 3 \end{bmatrix}$

12. $R = 4$

21. Rs. 21/90

22. (*i*) Rs. 1801/53 (*ii*) Rs. 9450

23.
$$\begin{matrix} \text{steel} & \text{wood} & \text{glass} & \text{paint} & \text{labour} \\ [146 & 526 & 260 & 158 & 388] \end{matrix}$$

24. (*i*) For type *I* Rs. 492
    For type *II* Rs. 528
    For type *III* Rs. 465

25. [6.3, 3.3., 3.6, 5.0], $\begin{bmatrix} 15 \\ 13 \\ 33 \end{bmatrix}$, Rs. 4/69

26. *RP* is a 3 × 1 matrix whose components represent profit for goods *A*, *B*, *C* respectively
    $\begin{bmatrix} 1 \\ 2 \\ 3 \end{bmatrix}$ method 2 is most profitable
    $\begin{bmatrix} 10 \\ 8 \\ 7 \end{bmatrix}$ method 3 is most profitable

6. ELEMENTARY OPERATIONS

Consider the matrices

$$A = \begin{bmatrix} 1 & 2 & 3 \\ 4 & 5 & 6 \end{bmatrix}, \quad B = \begin{bmatrix} 4 & 5 & 6 \\ 1 & 2 & 3 \end{bmatrix}$$

Matrix *B* is obtained from *A* by interchange of first and second row.

$$\text{Consider } C = \begin{bmatrix} 2 & 1 & 3 \\ 3 & 4 & 5 \end{bmatrix}, \quad D = \begin{bmatrix} 6 & 3 & 9 \\ 3 & 4 & 5 \end{bmatrix}$$

Matrix *D* is obtained from *C* by multiplying first row by 3.

$$\text{Consider } E = \begin{bmatrix} 2 & 3 & 4 \\ 1 & 3 & 2 \end{bmatrix}, F = \begin{bmatrix} 2 & 3 & 4 \\ 7 & 12 & 14 \end{bmatrix}$$

Matrix *F* is obtained from *E* by multiplying first row of *E* by 3 and adding it to second row.

Such operations on rows of a matrix as described above are called *Elementary row operations.*

Similarly, we define *Elementary column operations.*

An elementary operation is either elementary row operation or elementary column operation and is of the following three types:

Type I. The interchange of any two rows (or column).

Type II. The multiplication of any row (or column) by a non-zero number.

Type III. The addition of multiple of one row (or column) to another row (or column).

We shall use the following notations for three types of Elementary operations.

The interchange of *i*th and *j*th rows (columns) will be denoted by $R_i \leftrightarrow R_j\,(C_i \leftrightarrow C_j)$.

The multiplication of *i*th row (column) by non-zero number *k* will be denoted by $R_i \to k\,R_i\,(C_i \to k\,C_i)$.

The addition of *k* times the *j*th row (column) to *i*th raw (column) will be denoted by $R_i \to R_i + kR_j\,(C_i \to C_i + kC_j)$.

7. ELEMENTARY MATRICES

A matrix obtained from identity matrix by a single elementary operation is called **Elementary matrix.**

$$\text{For example} \begin{bmatrix} 0 & 1 & 0 \\ 1 & 0 & 0 \\ 0 & 0 & 1 \end{bmatrix}, \begin{bmatrix} 2 & 0 & 0 \\ 0 & 1 & 0 \\ 0 & 0 & 1 \end{bmatrix}$$

are elementary matrices, the first is obtained by $R_1 \leftrightarrow R_2$ and the second by $C_1 \to 2C_1$ on the identity matrix.

We state the following result without proof:

"*An elementary row operation on product of two matrices is equivalent to elementary row operation on prefactor.*"

It means that if we make elementary row operation in the product *AB*, then it is equivalent to making same elementary row operation in *A* and then multiplying it with *B*.

$$\text{Let } A = \begin{bmatrix} 1 & 2 & 3 \\ 2 & 3 & 4 \end{bmatrix}, \quad B = \begin{bmatrix} 1 & 2 \\ 1 & 1 \\ 2 & 3 \end{bmatrix}$$

$$\text{Then } AB = \begin{bmatrix} 9 & 13 \\ 13 & 19 \end{bmatrix}$$

Suppose we interchange first and second row of *AB*.
Then the matrix we get is

$$C = \begin{bmatrix} 13 & 19 \\ 9 & 13 \end{bmatrix}$$

Now interchange first and second row of A and get new matrix

$$D = \begin{bmatrix} 2 & 3 & 4 \\ 1 & 2 & 3 \end{bmatrix}$$

Multiply D with B to get

$$DB = \begin{bmatrix} 2 & 3 & 4 \\ 1 & 2 & 3 \end{bmatrix} \begin{bmatrix} 1 & 2 \\ 1 & 1 \\ 2 & 3 \end{bmatrix} = \begin{bmatrix} 13 & 19 \\ 9 & 13 \end{bmatrix}$$

So, $\quad DB = C.$

8. REDUCTION OF A MATRIX TO ECHELON FORM

Consider $A = \begin{bmatrix} 1 & 2 & 3 & 4 \\ 2 & 1 & 3 & 2 \\ 3 & 1 & 2 & 4 \end{bmatrix}$

Apply the following elementary row operations on A.

$$R_2 \to R_2 - 2R_1, \quad R_3 \to R_3 - 3R_1$$

and obtain a new matrix.

$$B = \begin{bmatrix} 1 & 2 & 3 & 4 \\ 0 & -3 & -3 & -6 \\ 0 & -5 & -7 & -8 \end{bmatrix}$$

Apply $\quad R_2 \to -\frac{1}{3} R_2$ on B to get

$$C = \begin{bmatrix} 1 & 2 & 3 & 4 \\ 0 & 1 & 1 & 2 \\ 0 & -5 & -7 & -8 \end{bmatrix}$$

Apply $\quad R_3 \to R_3 + 5R_2$ on C to get

$$D = \begin{bmatrix} 1 & 2 & 3 & 4 \\ 0 & 1 & 1 & 2 \\ 0 & 0 & -2 & 2 \end{bmatrix}$$

The matrix D is in *Echelon form* (*i.e.*, elements below the diagonal are zero).

We thus find elementary row operations reduce Matrix A to Echelon form.

In fact, *any matrix can be reduced to Echelon form by elementary row operations.* The procedure is as follows:

Step I. Reduce the element in (1, 1)th place to unity by some suitable elementary row operation.

Step II. Reduce all the elements in 1st column below 1st row to zero with the help of unity obtained in first step.

Step III. Reduce the element in (2, 2)th place to unity by suitable elementary row operations.

Step IV. Reduce all the elements in 2nd column below 2nd row to zero with the help of unity obtained in Step *III*.

Proceeding in this way, any matrix can be reduced to the Echelon form.

Example 21. *Reduce* $A = \begin{bmatrix} 3 & -10 & 5 \\ -1 & 12 & -2 \\ 1 & -5 & 2 \end{bmatrix}$ *to Echelon form.*

Step I. Apply $R_1 \leftrightarrow R_3$ to get

$$\begin{bmatrix} 1 & -5 & 2 \\ -1 & 12 & -2 \\ 3 & -10 & 5 \end{bmatrix}$$

Step II. Apply $R_2 \to R_2 + R_1, R_3 \to R_3 - 3R_1$ to get

$$\begin{bmatrix} 1 & -5 & 2 \\ 0 & 7 & 0 \\ 0 & 5 & -1 \end{bmatrix}$$

Step III. Apply $R_2 \to \frac{1}{7} R_2$ to get

$$\begin{bmatrix} 1 & -5 & 2 \\ 0 & 1 & 0 \\ 0 & 5 & -1 \end{bmatrix}$$

Step IV. Apply $R_3 \to R_3 - 5R_2$ to get

$$\begin{bmatrix} 1 & -5 & 2 \\ 0 & 1 & 0 \\ 0 & 0 & -1 \end{bmatrix}$$ which is a matrix in Echelon form.

Example 22. *Reduce* $A = \begin{bmatrix} 2 & 2 & 4 & 4 \\ 2 & 3 & 4 & 5 \\ 3 & 4 & 5 & 6 \\ 4 & 5 & 6 & 7 \end{bmatrix}$ *to Echelon form.*

Step I. Apply $R_1 \to \frac{1}{2} R_1$ to get

$$\begin{bmatrix} 1 & 1 & 2 & 2 \\ 2 & 3 & 4 & 5 \\ 3 & 4 & 5 & 6 \\ 4 & 5 & 6 & 7 \end{bmatrix}$$

Step II. Apply $R_2 \to R_2 - 2R_1, R_3 \to R_3 - 3R_1, R_4 \to R_4 - 4R_1$ to get

$$\begin{bmatrix} 1 & 1 & 2 & 2 \\ 0 & 1 & 0 & 1 \\ 0 & 1 & -1 & 0 \\ 0 & 1 & -2 & -1 \end{bmatrix}$$

Step III. (2, 2)th place is already unity.

Step IV. Apply $R_3 \to R_3 - R_2, R_4 \to R_4 - R_2$ to get

$$\begin{bmatrix} 1 & 1 & 2 & 2 \\ 0 & 1 & 0 & 1 \\ 0 & 1 & -1 & -1 \\ 0 & 0 & -2 & -2 \end{bmatrix}$$

Step V. Apply $R_3 \to (-1) R_3$ to get

$$\begin{bmatrix} 1 & 1 & 2 & 2 \\ 0 & 1 & 0 & 1 \\ 0 & 0 & 1 & 1 \\ 0 & 0 & -2 & -2 \end{bmatrix}$$

Step VI. Apply $R_4 \to R_4 + 2R_3$ to get

$$\begin{bmatrix} 1 & 1 & 2 & 2 \\ 0 & 1 & 0 & 1 \\ 0 & 0 & 1 & 1 \\ 0 & 0 & 0 & 0 \end{bmatrix}$$

which is a matrix in Echelon form.

Example 23. *Reduce* $A = \begin{bmatrix} 0 & 1 & 2 & 3 \\ 0 & 2 & 6 & 4 \\ 0 & 3 & 9 & 3 \\ 0 & 4 & 13 & 4 \end{bmatrix}$ *to Echelon form.*

Step I. Since all the elements in 1st column are zero Step *I* and Step *II* are not needed.

Step III. Apply $R_2 \to \frac{1}{2} R_2$ to get

$$\begin{bmatrix} 0 & 1 & 2 & 3 \\ 0 & 1 & 3 & 2 \\ 0 & 3 & 9 & 3 \\ 0 & 4 & 13 & 4 \end{bmatrix}$$

Step IV. Apply $R_3 \to R_2 - 3R_2, R_4 \to R_4 - 4R_2$ to get

$$\begin{bmatrix} 0 & 1 & 2 & 3 \\ 0 & 1 & 3 & 2 \\ 0 & 0 & 0 & -3 \\ 0 & 0 & 1 & -4 \end{bmatrix}$$

Step V. Apply $R_3 \leftrightarrow R_4$ to get

$$\begin{bmatrix} 0 & 1 & 2 & 3 \\ 0 & 1 & 3 & 2 \\ 0 & 0 & 1 & -4 \\ 0 & 0 & 0 & -3 \end{bmatrix}.$$

Step VI. Since elements below (3, 3)rd place are zero. Step *VI* is not needed.

Hence A is reduced to Echelon form.

EXERCISES

1. Apply the elementary row operation $R_1 \leftrightarrow R_3$ in each of the following matrices:

   (*i*) $\begin{bmatrix} 1 & 2 & 3 & 4 \\ 5 & 6 & 7 & 8 \\ 6 & 7 & 8 & 9 \end{bmatrix}$ (*ii*) $\begin{bmatrix} 1 \\ 2 \\ 3 \end{bmatrix}$ (*iii*) $\begin{bmatrix} 1 & 0 & 0 \\ 0 & 1 & 0 \\ 1 & 0 & 0 \end{bmatrix}$.

2. Apply the elementary row operation $R_1 \to 2R_1$ to each of the matrices in Question 1.

3. Apply the elementary row operation $R_2 \to R_2 + R_1 + R_3$ in each of the matrices in Question 1.

4. Let $A = \begin{bmatrix} 2 & -1 & 4 \\ -2 & 1 & 0 \end{bmatrix}$, $B = \begin{bmatrix} 1 & 2 & 3 \\ -1 & 0 & 1 \\ 0 & 1 & 2 \end{bmatrix}$

   verify that each of the following elementary row operation on AB is equivalent to the same elementary row operation on the pre-factor A.

   (*i*) $R_1 \leftrightarrow R_2$ (*ii*) $R_2 \to 2R_2$ (*iii*) $R_1 \to R_1 + R_2$.

5. Reduce each of the matrices given below to the Echelon form

(i) $\begin{bmatrix} 2 & 0 & -1 \\ 5 & 1 & 0 \\ 0 & 1 & 3 \end{bmatrix}$ (ii) $\begin{bmatrix} 1 & -1 & 1 \\ 4 & 1 & 0 \\ 8 & 1 & 1 \end{bmatrix}$

(iii) $\begin{bmatrix} -1 & -3 & 3 & -1 \\ 1 & 1 & -1 & 0 \\ 2 & -5 & 2 & -3 \\ -1 & 1 & 0 & 1 \end{bmatrix}$ (iv) $\begin{bmatrix} -1 & 0 & -2 & 2 \\ -2 & 1 & 0 & 1 \\ 1 & 0 & 2 & -1 \\ -4 & 1 & -3 & 1 \end{bmatrix}$

(v) $\begin{bmatrix} 1 & 2 & 3 \\ 2 & 3 & 4 \\ 3 & 4 & 5 \\ 4 & 5 & 6 \end{bmatrix}$ (vi) $\begin{bmatrix} 1 & -1 & 3 & 6 \\ 1 & 3 & -3 & -4 \\ 5 & 3 & 3 & 11 \end{bmatrix}$

(vii) $\begin{bmatrix} 2 & 3 & -1 & -1 \\ 1 & -1 & -2 & -4 \\ 3 & 1 & 3 & -2 \\ 6 & 3 & 0 & -7 \end{bmatrix}$ (viii) $\begin{bmatrix} 3 & 2 & -1 & 5 \\ 5 & 1 & 4 & -2 \\ 1 & -4 & 11 & -19 \end{bmatrix}$

(ix) $\begin{bmatrix} 1 & 2 & 1 \\ -1 & 0 & 2 \\ 2 & 1 & -3 \end{bmatrix}$ (x) $\begin{bmatrix} 1 & 3 & 3 \\ 1 & 4 & 3 \\ 1 & 3 & 4 \end{bmatrix}$

ANSWERS

1. (i) $\begin{bmatrix} 6 & 7 & 8 & 9 \\ 5 & 6 & 7 & 8 \\ 1 & 2 & 3 & 4 \end{bmatrix}$ (ii) $\begin{bmatrix} 3 \\ 2 \\ 1 \end{bmatrix}$ (iii) $\begin{bmatrix} 1 & 0 & 0 \\ 0 & 1 & 0 \\ 1 & 0 & 0 \end{bmatrix}$

2. (i) $\begin{bmatrix} 2 & 4 & 6 & 8 \\ 5 & 6 & 7 & 8 \\ 6 & 7 & 8 & 9 \end{bmatrix}$ (ii) $\begin{bmatrix} 2 \\ 2 \\ 3 \end{bmatrix}$ (iii) $\begin{bmatrix} 2 & 0 & 0 \\ 0 & 1 & 0 \\ 1 & 0 & 0 \end{bmatrix}$

3. (i) $\begin{bmatrix} 1 & 2 & 3 & 4 \\ 12 & 15 & 18 & 21 \\ 6 & 7 & 8 & 9 \end{bmatrix}$ (ii) $\begin{bmatrix} 1 \\ 6 \\ 3 \end{bmatrix}$ (iii) $\begin{bmatrix} 1 & 0 & 0 \\ 2 & 1 & 0 \\ 1 & 0 & 0 \end{bmatrix}$

5. (i) $\begin{bmatrix} 1 & 0 & -\frac{1}{2} \\ 0 & 1 & \frac{5}{2} \\ 0 & 0 & \frac{1}{2} \end{bmatrix}$ (ii) $\begin{bmatrix} 1 & -1 & 1 \\ 0 & 1 & -\frac{1}{5} \\ 0 & 0 & \frac{1}{5} \end{bmatrix}$

$$(iii)\ \begin{bmatrix} 1 & 1 & -1 & 0 \\ 0 & 1 & -1 & \frac{1}{2} \\ 0 & 0 & 1 & -\frac{1}{6} \\ 0 & 0 & 0 & \frac{1}{6} \end{bmatrix} \quad (iv)\ \begin{bmatrix} 1 & 0 & 2 & -1 \\ 0 & 1 & 4 & -1 \\ 0 & 0 & 1 & -2 \\ 0 & 0 & 0 & 1 \end{bmatrix} \quad (v)\ \begin{bmatrix} 1 & 2 & 3 \\ 0 & 1 & 2 \\ 0 & 0 & 0 \\ 0 & 0 & 0 \end{bmatrix}$$

$$(vi)\ \begin{bmatrix} 1 & -1 & 3 & 6 \\ 0 & 1 & -\frac{3}{2} & -\frac{5}{2} \\ 0 & 0 & 0 & 1 \end{bmatrix} \quad (vii)\ \begin{bmatrix} 1 & -1 & -2 & -4 \\ 0 & 1 & \frac{3}{5} & \frac{7}{5} \\ 0 & 0 & 1 & \frac{2}{3} \\ 0 & 0 & 0 & 0 \end{bmatrix}$$

$$(viii)\ \begin{bmatrix} 1 & -4 & 11 & -19 \\ 0 & 1 & -\frac{17}{7} & \frac{31}{7} \\ 0 & 0 & 0 & 0 \end{bmatrix} \quad (ix)\ \begin{bmatrix} 1 & 2 & 1 \\ 0 & 1 & \frac{3}{2} \\ 0 & 0 & -\frac{1}{2} \end{bmatrix} \quad (x)\ \begin{bmatrix} 1 & 3 & 3 \\ 0 & 1 & 0 \\ 0 & 0 & 1 \end{bmatrix}$$

9. SYSTEM OF LINEAR EQUATIONS

In this section we discuss a method to solve a system of linear equations with the help of elementary operations.

Consider the equations

$$a_{11}x + a_{12}y + a_{13}z = b_{11}$$
$$a_{21}x + a_{22}y + a_{23}z = b_{12}$$
$$a_{31}x + a_{32}y + a_{33}z = b_{13}$$

These equations can also be expressed as

$$\begin{bmatrix} a_{11} & a_{12} & a_{13} \\ a_{21} & a_{22} & a_{23} \\ a_{31} & a_{32} & a_{33} \end{bmatrix} \begin{bmatrix} x \\ y \\ z \end{bmatrix} = \begin{bmatrix} b_{11} \\ b_{12} \\ b_{13} \end{bmatrix} \text{ i.e. } AX = B$$

where A is the matrix obtained by writing the coefficients of x, y, z in three rows respectively, and B is the column matrix consisting of constants in RHS of given equations.

We reduce the matrix A to Echelon form and write the equations in the form stated earlier, and then solve. This will be made clear in the following examples. A system of equations is called *consistent* if and only if there exists a common solution to all of them, otherwise it is called *inconsistent*.

Example 24. *Solve the system of equations*

$$x - 3y + z = -1$$
$$2x + y - 4z = -1$$
$$6x - 7y + 8z = 7.$$

Solution. Let $A = \begin{bmatrix} 1 & -3 & 1 \\ 2 & 1 & -4 \\ 6 & -7 & 8 \end{bmatrix}$ $B = \begin{bmatrix} -1 \\ -1 \\ 7 \end{bmatrix}$

and assume that there exists a matrix

$$X = \begin{bmatrix} x \\ y \\ z \end{bmatrix}$$

Such that given system of equations becomes

$$AX = B$$

Then $$\begin{bmatrix} 1 & -3 & 1 \\ 2 & 1 & -4 \\ 6 & -7 & 8 \end{bmatrix} \begin{bmatrix} x \\ y \\ z \end{bmatrix} = \begin{bmatrix} -1 \\ -1 \\ 7 \end{bmatrix}$$

Apply $R_2 \to R_2 - 2R_1, R_3 \to R_3 - 6R_1$

$$\begin{bmatrix} 1 & -3 & 1 \\ 0 & 7 & -6 \\ 0 & 11 & 2 \end{bmatrix} \begin{bmatrix} x \\ y \\ z \end{bmatrix} = \begin{bmatrix} -1 \\ 1 \\ 13 \end{bmatrix}$$

Apply $R_2 \to \frac{1}{7} R_2$

$$\begin{bmatrix} 1 & -3 & 1 \\ 0 & 1 & -\frac{6}{7} \\ 0 & 11 & 2 \end{bmatrix} \begin{bmatrix} x \\ y \\ z \end{bmatrix} = \begin{bmatrix} -1 \\ \frac{1}{7} \\ 13 \end{bmatrix}$$

Apply $R_3 \to R_3 - 11R_2$

$$\begin{bmatrix} 1 & -3 & 1 \\ 0 & 1 & -\frac{6}{7} \\ 0 & 0 & \frac{80}{7} \end{bmatrix} \begin{bmatrix} x \\ y \\ z \end{bmatrix} = \begin{bmatrix} -1 \\ \frac{1}{7} \\ \frac{80}{7} \end{bmatrix}$$

Thus we have reduced coefficient matrix A to Echelon form. Note that each elementary row operation that we applied on A, was also applied on B simultaneously.

From the last matrix equation we have

$$x - 3y + z = -1$$
$$y - \frac{6}{7}z = \frac{1}{7}$$
$$\frac{80}{7}z = \frac{80}{7}$$

So, $z = 1, y = 1, x = 1$.

Hence given system of equations has a solution $(x = 1, y = 1, z = 1)$.

Example 25. *Solve the system of equations*

$$2x - 5y + 7z = 6$$
$$x - 3y + 4z = 3$$
$$3x - 8y + 11z = 11 \text{ if consistent}$$

Solution. Let $A = \begin{bmatrix} 2 & -5 & 7 \\ 1 & -3 & 4 \\ 3 & -8 & 11 \end{bmatrix}, B = \begin{bmatrix} 6 \\ 3 \\ 11 \end{bmatrix}$

So, given system of equations can be written as

$$\begin{bmatrix} 2 & -5 & 7 \\ 1 & -3 & 4 \\ 3 & -8 & 11 \end{bmatrix}\begin{bmatrix} x \\ y \\ z \end{bmatrix} = \begin{bmatrix} 6 \\ 3 \\ 11 \end{bmatrix}$$

Apply $R_1 \leftrightarrow R_2$

$$\begin{bmatrix} 1 & -3 & 4 \\ 2 & -5 & 7 \\ 3 & -8 & 11 \end{bmatrix}\begin{bmatrix} x \\ y \\ z \end{bmatrix} = \begin{bmatrix} 3 \\ 6 \\ 11 \end{bmatrix}$$

Apply $R_2 \to R_2 - 2R_1, R_3 - 3R_1$

$$\begin{bmatrix} 1 & -3 & 4 \\ 0 & 1 & -1 \\ 0 & 1 & -1 \end{bmatrix}\begin{bmatrix} x \\ y \\ z \end{bmatrix} = \begin{bmatrix} 3 \\ 0 \\ 2 \end{bmatrix}$$

Apply $R_3 \to R_3 - R_2$

$$\begin{bmatrix} 1 & -3 & 4 \\ 0 & 1 & -1 \\ 0 & 0 & 0 \end{bmatrix}\begin{bmatrix} x \\ y \\ z \end{bmatrix} = \begin{bmatrix} 3 \\ 0 \\ 2 \end{bmatrix}$$

$$\Rightarrow \quad \begin{aligned} x - 3y + 4z &= 3 \\ y - z &= 0 \\ 0 &= 2 \end{aligned}$$

Since $0 = 2$ is false, the given system of equations has no solution. So given system of equations is inconsistent.

Example 26. *Solve the system of equations*

$$\begin{aligned} x + y + z &= 7 \\ x + 2y + 3z &= 16 \\ x + 3y + 4z &= 22. \end{aligned}$$

Solution. Given system of equations in matrix form

$$\begin{bmatrix} 1 & 1 & 1 \\ 1 & 2 & 3 \\ 1 & 3 & 4 \end{bmatrix} \begin{bmatrix} x \\ y \\ z \end{bmatrix} = \begin{bmatrix} 7 \\ 16 \\ 22 \end{bmatrix}$$

Apply $R_2 \to R_2 - R_1, R_3 \to R_3 - R_1$

$$\begin{bmatrix} 1 & 1 & 1 \\ 0 & 1 & 2 \\ 0 & 2 & 3 \end{bmatrix} \begin{bmatrix} x \\ y \\ z \end{bmatrix} = \begin{bmatrix} 7 \\ 9 \\ 15 \end{bmatrix}$$

Apply $R_3 \to R_3 - 2R_1$

$$\begin{bmatrix} 1 & 1 & 1 \\ 0 & 1 & 2 \\ 0 & 0 & -1 \end{bmatrix} \begin{bmatrix} x \\ y \\ z \end{bmatrix} = \begin{bmatrix} 7 \\ 9 \\ -3 \end{bmatrix}$$

$$\Rightarrow \quad \begin{aligned} x + y + z &= 7 \\ y + 2z &= 9 \\ z &= 3 \end{aligned}$$

So, $z = 3, y = 3, x = 1$

The given system of equations has a solution (1, 3, 3).

Example 27. *Solve the system of equations*

$$\begin{aligned} x + y + z &= 2 \\ x + 2y + 3z &= 5 \\ x + 3y + 6z &= 11 \\ x + 4y + 10z &= 21. \end{aligned}$$

Solution. We have

$$\begin{bmatrix} 1 & 1 & 1 \\ 1 & 2 & 3 \\ 1 & 3 & 6 \\ 1 & 4 & 10 \end{bmatrix} \begin{bmatrix} x \\ y \\ z \end{bmatrix} = \begin{bmatrix} 2 \\ 5 \\ 11 \\ 21 \end{bmatrix}$$

Apply $R_2 \to R_2 - R_1, R_3 \to R_3 - R_1, R_4 \to R_4 - R_1$

Then $$\begin{bmatrix} 1 & 1 & 1 \\ 0 & 1 & 2 \\ 0 & 2 & 5 \\ 0 & 3 & 9 \end{bmatrix} \begin{bmatrix} x \\ y \\ z \end{bmatrix} = \begin{bmatrix} 2 \\ 3 \\ 9 \\ 19 \end{bmatrix}$$

Apply $R_3 \to R_3 - 2R_2, R_4 \to R_4 - 3R_2$

$$\begin{bmatrix} 1 & 1 & 1 \\ 0 & 1 & 2 \\ 0 & 0 & 1 \\ 0 & 0 & 3 \end{bmatrix} \begin{bmatrix} x \\ y \\ z \end{bmatrix} = \begin{bmatrix} 2 \\ 3 \\ 3 \\ 10 \end{bmatrix}$$

Apply $R_4 \to R_4 - 3R_3$

$$\begin{bmatrix} 1 & 1 & 1 \\ 0 & 1 & 2 \\ 0 & 0 & 1 \\ 0 & 0 & 0 \end{bmatrix} \begin{bmatrix} x \\ y \\ z \end{bmatrix} = \begin{bmatrix} 2 \\ 3 \\ 3 \\ 1 \end{bmatrix}$$

$\Rightarrow \quad x + y + z = 2, y + 2z = 3, z = 3, 0 = 1.$

This is absurd. So the given system is inconsistent.

Example 28. *Solve* $x - 3y - 3z = -10$

$3x + y - 4z = 0$

$2x + 5y + 6z = 13.$

Solution. We have

$$\begin{bmatrix} 1 & -3 & -8 \\ 3 & 1 & -4 \\ 2 & 5 & 6 \end{bmatrix} \begin{bmatrix} x \\ y \\ z \end{bmatrix} = \begin{bmatrix} -10 \\ 0 \\ 13 \end{bmatrix}$$

Apply $R_2 \to R_2 - 3R_1, R_3 \to R_3 - 2R_1$

$$\begin{bmatrix} 1 & -3 & -8 \\ 0 & 10 & 20 \\ 0 & 11 & 22 \end{bmatrix} \begin{bmatrix} x \\ y \\ z \end{bmatrix} = \begin{bmatrix} -10 \\ 30 \\ 33 \end{bmatrix}$$

Apply $R_2 \to \frac{1}{10} R_2$

$$\begin{bmatrix} 1 & -3 & -8 \\ 0 & 1 & 2 \\ 0 & 11 & 22 \end{bmatrix} \begin{bmatrix} x \\ y \\ z \end{bmatrix} = \begin{bmatrix} -10 \\ 3 \\ 33 \end{bmatrix}$$

Apply $R_3 \to R_3 - 11R_2$

$$\begin{bmatrix} 1 & -3 & -8 \\ 0 & 1 & 2 \\ 0 & 0 & 0 \end{bmatrix} \begin{bmatrix} x \\ y \\ z \end{bmatrix} = \begin{bmatrix} -10 \\ 3 \\ 0 \end{bmatrix}$$

$$\Rightarrow \qquad x - 3y - 8z = -10$$

$$y + 2z = 3$$

Let $\qquad z = k \Rightarrow y = 3 - 2k$ and $x = 9 - 6k + 8k - 10 = 2k - 1$

So, given system has infinite number of solutions of the form $x = 2k - 1, y = 3 - 2k, z = k$ where k is any number.

Example 29. *Solve* $x + 2y + 3z + 4w = 0$

$$8x + 5y + z + 4w = 0$$

$$5x + 6y + 8z + w = 0$$

$$8x + 3y + 7z + 2w = 0.$$

Solution. We have

$$\begin{bmatrix} 1 & 2 & 3 & 4 \\ 8 & 5 & 1 & 4 \\ 5 & 6 & 8 & 1 \\ 8 & 3 & 7 & 2 \end{bmatrix} \begin{bmatrix} x \\ y \\ z \\ w \end{bmatrix} = \begin{bmatrix} 0 \\ 0 \\ 0 \\ 0 \end{bmatrix}$$

Apply $R_2 \to R_2 - 8R_1, R_3 \to R_3 - 5R_1, R_4 \to R_4 - 8R_1$

$$\Rightarrow \quad \begin{bmatrix} 1 & 2 & 3 & 4 \\ 0 & -11 & -23 & -28 \\ 0 & -4 & -7 & -19 \\ 0 & -13 & -17 & -30 \end{bmatrix} \begin{bmatrix} x \\ y \\ z \\ w \end{bmatrix} = \begin{bmatrix} 0 \\ 0 \\ 0 \\ 0 \end{bmatrix}$$

Apply $R_2 \to -\frac{1}{11} R_2$

$$\Rightarrow \quad \begin{bmatrix} 1 & 2 & 3 & 4 \\ 0 & 1 & \frac{23}{11} & \frac{28}{11} \\ 0 & -4 & -7 & -19 \\ 0 & -13 & -17 & -30 \end{bmatrix} \begin{bmatrix} x \\ y \\ z \\ w \end{bmatrix} = \begin{bmatrix} 0 \\ 0 \\ 0 \\ 0 \end{bmatrix}$$

Apply $R_3 \to R_3 + 4R_2, R_4 \to R_4 + 13R_2$

$$\Rightarrow \begin{bmatrix} 1 & 2 & 3 & 4 \\ 0 & 1 & \frac{23}{11} & \frac{28}{11} \\ 0 & 0 & \frac{15}{11} & -\frac{97}{11} \\ 0 & 0 & \frac{112}{11} & \frac{34}{11} \end{bmatrix} \begin{bmatrix} x \\ y \\ z \\ w \end{bmatrix} = \begin{bmatrix} 0 \\ 0 \\ 0 \\ 0 \end{bmatrix}$$

Apply $R_3 \to \frac{11}{15} R_3$

$$\Rightarrow \begin{bmatrix} 1 & 2 & 3 & 4 \\ 0 & 1 & \frac{23}{11} & \frac{28}{11} \\ 0 & 0 & 1 & -\frac{97}{15} \\ 0 & 0 & \frac{112}{11} & \frac{34}{11} \end{bmatrix} \begin{bmatrix} x \\ y \\ z \\ w \end{bmatrix} = \begin{bmatrix} 0 \\ 0 \\ 0 \\ 0 \end{bmatrix}$$

Apply $R_4 = -\frac{112}{11} R_3$

$$\Rightarrow \begin{bmatrix} 1 & 2 & 3 & 4 \\ 0 & 1 & \frac{23}{11} & \frac{28}{11} \\ 0 & 0 & 1 & \frac{97}{15} \\ 0 & 0 & 0 & \frac{11374}{165} \end{bmatrix} \begin{bmatrix} x \\ y \\ z \\ w \end{bmatrix} = \begin{bmatrix} 0 \\ 0 \\ 0 \\ 0 \end{bmatrix}$$

$$\Rightarrow \begin{aligned} x + 2y + 3z + 4w &= 0 \\ y + \frac{23}{11} z + \frac{28}{11} w &= 0 \\ z - \frac{97}{15} w &= 0 \\ w &= 0 \end{aligned}$$

$\Rightarrow \quad x = 0, y = 0, z = 0, w = 0.$

Thus system has only one solution, namely $x = y = z = w = 0$.

10. GAUSS ELIMINATION METHOD

Suppose, we have a system of equations in the matrix form $AX = B$, where,

$$A = \begin{bmatrix} a_1 & b_1 & c_1 \\ a_2 & b_2 & c_2 \\ a_3 & b_3 & c_3 \end{bmatrix}, \; X = \begin{bmatrix} x \\ y \\ z \end{bmatrix}, \; B = \begin{bmatrix} d_1 \\ d_2 \\ d_3 \end{bmatrix}$$

The matrix

$$C = [A \mid B] = \left[\begin{array}{ccc|c} a_1 & b_1 & c_1 & d_1 \\ a_2 & b_2 & c_2 & d_2 \\ a_3 & b_3 & c_3 & d_3 \end{array}\right]$$

is called the augmented matrix of the given system of equations. Instead of writing the whole equation $AX = B$ and making elementary row transformations to it, we sometimes, work only on the augmented matrix and apply these operations on this matrix to get the solution. We explain this method by considering Example 26 done earlier. We have the system of equations

$$x + y + z = 7$$
$$x + 2y + 3z = 16$$
$$x + 3y + 4z = 22$$

which in the matrix form will be $AX = B$, where,

$$A = \begin{bmatrix} 1 & 1 & 1 \\ 1 & 2 & 3 \\ 1 & 3 & 4 \end{bmatrix}, \; X = \begin{bmatrix} x \\ y \\ z \end{bmatrix}, \; B = \begin{bmatrix} 7 \\ 16 \\ 22 \end{bmatrix}$$

Augmented matrix of this system of equations is

$$\left[\begin{array}{ccc|c} 1 & 1 & 1 & 7 \\ 1 & 2 & 3 & 16 \\ 1 & 3 & 4 & 22 \end{array}\right]$$

which becomes

$$\left[\begin{array}{ccc|c} 1 & 1 & 1 & 7 \\ 0 & 1 & 2 & 9 \\ 0 & 2 & 3 & 15 \end{array}\right] \; [R_2 \to R_2 - R_1, R_3 \to R_3 - R_1]$$

or,

$$\left[\begin{array}{ccc|c} 1 & 1 & 1 & 7 \\ 0 & 1 & 2 & 9 \\ 0 & 0 & -1 & -1 \end{array}\right] \; [R_3 \to R_3 - 2R_1]$$

Here, we get, $z = 3$, $y + 2z = 9$, $x + y + z = 7$

giving us the solution $x = 1$, $y = 3$, $z = 3$

Thus, we notice, it requires same operations as were used earlier. It is only a different way of expressing the same thing.

This method is called the *Gauss elimination method* of solving equations. Sometimes, we proceed further and reduce the augmented matrix to

$$\left[\begin{array}{ccc|c} 1 & 0 & -1 & -2 \\ 0 & 1 & 2 & 9 \\ 0 & 0 & -1 & -3 \end{array}\right] [R_1 \to R_1 - R_2]$$

$$\left[\begin{array}{ccc|c} 1 & 0 & -1 & -2 \\ 0 & 1 & 3 & 12 \\ 0 & 0 & -1 & -3 \end{array}\right] [R_2 \to R_2 - R_3]$$

$$\left[\begin{array}{ccc|c} 1 & 0 & 0 & 1 \\ 0 & 1 & 3 & 12 \\ 0 & 0 & -1 & -3 \end{array}\right] \text{ or } \left[\begin{array}{ccc|c} 1 & 0 & 0 & 1 \\ 0 & 1 & 0 & 3 \\ 0 & 0 & 1 & 3 \end{array}\right]$$

and the solution is $x = 1,\ y = 3, z = 3$.

This method is called *Gauss Jordan Reduction.*

NOTE: A matrix A is said to be in row echelon form if

(*i*) All rows which consist of only zeros are at the bottom of the matrix (such rows may or may not be there)

(*ii*) The first non zero entry in each (non zero) row is 1 (called the leading entry).

(*iii*) If kth and $(k + 1)$th rows are two consecutive rows (having some non zero entry) then the leading entry of the $(k + 1)$th row is to the right of the leading entry of the kth row.

Thus, the Gaussian elimination method requires the augmented matrix to be put in the row echelon form. If in addition to the above three conditions the matrix A also satisfies

(iv) If a column contains a leading entry of some row then all other entries in that column are zero. We say, then that A is in reduced row echelon form and this method is called Gauss-Jordan reduction. We thus realise that Gauss-Jordan reduction requires few extra steps than Gaussian elimination method. But in the former case the solution is obtained without any back substitution.

Example 30. *Solve the equations*

$$x + y + 2z = -1$$
$$x - 2y + z = -5$$
$$3x + y + z = 3$$

by using Gauss elimination method.

Solution. The matrix form of the equations is

$$\begin{bmatrix} 1 & 1 & 2 \\ 1 & -2 & 1 \\ 3 & 1 & 1 \end{bmatrix}\begin{bmatrix} x \\ y \\ z \end{bmatrix} = \begin{bmatrix} -1 \\ -5 \\ 3 \end{bmatrix}$$

Augmented matrix is

$$\left[\begin{array}{ccc|c} 1 & 1 & 2 & -1 \\ 1 & -2 & 1 & -5 \\ 3 & 1 & 1 & 3 \end{array}\right] \sim \left[\begin{array}{ccc|c} 1 & 1 & 2 & -1 \\ 0 & -3 & -1 & -4 \\ 0 & -2 & -5 & 6 \end{array}\right] \sim \left[\begin{array}{ccc|c} 1 & 1 & 2 & -1 \\ 0 & 1 & \frac{1}{2} & \frac{4}{3} \\ 0 & -2 & -5 & 6 \end{array}\right]$$

$$R_2 \to R_2 - R_1 \qquad\qquad R_2 \to R_2/-3$$
$$R_3 \to R_3 - 3R_1$$

$$\sim \left[\begin{array}{ccc|c} 1 & 1 & 2 & -1 \\ 0 & 1 & \frac{1}{3} & \frac{4}{3} \\ 0 & 0 & \frac{-13}{3} & \frac{26}{3} \end{array}\right] \sim \left[\begin{array}{ccc|c} 1 & 1 & 2 & -1 \\ 0 & 1 & \frac{1}{3} & \frac{4}{3} \\ 0 & 0 & 1 & -2 \end{array}\right]$$

$$R_3 \to R_3 + 2R_2$$

Hence, we get, $\quad z = -2$

$$y + \frac{1}{3}z = \frac{4}{3}$$

$$x + y + 2z = -1$$

giving $\qquad x = 1, \quad y = 2, \quad z = -2$

as the required solution.

Example 31. *Solve the above equations using Gauss-Jordan method.*

Solution. We get the augmented matrix reduced to $\left[\begin{array}{ccc|c} 1 & 1 & 2 & -1 \\ 0 & 1 & \frac{1}{3} & \frac{4}{3} \\ 0 & 0 & 1 & -2 \end{array}\right]$

as in above example. Reducing it further, we get

$$\left[\begin{array}{ccc|c} 1 & 1 & 2 & -1 \\ 0 & 1 & \frac{1}{3} & \frac{4}{3} \\ 0 & 0 & 1 & -2 \end{array}\right] \sim \left[\begin{array}{ccc|c} 1 & 0 & \frac{5}{3} & \frac{-7}{3} \\ 0 & 1 & \frac{1}{3} & \frac{4}{3} \\ 0 & 0 & 1 & -2 \end{array}\right]$$

$$R_1 \to R_1 - R_2$$

$$\sim \begin{bmatrix} 1 & 0 & 0 & 1 \\ 0 & 1 & \frac{1}{3} & \frac{4}{3} \\ 0 & 0 & 1 & -2 \end{bmatrix} \sim \begin{bmatrix} 1 & 0 & 0 & 1 \\ 0 & 1 & 0 & 2 \\ 0 & 0 & 1 & -2 \end{bmatrix}$$

$$R_1 \to R_1 - \frac{5}{3} R_3 \qquad R_2 \to R_2 - \frac{R_3}{3}$$

Hence, solution is $x = 1, y = 2, z = -2.$

Example 32. *Solve the following equations using Gauss elimination method*

$$x + 2y + 3z = 4$$
$$2x + 3y + 8z = 7$$
$$x - y - 9z = 1$$

Solution. Matrix form of the equations is

$$\begin{bmatrix} 1 & 2 & 3 \\ 2 & 3 & 8 \\ 1 & -1 & -9 \end{bmatrix} \begin{bmatrix} x \\ y \\ z \end{bmatrix} = \begin{bmatrix} 4 \\ 7 \\ 1 \end{bmatrix}$$

Augmented matrix is

$$\begin{bmatrix} 1 & 2 & 3 & 4 \\ 2 & 3 & 8 & 7 \\ 1 & -1 & -9 & 1 \end{bmatrix} \sim \begin{bmatrix} 1 & 2 & 3 & 4 \\ 0 & -1 & 2 & -1 \\ 0 & -3 & -12 & -3 \end{bmatrix}$$

$$R_2 \to R_2 - 2R_1$$
$$R_3 \to R_3 - R_1$$

$$\sim \begin{bmatrix} 1 & 2 & 3 & 4 \\ 0 & -1 & -2 & 1 \\ 0 & -3 & -12 & -3 \end{bmatrix} \sim \begin{bmatrix} 1 & 2 & 3 & 4 \\ 0 & 1 & -2 & 1 \\ 0 & 0 & -18 & 0 \end{bmatrix}$$

$$R_2 \to -R_2 \qquad R_3 \to R_3 + 3R_2$$

Thus we get, $\quad -18z = 0, \; y - 2z = 1, \; x + 2y + 3z = 4$

giving $\quad z = 0, \; y = 1, \; x = 2.$

Example 33. *Solve the above equations using Gauss-Jordan reduction.*

Solution. As in above example, we get the augmented matrix reduced to

$$\begin{bmatrix} 1 & 2 & 3 & 4 \\ 0 & 1 & -2 & 1 \\ 0 & 0 & -18 & 0 \end{bmatrix}$$

We further reduce it as

$$\left[\begin{array}{ccc|c} 1 & 2 & 3 & 4 \\ 0 & 1 & -2 & 1 \\ 0 & 0 & 1 & 0 \end{array}\right] \sim \left[\begin{array}{ccc|c} 1 & 0 & -1 & 2 \\ 0 & 1 & -2 & 1 \\ 0 & 0 & 1 & 0 \end{array}\right]$$

$$R_1 \to R_1 - 2R_2$$

$$\sim \left[\begin{array}{ccc|c} 1 & 0 & 0 & 2 \\ 0 & 1 & -2 & 1 \\ 0 & 0 & 1 & 0 \end{array}\right] \sim \left[\begin{array}{ccc|c} 1 & 0 & 0 & 2 \\ 0 & 1 & 0 & 1 \\ 0 & 0 & 1 & 0 \end{array}\right]$$

$$R_1 \to R_1 + R_3 \qquad\qquad R_2 \to R_2 + 2R_3$$

Hence, solution is $x = 2, \quad y = 1, \quad z = 0$.

Example 34. *The equilibrium conditions for two substitute goods are given by*

$$5P_1 - 2P_2 = 15$$
$$-P_1 + 8P_2 = 16$$

Find the equilibrium prices.

Solution. We write the given system of equations in the matrix form as

$$\begin{bmatrix} 5 & -2 \\ -1 & 8 \end{bmatrix} \begin{bmatrix} P_1 \\ P_2 \end{bmatrix} = \begin{bmatrix} 15 \\ 16 \end{bmatrix}$$

The augmented matrix is

$$\left[\begin{array}{cc|c} 5 & -2 & 15 \\ -1 & 8 & 16 \end{array}\right] \sim \left[\begin{array}{cc|c} 1 & \frac{-2}{5} & 3 \\ -1 & 8 & 6 \end{array}\right] \sim \left[\begin{array}{cc|c} 1 & \frac{-2}{5} & 3 \\ 0 & \frac{38}{5} & 19 \end{array}\right]$$

$$R_1 \to \frac{R_1}{5} \qquad\qquad R_2 \to R_2 + R_1$$

Solution is then given by

$$\frac{38}{5} P_2 = 19 \text{ and } P_1 - \frac{2}{5} P_3 = 3 \quad \textit{i.e.,} \quad P_1 = 4 \text{ and } P_2 = \frac{5}{2}.$$

Example 35. *An automobile company uses three types of steel s_1, s_2, s_3 for producing there types of cars c_1, c_2, c_3. Steel requirement (in tons) for each type of car is given as*

	c_1	c_2	c_3
s_1	2	3	4
s_2	1	1	2
s_3	3	2	1

Determine the number of cars of each type that can be produced using 29, 13 and 16 tons of steel of three types respectively.

Solution. Suppose x, y and z are the number of cars of each type that are produced. Then,

$$2x + 3y + 4z = 29$$
$$x + y + 2z = 13$$
$$3x + 2y + z = 16$$

This system of equations can be put in the matrix form as

$$\begin{bmatrix} 2 & 3 & 4 \\ 1 & 1 & 2 \\ 3 & 2 & 1 \end{bmatrix} \begin{bmatrix} x \\ y \\ z \end{bmatrix} = \begin{bmatrix} 29 \\ 13 \\ 16 \end{bmatrix}$$

Augmented matrix is

$$\left[\begin{array}{ccc|c} 2 & 3 & 4 & 29 \\ 1 & 1 & 2 & 13 \\ 3 & 2 & 1 & 16 \end{array}\right] \sim \left[\begin{array}{ccc|c} 1 & 1 & 2 & 13 \\ 2 & 3 & 4 & 29 \\ 3 & 2 & 1 & 16 \end{array}\right] \sim \left[\begin{array}{ccc|c} 1 & 1 & 2 & 13 \\ 0 & 1 & 0 & 3 \\ 0 & -1 & -5 & -23 \end{array}\right]$$

$R_2 \leftrightarrow R_1$ $\quad$ $R_2 \to R_2 - 2R_1$, $R_3 \to R_3 - 3R_1$

$$\sim \left[\begin{array}{ccc|c} 1 & 1 & 2 & 13 \\ 0 & 1 & 0 & 3 \\ 0 & 0 & -5 & -20 \end{array}\right]$$

$R_3 \to R_3 + R_2$

We thus have, $x + y + 2z = 13$

$$y = 3$$
$$-5z = -20$$

giving $\quad z = 4, y = 3, \text{ and } x = 2.$

The required number of cars produced.

Example 36. *There are three types of foods, Food I, Food II, Food III. Food I contains 1 unit each of the nutrients A, B, C. Food II contains 1 unit of nutrient A, 2 units of nutrient B and 3 units of nutrient C. Food III contains 1, 3, and 4 units of nutrients A, B, C. 7 units of A, 16 units of B and 22 units of nutrient C are required. Find the amount of three foods that will provide these.*

Solution. Suppose, x, y and z are the amounts of three foods to be taken so as to get required nutrients.

Then $\quad x + y + z = 7$

$$x + 2y + 3z = 16$$
$$x + 3y + 4y = 22$$

In matrix form we get,

$$\begin{bmatrix} 1 & 1 & 1 \\ 1 & 2 & 3 \\ 1 & 3 & 4 \end{bmatrix}\begin{bmatrix} x \\ y \\ z \end{bmatrix} = \begin{bmatrix} 7 \\ 16 \\ 22 \end{bmatrix}$$

Augmented matrix is

$$\left[\begin{array}{ccc|c} 1 & 1 & 1 & 7 \\ 1 & 2 & 3 & 16 \\ 1 & 3 & 4 & 22 \end{array}\right] \sim \left[\begin{array}{ccc|c} 1 & 1 & 1 & 7 \\ 0 & 1 & 2 & 9 \\ 0 & 2 & 3 & 15 \end{array}\right] \sim \left[\begin{array}{ccc|c} 1 & 1 & 1 & 7 \\ 0 & 1 & 2 & 9 \\ 0 & 0 & -1 & -3 \end{array}\right]$$

$$R_2 \to R_2 - R_1 \qquad R_3 \to R_3 - 2R_1$$
$$R_3 \to R_3 - R_1$$

which gives $\quad z = 3,\ y + 2z = 9,\ x + y + z = 7$

or that $\quad x = 1,\ y = 3,\ z = 3$

is the required solution.

Example 37. *A firm produces two products P_1 and P_2 passing through two machines M_1 and M_2 before completion. M_1 can produce either 10 units of P_1 or 15 units of P_2 per hour. M_2 can produce 15 units of either product per hour. Find daily production of P_1 and P_2 if the time available is 12 hours on M_1 and 10 hours on M_2 per day.*

Solution. Suppose, daily production of P_1 is x units and of P_2 it is y units. Then,

$$\frac{x}{10} + \frac{y}{15} = 12, \qquad \frac{x}{15} + \frac{y}{15} = 10$$

i.e.,
$$3x + 2y = 360$$
$$x + y = 150$$

Matrix representation is given by $\begin{bmatrix} 3 & 2 \\ 1 & 1 \end{bmatrix}\begin{bmatrix} x \\ y \end{bmatrix} = \begin{bmatrix} 360 \\ 150 \end{bmatrix}$.

Augmented matrix is

$$\left[\begin{array}{cc|c} 3 & 2 & 360 \\ 1 & 1 & 150 \end{array}\right] \sim \left[\begin{array}{cc|c} 1 & 1 & 150 \\ 3 & 2 & 360 \end{array}\right] \sim \left[\begin{array}{cc|c} 1 & 1 & 150 \\ 0 & -1 & -90 \end{array}\right]$$

$$R_1 \leftrightarrow R_2 \qquad R_2 \to 3R_1$$

i.e.,
$$x + y = 150$$
$$-y = -90$$

or that $x = 60$, $y = 90$ (daily production of P_1 and P_2).

EXERCISES

Solve the following equations:

1. $x + 2y + 3z = 14$
$3x + y + 2z = 11$
$2x + 3y + z = 11$

2. $2x - 4y - 5z = 10$
$2x - 11y + 10z = 36$
$4x - y + 5z = -6$

3. $5x + 3y + 7z = 4$
$3x + 26y + 2z = 9$
$7x + 2y + 10z = 5$

4. $x + 2y - z = 3$
$3x - y + 2z = 3$
$2x - 2y + 3z = 2$
$x - y + z = -1$

5. $x - y + 2z = 4$
$3x + y + 4z = 6$
$x + y + z = 1$

6. $2x + 3y + z = 9$
$x + 2y + z = 6$
$3x + y + 2z = 8$

7. $x + y + z = 3$
$3x - 5y + 2z = 8$
$5x - 3y + 4z = 14$

8. $3x + 2y - z - t = 0$
$x - y + 2z + 4t = 0$
$x + 3y + 3z - 2t = 0$
$3x + 6y - 7t = 0$

9. $3x + 4y - 5z + 7t = 0$
$2x + 3y + 3z - 2t = 0$
$4x + 11y - 13z + 16t = 0$
$7x - 2y + z + 3t = 0$

10. $x + y + z + t = 8$
$x - y - z - t = 6$
$3x + y + z + t = 22.$

ANSWERS

1. $x = 1, y = 2, z = 3$
2. $x = \frac{-15k - 34}{14},\ y = \frac{5k - 26}{7},\ z = k$
3. $x = \frac{7 - 16k}{11},\ y = \frac{3 + k}{11},\ z = k$
4. $x = -1, y = 4, z = 4$
5. $x = \frac{1}{2}(5 - 3k),\ y = \frac{1}{2}(-3 + k),\ z = k$
6. $x = \frac{35}{18}, y = \frac{29}{18}, z = \frac{5}{18}$
7. $x = \frac{23}{8} - \frac{7}{8}k,\ y = \frac{1}{8} - \frac{1}{8}k, z = k$
8. $x = -3k, y = 5k, z = -2k, t = 3k$
9. $x = y = z = t = 0$
10. $x = 7, y = 1 - l - k, z = l, t = k$

11. INVERSE OF A MATRIX

Consider the matrices

$$A = \begin{bmatrix} 2 & 0 & -1 \\ 5 & 1 & 0 \\ 0 & 1 & 3 \end{bmatrix},\quad B = \begin{bmatrix} 3 & -1 & 1 \\ -15 & 6 & -5 \\ 5 & -2 & 2 \end{bmatrix}$$

It can be easily seen that

$$AB = BA = I \text{ (unit matrix)}$$

In this case, we say, B is inverse of A. Infact, we have the following definition

"If A is a square matrix of order n, then a square matrix B of the same order n is said to be inverse of A if $AB = BA = I$ (unit matrix)."

NOTES:

(*i*) Inverse of a matrix is defined only for square matrices.

(*ii*) If B is an inverse of A, then A is also an inverse of B. [Follows clearly be definition.]

(*iii*) If a matrix A has an inverse, then A is said to be invertible.

(*iv*) Inverse of a matrix is unique.

For, let B and C be two inverses of A.

Then, $AB = BA = I$ and $AC = CA = I$

So, $\qquad B = BI = B(AC) = (BA)C = IC = C.$

Notation: Inverse of A is denoted by A^{-1}.

(*v*) Every square matrix is not invertible.

For, let $A = \begin{bmatrix} 1 & 1 \\ 1 & 1 \end{bmatrix}$

If A is invertible, let $B = \begin{bmatrix} x & x' \\ y & y' \end{bmatrix}$ be inverse of A.

Then $AB = I$ implies $\begin{bmatrix} x+y & x'+y' \\ x+y & x'+y' \end{bmatrix} = \begin{bmatrix} 1 & 0 \\ 0 & 1 \end{bmatrix}$

$\Rightarrow x + y = 1,\ x' + y' = 0,\ x + y = 0,\ x' + y' = 1$ which is absurd.

This proves our assertion.

(*vi*) The necessary and sufficient conditions for a matrix to be invertible will be discussed in next section.

In the present section, we give a method to determine the inverse of a matrix. Consider the identity $A = IA$.

We reduce the matrix A on left hand side to the unit matrix I by elementary row operations only and apply all those operations in same order to the prefactor I on the right hand side of the above identity. In this way, unit matrix I is reduced to some matrix B such that $I = BA$. Matrix B is then the inverse of A.

We illustrate the above method by the following examples.

Example 38. *Find the inverse of the matrix*

$$\begin{bmatrix} 1 & 3 & 3 \\ 1 & 4 & 3 \\ 1 & 3 & 4 \end{bmatrix}.$$

Solution. Consider the identity

$$\begin{bmatrix} 1 & 3 & 3 \\ 1 & 4 & 3 \\ 1 & 3 & 4 \end{bmatrix} = \begin{bmatrix} 1 & 0 & 0 \\ 0 & 1 & 0 \\ 0 & 0 & 1 \end{bmatrix} \begin{bmatrix} 1 & 3 & 3 \\ 1 & 4 & 3 \\ 1 & 3 & 4 \end{bmatrix}$$

Apply $R_2 \to R_2 - R_1$, then $R_3 \to R_3 - R_1$, we have

$$\begin{bmatrix} 1 & 3 & 3 \\ 0 & 1 & 0 \\ 0 & 0 & 1 \end{bmatrix} = \begin{bmatrix} 1 & 0 & 0 \\ -1 & 1 & 0 \\ -1 & 0 & 1 \end{bmatrix} \begin{bmatrix} 1 & 3 & 3 \\ 1 & 4 & 3 \\ 1 & 3 & 4 \end{bmatrix}$$

Apply $R_1 \to R_1 - 3R_2 - 3R_3$, we have

$$\begin{bmatrix} 1 & 0 & 0 \\ 0 & 1 & 0 \\ 0 & 0 & 1 \end{bmatrix} = \begin{bmatrix} 7 & -3 & -3 \\ -1 & 1 & 0 \\ -1 & 0 & 1 \end{bmatrix} \begin{bmatrix} 1 & 3 & 3 \\ 1 & 4 & 3 \\ 1 & 3 & 4 \end{bmatrix}$$

So, the desired inverse is

$$\begin{bmatrix} 7 & -3 & -3 \\ -1 & 1 & 0 \\ -1 & 0 & 1 \end{bmatrix}.$$

Example 39. *Find the inverse of the matrix*

$$\begin{bmatrix} 1 & 3 & -2 \\ -3 & 0 & -5 \\ 2 & 5 & 0 \end{bmatrix}$$

Solution. Consider the identity

$$\begin{bmatrix} 1 & 3 & -2 \\ -3 & 0 & -5 \\ 2 & 5 & 0 \end{bmatrix} = \begin{bmatrix} 1 & 0 & 0 \\ 0 & 1 & 0 \\ 0 & 0 & 1 \end{bmatrix} \begin{bmatrix} 1 & 3 & -2 \\ -3 & 0 & -5 \\ 2 & 5 & 0 \end{bmatrix}$$

Applying $R_2 \to R_2 + 3R_1$, $R_3 \to R_3 - 2R_1$, we have

$$\begin{bmatrix} 1 & 3 & -2 \\ 0 & 9 & -11 \\ 0 & -1 & 4 \end{bmatrix} = \begin{bmatrix} 1 & 0 & 0 \\ 3 & 1 & 0 \\ -2 & 0 & 1 \end{bmatrix} \begin{bmatrix} 1 & 3 & -2 \\ -3 & 0 & -5 \\ 2 & 5 & 0 \end{bmatrix}$$

Applying $R_3 \to 9R_3$ and then $R_3 \to R_3 + R_2$, we have

$$\begin{bmatrix} 1 & 3 & -2 \\ 0 & 9 & -11 \\ 0 & 0 & 25 \end{bmatrix} = \begin{bmatrix} 1 & 0 & 0 \\ 3 & 1 & 0 \\ -15 & 1 & 9 \end{bmatrix} \begin{bmatrix} 1 & 3 & -2 \\ -3 & 0 & -5 \\ 2 & 5 & 0 \end{bmatrix}$$

Applying $R_3 \to \frac{1}{25} R_3$, we have

$$\begin{bmatrix} 1 & 3 & -2 \\ 0 & 9 & -11 \\ 0 & 0 & 1 \end{bmatrix} = \begin{bmatrix} 1 & 0 & 0 \\ 3 & 1 & 0 \\ -\frac{3}{5} & \frac{1}{25} & \frac{9}{25} \end{bmatrix} \begin{bmatrix} 1 & 3 & -2 \\ -3 & 0 & -5 \\ 2 & 5 & 0 \end{bmatrix}$$

Applying $R_2 \to R_2 + 11R_3$, $R_1 \to R_1 + 2R_3$, we have

$$\begin{bmatrix} 1 & 3 & 0 \\ 0 & 9 & 0 \\ 0 & 0 & 1 \end{bmatrix} = \begin{bmatrix} -\frac{1}{5} & \frac{2}{25} & \frac{18}{25} \\ -\frac{18}{5} & \frac{36}{25} & \frac{99}{25} \\ -\frac{3}{5} & \frac{1}{25} & \frac{9}{25} \end{bmatrix} \begin{bmatrix} 1 & 3 & -2 \\ -3 & 0 & -5 \\ 2 & 5 & 0 \end{bmatrix}$$

Applying $R_2 \to \frac{1}{9} R_2$, we have

$$\begin{bmatrix} 1 & 3 & 0 \\ 0 & 1 & 0 \\ 0 & 0 & 1 \end{bmatrix} = \begin{bmatrix} -\frac{1}{5} & \frac{2}{25} & \frac{18}{25} \\ -\frac{2}{5} & \frac{4}{25} & \frac{11}{25} \\ -\frac{3}{5} & \frac{1}{25} & \frac{9}{25} \end{bmatrix} \begin{bmatrix} 1 & 3 & -2 \\ -3 & 0 & -5 \\ 2 & 5 & 0 \end{bmatrix}$$

Applying $R_1 \to R_1 - 3R_2$, we have

$$\begin{bmatrix} 1 & 0 & 0 \\ 0 & 1 & 0 \\ 0 & 0 & 1 \end{bmatrix} = \begin{bmatrix} 1 & -\frac{2}{5} & \frac{3}{5} \\ -\frac{2}{5} & \frac{4}{25} & \frac{11}{25} \\ -\frac{3}{4} & \frac{1}{25} & \frac{9}{25} \end{bmatrix} \begin{bmatrix} 1 & 3 & -2 \\ -3 & 0 & -5 \\ 2 & 5 & 0 \end{bmatrix}$$

So, the desired inverse is

$$\begin{bmatrix} 1 & -\frac{2}{5} & -\frac{3}{5} \\ -\frac{2}{5} & \frac{4}{25} & \frac{11}{25} \\ -\frac{3}{5} & \frac{1}{25} & \frac{9}{25} \end{bmatrix}.$$

Example 40. *Find the inverse of the matrix*

$$\begin{bmatrix} 1 & 2 & -1 \\ -4 & -7 & 4 \\ -4 & -9 & 5 \end{bmatrix}.$$

Solution. Consider the identity

$$\begin{bmatrix} 1 & 2 & -1 \\ -4 & -7 & 4 \\ -4 & -9 & 5 \end{bmatrix} = \begin{bmatrix} 1 & 0 & 0 \\ 0 & 1 & 0 \\ 0 & 0 & 1 \end{bmatrix} \begin{bmatrix} 1 & 2 & -1 \\ -4 & -7 & 4 \\ -4 & -9 & 5 \end{bmatrix}$$

Applying $R_2 \to R_2 + 4R_1$, $R_3 \to R_3 + 4R_1$, we have

$$\begin{bmatrix} 1 & 2 & -1 \\ 0 & 1 & 0 \\ 0 & -1 & 1 \end{bmatrix} = \begin{bmatrix} 1 & 0 & 0 \\ 4 & 1 & 0 \\ 4 & 0 & 1 \end{bmatrix} \begin{bmatrix} 1 & 2 & -1 \\ -4 & -7 & 4 \\ -4 & -9 & 5 \end{bmatrix}$$

Applying $R_1 \to R_1 + R_3$ then $R_3 \to R_3 + R_2$

$$\begin{bmatrix} 1 & 1 & 0 \\ 0 & 1 & 0 \\ 0 & 0 & 1 \end{bmatrix} = \begin{bmatrix} 5 & 0 & 1 \\ 4 & 1 & 0 \\ 8 & 1 & 1 \end{bmatrix} \begin{bmatrix} 1 & 2 & -1 \\ -4 & -7 & 4 \\ -4 & -9 & 5 \end{bmatrix}$$

Applying $R_1 \to R_1 - R_2$, we have

$$\begin{bmatrix} 1 & 0 & 0 \\ 0 & 1 & 0 \\ 0 & 0 & 1 \end{bmatrix} = \begin{bmatrix} 1 & -1 & 1 \\ 4 & 1 & 0 \\ 8 & 1 & 1 \end{bmatrix} \begin{bmatrix} 1 & 2 & -1 \\ -4 & -7 & 4 \\ -4 & -9 & 5 \end{bmatrix}$$

So, the desired inverse is

$$\begin{bmatrix} 1 & -1 & 1 \\ 4 & 1 & 0 \\ 8 & 1 & 1 \end{bmatrix}.$$

EXERCISES

Compute the inverse of each of the following matrices:

1. $\begin{bmatrix} -2 & 6 & 4 \\ 1 & -3 & 2 \\ 1 & 5 & 2 \end{bmatrix}$

2. $\begin{bmatrix} 8 & 4 & 2 \\ 2 & 8 & 4 \\ 1 & 2 & 8 \end{bmatrix}$

3. $\begin{bmatrix} a+ib & c+id \\ -c+id & a-ib \end{bmatrix}$ where $a^2 + b^2 + c^2 + d^2 = 1$

4. $\begin{bmatrix} 9 & 7 & 3 \\ 5 & -1 & 4 \\ 6 & 8 & 2 \end{bmatrix}$ 5. $\begin{bmatrix} 1 & 3 & -2 \\ -3 & 0 & -5 \\ 2 & 5 & 0 \end{bmatrix}$ 6. $\begin{bmatrix} 1 & 3 & 3 \\ 1 & 4 & 3 \\ 1 & 3 & 4 \end{bmatrix}$

7. $\begin{bmatrix} 9 & 7 & 6 \\ 7 & -1 & 8 \\ 3 & 4 & 2 \end{bmatrix}$ 8. $\begin{bmatrix} 0 & 2 & 1 & 3 \\ 1 & 1 & -1 & 2 \\ 1 & 2 & 0 & 1 \\ -1 & 1 & 2 & 6 \end{bmatrix}$ 9. $\begin{bmatrix} 0 & 1 & 0 & 0 \\ -1 & 0 & 1 & 0 \\ -1 & -1 & 0 & 1 \\ -1 & 1 & 0 & 0 \end{bmatrix}$

10. $\begin{bmatrix} 0 & 1 & 2 & 2 \\ 1 & 1 & 2 & 3 \\ 2 & 2 & 2 & 3 \\ 2 & 3 & 3 & 3 \end{bmatrix}$

ANSWERS

1. $\begin{bmatrix} -\frac{1}{4} & \frac{1}{8} & \frac{3}{8} \\ 0 & -\frac{1}{8} & \frac{1}{8} \\ \frac{1}{8} & \frac{1}{4} & 0 \end{bmatrix}$ 2. $\begin{bmatrix} \frac{1}{7} & -\frac{1}{14} & 0 \\ -\frac{3}{98} & \frac{31}{196} & -\frac{1}{14} \\ -\frac{1}{98} & -\frac{3}{98} & \frac{1}{7} \end{bmatrix}$

3. $\begin{bmatrix} a-ib & -c-id \\ c-id & a+ib \end{bmatrix}$ 4. $\begin{bmatrix} \frac{17}{35} & -\frac{1}{7} & -\frac{31}{70} \\ -\frac{1}{5} & 0 & \frac{3}{10} \\ -\frac{23}{35} & \frac{3}{7} & \frac{22}{35} \end{bmatrix}$

5. $\begin{bmatrix} 1 & -\frac{2}{5} & -\frac{3}{5} \\ -\frac{2}{5} & \frac{4}{25} & \frac{11}{25} \\ -\frac{3}{5} & \frac{1}{25} & \frac{29}{25} \end{bmatrix}$ 6. $\begin{bmatrix} 7 & -3 & 3 \\ -1 & 1 & 0 \\ -1 & 0 & 1 \end{bmatrix}$

7. $\begin{bmatrix} \frac{17}{25} & -\frac{1}{5} & -\frac{31}{25} \\ -\frac{1}{5} & 0 & \frac{3}{5} \\ -\frac{31}{50} & \frac{3}{10} & \frac{29}{25} \end{bmatrix}$ 8. $\begin{bmatrix} -1 & -3 & 3 & -1 \\ 1 & 1 & -1 & 0 \\ 2 & -5 & 2 & -3 \\ -1 & 1 & 0 & 1 \end{bmatrix}$

9. $\begin{bmatrix} 1 & 0 & 0 & -1 \\ 1 & 0 & 0 & 0 \\ 1 & -1 & 0 & -1 \\ 2 & 0 & 1 & -1 \end{bmatrix}$ 10. $\begin{bmatrix} -3 & 3 & -3 & 2 \\ 3 & -4 & 4 & -2 \\ -3 & 4 & -5 & 3 \\ 2 & -2 & 3 & -2 \end{bmatrix}$

12. DETERMINANTS

If A is a square matrix with entries from the field of complex numbers, then determinant of A is some complex number. This will be denoted by det A or $|A|$. If

$$A = \begin{bmatrix} a_{11} & a_{12} & \cdots & a_{1n} \\ a_{21} & a_{22} & \cdots & a_{2n} \\ \cdots & \cdots & \cdots & \cdots \\ a_{n1} & a_{n2} & \cdots & a_{nn} \end{bmatrix}$$

then det A will be denoted by

$$\begin{vmatrix} a_{11} & a_{12} & \cdots & a_{1n} \\ a_{21} & a_{22} & \cdots & a_{2n} \\ \cdots & \cdots & \cdots & \cdots \\ a_{n1} & a_{n2} & \cdots & a_{nn} \end{vmatrix}$$

NOTES: (*i*) det A or $|A|$ is defined for square matrix A only.

(*ii*) det A or $|A|$ will be defined in such a way that A is invertible iff det $A \neq 0$.

(*iii*) The determinant of an $n \times n$ matrix will be called determinant of order n.

13. DETERMINANT OF ORDER ONE

Let $A = (a_{11})$ be a square matrix of order one. Then det $A = a_{11}$.

By definition, if A is invertible, then $a_{11} \neq 0$ and so, det $A \neq 0$. Also, conversely if det $A \neq 0$, then $a_{11} \neq 0$ and so, A is invertible.

14. DETERMINANT OF ORDER TWO

Let $A = \begin{bmatrix} a_{11} & a_{12} \\ a_{21} & a_{22} \end{bmatrix}$ be a square matrix of order two. Then we define

det $A = a_{11}a_{22} - a_{12}a_{21}$

For example, if $A = \begin{bmatrix} 1 & 2 \\ 3 & 4 \end{bmatrix}$ then det $A = 1 \times 4 - 2 \times 3 = 4 - 6 = -2$.

Suppose $A = \begin{bmatrix} a_{11} & a_{12} \\ a_{21} & a_{22} \end{bmatrix}$ is invertible.

Then by definition there exists a matrix

$$B = \begin{bmatrix} x & y \\ z & w \end{bmatrix}$$ where x, y, z, w are complex numbers

such that $AB = I = BA$

The above identity implies

$$a_{11}x + a_{12}z = 1, \quad a_{11}y + a_{12}w = 0$$
$$a_{21}x + a_{22}z = 0, \quad a_{21}y + a_{22}w = 1$$

which in turn implies

$$\Delta x = a_{22}, \quad \Delta y = -a_{12}$$
$$\Delta z = -a_{21}, \quad \Delta w = a_{11}$$

where $\Delta = a_{11}a_{22} - a_{12}a_{21}$

Clearly $\Delta \neq 0$, for otherwise x, y, z, w will be indeterminate. This means that $\det A \neq 0$. Conversely, if A is a square matrix of order 2 such that $\det A \neq 0$, then A is invertible as

$$x = \frac{a_{22}}{\Delta}, \quad y = \frac{-a_{12}}{\Delta}, \quad z = \frac{-a_{21}}{\Delta}, \quad w = \frac{a_{11}}{\Delta}$$

will determine B uniquely satisfying $AB = I = BA$.

15. DETERMINANT OF ORDER THREE

Let $$A = \begin{bmatrix} a_{11} & a_{12} & a_{13} \\ a_{21} & a_{22} & a_{23} \\ a_{31} & a_{32} & a_{32} \end{bmatrix}$$ be a 3×3 matrix.

Then we define $\det A = a_{11}(a_{22}a_{33} - a_{32}a_{23}) - a_{12}(a_{21}a_{33} - a_{31}a_{23})$
$+ a_{13}(a_{21}a_{32} - a_{31}a_{22})$

The above definition may be explained as follows:

The first bracket is determinant of matrix obtained after removing first row and first column.

The second bracket is determinant of matrix obtained after removing first row and second column.

The third bracket is determinant of matrix obtained after removing first row and third column.

The elements before three brackets are first, second, third element respectively of first row with alternate positive and negative signs.

For eample, let $A = \begin{bmatrix} 1 & 2 & 3 \\ 4 & 5 & 6 \\ 7 & 8 & 9 \end{bmatrix}$

To find $\det A$.

The first bracket in the definition of $\det A$ is determinant of

$$\begin{bmatrix} 5 & 6 \\ 8 & 9 \end{bmatrix} = 45 - 48 = -3.$$

The second bracket is determinant of

$$\begin{bmatrix} 4 & 6 \\ 7 & 9 \end{bmatrix} = 36 - 42 = -6.$$

The third bracket is determinant of

$$\begin{bmatrix} 4 & 5 \\ 7 & 8 \end{bmatrix} = 32 - 35 = -3.$$

So, $\det A = 1(-3) - 2(-6) + 3(-3) = -3 + 12 - 9 = 0.$

It can be seen that if A is a square matrix of order 3, then A is invertible iff $\det A \neq 0$.

16. DETERMINANT OF ORDER FOUR

Let $$A = \begin{bmatrix} a_{11} & a_{12} & a_{13} & a_{14} \\ a_{21} & a_{22} & a_{23} & a_{24} \\ a_{31} & a_{32} & a_{33} & a_{34} \\ a_{41} & a_{42} & a_{43} & a_{44} \end{bmatrix}$$

Then we define det

$$A = a_{11} \times \det \begin{bmatrix} a_{22} & a_{23} & a_{24} \\ a_{32} & a_{33} & a_{34} \\ a_{42} & a_{43} & a_{44} \end{bmatrix} - a_{12} \times \det \begin{bmatrix} a_{21} & a_{23} & a_{24} \\ a_{31} & a_{33} & a_{34} \\ a_{41} & a_{43} & a_{44} \end{bmatrix}$$

$$+ a_{13} \times \det \begin{bmatrix} a_{21} & a_{22} & a_{24} \\ a_{31} & a_{32} & a_{34} \\ a_{41} & a_{42} & a_{44} \end{bmatrix}$$

$$- a_{14} \times \det \begin{bmatrix} a_{21} & a_{22} & a_{23} \\ a_{31} & a_{32} & a_{33} \\ a_{41} & a_{42} & a_{43} \end{bmatrix}$$

REMARK: A determinant $\begin{vmatrix} a_1 & b_1 \\ a_2 & b_2 \end{vmatrix}$ of order 2 can also be obtained when we eliminate x, y from $a_1x + b_1y = 0$, $a_2x + b_2y = 0$ provided one of x, y is non-zero. Similarly determinant of order 3 can be obtained by eliminating x, y, z from

$$a_1x + b_1y + c_1z = 0$$
$$a_2x + b_2y + c_2z = 0$$
$$a_3x + b_3y + c_3z = 0$$

provided one of x, y, z is non-zero.

17. PROPERTIES OF DETERMINANTS

We list below some imortant properties of determinants.

1. If two rows (or columns) are interchanged in a determinant it retains its absolute value but changes its sign.

i.e. $$\begin{vmatrix} a_1 & a_2 & a_3 \\ b_1 & b_2 & b_3 \\ c_1 & c_2 & c_3 \end{vmatrix} = -\begin{vmatrix} b_1 & b_2 & b_3 \\ a_1 & a_2 & a_3 \\ c_1 & c_2 & c_3 \end{vmatrix}$$

2. If rows are changed into columns and columns into rows the determinant remains unchanged.

i.e. $$\begin{vmatrix} a_1 & a_2 & a_3 \\ b_1 & b_2 & b_3 \\ c_1 & c_2 & c_3 \end{vmatrix} = \begin{vmatrix} a_1 & b_1 & c_1 \\ a_2 & b_2 & c_2 \\ a_3 & b_3 & c_3 \end{vmatrix}$$

3. If two rows (or columns) are identical in a determinant it vanishes.

i.e. $$\begin{vmatrix} a_1 & a_2 & a_3 \\ a_1 & a_2 & a_3 \\ c_1 & c_2 & c_3 \end{vmatrix} = 0$$

4. If any row (or column) is multiplied by a complex number k, the determinant so obtained is k times the original determinant.

i.e. $$\begin{vmatrix} a_1 & a_2 & a_3 \\ kb_1 & kb_2 & kb_3 \\ c_1 & c_2 & c_3 \end{vmatrix} = k\begin{vmatrix} a_1 & a_2 & a_3 \\ b_1 & b_2 & b_3 \\ c_1 & c_2 & c_3 \end{vmatrix}$$

5. If to any row (or column) is added k times the corresponding elements of another row (or column), the determinant remains unchanged.

i.e. $$\begin{vmatrix} a_1 + kb_1 & a_2 + kb_2 & a_3 + kb_3 \\ b_1 & b_2 & b_3 \\ c_1 & c_2 & c_3 \end{vmatrix} = \begin{vmatrix} a_1 & a_2 & a_3 \\ b_1 & b_2 & b_3 \\ c_1 & c_2 & c_3 \end{vmatrix}$$

6. If any row (or column) is the sum of two or more elements, then the determinant can be expressed as sum of two or more determinants.

i.e. $$\begin{vmatrix} a_1 + k_1 & a_2 + k_2 & a_3 + k_3 \\ b_1 & b_2 & b_3 \\ c_1 & c_2 & c_3 \end{vmatrix} = \begin{vmatrix} a_1 & a_2 & a_3 \\ b_1 & b_2 & b_3 \\ c_1 & c_2 & c_3 \end{vmatrix} + \begin{vmatrix} k_1 & k_2 & k_3 \\ b_1 & b_2 & b_3 \\ c_1 & c_2 & c_3 \end{vmatrix}$$

7. If determinant vanishes by putting $x = a$, then $(x - a)$ is a factor of the determinant.

e.g., $\begin{vmatrix} 1 & 1 & 1 \\ a & b & c \\ a^2 & b^2 & c^2 \end{vmatrix}$ has $(a - b)$ as one of its factors (for by putting $a = b$, first and second columns become identical).

8. If k rows or columns become identical by putting $x = a$ then $(x - a)^{k-1}$ is a factor of the determinant.

   For example in the following determinant:

$$\begin{vmatrix} (b+c)^2 & a^2 & a^2 \\ b^2 & (c+a)^2 & b^2 \\ c^2 & c^2 & (a+b)^2 \end{vmatrix}$$

all the three rows become identical by putting $a + b + c = 0$. So, $(a + b + c)^2$ is one of the factors of the given determinant.

Example 41. *Show that*

$$\begin{vmatrix} 1 & a & b+c \\ 1 & b & c+a \\ 1 & c & a+b \end{vmatrix} = 0.$$

Solution. Now

$$\begin{vmatrix} 1 & a & b+c \\ 1 & b & c+a \\ 1 & c & a+b \end{vmatrix}$$

$$= \begin{vmatrix} 1 & 1 & 1 \\ a & b & c \\ b+c & c+a & a+b \end{vmatrix} \quad \text{[interchanging rows and columns]}$$

Apply $C_2 \to C_2 - C_1, C_3 \to C_3 - C_1$

$$= \begin{vmatrix} 1 & 0 & 0 \\ a & b-a & c-a \\ b+c & a-b & a-c \end{vmatrix}$$

$$= (a-b)(a-c)\begin{vmatrix} 1 & 0 & 0 \\ a & -1 & -1 \\ b+c & 1 & 1 \end{vmatrix} = 0 \text{ by property 3.}$$

Example 42. *Show that*

$$\begin{vmatrix} a-b & b-c & c-a \\ b-c & c-a & a-b \\ c-a & a-b & b-c \end{vmatrix} = 0.$$

Solution. $\begin{vmatrix} a-b & b-c & c-a \\ b-c & c-a & a-b \\ c-a & a-b & b-c \end{vmatrix}$

Apply $R_1 \to R_1 + R_2 + R_3$

$$= \begin{vmatrix} 0 & 0 & 0 \\ b-c & c-a & a-b \\ c-a & a-b & b-c \end{vmatrix} = 0.$$

Example 43. *Prove that*

$$\begin{vmatrix} 1 & 1 & 1 \\ a & b & c \\ a^2 & b^2 & c^2 \end{vmatrix} = (a-b)(b-c)(c-a).$$

Solution. $\begin{vmatrix} 1 & 1 & 1 \\ a & b & c \\ a^2 & b^2 & c^2 \end{vmatrix} = \begin{vmatrix} 1 & 0 & 0 \\ a & b-a & c-a \\ a^2 & b^2-a^2 & c^2-a^2 \end{vmatrix}$

(Apply $C_2 \to C_2 - C_1$ and $C_3 \to C_3 - C_1$)

$$= (b-a)(c-a)\begin{vmatrix} 1 & 0 & 0 \\ a & 1 & 1 \\ a^2 & b+a & c+a \end{vmatrix}$$

$$= (b-a)(c-a)(c+a-b-a)$$

$$= (b-a)(c-a)(c-b)$$

$$= (a-b)(b-c)(c-a).$$

Example 44. *Prove that*

$$\begin{vmatrix} a-b-c & 2a & 2a \\ 2b & b-c-a & 2b \\ 2c & 2c & c-a-b \end{vmatrix} = (a+b+c)^3.$$

Solution. $\begin{vmatrix} a-b-c & 2a & 2a \\ 2b & b-c-a & 2b \\ 2c & 2c & c-a-b \end{vmatrix}$

Apply $R_1 \to R_1 + R_2 + R_3$

$$= \begin{vmatrix} a+b+c & a+b+c & a+b+c \\ 2b & b-c-a & 2b \\ 2c & 2c & c-a-b \end{vmatrix}$$

$$= (a+b+c) \begin{vmatrix} 1 & 1 & 1 \\ 2b & b-c-a & 2b \\ 2c & 2c & c-a-b \end{vmatrix}$$

Apply $C_2 \to C_2 - C_1$, $C_3 \to C_3 - C_1$

$$= (a+b+c) \begin{vmatrix} 1 & 0 & 0 \\ 2b & (a+b+c) & 0 \\ 2c & 0 & -(a+b+c) \end{vmatrix}$$

$$= (a+b+c)(a+b+c)^2 = (a+b+c)^3.$$

Example 45. $\begin{vmatrix} 1+a & 1 & 1 \\ 1 & 1+b & 1 \\ 1 & 1 & 1+c \end{vmatrix} = abc\left(1+\dfrac{1}{a}+\dfrac{1}{b}+\dfrac{1}{c}\right)$

Solution. $\begin{vmatrix} 1+a & 1 & 1 \\ 1 & 1+b & 1 \\ 1 & 1 & 1+c \end{vmatrix} = abc \begin{vmatrix} 1+\dfrac{1}{a} & \dfrac{1}{a} & \dfrac{1}{a} \\ \dfrac{1}{b} & 1+\dfrac{1}{b} & \dfrac{1}{b} \\ \dfrac{1}{c} & \dfrac{1}{c} & 1+\dfrac{1}{c} \end{vmatrix}$

Apply $R_1 \to R_1 + R_2 + R_3$

$$= abc \begin{vmatrix} 1+\dfrac{1}{a}+\dfrac{1}{b}+\dfrac{1}{c} & 1+\dfrac{1}{a}+\dfrac{1}{b}+\dfrac{1}{c} & 1+\dfrac{1}{a}+\dfrac{1}{b}+\dfrac{1}{c} \\ \dfrac{1}{b} & 1+\dfrac{1}{b} & \dfrac{1}{b} \\ \dfrac{1}{c} & \dfrac{1}{c} & 1+\dfrac{1}{c} \end{vmatrix}$$

$$= abc\left(1+\frac{1}{a}+\frac{1}{b}+\frac{1}{c}\right)\begin{vmatrix} 1 & 1 & 1 \\ \frac{1}{b} & 1+\frac{1}{b} & \frac{1}{b} \\ \frac{1}{c} & \frac{1}{c} & 1+\frac{1}{c} \end{vmatrix}$$

Apply $C_2 \to C_2 - C_1, C_3 \to C_3 - C_1$

$$= abc\left(1+\frac{1}{a}+\frac{1}{b}+\frac{1}{c}\right)\begin{vmatrix} 1 & 0 & 0 \\ \frac{1}{b} & 1 & 0 \\ \frac{1}{c} & 0 & 1 \end{vmatrix}$$

$$= abc\left(1+\frac{1}{a}+\frac{1}{b}+\frac{1}{c}\right).$$

Example 46. *Prove that $x = 2$ and $x = 3$ are roots of the equation*

$$\begin{vmatrix} x-5 & 2 \\ -3 & x \end{vmatrix} = 0.$$

Solution. Now $\begin{vmatrix} x-5 & 2 \\ -3 & x \end{vmatrix} = 0$

$\Rightarrow \quad x^2 - 5x + 6 = 0$

$\Rightarrow \quad (x-3)(x-2) = 0$

$\Rightarrow \quad x = 3, x = 2$ are roots of the given equation.

EXERCISES

1. Evaluate (without expanding) the following: $\begin{vmatrix} 265 & 240 & 219 \\ 240 & 225 & 198 \\ 219 & 198 & 181 \end{vmatrix}$.

2. Find the value of $\begin{vmatrix} 1 & \omega & \omega^2 \\ \omega & \omega^2 & 1 \\ \omega^2 & 1 & \omega \end{vmatrix}$

   where ω is one of the imaginary cube roots of unity.

3. Prove that $\begin{vmatrix} x+a & b & c \\ a & x+b & c \\ a & b & x+c \end{vmatrix} = x^2(x + a + b + c).$

4. Prove that $\begin{vmatrix} a & b & c \\ a-c & b-c & c-a \\ b+c & c+a & a+b \end{vmatrix} = a^2 + b^2 + c^3 - 3abc.$

5. Show that $\begin{vmatrix} 1 & 1 & 1 \\ a & b & c \\ a^3 & b^3 & c^3 \end{vmatrix} = (b - c)(c - a)(a - b)(a + b + c).$

6. Show that $\begin{vmatrix} a+b & b+c & c+a \\ b+c & c+a & a+b \\ c+a & a+b & b+c \end{vmatrix} = 2\begin{vmatrix} a & b & c \\ b & c & a \\ c & a & b \end{vmatrix}.$

7. Show that $\begin{vmatrix} b^2c^2 & bc & b+c \\ c^2a^2 & ca & c+a \\ a^2b^2 & ab & a+b \end{vmatrix} = 0.$

8. Show that $\begin{vmatrix} a & a-c & a-b \\ b & c+a & b-a \\ c & c-a & a+b \end{vmatrix} = 4\,abc.$

9. Show that $\begin{vmatrix} (a+b)^2 & ca & bc \\ ca & (b+c)^2 & ab \\ bc & ab & (a+c)^2 \end{vmatrix} = 2abc(a + b + c)^3.$

10. Prove that $x = 1$ and $x = -9$ are roots of the equation

$$\begin{vmatrix} x+1 & 3 & 5 \\ 2 & x+2 & 5 \\ 2 & 3 & x+4 \end{vmatrix} = 0.$$

Solve the equations

11. $\begin{vmatrix} 3x-8 & 3 & 3 \\ 3 & 3x-8 & 3 \\ 3 & 3 & 3x-8 \end{vmatrix} = 0.$

12. $\begin{vmatrix} a & a & x \\ m & m & m \\ b & x & b \end{vmatrix} = 0 \ (m \neq 0).$

13. $\begin{vmatrix} 15-2x & 11 & 10 \\ 11-3x & 17 & 16 \\ 7-x & 14 & 13 \end{vmatrix} = 0.$

14. $\begin{vmatrix} x-2 & 2x-3 & 3x-4 \\ x-4 & 2x-9 & 3x-16 \\ x-8 & 2x-27 & 3x-64 \end{vmatrix} = 0.$

15. $\begin{vmatrix} p+x & q+x & r+x \\ q+x & r+x & p+x \\ r+x & p+x & q+x \end{vmatrix} = 0.$

16. Prove that $\begin{vmatrix} n! & (n+1)! & (n+2)! \\ (n+1)! & (n+2)! & (n+3)! \\ (n+2)! & (n+3)! & (n+4)! \end{vmatrix} = 0.$

17. Prove that $\begin{vmatrix} a_1 & a_2 & a_3 \\ a_3 & a_1 & a_2 \\ a_2 & a_3 & a_1 \end{vmatrix} = (a_1 + a_2 + a_3)(a_1 + a_2 w + a_3 w^2)(a_1 + a_2 w^2 + a_3 w)$

where w is a cube root of unity.

ANSWERS

1. 0
2. 0
11. $\left[\frac{11}{3}, \frac{11}{3}, \frac{2}{3}\right]$
12. $x = a$ or b
13. $x = 4$
14. $x = 4$
15. $-\frac{1}{3}(p+q+r)$

18. MULTIPLICATION OF TWO DETERMINANTS

Consider two 2 × 2 matrices $A = \begin{bmatrix} a_1 & b_1 \\ a_2 & b_2 \end{bmatrix}$

and $B = \begin{bmatrix} c_1 & d_1 \\ c_2 & d_2 \end{bmatrix}$

Now $AB = \begin{bmatrix} a_1c_1 + b_1c_2 & a_1d_1 + b_1d_2 \\ a_2c_1 + b_2c_2 & a_2d_1 + b_2d_2 \end{bmatrix}$

$$\Rightarrow |AB| = (a_1c_1 + b_1c_2)(a_2d_1 + b_2d_2) - (a_1d_1 + b_1d_2)(a_2c_1 + b_2c_2)$$
$$= a_1c_1b_2d_2 + b_1c_2a_2d_1 - a_1b_2c_2d_1 - b_1d_2a_2c_1$$
$$= (a_1b_2c_1d_2 - b_1a_2d_2c_1) - (a_1b_2c_2d_1 - b_1a_2c_2d_1)$$
$$= (a_1b_2 - a_2b_1)c_1d_2 - (a_1b_2 - a_2b_1)c_2d_1$$
$$= (a_1b_2 - a_2b_1)(c_1d_2 - c_2d_1) = |A| \cdot |B|$$

Thus we have proved that product of two determinants of order 2 is a determinant of order 2, and rule for multiplication is same as that for the corresponding matrices.

In a similar manner we can prove that product of two determinants of order 3 is a determinant of order 3 and rule for multiplication remains same as that of corresponding matrices. In this process we have also proved that $|AB| = |A| \quad |B|$.

REMARK: Indeed the result stated above holds for determinants of all orders.

Example 47. *Prove that*

$$\begin{vmatrix} a_1 & b_1 \\ a_2 & b_2 \end{vmatrix}^2 = \begin{vmatrix} a_1^2 + b_2^2 & a_1b_1 + a_2b_2 \\ a_1b_1 + a_2b_2 & b_1^2 + b_2^2 \end{vmatrix}$$

Solution. LHS $= \begin{vmatrix} a_1 & b_1 \\ a_2 & b_2 \end{vmatrix} \begin{vmatrix} a_1 & b_1 \\ a_2 & b_2 \end{vmatrix}$

$$= \begin{vmatrix} a_1 & a_2 \\ b_1 & b_2 \end{vmatrix} \begin{vmatrix} a_1 & b_1 \\ a_2 & b_2 \end{vmatrix} \quad \text{property 2}$$

$$= \begin{vmatrix} a_1 \cdot a_1 + a_2 \cdot a_2 & a_1 \cdot b_1 + a_2 \cdot b_2 \\ b_1 \cdot a_1 + b_2 \cdot a_2 & b_1 \cdot b_1 + b_2 \cdot b_2 \end{vmatrix}$$

$$= \begin{vmatrix} a_1^2 + a_2^2 & a_2b_1 + a_1b_2 \\ a_1b_1 + a_2b_2 & b_1^2 + b_2^2 \end{vmatrix}.$$

Example 48. *Prove that*

$$\begin{vmatrix} b^2 + c^2 & ab & ac \\ ba & c^2 + a^2 & bc \\ ca & cb & b^2 + a^2 \end{vmatrix} = \begin{vmatrix} 0 & c & b \\ c & 0 & a \\ b & a & 0 \end{vmatrix}^2 = 4a^2b^2c^2.$$

Solution. $\begin{vmatrix} 0 & c & b \\ c & 0 & a \\ b & a & 0 \end{vmatrix}^2 = \begin{vmatrix} 0 & c & b \\ c & 0 & a \\ b & a & 0 \end{vmatrix} \begin{vmatrix} 0 & c & b \\ c & 0 & a \\ b & a & 0 \end{vmatrix}$

$$= \begin{vmatrix} 0 + c^2 + b^2 & 0 + 0 + ba & 0 + ca + 0 \\ 0 + 0 + ab & c^2 + 0 + a^2 & cb + 0 + 0 \\ 0 + ac + 0 & ba + 0 + 0 & b^2 + a^2 + 0 \end{vmatrix}$$

$$= \begin{vmatrix} b^2 + c^2 & ab & ac \\ ab & c^2 + a^2 & bc \\ ca & cb & b^2 + a^2 \end{vmatrix}$$

Again $\begin{vmatrix} 0 & c & b \\ c & 0 & a \\ b & a & 0 \end{vmatrix} = -c \begin{vmatrix} c & a \\ b & 0 \end{vmatrix} + b \begin{vmatrix} c & 0 \\ b & a \end{vmatrix}$

$$= -c(-ab) + bca = 2abc$$

Hence the result follows.

19. MINORS AND COFACTORS

Let
$$\Delta = \begin{vmatrix} a_1 & b_1 & c_1 \\ a_2 & b_2 & c_2 \\ a_3 & b_3 & c_3 \end{vmatrix}$$

The 2 × 2 determinant obtained by cancelling 1st row and 1st column is called Minor of a_1 and is denoted by A_1

Thus
$$A_1 = \begin{vmatrix} b_2 & c_2 \\ b_3 & c_3 \end{vmatrix} = b_2c_3 - b_3c_2$$

Similarly
$$B_1 = \begin{vmatrix} a_2 & c_2 \\ a_3 & c_3 \end{vmatrix} = a_2c_3 - a_3c_2,$$
$$C_1 = a_2b_3 - a_3b_2,\ A_2 = b_1c_3 - b_3c_1 \text{ etc.}$$

One notices at once that
$$\Delta = a_1A_1 - b_1B_1 + c_1C_1$$
$$= a_1A_1 - a_2A_2 + a_3A_3$$

whereas $a_2A_1 - b_2B_1 + c_2C_1$
$$= a_2(b_2c_3 - b_3c_2) - b_2(a_2c_3 - a_3c_2) + c_2(a_2b_3 - a_3b_2)$$
$$= 0$$

We have a simple rule:

If elements of 1st row (or 1st column) are multiplied by their minors and added with plus and minus sign alternatively (starting from plus sign), the algebraic sum is equal to the determinant, whereas if the same operation is performed with the minors of elements of 2nd row or those of third row (2nd column or 3rd column, in case of elements of 1st column) the sum is zero.

Since
$$-\Delta = \begin{vmatrix} a_2 & b_2 & c_2 \\ a_1 & b_1 & c_1 \\ a_3 & b_3 & c_3 \end{vmatrix} = a_2A_2 - b_2B_2 + c_2C_2$$
$$\Delta = -a_2A_2 + b_2B_2 - c_2C_2$$

Thus for expansion in turn of elements of 2nd row is done in similar manner except for multiplication by – 1. Second assertion remains true *e.g.* $a_2A_1 - b_2B_1 + c_2C_1 = a_2A_3 - b_2B_3 + c_2C_3 = 0$.

Cofactor of any element = $(-1)^{r+c}$ × (its Minor) where r is the number of row and c is the number of column in which that element lies. Cofactors are denoted by capital letter with a dash.

Thus cofactor of $a_1 = A_1' = (-1)^{1+1}A_1 = A_1$

cofactor of $c_2 = C_2' = (-1)^{2+1}C_2 = -C_2$

In terms of cofactor, the above stated results reduce to

$$a_1A_1' + b_1B_1' + c_1C_1' = a_1A_1' + a_2A_2' + a_3A_3' = \Delta$$

and
$$a_1A_2' + b_1B_2' + c_1C_2' = a_1A_3' + b_1B_3' + c_1C_3' = 0.$$

REMARK: Observe that in case of cofactors there is no negative sign.

20. CRAMER'S RULE FOR SOLUTION OF LINEAR EQUATIONS

Let
$$a_1x + b_1y + c_1z = d_1$$
$$a_2x + b_2y + c_2z = d_2$$
$$a_3x + b_3y + c_3z = d_3$$

Multiplying 1st Equation by A_1', 2nd by A_2' and 3rd by A_3' and adding we get

$$(a_1A_1' + a_1A_2' + a_3A_3')\,x + (b_1A_1' + b_2A_2' + b_3A_3')\,y + (c_1A_1' + c_2A_2' + c_3A_3')\,z = dA_1 + dA_2' + dA_3'$$

where A_1', A_2', A_3' are cofactors of a_1, a_2 and a_3 respectively, in determinant

$$\Delta = \begin{vmatrix} a_1 & b_1 & c_1 \\ a_2 & b_2 & c_2 \\ a_3 & b_3 & c_3 \end{vmatrix}$$

By properties of cofactors, we get

$$\Delta x = \begin{vmatrix} d_1 & b_1 & c_1 \\ d_2 & b_2 & c_2 \\ d_3 & b_3 & c_3 \end{vmatrix}$$

Suppose $\Delta \neq 0$, then

$$x = \frac{1}{\Delta}\begin{vmatrix} d_1 & b_1 & c_1 \\ d_2 & b_2 & c_2 \\ d_3 & b_3 & c_3 \end{vmatrix}$$

Similarly multiplying the three equations by B_1', B_2' and B_3' respectively and adding, we get

$$y = \frac{1}{\Delta}\begin{vmatrix} a_1 & d_1 & c_1 \\ a_2 & d_2 & c_2 \\ a_3 & d_3 & c_3 \end{vmatrix}$$

Finally multiply the three equations by C_1', C_2' and C_3' and add to get

$$z = \frac{1}{\Delta}\begin{vmatrix} a_1 & b_1 & d_1 \\ a_2 & b_2 & d_2 \\ a_3 & b_3 & d_3 \end{vmatrix}$$

Thus we have the following rule (known as Cramer's rule)

$$\frac{x}{\begin{vmatrix} d_1 & b_1 & c_1 \\ d_2 & b_2 & c_2 \\ d_3 & b_3 & c_3 \end{vmatrix}} = \frac{y}{\begin{vmatrix} a_1 & d_1 & c_1 \\ a_2 & d_2 & c_2 \\ a_3 & d_3 & c_3 \end{vmatrix}} = \frac{z}{\begin{vmatrix} a_1 & b_1 & d_1 \\ a_2 & b_2 & d_2 \\ a_3 & b_3 & d_3 \end{vmatrix}} = \frac{1}{\Delta}$$

$$\frac{x}{D_1} = \frac{y}{D_2} = \frac{z}{D_3} = \frac{1}{\Delta}$$

where D_1 is obtained by replacing 1st column of Δ with d_1, d_2, and d_3; D_2 is obtained by replacing 2nd column of Δ with d_1, d_2 and d_3 and D_3 is obtained by replacing 3rd column of Δ with d_1, d_2 and d_3.

REMARK: Cramer's rule can be fruitfully applied in case $\Delta \neq 0$, when $\Delta = 0$, we take help of matrices in solving the problem.

Example 49. *Solve with the help of determinants*

$$5x - 6y + 4z = 15$$
$$7x + 4y - 3z = 19$$
$$2x + y + 6z = 46.$$

Solution. Here

Here $$\Delta = \begin{vmatrix} 5 & -6 & 4 \\ 7 & 4 & -3 \\ 2 & 1 & 6 \end{vmatrix} = 419 \neq 0$$

$$D_1 = \begin{vmatrix} 15 & -6 & 4 \\ 19 & 4 & -3 \\ 46 & 1 & 6 \end{vmatrix} = 1257$$

$$D_2 = \begin{vmatrix} 5 & 15 & 4 \\ 7 & 19 & -3 \\ 2 & 46 & 6 \end{vmatrix} = 1676$$

$$D_3 = \begin{vmatrix} 5 & -6 & 15 \\ 7 & 4 & 19 \\ 2 & 1 & 46 \end{vmatrix} = 2514$$

Hence $\dfrac{x}{D_1} = \dfrac{y}{D_2} = \dfrac{z}{D_3} = \dfrac{1}{\Delta} \Rightarrow x = \dfrac{D_1}{\Delta} = \dfrac{1257}{419} = 3.$

$$y = \frac{D_2}{\Delta} = \frac{1676}{419} = 4 \text{ and } z = \frac{D_3}{\Delta} = \frac{2514}{419} = 6.$$

Example 50. *Solve with the help of determinants*

$$x + y + z = 9$$
$$2y + 5y + 7z = 52$$
$$2x + y - z = 0.$$

Solution. Here $\Delta = \begin{vmatrix} 1 & 1 & 1 \\ 2 & 5 & 7 \\ 2 & 1 & -1 \end{vmatrix} = -4 \neq 0$

$$D_1 = \begin{vmatrix} 9 & 1 & 1 \\ 52 & 5 & 7 \\ 0 & 1 & -1 \end{vmatrix} = -4$$

$$D_2 = \begin{vmatrix} 1 & 9 & 1 \\ 2 & 52 & 7 \\ 2 & 0 & -1 \end{vmatrix} = -12$$

and $$D_3 = \begin{vmatrix} 1 & 1 & 9 \\ 2 & 5 & 52 \\ 2 & 1 & 0 \end{vmatrix} = -20$$

Hence $x = \dfrac{D_1}{\Delta} = 1,\; y = \dfrac{D_2}{\Delta} = 3$ and $z = \dfrac{D_3}{\Delta} = 5.$

EXERCISES

1. Prove that if

$$\Delta = \begin{vmatrix} a_1 & b_1 & c_1 \\ a_2 & b_2 & c_2 \\ a_3 & b_3 & c_3 \end{vmatrix} \neq 0$$

then $\begin{vmatrix} A_1' & B_1' & C_1' \\ A_2' & B_2' & C_2' \\ A_3' & B_3' & C_3' \end{vmatrix} = \Delta^2$, where A_i', B_i', C_i'.

(i = 1, 2, 3) have usual meanings.

[**Hint.** Compute $\Delta \quad \Delta'$ where

$$\Delta' = \begin{vmatrix} A_1' & B_1' & C_1' \\ A_2' & B_2' & C_2' \\ A_3' & B_3' & C_3' \end{vmatrix}$$ and use properties of cofactors.]

2. Prove that

$$\begin{vmatrix} a^2 - bc & b^2 - ca & c^2 - ab \\ c^2 - ab & a^2 - bc & b^2 - ca \\ b^2 - ca & c^2 - ab & a^2 - bc \end{vmatrix} = \begin{vmatrix} a & b & c \\ c & a & b \\ b & c & a \end{vmatrix}^2$$

3. Show that the square of the determinant

$$\begin{vmatrix} 0 & \cos x & -\sin x \\ \sin x & 0 & \cos x \\ \cos x & \sin x & 0 \end{vmatrix}$$ can be written in the form:

$$\begin{vmatrix} 1 & \lambda & -\lambda \\ \lambda & 1 & -\lambda \\ -\lambda & -\lambda & 1 \end{vmatrix}$$ where $\lambda = -\sin x \cos x$.

4. Solve the following equations with the help of determinants

(*i*) $x + y + z = 3$, $2x - y + 4z = 5$, $x - 3y - 9z = -11$

(*ii*) $2x + y + 7z = -28$, $x - y + 3z = -15$, $3x + 2y - z = 5$

(*iii*) $2x + y + 2z = 10$, $x - y + 2z = 5$, $x + y + z = 6$

(*iv*) $x - 2y + z = 4$, $2x - 3y + 2z = 7$, $4x + y + 8z = 19$.

ANSWERS

4. (*i*) $x = y = z = 1$ (*ii*) $x = -1,\ y = 2,\ z = -4$

(*iii*) $x = 1,\ y = 2,\ z = 3$ (*iv*) $x = y = -1,\ z = 3$

21. ADJOINT OF A MATRIX

We now give another method to find inverse of a matrix. Before we come to the second method, we give:

Definition: *Cofactor Matrix.* It is defined to be the matrix obtained by replacing every number a_{ij} of the given matrix A by its cofactor in the determinant of A.

As an example, let

$$A = \begin{bmatrix} 1 & 2 & 3 \\ 4 & 5 & 0 \\ 2 & 1 & 4 \end{bmatrix}$$

then cofactor matrix of A is the matrix

$$\begin{bmatrix} \begin{vmatrix} 5 & 0 \\ 1 & 4 \end{vmatrix} & -\begin{vmatrix} 4 & 0 \\ 2 & 4 \end{vmatrix} & \begin{vmatrix} 4 & 5 \\ 2 & 1 \end{vmatrix} \\ -\begin{vmatrix} 2 & 3 \\ 1 & 4 \end{vmatrix} & \begin{vmatrix} 1 & 3 \\ 2 & 4 \end{vmatrix} & -\begin{vmatrix} 1 & 2 \\ 2 & 1 \end{vmatrix} \\ \begin{vmatrix} 2 & 3 \\ 5 & 0 \end{vmatrix} & -\begin{vmatrix} 1 & 3 \\ 4 & 0 \end{vmatrix} & \begin{vmatrix} 1 & 2 \\ 4 & 5 \end{vmatrix} \end{bmatrix} = \begin{bmatrix} 20 & -16 & -6 \\ -5 & -2 & 3 \\ -15 & 12 & -3 \end{bmatrix}$$

Adjoint of a matrix: Let A be a matrix and let C be its cofactor matrix, then the transpose C' of C is called the *adjoint* of A (to be written, in short as Adj A)

Thus in the above example

$$\text{Adj } A = \begin{bmatrix} 20 & -5 & -15 \\ -16 & -2 & 12 \\ -6 & 3 & -3 \end{bmatrix}$$

22. PROPERTIES OF THE ADJOINT OF A MATRIX

One can show that for square matrices A, B

(*i*) $A\,(\text{Adj } A) = (\text{Adj } A)A = |A|\,I$

(*ii*) $\text{Adj }(A') = (\text{Adj } A)'$

(*iii*) $\text{Adj }(AB) = (\text{Adj } B)\,(\text{Adj } A)$

We take up few examples to verify these results.

Example 51. *For the matrix* $A = \begin{bmatrix} 1 & 2 & 3 \\ 3 & 1 & 2 \\ 2 & 3 & 1 \end{bmatrix}$ *verify that*

Adj $A' = (\text{Adj } A)'$

Solution. Co-factor matrix of A is

$$\begin{bmatrix} \begin{vmatrix} 1 & 2 \\ 3 & 1 \end{vmatrix} & -\begin{vmatrix} 3 & 2 \\ 2 & 1 \end{vmatrix} & \begin{vmatrix} 3 & 1 \\ 2 & 3 \end{vmatrix} \\ -\begin{vmatrix} 2 & 3 \\ 3 & 1 \end{vmatrix} & \begin{vmatrix} 1 & 3 \\ 2 & 1 \end{vmatrix} & -\begin{vmatrix} 1 & 2 \\ 2 & 3 \end{vmatrix} \\ \begin{vmatrix} 2 & 3 \\ 1 & 2 \end{vmatrix} & -\begin{vmatrix} 1 & 3 \\ 3 & 2 \end{vmatrix} & \begin{vmatrix} 1 & 2 \\ 3 & 1 \end{vmatrix} \end{bmatrix} = \begin{bmatrix} -5 & 1 & 7 \\ 7 & -5 & 1 \\ 1 & 7 & -5 \end{bmatrix}$$

$$\therefore \quad \text{Adj } A = \begin{bmatrix} -5 & 7 & 1 \\ 1 & -5 & 7 \\ 7 & 1 & -5 \end{bmatrix}$$

Now $A' = \begin{bmatrix} 1 & 3 & 2 \\ 2 & 1 & 3 \\ 3 & 2 & 1 \end{bmatrix}$

Cofactor matrix of A' is $\begin{bmatrix} \begin{vmatrix} 1 & 3 \\ 2 & 1 \end{vmatrix} & -\begin{vmatrix} 2 & 3 \\ 3 & 1 \end{vmatrix} & \begin{vmatrix} 2 & 1 \\ 3 & 2 \end{vmatrix} \\ -\begin{vmatrix} 3 & 2 \\ 2 & 1 \end{vmatrix} & \begin{vmatrix} 1 & 2 \\ 3 & 1 \end{vmatrix} & -\begin{vmatrix} 1 & 3 \\ 3 & 2 \end{vmatrix} \\ \begin{vmatrix} 3 & 2 \\ 1 & 3 \end{vmatrix} & -\begin{vmatrix} 1 & 2 \\ 2 & 3 \end{vmatrix} & \begin{vmatrix} 1 & 3 \\ 2 & 1 \end{vmatrix} \end{bmatrix} = \begin{bmatrix} -5 & 7 & 1 \\ 1 & -5 & 7 \\ 7 & 1 & -5 \end{bmatrix}$

Hence $$\text{Adj } A' = \begin{bmatrix} -5 & 1 & 7 \\ 7 & -5 & 1 \\ 1 & 7 & -5 \end{bmatrix} = (\text{Adj } A)'$$

Example 52. *Show that for matrix* $A = \begin{bmatrix} 1 & -1 & 1 \\ 2 & 3 & 0 \\ 18 & 2 & 10 \end{bmatrix}$

$$A\,(\text{Adj } A) = 0$$

Solution. Cofactor matrix of A is

$$\begin{bmatrix} \begin{vmatrix} 3 & 0 \\ 2 & 10 \end{vmatrix} & -\begin{vmatrix} 2 & 0 \\ 18 & 10 \end{vmatrix} & \begin{vmatrix} 2 & 3 \\ 18 & 2 \end{vmatrix} \\ -\begin{vmatrix} -1 & 1 \\ 2 & 10 \end{vmatrix} & \begin{vmatrix} 1 & 1 \\ 18 & 10 \end{vmatrix} & -\begin{vmatrix} 1 & -1 \\ 18 & 2 \end{vmatrix} \\ \begin{vmatrix} -1 & 1 \\ 3 & 0 \end{vmatrix} & -\begin{vmatrix} 1 & 1 \\ 2 & 0 \end{vmatrix} & \begin{vmatrix} 1 & -1 \\ 2 & 3 \end{vmatrix} \end{bmatrix} = \begin{bmatrix} 30 & -20 & -50 \\ 12 & -8 & -20 \\ -3 & 2 & 5 \end{bmatrix}$$

Hence $\text{Adj } A = \begin{bmatrix} 30 & 12 & -3 \\ -20 & -8 & 2 \\ -50 & -20 & 5 \end{bmatrix}$

and so $A\,(\text{Adj } A) = \begin{bmatrix} 1 & -1 & 1 \\ 2 & 3 & 0 \\ 18 & 2 & 10 \end{bmatrix} \begin{bmatrix} 30 & 12 & -3 \\ -20 & -8 & 2 \\ -50 & -20 & 5 \end{bmatrix}$

$$= \begin{bmatrix} 30+20-50 & 12+8-20 & -3-2+5 \\ 60-60+0 & 24-24+0 & -6+6+0 \\ 540-40-50 & 216-16-200 & -54+4+50 \end{bmatrix}$$

$$= \begin{bmatrix} 0 & 0 & 0 \\ 0 & 0 & 0 \\ 0 & 0 & 0 \end{bmatrix} \text{ the zero matrix}$$

Example 53. *Verify that for the matrix* $A = \begin{bmatrix} 1 & 2 & 3 \\ 1 & 3 & 4 \\ 1 & 4 & 3 \end{bmatrix}$

$$A\,(Adj\,A) = (Adj\,A)A = |A|\,I_3$$

Solution. Cofactor matrix of A is

$$\begin{bmatrix} \begin{vmatrix} 3 & 4 \\ 4 & 3 \end{vmatrix} & -\begin{vmatrix} 1 & 4 \\ 1 & 3 \end{vmatrix} & \begin{vmatrix} 1 & 3 \\ 1 & 4 \end{vmatrix} \\ -\begin{vmatrix} 2 & 3 \\ 4 & 3 \end{vmatrix} & \begin{vmatrix} 1 & 3 \\ 1 & 3 \end{vmatrix} & -\begin{vmatrix} 1 & 2 \\ 1 & 4 \end{vmatrix} \\ \begin{vmatrix} 2 & 3 \\ 3 & 4 \end{vmatrix} & -\begin{vmatrix} 1 & 3 \\ 1 & 4 \end{vmatrix} & \begin{vmatrix} 1 & 2 \\ 1 & 3 \end{vmatrix} \end{bmatrix} = \begin{bmatrix} -7 & 1 & 1 \\ 6 & 0 & -2 \\ -1 & -1 & 1 \end{bmatrix}$$

Hence $\quad \text{Adj } A = \begin{bmatrix} -7 & 6 & -1 \\ 1 & 0 & -1 \\ -1 & -2 & 1 \end{bmatrix}$

Thus $A\,(\text{Adj } A) = \begin{bmatrix} 1 & 2 & 3 \\ 1 & 3 & 4 \\ 1 & 4 & 3 \end{bmatrix} \begin{bmatrix} -7 & 6 & -1 \\ 1 & 0 & -1 \\ 1 & -2 & 1 \end{bmatrix} = \begin{bmatrix} -2 & 0 & 0 \\ 0 & -2 & 0 \\ 0 & 0 & -2 \end{bmatrix} = -2I_3$

$$(\text{Adj } A)A = \begin{bmatrix} -7 & 6 & -1 \\ 1 & 0 & -1 \\ 1 & -2 & 1 \end{bmatrix} \begin{bmatrix} 1 & 2 & 3 \\ 1 & 3 & 4 \\ 1 & 4 & 3 \end{bmatrix} = \begin{bmatrix} -2 & 0 & 0 \\ 0 & -2 & 0 \\ 0 & 0 & -2 \end{bmatrix} = -2I_3$$

$$|A| = (9-16) - 2(3-4) + 3(4-3) = -2$$

Hence $A(\text{Adj } A) = (\text{Adj } A)A = |A|\,I_3$

Example 54. *For matrices* $A = \begin{bmatrix} 4 & 1 \\ -1 & 5 \end{bmatrix}$ *and* $B = \begin{bmatrix} 5 & -2 \\ 3 & -2 \end{bmatrix}$

verify that $Adj\,AB = (Adj\,B)\,(Adj\,A)$

Solution. Cofactor matrix of A is $\begin{bmatrix} 5 & 1 \\ -1 & 4 \end{bmatrix}$

$$\therefore \qquad Adj\ A = \begin{bmatrix} 5 & -1 \\ 1 & 4 \end{bmatrix}$$

cofactor matrix of B is $\begin{bmatrix} -2 & -3 \\ 2 & 5 \end{bmatrix}$

$$\therefore \qquad \text{Adj } B = \begin{bmatrix} -2 & 2 \\ -3 & 5 \end{bmatrix}$$

$$\text{Hence Adj } B \text{ Adj } A = \begin{bmatrix} -2 & 2 \\ -3 & 5 \end{bmatrix}\begin{bmatrix} 5 & -1 \\ 1 & 4 \end{bmatrix} = \begin{bmatrix} -10+2 & 2+8 \\ -15+5 & 3+20 \end{bmatrix}$$

$$= \begin{bmatrix} -8 & 10 \\ -10 & 23 \end{bmatrix}$$

$$\text{Now} \qquad AB = \begin{bmatrix} 4 & 1 \\ -1 & 5 \end{bmatrix}\begin{bmatrix} 5 & -2 \\ 3 & -2 \end{bmatrix}$$

$$= \begin{bmatrix} 20+3 & -8-2 \\ -5+15 & 2-10 \end{bmatrix} = \begin{bmatrix} 23 & -10 \\ 10 & -8 \end{bmatrix}$$

$$\text{cofactor matrix of} \quad AB = \begin{bmatrix} -8 & -10 \\ 10 & 23 \end{bmatrix}$$

$$\text{Thus} \qquad \text{Adj } AB = \begin{bmatrix} -8 & 10 \\ -10 & 23 \end{bmatrix}$$

$$\text{Hence} \qquad \text{Adj } AB = (\text{Adj } B)(\text{Adj } A).$$

In the following examples, we illustrate how to find inverse of a matrix by using Adj of the matrix.

Example 55. *Find adjoint and then inverse of the matrix*

$$A = \begin{bmatrix} 1 & -2 & 3 \\ -2 & -1 & 0 \\ 4 & -2 & 5 \end{bmatrix}$$

Solution. We notice here that

$$|A| = 1(-5+0) + -(-10-0) + 3(4+4)$$

$$= -1 \neq 0$$

Now cofactor matrix of A is

$$\begin{bmatrix} \begin{vmatrix} -1 & 0 \\ -2 & 5 \end{vmatrix} & -\begin{vmatrix} -2 & 0 \\ 4 & 5 \end{vmatrix} & \begin{vmatrix} -2 & -1 \\ 4 & -2 \end{vmatrix} \\ -\begin{vmatrix} -2 & 3 \\ -2 & 5 \end{vmatrix} & \begin{vmatrix} 1 & 3 \\ 4 & 5 \end{vmatrix} & -\begin{vmatrix} 1 & -2 \\ 4 & -2 \end{vmatrix} \\ \begin{vmatrix} -2 & 3 \\ -1 & 0 \end{vmatrix} & -\begin{vmatrix} 1 & 3 \\ -2 & 0 \end{vmatrix} & \begin{vmatrix} 1 & -2 \\ -2 & -1 \end{vmatrix} \end{bmatrix} = \begin{bmatrix} -5 & 10 & 8 \\ 4 & -7 & -6 \\ 3 & 6 & -5 \end{bmatrix}$$

Hence $$\text{Adj } A = \begin{bmatrix} -5 & 4 & 3 \\ 10 & -7 & 6 \\ 8 & -6 & -5 \end{bmatrix}$$

Also $$A^{-1} = \frac{1}{|A|} \text{Adj } A$$

$$= -1 \begin{bmatrix} -5 & 4 & 3 \\ 10 & -7 & 6 \\ 8 & -6 & -5 \end{bmatrix} = \begin{bmatrix} 5 & -4 & -3 \\ -10 & 7 & -6 \\ -8 & 6 & 5 \end{bmatrix}$$

Example 56. *Let* $A = \begin{bmatrix} a_{11} & a_{12} & a_{13} \\ a_{21} & a_{22} & a_{23} \\ a_{31} & a_{32} & a_{33} \end{bmatrix}$ *be a matrix s.t.,* $|A| \neq 0$.

Show that $A^{-1} = \dfrac{\text{Adj } A}{|A|}$.

Solution. Cofactor matrix of A is $\begin{bmatrix} c_{11} & c_{12} & c_{13} \\ c_{21} & c_{22} & c_{23} \\ c_{31} & c_{32} & c_{33} \end{bmatrix}$ (see under minors and cofactors) and thus Adj $A = \begin{bmatrix} c_{11} & c_{21} & c_{31} \\ c_{12} & c_{22} & c_{32} \\ c_{13} & c_{23} & c_{33} \end{bmatrix}$

Hence A (Adj A)

$$= \begin{bmatrix} a_{11}c_{11} + a_{12}c_{12} + a_{13}c_{13} & a_{11}c_{21} + a_{12}c_{22} + a_{13}c_{23} & a_{11}c_{31} + a_{12}c_{32} + a_{13}c_{33} \\ a_{21}c_{11} + a_{22}c_{12} + a_{23}c_{13} & a_{21}c_{21} + a_{22}c_{22} + a_{23}c_{23} & a_{21}c_{31} + a_{22}c_{32} + a_{23}c_{33} \\ a_{31}c_{11} + a_{32}c_{12} + a_{33}c_{13} & a_{31}c_{21} + a_{32}c_{22} + a_{33}c_{23} & a_{31}c_{31} + a_{32}c_{32} + a_{33}c_{33} \end{bmatrix}$$

$$= \begin{bmatrix} |A| & 0 & 0 \\ 0 & |A| & 0 \\ 0 & 0 & |A| \end{bmatrix} = |A| \begin{bmatrix} 1 & 0 & 0 \\ 0 & 1 & 0 \\ 0 & 0 & 1 \end{bmatrix} = |A| I$$

Hence $\dfrac{A(\text{Adj } A)}{|A|} = 1$

Giving $A^{-1} = \dfrac{\text{Adj } A}{|A|}$ $\quad (|A| \neq 0)$

Solution of Equations using the inverse

Suppose we have a matrix equation

$$AX = B$$

then if A^{-1} exists, we get

$$A^{-1}AX = A^{-1}B$$

$\Rightarrow$ $IX = A^{-1}B$ where I is unit matrix

$\Rightarrow$ $X = A^{-1}B$

we illustrate the method through

Example 57. *Solve the equations*

$$5x - y + z = 4$$
$$3x + 2y - 5z = 2$$
$$x + 3y - 2z = 5$$

by finding inverse of the coefficient matrix.

Solution. The matrix form of the given equation is

$$\begin{bmatrix} 5 & -1 & 1 \\ 3 & 2 & -5 \\ 1 & 3 & -2 \end{bmatrix} \begin{bmatrix} x \\ y \\ z \end{bmatrix} = \begin{bmatrix} 4 \\ 2 \\ 5 \end{bmatrix} \text{ i.e., } AX = B$$

Hence $|A| = 5(-4+15) + 1(-6+5) + (9-2) = 61 \neq 0$

Cofactor matrix of A is

$$\begin{bmatrix} \begin{vmatrix} 2 & -5 \\ 3 & -2 \end{vmatrix} & -\begin{vmatrix} 3 & -5 \\ 1 & -2 \end{vmatrix} & \begin{vmatrix} 3 & 2 \\ 1 & 3 \end{vmatrix} \\ -\begin{vmatrix} -1 & 1 \\ 3 & -2 \end{vmatrix} & \begin{vmatrix} 5 & 1 \\ 1 & -2 \end{vmatrix} & -\begin{vmatrix} 5 & -1 \\ 1 & 3 \end{vmatrix} \\ \begin{vmatrix} -1 & 1 \\ 2 & -5 \end{vmatrix} & -\begin{vmatrix} 5 & 1 \\ 3 & -5 \end{vmatrix} & \begin{vmatrix} 5 & -1 \\ 3 & 2 \end{vmatrix} \end{bmatrix} = \begin{bmatrix} 11 & 1 & 7 \\ 1 & -11 & -16 \\ 3 & 28 & 13 \end{bmatrix}$$

Thus $\quad \text{Adj } A = \begin{bmatrix} 11 & 1 & 3 \\ 1 & -11 & 28 \\ 7 & -16 & 13 \end{bmatrix}$

$$A^{-1} = \frac{1}{|A|} \text{ Adj } A = \frac{1}{61}\begin{bmatrix} 11 & 1 & 3 \\ 1 & -11 & 28 \\ 7 & -16 & 13 \end{bmatrix}$$

Hence, as $X = A^{-1} B$, we get

$$\begin{bmatrix} x \\ y \\ z \end{bmatrix} = \frac{1}{61}\begin{bmatrix} 11 & 1 & 3 \\ 1 & -11 & 28 \\ 7 & -16 & 13 \end{bmatrix}\begin{bmatrix} 4 \\ 2 \\ 5 \end{bmatrix}$$

$$= \frac{1}{61}\begin{bmatrix} 44+2+15 \\ 4-22+140 \\ 28-32+65 \end{bmatrix} = \frac{1}{61}\begin{bmatrix} 61 \\ 122 \\ 61 \end{bmatrix} = \begin{bmatrix} 1 \\ 2 \\ 1 \end{bmatrix}$$

The required solution is, therefore,

$$x = 1, y = 2, z = 1$$

Example 58. *Solve the following equations*

$$x + 2y + 3z = 14$$
$$3x + y + 2z = 11$$
$$2x + 3y + z = 11$$

by finding inverse of the coefficient matrix.

Solution. Matrix form of the equations is

$$\begin{bmatrix} 1 & 2 & 3 \\ 3 & 1 & 2 \\ 2 & 3 & 1 \end{bmatrix}\begin{bmatrix} x \\ y \\ z \end{bmatrix} = \begin{bmatrix} 14 \\ 11 \\ 11 \end{bmatrix} \quad \text{or} \quad AX = B$$

Here $|A| = 1(1-6) - 2(3-4) + 3(9-2) = -5 + 2 + 21 = 18 \neq 0$

Hence A^{-1} exists.

The cofactor matrix is given by

$$\begin{bmatrix} \begin{vmatrix} 1 & 2 \\ 3 & 1 \end{vmatrix} & -\begin{vmatrix} 3 & 2 \\ 2 & 1 \end{vmatrix} & \begin{vmatrix} 3 & 1 \\ 2 & 3 \end{vmatrix} \\ -\begin{vmatrix} 2 & 3 \\ 3 & 1 \end{vmatrix} & \begin{vmatrix} 1 & 3 \\ 2 & 1 \end{vmatrix} & -\begin{vmatrix} 1 & 2 \\ 2 & 3 \end{vmatrix} \\ \begin{vmatrix} 2 & 3 \\ 1 & 2 \end{vmatrix} & -\begin{vmatrix} 1 & 3 \\ 3 & 2 \end{vmatrix} & \begin{vmatrix} 1 & 2 \\ 3 & 1 \end{vmatrix} \end{bmatrix} = \begin{bmatrix} -5 & 1 & 7 \\ 7 & -5 & 1 \\ 1 & 7 & -5 \end{bmatrix}$$

Thus adjoint of A is $\begin{bmatrix} -5 & 7 & 1 \\ 1 & -5 & 7 \\ 7 & 1 & -5 \end{bmatrix}$

A^{-1} is now given by $\frac{1}{|A|}$ Adj A

$$= \frac{1}{18}\begin{bmatrix} -5 & 7 & 1 \\ 1 & -5 & 7 \\ 7 & 1 & -5 \end{bmatrix}$$

Since $X = A^{-1} B$, we get

$$\begin{bmatrix} x \\ y \\ z \end{bmatrix} = \frac{1}{18}\begin{bmatrix} -5 & 7 & 1 \\ 1 & -5 & 7 \\ 7 & 1 & -5 \end{bmatrix}\begin{bmatrix} 14 \\ 11 \\ 11 \end{bmatrix}$$

$$= \frac{1}{18}\begin{bmatrix} -70+77+11 \\ 14-55+77 \\ 98+11-15 \end{bmatrix} = \frac{1}{18}\begin{bmatrix} 18 \\ 36 \\ 54 \end{bmatrix} = \begin{bmatrix} 1 \\ 2 \\ 3 \end{bmatrix}$$

Hence solution is $x = 1, y = 2, z = 3$

Example 59. *Solve the following equations by using matrix inversion*

$$x + 2y - z = 3$$
$$3x - y + 2z = 1$$
$$2x - 2y + 3z = 2$$

Solution. Matrix form of the equations is

$$\begin{bmatrix} 1 & 2 & -1 \\ 3 & -1 & 2 \\ 2 & -2 & 3 \end{bmatrix}\begin{bmatrix} x \\ y \\ z \end{bmatrix} = \begin{bmatrix} 3 \\ 1 \\ 2 \end{bmatrix} \quad \text{or} \quad AX = B$$

Here $|A| = -5 \neq 0$

The cofactor matrix is given by

$$\begin{bmatrix} \begin{vmatrix} -1 & 2 \\ -2 & 3 \end{vmatrix} & -\begin{vmatrix} 3 & 2 \\ 2 & 3 \end{vmatrix} & \begin{vmatrix} 3 & -1 \\ 2 & -2 \end{vmatrix} \\ -\begin{vmatrix} 2 & -1 \\ -2 & 3 \end{vmatrix} & \begin{vmatrix} 1 & -1 \\ 2 & 3 \end{vmatrix} & -\begin{vmatrix} 1 & 2 \\ 2 & -2 \end{vmatrix} \\ \begin{vmatrix} 2 & -1 \\ -1 & 2 \end{vmatrix} & -\begin{vmatrix} 1 & -1 \\ -2 & 3 \end{vmatrix} & \begin{vmatrix} 1 & 2 \\ 3 & -1 \end{vmatrix} \end{bmatrix} = \begin{bmatrix} 1 & -5 & -4 \\ -4 & 5 & 6 \\ 3 & -5 & -7 \end{bmatrix}$$

$$\therefore \quad \text{Adj}\, A = \begin{bmatrix} 1 & -4 & 3 \\ -5 & 5 & -5 \\ -4 & 6 & -7 \end{bmatrix} = \text{transpose of the above matrix}$$

Hence inverse is given by

$$A^{-1} = \frac{1}{|A|} \text{Adj } A = \frac{1}{5}\begin{bmatrix} 1 & -4 & 3 \\ -5 & 5 & -5 \\ -4 & 6 & -7 \end{bmatrix}$$

Thus as $X = A^{-1}B$, we get

$$\begin{bmatrix} x \\ y \\ z \end{bmatrix} = -\frac{1}{5}\begin{bmatrix} 1 & -4 & 3 \\ -5 & 5 & -5 \\ -4 & 6 & -7 \end{bmatrix}\begin{bmatrix} 3 \\ 1 \\ 2 \end{bmatrix} = -\frac{1}{5}\begin{bmatrix} 3-4+6 \\ -15+5-10 \\ -12+6-14 \end{bmatrix}$$

$$= -\frac{1}{5}\begin{bmatrix} 5 \\ -20 \\ -20 \end{bmatrix} = \begin{bmatrix} -1 \\ 4 \\ 4 \end{bmatrix}$$

or that $x = -1, y = 4, z = 4$ is the required solution.

Example 60. *To control a crop disease it is necessary to use 8 units of chemical A, 14 units of chemical B and 13 units of chemical C. One barrel of spray P contains one unit of A, 2 units of B and 3 units of C. One barrel of spray R contains 1 unit of A, 2 units of B and 2 units of C. Find how many barrels of each type of spray be used to just meet the requirements.*

Solution: We can formulate the above problem in the following matrix equation

$$\begin{array}{c} \\ A \\ B \\ C \end{array}\begin{array}{c} \begin{matrix} P & Q & R \end{matrix} \\ \begin{bmatrix} 1 & 2 & 1 \\ 2 & 3 & 2 \\ 3 & 2 & 2 \end{bmatrix} \end{array}\begin{bmatrix} x \\ y \\ z \end{bmatrix} = \begin{bmatrix} 8 \\ 14 \\ 13 \end{bmatrix}$$

where x, y, z are number of barrels (to be used) of spray P, Q, R, respectively.

The above matrix equation becomes

$$\begin{bmatrix} x \\ y \\ z \end{bmatrix} = \begin{bmatrix} 2 & -2 & 1 \\ 2 & -1 & 0 \\ -5 & 4 & -1 \end{bmatrix}\begin{bmatrix} 8 \\ 14 \\ 13 \end{bmatrix} \qquad \text{(by finding inverse)}$$

$$= \begin{bmatrix} 16-28+13 \\ 16-14+0 \\ -40+56-13 \end{bmatrix} = \begin{bmatrix} 1 \\ 2 \\ 3 \end{bmatrix}$$

and hence we need 1 barrel of spray P, 2 barrels of spray Q and 3 barrels of spray R to just meet the requirements

Example 61. *In a market survey three commodities A, B and C were considered. In finding out the index number some fixed weights were assigned to three varieties in each of the commodities. The table below provides the information regarding the consumption of three commodities according to three varieties and also the total weight received by the commodity:*

Commodity	*Variety*			*Total weight*
	I	*II*	*III*	
A	*1*	*2*	*3*	*11*
B	*2*	*4*	*5*	*21*
C	*3*	*5*	*6*	*27*

Find the weights assigned to the three varieties by using matrix-inverse method, given that the weights assigned to a commodity are equal to the sum of weights of the various varieties multiplied by the corresponding consumption.

Solution. Let x, y, z be the weights assigned to A, B, C, respectively. Then we have

$$\begin{aligned} x+2y+3z &= 11 \\ 2x+4y+5z &= 21 \\ 3x+5y+6z &= 27 \end{aligned}$$

which, in matrix notation, reads as

$$\begin{bmatrix} 1 & 2 & 3 \\ 2 & 4 & 5 \\ 3 & 5 & 6 \end{bmatrix}\begin{bmatrix} x \\ y \\ z \end{bmatrix} = \begin{bmatrix} 11 \\ 21 \\ 27 \end{bmatrix}$$

Let $$A = \begin{bmatrix} 1 & 2 & 3 \\ 2 & 4 & 5 \\ 3 & 5 & 6 \end{bmatrix}$$

then $$|A| = \begin{vmatrix} 1 & 2 & 3 \\ 2 & 4 & 5 \\ 3 & 5 & 6 \end{vmatrix} = \begin{vmatrix} 1 & 2 & 3 \\ 0 & 0 & -1 \\ 0 & -1 & -3 \end{vmatrix} = -1.$$

It is easy to see that

$$\text{Adj } A = \begin{vmatrix} -1 & 3 & -2 \\ 3 & -3 & 1 \\ -2 & 1 & 0 \end{vmatrix}$$

Hence $\quad A^{-1} = \dfrac{1}{|A|} \text{Adj}\, A$

$$= \frac{1}{-1}\begin{bmatrix} -1 & 3 & -2 \\ 3 & -3 & 1 \\ -2 & 1 & 0 \end{bmatrix} = \begin{bmatrix} 1 & -3 & 2 \\ -3 & 3 & -1 \\ 2 & -1 & 0 \end{bmatrix}$$

Hence $\quad \begin{bmatrix} x \\ y \\ z \end{bmatrix} = A^{-1}\begin{bmatrix} 11 \\ 21 \\ 27 \end{bmatrix} = \begin{bmatrix} 1 & -3 & 2 \\ -3 & 3 & -1 \\ 2 & -1 & 0 \end{bmatrix}\begin{bmatrix} 11 \\ 21 \\ 27 \end{bmatrix}$

$$= \begin{bmatrix} 11 & -63 & +54 \\ -33 & +63 & -27 \\ & 22 & -21 \end{bmatrix} = \begin{bmatrix} 2 \\ 3 \\ 1 \end{bmatrix}.$$

Hence $\quad x = 2, y = 3, z = 1$

are the required weights assigned to *A*, *B* and *C*.

Example 62. *Given the following equations for two related markets (A) and (B) find the equilibrium conditions for each market. Also find the equilibrium price for each market.*

$$x_d(A) = 82 - 3p_A + P_B \qquad x_d(B) = 92 + 2p_A - 4p_B$$

$$x_s(A) = -5 + 15p_A \qquad x_s(B) = -6 + 32p_B$$

where x_d and x_s denote quantity demanded and quantity supplied respectively.

Solution. Equilibrium in supply and demand analysis occurs when $x_s = x_d$.

Thus, we have, for market (*A*)

$$82 - 3p_A + p_B = -5 + 15p_A$$

$$\Rightarrow \qquad 18p_A - p_B = 87 \qquad \text{... (1)}$$

Again for equilibrium in market (*B*)

$$92 + 2p_A - 4p_B = -6 + 32p_B$$

$$\Rightarrow \qquad 36p_B - 2p_A = 98 \qquad \text{... (2)}$$

(1) and (2) are the required equilibrium conditions for the two markets. To find the equilibrium price for each market we solve the equations (1) and (2)

In matrix form, we have

$$\begin{bmatrix} 18 & -1 \\ -2 & 36 \end{bmatrix}\begin{bmatrix} p_A \\ p_B \end{bmatrix} = \begin{bmatrix} 87 \\ 98 \end{bmatrix}$$

or $$AX = B$$

We have $$|A| = 646$$

and $$\text{Adj } A = \begin{bmatrix} 36 & 1 \\ 2 & 18 \end{bmatrix}$$

$$\text{thus } A^{-1} = \frac{1}{646}\begin{bmatrix} 36 & 1 \\ 2 & 18 \end{bmatrix} = \begin{bmatrix} \frac{18}{323} & \frac{1}{646} \\ \frac{1}{323} & \frac{9}{323} \end{bmatrix}$$

$$\Rightarrow \quad X = \begin{bmatrix} \frac{18}{323} & \frac{1}{646} \\ \frac{1}{323} & \frac{9}{323} \end{bmatrix}\begin{bmatrix} 87 \\ 98 \end{bmatrix} = \begin{bmatrix} 5 \\ 3 \end{bmatrix}.$$

Hence $p_A = 5, p_B = 3$ are required equilibrium prices.

We now, prove

Theorem. A necessary and sufficient condition for a matrix (square) A to be invertible is that $|A| \neq 0$.

Proof. Suppose A is an invertible matrix and suppose B is its inverse.

Then $AB = I$

$$\Rightarrow \quad |AB| = |I|$$

$$\Rightarrow \quad |A||B| = 1$$

$$\Rightarrow \quad |A| \neq 0$$

hence necessity follows.

Sufficiency: Let $|A| = 0$

Take $$B = \frac{1}{|A|}\text{ Adj } A$$

Then $$AB = A\left(\frac{1}{|A|}\text{Adj } A\right) = \frac{1}{|A|}(A \text{ Adj } A)$$

$$= \frac{1}{|A|}|A| = I = I$$

Again $$AB = \left(\frac{1}{|A|}\text{Adj } A\right)A = \frac{1}{|A|}[(\text{Adj})A)A]$$

$$= \frac{1}{|A|}\cdot|A|I = I.$$

Hence B is inverse of A and our assertion follows.

Example 63. *The prices of three commodities X, Y and Z are x, y and z per unit respectively. A purchases 4 units of Z and sells 3 units of X and 5 units of Y. B purchases 3 units of Y and sells 2 units of X and 1 unit of Z. C purchases 1 unit of X and sells 4 units of X and sells 4 units of Y and 6 units of Z. In the process A, B, C earn Rs. 6,000, 5,000 and 13,000 respectively. Using matrices, find the prices per unit of the three commodities. (Note that selling the units is positive earning and buying the units is negative earning).*

Solution. A sells 3 units of X and 5 units of Y so his earnings from X and Y are $3x$ and $5y$ respectively.

Again, A buys 4 units of Z and thus his earning from Z is $-4z$.

Thus total earnings of A are given by

$$3x + 5y - 4z$$

By hypothesis, $3x + 5y - 4z = 6000$

Similarly, we get the equations (giving earnings of B and C) as

$$2x - 3y + z = 5000$$
$$-x + 4y + 6z = 13000$$

Corresponding matrix equation is

$$\begin{bmatrix} 3 & 5 & -4 \\ 2 & -3 & 1 \\ -1 & 4 & 6 \end{bmatrix}\begin{bmatrix} x \\ y \\ z \end{bmatrix} = \begin{bmatrix} 6000 \\ 5000 \\ 13000 \end{bmatrix}$$

Augmented matrix is

$$\begin{bmatrix} 3 & 5 & -4 & : & 6000 \\ 2 & -3 & 1 & : & 5000 \\ -1 & 4 & 6 & : & 13000 \end{bmatrix}$$

Apply $R_1 \to R_1 + 3R_3,\ R_2 \to R_2 + 2R$ to get

$$\begin{bmatrix} 0 & 17 & 14 & : & 45000 \\ 0 & 5 & 13 & : & 31000 \\ -1 & 4 & 6 & : & 13000 \end{bmatrix} \text{ Apply } R_1 \to R_1 - \frac{17}{5}R_2$$

$$\begin{bmatrix} 0 & 0 & \frac{-151}{5} & : & -60400 \\ 0 & 5 & 13 & : & 31000 \\ -1 & 4 & 6 & : & 13000 \end{bmatrix}$$

Giving $\quad \dfrac{-151}{5}z = -60400 \Rightarrow z = 2000$

$$5y + 13z = 31000 \Rightarrow y = 1000$$

$$-x + 4y + 6z = 13000 \Rightarrow x = 3000$$

which give the required prices of the three commodities.

EXERCISES

Compute the inverse of each of the following matrices

1. $\begin{bmatrix} -2 & 6 & 4 \\ 1 & -3 & 2 \\ 1 & 5 & 2 \end{bmatrix}$. 2. $\begin{bmatrix} 8 & 4 & 2 \\ 2 & 8 & 4 \\ 1 & 2 & 8 \end{bmatrix}$.

3. $\begin{bmatrix} a+ib & c+id \\ -c+id & a-ib \end{bmatrix}$, where $a^2 + b^2 + c^2 + d^2 = 1$.

4. $\begin{bmatrix} 9 & 7 & 3 \\ 5 & -1 & 4 \\ 6 & 8 & 2 \end{bmatrix}$. 5. $\begin{bmatrix} 4 & 1 & -5 \\ -2 & 3 & 1 \\ 3 & -1 & 1 \end{bmatrix}$.

6. $\begin{bmatrix} 4 & 2 & 5 \\ 3 & 1 & 8 \\ 9 & 6 & 7 \end{bmatrix}$. 7. $\begin{bmatrix} 9 & 7 & 6 \\ 7 & -1 & 8 \\ 3 & 4 & 2 \end{bmatrix}$.

8. $\begin{bmatrix} 0 & 2 & 1 & 3 \\ 1 & 1 & -1 & 2 \\ 1 & 2 & 0 & 1 \\ -1 & 1 & 2 & 6 \end{bmatrix}$. 9. $\begin{bmatrix} 0 & 1 & 0 & 0 \\ -1 & 0 & 1 & 0 \\ -1 & -1 & 0 & 1 \\ -1 & 1 & 0 & 0 \end{bmatrix}$.

10. $\begin{bmatrix} 0 & 1 & 2 & 2 \\ 1 & 1 & 2 & 3 \\ 2 & 2 & 2 & 3 \\ 2 & 3 & 3 & 3 \end{bmatrix}$. 11. $\begin{bmatrix} 2 & 0 & -1 \\ 5 & 1 & 0 \\ 0 & 1 & 3 \end{bmatrix}$.

12. Solve the equations

$$x + 2y + 3z = 14$$
$$3x + y + 3z = 11$$
$$2x + 3y + z = 11$$

by finding inverse of the coefficient matrix.

13. Solve the equations

$$x + y + z = 7$$
$$x + 2y + 3z = 16$$
$$x + 3y + 4z = 22$$

by finding inverse of the coefficient matrix.

14. An amount of Rs 5000 is put into three investments at rates of 6, 7 and 8 per cent per annum respectively. The total annual income is Rs 358. The combined income from the first two investments is Rs 70 more than the income from the third investment. Find the amount of each investment.

15. The equilibrium conditions for three related markets are given by the equations

$$3p_1 - p_2 + p_3 = 2$$
$$-15p_1 + 6p_2 - 5p_3 = 5$$
$$5p_1 - 2p_2 + 2p_3 = 3.$$

Find equilibrium price for each market

16. A salesman has the following record of sales during three months for three items *A*, *B* and *C* which have different rates of commission:

Months	*Sales of units* A	B	C	*Total commission drawn (in Rs.)*
January	90	100	20	800
February	130	50	40	900
march	60	100	30	850

Find out the rates of commission on items *A*, *B* and *C*.

17. Find the equilibrium prices and quantities for two commodity market models:

$$x_{d_1} = -2 - p + q, \qquad x_{s_2} = -2 - q$$
$$xd_2 = -3 - p - q, \qquad x_{s_2} = -9 + p + q$$

where p is price and q is quantity.

ANSWERS

1. $\begin{bmatrix} -\frac{1}{4} & \frac{1}{8} & \frac{3}{8} \\ 0 & -\frac{1}{8} & \frac{1}{8} \\ \frac{1}{8} & \frac{1}{4} & 0 \end{bmatrix}$

2. $\begin{bmatrix} \frac{1}{7} & -\frac{1}{14} & 0 \\ -\frac{3}{98} & \frac{31}{196} & -\frac{1}{14} \\ -\frac{1}{98} & -\frac{3}{98} & \frac{1}{7} \end{bmatrix}$

3. $\begin{bmatrix} a-ib & -c-id \\ c-id & a+ib \end{bmatrix}$

4. $\begin{bmatrix} \frac{17}{35} & -\frac{1}{7} & -\frac{31}{70} \\ -\frac{1}{5} & 0 & \frac{3}{10} \\ -\frac{23}{35} & \frac{3}{7} & \frac{22}{35} \end{bmatrix}$

5. $\frac{-1}{98}\begin{bmatrix} 13 & 1 & 16 \\ 11 & 31 & 6 \\ -7 & 7 & 14 \end{bmatrix}$

6. $\begin{bmatrix} \frac{41}{17} & -\frac{16}{17} & -\frac{11}{17} \\ -3 & 1 & 1 \\ -\frac{9}{17} & \frac{6}{17} & \frac{2}{17} \end{bmatrix}$

7. $\begin{bmatrix} \frac{17}{25} & -\frac{1}{5} & -\frac{31}{25} \\ -\frac{1}{5} & 0 & \frac{3}{5} \\ -\frac{31}{50} & \frac{3}{10} & \frac{29}{25} \end{bmatrix}$ 8. $\begin{bmatrix} -1 & -3 & 3 & -1 \\ 1 & 1 & -1 & 0 \\ 2 & -5 & 2 & -3 \\ -1 & 1 & 0 & 1 \end{bmatrix}$

9. $\begin{bmatrix} 1 & 0 & 0 & -1 \\ 1 & 0 & 0 & 0 \\ 1 & -1 & 0 & -1 \\ 2 & 1 & 0 & -1 \end{bmatrix}$ 10. $\begin{bmatrix} -3 & 3 & -3 & 2 \\ 3 & -4 & 4 & -2 \\ -3 & 4 & -5 & 3 \\ 2 & -2 & 3 & -2 \end{bmatrix}$

11. $\begin{bmatrix} 3 & -1 & 1 \\ -15 & 6 & -5 \\ 5 & -2 & 2 \end{bmatrix}$

12. $x = 1, y = 2, z = 3$ 13. $x = 1, y = 3, z = 3$
14. 1000, 2200, 1800 15. $p_1 = 3,\ p_2 = 15,\ p_3 = 8$
16. Commissions on items A, B, C are respectively Rs 2, Rs 4 and Rs 11.
17. $p = 2, q = 1$

23. INPUT-OUTPUT ANALYSIS (LEONTIEF'S MODELS)

In an input-output model, we deal with that part of economy in which consumption equals production, *i.e.*, all that is produced is consumed. Broadly speaking there are two types of input-output models (*i*) closed and (*ii*) open.

Closed Input-output Model. In a closed input-output model, whatever is produced is supposed to be consumed by the producers themselves. No one except those who participate in the production are benefited. Consider

Example 64. *Suppose a society consists of three producers A, B and C, and suppose further that whatever they produce is consumed among themselves. Let A consume 20% of what he produces and B, 60% of A's production and the remaining is consumed by C. Again, let production of B be shared by A, B, C in the ratio 3 : 4 : 3. Finally, let A consume 10% of C's production, B 20% and C the remaining 70%.*

Then this is an example of a closed model. We find the ratios of incomes of A, B and C.

Solution. We can represent the above information by the following 3 × 3 matrix (here we assume that total production is unity).

$$\begin{array}{c} \textbf{Production} \\ \begin{array}{ccc} P_A & P_B & P_C \end{array} \end{array}$$

$$\text{Consumption}\ \begin{matrix} A \\ B \\ C \end{matrix}\begin{bmatrix} .2 & .3 & .1 \\ .6 & .4 & .2 \\ .2 & .3 & .7 \end{bmatrix}$$

The columns in this matrix represent the production of A, B and C respectively. Notice that sum of the terms in each column is unity (we have already assumed that production in each case is unity).

Elements of the first row represent the fractions of total amount consumed by A, but produced by A, B and C respectively. Similarly, second and third rows are interpreted.

Let x_1, x_2, x_3 be the total incomes of A, B and C respectively. The amount x_1 comes from sale of A's product. Looking at the expenditure of A, we observe, he consumes 20 % of his produce *i.e.*, he spends $\frac{x_1}{5}$ on his product.

Again A spends $\frac{3x_2}{10}$ on B's product and $\frac{1}{10}x_3$ on C's product.

Thus total expenditure of A is

$$\frac{x_1}{5}+\frac{3x_2}{10}+\frac{x_3}{10}$$

Similarly, by looking at expenditures of B and C we get the equations

$$x_2=\frac{3}{5}x_1+\frac{2}{5}x_2+\frac{1}{5}x_2$$

$$x_3=\frac{1}{5}x_1+\frac{3}{10}x_2+\frac{7}{10}x_3$$

The three equations simplify to

$$\frac{4x_1}{5}-\frac{3x_2}{10}-\frac{x_3}{10}=0; \qquad -\frac{3x_1}{5}+\frac{3}{5}x_2-\frac{1}{5}x_3=0$$

$$-\frac{1}{5}x_1-\frac{3}{10}x_2+\frac{3}{10}x_3=0$$

which in the matrix notation reads

$$\begin{bmatrix} \frac{4}{5} & -\frac{3}{10} & -\frac{1}{10} \\ -\frac{3}{5} & \frac{3}{5} & -\frac{1}{5} \\ -\frac{1}{5} & -\frac{3}{10} & \frac{3}{10} \end{bmatrix}\begin{bmatrix} x_1 \\ x_2 \\ x_3 \end{bmatrix}=\begin{bmatrix} 0 \\ 0 \\ 0 \end{bmatrix} \qquad \text{... (1)}$$

The matrix

$$A=\begin{bmatrix}\frac{4}{5} & -\frac{3}{10} & -\frac{1}{10}\\ -\frac{3}{5} & \frac{3}{5} & -\frac{1}{5}\\ -\frac{1}{5} & -\frac{3}{10} & \frac{3}{10}\end{bmatrix}$$

is called **Leontief matrix** for the given system.

We solve equation (1).

Applying $R_1 \to 10R_1,\ R_2 \to 5R_2,\ R_3 \to 10R_3$, we get

$$\begin{bmatrix}8 & -3 & -1\\ -3 & 3 & -1\\ -2 & -3 & 3\end{bmatrix}\begin{bmatrix}x_1\\ x_2\\ x_3\end{bmatrix}=\begin{bmatrix}0\\0\\0\end{bmatrix}$$

Again applying $R_2 \to R_2 - R_1,\ R_3 \to R_3 + 3R_1$ we get

$$\begin{bmatrix}8 & -3 & -1\\ -11 & 6 & 0\\ 22 & -12 & 0\end{bmatrix}\begin{bmatrix}x_1\\ x_2\\ x_3\end{bmatrix}=\begin{bmatrix}0\\0\\0\end{bmatrix}$$

Applying $R_3 \to R_3 + 2R_2$ we get

$$\begin{bmatrix}8 & -3 & -1\\ -11 & 6 & 0\\ 0 & 0 & 0\end{bmatrix}\begin{bmatrix}x_1\\ x_2\\ x_3\end{bmatrix}=\begin{bmatrix}0\\0\\0\end{bmatrix}$$

which gives $8x_1 - 3x_2 - x_3 = 0$

$$-11x_1 + 6x_2 = 0$$

$$\Rightarrow \qquad x_1 = \frac{6x_2}{11}$$

Putting in first, we get $\frac{48}{11}x_2 - 3x_2 - x_3 = 0$ or $x_3 = \frac{15}{11}x_2$

Hence $x_1 : x_2 : x_3$ is $6 : 11 : 15$

which gives us the required ratio of incomes of A, B and C.

REMARK. In general, an input-output matrix for a closed Leontief Model is of the form.

$$\begin{bmatrix}a_{11} & a_{12} & a_{13} & \dots & a_{1n}\\ a_{21} & a_{22} & a_{23} & \dots & a_{2n}\\ \dots & \dots & \dots & \dots & \dots\\ a_{n1} & a_{n2} & a_{n3} & \dots & a_{nn}\end{bmatrix}$$

where a_{ij} stands for the fractional amount of product consumed by i and produced by j. The sum of entries in any column would always be one, as we assume (in a closed model) that the consumption is completely by the producers themselves. Note any column represents the complete production by any one producer and we have assumed production to be unique.

Also, of course, then $0 \leq a_{ij} \leq 1 \ \forall \ i, j$.

Open Model. In the open input-output model, a part of the production is consumed by those who produce it and the rest is utilized by external bodies. It being, of course, assumed that whatever is produced is consumed (i.e., input equals output). In this model we are interested in finding the amount of production needed so that an expected demand of future is fulfilled when the present demand is known. We take up a few examples to illustrate this model.

Example 65. *Suppose there are two industries A and B, each one producing a single product. It is further assumed that whatever is produced by A is consumed (in parts) by A and B and the rest by outside agencies (consumers). Similarly, production of B is utilized. The following table gives the information as to how much is produced by each and how much is consumed by whom:*

	A	*B*	*Current consumer demand*	*Total output*
A	*30*	*40*	*60*	*130*
B	*20*	*10*	*40*	*70*

Solution. The first row shows that *A* produces 130 units of a certain good out of which 30 are consumed by *A* itself, 40 are consumed by *B* and the rest are other consumers.

Similarly, the second row represents the figures of industry *B*.

The current consumer demand is represented by the demand vector $\begin{bmatrix} 60 \\ 40 \end{bmatrix}$.

Suppose now that after the lapse of a certain time period, the demand of the goods is expected to be $\begin{bmatrix} 80 \\ 40 \end{bmatrix}$ (*i.e.*, demand for *A's* product will go up, whereas it will remain same for *B's* product). Then what should be the total output of each industry (to meet this demand)?

By the given information, we notice that, to meet the consumer's demand of 60 units, A has to actually produce 130 units of its product and in the process it consumes 30 units of its own product and also 20 units of B's product. Thus to produce 1 unit of A's product, it is essential to have $\frac{30}{130}$ units of A's product and $\frac{20}{130}$ units of B's product, similarly to produce 1 unit of B's product, it is essential to have $\frac{40}{70}$ units of A's and $\frac{10}{70}$ units of B's product.

The input-output matrix is then

$$\begin{bmatrix} \frac{30}{130} & \frac{40}{70} \\ \frac{20}{130} & \frac{10}{70} \end{bmatrix} \quad \text{or} \quad \begin{array}{c} \\ A \\ B \end{array} \begin{array}{c} \begin{array}{cc} A & B \end{array} \\ \begin{bmatrix} \frac{3}{13} & \frac{4}{7} \\ \frac{2}{13} & \frac{1}{7} \end{bmatrix} \end{array}$$

Where column 1 represents the amount of units to be produced by A and B for production of 1 unit of A and column 2 represents the amount of units to be produced by A and B for production of 1 unit of B's product.

The above input-output matrix is called the *matrix of technical coefficients or the technology matrix.*

In general, we can say that in this matrix, term a_{ij} represents the fraction of total units produced by j, needed in getting one unit of i.

We also notice that total of entries in each column is strictly less than unity as some outside agency is also using the product.

Let now x_1, x_2 be the total outputs of A and B respectively to meet the new (future) demand $\begin{bmatrix} 80 \\ 40 \end{bmatrix}$.

To produce x_1 units of $A's$ product, $\frac{3}{13}x_1$ units of $A's$ product are needed and to produce x_2 units of $B's$ product, $\frac{4}{7}x_2$ units of $A's$ product are needed. Again 80 units of $A's$ product are to be sold to outside agencies.

Hence $x_1 = \frac{3}{13}x_1 + \frac{4}{7}x_2 + 80$

Similarly, we get $x_2 = \frac{2}{13}x_1 + \frac{1}{7}x_2 + 40$

The two equations simplify to

$$\frac{10}{13}x_1 - \frac{4}{7}x_2 = 80$$

$$-\frac{2}{13}x_1 + \frac{6}{7}x_2 = 40$$

These are called *balance equations* for the demand vector $\begin{bmatrix} 80 \\ 40 \end{bmatrix}$.

Putting in the matrix form, we have

$$\begin{bmatrix} \frac{10}{13} & -\frac{4}{7} \\ -\frac{2}{13} & \frac{6}{7} \end{bmatrix} \begin{bmatrix} x_1 \\ x_2 \end{bmatrix} = \begin{bmatrix} 80 \\ 40 \end{bmatrix}.$$

Apply $R_1 \to R_1 + 5R_2$, and we get

$$\begin{bmatrix} 0 & \frac{26}{7} \\ -\frac{2}{13} & \frac{6}{7} \end{bmatrix} \begin{bmatrix} x_1 \\ x_2 \end{bmatrix} = \begin{bmatrix} 280 \\ 40 \end{bmatrix}$$

$$\Rightarrow \quad \frac{26}{7}x_2 = 280 \Rightarrow x_2 = \frac{980}{13}$$

$$-\frac{2}{13}x_1 + \frac{6}{7}x_2 = 40$$

$$-\frac{2}{13}x_1 + \frac{6}{7} \times \frac{980}{13} = 40 \Rightarrow x_1 = 160.$$

Hence total output by A and B should be 160 and $\frac{980}{13}$ respectively.

REMARKS. (*i*) The matrix $\begin{bmatrix} \frac{10}{13} & -\frac{4}{7} \\ -\frac{2}{13} & \frac{6}{7} \end{bmatrix}$ above is called *Leontief matrix.*

(*ii*) If $M = \begin{bmatrix} \frac{3}{13} & \frac{4}{7} \\ \frac{2}{13} & \frac{1}{7} \end{bmatrix}$ is the input-output matrix, and $X = \begin{bmatrix} x_1 \\ x_2 \end{bmatrix}$ is column matrix representing the production of each industry and $D = \begin{bmatrix} 80 \\ 40 \end{bmatrix}$ is representing future demand then the balance equations can be written down as

$$X = MX + D$$

or $$X - MX = D$$

or $$(I - M)X = D$$

or $$X = (I - M)^{-1}D$$

It is some times easy to use this form, while solving the problems.

Note if M is the matrix of technical coefficients then $I - M$ is the corresponding *Leontief matrix*.

Example 66. *Determine the total demand for industries 1, 2, 3, given the matrix of technical coefficients A and the final demand vector D as below*

$$A = \begin{bmatrix} \cdot 2 & \cdot 3 & \cdot 2 \\ \cdot 4 & \cdot 1 & \cdot 3 \\ \cdot 3 & \cdot 5 & \cdot 2 \end{bmatrix} \quad D = \begin{bmatrix} 150 \\ 200 \\ 210 \end{bmatrix}$$

Solution. We know that

$$X = (I - A)^{-1}B$$

where X is the total demand vector.

Now
$$I - A = \begin{bmatrix} 1 & 0 & 0 \\ 0 & 1 & 0 \\ 0 & 0 & 1 \end{bmatrix} - \begin{bmatrix} \cdot 2 & \cdot 3 & \cdot 2 \\ \cdot 4 & \cdot 1 & \cdot 3 \\ \cdot 3 & \cdot 5 & \cdot 2 \end{bmatrix}$$

$$= \begin{bmatrix} \cdot 8 & -\cdot 3 & -\cdot 2 \\ -\cdot 4 & \cdot 9 & -\cdot 3 \\ -\cdot 3 & -\cdot 5 & \cdot 8 \end{bmatrix}$$

by using earlier methods we find

$$(I - A)^{-1} = \frac{1}{\cdot 239} \begin{bmatrix} \cdot 57 & \cdot 34 & \cdot 27 \\ \cdot 41 & \cdot 58 & \cdot 32 \\ \cdot 47 & \cdot 49 & \cdot 60 \end{bmatrix}$$

Hence
$$X = \frac{1}{\cdot 239} \begin{bmatrix} \cdot 57 & \cdot 34 & \cdot 27 \\ \cdot 41 & \cdot 58 & \cdot 32 \\ \cdot 47 & \cdot 49 & \cdot 60 \end{bmatrix} \begin{bmatrix} 150 \\ 200 \\ 210 \end{bmatrix}$$

$$= \frac{1}{\cdot 239} \begin{bmatrix} 210 \cdot 2 \\ 244 \cdot 7 \\ 294 \cdot 5 \end{bmatrix} = \begin{bmatrix} 874 \cdot 5 \\ 1023 \cdot 85 \\ 1232 \cdot 22 \end{bmatrix}$$

which give the total demand.

Example 67. *For the following input-output table, calculate the technology matrix and also write the balance equations for the two vectors:*

Sector	*A*	*B*	*Final Demand*
A	*50*	*150*	*200*
B	*100*	*75*	*100*

Solution: Total output of sector A is $50 + 150 + 200 = 400$

Total output of sector B is $100 + 75 + 100 = 275$

Hence the technology matrix is $\begin{bmatrix} \frac{50}{400} & \frac{150}{275} \\ \frac{100}{400} & \frac{75}{275} \end{bmatrix}$ or $\begin{bmatrix} \frac{1}{8} & \frac{6}{11} \\ \frac{1}{4} & \frac{3}{11} \end{bmatrix}$.

Let x_1 and x_2 be the total outputs of sectors A and B respectively to meet the internal and external demands.

The balance matrix equation for the two sectors is

$$\begin{bmatrix} \frac{1}{8} & \frac{6}{11} \\ \frac{1}{4} & \frac{3}{11} \end{bmatrix} \begin{bmatrix} x_1 \\ x_2 \end{bmatrix} + \begin{bmatrix} 200 \\ 100 \end{bmatrix} = \begin{bmatrix} x_1 \\ x_2 \end{bmatrix}$$

or
$$\frac{1}{8}x_1 + \frac{6}{11}x_2 + 200 = x_1$$
$$\frac{1}{4}x_1 + \frac{3}{11}x_2 + 100 = x_2$$

Thus the balance equation for sector A is

$$\frac{7}{8}x_1 - \frac{6}{11}x_2 = 200$$

and for sector B is

$$-\frac{1}{4}x_1 + \frac{8}{11}x_2 = 100.$$

Example 68. *Given the following transaction matrix, find the gross output to meet the final demand of 200 units of Agriculture and 800 units of Industry.*

Producing sector	*Purchasing Sector*		*Current*
	Agriculture	*Industry*	*Demand*
Agriculture	*300*	*600*	*100*
Industry	*400*	*1200*	*400*

Solution. To obtain the matrix of technical coefficients we have

	A	*I*	*Current consumer Demand*	*Total output*
A	300	600	100	1000
I	400	1200	400	2000

and the new demand vector is $\begin{bmatrix} 200 \\ 800 \end{bmatrix}$.

The matrix of technical coefficients is therefore given by

$$M = \begin{bmatrix} \frac{300}{1000} & \frac{600}{2000} \\ \frac{400}{1000} & \frac{1200}{2000} \end{bmatrix} \text{ or } \begin{bmatrix} \frac{3}{10} & \frac{3}{10} \\ \frac{2}{2} & \frac{3}{5} \end{bmatrix}.$$

The Leontief matrix is thus $\begin{bmatrix} 1-\frac{3}{10} & 0-\frac{3}{10} \\ 0-\frac{2}{5} & 1-\frac{3}{5} \end{bmatrix}$ *i.e.,* $\begin{bmatrix} \frac{7}{10} & \frac{3}{10} \\ -\frac{2}{5} & \frac{2}{5} \end{bmatrix}$

The balance equations are thus given by

$$\begin{bmatrix} \frac{7}{10} & -\frac{3}{10} \\ -\frac{2}{5} & \frac{2}{5} \end{bmatrix} \begin{bmatrix} x_1 \\ x_2 \end{bmatrix} = \begin{bmatrix} 200 \\ 800 \end{bmatrix}$$

Apply $R_1 \to 10R_1, R_2 \to 5R_2$

$$\begin{bmatrix} 7 & -3 \\ -2 & 2 \end{bmatrix} \begin{bmatrix} x_1 \\ x_2 \end{bmatrix} = \begin{bmatrix} 2000 \\ 4000 \end{bmatrix}$$

Apply $R_1 \to 2R_1$ and then $R_1 \to R_1 + 7R_2$

$$\begin{bmatrix} 0 & 8 \\ -2 & 2 \end{bmatrix} \begin{bmatrix} x_1 \\ x_2 \end{bmatrix} = \begin{bmatrix} 32000 \\ 4000 \end{bmatrix}$$

$$\Rightarrow \qquad 8x_2 = 32000 \quad \Rightarrow x_2 = 4000$$

$$-2x_1 + 2x_2 = 4000 \quad \Rightarrow x_1 = x_2 - 2000 = 2000.$$

Hence $x_1 = 2000$ and $x_2 = 4000$ is the gross output to meet the final demand.

EXERCISES

1. Suppose a society consists of a farmer (who produces food), a builder (who constructs homes) and a tailor (who provides clothes). Suppose the farmer consumes one half of the food he grows, while the remainder is consumed equally by the builder and the tailor. Suppose the production of the builder is shared equally by the farmer, builder and tailor. Finally, suppose all of the clothing is consumed so that 40% is consumed by both the farmer and builder and 20% by the tailor. Find the ratios of the incomes of the farmer, builder and the tailor.
2. Find the income ratios of each person for the closed input-output matrices

$$(i)\begin{bmatrix} \frac{1}{2} & \frac{1}{3} & \frac{1}{4} \\ \frac{1}{4} & \frac{1}{3} & \frac{1}{4} \\ \frac{1}{4} & \frac{1}{3} & \frac{1}{4} \end{bmatrix} \qquad (ii)\begin{bmatrix} \cdot 4 & \cdot 3 & \cdot 2 \\ \cdot 2 & \cdot 3 & \cdot 3 \\ \cdot 4 & \cdot 4 & \cdot 5 \end{bmatrix}$$

3. Determine the total demand for industries *A*, *B*, *C* given the matrix of technical coefficients *M* and the final demand vector *D* as follows:

$$M = \begin{bmatrix} \cdot 3 & \cdot 4 & \cdot 1 \\ \cdot 5 & \cdot 2 & \cdot 6 \\ \cdot 1 & \cdot 3 & \cdot 1 \end{bmatrix} \quad D = \begin{bmatrix} 20 \\ 10 \\ 30 \end{bmatrix}$$

4. Suppose the matrix of technical coefficients for three industries *A*, *B*, *C* is given by

$$M = \begin{bmatrix} \cdot 4 & \cdot 3 & \cdot 1 \\ \cdot 2 & \cdot 2 & \cdot 3 \\ \cdot 2 & \cdot 4 & \cdot 2 \end{bmatrix}$$

and let the final demand vector be

$$\begin{bmatrix} 140 \\ 220 \\ 180 \end{bmatrix}.$$

If the forecast demand in three years is given by

$$\begin{bmatrix} 170 \\ 205 \\ 145 \end{bmatrix}.$$

What is the total output *X* given by?

5. Suppose the inter-relationships between the production of three industries *A*, *B*, *C* in a year is given by

	A	*B*	*C*	*Current demand*	*Total output*
A	50	20	40	70	180
B	20	30	20	90	160
C	30	20	20	50	120

Find the total output of each industry required to meet future demand

$$\begin{bmatrix} 60 \\ 110 \\ 60 \end{bmatrix}$$

6. If the input-output coefficient matrix is

$$\begin{bmatrix} \cdot 2 & \cdot 3 & \cdot 2 \\ \cdot 4 & \cdot 1 & \cdot 2 \\ \cdot 1 & \cdot 3 & \cdot 2 \end{bmatrix}$$

Find the demand vector D which is consistent with the output vector

$$\begin{bmatrix} 25 \\ 21 \\ 18 \end{bmatrix}$$

7. For the following transaction matrix, find the total output for each industry if the new final demands are 180 and 440 units respectively.

Industry	*Input to* 1	2	*Final demand*
1	160	200	40
2	80	400	320

8. Suppose the inter-relationship between the production of two industries *A*, *B* in a year is given by

	A	*B*	*Current demand*	*Total output*
A	20	30	50	100
B	10	20	30	60

Find the total output of each industry required to meet a future demand

$$\begin{bmatrix} 60 \\ 10 \end{bmatrix}.$$

ANSWERS

1. 8 : 6 : 5

2. (*i*) 4 : 3 : 4 (*ii*) 23 : 22 : 36

3. $\begin{bmatrix} 160\cdot 93 \\ 201\cdot 99 \\ 118\cdot 54 \end{bmatrix}$

4. $\begin{bmatrix} 767\cdot 79 \\ 723\cdot 88 \\ 735\cdot 14 \end{bmatrix}$

5. 178·322, 187·811, 135·969

6. $\begin{bmatrix} 10\cdot 1 \\ 5\cdot 3 \\ 5\cdot 6 \end{bmatrix}$

7. 1240, 1128

8. 93·1, 24·8

24. RANK OF A MATRIX

Suppose we have a 3×4 matrix

$$A = \begin{bmatrix} 1 & 2 & 3 & 4 \\ 5 & 6 & 7 & 8 \\ 9 & 10 & 11 & 12 \end{bmatrix}$$

If we delete any one column from it we get corresponding 3×3 sub matrix. The determinant of any one of these is called a minor of the matrix A. Thus

$$\begin{vmatrix} 1 & 2 & 3 \\ 5 & 6 & 7 \\ 9 & 10 & 11 \end{vmatrix}, \begin{vmatrix} 1 & 2 & 4 \\ 5 & 6 & 8 \\ 9 & 10 & 12 \end{vmatrix}, \begin{vmatrix} 1 & 3 & 4 \\ 5 & 7 & 8 \\ 9 & 11 & 12 \end{vmatrix}, \begin{vmatrix} 2 & 3 & 4 \\ 6 & 7 & 8 \\ 10 & 11 & 12 \end{vmatrix} \text{ are all}$$

minors of A. These are 3×3 determinants (some times called 3-rowed minors)

Similarly if we delete any one row and two columns of A, we get corresponding 2-rowed minors.

Definition: Let A be an $m \times n$ matrix. We say rank of A is r if (*i*) at least one minor of order r is non zero and (*ii*) every minor of order $(r + 1)$ is zero.

Example 69. *Find rank of the matrix*

$$\begin{bmatrix} 1 & 2 & 4 \\ -1 & -2 & -4 \\ 2 & 4 & 8 \\ -3 & -6 & -9 \end{bmatrix}$$

Solution. Since it is 3×4 matrix, it cannot have a minor with order larger than 3×3.

Now 3×3 minors of this matrix are

$$\begin{vmatrix} 1 & 2 & 4 \\ -1 & -2 & -4 \\ 2 & 4 & 8 \end{vmatrix}, \begin{vmatrix} 1 & 2 & 4 \\ -1 & -2 & -4 \\ -3 & -6 & -9 \end{vmatrix}, \begin{vmatrix} 1 & 2 & 4 \\ 2 & 4 & 8 \\ -3 & -6 & -9 \end{vmatrix}, \begin{vmatrix} -1 & -2 & -4 \\ 2 & 4 & 8 \\ -3 & -6 & -9 \end{vmatrix}$$

one can check that all these are zero. So rank of A, is less than 3.

Again since a 2×2 minor $\begin{vmatrix} 4 & 8 \\ -6 & -9 \end{vmatrix} \neq 0$

We find rank is ≥ 2 i.e., rank of A is 2.

Example 70. *Find rank of the matrix*

$$A = \begin{vmatrix} 0 & i & -i \\ -i & 0 & i \\ i & -i & 0 \end{vmatrix}$$

Solution: We have $|A| = \begin{vmatrix} 0 & i & -i \\ -i & 0 & i \\ i & -i & 0 \end{vmatrix} = 0$

thus rank $A \leq 2$

Again as $\begin{vmatrix} 0 & i \\ -i & 0 \end{vmatrix} = -1 \neq 0$

rank $A \geq 2$ and hence rank $A = 2$.

REMARK:

(*i*) It is easy to see that if the given matrix A is $m \times n$ matrix then rank $A \leq \min(m, n)$.

(*ii*) If in A, every $r \times r$ determinant is zero then rank is less than or equal to $r - 1$.

(*iii*) If $\exists$ a non zero $r \times r$ determinant then rank is greater than or equal to r.

(*iv*) Rank of null matrix is taken as zero.

(*v*) If every r rowed minor is zero then every higher order minor would automatically be zero.

One can prove that rank of a matrix remains unchanged by elementary operations. In view of this result the process of finding rank can be simplified. We first reduce the given matrix to triangular form by elementary row operations and then find rank of the new matrix which is the rank of the original matrix. We illustrate this through following examples:

Example 71. *Find rank of the matrix*

$$A = \begin{bmatrix} 1 & -3 & 2 \\ -3 & 9 & -6 \\ 2 & -6 & 4 \end{bmatrix}$$

Solution: We have

$$A = \begin{bmatrix} 1 & -3 & 2 \\ -3 & 9 & -6 \\ 2 & -6 & 4 \end{bmatrix} \sim \begin{bmatrix} 1 & 0 & 0 \\ -3 & 0 & 0 \\ 2 & 0 & 0 \end{bmatrix}$$

using $C_2 \to C_2 + 3C_1$
$C_3 \to C_3 - 2C_1$

$$\sim \begin{bmatrix} 1 & 0 & 0 \\ 0 & 0 & 0 \\ 0 & 0 & 0 \end{bmatrix}$$

using $R_2 \to R_2 + 3R_1$, $R_3 \to R_3 - 2R_1$
So rank of A is 1.

Example 72. *Find rank of the matrix*

$$A = \begin{bmatrix} 2 & 3 & -1 & -1 \\ 1 & -1 & -2 & -4 \\ 3 & 1 & 3 & -2 \\ 6 & 3 & 0 & -7 \end{bmatrix}$$

Solution: We have

$$A \sim \begin{bmatrix} 2 & 3 & -1 & -1 \\ 1 & -1 & -2 & -4 \\ 6 & 1 & 3 & -2 \\ 0 & 0 & 0 & 0 \end{bmatrix} \sim \begin{bmatrix} 1 & -1 & -2 & -4 \\ 2 & 3 & -1 & -1 \\ 6 & 1 & 3 & -2 \\ 0 & 0 & 0 & 0 \end{bmatrix} \sim \begin{bmatrix} 1 & -1 & -2 & -4 \\ 0 & 5 & 3 & 7 \\ 0 & 7 & 15 & 22 \\ 0 & 0 & 0 & 0 \end{bmatrix}$$

$R_4 \to R_4 - R_3 - R_2 - R_1$, $R_1 \to R_2$ $R_2 \to R_2 - 2R_1, R_3 \to R_3 - 6R_1$

$$\sim \begin{bmatrix} 1 & -2 & -2 & -4 \\ 0 & 35 & 21 & 49 \\ 0 & 35 & 75 & 110 \\ 0 & 0 & 0 & 0 \end{bmatrix} \sim \begin{bmatrix} 1 & -1 & -2 & -4 \\ 0 & 35 & 21 & 49 \\ 0 & 0 & 54 & 61 \\ 0 & 0 & 0 & 0 \end{bmatrix}$$

$$\text{Here} \begin{vmatrix} 1 & -1 & -2 \\ 0 & 35 & 21 \\ 0 & 0 & 54 \end{vmatrix} \neq 0$$

Hence rank of this matrix is 3

Thus rank of A is 3.

Example 73. *Find rank of the matrix*

$$A = \begin{bmatrix} 5 & 3 & 14 & 4 \\ 0 & 1 & 2 & 1 \\ 1 & -1 & 2 & 0 \end{bmatrix}$$

Solution. Apply $R_1 \leftrightarrow R_3$, then

$$A \sim \begin{bmatrix} 1 & -1 & 2 & 0 \\ 0 & 1 & 2 & 1 \\ 5 & 3 & 14 & 4 \end{bmatrix} \sim \begin{bmatrix} 1 & -1 & 2 & 0 \\ 0 & 1 & 2 & 1 \\ 0 & 8 & 4 & 1 \end{bmatrix} \text{ By } R_3 \to R_3 - 5R_1$$

$$\sim \begin{bmatrix} 1 & -1 & 2 & 0 \\ 0 & 1 & 2 & 1 \\ 0 & 0 & -12 & -4 \end{bmatrix} \text{ using } R_3 \to R_3 - 8R_2$$

Since this reduced matrix has non zero 3-rowed minor

$$\begin{vmatrix} 1 & -1 & 2 \\ 0 & 1 & 2 \\ 0 & 0 & -12 \end{vmatrix}$$

Its rank is 3. Also there is no 4-rowed minor. Hence rank of given matrix is also 3.

EXERCISES

1. Find rank of the following matrices

(i) $\begin{bmatrix} 1 & 2 & 3 \\ 2 & 3 & 4 \\ 4 & 5 & 6 \end{bmatrix}$ (ii) $\begin{bmatrix} 1 & 1 & 1 & 1 \\ 1 & 3 & -2 & 1 \\ 2 & 0 & -3 & 2 \\ 3 & 3 & 0 & 3 \end{bmatrix}$

(iii) $\begin{bmatrix} 1 & 2 & 3 \\ 2 & 3 & 5 \\ 8 & 13 & 21 \end{bmatrix}$

(iv) $\begin{bmatrix} 1 & 4 & 3 & 2 \\ 1 & 2 & 3 & 4 \\ 2 & 6 & 7 & 5 \end{bmatrix}$ (v) $\begin{bmatrix} 1 & 1 & 1 & 1 \\ 1 & 3 & -2 & 1 \\ 2 & 0 & -3 & 2 \\ 3 & 3 & 0 & 3 \end{bmatrix}$

ANSWERS

1. (i) 2 (ii) 3 (iii) 2
(iv) 3 (v) 3

CHAPTER 30

VECTOR ALGEBRA

1. INTRODUCTION

We come across different quantities in the study of physical phenomena, such as mass or volume of a body, time, temperature, speed, etc. All these quantities are such that they can be expressed completely by their magnitude, *i.e.,* by a single number. For example, mass of a body can be specified by the number of grams and time by minutes etc. Such quantities are called *Scalars.* There are certain other quantities which cannot be expressed completely by their magnitude alone. Like velocity, acceleration, force, displacement, momentum, etc. These are quantities that can be expressed completely by their magnitude and direction. Such quantities are called *Vectors.*

2. REPRESENTATION OF VECTORS

The best way to represent a vector is with the help of a directed line segment. Suppose A and B are two points, then by the vector $\overrightarrow{AB}$, we mean a quantity whose magnitude is the length AB and whose direction is from A to B.

A and B are called the *end points* of the vector $\overrightarrow{AB}$. In particular A is called the *initial point* and B is called the *terminal point.*

Sometimes a vector $\overrightarrow{AB}$ is expressed by a single letter **a** (which is always written in **bold type,** to distinguish it from a scalar). Sometimes, however, we write the vector **a** as $\vec{a}$ or $\tilde{a}$.

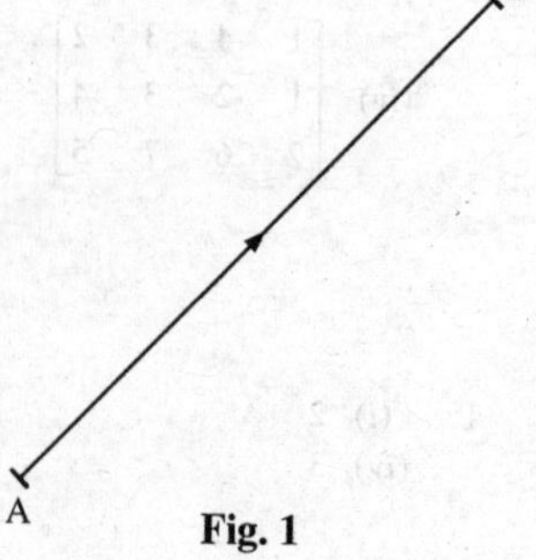

Fig. 1

We give below a few definitions.

3. DEFINITIONS

Modulus of a vector. The modulus or *magnitude* of a vector is the positive number measuring the length of the line representing it. It is also called the **vector's absolute value.** Modulus of vector **a** is denoted by | **a** | or by the corresponding letter *a* in italics.

Unit vector. A vector whose magnitude is unity is called a unit vector and is generally denoted by $\hat{a}$. We will always use the symbols **i, j, k** to denote the unit vectors along the *x, y* and *z*-axis in three dimensions.

If **a** is any vector, then $\mathbf{a} = a\hat{a}$ where $\hat{a}$ is a unit vector having same direction as that of **a**. (The idea would become more clear when we define the product of a vector with a scalar.)

Zero vector. A vector with zero magnitude (and any direction) is called a *zero vector* or a *null vector.* For example, if in Fig. 1 the point *B* coincides with the point *A*, the vector $\overrightarrow{AB}$ becomes the zero vector $\overrightarrow{AB}$. The zero vector is denoted by the symbol **0**.

Equality of two vectors. Two vectors are said to be equal if and only if they have same magnitude and same direction.

Negative of a vector. The vector which has same magnitude as that of a vector **a,** but opposite direction is called negative of **a** and is denoted by – **a.** Thus $\overrightarrow{AB} = -\overrightarrow{BA}$ for any vector $\overrightarrow{AB}$.

Free vectors. A vector is said to be a free vector (or a sliding vector) if its magnitude and direction are fixed but position in space is not fixed.

We shall be dealing, most of the time, with free vectors.

REMARK: When we defined equality of vectors, it was assumed that the vectors are free vectors. Thus two vectors $\overline{AB}$ and $\overline{CD}$ can be equal if $AB = CD$ and AB is parallel to CD (although they are not coincident).

So equality of two vectors does not mean that the two are equivalent in all respects. For example, suppose we apply a certain force in a certain direction at two different point of a body, then although the vectors are same still they may have varying effects on the body.

Localised vector is that whose position in space is also fixed.

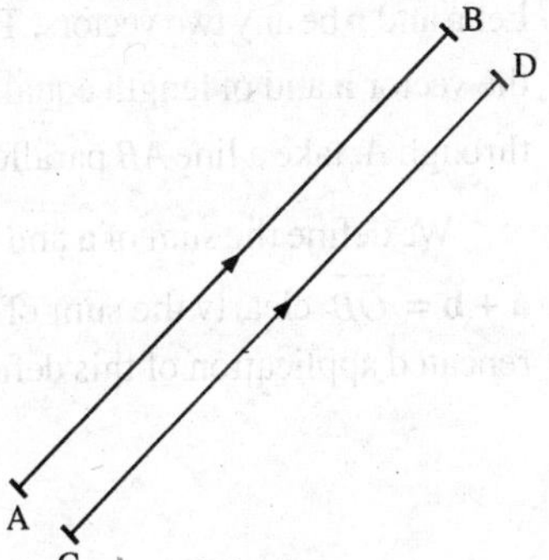

Fig. 2

Coinitial vectors. Vectors having the same initial point are called *coinitial vectors* or *concurrent vectors.*

4. ANGLE BETWEEN TWO VECTORS

Let $\overrightarrow{AB} = \mathbf{a}$ and $\overrightarrow{CD} = \mathbf{b}$ be any two vectors. Through a point O, take lines OA_1 and OC_1 parallel respectively to $\overrightarrow{AB}$ and $\overrightarrow{CD}$.

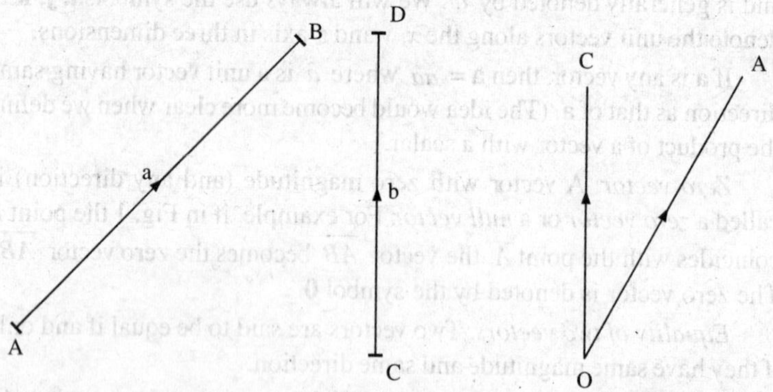

Fig. 3

The angle θ between the lines OA_1 and OC_1 is called the angle between the vectors **a** and **b**, where $0 \le \theta \le \pi$.

If $\theta = 0$ or π, the two vectors are said to be parallel. [Thus parallelism only requires that the two vectors have same or opposite direction, there being no necessary relation between the magnitudes.]

The vectors are said to be perpendicular if $\theta = \dfrac{\pi}{2}$.

5. ADDITION OF VECTORS

Let **a** and **b** be any two vectors. Through a point O, take a line OA parallel to the vector **a** and of length equal to a. Then $\overrightarrow{OA} = \mathbf{a}$ [by definition]. Again through A, take a line AB parallel to **b**, having length b, then $\overrightarrow{AB} = \mathbf{b}$.

We define the sum of **a** and **b** as **(a + b)** to be the vector $\overrightarrow{OB}$ and write $\mathbf{a} + \mathbf{b} = \overrightarrow{OB}$ clearly the sum of three or more vectors can be obtained by repeated application of this definition.

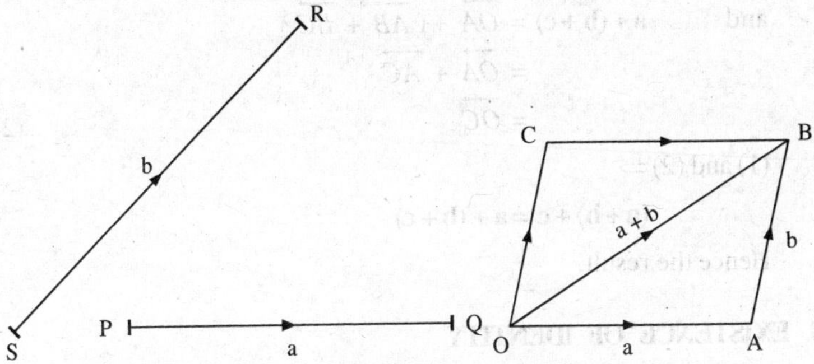

Fig. 4

REMARKS:

1. The process by which we obtained above an equal vector $\overrightarrow{OA}$ from **a** is sometimes referred to as translation of vectors. **[It is like moving the line segment of *a* from its original position to the new position *OA*, without disturbing the direction.]**
2. This method of addition is called *Parallelogram Law of Addition.*

6. VECTOR ADDITION IS COMMUTATIVE

Let **a** and **b** be any two vectors. We get

$$\overrightarrow{OB} = \mathbf{a}+\mathbf{b} \qquad \text{[refer to figure 4]}$$

Now complete the parallelogram *OABC*, then

$$\overrightarrow{OC} = \mathbf{b} \text{ and } \overrightarrow{CB} = \mathbf{a}$$

Also $\overrightarrow{OC} + \overrightarrow{CB} = \overrightarrow{OB}$ [by definition of addition]

$\Rightarrow$ $\mathbf{b}+\mathbf{a} = \overrightarrow{OB}$

Hence $\mathbf{a}+\mathbf{b} = \mathbf{b}+\mathbf{a} = \overrightarrow{OB}$

which proves the result.

7. VECTOR ADDITION IS ASSOCIATIVE

Let $\mathbf{a} = \overrightarrow{OA}$

$\mathbf{b} = \overrightarrow{AB}$

$\mathbf{c} = \overrightarrow{BC}$

be three vectors.

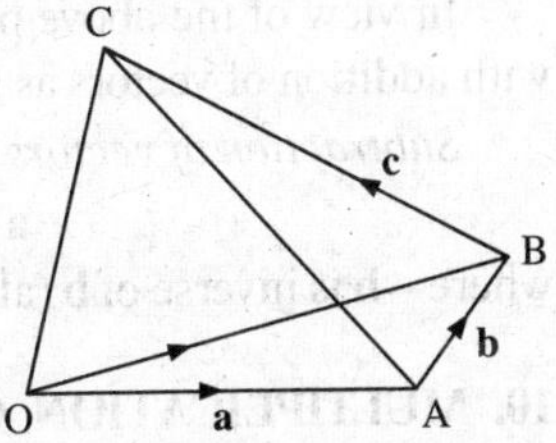

Fig. 5

Then

$$(\mathbf{a}+\mathbf{b})+\mathbf{c} = (\overrightarrow{OA} + \overrightarrow{AB}) + \overrightarrow{BC}$$

$$= \overrightarrow{OB} + \overrightarrow{BC} = \overrightarrow{OC} \qquad ...(1)$$

and $\mathbf{a}+(\mathbf{b}+\mathbf{c}) = \overrightarrow{OA} + (\overrightarrow{AB} + \overrightarrow{BC})$

$= \overrightarrow{OA} + \overrightarrow{AC}$

$= \overrightarrow{OC}$ ...(2)

(1) and (2) $\Rightarrow$

$$(\mathbf{a}+\mathbf{b})+\mathbf{c} = \mathbf{a}+(\mathbf{b}+\mathbf{c})$$

Hence the result.

8. EXISTENCE OF IDENTITY

If **a** is any vector and **0** is the zero vector then

$$\mathbf{a}+\mathbf{0} = \mathbf{a}$$

In the figure 4, if B coincides with A

then $\overrightarrow{AB} = \overrightarrow{AA} = \mathbf{0}$

By definition $\overrightarrow{OB} = \overrightarrow{OA} + \overrightarrow{AB}$

$\Rightarrow$ $\overrightarrow{OA} = \overrightarrow{OA} + \overrightarrow{AA}$

$\Rightarrow$ $\mathbf{a} = \mathbf{a}+\mathbf{0}$

Hence the result.

9. EXISTENCE OF INVERSE

If **a** is any vector then $\exists$ a vector $-\mathbf{a}$ (called *inverse* of **a**) such that

$$\mathbf{a}+(-\mathbf{a}) = \mathbf{0}$$

Let $\mathbf{a} = \overrightarrow{OA}$

Then by definition $-\mathbf{a} = \overrightarrow{AO}$

Clearly $\overrightarrow{OA} + \overrightarrow{AO} = \overrightarrow{OO}$ [definition of addition]

$\Rightarrow$ $\mathbf{a}+(-\mathbf{a}) = \mathbf{0}$

In view of the above properties we can say that the set V of vectors with addition of vectors as a binary composition forms an abelian group.

Subtraction of vectors. By $\mathbf{a}-\mathbf{b}$ we mean

$$\mathbf{a}+(-\mathbf{b})$$

where $-\mathbf{b}$ is inverse of **b** (also called negative of **b** as defined earlier).

10. MULTIPLICATION OF A VECTOR BY A SCALAR

Suppose **a** is a vector and n a scalar. By $n\mathbf{a}$ we mean, a vector, whose magnitude in $|n||\mathbf{a}|$, *i.e.*, $|n|$ times the magnitude of **a** and whose direction is that of **a** or opposite to that of **a** according as n is positive or negative.

Generally the scalar is written on the left of the vector, although one could write it on the right too.

Note also that we do not put any sign (. or ×) between n and **a** when we write $n\mathbf{a}$.

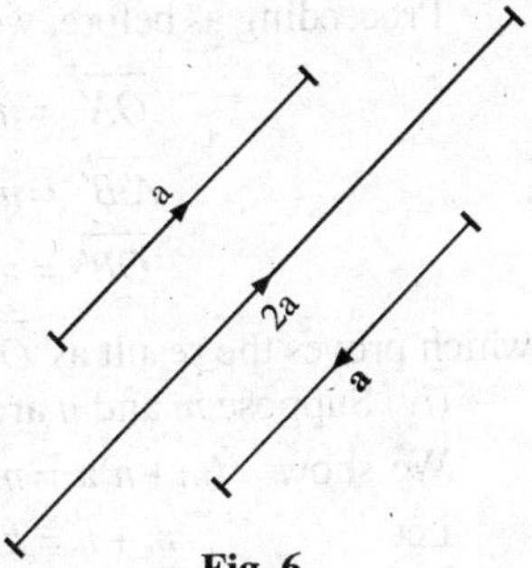

Fig. 6

The following results can be proved:

(*i*) $(mn)\,\mathbf{a} = m\,(n\mathbf{a})$

(*ii*) $0\mathbf{a} = \mathbf{0}$

(*iii*) $n(\mathbf{a}+\mathbf{b}) = n\mathbf{a} + n\mathbf{b}$

(*iv*) $(m+n)\,\mathbf{a} = m\mathbf{a} + n\mathbf{a}$

Proof. (*i*) and (*ii*) are direct consequence of the definition and hardly need any further proof.

(*iii*) Let n be positive.

Suppose $\mathbf{a} = \overrightarrow{OA}$, $\mathbf{b} = \overrightarrow{AB}$

then $\overrightarrow{OB} = \mathbf{a}+\mathbf{b}$

Let A', B' be points on OA and OB (or OA and OB produced) respectively such that

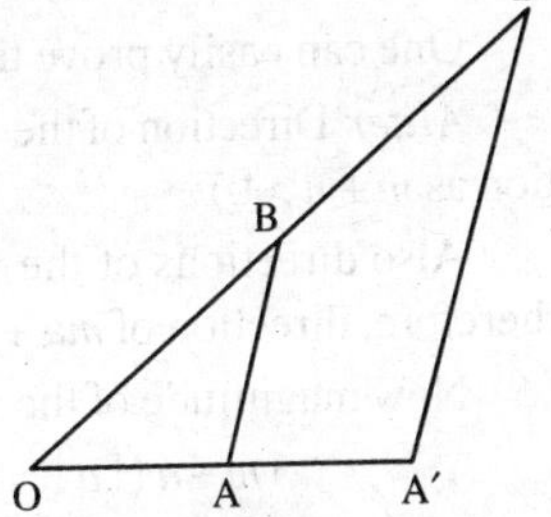

Fig. 7

$$OA' = n\,.\,OA$$

$$OB' = n\,.\,OB$$

then $\overrightarrow{OA'} = n\,\overrightarrow{OA} = n\mathbf{a}$

$\overrightarrow{OB'} = n\,\overrightarrow{OB} = n\,(\mathbf{a}+\mathbf{b})$

Also $A'B' = n\,AB$ [OAB and $OA'B'$ are similar triangles]

$\Rightarrow$ $\overrightarrow{A'B'} = n\,\overrightarrow{AB} = n\mathbf{b}$

Now $\overrightarrow{OB'} = \overrightarrow{OA'} + \overrightarrow{A'B'}$

$\Rightarrow$ $n\,(\mathbf{a}+\mathbf{b}) = n\mathbf{a} + n\mathbf{b}$

which proves our assertion.

When n is negative, the figure would change in this case as now A and A' will lie on the opposite sides of O.

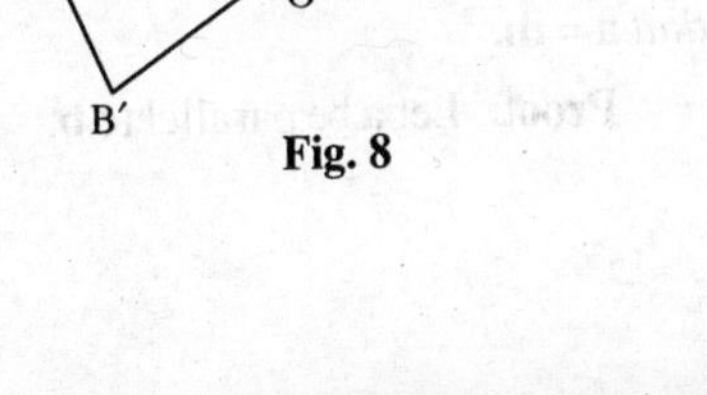

Fig. 8

Proceeding as before, we'll get

$$\overrightarrow{OA'} = n\mathbf{a}$$

$$\overrightarrow{A'B'} = n\mathbf{b}$$

$$\overrightarrow{OB'} = n(\mathbf{a}+\mathbf{b})$$

which proves the result as $\overrightarrow{OB'} = \overrightarrow{OA'} + \overrightarrow{A'B'}$

(*iv*) Suppose m and n are positive.

We show $(m+n)\mathbf{a} = m\mathbf{a} + n\mathbf{a}$

Let $m + n = k$, then

$$\text{LHS} = \mathbf{a}+\mathbf{a}+\mathbf{a}+...+\mathbf{a} \quad (k \text{ times})$$

Also

$$\text{RHS} = m\mathbf{a} + n\mathbf{a}$$

$$= \underset{\{m \text{ times}\}}{(\mathbf{a}+\mathbf{a}+...+\mathbf{a})} + \underset{\{n \text{ times}\}}{(\mathbf{a}+\mathbf{a}+...+\mathbf{a})}$$

$$= \mathbf{a}+\mathbf{a}+...+\mathbf{a} \ (m+n \text{ times}) \quad (= k \text{ times})$$

$\Rightarrow$ LHS = RHS

One can easily prove the result even if m or n is negative.

Aliter. Direction of the vector $(m+n)$ **a** is same as that of **a** (by definition as $m+n>0$)

Also directions of the vectors m**a** and n**a** are same as that of **a** and, therefore, direction of $m\mathbf{a} + n\mathbf{a}$ is also same as that of **a**.

Now magnitude of the vector $(m+n)$ **a** is

$$|m+n||a| = (m+n)\,a$$

$$= ma + na$$

$$= |m||\mathbf{a}| + |n||\mathbf{a}|$$

$$= |m\,\mathbf{a}| + |n\,\mathbf{a}| \text{ as they have same direction,}$$

$$= |m\,\mathbf{a} + n\,\mathbf{a}|$$

which is the magnitude of the vector $m\mathbf{a} + n\mathbf{a}$ *i.e.,* the vector on the RHS.

Thus the two vectors have same direction and magnitude and hence are equal.

The different cases when m or n is negative or both m and n are negative can be dealt with similarly.

11. THEOREM

Two non-zero vectors **a** *and* **b** *are parallel if and only if* $\exists$ *a scalar t such that* $\mathbf{a} = t\mathbf{b}$.

Proof. Let **a** be parallel to **b**.

$\Rightarrow$ Direction of **a** and **b** is same or opposite.

Suppose direction of **a** and **b** is same.

If $a = b$, where a, b are respectively the magnitudes of **a** and **b**, then $t = 1$ serves our purpose, because then

$$a = 1.b \Rightarrow \mathbf{a} = 1 \,.\, \mathbf{b}$$

If $a \neq b$, then we can always find a scalar t such that $a = tb$

[Property of real numbers, indeed we take $t = a/b$]

For this t, $\mathbf{a} = t\mathbf{b}$

So when direction of **a** and **b** is same, the result is true.

Let now direction of **a** and **b** be opposite. The same scalar will do the job except that in this case we will take t with the negative sign.

Conversely let **a** and **b** be two vectors such that $\mathbf{a} = t\mathbf{b}$ for some scalar t.

By definition of equality of vectors this implies that **a** and t**b** have same direction.

Again **b** and t**b** have same or opposite direction. [by definition of t**b**]

$\Rightarrow$ **a** and **b** are two vectors having same or opposite direction.

$\Rightarrow$ **a** and **b** are parallel.

Hence the result.

Example 1. *If ABC is a triangle and D is middle point of BC, show that* $\overrightarrow{BD} = \frac{1}{2}\overrightarrow{BC}$.

Solution. See Figure of example 2.

Now $\overrightarrow{BD}$ is a vector with magnitude $BD = \frac{1}{2} BC$ and $\overrightarrow{BC}$ is a vector with magnitude BC.

Since directions of vectors $\overrightarrow{BC}$ and $\overrightarrow{BD}$ are same it follows that

$$\overrightarrow{BD} = \frac{1}{2}\overrightarrow{BC}.$$

Example 2. *Show that the sum of the three vectors determined by the medians of a triangle directed from the vertices is zero.*

Solution. Let ABC be any triangle with AD, BE and CF as its medians.

We want to show that

$$\overrightarrow{AD} + \overrightarrow{BE} + \overrightarrow{CF} = 0$$

From triangle *ABD*, we have

$$\overrightarrow{AD} = \overrightarrow{AB} + \overrightarrow{BD}$$
$$= \overrightarrow{AB} + \frac{1}{2}\overrightarrow{BC}$$

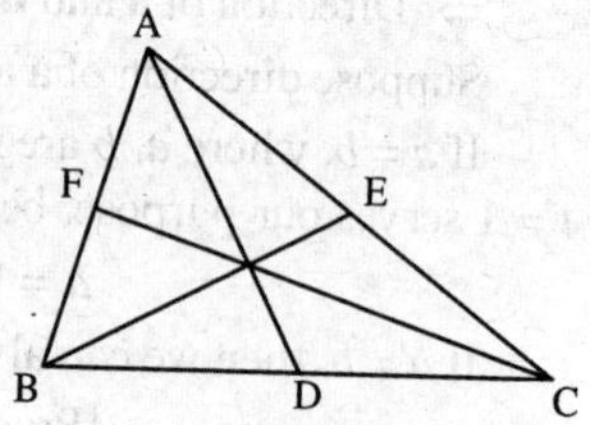

Fig. 9

Similarly $\overrightarrow{BE} = \overrightarrow{BC} + \frac{1}{2}\overrightarrow{CA}$

$$\overrightarrow{CF} = \overrightarrow{CA} + \frac{1}{2}\overrightarrow{AB}$$

Thus

$$\overrightarrow{AD} + \overrightarrow{BE} + \overrightarrow{CF} = \overrightarrow{AB} + \overrightarrow{BC} + \overrightarrow{CA} + \frac{1}{2}(\overrightarrow{AB} + \overrightarrow{BC} + \overrightarrow{CA})$$
$$= \vec{0}$$

as $\overrightarrow{AB} + \overrightarrow{BC} = \overrightarrow{AC}$

$\Rightarrow$ $\overrightarrow{AB} + \overrightarrow{BC} = -\overrightarrow{CA}$ $\Rightarrow$ $\overrightarrow{AB} + \overrightarrow{BC} + \overrightarrow{CA} = \vec{0}$.

Example 3. *Show that the vector equation*

$$\mathbf{a} + \mathbf{x} = \mathbf{b}$$

has a unique solution.

Solution. We note that

$$\mathbf{a} + [-\mathbf{a} + \mathbf{b}] = [\mathbf{a} + (-\mathbf{a})] + \mathbf{b} \quad \text{[Associativity]}$$
$$= \mathbf{0} + \mathbf{b} = \mathbf{b} \quad \text{[Identity]}$$

$\Rightarrow -\mathbf{a} + \mathbf{b}$ is a solution of $\mathbf{a} + \mathbf{x} = \mathbf{b}$.

Suppose now that $\mathbf{y}$ is any other solution of this equation.

Then $\mathbf{y} = \mathbf{0} + \mathbf{y} = [(-\mathbf{a}) + \mathbf{a}] + \mathbf{y}$

$$= (-\mathbf{a}) + (\mathbf{a} + \mathbf{y})$$
$$= -\mathbf{a} + \mathbf{b} \quad \text{as } \mathbf{y} \text{ is a solution}$$

$\Rightarrow -\mathbf{a} + \mathbf{b}$ is the unique solution.

EXERCISES

1. For any vector a, show that $-(-\mathbf{a}) = \mathbf{a}$.
2. Show that the sum of the three vectors determined by the sides of a triangle taken in order is the zero vector. Generalise this result for any closed polygon.
3. If G is the centroid of the triangle ABC and O is any point, show that $\overrightarrow{OA} + \overrightarrow{OB} + \overrightarrow{OC} = 3\,\overrightarrow{OG}$.
4. $ABCDEF$ is a regular hexagon. Forces $\overrightarrow{AB}, \overrightarrow{AC}, \overrightarrow{AD}, \overrightarrow{AE}$ and $\overrightarrow{AF}$ act at A. Show, that their resultant is $3\,\overrightarrow{AD}$. In other words, show that $\overrightarrow{AB} + \overrightarrow{AC} + \overrightarrow{AD} + \overrightarrow{AE} + \overrightarrow{AF} = 3\,\overrightarrow{AD}$.

5. Show, using vectors, that the line joining the middle points of two sides of a triangle is parallel to the third side and is half of it.
6. If *ABCD* is a quadrilateral, show that $\overrightarrow{AB} + \overrightarrow{DC} = \overrightarrow{AC} + \overrightarrow{DB}$
7. Show that $-(\mathbf{a} + \mathbf{b}) = -\mathbf{a} - \mathbf{b}$.

12. POSITION VECTOR

Let O be a fixed point (called *origin*). If P is any point in space and the vector $\overrightarrow{OP} = \mathbf{r}$, we say that position vector of P is $\mathbf{r}$ with respect to the origin O, and express this, in short, as $P(\mathbf{r})$.

Whenever we talk of some points with position vectors it is to be understood that all those vectors are expressed with respect to the same origin. We prove

If A and B are any two points with position vectors **a** *and* **b** *then*

$$\overrightarrow{AB} = \mathbf{b} - \mathbf{a}$$

If O is the origin then it is given that

$$\overrightarrow{OA} = \mathbf{a}$$

$$\overrightarrow{OB} = \mathbf{b}$$

Also then

$$\overrightarrow{OA} + \overrightarrow{AB} = \overrightarrow{OB}$$

[addition law]

$$\Rightarrow \quad \overrightarrow{AB} = \overrightarrow{OB} - \overrightarrow{OA}$$

$$\Rightarrow \quad \overrightarrow{AB} = \mathbf{b} - \mathbf{a}.$$

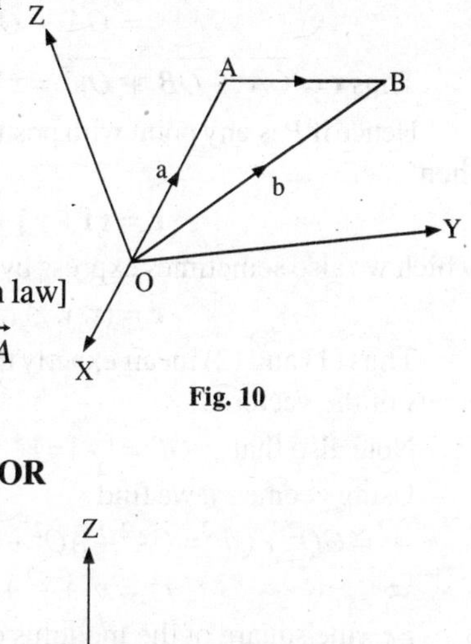

Fig. 10

13. COMPONENTS OF A VECTOR

Let P be any point in space with co-ordinates (x, y, z). Complete the parallelopiped as shown in Fig. 11.

Then co-ordinates of the points A, B, C, are respectively, $(x, 0, 0)$, $(0, y, 0)$, $(0, 0, z)$.

Suppose now that position vector of P is $\mathbf{r}$.

i.e., $\overrightarrow{OP} = \mathbf{r}$

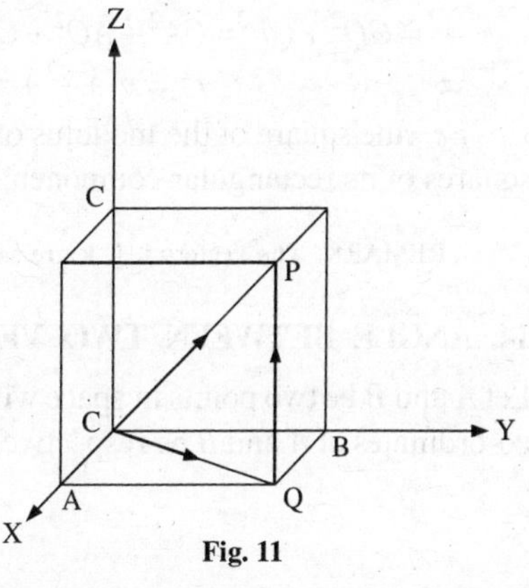

Fig. 11

Also let **i, j, k,** be the unit vectors along the three co-ordinate x, y and z-axis.

Now $$OA = x \Rightarrow \overrightarrow{OA} = x\mathbf{i}$$

Note that $x\,\mathbf{i}$ is a vector whose magnitude is $1.x = x$ and whose direction is that of the x-axis and this is precisely the vector $\overrightarrow{OA}$.

Similarly, $$\overrightarrow{OB} = y\,\mathbf{j}$$
$$\overrightarrow{OC} = z\,\mathbf{k}.$$

From the triangle OPQ,

$$\mathbf{r} = \overrightarrow{OP} = \overrightarrow{OQ} + \overrightarrow{QP}$$
$$= \overrightarrow{OQ} + \overrightarrow{OC}$$

Also from the triangle OPQ,

$$\overrightarrow{OQ} = \overrightarrow{OA} + \overrightarrow{AQ}$$
$$= \overrightarrow{OA} + \overrightarrow{OB}$$

Thus $\mathbf{r} = \overrightarrow{OA} + \overrightarrow{OB} + \overrightarrow{OC} = x\,\mathbf{i} + y\,\mathbf{j} + z\,\mathbf{k}.$

Hence if P is any point with position vector **r** and co-ordinates (x, y, z) then

$$\mathbf{r} = x\,\mathbf{i} + y\,\mathbf{j} + z\,\mathbf{k} \qquad ...(1)$$

which we also sometimes express by writing

$$\mathbf{r} = (x, y, z) \qquad ...(2)$$

Thus (1) and (2) mean exactly the same. x, y, z are called the *components* of the vector **r.**

Note also that $OP = |\mathbf{r}| = r$

Using geometry, we find

$$r^2 = OQ^2 + QP^2 = OA^2 + AQ^2 + QP^2 = OA^2 + OB^2 + OC^2$$

$$\Rightarrow \qquad r^2 = x^2 + y^2 + z^2$$

i.e., the square of the modulus of a vector is equal to the sum of the squares of its rectangular components.

REMARK: The vectors **i, j, k** are said to form an *orthonormal triad.*

14. ANGLE BETWEEN TWO VECTORS

Let A and B be two points in space with position vectors **a** and **b**. Also let co-ordinates of A and B be respectively (a_1, a_2, a_3) and (b_1, b_2, b_3).

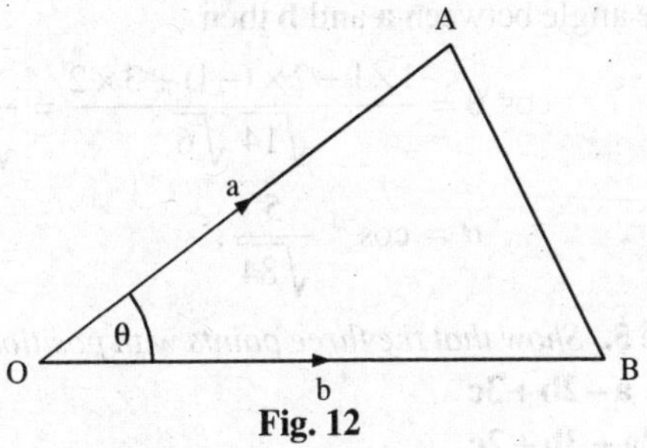

Fig. 12

Then $\mathbf{a} = \overrightarrow{OA} = a_1\,\mathbf{i} + a_2\,\mathbf{j} + a_3\,\mathbf{k}$

$\mathbf{b} = \overrightarrow{OB} = b_1\,\mathbf{i} + b_2\,\mathbf{j} + b_3\,\mathbf{k}$

$\Rightarrow$ $\mathbf{b} - \mathbf{a} = (b_1 - a_1)\,\mathbf{i} + (b_2 - a_2)\,\mathbf{j} + (b_3 - a_3)\,\mathbf{k}$

Also $\overrightarrow{AB} = \mathbf{b} - \mathbf{a}$

Thus $AB^2 = (b_1 - a_1)^2 + (b_2 - a_2)^2 + (b_3 - a_3)^2$ ...(1)

Let θ be the angle between **a** and **b** then θ is the angle between OA and OB and we have

$$AB^2 = OA^2 + OB^2 - 2\,OA\,.\,OB\cos\theta$$

$$\Rightarrow \quad \cos\theta = \frac{OA^2 + OB^2 - AB^2}{2\,OA\,.\,OB}$$

$$= \frac{(a_1^2 + a_2^2 + a_3^2) + (b_1^2 + b_2^2 + b_3^2) - \Sigma\,(b_1 - a_1)^2}{2\,a\,.\,b}$$

$$\Rightarrow \quad \cos\theta = \frac{a_1b_1 + a_2b_2 + a_3b_3}{\sqrt{a_1^2 + a_2^2 + a_3^2}\,\sqrt{b_1^2 + b_2^2 + b_3^2}}$$

because $a^2 = a_1^2 + a_2^2 + a_3^2$ and $b^2 = b_1^2 + b_2^2 + b_3^2$

as in the previous article.

Example. 4. *Find the angle between the vectors*

$$\mathbf{a} = \mathbf{i} + 2\mathbf{j} + 3\mathbf{k}$$
$$\mathbf{b} = \mathbf{i} - \mathbf{j} + 2\mathbf{k}.$$

Solution. We have

$\mathbf{a} = (1, 2, 3)$

$\mathbf{b} = (1, -1, 2)$

$\Rightarrow$ $a^2 = 1 + 4 + 9 = 14$

$b^2 = 1 + 1 + 4 = 6$

If θ is the angle between **a** and **b** then

$$\cos\theta = \frac{1\times 1 + 2\times(-1) + 3\times 2}{\sqrt{14}\sqrt{6}} = \frac{5}{\sqrt{84}}.$$

Hence $$\theta = \cos^{-1}\frac{5}{\sqrt{84}}.$$

Example 5. *Show that the three points with position vectors given by*

$$\mathbf{a} - 2\mathbf{b} + 3\mathbf{c}$$
$$-2\mathbf{a} + 3\mathbf{b} + 2\mathbf{c}$$
$$-8\mathbf{a} + 13\mathbf{b}$$

are collinear.

Solution. Let the three poins be A, B, C respectively.

Then $\overrightarrow{AB}$ = Position vector of B – Position vector of A [See Art. 12]

$$= (-2\mathbf{a} + 3\mathbf{b} + 2\mathbf{c}) - (\mathbf{a} - 2\mathbf{b} + 3\mathbf{c})$$
$$= -3\mathbf{a} + 5\mathbf{b} - \mathbf{c}$$

Similarly $\overrightarrow{BC} = (-8\mathbf{a} + 13\mathbf{b}) - (-2\mathbf{a} + 3\mathbf{b} + 2\mathbf{c})$

$$= 2(-3\mathbf{a} + 5\mathbf{b} - \mathbf{c}) = 2\,\overrightarrow{AB}.$$

$\Rightarrow \overrightarrow{BC}$ and $\overrightarrow{AB}$ are parallel [See Theorem 11]

which is possible only when A, B, C lie on one line. Hence the result.

Example 6. *If A, B, C are three points with position vectors given by*

$$\mathbf{a} = 2\mathbf{i} - \mathbf{j} + \mathbf{k}$$
$$\mathbf{b} = \mathbf{i} - 3\mathbf{j} - 5\mathbf{k}$$
$$\mathbf{c} = 3\mathbf{i} - 4\mathbf{j} - 4\mathbf{k}.$$

Show that they form a right triangle, right angled at C.

Solution. We have

$$\overrightarrow{AB} = \mathbf{b} - \mathbf{a} = (\mathbf{i} - 3\mathbf{j} - 5\mathbf{k}) - (2\mathbf{i} - \mathbf{j} + \mathbf{k}) = -\mathbf{i} - 2\mathbf{j} - 6\mathbf{k}$$

$$\overrightarrow{BC} = \mathbf{c} - \mathbf{b} = 2\mathbf{i} - \mathbf{j} + \mathbf{k}$$

$$\overrightarrow{AC} = \mathbf{c} - \mathbf{a} = \mathbf{i} - 3\mathbf{j} - 5\mathbf{k}$$

Giving $AB = \sqrt{1 + 4 + 36} = \sqrt{41}$

$$BC = \sqrt{4 + 1 + 1} = \sqrt{6}$$

$$AC = \sqrt{1 + 9 + 25} = \sqrt{35}$$

which shows $AB^2 = BC^2 + AC^2$.

$\Rightarrow ABC$ is a right triangle with right angle at C. (*Note* that $\overrightarrow{AB}$ and $\overrightarrow{BC}$ are not parallel, so A, B, C are non-collinear).

Aliter. To show that C is the right angle we observe

$$\cos C = \frac{AC^2 + BC^2 - AB^2}{2AC \cdot BC} = \frac{35 + 6 - 41}{2\sqrt{35}\sqrt{6}} = 0$$

$$\Rightarrow \qquad C = \frac{\pi}{2}.$$

15. SECTION FORMULA

To find the position vector of a point dividing the join of two given points in a given ratio.

Let A and B be the two given points with position vectors **a** and **b** respectively. Suppose the point R (**r**) divides AB in the ratio $m : n$.

i.e., $\qquad AR : RB = m : n$

Then $\qquad \dfrac{AR}{m} = \dfrac{RB}{n}$

or $\qquad nAR = mRB$

$\Rightarrow \qquad n\overrightarrow{AR} = m\overrightarrow{RB}$

$\Rightarrow \qquad n(\mathbf{r} - \mathbf{a}) = m(\mathbf{b} - \mathbf{r})$

$\Rightarrow \qquad nr + mr = m\mathbf{b} + n\mathbf{a}$

$\Rightarrow \qquad \mathbf{r} = \dfrac{n\mathbf{a} + m\mathbf{b}}{n + m}$

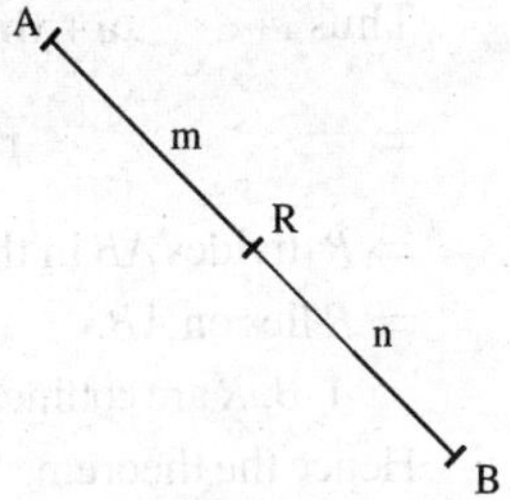

Fig. 13

which gives the required value of **r**.

Corollary. If R is the middle point of AB, then $\mathbf{r} = \dfrac{\mathbf{a} + \mathbf{b}}{2}$ as in this case $m = n$.

16. THEOREM

Three distinct points A, B, R with position vectors **a, b, r** *are collinear if and only if there exist three numbers x, y, z (not all zero) such that* $x\mathbf{a} + y\mathbf{b} + z\mathbf{c} = \mathbf{0}$ and $x + y + z = 0$.

Proof. Let the three points A, B, R be collinear.

The R divides AB in some ratio, say, $m : n$

we have as above $\quad \mathbf{r} = \dfrac{n\mathbf{a} + m\mathbf{b}}{n + m}$

$$\Rightarrow \quad (n+m)\,\mathbf{r} = n\mathbf{a} + m\mathbf{b}$$

or $\quad n\mathbf{a} + m\mathbf{b} - (n+m)\,\mathbf{r} = 0.$

Let $\quad x = n,\ y = m,\ z = -(n+m)$

then $\quad x\mathbf{a} + y\mathbf{b} + z\mathbf{r} = 0$

where $\quad x + y + z = n + m - (n+m) = 0.$

Clearly all x, y, z can't be zero.

Hence the result

Conversely. Suppose $\exists$ x, y, z not all zero such that

$$x\mathbf{a} + y\mathbf{b} + z\mathbf{c} = \mathbf{0}$$

and $\quad x + y + z = 0$

Let $z \neq 0$, now $x + y + z = 0$

$$\Rightarrow \quad x + y = -z$$

$$\Rightarrow \quad (x+y)\,\mathbf{r} = -z\mathbf{r}$$

Also $\quad -z\mathbf{r} = x\mathbf{a} + y\mathbf{b}$

Thus $\quad x\mathbf{a} + y\mathbf{b} = (x+y)\,\mathbf{r}$

$$\Rightarrow \quad \mathbf{r} = \frac{x\mathbf{a} + y\mathbf{b}}{x+y} \quad (\text{as } x + y \neq 0 \text{ otherwise } z = 0)$$

$\Rightarrow R$ divides AB in the ratio $x : y$

$\Rightarrow R$ lies on AB.

$\Rightarrow A, B, R$ are collinear.

Hence the theorem.

Example 7. *Show that the points with position vectors*

$3\mathbf{a} - 2\mathbf{b} + 4\mathbf{c}$

$\mathbf{a} + \mathbf{b} + \mathbf{c}$

$-\mathbf{a} + 4\mathbf{b} - 2\mathbf{c}$ *are collinear.*

Solution. The three points will be collinear if and only if we can find x, y, z (not all zero) such that

$$x\,(3\mathbf{a} - 2\mathbf{b} + 4\mathbf{c}) + y\,(\mathbf{a} + \mathbf{b} + \mathbf{c}) + z\,(-\mathbf{a} + 4\mathbf{b} - 2\mathbf{c}) = \mathbf{0} \quad \text{...(1)}$$

and $\quad x + y + z = 0 \quad$ ...(2)

equation (1) can be written as

$$(3x + y - z)\,\mathbf{a} + (-2x + y + 4z)\,\mathbf{b} + (4x + y - 2z)\,\mathbf{c} = \mathbf{0}$$

which gives

$$3x + y - z = 0$$

$$-2x + y + 4z = 0$$

$$4x + y - 2z = 0$$

Also we should have $x + y + z = 0$. One non-zero solution of these four equations is

$$x = z = 1, y = -2$$

hence we find the three given points are collinear.

Example 8. *Show that the medians of a triangle meet in a point that trisects them.*

Solution. Let ABC be any triangle with medians AD, BE and CF. See figure 9.

Let position vectors of A, B, C be respectively **a, b, c.**

Since D is middle point of BC, the position vector **d** of D is given by

$$\mathbf{d} = \frac{\mathbf{a} + \mathbf{b}}{2}$$

Let R be the point dividing AD in the ratio 2 : 1, then position vector **r** of R is given by

$$\mathbf{r} = \frac{\mathbf{a} + 2\left(\frac{\mathbf{b} + \mathbf{c}}{2}\right)}{1 + 2} = \frac{\mathbf{a} + \mathbf{b} + \mathbf{c}}{3}$$

Symmetry in **a, b,c** implies that R will also be the point that divides BE and CF in the ratio 2 : 1. This in turn yields that R is the required point where the three medians meet (and also it trisects them).

Example 9. *Show that the internal bisectors of the angles of a triangle are concurrent.*

Solution. Let ABC be any triangle with AD, BE, CF as the internal bisectors of the three angles. Suppose AD and BE meet in the point R. Let position vectors of the points A, B, C, D, E, F, R be respectively, **a, b, c, d, e, f, r.**

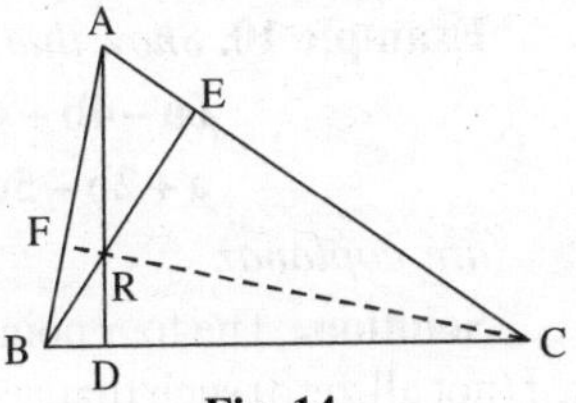

Fig. 14

Also let $AB = u$

$BC = v$

$CA = w$

Now E divides CA in the ratio $BC : AB$ *i.e.*, $u : w$

Thus by section formula $\mathbf{e} = \dfrac{u\mathbf{a} + w\mathbf{c}}{u + w}$ ...(1)

Also $\dfrac{CE}{EA} = \dfrac{u}{w}$

$$\Rightarrow \quad \frac{CE}{u} = \frac{EA}{w} = \frac{CE + EA}{u + w} = \frac{CA}{u + w} = \frac{v}{u + w}$$

$$\Rightarrow \quad EA = \frac{vw}{u + w}$$

Again from triangle ABE, as R divides BE in the ratio $AB : AE$.

i.e., $w : \frac{vw}{u + w}$ we get

$$\mathbf{r} = \frac{w\mathbf{e} + \frac{vw}{u + w}\mathbf{b}}{w + \frac{vw}{u + w}}$$

$$\Rightarrow \quad \mathbf{r} = \frac{u\mathbf{a} + v\mathbf{b} + w\mathbf{c}}{u + v + w} \qquad \text{[using (1)]}$$

Similarly if we find the position vector of the point of intersection of AD and CF, we'll get the same result. (Because of symmetry in **a, b, c** and u, v, w).

Hence R is the point where the three bisectors AD, BE and CF meet.

17. COPLANAR POINTS

It can be proved that four points with position vectors **a, b, c, d** are coplanar if and only if we can find scalars (not all zero) x, y, z, t such that

$$x\mathbf{a} + y\mathbf{b} + z\mathbf{c} + t\mathbf{d} = \mathbf{0}$$
$$x + y + z + t = 0$$

Example 10. *Show that the points with position vectors*

$$6\mathbf{a} - 4\mathbf{b} + 4\mathbf{c}, \quad -\mathbf{a} - 2\mathbf{b} - 3\mathbf{c},$$
$$\mathbf{a} + 2\mathbf{b} - 5\mathbf{c}, \quad -4\mathbf{c}$$

are coplanar.

Solution. The four points will be coplanar if we can find scalars x, y, z, t (not all zero) such that

$$x(6\mathbf{a} - 4\mathbf{b} + 4\mathbf{c}) + y(-\mathbf{a} - 2\mathbf{b} - 3\mathbf{c}) + z(\mathbf{a} + 2\mathbf{b} - 5\mathbf{c}) + t(-4\mathbf{c}) = \mathbf{0}$$

and $\quad x + y + z + t = 0$

The first equation suggests

$$6x - y + z = 0$$
$$-4x - 2x + 2z = 0$$
$$4x - 3y - 5z - 4t = 0$$

Also we should have $x + y + z + t = 0$

which give $x = 0, y = 1, z = 1, t = -2.$

which is a non-zero solution of the equations and thus the four points are coplanar.

EXERCISES

1. If $\mathbf{a} = \mathbf{i} + \mathbf{j} + \mathbf{k}$, $\mathbf{b} = 2\mathbf{i} + 2\mathbf{j} - \mathbf{k}$

   Find (*i*) $\mathbf{a} + \mathbf{b}$, (*ii*) $\mathbf{a} - \mathbf{b}$, (*iii*) $\mathbf{a} + 3\mathbf{b}$

2. Find the cosine of the angle between the vectors

   (*i*) $3\mathbf{i} + \mathbf{j} + 2\mathbf{k}$ and $2\mathbf{i} - 2\mathbf{j} + 4\mathbf{k}$

   (*ii*) $\mathbf{i} + \mathbf{j} + \mathbf{k}$ and $\mathbf{i} - \mathbf{j} - \mathbf{k}$

   (*iii*) $2\mathbf{i} + \mathbf{j} + \mathbf{k}$ and $\mathbf{i} + \frac{1}{2}\mathbf{j} + \frac{1}{2}\mathbf{k}$

3. Show that the vectors $\mathbf{a} = \mathbf{i} + 4\mathbf{j} + 3\mathbf{k}$ and $\mathbf{b} = 4\mathbf{i} + 2\mathbf{j} - 4\mathbf{k}$ are perpendicular.

4. The position vectors of the points *A, B, C, D* are given by

$$\mathbf{a} = 3\mathbf{i} + 4\mathbf{j} + 5\mathbf{k}$$
$$\mathbf{b} = 4\mathbf{i} + 5\mathbf{j} + 6\mathbf{k}$$
$$\mathbf{c} = 7\mathbf{i} + 9\mathbf{j} + 3\mathbf{k}$$
$$\mathbf{d} = 4\mathbf{i} + 6\mathbf{j}.$$

   Show that *AB* and *CD* are parallel.

5. Position vectors of the vertices of a triangle are

$$\mathbf{a} = 2\mathbf{i} + 4\mathbf{j} - \mathbf{k}$$
$$\mathbf{b} = 4\mathbf{i} + 5\mathbf{j} + \mathbf{k}$$
$$\mathbf{c} = 3\mathbf{i} + 6\mathbf{j} + 3\mathbf{k}$$

   Show that it is a right triangle.

6. Show that the points with position vectors $\mathbf{a}$, $\mathbf{b}$, $3\mathbf{a} - 2\mathbf{b}$ are collinear.

7. Show that the point with position vectors $3\mathbf{a} - 2\mathbf{b} + 4\mathbf{c}$, $\mathbf{a} + \mathbf{b} + \mathbf{c}$, $-\mathbf{a} + 4\mathbf{b} - 2\mathbf{c}$ are collinear.

8. Show that the diagonals of a parallelogram bisect each other.

9. If the diagonals of a quadrilateral bisect each other, show that it is a parallelogram.

10. *ABCD* is a parallelogram. *E, F* are the mid-points of the sides *AB* and *BC*. Show that *DE* and *DF* trisect the diagonal *AC*.

11. *A* and *B* are points with position vectors $\mathbf{a} = \mathbf{i} + \mathbf{j} + \mathbf{k}$, $\mathbf{b} = \mathbf{i} - \mathbf{j} - \mathbf{k}$. Find the position vector of the point *R* dividing *AB* in the ratio 1 : 2.

12. Show that the line joining the vertices of a tetrahedron to the centroids of the opposite faces meet in a point.

13. Show that the line joining the midpoints of two non-parallel sides of a trapezium is parallel to the parallel sides and is half of their sum.

14. Show that the line joining the mid-points of opposite edges of a tetrahedron are concurrent and bisect each other.

15. Show that the following points with position vectors **2a** – **b** + **c**, **a** + 2**b** – **c**, 3**a** + **b** – **c**, – **a** – 2**b** + 3**c** are coplanar (where **a, b, c** are non-coplanar vectors)
16. Show that the points with position vectors given by 3**a** + 2**b** – 5**c**, **a** + 4**b** – 3**c**, – 3**a** + 2**b** + **c**, 3**a** + 8**b** + 5**c** are not coplanar.

ANSWERS

1. (*i*) 3**i** + 3**j** (*ii*) – **i** – **j** – 2**k** (*iii*) 7**i** + 7**j** – 2**k**
2. (*i*) $\sqrt{\frac{3}{7}}$ (*ii*) $-\frac{1}{3}$ (*iii*) 1

11. $\mathbf{i}+\frac{1}{3}\mathbf{j}+\frac{1}{3}\mathbf{k}$

18. PRODUCT OF TWO VECTORS

Product of two vectors is defined in two ways, called respectively, the *scalar product and vector product.*

19. SCALAR PRODUCT (OR DOT PRODUCT)

If **a** and **b** are two vectors then their scalar product **a** . **b** (read as **a** dot **b**) is defined by

$$\mathbf{a}.\mathbf{b} = ab \cos \theta$$

where *a, b* are the magnitudes of the vectors **a** and **b** respectively and θ is the angle between the vectors **a** and **b**.

It is clear from definition that dot product of two vectors is a scalar quantity.

20. SCALAR PRODUCT IS COMMUTATIVE

$$\mathbf{a}.\mathbf{b} = ab \cos \theta = ba \cos \theta$$
$$= \mathbf{b}.\mathbf{a}$$

21. THEOREM

Two non-zero vectors **a** *and* **b** *are perpendicular if and only if*

$$\mathbf{a}.\mathbf{b} = 0.$$

Proof. Let **a** and **b** be two non-zero perpendicular vectors. Then

$$\mathbf{a}.\mathbf{b} = ab \cos 90 = 0$$

Conversely. Let **a** . **b**=0

$\Rightarrow$ $ab \cos \theta = 0$

where θ is the angle between **a** and **b**

$\Rightarrow \qquad \cos\theta = 0$ [as **a** and **b** are non-zero]

$\Rightarrow \qquad \theta = \dfrac{\pi}{2}$

$\Rightarrow$ **a** and **b** are perpendicular.

The following results are trivial:

$$\mathbf{i}\cdot\mathbf{i} = \mathbf{j}\cdot\mathbf{j} = \mathbf{k}\cdot\mathbf{k} = 1$$

$$\mathbf{i}\cdot\mathbf{j} = \mathbf{j}\cdot\mathbf{k} = \mathbf{k}\cdot\mathbf{i} = 0.$$

Definition. By $\mathbf{a}^2$ we will always mean **a. a.**

Thus $\qquad \mathbf{a}^2 = a.\,a\cos 0 = a^2.$

Example 11. *Show that* $\mathbf{a}(-\mathbf{b}) = -\mathbf{a}\cdot\mathbf{b}.$

Solution. We have

$$\mathbf{a}.(-\mathbf{b}) = ab\cos(\pi - \theta) \text{ when } \theta \text{ is angle between } \mathbf{a} \text{ and } \mathbf{b}$$
$$= -ab\cos\theta = (-\mathbf{a})\,.\,\mathbf{b}$$

22. DISTRIBUTIVE LAW

Prove that

$$\mathbf{a}\cdot(\mathbf{b}+\mathbf{c}) = \mathbf{a}\cdot\mathbf{b} + \mathbf{a}\cdot\mathbf{c}$$

Let $\overrightarrow{OA} = \mathbf{a}$

$\overrightarrow{OB} = \mathbf{b}$

$\overrightarrow{BC} = \mathbf{c}$

Let *BL* and *CM* be perpendiculars from *B* and *C* on $\overrightarrow{OA}$ respectively and *BK* be perpendicular from *B* on *CM*.

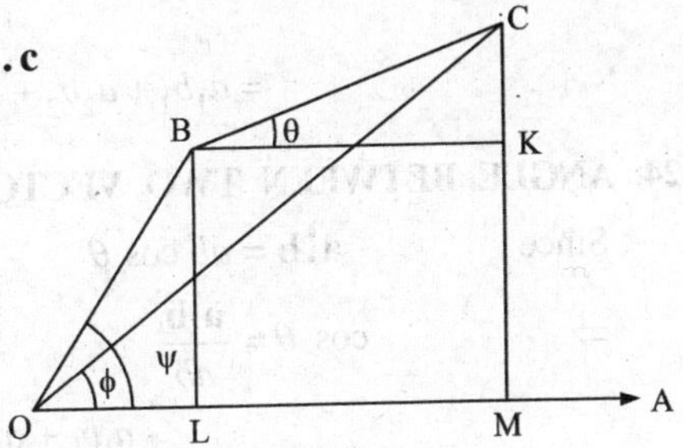

Fig. 15

Then $\qquad \mathbf{a}\cdot\mathbf{b} = ab\cos\psi = a\,.\,OL$

$\mathbf{a}\cdot\mathbf{c} = ac\cos\theta = a\,.\,BK = a\,.\,LM$

$\Rightarrow \qquad \text{RHS} = \mathbf{a}\cdot\mathbf{b} + \mathbf{a}\cdot\mathbf{c} = a\,.\,OL + a\,.\,LM = a\,(OL + LM)$

$= a\,.\,OM$

Again $\qquad \overrightarrow{OB} + \overrightarrow{BC} = \overrightarrow{OC}$

$\Rightarrow \qquad \mathbf{b} + \mathbf{c} = \overrightarrow{OC}$

$\Rightarrow \qquad \text{LHS} = \mathbf{a}(\mathbf{b}+\mathbf{c}) = \mathbf{a}\,.\,\overrightarrow{OC}$

$= a\,.\,OC\cos\phi = a\,.\,OM.$

Hence the result follows.

An immediate consequence of the above result is

$$\begin{aligned}(\mathbf{a}+\mathbf{b})^2 &= (\mathbf{a}+\mathbf{b}).(\mathbf{a}+\mathbf{b}) \\ &= \mathbf{a}.\mathbf{a}+\mathbf{a}.\mathbf{b}+\mathbf{b}.\mathbf{a}+\mathbf{b}.\mathbf{b} \\ &= \mathbf{a}^2+\mathbf{a}.\mathbf{b}+\mathbf{a}.\mathbf{b}+\mathbf{b}^2 \\ &= \mathbf{a}^2+2\,\mathbf{ab}+\mathbf{b}^2\end{aligned}$$

Similarly, we can prove

$$(\mathbf{a}-\mathbf{b})^2 = \mathbf{a}^2-2\mathbf{ab}+\mathbf{b}^2$$

$$(\mathbf{a}+\mathbf{b}).(\mathbf{a}-\mathbf{b}) = \mathbf{a}^2-\mathbf{b}^2.$$

23. SCALAR PRODUCT IN TERMS OF THE COMPONENTS

Let

$$\mathbf{a} = (a_1, a_2, a_3) = a_1\,\mathbf{i} + a_2\,\mathbf{j} + a_3\,\mathbf{k}$$

$$\mathbf{b} = (b_1, b_2, b_3) = b_1\,\mathbf{i} + b_2\,\mathbf{j} + b_3\,\mathbf{k}$$

be any two vectors. Then

$$\begin{aligned}\mathbf{a}.\mathbf{b} &= (a_1\,\mathbf{i}+a_2\,\mathbf{j}+a_3\,\mathbf{k}).(b_1\,\mathbf{i}+b_2\mathbf{j}+b_3\,\mathbf{k}) \\ &= a_1b_1\,\mathbf{i}.\mathbf{i}+a_2b_2\,\mathbf{j}.\mathbf{j}+a_3b_3\,\mathbf{k}.\mathbf{k}\end{aligned}$$

[other terms being zero]

$$= a_1b_1 + a_2b_2 + a_3b_3.$$

24. ANGLE BETWEEN TWO VECTORS

Since

$$\mathbf{a}.\mathbf{b} = ab\cos\theta$$

$$\Rightarrow \quad \cos\theta = \frac{\mathbf{a}.\mathbf{b}}{ab}$$

$$= \frac{a_1b_1 + a_2b_2 + a_3b_3}{\sqrt{a_1^2 + a_2^2\; a_3^2}\;\sqrt{b_1^2 + b_2^2 + b_3^2}}$$

a formula that we obtained earlier.

Example 12. *Show that the vectors* **a, b, c** *given by*

$$7\mathbf{a} = 2\mathbf{i} + 3\mathbf{j} + 6\mathbf{k}$$

$$7\mathbf{b} = 3\mathbf{i} - 6\mathbf{j} + 2\mathbf{k}$$

$$7\mathbf{c} = 6\mathbf{i} + 2\mathbf{j} - 3\mathbf{k}$$

are of unit length and are mutually perpendicular.

Solution. The three vectors are

$$\mathbf{a} = \left(\frac{2}{7}, \frac{3}{7}, \frac{6}{7}\right)$$

$$\mathbf{b} = \left(\frac{3}{7}, \frac{-6}{7}, \frac{2}{7}\right)$$

$$\mathbf{c} = \left(\frac{6}{7}, \frac{2}{7}, \frac{-3}{7}\right)$$

Now,
$$a = \sqrt{\left(\frac{2}{7}\right)^2 + \left(\frac{3}{7}\right)^2 + \left(\frac{6}{7}\right)^2} = \frac{1}{7}\sqrt{4+9+36}$$
$$= 1$$

$$b = \sqrt{\left(\frac{3}{7}\right)^2 + \left(\frac{-6}{7}\right)^2 + \left(\frac{2}{7}\right)^2} = 1$$

$$c = \sqrt{\left(\frac{6}{7}\right)^2 + \left(\frac{2}{7}\right)^2 + \left(\frac{-3}{7}\right)^2} = 1$$

This shows that the given vectors are of unit length.

Again

$$\mathbf{a}.\mathbf{b} = \frac{2}{7}\times\frac{3}{7} + \frac{3}{7}\times\left(\frac{-6}{7}\right) + \frac{6}{7}\times\frac{2}{7} = \frac{1}{49}[6 - 18 + 12] = 0$$

$\Rightarrow$ **a** and **b** are perpendicular.

$$\mathbf{b}.\mathbf{c} = \frac{3}{7}\times\frac{6}{7} + \left(\frac{-6}{7}\right)\times\frac{2}{7} + \frac{2}{7}\times\left(\frac{-3}{7}\right) = \frac{1}{49}[18 - 12 - 6] = 0$$

$$\mathbf{c}.\mathbf{a} = \frac{6}{7}\times\frac{2}{7} + \frac{2}{7}\times\frac{3}{7} + \left(\frac{-3}{7}\right)\times\frac{6}{7} = \frac{1}{49}[12 + 6 - 18] = 0.$$

This implies that **b** is perpendicular to **c** and **c** is perpendicular to **a**.

Example 13. *Show that the altitudes of a triangle meet in a point.*

Solution. Let ABC be any triangle and let the altitudes AD and BE meet in a point R. We show that the third altitude CF also passes through R.

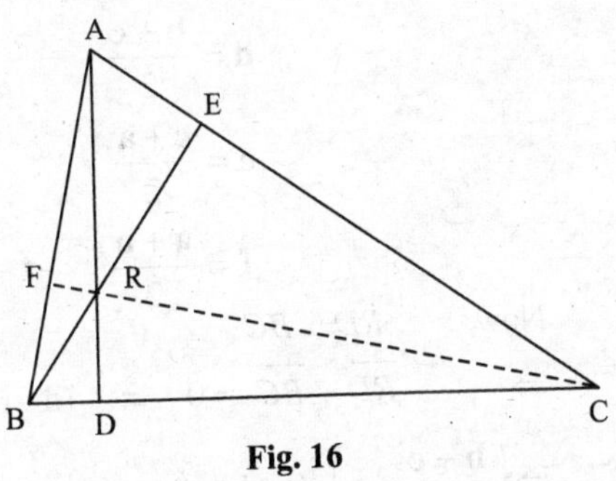

Fig. 16

Let **a, b, c, d, e, f, r** be the position vectors of the points A, B, C, D, E, F, R respectively.

Since $\quad AR \perp BC$

we have $\overrightarrow{AR} \cdot \overrightarrow{BC} = 0$

$\Rightarrow \quad (\mathbf{r}-\mathbf{a}) \cdot (\mathbf{c}-\mathbf{b}) = 0 \quad ...(1)$

Agin BR is perpendicular to CA.

$\Rightarrow \quad \overrightarrow{BR} \cdot \overrightarrow{CA} = 0$

$\Rightarrow \quad (\mathbf{r}-\mathbf{b}) \cdot (\mathbf{a}-\mathbf{c}) = 0 \quad ...(2)$

Adding (1) and (2) we'll get

$(\mathbf{r}-\mathbf{c}) \cdot (\mathbf{a}-\mathbf{b}) = 0$

$\Rightarrow \quad \overrightarrow{CR} \cdot \overrightarrow{BA} = 0$

$\Rightarrow \quad CR \perp BA$

$\Rightarrow$ CR is coincident with CF (the altitude through C).

Hence the three altitudes meet in a point.

Example 14. *Show that the perpendicular bisectors of the sides of a triangle are concurrent.*

Solution. Let ABC be any triangle and D, E, F be the middle points of the three sides AB, BC, CA respectively.

Let the perpendicular bisectors through D,E meet in the point R.

We show that the bisector through F also passes through R.

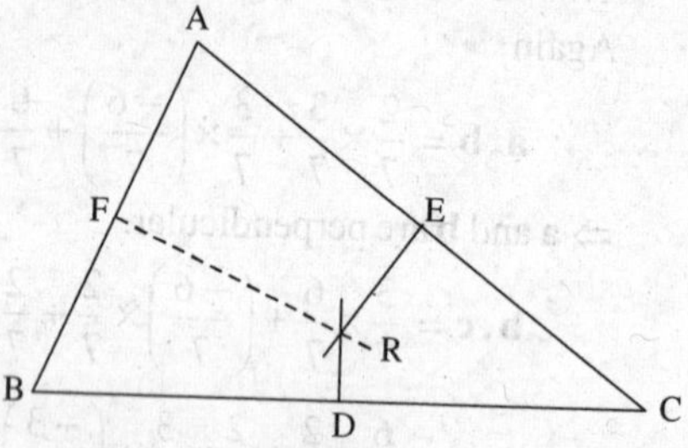

Fig. 17

Let **a, b, c, r** be the position vectors of the points A, B, C, R respectively.

Position vectors **d, e, f** of the points D, E, F are given by

$$\mathbf{d} = \frac{\mathbf{b}+\mathbf{c}}{2}$$

$$\mathbf{e} = \frac{\mathbf{c}+\mathbf{a}}{2}$$

$$\mathbf{f} = \frac{\mathbf{a}+\mathbf{b}}{2}$$

Now $\quad RD \perp BC$

$\Rightarrow \quad \overrightarrow{RD} \cdot \overrightarrow{BC} = 0 \Rightarrow (\mathbf{d}-\mathbf{r}) \cdot (\mathbf{c}-\mathbf{b}) = 0$

$\Rightarrow \left(\frac{\mathbf{b}+\mathbf{c}}{2} - \mathbf{r}\right) \cdot (\mathbf{c}-\mathbf{b}) = 0 \quad ...(1)$

Similarly, $RE \perp CA$

$\Rightarrow \quad (\mathbf{e}-\mathbf{r}) \cdot (\mathbf{a}-\mathbf{c}) = 0$

$$\Rightarrow \left(\frac{\mathbf{c}+\mathbf{a}}{2} - \mathbf{r}\right) \cdot (\mathbf{a}-\mathbf{c}) = 0 \qquad ...(2)$$

(1) and (2) on addition give

$$\left(\frac{\mathbf{a}+\mathbf{b}}{2} - \mathbf{r}\right) \cdot (\mathbf{a}-\mathbf{b}) = 0$$

$\Rightarrow \quad \overrightarrow{RE} \cdot \overrightarrow{BA} = 0 \quad \Rightarrow \overrightarrow{RF} \perp \overrightarrow{BA} \quad \Rightarrow RF \perp BA$

$\Rightarrow$ RF is the right bisector through F.

$\Rightarrow$ The three bisectors meet in the point R.

25. VECTOR PRODUCT (OR CROSS PRODUCT)

If **a** and **b** are two vectors then their vector product **a** × **b** (read as **a** cross **b**) is defined by

$$\mathbf{a} \times \mathbf{b} = ab \sin \theta \, \hat{n}$$

where a, b are the magnitudes of the vectors **a** and **b**, θ is the angle between **a** and **b** and $\hat{n}$ is a unit vector whose direction is along the normal to the plane of **a** and **b** in the direction from which rotation of **a** to **b** looks anti-clockwise (or, in other words, direction of $\hat{n}$ is towards that side to which a right handed screw will move if **a** is rotated towards **b**).

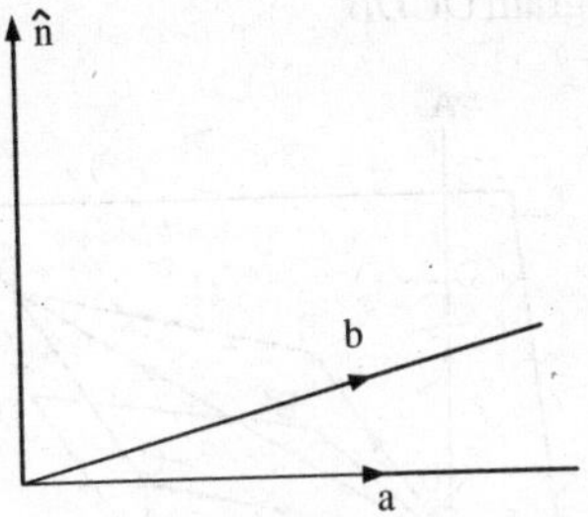

Fig. 18

So if **a** and **b** lie in plane of the paper as shown in the figure 18, then direction of $\hat{n}$ is along the normal to the plane of the paper pointing towards the reader.

We thus note (from the definitions) that the vector (or cross product) of two vectors is a vector.

Again it is clear from the definition that **a** × **b** and **b** × **a** will have the same magnitude $ab \sin \theta$, but in opposite directions.

Hence $\quad \mathbf{a} \times \mathbf{b} = -\mathbf{b} \times \mathbf{a}.$

Thus vector product is not **commutative**.

Also for any vector **a**

$$\mathbf{a} \times \mathbf{a} = a \cdot a \sin 0. \, \hat{n} = \mathbf{0}$$

The following results are direct consequence of the definition.

$$\mathbf{i}\times\mathbf{i}=\mathbf{j}\times\mathbf{j}=\mathbf{k}\times\mathbf{k}=\mathbf{0}$$

$$\mathbf{i}\times\mathbf{j}=\mathbf{k} \qquad \mathbf{j}\times\mathbf{i}=-\mathbf{k}$$

$$\mathbf{j}\times\mathbf{k}=\mathbf{i} \qquad \mathbf{k}\times\mathbf{j}=-\mathbf{i}$$

$$\mathbf{k}\times\mathbf{i}=\mathbf{j} \qquad \mathbf{i}\times\mathbf{k}=-\mathbf{j}.$$

Example 15. *Show that* $(m\mathbf{a})\times\mathbf{b}=\mathbf{a}\times(m\mathbf{b})=m(\mathbf{a}\times\mathbf{b})$.

Solution. We have

$$(m\mathbf{a})\times\mathbf{b} = mab\sin\theta\,\hat{n} = amb\sin\theta\,\hat{n} = \mathbf{a}\times(m\mathbf{b})$$

Similarly $\quad (m\mathbf{a})\times\mathbf{b} = m(\mathbf{a}\times\mathbf{b})$.

26. DISTRIBUTIVE LAW

We show that $\mathbf{a}\times(\mathbf{b}+\mathbf{c})=\mathbf{a}\times\mathbf{b}+\mathbf{a}\times\mathbf{c}$

Through a point O, take vectors $\overrightarrow{OA}=\mathbf{a}$, $\overrightarrow{OB}=\mathbf{b}$ and $\overrightarrow{OC}=\mathbf{c}$. Let S be a plane through O and perpendicular to $\overrightarrow{OA}$. Complete the parallelogram $OCDB$,

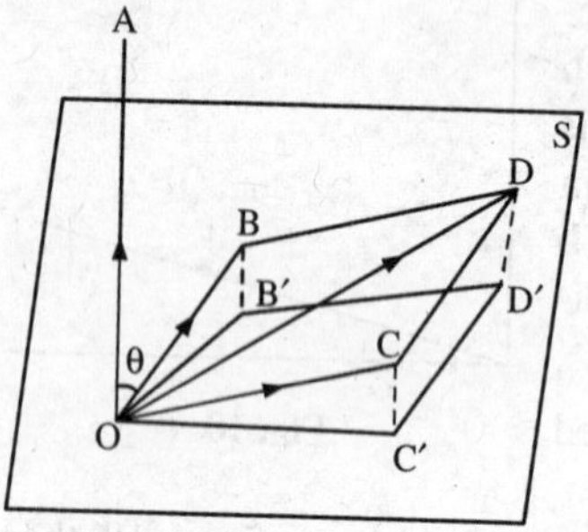

Fig. 19

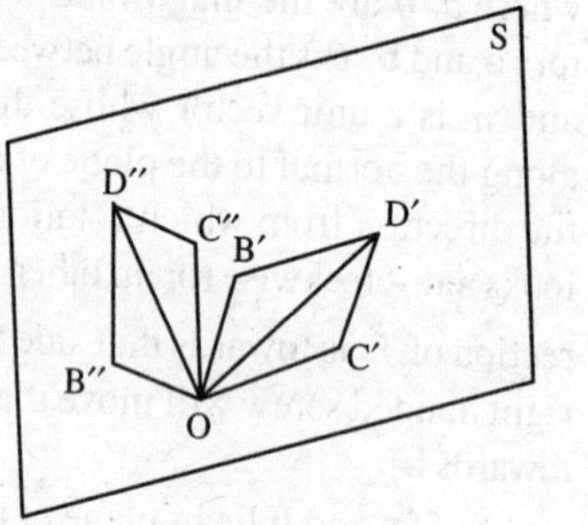

Fig. 20

So that $\quad \overrightarrow{OD}=\mathbf{b}+\mathbf{c}$

Let B', C', D' be the feet of perpendiculars from B, C, D respectively on the plane S.

Let $\quad \angle AOB=\theta$

Then $\quad \mathbf{a}\times\mathbf{b}=ab\sin\theta\,\hat{n}$

where $\hat{n}$ is a unit vector perpendicular to both OA and OB in the direction determined by motion of right handed screw.

Now $\quad \angle BOB'=\dfrac{\pi}{2}-\theta$

Thus if $\mathbf{b}' = \overrightarrow{OB'}$, then

$$|\mathbf{b}'| = b' = OB' = OB\cos\left(\frac{\pi}{2} - \theta\right) = b\sin\theta$$

Again since *OA, OB, OB′* are in the same plane *AOB′ B;* unit vector perpendicular to **a** and **b** is same as unit vector perpendicular to **a** and **b′**.

Thus $\quad \mathbf{a} \times \mathbf{b}' = ab' \sin 90^\circ\ \hat{n}$

$$= ab\sin\theta\,\hat{n} = \mathbf{a} \times \mathbf{b}$$

Similarly, $\quad \mathbf{a} \times \mathbf{c} = \mathbf{a} \times \mathbf{c}'$ where $\mathbf{c}' = 0\overrightarrow{OC'}$

and $\quad \mathbf{a} \times (\mathbf{b} + \mathbf{c}) = \mathbf{a} \times \overrightarrow{OD} = \mathbf{a} \times \overrightarrow{OD'}$.

Since *OA* is perpendicular to plane *S* and *OD′* lies in it, the unit vector perpendicular to both $\overrightarrow{OA}$ and $\overrightarrow{OD'}$ will lie in the plane *S*, say along *OD″*. So *OD″* lies in the plane *S* and is perpendicular to both *OA* and *OD′*.

Draw lines $\quad OB'' \perp OB'$

$$OC'' \perp OC'$$

such that $\quad OB'' = OA\,.\,OB'$

$$OC'' = OA\,.\,OD''$$

Also cut off $\quad OD'' = OA\,.\,OD'$

Then

$$\mathbf{a} \times \mathbf{b}' = \overrightarrow{OA} \times \vec{OB'} = \vec{OB''}$$

$$\mathbf{a} \times \mathbf{c}' = \overrightarrow{OA} \times \vec{OC'} = \vec{OC'}$$

$$\mathbf{a} \times \overrightarrow{OD'} = \overrightarrow{OA} \times \overrightarrow{OD'} = \vec{OC''}$$

Also *OC″D″ B″* will be a parallelogram as *OC′ D′B′* is a parallelogram. Hence

$$\overrightarrow{OD''} = \overrightarrow{OB''} + \overrightarrow{OC''}$$

i.e., $\quad \mathbf{a} \times \overrightarrow{OD'} = \mathbf{a} \times \mathbf{b}' + \mathbf{a} \times \mathbf{c}'$

i.e., $\quad \mathbf{a} \times (\mathbf{b} + \mathbf{c}) = \mathbf{a} \times \mathbf{b} + \mathbf{a} \times \mathbf{c}$

from the results proved earlier.

The above is sometimes referred to as the geometrical proof of the distributive law. Another proof of this result will be given later.

27. VECTOR PRODUCT IN TERMS OF COMPONENTS

Let $\quad \mathbf{a} = (a_1, a_2, a_3) = a_1\mathbf{i} + a_2\mathbf{j} + a_3\mathbf{k}$

$$\mathbf{b} = (b_1, b_2, b_3) = b_1\mathbf{i} + b_2\mathbf{j} + b_3\mathbf{k}$$

be any two vectors. Then

$$\mathbf{a}\times\mathbf{b} = (a_1\mathbf{i}+a_2\mathbf{j}+a_3\mathbf{k})\times(b_1\mathbf{i}+b_2\mathbf{j}+b_3\mathbf{k})$$

$$= a_1b_1\mathbf{i}\times\mathbf{i}+a_1b_2\mathbf{i}\times\mathbf{j}+a_1b_3\mathbf{i}\times\mathbf{k}+a_2b_1\mathbf{j}\times\mathbf{i}$$

$$+a_2b_2\mathbf{j}\times\mathbf{j}+a_2b_3\mathbf{j}\times\mathbf{k}+a_3b_1\mathbf{k}\times\mathbf{i}+a_3b_2\mathbf{k}\times\mathbf{j}+a_3b_3\mathbf{k}\times\mathbf{k}$$

$$= a_1b_2\mathbf{k}-a_1b_3\mathbf{j}-a_2b_1\mathbf{k}+a_2b_3\mathbf{i}+a_3b_1\mathbf{j}-a_3b_2\mathbf{i}$$

$$= \mathbf{i}(a_2b_3-a_3b_2)+\mathbf{j}(a_3b_1-a_1b_3)+\mathbf{k}(a_1b_2-a_2b_1)$$

$$= \begin{vmatrix} \mathbf{i} & \mathbf{j} & \mathbf{k} \\ a_1 & a_2 & a_3 \\ b_1 & b_2 & b_3 \end{vmatrix}$$

Example 16. *Show that*

$$(\mathbf{a}\times\mathbf{b})^2 = \mathbf{a}^2\mathbf{b}^2-(\mathbf{ab})^2$$

Solution. We have

$$(\mathbf{a}\times\mathbf{b})^2 = (\mathbf{a}\times\mathbf{b}).(\mathbf{a}\times\mathbf{b}) = (ab\sin\theta\,\hat{n}).(ab\sin\theta\,\hat{n})$$

$$= a^2b^2\sin^2\theta(\hat{n}.\hat{n}) = a^2b^2\sin^2\theta$$

$$= a^2b^2(1-\cos^2\theta)$$

$$= a^2b^2-a^2b^2\cos^2\theta$$

$$= a^2b^2-(ab\cos\theta)^2$$

$$= \mathbf{a}^2\mathbf{b}^2-(\mathbf{a}.\mathbf{b})^2$$

Example 17. *If* $\mathbf{a} = 2\mathbf{i}-\mathbf{j}+\mathbf{k}$, $\mathbf{b} = 3\mathbf{i}+4\mathbf{j}-\mathbf{k}$, *verify that* $\mathbf{a}\times\mathbf{b}$ *represents a vector perpendicular to both* **a** *and* **b**.

Solution. We have

$$\mathbf{a}\times\mathbf{b} = \begin{vmatrix} \mathbf{i} & \mathbf{j} & \mathbf{k} \\ 2 & -1 & 1 \\ 3 & 4 & -1 \end{vmatrix} = -3\mathbf{i}+5\mathbf{j}+11\mathbf{k}$$

Now $\quad \mathbf{a}.(\mathbf{a}\times\mathbf{b}) = (2\mathbf{i}-\mathbf{j}+\mathbf{k}).(-3\mathbf{i}+5\mathbf{j}+11\mathbf{k})$

$$= 2.(-3)+(-1).5+1.11 = 0$$

$\Rightarrow$ **a** is perpendicular to $\mathbf{a}\times\mathbf{b}$.

Similarly we can show that **b** is also perpendicular to $\mathbf{a}\times\mathbf{b}$.

Example 18. *If* $\quad \mathbf{a} = 2\mathbf{i}-\mathbf{j}+2\mathbf{k}$

$$\mathbf{b} = 10\mathbf{i}-2\mathbf{j}+7\mathbf{k}$$

find $\mathbf{a}\times\mathbf{b}$. *Find also the unit vector perpendicular to both.*

Solution.

$$\mathbf{a}\times\mathbf{b} = \begin{vmatrix} \mathbf{i} & \mathbf{j} & \mathbf{k} \\ 2 & -1 & 2 \\ 10 & -2 & 7 \end{vmatrix}$$

$$= \mathbf{i}(-7+4) - \mathbf{j}(14-20) + \mathbf{k}(-4+10)$$

$$= -3\mathbf{i} + 6\mathbf{j} + 6\mathbf{k}$$

Since $\mathbf{a}\times\mathbf{b}$ is a vector perpendicular to both **a** and **b** (by definition of $\mathbf{a}\times\mathbf{b}$), so to get a unit vector perpendicular to both **a** and **b**, we divide the vector $\mathbf{a}\times\mathbf{b}$ by its magnitude.

Now

$$|\mathbf{a}\times\mathbf{b}| = \sqrt{9+36+36} = 9$$

Thus required unit vector perpendicular to **a** and **b** is

$$-\frac{3}{9}\mathbf{i} + \frac{6}{9}\mathbf{j} + \frac{6}{9}\mathbf{k} \quad \text{or} \quad -\frac{1}{3}\mathbf{i} + \frac{2}{3}\mathbf{j} + \frac{2}{3}\mathbf{k}$$

Example 19. *If* $\mathbf{a} = 2\mathbf{i} + 3\mathbf{j} - 5x$ *and* $\mathbf{b} = -3\mathbf{i} + \mathbf{j} + 2\mathbf{k}$, *find the value of* $\mathbf{a}.\mathbf{b}$ and $\mathbf{a}\times\mathbf{b}$.

Solution. We have

$$\mathbf{a}.\mathbf{b} = 2\times -3 + 3\times 1 + (-5)\times 2 = -6 + 3 - 10 = -13$$

Also

$$\mathbf{a}\times\mathbf{b} = \begin{vmatrix} \mathbf{i} & \mathbf{j} & \mathbf{k} \\ 2 & 3 & -5 \\ -3 & 1 & 2 \end{vmatrix} = \mathbf{i}(6+5) - \mathbf{j}(4-15) + \mathbf{k}(2+9)$$

$$= 11\mathbf{i} + 11\mathbf{j} + 11\mathbf{k}.$$

Example 20. *If* $\mathbf{a} = (a_1, a_2, a_3)$ *and* $\mathbf{b} = (b_1, b_2, b_2)$ *are two vectors and* θ *is the angle between, them then show that*

$$\sin^2\theta = \frac{(a_2b_3 - a_3b_2)^2 + (a_1b_3 - a_3b_1)^2 + (a_1b_2 - a_2b_1)^2}{\left(a_1^2 + a_2^2 + a_3^2\right)\left(b_1^2 + b_2^2 + b_3^2\right)}.$$

Solution. We have shown earlier that

$$\mathbf{a}\times\mathbf{b} = (a_2b_3 - a_3b_2)\mathbf{i} + (a_3b_1 - a_1b_3)\mathbf{j} + (a_1b_2 - a_2b_1)\mathbf{k}$$

$$\Rightarrow \quad (\mathbf{a}\times\mathbf{b})^2 = (a_2b_3 - a_3b_2)^2 + (a_3b_1 - a_1b_3)^2 + (a_1b_2 - a_2b_1)^2 \qquad ...(1)$$

Also $\quad \mathbf{a}\times\mathbf{b} = ab\sin\theta\,\hat{n}$

where $\quad a = \sqrt{a_1^2 + a_2^2 + a_3^2}$

$$b = \sqrt{b_1^2 + b_2^2 + b_3^2}$$

$$\Rightarrow \qquad (\mathbf{a}\times\mathbf{b})^2 = a^2b^2\sin^2\theta \text{ as } \hat{n}\,.\,\hat{n} = 1$$

$$= \left(a_1^2 + a_2^2 + a_3^2\right)\left(b_1^2 + b_2^2 + b_3^2\right)\sin^2\theta \qquad ...(2)$$

(1) and (2) $\Rightarrow$

$$\sin^2\theta = \frac{(a_2b_3 - a_3b_2)^2 + (a_1b_3 - a_3b_1)^2 + (a_1b_2 - a_2b_1)^2}{\left(a_1^2 + a_2^2 + a_3^2\right)\left(b_1^2 + b_2^2 + b_3^2\right)}$$

Example 21. *Find the sine of the angle between the vectors* $3\mathbf{i} + \mathbf{j} + 2\mathbf{k}$ and $2\mathbf{i} - 2\mathbf{j} + 4\mathbf{k}$.

Solution. We have $(a_1, a_2, a_3) = (3, 1, 2)$

$$(b_1, b_2, b_3) = (2, -2, 4)$$

Thus

$$\sin^2\theta = \frac{(1\times4 - 2\times(-2))^2 + (3\times4 - 2\times2)^2 + (3\times(-2) - 1\times2)^2}{(9+1+4)\,(4+4+16)}$$

$$= \frac{(4+4)^2 + (12-4)^2 + (-6-2)^2}{14\times24}$$

$$= \frac{64+64+64}{336} = \frac{192}{336}$$

$$\Rightarrow \qquad \sin\theta = \sqrt{\frac{192}{336}} = \frac{2}{\sqrt{7}}.$$

28. THEOREM

Two vectors $\mathbf{a} = (a_1, a_2, a_3)$ *and* $\mathbf{b} = (b_1, b_2, b_3)$ *are parallel if and only if*

$$\frac{a_1}{b_1} = \frac{a_2}{b_2} = \frac{a_3}{b_3}.$$

Proof. Let **a** and **b** be parallel.

$\Rightarrow$ angle θ between them is zero

$$\Rightarrow \qquad \sin\theta = 0$$

$$\Rightarrow \qquad \mathbf{a}\times\mathbf{b} = \mathbf{0}$$

$$\Rightarrow \qquad \begin{vmatrix} i & j & k \\ a_1 & a_2 & a_3 \\ b_1 & b_2 & b_3 \end{vmatrix} = 0$$

$$\Rightarrow \qquad (a_2b_3 - a_3b_2)\,\mathbf{i} + (a_3b_1 - a_1b_3)\,\mathbf{j} + (a_1b_2 - a_2b_1)\,\mathbf{k} = 0$$

$$= 0\mathbf{i} + 0\mathbf{j} + 0\mathbf{k}$$

$$\Rightarrow \quad a_2b_3 - a_3b_2 = 0$$
$$a_3b_1 - a_1b_3 = 0$$
$$a_1b_2 - a_2b_1 = 0$$

$$\Rightarrow \quad \frac{a_1}{b_1} = \frac{a_2}{b_2} = \frac{a_3}{b_3}$$

Converse follows by simply retracing the steps back.

29. VECTOR PRODUCT AS AREA

Let *OABC* be a parallelogram such that

$$\overrightarrow{OA} = \mathbf{a}$$
$$\overrightarrow{OC} = \mathbf{b}$$

and let θ be the angle between **a** and **b.**

Now area of the parallelogram *OABC*

$= OA \,.\, CK$ (where $CK \perp OA$)

$= ab \sin \theta$

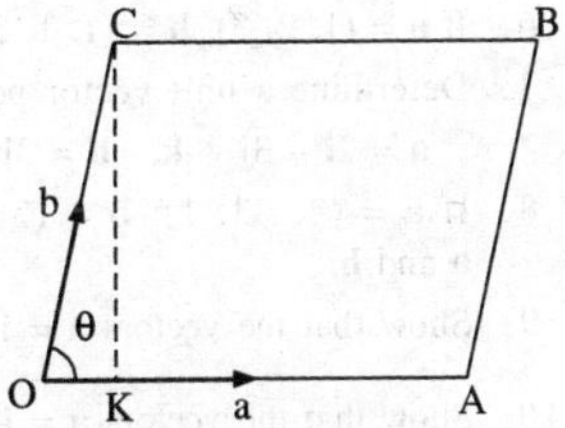

Fig. 21

Also $\mathbf{a} \times \mathbf{b} = (ab \sin \theta)\ \hat{n}$

Comparing the two we note that $\mathbf{a} \times \mathbf{b}$ = area of the parallelogram *OABC*

i.e., the magnitude of the vector product of two vectors is the area of the parallelogram whose adjacent sides are represented by these vectors.

Corollary. It is easy to see that the area of the triangle *OAC* is

$$\frac{1}{2}\ \mathbf{a} \times \mathbf{b}$$

Example 22. *Find the area to the parallelogram whose adjacent sides are determined by the vectors* $\mathbf{a} = \mathbf{i} + 2\mathbf{j} + 3\mathbf{k}$

$$\mathbf{b} = 3\mathbf{i} - 2\mathbf{j} + \mathbf{k}.$$

Solution. Required area $= |\, \mathbf{a} \times \mathbf{b} \,|$

Now $\quad \mathbf{a} \times \mathbf{b} = \begin{vmatrix} i & j & k \\ 1 & 2 & 3 \\ 3 & -2 & 1 \end{vmatrix}$

$$= \mathbf{i}\,(2+6) - \mathbf{j}\,(1-9) + \mathbf{k}\,(-2-6)$$
$$= 8\,(\mathbf{i} - \mathbf{j} - \mathbf{k})$$

$\Rightarrow \quad \mathbf{a} \times \mathbf{b} = \sqrt{64 + 64 + 64} = 8\sqrt{3}$ is the required area.

EXERCISES

1. Find the scalar product of the vectors $\mathbf{a} = \mathbf{i} + \mathbf{j} + \mathbf{k}$, $\mathbf{b} = \mathbf{i} - \mathbf{j} - \mathbf{k}$. Also find the cosine of the angle between them.
2. If m is any scalar, show that $(m\mathbf{a}) . \mathbf{b} = m(\mathbf{a} . \mathbf{b}) = \mathbf{a} . (m\mathbf{b})$
3. Find the angle between the vectors $\mathbf{a} = (1, 2, 3)$, $\mathbf{b} = (1, 1, 2)$
4. Show that the middle point of the hypotenuse of a right triangle is equidistant from its vertices.
5. Prove the cosine formula in a triangle ABC $c^2 = a^2 + b^2 - 2ab \cos C$ where letters have their usual meaning.
6. If $\mathbf{a} = (1, 2, 3)$, $\mathbf{b} = (1, 1, 2)$. Find $\mathbf{a} \times \mathbf{b}$.
7. Determine a unit vector perpendicular to each of the vectors
   $\mathbf{a} = 2\mathbf{i} - 3\mathbf{j} + \mathbf{k}$, $\mathbf{b} = 3\mathbf{i} + \mathbf{j} - 2\mathbf{k}$.
8. If $\mathbf{a} = (2, -3, 1)$, $\mathbf{b} = (3, 1, -2)$, find $\sin \theta$, where θ is the angle between $\mathbf{a}$ and $\mathbf{b}$.
9. Show that the vectors $\mathbf{a} = \mathbf{i} + 4\mathbf{j} + 3\mathbf{k}$ and $\mathbf{b} = 4\mathbf{i} + 2\mathbf{j} - 4\mathbf{k}$ are perpendicular.
10. Show that the vectors $\mathbf{a} = \mathbf{i} + 4\mathbf{j} + 3\mathbf{k}$ and $\mathbf{b} = \frac{1}{2}\mathbf{i} + 2\mathbf{j} + \frac{3}{2}\mathbf{k}$ are parallel.
11. Does $\mathbf{a} \times \mathbf{b} = \mathbf{a} \times \mathbf{c}$ imply $\mathbf{b} = \mathbf{c}$? Justify your answer.
12. Find the unit vectors perpendicular to each of the vectors $(2, -1, 1)$ and $(3, 4, -1)$. Find also the sine of the angle between these.
13. Find the area of the triangle whose adjacent sides are determined by the vectors $\mathbf{a} = 3\mathbf{i} + 4\mathbf{j}$, $\mathbf{b} = -5\mathbf{i} + 7\mathbf{j}$.
14. Show that $\mathbf{a} \times (\mathbf{b} + \mathbf{c}) + \mathbf{b} \times (\mathbf{c} + \mathbf{a}) + \mathbf{c} \times (\mathbf{a} + \mathbf{b}) = \mathbf{0}$.
15. Prove that the vector area of the triangle whose vertices are the points $\mathbf{a}, \mathbf{b}, \mathbf{c}$, is $\frac{1}{2}(\mathbf{b} \times \mathbf{c} + \mathbf{c} \times \mathbf{a} + \mathbf{a} \times \mathbf{b})$.
16. Show that $(\mathbf{a} - \mathbf{b}) \times (\mathbf{a} + \mathbf{b}) = 2\mathbf{a} \times \mathbf{b}$.
17. (*i*) $(\mathbf{a} + \mathbf{b}) \times \mathbf{c} = \mathbf{a} \times \mathbf{c} + \mathbf{b} \times \mathbf{c}$
    (*ii*) $(\mathbf{a} - \mathbf{b}) \times \mathbf{c} = \mathbf{a} \times \mathbf{c} - \mathbf{b} \times \mathbf{c}$
    (*iii*) $\mathbf{a} \times (\mathbf{b} \times \mathbf{c}) = \mathbf{a} \times \mathbf{b} - \mathbf{a} \times \mathbf{c}$.

ANSWERS

1. -1 ; $-\frac{1}{3}$
3. $\cos^{-1}\frac{9}{\sqrt{84}}$
6. $(1, 1, -1)$
7. $\frac{5\mathbf{i} + 7\mathbf{j} + 11\mathbf{k}}{\sqrt{195}}$
8. $\frac{\sqrt{195}}{14}$
12. $\frac{-3\mathbf{i} + 5\mathbf{j} + 11\mathbf{k}}{\sqrt{155}}$; $\sqrt{\frac{155}{156}}$
13. $4\frac{1}{2}$

30. SCALAR TRIPLE PRODUCT

Suppose **a, b, c** are three vectors. Then $\mathbf{b} \times \mathbf{c}$ is again a vector and thus we can talk of $\mathbf{a} \cdot (\mathbf{b} \times \mathbf{c})$, which would, of course, be a scalar. This is called *scalar triple product* (of three vectors).

Let $\mathbf{a} = (a_1, a_2, a_3)$

$\mathbf{b} = (b_1, b_2, b_3)$

$\mathbf{c} = (c_1, c_2, c_3)$

Then $\mathbf{b} \times \mathbf{c} = (b_2c_3 - b_3c_2,\ b_3c_1 - c_3b_1,\ b_1c_2 - b_2c_1)$

$= (d_1, d_2, d_3), = \mathbf{d}$ (say)

Thus

$$\mathbf{a} \cdot (\mathbf{b} \times \mathbf{c}) = \mathbf{a} \cdot \mathbf{d} = a_1d_1 + a_2b_2 + a_3d_3$$

$$= a_1(b_2c_3 - b_3c_2) + a_2(b_3c_1 - c_3b_1) + a_3(b_1c_2 - b_2c_1)$$

$$= \begin{vmatrix} a_1 & a_2 & a_3 \\ b_1 & b_2 & b_3 \\ c_1 & c_2 & c_3 \end{vmatrix} \quad ...(1)$$

so this is the value of the scalar triple product $\mathbf{a} \cdot (\mathbf{b} \times \mathbf{c})$

Suppose we had started with $\mathbf{b} \cdot (\mathbf{c} \times \mathbf{a})$, it is easy to see that the resulting determinant would have been

$$\begin{vmatrix} b_1 & b_2 & b_3 \\ c_1 & c_2 & c_3 \\ a_1 & a_2 & a_3 \end{vmatrix}$$

which is same as (1) [See properties of determinants] and so

$$\mathbf{a} \cdot (\mathbf{b} \times \mathbf{c}) = \mathbf{b} \cdot (\mathbf{c} \times \mathbf{a})$$

Similarly $\mathbf{b} \cdot (\mathbf{c} \times \mathbf{a}) = \mathbf{c} \cdot (\mathbf{a} \times \mathbf{b})$

$\Rightarrow$ $\mathbf{a} \cdot (\mathbf{b} \times \mathbf{c}) = \mathbf{c} \cdot (\mathbf{a} \times \mathbf{b}) = (\mathbf{a} \times \mathbf{b}) \cdot \mathbf{c}$ [commutativity]

Thus dot and cross can be interchanged in a scalar triple product and we write the scalar triple product as **[a, b, c]** or **[abc]** where it is to our choice as to where we put cross and dot.

NOTE. It can be verified that

[**abc**] = – [**bac**]

and [**abc**] = [**bca**] = [**cab**].

Example 23. *Prove the distributive law*

$$\boldsymbol{a} \times (\boldsymbol{b} + \boldsymbol{c}) = \boldsymbol{a} \times \boldsymbol{b} + \boldsymbol{a} \times \boldsymbol{c}$$

using scalar triple product.

Solution. Let $\mathbf{d} = \mathbf{a} \times (\mathbf{b} + \mathbf{c}) - \mathbf{a} \times \mathbf{b} - \mathbf{a} \times \mathbf{c}$

we show that $\mathbf{d} = \mathbf{0}$

Let **e** by any vector, then

$$\mathbf{e} . \mathbf{d} = \mathbf{e} . [\mathbf{a} \times (\mathbf{b} + \mathbf{c})] - \mathbf{e} . (\mathbf{a} \times \mathbf{b}) - \mathbf{e} . (\mathbf{a} \times \mathbf{c})$$
$$= (\mathbf{e} \times \mathbf{a}) . (\mathbf{b} + \mathbf{c}) - (\mathbf{e} \times \mathbf{a}) . \mathbf{b} - (\mathbf{e} \times \mathbf{a}) . \mathbf{c}$$

Interchanging dot and cross in the scalar triple products

$$= (\mathbf{e} \times \mathbf{a}) . [(\mathbf{b} + \mathbf{c}) - \mathbf{b} - \mathbf{c}] \text{ distributivity of scalar product}$$
$$= (\mathbf{e} \times \mathbf{a}) . \mathbf{0} = 0$$

$\Rightarrow$ $\mathbf{e} . \mathbf{d} = 0$ for *all* vectors **e**

$\Rightarrow$ $\mathbf{d} = \mathbf{0}$ [as we can take **e** to be a non-zero vector, not perpendicular to **d**]

Hence the result follows.

31. VECTOR TRIPLE PRODUCT

A product of the type $\mathbf{a} \times (\mathbf{b} \times \mathbf{c})$ is called a *Vector Triple Product.*

We show

$$\mathbf{a} \times (\mathbf{b} \times \mathbf{c}) = (\mathbf{a} . \mathbf{c})\, \mathbf{b} - (\mathbf{a} . \mathbf{b})\, \mathbf{c}$$

Let $\mathbf{a} = (a_1, a_2, a_3)$

$\mathbf{b} = (b_1, b_2, b_3)$

$\mathbf{c} = (c_1, c_2, c_3)$

Then $\mathbf{b} \times \mathbf{c} = (b_2c_3 - b_3c_2,\ b_3c_1 - b_1c_3,\ b_1c_2 - b_2c_1)$

$= (d_1, d_2, d_3) = \mathbf{d}$ (say)

Then

$$\mathbf{a} \times (\mathbf{b} \times \mathbf{c}) = \mathbf{a} \times \mathbf{d}$$
$$= (a_2d_3 - a_3d_2, a_3d_1 - a_3d_1, a_1d_2 - a_2d_1)$$
$$= (a_2d_3 - a_3d_2)\,\mathbf{i} + (a_3d_1 - a_1d_3)\,\mathbf{j} + (a_1d_2 - a_2d_1)\mathbf{k}$$
$$= \Sigma\, (a_2d_3 - a_3d_2)\,\mathbf{i}$$
$$= \Sigma\, [a_2(b_1c_2 - b_2c_1) - a_3\,(b_3c_1 - b_1c_3)]\,\mathbf{i}$$
$$= \Sigma\, [a_2b_1c_2 - a_2b_2c_1 - a_3b_3c_1 + a_3b_1c_3 + a_1b_1c_1 - a_1b_1c_1)]\,\mathbf{i}$$

[adding and subtracting $a_1b_1c_1$]

$$= \Sigma[b_1(a_1c_1 + a_2c_2 + a_3c_3) - c_1\,(a_1b_1 + a_2b_2 + a_3b_3)]\,\mathbf{i}$$
$$= [b_1(a_1c_1 + a_2c_2 + a_3c_3) - c_1\,(a_1b_1 + a_2b_2 + a_3b_3)]\,\mathbf{i}$$
$$+ [b_2(a_1c_1 + a_2c_2 + a_3c_3) - c_2\,(a_1b_1 + a_2b_2 + a_3b_3)]\mathbf{j}$$
$$+ [b_3(a_1c_1 + a_2c_2 + a_3c_3) - c_3\,(a_1b_1 + a_2b_2 + a_3b_3)]\,\mathbf{k}$$

$$= (a_1c_1 + a_2c_2 + a_3c_3)(b_1\mathbf{i} + b_2\mathbf{j} + b_3\mathbf{k}) - (a_1b_1 + a_2b_2 + a_3c_3)(c_1\mathbf{i} + c_2\mathbf{j} + c_3\mathbf{k})$$

$$= (\mathbf{a}\,.\,\mathbf{c})\,\mathbf{b} - (\mathbf{a}\,.\,\mathbf{b})\,\mathbf{c}$$

which proves our assertion.

NOTE. There is neither a cross nor a dot between (**a . c**) and **b** in (**a . c**) **b**.

Reason why !

Example 24. *Prove that*

$$a \times (b \times c) + b \times (c \times a) + c \times (a \times b) = 0$$

Solution. We know that

$$\mathbf{a} \times (\mathbf{b} \times \mathbf{c}) = (\mathbf{a}\,.\,\mathbf{c})\,\mathbf{b} - (\mathbf{a}\,.\,\mathbf{b})\,\mathbf{c}$$

$$\mathbf{b} \times (\mathbf{c} \times \mathbf{a}) = (\mathbf{b}\,.\,\mathbf{a})\,\mathbf{c} - (\mathbf{b}\,.\,\mathbf{c})\,\mathbf{a}$$

$$\mathbf{c} \times (\mathbf{a} \times \mathbf{b}) = (\mathbf{c}\,.\,\mathbf{b})\,\mathbf{a} - (\mathbf{c}\,.\,\mathbf{a})\,\mathbf{b}$$

Addition gives the result.

32. VECTOR PRODUCT OF FOUR VECTORS

For the four vectors **a, b, c, d,** we can talk of the vector $(\mathbf{a} \times \mathbf{b}) \times (\mathbf{c} \times \mathbf{d})$

Let $\mathbf{e} = (\mathbf{a} \times \mathbf{b})$

Then

$$(\mathbf{a} \times \mathbf{b}) \times (\mathbf{c} \times \mathbf{d}) = \mathbf{e} \times (\mathbf{c} \times \mathbf{d})$$

$$= (\mathbf{e}\,.\,\mathbf{d})\,\mathbf{c} - (\mathbf{e}\,.\,\mathbf{c})\,\mathbf{d}$$

$$= (\mathbf{a} \times \mathbf{b}\,.\,\mathbf{d})\,\mathbf{c} - (\mathbf{a} \times \mathbf{b}\,.\,\mathbf{c})\,\mathbf{d}$$

$$= [\mathbf{abd}]\,\mathbf{c} - [\mathbf{abc}]\,\mathbf{d} \qquad ...(1)$$

Now suppose $\mathbf{c} \times \mathbf{d} = \mathbf{r}$

Again $(\mathbf{a} \times \mathbf{b}) \times (\mathbf{c} \times \mathbf{d}) = (\mathbf{a} \times \mathbf{b}) \times \mathbf{r}$

$$= -\,\mathbf{r} \times (\mathbf{a} \times \mathbf{b})$$

$$= -\,[(\mathbf{r}\,.\,\mathbf{b})\,\mathbf{a} - (\mathbf{r}\,.\,\mathbf{a})\,\mathbf{b}]$$

$$= (\mathbf{r}\,.\,\mathbf{a})\,\mathbf{b} - (\mathbf{r}\,.\,\mathbf{b})\,\mathbf{a}$$

$$= (\mathbf{cda})\,\mathbf{b} - [\mathbf{cdb}]\,\mathbf{a} \qquad ...(2)$$

Equating (1) and (2), we get

$$[\mathbf{bcd}]\,\mathbf{a} - [\mathbf{acd}]\,\mathbf{b} + [\mathbf{abd}]\,\mathbf{c} - [\mathbf{abc}]\,\mathbf{d} = 0$$

which is called a *linear relation* in four vectors.

Example 25. *Prove that*

$$[\mathbf{a} \times \mathbf{b} \quad \mathbf{b} \times \mathbf{c} \quad \mathbf{c} \times \mathbf{a}] = [\mathbf{abc}]^2$$

Solution. We have the left hand side

$$= (\mathbf{a}\times\mathbf{b}) . [(\mathbf{b}\times\mathbf{c})\times(\mathbf{c}\times\mathbf{a})]$$

$$= (\mathbf{a}\times\mathbf{b}) . \{[\mathbf{bca}]\,\mathbf{c} - [\mathbf{bcc}]\,\mathbf{a}\} \text{ (as above).}$$

But $[\mathbf{bcc}] = \mathbf{b} . (\mathbf{c}\times\mathbf{c}) = 0$ as $\mathbf{c}\times\mathbf{c} = \mathbf{0}$ for any vector $\mathbf{c}$

Thus

$$\text{LHS} = (\mathbf{a}\times\mathbf{b}) . [\mathbf{bca}]\,\mathbf{c}$$

$$= (\mathbf{a}\times\mathbf{b} . \mathbf{c})\,[\mathbf{bca}]$$

$$= [\mathbf{abc}]\,[\mathbf{abc}] = [\mathbf{abc}]^2 = \text{RHS.}$$

Example 26. *Show that*

$$[\mathbf{a}+\mathbf{b}, \mathbf{b}+\mathbf{c}, \mathbf{c}+\mathbf{a}] = 2[\mathbf{a}, \mathbf{b}, \mathbf{c}]$$

Solution.

$$\text{LHS} = (\mathbf{a}+\mathbf{b}) . [(\mathbf{b}+\mathbf{c})\times(\mathbf{c}+\mathbf{a})]$$

$$= (\mathbf{a}+\mathbf{b}) . [\mathbf{b}\times\mathbf{c}+\mathbf{b}\times\mathbf{a}+\mathbf{c}\times\mathbf{a}+\mathbf{c}\times\mathbf{c}]$$

But $\mathbf{c}\times\mathbf{c} = \mathbf{0}$

$$= \mathbf{a} . (\mathbf{b}\times\mathbf{c}) + (\mathbf{b}\times\mathbf{a}) . \mathbf{a} + (\mathbf{c}\times\mathbf{a}) . \mathbf{a} + \mathbf{b} . (\mathbf{b}\times\mathbf{c}) + \mathbf{b} . (\mathbf{b}\times\mathbf{a}) + \mathbf{b} . (\mathbf{c}\times\mathbf{a})$$

$$= \mathbf{a} . (\mathbf{b}\times\mathbf{c}) + \mathbf{b} . \mathbf{c}\times\mathbf{a}$$

$$= [\mathbf{abc}] + [\mathbf{bca}]$$

$$= [\mathbf{abc}] + [\mathbf{abc}]$$

$$= 2\,[\mathbf{a}, \mathbf{b}, \mathbf{c}] = \text{RHS}$$

[all others being zero] e.g., $(\mathbf{b}\times\mathbf{a}) . \mathbf{a} = \mathbf{b} . (\mathbf{a}\times\mathbf{a}) = 0$ [as $\mathbf{a}\times\mathbf{a} = 0$]

Example 27. *Show that*

$$(\mathbf{a}\times\mathbf{b}) . (\mathbf{c}\times\mathbf{d}) = \begin{vmatrix} \mathbf{a}\cdot\mathbf{c} & \mathbf{a}\cdot\mathbf{d} \\ \mathbf{b}\cdot\mathbf{c} & \mathbf{b}\cdot\mathbf{d} \end{vmatrix}$$

Solution.

$$(\mathbf{a}\times\mathbf{b}) . (\mathbf{c}\times\mathbf{d}) = \mathbf{a} . \{\mathbf{b}\times(\mathbf{c}\times\mathbf{d})\}$$

$$= \mathbf{a} . \{(\mathbf{b} . \mathbf{d})\,\mathbf{c} - (\mathbf{b} . \mathbf{c})\,\mathbf{d}\}$$

$$= (\mathbf{b} . \mathbf{d})(\mathbf{a} . \mathbf{c}) - (\mathbf{b} . \mathbf{c})(\mathbf{a} . \mathbf{d})$$

$$= \begin{vmatrix} \mathbf{a}\cdot\mathbf{c} & \mathbf{a}\cdot\mathbf{d} \\ \mathbf{b}\cdot\mathbf{c} & \mathbf{b}\cdot\mathbf{d} \end{vmatrix}$$

EXERCISES

1. Show that $\mathbf{a}\times(\mathbf{b}\times\mathbf{c}) = (\mathbf{a}\times\mathbf{b})\times\mathbf{c}$ if and only if $(\mathbf{a} . \mathbf{b})\,\mathbf{c} = (\mathbf{b} . \mathbf{c})\mathbf{a}$.
2. Show that

$$(\mathbf{a}\times\mathbf{b}) . (\mathbf{c}\times\mathbf{d}) + (\mathbf{b}\times\mathbf{c}) . (\mathbf{a}\times\mathbf{d}) + (\mathbf{c}\times\mathbf{a}) . (\mathbf{b}\times\mathbf{d}) = 0.$$

3. Show that

$$\mathbf{a}\times\{\mathbf{b}\times(\mathbf{c}\times\mathbf{d})\} = [\mathbf{acd}]\mathbf{b} - (\mathbf{a} . \mathbf{b}) . (\mathbf{c}\times\mathbf{d}).$$

4. Show that

$$[\mathbf{a} \times \mathbf{b}, \mathbf{c} \times \mathbf{d}, \mathbf{e} \times \mathbf{f}] = [\mathbf{a}, \mathbf{b}, \mathbf{d}][\mathbf{c}, \mathbf{e}, \mathbf{f}] - [\mathbf{a}, \mathbf{b}, \mathbf{c}][\mathbf{d}, \mathbf{e}, \mathbf{f}]$$
$$= [\mathbf{a}, \mathbf{b}, \mathbf{e}]\,[\mathbf{f}, \mathbf{c}, \mathbf{d}] - [\mathbf{a}, \mathbf{b}, \mathbf{f}]\,[\mathbf{e}, \mathbf{c}, \mathbf{d}]$$
$$= [\mathbf{c}, \mathbf{d}, \mathbf{a}]\,[\mathbf{b}, \mathbf{e}, \mathbf{f}] - [\mathbf{c}, \mathbf{d}, \mathbf{b}]\,[\mathbf{a}, \mathbf{e}, \mathbf{f}]$$

5. Show that

$$(\mathbf{a} + \mathbf{b}) \cdot [(\mathbf{b} + \mathbf{c}) \times (\mathbf{c} + \mathbf{a})] = 2[\mathbf{a}, \mathbf{b}, \mathbf{c}].$$

6. Prove that

$$(\mathbf{a} \times \mathbf{b}) \times (\mathbf{a} \times \mathbf{c}) \cdot \mathbf{d} = \mathbf{a} \cdot \mathbf{d}\,[\mathbf{a}, \mathbf{b}, \mathbf{c}]$$

7. Prove that

$$[\mathbf{a}, \mathbf{b}, \mathbf{c}]\,[\mathbf{p}, \mathbf{q}, \mathbf{r}] = \begin{vmatrix} \mathbf{ap} & \mathbf{aq} & \mathbf{ar} \\ \mathbf{bp} & \mathbf{bq} & \mathbf{br} \\ \mathbf{cp} & \mathbf{cq} & \mathbf{cr} \end{vmatrix}$$

[**Hint.** Use the linear relation between the four vectors **a**, **b**, **c**, **p** × **q**].

CHAPTER 31

LINEAR PROGRAMMING

1. LINEAR PROGRAMMING

This is one of the recently developed branches of mathematics which is being applied to Commerce, Industry and other Social Sciences. In the post-war era, need for such a science in Military Strategies, Business Organisation etc. was felt badly and the methods of Operation Research were introduced. In the middle of 20th century, expansion of knowledge took place and operation research was further divided into different branches like Linear and Non-linear programing, Dynamic programming, Queueing theory, Theory of games etc. With the passage of time each one of these became a fully developed subject in itself. Though Hitckcock in 1941 formulated a particular type of linear programming problem, it was Dantzig who is considered the father of the subject. He not only gave several algorithms and techniques to solve such problems but also was instrumental in giving full stature to the subject as an important branch of *Applied Mathematics.*

To have a better understanding of linear programming problems, we start with a few examples.

In the following examples we shall illustrate how the examples are formulated mathematically (and will not, for the time being attempt to solve them).

Example 1. *A small metal part manufacturing company most of whose business comes from special orders, has decided to make use of the idle time of the equipment (i.e., the time when the equipment is not in use). The company has determined that two particular parts A and B could readily be sold at per unit profits of Rs 30 and Rs 20 respectively, in quantities upto 12 dozens of each part per day. In order to make each unit of part A, 5 minutes are required on a lathe, 7 minutes on a mill and 4 minutes on a grinder. To make each unit of part B, 3, 9, 7 minutes are required respectively on a lathe, mill and grinder. The company has one* *machine of each type available. Lathe is currently idle for 85 minutes per day; Mill, 130 minutes and grinder 100 minutes per day.*

How many parts of types A and B, if any, should the company produce in order to make maximum use (in terms of profit) of the idle time of its equipment?

Solution. Let us now see, how we reformulate this problem mathematically

Let x = number of parts of type A to be produced, and

y = number of parts of type B to be produced.

Total profit is $z = 30x + 20y$. ...(1)

The company does not wish to produce more than 144 (12 dozens) of each part, so

$$x \leq 144 \quad \text{...(2)}$$

$$y \leq 144 \quad \text{...(3)}$$

Total number of minutes required on the lathe to produce x units of part A and y units of part B are $5x + 3y$ and this quantity cannot exceed the available time on the lathe *i.e.*, 85 minutes.

Thus, $5x + 3y \leq 85$ ...(4)

Considering the availability of time for the mill and the grinder, we get,

$$7x + 9y \leq 130 \quad \text{...(5)}$$

$$4x + 7y \leq 100 \quad \text{...(6)}$$

obviously, also $x \geq 0, y \geq 0$ ...(7)

Hence, the given problem is reformulated as:

Maximize $z = 30x + 20y$

subject to the constraints

$$5x + 3y \leq 85$$
$$7x + 9y \leq 130$$
$$4x + 7y \leq 100$$
$$0 \leq x \leq 144, \quad 0 \leq y \leq 44.$$

Definition: Inequalities (2) to (7) above are called *Constraints* and right hand side of equation (1) is called *Objective function*.

REMARK: Note that in all the constraints, each term involving x and y is of degree one. Such constraints are called *linear*. This is the reason that a problem of the above type is called a *Linear Programming Problem.*

Notation: We shall use *LPP* for Linear Programming Problem, in future.

We consider now another example.

Example 2. *A farmer wants to make sure that his herd gets the maximum daily requirement of three basic nutrients A, B and C. Daily requirements are 15 units of A, 20 of B and 30 of C. Product L has 2 units of A and one unit each of B and C; product M has one unit each of A and B and 3 units of C. The cost of L is Rs 12 per gram and that of M is Rs 18 per gram. What should be the composition of the mixture of L and M so that the cost is minimum?*

Solution. The formulation of this problem could be done as:

Let x gms. of product L be mixed with y gms. of product M. Then we have to minimize the objective function

$$z = 12x + 18y$$

Total units of A available in this mixture will be $2x + y$. By hypothesis

$$2x + y \geq 15.$$

Considering the minimum requirement of the nutrient B and C, we get the inequalities

$$x + y \geq 20.$$

$$x + 3y \geq 30$$

$$x, y \geq 0.$$

NOTE: In the first example, the objective function is to be maximized whereas in the second example, it is to be minimized. Thus, according to the nature of the problem an objective function is either to be maximized or minimized. We shall use the word "*Optimized*" for both maximized and minimized.

Definition. A solution to the linear constraints (together with constraints that all variables are to be non-negative) is called a *Feasible Solution.*

Also then, a feasible solution which optimizes the objective function is called an *optimal solution*, and value of z for optimum solution is called *optimum value* or *Optimal value*.

Example 3. *The manager of an oil refinery must decide the optimal mix of the possible blending process of which the input and output per production run are as under:*

	Input (units)		*Output (units)*	
Process	*Crude A*	*Crude B*	*Gasoline X*	*Gasoline Y*
1	*5*	*3*	*5*	*8*
2	*4*	*5*	*4*	*4*

The maximum amounts available of crude A and B are 200 units and 150units respectively. Market requirements show that at least 100 units of Gasoline X and 80 units of Gasoline Y must be produced. The profits per production run for process 1 and process 2 are Rs 300 and Rs 400 respectively. Solve the problem.

Solution. Let x and y be the amounts produced in the two processes.

Profit z is given by $z = 300x + 400y$

Amount of crude A used is $5x + 4y$ units, which should naturally be less than or equal to the amount available

Hence, $5x + 4y \le 200,$

similarly for crude B, we obtain

$$3x + 5y \le 150.$$

Gasoline X produced in two processes is $5x + 4y$ units.

Because of market requirements $5x + 4y \ge 100$ considering the amount of Gasoline Y produced in two processes, we get

$$8x + 4y \ge 80 \quad \text{or} \quad 2x + y \ge 20$$

Also, of course, $x, y \ge 0.$

Thus, the mathematical formulation of the given *LPP* is

maximize $z = 300x + 400y$

subject to
$$5x + 4y \le 200$$
$$3x + 5y \le 150$$
$$5x + 4y \ge 100$$
$$2x + y \ge 20$$
$$x, y \ge 0.$$

Example 4. *A ship has three cargo loads – forward, aft and centre. The capacity limits are:*

	Weight in kgs.	*Volume in cu. cms.*
Forward	*2000*	*100,000*
Centre	*3000*	*135,000*
Aft	*1500*	*30,000*

The following cargos are offered. The ship owner may accept all or any part of each commodity.

Commodity	Weight in kgs.	Volume in cu. cms.	Profit in Rs per kg.
A	6000	60	60
B	4000	50	80
C	2000	25	50

In order to preserve the trim of the ship, the weight in each hold must be proportional to the capacity in kgs. The cargo is to be distributed so as to maximize the profit.

Solution. Let a_1, a_2, a_3, be the weights of the commodity A to be accommodated in forward, centre and aft portions respectively. Similarly, let b_1, b_2, b_3, and c_1, c_2, c_3 be the corresponding weights for B and C.

We are to maximize

$$z = 60(a_1 + a_2 + a_3) + 80\,(b_1 + b_2 + b_3) + 50\,(c_1 + c_2 + c_3)$$

subject to

$$a_1 + a_2 + a_3 \le 6000$$
$$b_1 + b_2 + b_3 \le 4000$$
$$c_1 + c_2 + c_3 \le 2000$$
$$a_1 + b_1 + c_1 \le 2000$$
$$a_2 + b_2 + c_2 \le 3000$$
$$a_3 + b_3 + c_3 \le 1500$$
$$60a_1 + 50b_1 + 25c_1 \le 100{,}000$$
$$60a_2 + 50b_2 + 25c_2 \le 135{,}000$$
$$60a_3 + 50b_3 + 25c_3 \le 30{,}000$$
$$a_i, b_i, c_i \ge 0, \qquad i = 1, 2, 3.$$

EXERCISES

Formulate the following LPPs mathematically.

1. A pine-apple firm produces two products canned pine-apple and canned juice. The specific amount of material, labour and equipment required to produce each product and the availability of each of the resource is shown as under

	Canned Juice	Canned Pine-apple	Available resource
Labour (man hours)	3	2	12
Equipment (machine hours)	1	2.3	6.9
Material (unit)	1	1.4	4.9

Assuming one unit each of canned juice and pine-apple has profit margin of Rs 2 and Re 1 respectively. Determine the product mix that will maximize the profit.

2. A manufacturing firm has discontinued production of a certain unprofitable product line, and this has created considerable excess production capacity. Management is considering to devote this excess capacity to produce one or more of the products 1, 2, and 3. The available excess capacity on the machines which might limit output, is summarised in the following table:

Machine type	*Available excess capacity (in Machine hours per week)*
Milling Machine	250
Lathe	150
Grinder	50

The number of machine hours required for each unit of the respective product is given below:

	Capacity Requirement (in Machine hours per week)		
Machine Type	*Product 1*	*Product 2*	*Product 3*
Milling Machine	8	2	3
Lathe	4	3	0
Grinder	2	0	1

The per unit contribution would be Rs 20, Rs 6 and Rs 8 respectively for products 1, 2 and 3.

3. A supplier of feed for poultry-raisers wishes to formulate a least-cost feed. Each chicken requires at least 250, 150 and 400 units of certain nutritive element, say α, β and γ per day. It is also known that there are four possible neutral feed materials *A*, *B*, *C* and *D*; that he can use to feed the chickens.

Following table shows how many units of each of these nutritive elements is contained in one kilogram of feed material. The cost of a kilogram of each of these feeds materials is also given.

Nutritive element	*Feed Material*				*Min. daliy requirement*
	A	B	C	*D*	
α	20	15	10	30	250
β	25	15	20	25	150
γ	25	20	20	30	400
Unit cost	3	1	2	4	

How much each of the four materials he should blend together to minimize cost?

4. A firm manufactures toilet soap, washing soap and shaving soap. The profit per soap cake is Rs 4, Rs 2 and Rs 3 respectively. The time required to manufacture one soap cake of each type and the daily capacity of two machine *A* and *B* is given below:

	Time per cake			
	Toilet soap	*Washing soap*	*Shaving soap*	*Machine capacity (in hours) per day*
Machine *A*	5	5	6	4
Machine *B*	3	4	7	6

Determine the daily number of units to be manufactured for each product. The firm must manufacture at least 1000 toilet soap cakes, 1500 washing soap cakes and 2000 shaving soap cakes. Also it cannot produce more than 3000 cakes of toilet soap due to some management problem. It is assumed that all the cakes produced are consumed in the market.

5. A company makes three products x, y, and z which flow through three department: Drill, Lathe and Assembly. The hours of department time required by each of the products, the hours available in each of the departments, the marginal contribution of each of the products, and the estimated incremental cost of idle time per hour are given in following table:

Products	*Department*		*(Hours unit) Assembly*	*Marginal contribution unit (Rs)*
	Drill	*Lathe*		
x	3	3	8	10
y	6	5	10	150
z	7	4	12	200
Hours available	180	240	860	
Incremental cost of idle time/hour	85	115	130	

6. An automobile manufacturing company has five assembly plants and six dealers located throughout the country. The company would like to determine which plants should assemble the automobiles for each dealer in order to minimize the transport costs. The following information is available:

Dealer numbers	1	2	3	4	5	6
No. of cars ordered	35	28	52	33	62	61
Assembly plant	*A*	*B*	*C*	*D*	*E*	
Capacity (cars)	100	90	120	80	90	

Transport Charges (per car) in hundred of Rupees

From/To	*1*	*2*	*3*	*4*	*5*	*6*
A	25	36	31	20	27	33
B	37	23	28	35	19	31
C	26	19	17	28	27	36
D	42	25	15	33	23	33
E	19	31	45	31	34	32

Each dealer requires a certain number of cars, and each assembly plant can provide cars upto its capacity. Also each dealer can receive cars from more than one assembly plant, if this procedure would reduce the overall costs.

7. The investment counsellor of a bank has given 1.5 million rupees to invest for a period of 3 years. The counsellor has determined that there are three reasonably attractive investment opportunities available currently: investment *A* yields an annual rate of return of 7%, investment *B* yields 5% the first year and 8% per annum thereafter; investment *C* yields a flat 20% at the end of third year and may not be invested in after this year. The counsellor has also learned that at beginning of the second year (only) a new investment opportunity, investments *D*, will become available yielding 16% at the end of the third year. The investment counsellor wishes to determine how much money to invest – and when – in each of the possible investments so that the amount of money he will have at the beginning of the fourth year is a maximum.

8. A city hospital has the following minimal daily requirement for nurses:

Period	*Clock-time (24 hours day)*	*Minimal Number of Nurses required*
1	6 A.M. – 10 A. M.	2
2	10 A.M. – 2 P. M.	7
3	2 P.M. – 6 P. M.	15
4	6 P.M. – 10 P. M.	8
5	10 P.M. – 2 A. M.	20
6	2 A.M. – 6 A. M.	6

Nurses report to the hospital at the beginning of each period and work for 8 consecutive hours. The hospital wants to determine the minimal number of nurses available for each period. Formulate this as LPP by setting up appropriate constraints and objective function.

2. SOLUTION BY GRAPHICAL METHOD

So far we have been talking about the mathematical formulation of the problem. We now come to the next part *i.e.*, the actual solution of the problem. In this section, we describe the graphical method of solving an LPP involving only two variables. The technique can be divided into three steps.

Step I. Convert each inequality into an equation. The equation being linear, its graph will be a line. If the line is not parallel to x-axis, $X'OX$, the given inequality will represent the portion of the plane either 'on left' or 'on right' according to the sign of the inequality. If the line is parallel to x-axis, the corresponding inequality will represent portion of the plane 'above' or 'below' the line according to the sign of the inequality.

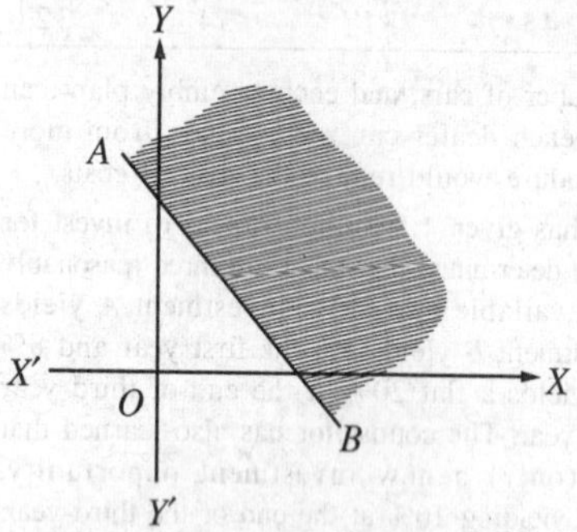

Fig. 1.

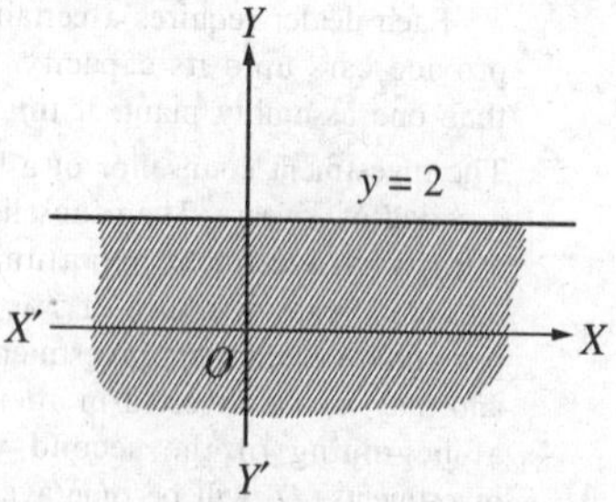

Fig. 2.

Consider, for example, $x + y \geq 1$. This represents the shaded portion (lying on the right of line $x + y = 1$).

Similarly, $x + y \leq 1$ represents the portion of the plane on the left of the line $x + y = 1$.

Again, consider the inequality $y \geq 2$.

It represents portion of the plane above the line $y = 2$. Similarly, $y \leq 2$ represents portion lying below this line, shown by shaded portion in Fig. 2.

Step II. Shade the common portion of all the regions represented by all constraints in the first quadrant (recall that $x \geq 0, y \geq 0$).

Two cases arise:

Case (*i*) The shaded portion is a figure bounded by a convex polygon.

Case (*ii*) The shaded portion is unbounded.

For case (*i*), we use **Extreme point theorem** which states: *If an optimal solution of an LPP exists then the solution will be found among the co-ordinates of the vertices (corners) of the bounding polygon.* The proof of this theorem being beyond the scope of this book will be omitted.

For case (*ii*), if the problem is of maximization of the objective function, the solution is unbounded. In other words, no finite solution exists. But if in this case the problem is of minimization, the optical value will be obtained as in case (*i*).

Step III. In case (*i*), or (*ii*) (if the problem is of minimization of the objective function), we substitute the co-ordinates of the corner points one by one in the objective function. Since the number of constraints (that we will be dealing with) is always finite, the corners are finite in number and hence we can easily detect the corner whose co-ordinates optimize the objective function.

REMARKS: To see which sign of inequality $\geq$ or $\leq$ represents the left or the right side of a line, not parallel to the *x*-axis, we proceed as under:

Let $ax + by \geq c$ be a linear inequality $a \neq 0, c \neq 0$ plot the line $ax + by = c$. Then check from the figure whether the origin lies on the left or right of this line. Now, substitute $x = 0, y = 0$ in the given linear inequality. If this inequality is satisfied, then the origin will be lying in the area denoted by $ax + by \geq c$. (*i.e.*, $ax + by \geq c$ represents that side on which origin lies). If the inequality is not satisfied, origin is on the opposite side to the area represented by the inequality.

If $c = 0$, origin lies on the line $ax + by = c$. Then check the position of some other known point, which is not on the line $ax + by = c$.

If $a = 0$, the line is parallel to *x*-axis. Here again, with the help of relative position of the origin, we can determine the region denoted by the given inequality.

REMARK: Since, we have $x \geq 0$, $y \geq 0$, it means that we shall be working in the first quadrant only.

We now illustrate the graphical method of solving LPP with the help of a few examples.

Example 5. *Maximize* $z = 20x + 10y$

Subject to $4x + 3y \leq 48$

$3x + 5y < 60$

$x \leq 9,\ x,\ y \geq 0$

Solution. We first plot the lines

$$4x + 3y = 48 \quad \text{... } (i)$$

$$3x + 5y = 60 \quad \text{... } (ii)$$

$$x = 9 \quad \text{... } (iii)$$

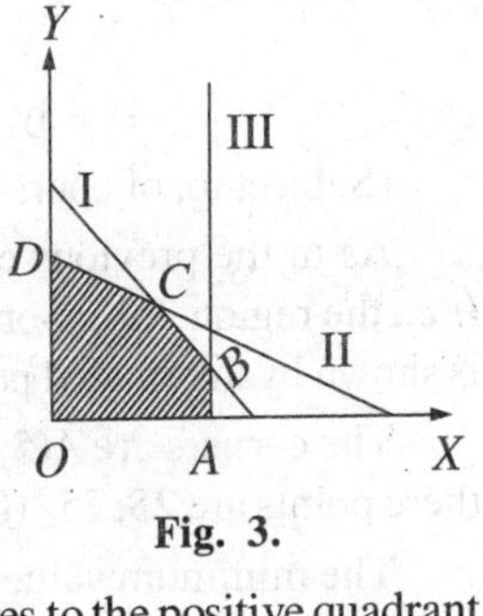

Fig. 3.

We shall, because of $x, y \geq 0$, confine ourselves to the positive quadrant only.

From Fig. 3, it is clear that the origin lies on the left of line (*i*).

Now $4.0 + 3.0 = 0 \leq 48$, so $4x + 3y \leq 48$ represents the region which consists of points lying on the left of line (*i*) and on the line (*i*).

Similarly, we can check that $3x + 5y \leq 60$ represents the region that consists of points lying on the left of line (*ii*) and on it.

Finally, $x \leq 9$ represents the points on it and on the left of $x = 9$.

The common region (corresponding to feasible solution), is shown by shaded portion in the figure.

This is bounded by the polygon *OABCD*. Its corners are $A(9, 0)$, $B(9, 4)$, $C\left(\frac{60}{11}, \frac{96}{11}\right)$, $D(0, 12)$ and $O(0, 0)$. Co-ordinates of *A* and *D* are obtained by putting $y = 0$ and $x = 0$ respectively in (*iii*) and (*ii*). *C* is the point of intersection of lines (*i*) and (*ii*) and *B* is the point of intersection of lines (*i*) and (*iii*).

Values of z at these points are respectively equal to 180, 220, $196\frac{4}{11}$, 120, 0.

Clearly $B(9, 4)$ gives maximum value of z.

Hence, optimal solution is $x = 9, y = 4$, optimal $z = 220$.

Example 6. *Find the minimum value of* $z = 5x + 7y$

Subject to

$$x + 2y \leq 20$$
$$3x + y \geq 15$$
$$4x + 3y \leq 60$$
$$x, y \geq 0$$

Solution. We plot the three lines

$$x + 2y = 20 \quad \text{... } (i)$$
$$3x + y = 15 \quad \text{... } (ii)$$
$$4x + 3y = 60 \quad \text{... } (iii)$$

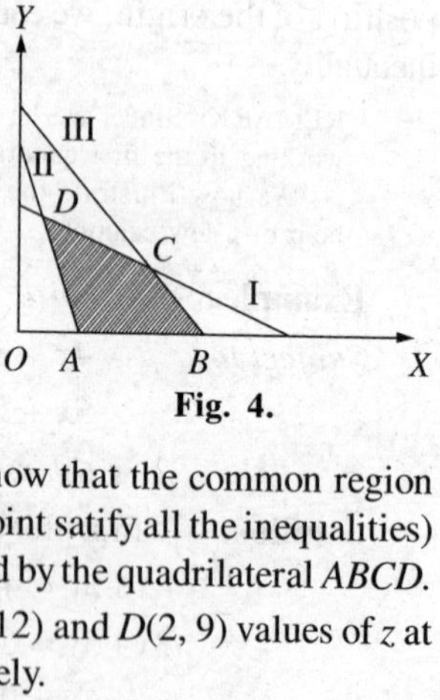

Fig. 4.

(Subject to, of course, $x, y \geq 0$)

As in the previous example, we can show that the common region (*i.e.*, the region, the co-ordinates of whose point satify all the inequalities) is shown by the shaded portion. It is bounded by the quadrilateral *ABCD*.

The corners are $A(5, 0)$, $B(15, 0)$, $C(4, 12)$ and $D(2, 9)$ values of z at these points are 25, 75, 104 and 73 respectively.

The minimum value of z is thus given by co-ordinates of *A*.

Hence, optimal solution is

$$x = 5, \quad y = 0; \text{ optimal value of } z \text{ is } 25.$$

Example 7. *Maximize* $z = 3x + 4y$
subject to conditions $x - y \le -1$
$-x + y \le 0$
$x, y \ge 0$

Solution. We plot the lines

$$x - y = -1 \qquad \text{... (i)}$$
$$-x + y = 0 \qquad \text{... (ii)}$$

The shaded portion denotes the region $x - y \le -1$ and $-x + y \le 0$.

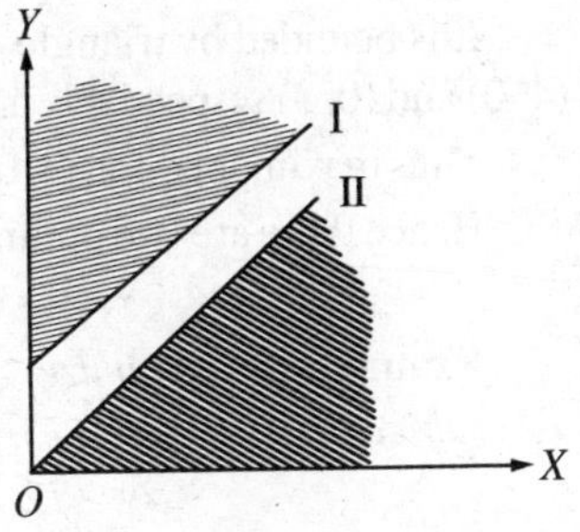

Fig. 5.

As is clear from Fig. 5 these two portions are disjoint. In other words, we cannot find a single point (x_1, y_1) *s.t.*,

$$x_1 - y_1 \le -1 \text{ and } -x_1 + y_1 \le 0,$$
$$x_1, y_1 \le 0$$

Hence, the given LPP has no optimal solution.

Example 8. *Maximize* $z = 4x + 5y$
subject to $x + y \ge 1$
$-2x + y \le 1$
$4x - 2y \le 1$
$x, y \ge 0.$

Solution. Draw the lines

$$x + y = 1 \qquad \text{... (i)}$$
$$-2x + y = 1 \qquad \text{... (ii)}$$
$$4x - 2y = 1 \qquad \text{... (iii)}$$

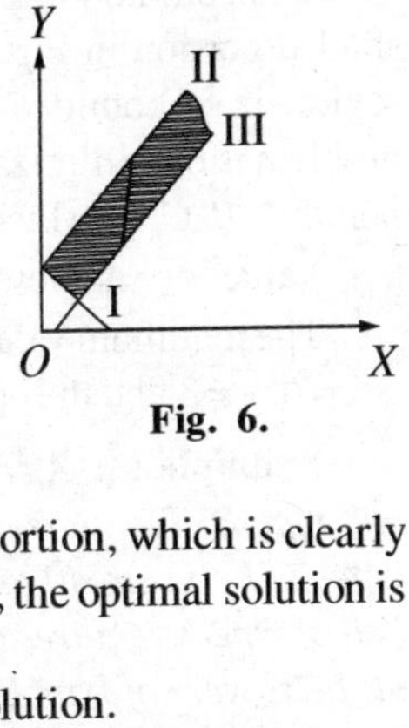

Fig. 6.

The common region is shown by the shaded portion, which is clearly unbounded. Since the problem is of maximization, the optimal solution is unbounded.

In other words the given LPP has no finite solution.

Example 9. *Maximize* $z = 15x + 20y$
subject to $3x + 4y \le 12,$
$x \ge 0,$
$y \ge 0$

Solution. Plot the line $3x + 4y = 12$

The feasible portion is shown by the shaded portion in Fig. 7.

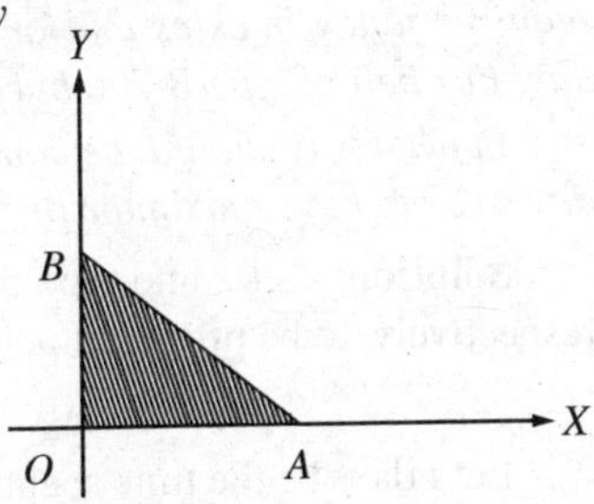

Fig. 7.

It is bounded by triangle OAB the co-ordinates of O, A, B, are (0,0), (4, 0) and (0, 3) respectively and values of z at these points are 0, 60, 60

Thus maximum z is at (4, 0) and (0, 3).

Hence there are two optimal solutions, namely,

$$x=4,\ y=0 \text{ and } x=0,\ y=3 \text{ and optimal value is } 60.$$

Example 10. *Minimize* $z = 30x + 50y$

subject to $3x + y \geq 15.$

$x + 2y \geq 12.$

$3x + 2y \geq 24,$

$x, y \geq 0.$

Solution. Plot the lines

$$3x+y=15 \quad \text{... } (i)$$

$$x+2y=12 \quad \text{... } (ii)$$

$$3x+2y=24 \quad \text{... } (iii)$$

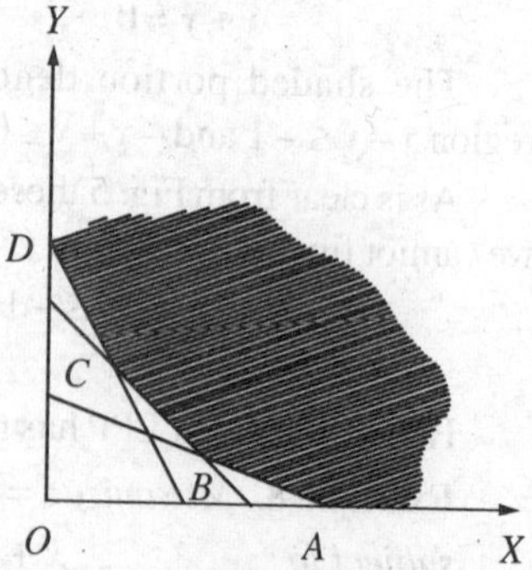

Fig. 8.

The common region is shown by shaded portion in Fig. 8. Clearly this region is unbounded. However, the problem is of minimization, so we compute the co-ordinates of the corner points A, B, C, D, which are respectively, (12, 0), (6, 3), (2, 9) and (0, 15).

Values of z at these points are respectively, 360, 330, 510 and 750.

The minimum value corresponds to $x=6$, $y=3$. Hence optimal solution is $x=6$, $y=3$ and the optimal value is 330.

Example 11. *A company produces two types of leather belts, type A and type B. Type A is of superior quality than type B. Profits on the two types of belts are 40 and 30 paise per belt respectively. Producing each belt of type A requires twice as much time as required by that of type B. If all belts were of type B, the company could produce 1000 belts per day. But the supply of leather is sufficient only for 800 belts per day. Type A requires fancy buckles and only 400 fancy buckles are available per day. For belt of type B 700 buckles are available per day.*

In what way should the company manufacture two types of belts per day so as to have maximum profit.

Solution. Let x and y be the number of belts of type A and type B respectively, to be produced per day. Profit per day is given by

$$z = 40x + 30y \text{ paise.}$$

Let t days be the time spent in production of one belt of type B, then $2t$ is the time spent in the production of one belt of type A.

Thus $2xt + yt \le 1$

or $$2x + y \le \frac{1}{t} \qquad \text{... (1)}$$

But, by hypothesis, only 1000 belts of type *B* can be manufactured in one day

i.e., $1000t = 1$

i.e., $t = \frac{1}{1000}$.

So (*i*) reduces to $2x + y \le 1000$.

Again total number of belts per day cannot exceed 800, and so $x + y \le 800$

Further, number of fancy buckles is less than or equal to 400 and hence $x \le 400$.

as each belt of type *A* needs a fancy buckle.

Similarly, $y \le 700$.

Consequently, mathematical formulation of the given *LPP* is as follows:

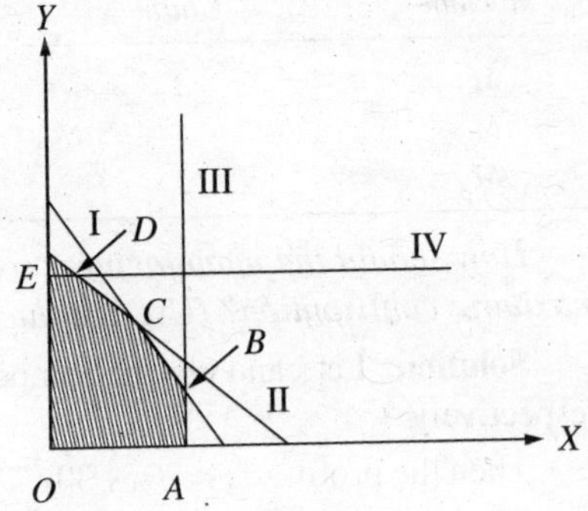

Fig. 9.

Maximize $z = 40x + 30y$

subject to $2x + y \le 1000$

$x + y \le 800$

$x \le 400,\ y \le 700,\ x, y \ge 0.$

Plot now, the lines

$2x + y = 1000$ ... (*i*)

$x + y = 800$ ... (*ii*)

$x = 400$ ... (*iii*)

$y = 700$ ... (*iv*)

The feasible region is shown by the shaded portion in Fig. 9. It is bounded by the polygon *OABCDE*.

Corners are *O* (0, 0); *A* (400, 0), *B* (400, 200), *C* (200, 600), *D* (100, 700), *E* (0, 700).

Values of *z* at these points are respectively, 0, 16000, 22000, 26000, 25000, and 21000 clearly, $x = 200, y = 600$ gives maximum value 26000 of *z*.

Hence optimal solution is $x = 200, y = 600$ and optimal value is 26000 paise or 260 Rupees.

In other words, 200 belts of type A and 600 belts of type B should be produced per day to get maximum profit, which will then be Rs 260.

Example 12. *A firm makes two types of furniture: chairs and tables. The contribution for each product as calculated by the accounting department is Rs 20 per chair and Rs 30 per table. Both products are processed on three machines M_1, M_2 and M_3. The time required in hours per week on each machine is as follows:*

Machine	*Chair*	*Table*	*Available Time*
M_1	3	3	36
M_2	5	2	50
M_3	2	6	60

How should the manufacturer schedule his production in order to maximize contribution? (Use graphic method only)

Solution. Let x and y be the number of chairs and tables manufactured respectively.

Then the profit $\quad z = 20x + 30y$

Machine M_1 will be busy for $3x + 3y$ hours

By hypothesis $\quad 3x + 3y \leq 36$

or $\quad x + y \leq 12.$

Similarly, considering availability of M_2 and M_3, we get

$$5x + 2y \leq 50.$$

Finally $\quad 2x + 6y \leq 60$

or $\quad x + 3y \leq 30.$

Thus the corresponding LPP is

Maximize $\quad z = 20x + 30y$

Subject to constraints $x + y \leq 12$

$$5x + 2y \leq 50$$
$$x + 3y \leq 30$$

and $\quad x, y, z \geq 0.$

We first plot the lines

$$x + y = 12 \quad \text{... (i)}$$
$$5x + 2y = 50 \quad \text{... (ii)}$$
$$x + 3y = 30 \quad \text{... (iii)}$$

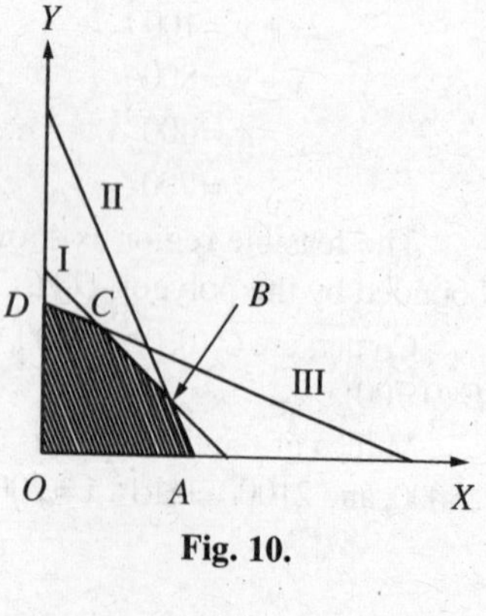

Fig. 10.

Note that (*i*) cuts the axes at the points (12, 0) and (0, 12). (*ii*) at (10, 0) and (0, 25) and (*iii*) meets the axes at (30, 0) and (0, 10).

The inequalities $x + y \le 12,\ \ x, y \ge 0$ denote the portion of 1st quadrant below (*i*).

Similarly, second inequality and $x, y \ge 0$ represent portion below (*ii*) and third inequality with feasibility condition represents region of 1st quadrant below (*iii*).

The common portion is bounded by polygon *OABCD* where *O* is the origin (0, 0), *A* is (10, 0), *D* is (0, 10) and *B* & *C* are the points of intersection of lines (*i*) and (*ii*), and (*i*) and (*iii*) respectively.

Solving $\quad x + y = 12$ and $5x + 2y = 50$

we get $\quad x = \dfrac{26}{3},\ y = \dfrac{10}{3}.$

Thus the point *B* is $\left(\dfrac{26}{3}, \dfrac{10}{3}\right)$.

Again solving $\quad x + y = 12$ and $x + 3y = 30$

we get $\quad x = 3$ and $y = 9$

i.e., point *C* is (3, 9).

We know that objective function is optimal at corners *O*, *A*, *B*, *C*, *D*, so we calculate values of *z* at these points.

At *O*, $\quad z = 20 \times 0 + 30 \times 0 = 0$

At *A*, $\quad z = 20 \times 10 + 30 \times 0 = 200$

At *B*, $\quad z = 20 \times \dfrac{26}{3} + 30 \times \dfrac{10}{3} = 273\dfrac{1}{3}.$

At *C*, $\quad z = 20 \times 3 + 30 \times 9 = 330$

At *D*, $\quad z = 20 \times 0 + 30 \times 10 = 300$

Hence point *C* gives maximum value of *z* and thus for maximum contribution $x = 3, y = 9$, *i.e.*, 3 chairs and 9 tables.

EXERCISES

1. Maximize $\quad z = 24x + 8y,$
   subject to $\quad 2x + 5y \le 40$
   $4x + y \le 20$
   $2x + y \le 12,\ \ x, y \ge 0.$

2. Maximize $\quad z = 5x + 3y,$
   subject to $\quad 3x + y \le 12$
   $x + 2y \le 14$
   $x + y \le 8,\ \ x, y \ge 0.$

3. Minimize $z = -x + 2y,$
subject to $-x + 3y \le 10$
$x + y \le 6$
$x - y \le 2, \quad x, y \ge 0.$

4. Minimize $z = 3x + 4y,$
subject to $2x + 3y \ge 36$
$2x + y \ge 14$
$4x + y \ge 16, \quad x, y \ge 0.$

5. Minimize $z = 4x + 5y,$
subject to $2x + y \ge 14$
$2x + 3y \ge 30$
$y \ge 4, \quad x, y \ge 0.$

6. Maximize $z = 3x + 2y,$
subject to $x - y \le 1$
$x + y \ge 3$
$x, y \ge 0.$

7. Maximize $z = 4x + 5y$
subject to $x + y \ge 1$
$-2x + y \le 1$
$4x - 2y \le 1, \quad x, y \ge 0.$

8. Maximize $z = 6x + 4y,$
subject to $-2x + y \le 2$
$x - y \le 2$
$3x + 2y \le 9, \quad x, y \ge 0.$

9. Maximize $z = x + y$
subject to $x + y \le 1$
$-3x + y \ge 3$
$x, y \ge 0.$

10. Maximize $z = 4x + 6y$
subject to $x + 4y \le 110$
$2x + 3y \le 160, \quad x, y \ge 0.$

11. A horticulturist, wishes to mix fertiliser that will provide a minimum of 15 units of potash, 20 units of nitrates and 24 units of phosphate. *Brand I* provides 3 units of potash, 1 unit of nitrate and 3 units of phosphate; it costs Rs 120. *Brand II* provides, 1 unit of potash, 5 units of nitrates and 2 units of phosphate; it costs Rs 60. Find the quantities of two brands, which should be mixed such that the cost is minimum. Find also the minimum cost.

12. A company sells two different products *A* and *B*. The company makes a profit of Rs 40 and Rs 30 per unit on products *A* and *B* respectively. The two products are produced by common production process and one sold in two different markets. The production process has a capacity of 30,000 man-hours. It takes 3 hours to produce one unit of *A* and one hour to produce one unit of *B*. The market has been surveyed, and company officials feel that the maximum number of units *A* that can be sold is 8000 and that of *B* is 12000. Subject to these limitations the products can be sold in any convex combination. Formulate the above as LPP and solve it by the graphical method.

ANSWERS

1. $x = 4, y = 4, z = 128.$
2. $x = 2, y = 6, z = 28.$
3. $x = 2, y = 0, z = -2.$
4. $x = 3/2, y = 11.$
5. $x = 3, y = 8, z = 52.$
6. Unbounded solution.
7. Unbounded solution
8. $x = \frac{13}{5}, y = \frac{3}{5}$ or $x = \frac{5}{7}, y = \frac{24}{7}, z = 18$
9. No solution.
10. Two optimal solutions $x = 80, y = 0$ and $x = 62, y = 12$ optimal value $z = 320.$
11. $x = 2, y = 9, z = 780.$
12. $x = 6000, y = 12000, z = 96000.$

3. SIMPLEX METHOD

When number of variables is more than two, the graphical method cannot be used. Dantzig developed an algorithm for solving such LPP's. In this method, properties similar to those of a rectilinear figure having least number of vertices, called '*simplex*' are exploited and this is the reason that this method is called the simplex method.

We first introduce the concept of *slack* and *surplus variables.*

A general linear constraint can be of three types:

$$\sum_{i=1}^{n} a_i x_i = b \quad \text{or} \quad \sum_{i=1}^{n} a_i x_i \le b$$

or

$$\sum_{i=1}^{n} a_i x_i \ge b.$$

Without loss of generality we can assume that $b \ge 0$, otherwise we multiply the equation or the inequality by -1. In such a situation the three constraints will be transformed to $\sum_{i=1}^{n} (-a_i) x_i = -b$ and $\sum_{i=1}^{n} (-a_i) x_i \ge -b$ and $\sum_{i=1}^{n} (-a_i) x_i \le -b$ respectively and here $-b \ge 0$.

In the second type of the linear constraint $\sum_{i=1}^{n} a_i x_i \le b$, if we add a new suitable variable, say x_{n+1} (≥ 0) we get an equation

$$\sum_{i=1}^{n} a_i x_i + x_{n+1} = b.$$

This new variable x_{n+1} is called a *slack variable.*

Again, in the third type $\sum_{i=1}^{n} a_i x_i \ge b$, if we subtract a suitable new variable, say x_{n+2} (≥ 0) we get

$$\sum_{i=1}^{n} a_i x_i - x_{n+2} = b.$$

This new variable x_{n+2} is called a *surplus variable*. Consequently we notice that any linear constraint can be converted to a linear equation (with the introduction of a slack or a surplus variable).

Definition: An LPP in which all constraints are in the form of equations is called a *Standard Linear Programming Problem* (SLPP).

In view of the above discussion, we notice that every LPP can be converted into SLPP, provided the objective function is modified suitably.

The LPPs which we shall be discussing in this book are mainly of two types.

Type I: Objective function is to be *maximized* and all constraints (except for $x \geq 0, y \geq 0$) are of the type $\leq$.

Type II: Objective function is to be *minimized* and all constraints are of the type $\geq$.

Type I. Suppose $z = \sum_{i=1}^{n} c_i x_i$ is to be maximized subject to constraints

$$\sum_{j=1}^{n} a_{1j} x_j \leq b_1$$

$$\sum_{j=1}^{n} a_{2j} x_j \leq b_2$$

...

...

$$\sum_{j=1}^{n} a_{mj} x_j \leq b_m$$

with $b_1, b_2, ..., b_m \geq 0$.

We change this LPP to SLPP by introducing slack variables x_{n+1}, $x_{n+2}, ..., x_{n+m}$.

The new LPP will then be:

Maximize $$z = \sum_{j=1}^{n} c_i x_i + 0x_{n+1} + 0x_{n+2} + ... + 0x_{n+m}$$

subject to
$$\left.\begin{aligned} &\sum_{j=1}^{n} a_{1jx_j} + x_{n+1} = b_1 \\ &\sum_{j=1}^{n} a_{2jx_j} + x_{n+2} = b_2 \\ &... \\ &... \\ &\sum_{j=1}^{n} a_{mjx_j} + x_{n+m} = b_m \end{aligned}\right\} \quad ...(1)$$

$x_j \geq 0, j = 1, 2, ..., n+m.$

Definition: The matrix $\begin{bmatrix} c_1 \\ c_2 \\ \vdots \\ c_n \end{bmatrix}$ is called *cost vector*. Each c_i is called *cost* associated with the variable x_i.

We now discuss the simplex method for **Type I,** LPP. First we form an $m \times (n+m+3)$ table, (called **Simplex Table I.**) This table is also known as *First Iteration Table.*

Table 31.1

Y_B	C_B	X_B	y_1	y_2	y_3	...	y_n	y_{n+1}	y_{n+2}	...	y_{n+m}
y_{n+1}	0	b_1	a_{11}	a_{12}	a_{13}	...	a_{1n}	1	0	...	0
y_{n+2}	0	b_2	a_{22}	a_{21}	a_{23}	...	a_{2n}	0	1	...	0
...	...	...	...	...	...	...	...	...	...	...	...
y_{n+m}	0	b_m	a_{m1}	a_{m2}	a_{m3}		a_{mn}	0	0		1
		$C_B \rightarrow$	c_1	c_2	c_3	...	c_m	0	0	...	0
		$\Delta_B \rightarrow$	$-c_1$	$-c_2$	$-c_3$	...	$-c_n$	0	0	...	0

The column headed by Y_B consists of slack variables (x replaced by y). Column 'C_B' *denotes* the costs associated with slack variables. Column 'X_B' consists of constants $b_1, b_2, ..., b_m$ (all ≥ 0). Columns $y_1, y_2, .., y_{n+m}$ are the columns of the coefficient matrix of the system of equation (1); y_i representing i^{th} column.

Row representing C_B denotes the costs associated with all the variables (actual and slack). Row represented by Δ_B denotes the elements Δ_j ($j = 1, 2, ..., m+n$) obtained by multiplying column C_B with column y_j (element wise) and then subtracting c_j. Thus

$$\Delta_1 = 0.a_{11} + 0.a_{21} + ... + 0.a_{m1} - c_1$$
$$\Delta_2 = 0.a_{12} + 0.a_{22} + ... + 0.a_{m2} - c_2$$
$$\Delta_3 = 0.a_{13} + 0.a_{23} + ... + 0.a_{m3} - c_3$$
$$\dots\dots\dots\dots\dots\dots\dots\dots$$

and $$\Delta_{m+n} = 0.0 + 0.0 + ... + 0.1 - 0 \text{ as } c_{m+n} = 0.$$

The matrix with columns $X_B, y_1, y_2, ..., y_{n+m}$ plays key role in the simplex method. **Whenever we refer to any row operation, we shall have this matrix in our mind**. We shall for convenience sake, call it **Activity Matrix**. If each entry in Δ_B row is ≥ 0, this table is final table and solution is obtained by *equating* entries in column Y_B with corresponding entries in column X_B. The variables *not occurring* in column Y_B are given zero values. Thus if all $-c_1, -c_2, ..., -c_n$ are ≥ 0 the optimal solution is $x_1 = x_2 = ... = x_n = 0$ (note that y replaces x and none of $y_1, y_2, ..., y_n$ appears in column Y_B). Optimal solution is given by $C'_B X_{B1}$, C'_B being transpose of column matrix C_B.

Hence optimal value in the above case will be $0.c_1 + 0.c_2 + ... + 0.c_n = 0$.

If any one of Δ_B is strictly negative then we select the smallest of all entries of Δ_B. Let us suppose that $\Delta_j = C'_B Y_j - c_j$ is the smallest strictly negative entry. By smallest strictly negative entry we mean $\Delta_j \leq \Delta_i$ for all $i = 1, 2, ..., n + m$. The column y_j will be termed as an **incoming** vector (recall that a column or a row matrix is often referred to as a vector). We shall put an arrow of type ↑ below Δ_f to indicate that this column will enter in the second table to be constructed just after. Consider all entries of column y_j namely $a_{1j}, a_{2j}, ..., a_{mj}$. We compute the ratios $\frac{b_1}{a_{1j}}, \frac{b_2}{a_{2j}}, ..., \frac{b_m}{a_{mj}}$ only for those a_{1j}'s $(i = 1, 2, ..., m)$ which are strictly positive. (If all $a_{1j}, a_{2j}, ..., a_{mj}$ are ≤ 0, we shall say that the solution is **unbounded**).

Let minimum of $\left\{\frac{b_1}{a_{1j}}, \frac{b_2}{a_{2j}}, ..., \frac{b_m}{a_{mj}}, a_{1j} > 0\right\}$ be $\frac{b_k}{a_k}$. Then y_{n+m} will be termed as **outgoing** vector in the next table to be constructed just after we put an arrow of type → to the right of kth row of the simplex table (1). The entry a_{kj} (*i.e.*, the entry at the intersection of incoming and outgoing vectors is called the **Pivot Element.** We shall encircle it; with the help of the pivot element we shall be able to fill the entries of the second table. We make all the entries of incoming vector y_j as zero except the kth entry which we reduce to **one**. For this purpose we apply the row transformations in the activity matrix as under.

$$R_1 \to R_1 - \frac{a_{1j}}{a_{kj}} R_k, R_2 \to R_2 - \frac{a_{2j}}{a_{kj}} R_k, ...,$$

$$R_{k-1} \to R_{k-1} - \frac{a_{k-1,\,j}}{a_{kj}} R_k, R_k \to \frac{1}{a_{kj}} R_k, R_{k+1} \to$$

$$R_{k+1} - \frac{a_{k+1,\,j}}{a_{kj}} R_k, \text{... and } R_m \to R_m - \frac{a_{mj}}{a_{kj}} R_k$$

After these operations we get the activity matrix of the second table.

Table 2 is similar to Table 1 as far as Column's and Row's headings are concerned. The difference will be as under.

(1) In column Y_B, y_{n+k} will be replaced by y_j, the entry in kth row, the cost associated with y_{n+k} will be replaced by c_j, the cost associated with y_j.

(2) Activity matrix of Table 1 is replaced by the new matrix obtained after applying above said row operations.

We compute the entries of the row represented by Δ_B (note that row represented by C_B is unaffected). These entries will generally be changed. If all entries of this row are ≥ 0, we get optimal solution at this stage. Solution is to be read as in the case of Table 1. Otherwise we repeat the whole process and prepare third table and so on.

REMARKS:

1. If there are more than one vector chosen for entry (for example when for two values of j, say $j_1 \neq j_2$, $\Delta_{j1} = \Delta_{j2}$ is the smallest strictly negative entry) we can select any one of these vectors as in coming vectors. Solution is not affected.
2. If there are more than one pivot elements *i.e.*, the minimum of

$$\left\{\frac{b_1}{a_{1j}}, \frac{b_2}{a_{2j}}, \ldots, \frac{b_m}{a_{mj}}, a_{1j} > 0\right\}$$

is not unique, we get the so-called **Degeneracy case**. We shall not discuss, in this book, the methods of solution of degeneracy cases.

3. We shall write d for 1×1 matrix (d).

The following examples will make the method clear.

Example 13. *Maximize* $z = 6x_1 + 4x_2$

subject to

$$-2x_1 + x_2 \leq 2$$
$$x_1 - x_2 \leq 2$$
$$3x_1 + 2x_2 \leq 9$$
$$x_1, x_2 \geq 0$$

Solution. Corresponding SLPP is

Maximize $z = 6x_1 + 4x_2 + 0x_3 + 0x_4 + 0x_5$

Subject to

$$-2x_1 + x_2 + x_3 = 2$$
$$x_1 - x_2 + x_4 = 2$$
$$3x_1 + 2x_2 + x_5 = 9$$
$$x_1, x_2, x_3, x_4, x_5 \geq 0$$

Our first iteration table is:

y_B	c_B	x_B	y_1	y_2	y_3	y_4	y_5	
y_3	0	2	– 2	1	1	0	0	
y_4	0	2	(1)	– 1	0	1	0	→
y_5	0	9	3	2	0	0	1	
		C_B	6	4	0	0	0	
		Δ_B	–6	–4	0	0	0	
			↑					

Entries of Δ_B row are respectively – 6, – 4, 0, 0, 0. All entries are not ≥ 0. We choose the least negative entry *i.e*, – 6.

The only strictly positive entries of y_1 are $a_{21} = 1$, $a_{31} = 3$,

$$\text{Min}\left\{\frac{b_2}{a_{21}}, \frac{b_3}{a_{31}}\right\} = \text{Min}\left\{\frac{2}{1}, \frac{9}{3}\right\} = 2$$

This corresponds to second row, the row headed by y_4. So y_4 is outgoing vector, pivot element is 1 and thus y_1 will replace y_4 in second table.

Apply operations

$$R_1 \to R_1 + 2R_2, \quad R_3 \to R_3 - 3R_2$$

The second iteration table is:

y_B	c_B	x_B	y_1	y_2	y_3	y_4	y_5	
y_3	0	6	0	– 1	1	2	0	
y_1	6	2	1	– 1	0	1	0	
y_5	0	3	0	(5)	0	– 3	1	→
		C_B	6	4	0	0	0	
		Δ_B	0	–10	0	6	0	
				↑				

Again one entry in Δ_3 row is –ve. So it gives the incoming vector namely y_2.

Now the only strictly positive entry of this column is a_{32}. So the row to which this belongs, *i.e.*, y_5 row is outgoing vector. It is to be replaced by y_2 for the third table. Also the pivot element is 5.

Apply

$$R_1 \to R_1 + \frac{1}{5} R_3, \quad R_2 \to R_2 + \frac{1}{5} R_3, \quad R_3 \to \frac{1}{5} R_3$$

The third iteration table is:

y_B	c_B	x_B	y_1	y_2	y_3	y_4	y_5
y_3	0	$\frac{33}{5}$	0	0	1	$\frac{7}{5}$	$\frac{1}{5}$
y_1	6	$\frac{13}{5}$	1	0	0	$\frac{2}{5}$	$\frac{1}{5}$
y_2	4	$\frac{3}{5}$	0	1	0	$-\frac{3}{5}$	$\frac{1}{5}$
		C_B	6	4	0	0	0
		Δ_B	0	0	0	0	2

In this table all Δ_j's are ≥ 0.

Hence the optimal solution is $x_1 = 6, x_2 = 4,\ x, x_3 = \frac{13}{5}$

As we are not now concerned with variable that we introduced,

we shall write $x_1 = 6, x_2 = 4\ \frac{3}{5}$ the optimal solution.

Optimal value $= C_B' x_B$ (for the third table)

$$= 0.\ \frac{33}{5} + 6. + \frac{13}{5} + 4.\frac{3}{5} = \frac{78}{5} + \frac{12}{5} = 18.$$

Example 14. *Maximize* $z = 3x_1 + 4x_2 + 2x_3$

subject to $x_1 - 2x_2 + 4x_3 \leq 36$

$2x_1 + 3x_2 - 5x_3 \leq 40$

$3x_1 + 2x_2 + x_3 \leq 28$

$x_1, x_2, x_3 \leq 0$

Solution. The corresponding SLPP is

Maximize $z = 3x_1 + 4x_2 + 2x_3 + 0x_4 + 0x_5 + 0x_6$

subject to $x_1 - 2x_2 + 4x_3 + x_4 = 36$

$2x_1 + 3x_2 - 5x_3 + x_5 = 40$

$3x_1 + 2x_2 + x_3 + x_6 = 28$

$x_i \geq 0, i = 1, 2, ..., 6$

Table I

y_B	c_B	x_B	y_1	y_2	y_3	y_4	y_5	y_6	
y_4	0	36	1	−2	4	1	0	0	
y_5	0	40	2	(3)	−5	0	1	0	→
y_6	0	28	3	2	1	0	0	1	
		C_B	3	4	2	0	0	0	
		Δ_B	−3	−4	−2	−0	0	0	
				↑					

Apply $R_1 \to R_1 + \frac{2}{3}R_2$, $R_2 \to \frac{1}{3}R_2$, $R_3 \to R_3 - \frac{2}{3}R_2$, we get

Table II

y_B	c_B	x_B	y_1	y_2	y_3	y_4	y_5	y_6	
y_4	0	$\frac{188}{3}$	$\frac{7}{3}$	0	$\frac{2}{3}$	1	$\frac{2}{3}$	0	
y_2	4	$\frac{40}{3}$	$\frac{2}{3}$	1	$-\frac{5}{3}$	0	$\frac{1}{3}$	0	→
y_6	0	$\frac{4}{3}$	$\frac{5}{3}$	0	($\frac{13}{3}$)	0	$-\frac{2}{3}$	1	
		C_B	3	4	2	0	0	0	
		Δ_B	$-\frac{1}{3}$	0	$-\frac{26}{3}$	0	$\frac{4}{3}$	0	
					↑				

Again apply $R_1 \to R_1 - \frac{2}{13}R_3$, $R_2 \to R_2 + \frac{5}{13}R_3$,

$R_3 \to \frac{3}{13}R_3$, we get

Table III

y_B	c_B	x_B	y_1	y_2	y_3	y_4	y_5	y_6
y_4	0	$\frac{812}{13}$	$\frac{27}{13}$	0	0	1	$\frac{10}{13}$	$-\frac{2}{13}$
y_2	4	$\frac{180}{13}$	$\frac{17}{13}$	1	0	0	$\frac{1}{13}$	$\frac{5}{13}$
y_3	2	$\frac{4}{13}$	$\frac{5}{13}$	0	1	0	$-\frac{2}{13}$	$\frac{3}{13}$
		C_B	3	4	2	0	0	0
		Δ_B	$\frac{39}{13}$	0	0	0	0	2

since all entries in Δ_B row are ≥ 0, we get the optimal solution as $x_1 = 0$ (y_1 does not appear in column y_B)

$$x_2 = \frac{180}{13},\ x_3 = \frac{4}{13}.$$

Optimal value is $0.\frac{812}{13} + 4.\frac{180}{13} + 2.\frac{4}{13} = \frac{728}{13} = 56.$

Example 15. *Maximize* $z = x_1 - x_2 + 3x_3$

subject to

$$x_1 + x_2 + x_3 \leq 10$$
$$2x_1 - x_3 \leq 2$$
$$2x_1 - 2x_2 + 3x_3 \leq 0$$
$$x_1, x_2, x_3 \leq 0.$$

Solution. Corresponding SLPP is

Maximize $z_1 = x_1 - x_2 + 3x_3 + 0x_4 + 0x_5 + 0x_6$

subject to

$$x_1 + x_2 + x_3 + x_4 = 10$$
$$2x_1 - x_3 + x_5 = 2$$
$$2x_1 - 2x_2 + 3x_3 + x_6 = 0$$
$$x_1, \geq 0, i = 1, 2, ..., 6.$$

The following tables help us with the solution

Table I

y_B	c_B	x_B	y_1	y_2	y_3	y_4	y_5	y_6	
y_4	0	10	1	1	1	1	0	0	
y_5	0	2	2	0	–1	0	1	0	→
y_6	0	0	2	–2	(3)	0	0	1	
		C_B	1	–1	3	0	0	0	
		Δ_B	–1	1	–3	0	0	0	
					↑				

Apply transformations $R_1 \to R_1 - \frac{1}{3} R_3$; $R_2 \to R_2 + \frac{1}{3} R_3$

and $R_3 \to \frac{1}{3} R_3$, we have

Table II

y_B	c_B	x_B	y_1	y_2	y_3	y_4	y_5	y_6
y_4	0	10	$\frac{1}{3}$	$\frac{5}{3}$	0	1	0	$-\frac{1}{3}$
y_5	0	2	$\frac{8}{3}$	$-\frac{2}{3}$	0	0	1	$\frac{1}{3}$
y_3	3	0	$\frac{2}{3}$	$-\frac{2}{3}$	1	0	0	$\frac{1}{3}$
		C_B	1	–1	3	0	0	0
		Δ_B	1	–1	0	0	0	1

Again apply $R_1 \to \frac{3}{5} R_1$; $R_2 \to R_2 + \frac{2}{5} R_1$ and

$R_3 \to R_3 + \frac{2}{5} R_1$, we have

Table III

y_B	c_B	x_B	y_1	y_2	y_3	y_4	y_5	y_6
y_2	-1	6	$\frac{1}{5}$	1	0	$\frac{3}{5}$	0	$-\frac{1}{5}$
y_5	0	6	$\frac{14}{5}$	0	0	$\frac{2}{5}$	1	$\frac{1}{5}$
y_3	3	4	$\frac{4}{5}$	0	1	$\frac{2}{5}$	0	$\frac{1}{5}$
		C_B	1	-1	3	0	0	0
		Δ_B	$\frac{6}{5}$	0	0	$\frac{3}{5}$	0	$\frac{4}{5}$

all Δ_j's are ≥ 0, hence this table gives optimal solution as

$$x_1 = 0, x_2 = 6, x_3 = 4,$$

optimal value is $\quad -1.6 + 0.6 + 3.4 = -6 + 12 = 6.$

EXERCISES

Use simplex method to solve the following *LPP's*:

1. Maximize $z = 7x_1 + 5x_2$
   subject to
   $$x_1 + 2x_2 \leq 5$$
   $$4x_1 + 3x_2 \leq 12$$
   $$x_1, x_2 \geq 0.$$

2. Maximize $z = 4x_1 + 10x_2$
   subject to
   $$2x_1 + x_2 \leq 50$$
   $$2x_1 + 5x_2 \leq 100$$
   $$2x_1 + 3x_2 \leq 90$$
   $$x_1, x_2 \geq 0.$$

3. Maximize $z = x_1 + x_2 + 3x_3$
   subject to
   $$3x_1 + 2x_2 + x_3 \leq 3$$
   $$2x_1 + x_2 + 2x_3 \leq 2$$
   $$x_1, x_2, x_3 \geq 0.$$

4. Maximize $z = -x_1 + 3x_2 - 2x_3$
   subject to
   $$3x_1 - x_2 + 2x_3 \leq 7$$
   $$-x_1 + 2x_2 \leq 6$$
   $$-4x_1 + 3x_2 + 8x_3 \leq 10$$
   $$x_i, \geq 0 \ \forall\ i = 1, 2, 3.$$

5. Maximize $z = 3x_1 + 2x_2 + 5x_3$
subject to
$$x_1 + 2x_2 + x_3 \leq 430$$
$$3x_1 + 2x_3 \leq 460$$
$$x_1 + 4x_2 \leq 420$$
$$x_i \geq 0 \quad (i = 1, 2, 3).$$

6. Maximize $z = 30x_1 + 24x_2 + 60x_3$
subject to
$$6x_1 + 3x_2 + 5x_3 \leq 30$$
$$x_1 + x_2 + 5x_3 \leq 25$$
$$x_1, x_2, x_3 \geq 0.$$

7. A television company has three major departments for its manufacture of two models *A* and *B*.

Monthly capacities are given as:

Per unit time requirements (hour)

	Model A	*Model B*	*Hours available this month*
Department I	4.0	2.0	1,600
Department II	2.5	1.0	1,200
Department III	4.5	1.5	1,600

The marginal profit of model *A* is Rs 400 each and that of model *B* is Rs 100 each. Assuming that the company can sell any quantity of either product due to favourable market conditions determine the optimum output for both models, highest possible profit for this month and slack time in three departments.

ANSWERS

1. $x_1 = 3, x_2 = 0$, Max. $z = 21$.
2. $x_1 = 0, x_2 = 20$, Max. $z = 200$.
3. $x_1 = x_2 = 0, x_3 = 1$, Max. $z = 3$.
4. $x_1 = 4, x_2 = 5, x_3 = 0$, Max. $z = 11$.
5. $x_1 = 0, x_2 = 100, x_3 = 23$, Max. $z = 1350$.
6. $x_1 = 0, x_2 = 5/2, x_3 = 9/2$, Max. $z = 330$.
7. 800/3 units of both *A* and *B*. Maximum profit Rs 13333.

4. DUALITY PRINCIPLE

Let a given LPP be

Minimize $z = c_1x_1 + c_2x_2 + ... + c_nx_n$

subject to
$$a_{11}x_1 + a_{12}x_2 + ... + a_{1n}x_n \geq b_1$$
$$a_{21}x_1 + a_{22}x_2 + ... + a_{2n}x_n \geq b_2$$
$$\cdots \quad \cdots \quad \cdots$$
$$a_{m1}x_1 + a_{m2}x_2 + ... a_{mn}x_n \geq b_m$$
$$x_i \geq 0 \quad \forall i = 1, 2, ..., n$$

The method discussed in the earlier section cannot be used here. In such a situation we transform the given LPP to a new LPP as under:

Maximize $w = b_1y_1 + b_2y_2 + ... + b_my_m$

subject to

$$a_{11}y_1 + a_{21}y_2 + ... + a_{m1}y_m \le c_1$$
$$a_{12}y_1 + a_{22}y_2 + ... + a_{m2}y_m \le c_2$$
$$...$$
$$...$$
$$a_{1n}y_1 + a_{2n}y_2 + ... + a_{mn}y_m \le c_n$$
$$y_i \ge 0 \quad \forall i = 1, 2, ... m.$$

This new LPP is called *dual* to the first LPP. The former LPP is called *primal* to the latter. The dual can now be solved by means of the simplex method described earlier.

In matrix notation, the primal can be written as:

Minimize $z = C'X$

where $C = \begin{bmatrix} c_1 \\ c_2 \\ \vdots \\ c_n \end{bmatrix}$, $X = \begin{bmatrix} x_1 \\ x_2 \\ \vdots \\ x_n \end{bmatrix}$ and C' is transpose of C

subject to $AX \ge B,\ X \ge O_{n1}$

where $A = \begin{bmatrix} a_{11}\ a_{12} ... a_{1n} \\ a_{21}\ a_{22} ... a_{2n} \\ ... \\ a_{m1}\ a_{m2} ... a_{mn} \end{bmatrix}$ is coefficient matrix

and $B = \begin{bmatrix} b_1 \\ b_2 \\ \vdots \\ b_m \end{bmatrix}$ and O_{n1} is $n \times 1$ zero matrix.

Also if $P = (p_{ij})$ and $Q = (q_{ij})$ are $m \times n$ matrices over real numbers then by $P \le Q$ (or $P \ge Q$) we mean $P_{ij} \le q_{ij}$ (or $p_{ij} \ge q_{ij}$) $\forall\ i, j$.

In terms of matrices, dual can be written as
Maximize $W = B'Y$

where $$Y = \begin{bmatrix} y_1 \\ y_2 \\ \vdots \\ y_m \end{bmatrix} \text{ subject to } A'Y \le C,\ Y \ge O_{m1}$$

We shall, often be using the following theorem (sometimes referred to as Duality Principle).

Theorem: Primal has optimal solution if and only if Dual has optimal solution and further

$$\text{Minimum } z = \text{Maximum } w$$

Using the duality principle, we can, by means of simplex method, solve LPP's of type II.

Remark: Note that we can solve the dual problem by the method discussed for type 1, LPP provided $C \ge O_{n1}$.

Example 16. *Minimize* $z = 2x_1 + 4x_2$
subject to
$$2x_1 + x_2 \ge 14$$
$$x_1 + x_2 \ge 12$$
$$x_1 + 3x_2 \ge 18$$
$$x_1, x_2 \ge 0.$$

Solution. Dual LPP will be

Maximize $$w = 14y_1 + 12y_2 + 18y_3$$
subject to
$$2y_1 + y_2 + y_3 \le 2$$
$$y_1 + y_2 + 3y_3 \le 4$$
$$y_1, y_2, y_3 \ge 0$$

using the simplex method we can now solve it.

We get the following tables

Table I

z_B	c_B	y_B	z_1	z_2	z_3	z_4	z_5	
z_1	0	2	2	1	1	1	0	→
z_5	0	4	1	1	(3)	0	1	
		C_B	14	12	18	0	0	
		Δ_B	−14	−12	−18	0	0	
					↑			

Table II

z_B	c_B	y_B	z_1	z_2	z_3	z_4	z_5	
z_4	0	$\frac{2}{3}$	$\frac{5}{3}$	$\frac{2}{3}$	0	1	$-\frac{1}{3}$	→
z_5	18	$\frac{4}{3}$	$\frac{1}{3}$	$\frac{1}{3}$	1	0	$\frac{1}{3}$	
		C_B	14	12	18	0	0	
		Δ_B	-8	-6	0	0	6	
					↑			

Table III

z_B	c_B	y_B	z_1	z_2	z_3	z_4	z_5	
z_1	14	$\frac{2}{5}$	1	$\frac{2}{5}$	0	$\frac{3}{5}$	$-\frac{1}{5}$	→
z_3	18	$\frac{6}{5}$	0	$\frac{1}{5}$	1	$-\frac{1}{5}$	$\frac{2}{5}$	
		C_B	14	12	18	0	0	
		Δ_B	0	$-\frac{14}{5}$	0	$\frac{4}{5}$	$\frac{22}{5}$	
				↑				

Table IV

z_B	c_B	y_B	z_1	z_2	z_3	z_4	z_5
z_1	12	1	$\frac{5}{2}$	1	0	$\frac{3}{2}$	$-\frac{1}{2}$
z_3	18	1	$-\frac{1}{2}$	0	1	$-\frac{1}{2}$	$\frac{1}{2}$
		C_B	14	12	18	0	0
		Δ_B	7	0	0	9	3

All the entries in the Δ_B row are ≥ 0.

Hence the optimal solution for the dual LPP is $z_1 = 0, z_2 = 1, z_3 = 1$ and maximal value $= 12.1 + 18.1 = 30$.

By duality principle, minimal value of primal is 30. Optimal solution to primal is obtained by Δ_4 and Δ_5 (*i.e.*, Δ. value for slack variables) in the final table. Here they are 9 and 3.

Thus optimal solution of primal is $x_1 = 9$ and $x_2 = 3$.

Example 17. *Minimize* $z = 2x_1 + 9x_2 + x_3$
subject to
$$x_1 + 4x_2 + 2x_3 \geq 5$$
$$3x_1 + x_2 + 2x_3 \geq 4$$
$$x_1, x_2 x_3 \geq 0$$

Solution. Dual of the given LPP is

Maximize $w = 5y_1 + 4y_2$
subject to
$$y_1 + 3y_2 \leq 2$$
$$4y_1 + y_2 \leq 9$$
$$2y_1 + 2y_2 \leq 1$$
$$y_1, y_2 \geq 0$$

Proceeding as before, we get the following tables:

Table I

z_B	c_B	y_B	z_1	z_2	z_3	z_4	z_5	
z_3	0	2	1	3	1	0	0	
z_4	0	9	4	1	0	1	0	→
z_5	0	1	(2)	2	0	0	1	
		c_B	5	4	0	0	0	
		Δ_B	–5	–4	0	0	0	
				↑				

Table II

z_B	c_B	y_B	z_1	z_2	z_3	z_4	z_5
z_4	0	$\frac{3}{2}$	0	2	1	0	$-\frac{1}{2}$
z_5	0	7	0	–3	0	1	–2
z_1	5	$\frac{1}{2}$	1	1	0	0	$\frac{1}{2}$
		c_B	5	4	0	0	0
		Δ_B	0	1	(0)	(0)	($\frac{5}{2}$)

Thus the optimal solution for the dual is

$$y_1 = \frac{1}{2},\ y_2 = 0,\ y_3 = 0$$

and maximum value is $5 \cdot \frac{1}{2} = \frac{5}{2}$.

By duality principle, optimal value of primal is $\frac{5}{2}$ and optimal solution is $x_1 = 0,\ x_2 = 0,\ x_3 = \frac{5}{3}$.

Example 18. *A diet for a sick person must contain at least 4000 units of vitamins, 50 units of minerals and 1400 calories. Two foods A and B are available at a cost of Rs 4 and Rs 3 per unit respectively. If one unit of A contains 200 units of vitamins, 1 unit of minerals and 40 calories whereas one unit of food B contains 100 units of vitamins, 2 units of minerals and 40 calories. Find by simplex method, what combination of foods be used so as to have least cost.*

Solution. Let x_1 units of A and x_2 units of B be used. Then cost

$$z = 4x_1 + 3x_2$$

No. of units of vitamins in the combined food are

$$200x_1 + 100x_2$$

No. of units of minerals will be $x_1 + 2x_2$ and No. of calories is

$$40x_1 + 40x_2$$

By hypothesis, $200x_1 + 100x_2 \geq 4000$

or $2x_1 + x_2 \geq 40$

and $x_1 + 2x_2 \geq 50$

$40x_1 + 40x_2 \geq 1400$ and, of course,

$$x_1, x_2 \geq 0$$

Thus the primal problem is

Minimize $z = 4x_1 + 3x_2$

subject to $2x_1 + x_2 \geq 40$

$x_1 + 2x_2 \geq 50$

$x_1 + x_2 \geq 35,\ x_1, x_2 \geq 0.$

Dual problem will be

Maximize $w = 40y_1 + 50y_2 + 35\,y_3$

subject to $2y_1 + y_2 + y_3 \leq 4$

$$y_1 + 2y_2 + y_3 \leq 3$$

$$y_1, y_2, y_3 \geq 0.$$

Table I

z_B	c_B	y_B	z_1	z_2	z_3	z_4	z_5	
z_4	0	4	2	1	1	1	0	
z_5	0	3	1	(2)	1	0	1	→
		C_B	40	50	35	0	0	
		Δ_B	–40	–50	–35	0	0	
				↑				

Table II

z_B	c_B	y_B	z_1	z_2	z_3	z_4	z_5	
z_4	0	$\frac{5}{2}$	$\left(\frac{3}{2}\right)$	0	$\frac{1}{2}$	1	$-\frac{1}{2}$	
z_2	50	$\frac{3}{2}$	$\frac{1}{2}$	1	$\frac{1}{2}$	0	$\frac{1}{2}$	→
		C_B	40	50	35	0	0	
		Δ_B	–15	0	–10	0	25	
				↑				

Table III

z_B	c_B	y_B	z_1	z_2	z_3	z_4	z_5	
z_5	40	$\frac{5}{3}$	1	0	$\frac{1}{3}$	$\frac{2}{3}$	$-\frac{1}{3}$	
z_2	50	$\frac{2}{3}$	0	1	$\frac{1}{3}$	$-\frac{1}{3}$	$\frac{2}{3}$	→
		C_B	40	50	35	0	0	
		Δ_B	0	0	– 5	10	20	
				↑				

Table IV

z_B	c_B	y_B	z_1	z_2	z_3	z_4	z_5
z_1	40	1	1	–1	0	1	–1
z_3	35	2	0	3	1	–1	2
		C_B	40	50	35	0	0
		Δ_B	0	15	0	(5)	(30)

Thus the optimal solution for the dual is $y_1 = 1,\ y_2 = 0,\ y_3 = 2$, and optimal vale is $40.1 + 35.2 = 110$.

By duality, optimal value of primal is 110 and optimal solution is

$$x_1 = 5, x_2 = 30.$$

EXERCISES

1. Minimize $z = 2x_1 + 3x_2$

   subject to
   $$7x_1 + x_2 \geq 6$$
   $$x_1 + 2x_2 \geq 4$$
   $$x_1 + x_2 \geq 5; \quad x_1, x_2 \geq 0.$$

2. Minimize $z = 6x_1 + 8x_2 + x_3$

   subject to
   $$3x_1 + 5x_2 + 3x_3 \geq 20$$
   $$x_1 + 3x_2 + 2x_3 \geq 9$$
   $$6x_1 + 2x_2 + 5x_3 \geq 30.$$
   $$x_1, x_2, x_3 \geq 0.$$

3. Minimize $z = 6x_1 + 3x_2$

   subject to
   $$x_1 + x_2 \geq 4$$
   $$3x_1 + 4x_2 + \geq 12$$
   $$x_1, x_2, \geq 0.$$

4. Minimize $z = x_1 + 2x_2 + x_3$

   subject to
   $$x_1 - 3x_2 + 4x_3 \geq 12$$
   $$3x_1 + x_2 + 20x_3 \geq 10$$
   $$x_1 - x_2 - x_3 \leq -8$$
   $$x_1, x_2, x_3 \geq 0.$$

   [Hint: First multiply third inequality by – 1]

5. Minimize $z = 3x_1 + 3x_2 + 4x_3$

   subject to
   $$x_1 - 2x_2 - 2x_3 \leq -2$$
   $$x_1 + x_2 + x_3 \geq 2$$
   $$2x_1 + x_3 \geq 3$$
   $$x_1, x_2, x_3 \geq 0.$$

6. A manufacturer of leather belts makes three types of belts A, B, and C which are processed on machines M_1, M_2 and M_3. Belt A requires 2 hours on machine M_1 and 3 hours on machine M_3. Belt B requires 3 hours on M_1, and 2 hours on M_2 and M_3 each. Belt C requires 5 hours on M_2 and 4 hours on M_3. There are 8 hours of time per day available on machine M_1, 10 hours per day on M_2 and 15 hours on M_3. The profit gained from belt A is Rs 3 per unit, form belt B is Rs 5 per unit and from belt C is Rs 4 per unit. What should be the daily production of each type of belt so as to have maximum profit.
7. A firm makes two types of furniture: chairs and tables. Profits are Rs 20 per chair and Rs 30 per table. Both products are processed on three machines M_1, M_2 and M_3. The time required for each product in hour and total time available in hours on each machine are as follows:

Machine	*Chair*	*Table*	*Available time*
M_1	3	3	36
M_2	5	2	50
M_3	2	6	60

(*a*) Formulate the above problem as a linear programming problem to maximise profit; (*b*) write its dual; and (*c*) solve the primal problem by simplex method.

8. A manufacturer produces three products A, B and C. Each product can be produced on either of the two machines I or II. The time required to produce I unit of each product on a machine is as follows:

Time to produce 1 unit (in hours) on

Product	*Machine I*	*Machine II*
A	.5	.6
B	.7	.8
C	.9	1.05

There are 85 hours available on each machine; the operating cost is Rs 5 per hour for machine I and Rs 4 per hour for machine II. The product requirements are at least 90 units of A, at least 80 units of B and at least 60 units of C. The manufacturer wishes to meet the requirements at minimum cost.

Solve the given linear programming problem by the simplex method.

9. A farmer has 1000 acres of land on which he can grow corn, wheat or soybeans. Each acre of corn costs Rs 100 for preparation, requires 7 man days of work and yields a profit of Rs 30. An acre of wheat costs Rs 120 to prepare, requires 10 man days of work and yields a profit of Rs 40. An acre of soyabean costs Rs 70 to prepare, requires 8 man days of work and yields a profit of Rs 20. If the farmer has Rs 1,00,000 for preparation and can count on 8000 man days work, how many acres should be allocated to each crop to maximize the total profit?

ANSWERS

1. $x_1 = 5, x_2 = 0$, optimal $z = 10$.
2. $x_1 = x_2 = 0,\ x_3 = \frac{20}{3}$, optimal $z = \frac{20}{3}$.
3. $x_1 = 0,\ x_2 = 4,\ z = 12$.
4. $x_1 = x_2 = 0,\ x_3 = 85,\ z = 8$.
5. $x_1 = 2,\ x_2 = x_3 = 0,\ z = 4$
6. $x_1 = \frac{89}{41}$, $x_2 = \frac{50}{41}$, $x_3 = \frac{62}{41}$ and $z = \frac{765}{41}$.
7. 3 chairs and 9 tables.
8. 64 hours on machine II, no time on machine I, min. cost Rs 256.
9. Corn 250 acres, wheat 625 acres, soyabean 0 acres, profit Rs 3,25,00.

Index

TABLES
LOGARITHMS

	0	1	2	3	4	5	6	7	8	9	1	2	3	4	5	6	7	8	9
10	0000	0043	0086	0128	0170						5	9	13	17	21	26	30	34	38
						0212	0253	0294	0334	0374	4	8	12	16	20	24	28	32	36
11	0414	0453	0492	0531	0569						4	8	12	16	20	23	27	31	35
						0607	0645	0682	0719	0755	4	7	11	15	18	22	26	29	33
12	0792	0828	0864	0899	0934						3	7	11	14	18	21	25	28	32
						0969	1007	1038	1072	1106	3	7	10	14	17	20	24	27	31
13	1139	1173	1206	1239	1271						3	6	10	13	16	19	23	26	29
						1303	1335	1367	1399	1430	3	7	10	13	16	19	22	25	29
14	1461	1492	1523	1553	1584						3	6	9	12	15	19	22	25	28
						1614	1644	1673	1703	1732	3	6	9	12	14	17	20	23	26
15	1761	1790	1818	1847	1875						3	6	9	11	14	17	20	23	26
						1903	1931	1959	1987	2014	3	6	8	11	14	17	19	22	25
16	2041	2068	2095	2122	2148						3	6	8	11	14	16	19	22	24
						2175	2201	2229	2253	2279	3	5	8	10	13	16	18	21	23
17	2304	2320	2355	2380	2405						3	5	8	10	13	15	18	20	23
						2430	2455	2480	2504	2529	3	5	8	10	12	15	17	20	22
18	2553	2577	2601	2625	2648						2	5	7	9	12	14	17	19	21
						2672	2695	2718	2742	2765	2	4	7	9	11	14	16	18	21
19	2788	2810	2833	2856	2878						2	4	7	9	11	13	16	18	20
						2900	2923	2945	2967	2989	2	4	6	8	11	13	15	17	19
20	3010	3032	3054	3075	3096	3118	3139	3160	3181	3201	2	4	6	8	11	13	15	17	19
21	3222	3243	3263	3284	3304	3324	3345	3365	3385	3404	2	4	6	8	10	12	14	16	18
22	3424	3444	3464	3483	3502	3522	3541	3560	3579	3598	2	4	6	8	10	12	14	15	17
23	3617	3636	3655	3674	3692	3711	3729	3747	3766	3784	2	4	6	7	9	11	13	15	17
24	3802	3820	3838	3856	3874	3892	3909	3927	3945	3962	2	4	5	7	9	11	12	14	16
25	3979	3997	4014	4031	4048	4065	4082	4099	4116	4133	2	3	5	7	9	10	12	14	15
26	4150	4166	4183	4200	4216	4232	4249	4265	4281	4298	2	3	5	7	8	10	11	13	15
27	4314	4330	4346	4362	4378	4393	4409	4425	4440	4456	2	3	5	6	8	9	11	13	14
28	4472	4487	4502	4518	4533	4548	4564	4579	4594	4609	2	3	5	6	8	9	11	12	14
29	4624	4639	4654	4669	4683	4698	4713	4728	4742	4757	1	3	4	6	7	9	10	12	13
30	4771	4786	4800	4814	4829	4843	4857	4871	4886	4900	1	3	4	6	7	9	10	11	13
31	4914	4928	4942	4955	4969	4983	4997	5011	5024	5038	1	3	4	6	7	8	10	11	12
32	5051	5065	5079	5092	5105	5119	5132	5145	5159	5172	1	3	4	6	7	8	10	11	12
33	5185	5198	5211	5224	5237	5250	5263	5276	5289	5302	1	3	4	5	6	8	9	10	12
34	5315	5328	5340	5353	5366	5378	5391	5403	5416	5428	1	3	4	5	6	8	9	10	11
35	5441	5453	5465	5478	5490	5502	5514	5527	5539	5551	1	2	4	5	6	7	9	10	11
36	5563	5575	5587	5599	5611	5623	5635	5647	5658	5670	1	2	4	5	6	7	8	10	11
37	5682	5694	5705	5717	5729	5740	5752	5763	5775	5786	1	2	3	5	6	7	8	9	10
38	5798	5809	5821	5832	5843	5855	5866	5877	5888	5899	1	2	3	5	6	7	8	9	10
39	5911	5922	5933	5944	5955	5966	5977	5988	5999	6010	1	2	3	4	5	7	8	9	10
40	6021	6031	6042	6053	6064	6075	6085	6096	6107	6117	1	2	3	4	5	6	8	9	10
41	6128	6138	6149	6160	6170	6180	6191	6201	6212	6222	1	2	3	4	5	6	7	8	9
42	6232	6243	6253	6263	6274	6284	6294	6304	6314	6325	1	2	3	4	5	6	7	8	9
43	6335	6345	6355	6365	6375	6385	6395	6405	6415	6425	1	2	3	4	5	6	7	8	9
44	6435	6444	6454	6464	6474	6484	6493	6503	6513	6522	1	2	3	4	5	6	7	8	9
45	6532	6542	6551	6561	6571	6580	6590	6599	6609	6618	1	2	3	4	5	6	7	8	9
46	6628	6637	6646	6656	6665	6675	6684	6693	6702	6712	1	2	3	4	5	6	7	7	8
47	6721	6730	6739	6749	6758	6767	6776	6785	6794	6803	1	2	3	4	5	5	6	7	8
48	6812	6821	6830	6839	6848	6857	6866	6875	6884	6893	1	2	3	4	4	5	6	7	8
49	6902	6911	6920	6928	6937	6946	6955	6964	6972	6981	1	2	3	4	4	5	6	7	8

LOGARITHMS

	0	1	2	3	4	5	6	7	8	9	1	2	3	4	5	6	7	8	9
50	6990	6998	7007	7016	7024	7033	7042	7050	7059	7067	1	2	3	3	4	5	6	7	8
51	7076	7084	7093	7101	7110	7118	7126	7135	7143	7152	1	2	3	3	4	5	6	7	8
52	7160	7168	7177	7185	7193	7202	7210	7218	7226	7235	1	2	3	3	4	5	6	7	7
53	7243	7251	7259	7267	7275	7284	7292	7300	7308	7316	1	2	2	3	4	5	6	6	7
54	7324	7332	7340	7348	7356	7364	7372	7380	7388	7396	1	2	2	3	4	5	6	6	7
55	7404	7412	7419	7427	7435	7443	7461	7459	7466	7474	1	2	2	3	4	5	5	6	7
56	7482	7490	7497	7505	7513	7520	7528	7536	7543	7551	1	2	2	3	4	5	5	6	7
57	7559	7566	7574	7582	7589	7597	7604	7612	7619	7627	1	2	2	3	4	5	5	6	7
58	7634	7642	7649	7657	7664	7672	7679	7686	7694	7701	1	1	2	3	4	4	5	6	7
59	7709	7716	7723	7731	7738	7745	7752	7760	7767	7774	1	1	2	3	4	4	5	6	7
60	7782	7789	7796	7803	7810	7818	7825	7832	7839	7846	1	1	2	3	4	4	5	6	6
61	7853	7860	7868	7875	7882	7889	7896	7903	7910	7917	1	1	2	3	4	4	5	6	6
62	7924	7931	7938	7945	7952	7959	7966	7973	7980	7987	1	1	2	3	3	4	5	6	6
63	7993	8000	8007	8014	8021	8028	8035	8041	8048	8055	1	1	2	3	3	4	5	5	6
64	8062	8069	8075	8082	8089	8096	8102	8109	8116	8122	1	1	2	3	3	4	5	5	6
65	8129	8136	8142	8149	8156	8162	8169	8176	8182	8189	1	1	2	3	3	4	5	5	6
66	8195	8202	8209	8215	8222	8228	8235	8241	8248	8254	1	1	2	3	3	4	5	5	6
67	8261	8267	8274	8280	8287	8293	8299	8306	8312	8319	1	1	2	3	3	4	5	5	6
68	8325	8331	8338	8344	8351	8357	8363	8370	8376	8382	1	1	2	3	3	4	4	5	6
69	8388	8395	8401	8407	8414	8420	8426	8432	8439	8445	1	1	2	2	3	4	4	5	6
70	8451	8457	8463	8470	8476	8482	8488	8494	8500	8506	1	1	2	2	3	4	4	5	6
71	8513	8519	8525	8531	8537	8543	8549	8555	8561	8567	1	1	2	2	3	4	4	5	6
72	8573	8579	8585	8591	8597	8603	8609	8615	8621	8627	1	1	2	2	3	4	4	5	5
73	8633	8639	8645	8651	8657	8663	8669	8675	8681	8686	1	1	2	2	3	4	4	5	5
74	8692	8698	8704	8710	8716	8722	8727	8733	8739	8745	1	1	2	2	3	4	4	5	5
75	8751	8756	8762	8768	8774	8779	8785	8791	8797	8802	1	1	2	2	3	3	4	5	5
76	8808	8814	8820	8825	8831	8837	8842	8848	8854	8859	1	1	2	2	3	3	4	5	5
77	8865	8871	8876	8882	8887	8893	8899	8904	8910	8915	1	1	2	2	3	3	4	5	5
78	8921	8927	8932	8938	8943	8949	8954	8960	8965	8971	1	1	2	2	3	3	4	4	5
79	8976	8982	8987	8993	8998	9004	9009	9015	9020	9025	1	1	2	2	3	3	4	4	5
80	9031	9036	9042	9047	9053	9058	9063	9069	9074	9079	1	1	2	2	3	3	4	4	5
81	9085	9090	9096	9101	9106	9112	9117	9122	9128	9133	1	1	2	2	3	3	4	4	5
82	9138	9143	9149	9154	9159	9165	9170	9175	9180	9186	1	1	2	2	3	3	4	4	5
83	9191	9196	9201	9206	9212	9217	9222	9227	9232	9238	1	1	2	2	3	3	4	4	5
84	9243	9248	9253	9258	9263	9269	9274	9279	9284	9289	1	1	2	2	3	3	4	4	5
85	9294	9299	9304	9309	9315	9320	9325	9330	9335	9340	1	1	2	2	3	3	4	4	5
86	9345	9350	9355	9360	9365	9370	9375	9380	9385	9390	1	1	2	2	3	3	4	4	5
87	9395	9400	9405	9410	9415	9420	9425	9430	9435	9440	1	1	1	2	2	3	3	4	4
88	9445	9450	9455	9460	9465	9469	9474	9470	9484	9489	0	1	1	2	2	3	3	4	4
89	9494	9499	9504	9509	9515	9518	9523	9528	9533	9538	0	1	1	2	2	3	3	4	4
90	9542	9547	9552	9557	9562	9566	9571	9576	9581	9586	0	1	1	2	2	3	3	4	4
91	9590	9595	9600	9605	9609	9614	9619	9624	9628	9633	0	1	1	2	2	3	3	4	4
92	9638	9643	9647	9652	9657	9661	9666	9671	9675	9680	0	1	1	2	2	3	3	4	4
93	9685	9689	9694	9699	9703	9708	9713	9717	9722	9727	0	1	1	2	2	3	3	4	4
94	9731	9736	9741	9745	9750	9754	9759	9763	9768	9773	0	1	1	2	2	3	3	4	4
95	9777	9782	9736	9791	9795	9800	9805	9809	9814	9818	0	1	1	2	2	3	3	4	4
96	9823	9827	9832	9836	9841	9845	9850	9854	9859	9863	0	1	1	2	2	3	3	4	4
97	9868	9872	9877	9881	9886	9890	9894	9899	9903	9908	0	1	1	2	2	3	3	4	4
98	9912	9917	9921	9926	9930	9934	9939	9943	9948	9952	0	1	1	2	2	3	3	4	4
99	9956	9961	9965	9969	9974	9978	9983	9987	9991	9996	0	1	1	2	2	3	3	4	4

ANTILOGARITHMS

	0	1	2	3	4	5	6	7	8	9	1	2	3	4	5	6	7	8	9
.00	1000	1002	1005	1007	1009	1012	1014	1016	1019	1021	0	0	1	1	1	1	2	2	2
.01	1023	1026	1028	1030	1033	1035	1038	1040	1042	1045	0	0	1	1	1	1	2	2	2
.02	1047	1050	1052	1054	1057	1059	1062	1064	1067	1069	0	0	1	1	1	1	2	2	2
.03	1072	1074	1076	1079	1081	1084	1086	1089	1091	1094	0	0	1	1	1	1	2	2	2
.04	1096	1099	1102	1104	1107	1109	1112	1114	1117	1119	0	1	1	1	1	2	2	2	2
.05	1123	1125	1127	1130	1132	1135	1138	1140	1143	1146	0	1	1	1	1	2	2	2	2
.06	1148	1151	1153	1156	1159	1161	1164	1167	1169	1172	0	1	1	1	1	2	2	2	2
.07	1175	1178	1180	1183	1186	1189	1191	1194	1197	1199	0	1	1	1	1	2	2	2	2
.08	1202	1205	1208	1211	1213	1216	1219	1222	1225	1227	0	1	1	1	1	2	2	2	3
.09	1230	1233	1236	1239	1242	1245	1247	1250	1253	1256	0	1	1	1	1	2	2	2	3
.10	1259	1262	1265	1268	1271	1274	1276	1279	1282	1285	0	1	1	1	1	2	2	2	3
.11	1288	1291	1294	1297	1300	1303	1306	1309	1312	1315	0	1	1	1	2	2	2	2	3
.12	1318	1321	1324	1327	1330	1334	1337	1340	1343	1346	0	1	1	1	2	2	2	2	3
.13	1349	1352	1355	1358	1361	1365	1368	1371	1374	1377	0	1	1	1	2	2	2	3	3
.14	1380	1384	1387	1390	1393	1396	1400	1403	1406	1409	0	1	1	1	2	2	2	3	3
.15	1413	1416	1419	1422	1426	1429	1432	1435	1439	1442	0	1	1	1	2	2	2	3	3
.16	1445	1449	1452	1455	1459	1462	1466	1469	1472	1476	0	1	1	1	2	2	2	3	3
.17	1479	1483	1486	1489	1493	1496	1500	1503	1507	1510	0	1	1	1	2	2	2	3	3
.18	1514	1517	1521	1524	1528	1531	1535	1538	1542	1545	0	1	1	1	2	2	2	3	3
.19	1549	1552	1556	1560	1563	1567	1570	1574	1578	1581	0	1	1	1	2	2	3	3	3
.20	1585	1589	1592	1596	1600	1603	1607	1611	1614	1618	0	1	1	1	2	2	3	3	3
.21	1622	1626	1629	1633	1637	1641	1644	1648	1652	1656	0	1	1	2	2	2	3	3	3
.22	1660	1663	1667	1671	1675	1679	1683	1687	1690	1694	0	1	1	2	2	2	3	3	3
.23	1698	1702	1706	1710	1714	1718	1722	1726	1730	1734	0	1	1	2	2	2	3	3	4
.24	1738	1742	1746	1750	1754	1758	1762	1766	1770	1774	0	1	1	2	2	2	3	3	4
.25	1778	1782	1786	1791	1795	1799	1803	1807	1811	1816	0	1	1	2	2	3	3	3	4
.26	1820	1824	1828	1832	1837	1841	1845	1849	1854	1858	0	1	1	2	2	3	3	3	4
.27	1862	1666	1871	1875	1879	1884	1888	1892	1897	1901	0	1	1	2	2	3	3	3	4
.28	1905	1910	1914	1919	1923	1928	1932	1936	1941	1945	0	1	1	2	2	3	3	4	4
.29	1950	1954	1959	1963	1968	1972	1977	1982	1986	1991	0	1	1	2	2	3	3	4	4
.30	1995	2000	2004	2009	2014	2018	2023	2028	2032	2037	0	1	1	2	2	3	3	4	4
.31	2042	2046	2051	2056	2061	2065	2070	2075	2080	2084	0	1	1	2	2	3	3	4	4
.32	2089	2094	2099	2104	2109	2113	2118	2123	2128	2133	0	1	1	2	2	3	3	4	4
.33	2138	2143	2148	2153	2158	2163	2168	2173	2178	2183	0	1	1	2	2	3	3	4	4
.34	2188	2193	2198	2203	2208	2213	2218	2223	2228	2234	1	1	2	2	3	3	4	4	5
.35	2239	2244	2249	2254	2259	2265	2270	2275	2280	2286	1	1	2	2	3	3	4	4	5
.36	2291	2296	2301	2307	2312	2317	2323	2328	2333	2339	1	1	2	2	3	3	4	4	5
.37	2344	2350	2355	2360	2366	2371	2377	2382	2388	2393	1	1	2	2	3	3	4	4	5
.38	2399	2404	2410	2415	2421	2427	2432	2438	2443	2449	1	1	2	2	3	3	4	4	5
.39	2455	2460	2466	2472	2477	2483	2489	2495	2500	2506	1	1	2	2	3	3	4	5	5
.40	2512	2518	2523	2529	2535	2341	2547	2553	2559	2564	1	1	2	2	3	4	4	5	5
.41	2570	2576	2582	2588	2594	2600	2606	2612	2618	2624	1	1	2	2	3	4	4	5	5
.42	2630	2636	2642	2649	2655	2661	2667	2673	2679	2685	1	1	2	2	3	4	4	5	6
.43	2692	2698	2704	2710	2716	2723	2729	2735	2742	2748	1	1	2	3	3	4	4	5	6
.44	2754	2761	2767	2773	2780	2786	2793	2799	2805	2812	1	1	2	3	3	4	4	5	6
.45	2818	2825	2831	2838	2844	2851	2858	2864	2871	2877	1	1	2	3	3	4	5	5	6
.46	2884	2891	2897	2904	2911	2917	2924	2931	2938	2944	1	1	2	3	3	4	5	5	6
.47	2951	2958	2965	2972	2979	2985	2992	2999	3006	3013	1	1	2	3	3	4	5	5	6
.48	3020	3027	3034	3041	3048	3053	3062	3069	3076	3083	1	1	2	3	4	4	5	6	6
.49	3090	3097	3105	3112	3119	3126	3133	3141	3148	3155	1	1	2	3	4	4	5	6	6

ANTILOGARITHMS

	0	1	2	3	4	5	6	7	8	9	1	2	3	4	5	6	7	8	9
.50	3162	3170	3177	3184	3192	3199	3206	3214	3221	3228	1	1	2	3	4	4	5	6	7
.51	3236	3243	3251	3258	3266	3273	3281	3289	3296	3304	1	2	2	3	4	5	5	6	7
.52	3311	3319	3327	3334	3342	3350	3357	3365	3373	3381	1	2	2	3	4	5	5	6	7
.53	3388	3396	3404	3412	3420	3428	3436	3443	3451	3459	1	2	2	3	4	5	6	6	7
.54	3467	3475	3483	3491	3499	3508	3516	3524	3532	3540	1	2	2	3	4	5	6	6	7
.55	3548	3556	3565	3573	3581	3589	3597	3606	3614	3622	1	2	2	3	4	5	6	7	7
.56	3631	3639	3648	3656	3664	3673	3681	3690	3698	3707	1	2	3	3	4	5	6	7	8
.57	3715	3724	3733	3741	3750	3758	3767	3776	3784	3793	1	2	3	3	4	5	6	7	8
.58	3802	3811	3819	3828	3837	3846	3855	3864	3873	3882	1	2	3	4	4	5	6	7	8
.59	3890	3899	3908	3917	3926	3936	3945	3954	3963	3972	1	2	3	4	5	5	6	7	8
.60	3981	3990	3999	4009	4018	4027	4036	4046	4055	4064	1	2	3	4	5	6	6	7	8
.61	4074	4083	4093	4102	4111	4121	4130	4140	4150	4159	1	2	3	4	5	6	7	8	9
.62	4169	4178	4188	4198	4207	4217	4227	4236	4246	4256	1	2	3	4	5	6	7	8	9
.63	4266	4276	4285	4295	4305	4315	4325	4335	4345	4355	1	2	3	4	5	6	7	8	9
.64	4365	4375	4385	4395	4406	4416	4426	4436	4446	4457	1	2	3	4	5	6	7	8	9
.65	4467	4477	4487	4498	4508	4519	4529	4539	4550	4560	1	2	3	4	5	6	7	8	9
.66	4571	4581	4592	4603	4613	4624	4634	4645	4656	4667	1	2	3	4	5	6	7	9	10
.67	4677	4688	4699	4710	4721	4732	4742	4753	4764	4775	1	2	3	4	5	7	8	9	10
.68	4786	4797	4808	4819	4831	4842	4853	4864	4875	4887	1	2	3	4	6	7	8	9	10
.69	4893	4909	4920	4932	4943	4955	4966	4977	4989	5000	1	2	3	5	6	7	8	9	10
.70	5012	5023	5035	5047	5058	5070	5082	5093	5105	5117	1	2	4	5	6	7	8	9	11
.71	5129	5140	5152	5164	5176	5188	5200	5212	5224	5236	1	2	4	5	6	7	8	10	11
.72	5248	5260	5272	5284	5297	5309	5321	5333	5346	5358	1	2	4	5	6	7	9	10	11
.73	5370	5383	5395	5408	5420	5433	5445	5458	5470	5483	1	3	4	5	6	8	9	10	11
.74	5495	5508	5521	5534	5546	5559	5572	5585	5598	5610	1	3	4	5	6	8	9	10	12
.75	5623	5636	5649	5662	5675	5689	5702	5715	5728	5741	1	3	4	5	7	8	9	10	12
.76	5754	5768	5781	5794	5808	5821	5834	5848	5861	5875	1	3	4	5	7	8	9	11	12
.77	5888	5908	5916	5929	5943	5957	5970	5984	5998	6012	1	3	4	5	7	8	10	11	12
.78	6026	6039	6053	6067	6081	6095	6109	6124	6138	6152	1	3	4	6	7	8	10	11	13
.79	6166	6180	6194	6209	6223	6237	6252	6266	6281	6295	1	3	4	6	7	9	10	11	13
.80	6310	6324	6339	6353	6368	6383	6397	6412	6427	6442	1	3	4	6	7	9	10	12	13
.81	6457	6471	6486	6501	6516	6531	6546	6561	6577	6592	2	3	5	6	8	9	11	12	14
.82	6607	6622	6637	6653	6668	6683	6699	6714	6730	6745	2	3	5	6	8	9	11	12	14
.83	6761	6776	6792	6808	6823	6839	6855	6871	6887	6902	2	3	5	6	8	9	11	13	14
.84	6918	6934	6950	6966	6982	6998	7015	7031	7047	7063	2	3	5	6	8	10	11	13	15
.85	7079	7096	7112	7129	7145	7161	7178	7194	7211	7228	2	3	5	7	8	10	12	13	15
.86	7244	7261	7278	7295	7311	7328	7345	7362	7379	7396	2	3	5	7	8	10	12	13	15
.87	7413	7430	7447	7464	7482	7499	7516	7534	7551	7568	2	3	5	7	9	10	12	14	16
.88	7586	7603	7621	7638	7656	7674	7691	7709	7727	7745	2	4	5	7	9	11	12	14	16
.89	7762	7780	7798	7816	7834	7852	7870	7889	7907	7925	2	4	5	7	9	11	13	14	16
.90	7943	7962	7980	7998	8017	8035	8054	8072	8091	8110	2	4	6	7	9	11	13	15	17
.91	8128	8147	8166	8185	8204	8222	8241	8260	8279	8299	2	4	6	8	9	11	13	15	17
.92	8318	8337	8356	8375	8395	8414	8433	8453	8472	8492	2	4	6	8	10	12	14	15	17
.93	8511	8531	8551	8570	8590	8610	8630	8650	8670	8690	2	4	6	8	10	12	14	16	18
.94	8710	8730	8750	8770	8790	8810	8831	8851	8872	8892	2	4	6	8	10	12	14	16	18
.95	8913	8933	8954	8974	8995	9016	9036	9057	9078	9099	2	4	6	8	10	12	15	17	19
.96	9120	9141	9162	9183	9204	9226	9247	9268	9290	9311	2	4	6	8	11	13	15	17	19
.97	9333	9354	9376	9397	9419	9441	9462	9484	9506	9528	2	4	7	9	11	13	15	17	20
.98	9550	9572	9594	9616	9638	9661	9683	9705	9727	9750	2	4	7	9	11	13	16	18	20
.99	9772	9795	9817	9840	9863	9886	9908	9931	9954	9977	2	5	7	9	11	14	16	18	20

NATURAL SINES

Degrees	0′ 0°.0	6′ 0°.1	12′ 0°.2	18′ 0°.3	24′ 0°.4	30′ 0°.5	36′ 0°.6	42′ 0°.7	48′ 0°.8	54′ 0°.9	Mean Differences 1	 2	 3	 4	 5
0	.0000	0017	0035	0052	0070	0087	0105	0122	0140	0157	3	6	9	12	15
1	.0175	0192	0209	0227	0244	0263	0279	0297	0314	0332	3	6	9	12	15
2	.0349	0366	0384	0401	0419	0436	0454	0471	0488	0506	3	6	9	12	15
3	.0523	0541	0558	0576	0593	0610	0628	0645	0663	0680	3	6	9	12	15
4	.0698	0715	0732	0750	0767	0785	0802	0819	0837	0854	3	6	9	12	15
5	.0872	0889	0906	0924	0941	0958	0976	0993	1011	1028	3	6	9	12	14
6	.1045	1063	1080	1097	1115	1132	1149	1167	1184	1201	3	6	9	12	14
7	.1219	1236	1253	1271	1288	1305	1323	1340	1357	1374	3	6	9	12	14
8	.1392	1409	1426	1444	1461	1478	1495	1513	1530	1547	3	6	9	12	14
9	.1564	1582	1599	1616	1633	1650	1668	1685	1702	1719	3	6	9	12	14
10	.1736	1754	1771	1788	1805	1822	1840	1857	1874	1891	3	6	9	12	14
11	.1908	1925	1942	1959	1977	1994	2011	2028	2045	2062	3	6	9	11	14
12	.2079	2096	2113	2130	2147	2164	2181	2198	2215	2232	3	6	9	11	14
13	.2250	2267	2284	2300	2317	2334	2351	2368	2385	2402	3	6	8	11	14
14	.2419	2436	2453	2470	2487	2504	2521	2538	2554	2571	3	6	8	11	14
15	.2588	2605	2622	2639	2656	2672	2689	2706	2723	2740	3	6	8	11	14
16	.2756	2773	2790	2807	2823	2840	2857	2874	2890	2907	3	6	8	11	14
17	.2924	2940	2957	2974	2990	3007	3024	3040	3057	3074	3	6	8	11	14
18	.3090	3107	3123	3140	3156	3173	3190	3206	3223	3239	3	6	8	11	14
19	.3256	3272	3289	3305	3322	3338	3355	3371	3387	3404	3	5	8	11	14
20	.3420	3437	3453	3469	3486	3502	3518	3535	3551	3567	3	5	8	11	14
21	.3584	3600	3616	3633	3649	3665	3681	3697	3714	3730	3	5	8	11	14
22	.3746	3762	3778	3795	3811	3827	3843	3859	3875	3891	3	5	8	11	14
23	.3907	3923	3939	3955	3971	3987	4003	4019	4035	4051	3	5	8	11	14
24	.4067	4083	4099	4115	4131	4147	4163	4179	4195	4210	3	5	8	11	13
25.	.4226	4242	4258	4274	4289	4305	4321	4337	4352	4368	3	5	8	11	13
26.	.4384	4399	4415	4431	4446	4462	4478	4493	4509	4524	3	5	8	10	13
27	.4540	4555	4571	4586	4602	4617	4633	4648	4664	4679	3	5	8	10	13
28	.4695	4710	4726	4741	4756	4772	4787	4802	4818	4833	3	5	8	10	13
29	.4848	4863	4879	4894	4909	4924	4939	4955	4970	4985	3	5	8	10	13
30	.5000	5015	5030	5045	5060	5075	5090	5105	5120	5135	3	5	8	10	13
31	.5150	5165	5180	5195	5210	5225	5240	5255	5270	5284	2	5	7	10	12
32	.5299	5314	5329	5344	5358	5373	5388	5402	5417	5432	2	5	7	10	12
33	.5446	5461	5476	5490	5505	5519	5534	5548	5563	5577	2	5	7	10	12
34	.5592	5606	5621	5635	5650	5664	5678	5693	5707	5721	2	5	7	10	12
35	.5736	5750	5764	5779	5793	5807	5821	5835	5850	5864	2	5	7	10	12
36	.5878	5892	5906	5920	5934	5948	5962	5976	5990	6004	2	5	7	9	12
37	.6018	6032	6046	6060	6074	6088	6101	6115	6129	6143	2	5	7	9	12
38	.6157	6170	6184	6198	6211	6225	6239	6252	6266	6280	2	5	7	9	11
39	.6293	6307	6320	6334	6347	6361	6374	6388	6401	6414	2	4	7	9	11
40	.6428	6441	6455	6468	6481	6494	6508	6521	6534	6547	2	4	7	9	11
41	.6561	6574	6587	6600	6613	6626	6639	6652	6665	6678	2	4	7	9	11
42	.6691	6704	6717	6730	6743	6756	6769	6782	6794	6807	2	4	6	9	11
43	.6820	6833	6845	6858	6871	6884	6896	6909	6921	6934	2	4	6	8	11
44	.6947	6959	6972	6984	6997	7009	7022	7034	7046	7059	2	4	6	8	10
45	.7071	7083	7096	7108	7120	7133	7145	7157	7169	7181	2	4	6	8	10

NATURAL SINES

Degrees	0′	6′	12′	18′	24′	30′	36′	42′	48′	54′	Mean Differences				
	0°.0	0°.1	0°.2	0°.3	0°.4	0°.5	0°.6	0°.7	0°.8	0°.9	1	2	3	4	5
46	.7193	7206	7218	7230	7242	7254	7266	7278	7290	7302	2	4	6	8	10
47	.7314	7325	7337	7349	7361	7373	7385	7396	7408	7420	2	4	6	8	10
48	.7431	7443	7455	7466	7478	7490	7501	7513	7524	7536	2	4	6	8	10
49	.7547	7558	7570	7581	7593	7604	7615	7627	7638	7649	2	4	6	8	9
50	.7660	7672	7683	7694	7705	7716	7727	7738	7749	7760	2	4	6	7	9
51	.7771	7782	7793	7804	7815	7826	7837	7848	7859	7869	2	4	5	7	9
52	.7880	7891	7902	7912	7923	7934	7944	7955	7965	7976	2	4	5	7	9
53	.7986	7997	8007	8018	8028	8039	8049	8059	8070	8080	2	3	5	7	9
54	.8090	8100	8111	8121	8131	8141	8151	8161	8171	8181	2	3	5	7	8
55	.8192	8202	8211	8221	8231	8241	8251	8261	8271	8281	2	3	5	7	8
56	.8290	8300	8310	8320	8329	8339	8348	8358	8368	8377	2	3	5	6	8
57	.8387	8396	8406	8415	8425	8434	8443	8453	8462	8471	2	3	5	6	8
58	.8480	8490	8499	8508	8517	8526	8536	8545	8554	8563	2	3	5	6	8
59	.8572	8581	8590	8599	8607	8616	8625	8634	8643	8652	1	3	5	6	7
60	.8660	8669	8678	8686	8695	8704	8712	8721	8729	8738	1	3	4	6	7
61	.8746	8755	8763	8771	8780	8788	8796	8805	8813	8821	1	3	4	6	7
62	.8829	8838	8846	8854	8862	8870	8878	8886	8894	8902	1	3	4	5	7
63	.8910	8918	8926	8934	8942	8949	8957	8965	8973	8980	1	3	4	5	6
64	.8988	8996	9003	9011	9018	9026	9033	9041	9048	9056	1	3	4	5	6
65	.9063	9070	9078	9085	9092	9100	9107	9114	9121	9128	1	2	4	5	6
66	.9135	9143	9150	9157	9164	9171	9178	9184	9191	9198	1	2	3	5	6
67	.9205	9212	9219	9225	9232	9239	9245	9252	9259	9265	1	2	3	4	6
68	.9272	9278	9285	9291	9298	9304	9311	9317	9323	9330	1	2	3	4	5
69	.9336	9342	9348	9354	9361	9367	9373	9379	9385	9391	1	2	3	4	5
70	.9397	9403	9409	9415	9421	9426	9432	9438	9444	9449	1	2	3	4	5
71	.9455	9461	9466	9472	9478	9483	9489	9494	9500	9505	1	2	3	4	5
72	.9511	9516	9521	9527	9532	9537	9542	9548	9553	9558	1	2	3	3	4
73	.9563	9568	9573	9578	9583	9588	9593	9598	9603	9608	1	2	2	3	4
74	.9613	9617	9622	9627	9632	9636	9641	9646	9650	9655	1	2	2	3	4
75	.9659	9664	9668	9673	9677	9681	9686	9690	9694	9699	1	1	2	3	4
76	.9703	9707	9711	9715	9720	9724	9728	9732	9736	9740	1	1	2	3	3
77	.9744	9748	9751	9755	9759	9763	9767	9770	9774	9778	1	1	2	3	3
78	.9781	9785	9789	9792	9796	9799	9803	9806	9810	9813	1	1	2	2	3
79	.9816	9820	9823	9826	9829	9833	9836	9839	9842	9845	1	1	2	2	3
80	.9848	9851	9854	9857	9866	9863	9866	9869	9871	9874	0	1	1	2	2
81	.9877	9880	9882	9885	9888	9890	9893	9895	9898	9900	0	1	1	2	2
82	.9903	9905	9907	9910	9912	9914	9917	9919	9921	9923	0	1	1	2	2
83	.9925	9928	9930	9932	9934	9936	9938	9940	9942	9943	0	1	1	1	2
84	.9945	9947	9949	9951	9952	9954	9956	9957	9959	9960	0	1	1	1	2
85	.9962	9963	9965	9966	9968	9969	9971	9972	9973	9974	0	0	1	1	1
86	.9976	9977	9978	9979	9980	9981	9982	9983	9984	9985	0	0	1	1	1
87	.9986	9987	9988	9989	9990	9990	9991	9992	9993	9993	0	0	0	1	1
88	.9994	9995	9995	9996	9996	9997	9997	9997	9998	9998	0	0	0	0	0
89	.9998	9999	9999	9999	9999	1.000	1.000	1.000	1.000	1.000	0	0	0	0	0
90	1.0000														

NATURAL COSINES

[*Numbers in difference columns to be subtracted, not added.*]

Degrees	0′	6′	12′	18′	24′	30′	36′	42′	48′	54′	Mean Differences				
	0°.0	0°.1	0°.2	0°.3	0°.4	0°.5	0°.6	0°.7	0°.8	0°.9	1	2	3	4	5
0	1.000	1.000	1.000	1.000	1.000	1.000	.9999	9999	9999	9999	0	0	0	0	0
1	.9998	9998	9998	9997	9997	9997	9996	9996	9995	9995	0	0	0	0	0
2	.9994	9993	9993	9992	9991	9990	9990	9989	9988	9987	0	0	0	1	1
3	.9986	9985	9984	9983	9982	9981	9980	9979	9978	9977	0	0	1	1	1
4	.9976	9974	9973	9972	9971	9969	9968	9966	9965	9963	0	0	1	1	1
5	.9962	9960	9959	9957	9956	9954	9952	9951	9949	9947	0	1	1	1	2
6	.9945	9943	9942	9940	9938	9936	9934	9932	9930	9928	0	1	1	1	2
7	.9925	9923	9921	9919	9917	9914	9912	9910	9907	9905	0	1	1	2	2
8	.9903	9900	9898	9895	9893	9890	9888	9885	9882	9880	0	1	1	2	2
9	.9877	9874	9871	9869	9866	9863	9860	9857	9854	9851	0	1	1	2	2
10	.9848	9845	9842	9839	9836	9833	9829	9826	9823	9820	1	1	2	2	3
11	.9816	9813	9810	9806	9803	9799	9796	9792	9789	9785	1	1	2	2	3
12	.9781	9778	9774	9770	9767	9763	9759	9755	9751	9748	1	1	2	3	3
13	.9744	9740	9736	9732	9728	9724	9720	9715	9711	9707	1	1	2	3	3
14	.9703	9699	9694	9690	9686	9681	9677	9673	9668	9664	1	1	2	3	4
15	.9659	9655	9650	9646	9641	9636	96312	9627	9622	9617	1	2	2	3	4
16	.9613	9608	9603	9598	9593	9588	9583	9578	9573	9568	1	2	2	3	4
17	.9563	9558	9553	9548	9542	9537	9532	9527	9521	9516	1	2	3	3	4
18	.9511	9505	9500	9494	9489	9483	9478	9472	9466	9461	1	2	3	4	5
19	.9455	9449	9444	9438	9432	9426	9421	9415	9409	9403	1	2	3	4	5
20	.9397	9391	9385	9379	9373	9367	9361	9354	9348	9342	1	2	3	4	5
21	.9336	9330	9323	9317	9311	9304	9298	9291	9285	9278	1	2	3	4	5
22	.9272	9265	9259	9252	9245	9239	9232	9225	9219	9212	1	2	3	4	6
23	.9205	9198	9191	9184	9178	9171	9164	9157	9150	9143	1	2	3	5	6
24	.9135	9128	9121	9114	9107	9100	9092	9085	9078	9070	1	2	4	5	6
25	.9063	9056	9048	9041	9033	9026	9018	9011	9003	8996	1	3	4	5	6
26	.8988	8980	8973	8965	8957	8949	8942	8934	8926	8918	1	3	4	5	6
27	.8910	8902	8894	8886	8878	8870	8862	8854	8846	8838	1	3	4	5	7
28	.8829	8821	8813	8805	8796	8788	8780	8771	8763	8755	1	3	4	6	7
29	.8746	8738	8729	8721	8712	8704	8695	8686	8678	8669	1	3	4	6	7
30	.8660	8652	8643	8634	8625	8616	8607	8599	8590	8581	1	3	4	6	7
31	.8572	8563	8554	8545	8536	8526	8517	8508	8499	8490	2	3	5	6	8
32	.8480	8471	8462	8453	8443	8434	8425	8415	8406	8396	2	3	5	6	8
33	.8387	8377	8368	8358	8348	8339	8329	832	8310	8300	2	3	5	6	8
34	.8290	8281	8271	8261	8251	8241	8231	8221	8211	8202	2	3	5	7	8
35	.8192	8181	8171	8161	8151	8141	8131	8121	8111	8100	2	3	5	7	8
36	.8090	8080	8070	8059	8049	8039	8028	8018	8007	7997	2	3	5	7	9
37	.7986	7976	7965	7955	7944	7934	7923	7912	7902	7891	2	4	5	7	9
38	.7880	7869	7859	7848	7837	7826	7815	7804	7793	7782	2	4	5	7	9
39	.7771	7760	7749	7738	7727	7716	7705	7694	7683	7672	2	4	6	7	9
40	.7660	7649	7638	7627	7615	7604	7593	7581	7570	7559	2	4	6	8	9
41	.7547	7536	7524	7513	7501	7490	7478	7466	7455	7443	2	4	6	8	10
42	.7431	7420	7408	7396	7385	7373	7361	7349	7337	7325	2	4	6	8	10
43	.7314	7302	7290	7278	7266	7254	7242	7230	7218	7206	2	4	6	8	10
44	.7193	7181	7169	7157	7145	7133	7120	7108	7096	7083	2	4	6	8	10
45	.7071	7059	7046	7034	7022	7009	6997	6984	6972	6959	2	4	6	8	10

NATURAL COSINES

Degrees	0′ 0°.0	6′ 0°.1	12′ 0°.2	18′ 0°.3	24′ 0°.4	30′ 0°.5	36′ 0°.6	42′ 0°.7	48′ 0°.8	54′ 0°.9	1	2	3	4	5
46	.6947	6934	6921	6909	6896	6884	6871	6858	6845	6833	2	4	6	8	11
47	.6820	6807	6794	6782	6769	6756	6743	6730	6717	6704	2	4	6	9	11
48	.6691	6678	6665	6652	6639	6626	6613	6600	6587	6574	2	4	7	9	11
49	.6561	6547	6534	6521	6508	6494	6481	6468	6455	6441	2	4	7	9	11
50	.6428	6414	6401	6388	6374	6361	6347	6334	6320	6307	2	4	7	9	11
51	.6293	6280	6266	6252	6239	6225	6211	6198	6184	6170	2	5	7	9	11
52	.6157	6143	6129	6115	6101	6088	6074	6060	6046	6032	2	5	7	9	12
53	.6018	6004	5990	5976	5962	5948	5934	5920	5906	5892	2	5	7	9	12
54	.5878	5864	5850	5835	5821	5807	5793	5779	5764	5750	2	5	7	9	12
55	.5736	5721	5707	5693	5678	5664	5650	5635	5621	5606	2	5	7	10	12
56	.5592	5577	5563	5548	5534	5519	5505	5490	5476	5461	2	5	7	10	12
57	.5446	5432	5417	5402	5388	5373	5358	5344	5329	5314	2	5	7	10	12
58	.5299	5284	5270	5255	5240	5225	5210	5195	5180	5165	2	5	7	10	12
59	.5150	5135	5120	5105	5090	5075	5060	5045	5030	5015	3	5	8	10	13
60	.5000	4985	4970	4955	4939	4924	4909	4894	4879	4863	3	5	8	10	13
61	.4848	4833	4818	4802	4787	4772	4756	4741	4726	4710	3	5	8	10	13
62	.4695	4679	4664	4648	4633	4617	4602	4586	4571	4555	3	5	8	10	13
63	.4540	4524	4509	4493	4478	4462	4446	4431	4415	4399	3	5	8	10	13
64	.4384	4368	4352	4337	4321	4305	4289	4274	4258	4242	3	5	8	11	13
65	.4226	4210	4195	4179	4163	4147	4131	4115	4099	4083	3	5	8	11	13
66	.4067	4051	4035	4019	4003	3987	3971	3955	3939	3923	3	5	8	11	14
67	.3907	3891	3875	3859	3843	3827	3811	3795	3778	3762	3	5	8	11	14
68	.3746	3730	3714	3697	3681	3665	3649	3633	3616	3600	3	5	8	11	14
69	.3584	3567	3551	3535	3518	3502	3486	3469	3453	3437	3	5	8	11	14
70	.3420	3404	3387	3371	3355	3338	3322	3305	3289	3272	3	5	8	11	14
71	.3256	3239	3223	3206	3190	3173	3156	3140	3123	3107	3	6	8	11	14
72	.3090	3074	3057	3040	3024	3007	2990	2974	2957	2940	3	6	8	11	14
73	.2924	2907	2890	2874	2857	2840	2823	2807	2790	2773	3	6	8	11	14
74	.2756	2740	2723	2700	2689	2672	2656	2639	2622	2605	3	6	8	11	14
75	.2588	2571	2554	2538	2521	2504	2487	2470	2453	2436	3	6	8	11	14
76	.2419	2402	2385	2368	2351	2334	2317	2300	2284	2267	3	6	8	11	14
77	.2250	2233	2215	2198	2181	2164	2147	2130	2113	2096	3	6	9	11	14
78	.2079	2062	2045	2028	2011	1994	1977	1959	1942	1925	3	6	9	11	14
79	.1908	1891	1874	1857	1840	1822	1805	1788	1771	1754	3	6	9	11	14
80	.1736	1719	1702	1685	1668	1650	1633	1616	1599	1583	3	6	9	12	14
81	.1564	1547	1530	1513	1495	1478	1461	1444	1426	1409	3	6	9	12	14
82	.1392	1374	1357	1340	1323	1305	1288	1271	1253	1236	3	6	9	12	14
83	.1219	1201	1184	1167	1149	1132	1115	1097	1080	1063	3	6	9	12	14
84	.1045	1028	1011	0993	0976	0958	0941	0924	0906	0889	3	6	9	12	14
85	.0872	0854	0837	0819	0802	0785	0767	0750	0732	0715	3	6	9	12	15
86	.0698	0680	0663	0645	0628	0610	0593	0576	0558	0541	3	6	9	12	15
87	.0523	0506	0488	0471	0454	0436	0419	0401	0384	0366	3	6	9	12	15
88	.0349	0332	0314	0297	0279	0262	0244	0227	0209	0192	3	6	9	12	15
89	.0175	0157	0140	0122	0105	0087	0070	0052	0035	0017	3	6	9	12	15
90	.0000														

NATURAL TANGENTS

Degrees	0′ 0°.0	6′ 0°.1	12′ 0°.2	18′ 0°.3	24′ 0°.4	30′ 0°.5	36′ 0°.6	42′ 0°.7	48′ 0°.8	54′ 0°.9	Mean Differences 1	2	3	4	5
0	.0000	0017	0035	0052	0070	0087	0105	0122	0140	0157	3	6	9	12	15
1	.0175	0192	0209	0227	0244	0262	0279	0297	0314	0332	3	6	9	12	15
2	.0349	0367	0384	0402	0419	437	0454	0472	0489	0507	3	6	9	12	15
3	.0524	0542	0559	0577	0594	0612	0629	0647	0664	0682	3	6	9	12	15
4	.0699	0717	0734	0752	0769	0787	0805	0822	0840	0857	3	6	9	12	15
5	.0875	0892	0910	0928	0945	0963	0981	0998	1016	1033	3	6	9	12	15
6	.1051	1069	1086	1104	1122	1139	1157	1175	1192	1210	3	6	9	12	15
7	.1228	1246	1263	1281	1299	1317	1334	1352	1370	1388	3	6	9	12	15
8	.1405	1423	1441	1459	1477	1495	1512	1530	1548	1566	3	6	9	12	15
9	.1584	1602	1620	1638	1655	1673	1691	1709	1727	1745	3	6	9	12	15
10	.1763	1781	1799	1817	1835	1853	1871	1890	1908	1926	3	6	9	12	15
11	.1944	1962	1980	1998	2016	2035	2053	2071	2089	2107	3	6	9	12	15
12	.2126	2144	2162	2180	2199	2217	2235	2254	2272	2290	3	6	9	12	15
13	.2309	2327	2345	2364	2382	2401	2419	2438	2456	2475	3	6	9	12	15
14	.2493	2512	2530	2549	2568	2586	2605	2623	2642	2661	3	6	9	12	16
15	.2679	2698	2717	2736	2754	2773	2792	2811	2830	2849	3	6	9	13	16
16	.2867	2886	2905	2924	2943	2962	2981	3000	3019	3038	3	6	9	13	16
17	.3057	3076	3096	3115	3134	3153	3172	3191	3211	3230	3	6	10	13	16
18	.3249	3269	3288	3307	3327	3346	3365	3385	3404	3424	3	6	10	13	16
19	.3443	3463	3482	3502	3522	3541	3561	3581	3600	3620	3	7	10	13	16
20	.3640	3659	3679	3699	3719	3739	3759	3779	3799	3819	3	7	10	13	17
21	.3839	3859	3879	3899	3919	3939	3959	3979	4000	4020	3	7	10	13	17
22	.4040	4061	4081	4101	4122	4142	4163	4183	4204	4224	3	7	10	14	17
23	.4245	4265	4286	4307	4327	4348	4369	4390	4411	4431	3	7	10	14	17
24	.4452	4473	4494	4515	4536	4557	4578	4599	4621	4642	4	7	11	14	18
25	.4663	4684	4706	4727	4748	4770	4791	4813	4834	4856	4	7	11	14	18
26	.4877	4899	4921	4942	4964	4986	5008	5029	5051	5073	4	7	11	15	18
27	.5095	5117	5139	5161	5184	5206	5228	5250	5272	5295	4	7	11	15	18
28	.5317	5340	5362	5384	5407	5430	5452	5475	5498	5520	4	8	11	15	19
29	.5543	5566	5589	5612	5635	5658	5681	5704	5727	5750	4	8	12	15	19
30	.5774	5797	5820	5844	5867	5890	5914	5938	5961	5985	4	8	12	16	20
31	.6009	6032	6056	6080	6104	6128	6152	6176	6200	6224	4	8	12	16	20
32	.6249	6273	6297	6322	6346	6371	6395	6420	6445	6469	4	8	12	16	20
33	.6494	6519	6544	6569	6594	6619	6644	6669	6694	6720	4	8	13	17	21
34	.6745	6771	6796	6822	6847	6873	6899	6924	6950	6976	4	9	13	17	21
35	.7002	7028	7054	7080	7107	7133	7159	7186	7212	7239	4	9	13	18	22
36	.7265	7292	7319	7346	7373	7400	7427	7454	7481	7508	5	9	14	18	23
37	.7536	7563	7590	7618	7646	7673	7701	7729	7757	7785	5	9	14	18	23
38	.7813	7841	7869	7898	7926	7954	7983	8012	8040	8069	5	9	14	19	24
39	.8098	8127	8156	8185	8214	8243	8273	8302	8332	8361	5	10	15	20	24
40	.8391	8421	8451	8481	8511	8541	8571	8601	8632	8662	5	10	15	20	25
41	.8693	8724	8754	8785	8816	8847	8878	8910	8941	8972	5	10	16	21	26
42	.9004	9036	9067	9099	9131	9163	9195	9228	9260	9293	5	11	16	21	27
43	.9325	9358	9391	9424	9457	9490	9523	9556	9590	9623	6	11	17	22	28
44	.9657	9691	9725	9759	9793	9827	9861	9896	9930	9965	6	11	17	23	29
45	1.0000	0035	0070	0105	0141	0176	0212	0247	0283	0319	6	12	18	24	30

NATURAL TANGENTS

Degrees	0′	6′	12′	18′	24′	30′	36′	42′	48′	54′	Mean Differences				
	0°.0	0°.1	0°.2	0°.3	0°.4	0°.5	0°.6	0°.7	0°.8	0°.9	1	2	3	4	5
46	1.0355	0392	0428	0464	0501	0538	0575	0612	0649	0686	6	12	18	25	31
47	1.0724	0761	0799	0837	0875	0913	0951	0990	1028	1067	6	13	19	25	32
48	1.1106	1145	1184	1224	1263	1303	1343	1383	1423	1463	7	13	20	27	33
49	1.1504	1544	1585	1626	1667	1708	1750	1792	1833	1875	7	14	21	28	34
50	1.1918	1960	2002	2045	2088	2131	2174	2218	2261	2305	7	14	22	29	36
51	1.2349	2393	2437	2482	2527	2572	2617	2662	2708	2753	8	15	23	30	38
52	1.2799	2846	2892	2938	2985	3032	3079	3127	3175	3222	8	16	24	31	39
53	1.3270	3319	3367	3416	3465	3514	3564	3613	3663	3713	8	16	25	33	41
54	1.3764	3814	3865	3916	3968	4019	4071	4124	4176	4229	9	17	26	34	43
55	1.4281	4335	4388	4442	4496	4550	4605	4659	4715	4770	9	18	27	36	45
56	1.4826	4882	4938	4994	5051	5108	5166	5224	5282	5340	10	19	29	38	48
57	1.5399	5458	5517	5577	5637	5697	5757	5818	5880	5941	10	20	30	40	50
58	1.6003	6066	6128	6191	6255	6319	6383	6447	6512	6577	11	21	32	43	53
59	1.6643	6709	6775	6842	6909	6977	7045	7113	7182	7251	11	23	34	45	56
60	1.7321	7391	7461	7532	7603	7675	7747	7820	7893	7966	12	24	36	48	60
61	1.8040	8115	8190	8205	8341	8418	8495	8572	8650	8728	13	26	38	51	64
62	1.8807	8887	8967	9047	9128	9210	9292	9375	9458	9542	14	27	41	55	68
63	1.9626	9711	9797	9883	9970	2.0057	2.0145	2.0233	2.0323	2.0413	15	29	44	58	73
64	2.0503	0594	0686	0778	0872	0965	1060	1155	1251	1348	16	31	47	63	78
65	2.1445	1543	1642	1742	1842	1943	2045	2148	2251	2355	17	34	51	68	85
66	2.2460	2566	2673	2781	2889	2998	3110	3220	3332	3445	18	37	55	73	92
67	2.3559	3673	3789	3906	4023	4142	4262	4383	4504	4627	20	40	60	79	99
68	2.4751	4870	5002	5129	5257	5386	5517	5649	5782	5916	22	43	65	87	108
69	2.6051	6187	6325	6464	6605	6746	6889	7034	7179	7326	24	47	71	95	119
70	2.7475	7625	7776	7929	8083	8239	8397	8556	8716	8878	26	52	78	104	131
71	2.9042	9208	9375	9544	9714	9887	3.0061	3.0237	3.0415	3.0595	29	58	87	116	145
72	3.0777	0961	1146	1334	1524	1716	1910	2106	2305	2506	32	64	96	129	161
73	3.2709	2914	3122	3332	3544	3759	3977	4197	4420	4646	36	72	108	144	180
74	3.4874	5105	5339	5576	5816	6059	6305	6554	6806	7062	41	81	122	163	204
75	3.7321	7583	7848	8118	8391	8667	8947	9232	9520	9812	46	93	139	186	232
76	4.0108	0408	0713	1022	1335	1653	1976	2303	2635	2972	53	107	160	213	207
77	4.3315	3662	4015	4374	4737	5107	5483	5864	6252	6646					
78	4.7046	7453	7867	8288	8716	9152	9594	5.0045	5.0504	5.0970					
79	5.1446	1929	2422	2924	3435	3955	4486	5026	5578	6140					
80	5.6713	7297	7894	8502	9124	9758	6.0405	6.1066	6.1742	6.2432					
81	6.3138	3859	4596	5350	6122	6912	7720	8548	9395	7.0264					
82	7.1154	2066	3002	3962	4947	5958	6996	8062	9158	8.0285					
83	8.1443	2636	3863	5126	6427	7769	9152	9.0579	9.2052	9.3572					
84	9.5144	9.677	9.845	10.02	10.20	10.39	10.58	10.78	10.99	11.20					
85	11.43	11.66	11.91	12.16	12.43	12.71	13.00	13.30	13.62	13.95					
86	14.30	14.67	15.06	15.46	15.89	16.35	16.83	17.34	17.89	18.46					
87	19.08	19.74	20.45	21.20	22.02	22.90	23.86	24.90	26.03	27.27					
88	28.64	30.14	31.82	33.69	35.80	38.19	40.92	44.07	47.74	52.08					
89	57.29	63.66	71.62	81.85	95.49	114.6	143.2	191.0	286.5	573.0					
90	∞														

Mean difference cease to be sufficiently accurate